GLADSTONE

* * *

1809–1898

Gladstone aged thirty-three. *Drawing by George Richmond (1843) for the series commissioned by Grillion's Club*

GLADSTONE

***

1809–1898

H. C. G. MATTHEW

CLARENDON PRESS · OXFORD

1997

Oxford University Press, Great Clarendon Street, Oxford OX2 6DP

Oxford New York

Athens Auckland Bangkok Bogota Bombay
Buenos Aires Calcutta Cape Town Dar es Salaam
Delhi Florence Hong Kong Istanbul Karachi
Kuala Lumpur Madras Madrid Melbourne
Mexico City Nairobi Paris Singapore
Taipei Tokyo Toronto Warsaw

and associated companies in
Berlin Ibadan

Oxford is a trade mark of Oxford University Press

Published in the United States
by Oxford University Press Inc. New York

British Library Cataloguing in Publication Data
Data available

Library of Congress Cataloging in Publication Data
Data Applied for

ISBN 0-19-820696-8

1 3 5 7 9 10 8 6 4 2

Typeset by Joshua Associates Ltd.
Printed in Great Britain
on acid-free paper by
J. W. Arrowsmith Ltd., Bristol

TO
SUE, DAVID, LUCY, OLIVER

Preface

WILLIAM EWART GLADSTONE was elected to the Commons in 1832 at the age of 22, was first in office in 1834, left office for the last time in 1894, and retired from the Commons in 1895. He continued to speak in public until 1897, the year before his death. He was 88 when he died (it may be helpful for the reader to note that to calculate Gladstone's age in relation to a nineteenth-century date, subtract ten, except for the last three days of December: he was born on 29 December 1809). Gladstone heard the guns fire from Edinburgh Castle to announce the abdication of Napoleon almost at the start of the century and he lived to make recordings of his voice and to conduct business by telephone almost at the end of it. It is as if, in our own times, a man first in office in Ramsay MacDonald's National Government had been fairly constantly in Cabinet since 1943 and had, in 1996, only recently resigned from his fourth term as Prime Minister. In comparison with Gladstone's span of 60 years in and out of office, Palmerston notched up 57 years (1808–1865) and Winston Churchill 50 years (1905–1955). These political careers have no later equivalents, nor are likely to have. Throughout his huge career, Gladstone spoke constantly, wrote books and articles copiously and kept most of his enormous correspondence, as well as writing about 25,200 daily entries in his diary. Consequently, it would have not have been difficult, indeed it would have been much easier, to have made this book twice or five times its present length.

The book is an introduction to Gladstone, an extended biographical essay; it makes no claim to be exhaustive or definitive. Indeed, such a claim with respect to so Protean a person as Gladstone would be silly. This volume brings together, largely unaltered, *Gladstone *1809–1874* (1986) and *Gladstone **1875–1898* (1995). My many debts and obligations are acknowledged in their prefaces. Those two volumes, in their turn, largely comprised the Introductions which I wrote between 1973 and 1994 to volumes of *The Gladstone Diaries with Cabinet Minutes and Prime-Ministerial Correspondence*.

* * *

Coming to terms with an historical personality, especially a personality as powerful and wide-ranging as Gladstone, is not easy. The Victorian period seems close because it is close chronologically. But it was a phase, and a phase that has passed. We live with its consequences, but we do not live with it itself. Our distance from it is a loss and a gain; what we gain in

perspective, we lose in understanding. I have tried to understand Gladstone, and to be fair. But it is good to sense the distance and also to keep in
mind his own view and that of one of his 'four Doctors':

Every secret which is disclosed, every discovery which is made, every new effect
which is brought to view, serves to convince us of numberless more which remain
concealed.

(Joseph Butler, 'Upon the Ignorance of Man')

There is scarcely a single moral action of a single man of which other men can have
such a knowledge, in its ultimate grounds, its surrounding incidents, and the real
determining causes of its merits, as to warrant their pronouncing a conclusive
judgment upon it.

(Gladstone on Leopardi)

Oxford   COLIN MATTHEW
1996

Contents

List of Illustrations   xi

PART I

Prologue   1

I   Liverpool, Eton, and Oxford   3

II   Gladstonian Conservatism: from Oxford to Westminster   24

III   Church, State, and Free Trade: the Public Crisis of the 1840s   59

IV   Religion, Family, and Sex: the Private Crisis of the 1840s   87

V   Chancellor of the Exchequer: Free Trade, Budgets, and Franchise Reform   103

VI   Travel, Family, and Affairs in the 1860s   149

VII   The First Government: Ireland, Education, and External Policy   170

VIII   The First Government: Disintegration and Downfall   207

IX   A Prime Minister's Private Life   233

PART II

I   Retirement, Religious Nationality, and the Eastern Question   253

II   The Midlothian Campaign   293

III   Private Life in Retirement   313

IV   Gladstone at 70: a Review and a Retrospect   330

V   The Second Gladstone Government, 1880–1885: Retirement, Cabinet, and Party   351

VI   Colonial, Foreign, and Defence Policy, 1880–1885   374

VII   Domestic Policy in the 1880s   414

VIII   Gladstone and Ireland 1875–1885   435

IX   Towards Home Rule   463

X   Home Rule, Land, and the Proposed Pacification of Ireland
    1886   491

XI   The Daily Round: Court, Patronage, and the Commons   511

XII   Behind the Scenes   527

XIII   An Energetic Octogenarian   549

XIV   Leading the Liberal Party, 1887–1892   558

XV   The Fourth Gladstone Government, 1892–1894   579

XVI   'Successive snapping of the threads'   608

     Epilogue   639

     References   647

     Gladstone's Papers   655

     Chronology   657

     Index   665

Illustrations

Frontispiece   Gladstone aged thirty-three (*drawing by George Richmond for Grillion's Club*)

between pp. 242 and 243

1. Gladstone in 1833 (*oil sketch by George Hayter*)

2. Sir John Gladstone in old age (*calotype by D. Hill and R. Adamson*)

3. Catherine Gladstone (*watercolour of 1843 by George Richmond*)

4. 'The Flight of Daedalus and Icarus!' (*cartoon by H.B. (John Doyle*))

5. Gladstone in 1858 (*from Maull and Polyblank's* Photographic Portraits of Living Celebrities)

6. Tenniel's cartoon, 'Critics' (*from* Punch, *14 May 1870*)

7. Agnes, Catherine Jessy, Mary, and Herbert John Gladstone (*drawing by G. Richmond, portrait by G. Hayter and photographs at Hawarden*)

8. Gladstone's diary of his tour of Lancashire, 1864 (*facsimile of Lambeth MS 1438, f. 61*)

9. 'The House of Commons debating the French Treaty of 1860' (*mezzotint by T. O. Barlow after the oil painting by John Phillip*)

10. Gladstone's First Cabinet (*group portrait by Lowes Dickinson*)

11. (a) Gladstone speaking at Blackheath, 28 October 1871

    (b) Speech at Blackheath, 28 January 1874 (*Illustrated London News, 7 February 1874*)

12. (a) Two views of Laura Thistlethwayte (*miniature by Girard in the Wallace Collection; carte de visite*)

    (b) Harriet, Dowager Duchess of Sutherland (*bust by J. Noble*)

    (c) William and Catherine Gladstone in the 1860s

13. (a) Gladstone in the 1860s

    (b) Gladstone in Privy Councillor's uniform

    (c) Sir Stephen Glynne

14. (a) Gladstone to his bookseller (*facsimile of letter of 1 February 1858*)

    (b) A holiday snap at Penmaenmawr, August 1874

15. (a) W. H. and W. E. Gladstone *à la mode* (*Tailor and Cutter*, 18 June 1870)

    (b) Gladstone at Edgware Road Station, 24 May 1862

16. Gladstone as Prime Minister

between pp. 466 and 467

17. Catherine Gladstone (*photograph by Miss Sarah Acland, Oxford, 25 October 1892*)

18. Gladstone and his Private Secretaries

19. Gladstone in the 'Temple of Peace', Hawarden Castle, 6 June 1884 (*from J. P. Mayall*, Artists at Home)

20. (a) Gladstone's plan of Cabinet seating, June 1885, revised 1886

    (b) The Cabinet in July 1883

21. (a) Electioneering at Warrington, 28 November 1885

    (b) 'Mr Gladstone's Collars' (*Harry Furniss' cartoon in* Punch)

    (c) A Unionist chamberpot

22. (a) Studio photograph by Rupert Potter, 28 July 1884

    (b) Millais's portrait of Gladstone, 1885, for Christ Church, Oxford

23. The Gladstones planting a tree at Newnham College, Cambridge, 31 January 1887

24. (a) 'Enemies on his flank' (*cartoon by F. Carruthers Gould*)

    (b) 'Sitting out a debate' (*cartoon of Lord Salisbury by F. Carruthers Gould*)

25. Whigs all: Granville, Spencer, Lord Frederick Cavendish, Lord Hartington (*photographs in G. Barnett Smith*, Life and times of ... Gladstone (*illustrated edition, n.d.*))

26. (a) 'Salisbury, Gladstone and Chamberlain' (*cartoon by F. Carruthers Gould*)

    (b) 'Over the hills and far away' (*Tenniel's cartoon of Gladstone in the Highlands, September 1893, in* Punch)

27. Gladstone, W. H. Gladstone and the family treefelling at Hawarden in the 1880s

28. (a) Gladstone in Munich, 13 October 1879 (*photograph by F. von Lenbach*)

    (b) Herbert Gladstone

29. (a) Gladstone and Döllinger, September 1886 (*unfinished portrait by F. von Lenbach*)

    (b) Gladstone, Döllinger, Acton, and others at Tegernsee, 1886

30. (a) Gladstone reading (*drawing by George Howard, M.P., 5 June 1879*)

    (b) W. B. Richmond's drawing of Gladstone dead, 21 May 1898

(c) The Gladstones' visit to J. J. Colman in Norfolk, 19 May 1890

31. Last entry in Gladstone's diary, 29 December 1896

32. Gladstone, dead, laid out in his doctoral robes in the 'Temple of Peace', Hawarden Castle

*

Thanks for permission to reproduce these illustrations are due to the Archbishop of Canterbury, the Trustees of the British Library, the British Museum, the Wallace Collection, the National Portrait Gallery, the Scottish National Portrait Gallery, the Governing Bodies of Christ Church, Oxford and Newnham College, Cambridge, Clwyd Record Office, the Lenbachhaus, Munich, the Gernsheim Collection, Texas, B.B.C. Hulton Picture Library, Sir Richard Acland, Mr. Robin Crompton, Sir William Gladstone, and the Hon. Simon Howard. Several of the illustrations are from my own collection.

Prologue

'MEN make their own history, but not of their own free will; not under circumstances they themselves have chosen but under the given and inherited circumstances with which they are directly confronted.' Of few can Marx's truism be truer than of William Ewart Gladstone. His epic public career—first in office in 1834, last in 1894—confronted the prime of Britain as the first industrial nation. The agenda of free trade and imperialism was dictated by forces far beyond the control of individuals acting as such. Yet the interpretation and execution of the agenda was achieved by the decisions and actions of individuals and explained through their speeches and writings. In this interpretation, execution, and explanation, Gladstone's career holds a central place. In the process through which the British governing class came to terms with its new commercial and industrial destiny, Gladstone was a vital agent.

Forged by an education essentially pre-industrial, Gladstone mirrored his times in adapting politically, religiously, and socially to new circumstances. 'He'll shape his old course in a country new' (*King Lear*) was the motto he placed on the cover of his 1865 *Speeches and Addresses*, and it fairly describes what came to be his intentions and his actions. A radical conservatism, which fused at times with an advanced liberalism, was Gladstone's method. It was a method which deeply perplexed Conservatives, and often disappointed Liberals. For the former, it was almost always too much, too soon; for the latter, it was sometimes too little, too late. But it came to give Gladstone a curious position of great power in the centre of British politics, the power of surprise, of resource, of stability, and of an appeal, after the 1830s, that history and time were on his side.

Allied to this was an intuitive appreciation of the requirements and possibilities of modern politics, of the availability to the politician of a whole new forum of public debate made possible by the development of the public meeting and the national exchange of debate fostered by an integrated London and provincial press. In this process of directly addressing the people in great meetings, Gladstone confronted the popular politics of his day, but he also to an extent directed and controlled them. He was both their creature and creator.

In all this, the fixed point for Gladstone was his Christian faith, the preservation of the Church and the triumph of Christian values. Christianity gave Gladstone a powerful sense of his destiny, both in general and in particular situations. A man of intense temper and sexuality, he used his Christianity to maintain self-control. He also was required by it to be truthful. Truthfulness in representative government is never an easy business: as he wrote in 1896 in almost the last entry of his lifelong journal, 'It is so easy to write, but to write honestly nearly impossible.' Gladstone tried to meet the problem of honesty in public life first, by not telling untruths, and, second, by living for the record. Nobody has more assiduously compiled materials for the benefit of history, including the careful preservation of a private journal intended to show its author to be 'the chief of sinners'. Gladstone had high standards and expectations of himself, and so have had historians, always eager for a slip or an inconsistency. On the whole, he has proved an awkward fellow to catch out. 'Terrible in the rebound' was Lord Aberdeen's comment on his *protégé*, and, like contemporaries, historians have often found the same.

As a chief representative of the Victorian age, Gladstone's career displays the strengths and weaknesses of a liberal democracy at the height of its self-confidence. The powerful individualism, the executive competence, the capacity for a sense of history, a feel for 'ripeness' and for national development; against these may be balanced, for all the introspection, a curious lack of self-awareness.

This book describes Gladstone's attempts to explain and to justify his age and its place in history to himself and to his contemporaries; his efforts to help it to prune and to consolidate, to adapt and to reform itself politically, administratively, ecclesiastically, and intellectually; and his strivings to harness his will and his passions to the service of God.

CHAPTER I

Liverpool, Eton, and Oxford

Family and Fortune—An Evangelical Family—An Eton Boy—
A House Man

My [twenty-first] birthday. Surely to me a day of pain in as far as it was a day of reflection: to others perhaps (God bless them) of joy. As to *idleness* one of my great foes, there has been *less* of it thank God during the past year: but the only redeeming portion was the Long Vacation—and then it was owing to my close contact with industrious persons.

This has been my Debating Society year: now I fancy done with. Politics are fascinating to me. perhaps too fascinating. . . .

I have thank God enjoyed much in Society. But as to real progress in religion: that is in the practical part of religion—the subjugation of the will & affections—I see no progress: though I may have clearer notions perhaps: which if so increase guilt.—

May God keep me during the coming year & from day to day may I approach more a practical belief that *he* is my friend, I mine enemy.

Family and Fortune

The earliest document in the Gladstone family papers is dated 1550; none the less, John Gladstone, the Prime Minister's father, was a self-made man. His career epitomized the entrepreneurial drive which made British commerce the dominant influence in world trade in the first half of the nineteenth century. His father, Thomas Gladstones, was a middle-ranking corn dealer in Edinburgh and Leith, the family having moved to the capital from the village of Biggar in the Scottish Borders. John Gladstone, born in Leith in 1764, soon saw the limitations of east coast trade, and moved west. Ignoring the difficulties of the French and American wars, and indeed turning those difficulties to advantage by surefooted anticipation of shortages, he assembled a huge fortune, travelling widely in North America and the Baltic in pursuit of purchases. On the basis of the transatlantic grain trade, which fed the rapidly growing population of Lancashire, and of diversification into property, shipping and West Indian sugar, cotton and slavery, his fortune rose from about £15,900 in 1795, to £40,700 in 1799, £333,600 in 1820, £502,550 in 1828.[1] In 1860 Samuel Smiles told William Gladstone, then Chancellor of the Exchequer, that he hoped to write John Gladstone's biography. Though William encouraged Smiles, nothing came of the proposal because of a dispute within the Gladstone family about it.² This was unfortunate, for John Gladstone was a classic Smilesian character, mixing duty, probity, and religion with materialism, initiative, and a strong drive for worldly success.

Of Lowland Scottish Presbyterian stock, John Gladstone made his way from Leith to Liverpool, from Whig to Tory, and from the Church of Scotland to the Church of England, dropping the 's' at the end of his name on the way. By his second marriage, to Anne Mackenzie Robertson—his first wife, Jane, died childless in 1798—he linked himself with a minor line of Highland gentry, William Gladstone recalling his grandmother as 'stoutly Episcopalian and Jacobite'.³ He began to translate his money into social prestige through land, buying the Seaforth estate by Sefton then in the countryside outside Liverpool, and, in 1830, when his six children's education was nearing completion, buying the house and estate of Fasque, in the Mearns between Aberdeen and Montrose on the east coast of Scotland. In 1846, on the fall of the Peel government, he became Sir John Gladstone, baronet, of Fasque and Balfour. Sir Thomas Gladstone, the Prime Minister's elder brother, inherited the title and the estate of Fasque, but took no significant part in commerce.

John Gladstone also attempted to use his money politically, sitting in the Commons from 1818 to 1827 for a series of corrupt boroughs: Lancaster from 1818–20, Woodstock 1820–6 (bought cheaply from the Duke of Marlborough), Berwick-on-Tweed 1826–7 (unseated on petition). He was, therefore, one of those representatives of the new commercial class in the north of England who paid their way into the unreformed House of Commons. He was the sort of man who, in the eyes of the Canningites—the following of George Canning, Foreign Secretary and MP for Liverpool—demonstrated that the Constitution needed no reform since it was capable of representing new interests in an old system, or, alternatively, the sort of man who in the eyes of the ultra-Tories—the extreme defenders of the Protestant constitution—represented the corruption of the constitution by money. John Gladstone had thrived in unreformed Britain. His desire for continuing social stability, his distrust of speculative thought, and his respect for established religion, made him a natural supporter of the administrations of Lord Liverpool in the 1820s, and especially of the style of modest fiscal and administrative reform pursued by Canning, Huskisson, and Peel which justified by works the anomalies of the British representative system.

Thus, in brief, was forged the family context in which the fifth child, and fourth son, William Ewart Gladstone, was raised. His brothers and sisters were of very varied character. Anne, the first child, born in 1802, was an invalid like her mother and died unmarried at the age of 26. Her important religious influence on her brother will be discussed later. Tom, the oldest of the boys, tried hard to carry the burden of expectation which his father placed upon him, and preceded William at Eton and Christ Church, Oxford. He lacked the ability to capitalize on his advantages and never rose beyond the level of a Tory backbench MP. Robertson, born in 1805, was taken from Eton by his father and moved into the family business. A huge fat man when in his prime, he was for most of his life an able businessman, active in radical Liverpool politics, becoming Mayor of Liverpool and President of the Financial Reform Association before disintegrating mentally in his later years. John Neilson, the third son, refused to accept his father's wishes and with great character followed the naval career on which he was determined. He was for a time a Conservative MP and ended as High Sheriff for Wiltshire, the county in which he settled. Next came William Ewart, named from John Gladstone's political friend in Liverpool (the families quarrelled over the Ewarts' increasing radicalism in the 1831 election[4]), and last, Helen Jane, born in 1814. Like her sister and mother she was as a child often ill, but lived till 1880. A woman of high intelligence, she enjoyed a period of considerable intimacy with her brother William in the late 1820s and early 1830s. Her subsequent tragic life will punctuate the chapters of this book.

This was, then, a family of character, variety, and strong personalities. It was clearly upwardly-mobile and politically ambitious, but its huge correspondence—for all the members wrote regularly to each other, sometimes even when in the same house—is characterized by gentility. The code of the English gentleman—the assumptions of honour, of duty, of charity, and of an easy acceptance of a social superiority which it would be bad manners to assert—was quickly assimilated by the male Gladstone children; the corresponding role of the pure but supine woman was exemplified by the mother and Anne, but not by Helen Jane, whose life was to be a series of rebellions.

Money, clearly, was never a problem. In the dangerous world of speculation, slumps, and gluts which characterized Regency Britain, John Gladstone moved adroitly and successfully. The bankruptcies which so shook the families of John Henry Newman and Henry Edward Manning, unsettling their confidence in the social arrangements of English society, did not disturb the Gladstones, and as a young man William Gladstone never had to consider money seriously. There was, however, a certain social uncertainty about the Gladstone household. In Britain money tempered by gentility could buy status, and in John Gladstone's case it certainly did, but it could not altogether buy recognition. In most obvious senses the career of John Gladstone represented a classic demonstration of the openness of the British ruling élite. But there was, none the less, a certain restlessness about his position, compounded by the chronic illnesses of his wife and daughters, which from the mid-1820s prevented entertaining and required frequent peregrinations to watering-places: a rather isolated residence in Leamington Spa was not really a fitting reward for a merchant prince. His political disappointments, and especially his inability to gain selection as Canning's running-mate in the two-member constituency of Liverpool, rankled personally, and the move to the then remote estate at Fasque constituted an exile from the mainstream of British public life from which John Gladstone never returned, active though he remained in correspondence to the press, in commerce, and in local affairs.

An Evangelical Family

When William Ewart Gladstone was born on 29 December 1809 in Rodney Street, Liverpool, his father was forty-six and his mother thirty-eight. The atmosphere of the home was moderately Evangelical, with the Evangelicals' strong emphasis on the reading of the Bible and on personal duty, family obligation, sin and atonement. Religion brought joy to the Gladstone women, but it weighed heavily upon the men, and especially upon William. William's mother believed that he had been 'truly converted to God' when he was about ten.[5] But there is little direct evidence of this: certainly it was not a vivid transformation such as that experienced by J. H. Newman, who kept the anniversary of his conversion to the end of his life. Indeed, as we shall see, the question of conversion came to preoccupy William in his student days.

Strong paternalism was a characteristic of evangelical families, and in the Gladstones' case this was reinforced by the contrast of the rude vigour of the tall, dark-suited husband with the sickliness of the mother and her elder daughter. An innate respect for male authority, and for the institutions that reflected it, was thus inherent in both a moral and a physical sense in William Gladstone's upbringing. The physical helplessness of the two Anne Gladstones made a permanent impression on the young William, who throughout his life saw women essentially as potentially noble creatures to be helped and lifted to a moral state as pure as that of his mother and his elder sister. When his mother died in 1835, Gladstone wrote of her:

Sin was the object of her hatred—and she can now sin no more. Sin is the cause of all the sorrow in the world: she can now no more add to the sin nor to the sorrow.... She departed in seraphic peace, like the gentleness of her own disposition.... She was eminent in the discharge of every duty: she sorrowed for sin: she trusted in the atonement of Christ. But this was not all: these elementary sentiments of religion were matured in her by the power of God, and she was made partaker of the nature and very life of the Redeemer, and her will conformed to his. Therefore, being, like Him, perfected through suffering, she had no new thing to learn, no fresh character to assume, upon translation to the world of spirits.... Two only have been taken from our family: and both are angels in heaven.[6]

He annually marked the birthday of the other 'angel in heaven', his sister Anne, who was also his godmother, remembering it as a special day of religious observance, rather in the manner that Newman remembered his experience of conversion. For Gladstone, the memory of his sister's 'ascendancy to Heaven' served almost as a vicarious conversion. His mother and sister, in fact, possessed that Evangelical religious assurance, repose, and sense of grace which Gladstone never throughout his life gained. For him, awareness of sin—certainly one of the Evangelical attributes—was always uppermost, never its atoning opposite. His mother and his sister represented to him, therefore, a quality of holiness which both inspired him and intensified his sense of inadequacy. Despite this, however, his extensive early writings on religion do not show any particular personal awareness or fear of hell of the sort exemplified for his generation by Thomas Chalmers, the Scottish presbyterian Evangelical and a family friend.

Another aspect of the Evangelical home was its very powerful emphasis on retribution for particular actions—the lazy moment, the naughty thought, the small, cheating trick—each must be marked, atoned for, and the appropriate lesson for the future learned. And not only this: such sins must inwardly be continually sought for, searched out, even when perhaps they were non-existent. This sense of permanent accountability, this searching oneself for sin, this acute awareness of God's immanence in watching for a chance for retribution, became a deep, perhaps the most profound, element in Gladstone's character. This inward searching, leading to a developed awareness of sin, led many Evangelicals to keep journals, and it was in this spirit that William Gladstone continued the journal which he began at Eton in 1824 or 1825—the date of the first surviving entry is 16 July 1825—as a simple, very brief record of work and events. He maintained it daily in over 25,000 entries with only the odd break until almost the end of his life. William Wilberforce, the archetypal lay Evangelical, noted of his own journal: 'I put these things down, that I may fix and ascertain, and re-consider my own corruptions and the deceitful working of my mind and passions.' Similarly Gladstone wrote his to 'tell, amidst the recounting of numberless mercies, . . . a melancholy tale of my own inward life'.[7]

But if Evangelicalism was the dominant ethos in the Gladstone home, it was not the exclusive influence. Gladstone's mother's Episcopalian background naturally linked her once she had come to Liverpool to the Church of England, and William Gladstone was baptized an Anglican. Though the two churches built by the Gladstones increased the Evangelical presence in the Liverpool area from one to three, their membership of the Church of England linked them with various wider and differing traditions, and both the Anne Gladstones—and especially the daughter—were familiar with the 'standard divines of the English Church',[8] including Richard Hooker's *Ecclesiastical Polity*. More importantly, from the point of view of William

Gladstone's later development, his family's membership of the Church of England meant that their Evangelicalism was nurtured in the context of an episcopal form of church government, very different from the democratic presbyterianism of John Gladstone's youth. Evangelicals generally took a somewhat 'low' view of episcopacy and of the national and established role of the Church of England; none the less their continuing membership—a deliberate choice in that many Evangelicals left it—meant a self-conscious association with a national church whose bishops were appointed by the Prime Minister and whose governing body, as far as it had one, was the Crown in Parliament. Membership of the Church of England, for an Evangelical, represented an integrative political act as well as a set of religious beliefs.

Politics no doubt played a part of some importance in John Gladstone's Church of Englandism. Like the Wilberforce family, the young Gladstones were brought up in an atmosphere of close interest in national politics, politicians, and the commercial world. As William Gladstone later remembered, 'the Evangelical movement . . . in lay life . . . did not ally itself with literature, art and general cultivation; but it harmonized very well with the money-getting pursuits'. Accompanying his father on business expeditions, the young Gladstone gained a very early experience of British geography. Despite the difficulty of movement in the pre-railway age—he was almost always sick in the coach—by the time he was eleven William Gladstone not only knew Lancashire well, but had visited Dingwall, Edinburgh, Cambridge, and London. It was in Edinburgh that he heard, as he later recalled, the 'rattling of the windows when the guns were fired on some great occasion, probably the abdication of Napoleon'.[9]*

From the start, Gladstone was familiar with the great, and ready to argue with them. One of his earliest memories was, at the age of two, being taken into the dining-room of his father's house when George Canning was a guest. Dressed in a red frock, 'I was set up on one of the chairs, standing, and directed to say to the company: "Ladies and gentlemen". I am sorry to add that I remember showing in boyhood an uncivilised nature by contending that it ought to be "gentlemen and ladies"'.[10] As a boy in Liverpool he was acquainted with the great political figures of the town, especially those in Tory circles, and on several occasions the family spent the

---

* Gladstone had what he called an excellent 'local memory' (i.e. for places) and the fragments—extensively used by Morley and now printed in *The Prime Minister's Papers* series—which he wrote in the 1890s on his early life in preparation for an autobiography were, considering the length of time which had elapsed and the extraordinary range of his public activities, unusually accurate. Gladstone had the chronology of his career very accurately in his head and when recalling a political event in conversation or on paper he was rarely more than a week or so out. None the less, an accurate factual memory is not necessarily a completely reliable guide to opinion and these 'autobiographica', as Gladstone called them, must be used with caution, the more so as they so often quite closely *approximate* to what can be shown from other contemporary sources to have been his opinion as expressed at the time.

parliamentary sessions in London. John Gladstone intended that as many of his sons as possible should consolidate this acquaintance with the political world, and so he sent them to Eton and to Christ Church, Oxford; their education would thus be that of George Canning.

An Eton Boy

When sent to Eton in 1821, at the age of eleven (rather older than was the custom), William Gladstone brought with him a curious intellectual and emotional baggage: a mixture of worldly experience through his father and from his mother a degree of religious separateness which, as we have seen, was not as sternly Evangelical as it could have been but which none the less set him apart from other boys. This blend was to stand him in good stead as he met the world of affairs which Eton represented. Gladstone came to Eton with little in the way of learning. He had been taught at the rather carefree school run by William Rawson on the sands at Bootle on the Mersey. Rawson was a moderate Evangelical brought to the Liverpool area by John Gladstone on the advice of Charles Simeon, the famous Cambridge preacher. At his school, Gladstone 'shirked my work as much as I could. I went to Eton in 1821 after a pretty long spell in a very middling state of preparation, and wholly without any knowledge or other enthusiasm, unless it were a priggish love of argument which I had begun to develop.'[11] This lack of preparation was not any great disadvantage. The formal education at Eton was largely mechanical: Latin and Greek—but mainly Latin—grammar, translation, and construing. 'Gladstone *mi*.'—for his brother Tom, for whom he fagged, was already at the school—had, with his control of detail and his excellent memory, little difficulty in mastering the system. Such stimulation beyond the technical competence required for such exercises came from the weekly 'Verses', a composition in Latin on an original subject but with little advice or assistance. Gladstone kept his fair copies of many of these; they are largely uncorrected by the schoolmaster, but have a laconic 'Well' (or sometimes 'Very Well') written at the end in the master's hand.[12]

In addition to classics, some modern languages were taught, and Gladstone clearly benefited considerably from M. Berthomier, his French instructor, who introduced him to French drama and especially Molière, an unusual interest for the time (shared incidentally with Disraeli) and one which he maintained throughout his life. Though Gladstone at the end of his life stated that the 'system was without merit', on reflection he believed that 'in one point it was admirable. I mean its rigid, inflexible, and relentless accuracy . . . it has been my habit to say that at Eton in my day a boy might if he chose learn something, or might if he chose learn nothing, but that one thing he could not do, and that was to learn anything inaccurately.'[13]

John Gladstone had not sent his son to Eton to acquire proficiency in the hexameter. Attending Eton was a confirmation of the Gladstones' arrival in the upper echelon of British society and was also the means of penetration to its centre, the House of Commons, and the London professions. The curious structure of Eton, with its College and its Oppidans, its self-employed housemasters, its private tutors and its Dames, was a microcosm of the British ruling élite: at first glance a fairly clearly identifiable body of people, at second glance an extraordinarily complex organism with rules and conventions known fully only to those brought up within it, and only very rarely penetrated successfully from outside (as, for example, by Disraeli).* It was to be brought up in these ways of thinking, and to be part of the class that thought that way, that John Gladstone sent three of his sons (Tom, Robertson (briefly), and William) to Eton.

The absence of general education at the school assisted this process, if a boy had character and ability. Such boys made their own education, and William Gladstone quite quickly found a place among them. In 1825 he was elected to the Eton Society (also known as the 'Literati' and later as 'Pop'), founded in 1811 by Charles Fox Townshend to give the boys an organization in which intellectual discussion and debate could develop. The success of the society, after a poor period about 1820, meant that by Gladstone's day membership was one of the chief glittering prizes which the school had to offer and the blackballing election system—mirroring the London political clubs—was taken most seriously. The society was small, self-electing, and wholly independent of the masters. Former pupils of the school continued for a time to be members, and in Gladstone's day the membership included eight MPs.[14] It also included, unbeknown at the time to him, his future brother-in-law and his best man, Stephen Glynne and Francis Doyle. Members read papers for discussion, and debated motions on aesthetic and political topics; 'Our Society men are great politicians in a small way'.[15] A 'fifty year rule' excluded motions on contemporary politics, but this could be got around, Catholic Emancipation, for example, being debated in 1826 in the form of a motion on the right of the former Polish government to exclude Protestants from the civil service. As the political tension rose in the 1820s with the gradual disintegration of Liverpool's Tory Party, private debates, ancillary to the Society, became common, Catholic emancipation and political reform being naturally among the topics. The effect of the 'fifty year rule' was to encourage historical knowledge and an identification with the parties and factions of pre-industrial Britain, for many of the

---

* Eton's complex structure contrasted markedly with that of the reformed public schools later in the century where the emphasis was on a simple, authoritarian structure based on school and house prefects and with clear lines of demarcation of authority.

motions involving Britain were on Reformation or Civil War topics, the rest being mainly on classical issues. The terms in which these youths learned to discuss politics were therefore those of the Greek–Roman period and those of the making of the Protestant constitution and nation-state in what would now be called the early-modern period. The atmosphere within the Society was both friendly and competitive, with an especial emphasis on prowess of presentation of argument.

Gladstone formed two friendships of particular importance, as well as a wide circle of acquaintances many of which relationships he maintained by letter, despite political differences, until the death of the correspondent (for he outlived them all). James Milnes Gaskell was, Gladstone wrote at the time, 'a very clever fellow . . . [with] by far the most extensive political knowledge and intimate acquaintance with English history of any boy that I ever saw'; he recalled him seventy-two years later as 'that rare and most precious thing, an enthusiast'.[16] Gaskell's enthusiasm was for the minutiae of politics, the division lists, the journals, the details of the conventions: he 'inoculated us all with a love for politics'.[17] That mastery of the detail of debating procedures, so formidable a weapon throughout his career in the Commons, Gladstone learned with the enthusiastic Gaskell. For Gaskell, politics was a process justified in its own terms, an endless game in which knowing the rules was more important than winning. When Gladstone later referred to politics as being both a game and a high art,[18] he referred to a sport whose rules he had learnt very early.

The chief love of Gladstone's schooldays was Arthur Henry Hallam, son of the Whig historian and subject of Tennyson's great elegy, *In Memoriam*. This relationship with Arthur Hallam was certainly not the usual 'crush' developed between boarding-school boys living in close proximity, for Hallam was tutored by F. C. Hawtrey, while Gladstone's tutor was H. H. Knapp, and 'messing' (i.e. eating) between boys in different houses was most unusual.[19] None the less the relationship was intense, though not directly sexual, and prefigured several such relationships, with both sexes, in Gladstone's later life. It developed chiefly within the Eton Society where competition for affection as well as for superiority was often overt as well as covert. Hallam wrote to his sister in 1826: 'walking out a good deal, & running the changes on Rogers, Gladstone, Farr and Hanmer'.[20] What heartaches for the others lie buried in that simple phrase, 'running the changes'! It shows Hallam to have had a cool edge to his brilliant personality. Despite this, he certainly captivated Gladstone emotionally, though not intellectually, in the way we shall see Manning and James Hope doing in later years. Hallam was, like his father, a steadfast Whig: he put the case for political reform to Gladstone in a letter of astonishing maturity, but he did not convince him.[21] In 1829, when Hallam was at Cambridge with Tennyson and Gladstone was at Oxford, the latter noted a brief history of his relationship with Hallam:

The history of my connection with [Hallam] is as follows.
It began late in 1824, more at his seeking than mine.
It slackened soon: more on my account than his.
It recommenced in 1825, late, more at my seeking than his.
It ripened much from the early part of 1826 to the middle.
In the middle, [Farr?] *rather* took my place.
In the latter end [of 1826], it became closer & stronger than ever.
Through 1827, it flourished most happily, to my very great enjoyment.
Beginning of 1828, [Hallam] having been absent since he left Eton, it varied but very slightly.
Middle of 1828, [Hallam] returned, and thought me cold. (I did not increase my *rate* of letters as under the circumstances I ought to have done.)
Early in 1829, there was friendly expostulation (unconnected with the matter last alluded to) and affectionate reply.
Illness in [spring and summer of 1829].
At present, almost an uncertainty, very painful, whether I may call [Hallam] my friend or not.

Clearly, for Gladstone 1827 was the best year. In 1828, Gaskell and Hallam were both in Italy, and both fell in love with Anna Wintour. Gladstone indirectly came to know of the affair, but almost certainly not of the depth of the passion in both men.[22] How far this upset the delicate balance of his friendship with Hallam can probably not now be known. From Hallam, Gladstone not only gained a direct and intimate confrontation with Whig arguments, but also encouragement towards a powerful aesthetic sense, for it was in aesthetics and Italian literature that Hallam's real interests came to lie; and he had little interest or ability in the feats of memory required to produce accurate Greek and Latin verse and prose.[23] Gladstone brought to Hallam, clearly a rather sophisticated youth, a quality of innocence blended with intellect which Hallam, writing in May 1829 when the height of the friendship's intensity had passed, captured in a powerful line:

... the father of good
On my early spring one perfect gem bestowed.[24]

The Eton Society also gave the stimulus to the *Eton Miscellany*, jointly edited by Gladstone as 'Bartholomew Bouverie' and George Selwyn, later the tractarian Bishop of New Zealand. Like most schoolboy journalism, there was a good deal of wrangling about late entries, and some of the result was rather precious. None the less, the various numbers, which were collected into a volume, have a natural authority about them. As with the contributors' correspondence, a reader coming across it unawares would probably not realize it was written by schoolboys.

In the debates with his friends, Gladstone on the whole took a Tory line, but, as in his Oxford days and in the early 1830s, his conservatism had some unusual elements to it. Predictably enough, he spoke for the Norman Conquest against Hallam, but he voted at first, somewhat indecisively, and perhaps reflecting his mother's influence, for the 'Stewarts' in the 1745 Rebellion, which most Liverpool Conservatives in the 1820s would have regarded as merely quixotic and irresponsible romanticism, wedded as they had become to the Hanoverian constitution. Further study and conversation led to his 'getting a new light on subject of Stuarts, 1745 &c.' He was undecided whether it could be said that the Whigs in the reign of Anne had deserved well of their country, and initial hostility and a vote against that greatest of the Whigs, Sir Robert Walpole, changed to a favourable vote, with the comment: 'there were surely considerable blots,—but nothing to *over*-balance, or to equal, the great merit of being the bulwark of the Protestant Succession—and his commercial measures—& (*in general*) his Pacific Policy'.[25]

These positions were not lightly taken. Though high-spirited, the members of the Eton Society were fully aware of their political destinies, and flippancy in debate was severely disapproved of, by none more so than Gladstone, later remembered by Francis Doyle in his poem 'The Poetaster's plea: a familiar epistle to W. E. Gladstone, Esq., M.P.':

> To one I turn—the monarch of debate,
> President Minos of our little state,
> Who, when we met to give the world the law
> About Confucius, Caesar or Jack Straw,
> Saw with grave face the unremitting flow
> Of puffs and jellies from the shop below;
> At the right moment called us to forsake
> Intrusive fruit, and unattending cake;
> And if unheeded, on the stroke of four,
> With rigid hand closed the still-opening door.[26]

'To give the world the law' was a fair description of the Eton Society's members' ambition and expectation. They had an innate awareness of their natural membership of 'the clerisy', the phrase coined at this time by Coleridge to describe what would now in Gramsci's terminology be called the hegemonic class.

One law much in contention because of its abolition's potential effect on the Anglican nature of that clerisy—indeed its abolition in 1829 was the stimulant to Coleridge's definition—was the law excluding Roman Catholics from full British citizenship, and especially from holding public office. Gladstone seems to have been consistently in favour of Catholic Emancipation, in contrast with many Tories, but in harmony with his father and George Canning. In 1827 he noted: 'Received the horrid news of the defeat of [Burdett's motion in the Commons on] the Catholics. I trust it is all for the best; but the prospect is awful.'[27] This last phrase suggests it was the prospect of disorder which concerned William Gladstone, at this stage following his father in seeing 'emancipation' in the light of prudence rather than of right.

Tory though Gladstone saw himself to be, his experience at Eton was essentially Whiggish, in the sense that it taught him to see society in terms of politics, and to see the history of Britain in terms of development and of the centrality to that development of constitutional politics rather narrowly defined. The framework of discussion, even for those in disagreement with aspects of it, was determined by the Whig view of history. For what was the constitution so steadfastly maintained by the Tories of the 1820s, but the Whig settlement of 1688? Ready to abandon the Tory settlement of the 1660s by repealing the Test and Corporation Acts and the acts restricting Roman Catholics, the Tories regathered to defend the parliamentary constitution of the late seventeenth and early eighteenth century Whigs. Catholic Emancipation passed shortly after Gladstone left Eton, and its passing opened a new political era, the reforming decade of the thirties in which the young Gladstone attempted to forge his Toryism into a doctrine.

We have seen the social and political influences of Eton on him: what of the intellectual and religious?

Gladstone read widely at school, ranging far outside the required texts. He began his life-long practice of noting all his reading (except newspapers) in his daily journal entry. He read much modern British history—Clarendon, Burnet, Coxe's *Walpole*, Tomline's *Pitt*—he read most of the plays of Shakespeare, and he read Scott. In this, perhaps, he built on an earlier enthusiasm for Ossian (in an early letter home from Eton he requested the sending on of his Ossian, and he continued to be interested in the controversy). For it was the Scottish works of Scott that attracted him as a schoolboy— *Waverley* (read for the second time when he was sixteen), *Old Mortality* ('in the first rank of Waverley Novels, me judice'), *Heart of Midlothian*, *Legend of Montrose*, *Rob Roy*, *Chronicles of the Canongate*, and *Tales of a Grandfather*. For the rest of his life Scott was to be 'a treat', not written about or analysed, but absorbed. Gladstone can hardly have been unaffected by the central theme of Scott's Scottish novels, how society progresses in an irreversible direction and how those individuals who fail to progress with it, while particularly attractive and fascinating, are ultimately quaint. Not to have met Scott before he died in 1832—there was a chance in Rome in April 1832 'but we could not find him out'—was one of the regrets of Gladstone's life.

Important parts of Gladstone's schoolboy reading were prompted by the topics chosen for debate in the Eton Society. Debating preparation launched him on Milton, Clarendon, and Hume. In each case he continued his reading after the context of the debate and its subsequent discussions had passed.

Gibbon was begun in November 1825, returned to for a debate in 1827, and then completed. Not surprisingly, Gladstone thought the 'style . . . beautiful, but much sneering at Christian religion, partially disguised',[28] but his general view of the work was more favourable than might have been expected from one of his background. He made one of his detailed 'Epitomes' (a digest of the argument written on long thin strips of paper). He found 'Gibbon's style diffuse; sometimes very beautiful, sometimes too highly ornamented'. He preferred David Hume's *History of England*, of which he also made an Epitome: 'Hume *me judice* a greater historian', and 'Finished Gibbon. Elegant and acute as he is, he seems to me not so clear, so able, nor so attractive as Hume: does not impress my mind so much.' This enthusiasm for Hume ('a delightful history—barring the religious principles'[29]) was important in conditioning Gladstone's youthful view of the lack of a correlation between liberty and democracy.

Gladstone discounted the scepticism of Gibbon and Hume without much difficulty. He read many other works at school which might have surprised his mother: 'read [on a Sunday] . . . a little Locke on Toleration, but found much Repetition, so began [his] Reasonableness of Christianity'.[30] The whole of his Eton experience built upon the outward-looking aspects of his family's religion, but usually in a secular way. At Eton, Gladstone's religion was privately practised. He learned to observe his religion regardless of a largely indifferent surrounding, and without making a fuss. This was a valuable lesson. Throughout his life he was to be able to exist in close and happy relationship in male society with those—like Lord Granville— who shared none of his religiosity. He does not seem to have behaved in the school or in the Eton Society as in any way an overt Evangelical; he did not try to convert his friends, and his letters to them attempt to match the jocular tone of Hallam and Gaskell. He sometimes argued about religion with them ('stiff arguments with Hallam, as usual on Sundays, about Articles, Creeds &c.') but this was probably on their legal and political role, rather than as questions of faith. In such discussions he took a Cavalier's view of the seventeenth century church, defending Charles I for 'saving our religion', and relying on the authority of Clarendon's *History of the Rebellion*: 'it is astonishing how your Cavalier spirit runs away with you' complained the strongly Parliamentarian Hallam.[31]

Privately, however, in the manner of his family, Gladstone read the Bible daily and extensively on Sundays, sometimes in Greek; in his last year he read through the Gospels using the High-Church commentary by D'Oyly and Mant.[32] He was also an avid sermon-reader. Some of his choices—the sermons of the moderate Evangelical J. B. Sumner and the sermons and discourses of Thomas Chalmers, the Scottish Evangelical and a family friend—were predictable. But he also made a prolonged study of the sermons of the moderate Presbyterian Hugh Blair, a prominent figure in the Scottish Enlightenment and a friend of Adam Smith and David Hume. Gladstone found him, eventually, 'more flowery than solid', hardly a strong reaction to the Enlightenment.[33] This, and his voluntary reading of William Paley's *Evidences of Christianity* with its argument from Design, suggests, when taken together with Mant's commentary, a considerable eclecticism and a curiosity to move well beyond the simplicities of Biblical evangelicalism, together with an embryonic High-Churchmanship as yet historical in form and only partially integrated into his developing religious persona.

To describe Gladstone at Eton simply as an Evangelical would therefore be at the least an over-simplification. The most surprising item in his religious studies at Eton is his Sunday reading of 'the Roman Catholic Prayer Book' in 1826:[34] in the Evangelical world of Gladstone's upbringing, knowledge of and interest in the details of the bishop of Rome's church was regarded as little short of Satanism.

In his last year at Eton, after a brief preparation, Gladstone was confirmed 'according to the apostolical rite preserved in the Church of England',[35] a turn of phrase pointing quite clearly to the developments of the 1830s. As in most Anglican churches in the 1820s, the Sacrament was not often celebrated at Eton, but by the end of the year Gladstone had communicated six times.

He left Eton at the end of 1827, a noted figure among a notable coterie, 'no ordinary individual', as Milnes Gaskell observed.[36] His time there was happy: 'if any thing mortal is sweet, my Eton years, excepting anxieties at home, have been so!'[37] His experience there had been enlarging, had taught him self-reliance socially and intellectually, and had, as John Gladstone had intended, associated him with the mainstream of English public life. His time there had also been fun: sculling on the river with Hallam, playing cricket, drinking with the Salt Hill Club which 'went up to Salt Hill to bully the fat waiter, eat toasted cheese, and drink egg-wine'; within the club Gladstone went by the name of 'Mr. Tipple'.[38] In the habit of English boarding-school former pupils, Gladstone became nostalgic about Eton, despite its pedagogic inadequacies.

A House Man

John Gladstone next sent his son to Christ Church—Aedes Christi, the 'House'—the dominant college, politically, intellectually, and socially, of the University of Oxford.* Under Cyril Jackson, the great reforming Dean who retired in 1809 but whose nominees still ran the college, Christ Church had since the late eighteenth century become the college most linked to the world of affairs. Jackson had deliberately and successfully made Christ Church a forerunner of the French *écoles*, a college intimately linked with

---

* This step had been planned at least as early as 1824, when the expectation was that William Gladstone would take his degree, then study law in London prior to entering political life.[39]

politics and administration, with the explicit purpose of creating a governing élite of the highest quality. It was under the influence of Jackson and Christ Church that the highly competitive system of examination by classes had been introduced in a series of Statutes beginning in 1800. The college still had a rowdy element for, as is often the case with educational reform, the peer group's standards were slow to adapt to change, and there were still those who were not 'reading' men (i.e. did not intend to take an honours degree). It was, no doubt, some of these undergraduates who entered Gladstone's room on 23 March 1830 and beat him up. None the less, in so far as a large Oxford college could at that time be a centre of intellectual endeavour, Christ Church was. When Gladstone took the 'Schools' in December 1831 (the examination for honours), of the ten First Classes awarded, five went to Christ Church men. Jackson's move from Whiggery into Toryism mirrored the tendency of many of the propertied class in the French Revolutionary years and though the college still had its Whigs the dominant ethos was that of Lord Liverpool's Toryism, exemplified by the most noted of the college's *alumni*, Liverpool himself, George Canning, and Robert Peel. These men reflected an emphasis on 'practicability', administrative reform and the linking of the aristocracy with commerce and manufacturing.

The college had a certain grand reserve which characterized the inmates as well as the buildings:

The etiquette of introduction is here as strict as in general society, or even more so, I think; which seems to have something absurd in it: though when it is considered how great an advantage it is to be kept *free*, it seems on the whole, to me at least, right. It is, I think, one of the greatest advantages attending a large college like Christ Church, that you are not under obligation to any acquaintance with a person merely because he belongs to the same establishment. In a small one, each individual is much more thrown into contact with every one of the rest: and of course it must be very unpleasant & injurious in many cases to be thus obliged either to put up with indifferent associates at least those who are not to one's mind or to give offence by avoiding their company. There are people in Oxford, in small colleges, who are much abused, because they *cannot* enter into the society of & the same course of life with, those around them. Here, each individual is, more or less, insignificant in regard to the mass. . . .[40]

It was, in fact, the sort of college which required undergraduates to act as if they were already in the metropolitan polite society for which so many of them were destined.

The education provided in Christ Church was not significantly different from that of Eton, but it was better done. Jackson had reformed the examination system of the University, introducing a strongly competitive classified hierarchy of classes (from 'First' to 'Fifth', i.e. the Pass School), into which each undergraduate was placed if he was to take a degree (a considerable number in the University as a whole did not, but most Christ Church men did). On the other hand, Jackson had not strenuously sought to reform the syllabus. Changes introduced, particularly under the influence of R. D. Hampden and 'the Noetics', at Easter, 1831, opened the syllabus a little more to recent writing, but these were made too late to affect Gladstone's undergraduate studies. Moreover, though Oxford was open to talent, it was not open to non-Anglicans: unlike Cambridge, all undergraduates had to subscribe to the Thirty Nine Articles at the time of matriculation, as Gladstone did on 23 January 1828: 'matriculated, taking the oaths, & subscribing to the Articles & Statutes'. Although the English governing class avoided becoming a caste in the French mode, the restriction of the Articles was pushing Oxford towards becoming one in education. The University faced the question, could it be both national and Anglican? It never itself succeeded in providing an answer. Eventually, Gladstone himself reluctantly cut the knot, repealing the 'Tests' in 1871.

A classical education with some compulsory theology, and with mathematics as an afterthought (for under the recent reforms the mathematics and physics examination could only be taken as a postscript to Literae Humaniores), was thus thought to be the best training for the Anglican clerisy. To the many criticisms which came from utilitarians on the one hand and some theologians on the other, arguing either that a classical education was of little value to an increasingly commercially-oriented society or that the Anglican priesthood (easily the largest professional destination of Oxford graduates) required a much more specifically theological training, Gladstone responded vigorously shortly after leaving the University:

It will be attempted to prove that one and all of these objections are futile: that there is no fair presumptive argument for change in our educational systems, as regards their fundamental principles, from the changes which have taken place in military tactics, in popular science, in manufacture ... the errors of a pagan are not only not more, but are far less likely to entrap and mislead us, than those of that mass of modern writers, who bear the badge, and profess the principles of Christianity, while their real principles rise no higher than the level of the common opinions of society ... not only do the classics quicken our views of Christianity by the force of contrast, and enlarge our knowledge of human nature by augmenting the stock of experimental facts whence our inductions are to be drawn: but further, that they are the best school for a study of human nature.

As Newman wrote in his Anglican days: 'put faith first and knowledge second, and Aristotle changes into Butler'.[41]

Gladstone was thus a product and a defender of liberal education in its purest form. But in contrast to the usual argument for a liberal education, that it encourages individual development and safeguards a pluralistic system of values, Gladstone believed that it would reinforce orthodox Anglican Christianity.

The deficiencies of his Eton education, especially in Mathematics, had been to some extent compensated by a rather unsatisfactory interim spell with a crammer, the Revd J. M. Turner of Wilmslow, another moderate Evangelical.[42] For most of his time at Christ Church, Gladstone worked hard, but not very hard:* he did not have to, until a spurt in his last year. Then he worked very hard indeed. His obvious ability was marked by his elevation by Dean Smith to a Studentship of the College in 1829. The only set-backs of his academic career were his failure to win the Dean Ireland Scholarship for which he entered in 1830 and 1831 (coached by Charles Wordsworth), the Craven in 1830 (being defeated on each occasion by a member of the Shrewsbury School coterie of textual analysts), and his entry 'Tyre' for the latin verse prize was unsuccessful; however, his memory in old age that he had entered for the Newdigate Poetry Prize was erroneous.

Milnes Gaskell noted 'He is among the very few who are thought sure of his class',[43] and the expected Double First (in Literae Humaniores and Mathematics and Physics) was obtained in December 1831,† despite alarms about the Mathematics, which a year earlier his father had agreed he need not offer, and despite a substantial amount of time in the summer term before the examinations being spent in organizing the Oxford petition against the Reform Bill and writing a long pamphlet (never published) opposing it. Naturally, such an achievement was accompanied by nervous strain: one Oxford School in a month is enough for most undergraduates! But arduous though Gladstone found the ordeal, he kept control, helped by his friends and some sedatives. It was a performance to be repeated many times in his life: for the work of assembling the budget and presenting it to the Commons, the concentrated effort of his oral examination before R. D. Hampden in the

---

* His formal timetable, undated but probably in 1829, may be of interest:[44]

Sunday	Church
	Divinity Lect I (6pm)
Monday	Mathematics 11
	Evening Lecture 7
Tuesday	Thucydides 11
	Romans in Second Century 12
Wednesday	Mathematics 11
	Evening Lecture 7
Thursday	Thucydides 11
	Romans in Second Century 12
Friday	Mathematics 11
	Juvenal 12
Saturday	Romans in Second Century 12
	Hall 2

† At that time, an undergraduate could offer himself for examination, with very little notice, when he felt ready, the examinations being provided several times a year.

Schools was—with many friends and others present—a good training. Gladstone found the preparation valuable:

Term is now approaching, and the critical time too. Taking into consideration *together* the amount of mental labour and of physical trial, and the anxiety arising from uncertainty of results, it is a sort of thing which ought not I think to come more than once in one's life, though for once it is very well, and the benefits certainly, as I think, exceedingly great: I doubt whether the intellect of the nineteenth century will ever set up a system of education more fundamentally sound.[45]

Years later, he disputed the value of such examinations with John Ruskin, who a decade after Gladstone had broken down during his preparation at Christ Church and could not take the honours examination: 'Gladstone gave, as a strong argument, *pro* the value of the sudden strain and effort, the vast concentration of mind, the hasty calling into play of all the intellectual powers, as a training for political life'.[46]

The set books a student reads, if taught properly as texts and not via commentaries,* stay with him or her throughout life: they have a peculiar grounding quality which is unequalled by later reading. This was certainly the case with Gladstone's undergraduate studies. The set books at Oxford were prescribed under the general rubric of 'a sufficient acquaintance with the Greek and Latin language and ancient history … and Moral and Political Science, as derived from the ancient Greek and Roman authors, and illustrated, if need be, from modern authors.' They introduced him, amongst others, to Homer, Plato's *Phaedo*, Aristotle's *Ethics* and *Rhetoric*, Joseph Butler's *Analogy* and Thucydides' *History* (partly studied via Thomas Hobbes's 'Summary'): this last may be a clue, because of these, only Thucydides did not become a lifelong influence.† These and other books were exhaustively studied.

Gladstone's method of learning was, as at Eton, the detailed Epitome, and the way he made these Epitomes shows that he learned his set books while making a direct relationship between them and his own times. For example, his Epitome of Aristotle's *Rhetoric* is written on the right-hand side of the page; on the left are given examples from contemporary Parliamentary speeches by such as Canning, Peel, and Palmerston to illustrate the Aristotelian categories.[47] Of course, the full significance of these works was not apparent to him at the age of 21, when he took the Schools, but their categories were his instinctive points of reference for the rest of his life.

* It is interesting that on this ground Gladstone disapproved even of the introduction—after his time—of the aid of Liddell and Scott's *Greek Lexicon*: 'I had to make my own Homeric Lexicon, and the labour did me good.'[48]

† In the course of the Literae Humaniores examination—oral and written—Gladstone recorded being examined in Rhetoric, Ethics, Butler's *Analogy*, Plato's *Phaedo*, Homer's *Iliad* and *Odyssey*, Virgil, Persius, Aristophanes, Herodotus, Thucydides; he was prepared for, but was not examined in, Hellenics, Livy, Polybius, Select Orations, Horace, Juvenal, Aeschylus, Sophocles; he added 'I fear that unless they alter this, no one will get up his books' (17 Nov. 31).

It will be noted that Gladstone's set books offered him a number of models of how the world should work or had worked, but none of how it actually did work. Everything was by analogy and inference: parallels and analyses of the modern world were drawn by comparisons with the working of human nature and institutions in the ancient. Butler's *Analogy*, which itself of course reinforced this method of thinking by comparison, was the only set book for Literae Humaniores written after the first century.

The ways of thinking offered to the undergraduate were thus all preindustrial, and prior to that body of writing on political economy which by the 1820s was well-established and considerable. None of the Oxford teaching dealt with political economy except through Aristotle, an author profoundly hostile to the division of labour both as a fact and as a means of social organization (except in the crude division between citizens, women, and slaves). Gladstone had thus no awareness of the Smithian revolution in political and economic thought which was already prescribed reading in the Scottish universities. There was no objection in itself to secular authors, for he was taught secular, classical authors as a contrast to Christianity, but the extensive debate as to whether Christianity and political economy were compatible passed him by. The laws of the market, the division of labour and the consequent concept of a world free trade market were to dominate the politics and intellectual life of Gladstone's century, but he finished his university studies with nothing more than a third-hand Malthusianism.

Though Gladstone's formal education at Oxford was much more rewarding than that of Eton, a good deal of the value of his time there sprang from what were really extensions of the Eton Society: the university Debating Society (which soon became the Oxford Union) and the Essay Club which he and others founded in Christ Church in October 1829. The intention of the founders of the Essay Club was to provide an Oxford equivalent of the Cambridge Apostles, of which Hallam was a member, and which gave Gladstone the idea of the Club.[49] It often met in his rooms in Canterbury, the small, 'very *fashionable*'[50] quadrangle—then a new building—built with money from Richard Robinson, late Archbishop of Armagh, and the Club became known by his initials, the WEG.* The club does not long seem to have survived his time at Oxford. Certainly the aim of an elitist, intercollegiate, private but notorious intellectual club, which would be self-perpetuating, was not achieved. In the Union, a mirror of

* The names of the members give an impression of Gladstone's Oxford circle; original members were: T. D. and A. H. D. Acland, J. Anstice, F. and O. B. Cole, F. H. Doyle, J. Milnes Gaskell, Gladstone, Benjamin Harrison, J. T. Leader, H. Moncrieff, Frederic Rogers later Lord Blachford, H. Seymer, E. H. Grimston; members joining later, Lord Abercorn, I. and J. Bruce, T. Egerton, H. G. Liddell, Lord Lincoln, H. Lushington, F. D. Maurice, N. Oxnam, C. Thornton, H. H. Vaughan, C. Marriott. The last recorded meeting was the 56th, in June 1832, with H. G. Liddell as secretary (Add MS 44804).

Parliament of which Gladstone became President for 1830, the same enthusiasm for political conventions as had dominated the Eton Society trained its active members for the debates in the Commons; it differed from the Eton Society in being generally open to membership and in being able to debate contemporary politics.

In these contexts Gladstone continued old friendships with Etonians, but made no burning new ones. He enlarged his circle of friends, naturally, but his contacts with his contemporaries—as varied as Lord Lincoln, F. D. Maurice, the Acland brothers, Sidney Herbert, Robert Phillimore, Walter Kerr Hamilton, Henry Manning—were amicable but not intense, though a number of them became so in later years. Intimacy was encouraged amongst those who regularly received Communion (in addition to the chapel-going which was compulsory for all undergraduates). This group was, Gladstone felt, deplorably small. He noted on 1 November 1829: 'Sacrament. Drake, Anstice, [Benjamin] Harrison, Ld Grimston & his brother, the two Aclands, [Martin] Tupper—& perhaps the servitor—I did not observe'; and again on 6 December 1829: 'Sacrament: as cold and unprepared as usual. Ld Grimston & his brother, Acland jun., Tupper, Anstice, [Penry] Williams(sen) & myself.' Several of these were members of the WEG. Gladstone felt a special bond with them, nurtured by the intensity common in an undergraduate group which feels itself besieged—as Gladstone certainly did by the general want of religious fervour which he identified as characteristic of the Oxford of his time. Tupper, later the author of the best-selling *Proverbial Philosophy*, was not a member of the WEG, but, despite finding him in later years rather tedious, Gladstone kept up with him even when he had fallen on hard times, sometimes giving him small 'loans' without expectation of repayment and eventually, in 1873, securing him a Civil List pension.

Of this group, Joseph Anstice and the Acland brothers were the closest to him. Anstice and Gladstone, together with Walter Kerr Hamilton, spent some time in the summer of 1830 at Cuddesdon, near Oxford, on a reading party supervised by A. P. Saunders. All three of these undergraduates were brought up under an Evangelical influence and moved in the 1830s towards a Tractarian or High Church position. It was in conversation with Anstice on 3 August 1830, as they walked back to Cuddesdon from a visit to Oxford, that thoughts 'first spring up in my soul (obvious as they may appear to many) which may powerfully influence my destiny'. Gladstone shared with Anstice 'that awful subject which has lately engrossed my mind'—the possibility of becoming a clergyman, whose full context and consequence will be discussed shortly. Thomas and Arthur Acland joined with Gladstone in the 1840s to found 'the Engagement', a laymen's substitute for clericalism, as no doubt Anstice, who also settled in London, would have done had he not died in 1836. At that time Gladstone noted: 'Heard to my deep sorrow of Anstice's death on Monday. His friends—his young widow—the world can spare him ill: so at least says the flesh'; next day he wrote some verses in his memory.

Though Christ Church reflected the self-confidence of a ruling class which had successfully beaten the French and avoided revolution at home (Gladstone's first Union speech defended Pitt's repressive legislation of 1795, an 'exceedingly easy' subject[51]), the Oxford of Gladstone's day had an undertone of unease. The dynamic entrepreneurial spirit of the north of England was not reflected in the south. Certain sections of the University maintained the old Tory non-juring tradition and a number of the younger dons, though not part of that tradition, were, like J. H. Newman, vicar of the University Church of St Mary, tinged with cultural pessimism.

As the Church of England in the 1820s began to appreciate the sheer scale of the reforming problem that it faced if it hoped in any real way to retain its position as the national Church, Oxford, the chief nursery of its incumbents, was neither buoyant nor energetic. The University saw itself threatened at almost every level—intellectually, politically, ecclesiastically, and constitutionally—a threat supposedly confirmed by the disintegration of the Tory party, the passing of Catholic Emancipation, and the victory of the Whigs in the General Election of 1830. Those who tried to sponsor internally generated constitutional reform to broaden the basis of the University by abandoning the requirement to subscribe to the Articles got short shrift from their colleagues, and in a panic of spurious orthodoxy R. D. Hampden, Principal of St Mary's Hall, was censured for rationalism in 1836–7 when Melbourne appointed him Regius Professor of Divinity. But for Parliamentary business, Gladstone would have gone to Oxford to vote against Hampden, an intention he later regretted.[52]

For any thinking member of the Church of England, the 1830s was to be a decade of ferment as groups within the Church of England and the University sought to regain the initiative for Anglicanism. Gladstone was to find himself a leading protagonist of this movement. While contemplating his future in 1831, he told his father: 'One of the most formidable features in the present frightful circumstances of the country is, that we have so long been blessed, contrary to our deserts, with ease and peace & settled habits, that the upper classes in this country cannot bring themselves to believe they are about to be wrested from them, and in consequence sit with hands folded and look on while the Revolution is in progress, instead of making strenuous exertions.'[53] Gladstone never sat with hands folded. His strenuous exertions were to form an unusual episode in the history of British Conservatism.

CHAPTER II

Gladstonian Conservatism: from Oxford to Westminster

*A Young Conservative—A Serious Call?—The Tories' Rising Hope—
Towards a 'Science of Government': Plato and Aristotle—Church Principles—
Political Action—Wooed and Married and All—Money and Morality—
A Confident Conservative?*

The time and circumstances are difficult in which I have to steer my little boat: but the pole-star is clear. Reflection shows me that a political position is mainly valuable as instrumental for the good of the Church: & under this rule every question becomes one of detail only.[1]

A Young Conservative

Gladstone left Oxford University after dramatically carrying in the Union an amendment stiffening a motion opposing the Reform Bill. In the manner of his time, he then made an extended visit to the Continent, travelling widely in France and Italy. While he was abroad, the Duke of Newcastle, father of his Christ Church acquaintance Lord Lincoln—and at the latter's instigation, for he was much struck by Gladstone's anti-Reform speech—approached John Gladstone with the proposal that William should sit for Newark, a town in which the Duke had influence, though not an exclusive influence. It was a good example of that 'representation of mind, for the political training of youth upwards, of the most capable material of the country' through the pocket borough system, a system which for that reason Gladstone always defended.[2] Rather to his surprise, Gladstone found himself in the new post-Reform Commons.*

This political destination in retrospect seems natural, and it seemed natural at the time to Gladstone's friends and to his father. To see why it came to seem appropriate to him, we must look in more detail at certain aspects of his life in early manhood.

The young Gladstone was a Tory. If we look at his letters, writings, and speeches in the late 1820s and early 1830s, it is not difficult to portray him as

---

* He also guarded himself against subsequent failure by eating a few of the dinners required by Lincoln's Inn for joining the bar—the original plan he and his father had devised, and a common one for young men in his position.

a very hard-nosed Tory indeed. Like many of his generation, he shared, at certain moments and especially in 1831–2, a millenarian feeling that European society stood on the brink of revolution and moral disaster.

... The signs of the times are so appalling. ... Who can look abroad and say what the morrow shall bring forth, or hope that the dove of peace may find where to rest her foot amidst the deluge that is spreading ... society seems, by the promulgation of new, pestilent, impracticable theories, shaken to its very foundations ... this country is the main remaining home and hope of the cause of order throughout the world and even this last bulwark is assailed from within as well as from without.

The Reform Bill was 'the monstrous Bill which Ministers have introduced. It seems to me that they come nearer to deserving impeachment than any Ministry this country has had since the Revolution.'[3]

This view was not confined to the Reform Bill. In 1835, as the fall of the brief Peel government loomed, Gladstone told his mother: 'if we are beaten tonight as we are humanly certain to be, Sir Robert Peel will resign tomorrow, and with him will depart not indeed the last hope, for God still reigns, but (in my mind) the last ordinary, available, natural resource against the onset of Revolution'. Like others at the time, and especially those seeking a development from Evangelicalism, Gladstone was interested in Edward Irving's apocalyptic Catholic Apostolic Church, but when he visited it he found 'a scene pregnant with melancholy instruction', and Irving 'little short of madness'.[4] Gladstone's concern about what he saw as revolution was genuine but it was not cranky, that is, it was a concern conceived within the established categories of English political analysis. It is interesting that several of Gladstone's most urgent analyses—including that quoted above—were made in the context of a defence of rational exposition as against a flight to Pentecostalism by such as Bulteel and Irving as the means of responding to the crisis of the epoch. The change Gladstone feared was a constitutional, parliamentary revolution carried through by a Whig government; he showed no sign of alarm at the possibility of popular revolution. It was this constitutional revolution, a betrayal of its role by the aristocracy, that Gladstone worked to prevent.

As an undergraduate and as a young MP his votes, with the important exception of Catholic emancipation, were hostile to Whiggish and radical causes: political and church reform, abolition of Jewish civil disabilities, and abolition of hanging and flogging. His organization of the very strongly worded Oxford petition against reform and his newspaper articles written in 1833 in his early days as an MP suggest a simplistic stridency and a lack of qualification uncharacteristic of his later career. Gladstone later regarded this phase of his political life as one of 'folly', the problem being that he had not yet learned 'the great fact that liberty is a great and precious gift of God, and that human excellence cannot grow up in a nation without it'.[5] This recollection of 1892 is a little misleading. In certain small respects Gladstone was antilibertarian—for example, he several times tried to get the utilitarian *Westminster Review* struck off the Oxford Union's list of purchases—but he was never antilibertarian in a thoroughgoing way and, in the Protestant tradition, he always allowed for scruples of conscience. Rather, he held a view similar to that put forward as a main theme of David Hume's *History of England*, to which as we have seen he paid close attention as a schoolboy, the view that there was no necessary correlation between liberty and parliamentary institutions, and that liberty was more a judicial than a political concept. The exercise of such liberties was the fulfilment of an obligation rather than the exercise of a right. In the sense that Gladstone did not think in terms of rights, he was certainly fundamentally separated from the secular liberal tradition exemplified in his day by the *Westminster Review* and the Mills. Gladstone's view of society, rather, was of a social order whose gradations were related to each other by duties, and whose legitimacy derived from Providence. 'Man . . . comes into the world under a debt to society [and] to his parents', Gladstone told the WEG Club in answer to Moncrieff's support for the view that liberty was the end of government.[6]

The function of the British constitution was thus to permit the living of a Christian life: it had no other legitimacy, and certainly no natural rights inherent in it. Property, in Gladstone's view, had duties but no absolute rights. Its tenure was a convenient and on the whole beneficial social arrangement which could be changed. Society should be a community of believers, not of property-owners, and above all society existed for discipline. As he put it a little later:

The whole experience of life, all that befalls and belongs to him [mankind] in it, his domestic position, his social position, whatever is his, whatever lies around him, is one comprehensive system of discipline, devised by Divine Wisdom for the purpose of contributing to the accomplishment of that great design, the renovation of the nature of God in a race that had fallen away.

So Gladstone was a Tory. But we must take care not to make him too Tory.* He recognized that the political and ecclesiastical aspects of the constitution as it existed in the 1820s contained major 'anomalies' which neither could nor should be absolutely defended. Though influenced by Burke's organic analysis of the social and political order, he did not at that time take a Burkean view of 'prescriptive rights' and he did not, as many in Oxford increasingly did, argue that the Church had inviolate rights of a temporal kind unassailable by the State. He was, therefore, never an 'ultra', as the last ditchers in 1828–32 were called. Having consistently supported

* The terms Conservative and Tory were both used in the 1830s; Gladstone usually, but not always, used the former.

Catholic emancipation while a schoolboy, in Oxford he came out boldly against Wellington's administration when the duke declared against all Parliamentary reform at the end of 1830. The evening he was elected president of the Oxford Union, 11 November 1830, he moved and carried by one vote a motion of no confidence in the duke's government. He accepted the need in the regrettable circumstances—as the Huskisson group saw them—for modest political reform. As he put it in an unpublished pamphlet written in July 1831, a measure might have been introduced 'to restore as completely as possible the balance of the principles' of the constitution, achievable by a variety of means: modest redistribution, franchise reform, corrupt practices reform. If this had been done, 'though all might not have adopted the whole of these opinions, rational men would in general have admitted that the object was fair and attainable and that the means proposed did not necessarily imply the action of any destructive principle'. As it was, the thoroughgoing, wholesale reconstruction of the electoral system, even, as Gladstone saw it, of the constitution itself—'a revolution bill and *not* a Reform Bill' he called it—which the Whigs proposed in 1831 and eventually carried, threw him off balance, and kept him off balance for the rest of the decade.[7]*

Gladstone's very strong political reaction to the Whigs' reform proposals in 1831 mirrored his alarm at what he saw as the appalling state of religion at Oxford. He was shocked that 'a seminary for furnishing with ministers a reformed and Apostolical Church' should, given all its advantages of wealth, learning, and reputation, be so sterile: 'Here irreligion is the rule, religion is the exception.'[8] Neither the moral virtues of a classical education nor the proper qualities of the national priesthood could be achieved if the Church in Oxford, and generally, did not revive itself. Given the central importance in the nation's morale which Gladstone accorded to Oxford, the situation he believed he had found there amounted to a national disaster, calling for thoroughgoing remedies. Gladstone tried to respond to the situation at two levels, the personal, by considering whether he should himself become a clergyman, and the national, by trying to develop an active conservatism in public affairs.

A Serious Call?

A linear move from strict Evangelicalism to a High Church position has commonly been seen as characterizing Gladstone's religious 'development' in the 1820s and 1830s. This is an oversimple view. As has already been shown, it would be misleading to describe him simply as an Evangelical in his schooldays, even though he retained some Evangelical qualities

* In 1865 he recalled: 'The Reform bill frightened me in 1831, and drove me off my natural and previous bias. Burke and Canning misled many on that subject, and they misled me'; Morley, i. 70.

throughout his life. At Oxford, in a context he clearly felt religiously unsympathetic whatever its other strengths, he sought to stabilize his religious opinions. He found strict Evangelicalism inadequate though he often used Evangelical terminology. But he also seems to have felt that he ought to be able to respond better than he did to the Evangelical challenge. Confronted by 'national apostacy', he felt it his duty in 1830 to offer himself as a potential clergyman; his tutor, Biscoe, had earlier asked him if he was considering the clerical profession.[9] But the way he made this offer was most curious.

During the reading party at Cuddesdon in July–August 1830, Gladstone worked not only on the classics but on the Old Testament with Anstice. In a conversation, Anstice stressed 'the love of God, *not* selfishness' as the motive for actions. Gladstone was filled with remorse for his own inadequacy: 'I should have been in ecstasy to hear such an avowal of grand and high truths: but as it was the working[s] of my Satanic heart were far otherwise, as the day of judgment will show.' Fearful for the salvation of mankind, 'I ask myself the question why I am slumbering and trifling over matters which have at best but an indirect connection with religion, while souls throughout the world are sinking daily into death?' He felt a powerful duty to offer himself as a clergyman, but also a duty to ask his father's permission to do so. He wrote asking this permission already knowing that his father was hostile to the suggestion. He told John Gladstone: 'I do not now see my own view can or ought to stand for a moment in the way of your desires. In the hands of my parents therefore I am left.' Since John Gladstone had educated him to go into the law with a view to a career in politics, only one answer was likely.

Gladstone's attempt to become a clergyman had none of the committed determination of his brother John's wish to become a sailor. William Gladstone felt he *ought* to be a clergyman—it was his duty to God to offer himself—but he had had no clear call. 'O that, whithersoever he calls, I may follow!' Gladstone wrote in his diary when writing to his father and while 'much distracted with doubts as to my future line of conduct'. But God did not call. If Gladstone had had a clear call, if he had seen his way instead of being 'utterly blind', God's authority would have trumped his father's. There was relief rather than disappointment when John Gladstone's temperate reply urged public life as a broader profession, and counselled delay in making a decision: 'Had a most kind letter from my father for which I ought to be very thankful.'[10]

If Gladstone had not had a call, so also had he not experienced a conversion in the strict Evangelical sense, and this separated him from the Calvinist predestinarianism which he found in the Oxford Evangelicals, represented by the St Edmund Hall set and the Revd H. B. Bulteel, whose church and sermons Gladstone quite often attended. He wrote a long memorandum, 'The Doctrine of Conversion', to show that conversion was wrongly understood when measured by 'signs commonly arbitrary and frequently erroneous and improper' described, in a caricature of the Evangelical experience, as 'ideas of inspiration sudden and sensible, of bodily convulsions, of wild and idle speculations and imaginations'. Conversion was a '"turning" . . . so far from being the work of a moment that it cannot even be considered as the work of a life'. It was thus a lifelong process, involving a 'turning-point' when the balance tipped between one 'general ascendancy' and another, but it was a 'turning-point' invisible to man.[11]

This was at most a very moderately Evangelical view of conversion. Gladstone found himself turning to a less inward-looking religious stance and more to the Church as a body of believers, 'the Church militant here on earth', the institutional representation of Christ on earth. When he came again to declare his intended profession, it was again in the form of a letter to his father, written in January 1832 in the light of the reform crisis of the second half of 1831:

I cannot help believing, from circumstances around me, that the human race, or at least the civilized world, is rapidly approaching its crisis: that no great number of years will in their revolutions bring the time when the whole fabric of human society shall be rocked to its very foundations. . . .

The consequence was a duty to enter 'what is called public life' with a view to resisting social disintegration, since 'intercourse *with subordination* forms the essence of what we understand by "society" in its largest sense'. The first symptom of the destructive 'new philosophy' which was spreading, 'a kind of calculation of interests', was the attack (as Gladstone saw it) on the Church, an attack which, he believed, could ultimately lead 'through the degradation of the British nation to wide and irremediable ruin through the world'.[12]

*The Tories' Rising Hope**

Religion led Gladstone to 'public life' and his attitude to it thus focussed on two related points: the stability of society and the well-being of the Church. The attempt to define, to relate, and to justify the importance of these two foci was to be his chief preoccupation of the 1830s, and, in various complex restatements, of the rest of his life. This preoccupation reflected his movement away from a rather inward-looking, self-directed, faith to a much more ecclesiological and institutional position.

'Society', 'State', and 'Church' were all in the 1830s 'essentially contested

* Macaulay's famous comment, often misquoted, that Gladstone was 'the rising hope of those stern and unbending Tories', was added in the margin of the draft for his *Edinburgh Review* article on Gladstone's book; his first deleted formulation appears to read 'the darling hope of those stern and uncompromising Tories'. I am obliged to Mr William Thomas for drawing my attention to this.

concepts': that is, they were those terms which lay at the centre of ideological and political dispute, used by different groups to mean different things, but commonly agreed to be the focal points of argument. The intellectual debate of the age therefore centred on their definition. The Whig cabinets in office between 1830 and 1841 (with the brief caesura of the Wellington–Peel minority government of 1834–5 in which Gladstone gained office for the first time) marked a sharp change of direction from the financial and administrative reforms of the Tories in the 1820s. The Whigs were primarily institutional reformers, unafraid of facing head-on the difficulties of definition which major institutional reforms raised in a stark, confrontational form. The Whigs thus reformed the representative system of the constitution both nationally and locally, and attempted a reconstruction of the national church and its allied educational system. Sometimes dismissed as foppish cynics, the dominant Whigs of the 1830s in fact represented Broad-Churchmanship in action, with a clearly-defined ideology, owing much to Richard Whately and Thomas Arnold, which was integrative and anti-dogmatic.[13]

Young Tories such as Gladstone thus found themselves faced with 'a gigantic scheme of speculative amelioration',[14] an ideological as well as a legislative challenge. Beyond the Whigs was seen an even more dangerous menace, a thoroughgoing secular utilitarianism represented in the Commons by the Radicals on whom, with O'Connell's Roman Catholics, the Whig government was dependent for votes after 1835. Tories such as Gladstone saw the Whigs as sometimes their abettors, sometimes their dupes. In discussing Gladstone's reaction to this situation, it is important to remember the wider context. The government's legislation in the 1830s, together with a general awareness (expressed inside and outside Parliament) of the fundamental shift in British society which industrialization and urbanization were producing, encouraged widespread questioning and justifying of values and assumptions hitherto taken to be so self-evidently right as not to need contemporary systematic justification. As Gladstone observed, 'Do we not live in an age when everything is made a subject of question and doubt. . . . It is the critical period in the history of nations, when men begin to question themselves respecting everything around them. . . .'[15]

Often such investigations, originally conceived in a defensive spirit, came to have radical consequences, as many of the leading authors of the Tracts for the Times, begun by J. H. Newman in Oxford in 1833, discovered. Works such as William Palmer's High-Church Treatise on the Church of Christ and F. D. Maurice's Platonic Broad-Church The Kingdom of Christ, both published in 1838 at almost the same time as Gladstone's The State in its Relations with the Church, reflected this general concern. The problem was one confronting any nation state with a liberal constitution, as was shown in the French case by Lamennais' rather earlier De la religion con-

sidérée dans ses rapports avec l'ordre politique et civil (1825–6):[16] what was authority and legitimacy in the modern state, and how justified was the Church of England (in the English case) in claiming that authority?

It is proper to discuss Gladstone's position in this intellectual context. As a young MP he was of course involved in routine parliamentary duties, for example sitting on Select Committees on bribery petitions, but it is clear from his diary and from the voluminous memoranda written throughout the 1830s that the chief direction of his energies lay in intellectual pursuits.[17]

None the less, his obvious political abilities were quickly recognized. After his first speech in Newark following the hustings in 1832, the *Nottingham Journal* concluded, 'he is a young gentleman of amicable manners and the most extraordinary talent; and we venture to predict, without the slightest exaggeration, that he will one day be classed among the most able statesmen in the British Senate'.[18] Gladstone made his inaugural speech, on slavery in the West Indies—he had hoped to make it on the Irish Church Bill—in June 1833: 'House 5–1. Spoke. my first time— for 50 min. My leading desire was, to benefit the cause of those, who are now so sorely beset. The House heard me very kindly, and my *friends* were satisfied. Tea afterwards at the Carlton.' Two days later 'Sir R. Peel came up to me most kindly & praised the affair of Monday night.'[19] Gladstone's attacks on the terms of emancipation of the slaves—but not on the principle—and his defence of the church establishment in Oxford, England, and Ireland, gained him a place in the minority Tory government of 1834–5 as a Commissioner of the Treasury (usually known as a Junior Lord of the Treasury) with routine responsibilities, and on 26 January 1835, Peel 'offered me the Colonial Under Secretaryship. I accepted this great responsibility.' Less than a month later the government was defeated on the election of the Speaker, and its end was certain: 'Of the state, of wh. this div. is a symptom, I can form but one opinion.' On 18 April 1835, he 'bade farewell to the Colonial Office', ending his time there with a partial disagreement with his superior, Lord Aberdeen, over West Indian education, Gladstone wishing that any educational scheme for the ex-slaves there should be explicitly Anglican.

This sort of difficulty with a much respected fellow Tory, which, had it been brought to a head 'would have been extremely painful', encouraged Gladstone in the view that his intellectual position required deepening and systematizing. In the long recess in the winter following the return of the Whig government in 1835, he went to Fasque and undertook what represented, in scope and intensity, almost a second education. His mother's death and his own unrequited love for a society beauty, Caroline Farquhar, sister of one of his college and political friends, seem to have intensified rather than deflected him from his studies. He read, amongst others,

Hume's *History* (again), beginning at the Commonwealth, Locke's *Essay Concerning Human Understanding*, Augustine's *Civitas Dei*, Tocqueville's *Democracy in America*, Thomas Chalmer's *Bridgewater Treatise*, Bolingbroke, Blackstone, Dante, and especially Aristotle's *Politics* which rather curiously had not formed a chief part of his Aristotelian studies at Oxford; he found it 'a book of immense value for all governors and public men'. This programme of reading was buttressed before and after the recess by Gladstone's usual wide-ranging studies. The reading of Augustine and Dante, and especially the thorough study of the latter, gave a catholic balance to the list, and Gladstone maintained his reading, finishing 'the dear Paradiso' for the first of many times in March 1836.[20]

The striking feature of much of this reading is its theoretical nature. As a young MP, Gladstone sought right rather than results. Unlike many in his position, he did not try to make himself an authority on some particular topic, though because of his father's business interests he found himself speaking frequently in defence of the West Indian plantation owners in the period of 'apprenticeship' which intervened between abolition of slavery in principle and abolition in practice, and his experience as Colonial Under-Secretary added some authority to his interventions on imperial affairs, especially with respect to Canada, in the later years of the Melbourne government. The many private papers which he wrote in the 1830s are almost wholly theoretical (in the sense of abstract) in tone; they deal with the nature of obligation in State and Church, and usually with little or no reference to the circumstances of the day, except by implication by way of comment on periods of earlier constitutional crisis.

While revising for his Oxford examinations in 1831, Gladstone had 'an idea . . . of gathering during the progress of my life, notes & materials for a work embracing three divisions—Morals—Politics—Education'. He kept some such notion of a book in his mind, recording it in 1835 during his period of reflection at Fasque as 'Idea of the Church. What the Church is: idea as it should be.' After a good deal of preparatory writing in 1837 it had by March 1838 taken a rather different form: 'I spoke to Mr. G. after dinner on the point I opened to Mahon at B[ridgwater] H[ouse]—viz. a definite principle on religious matters in the event of any C[onservative] Govt being formed.' Thus a work originally conceived in rather secular, classical categories (though obviously their treatment if it had any contemporary content would have involved religion), had become more explicitly religious in direction and more directly linked to the principles on which conservatism should act. If 'the science of Government', he told the Commons in 1835, was to exclude 'the consideration of religion—the most vital of all subjects to our permanent happiness and advancement', the result would be that 'so far from the science of politics being, as the greatest philosophers of antiquity fondly proclaimed it, the queen and mistress of all other arts, and discharging the noble functions of the mind, it will be an occupation degrading in its practice, and fitted rather for the very helots of society'. The Aristotelian good life of the property-owning gentleman must be conditioned and legitimized by the Anglican Church. Gladstone thought 'this matter of speaking is really my strongest religious exercise'.[21]

He published his views on this question in two books, *The State in its Relations with the Church*, published in December 1838, and *Church Principles Considered in their Results*, published in November 1840, which together represent the political and theological position reached by Gladstone in his twenties.

Three areas of influence bore upon Gladstone as he faced the controversies of the 1830s and attempted to forge conservatism for his generation: first, intellectual, the classical legacy of his education; second, ecclesiastical and theological, his increasing interest in the question of authority within the church; third, political, the participation in the political debates of the 1830s.

Towards a 'Science of Government': Plato and Aristotle

Gladstone was, as we have seen, steeped in the classics. But the classical school, though it suggested the basis for an analysis of society by analogy, in itself suggested no single view. Gladstone found himself attracted to both its two chief combatants, Plato and Aristotle. Unlike many of his contemporaries he was not simply a Platonist or an Aristotelian. The comment 'Optime' in the Christ Church Collection [Report] book on his work on both Plato and Aristotle reflected his balanced approach. From Aristotle Gladstone gained categories of analysis—the family, the local community, the state—which encouraged him to analyse society as a natural organism. From Plato he gained the concept of a vision of human society not yet realized. He found himself unable to decide decisively in the long battle between these two philosophers and their supporters. Aristotle's *Ethics* took no account of the fallen nature of man or of the possible reward of a future life; they were therefore deficient and feeble in lacking the concepts of retribution and reward. Looked at as to character Plato seemed superior: 'The *motives* are the main spring of every ethical system. Aristotle's are common: Plato's exalted: an approach far more in character to those proposed to us in the Word of God.'* Thus Gladstone concluded an essay comparing the two offered to the WEG Club. None the less, Aristotle's supposed 'practicality' appealed: 'It seems to me therefore that no one would deny the ἰδέα [nature, form] of Plato's scheme to be

---

* Plato's *Phaedo*, the main Platonic text for undergraduates, was, with its stress on an afterlife and on the fallen nature of man, the most convenient of Plato's works for instruction in a university whose tutors and students all subscribed to the Thirty Nine Articles; Gladstone and his generation were thus given a very unbalanced view of Plato.

finer, *except* possibly from the supposition that Aristotle's is more practical.'[22] It is clear that Gladstone's chief interest in making this comparison was in its political consequences; he was not interested in the more philosophical aspects of the debate. In refusing to side with one rather than the other, he was, for his time, rather unusual, and this refusal reflects a very general eclecticism in his intellectual position. Quotations can always be found with which to pin Gladstone to a particular school, political, ecclesiastic, or philosophical, but they always misrepresent the gallimaufrous nature of his mind, taken as a whole.

Gladstone took from Aristotle an analysis of society which was stable, almost static, each individual in his or her natural place, fulfilling social and political obligations rather than exercising rights. Thus his starting point for writing 'On the Principle of Government', written shortly after his essay comparing Aristotle and Plato, was strongly Aristotelian in its stress on natural status:

A state of graduated subordination is the natural law of humanity. . . . Civil government then is not a matter of option but of nature. . . . It is the prevailing error of all times, and particularly of the present ones, that men are looking at the power of self-government as intrinsically and essentially a good: whereas I think any reasoning lover of freedom would admit that it was not necessarily a good *when alone*, although he might contend for it as not only *a condition* but a *part* of the chief good. People talk and act as if the faculty of choice was the one thing needful—instead of the disposition to choose rightly.

This 'disposition' would be paternally encouraged and consequently

the right principle seems to me to be, not to give as much political liberty to the subjects as can be conceded compatibly with the maintenance of public order, but as little. A minimum of representation and not a maximum is I think the first object to be desired.[23]

Gladstone's detailed study of Aristotle's *Politics* in 1834–5 deepened his view that the social order was both natural and, when Christian revelation was added to Aristotle, divinely orchestrated; for of course Gladstone believed that classical authors could only offer a partial truth, to be modified and illuminated by revelation. At Fasque he wrote a long paper 'Of the Law of Social Obligation':

Society possesses, both from the *nature of the objects* it contemplates, and from the *debt which by benefits conferred* it has imposed upon every one of us, has a natural and binding right to our allegiance, anterior to, and wholly independent of, any individual conviction on our parts . . . this right, not having its *formation* and origin in the will of society, or of any member of it, is not determinable in its specific requisition by individual members of the community . . . though distinct from absolute right, and capable of deviation from absolute wisdom, it has a Divine sanction as well as a human reasonableness. . . . We are therefore placed in our nation, as in our family: and must discharge our social, as our domestic duties, in deference and subordination to naturally that is Divinely constituted ordinance.[24]

This Aristotelian viewpoint offered the basis for an attack on the idea of 'original contract, as advocated by Hooker, Locke, the Whigs of 1688, and Mr. Burke' and on 'original contract as held by Rousseau'. This long paper entitled 'Prevalent theories of government', written in December 1835, disposed of all these, and of absolute and indefeasible hereditary monarchies, and of the will and numbers (i.e. *vox populi*) as a basis for a constitution, and it concluded in a passage headed 'The true position of Will in Government':

We have striven to overthrow the persuasion, which in various shapes of prejudice, habit, opinion, affection, and even conviction, is so popular, that human will is a rightful and original arbiter in the main and essential matters of government. . . . The doctrine is in itself so totally unable to bear the light of investigation, that in no form of government can it be acceptable to the inquiring mind: it hides from view and takes refuge in some artifice, as that the king's will is wiser than the people's, or the people's than the king's, but from thence to the occasion of action, and in the excitement of selflove, it is ever ready to come forth again and animate the crowd of tumultuous passions which a single moment can evoke, and become, even though unconsciously, the governing motive of men or bodies of men. Such is the subtlety of evil. It is therefore our duty in the security of study and contemplation, firmly to grasp by the understanding, the truth that human will, as will, though it has power has not authority, in the fundamental matters of government: nor can we more forcibly concentrate the sentiments which belong to this proposition, than in the nervous declaration of Aristotle 'οὐκ ἐῶμεν ἄρχειν ἀνθρωπον'.* For it is against *man*, against king, nobles, people, all alike, when considered as creatures of mere will, that our objections and accusations lie.

In his reflections about society, Aristotle was the predominant influence in the early 1830s, though Gladstone's many notes on him often express qualification or objection. Aristotle explained why society was what it was; he did not say what it could become. Here Plato's *Republic*, begun in August 1832 (i.e. after leaving Oxford), offered an image of perfection: 'Aristotle built upon the practical unity of φιλία [family affection] (on which a larger unity may however be raised)—Plato wrought synthetically & removed existing instincts and affections to substitute one visionary in great measure.'[25]

Gladstone offered a self-confident hierarchical conservatism abstractly defended. When linked with a visionary view of what Christianity could become, it was to be a heady mixture. The difficulty with it was that while it offered an analysis of the present and a prescription for the future, it did

---

* 'This is why we do not allow a *man* to rule, but rational principle, because a man behaves thus in his own interests and becomes a tyrant', *Nichomachean Ethics* (1134 a. 35); Add MS 44725; paper of 11 December 1835.

not offer either a means or a method. It might be a science of society, but it was not a science of government.

Church Principles

Parallel to this analysis of society, related to it but never wholly fused with it, Gladstone in the early 1830s developed his views of the Church. He completed his formal education in the usual way, a tour of the Continent, made in 1832 with his brother John. This tour awakened his international-ism but also strengthened his nationalism—a duality which he retained throughout his life. Raised, as was his generation, to instinctive but largely uninformed hostility to Continental liberalism and the French Revolu-tion,* he experienced on visiting the field of Waterloo a curious mixture of emotions, of patriotic separation, anti-popery, and prudent reformism:

The sight of this field, especially under the present aspect of circumstances, suggests many recollections of an overwhelming interest. How dearly the honours and the benefits of that field were brought: and how does the very grandeur of the victory itself bear a melancholy witness to the intensity of the struggle. If indeed that battle were fought in a wrong cause, how painful has been our guilt: if in a right one, and if in accordance with the commands of God, yet with how much alloy of baser motives has the great enterprise been prosecuted! Yet after all, if the cause were good, this is indeed a spot where an Englishman's heart should beat high with exultation.

But what if the tide of our national destiny is turned, and if we are now about to go hand in hand with those alien principles, against which we once waged an implacable war? God forbid, and direct all for good. And indeed in the grand division of continental parties, it is very much easier to predicate evil of one side, than good of the other. It may be painful to see Church Establishments over-thrown—but who would wish for the renewal of the Empire of Popery in all its pride? It may shock our feelings to see the kingly office first misunderstood and misdefined, and then degraded, yet who can say that the ancient despotism was a wholesome government for France?[26]

This duality was strengthened in another dimension by Gladstone's experiences of religion in Italy. While at Oxford he had developed his earlier interest in Roman Catholicism by making an extended analysis of 'Roman Catholic Doctrines and Ceremonies'. In March 1832 he experi-enced Roman Catholicism at first hand—for he knew no English Roman Catholics—when he made the first of many crossings of the Alps into Italy, then a patchwork of states, most of them ruled by the Hapsburgs, the Bourbons, or the Pope. He immediately made a pilgrimage to the valley of the Vaudois, Milton's 'slaughtered saints' in whom he had been interested

---

* Gladstone's tour made him aware of his ignorance; on his return he noted: 'I find so much the want of knowledge in detail of the French Revolution, that I begin Scott's account of it [in his *Life of Napoleon*]', so as to be able to evaluate the French authors such as Sarrans and de Bourrienne whose works he had recently begun.

since Eton, and was dismayed to find those legendary Protestants to be rather ordinary and undistinguished.[27] Travelling south towards the Papal States, he was soon fascinated by the Roman Catholic church services, in his view a curious mixture of beauty and inaudibility. He formed contempt for the temporal power of the Pope—'there seems to be every absurdity involved in the idea of an ecclesiastical sovereign—whether legislative or executive'—and his instinctive reaction to seeing St Peter's for the first time was to note 'my humble homage is reserved for that Gothic style, which prevails in our own English cathedrals'. None the less, he soon 'experienced the truth of the universal opinion, that St. Peter's grows upon one's continuing contemplations'. And not only architecturally:

In entering such a Church as this, most deeply does one feel the pain and shame of the schism which separates us from Rome—whose guilt (for guilt I at least am well persuaded there always is where there is schism,) surely rests not upon the Venerable Fathers of the English Reformed Church, but upon Rome itself—yet whose melancholy effects the mind is doomed to feel, when you enter this magnificent temple, and behold on its walls the images of Christian saints and the words of Everlasting Truth. . . . May God bind up the wounds of his bleeding Church.

This visit to St Peter's made an abiding impression. When he visited Rome again in 1838, he noted of his visit to St Peter's: 'Here I remember almost to have experienced the first conception of unity in the Church—acquired alas! by the existing contrasts—and first to have longed for its visible attainment: an object in every human sense hopeless: but not therefore the less to be desired. . . . That idea has been upon the whole, I believe the ruling one of my life during the period which has since elapsed.'[28]

Gladstone's first direct experience of Roman Catholicism in its majesty thus both attracted and repelled him. It opened a vision of what Christendom might be and it exposed the worm in the bud. As he attended the Palm Sunday Service in the Sistine Chapel, in the presence of the Pope, he felt: 'its principle of life, has left it. Even so stood before us the great members of the papal system, as the cold and pale spectres of the highest and most powerful domination the world has ever beheld.'[29]

The dualism of Gladstone's reaction to Rome not surprisingly encouraged inquiry into the Church of England's place—or potential place—in the religious world order, an inquiry reinforced by the ignorance of the Church of England which he discovered in Italy. He began to look at 'some of the details of the system of the English Church, as set forth in the Prayerbook, with which I was before less acquainted'. His experience in Roman Catholic countries gave him 'an idea' of the nature of a Church 'very much higher & more important than I had previously any conception of'.[30]

This concept of 'an idea', a vision, an image, was of growing importance. In opposing Whig reforms of the Church of England and Ireland in 1835, Gladstone showed himself a more than competent combatant at the

statistical level, using the old device of quoting the opposite side's figures
to refute its arguments. At one level this was satisfactory and effective. But
it was not in itself adequate. Like many of his generation of Oxford men,
Gladstone found a decade of Whig reforms driving him increasingly to look
for a more systematic defence of the establishment and claims of the
Church of England. He sought a more thoroughgoing explanation of the
State's relationship to it than 'commonsense' conservatism of the sort
offered by, for example, Sir Robert Inglis, the successor to Peel in one of
the Oxford University seats, and by Peel himself in the buffer device of the
Ecclesiastical Commissioners set up during the 1834–5 minority Conservative government and continued subsequently by the Whigs. Gladstone did
not oppose this sort of reform, though he strongly opposed some of its subsequent recommendations, but his writings, his reading, and his demea-
nour in the 1830s reflect a yearning for a more theoretical base.[31] He always
despised 'the miserable policy of mere resistance to change, and of tenacious adherence to civil privilege'.

Unlike some of his Oxford contemporaries, Gladstone was not led by
this process to question or to test the legitimacy of the Church of England,
but rather to inquire into what should be the relationship of the State
towards it. On the contrary, the 1830s brought to him an increasing awareness of, and devotion to, the Church of England. His continental experiences in 1832, and his subsequent reading, coming at a time when he was
beginning to be interested in 'system' in the Church, convinced him of two
things. First, that there is 'a real and not merely supposititious personality
of nations, which entails likewise its own religious responsibilities' and,
second, that the Church of England represented truth and thus, in its geographical context (i.e. England, Wales, Ireland, and the Colonies, but not
Scotland), represented the 'religious responsibility' incumbent on the
state, and was also the criterion of deciding, in Aristotelian terms, what the
disposition of a good citizen should be.

From these two beliefs sprang that concept of 'religious nationality'
which was fundamental to Gladstone's view of the state, whether English,
British, or elsewhere.[32] In certain respects, this placed Gladstone close to
the Noetics of Oxford.* His elevated view of nationalism (at this stage, it
should be noted, owing little to Liberal views of self-determination) related
him to the nationalism of Thomas Arnold's *Principles of Church Reform*
(1833), the classic advocacy of antidogmatism in the Church in order to
achieve the confessional state.[33] The idealism which permeated Gladstone's views on the State in the late 1830s was mainly derived from

___

* It is interesting that his specific complaint against Richard Whately, the doyen of the Noetics,
several of whose sermons he attended as an undergraduate, was about 'his antisabbatical doctrine
. . . as mischievous as it is unsound' (18 Sept. 1831). Gladstone might have been expected to have
been much more quickly and more generally hostile.

Coleridge's *On the Constitution of the Church and State According to the Idea of Each*, the classic defence of the confessional state. Both Arnold and Coleridge held out an Ideal, derived through the inspiration of Plato, against which present-day institutions might be measured, Coleridge arguing, in a famous phrase, that the congruity of the English state and the Church of England was a 'blessed accident', enabling the Ideal to be observed in actuality. In notes made in 1837 on Coleridge's *Church and State*, Gladstone commented: '*We* do not claim to be the Universal Church of the whole earth—but we claim to be the Church of this realm corresponding in all material laws with that model which was established and intended to be universal.' Coleridge's book was published in 1830. Gladstone did not read it until 1837—he had earlier read other of his works—but when he did read it he read it very carefully, as the annotations in his copy show.[34] Similarly, though he had read Plato's dialogues as an undergraduate, he did not read the *Republic* until late in 1832. He turned energetically to Idealist authors, and especially Coleridge, from 1836 onwards. 'Finished Coleridge's Idea' is, significantly, the way Gladstone refers to the end of his study of Coleridge's book—not the short title by which it was or is usually known. Not surprisingly, therefore, Arnold saw Gladstone as a quasi-ally.*

This rather unsystematic contact with the Idealist tradition was important. We have seen Gladstone, both deeply trained at university and by his own subsequent studies in the 'practical' Aristotle, dissatisfied with the inadequacy of 'low' defences of the Church. Seeing the established Church as useful rather than transcendental played into the hands of its opponents. Plato and Coleridge gave Gladstone an intellectually perhaps rather dangerous means of expressing and developing his already half-thought-out views about the relationship of the State to the Church.

Gladstone was also concerned about what he saw as the increasing materialism of the age: 'There is danger when we are led to fix our thoughts on possession, rather than use. Here one [?our] peril arising from money's becoming the basis of all relations: because it has no intrinsic value.'[35] Such materialism, an obvious, even a defining feature of industrial Britain, could only be met by a national antithesis. Those like Thomas Chalmers who met political economy on its own ground and stressed the central role of the moral autonomy of the individual consequently, in Gladstone's view, neglected the high place of a national Church based on an apostolic ministry. Gladstone was completing a draft of a work on 'Ch & St.'

* Thomas Arnold, *Introductory Lectures on Modern History* (1842), 51: 'I would unite one half of the Archbishop of Dublin's [Whately] theory with one half of Mr. Gladstone's; agreeing cordially with Mr. Gladstone in the moral theory of the state, and agreeing cordially with the Archbishop in what I will venture to call the Christian theory of the Church, and deducing from the conclusion, that the perfect state and the perfect church are identical.'

previously worked on in 1837 and perhaps earlier,* when he attended
lectures on establishment given in London by Chalmers in the spring of
1838. Stung by Chalmers's low view of apostolicity and the corporate
Church, he refurbished his draft to stress the importance of these factors.

Gladstone's acquaintance with the 'high' Idealist image of perfection
seemed to give him the analytical tool he needed. Coleridge offered an
argument 'alike beautiful and profound', and Gladstone was especially
drawn to Coleridge's argument that the '*cultivation* of the inward man,
which is the root, the corrective, and the safeguard of *civilization*' should
be nourished as 'a paramount ingredient of national life' by a 'natural
"clerisy" of a state'. Of the various writers whose views on the relationship of State and Church Gladstone surveyed—Hooker, Warburton,
Paley, Chalmers, Hobbes, Bellarmine, Coleridge—it was the last whose
definition was the most acceptable, its deficiency being that 'he does not
carry his conceptions into detail'.[36] Gladstone concluded his public statement of his views, his book *The State in its Relations with the Church* (1838),
with quotations from two of the high priests of the Idealist movement,
Herder and Plato.

Gladstone was concerned to develop a view of a confessional State on a
'high' ground. He was equally concerned to assert not merely the Anglican
Church's function within such a State, but what was regarded as a High-
Church view of the nature of that Church. 'Church principles' involved a
strong stress on 'the divine constitution of the visible Church' as exemplified by bishoprics and the apostolic succession. Thus, while the confessional, national aspect of Gladstone's view of the State seemed to point
towards Arnold's antidogmatic, integrative reforms, his view of the Church
led him towards a rather narrow apostolicity which linked him clearly both
with the older High-Churchmen such as William Palmer, whose *Treatise*
came out too late to have much impact on the first edition of Gladstone's
book, and with the Puseyite element of the Oxford Movement, or Tractarians as its members were known. Faced with a choice, Gladstone always
put Anglican apostolical purity first. For the Greek tradition of civic
humanism, important though it was, was not enough and Aristotle and
Plato were merely 'pagans': 'great as is the importance of our civil and
social life, it is not an essential but an instrumental importance: it is
important for what it yields and generates, not for that which it is. . . . It is in
the history of the Church that we have the final consummation of all human
destinies.'[37] *Church Principles* attracted much less attention than *The State in
its Relations with the Church*. But it was, from the author's point of view, a
more comfortable book. It did not have the awkwardness of Glad-

* The absence of the MSS of the early drafts of *The State in its Relations with the Church* makes it
difficult to be sure how the bouts of writing on this subject, mentioned in the diary from 1836 onwards, relate to the final version.

stone's attempt in *The State* to meld the Aristotelian with the Platonic–Coleridgean way of thought.

Gladstone's stress in both his books on the legitimacy of the Church of England meant that he was strongly hostile to concurrent endowment (i.e. the notion that the State should take religions as it found them and organize education through whatever denominations, Roman Catholic or Protestant, might be found to exist side-by-side with Anglicanism). After formulating this view in the 1830s he subsequently always preferred no State patronage to mixed, pluralist State patronage in religion and education, a situation he described as prevalent in Prussia and in France, where, despite the predomination of Roman Catholicism in the latter, 'the principle of national religion has been essentially surrendered, and the state joins hands with all creeds alike—a marked and memorable result of her first Revolution'.[38] Gladstone did not argue that the Church of England was in an absolute sense the representative of true religion in the areas where it was established, but, following Bishop Butler's view of probability, he argued that the government maintained it as 'that form of belief which it conceives to contain the largest portion of the elements of truth with the smallest admixture of error'.[39] Thus Gladstone disagreed sharply with some of William Palmer's less qualified statements, such as his view that Nonconformists were outside the Church and therefore beyond salvation.[40]

In the British case, Gladstone thought, 'we still seem to have ground which is defensible, and which is worth defending'. 'Our country', he believed, 'seems to promise at least a more organised, tenacious, and determined resistance to the efforts against national religion as well as to the general principles of democracy, than any in the civilized world.'[41] In thinking this, in the light of the difficulties of Romanism, Socialism, paganism, and dissent of which he showed himself well aware, Gladstone revealed himself as an optimist. In this sense, his Idealist phase placed him in a different position than the High-Churchmen of the Palmer sort, who defined and guarded the Anglican tradition and deplored the Roman drift of the Newmanites, but offered little that was positive or forward looking.

The State in its Relations with the Church and *Church Principles*, as we have seen, were amongst other things deliberately intended as a guide to Conservatives as they prepared for office. This was, probably, the last point at which a general defence of Anglican hegemonic nationalism could be attempted. If conservatism was to be more than a Fabian defence against, and consequently a pragmatic accommodation of the liberal, pluralist, and industrial state—if it was to be an ideology rather than a reaction—Gladstone's position, or something like it, had to be held. Gladstone contributed to the very high expectations which Conservatives placed upon the coming Peel government, an almost apocalyptic expectation which by its very existence added to the difficulties of that government and to its failure and the subsequent disintegration of the Conservative Party. Ultra Tories looked to him, as they were to do in 1845, but they looked ultimately in vain. Gladstone's Canningism seemed suspended in the 1830s, but it was not dead.

The difficulties into which Gladstone's first book led him in the 1840s will be considered in the next chapter. In the context of Conservatism of the 1830s, it is worth noting two points. First, his view of Anglicanism denied the 'subjective immobility' of any religious system and accepted that each age produces 'particular modifications', with doctrine therefore being essentially secondary. Though cautious and conservative, his position therefore accepted renovation and growth: an analogy with Aristotle's view of the organic growth of society from family to State is supported by Gladstone's use in the Church context of the famous Aristotelian simile used in the *Politics*, 'as an oak unfolds the life which it has carried seminally within it from the acorn'.[42] The function of the conservative was to locate, by historical awareness, where on this path of growth the present stood. However cautiously applied, and however different the intended conclusion, Gladstone's use of development associated him with the dominant progressivism of the age. Second, Gladstone was, even with respect to fundamentals, sometimes less confident about his party position than his public persona suggested. In 1836 he privately surveyed the positions of the two main parties (without naming them); the one, he thought, was based on the 'major principle that control and restraint are in themselves good for human nature and are not to be accepted merely as disadvantages necessarily entailed by a social status', that power was 'in itself intoxicating' and must be curtailed by 'that passionless agency of Law and fixed institution which most restricts individual caprice and lowers pride'. The other party assumes 'that the right of government finally resides in the mass: that man is the best judge of his own interests in political as much as in private matters: that the principle of birth and wealth are rather the tolerable accidents, than the valuable auxiliary, of social excellence . . .'. It would appear obvious which side Gladstone was on—and it is interesting to note that he assumed party was based on fundamentally differing principles—but his conclusion was more tentative than might be expected:

Who may be right and who wrong in this fundamental principle lying at the root of party distinctions, is a deep and difficult question, and one in which we must perhaps rely mainly upon perceptions and persuasions incapable of analysis and ranking among the ultimate facts of our nature. The details of Revealed truth seem to me to bear out the choice which my mind has made: to indicate that we are as children and pupils, seeing in a glass darkly, appointed to self-government for the purpose of growth and strength, but not intended to regard it as an end valuable in itself: and as on the other hand necessary, but *less* necessary, than the counterpoising principle of obedience, while the two together as the active and the passive principle form the harmony of our nature.[43]

As Gladstone's life progressed, he was to find harmony difficult to achieve, for in his nature the active clearly dominated the passive.

Political Action

Following Bishop Butler, Gladstone saw man as an agent, with the need to act. Man was not an observer, but a participant: a participant participates, as best he can, in situations given by history. Taking decisions involves the risk, even the expectation, of being wrong, and much effort must be taken to minimize error. It was to try to establish the best criteria for right action that Gladstone's works and speeches in the 1830s were devoted.

In 1835, he described how a politician should approach the business of politics. The passage sums up very well his own approach to his Parliamentary activities—it being always remembered that he only saw these as a partial fulfilment of his calling to 'public life'—and is worth quoting at length:

In that gradation of instruments through means of which this lofty standard is applied to the varieties of practice in the government of human societies, next to the standard itself are those contemplative and philosophical faculties by which we handle the grounds and principles of the highest sciences. Partly analytical and discriminative: partly such as generalise and compare. The union of these two great branches of intellectual power is perhaps nowhere more necessary than in the politician, who has for his object not to delineate an ideal picture, but to frame a practical system, which embodying many principles of Divine wisdom from which human depravity is averse, shall nevertheless be adapted to operate upon the masses of human beings without violence, to change their opinions and habits for the better, without arraying those opinions and habits against itself. He is to give every consideration, like the ethical teacher, to the needs and frailties of human nature, to combine the indulgence of sympathy with allegiance to everlasting truth. He ought therefore to be familiar with each of those two mental moods so rarely found in union, analytical disquisitiveness, and creative contemplation. In his observation which has amassed, in his judgment which classifies his experimental facts, and in his reason which contemplates the fixed principles of human nature and Divine Will . . . we find a copy as it were of that Divine Will as regarding human societies: faint and dim and mutilated, but still the best which our capacities can attain, and therefore the most authentic evidence of political right, which is to be found on earth.[44]

Being an MP obviously suggested activity, even if it was only participation in the process of politics by voting in the lobbies. For Gladstone, the presupposition was always that it would mean speaking as well. He had written on 'Rhetoric' for the *Eton Miscellany*, and he wrote a further article (unpublished) on 'Public Speaking' in 1836. His education had been in large measure a training in and through rhetoric. Involvement in rational debate—winning the argument—was always for him a central function of political activity, for from the winning of the argument, if it was a right argument, would come political success. Thus the argument that the Church of England represented truth rather than numbers was always his point of departure. In England, there was—or was thought to be—a congruence between truth and numbers; in Ireland there was not. The point of defence thus became the establishment of the Church in Ireland. The Church in Ireland deserved to be established there because it represented true religion. The failure of the Roman Catholics there to recognize this implied, not disestablishment or concurrent endowment, but inadequacy in the presentation of this truth to the Irish peasantry. Thus Gladstone consistently defended the Irish establishment, and church rates generally, and worked towards a refurbished system of Anglican education in Ireland.

'The Protestant faith', he told his constituents in Newark in 1835, 'is held good for us, and what is good for us is also good for the population of Ireland.' But this depended on a peculiarly English view of British nationality, already, by the establishment of Presbyterianism in Scotland, in fact and in law pluralist in character. Gladstone accepted this with respect to Scotland. There, despite his strong reservation about the Presbyterians' supposed want of apostolicity, he found a form of national religion perhaps purer than in England: 'I have myself found in the nationality of Scottish religion . . . a cause of its comparative purity.' It might not seem a large step to recognize that the Episcopalian Church in Ireland was no more 'national' than it was in Scotland. Yet in the context of the parliamentary politics of the 1830s it was a huge step, and with huge consequences. Defending the Irish Church, Gladstone found himself unable to explain how that Church could become more broadly based, even if great abuses in it were conceded to exist. He was forced back on consequential arguments—more consequential than at the time he can have realized: 'we have abundant reasons, even of a political complexion, for maintaining that Church: after its destruction we should not long be able to resist the repeal of the Union, partly by loss of strength, and more from abandonment of our principles'.[45] This was not simply a question of numbers—the Anglicans' lack of support. Gladstone could be appealed to on more positive grounds, and in 1839, as he sat waiting 'to obey my superiors' by answering the Whigs in an Irish debate, and as the Tories began to anticipate a return to office, a remark of Lord John Russell's struck Gladstone 'ineffaceably', as he recalled thirty-one years later: 'You [Russell] said, "The true key to our Irish debates was this: that it was not properly borne in mind that as England is inhabited by Englishmen, and Scotland by Scotchmen, so Ireland is inhabited by Irishmen."'[46] Parliamentary action to defend the Anglican establishment in Ireland was becoming problematical.

The active side of Gladstone's nature also led him in the later 1830s to a number of practical initiatives, mostly in the religious sphere. He was closely associated with Bishop Blomfield's Metropolis Churches Fund, founded in 1836 to supply by subscription what the State declined to pay for by taxation, and in 1838 on Blomfield's invitation he joined the council of the National Society for the Education of the Poor in the Principles of the Established Church, and from this position he energetically opposed the Whigs' programme for a permanent committee of the Privy Council to promote education on the principle of concurrent endowment. He was prominent in the founding in 1837 of the Additional Curates Society, a High Church breakaway group from the evangelical Church Pastoral-Aid Society.[47] Developing the High Church or Tractarian side of his interests, he co-operated with E. B. Pusey in promoting reform along the lines of Pusey's pamphlet, 'Remarks on the prospective and past benefits of Cathedral institutions' (1833): 'Breakfast with Acland [in May 1838] to meet Dr. Pusey: conversation on Ch. Govt of Cathl question—wh is now fermenting in my mind.' The association between Gladstone and Pusey was a natural one, for they shared an Anglo-Catholicism which was thoroughly non-Roman, however much their willingness to go beyond High Church passivity might be misunderstood by many of their contemporaries.[48]

Initiatives such as these placed Gladstone at the front of the young Conservative MPs, a number of whom were, like him, associated with the Tractarian movement while not really part of it. His Puseyism dismayed some of the older MPs, always extremely cautious of any implication of a concession to Roman Catholicism, but it was not necessarily a disadvantage with his own Tory generation. In 1839 J. S. Mill, not a sympathetic observer, made a sharp analysis of 'the Oxford School . . . a new Catholic school without the Pope . . . one of the forms, & the best forms hitherto, of the *reaction* of Anglicanism against Methodism, incredulity & rationalism'. Mill concluded, echoing Macaulay's famous phrase: 'Among others of their proselytes it is said that Gladstone, the only rising man among the Tories, is one; the man who will probably succeed Peel as the Tory leader, unless this prevents him.'[49]

Gladstone's conservatism in the 1830s was highly romantic, even Utopian, much more so than that of the Young England movement of the 1840s which it anticipated. It was also much more systematically worked out than that exotic initiative; Gladstone's timing was poor—he was at least a generation too late—but it was not as poor as Disraeli's.

His highminded view of the functions of Conservatism contrasted markedly with the realities of electioneering in the two-member constituency of Newark, where he was returned in the general elections of 1832, 1835, and 1837 (in the last two of which he was unopposed), and 1841. It was not that Gladstone was ignorant. In Newark, bribery and 'treating' (i.e. free drink) were, as in most constituencies at the time, the accepted means of political persuasion and elections were extremely rumbustious. On his first appearance on the hustings, in 1832, his elaborate speech was totally inaudible: 'Mr. Gladstone then endeavoured to address the electors, but an outrageous noise, in groaning, hissing, and shouting, prevented him proceeding'; Gladstone struggled on for fifteen minutes undaunted—but he could not be heard. At the 1835 election, his attempts at a complex statement of belief were cut down to a brief broadsheet manifesto (though this was partly because of the absence of an opponent). Working for a Tory in a by-election in Westminster in 1835 he noted: 'A stormy scene. Got cut over the nose with a piece of wood.' The negotiations he had to carry on between the Duke of Newcastle, his father, and the Tory political agent about overspending in the elections reinforced the knowledge he gained from sitting on Commons committees inquiring into bribery in other constituencies. Not surprisingly, Gladstone concluded that the 'most singular argument' he found in his Aristotelian studies in the 1830s was the view that 'the clubbed intellects of the multitude may render them fitter to govern than the few'.

So it was not that Gladstone was ignorant of the realities of constituency politics. It was rather that, as yet, he did not think the rank-and-file elector capable of sophisticated political judgement. As he told the House of Commons soon after joining it, 'in what did the heinousness of bribery consist? Was it not in the bartering of a man's conscience? . . . those in the humbler walks of life could not be supposed to have very correct abstract opinions upon the nature of bribery. The utmost, perhaps, that could be reasonably expected from them would be, that they should consistently adhere to one political creed.'[50] But it was largely Church questions which were at issue at the hustings and which were being decided by a bribery which Gladstone accepted was understandable enough and perhaps rational from the individual voter's point of view. This suggested a curious process of electing the body which was in effect the synod of the Church of England and Ireland. Of course, this had been one of the Tories' objections to reform in 1830. But since the Church must be a community of self-aware believers, where then did this leave 'Church Principles' a decade later? For a national Church could not be national unless it had men as well as officers.

His view of Conservatism also left Gladstone curiously dissociated from his own mercantile origins. In an article written in 1834, but never published, he observed: 'A new population has sprung up in the manufacturing districts, with new habits, wants and wishes, and has greatly diverged from the ancient and indigenous national character.'[51] This was an uneasy position for John Gladstone's son to hold. None the less, it was a common view in the Tory circle—often Oxonians living in London—in which Gladstone moved. His two close friendships of the 1830s, with Henry Edward Manning (a man of rather similar origins) and James Hope, were formed in 1836 in the context of his idealistic High Church Conservatism. Like Gladstone, Manning (Balliol) and Hope (Christ Church) had been privately tutored by Charles Wordsworth; both had become Fellows of Merton College. Again, like Gladstone, Hope, a Scottish Episcopalian, had thought of taking Orders, but became a lawyer; Manning, of Evangelical upbringing, served briefly in the Colonial Office, but took Orders in 1832: both specialized in a rather arid legalism. Gladstone knew them as undergraduates, but not intimately. On reading Arthur Hallam's *Remains* in 1834, Gladstone had noted, 'if I were *now* to meet one such, still the old affection might be initiated but could not be renewed'.[52] He was to be surprised. In his rather lonely bachelor life in London he found with Hope, especially, a congruence of personal and intellectual attraction which was irresistible, as great perhaps, and certainly longer lasting, than that of Hallam. From today's perspective it is hard to understand the fascination exercised by Hope, who was high-minded but rather limited. But fascination there undoubtedly was with both Hope and Manning, and their apostasy to Roman Catholicism in 1851 contributed greatly to Gladstone's nervous sexual crisis of the early 1850s.

The friendship with Hope and Manning brought joy for the time being. They helped with advice about the writing of *The State in its Relations with the Church*, a time of enthusiasm and friendship as well as energetic intellectual work. In 1838 Manning was with Gladstone in Rome where they compared the Church of England to the Church of Rome and, fatefully, Gladstone 'took Manning to Wiseman's'. Wiseman, the leader of the English Roman Catholics, arranged for them to go to the English College to attend Mass 'with the parts of which I am beginning to acquire a little acquaintance'. Gladstone, at least, was 'confirmed in the idea that the mass implies & carries less of active mental participation than the English Liturgy'. Also in 1838 Gladstone drew up plans for a 'Third Order' in which clergy and laymen would share their religious thoughts and charitable activities, and the sort of spiritual, religious affinity which Gladstone felt for his friends would be given an institutional setting.[53] In the 1840s, as we shall see, something of the sort was achieved by the 'Engagement'. Religion in the male context—and the religious revival of the 1830s was very male-orientated—was thus for Gladstone personally uplifting.

It was also disturbing. Two of the three dreams recorded by Gladstone in the course of a lifetime of self-analysis date from just before this time. They were both dreams about Christ, the second apocalyptic and similar to the visions of the then fashionable artist, John Martin. Gladstone, in character, drew a moral lesson from each. Their interpretation must be hazardous, but the reader may like to have Gladstone's own account of them. First, on 19 July 1834, while in London during the Session:

Had last night a very curious dream of an appearance of our Saviour. Oh that he were ever present to the eye of my mind, as other visions often are.

Second, on 25 August 1834 while at Fasque and after writing the previous day (a Sunday) on 'God is love':

This morning I had a painful and appalling dream. I stood with ——, looking out towards the S. and E.—Over the sea there arose a light strange in colour, between blue and green, indescribably clear—it extended its arch upon the heaven: 'look, look, look!' and as we looked, it brightened into a clear flame, a white consuming flame, masses appeared to [be] crackling and dissolving in it: its advance was steady and rapid over the intervening space, it gathered up and devoured all the rival elements on its way: the truth flashed upon me, it is the coming of the Son of Man! I turned and saw one drawn by a resistless power, in convulsive struggles down, down to the ground, and under the ground: my tongue said mechanically, Glory to thee, O God! but I felt within me the mass of sin, of flesh, of self, a death from which I could not escape and along with which I too must surely and how deservedly be destroyed—but here my vision ended, I awoke. It should be useful: may it be.

Wooed and Married and All

Relationships with women were much more problematical than with men such as Hope, which followed a code well-established at school and university. For men with an Evangelical upbringing, the psychological pressures to marry were very strong. Some, like Newman, countered this by developing an ethos of celibacy, but Gladstone always seems to have seen marriage as his natural destiny. His education had left him with hardly any day-to-day experience of women of his own age, save for his sisters during the holidays. In the wholly male society of Eton and Christ Church—his Eton Dame was the only woman who played any part in his formal education—he developed a tendency to masturbate. This was in the circumstances natural enough, but like almost every male in his century who underwent a similar education, Gladstone saw it as a sin requiring forgiveness, a desire to be suppressed, even while recognizing it as a 'natural (& vigorous)' tendency. He was tantalized by this temptation through the 1830s and perhaps beyond. From an early age he began to counter it by (in the 1830s) occasional approaches to women in the street who were either destitutes or prostitutes, and with these he would hold religious conversations and sometimes give a charitable donation.

Living as a bachelor in London, he was left to make his own way, and this amounted to meetings with society women during the elaborate rituals of Conservative political society: 'dined at Sir E. Kerrison's—& sung! at Lady Salisbury's'. For a vulnerable youth with a tendency to introspection such opportunities cannot have been easy to take. Always anxious as a young man about the rightness of amusement and relaxation, Gladstone cannot have been at ease on such occasions. As always, he saw retribution hovering, and he agonized over the propriety of his attending balls and parties.

All three of the women to whom Gladstone proposed marriage were daughters of the aristocracy. Each was therefore socially superior to his father (though less so to his deceased mother) and each fell within the class whose value to the constitution Gladstone particularly revered. In his approach to marriage, Gladstone—no doubt subconsciously—sought to consolidate the social position to which his education had accustomed him.

His first two attempts at proposals were disastrous. Caroline Farquhar was well-known in society for her beauty. She was the daughter of Sir Thomas Farquhar, the sister of Walter Farquhar, an Eton and Christ Church friend, and a cousin of W. K. Hamilton, also of the House. She was clearly bewildered by the Gladstonian barrage, episodically maintained in 1835 and 1836 and probably exacerbated by his brother Robertson's marriage—albeit in an Anglican church—to a Unitarian in January 1836. Religious difficulties and differences were compounded by an absence of attraction on Miss Farquhar's part, Walter Farquhar telling Gladstone bluntly after some eight months of courtship, mostly by letter: 'The barrier you have to overcome is the obtaining of my sister's affections.'[54] Aged twenty-seven at this time, Gladstone began to brood about marriage, and in a melancholy mood:

> I know not whether any other boon
> Except the holy treasure of a wife
> Could make me love this anxious load of life
> Or think if now I died, I died too soon.[55]

This despondent frame of mind probably explains his sudden proposal to Lady Frances Douglas, daughter of the Earl of Morton. Having met her two years earlier, he courted her during a brief visit in November 1837 to her father's house, Dalmahoy, near Edinburgh. E. B. Ramsay, the famous Episcopalian dean of Edinburgh, acted as an intermediary, but achieved nothing, having to send Gladstone 'a crushing letter'.[56] Ramsay continued to intercede on Gladstone's behalf, but on 31 January 1838 he 'heard conclusively from Mr. Ramsay'—the Mortons had ordered an end to the correspondence.

These two attempts at marriage left Gladstone uncertain and disorientated. For the only time in his adult life he experienced something like despair. To gain a change of scene he asked his father to let him make a voyage to the West Indies so as personally to investigate the controversial plantations. The request was refused. The diary in 1838 has a number of mournful entries: 'The world outside me seems somehow dismantled now, because of the icy coldness of my heart. . . . This results from a few very bitter things which have gone the wrong way for me'[57] '. . . the daily sadness that is upon me in the midst of this painted life of inward trouble' '. . .I live almost perpetually restless & depressed.'[58] The tone is Byronic; *Childe Harold* had offered a model of romantic restlessness to Gladstone's generation, and he read it as the fruitlessness of his suit of Caroline Farquhar began to be apparent.[59] His depression partly reflected distress at the state of public affairs, for Gladstone was finishing the manuscript of his book in a mood less optimistic than its pages suggest: 'Conversation with Pusey. I told him for himself only—I thought my own Church & State principles within one stage of becoming hopeless as regards success in this generation.' But no public developments could entirely account for this inward malaise. With relief, Gladstone left for the Continent as soon as the Session ended. He went in the company of Arthur Kinnaird, a Liberal MP 'at once frank and gentle, and set singly upon the truth'.[60]

A few days before leaving, he met Catherine and Mary Glynne, sisters of his Eton and Christ Church acquaintance, Sir Stephen Glynne. The Glynnes were also bound for Italy. Gladstone had stayed a weekend at their family seat, Hawarden Castle in Flintshire (now Clwyd) in January 1836,[61]—immediately after his brother Robertson's controversial wedding and while he was courting Caroline Farquhar by letter. At that time he made no note of either of the Glynne sisters in his diary, though he found time to commend the sermon of Henry Glynne, their brother and Rector of Hawarden.

The Glynnes were an old Flintshire family—Sir Stephen was the ninth baronet—modestly well-off and attempting to sustain its position by associating itself with industrial development in the area—a move whose disastrous consequences were already becoming apparent with respect to the over-extended Oak Farm brick company in Staffordshire. Sir Stephen was Whig MP for Flintshire. He was a remnant of those Pittite Whigs who had not begun to call themselves Tories; Pitt the Younger was Catherine Glynne's first cousin twice removed and the family was linked to the Grenvilles and the Braybrookes. Glynne's obvious conservatism both impressed Gladstone and, as was the case with his travelling companion Kinnaird, flew in the face of his adversarial view of party relationships in the 1830s. Glynne was also a pillar of the Church of England in Wales and his huge collection of notes on all the old churches in Wales is a major achievement of nineteenth century antiquarianism, as well as showing the enthusiasm for Wales (and its ancient apostolic Christianity) characteristic of many of the Welsh gentry, so often dismissed as an alien presence by the Nonconformists. On the Italian journey he was a charming and knowledgeable companion, quite apart from the attraction Gladstone felt for his sister

Catherine. Gladstone took his own sister, Helen, to Ems on a cure for her health, but moved on quickly to Italy with Kinnaird to fall in with the Glynne party. While on this journey, he had a long conversation at Milan with Manzoni, the author of *I Promessi Sposi* which he had read earlier; Gladstone found him 'a man of rather strong Transalpine principles, but of fervent piety and charity'. The party visited Rome and Naples, Gladstone correcting the proofs of his book on the wing. Gladstone and Kinnaird went on for a month's tour of Sicily.

On returning to Rome, Gladstone renewed his courting of Catherine Glynne, almost bringing himself to a proposal in the moonlight in the Colosseum. For the first time his attentions were received with understanding. On 17 January 1839 he proposed by letter,[62] even though he was frequently in the Glynnes' company. The statement of important feelings by letter rather than word was common at this time both generally and in the Gladstone household. An extra reason on this occasion was Gladstone's wish to avoid the 'precipitancy' which he believed had spoilt his chances on earlier occasions.

Love for Catherine partially dispelled the malaise characteristic of the first part of the year. The change from the private diary to a travel diary written to be read at home and even more widely—the Sicilian sections were later rewritten to form the relevant part of Murray's *Handbook for Sicily*—means that the course of Gladstone's wooing and depression both go unrecorded. On resuming the private diary in February 1839, he noted:

In my accustomed review at the end of the past year [1838] I found that I had passed through more real depression in the earlier part of it, than ever before. . . . The truth is I believe my affections are more worthless than ever. Poured forth more than once & more than once repudiated they have become stale and unprofitable; and I am strangely divided between the pain of solitude in the heart and the shame of soliciting a love which I sometimes fear it is impossible for me to repay. I am so deadened and exhausted by what has taken place. . . . And yet I suffered more & more from being *inwardly* alone . . . in my circumstances a nature truly noble would probably come to the conclusion that it had nothing left to give which would be worthy of any woman herself such as to be worthy of its attachment.—I offer myself therefore with many conflicting feelings: but this time must I suppose be the last, were it only for shame's sake.

In her C.G. I saw what I desired, as I think distinctly developed: the admiration of sacrifice made for great objects—and a gentle not unwomanly contempt for the luxurious pleasures of the world.[63]

Faced with the prospect of permanent union with a man whose character was transparently extraordinary, Catherine Glynne asked for time. A week later Gladstone and Sir Stephen Glynne returned from Rome to London for the opening of the Session. Courtship continued with the return of Catherine and Mary Glynne to London in May, Gladstone eventually telling his father of his suit, 'concealment became too heavy for me'. At last, on 8 June 1839, during a walk by the river at Lady Shelley's house near Fulham, Catherine Glynne accepted him. Both saw the marriage in intensely religious terms:

We walked apart, and with an effort she said that all doubt on my part might end. I intreated her to try & know me well: I told her what was my original destination & desire in life, in what sense & manner I remained in connection with politics—all this produced no revulsion in her pure and lofty spirit. She asked for the earliest Communion, that we might go together to the altar of Christ.

Purity of behaviour was further established by an exchange of information about each other's earlier suits, Gladstone wanting 'to show her the letter of September 1835, and explain to her, at the least, that subject', i.e. the Caroline Farquhar affair. In his diary he noted, using Greek letters, the names—a considerable list—of her suitors, commenting, 'I could not fail to become more and more attracted by such goodness':

σημερνεναρκίλλϝαυάνὲγερτονὰνϛονάρκουρτλενιϛμορδαυντ[64]*

The couple were very quickly married on 25 July 1839 in Hawarden parish church with Francis Doyle as best man in a double wedding with Mary Glynne and George, Lord Lyttelton, whose engagement was even shorter. 'It has been more of heaven than of earth today' wrote Gladstone on his wedding day. But, characteristically, he qualified the joy: 'it has had its warning voice'; the brooding figure of Lady Glynne, too depressed to attend the ceremony, was a reminder of 'the contrasts of this mortal life'.

Gladstone was almost certainly a virgin when he married. Always highly susceptible to beauty, he had often been tempted and his diary contains many scattered references to sins of temptation of an unspecified sort. In his usual way of being precise without being explicit, Gladstone noted on the day Mary Glynne became engaged to George Lyttelton: 'I now know enough to be convinced that not without the faithful Providence of God have I been reserved for access to a creature so truly rare and consummate as my Catherine.'[65]

Catherine Glynne was a strong-minded, healthy, independent, and beautiful woman with, as her husband noticed after their wedding night, 'a pure, enduring brightness'. She had Gladstone's mother's sense of repose but combined it with a life of energy and action directed at the family and at charities for the service of children, estate workers, and, later, East-Enders. She thus stood somewhat outside Gladstone's conception of womanhood as exemplified by his mother and his sister Anne. For all his adoration of them, he did not marry their image. 'What am I', wondered Gladstone, 'to charge myself with the care of such a being, and to mix her destiny in mine.'[66] Catherine Glynne must have been aware at the time of her

* i.e. Seymer, Newark, Hill, Vaughan, Egerton, Anson, Harcourt, Lewis, Mordaunt.

marriage of the extraordinary potential of her husband's public life. She can hardly have anticipated its astonishing private developments.

Money and Morality

The Gladstones were a comfortably-off couple, in every sense. Well connected, their honeymoon was a tour of great houses in England and Scotland. Marriage to Catherine brought a wide range of contacts with every level of the aristocracy save the very top, and their life-style in London reflected this. Marriage also placed her husband in a curious relationship to the great social classes of the country. Never actively in business, commerce, or the professions, Gladstone was none the less 'middle class' and always regarded himself as such, though his use of the preposition 'still' in the following quotation suggests his recognition of ambiguity: 'I ... with the family of which I am a member, still claim to belong to that middle class',[67] he told the citizens of Liverpool in 1843. On the other hand, though not landed himself, he soon found himself, through marriage and through Sir Stephen Glynne's financial incompetence, the effective head of the Hawarden estates, with a country as well as a town base. Gladstone was, in fact, ideally placed in social terms later to develop the position which gave him such power in British politics, the arbitrator and mediator between the aristocracy and the middle class.

Catherine Glynne brought with her, by her husband's calculation, £10,716. 13s. 4d.[68] This roughly balanced what William Gladstone already had. His father had launched him on his career as an MP with a gift of £10,000, with further gifts of East India stock in 1837, valued at £2,150, and of £2,000 in 1840. To this was added an annual allowance of £2,500 and various generous gifts towards furnishing and day-to-day expenses such as 'Linen, Books, Carriages, Plate &c.'. To have a carriage was important in London society: it was the demarcating line between the wealthy and the pretenders.

As a bachelor MP, Gladstone lived in L2 in the Albany, off Piccadilly. When he married he bought the lease of 13 Carlton House Terrace on a mortgage of £6,500 paid at 6 per cent. Both these addresses were impeccable. Always a stickler for form—far more so than his wife—Gladstone's choice of houses reflected not merely convenience, but a desire for the best that orthodox London society could offer.

Apart from his salary during his brief period of office in 1834–5, Gladstone had earned not a penny of his wealth, which he valued in 1840 (including the mortgaged house and his wife's money) at £34,270. Given his view that society was based on obligations and duties rather than on rights, Gladstone naturally took his money seriously, though he was never embarrassed by it:

We ought to care about money: as a means, to be utterly regardless of it, as an end. We ought to be careful 1. to spend it—always to have either a) a present or

b) a prospective purpose for it. 2. *so* to spend it, that we may be the better able to open our books of pecuniary account, along with the rest of our proceedings, before God at the day of judgement.[69]

Consequently, Gladstone was exact about his charitable donations, the usual way of demonstrating proper stewardship. While an undergraduate, he reckoned that he had about £35. 10s. 6d. for 'Charity and Religion', and that this was 'under 1/11th' of his income (not of overall wealth); this had risen by 1835 to £211. 8s. 0d. ('about 1/9th'): for the years 1831–40, the average was, he calculated, 1/8th, or a total of £1,887. 1s. 0d. It is a little surprising that Gladstone seems to have seen these sums as residues after expenditure had been subtracted from income, rather than as sums set by forward planning. None the less, he had, in fact, done rather better than the Biblical tithe or tenth often used as the guide for personal charitable donations. In 1840 he planned in future to give 1/6th of his income. Later in the 1840s he partly separated charitable donations from his own expenditure pattern by setting up a separate charity fund, especially invested and generating its own income. In 1885 he calculated that, since 1831, he had given £52,113 to 'Charity & Religion'.

The Gladstone household was run religiously. The married couple read the Bible together, and household prayers—that Evangelical habit which in the early 1840s was becoming widespread—were regularly held. William Gladstone wrote a remarkable series of sermons which he read to the servants on Sundays, a habit he had developed while a bachelor—the series runs from 1834 to 1866.[70] On Sundays Gladstone always also privately read some printed sermons. As the 1830s progressed these tended to become High Church or Tractarian in tone: sixteenth-century divines such as John Jewell (Hooker's patron), Arminian and Caroline divines such as William Laud and Jeremy Taylor, or Tractarians such as Keble, Newman, and Pusey. As an undergraduate, Gladstone often read Thomas Arnold's moralistic sermons, but as the 'church party' tension of the 1830s developed and Arnold denounced the Tractarians as 'Oxford Malignants', he figures less in Gladstone's reading. Even so, this reading never became exclusively devoted to writers in the apostolic tradition.

In worship, Gladstone became increasingly Tractarian. For the time, he communicated very regularly, regarding 'the Eucharist, as representing food rather than remembrance'.[71] He made private notes for regular use in preparation for communion, one of his Eucharistic verses later finding its way into *The English Hymnal* as hymn 322. He usually attended his local parish church—St James's, Piccadilly, when living in the Albany, St Martin-in-the-Fields after his marriage—but he felt strongly drawn to the new ecclesiological and Tractarian developments in worship. In a paper written in 1839 on the need for beauty and veneration in worship, he wrote:

There is a true wisdom—varying in its application through a thousand degrees according to temperaments and circumstances—in the tinted lights, the rich and solemn architecture, in the plaintive chanted prayer, in the many voiced celestial organ: because they do for certain portions of our complex nature (instrumentally under God) what mental effort does for certain other portions.[72]

This view places Gladstone, as do his private devotional habits as developed in the 1840s, very much in the Puseyite tradition, however cautious publicly he was about some of its tendencies.

A Confident Conservative?

In concluding this review of Gladstone's years of high-Conservatism, it would be wrong to argue that his position was either clear or easy. Even in his chosen area of State–Church relationships, there was a wide range of influences pulling in differing directions. Two of these—the Broad Church nationalism of Coleridge and Arnold, and the apostolic semi-separatism of the Tractarians—both led in the context of the century to Liberalism, though for very different reasons. It was a great irony that almost all those Oxonians of Gladstone's generation who in the 1830s wrote books and pamphlets to counteract the dangerous tendencies of Liberal intellectualism and Liberal politics—Gladstone, Pusey, Manning, Newman—later found themselves its political beneficiaries.

None the less, Gladstone's Conservatism was characterized by boldness. That guarded qualification typical of the later Gladstone was already present, but it was not dominant. In the 1840s Gladstone came to prefer the 'lean and stunted affirmations' of Bishop Butler as he used probability as his guide to conduct. In the 1830s 'probability' lurked in the small print; Gladstonian Conservatism appeared certain and unyielding.

In certain important aspects of Conservatism Gladstone showed no interest. In particular, on the great question of fiscal policy he had as yet no well worked-out views of the sort that he had on Church questions. Brought up a Huskissonian moderate tariff reformer, he remained so during the 1830s, but without much scrutiny of his position. There are a few clues. Gladstone's method was already clear. In the second order world of fiscal arrangements he judged by facts rather than by abstract, a priori premises and deductions. In 1826, aged 16, he defended his Huskissonian position on the Corn Laws in anonymous letters to the *Liverpool Courier*, arguing he was 'as much opposed to the Levellers and visionaries of the one side, as to the Bigots and Monopolists of the other'. 'I admit facts, and abstract principles only in subservience to facts, as the true standard of Agricultural, Commercial and Financial Legislation' he told the electors in his election address in 1832, without mentioning the

Corn Laws. In the 1830s, these facts were thought to support the modified Corn Laws:

surely we are aware that if they were repealed, the landlords would be impoverished: no rents would remain . . . the landlords would become farmers themselves . . . the farmers would become labourers; and the labourers . . . must be contented with such wages as foreign countries give.

This comment, written in a draft pamphlet on the dismissal of the Whigs in 1834, Gladstone chose not to publish, and it is, among his many statements about the politics of the 1830s, almost a lone comment on the contemporary situation.[73] Early in 1841 he had an interesting confrontation with Richard Cobden on the Anti-Corn Law League. Cobden, not yet himself an MP, campaigned for the League at a by-election at Walsall, where J. N. Gladstone was the Tory candidate. Gladstone campaigned for his brother, and made a speech. Cobden wrote to complain at Gladstone's claim in his speech that 'this Anti-Corn Law League was no better than a big borough-mongering association', and challenged him to a public debate. 'I propose to show', Cobden wrote,

that the corn and provision laws are partial and unjust, that they are calculated for the temporary enrichment of a small part of the community, at the expense of the millions who subsist by honest industry, that they are an interference with the dispensation of divine Providence as proved by the revealed word of God and the obvious laws of nature, and that therefore they ought to be totally & immediately repealed.

This assault by the Anglican Cobden used a terminology which would have appealed to Gladstone, though he would not himself at any stage have made such a mechanical link between Providential dispensation and the need for repeal. It caught Gladstone slightly off-balance, and, declining the debate, he replied by separating the League from the Laws and attacking the former:

You desire me to meet you in discussion not upon the League but upon the Corn Law. I cannot imagine two subjects more distinct. I admit the question of the repeal of the Corn Law to be a subject fairly open to discussion although I have a strong opinion against it. But as to the Anti-Corn Law League I do not admit that any equitable doubt can be entertained as to the character of the proceedings: &, excepting a casual familiarity of phrase, I adhere rigidly to the substance which I have expressed.

Not surprisingly, he concluded in 1841 that 'Cobden will be a worrying man on corn'.[74]

A tariff structure implies, to a degree, a managed economy. In that sense, it was not incompatible with the confessional State which Gladstone spent much of the 1830s contemplating. Indeed, in the twentieth century, advocates of a confessional State have often been explicitly corporatist in their view of the economy. But Gladstone drew no such conclusion. He made no attempt to link a national economy with a national religion. When in 1843 he commented on a pamphlet by Friedrich List, the chief apologist of a national economy in the nineteenth century, he attacked 'those anti-commercial ideas which have lately been propagated in Germany by Dr. Liszt [*sic*]'. In keeping with the traditions of his education, he did not connect political thought with political economy: indeed, as we have seen, he was largely ignorant of the latter. Like most of his generation, nurtured on the supposed evils of the national debt incurred during the wars against France, he was an instinctive retrencher. From his first manifesto in Newark in 1832, Gladstone declared himself an economic reformer, i.e. in favour of the curtailment of government spending. This meant that he did not support the plans put forward by Sir Robert Inglis and some other Tories for extensive grants to the Church of England for its expansion into the areas of new population. The means of achieving 'national religion' were, therefore, in Gladstone's view to be voluntary means: the modern state should have a national church, but without it being paid for from government revenue.

There was in all this the embryo of a method, but no developed view. Partly this may be explained by the fact that for most of the decade fiscal policy was, compared with constitutional reform and Church questions, relatively unimportant: 'from 1833 to 1841, was a period the most inactive we believe in the improvement of our commercial legislation, since the peace of 1815', wrote Gladstone in 1843 when he had turned to consider such matters.[75] It was possible for a young MP living in the Albany not to have to be confronted by the practical consequences of industrialization in any very direct way. Yet it remains curious that Gladstone gave little attention to the social and economic organization that would have to underpin 'national religion', particularly as the role of the landed aristocracy in his system was bound to be prominent.

As with many of his contemporaries who looked to the Tory Party as their best hope, Gladstone lacked the intellectual categories with which to discuss such issues. The language of Toryism did not embrace concepts such as industrialization and modernization. The vague notion of 'improvement' to which Gladstone subscribed was an insufficient guide. At certain moments in the decade, Gladstone yearned for a fusion of intellect and religious zeal. He tried to see them as complementary rather as Coleridge in the social and political area saw the concepts of 'progress' and 'permanence', and in general attempted a fusion of knowledge and belief. Gladstone hoped to 'direct the mental eye of man in a course intermediate between speculation and idolatry', and he used the image of the steam engine to describe his vision:

It is true that we have hitherto seen but too often the principle of intellectual excellence & the spirit of religious zeal in collision rather than in harmony, but let us hope that it may be otherwise, even as the elements of fire and water . . . now are blended to accelerate the passage of man over the wide ocean.[76]

It was, of course, just such a fusion that the Oxford Noetics were attempting with respect to philosophy, theology, political economy, and social organization. The experience of the Peel government of 1841–6 was to provide the shock which completed the first phase of Gladstone's education, and then in the very un-Noetical direction of a disaggregation of functions: Church and State, government and economy, was each to ride its different way.

The 1830s as a decade turned out to be something of a red herring for Gladstone. He later believed that the 1832 Reform Act delayed the repeal of the Corn Laws by a decade. A similar delay may be suggested in his own development with respect to Church–State relations. But the reasons for both were the same. It was not generally apparent in the 1830s that intellectual, administrative, economic, demographic, and political pressures were all pointing towards a free-trading solution. Nor was it apparent, though it was perhaps easier to see, that similar pressures were rendering redundant both the Tory and the Whig versions of 'national religion'.

Learning this was to be a hard lesson, with permanent consequences.

CHAPTER III

Church, State, and Free Trade: the Public Crisis of the 1840s

*Gladstone in the 1840s — 'A book upon a portion of political science' —
National Religion — Peel's Government — Idealism versus Practicability: the
Maynooth Grant and Resignation — Maynooth and the Oxford Movement —
Church Affairs — Free Trade and Experience — International Morality —
Liberalism and Politics in the Early 1850s — A 'Mixed Government':
the Aberdeen Coalition*

The last years have woven strong cords upon me that I had not before: but my vocation does not seem as yet to struggle against them. I am older than was the Redeemer in the flesh. Is He in any sense my pattern, in any sense that is not a mockery? Have I made any true progress in the work of salvation? Habitually my hope preponderates over fear: but it is not free itself from the fear that it may be a sin-wrought delusion.

Gladstone in the 1840s

Thus Gladstone wrote in his diary (or journal, as he always called it) on his birthday, 29 December 1844, as he prepared to resign from Peel's cabinet on the Maynooth question. And indeed strong cords were being both woven around him and released, cords which, partly by his own tying and partly by the developments of the day, came to bind him to political and intellectual positions which in the 1830s he would have regarded as inconceivable, even satanic. The predominant features of Gladstone's life in the 1840s are those of sharp change and sometimes painful consolidation: change in domestic, political, and intellectual affairs; consolidation in the gradual establishment of life-long attitudes and commitments.

Domestically, Gladstone's marriage in 1839 marked the start of wide-ranging responsibilities and changes. The 1840s and early 1850s saw the birth of all his children and the death of one of them, the death of his father, the apostasy of his sister and of some of his closest friends, and the start of his regular attempts at the redemption of prostitutes. His marriage involved him in the bankruptcy of the Oak Farm company, the consequent mortgaging of his wife's family estates at Hawarden, and his life-long commitment to their rescue. These domestic developments, together with the stress of public life, forced upon him a severe psychological crisis whose expression took a sexual form. He risked ruin 'all'anima ed al corpo' (to the soul and body).

They made for Gladstone a personal and sometimes intrusive background for the dramatic public developments of the 1840s. The resurgence of the Tory party ended in 1846 in one of the three major schisms of modern British politics, causing party instability and long-standing personal bitterness. The Oxford (Tractarian) movement had a development *pari passu*, of influence, defeat, and disintegration. The government and the governing class came to terms with the social, economic, and political problems of the most industrialized nation in the world, and tried to deal with those of its regional antithesis, rural Ireland.

The years between 1840 and 1855 were one of those periods which force men from their courses, and of no figure is this more true than of Gladstone; they have, at least between 1840 and 1848, a sustained and heightened feel of political crisis not again met until the 1880s. In those years Gladstone reached the Cabinet (and resigned from it) and held three offices in it, two of them of central and even decisive importance: President of the Board of Trade (1843–5), Secretary of State for War and the Colonies (1845–6), and Chancellor of the Exchequer (1852–5). The 'swan, very white and tender, and stuffed with truffles' which Disraeli observed at a dinner party in 1835, spread its wings and dirtied its feathers: the Tory Tractarian became the nation's leading financial statesman, and the colleague in Cabinet of the radical Utilitarian Sir William Molesworth. Intellectually and ecclesiastically the author of *The State in its Relations with the Church* witnessed the collapse of his political and ecclesiastical system and built anew on the basis of free trade, a colonial empire and, however reluctantly, an increasingly secularized State.

These years were, therefore, of central and pivotal significance for Gladstone's political, intellectual, and ecclesiastical development. His diary chronicles them and their consequences relentlessly, sometimes in the form of passages of reflection, always in the form of detailed records of reading and correspondence which show the changing pattern of his social and political involvements and intellectual interests.

Though by 1840 well established as a political figure, Gladstone never saw himself as merely a politician; he saw, or tried to see, political life as merely a function of a more general calling. As he put it: 'it is especially true that he who holds office of public trust runs a thousand hazards of sinking into a party man, instead of a man employing party instrumentally for its ulterior purposes; into a politician, instead of a man in politics; into an administrator, instead of a man in administration'. When in 1840 he drew up a list of 'plans at present in view', all were extraparliamentary and only two were concerned with politics, and those very obliquely.* In principle and in theory, therefore, withdrawal from political life would be a natural enough move, and he considered it on several occasions during these years. The reader may judge for himself whether, having experienced real power, Gladstone found a satisfactory alternative in his out-of-office pursuits.

'A book upon a portion of political science'

Like George Eliot's Dorothea in *Middlemarch*, Gladstone's mind was 'theoretic, and yearned by its nature after some lofty conception of the world'. Throughout his life and to an extent far beyond that of any other British politician who was regularly in office, he spent much time yearning after such a conception, and attempting to define it in such a way as would be true and at the same time applicable to the realities of British public life. Gladstone approached problems in two ways. First by massive and detailed analysis resulting in a practical solution advanced and defended by overwhelming empirical argument, laborious correspondence, and dextrous use of institutional manipulation; second, if the problem moved him sufficiently, by a reflective article or book review, or, in a major instance, by a book. Thus his response to the Reform Bill of 1832 and its Whiggish aftermath was *The State in its Relations with the Church*; to university reform and the justification of classical studies as the basis of a Christian education, *Studies on Homer and the Homeric age*, to the general problem of right conduct in public life, his edition of Joseph Butler and his *Studies subsidiary to Butler's works*, begun in 1845.

We shall not, therefore, get far in understanding Gladstone's behaviour without considering the background: *The State in its Relations with the Church*, first published in 1838, twice reprinted, with a second edition in two volumes in 1841, and its companion volume *Church Principles considered in their Results* (1840). For these, and especially the first, intended as 'a book upon a portion of political science', sum up what he thought, *circa* 1840, the essentials of public life and social order ought to be. The consequences of the discovery of the impracticability of this approach, the crisis which this forced upon him, and his attempts to resolve that crisis, constitute the framework for the reading, correspondence, and self-analysis which provide the bulk of the entries in his diaries. An examination in some detail of the arguments and implications of these volumes is therefore necessary.

* '1. Publication of my book on Church principles.
  2. Enlargement of my book on Church & State.
  3. Scotch College [i.e. Glenalmond].
  4. Church at the Oak Farm.
  5. Certain rules to be established at my Father's new Church in Liverpool.
  6. A new School & a Board of Education at Newark.
  7. To concentrate & reorganise those operations now carried on through 'Societies'.
  8. Church at Fasque.'

Gladstone's first two books, certainly the most remarkable of British Prime Ministers' publications, cannot be dismissed as *jeux d'esprit*, youthful aberrations whose theories were either painlessly or quickly abandoned.* We have seen in the previous chapter the extensive reading and emotional energy through which Gladstone in the 1830s developed his intellectual and religious position. Of the books, *The State in its Relations with the Church* is the more important of the two, for *Church Principles* largely derives from its premisses. Though described famously and wrongly by Macaulay, followed by Morley and many others, as *Church and State*, the emphasis falls on the State, and this constitutes its chief interest. Though intended as a contribution to the revival of Anglicanism in the form of the Oxford movement, the work is not a characteristic Tractarian production. It relies strongly on Hooker for its approach to the Church, but on Burke and Coleridge for the State. Based on the Coleridgian concept of the Ideal, Gladstone defined the State as an 'organic body' in which persons were to be considered 'not as individuals, but only as constituents of the active power of that life . . . the state is the self-governing energy of the nation made objective'. Thus the State was not merely an aggregation of individuals, but an organic whole with 'a national conscience . . . formed upon a pure and comprehensive idea of right and wrong'. Definition of right and wrong was the function of the Church: 'religion is directly necessary to the right employment of the energies of the state as a state'. From this derived the role of the Established Church and the necessity for its preservation.

These arguments from within the Idealistic tradition implied strong hostility to the Utilitarian position, and Gladstone denounces 'the philosophy which holds that the latter [the individual man] will do best to choose his actions by a consideration of their general consequences, and which maintains that presumed advantage is to the human mind the best and most available criterion of right'. 'The injurious legacy of Locke' had spawned 'the twin sister of that degraded system of ethics or individual morality' which reached its full development in Bentham and James Mill.

Gladstone had made very bold claims for the theoretical authority of the State—bolder perhaps than he knew. For, as Macaulay observed in his famous attack in the *Edinburgh Review*, he had developed a major premiss to support a minor. Gladstone had no time for the old High Tory Establishment arguments of convenience and social stability, a

---

* Gladstone's reaction to criticism was to expand to two volumes, not disavow, his book. Historians have tended to isolate the comment in 'A chapter of autobiography', 'scarcely had my work issued from the press when . . . I found myself the last man on the sinking ship', without heed to the subsequent time-span. Morley does not meet head-on the role which *The State in its Relations with the Church* and its aftermath played in the development of the intellectual aspects of Gladstone's views on politics. The condition of the Liberal party, the debate about the nature of Liberalism 1899–1902, and Morley's own difficulties about making a systematic analysis of political Liberalism may well have discouraged him from this confrontation.

kind of Protestantism, with which I have no sympathy whatever ... which grew into fashion during the last century and has not quite grown out of it: that hated everything in religion which lived and moved: which lowered and almost paganised doctrine: loosened and destroyed discipline, and much defaced, in contempt of law, the decent and beautiful order of the Church: which neglected learning, coolly tolerated vice ... heaped up abuses mountain-high in the shape of plurality, non-residence, simony, and others more than I can tell ... made the Church of England, I say it with deliberate sorrow, instead of being the glory, in many respects the shame of Christendom.

The object of the book was to erect a framework of justification for establishment in theoretical terms strong enough to outweigh the objections—legitimate as Gladstone thought—to High Tory practice and expediency. Hence the very strong major premiss. The implications of the major premiss of the organic State are not worked out. Indeed, when he came to consider the rights of individuals and the historic position of the right of dissenters to exist without persecution, Gladstone was forced back upon that utilitarian tradition which he had earlier in the book so vehemently condemned. Notwithstanding his claims for the State, Gladstone asserted that 'the individual man, in virtue of his rational understanding and free agency, is entitled and bound in the sight of God to be in the last resort the arbiter of his religious creed, subject to his own full responsibility for employing the means most calculated to put him in possession of the truth';* and he mentions Locke's *Letters on toleration* as merely a step towards the goal. Thus at the heart of the book lay a profound contradiction, the result of the attempt to use two quite separate philosophical traditions to justify first an Ideal of society, then practical anomalies to that Ideal which already existed. There was, therefore, a lifeline to utilitarianism and consequently pluralism when the ship sank.

National Religion

Before considering the practical implications of these ideas, two other characteristics of the volume may be noted. Most striking is the high role given to nationality and its definition. The organic definition of the State and its close marriage to the Church would reflect the national character: 'national religion is the vivifying and ennobling principle of all national life'. 'National organization is evidently of divine appointment ... nations are the families into which the human race has what may be termed its primary distribution.' Keble, in his review in the *British Critic*, regarded the passage on the nationality of Anglicanism as the most original section of the book. The State, 'the natural organ of the nation', must choose the religion, guided by its ruling élite, which in Gladstone's view should resemble Coleridge's clerisy. Thus embodying their various national

* An aim of religion is 'the greatest holiness of the greatest number'.

characteristics, the English élite chose Anglicanism, the Mohammedans Mohammedanism, the United States a diversity of beliefs. Though the two last fell short of the ideal, they were acting not wrongly but naturally: the national Church reflected the innate characteristics of the nation it served. This belief was to be crucial when Gladstone came in later years to confront the problem of nationality in the Empire and in America. An expression of this view and of the practical application of what Gladstone called 'religious nationality' can be seen in his denunciation in 1851 of the Whigs' anti-Buddhist policy in Ceylon. In the Anglican context, therefore, the consequence was that the laws of Church and State, though of great importance, were merely the legal expression of English 'religious nationality': 'the union of the Church and the State is not a law of a primary kind, but a consummatory result of the development of Christianity in a people'. Believing this, Gladstone naturally had difficulty in justifying the Anglican establishment in Ireland, and the passages defending it in his book are much more mechanistic and less organic in tone than those on England. This emphasis on national religion, on locality, and separate traditions, distanced Gladstone somewhat from the Newmanite group within the Tractarians, and associated him rather with the High-Churchmen such as William Palmer, a group increasingly concerned about the 'Romanizing' tendencies of Newman's circle.

Because of this deeply-rooted belief that the form of religion was conditioned by nationality, Gladstone was never inclined to Roman Catholicism, whatever the Protestant press maintained. Of all those regarded as Tractarians he was perhaps most personally appalled at the progressive apostasy which overtook that movement, and no layman can have done more by correspondence and admonition to try to prevent it. For Gladstone already regarded Roman Catholicism as, at least in the nineteenth century, necessarily ultramontanist. He regarded what he saw as the Liberal Catholic Montalembert's failure to put truthful statement of fact and argument as a necessary and 'crucial instance of that fundamental antipathy between ultramontanism and freedom which at this moment constitutes one of the darkest omens for the future of Christendom', and he regarded Montalembert's Liberal Catholicism an 'imposture . . . he little knows what freedom means'. Gladstone naturally found 'startling' the 'general view of the ulterior section of the Oxford writers and their friends', for the ultimately ultramontanist position of the supporters of Newman's Tract XC seemed to him unnecessary, unhistorical, and deplorable, as he pointed out in drafting an anonymous letter to *The Times* in 1842 (though he thought better of sending it).

Another pronounced feature of *The State in its Relations with the Church* is its preoccupation with moral progress in this world. Coleridge's *Essay on the Constitution of Church and State* (1830), which, as we have seen, influenced

Gladstone from the mid-1830s, was ethical in tone and Gladstone was very much concerned with the ethics of the clerisy, an intellectual élite 'inherent in every well-constituted body politic', and with the morality of the nation as a whole. (His interest in the clerisy—a 'class . . . sufficiently supported . . . freed from corroding want and care'—led naturally to his later enthusiasm for the administrative grade of the civil service.) Though he spent much time himself on personal analysis, he was less concerned than other Tractarians with individual spirituality; the world of affairs not John Keble's Hursley vicarage was his natural home. Indeed Keble, in a review whose nuances are today of more interest than Macaulay's sledge-hammer blows, found Gladstone's book deficient in a number of Tractarian virtues. It had an 'unconscious tinge, we will not say of Erastianism, but of state as distinct from Church policy'; Gladstone had failed 'to keep his language clear of a certain utilitarian tone'; he should have given 'less encouragement to the enemies of Christian discipline'.

Peel's Government: Idealism versus Practicality

These then were the high aims of the young Tory of the early 1840s: the dream of a moral State married to a cleansed Church together countering 'the moral movement . . . of the day, away from religion and towards infidelity' and so achieving a peculiarly English and nationalistic form of ethical and religious progress. Other countries were seen in terms of Britain's salvation. Thus when in 1840 he spoke strongly against the infliction of the opium trade upon China, Gladstone was motivated partly by sympathy for the Chinese but also he was 'in dread of the judgment of God upon England for our national iniquity towards China'. Similarly, Ireland in 1845 was 'that cloud in the West, that coming storm, the minister of God's retribution upon cruel and inveterate and but half-atoned injustice!'* But national virtue depended on individual conviction. Individual and institutional leadership was therefore vital to establish a context of moral progress: 'the people must recover their moral health as individuals (in a polity where they exercise a main controul) before they can enjoy its consequences as a combination'. Gladstone continually stressed, in a characteristically Anglican way, the superior advantages of the Church of England as an effective compromise, in which all reasonable persons might find a mansion.

Individual leadership was provided by individual Tractarians; institutional leadership would come from the Tory party and the Anglican establishment secured by that party. Tactical success thus depended, as Gladstone and Keble both observed, on the Tory party as the guardians of

* Letter of 12 October 1845, in A. Tilney Bassett, *Gladstone to his wife* (1936), 64; the context of this famous quotation appears to refer to the Church question, not to the famine, but the nature of the 'injustice' is not made clear.

the Establishment and on the 'chosen band' of Tractarians within it 'to assert those principles'. The role of the Tory party was therefore crucial to the Gladstonian conception of State–Church politics, for the Whigs and Radicals were certain to act against it. But the idea of the chosen Tractarian band persuading the Tory country worthies to lead the nation along Tractarian paths of spiritual, ethical, and ecclesiastical progress seems odd enough, as some Tractarians, such as Newman, had already recognized by the late 1830s. As the prospect of office in 1841 became a certainty, Gladstone began to question the practicability of his concept, a matter of fundamental importance to his political life, for if the Tories failed to live up to their role, he would have to reconsider his own function and position in politics. 'Supposing the party abandon altogether the recognition of the Church, I mean of the Church as *the* Church', Gladstone wrote in May 1841, then he would have to 'accept the conditions of the age', 'leave a way which is hopelessly barred' and perhaps abandon parliamentary action altogether.

The recognition that the way to the realization of his dream was indeed barred by 'the conditions of the age' was to be slow, painful, and critical. During the collapse of the Whig ministry in the summer of 1841, Gladstone was included in Peel's meetings to discuss Tory tactics. His hope of the Cabinet and of a post in Ireland—for 'since the Address meetings the idea of Ireland had nestled imperceptibly in my mind'—were unrealized. (The Anglican establishment was most obviously vulnerable in Ireland.) Reluctantly, and with qualifications about the morality of British policy towards China, he accepted the vice-presidency of the Board of Trade. At first he regarded this as a limited and technical activity which left him 'morally free' (because he was outside the Cabinet) with respect to the administration's general policy. He immersed himself in minutes, tariff and corn law revision, and reading on economic questions. Peel had chosen wisely. In the Board of Trade Gladstone, from the start virtually its president as the records of the minute books show, discovered an absorbing fascination with the details of administration. Despite his self-confessed earlier ignorance, Gladstone was soon sufficiently informed and self-confident to challenge Peel—the accepted financial expert of the age—on the details of corn law revision, even to the point of threatening resignation. In a few months Gladstone had advanced from having 'no general knowledge of trade whatever' to being one of the few who had mastered the labyrinthine detail of British tariffs, even allowing himself to draw some comfort from his new-found abilities, the more so as he realized that Ripon's lethargy as president hampered the Board of Trade's effectiveness at Cabinet level.

Peel remedied this in 1843 when Ripon retired by offering Gladstone, then aged thirty-three, the presidency with a seat in the Cabinet. Peel was

careful in discussing the matter to mention 'the compromises and adjustments of opinion necessary to ensure the cooperation of a Cabinet composed of any fourteen men'. Gladstone raised difficulties about the opium
trade, Graham's proposed Education Clauses for the Factory Bill, and the
amalgamation of bishoprics in North Wales to provide a new see for Manchester. He wavered between entering the Cabinet and retiring altogether
('at least such is probably the second alternative'). Guided by the 73rd
Psalm—the set Psalm for the relevant Sunday—and a conversation with
Hope and Manning who urged acceptance despite the narrow issue of the
bishoprics, he accepted the presidency and joined the Cabinet. 'My first
Cabinet', on 15 May 1843, was on O'Connell's movement for the repeal of
the Act of Union.

As president, Gladstone quickly developed his remarkable facility for
combining in a bill both immediate and anticipatory elements. Thus his
Railway Bill of 1844 tidied up the procedure for handling the mass of
private bills necessary for developing a railway network sponsored by
private capital, and reserved the State's rights to intervene in the concerns
of the railway companies. It provided for the needs of the working-class
family through the 'parliamentary train'—one train to run each day at the
minimum charge of 1d. per mile. Gladstone also anticipated that private
enterprise might not produce an adequate railway system, and so provision
was made for the preservation of the national interest by allowing for the
ultimate acquisition of the railways by the public under certain stated terms
of compensation, a provision which reflected Gladstone's general attitude
to the limitations on the privateness of property, his natural *étatisme* and, it
may be said, his common sense.

The implications of this realization of the beauty, joy, and technical
satisfaction of departmental work were profound for Gladstone's general
approach to politics. For it launched him on that life-long passionate effort
of 'working the institutions of the country', and of explaining and defending the details of administration in the Commons. The growth of this technical fascination can be seen throughout the years 1841–5. By 1845 time
spent on 'business' was counted with study and devotion as time spent in a
Godly way (measured daily by the hour and recorded in the diary). Though
Gladstone sometimes regretted his absence from church through the pressures of administration, he never regarded the latter as unworthy, however
routine the activity. His diary testifies continually to the energy with which
he absorbed speeches, correspondence, reports, books, and pamphlets
which allowed him to speak, write, and act on such a variety of topics.

This absorption in the realities of administration forced Gladstone to
recognize that as 'a man in politics' he might have a wider function than the
ethical role he had accorded himself in the 1830s and the governing élite in
his book. It also brought into sharp focus the excessively theoretical nature

of his earlier views. The success of political Tractarianism had depended on infiltration and control of the Tory party. But it was soon clear that the Tory party in office, and perhaps especially its Cabinet, would fall far short of the high role accorded it by Gladstone. By 1842 he noted that he had ceased to believe that in 'the adjustment of certain relations of the Church to the State . . . the action of the latter can be harmonised to the laws of the former. We have passed the point at which that was possible. . . . The materials waste away daily.' But he hoped a Tory Cabinet would at least avoid worsening the Church's position and that under the Tories 'the State would honestly aim at enabling the Church to develop her own intrinsic means'. At the end of 1843 he noted: 'of public life I certainly must say every year shows me more & more that the idea of Christian politics can not be realised in the State according to its present conditions of existence'. None the less some cause for optimism remained, and the impracticability of Gladstone's State and Church theory had not yet been fully demonstrated. Moreover he was directly involved in its defence by his promotion to the Cabinet: he could no longer claim the moral freedom of mere departmental responsibility.

The tortuous and technical questions which lay behind the 1844 Dissenters Chapels Bill did not prevent Gladstone from supporting it enthusiastically on 'general principles of equity and justice'. This view dismayed Tory Establishmentarians of the old school and prompted R. L. Sheil, the Irish MP, to a perceptive if slowly realized prophecy: Gladstone, 'the champion of free trade, will ere long become the advocate of the most unrestricted liberty of thought'. But Gladstone's support for this bill sprang from the awkward historicism of his general support in his book for Dissenters' rights. It did not strike at the roots of his theory, or at any rate at that section of his book which justified the apparent anomaly of Dissenters' rights by arguments of utilitarianism and historicism.

The Maynooth Grant and Resignation

The crisis, however, soon came, and on what was for Gladstone the central point of principle, perhaps because it was more significant symbolically than practically, he found the cabinet wanting in steadfast principle. Hostility to the endowment and increase of the educational grant to the Roman Catholic college of Maynooth, near Dublin, seriously proposed in January 1844, became for Gladstone the touchstone of orthodoxy, for what was this but Whiggish concurrent endowment by the back door, which his book committed him to oppose?* On the question of English education he was ready to take, once in the cabinet, a position of administrative convenience. But Maynooth he saw as the battleground for 'National Religion', and it was in that 'Serbonian bog' that Gladstone's model for State and Church sank to its axles.

* In 1842 he supported the grant before its increase, 'reluctant but convinced'.

The battle between Gladstone and the cabinet was prolonged—from February 1844 to his resignation in January 1845—but the result was never in doubt. The impracticality of Maynooth as a battle-cry was merely a measure of the impracticality of the theory it symbolized. With his recent training in Peelite techniques of administration Gladstone soon saw this. Principle rejected the Maynooth grant: good government demanded it. Thus Gladstone both resigned from the cabinet and voted for the grant: the man of theory and the man of government.

Gladstone's resignation was popular amongst many Tories, churchmen, and even Nonconformists, who looked to Gladstone as the natural leader of the opposition to Peel—and as a much more substantial and reputable focus of opposition than Disraeli. Strong pressure was put upon him to lead the opposition to the grant. Ministerial fears that the government might fall on the issue reflected strong anti-Catholicism in the constituencies, and the petitions and deputations against the bill presaged the better known demonstrations against the establishment of Roman Catholic sees in 1850-1. It was not Gladstone's resignation, but his subsequent support for the grant which seemed perplexing and casuistic.

Idiosyncratic and perverse though Gladstone's action seemed to contemporaries, it was for him a pivotal and purgative experience. Never again (except perhaps in his last officially significant act in 1894) did he resign purely on principle, never again did he invest government or party with the high ethical status of *The State in its Relations with the Church*. The crisis foreseen in 1841 had occurred; the basic assumptions of his political life had been shown impracticable. He had, he told Newman, 'clung to the notion of a conscience, in the State, until that idea has become in the general mind so feeble as to be absolutely inappreciable in the movement of public affairs'. The experience was a 'nightmare' for him for several months, but it had one immediate dividend. He met the split of the Tory party in 1846 with relative equanimity; for Gladstone and for many lesser Tractarians at Westminster, in country vicarages, and in Oxford colleges, it had already abandoned its elevated function.

Maynooth and the Oxford Movement: 'the Parting of Friends'

The personal problem facing Gladstone in the years after Maynooth was: should he remain in politics and could anything be salvaged from the wreck of his theories? Gladstone told Stanley during the Maynooth crisis that 'the lower ends of a State ought to be fulfilled even when the higher ones should have become impractical', and he had only momentary doubts about continuing as an MP. His own problem of ideological reconstruction was much more complex. It was to some extent simplified by the collapse of the Oxford movement during the 1840s. One by one the friends parted, each with his own Maynooth, but all going further than Gladstone ever contemplated by joining the Church of Rome. Newman, Hope, Manning, all the Wilberforces save Samuel, and many of lesser fame took the step against which Gladstone so anxiously watched, argued, and prayed. The apostasy of Hope and Manning in 1851 was, on both sides, a bar to further intimacy; it left Gladstone 'unmanned and unnerved' though with 'total freedom from doubts' and brought on a period of severe spiritual loneliness expressed in part in a sexual crisis when he found 'my trusts are Carnal'.*

Thus was gradually broken up the circle of friends who from the mid-thirties had been Gladstone's closest confidants, to whom he had naturally turned even on political matters. If this left Gladstone without many friends with whom he could discuss his intellectual problems—James Hope is the only man outside the family given an albeit self-conscious nickname—it meant that those who were his friends were more political in outlook and commitment and less clerical in occupation than previously. Lord Lincoln and Sidney Herbert (both Tractarians) in political, Samuel Wilberforce increasingly in ecclesiastical matters, became reliable friends, but these were not intellectual friendships of the burning intensity shared with Manning and James Hope. In old age Gladstone recalled of Manning, 'I can only look at him as a man looks at the stars', and of Hope, 'he possessed that most rare gift, the power of fascination, and he fascinated me'.

There could be no expectation of an imminent resurgence of the Oxford movement, or of that great burst of progress in English religion to which Gladstone had looked to make his theory possible: after Maynooth he concluded 'that any man, in any country, can in this age of the world, give full effect to Christian principles in the work of Government, is alas! very far beyond my belief'. The direct consequence of this realization was an alteration of position on issues affecting the legal relationship of Church and State. Gladstone never again directly defended Irish Establishment, though it was many years before he publicly supported its abolition. But already by 1847 he was privately unable to give an assurance to Phillimore while 'I can in my own mind entertain so much as a suspicion that I may some years hence be forced to abandon it. . . . We are no longer in a condition to occupy high and secure ground in arguing for the integrity of the Irish Church Temporalities.'†

Gladstone returned to the Commons in December 1847 as one of the two burgesses (MPs) for Oxford University. His success in the election against C. G. Round showed the extent to which he and his group of Oxonian Tories had moved since the 1830s. For his vote (from the constituency of all Oxford MAs whether resident or not) was made up of an

---

* See below, p. 93, for further discussion of this. Gladstone's grief at his friends' apostasy became intermingled with his work for, and temptation by, prostitutes. When James ('Jim')Hope joined the Roman Catholic Church, Gladstone immediately struck off Hope's name as an executor of his will.

† Letters to Phillimore in this and subsequent paragraphs are in the Phillimore MSS in Christ Church.

alliance between Anglo-Catholics of one sort or another—Tractarians and High-Churchmen—and Liberals. At the university level, his supporters agreed that the history of the University between the Hampden affair in 1836—when the Tractarians were ascendant—and the degradation of W. G. Ward in 1845—when they lost, Newman almost being stripped of his MA at the same time as Ward—showed that reform was essential. Gladstone's membership for Oxford thus represented and accepted a desire for change, and in a Liberal direction.

Gladstone was at this time commonly regarded as a Tractarian, and we have seen that in several respects it is quite fair to call him that. Keble described him in 1847 as 'Pusey in a blue coat: and what can be said more for any layman? . . . I am so sure of him that I don't at all mind here and there a speech or vote which I can't explain.'*

The University contests produced much vituperative literature; indeed, their campaigns, in which the candidates took no direct part, were carried on at a lower level of argument than many of the other constituencies. This Evangelical squib represents the better side of Oxford election wit, and it captures something of Gladstone's Puseyite image:

> Swell'd with his honours from the classic school,
> See Gladstone! as a legislator rule!
> A second Canning! yes, with like conceit,
> But tithing not his eloquence and wit:
> A second Wilberforce! he wrote a book,
> But, for the Gospel, Puseyism mistook!
> 'The Protestant' (our pure Reformed Faith)
> 'Is but a *negative*' wise Gladstone saith,
> 'The Roman Catholic, the *positive*,
> 'Which only, can the Christian blessings give.'
> Gladstone! what honest sect, does this betoken?
> Words, only fit, for Roman to have spoken!
> Did'st thou, from science of the loadstone speak,
> Or some recondite Hebrew, Latin, Greek!
> Was it St. Stephen's dome inspired the rant,
> Or did'st thou not know what was Protestant?
> Wou'dst thou call *virtue, negative* of vice,
> Or *courage, negative* of cowardice?
> Thou'rt not too old to learn, if not too wise;
> Oh, do not then, our humble muse despise,
> Go back to school, and learn thy Catechism;
> Add not this folly, to thy other schism!
> Can we not grave authority advance,
> How Cato Greek learnt,—Socrates to dance—

* Quoted in the useful analysis of the Oxford constituency which I have relied on for the previous paragraph: W. R. Ward, 'Oxford and the origins of Liberal Catholicism in the Church of England' in *Studies in Church History*, i (1964).

Recant! recant! ere thou presumest to be
A Candidate for the University!
Your Popish tricks shall prove impotent spell,
If Oxford-sons perform their duty well.*

Gladstone regarded himself as, and was, primarily a Church of England man; he personally disliked church-party labels, and went out of his way to avoid direct association. He told Phillimore in 1847: 'With respect to Tractarianism, it is true, but I suppose of no use to say, that I have not read the Tracts ... I do not find people denounce me as a Tractarian from my books. It is chiefly on the ground of the vote with Ward.' (Gladstone strongly attacked, in an article in the *Quarterly*, W. G. Ward's views as expressed in the *Idea of a Christian Church*, but he went to Oxford to vote against his losing his MA.) In a second letter to Phillimore he developed his point about parties: 'I must firmly say I have committed myself to no party in the Church and no party has a right to reckon me among its members. . . . It is then certainly not *e confessio* that I belong to a party.' It was true that Gladstone had not read the ninety *Tracts for the Times*, but he had read some of them, and a fair collection were to be found in the library at Hawarden. It was true that Gladstone's published works on religion reflect a wide range of influences, but it was also true that his private religious observances were markedly Tractarian in character. If Keble, the originator of 'the engagement', could find Gladstone 'Pusey in a blue coat' it would seem fair to describe him as a Tractarian, while bearing in mind his own reservations, and that the label 'Tractarian', especially by the 1840s, covers quite a wide spectrum of opinion. In terms of his constituency, Gladstone gained and lost from the label. It associated him with an important and well-organized but waning group within the University, it estranged him from the Evangelicals, and it raised problems about his relationship with the Liberals, who were finding common cause with him on non-religious matters.

On his return to the Commons, his first act found him reflecting his new political position and the changing opinions of those who had supported him: he voted for the Whigs' bill to permit Jews to take a different oath and thus become MPs. This was 'a painful decision to come to. But the only substantive doubt it raises is about remaining in Parliament.' His speech and vote were given shortly after Sir Robert Inglis, the other Oxford University Member who was returned unopposed, had presented a petition of Convocation against the bill. Gladstone's relationship with some of his university constituents was thus from the first acerbic, and opposition to him at the next election was assured. His vote on Jewish disabilities marked his new awareness of the necessity of pragmatic adjustment and the relativity of theory: 'the application of the immutable principles of justice to the

* From *The Newmania; or, Puseyism Unmasked* (1847).

shifting relations of society must be determined by successive generations for themselves, according to their several diversities'. He admitted that his book had 'strained the facts of the case' and that members of the University and politicians must recognize 'the political temper of the age'.

This feeling for the practical, and his unwillingness again to expose himself to a practically untenable position, can also be seen in his handling of the Gorham crisis of 1850, when the State reversed a patronage decision of an ecclesiastical court. Dismayed though he was privately by the judgement,* which for some Tractarians such as Manning was the occasion for apostasy, and though at first 'resolved to try some immediate effort' he declined to take a public stance, argued that it was for the bishops to lead the Church, and refused to sign a Declaration (for which refusal he was described as Judas, so central was the issue to Tractarians) and later tried to delay further action. He argued in his pamphlet, 'Remarks on the Royal Supremacy' (1850), that the Church of England as established at the Reformation was historically justified (Manning at this time concluded that it was not), but that the constitutional basis of the Gorham judgement was not so. Maynooth had taught Gladstone not only pragmatism but political tact.

But Gladstone had not admitted, and never admitted, that his theoretical conception as expressed in *The State in its Relations with the Church* was wrong. His subsequent writing and behaviour recognized its impracticality on specifically allied topics, but a larger question remained—could something more positive be achieved, could aspects of it be made practical by other means? The decade after 1845 shows his attempt to reach an alternative if less elevated synthesis. In addition to his movement towards acceptance of an increasingly secularized Parliament, Gladstone tried to construct this in three ways: colonial affairs, the morality of free trade and finance, and the morality of international affairs.

Colonial Affairs

Despite his resignation over Maynooth and his lowered view of politics, Gladstone remained eager for office in 1845 and became colonial secretary after the political crisis of December 1845, when Peel attempted to resign when his cabinet would not follow him over suspension of the Corn Laws and Russell declined to accept the 'poisoned chalice'. His tenure of office could not but be brief, and he began no large-scale plans. He dealt firmly with West Indian questions, on which he was already well-informed. More important, however, was his involvement in constitution-making in the white settlement colonies. For here was a new interest, much developed in the years after 1846, though in the 1830s he had spoken on Canadian and New Zealand affairs.

* When the case started he told Phillimore, 3 December 1847: 'O Newman! without thee we never should have had a Gorham case showing its face among us.'

Gladstone's understanding of nationality as organic, something much more than an aggregation of individuals, led him to interest in the British nation transplanted (and transported) abroad. He was much influenced by Gibbon Wakefield and by Cornewall Lewis's *Essay on the government of dependencies* (1841). Although a Whig, Lewis was, like Gladstone, a product of Christ Church and the Oxford classical tradition and his *Essay* gave an historical dimension to Gladstone's thinking. Gladstone's speeches on overseas colonies were in substance and sentiment adapted from Lewis's *Essay*. Lewis wrote that 'On reviewing the history of the Greek colonies . . . it will be seen that the advancement of mankind is to be expected rather from the diffusion of civilized nations than from the improvement of barbarous or half-civilized tribes.' Colonies were thus one of the 'best means of advancing and diffusing civilization'; the object of colonization, Gladstone thought, was 'the creation of so many happy Englands'. Greek colonies had set the right example by being founded not in dependency but in 'the union of heart and character'. It was no coincidence that Gladstone's increased interest in colonial affairs in the late 1840s coincided with his first burst of constructive work on Homer, for was not Homer essentially the story of the early development of 'the greatness of our race'?*

'Happy Englands' were for Gladstone Tractarian Englands: if the Anglican Church could not play its full role in England, perhaps it could in the colonies. Thus Gladstone saw systematic colonization as a means to systematic Tractarianism. His personal effort in the years 1846–52 was in the establishment first of colonial bishoprics, then of the emancipation of colonial sees from metropolitan control. To this end he introduced a series of private bills, none of which was passed in the form he intended. Though unsuccessful, Gladstone was led by these legislative attempts and by his analogies from Greek history to an important conclusion: local independence and responsible government were of vital importance to a colony. Locally churches should be supported by synods involving clergy and laity—a development he also advocated for Scotland in 'The functions of laymen in the Church' (1852). Colonies likewise must have responsible assemblies.

In his attempt to reconstruct the means towards moral progress, Gladstone certainly moved more quickly in colonial than in domestic affairs. As colonial secretary he moved much more rapidly than Stanley, his predecessor, towards self-government for New Zealand, and his good relations with Gibbon Wakefield helped bring the New Zealand company and the Colonial Office together. He was, if necessary, ready to partition the colony to achieve immediate self-government, which he thought should include local control of native affairs. His diary, when at the Colonial Office in 1846, shows his frequent contacts with Wakefield and he subsequently

---

* *Studies on Homer and the Homeric age* (1858), iii. 615 (conclusion).

became a chief, if not wholly orthodox, supporter of systematic colonization. Though he did not join the Colonial Reform Association, for he wished to assert the primary importance of his own Colonial Church Bills, he was deeply involved in its manœuvres, and he worked with his wife's brother-in-law, Lyttelton (whom he had made under-secretary when he was at the Colonial Office), J. R. Godley and Gibbon Wakefield to establish the Tractarian colony at Canterbury in New Zealand.

This developing interest in colonization ('planting a society of Englishmen') by 'the Anglo-Saxon race' had two important consequences. It was the political means by which, together with free trade, Gladstone found himself allied with Liberals and Radicals such as Molesworth and Roebuck. His views on colonial subjects gave a wider, more institutional, and more directly political dimension to the implied Liberalism of his free-trade ideas, discussed below. In the years after 1846 he found himself more radical than and in frequent conflict with Grey, the Whigs' colonial secretary, and it was on Gladstone's encouragement that Adderley put forward for the Colonial Reform Association the motion which effectively caused the resignation of the Russell administration in February 1852, 'of course to escape the Cape motion'. Thus on the formation of the coalition ministry in December 1852, Gladstone was an obvious candidate for colonial secretary, and was pressed as such at court by Aberdeen, but it is hard to see how he could have sat as such in a cabinet with Grey had Aberdeen persevered.

Free Trade and Experience

As a colonial reformer Gladstone was separated from the Cobdenite Radicals who had no interest in exported nationalism. He was also at first separated from them in his free trade views, though the gap narrowed as Gladstone more and more came to see free trade as an alternative, or at least a supplement, to the Church as the means by which the conscience of the State could be expressed and the relationships of an industrial society fairly adjusted.

Gladstone approached the problem of protection through the work of the Board of Trade, that is, through the administration of the vast corpus of tariffs for which the department was responsible. His primary concern was therefore with the supply of raw materials for manufacturing, with the export of manufactured goods and with the whole framework of trade treaties with other nations. In this context the question of the Corn Law was secondary, though clearly important. Gladstone's progressive conviction that the windows of 'the hothouses of protection' should be further and further opened was thus formed partly for administrative and partly for general commercial reasons. Reductions of tariffs could be achieved progressively but gradually by good administration from within the existing system. A general movement towards free trade across the board, rather than a localized interest in the Corn Law was therefore his chief interest. This was not to say that he did not admit a strong case against the Corn Law; in 1842 he felt the old law to have been 'a very stringent and severe one' and proposed resignation when he felt it had been insufficiently alleviated. But he did not support repeal at a stroke. As he told his father, 'I viewed the Corn Law as defensible only on the ground that the agriculturist had a claim to very gradual and cautious transition out of the artificial state in which law had placed him.' He therefore showed no enthusiasm for the social and political aims implicit in the programme of 'the notorious League' which, in 1843, he thought basically ingenuous:

An enormous credulity, as it appears to us, is essentially required before a man can raise himself to the level of that dogmatic faith, wherewith some of the opponents of the corn laws appear really to believe, that the removal of the restrictions upon the trade in grain is to remove all suffering, to obviate all risks, and to introduce in short a commercial millennium.*

Gladstone at the end of 1845, rejoining the Cabinet during a political crisis, saw the Corn Law question in terms firstly of political pledges given in 1841 at the election, secondly in terms of the immediate Irish crisis. At the time he showed little interest in the law as a symbol, and he deplored the symbolic tone of Peel's famous tribute to Cobden in 1846. Experience, and the balance of the evidence, rather than a conversion to Ricardian comparative advantage theories, in the first instance made Gladstone a free trader.

With an interest in general tariff reduction Gladstone was coming to see free trade not, as the Leaguers saw it, as the field for a battle fought between two classes on the issue of the Corn Laws, but rather as the class-integrating factor in the organic state. As his system of State and Church collapsed in 1845, Gladstone, searching for a substitute, came to invest the general concept of free trade with the moral role in the nation's ethical progress earlier attributed to the Established Church. In this sense the 1853 budget was the answer to the Maynooth grant. Gladstone's search for a role was over: fiscal probity became the new morality.

Practical experiences at the Board of Trade made Gladstone consider the relationship of religion to commerce; he squarely faced the question 'whether the system of modern industry is . . . fundamentally and essentially at variance with the principles of the gospel'. He concluded 'that this question must be deliberately answered in the negative'. This was of fundamental importance, since 'religion and Christian virtue, like the faculty of taste and the perception of beauty, have their place, aye and that the first place, in political economy, as the means of creating and preserving wealth' and he quoted John Wesley to prove it.†

---

* 'Course of Commercial Policy at Home and Abroad', *Foreign and Colonial Quarterly Review*, i. 252 (January 1843).
† Ibid., 253.

Gladstone thus saw economic progress linked to religion in achieving moral and social development. A central function of government was to facilitate this. Gladstone believed the Board of Trade and the Exchequer had in 1841–5 achieved progress of this sort: existing departments were efficient, and could be made more so by and within the existing political structure. He therefore did not see any urgent need for further political reform and though not opposed to it in principle was certainly not its protagonist in the Aberdeen administration of 1852. In this merging of religion, ethics, and economic progress, Gladstone owed much to Thomas Chalmers, whose lectures in the 1830s had in part occasioned *The State in its Relations with the Church*. Chalmers' works on commerce are often referred to in the diary, though not always with unqualified praise.

In his changing political situation in the mid-forties, free trade became more and more the touchstone of Gladstone's political action. The Aristotelian notion of a balanced society based on obligation and duty gave way (though it did not wholly disappear) to a society in which the assertion of economic individualism gained predominance, conditioned though Gladstone hoped it would be by probity, self-control, and Christian morality. Though Gladstone sometimes continued to use the language of a preindustrial social hierarchy (especially when discussing the duties of landowners), his political actions increasingly in fiscal matters coincided (though he did not see them fusing) with the atomistic individualism of political economy. He read the political economists fully and repeatedly. His hostility to the Mills in the late thirties changed to an increasing reliance on them for technical competence in fiscal matters. His notes and jottings show him teaching himself Millite political economy at first at a very simplistic level. It would go too far to say that Gladstone became at any stage in his career in any full sense a utilitarian, but those utilitarian aspects of his approach to society, noted above and criticized by Keble, certainly became more pronounced.

State and Church being out of the way as the pivot of his political relationship, he found fiscal rectitude the chief bar to a return to the Tory party. Disraeli's supposed flippancy and slackness in fiscal matters and his irreverence towards fiscal canons appalled Gladstone in the same way as the approach of the Whigs and Radicals to the Irish Church had in the 1830s.

Because at first Gladstone saw tariff reduction as primarily an administrative problem, his movement towards free trade was not in the early 1840s politically dramatic, and as late as 1848–9 he spoke against complete abolition of the Navigation Acts, favouring safeguards during a transitional period for the merchant navy, and some control over colonial trade relations with foreign powers. But rather than endanger the overall success of repeal of the Acts, he did not press his scheme, much to the disappointment of Disraeli. His proposal had become futile when 'the ship owners and their friends ... would not adopt a plan upon the basis I propose'. Thus, despite occasional questionings of timing, the change in his position was, at bottom, firm and irrevocable. As such, it involved a quarrel with his father, who had supported Huskisson but would move no further in the 1840s, and opposed repeal of the Corn Laws and of the Navigation Acts in long letters from Fasque. The quarrel was especially distressing to both, for it occurred during the attempts to rescue Helen Gladstone from the drug addiction following her conversion to Roman Catholicism.

When his father in 1849 accused him of having made Peel a free trader Gladstone wrote this account of his position:

As respects my 'having made Peel a free trader', I had never seen that idea expressed anywhere and I think it is one which does great injustice to the character and power of his mind. In every case, however, the head of a Government may be influenced more or less in the affairs of each department of State by the person in charge of that department. If, then, there were any influence at all upon Peel's mind proceeding from me between 1841 and 1845, I have no doubt it may have tended on the whole towards Free Trade: I can recollect many cases in which my endeavour was to lead the Government onwards in the path of progressive & gradual relaxation, than to keep it back. In 1842 for instance it was my wish individually to have made a somewhat greater reduction of the corn duties.... But all this ceased with the measures of 1845 when I left office. It was during the alarm of a potato famine in the autumn of that year [that] the movement in the Government about the Corn Laws began. I was then on the continent, looking after Helen....

... I myself had invariably, during his [Peel's] Government, spoken of Protection not as a thing good in principle but to be dealt with as tenderly and cautiously as might be according to circumstances, always running in the direction of Free Trade. It *then* appeared to me that the case was materially altered by events: it was no longer open to me to pursue that cautious course: a great struggle was imminent in which it was plain that two parties only could really find place, on the one side for repeal, on the other side for the *permanent* maintenance of a corn law and a protective system generally & on principle. It would have been more inconsistent in me, even if consistency had been the rule, to join the latter party than the former. But independently of that, I thought, & still think that the circumstances of the case justified and required the change: I should have preferred rather a different form, that is to say a low fixed duty of 4/- or 5/- per quarter to last for a greater number of years; but that was decided otherwise....

So far then as relates to the final change in the Corn Law you will see that no influence proceeded from me, but rather that events, over which I had no controul, and steps taken by Sir R. Peel while I was out of the Government, had an influence upon me, in inducing me to take office.

Gladstone's separation from the Tory party was initially on the tariff issue, but it slowly broadened into a difference on fiscal policy generally, culminating in his violent and devastatingly successful attack on Disraeli's budget on 17 December 1852. This was due in part to a personal dislike of Disraeli and regret at not having been able to defend Peel in Parliament in 1846 (Disraeli would not have been able to dismiss Gladstone, as he had Sidney Herbert, with jokes about valets). Gladstone's diary and correspondence show mounting irritation and dislike of Disraeli, without the usual charitable qualifications which accompany Gladstone's remarkably rare personal censures. By 1849 Gladstone felt 'it is a very unsatisfactory state of things to have to deal with a man whose objects appear to be those of personal ambition and who is not thought to have any strong convictions of any kind upon public matters'. By 1852 he was glad not to have to speak in direct answer to him, and even to do so indirectly gave him an unwonted sleepless night. After his great personal triumph over Disraeli in December 1852, his only regret, which kept him up most of the night, was that he had 'mismanaged a material point (by omission)'—this in an overwhelmingly successful speech, which immediately preceded the defeat of the government.

But it would be unwise to attribute to as politically complex a character as Gladstone a position based purely on personal antipathy, important though that was in this instance, at least as an immediate spur. Since the Peel government's fall in 1846 little had been done, save the repeal of the Navigation Acts, to further that great plan of gradual but progressive reduction of tariffs across the board. Nor had the question of the theoretically temporary but continually renewed income tax of 1842 been tackled. Nor did either a Whig or a Tory ministry show itself likely to tackle these problems thoroughly. To the tariff question therefore was added the income tax question; the two come together in the 1853 budget, essentially an expanded version of that of 1842, but going far beyond it in general social significance and future planning. The 1853 budget was, as well as the saving of the coalition, the summit of Gladstone's early political and administrative career; it was the moment at which he became a national as well as a parliamentary figure, and one clearly marked out for leadership. Had those who heard it been aware of the highly effective tactical battle which Gladstone had fought in cabinet to maintain it intact, they would have been the more impressed. This developing view of the importance of fiscal responsibility was therefore the background to Gladstone's decision to join the coalition in December 1852, despite his lingering affection for the Tories as a party, and his antipathy to the Whigs as promoters of the Ecclesiastical Titles Bill.

International Morality

Right relations with the colonies and fiscal responsibility thus formed the two chief interests of Gladstone during his attempt to find a political role following the collapse of his State and Church structure. To these must be added spasmodic interest in international morality. China in the late thirties and early forties, Don Pacifico in 1850, Italy in 1851–2 were questions taken up with great, even violent passion and then dropped almost as suddenly, at least for a time, though Italy was a slow-burning fuse. Little attempt seems to have been made to integrate them into a coherent view of international affairs and Gladstone did nothing when Chancellor of the Exchequer after 1852 to resolve Neapolitan problems, apart from acts of personal charity towards the political prisoners. None the less his interventions in these questions made him a figure of European note even before he became, as chancellor, a first-rank politician in his own country.

Gladstone's two visits to Italy in these years were both fortuitous. The first, in 1849, was in pursuit of Lady Lincoln who had fled thither with her lover. Gladstone finally found the villa near Lake Como and entered the grounds disguised as a guitarist to get the evidence needed for Lincoln to divorce her by private bill. He later gave evidence in the House of Lords on this, an action which he had some difficulty in explaining when he vehemently opposed the bill which made divorce generally available in 1857. The general importance of this visit was that during it Gladstone began to read Leopardi, whose works he reviewed in the *Quarterly* on his return.

The second visit was in 1850–1, made for the benefit of his daughter Mary's eyesight. It was, as we shall shortly see, to have important political consequences. Neither visit, therefore, was the result of direct curiosity about Italian developments. However, their timing was important. In Italy, and especially in the Bourbon kingdom of the Two Sicilies, the thoughts about right social relations in British domestic and imperial affairs which had preoccupied Gladstone in the 1840s were brought into sharp focus. For in Naples he found a society where right relationships had manifestly not been established, and by a government indisputably conservative. The arbitrary arrests and managed trials of respectable lawyers, the realization that 'a portion' of the Roman Catholic priesthood could be informers and perjurers, the appreciation that normal British standards of justice and governmental conduct—let alone representative institutions—were regarded as liberal and thus damned, gradually forced Gladstone to the conclusion that action must be taken, privately at first, publicly if necessary: 'one grows wild at being able to do nothing' against 'the Government of Naples which I believe to be one of the most purely Satanic agencies upon earth'.

Visits a few days before leaving Naples to the prisons of the Vicaria and the Nisida, and in particular a talk with Carlo Poerio outside the latter, ensured that Gladstone reached London ardent for action. Somewhat to the embarrassment of their recipient, Gladstone published two *Letters to the Earl of Aberdeen*, the first of which described Bourbon rule in Italy as 'the negation of God erected into a system of government', the first of Gladstone's famous phrases which punctuate the century. The reaction to the *Letters* reflected at a European level the position which Gladstone had already reached in British politics. Whatever his motives, he found himself unavoidably associated with the Liberals: European Conservatives in Britain and throughout Europe, with hardly an exception, deplored his initiative. In the third of his pamphlets on Naples, Gladstone ended by extolling the mid-century Liberal solution: 'free and unrestricted exchange ... with all the nations of the world', with Britain 'the standard bearer of the nations upon the fruitful paths of peace, industry and commerce'. Thus the 1853 budget was also the answer to King Bomba. Conservative he might still feel himself, Liberal his language was certainly becoming.

Liberalism and Politics in the early 1850s

By the early 1850s, therefore, Gladstone had shed many of his Tractarian Tory political, though not necessarily social, predilections of the 1830s. In this sense the decade 1841–51 is the crucial period of his political development. In place of his earlier views he had developed a number of interests, which were not yet necessarily coherently interlocked but which, taken as a whole, made it increasingly difficult for him to co-operate with the Tory rump.

His aim had been not to reconstruct an abstract theory of the sort given in *The State in its Relations with the Church*, but to arrive at a series of practical positions which would further national moral progress. He had developed a 'thorough Sir Robert Peelian horror of *abstract* resolutions' and he never again attempted, as he had in his book, first to state an abstract principle, then to work it out in politics. Subsequently he invested practical measures with abstract principle; here lay one of the secrets of his great public success.

To say whether this constituted Liberalism is to measure him against an undefined standard. But it can be said that it placed him with the political economists on fiscal policy (Liberals to a man)—with the Whigs on civil liberties—with the Radicals Molesworth and Roebuck on colonial affairs, and—whether he liked it or not—with the moderates of European Liberalism on the Italian question. On the topics which had become central to his political interests, therefore, he found himself in each case allied with groups which, whatever they were, were not predominantly Tory.* For a politician of Gladstone's type, the change in personal relationships follows the change of opinion. Of all the leading Peelites he had become the most

---

* The Ecclesiastical Titles Bill of 1851 and the Don Pacifico debate of 1850 were partial exceptions to this; but on the first, Gladstone defended a pluralist position which was essentially Liberal rather than Whiggish or Conservative, and in the second his speech against Palmerston on international morality was far more characteristic of Bright than of Disraeli, though Gladstone found himself in the lobby with the Conservatives.

Liberal, on many topics, in the sense of policy, but remained the most enthusiastic for a rejuvenated Conservative party permeated and controlled by the Peelite group. 'Junction with the liberals' in 1852 would be 'our least natural position'; the function of the Peelites was 'working out a liberal policy through the medium of the Conservative party'. But in saying this, Gladstone already believed that in terms of issue and policy he would find great difficulty in supporting Derby's Conservative government at least until its protectionist proposals had been defeated. Then the Peelites would be 'free & ready to pursue whatever course in point of party connection the interests of the country might seem to require'.

A 'Mixed Government': the Aberdeen Coalition

Gladstone played his part in the defeat of the minority Conservative government. Quite handsomely returned for Oxford University in the General Election of July 1852, he attended the opening of the Session in November in a state of high nervous excitement marked by a bout of self-flagellation. He contributed to the defeat of protection on 26 November: 'Divided in 336:256 and in 458:53. So ends the great controversy of Free Trade. Nervous excitement kept me very wakeful: the first time (after speaking) for many years.' But that was not all, for, on the night of 16–17 December 1852, as he noted laconically: 'Rose at one & spoke till past 3 in answer to Disraeli.' As the thunder shook the windows of the newly finished Palace of Westminster, the Peelites made clear what had been implicit in their behaviour since 1846 and virtually explicit since their refusal to join Derby in February 1852: their support for the Tory party was on conditions it could not meet, even by giving up protection. The subject was the budget; the issue, Disraeli's intention to overstep the traces of orthodox Peelite views about taxation. Gladstone's attack was, most unusually, made after Disraeli had wound up the debate in a brilliant, mesmeric speech. But certain comments about personalities had left Disraeli open to a reply. Gladstone's response, first a ticking off of the chancellor for want 'of discretion, of moderation, and forbearance', then an assault on the deficiencies of the budget, gained the hearing of an initially rowdy House. The attack appeared to be an impassioned, impromptu effort. Gladstone's diary shows most of it to have been, like most spontaneous successes, well-researched and thoroughly prepared.

Gladstone did not bring down the ministry single-handed. The General Election and the regrouping of the supporters of the previous Whig government had Disraeli already wriggling in the Commons. But his intervention, at a moment when it looked as if Disraeli's 'unorthodox' views on taxation were attracting some support, appeared decisive; it certainly showed Gladstone holding the dagger which slew the government, and it marked him out as the chief antagonist of Disraeli.* The consequence of the ministry's subsequent resignation, Gladstone concluded, was that 'the only remaining alternative would therefore seem to be a mixed Government'. Two days later he avoided a 'lion's den' in the Carlton Club only by physically removing himself from that Tory stronghold.

Aberdeen went to Windsor to kiss hands and mentioned Gladstone for either the Exchequer or his old post at the Colonial Office. According to Prince Albert, the Crown tipped the balance in favour of the Exchequer. Thus was Gladstone launched on what were to be a series of 'mixed governments' (he preferred this term to 'coalition') on the progressive side of British politics, eventually and in no very certain or deliberate way developing into the Liberal party.

In the Aberdeen coalition, as the ministry of 1852 is usually called, Gladstone found himself playing a central political role. The most effective of the Peelites in the Commons, he was also the most successful departmentally, and in two very different directions. As Chancellor of the Exchequer, he held the office whose former incumbents' proposals (Wood for the Whigs, Disraeli for the Tories) had led to disaster. What was needed, first, therefore, was a safe pair of hands. Gladstone perhaps rather surprised his contemporaries, accustomed as they were to his Tractarianism, by being in peacetime first, foremost, and *almost* always, a safe chancellor. He did not make mistakes, and he did not have to take things back. He thus provided, at the least, stability and control, qualities which were important in the very uncertain circumstances of British politics in the early 1850s. Of course, he also provided a great deal more, and it will be convenient to examine his work as a mid-Victorian chancellor in a later chapter (Chapter V).

University reform was an inevitable duty of the government. The Royal Commission on Oxford University set up by the Whigs (and opposed by Gladstone) in 1850 had in 1852 produced a powerful statement of the Liberal case. The arguments of the Tories in the 1830s, including Gladstone, that the University could and would, given time, reform itself institutionally, had been seen to be fruitless. The issue was not whether but how Parliament would reshape Oxford. As MP for the University, with a vote awkwardly, as we have seen, composed of Liberals, Tractarians, and many of the leading scholars resident in Oxford, but opposed by Tories, Evangelicals, and many of the country clergy, it naturally largely fell to Gladstone to produce the government's response to the Royal Commission,

* The intensity of the personal antagonism between the two men—rare on each side—was reflected in a tetchy exchange of letters, much of it in the third person, after Gladstone had succeeded Disraeli as chancellor, the issue being the value of the furniture in No. 11 Downing Street (the chancellor's house) and the handing over of what was thought to be Pitt's chancellor's robe, traditionally sold by one chancellor to the next; despite his support for tradition and precedent, Disraeli held on to it. Gladstone noted about one of his letters, written on a Sunday: 'Wrote (draft) to Mr. Disraeli: (I did it purposely *today*).'

for if he surrendered control of the bill, he would have effectively surrendered control of his constituency as well. The details of the bill concern Oxford more than Gladstone, but its general form is revealing about his approach to institutions and his relationship with the various political groups. The Liberals wanted a rationalized university, the traditional autonomy of the colleges broken by a powerful professoriate: a movement towards a departmental rather than a collegiate system. They expected Gladstone would back them. He did not. His bill, he told Bonamy Price, was framed on 'the principle of working with the materials which we possess, endeavouring to improve our institutions through the agency they themselves supply, and giving to reform in cases where there is a choice the character of return and restoration'.*

This method, the use of Parliament to permit regeneration rather than to impose novelty, to work from within a set of historic institutions rather than from an a priori plan, characterized the mid-century Gladstone. When the Liberals complained, he reacted sharply: 'these gentlemen, whatever they may be as irrigators are as respects Parliament merely dreamers. An English legislature would not, even if we were to ask it, force their "spick and span" Professoriate upon Oxford any more than they would adopt a constitution out of the pigeon holes of Abbé Sieyès.'† The bill was one of radical conservatism. As usual, Gladstone's conservative intentions—pruning off the rotten branch, as he later said of compulsory church rates—were misunderstood by the Conservatives; Dean Gaisford of Christ Church, for example, found the bill 'unjust and tyrannical'.

The bill secured a viable solution by borrowing something from the Liberals, and by reflecting the aims of the moderately reforming Tutors' Association; it gained support for a fundamentally conservative solution by readily giving up obvious but superficial conservative totems. Having decided on his line of action, Gladstone was determined and thoroughgoing in achieving it, and saw to its completion by insisting on the provision of commissioners to supervise its execution. The Liberals were disappointed, but the Tories were shocked. In this sense, Gladstone's making of the Oxford University Bill epitomized his relationship to British politics.

Gladstone's work on the bill involved him in a huge correspondence—again, a characteristic of his methods of preparing legislation. Springing from this, on the urging of the Broad-Churchmen Temple and Jowett, he requested Northcote (formerly his secretary) and Sir Charles Trevelyan of the Treasury to report on recruitment to the civil service. Skilful use of their brief report supporting competitive examinations through a central board made it one of the most famous British documents of the century.

* Quoted in E. G. W. Bill, *University reform in nineteenth-century Oxford* (1973), 151.
† Quoted in ibid., 160. The bill was introduced in the Commons by Russell who acknowledged Gladstone's predominance in its construction; Gladstone then worked it through the Commons.

Gladstone saw competitive examination as the means of achieving the ascendancy of a Coleridgean clerisy in the secular world. The almost absolute distinction between the administrative grade and the rest of the service, with admission to the administrative grade via examinations which were effectively a repeat of the Oxford and Cambridge degree examinations, would tend 'to strengthen and multiply the ties between the higher classes and the possession of administrative power'.* A civil service hitherto appointed by patronage and influence would give way to a non-political administrative class educated in the moral values of a liberal education further developed by a reformed Oxford and Cambridge. It was a means of extending, confirming, cleansing, and legitimizing an existing élite. Whereas, Gladstone thought, the seventeenth century had been an age of rule by prerogative, and the eighteenth by patronage, the nineteenth would become a rule by virtue. For a liberal education attempted, above all, to produce citizens who were morally good, and such it was that would succeed in the examinations. In this objective, the Peelites were at one with the Liberals, though not with the Whigs. What the Liberals failed to gain in Oxford, the gradual implementation of competitive examinations (fully effected in 1870) gave them in the British Establishment as a whole.

'I fear', Russell wrote to Gladstone in March 1854, 'my mind is exclusively occupied with the war and the Reform Bill, and yours with university reform.'† Certainly Gladstone, though he had to raise the money to pay for it, was only marginally involved in the Cabinet's move towards war with Russia. But his position was clear and resolute: he accepted the need for British intervention in the general cause of peace, and he stiffened Aberdeen's will as the moment arrived in February 1854:

He [Aberdeen] said how could he bring himself to fight for the Turks? I replied we were not fighting for the Turks, but we were warning Russia off the forbidden ground.... We stand I said upon the ground that the Emperor has invaded countries not his own, inflicted wrong on Turkey & what I feel much more most cruel wrong on the wretched inhabitants of the Principalities [of Moldavia and Wallachia]: that war had ensued and was raging with all its horrors: that we had procured for the Emperor an offer of honourable terms of peace which he had refused: that we were not going to extend the conflagration (but I had to correct myself as to the Baltic) but to apply more power for its extinction: and this I hoped in conjunction with all the Great Powers of Europe: that I for one could not shoulder the musket against the Christian subjects of the Sultan: and must there take my stand.

Gladstone came to oppose aspects of the conduct of the war and of the negotiations to end it, but his view of its initial necessity as an act of public

* See J. B. Conacher, *The Aberdeen Coalition* (1968), chapter 13 for this, and for the wrangles with the Whigs which, with the onset of war and the break-up of the government, led to the loss of the proposed legislation.

† Morley, i. 500.

control remained an important point of departure for his interventionism in the Eastern Question later in the century.

The Aberdeen coalition rescued Gladstone. The private torments, which will be discussed in the next chapter, largely fell away. The public promise, sketched in his Tory career but cast in shadow by the confusion of the Maynooth resignation and vote and the disintegration of his party, was now confirmed on a wider canvass. The coalition gave Gladstone his chance at the top level of British politics, and he took it.

CHAPTER IV

Religion, Family, and Sex: the Private Crisis of the 1840s

Religion and Family Finances—Sex, Prostitutes, and the Oxford Movement—
Gleanings from the Journal in the 1840s and Early 1850s—Taking Leave of the
Early Gladstone

When I compare my convictions in religion, and the mercies that have been poured upon me, with the extraordinary tenacity of the evil in me, the fruit without doubt of indulgence, I cannot but deeply believe that my debt to the justice of God is the very heaviest that can be conceived: for have I not after all suffered that sin which I have described to have its habitation & to find its food in me, and could it have been covered by such flimsy pretexts but for an extreme corruption?

The pursuit of knowledge, the desire of estimating different periods & states of the moral and religious life of man, the hope of doing good to the persons living in sin: of all these I had utterly failed to discern the proper bounds, and had sometimes perhaps often lost even these from view when once upon the train of thought on imagery of which they might have first effected the introduction. Further if at any time I had discerned those bounds, the vision of them became dim & ineffectual at the time of need, even if resolutions of a solemn kind had been formed, & formed at the most solemn hour—before the Altar.

Looking back then over more than twenty years since this plague began, I can discern two periods at which the evil was so to speak materially limited but it may also have been formally, essentially, enhanced. First the period of marriage: and secondly that period of general recollection and prevision, which was vouchsafed me in my retired life at Baden [in 1845] . . . though I might persuade myself that in my inner heart I carried along with me a perfect hatred and disgust towards the fruit & work of lust, yet this was not genuine, or, if genuine was too weak to defend mind and body from the infection, especially in a case like mine, when the habits of my life, such as being out at all hours, place me peculiarly in the way of contact with exciting causes.*

Religion and Family Finances

The great crisis of Conservatism and of the Conservative party in the 1840s was in part the consequence of the very high expectations of the Church–

* 19 July 1848.

State Conservatives, of whom Gladstone was a prominent member. They brought to politics expectations which the normal political process could not satisfy. The Whig–Liberal coalition expected less and was consequently better able to overcome disappointment. Like the Conservatives in 1846, Whig governments tended to disintegration, but, unlike the Conservatives, they knew how to regroup.

For the Conservative party, hitherto so bold, so assured, so knowing about the deficiencies of its opponents, the twenty years after 1846 were to be years of exclusion, ideological sterility, and a gradual acceptance of Peel–Gladstone fiscal policy. For Gladstone, as we have seen in the previous chapters, the 1840s were an education in the practicalities of politics and policies.

This reformation of political role and belief was not achieved without a price. The diary for the years after 1846 is a strange mixture of solid plodding and masked, sometimes open, anxiety. Gladstone the administrator is seen supervising a series of estate developments, railway wrangles, and reforms in voluntary institutions. In the most dramatic situations Gladstone could reinforce himself by routine actions—witness his reading Mayhew 'on the Street folk' outside the room where his father lay dying. Gladstone the thinker involves himself in petty projects such as his dictionary of 'homoionyms', as well as his classical studies, his reviews, and correspondence. All this without apparent care at his loss of office and the uncertainty of his political position, though he was much relieved to be back in the Commons in 1847 and in 1848 noted about his attendance on his father, 'this & what I have towards my wife's family must for the present stand instead of much else'. Yet there is an underlying restlessness expressed most obviously in his bizarre solo journeys to the Continent in pursuit of his sister Helen in 1845, and of the eloping Lady Lincoln in 1849, and in the start of his rescue work with prostitutes.

Before the prostitutes are considered, some account must be made of the overwhelming family disaster of these years—the failure in 1847 of the Oak Farm works, for which Gladstone was examined in the Birmingham court of bankruptcy in 1848. Gladstone became involved in the works by marriage into the Glynne family, but he soon became an important influence in its management, advising his wife's brother-in-law, George Lyttelton, not to sell his share in it in 1840. Characteristically his chief interest was to build a church for the employees in the iron works.

John Gladstone had made a fortune as a merchant; he had never been a manufacturer. He had taught his son William much about the principles of financial success, but little of the specific and technical skills on which his success was based. William had never served even a brief turn in the family offices; it was his brother Robertson who was given the role of business successor to John Gladstone. The Oak Farm was a brick and iron works near Stourbridge, in which the Glynne family was heavily involved. Its business was closely interlocked with the many other small and medium-sized works in that area. On no basis of experience and despite his father's cautions, Gladstone supported Boydell, the manager, in his over-expansion of the iron works, until the general financial crisis of 1846–7 made it too late to withdraw. The subsequent bankruptcy and mortgages, for which Boydell was blamed, but for which Gladstone must bear a share of the responsibility, forced the Glynne family for a time out of Hawarden Castle, and occupied Gladstone until the 1880s. The affair is of general interest to his career mainly because of the anxiety it caused him, which, on occasion, took a sexual form of expression.

Acute anxiety was also caused by his sister Helen with whom his relationship was close though ill-natured. He had political as well as personal reasons for regretting her conversion to Roman Catholicism (she was one of the first casualties of the Oxford movement) but his concern about her drug addiction was more important. Gladstone saw in his sister what could happen when the powerful emotions to which he was also heir broke loose from the tight middle-class conventions to which his family subscribed, despite their aristocratic marriages and purchases of landed estates. He had played some part in the development of her condition. When she joined the Roman Catholic Church he advised his father to expel her from his house and was dismayed when the old man's 'paternal affection' prevented this. For a time he forbad her to see his children. Gladstone visited Baden in October 1845 to try to persuade Helen to give up her laudanum if not her Roman Catholicism, and witnessed appalling scenes as she became paralysed by the drug and was 'held down by force to have leeches put on'; 'she stipulated I was not to touch her'. It was in this context that, already ravaged that year by the 'nightmare' of Maynooth and the demise of the State and Church system, Gladstone drew up the extraordinary list of remedies and categories of temptation which is discussed later in this chapter.

Sex, Prostitutes, and the Oxford Movement

Helen Gladstone's self-control had snapped; her brother William's came very close to doing the same. Gladstone was a man of intense, and, in the 1840s, apparently increasing, sexuality. At first it was contained by his marriage, but this also, he believed, may have 'formally, essentially, enhanced' it. His wife was nine times pregnant and recovering from childbirth or miscarriage in fourteen years. There is no indication in the diary or elsewhere of any sexual incompatibility between the two, but it is clear that there were considerable periods of enforced sexual abstinence, caused by the Victorian middle-class convention of abstaining from sexual relations during most of pregnancy, nursing, and menstruation. Moreover, it may well have been that the Gladstones, in common with many Victorian religious families, took literally the implication for the marriage bed of the Prayer Book's statement that marriage was 'first . . . for the procreation of children'. The comment on 'the ideal above the ordinary married state' in the diary at 22 April 1849 perhaps refers to this. Certainly, Gladstone told his daughter Mary in the 1880s that he hated birth control as much as he hated anything. What is definite is that Catherine Gladstone was often absent from her husband, with children or relatives at Hagley or Hawarden. It was usually during these periods that Gladstone's rate of rescue work increased, and it was certainly during her absence that nervous crises occurred in October 1845, July 1848, April 1849, and especially in the critical period of July 1851.

Anxiety about his political work, his friends' religion, the Oak Farm finances, and his personal problems, aggravated Gladstone's feelings. At first, during the 1840s, he relieved them by reading what he regarded as pornography—mostly Restoration poems, classical authors such as Petronius, and *fabliaux* (French verse fables, some of them extremely bawdy). These were all readily available in bookshops and in the libraries of friends such as Thomas Grenville.* To pornography he later added conversations with prostitutes, some of whom he found beautiful and physically attractive.

At first the 'rescue work' (as he called it) was an act of conventional charity done within the context of the 'engagement'. The 'engagement' was a lay Tractarian brotherhood organized by the Acland brothers on advice from Keble. It had a thoroughly Tractarian ethos. Gladstone was associated with its planning in 1844 and began to attend it early in 1845. It had obvious associations with the 'Third Order' which he had sketched in 1838, and several of its members had first come together in the WEG Club at Oxford. Its membership of fifteen, which met in the Margaret Chapel and included Frederic Rogers, J. T. Coleridge, Roundell Palmer, and the architect William Butterfield, was subject to twelve rules, of which the first was to perform 'some regular work of charity'.† Gladstone fulfilled this rule in the early days of 'the engagement' by work with destitutes, male and female, who were in or dependent on the House of St Barnabas (the 'engagement's' patron saint) in Rose Street, Soho. But by 1848 he found

---

* His friend Monckton Milnes had a well-known and outstanding library of pornography, though Gladstone does not mention it.

† Its rules were: '1 Some regular work of charity, 2 Attendance on the daily service, 3 Observance of the fasts of the church, 4 Observance of the hours of prayer (9, 12, 3), 5 Special prayers for the unity of the church and conversion of unbelievers at some hour: also for the other persons engaged, 6 Rule of number of hours to be spent in sleep and recreation, 7 Meditation with morning prayers—self-examination with evening, 8 To fix a portion of income for works of mercy and piety, 9 To consider with a practical view the direction of the church concerning confession and absolution, 10 Failing any spiritual director, to follow the judgement of one or more of those co-engaged in the case of breach of rule, 11 If unable to perform (1) contribute funds instead, 12 To meet, compare results, and consider amendments.'

this work 'less suitable than it was' and told Acland it was too time-consuming.

In May 1849, under stress from Oak Farm affairs and the Clergy Relief Bill, he began meeting prostitutes on the streets late at night.* In the Session, he was often in the Commons till midnight. In July 1850, following the Pacifico debate and the death of Peel, when his wife was away at Hagley, and perhaps prompted by an article in the *Westminster Review*,† he began regular meetings with prostitutes in the vicinity of the notorious Argyll Rooms, and the names of individual prostitutes start to be regularly noted in the diary.

The rescue work was at one level exactly that—the attempt to rescue prostitutes from the streets and rehabilitate them in suitable employment, or by marriage, or by emigration, after a time of training. This was done at the House of Mercy at Clewer, by Windsor, where the keeper in the early 1850s was Mariquita Tennant whom Gladstone had known since 1843. Much time was spent in persuasion and in arranging transport and subsequent employment. Catherine Gladstone was well informed about these activities and prostitutes were, almost from the start, invited to the Gladstones' house. But it is also clear that for Gladstone rescue work became not merely a duty but a craving; it was an exposure to sexual stimulation which Gladstone felt he must both undergo and overcome. As he admitted to himself, he deliberately 'courted evil'.

The redemption of prostitutes was an activity which, in principle, had an obvious Christian justification. But for Gladstone it also involved temptation. Was the danger to his spiritual well-being balanced by the good he was doing? In his talks with prostitutes he 'trod the path of danger' as regards himself, while at the same time having little success in proselytizing. By January 1854 he had spoken, 'indoors or out', to between eighty and ninety prostitutes, but 'among these there is but one of whom I know that the miserable life has been abandoned *and* that I can fairly join that fact with influence of mine'. The lack of success was not surprising, for the discipline during rehabilitation at the Houses of Mercy at Clewer and Rose Street, Soho, was stronger than that of any Victorian boarding school. Jane Bywater, a partially rescued prostitute, wrote to Gladstone in 1854 after a short spell in the House of Mercy: 'I have no doubt that you wished to do me some service, but I did not fancy being shut up in such a place as that for perhaps twelve months. I should have committed suicide.'

Gladstone completely ignored the political danger attending his rescue work. When a Scot named Wilson attempted blackmail by threatening to expose him to the *Morning Herald* for speaking to a prostitute shortly after

---

* There had been some rescue work done earlier, but not systematically.

† He was familiar with Parent Duchâtelet's work on prostitution in Paris, *De la prostitution dans la ville de Paris*, 2 vols. (1836).

the 1853 budget, Gladstone met the threat with resolute indifference, exposing it to the police and the courts without hesitation. He was well aware that 'these talkings of mine are certainly not within the rules of worldly prudence' but this was not, for him, of importance. The crucial question was whether 'Christian prudence sanctions them for such an one as me'. Despite his awareness both of spiritual danger and lack of success, the work continued.

His predilection for pornography has been noted above. In 1849 Gladstone began to scourge himself to counter stimulation from it. By 1851 he was also scourging himself after conversations with prostitutes during which he felt he had allowed himself to be excessively excited. Sometimes he went to their homes or lodging houses for talks long into the night, sometimes for tea. On occasion he was moved to almost lyrical praise of their beauty, noted in Italian.* So far as we know, and there is no evidence to the contrary, he managed to remain, in the end, self-controlled and self-critical.

Beginning in October 1845 during his visit to his sister Helen in Germany, Gladstone analysed his feelings about both pornography and prostitutes in a series of remarkable passages, some in the diary, some on separate sheets of paper which were folded and enclosed with the diary. He kept records of his temptations and of his measures to overcome them. These were listed as 'Channels', 'Incentives', 'Chief actual dangers', and 'Remedies', each broken down into several sub-headings and categories. The presence of the Aristotelian philosophical tag πρός τι (in respect of things of a certain kind) and the abstract form of the other categories shows the pervading influence of the Oxford Schools even on Gladstone's most private thoughts. It is a curious footnote to G. M. Young's observation of the basic importance of their Oxford training to both Gladstone and Newman.†

Notes of his self-scourgings were kept first on the separate sheet, later in lists in the diary, and then day by day by signs in the diary entries. The last started the day he read Froude's *Nemesis of Faith*. This series of lists, explanations, and entries must be regarded as a classic of mid-Victorian self-analysis of guilt. It is also very characteristically Gladstonian; a strange mixture of detail, thoroughness, generality, and principle, carried through with cool efficiency, passion, self-confidence, and religious repentance. A small part of one of the passages is quoted at the head of this chapter.

Gladstone's self-analysis of an explicitly sexual topic was made in

---

* As W. Acton noted, prostitutes in central London were 'generally pretty and elegant—oftener painted by Nature than by art' (*Prostitution* (1857), 53). In 1841 the Metropolitan Police estimated that in the St James's–Regent Street–Soho area there were 152 brothels and 318 prostitutes; in the Westminster–Chelsea area, 153 brothels and 514 prostitutes; ibid. 16.

† G. M. Young, 'The Schoolman in Downing Street', *Victorian essays* (1962), 86–7.

language which treated it implicitly. In this, despite the privacy of his diary and the various codes and foreign languages available to him, he remained within Victorian public conventions. Thus it is impossible to know the exact nature of Gladstone's relationship with the prostitutes he visited. The language is guarded, but occasionally suggestive. In 1896, seventeen months before he died, he assured his son and pastor, Stephen, that he had never 'been guilty of the act which is known as that of infidelity to the marriage bed'; he specifically limited himself 'to this negation', a precise and obviously qualified declaration.*

What is clear is that on occasion these confrontations were followed by self-scourging. Gladstone's use of the scourge or discipline is marked in the diary or on his lists by the sign ♭, presumably because of its resemblance to a whip. An entry characteristic of its use, and of the oblique references to what may seem to be some form of limited physical encounter, is that of 13 July 1851, in the crisis of Hope and Manning's apostasy, which literally 'demoralized' him. In the urgency of the crisis—a crisis as Gladstone saw it of national as well as of personal identity—he lost for a time his moral sense. Numbed, disorientated, overwhelmed by a development he had failed to anticipate, he

Went with a note to E[lizabeth] C[ollins]'s—received (unexpectedly) & remained 2 hours: a strange & humbling scene—returned & ♭.

This and all other entries when a prostitute was involved suggest that the flagellation was self-administered in private, following, not during, the meeting.

It is true that flagellation was known as 'the English vice' and doubtless figured in the pornography which Gladstone read.† None the less, the idea of its use for what was intended as a punishment for sin probably came to him in a Tractarian context. Newman certainly used a scourge and described it in his novel, *Loss and gain*, as 'an iron discipline or scourge, studded with nails'. E. B. Pusey asked Gladstone's closest friend, James Hope, to bring him a discipline from the Continent, and hoped that Keble, his confessor, would advise him to use it. Gladstone may well have found the discipline being used by brother members of the 'engagement', rule ten of which would have allowed for mutual instruction in this, though there is no evidence found that this was so.

From the diary it seems that Gladstone used the scourge without consultation. In 1840 he contemplated 'voluntary periodical confession', recognizing that 'for many consciences I should not think it necessary in any

* During the Wright case in 1927 (a libel case between Captain Wright and Herbert Gladstone which turned on the truth or falsity of Wright's allegations about the Prime Minister's private life) the Gladstone brothers felt on counsels' advice that, because of this specific limitation, the declaration could not be used as evidence on their side.

† I. Bloch, *Sexual life in England* (1901), *passim*, and S. Marcus, *The Other Victorians* (1960), 103.

degree; but for mine it is a question to be pondered'. When considering a paper by Keble planning the 'engagement' in 1844 which provided for group confession, he wrote: 'it often occurs to me what a blessing it will be to our children if they can be brought up in the habit of constantly disclosing the interior of their minds'. It is perhaps remarkable in view of this, and of his apparent Anglo-Catholicism, that he neither practised sacramental confession, as a number of his friends did, nor sought the advice of a spiritual director, lay or clerical, in these times of temptations. It is also interesting, although perhaps not surprising, that his wife is never mentioned in this context of self-examination: there is no hint in the diary or in their correspondence that she knew anything specific of these temptations, although she was involved even with those rescue cases which tempted him most. Indeed Gladstone deliberately kept his difficulties from her, as is shown by this melancholy passage from a letter which he wrote to her in July 1851—she was at Hagley—just after the high pitch of temptation with Elizabeth Collins had been reached and overcome by scourging:

When you say I do not know half the evil of your life, you say that which I believe in almost every case is true between one human being and another; but it sets me thinking how little you know the evil of mine of which at the last day I shall have a strange tale to tell.

Throughout his life Gladstone was essentially secretive (though he had in principle no political secrets from his wife) while at the same time living for the record—but the record was to be read by posterity; his diary and his many memoranda were used to clarify his thoughts and as a means of 'self-rebuke' and self-confession. In this crisis of his early middle-age (he was forty-one at the height of this bout of sexual temptation), he worked out his own salvation less like a Tractarian than an Evangelical or Nonconformist.

The use of the discipline and the other 'mechanical' means developed by Gladstone seem to have been helpful with the pornography, less so with the prostitutes. No doubt many today will find it risible that the Chancellor of the Exchequer should so have relieved his tensions rather than by taking a mistress. But Gladstone knew his own character. He was aware of his 'deadly foe' which was 'the subtle and blinding influences of corrupt sophism' and he must have realized that these passions, once fully liberated, must have destroyed his family and himself. Priggish and hypocritical he may have seemed to enemies, foolhardy to friends, but his struggles with his body and his conscience, when seen in the diary in the context of his religious, political, and family life, cannot but seem noble.

Gladstone's involvement with prostitutes was therefore in no way casual, nor was it merely charitable work which might equally have taken another form. The space taken to discuss it here reflects the time and concern Gladstone devoted to it, 'the chief burden of my soul'. The time spent on it, the obvious intensity of many of the encounters, the courting of evil, show how at the centre of a Victorian family and religious life was a sexual situation of great tension. It is tempting to see Gladstone, because of his religious and political prominence, as exceptional in these matters, but perhaps if more middle-class Victorians had recorded their secret lives so assiduously and honestly he would not seem so; indeed he might seem, rather than a curiosity, predominantly an abstainant.

Gleanings from the Journal in the 1840s and Early 1850s

We should not see Gladstone merely as a politician wrestling with an intellectual crisis or a Tractarian flagellating his sinful body. For perhaps his most remarkable ability was that of living life with equal intensity at many levels, and, in these years, without being fully committed to any. It was this ability to change levels, to design railways for the Hawarden estate, to denounce at length Montalembert's *Des Intérêts Catholiques au XIVe Siècle* in the *Quarterly Review*, to translate Farini's *Lo Stato Romano* and to produce the most famous budget of the century, all within the space of a year, 1853, which gave Gladstone his great public weapon—surprise, and his great private resource—variety.

Despite the intensity of his feelings about his sexuality, his life with his family never seems to have been less than happy. The diary incidentally records the life of a fairly normal wealthy Victorian family, with problems about the governesses, difficulties with the servants, the self-inflicted anguish of sending off the boys to boarding schools. The seven children who lived were raised to adulthood without the sort of casualty which Helen, Gladstone's sister, had been for her generation. Doubtless much of this was the result of Catherine Gladstone's balance and resilience, which seems to have been taken so much for granted that references to her in the diary are very rarely expansive.*

Gladstone's health in the 1840s was, on the whole, good. His eyesight gave trouble, and an exhaustive series of rules was drawn up to improve it, with some success. Illness was occasional: a bad attack of erysipelas in September and October 1847, which he caught from his daughter Agnes, who nearly died from it, recurred in September 1853. On the first occasion his arms were 'more or less disabled'; on the second, 'an apparent return of my erysipelatous inflammations' at Dunrobin, the Duchess of Sutherland passed the time by reading to him, 'full of the utmost kindness and simplicity', thus beginning a relationship of increasing importance to both. The male side of the family was little troubled by illness—none of the four boys was seriously ill in these years. The girls were less fortunate. Agnes, as we have seen, had severe erysipelas, Mary's sight was so bad that in 1850

---

* When apart, Gladstone wrote to his wife very frequently, and at great length, almost always signing himself 'Ever your afft. W.E.G.'

her parents had to take her to Naples for a change of climate, a journey with results far beyond the improvement of her eyes, and Jessy suffered an appalling death from meningitis, aged 5, on 9 April 1850. Her parents could but sit and watch her die. Gladstone's response to distress and crisis was activity; the long biography of Jessy begun that day and the twenty-five letters written testify to the depth of his reaction. By himself, he took her coffin by train and coach to Fasque and saw her buried in the family vault.

Life for Gladstone was not especially hard, but it was earnest, and earnestness is the dominant characteristic of the diary. There is much material about holidays, but even on these Gladstone worked hard at relaxing. Miles walked, feet climbed, churches seen, sermons (never enough) heard, conversations held with unreliable foreigners when abroad, charitable visits to tenants (marked +), are all carefully noted, with Victorian obsession for detail and record as valuable in themselves. Even the casualties of relaxation, such as the top of his left forefinger blown off while shooting in 1842, taught a moral as well as a technical lesson: 'a foolish conceit secretly' had intruded into his shooting, 'in being or seeming able to do what others do. This silly & carnal temper has I hope received a rebuke from the Divine mercy.... I really wanted some lesson however little in bodily pain lest I should forget or hold only a dead remembrance of that part of the lot of mortality.'

Gladstone carefully recorded his religious observances. He almost always attended church twice, sometimes three times, on Sundays, and tried to go once each weekday, usually to an early evensong. To maintain the regularity of his attendance in Scotland, he would go if necessary to a Presbyterian church. His churchgoing in London was to some extent conditioned by easy access from Westminster, but it is clear that he gained most from Frederick Oakeley's Anglo-Catholic Margaret Chapel, where he found an 'atmosphere of devotion ... which I know not where else to look for'. The chapel was rebuilt after Oakeley's apostasy in 1845 as All Saints, Margaret Street, by Butterfield, a member of the 'engagement', many of whose members worshipped there.

Gladstone took communion usually each Sunday, drawing great sustenance from it. His lack of worthiness for receiving it was the immediate cause of the great passage of self-analysis of July 1848 quoted earlier. His communicating was accompanied by elaborate, self-devised preparation and subsequent contemplation, which he noted as 'Secreta Eucharistica', revised at intervals throughout his life. But while his churchgoing was in many respects that of an Anglo-Catholic, in choice of church and in sacramental regularity, it continued to have a strong Evangelical underpinning. We have already noticed Gladstone's reluctance to turn to confession in times of temptation. In a more positively Protestant way he relied strongly on the old custom of waiting on the Bible to 'speak' to him, almost after the fashion of Balfour of Burley, the Covenanter in Scott's *Old Mortality*, one of his favourite novels. The Psalms, he felt, were regularly a present help in time of trouble and decision, both personal and political. Thus in 1843, when deciding whether to enter the Cabinet, he noted: 'in the occurrence of the 73rd Psalm among the services of this day I see another of those minute but striking Providential adjustments which I have often had to remark'. On 9 May 1854 he made a survey in his diary of some of the occasions on which the Psalms had providentially confirmed—never it seems altered—his inclinations.

Personal devotions were for Gladstone no haphazard matter. His morning and evening prayers were carefully planned, with long lists of persons, projects, and categories to be remembered, from the Queen, through his family, the members of the 'engagement', widows, and apostates, to the tenants of Fasque. The children were from the earliest possible age regularly instructed in the Bible, which he tried to read regularly aloud with his wife. Sunday reading was largely spiritual or ecclesiastical. There were clear rules for religious observance in the household, and for household prayers Gladstone made an abstract of the Prayer Book, which he published in 1845. He continued each week to read one of his own sermons to the servants. Though often generalized homilies on a scriptural theme, these sometimes discussed in a straightforward, fairly simple way, some contemporary event; there are some of great interest explaining the Irish famine as a consequence of Providential judgement.

Though his main personal charitable efforts were given to dealings with prostitutes, Gladstone spent much time in the mid-1840s on a project to build a church in Leicester Square, which was eventually unsuccessful. Instead, he and Sir Walter James used the funds to establish a chapel of ease in Bedfordbury in a small upstairs room, behind what is now the London Coliseum Theatre. Gladstone and James paid for a part-time curate, in breaks from the Commons they taught at the ragged school held in it, and they sometimes took the services as well. Saint Andrew's Chapel, in the grounds of Fasque but available to the villagers, and Trinity College, Glenalmond, the school through which the Gladstones hoped to Anglicize, or at any rate Episcopalianize the Scots, were larger examples of institutional proselytization.

Beyond these, Gladstone was involved in many examples of voluntary work; he was one of the chief founders of the Metropolitan Visiting Association (the chief mid-century charity caring for London destitutes), of Saint Barnabas, the House of Mercy still active in Rose Street, Soho, and of the Clewer House of Mercy (also still active), and he played an important role on other religious and secular committees. He was an active member of whatever body he joined, and he joined many. In addition to his parliamentary duties, he was one of those journeymen who work the institutions of the Establishment from the inside, and make them run. Among many such posts, he was an active trustee of the British Museum, a founder of the London Library, chairman for almost thirty years of the Radcliffe Trust which at that time ran the Radcliffe Camera and other property in Oxford, a governor of the Charterhouse and of King's College, London, a trustee of the National Portrait Gallery and of the Colonial Bishoprics Trust, and an often rather parsimonious Commissioner of the 1851 Exhibition, as well as being, when in office, *ex officio* on the governing body of a variety of institutions. Oxford and the Church of England are the important links between many of these, and certainly Gladstone was one of the chief effective Anglican laymen of his time: he earned his right to tell his Church how it should develop.

Despite his many activities, Gladstone found time, spasmodically, for his growing family. Always a cheerful, even a boisterous *pater familias*, he managed in the family circle to forget, or ignore, the public and private pressures and temptations which beset him. Away from his family, Gladstone was often forgetful of birthdays and other events; with them he was part father, part tutor. It is in the latter role that he usually presents himself in the diary. Willy, the eldest of the four boys, bore the brunt of this. Aged three and a third, he was given a course of lessons 'respecting our Saviour'. Perhaps naturally for his age, 'his interest fixes itself upon His being placed upon the cross'. Willy's Latin verses improve over the years, but only after much instruction and, on one occasion, a whipping by his father after a row with his tutor, the local priest. His preparation for confirmation gave his father much pleasure, but Willy may have looked back with more affection to the bonfire on 5 November 1849 when his family was gathered together at Fasque. His father noted: 'Poor Willy's Guy Faux in the evening had an unfortunate effect. I confessed to Aunt J[oanna] the excess into which I was betrayed.'

In the 1840s and 1850s, Gladstone's reading, which he listed with occasional commentary, continues to impress by its range. A new feature in these years is that much of it was done in preparation for a public statement of view in the form of a pamphlet or book review. His book reviews, issued in a steady stream from 1843, were at first for ecclesiastical periodicals such as the *Foreign and Colonial Quarterly Review* or for the Tory *Quarterly Review*. An important development, symptomatic of his developing Liberalism and inconceivable in the 1830s, was a review in 1852 for the Whiggish *Edinburgh Review*, a review, amongst other works, of his own translation in four volumes of L. C. Farini's attack on the Pope's temporal power, *Lo Stato Romano*.

The records of his reading indicate when and through what sources he became interested in specific topics, and what sources were used to resolve the questions raised. In 1852, for example, his reading (apart from sermons) was mostly on colonies, the United States, and Oxford reform until November when he read an article by Cardwell on finance and J. G. Hubbard's pamphlet on the income tax. From then until his budget in 1853 he read all the current pamphlets and reports on the tax, including material from other countries and from the eighteenth century.

On the Crimean war, which did much to frustrate the success of the income-tax measures of the 1853 budget, Gladstone read more patchily. In the summer of 1853, after the budget and before his involvement with the Oxford Bill, he informed himself of the historical and legal background of the eastern question from Marmont's *State of the Turkish empire* (1839) and Phillimore's study of international law, *Russia and Turkey* (1853). But despite further reading in Greek and French, it is clear that there is never that depth and urgency which characterized his reading on a problem in which he felt fully involved. The war appears in the diary mainly in the form of the mass of financial detail it required. Gladstone had firm views on how the war should be financed and fought—on the Foreigners Enlistment Bill he 'never before heard the announcement of a majority in which I had myself voted with such doubtful (if indeed doubtful) feelings'—but he does not seem to have doubted that there was any option but to fight it. He greeted the news of the Alma patriotically and got much more heated over his row with Lord John Russell about the dismissal of a Whig civil servant, Kennedy, than about the departmental reorganization occasioned by the war. The 'brute passions' aroused by the Kennedy affair created 'overflowing disgust at the conduct of Ld J[ohn] & the degradation of the Cabinet' and endangered Gladstone's relationship with the Whigs, though in the end it was probably Aberdeen who suffered most from the 'feud'.

In addition to reading on particular topics of the moment, Gladstone read steadily the literature of the day. *Uncle Tom's Cabin* 'scarcely denies exaggeration', though he thought it of sufficient value to distribute to prostitutes; *Jane Eyre* he found 'a very remarkable but jarring book', as well he might if it is compared to the minor Tractarian novels which provided, especially in the 1840s, a steady supply of undemanding sanctimony.

These brief gleanings from the diary may perhaps encourage the reader to seek out its printed volumes. Its range, political, literary, religious, social, and personal, is extraordinary. No-one will find it light work, and those seeking an easy read will be disappointed. The eclectic complexity and interrelated nature of Victorian culture pervades every entry. The reader approaching the diary will find it looming like some vast rock face seen from far off, some of it sunny and appealing, much of it bleak and uninviting. But closer inspection reveals a different aspect; it is, after all, a climbable face. The ascent is arduous, but reveals on the way a vast mosaic of events, views, descriptions, analyses, reports, changing social and intellectual relationships. As the end is gained, the pattern as a whole becomes clear.

Taking Leave of the Early Gladstone

Two figures emerge as dominating in these early political years: Sir John Gladstone and Sir Robert Peel. John Gladstone, given his baronetcy by Peel in 1846 despite his hostility to Corn Law repeal, had a business as much as a personal relationship with his son. None the less it was he who was largely responsible for creating the framework by which Gladstone reached the Cabinet. He had provided the education of his choice, he had steered 'son William' (as he docketed all his letters) away from the Church as a career; he provided the house and the income which made his son's glittering social and political success possible. The success of many of the projects close to William Gladstone's heart depended on his father's support: he made possible the building of the Scottish Episcopalian boarding school, Trinity College, Glenalmond, and of St Andrew's Episcopalian chapel at Fasque, and provided the bulk of the funds for saving the Hawarden estate, the three material successes which in these years probably pleased Gladstone most. In return Sir John expected attention and attendance. Hence the long journeys to Fasque, Sir John's estate in the Mearns, south of Stonehaven, so dramatically eased by the coming of the railway, and the long sojourns there, out of touch with religious and political developments. Games of whist and piquet, constant arguments about the evils of Anglo-Catholicism and of free trade ('stood two batteries on Free Trade' is characteristic), were the price Gladstone paid for his father's assistance. Not a high price to pay, but one which until his father's death in 1851 was being paid frequently. When with his father, he acted as secretary, a duty which irked him, forcing him to display 'inward & even outward impatience'. Gladstone enjoyed the countryside around Fasque but his service to his father and the need for constant self-containment in the face, especially in the late forties, of persistent harangues, bore heavily upon him, though he tried to turn it to didactic advantage, 'in teaching patience & a humble mind'. Catherine Gladstone must have found life at Fasque very trying, dealing both with the kind but cantankerous Sir John, and with the unpredictable Helen, often drugged and quarrelling with her brother or the servants.

His family around him, the tough old man died aged eighty-seven, in December 1851, refusing the doctor and the holy communion—the latter to William's distress—and calling for porridge. There is some indication of a craving for affection, or at least for recognition, by William at the deathbed, but he met his father's death with equanimity, carefully noting the details of the final stages, concluding with an argument with his brothers about the sacrament, the property, and free trade, and a poignant reminder of a relationship in which, though both had prospered, neither had found much more than a business intimacy: 'I kissed thrice my Father's cheek & forehead before & after his death: the only kisses that I can remember.'

With the death of Sir John, Fasque passed to the eldest brother Tom, and Gladstone took his 'final adieu to Fasque as a home'; despite all the quarrelling, Fasque had become his instinctive home, to which he had taken the body of his dead child Jessy to lie in the family vault. His suggestion that he rather than Tom should take over Fasque came to nothing. Hawarden, reopened after the financial difficulties of 1847 largely as a result of Sir John's generosity, replaced Fasque: Gladstone's 5,000 books were moved to Hawarden and the metamorphosis of the Gladstones of Biggar, so carefully designed by Sir John, was complete: 'son William' was in all but name the owner of an aristocratic estate, walking with pride from Chester to Hawarden castle 'thro' my land'.*

Sir Robert Peel, the nation's 'greatest statesman', had died eighteen months before Sir John, thrown from his horse two days after Gladstone's great speech in the Don Pacifico debate. Gladstone remembered 'with joy with how pure true and vigilant a conscience he always seemed to act'. The diary is a continual witness to the influence of Peel. Peel's very different view of Anglicanism led to disagreements, but Gladstone realized that in the 1841 ministry he was receiving the sort of governmental education which few had the luck to get. If Aberdeen taught Gladstone gentleness, generosity, and justice in politics, Peel taught him method. It was on this method that Gladstone's political success depended, for it provided an indestructible base to which he could return from the ideological forays which many of his political colleagues found extraordinary. Thus on a speech in 1848, 'Peel was gratified & that was enough for me'.

A final word may be said about Gladstone's political development in his Peelite years. It took place within a clearly defined social and parliamentary environment, which, if anything, narrowed as the years passed. As MP for Newark until 1845 Gladstone had some contact, at elections, in correspondence, and through occasional visits to his constituency, with ordinary citizens otherwise unconnected with him. As burgess for Oxford University after 1847 he was, by custom, prevented from direct electioneering, and his constituents were all, by definition, graduates, many of them priests. His fellow-Peelite, Sir James Graham, already felt that Oxford excessively muzzled him, telling Aberdeen in 1853: 'the defeat of Gladstone at Oxford at this precise juncture would be a misfortune; but for his own sake hereafter, Emancipation from the Thraldom of that Constituency would be a blessing'. This may have been true on some issues, but it does

---

* Gladstone technically only owned Hawarden for a few months in 1875 but he and his wife regarded their eldest son from birth as the probable heir. Gladstone bought in his own name considerable property around the Hawarden estate.

not seem to have restricted Gladstone at this time. For Oxford controversies were either of the symbolic sort, such as the feeling about the Jewish Disabilities Bill, or progressively inward-looking. In developing his ideas on the major imperial and national issues of the day Gladstone was largely free, in the 1840s and 1850s, from the normal constituency pressures which affected even other Peelites, themselves an unusually cushioned group in their choice of seats. Rarely can a politician undergoing an intellectual crisis have had more like-mindedly perplexed constituents than Gladstone and the Oxford MAs in the decade between the degradation of W. G. Ward in 1845 and the Oxford Reform Bill of 1854.

At the Board of Trade Gladstone had met many deputations of manufacturers, but he seems to have been influenced less by them than by his reading and by the views of permanent members of the department. Thus his contacts, apart from those with prostitutes and tenants, and his correspondence were overwhelmingly with MPs, civil servants, clergymen (mostly Anglican), lawyers, and gentry.* Nonconformists, Chartists, even ordinary electors, made little impact on his diary and impinged on Gladstone only indirectly, in the pages of reports and pamphlets on their condition.† An exception was Gladstone's visit to Manchester in October 1853, when he made his first important extra-parliamentary speech as a Cabinet minister, and his first speech to a large audience since the 1841 election. It was the first of those great public orations before an 'enormous auditory' of which he later became the master, and perhaps also the slave. In Manchester he unveiled a statue of Peel, making a speech to a large crowd in the open air, and then made an important declaration to local dignitaries in the Town Hall on government policy towards the Crimea. The speech at the unveiling of the statue—the shorter of the two—was made 'before a great assemblage—of *men* almost exclusively, & working men. There I spoke to the cracking of my voice.' Gladstone clearly enjoyed the occasion; it was a portent for the future.

---

* His correspondence with West Midlands creditors of the Oak Farm—mostly small manufacturers—was an exception to this.

† He was a special constable against the Chartists in 1848 and wrote an anti-Chartist declaration of loyalty to the Crown; however, he helped the Spitalfields ballast heavers in 1843 and at the Board of Trade he introduced an employment register for London coalwhippers, and he addressed a meeting of Shadwell coalwhippers. His work with prostitutes gave him a thorough knowledge of a specialized aspect of working-class life, though it did not lead him to attempt its systematic prevention or alleviation, save by voluntary effort.

CHAPTER V

Chancellor of the Exchequer: Free Trade, Budgets, and Franchise Reform

A Peelite and mid-Victorian Politics—Gladstone as Chancellor—
The Politicization of the Chancellorship—The Social Contract of the
mid-Victorian State—Income Tax, Virtual Representation, and Franchise
Reform—The Emergence of a National Politician: Regionalism, Speech-making,
Class, Trade Unions—The 'People's William' and the Press—A Broadening
Political Base—A 'smash . . . without example': Franchise Reform 1866–7—
Regaining the Initiative: Ireland and the Premiership

But I feel like a man under a burden under which he must fall and be crushed if he looks to the right or left, or fails from any cause to concentrate mind and muscle upon his progress step by step. This absorption, this excess, this constant ἄγαν is the fault of political life with its insatiable demands which do not leave the smallest stock of moral energy unexhausted and available for other purposes.

They certainly however have this merit: they drive home the sense that I am poor, and naked, and blind and miserable: and they make forgetfulness of God not a whit less unintelligible than it is excusable, though it is one thing to remember and another to obey.

Swimming for his life, a man does not see much of the country through which the river winds, and I probably know little of these years through which I busily work and live, beyond this, how sin and frailty deface them, and how mercy crowns them.*

A Peelite and mid-Victorian Politics

Thus Gladstone, twenty-six days after kissing hands in 1868 as first lord of the Treasury for the first time, celebrated his arrival at 'the top of the greasy pole'. It had not for him been a difficult climb, though there had been the odd slip and loss of grip. Nor had the conditions been especially arduous in the decade since the Crimean War. The crises of 'the hungry forties' gave way to the spectacular prosperity of the 1850s and 1860s. Britain moved towards democracy by the rule book, recalcitrant theorists proving a worse problem for the government than the demonstrations of loyal artisans, eager to ally themselves with political democracy. Problems of public

* 31 December 1868.

order, the chief feature of the earlier years of Gladstone's career, gave way to the limited adjustment of relationships between unalienated groups: whereas the Chartists had wished to overturn the political order, the Reform League merely wished to associate itself with it.

The 1850s and early 1860s showed the Victorian constitution working in its most characteristic form, in a context of economic progress at which contemporaries wondered, though without complacency. By the late 1860s the propertied classes were becoming disconcerted by the re-emergence of those 'great social forces' which suggested that the mid-Victorian settlement might not, after all, hold. But the early 1860s—the 'Age of Equipoise' in W. L. Burn's phrase—were years in which the achievement of progress—material, moral, intellectual—seemed to be Britain's contribution to an envious and admiring world. 'Greater World' was Gladstone's slip of the pen when Dilke's 'Greater Britain' was intended: it characterized a generation.

For Gladstone personally most of these years offered a similar tranquillity. The great crises of his public and private life which characterized the 1840s and early 1850s had been largely resolved. The tensions in what he saw as political and sexual temptations became the tensions of tactical not of strategic decision: the path of his life seemed finally charted, the set of his thought consolidated.

This is not to say that the problems of political tactics were not extremely complex, as we shall see; but the great questions for Gladstone of the 1830s and 1840s, of whether politics was for him a legitimate career, of the nature of the Christian State, and of the relationship between ambition and duty, no longer form the central themes of his diary.

Politically, the diary of these years records a series of decisions and manœuvres whose context is quite different from that in which Gladstone could seriously offer to Peel the amalgamation of two Welsh sees as a reason for not joining the Cabinet. For Gladstone, the relationships of Church and State had ceased to be a chief point of theoretical controversy: his decisions in 1868 about the abolition of compulsory church rates and Irish disestablishment were decisions about timing and tactics, no longer about great moral issues; the latter, he believed, had already been settled by the failure of the Oxford movement in the 1840s to convert the nation.

However, in purely tactical political terms, the years 1855–9 were the most personally complex in Gladstone's career. The success of the Peelite–Liberal coalition of 1852 was, from Gladstone's point of view, broken by the events of January and February 1855, which he records in very great detail. But no great ideological difference separated Gladstone from the Palmerston government (in which some Peelites, notably Argyll, continued to serve) except the character of its leader. On the other hand, no great question of policy seemed to bar his return to the Tory party. As he put it, anonymously, in the *Quarterly Review* in 1856:

The interval between the two parties has, by the practical solution of so many congested questions, been very greatly narrowed. He who turns from Pall Mall towards the Park between the Reform and Carlton Clubs will perceive that each of those stately fabrics is mirrored in the windows of the other, and it may occur to him, with horror and amusement, according to his temper, that those mutual reflections of images set up in rank antagonism to one another, constitute a kind of parable, that offers to us its meaning as we read with conscience and intelligence the history of the time.*

The Peelites found themselves standing in the street, exiles from one club, fearful to join the other, though willing to visit it.

Thus while there was a tendency to co-operation with the Liberal party, as in 1852, when, as Gladstone told Aberdeen in 1857, 'the act was done, which would probably have led to a real & final amalgamation with the Liberal party', there was also a tendency to reunion with the mass of the Conservatives who appeared to have abandoned the fiscal views which after 1846 had made continued co-operation with them impossible.

In his attempt to reassess his notion of a moral organic society, Gladstone had in the late 1840s travelled a very considerable distance in certain aspects of his thought towards a liberal position. His difficulty was that politics had not continued to divide on the question of free trade on which this liberalism was founded, and the national dedication to free trade seemed belied by the later stages of the Crimean war and the disasters of the general election in 1857 in which many of the free trade Radicals lost their seats. Foreign policy during Palmerston's government of 1855 to 1858 had certainly not followed what Gladstone regarded as moral policies, and that government had in his view also been misguided in its financial and immoral in its divorce policy. Gladstone thus found it easier to work on some questions with the Radicals, on others with the Conservatives, but rarely with the Whigs.

However, the position of a politician assessing motion by motion on its merits was not congenial to Gladstone's executive turn of mind: 'He must be a very bad minister indeed, who does not do ten times the good to the country when he is in office, that he would do when he is out of it.' The Radicals he found irresponsible, in the sense that they were critics with no desire to become actors. He could work with them on specific issues, but they could offer no solution to the question of the execution of policy. Similarly the Conservatives, much though he might appreciate Derby's

---

* [W. E. Gladstone], 'The declining efficiency of parliament', *Quarterly Review*, xcix. 562 (September 1856); this important and neglected article, an expansion of a letter to Aberdeen, written in the light of his 'memorandum on finance' of 15 February 1856, gives a clear and revealing account of Gladstone's views about the proper development of British politics.

probity, offered no prospect of a satisfactory executive position, for Gladstone believed, very probably rightly, that the Peelites did not constitute a political grouping substantial enough to assist the Conservatives to a working majority in the Commons. Moreover, Gladstone found that co-operation with the Conservatives on financial matters broke down on the important question of the social implications of different types of taxation, an issue which in 1856 raised the question whether the apparent agreement between the Peelites, the Radicals, and the Conservatives on the defects of Cornewall Lewis's financial policy, could in the long term be maintained.*

Gladstone had become essentially an executive politician. As he told Samuel Wilberforce in 1857, 'I greatly felt being turned out of office, I saw great things to do. I longed to do them. I am losing the best years of my life out of my natural service. . . .' This was by no means a characteristic attitude for a mid-Victorian politician. Even more uncharacteristic was Gladstone's action in drawing up in opposition (in February 1856) a great programme of measures to be passed through when next in office.

This programme of twenty-one financial measures included, amongst others, what became the Exchequer and Audit Act of 1866, the assertion of treasury control over all other departments, a reappraisal of the role and profits of the Bank of England, the abolition of the paper duties, the reduction of the wine, malt, sugar, coffee, insurance, and stamp duties, the reform of the taxation system by 'the extension and increase of the House Duty upon the determination of the Income Tax', and a series of technical measures. Where Peel had moved hesitantly and experimentally, Gladstone codified a large but miscellaneous body of fiscal and departmental reforms into a coherent plan for an all-powerful 'ministry of finance', and one which only his formidable political will was likely to be able to translate into legislative and administrative reality.

Not surprisingly, therefore, Gladstone regarded his period of opposition after 1855 as an anomaly to be ended by entry to the Cabinet of either a Whig–Liberal or a Conservative administration. Although he does not say so, he must have realized that his choice of party must now be final: he could hardly expect forgiveness from either side a second time. This may well account for his caution. His personal inclination in the period 1855 to 1859 lay on the whole with the Conservatives, whom he saw as less capricious than Palmerston; but, apart from Derby and Spencer Walpole, he had little intimacy with Conservatives of Cabinet rank. The Conservatives, for their part, while keen to capture Gladstone, made it clear to him that the extent of demand for office within their own party would leave no room for a general occupancy of senior Cabinet posts by the Peelite group.

* Gladstone's argument that finance benefited from having the Conservatives in office because the Liberals were more effective retrenchers when in opposition hardly offered a long-term solution.

Gladstone, however, consistently argued that the problem of party after the break-up of the coalition in 1855 could not be solved by men, but by measures. By measures, he meant the fulfilment of the programme of financial reform which he worked out in February 1856. Other Peelites, however, without exception worked to push him away from Derby and appear on several occasions to have exercised at least a decisive negative influence upon him. His failure to join Derby in 1858 was crucial, for, if he was again to hold office, there was no alternative left for him but to join the government of 1859, consequent upon the overthrow of the Derby Cabinet.

The Ionian Islands commissionership extraordinary, held by Gladstone in 1858–9 at the request of the Conservative government, was not from his point of view a move towards the Tories, though it was so intended by them. Gladstone had never, by his votes or speeches in the 1850s, hidden his view that the Conservatives deserved respect and, when possible, support. Though accepting the position from a Conservative ministry might seem to suggest a movement towards holding domestic office in that ministry, this was not the consequence seen by Gladstone's subtle mind. In Gladstone's analysis of the political situation it added nothing and subtracted nothing: it did not involve the Peelites as a group, and it did not involve 'measures'. If he had found insufficient reason to join the Derby ministry at its outset, there was no further reason to contemplate joining later, for the life of the ministry was agreed by all to be certain to be short. The Ionian interlude is certainly of interest, but not in the party political context; it will be discussed later.

There was also 'the difficulty of Disraeli', by the late 1850s firmly established as the leading Conservative in the Commons and the probable Leader of the House in any Conservative ministry. As Sir James Graham said to Gladstone, the Peelites could not expect Derby to throw Disraeli away 'like a sucked orange'. Gladstone personally felt 'unable to enter into any squabble or competition with him for the possession of a post of prominence'. To join with Disraeli was, in the Peelites' view, to place political morality at the service of chicanery, though in Gladstone's opinion Palmerston was not much better, despite being like himself a Canningite in origin, having 'dishonour as the great characteristic of [his] Government'.

By biding his time and accepting Peelite cautions against Conservatism, Gladstone solved the problem by elimination. Always reluctant to admit the role of ambition in politics, Gladstone was none the less aware of his abilities and their lack of application since 1855; his entry to Palmerston's Cabinet in 1859 thus involved no great moral choice and produced no great passage of self-analysis in the diary.* It was the hard-headed response of an able politician with a programme for action, invited to join a Cabinet at the

---

* The aftermath of the general election of April–May 1859 did, however, occasion one night of self-flagellation and a half-sleepless night.

outset of its formation.* In discussing political contingencies in 1856 with the other MP for Oxford University, Sir William Heathcote, Gladstone remarked:

That as to union, it was quite impossible to treat it as a matter of mere choice or will: whether it were a question of rejoining our late colleagues, or any other persons, our proceeding to be warrantable, must be founded on convictions of the public interest & on community of views evinced to the world by co-operation on great questions of the day which as they arose would speak for themselves & would open the path of duty.

Robertson Gladstone, by now Mayor of Liverpool and a leader of Lancastrian Radicalism , put the political point more directly:

No one, who knows you, if he ever thinks, can suppose, that you would coalesce with D'Israeli: when *you* join with another, that move, we know, will have some sort of principle, at least, to boast of.

Italy was, or could be made to seem, such a question in 1859. But in the general context of Gladstone's position in the years after 1855, of his failure to find a similar basis for co-operation with the Conservatives despite his violent and publicly voiced hostility to Whig foreign policy, of his persistently expressed criticisms of the financial policies of successive governments, of his own solution to financial ills, and of his demand in 1859 for the Exchequer alone, it is hard to see Italy as more than a convenient issue on which to combine with the Whigs on their own ground of foreign policy. This is not to say that Gladstone was using the Italian question deceitfully: he undoubtedly believed in the policy to which in the latter part of 1859 he contributed, but he can hardly have seen Italy as the basis for a government, and it did not figure in the list of public questions which he believed in 1857 to be of primary parliamentary significance.

Gladstone's visit to Venetia and Piedmont in the spring of 1859 on his way back from the Ionian islands undoubtedly quickened his interest in the subject, though his view of what should happen there was largely negative and even anti-Piedmontian: Austria should be removed, but not to Piedmont's advantage, and the temporal power of the Pope diminished. Despite his opportunities, Gladstone did not much encourage the Italianate sympathies of the English radicals, with their republican over-

---

* Palmerston had been confident Gladstone would join, and hopeful that he could be kept out of the Exchequer. On 30 March 1859 he had listed Gladstone for the Colonial Office, as he also did on an undated list, and for the India Office on another (undated) list. On these lists he had put Lewis down for the Exchequer. But Gladstone apparently saw Palmerston, knowing that Lewis would cede the Exchequer to him; see A. Hayward (to his sisters, 16 June 1859) *Correspondence* (1886) ii. 34: 'It was through me that Sir George Lewis communicated to Gladstone his readiness to give up the Chancellorship of the Exchequer to him if he wished and it was I who first told Lord Palmerston that Gladstone would join.' This is probably the meeting recorded by Gladstone on 2 June 1859, i.e. before the vote of 10 June which felled Derby's government, in which Gladstone voted against the motion of want of confidence. Gladstone told Herbert he would only have accepted the Exchequer.

tones, and his behaviour during Garibaldi's visit to England in 1864 can only be described as shuffling. Despite his later claims, Gladstone played an important part in persuading Garibaldi to abandon his planned provincial tour.

Appalling though Gladstone believed Palmerston's policies to have been between 1855 and 1858, their direction had advantages from his point of view. Gladstone argued that Palmerston's

stock in trade as a Peace Minister was wholly inadequate, or rather nearly null. It followed that he could only be a Peace Minister by keeping alive the passions, maintaining the sentences, and thus ever walking on the giddy brink of war.

But, to last, a peace-time government must offer more than this; it must offer a substantial programme of domestic legislation. This Gladstone could provide. There was 'a policy going a'begging', already prepared in some detail, which could provide the basis for the domestic programme of the government. A prime minister whose chief interest was bound to be in the area of foreign policy could have advantages for a Chancellor of the Exchequer with his own programme of legislation, and a programme it was. Gladstone as chancellor between 1859 and 1866 introduced, step by step, the items of the programme he had drawn up in 1856, the last item, the Exchequer and Audit Act, being passed shortly before the government resigned in 1866. This was a remarkable, perhaps unique, achievement in Victorian politics, and one which showed that, at least for Gladstone, the construction of policy could be something more than the accidental product of the politics of personality.

Gladstone as Chancellor

Gladstone was Chancellor of the Exchequer from December 1852 to February 1855, and from June 1859 until July 1866, the latter the longest continuous tenure between Vansittart and Lloyd George.* It may be useful, therefore, to set out the context of what was probably the most satisfying period of his political career, and certainly his most sustained period of departmental success.

A Victorian chancellor was not much troubled by the sort of crises characteristic of British history since 1914; the only peace-time occasion on which Gladstone had to act unexpectedly was the 1866 financial crisis caused by the failure of Overend and Gurney's bank, and even this was, from the chancellor's point of view, intrusive only for a weekend: 'Although the case was perplexing at the onset, & will be so in the *hereafter*, yet when we obtained the facts of the operations of the day our course became at once perfectly clear.' For the most part the chancellor

* Gladstone beat Hicks Beach (1895–1902) by five days, and was beaten by Lloyd George (1908–15) by a month.

was concerned with strategy, with the construction of an efficient 'Ministry of Finance', as Gladstone usually called it, and with the measured preparation of the annual budget. This pattern was disturbed only by the spasmodic need for extra revenue for imperial exploits, and by sudden calls for extra domestic defence expenditure through last minute changes in the departmental estimates. As chancellor, Gladstone was rarely involved in the day-to-day activities of the Treasury. The sort of detailed work which at the Board of Trade he had done himself, such as the day-to-day correspondence with other departments, was the responsibility of the financial secretary to the Treasury. It would seem that Gladstone involved himself more in departmental matters than most chancellors, but even this involvement was chiefly in the area of contract negotiations, especially as they affected overseas communications, for example the Red Sea telegraph and the Galway packet contract for postal communication with North America.

Gladstone usually drew up the heads of his spring budget the previous Christmas, at Hawarden, and without any reference to the Treasury. On one occasion he began earlier, in August: 'I dreamt of the next Estimates: with a dour sense of the work I have to do.' He would then request information from the various departments, such as the Board of Inland Revenue and the national debt commissioners, about the likely effect on revenue of changes in taxation which he contemplated introducing. He did not consult the Treasury or the departments on questions of policy, but merely on administration, nor did the Treasury or the departments propose policy changes to him. Least of all did he involve his Cabinet colleagues. As he told Cornewall Lewis when Lewis succeeded him as chancellor in 1855: 'I advised him to keep his own Counsel & let the Cabinet as a whole not know his plans till his mind was made up in the main, & the time close at hand.'

As chancellor, therefore, Gladstone acted independently. He also acted aggressively. His years at the Treasury coincided with reform of that institution from within which Gladstone both shared and encouraged.* The Treasury was asserting its right to control the activities and personnel of the civil service as a whole; Gladstone asserted the political position of the chancellor in Cabinet, in Parliament, and hence in the country generally. Hitherto the Exchequer had either been held by a man of importance, but not of the first importance, or by the First Lord of the Treasury himself. Peel had, between 1841 and 1846, used Goulburn more as a financial secretary than a chancellor, and had prepared and introduced budgets almost without reference to his chancellor. Whig chancellors had been second rank men without aspirations to real power. Disraeli had been the first chancellor also to be the obvious second man in the government.

* See M. Wright, *Treasury control of the civil service, 1854–1874* (1969).

By deliberately asserting the overall suzerainty of the Treasury, Gladstone not surprisingly clashed with the spending departments, particularly the Admiralty and the War Office, for army and navy estimates constituted 43% of all government spending in 1861. Defence and the charges on the national debt together accounted for about three-quarters of central government expenditure, and were therefore the chief areas of concern for the chancellor on the expenditure side.* He battled with the Admiralty and the War Office about what he considered unnecessary expenditure, though always, to the distress of some of the Radicals on the back-benches, accepting the need for both an efficient army of considerable size and a large fleet. The debt, he attempted to deal with by conversion in 1853 and 1866–7 (a happy co-operation with Disraeli) and, to a lesser extent, by redemption.

In the Cabinet struggles of the early 1860s, Gladstone tried to force the defence departments to work within the Treasury's framework of taxation reform; that is, he appeared to give priority over imperial considerations to a financial programme of mainly domestic political importance. But this was to a considerable extent only appearance. Because Gladstone could not decide whether spending on imperialism was chronic or merely spasmodic, he failed to develop a policy to deal with it, save the negative one of making colonies of predominantly European settlement pay for their own defence. Thus he found himself treating each imperial crisis in non-white areas separately and in its own terms only, and, as each imperial action could be made to seem plausible, Gladstone, as Cobden so often complained, found himself raising funds for imperialism as effectively as any Whig or Tory.

The other contentious item was the plan to fortify the southern coast against French invasion. Here Gladstone had an alternative policy: the

* As % of total gross central government expenditure

	Debt charges	Defence	Civil government
1836–40	57.7	24.6	10.0
1841–5	54.5	25.8	10.4
1846–50	50.2	28.9	12.0
1851–5	48.8	27.9	12.2
1856–60	38.6	39.9	12.4
1861–5	37.7	39.4	15.4
1866–70	38.2	36.1	15.8
1871–5	38.1	33.1	17.2
1876–80	34.8	32.5	20.0
1881–5	34.4	31.3	21.7
1886–90	28.5	34.4	21.2
1891–5	24.3	34.7	19.8
1896–9	21.0	36.6	19.9
1900–3	12.3	56.5	19.9
1904–8	22.9	43.1	20.2
1909–13	11.7	38.0	31.2

Compiled from B. R. Mitchell and P. Deane, *Abstract of British Historical Statistics* (1971), tables 4 and 4a. The total to 100 is made up by administrative costs, Post Office, etc.

French commercial treaty of 1860, and on this question time proved him right. The fact that the war secretary was his close and already ailing friend, Sidney Herbert, made no difference to Gladstone, who relentlessly exposed Herbert to a full-scale battle by correspondence. But Herbert had behind him the Duke of Somerset, First Lord of the Admiralty, and, more important, Palmerston, one of the very few men who could equal Gladstone in political stamina.

In 1860 Gladstone pressed his hostility to the brink of resignation, but not over it. 'My resignation *all but* settled': the significance lay in the italics. Gladstone, unlike Randolph Churchill in 1886, never offered resignation formally. Moreover Palmerston, unlike Salisbury with Churchill, did not wish him to go, and despite their differences went to considerable lengths to keep him in the Cabinet, the Duke of Argyll acting as mediator. In these protracted struggles, each side convinced itself that it had won at least the odd battle. In the sense that imperialism was paid for and some of the fortifications built, the Admiralty and War Office gained most of their objectives. Gladstone pressed through the French treaty and, eventually, the repeal of the paper duties. He gained politically what he lost fiscally, and, by not resigning, remained to realize the programme of treasury control which, if apparently unsuccessful in the short term of the 1860s, in the long term seemed to triumph.

The Politicization of the Chancellorship *

Some of what the chancellor had to do was technical: the details of the small print of the handling of various taxes and of the national debt, though even these were never uncontroversial. Gladstone was very good at this sort of behind-the-scenes management, but it was not this that gained him his fame as chancellor. In 1857, when reacting to Cornewall Lewis's budget, he drew up a list of priorities:

> To maintain a steady surplus of income over expenditure—to lower indirect taxes when excessive in amount for the relief of the people and bearing in mind the reproductive power inherent in such operations—to simplify our fiscal system by concentrating its pressure on a few well chosen articles of extended consumption—and to conciliate support to the Income Tax by marking its temporary character & by associating it with beneficial changes in the laws: these aims have been for fifteen years the labour of our life.

The Peelites liked finance to be neat, regular, and seen to be so. The balanced budget, its income raised by a simple, pared-down structure of direct and indirect taxes, its expenditure given to a few absolutely necessary departments of government, exemplified a nation with its bowels in

---

* In this and the next section I have introduced some material originally quoted in my article 'Disraeli, Gladstone and the politics of mid-Victorian budgets', *Historical Journal* (1979), which has more detail on various aspects of Gladstone's chancellorship.

good working order. 'Finance is, as it were, the stomach of the country, from which all the other organs take their tone', Gladstone wrote in 1858. For this to be so, a high political profile for the chancellor and the Treasury was essential.

Gladstone aggressively and consistently politicized the chancellorship, through the preparation and prosecution of budgets. In 1853 he immediately established almost complete independence from his old department, the Board of Trade, remembering perhaps the way it had, under his direction, influenced budgetary preparation in the 1840s. The 1853 and 1860 budgets (especially the latter) were of course in large measure tariff budgets, but in their preparation the Board of Trade was consulted merely on technicalities.

The 1860 French treaty, a central feature of that year's budget, was negotiated almost independently of the Foreign Office, and largely independently of the Cabinet. The 1860 treaty was a quite deliberate interference in Whig foreign policy. It was presented politically as a further step towards free trade, though technically it was a reciprocity treaty and criticized as such by some theoretical free traders. Its financial importance was chiefly confined to its effect on the English silk and glove trades, and to Gladstone's plan to solve the drink problem by creating a nation of wine drinkers consuming their cheap 'Gladstone claret', as it came to be called, in decorous cafés which paid their licence fees to the government, instead of in public houses under the licence of local and often independently minded magistrates. The French treaty was the first of several such treaties in the 1860s, but it was the only one to which Gladstone attached much political importance. To counter Whig suspicions of France and the consequent construction of massive fortifications along the English south coast, Gladstone was determined to get a commercial treaty with France, at almost any cost. He told Cobden, who negotiated the treaty in Paris, of

... the great aim—the moral and political significance of the act, and its probable and desired fruit in binding the two countries together by interest and affection.

Neither you nor I attach for the moment any superlative value to this Treaty for the sake of the extension of British trade.... What I look to is the social good, the benefit to the relations of the two countries, and the effect on the peace of Europe.

Similarly the repeal of the paper duties in 1860 and 1861, involving the first major institutional row between the two Houses of Parliament since 1832, deliberately allied the chancellor with political radicalism in a way that Gladstone had been careful to avoid with respect to the 'taxes on knowledge' during his previous chancellorship in 1852–5. Both Gladstone's most famous budgets, of 1853 and 1860, were pressed through an unwilling Cabinet. We have already seen his finesse in getting eventual Cabinet acceptance for his 1853 budget. In 1860, on the paper duties question, he was only supported by Gibson and Argyll in the Cabinet, and in 1861 only by Gibson, yet he was eventually able to prevail. Moreover, since it became quite clear from the press, and from the behaviour of Palmerston in parliamentary debates, that paper duty repeal was at Cabinet level very much Gladstone's own policy, the political advantages to Gladstone of the eventual success of the repeal and of the outflanking of the House of Lords were all the greater.

Much of Gladstone's work as chancellor was self-consciously in the tradition of Peel, but it was executed in a political style more dramatic, more rhetorical, and less discreet than the Peelite reforms of the 1840s. This was not accidental or merely the result of personal differences. Gladstone believed that big bills and budgets were a necessary feature not merely of executive government but of post-1832 politics. He attacked Macaulay for articulating the eighteenth-century view that it was not the function of the Executive persistently to initiate legislation, and he denounced Palmerston between 1855 and 1858 for acting like the eighteenth-century Duke of Newcastle—a domestic programme of quiescence designed to placate placemen.

This was therefore not merely the Pitt–Peel argument that there were reforms to be done and abuses to be remedied, but a much more political argument that it was politically essential that reforms should persistently be seen to be done, for 'it is rapid growth in the body politic that renders stereotyped law intolerable'. 'Public opinion', Gladstone argued, 'is disposed to view with great favour all active and efficient government.' In this sense Gladstone's chancellorships represented the politicization of Peelism. For Gladstone, therefore, big bills and big budgets* represented a means of regular renewal of the legitimacy of Parliament and the political system; for Palmerston and the Whigs they represented a continuous threat to stability and moderation.

At first glance there was something of a paradox here: the less budgets and the fiscal system were intended to superintend or direct the national economy, the more they became the centre-pieces of the political year. But this was not really paradoxical because an important, indeed a central, feature of the mid-Victorian finance of which Gladstone was the dominant exponent was what may be called positive retrenchment. The direct relationship between government and the economy should be minimal, but the indirect relationship, through the setting up of a self-sustaining economy, would be considerable. The reduction of government superintendence of the economy by the abolition of the tariff structure and the maintenance of a low level of government spending was intended to have positive results. First, the economy would be self-regulating. This would

---

* Ironically, the Queen, later to be so alarmed by the Gladstonian habit of big bills, encouraged him in this direction, telling him in 1859 that a big budget was required.

have the economic benefit, it was thought, of allowing the maximum of capital accumulation in a free market; 'in giving legal freedom to the energy of capital and skill of Englishmen, we were adopting a true and powerful means of extending our commercial prosperity'.* It would also have the political benefit of dissociating government and Parliament from the need to bargain with economic pressure groups. 'Government' and 'the economy' would thus be quite separate entities—good citizenship would not be compromised by economic interest.† Indeed, a society in which the political process was mainly concerned to deal with such groups would be a corrupt society.

By 1880 Gladstone had come to see protection as a 'poison', sheltering nothing 'but the most selfish instincts of class against the just demands of the public welfare'; it armed producers with 'power and influence largely gotten at the expense of the community, to do battle, with a perverted prowess, against nature, liberty and justice'.‡

This stress on a concept of citizenship which discounted the economy would allow Parliament to be seen as 'fair' and dispassionate by all classes in the State.§ Consequently, although 'classes' would undoubtedly exist and indeed Gladstone's view of the distribution of taxation took direct account of them, politics would not appear essentially to be about class. By

---

* The success of this strategy was remarkable. At a time when, as Gladstone pointed out, the proportion of government spending to national wealth was rising rapidly in Continental nations, in Britain it remained both low (relative to a world power's responsibilities) and fairly constant (though falling markedly in the years of Gladstonian suzerainty, 1860–75), as the following table shows:

Proportion of Central Government Gross
Expenditure to Gross National Product

	Expenditure £m	G.N.P. £m	%
1853	55.3	642 (1855)	8.6
1860	70.0	702	10.0
1865	67.1	846	7.9
1870	67.1	953	7.0
1875	73.0	1136	6.4
1880	81.5	1101	7.4
1885	88.5	1120	7.9
1895	100.9	1459	6.9
1905	149.5	1814	8.2
1913	202.2	2322	8.7

Source: B. R. Mitchell and P. Deane, *Abstract of British Historical Statistics* (1971), Public Finance 4 and 4a, and C. H. Feinstein, *National Income, Expenditure and Output of the United Kingdom 1855–1965* (1972), Table 1.

† See G. Stedman Jones, *Languages of Class* (1983), 177–8, for the success of this strategy in countering Chartism.

‡ W. E. Gladstone, 'Free Trade, Railways, and the growth of Commerce', *Nineteenth Century* (February 1880), 377; in this article, he was careful to reserve his position on infant industries.

§ See Ross McKibbin, 'Why was there no Marxism in Great Britain?', *English Historical Review* (1984).

its wider ranging fiscal reforms, and especially its abolition of protective tariffs, the House of Commons had acted, Gladstone told it in his 1860 speech on the budget and the Cobden treaty,

on behalf of the masses of the people, and not on behalf of them alone, but on behalf of every class, on behalf of the Throne, and of the institutions of the country. . . . By pursuing such a course as this it will be in your power to scatter blessings among the people, and blessings which are among the soundest and most wholesome of all the blessings at your disposal; because in legislation of this kind, you are not forging mechanical supports and helps for men, nor endeavouring to do that for them which they ought to do for themselves; but you are enlarging their means without narrowing their freedom, you are giving value to their labour, you are appealing to their sense of responsibility, you are not impairing their temper of honourable self-dependence . . . [these sorts of laws] win more and more for the Throne and for the institutions of the country the gratitude, the confidence, and the love of an united people.

But the advantages were not merely domestic. Defending in 1853 the use of 'the mighty engine' of income tax, so essential to the financing of the war effort against the French Revolution and Napoleon, and now so valuable as the agent of free trade through commercial and fiscal reform, Gladstone claimed a world mission for the British model: 'in reforming your own fiscal and commercial system, you have laid the foundations of similar reforms—slow, perhaps, but certain in their progress—through every country of the civilized world'.

This view of the relationship of central government to the economy pre-supposed two premises, both of which turned out, in the long run, to be false. First, it presupposed that equilibrium in the economy would naturally be achieved at the full utilization of available resources, both capital and labour—that, as J. S. Mill put it, an excess of supply was, except in moments of temporary dislocation, an impossibility. Second, it pre-supposed the capacity of a vast network of voluntary organizations to superintend, through the participation of active citizens and in co-operation with local government, most of the range of moral, charitable, educational, and welfare services. The absence of initiative by central government in such areas was thus premissed on the vigorous involvement of the citizen in local affairs, in charitable giving and administration, in savings societies, and in the many religious organizations which aspired to offer a very wide range of services, many of which would today be regarded as outside the area of 'religion'. Gladstone himself, as we have seen, was active in a private capacity in exactly these sorts of endeavours. There was no divide between his public advice and his private thought and action. As an Anglican, however, he had a rather different perspective on such matters from a Nonconformist or a strict Liberal. Anglican welfarism necessarily had national objectives which implied, ultimately, national standards, coverage, and measurement. In this pattern of voluntary action, the Church of England must be included, for it was expected to raise its revenues by voluntary means. But it was not to be expected that its members could accept without reserve the aberrations which a voluntary system of welfare and education were bound to produce.

Consequently Gladstone's retrenchment ethos and his preference for a voluntarist society were tempered by an absence of dogma, a willingness to see problems in a national context, and a maintenance of executive authority. His programme of legislation was, as has been mentioned above, set out privately in 1856 and carried through between 1859 and 1866. Its aim was the construction of an independent and controlling Treasury, represented at Cabinet level by a powerful 'minister of finance', supported in the legislature by annual inquiry through the Public Accounts Committee, set up in 1861, and by a House of Commons dedicated to vigilance and retrenchment. The Public Accounts Committee checked abuses in expenditure retrospectively. Enthusiastic though he was for retrenchment, Gladstone was also very careful not to yield executive control of the planning of expenditure. At an early stage of its existence, in 1862, the Committee showed interest in prospective expenditure and its control. Gladstone explained in evidence to the Committee that if a spending department and the Treasury could not agree, 'they would go to the Cabinet, and the Cabinet would decide questions for that period'. He then considered another possibility: 'the other choice would be that of presenting the transaction to Parliament before it had become final, and while it was subject to modification. I think if it were to be presented in that way it must go to some Committee or to some separate body; it could not go to the House of Commons at large.' This opened the possibility in the working of such a Committee of an alliance between Parliament and the Treasury for the pursuit of retrenchment. But Gladstone, despite his wide-ranging plans for the extension of Treasury control, his frequent appeals for public demand for retrenchment, and his lament for the 'declining efficiency of Parliament', never advocated the setting up of such a Committee; control of prospective expenditure remained effectively and firmly in the hands of the executive, and in this he acted wholly in character.

Gladstone is well known for his phrase that money should 'fructify in the pockets of the people', but what he actually meant was that it should fructify in the deposit vaults of the National Debt Commissioners. Much though he extolled the virtues of self-help, his actions as chancellor were consistently *étatist*. While Gladstone often used pluralist free trade arguments to justify the use of exchange as an impartial arbiter of social morality, in practice as chancellor he often returned to the organic, almost corporatist view of the State which he had set out in his first book. The aim of his Post Office Savings Banks plan was to give the Treasury more independence from the Bank of England. His Working Class Annuities Act, passed against strong hostility from the Friendly Societies, was in direct competition with them, and denounced by them as quite contrary to the self-help ethos, but was welcomed by trade unionists anxious to associate themselves with the State.*

The aim of his Country Bank Notes Issue Bill, which had to be withdrawn, was to speed up the working of the issue centralizing clauses of the Bank Charter Act of 1844. But the strengthened Bank of England was to make less money from its role as the government's bank, and was to be less firmly entrenched as the pivot of fiscal crisis, for Gladstone contemplated a radical alteration to the 1844 Bank Act, by which an issue of bonds, controlled by the Treasury, would expand the money supply in times of crisis, controlled by an ever-increasing rate of interest. The failure of the Country Notes Bill showed the strength of the lobby for the existing banking system, and the plan for the revision of the 1844 Act, also strongly opposed within the Treasury, never became more than a privately canvassed proposal.

Gladstone's mistrust of the existing banking system stemmed from his experiences after his wife's family business had been bankrupted in the fiscal crisis of 1847. Partly as a result of this, partly in keeping with a general change of view characteristic of mid-Victorian Britain, Gladstone came to believe, at least in the 1860s, that market forces could not produce a just society. Moreover, he had never been an out-and-out Ricardian. His youthful Idealist approach to the organic nation had been in direct contrast to Ricardianism and though in the late 1840s he had abandoned as unworkable the view of State–Church relations set out in his first book, he had specifically not forsworn his view of the organic nature of the State.

As chancellor, Gladstone compared himself to an architect altering a fine but decaying eighteenth-century mansion to a form fitted for the industrial age, designing the new building, controlling its construction, modifying its form as the years passed. Technically put, the function of the chancellor was to create a model of international free trade and then to interfere at the margin of the domestic economy on grounds of social justice:

Once security has been taken that an entire society shall not be forced to pay an artificial price to some of its members for their production, we may safely commit the question [of cheapness of goods] to the action of competition among manufacturers, and of what we term the laws of supply and demand. As to the condition of the workpeople, experience has shown, especially in the case of the Factory Acts, that we should do wrong in laying down any abstract maxim as an invariable rule.

But this absence of 'abstract maxim' led in practice to considerable flexibility, for

---

* In practice, the response was disappointing; about 13,000 annuities *per annum* were taken up.

There is no one, I should imagine—at least I know of none—who thinks that savings banks, or the grant of annuities or assurances for the people, are matters with which it is desirable abstractedly for Government to deal. If it could be said that the operation of the great law of supply and demand is generally satisfactory and sufficient, and that the failures which occur are incidental to the principles on which commerce must be conducted, that would merely be a conclusive condemnation, not merely of the law you passed two years ago for Post Office Savings Banks . . . and also of the laws as to the grant of annuities and the old savings banks.

Government interference could be of three kinds:

The highest form in which it has been carried out is that of positive regulations requiring this thing and that thing to be done in the course of private commercial arrangements, for the sake of obviating social, moral or political evils . . . the second kind of Government interference . . . has been interference by sheer naked prohibition . . . the third and . . . mildest description of Government interference . . . [is] that by the interference of the Government you enjoin nothing and you prohibit nothing, but you offer to such members of the community as may be disposed to avail themselves of your proposal certain facilities for what I may call self-help.

The most notable exercise of Gladstone's *étatism* would have been the putting into effect of the 'nationalization' clauses of his 1844 Railways Act, which provided for the option of purchase by the State after twenty-one years (i.e. in 1865) of railways constructed in or since 1844.* Such State action would not have been in character with the age, but it was not wholly fanciful, as the Tory nationalization of the telegraph system in 1868 showed. If it was to be done, Gladstone noted, it would have to have 'the support of a general and impartial public opinion'.† Gladstone certainly toyed with the possibility of nationalization. As the moment for review of the 1844 Act came, he raised the matter (without mentioning the Act) with Palmerston, who showed himself by no means in principle opposed. Encouraged, Gladstone reminded him of the 1844 clauses and, in reply to further queries, wrote:

We suppose the Railways 1. To have been purchased and taken into possession by the State. 2. To be worked by commercial firms or companies as lessees from the State, in conveniently divided groups. And probably 3. To be superintended, as far as the State is concerned, by a Board or Department having a qualified independence from the Executive Government.

Palmerston, alarmed about cost, found this 'on the first Blush a wild and more than doubtful Project'. Gladstone backed off, pointing out that his scheme had been hypothetical, 'Upon the assumption of a certain state of things, not . . . showing that the state of things ought to exist.'‡ The matter

* See above, p. 67.

† 19 Dec. 64. For telegraph nationalization—a Tory Act following up a Liberal initiative—see J. L. Kieve, *The Electric Telegraph* (1973), chs. 7 and 8.

‡ See the correspondence between Gladstone and Palmerston in October–December 1864 in P. Guedalla, *Gladstone and Palmerston* (1928), 291–319.

was referred to a Royal Commission which Gladstone intended would make merely a factual inquiry which would not 'compromise or commit either ourselves or Parliament with any reference to any legislation upon a matter of this vast importance'.* The Commission, however, pronounced strongly against putting the 1844 option, or a developed version of it, into operation, and there the matter of State purchase effectively rested until the Labour party made nationalization one of its leading objectives.

It is not clear how committed Gladstone was to nationalization. In his correspondence with Palmerston and in his statements in the Commons he was careful not to be tied to executing his 1844 option; but he was equally careful not to forswear it. This was quite in line with his policy of not being publicly committed to general propositions which had no immediate prospect of becoming statutes. Cabinet considerations of the railway question coincided with a major row over defence expenditure. Although Gladstone's plan 'was one which would have created no debt in lieu of stock, and which only looked to a distant reversion', it may be that he was alarmed about the costs, or worried at Palmerston being given an opportunity to present himself as the retrencher and Gladstone the spender. He may have felt that public opinion would not be sufficiently favourable. Whatever the reason, or reasons, he did not raise the question again, and his own government after 1868 made no progress even on the relatively minor and probably less controversial issue of the nationalization of Irish railways. Had Gladstone pressed through the scheme he adumbrated which was very similar to the Liberals' solution in the 1920s for the coal industry—public ownership leased to private management—the administrative history of the nineteenth century and perhaps the political history of the early twentieth would have been very different.

The Social Contract of the Mid-Victorian State: Income Tax, Virtual Representation, and Franchise Reform

To permit movement towards freer trade for Britain, Peel's government had in 1842 imposed income tax: a spectacular departure, since the previous income tax had been a war measure, removed with indecent haste and with little concern for a fair balance of taxation, in 1816. At the Board of

---

* Gladstone's reply to Roebuck's question about the Royal Commission in *Hansard*, clxxvii. 232 (14 February 1865); for the Royal Commission's report, see *Parl. Papers* 1867, xxxviii. The Commission found it 'inexpedient at present to subvert the policy which has hitherto been adopted, of leaving the construction and management of railways to the free enterprise of the people, under such conditions as Parliament may think fit to impose for the general welfare of the public'. The Commission thought 'the Act of 1844 warns us of the extreme difficulty of making prospective arrangements to take effect after many years. Instead of facilitating the acquisition of the railways by the State, it has rendered the operation more difficult, and indeed almost impracticable with a due regard to the guarantees it has accorded to the railway companies.' This was a little hard, since if the 1844 Act had not existed, it is unlikely that the question would have had a serious airing in the 1860s.

Trade in 1842, Gladstone had regretted the imposition of income tax, favouring instead an increase in a different form of direct tax, the house tax. He had not, however, disagreed with Peel's view, that the balance of contributions to government revenue was too far weighted to the disadvantage of the indirect tax payers.

In the arguments about the income tax in the 1850s and 1860s, this concern for the balance between the direct and indirect tax payers had continued to be of central importance, and Gladstone's attempts to remove the income tax must always be seen in the context of that concern. In 1853 his chief aim had been to prevent the existing tax being discredited, as he saw it, by differentiation (that is, the taxation of different forms of income at different rates).

This he had triumphantly done. The Aberdeen coalition, defeated in the Commons three times in the week before the budget in 1853, was not again seriously threatened until the worst days of the Crimean war. Gladstone's budget in 1853 retained the income tax but did not reform it; his 1860 budget confirmed this position. In maintaining the income tax unreformed Gladstone strove to achieve a balance. On the one side, the Radicals through the Liverpool Financial Reform Association called for abolition of all indirect taxes and the raising of government revenue only through the income tax, but an income tax differentiated to accommodate the claims of 'precarious' professional income tax payers such as lawyers and doctors. On the other side the landed interest favoured indirect taxation and, if there was to be an income tax, one not altered to favour the professions. Gladstone's budgets struck a balance between the two.

Gladstone's first budget, a speech of four-and-three-quarter hours delivered on 18 April 1853, struck a keynote of energetic resolution which was repeated in his subsequent performances. He made finance and figures exciting, and succeeded in constructing budget speeches epic in form and performance, often with lyrical interludes to vary the tension in the Commons as the careful exposition of figures and argument was brought to a climax. The 1853 budget and its background thus deserve some attention.

The role of Peel's income and property tax of 1842 was ambiguous in character. It was introduced to balance the Whigs' deficit and to permit the remission of indirect taxes and protective tariffs. The understanding was that once the remission was made, the tax would be removed, but Peel never explicitly committed himself to this position. The tax limped on and a substantial demand for its reconstruction developed among articulate members of the propertied classes, who wanted differentiation for the benefit of the 'precarious incomes'. Wood, the Whig chancellor of the late 1840s, lost his budget of 1851 because of this, and Disraeli's ambitious attempt—too imaginative for its day—at the reconstruction of the tax was partly the cause and certainly the occasion of the minority Conservative

government's defeat. The existence of the tax and the question of its differentiation had become the focal point of fiscal and political controversy.
Gladstone realized, as had Disraeli in 1852, that whoever settled the
income tax question would earn his party and himself a great political
dividend.

This settlement was thus in 1853 'the corner stone of our whole financial
plan'. Gladstone continued the income and property tax for seven years
(the previous maximum had been three) and, following Disraeli, extended
it to Ireland, but with a step-by-step reduction intended to lead to its abolition in 1860. He thus offered hope both to those who wished to see the tax
abolished and, by the length of its renewal, to those direct taxers such as
the members of the Financial Reform Association and the Cobdenites who
wished to see it permanent. He dramatically increased the number of those
paying income tax by reducing the starting point from £150 to £100, thus
increasing its yield and broadening its social base. He strongly opposed
formal differentiation because of the anomalies it would produce, but, with
spectacular political finesse, he introduced an effective differentiation by
an exemption from tax of savings which took the form of premiums for life
insurance policies or deferred annuities. He thus aimed to meet the 'public
feeling' that 'relief should be given to intelligence and skill [i.e. the precarious incomes] as compared with property'. This exemption formed the
point of departure for one of the chief forms of saving in middle-class
families until it was abolished by the Conservatives in 1984.* Such families
were also conciliated by the development of the legacy duty. 'This', Gladstone told the Commons, 'is a tax which will leave wholly untouched the
intelligence and skill of the country. It is a tax that gives the relief, and more
than the relief that you aim at by the reconstruction of the income-tax, but
it does it without the danger which would necessarily attend that reconstruction.' It also offered for the future a permanent form of direct taxation
and a tax on capital held by Liberal economists such as Mill to be a fair
exception to the general rule of avoiding the taxation of capital.

The propertied classes were thus offered a more palatable income tax, a
tax more widely based in terms of numbers paying it, and a tax with a
planned redundancy. The working classes, and consumers generally, were
offered a substantial remission of indirect taxation by reduction and abolition of duties which it was hoped would, as in previous Peelite remissions,
ultimately pay for itself because the reduced duties would stimulate
demand and consequently a lower duty could raise as much as a higher.

In the budget, the propertied classes and the working classes confronted
each other in the distribution of taxation, and Gladstone as chancellor

---

* By the end of the century about a fifth of income-tax payers claimed the relief, commonly
spending 5% or more of their incomes on insurance; see L. Hannah, *Inventing Retirement* (1986), 5
and 154.

acted as broker between them. The result was the social contract of the Victorian State: the budget brought the direct and the indirect taxpayers face to face,* and, as we shall see shortly, it related them not only as payers of taxes, direct and indirect, but as voter and non-voter by fixing as £100 the level at which payment of income tax began. 'Declining [as Gladstone said] to draw any invidious distinction between class and class', the budget offered much to each. As the great economist Joseph Schumpeter observed in 1954, 'Gladstonian finance ... translated a social, political, and economic vision which was comprehensive as well as historically correct, into clauses of a set of co-ordinated fiscal measures.'†

In political terms the 1853 budget consolidated the Aberdeen coalition and provided a point of reference for Liberal politics for much of the rest of the century. For Gladstone, his technical triumph—for the budget had many neat but complex details of the sort the Victorian press admired—married with his understanding of the central, reconciling importance of taxation to 'right relations' between the great classes of the State to give him not only a prime position in the history of British finance, but a strong reserve of political capital.

Gladstone mistrusted and feared the peacetime income tax, but in all his years as chancellor he never abolished it. It played too central a role in the great taxation compromise which legitimized the Liberal State in Britain.

The effect of Gladstone's handling of the income tax was to entrench the ambiguity which, as we have seen, was inherent in Peel's reintroduction of it. This was reflected in the way that Gladstone's proposal of 1853 appealed both to those who wanted the tax continued and to those who wanted it abolished. The tax could not be reconstructed and differentiated because that would imply permanence to what was soon to be abolished (and the Peelites declined for this reason to sit on the 1851 Select Committee on the tax); on the other hand, the propertied classes must accept the unreconstructed tax so as to permit social and economic progress. Gladstone unconsciously caught the ambiguity in his summary of Peelite finance made in 1857; there, as already quoted, he aimed both 'to conciliate support to the Income Tax by marking its temporary character & by associating it with beneficial changes in the laws'. Was it possible for the same tax both to be marked by a 'temporary character' and to be associated with 'beneficial changes', for was not the character of those changes likely to be of an on-going, shifting nature? Gladstone's position implied that a permanent peacetime equilibrium of the state and its finances could be achieved. The

---

* Even if the abolition of income tax had been achieved in 1860, Gladstone planned to replace it with the direct tax he had originally favoured in 1842, the house duty, thus preserving the direct/indirect tax balance. He had a similar plan in 1874, on that occasion wishing to use the death duties.

† J. A. Schumpeter, *History of Economic Analysis* (1954), 403.

rest of the century was to be the battleground on which he fought the forces which prevented it.

It was not Gladstone's intention, but it was his achievement, that at the end of the century Britain had the income tax which the governments and progressive politicians of Germany, France, and the United States craved but could not gain. In the competition between the need for a fair ratio between the 'twin sisters' of direct and indirect taxation on the one hand and dislike of income tax on the other, Gladstone kept the tax to maintain the ratio.

In 1853 the phased reduction of the income tax to permit its abolition in 1860 was hedged about by many conditions. First, it assumed that the *pari passu* reduction and abolition of customs and excise duties would be offset by an increase in consumption by which those duties remaining—especially tea, drink, and sugar—would produce more revenue; in other words it assumed at the least no economic recession. Second, it assumed no intervening disaster requiring a large increase in government expenditure. Third, it assumed that the new succession duty, an alternative direct tax, would yield a substantial amount. Finally, it assumed a diminution of ordinary government expenditure.

It was unlikely that all of these conditions could be met, and they were not all met, even if the Crimean war is discounted. Faced in 1860 with continuing the income tax or substantially increasing the burden of indirect taxation as a necessary consequence of repealing the income tax, Gladstone unhesitatingly chose to continue the income and property tax, which at that time contributed about 13% of central government revenue. The switch to indirect taxation which its unilateral abolition would have involved would have been politically quite unacceptable to the Liberals.*

At the same time, maintaining and extending his Board of Trade work of the 1840s and the budget of 1853, Gladstone abolished, together with the changes resulting from the French treaty, the Customs and Excise duties and tariffs on nearly 400 articles. He thus left only about fifteen articles subject to duty and contributing a significant income. Virtually none of these remaining duties constituted a protective or differential tariff. Protection was all but eliminated from the British fiscal system (Gladstone's first government completed the process by abolishing the 1s. 0d. duty on corn left from 1846). Among the duties abolished was the excise duty on paper, thus providing for cheap newspapers and preferred in the budget to a reduction to a minimum of the duties on tea and sugar. The House of Lords rejected this proposal. In 1861 Gladstone consolidated all his financial measures in a single finance bill, the first time that this had been done. The Lords, faced with a single package of legislation, passed it, including the paper duty abolition.

* A position energetically taken by Palmerston in 1865; see Guedalla, op. cit., 321.

1860 was thus the last of what Gladstone later called 'the cardinal or organic years' of the introduction of 'the Free Trade factor'. The legislation of that year gave almost universal effect to two principles:

1. That neither on raw produce, nor on food, nor on manufactured goods, should any duty of a protective character be charged.
2. That the sums necessary to be levied for the purposes of revenue in the shape of Customs' duty should be raised upon the smallest possible number of articles.*

The British fiscal system was thus as open as it could be. The indirect taxes, reduced to a tiny number, were imposed on goods proportionately important for the working classes. The consumption of the goods on which these remaining duties fell—for example, tea, coffee, beer, spirits, sugar, tobacco—was held by some to be 'voluntary', so that those wage-earners who chose not to consume such articles would not have to pay any central government taxes at all.

This notion, widely held by mid-nineteenth-century political economists—more so than by Gladstone and the Peelites, who emphasized particularly the cheapness of administration and the high yield of these few taxes—was really a justificatory device, for if the labouring classes had acted 'voluntarily' so as not to pay taxes, the revenue would have been thrown into confusion. In fact, these items were so remunerative because they fell on goods culturally central to working-class budgets; in 1866 Gladstone remarked that 'undoubtedly not less than one-third, probably a good deal more than one-third, of the sixty-eight millions at which our revenue now stands, is contributed by the working population of this country. My belief is that the working man pays taxes in as high a proportion to his income as is borne by the wealthier classes.'†

The consequence of this limiting of the number of indirect taxes was that it made the raising of extra revenue much more controversial than if a wider tax base had been maintained, for extra central government revenue (beyond that created by increasing consumption and income) could be obtained only by raising the existing duties on food, drink, and tobacco,‡ or by controversially introducing new indirect taxes, or by raising direct taxes, i.e. the income and succession duty taxes. This limitation was quite deliberate; it was intended to shackle British peacetime governments to the minimum expenditure required by the minimum state. *Étatist* Gladstone certainly was, evolutionary in his view of politics and political policies he had learnt to become; but in his financial policy a different tone

* W. E. Gladstone, 'Free Trade, Railways, and the Growth of Commerce', *Nineteenth Century* (February 1880), 374.

† Speech in Liverpool, 6 April 1866, in *Speeches on Parliamentary Reform in 1866* (1866), 71.

‡ This was because the technique of reducing taxes to stimulate consumption of particular articles had obvious limits of elasticity; the technique had probably reached its limits by the end of the 1860s.

predominated: he aspired to a timeless equilibrium undisturbed by other than temporary dislocations.

The equilibrium never became timeless, but it was remarkably enduring, as the table on p. 115 shows. There was a difficulty as far as Gladstone's position was concerned. Once he had become a Liberal leader and especially once the franchise had been extended in 1867, any extra revenue-raising was, because of the narrow indirect tax base and the general Liberal predilection for improving the contribution of direct taxation, likely to be forced largely on to the income tax, making its abolition the less probable. His emphasis on retrenchment was thus reinforced.

The 1853 and 1860 budgets reflected, amongst other things, a close attention to the social balance of taxation. The years of Peel–Gladstone finance saw a slow but on the whole steady movement towards the equalization of the contribution from indirect and direct taxes.* Gladstone's attitude to income tax was always qualified by the need, if it were to be abolished, to replace it with some other form of direct tax and by its relationship to indirect taxation. In the years after the Crimean war, he consistently supported reduction of customs and excise duties. In 1857, during what was potentially the most successful of his various negotiations with the Conservative party in these years, he broke off the negotiation rather than give way on this point. In the Commons the difference between them was made clear: Disraeli moved the reduction of the income tax, Gladstone proposed to move the reduction of the tea and sugar duties. Derby told Gladstone that his Resolutions

not only point distinctly to an infraction of the *implied* engagement that the Income Tax should terminate in 1860 but also to an alteration of its positive enactment during the term of its continuance; and this, not to meet any sudden and unfore-

* Percentage of United Kingdom
exchequer revenue contributed by
indirect and direct taxation

	Indirect	Direct
1836–40	78.7	21.3
1841–5	75.2	24.8
1846–50	69.8	30.2
1851–5	69.2	30.8
1856–60	64.8	35.2
1860–5	64.9	35.1
1866–70	66.6	33.4
1871–5	65.4	34.6
1876–80	65.3	34.7
1881–5	59.3	40.7
1886–90	56.1	43.9
1891–5	56.0	44.0
1896–1900	52.4	47.6
1901–5	48.8	51.2
1906–9	48.3	51.7

1844 was the first full year of property and income tax returns; for details of the compilation of this table and of the indirect/direct tax question, see Matthew, art. cit., 638 ff.

seen emergency, but to enable the Government to reduce other Taxes, by again raising the Income Tax to its original amount.

As Chancellor of the Exchequer the need for a balanced reduction of direct and indirect taxation was one of Gladstone's chief concerns. But since the maintenance of the balance greatly increased the difficulty of abolishing income tax, and since its abolition depended on the substantial reduction of government expenditure, Gladstone determined to increase equally substantially the number of income-tax payers. For he believed that the more persons made to pay the tax, the greater would be the demand for the reduction in expenditure which would permit its eventual abolition. Hence the important reduction in 1853 from £150 to £100 as the amount at which incomes became liable to pay the tax, a drop which roughly doubled the number of income-tax payers on Schedule D. The £100 line was, Gladstone argued, 'the dividing line . . . between the educated and the labouring part of the community'. It was, as the statistician Dudley Baxter observed, 'the equatorial line of British incomes'.*

There was therefore intended to be a rough correlation between the income-tax payers and the electorate, which should consequently vote to hold down public expenditure. As Gladstone wrote in a public letter in 1859 to J. L. Tabberner, a propagandist for direct taxation: 'it is desirable in a high degree, when it can be effected, to connect the possession of the franchise with the payment in taxes'. This then was the social contract: the indirect taxes (now chiefly on items of working-class consumption) fell mainly on the non-electors or the 'labouring' section of the poulation, and the direct taxes (chiefly the income tax) on the 'educated' classes, those likely to be enfranchised. The £100 exemption thus represented the line at which the doctrine of trusteeship by the electorate on behalf of the unenfranchised wage-earners began. The wage-earners were, uniquely in Europe, virtually represented in Parliament by a self-taxing class of income-tax paying electors. Income tax thus reminded the propertied class not merely of its fiscal but of its political responsibilities; it united the two factors which Victorians regarded as cardinal to stability in the State: fiscal and political probity. It was for the electorate to support the chancellor in achieving probity by retrenchment.

The experiences of the 1857 general election, when Gladstone campaigned unsuccessfully on an anti-expenditure basis in Flintshire for his brother-in-law, Sir Stephen Glynne, and when most of the anti-expenditure Radicals lost their seats, and of the long battle with Palmerston and the service ministries over military and naval estimates between 1860 and 1863,

---

* The figures worked neatly; Gladstone calculated that to attain a £10 household qualification, an income of £96 p.a. was required, with the consequence that 'I do not think that a £10 franchise can in the fair meaning of the word be said to be within the reach of the working man' (*Speeches on Parliamentary Reform in 1866* (1866), 53).

showed that the House of Commons as then constituted was an unreliable check against government expenditure, however many of its electors also paid income tax. Moreover, Gladstone came to see income tax not as the restrainer of expenditure through its unpopularity, but as the creator of expenditure through the ease with which it could be levied, and the predictability of its return.

This left two possibilities: abolish the income tax, or reform the House of Commons. In the winter of 1863, Gladstone toyed with both. The arguments against income tax abolition had been resolved, and the contacts Gladstone had with trade unionist artisans during the preparation of the Government Annuities Bill in the spring of 1864 encouraged him in the view that a moderate increase in the electorate through the addition of articulate artisans would strengthen the economical wing of the Liberal party in the House of Commons. He also developed the view that the franchise should be related to taxation by arguing that, as working men contributed almost half of national income and, through payment of indirect taxes, a third or rather more of the government's revenue, it was fair that about a third of the borough seats should have a predominance of 'working class' voters.* Gladstone's 'pale of the constitution' speech of 1864, and his subsequent strict adherence to the £7 annual rental level of qualification in the Reform Bill crisis of 1866 and 1867, have therefore to be seen in the context of his views on the role of taxation in politics.

The effect of Disraeli's Reform Acts of 1867–8, which introduced a much wider (if still quite limited) urban franchise than the abortive Liberal Reform Bill of 1866 would have allowed, was to remove the basis of the 1860s settlement which Gladstone had helped to create. For the extended franchise of 1867 introduced problems of political communication, organization and policy of a quite new order. Gladstone's franchise proposals of 1866 were designed to consolidate an existing order; Disraeli's destroyed it.

The Emergence of a National Politician: Regionalism, Speech-making, Class, Trade Unions

Gladstone's budgets represented a compromise and a balance—a settlement in accord with the House of Commons as it was between the first and second Reform Acts. As such, they gave Gladstone a central place in the success of the Whig–Liberal ministries between 1859 and 1866. They also allowed him to construct a new kind of constituency in the country. Gladstone had no personal political base of the sort normal in post-1832 politics. He could not even get his brother-in-law elected in 1857 in the small county constituency in which they were together important land- and coal-owners. His position in his own university seat—which had no constituency in the normal sense of the word—was increasingly uncertain.

* Speech in Liverpool, 6 April 1866, in *Speeches on Parliamentary Reform in 1866* (1866).

After he joined Palmerston's ministry it was evident that his candidacy at Oxford would always be contested as it had been in 1853 (a contest in a university seat was in itself a grave mark of disfavour)* and few doubted it would soon be defeated. In 1860 Gladstone drafted an address stating his intention not to contest the Oxford seat again, though he did not send it. In the early 1860s he rejected a number of offers of alternative seats, though he did not wholly disavow his selection by the Liberals for the new, third, seat in South Lancashire, and his candidacy for Oxford in 1865 was, especially after his statement in 1865 on Irish disestablishment, virtually a challenge to the university to throw him out. Gladstone's rejection in 1865, and his famous arrival 'unmuzzled' in Lancashire, dramatized the role of popular politician which he had cultivated during the 1860s with considerable skill. Defeat in a wholly Anglican and largely clerical constituency also made Gladstone's position in the Liberal party much simpler. As he told Sir Walter James in July 1865:

These good people, my opponents, have been resolved, in their blind antagonism, to *force* me into the confidence of the Liberal party, and it really seems they are succeeding.

It has rightly been emphasized that changes in the nature of national and local politics in the 1850s and 1860s made possible the emergence of a new kind of popular politician.† We may notice here, however, Gladstone's own contribution to his success, since his emergence as the chief beneficiary of the changing political order was not accidental.

Gladstone had made himself a national politician in a literal sense. He travelled frequently, widely, and conspicuously, and he kept his friendships warm. There were few parts of the mainland of the United Kingdom with which he did not have intimate links and where he did not have powerful friends.

In Scotland the Gladstone family was, of course, well known. In this period, as first Rector of Edinburgh University from 1859 (elected by the undergraduates)‡ Gladstone made annual visits. Appointments to Chairs were made jointly by the university and the city corporation under the rector's chairmanship and he took his duties seriously. Gladstone in this capacity made several political friendships, and laid the base to which he returned for the Midlothian Campaign in 1879. He could, and did, remind his audiences of his family's roots in the Borders and Lothians and in the port of Leith. In Glasgow his stockbroker, Sir James Watson, was a powerful member of the corporation, and soon to be Lord Provost. In Wales,

---

* After Gladstone's defeat in 1865 there was no contest for either Oxford University seat at a general election until 1918, and only one at a by-election (1878).

† John Vincent, *The formation of the Liberal party* (1966), especially ch. 2.

‡ He was defeated when standing as Chancellor of Edinburgh University in 1868, the electors for the chancellorship being the graduates. His proposal (included in a permissive clause of the 1858 Universities (Scotland) Act) that the Scottish universities would use their resources more efficiently if they became colleges of one Scottish National University, was not popular.

Gladstone could and did show himself as an important landowner in a rich farming area, an encourager of industrial development in the Dee estuary, a well-known holiday-maker, and local personality.

In England, Gladstone's areas of contact were numerous. He could tell his Lancastrian audiences of his youth on the sandhills of the Mersey, and almost all his speeches in his Lancastrian campaigns showed local knowledge. In the Midlands his contacts with the Duke and Duchess of Sutherland, with the Earl of Dudley (his creditor in the Oak Farm disaster, also a Tractarian friend), his relationship to the Lytteltons of Hagley, and his links with sundry influential local solicitors (many started by Oak Farm correspondence but now maintained on a political basis), his experience with Midland capitalists during his arbitrations of railway disputes, all these made him familiar and prominent in the heartland of industrial expansion. In the capital Gladstone was a noted pedestrian by day and night, active in many of its institutions as well as being one of the best known lay Christians in the city, whose appearance in church could of itself abate an anti-ritualist riot, as at St George's in the East in October 1860, when Gladstone sat prominently in the churchwardens' pew with police in attendance.

Such a geographical range of interests might be forced upon a great Whig landlord by the accident of heredity. In Gladstone it was present largely by the assiduous nourishment of interests which, not being landed, would otherwise soon have withered. Railways allowed politicians to treat the British mainland as a single political constituency in a way physically impossible in the pre-railway age. But if Gladstone was the beneficiary of this new national political community, it was in large measure because he imposed himself upon public attention not merely in the metropolis, but also at many points on the periphery.

The nurturing of these regional acquaintances could encourage an impression of national reputation, but it could not bring that reputation to influence the practicalities of power. This could be done more directly first by the impact of things done at the periphery upon Westminster politics, second by astute use of the press, third by the control and demonstration of executive power. These three prerequisites of Gladstone's political success will now be discussed.

Gladstone's use of extra-parliamentary speech-making, dormant in the late 1850s save for addresses to societies such as the Society for the Propagation of the Gospel, was recommenced in 1862 with tours of Lancashire and Tyneside. Public orations increased his reputation in the regions in which he spoke, in the newspaper reading nation as a whole through verbatim reports of his speeches, and at Westminster, for one result of his platform speeches was to emphasize his separation from the conventional Whiggery of the rest of the ministry's leadership. The extent of Gladstone's platform activities of the 1860s should not be exaggerated—he turned down many more invitations to speak than he accepted—but they were large in comparison with his previous platform appearances, with his ministerial colleagues, and with his own behaviour as Prime Minister in his first ministry. By these speeches Gladstone, hitherto known mainly at West-minster, at Court, and amongst the intelligentsia, became a national figure, a household name among the middle-class families which attended the meetings or, a far larger number, read the six columns of closely-set type, reporting the speech in the morning newspapers.

Gladstone's relationship with the middle classes in the provinces, and also with the working classes, is to be seen, from his point of view, primarily in terms of his fiscal strategy. He visited factories and he marvelled at the achievement of the middle class: it was at this time that he hoped Samuel Smiles would write his father's biography. Similarly he assessed groups of working people according to the extent to which they complemented and buttressed that strategy, which to a considerable degree they did.

Viewed *en masse*, Gladstone found the working classes amorphous, obscure in their tendencies and potentially dangerous. He noted on Harrison Ainsworth's historical novel: 'Finished that singular and for the masses dangerous book Jack Sheppard',* and just after the débâcle of the Reform Bill in 1866 George Eliot's reconstruction of the riots in 1832 disconcerted him: 'Finished Felix Holt: a most inharmonious book. It jars and discomposes me.' But when 'the masses' were presented to him in an organized and particularized form, his reaction was almost always enthusiastic.

As chancellor, Gladstone received deputations from working people. As is well known, these deputations had a considerable effect upon his views on working-class 'responsibility'. What is rarely emphasized is that these were trade union deputations. In particular, the trade unions requested the privilege of using the new Post Office Savings Banks, a concession expressly conceded,† and in 1864 the well-known deputation in favour of the Annuities Bill, which spurred Gladstone to his 'pale of the constitution' speech, was a deputation from the 'Junta' offering the support of the new unionism for the government's proposals.

The consequence of this was that, when in 1867 and 1868 trade union-ism became a question of primarily political discussion, Gladstone defended the 'Junta' (the Liberal trade unionists led by Robert Apple-garth who turned their backs on Chartism) as being a useful adjunct to

---

* Another important source of contact with London artisans were the exhibitions organized by Newman Hall, the Congregationalist minister, and patronized by Gladstone.

† See S. and B. Webb, *The history of trade unionism* (1902 edn.), 245. An echo of this request is to be found in the only 'fancy franchise' of the Liberal Reform Bill of 1866—a right of registration for holders of a savings bank account of £50 for two years, in lieu of qualification through the property qualification; this would chiefly assist those in the counties whose houses were under the £14 qualification.

the consolidation of the 1860s economic settlement. In an important speech opening a Mechanics Institute in Oldham in 1867 he declared himself not hostile to the right to strike and while arguing an orthodox view of the wages fund, he did not 'deny, in principle, that it is perfectly fair, as an economical question, for the labouring man to get as good a share of it as he can'.* In saying this, Gladstone placed himself in an advanced position in the intense debate about the labour question in the late 1860s. But he did so believing that the 'Junta' and its moderate policy represented the likely development of the trade union movement; he rejected the more extreme demands of George Potter when Potter led a deputation hostile to what he saw as the moderation of the Oldham speech, and in his contacts with working-class support for the 1866 Reform Bill, he declined contact with the Potter faction.†

Gladstone confirmed his advanced position and his optimistic view of union moderation when he was chairman of a remarkable meeting of the National Association for the Promotion of Social Science in July 1868. At this meeting he stated his conclusion reached through his contacts with those of the 'Junta' who favoured co-operation rather than confrontation with capitalism: 'Experience convinces me that with respect to those from whom perhaps we might anticipate the greatest difficulties, viz. the artisans and skilled labourers of this country, we have only to approach these in the right way, in order to find them thoroughly amenable to reason.'‡

Gladstone's call, therefore, was for working people's allegiance to the economic order of a marginally modified free trade society. He sought exactly the allegiance reflected in these lines written in 1865 by Janet Hamilton, the blind working-class temperance poet of the Scottish lowlands, lines characteristic of the enthusiasm of at least the politically aware Liberal working class for the fiscal system:

> That gleg birkie, Gladstone, has weel dune his part;
> Exchequer's big pouches o' siller are fu',
> An' mony's the taxes that's dune awa' noo,
> An' labour's weel paid, an' the flour an' the meal
> At a wanworth—an' sae we micht fen unco weel.§

* On the other hand, Gladstone also argued that the capitalist should improve his machinery and 'make himself independent of those who resort to strikes', thus anticipating the 1871 Criminal Law Amendment Act. He also opposed 'restraint in industry' and restrictions on piece-work.

† Gladstone told Potter that the employer's right of dismissal was 'a natural mode ... of self defence in that friendly strife which must always go on between the capitalist and the labourer'.

‡ The remarkable assembly, in addition to 'advanced' employers such as A. J. Mundella and T. Brassey, included John Ruskin, W. Allen, R. Applegarth, Frederic Harrison, J. G. Holyoake, Lloyd Jones, and J. M. Ludlow; the meeting was to set up a committee, of which Gladstone was elected chairman, 'to diffuse information as to the natural laws regulating the rate of wages and the demand for and supply of labour, and to promote industrial partnership and the formation of courts of conciliation'.

§ Janet Hamilton, 'Rhymes for the Times, 1865' in her *Poems and Ballads* (1868).

Working-class movements that buttressed that economic order Gladstone encouraged, those that challenged it he disparaged. Thus he approved of co-operative ownership, because 'in the cooperative mill the operative becomes a capitalist', but the co-operative store could be commended only in so far as it encouraged a more competitive retail system, for the existence of the co-operative store could only be 'indicative of some defect, removal of which would restore things to their natural course' of capitalist entrepreneurship.

The great tours of Tyneside and Lancashire in 1862 and 1864 were celebrations of achievements, not campaigns for a better future: free trade, the French Treaty, the repeal of the paper duties, these were the themes of speeches which were already by 1868 retrospective. Criticism was confined to government expenditure, and the need for the new electorate to reduce it. As we have seen, Gladstone's call for reform in 1866 was for a carefully limited addition of frugally minded artisans to the franchise. Frustrated in this, he attempted to enrol the household suffrage of 1867 under the same colours: 'There are those who tell us that a Parliament more highly popularised would become more extravagant than parliaments resting upon a more limited suffrage. It depends upon you to falsify that adverse prediction (Cheers).'

The 'Cheers' may have caused a moment of optimism in the exchancellor's mind, but it was not to last. Gladstone believed that the extension of the franchise to thinking and articulate artisans would force the Commons to reduce expenditure; Cobden had likewise believed that it would reduce militarism. But the experiment was never tried, and Gladstone soon began to find after 1867 that appeals to frugality were incompatible with the *étatist* measures which as chancellor in the 1860s he had begun to introduce. His appointment of the rigidly orthodox Robert Lowe as his Chancellor of the Exchequer in 1868 suggests that he had already made his choice in favour of frugality.

'God knows I have not courted them: I hope I do not rely on them' recorded Gladstone after a Lancastrian tour in 1864. But the courting lay in the very existence of the tours. Many contemporaries supposed that the novelty of Gladstone's electioneering must also involve a novelty of message to the electorate. In fact Gladstone consistently used such occasions as an appeal for support for an already existing order;* only three times did he appeal for popular support for a novelty: in 1862, 1866, and 1867.

In 1862, on his visit to Newcastle, he made his famous claim that the Confederate leaders had 'made a nation'. Much repented and explained away later, this claim was both premeditated and popular. Gladstone had

---

* The 1868 election campaign was retrospective, in the sense that it requested popular support for an Irish Church policy already approved by the House of Commons.

used the same phrase three weeks before in a letter to Arthur Gordon,* and the same sentiments, less dramatically expressed, in a speech in Manchester in April. The speech was well received in Newcastle; Gladstone's view was not as heretical in Liberal and northern circles as was subsequently made out. If Gladstone's aim in making this speech was to use extra-parliamentary oratory to force the Cabinet into recognition of the confederacy, it was unsuccessful.

In 1866 Gladstone appealed at the Liverpool Amphitheatre for popular support for reform, but for reform as expressed in the very limited Bill with the £7 limit. He told his audience (shocking many of his fellow MPs): 'it is, to a great extent, in these great assemblies of our fellow countrymen, that the opinions and sentiments are formed, which become ultimately the guides of the public mind and public policy'. Even so, extra-parliamentary oratory had little effect on the Adullamites. Gladstone, though offered many opportunities, declined the next logical step, public collaboration with the Reform League.

In 1867, in his speech at Southport, he raised the general questions of Irish land and the Irish Church, but with no specific proposals, no personal commitment save by implication, but with an appeal for popular involvement and awareness: 'Ireland is at your doors. Providence placed her there; law and Legislature have made a compact between you; you must face these obligations: you must deal with them and discharge them.' The Southport speech and its exhortation suggested a departure from a mere appeal for consolidation but its consequences were not to be immediately apparent. Radical activity in the 1860s consisted chiefly of groups appealing for inclusion in the working of the political community. It was such groups that Gladstone addressed; it is not therefore surprising that his consolidatory appeals met so enthusiastic a response. It was his aim to encourage the disaffected Irish to behave similarly: 'What we want is that those sympathies in Ireland which now hang and float bewildered between law and lawlessness shall be brought into active alliance with it.'

Consolidatory though Gladstone's public appeal might be, his enunciation of it on platforms in industrial towns in vast speeches, nationally reported, created an unprecedented focus of popular interest in an executive politician, which in turn gave him in a parliamentary context a patina of strangeness, even of menace. As yet Gladstone had not tried to use his popular following against the Commons; but the threat existed, exemplified in the London crowds which followed him daily in the streets during the 1866 debates, that he might do so.

A further result of these speeches may be noted. They were the chief means by which free trade, for long associated with Radicalism and in

---

* '. . . it has long been (I think) clear that Secession is virtually an established fact & that Jeff. Davis & his comrades have made a nation.' Gladstone to Gordon, 22 September 1862.

a vaguer way with Whiggery, became an absolute article of faith for the Liberal party as a whole. It has been argued that the Liberal party was made up of groups whose chief point of identification was religious or parochial, that Liberalism was not an exact creed and that most Liberal MPs were not much more than men of good will.* None the less, the 1860s was the decade in which the Liberal party moved from being the party amongst which free traders were most likely to be found, to being the chief free trade party in European politics, with an absolute commitment to the doctrine which survived as the article of party faith virtually unchallenged until 1929.

Through Gladstone's chancellorships free trade became an administrative reality, but also something much more remarkable, for through his oratory the creed of the Cobdenites became the orthodoxy of the electorate. Further, the years of Gladstone's chancellorships came to be generally regarded as 'normal' years, the point of reference by which subsequent decades in the period before 1914 were measured. The early 1860s represented for the nineteenth century, as the 1950s did for the twentieth, the period in which the British economy behaved 'naturally', the years in which capitalism seemed to have created a balanced society.

The 'People's William' and the Press

Public appreciation of Gladstone as a new kind of executive politician had depended greatly on the rapidly expanding provincial and metropolitan daily press. Gladstone's awareness and use of the newspaper press was much more acute than has hitherto been allowed. He was, of course, the benefactor of the popular quality provincial and London dailies by his repeal of the paper duties in 1861, which made possible the development of the penny press. He exploited this advantage deliberately. When J. A. Froude wrote in 1861 to criticize Gladstone's handling of the press, he replied:

The whole subject of working through the press for the support of the measures of the financial departments is very new to me: I have commonly been too much absorbed in the business of the offices I have held to consider as much as I ought of the modes in which my proceedings or those of others could be commended favourably to the public notice. I will with your permission bear the subject in mind.

Gladstone found a remedy with little difficulty. The chief London paper to benefit from the repeal of the 'taxes on knowledge' was the *Daily Telegraph*, owned by the Levy-Lawson family. Virtually restarted as a penny daily in 1855, it had reached a circulation of nearly 200,000 by 1871, far outdistancing *The Times*. Gladstone had come in contact in 1860 with one of its

* See John Vincent, *The formation of the liberal party* (1966), *passim*.

reporters, Thornton Leigh Hunt, son of the essayist, J. H. Leigh Hunt. In 1861 they corresponded on the paper duty repeal. By 1862 Gladstone was helping Hunt gain access to details about the Ecclesiastical Commissioners, and a spasmodic but substantial flow of information passed from Gladstone to Hunt during the later years of Palmerston's government. In 1865, for example, Gladstone sent papers on the annuities legislation with encouragement to write on it, but with instructions about not disclosing the name of Scudamore, the source of the information. Hunt organized at Gladstone's request an Irish visit in 1866 by the eldest Gladstone boy, Willy, as a result of which some of Willy's articles on Ireland were published in the *Telegraph*.

During the Reform Bill crisis, Hunt's name is very frequently mentioned in the diary, as it is during the Irish Church resolutions and Church rate debates in 1868. The *Telegraph* was a strong supporter of Gladstone through the crises of the 1860s, and this appears to have been largely encouraged by his links with Hunt; certainly there is little evidence of contact with its proprietors.

The *Telegraph*'s view that Gladstone was the coming man was persistently pressed from at least 1862 onwards:

We have enshrined Free Trade at last in a permanent act. . . . The time must come, though patriotism wishes it far away, when the failing hand of the Premier will relinquish the helm of state. It would be ill for England, in prospect of such a day, if she had not one pilot at least to whom she could look with proud and happy confidence. She can, she does, so look to Mr. GLADSTONE, because in all a long career of public life he has never swerved from the path of manly and straightforward policy. His words and deeds alike have confuted the fools who hold that statesmanship is intrigue, and diplomacy chicanery. His words and deeds have alike confuted the cynics who think religion and morality are well in every place but a Cabinet. In his person it is not only a grand commercial theorem that has been triumphantly vindicated, but the sterling worth of veracity and the irresistible strength of honour.

Since much of the provincial press followed the *Telegraph*'s lead respecting Westminster politics, these contacts between Gladstone and the *Telegraph* are of great importance. As W. T. Stead pointed out, it was the *Telegraph* which created the 'People's William'.

Gladstone's attention to publicity in the 1860s was always exact, from instructions to his secretary about the release of budget figures, to his insistence on his photograph being sold for 6*d.* or under. That this was combined with an appearance of unworldliness was particularly irritating to opponents. Even during his commissionership in Ionia in 1858–9 the flow of copy for the press was undiminished, provoking Disraeli's exasperated complaint to Lytton, the colonial secretary: 'The daily advertisements respecting Gladstone, his intentions & movements, are becoming ridiculous. Pray give direction, that it should be stopped.' But this was a futile plea: Gladstone had reached that point when his own efforts as a publicist were no longer fundamental to his persistent appearance in the press: an action or a speech was news because he did or said it, regardless of its intrinsic interest. This enabled Gladstone sometimes to appear un-interested in publicity, but this unworldliness should not be allowed wholly to mask an acute and purposeful flair.

A Broadening Political Base

Gladstone's relationships with regional politics and the press were characteristic of a Radical; as such, they caused dismay and distrust among the leaders of the Whig–Liberal party; they were certainly not sufficient in themselves to carry him to the party leadership. The informal but tight group of Whig elders—if Palmerston may by the 1850s be so included—still played a role of great importance. But the ability of the Whigs to control the Liberal party fully was uncertain. In 1855, in the last great political crisis of the closet in the eighteenth-century style, the true Whigs had, between them, failed to form a ministry, thus letting in Palmerston. In 1859, a Liberal ministry only became a certainty after a party meeting. But if the Whigs' patronage was in decline and their hereditary right to rule in question, party had not yet risen in a formal sense. The prediction of divi-sions was risky, and a ministry could expect to be defeated quite frequently on minor questions and even, on occasion, on major ones, without being expected to resign or dissolve. Nor was the size of the electorate yet such as to require the strict party allegiance of individual MPs, many of whom still expected to be returned almost regardless of how they voted in the House.

Gladstone stood to benefit from this Parliamentary situation. By the 1860s, while not rivalling the Whigs in executive service, he was, of the non-Whig Cabinet members, much the most experienced. Italy had been the question which sustained the unity of the ministry at its formation, but Italy could not have more than a passing effect on party politics. Gladstonian finance pro-vided the staple legislation around which the Whig–Radical–Peelite coali-tion of 1859 could coalesce. The technical aspects of Gladstone's work as chancellor have already been discussed. Politically, his 1853 budget stabil-ized the Aberdeen coalition. The defection of the senior Peelites in 1855 was caused by the personal loyalty of Gladstone, Herbert, and Graham to Aber-deen and Newcastle, not by differences on general policy. The budgets of the 1860s and the gradual fulfilment of Gladstone's programme of treasury legis-lation constituted the main domestic achievement of Palmerston's govern-ment. Cobden told Gladstone in 1863, 'I consider that you alone have kept the party together so long by your great budgets.'

By his combination of administrative achievement and political moralis-ing, Gladstone appealed, not merely to the established Radicals such as

John Bright, but to the leaders of the coming generation of Liberal MPs, men of moderate but none the less firmly held Radicalism, such as H. A. Bruce, H. C. E. Childers, W. E. Forster, James Stansfeld, W. P. Adam, G. J. Shaw-Lefevre, Lyon Playfair: representatives of the moderate but committed readership of the *Telegraph*, men who were to epitomize the non-Whig element and to be the work-horses of the Liberal party in the 1870s. For his part, Gladstone gave these men their chance in his first administration. They were mostly men more interested in policy than in party, and this accorded with Gladstone's own view.

Gladstone's successes as chancellor balanced the mistrust which his Tractarianism caused amongst many of the Whigs. His Church policy was always liable to lead to conflict. In July 1857 he had prolonged the Session to prevent the Divorce Bill then being passed from forcing Anglican priests against their consciences to remarry divorced persons. But in Palmerston's 1859 ministry Gladstone avoided religious wrangles. His interference in episcopal appointments was cautious and he refrained from playing a public role in the Colenso case and in the outcry about the controversial Broad Church volume, *Essays and Reviews* (1860). Although Gladstone's personal beliefs remained resolutely 'catholic', in the sense that he used the word in his book on *Church Principles* (1840), he enlarged his experience by a series of meetings with Methodists and Congregationalists, organized by Christopher Newman Hall. Though Newman Hall carefully balanced the denominational membership of these meetings, Gladstone regarded them all as 'Dissenters': 'A conclave of Dissenters chiefly Ministers: the teeth and claws not very terrible.' These meetings did not encourage intimacy, but they developed respect on both sides. A potentially important barrier to Gladstone's party leadership was being removed. At a personal level, the many meetings at Penmaenmawr with Unitarian guests of Samuel Darbishire were of importance.

Developments within the coalition hierarchy fell favourably for Gladstone. Cornewall Lewis, the ablest of the younger Whigs of Cabinet rank, regarded by some as a likely successor to the Palmerston–Russell duumvirate, died in 1863. Of the Peelites, Lord Aberdeen died in 1860, Sidney Herbert and Sir James Graham (already retired) died in 1861, the Duke of Newcastle, the Lord Lincoln of Christ Church days, once regarded by Gladstone as a future Prime Minister, died in 1864, his mind, his family, and his estates in chaos.

With the death of Palmerston in 1865, this left only Russell and Gladstone in obvious contention for the premiership; Granville and Clarendon, the other possible candidates, would have to challenge in order to be considered. Some of Gladstone's friends had encouraged him to bid for the post-Palmerstonian leadership. But the circumstances of Palmerston's sudden death found Gladstone quite unprepared and 'giddy'; the Queen told Russell to be ready even before Palmerston died, and Gladstone, isolated at Clumber sorting out Newcastle's chaotic estate, sent an unsolicited letter of allegiance to Russell, who insisted on his taking the leadership of the Commons in addition to the chancellorship. Gladstone's position of heir-apparent to Russell was thus reached without any explicit struggle for power. His formidable political skills were known; they did not have to be directly employed.

A 'smash . . . without example': Franchise Reform 1866—7

The serious commitment of the Liberal Cabinet to a reform bill in the autumn of 1865 to some extent altered this. Gladstone's great measures of the 1850s and 1860s had all been carefully balanced compromises: the Oxford University Bill of 1854 which achieved a middle way between the Liberal reformers and the college traditionalists, the budgets of 1853 and 1860 which satisfied both Radicals and Whigs. Once Gladstone had achieved what he regarded as a balance, he stuck to it with obduracy. This was particularly noticeable in the case of the Taxation of Charities Bill of 1863. Gladstone believed that many charities were inefficient, corrupt, and misnamed, and that bequests by the dead which went untaxed encouraged posthumous vanity, while donations by the living, made regularly and unspectacularly, came out of income which was taxed. To round off his reform of the income tax, already extended in 1853 to Ireland, he wished to extend it to charities. Gladstone saw this as a reasonable and fair bill, a logical part of his great series of reforms; its failure was an unusual rebuff.

Gladstone saw the Reform Bill planned by Russell and himself early in 1866 in the same light. He had voted for Baines's Borough Franchise Bill in 1861, and had made a famous speech in 1864 in which he argued that every male 'who is not presumably incapacitated by some consideration of personal unfitness or of political danger, is morally entitled to come within the pale of the constitution', a declaration which caught the spirit of the Liberal press, infuriated the Prime Minister, Palmerston, and became one of the famous political quotations of the century. It was generally interpreted to herald a wide-ranging extension of the franchise. However, Gladstone explained that by 'capacity' he meant 'self-command, self-control, respect for order, patience under suffering, confidence in the law, regard for superiors'. The vote was a privilege granted to those with such qualities; it was not a right. Gladstone thought that a lowering of the borough franchise from £10 to an annual rental of £7 would bring within the constitution's pale a rather clearly defined group of men (and exclusively men) with rather clear qualities.

This was quite definitely not a call for what contemporaries called 'household suffrage' (a vote for all male heads of households). The £7 line was, despite the difficulties of the data, carefully calculated. Introducing the 1866 Bill, Gladstone told the Commons that a £6 rental qualification was too low: it 'would place the working class in a clear majority upon the constituency. Well . . . I do not think . . . we are called upon by any . . . sufficient consideration . . . to give over the majority of town constituencies into the hands of the working class. We propose, therefore, to take the figure next above . . . namely a clear annual rental of £7', which would represent 'an income very generally attainable by the artisans and skilled labourers of our towns'.* Like many mid-Victorians, Gladstone developed an acute sense of the labour aristocracy, and his bill was intended to complete its integration into the political community. In the context of the various schemes for parliamentary reform being discussed in the 1860s, it was, short of doing nothing, the minimum that could be proposed.

Gladstone's views reflected general contemporary ambivalence about 'class'. On the one hand, it was clearly recognized to exist, and the 1866 proposals made a carefully calculated distinction between the labour aristocracy and the rest. On the other hand, Gladstone believed—and it was a belief necessary and central to the Liberal case for parliamentary reform— 'that there is no proof whatever that the working classes, if enfranchised, would act together as a class'.† The thrust of the argument for incorporation through religion, education, fiscal fairness, and political reform, rested on this being so in the future. Certainly, in the 1860s Gladstone believed that such an incorporation was being achieved and that modest parliamentary reform would consolidate it. England's peculiar historical and geographical position, if wisely nurtured, cherished, and developed, would 'improve' her position 'for the sake of preserving it'. For England stood uniquely between the old world and the new, with aspects of both: 'she stands between those feudal institutions on the one side under which European states were formed, and which have given to England her hierarchy of classes, and on the other side, those principles of equality which form the base of society in the United States'. This blending of hierarchy and egalitarianism gave the English both their peculiar class structure and their chance for 'a forward and onward movement . . . an increase of attachment of the people to its laws, its institutions and its rulers'.‡

Gladstone's proposal for a limited extension of the franchise was based on arguments about the declining efficiency of Parliament and the virtues of the labour aristocracy which seemed to him self-evident: there were self-evident reasons why reform was needed, and self-evident reasons why reform should be limited to the £7 ratepayer. Moreover, this was just the sort of balanced measure which had stood the coalition well in the past.

* See F. B. Smith, *The Making of the Second Reform Bill* (1866), 67.
† Speech moving the Second Reading of the Reform Bill, 12 April 1866, in *Speeches on Parliamentary Reform in 1866* (1866), 109.
‡ Speech in Liverpool, 6 April 1866, ibid., 85.

This is not the place to trace the complex débâcle of the 1866 Reform Bill. Certain aspects of it as it affected Gladstone and his political position may however be noted. Unlike previous major legislative measures for which he had been responsible in the Commons, Gladstone had only partial control of the drawing up of the Bill. His usual exhaustive mustering of figures and facts gave way to confused discussions in a committee of Cabinet working with rushed and inaccurate data. It became clear to Gladstone at an early stage that the bill was in difficulties; he told his Tractarian friend and legal adviser Sir Robert Phillimore even before the bill was introduced: 'I cannot see how I am to succeed or how I am to be beaten.' He began to bring into play alternative political forces.

First, in early February 1866 he raised in Cabinet the question of a compromise on the long-standing Dissenter grievance on compulsory Church rates. By the time the Reform Bill was in serious difficulties, agreement had been reached with the Dissenters and a bill was introduced. Gladstone ran Church rates side by side with the reform question from the drafting of the Reform Bill early in 1866 until his Church Rates Bill emerged in its final form to confirm his links with Radicalism in 1868.*

Second, once the bill was seen to be in danger, he made two speeches in Liverpool attacking the Adullamite minority, an unprecedented extra-parliamentary appeal by a Cabinet minister on behalf of legislation before the Commons, ensuring that, whatever the fate of the Bill, he would have been popularly seen heading the 'fight for the future'. His support for dissolution and a 'purge' of the party, rather than resignation, in June 1866 followed from this activity. The Cabinet's overruling of Gladstone's and Russell's calls for dissolution saved Gladstone from what was potentially the biggest set-back of his career: a poor general election result, fought on an issue at that time intensely divisive for the Liberal party, might have created the circumstances for an organized opposition to his succession to Russell. Resignation, removal from British politics by a winter in Rome, and the extraordinary passage of the Derby–Disraeli bill in 1867, did not. Indeed, in the crisis of April 1867, it was Gladstone who considered writing a letter threatening resignation from the leadership in the Commons, while Granville and Brand, the Liberal chief whip, begged him not to send it.

The 'smash perhaps without example' of April 1867, when forty-five Liberals paired or voted against Gladstone's amendment to the Conservatives' bill, certainly was a 'smash' in the short term in the Commons. But what was smashed was not Gladstone's position of Liberal leader in the Commons, but rather his attempt to avoid household suffrage and keep

* For the details, see O. Anderson, 'Gladstone's abolition of compulsory church rates', *Journal of Ecclesiastical History*, xxv. 187 (1974); the Act was a characteristic compromise, seeming more radical than it was.

reform to the moderate £5 limit. Gladstone's political ferocity had been a
ferocity of consistent moderation. The effect of Disraeli's intricate
manœuvres was, as Gladstone told a 'Monster Deputation' of the Reform
Union after the 'smash', to cut Gladstone loose from moderation: 'my
proposal of the £5 is gone (cheers). I do not see the circumstances under
which I am likely to revive it. I must reserve to myself perfect liberty. . . .' It
was not difficult for Gladstone then to move quickly to support, before
Disraeli's unexpected acceptance of it, Hodgkinson's amendment which
seemed to lead the way to thoroughgoing household suffrage. Nor, given
the extraordinary complexity of the implications of the various amendments, incomprehensible to many MPs, let alone electors, was it difficult
for Gladstone to be presented in the country as the champion of the bill,
the man who forced reform upon the Commons. On the other hand at
Westminster he could be known as the proponent of that bill which the
Adullamite Whigs would have preferred if they could have seen the end at
the beginning. Disraeli's desire for any bill at any price so long as it was his
bill, for any amendment so long as it was not Gladstone's amendment,
could discompose the latter but not displace him.

Regaining the Initiative: Ireland and the Premiership

In December 1867 Russell announced his intention that he would not again
take office. By telling Gladstone a week before he told Granville, his
successor in the Lords, he effectively made Gladstone his heir. Gladstone
heard the news in bed at Hawarden, almost blinded by a stray splinter of
wood, a hazard of his hobby. Russell's parting gift to British radicalism
was a pamphlet series on the Irish Church, calling for not merely disestablishment but almost complete disendowment as well.

Gladstone's Irish Church Resolutions of 1868 had therefore an immediate and impeccable Whig as well as Radical pedigree: indeed in the
context of such proposals as Russell's and of those of the Liberation
Society, Gladstone could even present his Resolutions as being a compromise to save the Irish Church, rather than to break it. The Resolutions,
added to the Church Rates Bill already in the Commons, allowed Gladstone to continue to behave as he had behaved since the ministry's resignation in June 1866, as if he were a government minister rather than an
opposition leader. Gladstone's first ministry had in a legislative sense
started with the beginning of the autumn session of 1867, though he did not
return to office until December 1868. He brought forward and successfully
pressed through the Commons legislation and resolutions in 1868 as if he
were in office and sitting on the government rather than the opposition
front bench. He introduced his Suspensory Bill for the Irish Church
exactly as if he were leader of the House, and indeed it was soon assumed,
and has often been assumed since, that the Church Rates Bill was passed

by his government and that therefore his first ministry must have begun early in 1868, rather than in December.*

This appearance of competence and control consolidated Gladstone's position within his party. Disraeli was caught in his own web: he could not put Gladstone's confused position of 1867 quickly to an electoral test because the tail-ends of the reform legislation in 1868—Scottish and Irish Reform Bills, redistribution, corrupt practices—took as long to pass as the England and Wales Representation of the People Act on which most interest had been centred.

As soon as Derby resigned through ill-health in February 1868 and was succeeded by Disraeli, Gladstone began to consider 'the personnel of our party with a view to contingencies'. In July he reached what appear to have been amicable agreements with the Whig leaders—first Granville, then Clarendon—about the distribution of offices, Clarendon being promised the Foreign Office. These conversations insured, so far as possible, against any move by the Crown to form a Whig-led ministry.†

Such a move was unlikely. Gladstone's standing at Court was still good. During Albert's life he had been a Court favourite.‡ Certainly his reverential manner had been in marked contrast to that of Palmerston and Russell. After Albert's death he had had an important and intimate audience with the Queen. His account of it shows the start of that unbendingness which Disraeli so adroitly exploited. The reserve this caused on the part of Victoria was apparent to Gladstone at Osborne in 1865; but so great was his reverence for the institution of monarchy that he seems to have been unable to adapt himself to the needs of its holder. Gladstone had had considerable opportunities as minister in residence at Balmoral in 1863 and 1864. He seems to have got on well, but not very well. Lady Augusta Stanley recorded the effect: 'Mr. Gladstone left us today, to our sorrow. He is most pleasant, but perhaps a thought too systematic.' But these were as yet minor, largely personal difficulties. Gladstone had handled the batch of royal marriage financial settlements in the early 1860s with skill. He had been the leader of the 'peace' party in the Schleswig-Holstein affair, his Reform Bill had had strong royal support. The Queen disapproved of the Liberal party's Irish Church policy, but, since the whole party was committed to it, this was not a question on which the choice of leader could have an effect. The summons from the

* The fact that the Tory budget of 1867 was largely and admittedly based on Gladstone's debt proposals of the previous year reminded MPs of his executive importance even during his worst humiliations in the spring of 1867.

† The court was ignorant of these mid-summer talks and decisions, General Grey, the Queen's secretary, thinking in November 1868 in terms of preventing an offer of the Foreign Office to Clarendon.

‡ As a member of the 1851 Commission which met often throughout the 1850s, Gladstone maintained his contacts with Albert even when not in office.

Queen in December 1868* after the Liberal victory in the General Election was therefore surprising only in the sense that Disraeli's resignation without meeting the Commons was unprecedented. From the point of view of the Liberal party it merely recognized a supremacy unchallenged, if not universally welcomed.

Certainly Ireland had played a large part in consolidating that supremacy, and these observations on some of the aspects of Gladstone's political life in the 1860s may fittingly close with a comment on his Irish policy.

On 23 November 1868, when the general election was virtually over, Gladstone published 'A Chapter of Autobiography'. The 'Chapter' explained Gladstone's changing views about establishment, but it did so first, almost entirely in terms of the effect on Gladstone's political development in the late 1830s, Peel's ministry of 1841–6, and the Maynooth Grant of 1845, and second, almost entirely in terms of changes in the 1840s in Gladstone's own position on State and Church. We have seen earlier that by the late 1840s Gladstone had indeed significantly changed the orientation of his political views. It can easily be understood why the 'Chapter' was originally intended as an election tract: its effect was to concentrate discussion of the Irish establishment on Gladstone, on the Gladstone of the 1840s, and on the Oxford movement.

By its compelling prose—it is the best written of Gladstone's pamphlets, with several passages reminiscent of Newman's artful simplicity—'A Chapter of Autobiography' deflected attention from Ireland to England, and from the policies of the Liberal party in the 1860s to the problems of the Conservative party and the Oxford movement in the 1840s. Though it alluded to 'silent changes, which are advancing in the very bed and basis of modern society', it placed these changes in the England of the 1840s. But if, from the late 1840s 'that principle—the application of a true religious equality to Ireland—was biding its time', why was 1868 the moment when that time had come? 'A Chapter of Autobiography' gave no analysis of Gladstone's assessment of the 1860s, save for documentation of his statements in 1863 and 1865. It gave no clue to the part that the parliamentary situation, Fenianism, and agitation for tenant right, played in Gladstone's conclusion that Irish disestablishment had ceased to be 'a remote question'. 'A Chapter of Autobiography' answered the immediate political questions of the day as obliquely as Newman's *Apologia* answered Charles Kingsley.

Gladstone's spasmodic comments help to establish a chronology of his thinking about the Irish question. In 1857, rather surprisingly, he told Aberdeen that 'Ecclesiastical questions in Ireland' were one of the 'great

* Victoria appears to have summoned Gladstone immediately and without hesitation, being concerned more with keeping salacious Whigs—Clarendon and de Tabley—out of office than with Gladstone.

subjects of public policy, which may be said to lie within reach'. Before the election in 1865 Gladstone, apparently with the desire of not deceiving his Oxford constituents, made a statement that the Irish establishment was in principle indefensible, but he committed neither the government nor himself to any action. But as Gladstone had believed this since the late 1840s, standing in the meantime at three contested and three uncontested elections for the University constituency, his need to state it publicly must mean that he anticipated imminent circumstances in which secret belief would have to become public practice.* Three days after making this statement, Gladstone notes on the question of a select committee on Irish land tenure: 'We *persuaded* Lord Palmerston.' In 1865, therefore, Gladstone was moving towards an active policy on what he perceived were the twin remediable evils of the Irish question: the Church establishment and the land tenure system.

Gladstone was by no means unique in this; indeed he had hardly reached the position held by the Whigs since 1835, let alone that of the Radicals. The difference was that he alone held a position which could offer success on both wings of the policy; he could throw behind disestablishment—the question which would immediately involve public opinion—the widely based range of political skills discussed earlier, and behind a new land settlement—involving the dislocation of an interest group—the formidable executive capacity which his years as chancellor had demonstrated. In February 1866 a large 'Budget' of possible Irish legislation was sent to him by Chichester Fortescue, the Whig with whom at this time he had a close relationship second only to, and perhaps equal with, Granville. From this, Gladstone strongly pressed for a large-scale extension of the 1860 Irish Land Act, urging Fortescue, 'if progress can be made in such a question as Landlord and Tenant I quite think it should be done by a Bill'.

The 1866 Land Bill, caught in the breakdown of party business and discipline caused by the Reform Bill, had to be withdrawn, though Gladstone was seen publicly attached to it. Gladstone had therefore given priority to land over disestablishment, arguing that the latter was too contentious and 'unripe'. The heat of Fenianism seems to have caused a sufficient ripening of both points, bitter though they might be. Gladstone explained his views to Fortescue in December 1867:

I am going into Western Lancashire next week, & I have just had an intimation that the *Liberal* Farmers are for maintaining the Irish Church as it is! This I suppose is the tendency which Fenian manifestations make on stupid men. Of course I do not mean my constituents.

* His statement in his letter to Hannah, sent on 9 June 1865 (which Gladstone knew would be widely circulated if not immediately printed), that 'the question is remote, and apparently out of all bearing on the practical politics of the day' apparently showed little awareness of the activities of the Nonconformists and Irish, until it is noted that Gladstone wrote in 'A Chapter of Autobiography' that by 'remote' he meant 'Heaven knows, perhaps it will be five years, perhaps it will be ten'.

The Irish question which has long been grave is growing *awful*. In my opinion this Empire has but one danger. It is the danger expressed by the combination of the three names Ireland, United States and Canada. English policy should set its face two ways like a flint: to support public order, and to make the laws of Ireland such as they should be. This is what we must try: but I believe we shall have to go to martyrdom upon it, which is a graver consideration for men of your age than of mine.

. . . Maguire has given notice of his Resolution only to occupy the ground—so at least I understood him.

I hope you will use every effort to come to an understanding with him & with others perhaps through him, as to a new Land Bill. Except the quantities which may be afforded by loans of public money to the Landlords, I do not *know* in what the Bill of 1866 can be greatly improved.

It would have been with the utmost difficulty that we should have got that Bill well supported by the Cabinet & our friends and a more ultra measure would only mean more splitting.

Gladstone's views on Irish land in 1867–8 were thus only loosely formed and he was as yet engaged in the question in principle rather than in detail. Moreover, the tender condition of the Liberal party did not allow an attempt in opposition to bring forward land proposals: that could only be achieved with the full panoply of executive authority. Resolutions of principle on the Irish Church, however, both unified the party and were possible within the limitations of opposition. It was towards these that the Liberal leadership moved in the winter of 1867–8, Russell's pamphlet giving the clarion call.*

Gladstone summed up the position in February 1868 to Clarendon, who was well known for his caution on the land question:

I have not yet seen Lord Russell's pamphlet but it is in the act of being born. It recommends I understand distribution of the Irish Church Revenue among the different bodies—this may be reasonable, but it appears to me to be impossible. The Irish land question becomes more and more complicated with delay. I am afraid it is passing from the stage of compensation for improvement into the very dangerous and unsound one of fixity of tenure in some form or other. In truth the aspect of affairs is to my mind more gloomy than it has been for a quarter of a century.

Gladstone's Irish Church Resolutions of March 1868 should therefore be seen not merely as an individual initiative on a single Irish issue, but as part of a general move by the Liberal leadership to solve both their party and their policy problems, Gladstone wishing to preserve more of an equality of urgency between Church and land than the propertied Whigs.

In the General Election campaign in the autumn of 1868, Gladstone

* Russell also prepared, shortly before announcing his intention to retire, an initiative on education, in which Gladstone was not included. Gladstone would certainly not have been able to unify the party on the education issue.

made this clear. His last speech in Lancashire worked up to a mighty peroration linking the various proposals for Irish legislation to the fundamental evil of the Protestant ascendancy, alarming the Whigs and using the simile of the Upas tree, a fabulous Javanese tree so poisonous as to destroy all life in its vicinity:

The Church of Ireland . . . is but one of a group of questions. There is the Church of Ireland, there is the land of Ireland, there is the education of Ireland; there are many subjects, all of which depend on one greater than them all; they are all so many branches from one trunk, and that trunk is the tree of what is called the Protestant ascendancy. . . . We therefore, aim at the destruction of that system of ascendancy which, though it has been crippled and curtailed by former measures, yet still must be allowed to exist. It is still there like a tall tree of noxious growth, lifting its head to heaven and darkening and poisoning the land so far as its shadow can extend; it is still there, Gentlemen, and now at length the day has come when, as we hope, the axe has been laid at the root of that tree, and it nods and quivers from its root to its base. It wants, Gentlemen, one stroke more, the stroke of these elections.*

As anticipated, the strength of anti-popery in the area meant that the majority of the electors of south-west Lancashire kept their axes sheathed, but Gladstone had already been elected at Greenwich as a precaution. The electors, old and new, in the country as a whole reaffirmed the reunited Liberal party in power with a majority of 112.

This, then, was the background to the famous scene in Hawarden Park on 1 December 1868, witnessed by Evelyn Ashley, formerly Palmerston's secretary, and memorably described by him (though getting the date wrong) in 1898:

One afternoon of November, 1868, in the Park at Hawarden, I was standing by Mr. Gladstone holding his coat on my arm while he, in his shirt sleeves, was wielding an axe to cut down a tree. Up came a telegraph messenger. He took the telegram, opened it and read it, then handed it to me, speaking only two words, namely, 'Very significant', and at once resumed his work. The message merely stated that General Grey would arrive that evening from Windsor. This, of course, implied that a mandate was coming from the Queen charging Mr. Gladstone with the formation of his first Government. I said nothing, but waited while the well-directed blows resounded in regular cadence. After a few minutes the blows ceased and Mr. Gladstone, resting on the handle of his axe, looked up, and with deep earnestness in his voice, and great intensity in his face, exclaimed: 'My mission is to pacify Ireland.' He then resumed his task, and never said another word till the tree was down.†

The description rings true. But like most descriptions of a Gladstonian moment, it was a partial truth only. It reflected Gladstone's capacity to

---

* Speech in Wigan, *The Times*, 24 October 1868, 6c.
† Ashley's obituary of Gladstone in *National Review*, June 1898, mostly in Morley, ii. 252.

harness an issue and to personalize it. It obscured his political breadth and all-round strength, which allowed him so often to surprise his colleagues and opponents alike.

The same day, Gladstone wrote a memorandum, not on Irish disestablishment but on the welfare of the Irish poor, for whom some of the monies from disestablishment were used. In his journal, he wrote at the end of this notable day:

Ch. 8½ A.M. The Lessons, as usual in times of crisis, supplied all my need. 'The Lord shall give thee rest from thy sorrow, & from the hard bondage wherein thou wast made to serve. . . . The whole earth is at rest, & is quiet: they break forth into singing.['] Isa. 14. Blessed central peace! Tried a little revision of Homer: but only a little. Read Swift. The Ball in evg till 12. Much babblement: & saw divers.

Two days later he went by train to Slough on the scheduled service. Hearing that Victoria was out driving in her carriage, he visited his son Harry at Eton College and then walked unnoticed from the college to Windsor Castle, avoiding the large reception planned at Windsor railway station. He kissed the Queen's hands and formally began the work of forming a government.

CHAPTER VI

Travel, Family, and Affairs in the 1860s

*Weekends and Holidays—Homer and Civilization—Religion and 'rescue work':
Gladstone as Pre-Raphaelite Knight—Family Life and the Political Circle—
Abroad: Ionia and Italy—'A rebellion . . . against growing old'*

I am well past half a century. My life has not been inactive. But of what kind has been its activity? Inwardly I feel it to be open to this general observation: it seems to have been & to be a series of efforts to be and to do what is beyond my natural force. This of itself is not condemnation, though it is a spectacle effectually humbling when I see that I have not, according to Schiller's figure, enlarged with the circle in which I live and move. More condemnatory by far is the moral judgment: such snares of lurking unextracted sin in so many forms: and suspicion of secret sin that is secret only because conscience has become dull to it. In other quarters some better gleams of light. In the great hand of God I stand: how well that it is so.*

Weekends and Holidays

As a politician Gladstone was well known, even notorious, for hard work. His diary shows, however, that even a life lived at full stretch by the standards of the day left a considerable time for relaxation and activities not directly political—writing, holidaying, and weekending. By the 1860s the weekend had become an established form of relaxation, combining comfort in the great houses of England with the development of political relationships. Gladstone's weekends were spent almost entirely at Whig houses, particularly with the Sutherland family and their relations the Argylls, at their great houses of Chiswick and Cliveden; during the holidays he also visited Trentham, Dunrobin, and Inveraray. He was also a fairly frequent visitor to Lady Waldegrave and Chichester Fortescue at Strawberry Hill in Twickenham. The other main Whig houses visited were Chislehurst and Chatsworth (the Cavendishes), Mentmore Towers (the Rothschilds), Woburn (the Duke of Bedford), Brougham Hall (confirming an interesting friendship with Henry Brougham which developed in the late 1850s), Eaton Hall (the Grosvenors), Pembroke Lodge (Lord John Russell), and Broadlands (but only after Palmerston's death). The

---

* 29 December 1863.

only Tory roofs under which Gladstone slept in the 1860s were those of Lord Penrhyn in Wales, where courtships between Penrhyn's daughters and the Gladstone boys were proceeding, the Duke of Marlborough at Blenheim, an odd and unexplained visit in 1861, and, curiously, Lord Salisbury at Hatfield, where he stayed as his administration was being completed in December 1868.

Certainly politics was a chief reason for many of these visits but, especially at Chiswick and Cliveden, politics often took second place to religion and literature. A characteristic comment in the diary is 'Off with the Argylls and others to Cliveden. Conversation with Argyll on Future Punishment. We had a delightful evening.' Tennyson was also a friend of the Dowager Duchess of Sutherland and read his poems to the company. In keeping with this intellectual atmosphere, Gladstone contributed the Latin inscription for the frieze on the entablature of Cliveden House.

The Cliveden set of the 1860s represented Whiggery at its most high-minded and progressive. For Gladstone, this was an important political connection. Indeed, in the decade after 1858, Harriet, the Dowager Duchess, to a considerable extent took him in hand.* The Sutherlands were among the most influential, and were certainly the richest, of the great Whig families. In her day a great society beauty, Harriet linked the Sutherlands with the Howards and the Cavendishes; Lord Granville was a close relation on the Sutherland side (and consequently also Acton, his step-son); the Duke of Argyll was her son-in-law. The Dowager Duchess was perhaps the last of the Whigs to be on genuinely confidential terms with the Queen (she was Mistress of the Robes in various Whig governments until she retired in 1861). She was, therefore, a powerful political patron, and Gladstone's fairly successful movement into the Whig political circle in the 1860s probably owed a good deal to her shrewd management. He saw her frequently, both at the weekends at Cliveden, and in brief visits to Chiswick during the week. The link between the families was later consolidated when, after the Dowager Duchess's death, Willy Gladstone married her granddaughter Gertrude.

Life at Hawarden and holidays in North Wales constituted Gladstone's chief relaxation. In the autumn, he usually spent several months in the country. When chancellor, for example, he was away from London in 1863 between 31 July and 10 November, in 1864 from 2 August until 7 November. Business was conducted by letter from Hawarden, but heavy though the correspondence was—one day when his secretary was away Gladstone had to open forty-four envelopes—it could almost always be dealt with in the morning.

In mid-August the family usually took a house for three or four weeks

---

* Unfortunately, Gladstone's letters to her cannot now be found; Morley, however, printed a selection; Morley, ii. 183 ff.

on the North Wales coast at Penmaenmawr, near to where Dean Liddell of Christ Church, the father of 'Alice in Wonderland', owned a house for holidaying. At Penmaenmawr business was confined mainly to letters with leading politicians; administrative correspondence seems to have been occasional. While on holiday Gladstone worked on his classical studies, walked and swam daily—'I find it a very *powerful* agent'—noting the number of times, and days missed, in his diary. He liked the water astringent, complaining at Brighton that the sea on Whit Monday was 'over-warm'.

In North Wales Gladstone led his family great distances over the mountains of Snowdonia, though he suffered from vertigo, much to Henry Liddell's amusement (and perhaps relief in finding a chink in the armour). A crisis on the Great Orme ended with these two Christ Church dignitaries clutching each other on the heights, 'the Dean leading Mr. Gladstone along, with eyes closed, while the rest of the party formed a sort of buttress to protect him on the seaward side'. Gladstone also took his family frequently to church, in Penmaenmawr on occasion to a service in Welsh, though he was not impressed by the language. At Hawarden the boys joined in silviculture—mostly cutting, but also planting—a regular occupation from 1858. Cataloguing the already vast collection of books, pamphlets, and private papers, including 'a bonfire of papers on private business to 1866 inclusive', took up much time, as did the servicing of the porcelain collection, which was lent out to exhibitions. In the diaries 'worked on China' almost always refers in the 1850s and 1860s to the collection rather than the country, even at the height of the Canton crisis.

Gladstone did not try to make Hawarden a centre of political activity. There were some visitors of political importance. There was an important visit in 1855 from Lord Stanley, later 15th earl of Derby; the French Treaty was suggested by Cobden in the Hawarden garden, Bagehot made a visit in December 1865 to discuss the country banks issue question, Lord Clarence Paget came to arrange a compromise on the fortifications issue, an attempt at reconciliation with Northcote included a visit by the latter to Hawarden, Anderson of the Treasury came to discuss Treasury matters, and there were visits from Lancashire Liberal organizers such as George Melly. But Hawarden Castle was not on the great house circuit, and Gladstone did not attempt to put it there. Gladstone's many visits to the great houses of the Sutherlands and the Argylls were reciprocated only twice, in 1855 and 1867. Indeed he bore most visitors only with reluctance and because they pleased his brother-in-law, Sir Stephen Glynne, still the nominal owner of the Castle. Visitors whom he enjoyed were usually academic or ecclesiastical, or close friends such as Robert Phillimore and Sidney Herbert. Hawarden was a family home, with 'ordinarily a family song or dance after dinner', not, as yet, a political headquarters. Among the many family amusements was the writing of comic verses; these are two of Gladstone's contributions, written in 1862:

> There was an old woman of Ewloe
> Her habits were really too low;
> She drank like a fish
> And she ate off the dish
> This ill-mannered old woman of Ewloe.

> There was an old woman of Broughton
> Whose deeds were too bad to be thought on;
> She poisoned her brother
> And throttled another
> This flagitious old woman of Broughton.*

Gladstone built on to the Castle the famous 'Temple of Peace'—a library and working room—into which books were moved in October 1860, and it was at Hawarden that most of his literary work in these years was done. Before joining the Aberdeen coalition in 1852, Gladstone's books and articles had been very largely theological or at least ecclesiastical. Out of office in 1855, his attention turned to the classics, and in the subsequent decade he hardly published on church questions at all, though, as the diary shows, there was little slackening in his religious reading.† The exception was his extremely influential review of Seeley's *Ecce Homo*.

Homer and Civilization

Between 1855 and 1868 Gladstone published seven long articles on classical topics, a book of *Translations* (with Lord Lyttelton) of classical and romantic poetry, a three-volume work, *Studies on Homer and the Homeric Age* (1858), and prepared a popularized version of it, *Juventus Mundi*, published in 1869. Gladstone's abstinence from theological composition is to be accounted for partly by the fact that his earlier writings had led him into an impasse, partly perhaps because open conflict with the Liberalism of *Essays and Reviews* (1860) and Bishop Colenso's publications on the Pentateuch—the two theological storms of the 1860s—would have led to political complications, partly because, as his review of *Ecce Homo* showed, Gladstone had reached a position of some ambivalence on

---

* These would today be called Limericks; Gladstone called them 'Penmaenmawrs' after the resort he was visiting at the time. It may well be that this sort of nonsense verse was commonly called by its place of composition; Ewloe and Broughton are villages near Hawarden.

† Gladstone was publicly though not spectacularly involved in the Colenso case, being sued, as one of the trustees of the Colonial Bishopric Fund, by Colenso; the Fund had cut off his salary. He was involved in the case of Archdeacon Denison, found heretical on the eucharist; he wrote, with Phillimore, Denison's statement for appeal.

theological modernism, but partly also because he believed classical writings, and especially Homer, made a real and neglected contribution to European civilization.

He believed that the neglect of Homer at Eton and Oxford during his years there was similar and parallel to the neglect of true religion. In Gladstone's mind the two were inseparably linked. The ideal of the Christian gentleman was in his view not the erastian pentameter-construing cynic of the late eighteenth century, but the churchman suffused with the civic qualities of the Homeric world. His concern touched upon a fundamental problem for Victorian middle- and upper-class education: if the aim of education was to produce godliness and good living, how could the predominance, at school and university, of the study of a pagan society be justified?

Briefly put, Gladstone's argument was that civilization was 'a thing distinct from religion, but destined to combine and coalesce with it. The power derived from this source was to stand in subordinate conjunction to the Gospel, and to contribute its own share towards the training of mankind'. Thus the Old Testament was a guide to man's relationship to God, a 'master-relation'; it was not intended to present 'a picture of human society, or of our nature drawn at large'.* The earliest statement of the values and organization of a civilized society was to be found in ancient Greece, and especially in the works of Homer. Though he still worked on Aristotle, Gladstone came to find in Homer and his gods rather than in Aristotle's sophisticated secularism the most attractive parallel to a society based on a true revelation.

Gladstone's detailed work on Homer began in the years following the Crimean War (fought for control of the area of Homer's territory) and his own High Commissionership of the Ionian Islands. In trying to understand the origins of the world order which the Crimean War had questioned, he found Homer a much greater help than Abraham. Indeed Gladstone believed that, in understanding the earliest stages of civilization, 'the Holy Scriptures are like a thin stream', whereas the Homeric Poems were like 'a broad lake outstretched in the distance, which provide us with a mirror of one particular age and people'. From what Gladstone called the 'relative parallelism between the oldest Holy Scriptures and the works of Homer', the Homeric poems 'supplied materials for the intellectual and social portions of that European civilization, which derives its spiritual substance

* W. E. Gladstone, 'On the place of Homer in classical education and in historical inquiry', *Oxford Essays* (1857), 3–5. An examination of Gladstone's competence as a classicist and of his place in classical historiography will be found in Hugh Lloyd-Jones's paper, 'Gladstone on Homer', read to my seminar and reprinted in *The Times Literary Supplement*, 3 Jan. 1975 and in *Blood for the Ghosts* (1982).

from the Christian Faith'. The Homeric element in European civilization was vital, Gladstone thought, because it compensated for the narrow nationalism of the Jews. The Jews had been set aside by God, Gladstone argued, 'for a purpose, the most profound of all His wise designs' but with the result that they had been removed 'out of the family of nations'. The Jews thus 'had no world-wide vocation committed to them; they lay ensconced in a country which was narrow and obscure . . . an unhonoured and undistinguished race, simply elected to be the receivers of the Divine Word'. Consequently, Gladstone found the prevailing Victorian view—that the Jews should be considered 'the fountainhead of the Greek arts and letters'—to be 'childish': until the Incarnation of Christ, he thought, 'the world's history was without a centre'.

Gladstone believed that Homer wrote an accurate and in a sense historical description as well as great imaginative epic poetry. He thus gave an encomium—if a cautious one—to Heinrich Schliemann's description of his archaeological discoveries in the preface he wrote to Schliemann's *Mycenae* (1878); Schliemann dedicated the book to him. Gladstone believed that Homer had caught humanity at its Rousseauvian moment, innocent and uncorrupted. He was lyrical in his sense that Homer carries 'us back to the early morning of our race, the hours of its greater simplicity and purity, and more free intercourse with God'. And in that early morning were to be found 'the real first foundations of political science', purer and without the 'political exaggeration' of subsequent Greece. Homeric political institutions were marked, Gladstone believed, by 'two great instruments of government . . . namely, publicity and persuasion'. In this view, Gladstone contradicted the more constitutional approach of George Grote. More importantly in the longer term, in Homer's comments on publicity and persuasion he found two of the constituents of his own view of civilized politics, and found them just as his own political personality began to exemplify them. Whereas many Victorians found the origins of public life in the Anglo-Saxon Witenagemot, Gladstone found 'an original similitude' between Homer and 'the best ideas of our European and our British ancestry', consisting chiefly in the primacy of oratorical debate in each. Homeric speeches were not merely declamatory orations, but had 'the faculty of what in England is called "debate"'.

Even so, Homer and the society he described offered the Victorians no simple model or analogy. Homer was 'a schoolmaster to bring us to Christ, because it demonstrated our inability to tread the way of righteousness and pardon without the Redeemer'; corruption had necessarily followed the Homeric idyll. The role of Greece in what Gladstone called 'the providential order of the world' was thus to demonstrate a negative: even at 'the maximum of power' in the early days of the world 'the total inability of our race . . . to solve for ourselves the problem of our destiny' was apparent.

There was none of that sense, which so powerfully affected the many members of the Victorian intelligentsia who moved from faith to agnosticism, that the Greek past gave a model for the future. For Gladstone, the opposite was the case: the Greek past showed a decline from the relative purity of the Homeric period: there was, he argued, 'an uninterrupted aberration from the line of truth'.

These views were unusual in the context of mid-Victorian scholarship.* Gladstone's emphasis on Homer as an historical source—and this was more important to him than the question of whether Homer was a 'single author' or not—was contrary to the trend of much scholarly opinion. His view of the unique origin of an Homeric society, and the sharp divide he made between the relative purity of the Homeric period and a subsequent decline was an inversion of the usual Victorian approach, which shared Gladstone's moralism but Whiggishly inverted it.

Like many such works, Gladstone's writings on Homer tell us as much about the scholar as about the subject. Of especial interest is Gladstone's analysis of the role of oratory in Homer. Whereas the great poems of great modern poets, such as Milton and Wordsworth, cut across their epochs, great orators, he argued, necessarily reflected the character of the age. The orator's work is 'inextricably mixed up with practice. It is cast in the mould offered him by the mind of his hearers. It is an influence principally received from his audience (so to speak) in vapour, which he pours back upon them in a flood. The sympathy and concurrence of his time is with his own mind the joint parent of his work'. In Homer was to be seen the pure work of oratory, for it resulted, not in the crude measure of a statistical majority, but in the moral convictions of the audience. In Homer one man (the king) gathered popular opinion into 'one focus'; the implication for Gladstone's role in the modern age was clear.

Gladstone's belief that Homer represented almost a parallel revelation to that of the Old Testament (though lacking the latter's 'one invaluable code of Truth and Hope') was, to many Victorians, a shocking, startling, and almost blasphemous claim. As so often, Gladstone found himself closer than he expected to Broad-Churchmen such as Milman, who had so alarmed the Church by calling Abraham a 'Sheik or Emir'. Milman had shocked by demoting the Old Testament; Gladstone alarmed by elevating Homer to a prophet. It was not accidental that it was that Broad Church classicist, Connop Thirlwall, who read the proofs of *Studies on Homer*. Greece therefore had in Gladstone's view a special place in the 'providential order of the world', and it was the duty of those involved in the construction of a modern society to study and expand its lessons.

* See Frank Turner, *The Greek heritage in Victorian Britain* (1981).

Homeric writings were therefore not an alternative but a supplement to religious works. Gladstone noted on the day he finished the MS of *Studies on Homer*: 'If it were even tolerably done, it would be a good service to religion as well as to literature: and I mistrustfully offer it up to God.' Vast effort was lavished on these works, even when in office. A translation of the Iliad (never published), a translation of and concordance to Aristotle's Politics, and a 'Trochaic Version' of Homer, worked on 'even in Crewe waiting room at midnight' were attempted while Gladstone was chancellor. He noted: 'This attempt is of the utmost interest & attraction: it threatens to be a snare. I think of beginning to inhibit myself from touching it except after dinner. This will pretty well starve it.' But in 1864 he started work on the 'Shield of Achilles' instead. Not surprisingly, Gladstone was aware of the clash between his literary and political work: 'Worked on Translation in German & English: an agreeable way for a C. of E. to pass his time.' He was also aware why, as chancellor, he did it: 'Restlessness drives me to this.' In 1868 the preparation of *Juventus Mundi* was a clear antidote to rising political excitement as the result of the election became clear.

Classical studies were therefore both a vocation and a distraction. But they were doomed to fulfil the second role more effectively than the first. For Gladstone's studies of the society of the ancient world, while contributing to the eclecticism of Victorian culture, were not much more than an *ex post facto* justification of that culture. Gladstone used classicism to buttress religion: his habits of thought were at bottom apologetic (in the sense of being a vindication): he could never have seriously considered an intellectual framework alternative to Christianity. The implications of his views of comparative myth could have led him via the Broad-Churchmen towards *The Golden Bough*, but instead they did not amount to much more than a plea for more Homer at Eton and Oxford. *Studies on Homer* showed that John Gladstone had been wise in his choice of his son's profession.

Amid this prolonged period of classical studies, Gladstone's signed review in 1868 of J. B. Seeley's *Ecce Homo* (published anonymously in 1865) stands in lonely but interesting contrast. It is surprisingly favourable. Whereas most High Church/Tractarian and Evangelical comment was bitterly hostile, Gladstone's review was essentially a defence. Yet once more he was placed in association with the Broad-Churchmen. Carefully distinguishing the book from Strauss's *Das Leben Jesu* (which he had studied at length in the 1840s) and from Renan's *Vie de Jésu* (re-read for the review), he went to great lengths to show that the author was working in a tradition of exegesis scripturally defensible, and that the book was in its freshness and directness 'eminently suited' to 'the needs of our particular day and generation'.

The review represents, in fact, a recognition that the intellectual tide had turned against Christianity. The balance of intellectual presumption, thought to be so obviously favourable in the 1830s, was now uncertain: 'the evidences purely traditional have lost their command (among others) over those large classes of minds which, in their times, before a shock was given, or the tide of fashion turned, would perhaps most steadily and even blindly have received them'. Gladstone's own religious thought and practice remained unchanged, but he recognized that it was beginning to be a personal faith practised by a limited section of the community: the rest of the community was subject as it were to 'a distemper that infects for a time the moral atmosphere'.* Thus while he saw Strauss and Renan as intending to destroy, he saw Seeley, on the whole rightly, as intending to cleanse.

Religion and 'rescue work': Gladstone as Pre-Raphaelite Knight

If classical studies in the 1850s and 1860s represent an alternative to theological writings, Gladstone's religious activities after 1855 also show considerable change. While religious activity remained very important to him, religious experience appears to have become less intense. The diary for the 1850s and 1860s dwells little on preparation for communion, failures in observing Lent (though this was partly on doctor's orders), or on the obsessive distinctions between godly and worldly activity, hitherto a persistent characteristic of Gladstone's self-analysis. The dimension of the secret male fraternity of the 'engagement' has wholly disappeared. Of the lay Tractarian generation of the 1830s, only Sir Walter James continued in intimate contact with Gladstone, and even in this case, their fund for charitable work in Leicester Square was wound up in 1855. Contact was renewed with H. E. Manning and James Hope-Scott, the two catalysts of the great sexual crisis of the summer of 1851 but in 1861 with nostalgia rather than intensity:

Saw Manning: a great event: all was smooth: but quantum mutatus: Under external smoothness and conscientious kindness, there lay a chill indescribable. I hope I on my side did not affect him so. He sat where Kossuth sat on Friday: How different!

Liberal politics encouraged Manning and Gladstone to establish a working relationship, and this was done. But Manning's inflexible ultramontanism meant intimacy was impossible.

If less intense, Gladstone's religious observances were as regular as ever. Church daily, whenever possible, remained the rule; 'ejaculatory prayer' was to be secretly practised at odd moments, such as the striking

* *Gleanings*, iii. 41 ff.

of the clock. W. E. Heygate's *The Good Shepherd*, a popular Anglo-Catholic work of the period, whose subtitle, 'meditations for the clergy', is a reminder of Gladstone's youthful desire to be ordained, was read daily as he dressed in the morning and for dinner. Less obviously predictable is an interest in Jansenism; the works of Nicole, the sisters Agnès and Angélique Arnauld, and of others of the seventeenth century Port-Royal group were studied in French in considerable detail. Gladstone's Evangelical origins, still discernible in some of his notes ('The hours of our mirth are not the hours in which we live ... the hours in which we live are the hours of trial sorrow care evil & struggle'), may account for this interest in Jansenism, but his interest in ecumenicalism and his growing horror of ultramontanism in the 1850s and 1860s also led him to investigate any form of Catholicism which was unsullied by Rome. This was certainly the reason for his growing interest in the 1850s and 1860s in the Orthodox religion of the Eastern Churches.

As with politics, Gladstone appears to have become tougher and less vulnerable in religion. His religious charity work with prostitutes caused, or was the occasion for, much less highly charged encounters than between 1850 and 1853. The sign for flagellation occurs only once in the diary for the late 1850s, on 25 May 1859, as the political crisis of the fall of the Tory government developed, and the comments in the diary on prostitutes are on the whole formulaic and routine rather than agonized. This is not to say that there was any diminution in rescue work. It remained persistent and regular whenever Gladstone was in London, spasmodic but prominent when elsewhere, except at Hawarden. To a certain extent 'rescue work' had become a habit. If anything his success rate seems to have declined. Nowhere in the 1860s does Gladstone analyse its usefulness or its results, nor does he seem to have made any link between his own 'rescue work' which was conducted on strictly individualist principles, and his early and determined support in Cabinet for state control of dock-town prostitution through the Contagious Diseases Act.

Most of the girls to whom he talked appear to have been common prostitutes met on the streets and appealed to there. However, there were exceptions. On 30 July 1859 Gladstone met an artist's model named Summerhayes, who also seems to have been a courtesan, a common enough situation; she was 'full in the highest degree both of interest and of beauty'. After Gladstone returned from Hawarden in September, without his wife, although he realized his thoughts 'require to be limited and purged', there were several highly-charged meetings: 'a scene of rebuke not to be easily forgotten'. Miss Summerhayes was a striking beauty in the pre-Raphaelite style. Gladstone introduced her to his friend, the painter William Dyce, and arranged for her portrait to be painted. Dyce painted her as 'Lady with the Coronet of Jasmine'.* The picture certainly bears out Gladstone's remark that 'Altogether she is no common specimen of womanhood.' Later when she had changed her name and perhaps her station to Mrs Dale, Gladstone met her at a meeting of the Fine Arts Club held in his house, and their meetings continued fitfully until 1867.

Lucy Sinclair, also known as Phillips, was a courtesan of some substance—she had a housekeeper. Gladstone met her in August 1866. They appear to have got on convivially ('singing, luncheon'), but though on occasion they had a 'smart contest', Gladstone's feelings about her do not seem to have become intense. The same was true with H. Hastings, to whom he 'read the whole of [Tennyson's] Guinevere aloud' and Miss Rigby, to whom he 'gave Shakespeare' (*The Tempest*, perhaps?) 'for a practical purpose & advised to think of emigration'. Miss Cowper, a courtesan 'at the very top of the tree . . . she has driven her open carriage and pair daily all this year in the Park', did constitute a success, at least for a time. Gladstone arranged for her to go to Harriet Monsell's House at Clewer, the responsibility for the welfare of her King Charles spaniel falling upon the chancellor.

Laura Thistlethwayte was to prove a very different case. Gladstone probably met her in 1864, riding in Rotten Row where he often rode, and where she was well known. She was the daughter of Captain Bell of Bellbrook, county Antrim, and the wife of Augustus Frederick Thistlethwayte, a gentleman of means, with a house in Grosvenor Square a few doors from Lord Shaftesbury, a brother at Eton and Christ Church, and a lineage in Burke's *Landed Gentry*. Gladstone always referred to her in his diary as 'Mrs. Thistlethwayte', or 'Mrs. T.', not giving merely a surname (perhaps with an initial) as was done with regular rescue cases. She was not therefore a 'rescue case', but she had been well known, even notorious, in the *demi-monde*. In 1869 she wrote a lengthy autobiography to show Gladstone that her reputation had been unfairly treated, but unfortunately this work has not survived. It is clear, however, that, probably some time after her marriage in 1852, she experienced a religious conversion to a nondenominational ethical Christianity, about which she lectured at the London Polytechnic. Gladstone attended one of these lectures and noted: 'I do not much wish to repeat it.' After her conversion she became a friend of the Duke of Newcastle and Arthur Kinnaird, and it was in this context that her early conversations with Gladstone occurred. At first their relationship was one of interested acquaintance. They met and corresponded on occasion, but not very regularly. It was not until Gladstone was Prime Minister, in the autumn of 1869, that there occurred one of those Gladstonian emotional explosions of extraordinary

---

* This painting is reproduced in *The Gladstone Diaries*, V, plate 3.

force and danger. We shall meet Laura Thistlethwayte again, for she did not die until 1894, and the emotional crisis of 1869 was an important part of Gladstone's life as Prime Minister.

Through Gladstone's rescue work ran a strong pre-Raphaelite streak. He read 'The Princess' and 'Guinevere' to rescue cases; he compared Mrs Thistlethwayte to the second; he was reading Tennyson and Malory when he suggested that Miss Summerhayes should be painted as 'Lady with the Coronet of Jasmine'. The blend of duty and romance of the Arthurian knights was recreated in alleys, on street corners, and in Rotten Row. 'Lofty example in comprehensive forms is, without doubt, one of the great standing needs of our race' is Gladstone's opening comment in his review of Tennyson's *Idylls*.* London accommodated this easily enough. The controlled and perceivable relationships of provincial towns with their respectable nonconformity meant nothing there.

Together with the image of womanhood, Gladstone wondered at the image of London and the relationship in it of two worlds: 'the west and the east ... I wish that those who inhabit the western portions of this great metropolis could, each for himself, endeavour to realise their immense responsibilities towards the vast masses of population which are as completely unknown to the inhabitants of the magnificent squares and streets of London as if they were neither fellow-countrymen nor even fellow Christians. Aye, they might be better known if they inhabited the remotest quarters of the globe.' Courtesans, prostitutes, and servants lived in both these worlds, hence, in part, their fascination.

Gladstone agreed to Laura Thistlethwayte's request that she should have a veto on what he told his wife about their relationship: 'I shall say no more to my wife, except it be with your free and full concurrence, and approval.' This placed their relationship in the same category as the flagellating rather than the charitable side of the rescue work: the only topic on which Gladstone did not consult his wife. It is clear that his relationship with Catherine Gladstone, while stable and very affectionate, had a clear limit to intimacy. Gladstone spent a good deal of time away from her, and she from him. He noted that his weekends at Cliveden without her were 'selfish', but did not remedy this. He told Mrs Thistlethwayte: 'from morning to night, all my life is pressure, pressure to get on, to dispatch the thing I have in hand, that I may go to the next, urgently waiting for me. Not for years past have I written except in haste a letter to my wife. As for my children, they rarely get any.'

Quarterly Review, cvi. 465 (October 1859); this review is usually recalled for its criticism of 'Maud', but most of the review is a highly favourable appraisal of Tennyson's Arthurian poetry and of the Arthurian legend and its social implications: 'The Arthurian Romance has every recommendation that should win its way to the homage of a great poet. It is national: it is Christian ... and, though highly national, it is universal.'

Family Life and the Political Circle

Gladstone's expectations of his wife in her post-child-bearing years seem unclear. He noted in 1862 when he had been reading *Tannhäuser*: 'Dearest C's. birthday. How much might I say of her as a hero-woman.' Certainly she often offered advice, on politics as well as family affairs. She handled Arthur Gordon's proposal to Agnes and helped the boys with theirs. 'Walk with C.—now rare' exemplifies the references of Gladstone to his wife after twenty years of marriage: he took it for granted that she would be on hand when needed, valued her advice and energy, but did not go much out of his way on her behalf.

On the occasion of her great need—the lingering death of her sister Mary Lyttelton in 1857—Gladstone paid only fleeting visits to the Lytteltons' house at Hagley, remaining in London to oppose and amend the government's Divorce Bill. After Mary's death, Catherine suffered a severe breakdown in health, the doctor finding 'her whole system much deranged'. This may also have been linked to her menopause (she was forty-six in 1858), though Gladstone says nothing directly on this point. The decision to go to Ionia later in 1858 may have been influenced by a desire to improve Catherine's health, as the visit to Rome in 1850 had been to help his daughter Mary's.

By 1868 Willy Gladstone was twenty-eight, and Herbert, the youngest of the seven living children, sixteen. No serious illness afflicted the children in these years, and their upbringing was on the whole uneventful. Willy bore the brunt of his father's expectations as he worked his way through Eton and Christ Church, never short of admonition and instruction. Encouraged, even forced into a political career, he was not even allowed to write his own election address. 'Most satisfactory though taciturn', he acted as his father's secretary in 1865, as did his brother Stephen. Stephen at the age of eleven announced his intention to enter the church, and apparently never deviated from it; he was ordained deacon in 1868. Harry, aged twelve, said he would be a merchant, which he later became. Herbert already showed signs of an easy relationship with his father, whom he also puzzled: 'Herbert's [eighth] birthday: he will hardly be an ordinary man, seems to have both breadth and depth.'

The three girls, Agnes, Mary, and Helen, figure in the 1860s chiefly as objects of education—unlike the boys, they were educated entirely at home by governesses and by their father. Although Agnes, the eldest girl, was in her late twenties, there seems to have been only one (unsuccessful) proposal of marriage, that by Arthur Gordon, who had fallen in love with her when he was Gladstone's secretary in Ionia. Lucy Lyttelton, Catherine Gladstone's niece, became almost one of the family after her mother's death. She often stayed at Hawarden or Carlton House Terrace, rode with Gladstone in Rotten Row, and listened to his speeches in the Commons. Her marriage to Lord Frederick Cavendish, which was not without important political implications for the Gladstone family, was the chief moment of formal family rejoicing recorded in the 1860s.

Much more worrying than the immediate family were the affairs of the Glynnes and George Lyttelton. Lyttelton was melancholic after the death in 1857 of his wife Mary, who died almost certainly from bearing their twelfth child. Gladstone tried to draw him out of himself by joining him in authorship of a volume, *Translations*, published after several delays by Quaritch in 1861, and by encouraging him in his educational activities. Lyttelton found some consolation in a friendship with Sybella, wife of Humphrey St John Mildmay, the Liberal MP. The Gladstones did not discourage this, and Lyttelton married her after her husband's death.

Sir Stephen Glynne's business affairs improved at this time, but the prosperity hoped for from the coal-mines opened on the Hawarden estates in the late 1850s was not realized. However, the mining finances were conducted by Burnett, the agent, with none of the abandon of Boydell at the Oak Farm fifteen years earlier, and the estate finances were not over-extended. The residual problems of the Oak Farm disaster were no longer acute and by the 1860s the way to an eventual solution was clear, so much so that funds were available for the development of the estuary of the Dee.

More dramatic were the personal affairs of the widowed Henry Glynne, Catherine Gladstone's brother and rector of Hawarden, who became entangled first with a Miss Lowder, then with a Miss Rose, daughter of a local pit owner and for a time governess to his motherless daughters. Henry Glynne's remarriage was of great potential importance, for, should he have a male heir, Hawarden would not pass to the Gladstone family, and the intricate structure of mortgages and loans, constructed in the aftermath of the Oak Farm crash on the assumption that Willy Gladstone would ultimately inherit, would be overturned. The Gladstones were strongly opposed to a marriage to either lady, as becomes clear from the diary, though no reason for this hostility is given.

Unfortunately full documentation of the Lowder and the Rose affairs has not come to light. It seems, however, that a breach of promise action against Henry Glynne was only avoided by a payment by Gladstone to either Miss Lowder or Miss Rose, probably the latter. The affair was publicly referred to in the *Cork Constitution* in 1861 when the paper, trying to discredit the chancellor because of his part in cancelling the government contract with the Galway steamboat packet company for postal services to the United States, stated that he had paid £5000 to avoid summons as a co-respondent in a divorce case. Gladstone told his solicitor:

In the present case it happens that some circumstances have happened to a relative of mine which recently caused me to be the medium of transmitting to a lady through a London Bank a sum of money: it is possible that this may have grown without any intentional falsehood into the fiction we now have to deal with.

When your contradiction has been inserted into the *Cork Constitution* I should prefer not taking steps to inquire whether other papers have carried the paragraph. It seems to me that with a public denial my duty terminates, if the idea of legal punishment or redress is not to be entertained.

This was the end of the matter publicly and privately; there was no legal action, and Henry Glynne did not remarry.

Gladstone saw more of the Glynnes and the Lytteltons than he did of his own kin, who were met chiefly at deathbeds. His brother Robertson was an exception to this, though, already in decline, he played less of a part in Gladstone's electioneering in Lancashire than might have been expected from a former radical mayor of Liverpool. Two of Gladstone's brothers' wives died during these years, Elizabeth, wife of John Neilson Gladstone, and Mary Ellen, wife of Robertson Gladstone. John Neilson Gladstone did not long survive his wife. At her funeral in 1862 Gladstone noted: 'There I found my three brothers & sister. I think not assembled since my Father's death.'

Despite this family disintegration, two important relationships were restored. The visit of Sir Thomas Gladstone and his family to Hawarden in 1856 was reciprocated by a nostalgic trip to Fasque, now Thomas's house, in 1858; the brothers were not intimate, and Tom continued to vote against William at Oxford University elections, but the hostility of the early 1850s declined. Helen Gladstone, whose harrowing experiences consequent upon her apostasy were of such central importance to her brother William in the 1840s, and who had largely disappeared from the diary in the 1850s, appears in the the 1860s considerably restored: 'Helen's birthday. Well, it is brighter than once it was.' He visited her at St Helen's Convent on the Isle of Wight and she became quite a regular visitor to the family. She remained a source of political embarrassment, being the only convincing evidence for the many charges of Popery levelled at Gladstone in Lancashire, especially in the 1868 election campaign.

One figure on the fringe of the family circle deserves some attention: Frank Lawley. Lawley, a relative of Catherine Gladstone, resigned his seat and his position as Gladstone's secretary in 1854 after being caught gambling with the funds. This lapse of probity by no means discredited him with Gladstone who assisted in his financial rehabilitation and subsequently employed him as a less spectacular version of Disraeli's political factotum, Ralph Earle. Lawley sent information from Virginia about the attitude of the Confederate Cabinet during the Civil War and, on his return from America, he acted as Gladstone's intermediary with the Adullamites during the Reform Bill crises, during which Gladstone records seeing him almost daily. Gladstone clearly tried to use Lawley to counter the chief weakness in his political armoury: his relationship with the party in the Commons, and with its organization. But if he had identified a problem, he had not solved it.

Gladstone knew Cabinets and the executive machine and he had to a considerable extent outflanked the party by his development of extra-parliamentary appearances. But, though he accorded party an important, indeed crucial, constitutional role, he had given little attention to the details of its management.

It is true that he might be called the first psephologist, for in 1857 he calculated the median percentage swing for five polling stations in the Flintshire and Flint boroughs constituencies at the general election, but this was not an interest followed up in his post-Oxford elections. At Oxford, tradition compelled him not to interest himself directly in the details of political management. In Lancashire and Greenwich in 1865 and 1868, he was content to continue this practice, leaving the details of campaigning almost entirely to the local experts, in Lancashire to George Melly and the Heywood family, in Greenwich to Alderman Salomons.

Though he had thought about the nature of the new electorate, and though he had a perception and active awareness of the dynamic economic and social condition of the nation, Gladstone had not developed any view of the relationship of the Liberal party as such to it. His technique as chancellor had been to gather the party in Parliament and in the country around 'measures'. But the specific financial reform measures used for this purpose were now almost all achieved. 'Measures' could be divisive as well as integrative, as 1866 showed. Gladstone had not developed any countervailing force to this divisiveness; his solution was more but different 'measures', presented as Gladstonian initiatives. The Liberal whips of the period, Brand and G. G. Glyn, were, as members of great banking families now also landed, well placed to manage the parliamentary party of the 1860s. But they had no answer to the constituency problems implied by the Reform Act of 1867. Certainly Frank Lawley, Willy Gladstone, William Gurdon, Algernon West, and the others who formed the immediate group of personal assistants around Gladstone when he became Prime Minister were not the sort of men to answer or even to address themselves to this problem.

Abroad: Ionia and Italy

During periods of exclusion from parliamentary office in the mid-century years, Gladstone twice took his family on extended continental expeditions, the first on government business (to govern Ionia in 1858–9), the second to escape it (to Italy in the recess after the Reform Bill débâcle, 1866–7). Both are of considerable interest.

The Ionian Islands off the coast of Greece and Albania became a British Protectorate in 1815. In the confused political situation of the minority Derby government of 1858, Gladstone, as described earlier (see p. 107), went there to act as Commissioner Extraordinary alongside Sir John Young. Young was a Peelite of the second rank who had failed to deal constructively with the Risospast ('union with Greece') movement in the islands—the start of many British encounters with nationalism in the eastern Mediterranean.

The Gladstones travelled to Ionia via Dresden, Prague, and Vienna. While in Vienna, they learnt of the theft and publication in London of a dispatch written by Young the previous year proposing the transfer of all or most of the islands to Greece. Gladstone thus arrived in Corfu to find a situation of considerable political confusion. After meeting the local dignitaries—for Corfu had the full complement from an archbishop and a chief justice downwards—Gladstone quickly began a paper on the islands' future. He also recommended that Young should be replaced and Young was consequently recalled. Gladstone then acted briefly as lord high commissioner until Sir Henry Storks arrived to take his place.* His function was therefore to offer a means by which Young, regarded by Derby as incompetent well before Gladstone was sent, could be eased out without a scene, and to make recommendations about the future of a potentially important strategic Protectorate†—the islands being with Gibraltar and Malta the only British bases in the Mediterranean.

As well as their general strategic importance (limited for want of a good harbour), the islands were one of the many factors in the Eastern question; 'this small question', Gladstone correctly observed, 'is the narrow corner of a very great question, one no less, in all likelihood, than the reconstruction of all political society in South-Eastern Europe'. Gladstone's appointment thus directly confronted him with a problem involving questions of strategy, imperialism, and nationalism, and in a crisis in which he had to act. As so often, his instinct was consolatory. Though he went to the islands with some predisposition for their partial union with Greece, familiarization with the situation decided him in favour of

* Holding this office meant that Gladstone vacated his seat in the Commons; some Peelites indeed saw the whole Ionian episode as a Disraelian plot to draw Gladstone into a by-election which he would probably lose; consequently they saw to it that Storks's arrival was as speedy as possible; thus, by the time the writ for the by-election was moved, Gladstone was no longer lord high commissioner; he was returned unopposed in February 1859.

† Important in the sense of being denied to the Russians, though the union with Greece was regarded as dangerous because Greek politics were so unstable as to be unable to prevent Russian penetration of the islands, should they be annexed to Greece.

a bold attempt to convert 'the abstract sentiment of nationality', which he found to be 'universal', to an acceptance of the benefits of an imperial protectorate. This was to be achieved by 'Responsible Government', which 'may now be said to form the fixed rule of the policy of the British Empire' in all areas 'not stamped with an exceptional character, either as purely military Possessions, or as being in mere infancy, or as being too critically divided between dominant and subject races'. Nationalism, Gladstone argued, subsumed all grievances, whether strictly related to national feeling or not; approached, however, 'by reason rather than by reproach', nationalism could be contained, since 'free institutions' would create an educated class receptive to imperial considerations. Even after the loss of the islands was certain in 1863, he was anxious to avoid the Ionians being seen 'as "deciding" on their destiny'.

Not too much should be made of the obvious comparisons which can be drawn from this analysis; Ionian nationalism was pro-Greek and pre-imperial, rather than primarily anti-imperial and anti-British. None the less, Gladstone made it clear in a remarkable dispatch to Lytton that he saw the Ionian question in a general imperial context, and that comparisons with problems about the compatibility of nations within the United Kingdom were also in his mind. His analysis of Ionian nationalism was acute, and overran his conclusions in the earlier part of the dispatch: he did not succeed in showing that his proposals for constitutional reform were in practice likely to woo middle-class Ionians from their Risospast (unionist) position. It is unfortunate that Gladstone never attempted to set down in similar detail his thoughts on Irish nationalism which, as he hints, were in his mind as he wrote the dispatch. Had he done so, he would have had to think more exactly about the relationship of practical reform to nationalist sentiment in the United Kingdom, and about the precise meaning of the 'justice' he claimed for Ireland.

Ruritanian though the islands' society and politics sometimes seemed, Gladstone took his mission to Ionia seriously: no sense of irony is to be found in his observation that his work in the islands had absorbed him as much as any parliamentary business. But despite his pains and intensive lobbying, his proposals were completely rejected by the Ionian Assembly, which petitioned for union with Greece instead—an instructive lesson to which he seems to have paid little attention.

HMS *Terrible* was at the lord high commissioner's disposal and the Gladstones had a splendid time in the islands, with picnics at Homeric sites, expeditions by boat, dinners, speeches in classical Greek (incomprehensible to the audience, some of whom supposed them to be in English), and in Italian (the language used by the professional classes in the islands), and two visits to the mainland. The first of these was a stay of five days in Athens where they saw the classical sites and met the

British community and the Court, which used Gladstone's visit to encourage anti-Russian feeling by excluding pro-Russian Greeks from the proceedings. Gladstone was less excited by his visit to the Acropolis than might have been expected. Perhaps it was too rushed ('The view—the ruins—& the sculptures, taken together are almost too much for one day'), perhaps his dealings with the unpopular Court (the King was forced to abdicate in 1862) spoilt the atmosphere. The second visit was an overnight trip to Philiates in Albania, then part of the Ottoman Empire. His only visit to Turkish soil dismayed him:

Off at 11½ for Filates: 1½ h. steam, 3 h. hard walk. We were the guests of the Validi Jaffier Pacha. Visited the mosque, heard the muezzin, & went through the town. Turkish dinner, in rude abundance: after wh I smoked my first & last Chibouk. Conversation by interpreters with our hostess respecting her Son whom she wants me (!) to get appointed Pacha in Albania: & with the Moodir. Turkish night accommodation too. The whole impression is most saddening: it is all all indolence, decay, stagnation: the image of God seems as if it were nowhere.
But there is much of wild & picturesque.

While in the Mediterranean, Gladstone had much opportunity to observe the Greek Orthodox Church at work, which he had hitherto studied only theoretically. He was impressed by the fusion of the Church with the people, and in visiting the monastery on Corfu where Capodistria is buried he noted 'I have not in the Latin countries seen any monastery like this.' His view of Roman Catholicism was becoming increasingly pessimistic, and this sympathy for Orthodoxy was to have important consequences when the fate of the Orthodox Christian subjects of the Ottoman Empire became a central concern at the time of the Bulgarian atrocities in 1876.

While returning from Ionia in 1859, Gladstone passed through northern Italy, which was virtually in a state of war. In Milan he met Cavour and other Risorgimentist leaders who took him into their confidence about their plans, as a result of which Gladstone arrived in London sympathetic to change in Italy, a sympathy reflected in his article in the *Quarterly* and in his early activity in Palmerston's ministry. This sympathy was chiefly for moves against Austria and against the Pope's temporal power; in 1859 Gladstone did not in principle favour major increases in Sardinia's territory, though he shifted his view on this in 1861.

Gladstone visited Italy again in 1866, to recover and to distance himself from English reform politics. While in Rome he had two audiences with the Pope, observed the making of the Vatican Council of 1870, and was dismayed, a feeling shared by Sir John Acton, also in Rome at that time. During this visit, Gladstone's relationship with Acton considerably deepened. Hitherto it had centred round exchanges of letters and meetings in company at Gladstone's breakfast parties. When they had met more privately, as at Cliveden, Gladstone had been much impressed: 'the more I see the more I like. *Si sic omnes.*' Drives and dinner parties in Rome allowed Gladstone's opinion of Acton to be confirmed. One of Gladstone's aims in visiting Italy at this time was to assist his friend Father Tosti in saving the monastery of Monte Cassino, then in the process of being secularized. The exact details of Gladstone's part in the compromise reached are not clear; he raised the matter when visiting Florence (then the Italian capital) on his way home, when he also advised Scialoja on the preparation of the Italian Budget.

These two foreign journeys occasioned none of the emotional crises which characterized all Gladstone's previous expeditions abroad. They did however confront him with two of the problems which were to be in the forefront of his mind in the early years of his first ministry: nationalism and ultramontanism.

'A rebellion . . . against growing old'

Gladstone's diary in the 1860s contains no single theme to which the diarist returns, almost obsessively, as was the case in the 1840s. That there was no such theme accounts perhaps for Gladstone's feeling of suspension: 'the horizon enlarges, the sky drifts around me' and 'a man does not see much of the country through which the river winds'. In the 1850s and 1860s, Gladstone used his financial policy, interpreted in its widest sense, to stabilize and check this feeling of drift. He was remarkably successful in suggesting to himself and to his countrymen an illusion of stability and, following it in the second half of the 1860s, of change to consolidate that stability. Whether Gladstone's view of the State, a strange mixture of organic and pluralist practice and theory, could offer a permanent solution remains to be seen. What is clear is that Gladstone faced the world bleakly and increasingly alone:

There is a resistance to the passage of Time as if I could lay hands on it & stop it: as if youth were yet in me & life and youth were one.

All the world seems to lie before me, none behind.

I feel within me the rebellious unspoken word, I will not be old.

The strangest though not the worst of all in me is a rebellion (I know not what else to call it) against growing old.

Above all, the 1860s show Gladstone progressively isolated but persistently resilient. Resilient, in that the years after 1865 showed him flexible and inventive enough to move from the settled and predictable field of government trade and finance to a central point in the increasingly volatile and complex politics of British Liberal-Radicalism in such a way as both to encourage and control them. Isolated, in that he lived on, both the only survivor of the Tractarian politicians of the 1830s, and the chief relic of the Peelite Conservatives, still described in *Dod's Parliamentary Companion* (until 1870) as a Liberal-Conservative. He noted in 1864:

Newcastle's death removes the very last of those contemporaries who were also my political friends. How it speaks to me!
   'Be doing: and be done'.

To 'be doing' was never a problem for Gladstone; to 'be done' was to prove a painful process, for him and for others.

CHAPTER VII

The First Government: Ireland, Education, and External Policy

Gladstone and the Victorian State—Expectations of Office—Cabinet and Court—Foreign Policy: united Germany and re-united United States— The Colonies Old and New: free trade, retrenchment, and expansion—The Upas Tree: the Irish Church—The Upas Tree: Irish land—The Upas Tree: Irish education—Education in Scotland and England, 1869–70

'Truth, justice, order, peace, honour, duty, liberty, piety', these are the objects before me in my daily prayers with reference to my public function, which for the present commands (and I fear damages) every other: but this is the best part of me. All the rest is summed up in 'miserere'.

And so falls the curtain on another anxious and eventful year [1872]: probably the last of the present cares, and coming near the last of all.

The year [1873] ends as it were in tumult. My constant tumult of business makes other tumult more sensible. Upon me still continued blessings rain: but in return I seem to render nothing except a hope that a time may come when my spirit instead of grovelling may become erect, and look at God. For I cannot, as I now am, get sufficiently out of myself to judge myself, and unravel the knots of being and doing, of which my life seems to be full.

Gladstone and the Victorian State

That Gladstone regarded the premiership which began in December 1868 as his last as well as his first, can hardly be doubted by any reader of his journal. Anticipation of retirement is perhaps the most frequently reiterated theme in moments of recorded private reflection and in hints in private correspondence. The foreknowledge of the dramas of subsequent decades should not warp the reader's perspective on Gladstone's attitude of mind as he kissed hands as First Lord of the Treasury, thus becoming Prime Minister of the only world power.

Politically, Gladstone's view was consistent. For the previous two decades he had seen politics and policies from the perspective of the Treasury. As Chancellor of the Exchequer he had been the codifier, legislator, and guardian of the canons of Peelite finance. Under his suzerainty the Treasury had become the guarantor of the 'minimalist' State.

No industrial economy can have existed in which the State played a smaller role than that of the United Kingdom in the 1860s. Government had appeared to forswear responsibility for fiscal and economic management and it had abolished virtually all tariffs, save those non-protective duties required for revenue purposes. As yet, government responsibility for education existed only through its relationship with the Established Church and its schools and universities, and through small grants to non-established denominations. Government involvement in industrial relations and legislation was largely confined to labour relations in the royal dockyards and to the inspectorate created by the Factory Acts. The concept of social welfare in the twentieth-century sense did not exist. Government grudgingly accepted a 'last resort' responsibility in the specific areas of public health and pauperism, but this was a responsibility to prevent disease in the first case and death in the second, not a responsibility for any positive concern in the welfare of individuals.

Gladstone's part in the construction of this model had been self-conscious and deliberate. His Chancellorship had had as its first aim 'to complete the construction of a real department of Finance' and this had been achieved. There remained outstanding items, aspects of the great plan of 1856 which had not yet been executed, but their absence did not detract from the fundamental success of the plans of the 1850s and 1860s.

Even by the 1860s, the 'minimalist' State in Britain was under attack, both directly and by attrition. It was already clear that neither the Established Church nor voluntaryism could meet the demand for education. Gladstone himself had introduced, in direct and controversial competition with the friendly societies, state-guaranteed annuities which, although self-financing, voluntary, and in practice ineffective, pointed the way to National Insurance.

As a good Peelite, Gladstone had always accepted that the reserve powers of the executive must be retained. He did not accept constitutional devices which would impede executive spending should the policy for such spending be agreed upon, and his criticism of the Bank Act of 1844 was not that it was monopolistic, but that it was inefficient. One of his Cabinet's first acts was to consolidate the preceding Tory government's nationalization of the telegraph system. Gladstone's religion, his Peelism, and his innate political and executive activism prevented him from ever being a thoroughgoing *laisser-faire* Liberal. Indeed, as we have already seen, there was always a strong *étatist* element in Gladstone which lay ambivalently and uneasily side-by-side with his fiscal liberalism. For he certainly looked to free trade as providing, in the realm of secular affairs, what he regarded as a second-order political morality, his own first-order concept of a confessional, Anglican State having been set aside in the 1840s, though not wholly abandoned.

There were always, therefore, substantial qualifications both in Gladstone's mind and in the minds of most mid-Victorians to the view that minimal 'interference' was the best government. It is probably the case that, although the minimalist State was achieved in Victorian Britain in the fullest form compatible with the social requirements of an industrialized population, none the less, in these qualifications were contained the assumptions which were to lead to its gradual disintegration. But the consequences of these qualifications upon the minimalist State were as yet faint and ill-perceived. Though many of the measures of Gladstone's first administration prepared the ground for future developments, these were not intentionally pursued, at least at Cabinet level. For this was a Cabinet, not just a Prime Minister, in deadly earnest about retrenchment. In one area at least—that of the Poor Law now supervised, from 1871, by the new Local Government Board under G. J. Goschen—the administration could claim spectacular success in enforcing a dramatic reduction in supposedly sentimental and unsystematic outdoor poor relief, and in making, in co-operation with the Charity Organization Society (1869), the most sustained attempt of the century to impose upon the working classes the Victorian values of providence, self-reliance, foresight, and self-discipline.*

Looking at the architecture of the State in the late 1860s, Gladstone saw the grand design largely fulfilled. The odd cornice remained to be completed, but the foundations and superstructure were built. Gladstone saw his first government not as the new dawn of thoroughgoing liberalism emancipated by democracy, but as the setting of the sun at the end of the day of the building of the mid-century edifice. The long-term implication of the household suffrage was, no doubt, the destruction of this creation. But it must be remembered that, as we have seen, Gladstone had not sought the household suffrage of 1867, had resisted it until it was forced upon him, and had promoted limited franchise reform in 1866 as a means of consolidating the mid-century order of State, party, and politics, not of undermining it.

There is an interesting contrast between Gladstone and Disraeli. Disraeli, though relating the nineteenth century to an ideal model of a Tory constitution corrupted by Whiggery and now unattainable, saw the politics of his own day as a process, an endless series of contingencies, one leading on to the next. A part of Gladstone certainly shared this sense of contingency, also sharing the sense of a relationship to a past ideal now unattainable. When dealing with questions in which general principles related to particular legislative proposals—disestablishment, franchise reform, women's suffrage—Gladstone showed a subtle, perhaps an over-subtle,

* See M. E. Rose, 'The crisis of poor relief in England 1860–1880' in W. J. Mommsen, ed., *The emergence of the Welfare State in Britain and Germany* (1981) and C. L. Mowat, *The Charity Organization Society 1869–1913* (1961); Gladstone was associated with its first Report in 1870, ibid., p. 19.

understanding of the value of time. Privately held views required a sense of 'ripeness' of public opinion before their disclosure. There was a world of difference between an abstract resolution and its legislative expression in a Statute. Hence a political leader could use time as a solvent; the process of politics discouraged the expression of final positions with respect to the future.* But an important part of Gladstone did not share this sense of flux and impermanence. To an extent, bounded particularly by his financial and administrative policies, he sought a final settlement of the State, the establishment of modes of conduct which should require no fundamental review. Although placing himself on the side of historic development— 'time is on our side', the 'forward and onward movement' of social forces— Gladstone had no sense of the evolution of the fiscal or perhaps of the administrative State beyond his own time, and many of his boldest policies were intended to confirm the future in the mold of the present. Of course, we must not overemphasize this yearning for permanence; the active side of Gladstone's political nature assumed change and responded to it—few politicians could do so more formidably. None the less, Gladstone was unusual among British Prime Ministers in expecting the permanent settlement of some fundamental questions of economic policy.

Expectations of Office

Unlike 1859, Gladstone came into office in 1868 with no overall legislative programme. He entered office intent on making the existing structure of government work, improving it at the margin, and legislating on Ireland. No great lists of topics to be tackled were drawn up, and apart from the Irish Church, the programme for the first session ('Bankruptcy—Middle Schools—Scotch Education—Irish railways—Rating clauses') was modest. It was not, of course, the case that a government would play all its cards in its first session—and the Cabinet in 1868 could theoretically expect the norm of six years of office—but there seems little evidence that Gladstone in December 1868 had a clear view of the overall legislative future of his administration.

Of course, there was nothing unusual in this. Peel had been exceptional among Prime Ministers in being seen as the originator of many of the legislative measures of his administration. It would not have occurred to Melbourne, Aberdeen, or Palmerston that his duty as Prime Minister was personally to stimulate, far less personally to draw up, bills for Parliament, or that his government should be judged by legislative achievement. Russell's view in 1848 had characterized the epoch between the first two Reform Acts: 'It is not the sole or principal duty of a government to introduce legislative measures or to carry them through Parliament.'

* Gladstone's method (in this case with respect to women's suffrage) is well described in Ann Robson, 'A Bird's Eye View of Gladstone' in B. L. Kinzer, ed., *The Gladstonian Turn of Mind* (1985).

It was Gladstone's problem that his career had hitherto been unusually associated with great legislative successes, and that many of his supporters expected legislation of a dramatic sort to follow the 1867 Reform Act and the great electoral victory of 1868. Allied to this was Gladstone's view of the minimalist State, which was primarily fiscal. Fiscal policies for Gladstone always implied moral principles: he never took a narrow or mechanistic view of fiscal questions, but rather regarded them as being the political and administrative expression of a comprehensive set of moral beliefs. But the form of this expression was fiscal, a general Peelite emphasis, intensified for Gladstone by his long tenure of the Chancellorship of the Exchequer.

The curious dislocation of early Victorian politics had meant that fiscal liberalism had been achieved while political liberalism had been barely begun. Such had indeed been the Peelite objective: to show that fiscal liberalism was possible without political reform; equality of opportunity should be the gradual consequence of fiscal measures, not the result of deliberately pursued programmes of social and political reform. Gladstone by no means shared the view that free trade in tariffs should be mirrored by free trade in religion, or that the Burkean social structure of England should be disrupted save by the slow consequences of economic competition. He reminded his supporters of his move towards pluralism in the 1840s by publishing 'A Chapter of Autobiography' at the end of the election campaign in 1868, but in practice his interest in disestablishment was confined to Ireland. A politician might perceive a result to be politically probable, without having an onus personally to promote it. Indeed Gladstone seems in the late 1860s more sceptical about the value of political liberalism generally than he had been in the days of readjustment of theoretical questions of Church and State in the late 1840s.

Not so his supporters. Buoyed up by the great Nonconformist revival of the 1860s, Dissenters saw the victory of 1868 as the occasion for an assertion of the political priorities of Nonconformity: general disestablishment, abolition of university tests, a Burials Bill. The disestablishment of the Anglican Church would lead to social and political equality in the same way that Peelite finance had led to fiscal and economic equality. Allied to these proposals were those of the intellectuals, especially demanding educational reform, the abolition of university tests, the ballot, and equality of opportunity in entrance to the Civil Service. Most of these Gladstone regarded with caution, and some with hostility. He particularly disliked the complete repeal of university tests, which he succeeded in avoiding in its extreme form. He also regretted the introduction of the ballot which he came to see as unavoidable but with a 'lingering reluctance', and whose various delays he contemplated with some satisfaction, partly because the issue helped to hold the party together in 1871 and 1872. Certainly the days were over when, as in the later years of Palmerston, Gladstone had been regarded by many, not least by Palmerston himself, as almost a Radical. Given the completion of his radical fiscal programme, this was not surprising, but it came to surprise many who had seen in Gladstone's espousal of Irish disestablishment early in 1868 the implication of his general espousal of the Radical political programme.

The problems of Gladstone's personal relationship with Radicalism worked themselves out against the canvas of the electorate and constituencies created by the 1867–8 reform measures. The picture on this canvas was as yet like a preliminary charcoal sketch, of which only the vague outline was apparent. The household suffrage in the boroughs had expanded the electorate, more than Gladstone had wished, in practice less than many had expected. The 1868 election had taken place in considerable bureaucratic confusion, with registers hastily and often imperfectly drawn up, and constituency boundaries so new as to make identification with the candidate on the part of the elector difficult and confusing. It was certainly not clear that Conservative resurgence was to be a chief consequence of the Act. Acton's observation that 'by sinking a shaft through the Democratic drift they would come to a Conservative substratum' was coming to be understood in many an individual constituency, not least in Gladstone's own constituency of Greenwich; but its implications for the Liberal party at a national level were only slowly grasped. Indeed the party in a national, organizational sense, barely existed. It had no framework save the moderate discipline that the whips could exercise through the distribution of patronage and small sums of money; it had no permanent structure in many constituencies; and it had no membership.

No lead from the centre was given throughout this period of government as to how these problems could be solved. Glyn and A. W. Peel, successively the chief whips of the ministry, had nothing to contribute to the development of the Liberal party in an extended electorate. They saw their roles in strictly traditional terms. Gladstone had no John Gorst, nor did he look for one.* Neither was it the duty of the Cabinet to consider the party, save at moments of crisis. Though it was the only forum for joint discussion that the Liberals had, the Cabinet did not attempt to deal with the structure of the party; 'party' only intruded into its discussions when that structure had, in the Commons, disintegrated. Initiative, when it came, came from the provinces, and especially from Birmingham. Confusion in the constituencies and mismanagement and ill-discipline in the Commons were distinctive features of the administration, and the latter came to be predominant.

The dismantling of the patronage system in the previous fifty years

---

* The historian of Gladstone's own constituency (until 1880) observes: 'the Greenwich electoral register between 1870 and 1900 was largely a creation of the Conservative Party'; G. Crossick, *An Artisan Élite in Victorian Society* (1978), 213.

meant that the party in power had little of the 'pork-barrel' left to offer its followers save honours; as Gladstone correctly reminded Lowe in 1869, when the latter urged Cabinet discussion of the topic, the opening of the Civil Service to competition would critically change some of the functions of the whip's office: 'the change would affect more or less the basis of his [Glyn's] office, his *quid pro quo*'. Patronage in the Civil Service had been almost the last '*quid pro quo*' left of the old system of familial government; there remained after 1870 only the odd Lord-Lieutenancy, the Church, the colonies, and the Justices of the Peace. For Nonconformists, the first was as yet beyond their aspirations, the second impossible by definition, the third inimical and expensive, the fourth the preserve of a Lord Chancellor almost certain to be an Anglican. To the eighteenth-century Lord Chesterfield, patronage had been the 'pasture for the beasts we feed'; for Gladstone, the process of legislation became the sustenance of his followers, and he promised more of it in his election address in 1874.

But if legislation was the primary expectation of the backbenchers and party workers, it was by no means the only concern of the incoming premier. Indeed, the advantage of the Irish Church Bill was that it ensured at least a session of relative concord within the party. Unanimously supported at least as to its principle of disestablishment by the party before the election, confirmed by the electors, admitted as in some form legitimate by the opposition, opposed in full only by the Anglican Establishment in Ireland, but certain to provoke severe infighting in Commons and Lords on details, the Irish Church Bill offered a sure means of stabilizing the majority and preventing the dreadful disintegration which had followed victory in the 1865 general election. The future for the first Session could not but be bright in the main.

Cabinet and Court

But if the mass of the party looked to legislative achievement, the Prime Minister's immediate duties were more traditional: the making of a Cabinet and the management of the Court. The two were closely related. The Cabinet as formed in December 1868 had fifteen members; the Whigs predominated as a group with seven: Clarendon, Granville, Fortescue, Hartington, Kimberley, the Whiggish Hatherley, and Argyll (a Peelite/ Whig); three Whigs, Halifax, Russell, and Sir George Grey had declined to serve. There were two Peelites, Gladstone and Cardwell (Roundell Palmer, a Peelite, declined to serve), one Radical quasi-Peelite, de Grey (from 1871, Ripon), two contrasting Radicals, Lowe and Bright, and three Liberals, Childers, Goschen, and Bruce. All were nominally Anglicans, save Bright, a Quaker; only ten of the fifteen had been to university (four to Christ Church, Oxford, three to Trinity College, Cambridge), most were substantial landowners, and one, Bright, had some direct experience of industrial management. All, save Bright, had held at least minor office before, but, surprisingly, in view of the long predominance of Whig–Liberal governments, only just over half (eight) had sat in Cabinet before: Gladstone, Cardwell, Clarendon, Granville, Argyll, de Grey (Ripon), Goschen, and Hartington. The refusal of the three old Whigs to serve gave the Cabinet a fresh look—indeed five of its members were still in Cabinets in the mid-1890s, and one, Ripon, lived to sit in Campbell-Bannerman's Cabinet of 1905.

One general point about the assumptions of the Cabinet may be made. That the future government of Britain and the Empire was to lie with the 'Box and Cox' alternation of Liberals and Tories was by no means clear to contemporaries. 'The swing of the pendulum', as politicians at the end of the century came to call it, lay in the future: there may be a case for saying it began to swing in 1874, though 1880 or 1886 may be seen as its true start; in practice its arc was almost always irregular. 1868 may seem in retrospect to be the start of 'modern' party politics, but it was not seen as such then. The Cabinet represented a ruling political coalition whose only absence from office had been the result of internal disputes: since 1846, the Whig–Liberal–Peelite alliance had occasionally lost office, but never power. The Cabinet thus worked very much within assumptions to which it anticipated no serious challenge save that of spasmodic obstruction; it did not expect the reversal of policy or legislation, and it gave electoral considerations a low priority.

The assumption of most Liberals was that the worst that could follow the first Gladstone government would be another minority Tory administration, which would allow time for the party of progress to regroup and then again take power. That the Tories would replace the Gladstone government with a substantial majority in the Commons was beyond expectation; that the Tories would begin their administration in 1874 by reversing Liberal legislation was a precedent for the twentieth century, not a precept of the nineteenth. After losing the election of 1874, Gladstone complained about a Tory bill: 'This is the first instance on record, so far as I have been able to ascertain, of any deliberate attempt being made by a Ministry of retrogression.'* Adversary politics were on the doorstep, but the door was

---

* The Endowed Schools Amendment Act; it is worth having Gladstone's exposition (*H* ccxx. 1707): 'This is a Bill for undoing part of the work of the last Parliament. It is in that respect unusual. I do not wish to deny or to qualify or weaken the fact that the party which sits opposite possesses, after having been many years in a minority, a large majority. What I wish to point out is this, that the history of our country for the last 40 or 50 years, presents to us, as a general rule, this remarkable picture: The initiative of policy in almost every instance—I do not know of even one exception—both of administrative and legislative, was supplied by the Liberal party, and subsequently adopted in prudence and in honesty by the party which is called Conservative. Take the financial—take the colonial—take any of the Departments; and I venture to say that you will find that this is a true description of the history of which we have all been witnesses. When the Conservative Government came into power in 1834, and again in 1841, after the first Reform Act had been the

still closed. In certain respects, therefore, ministers simply did not think in those terms of party which were soon to become dominant. In other words, ministers were closer to the eighteenth than to the twentieth century in the way they saw their role.

Considering its obvious importance, and the place which Bagehot assigned it as the central and co-ordinating element of the British constitution, the Victorian Cabinet has been remarkably little studied. In part this has been the consequence of poor documentation. The documentation of Gladstone's Cabinets is far more thorough than that of any other Prime Minister until records began to be officially kept in 1916. For most Cabinets before 1916, the Prime Minister's letter reporting its transactions to the monarch is the chief regular source. But these letters have obvious and severe limitations, especially when they describe the affairs of a Cabinet to which the monarch was hostile. Gladstone's letters to the Queen were intended to instruct, Disraeli's to entertain; neither attempted to describe the details of Cabinets often lasting several hours. Gladstone's method was to tell the Queen of important decisions which the Cabinet had made, particularly in those areas of foreign and colonial policy which especially interested her. Cabinet discussions on prospective policy, on details of domestic policy, and on party matters and Commons business, are rarely alluded to. To take a random example: the letter reporting the Cabinet of 8 July 1871 only mentions the first of the five items discussed by the Cabinet, the state of play in the row about abolition of purchase.*

Gladstone is unique among Victorian Prime Ministers in keeping systematic records of his Cabinets. These records provide, at the least, a comprehensive guide to topics discussed. The Cabinet usually had a weekly meeting during the parliamentary session, several meetings in the autumn for the discussion of the Estimates and of business accumulating during the Recess, and several meetings for planning the work of the session and the preparation of the Queen's Speech; crises, political and foreign, required extra meetings as occasion demanded. The average number of Cabinet meetings for each year between 1869 and 1873 was about fifty. Gladstone's minutes provide information on almost all of these. Exceptions are those meetings at which he was absent through illness, in which case Granville presided, meetings held hurriedly in the Commons during great crises, such as the deadlock over the abolition of army purchase in 1871, and occasional meetings held in odd places, such as that of

subject of a long dispute and much contention, there was absolute security in the mind of the country and full conviction that the party coming into office would not be so unwise and so unpatriotic as to retrace the steps taken by their Predecessors.'

* 'There was no other subject treated by the Cabinet to-day which it is necessary for him [the Prime Minister] to bring before Your Majesty'; the other subjects discussed were proposals for a Law University, the cumulative vote in School Board elections, bishops' resignations, and Contagious Diseases Acts.

21 March 1871, when the Cabinet met in a GWR. railway carriage, 'to consider the Telegram on the U.S.', as its members returned from Windsor. Very occasionally, a Cabinet held in normal circumstances has no surviving minutes.* Although kept entirely on Gladstone's initiative, these minutes had some official standing, or could be used officially, for Granville wrote to General Schenck, the American minister in London during the crisis over the Alabama negotiations, of a Cabinet decision on Alabama 'as recorded in a minute by Mr. Gladstone'. Gladstone's minutes are almost always brief; they are in fact a combination of topics for discussion and consequent decisions for implementation.

This brevity is not to be explained merely by shortage of time. Gladstone had little interest in the gossip of politics. In all of his vast correspondence it would be hard to find a single letter, outside those dealing with family affairs, which could be called gossipy. The odd pleasantry from time to time occurs at the end of a letter, but it is rarely *ad hominem*, and never malicious. The spirit of futility about the usefulness or success of democratic politics which usually characterizes letters of political gossip was entirely lacking in Gladstone. His minutes and letters carry the same assumption of self-confident purpose.

This is not to say that Gladstone was naïve about the content of much of political life. Commenting on an obituary of the fourteenth Earl of Derby, Gladstone observed:

Politics are at once a game and a high art; he allowed the excitement of the game to draw him off from the sustained and exhausting efforts of the high art. But this was the occasional deviation of an honourable man, not the fixed mental habit of an unprincipled one.

Whether or not this description is true of Lord Derby, it is certainly the case that Gladstone saw politics as 'at once a game and a high art'. Much of their fascination for him sprang from the problems posed in working out the detailed consequences of great principles in the context of Cabinet and Parliament. Gladstone saw the process of politics as inseparable from its principles; nothing delighted him more than the evolving of a policy which was both internally coherent and at the same time outflanked the enemy. This combination of gamesmanship and morality gave Gladstone much of his power. He was as alert to political manœuvring as the most formidable of his opponents, as flexible and resourceful at defending or exploiting a position, and more than a match in stamina for any of his contemporaries when it came to a pitched battle. On the other hand, he appeared to act within a general context of moral objectives which allowed him to personify the moral imperatives of Victorian Liberal politics.

* Records also survive for some 'conclaves'; a 'conclave' was a meeting with non-Cabinet members present, usually for the purpose of discussing a specific problem or emergency, such as the Irish Church Bill's progress, or the state of the Alabama negotiation.

With respect to politics as a game, Gladstone's first ministry was in one sense not dramatic, for many of the players at Cabinet level were remarkably unambitious. Gladstone's position as Prime Minister was unassailable and unassailed, and his role as party co-ordinator was essential. None of the other Cabinet members made any persistent attempt to act as an alternative focus of power or influence within the Cabinet, save on certain specific issues: for example, the Whigs on Ireland and foreign policy, Bright on education.

Gladstone looked back in 1897 on this ministry as 'a Cabinet easily handled'. This was not rose-tinted nostalgia, for what Gladstone meant was that, despite the arguments, personal relationships within the Cabinet were easy: the presence of 'several members who were senior to myself' facilitated business. These older Whigs were unambitious but not embittered; they fought on policies much more than on personalities. Gladstone's happy relationship with Granville is well known, but he believed he also came to be on good terms with Clarendon (who died in June 1870), with Halifax (once the Charles Wood of the disastrous budget of 1851) and, to a lesser extent, with Kimberley, the leader of the younger Whigs. These Whigs were inclined to find 'Merrypebble', as Clarendon nicknamed Gladstone, in principle almost ridiculous, with his Tractarianism and his moralizing, but during the first ministry their personal relationships with him remained amiable, though they fought tooth-and-nail on policies. While their doubts about Gladstone's restlessness and unpredictability increased, these were, at Cabinet level, still doubts fairly easily contained within the existing structure of politics. When Kimberley believed the government was at an end after the defeat on the Irish University Bill in March 1873, he noted in his journal a judgement clearly relative to his experience of administrations since 1852: 'We have been wonderfully harmonious during our four years of office and power.'

The Whigs were a first and particular worry for Gladstone. Though a diminishing force in the country, they remained essential for government. They controlled the Foreign and Colonial Offices almost as by right, and with their great landholdings they dominated the Irish offices. They were an essential link between Court and Premier (here the appointment of Halifax as Lord Privy Seal in July 1870 was a shrewd move, creating a buffer between Queen and Prime Minister and taking some of the weight off the overworked Granville), and the support of the Whigs in the Lords was all the Liberals had. Disaffection among the leading Whigs would therefore bring rapid disaster; disaffection among some Whigs there certainly was, as will be shown below, but at Cabinet level the Whigs co-operated sufficiently to maintain the unity of the ministry. It is a moot point whether Russell outside the Cabinet was more trouble than he would have been inside it; Gladstone went to considerable lengths, especially in 1869–70, to keep him in touch, but he came to regard Russell's supposedly failing powers as irremediable.

At the other end of the Cabinet stood John Bright, ill, ineffective in administration, perhaps rather idle, but still a dominant force in non-official Liberalism, or at least regarded as such by Gladstone. Bright represented in Cabinet the old Liberalism of the Anti-Corn Law League but also something of the new Liberalism of the 1860s, the complex clutch of reforming urges round which Radicalism had clustered in the constituencies. To lose Bright, especially before the Education Bill was passed, would be to isolate official Liberalism, that body of men which formed the executive, still essentially the Aberdonian coalition of Whigs and Peelites, from the new enthusiasts.

Gladstone's letters to Bright testify to his persistence and, on the whole, to his success. He encouraged Bright by offering 'early friendly and confidential communication on subjects of great public interest'; he flattered him by praising his 'Herculean efforts'; he arranged for Bright to remain a Cabinet member though unable to attend for several months; he succeeded in delaying Bright's resignation, promised for late 1870, until January 1871, when the worst of the crisis of the Franco-Prussian war was over. In October 1871 Gladstone returned to the pursuit with flattery ('those who have official responsibility must ever feel a natural anxiety to arm themselves with the best assistance and advice'), arranging a visit by Bright to Hawarden, informing him of Cabinet details once he had ceased to be a member, and eventually succeeding in bringing him back into the Cabinet in September 1873 to strengthen the government after the sundry crises of the spring and summer of that year.

Next to the Queen, no one was more cosseted than John Bright. Whereas Lowe received a very sharp analysis of the attributes of his character, Bright's executive deficiencies passed without hostile comment, evoking merely sympathetic understanding. Gladstone began his brutally frank comments on Lowe's political failings by observing that 'I always hold that politicians are the men whom as a rule it is most difficult to understand i.e. understand completely; and for my own part, I never have thus understood or thought I understood above one or two, though here and there I may get hold of an isolated idea about others.' Gladstone's handling of Bright shows he had understood a good deal of the sentimental side of Victorian Radicalism.

In cosseting Bright, Gladstone cosseted Nonconformity; he was much more successful with the particular than the general. He ended with Bright back in the Cabinet but with Nonconformity at best apathetic, at worst openly hostile. Cabinet cohesion was a window-dressing which was intended to mask disintegration in the constituencies. Bright balanced the Cabinet, allowed Gladstone to appear in a more central and less exposed position than would have been the case with Bright absent: Bright had therefore a function *vis-à-vis* the Whigs and the Court as well as *vis-à-vis* the Nonconformists and constituency Radicals.

It was Court and Whig departmental business which formed the first course of the Cabinet's staple diet. Discussion of foreign and colonial business—especially the former—was the regular business of the Cabinet, and was often discussed as the first or second item of the agenda. The second regular function of the Cabinet was agreement on and supervision of the legislative programme. Third, particularly at certain times of the year, the Cabinet discussed finance and the Estimates. It also, naturally, dealt with miscellaneous problems as and when they occurred.

It is hard to disentangle the activities of a Prime Minister from the work of his ministry as a whole, but it is the aim of this and the next chapter to examine the part which Gladstone played in that administration, and to discuss those issues in which he involved himself, or was necessarily particularly involved by the nature of his office. Of course, as Prime Minister and Leader of the Commons, papers dealing with every aspect of the ministry's activities came before him, as they also came before the Queen. But some subjects, of importance for the ministry and its subsequent fate, such as legislation on the drink trade, largely passed him by, and are thus not discussed here.

It will be convenient to discuss Gladstone's involvement as Prime Minister under the headings outlined above: foreign and colonial policy; the legislative programme; the Court; the economy.

Foreign Policy: united Germany and reunited United States

Gladstone had not previously been directly and persistently involved in the making of foreign policy, though he had been Colonial Secretary in 1845–6. However, as Chancellor of the Exchequer, he had seen many Foreign Office dispatches, and he had of course been in Cabinet during both the Crimean and Schleswig-Holstein crises, and throughout the American Civil War. He had therefore been privy in general to the making of much of British foreign policy since 1852, and the Anglo-French Cobden Treaty of 1860 had been more his achievement than that of any other member of Palmerston's government.

For a Utopian and out-and-out free trader, foreign policy might seem in principle unnecessary: international free trade was to lead to international harmony which would replace the need for bargains between governments. But the way that British free trade had developed had not in fact been that of unilateral tariff abolition. Britain by the late 1860s was related to most European countries by a complex series of trade treaties, most of them most-favoured-nation treaties, a process which was still not completed. It was not until the Continental abrogation of freer trade in the 1870s that

British free trade existed quite independently of Continental attitudes. By the late 1860s the framework of the free trade treaty structure was built. Gladstone, as one of its architects, now looked to its defence; while happy to extend the system, he did not come to office with any intention of fundamentally changing it. His objective in the long negotiations over the renewal of the French Commercial Treaty after the 1870 war was essentially to save what he could of the 1860 Treaty; he stressed his 'unchanged adherence to the principles and objects of 1860 whatever force there may be in the consideration that the application of such principles must be subject to considerations of time, place, & circumstance'.

The same can be said of Gladstone's attitude to foreign policy generally. His acute sense of organic and historicist nationality exemplified in *The State in its Relations with the Church* meant that the acceptance of nationality was his starting-point. Foreign policy was not, as it was for the Radicals, corrupt dealings between landed castes,* but rather the means by which European nations communicated for the public good. It was, therefore, desirable and potentially beneficial. Amongst these nations Gladstone discerned a developing awareness of civil progress, based on the acknowledgement of mutual interests, through 'treaties of mutual benefit with every nation of earth; treaties not written on parchment, but based on the permanent wants and interests of man, kept alive and confirmed by the constant play of the motives which govern his daily life'.† It was the function of the British 'to found a moral empire upon the confidence of the several peoples'. His article in the *Edinburgh Review*, an extraordinary initiative for a Prime Minister, anonymously written and published at the height of the Franco-Prussian war, was intended to give public airing to views which could not be given an official imprimatur: 'the silence of a Government need not be copied by those who, not invested with authority, aim at assisting the public mind and conscience by discussion'. It concluded with an interesting and optimistic statement which is both retrospective and admonitory:

Certain it is that a new law of nations is gradually taking hold of the mind, and coming to sway the practice, of the world; a law which recognises independence, which frowns on aggression, which favours the pacific, not the bloody settlement of disputes, which aims at permanent and not temporary adjustment; above all, which recognises, as a tribunal of paramount authority, the general judgment of civilised mankind. It has censured the aggression of France; it will censure, if need arise, the greed of Germany. '*Securus judicat orbis terrarum.*'‡ It is hard for all nations to go

---

* Gladstone seems to have felt no particular irritation at the exemption of the Foreign Office from entry by competition, and he raised few complaints about the quality of the predominantly Whiggish British envoys abroad.

† 'Germany, France, and England', *Edinburgh Review*, October 1870, reprinted in *Gleanings*, iv, begun on 1 Sept. 70, the day of the battle of Sedan. Attempts to keep authorship 'absolutely secret' fairly quickly failed.

‡ 'The verdict of the whole world is conclusive.'

astray. Their ecumenical council sits above the partial passions of those, who are misled by interest, and disturbed by quarrel. The greatest triumph of our time, a triumph in a region loftier than that of electricity and steam, will be the enthrone-ment of this idea of Public Right, as the governing idea of European policy; as the common and precious inheritance of all lands, but superior to the passing opinion of any. The foremost among the nations will be that one, which by its conduct shall gradually engender in the mind of the others a fixed belief that it is just. In the competition for this prize, the bounty of Providence has given us a place of vantage; and nothing save our own fault or folly can wrest it from our grasp.

This passage exemplifies Gladstone's expectations and hopes for foreign policy. Its tone is certainly not thoroughgoingly Radical: the central quota-tion, St Augustine's famous maxim which drove J. H. Newman to Rome, resurrects the image of a Christian, homogeneous Europe. The comity of nations was to mirror the ecumencial councils of the Church.

This introduction of ecumenism at so vital a point reflects Gladstone's personal religious preoccupations of recent years. It also refers to his major preoccupation in foreign affairs in the first year of his ministry: the preparations for the Vatican Council and for the declaration of Infallibility. Gladstone's case against Infallibility was both personal and general: it ruined ecumenism in England, and it cast in doubt the civic allegiance of all Roman Catholic populations. It was 'civic individuality' which gave European nations the right to claim superiority in world affairs, and it was 'civic individuality' which was the guarantor of liberty both personal and national: 'Nothing can compensate a people for the loss of what we may term civic individuality. Without it, the European type becomes politically debased to the Mahometan and Oriental model.' Ultramontanism struck straight at 'civic individuality'; Gladstone's hope was that 'a combined action of the Governments' would strengthen 'the more moderate & right minded Bishops' and consequently either prevent or moderate a declara-tion of Infallibility; 'there may be an opportunity of helping to do what the Reformation in many things did: to save the Pope and the Roman Church from themselves'.

Gladstone's difficulty was first that Britain had no official diplomatic representation at Rome, thus finding it difficult to take the lead, and second, that the Whiggish and world-weary Clarendon, though thoroughly Erastian and anti-Papal, did not invest the controversy with the same ideological significance or urgency as his Prime Minister. The conscience of Europe stirred twice, in the Bavarian initiative of the spring of 1869, and in the French initiative of March 1870. Britain was not included in the Bavarian initiative, and only marginally in the French initiative. In the latter case, Clarendon persuaded the Cabinet, against Gladstone's wishes, to respond to the French appeal verbally, rather than by a note. The voice of Europe, when it spoke, fell on deaf ears, despite the fulfilment of Gladstone's wish that 'Pope & Ecclesiastics' should not be able 'to say with truth that they never received a friendly warning'.

The appeal of the Concert had been spectacularly unsuccessful in the case of the Roman Catholic Church. Its failure called into question Gladstone's hope that 'the general judgment of civilized mankind' would act as the guarantor of the European order. Gladstone realized this; once the Council was under way he hoped that the French would threaten to withdraw their troops, using the threat of leaving the Papacy at the mercy of the Italian Government as a means of containing the Pope's theological ambitions. He also felt this negative use of troops to be the only way of bringing effective pressure to bear: 'withdrawal of the troops is the only measure within the power of France to take which the Pope and his myrmidons care about . . . it is by threats and threats alone that the Court of Rome, as to its Roman & Church policy, is influenced: its whole policy is based in the rejection of reason'.

The success of ultramontanism seemed to Gladstone to mark a major crisis in the progress of 'civic individuality' in Europe, as well as in its effect on Anglican–Roman relations in England and on the Irish situation. It would be going only just too far to say that he regarded it as a worse blow than the Franco-Prussian war, which ended the Council peremptorily but with the French troops staying in Rome long enough to allow a declaration of Infallibility to be rushed through. He returned to the theme frequently in correspondence and speeches, and his attempt to include in his election manifesto in 1874 a passage admonishing vigilance to prevent the effects of ultramontanism on 'civil rights and equality of all' was only struck out at the last moment by the demands of the other members of the Cabinet. His response to ultramontanism was to be the obsession of his quasi-retirement and the occasion of his return to public dispute with the publication of *The Vatican Decrees* in November 1874.

Gladstone had intervened as enthusiastically as he could to stimulate the Concert to action on ultramontanism. He had been held back partly by Clarendon's reluctance but mainly by Britain's weak position: no official envoy in Rome, the lack of Roman Catholic representation in the official classes, and the unfortunate fact that the leader, whip, and wire-puller of the ultramontanists, 'the madmen of the Council', was his former intimate, the apostate H. E. Manning, Archbishop of Westminster, whose co-operation was thought central to the management of the Irish bishops and Liberal MPs and thus to the success of the government's Irish legislation. In such circumstances Britain was relatively uninfluential: 'I agree with you', Gladstone told Clarendon, 'that Dr. Döllinger expects far too much from anything we could say.'

Was this to be the case with the 'deluge of events' in the second half of 1870, the war between Prussia and France which 'unset, as it were, every joint of the compacted fabric of Continental Europe'? Starting from the assumption that 'the nations of Europe are a family', Gladstone saw British involvement in the quarrel as wholly natural: England's 'hand will not be unready to be lifted up, on every fit and hopeful occasion, in sustaining the general sense of Europe against a disturber of the public peace'.

Here he differed sharply from traditional Mancunian isolationism embodied in the Cabinet by John Bright. In addition to the precept of intervention, he supported a traditional priority of the 'national interest' view of Continental affairs. Right at the start of his ministry, he told Clarendon: 'A war between France and Germany would be sad but the compulsory or fraudulent extinction by annexation of the Free State of Belgium would be worse.' The careful qualifications characteristic of any Gladstonian letter show that he did not at that stage regard Belgium as an absolute commitment, and he soon made it clear that British interest was not in itself sufficient: 'I for one believe, but do not know, that the true public opinion of Belgium is possessed with a sense of nationality, & is resolved to struggle for its maintenance. That is the only possible standing point I apprehend for permanent resistance.' The 'dirt in the sky' which Gladstone saw early in 1869 was in large measure lost sight of as the immediate crisis of the Belgian railways passed.

'What pretext has he [Bismarck] for interfering in Bavaria?', Gladstone asked Clarendon in February 1870. By the summer, Bismarck had his pretext, and Gladstone made no complaint about Prussia's conduct in the outbreak of the war, but blamed France's 'folly, inconsistency, and temerity'. His analysis of French politics shows an understanding of the dynamic and unstable nature of the Second Empire, which the Cobden Treaty, in his view, had been intended, but had had insufficient time, to stabilize. He also showed an understanding of the internal dynamics of German nationalism and Prussian politics but made no direct link between them and the events of the first half of 1870. Gladstone could not object to the formation of 'our Teutonic cousins' into a single political nation. It is striking that he assumed that 'Germany' was what Bismarck made it: that is, 'Germany' for Gladstone meant the *Kleindeutsch* solution, and Prussia's policy was thus in his view teleologically directed and justified: 'the aggrandisement of Germany by consolidation from within her own frontiers, is not a matter of which other countries are entitled to take any hostile cognisance'.

Officially, Gladstone and the British government maintained a strictly neutral position, arranging the guarantee of Belgian neutrality by treaty. Privately, Gladstone acted quickly to make the War Office 'study the means of sending 20,000 men to Antwerp', while strongly resisting the use of the occasion for a general increase in military strength, which was 'the extreme susceptibility, on one side of the case, of some members of the

Cabinet'. Gladstone seems to have had no personal doubt about the maintenance of Belgian and consequently British neutrality, for when Consols fell he bought £2,500 at 90 on 18 July.

The defence of Belgium was achieved without the dual priorities of British national interest and the rights of peoples having to be disentangled by members of the Cabinet. The same was not the case with Alsace and Lorraine. Gladstone differed from his colleagues in the vehemence of his hostility to Bismarck's annexation. He discussed the question simultaneously with his old friend, the French free-trader Michel Chevalier, and with Friedrich Max Müller, the peregrinating philologist and apologist for German nationalism who was in 1870 a professor in Oxford. To Chevalier, he blamed the French for making their case against annexation on the basis of erecting 'the inviolability of soil into an abstract principle'; to Max Müller, he complained at the absence of 'previous proof' that 'the inhabitants generally are favourable' and that annexation was militarily necessary to Germany and that Germany would not use Alsatian fortifications against France. Unilateral annexation and lack of general discussion on the terms of the peace would, Gladstone believed, mean 'that Germany, crowned with glory & confident in her strength, will start on her new career ... without the sympathies of Europe', a mistake as 'ruinous' in its consequences as 'our going, or Mr. Pitt's going, to war in 1793'.

Gladstone was not opposed to flexibility of boundaries; what he required was legitimation of their change. An advance upon the 'old and cruel practice of treating the population of a civilised European country as mere chattels' had been achieved by references to local opinion in plebiscites or votes of assemblies; Gladstone proposed 'military neutralization' as an alternative to annexation in the case of Alsace-Lorraine, and requested the Cabinet's agreement for an appeal to other neutral nations for support. The Cabinet supported Granville's more anodyne suggestion, and a second attempt was drowned by the Gortchakoff circular on the Black Sea clauses of the 1856 Paris Treaty.

In neither the Vatican question nor the Franco-Prussian war had 'the mind of Europe' been as clearly or as forcefully expressed as Gladstone would have liked. His differences with his Cabinet should not, however, be exaggerated. In neither case was Gladstone suggesting more than verbal initiatives, and in both cases his initiatives were intended as homilies which would inform the Cabinet and, if accepted there, the civilized world, what ought to be done, rather than as policies which Gladstone believed had any real chance of success. He did not think that either the Papacy or Bismarck would change course; he felt that neither should be allowed to go against what he saw as the standards of civilization without remonstrances which might act as precedents for the future.

In both these great crises of the mind and shape of Europe, Britain's intervention depended on the attitude of other members of 'the family'. In neither case were the relatives likely to be co-operative, and in the Franco-Prussian war Russia showed that she at any rate would use a family row to take what she could get. In the case of British–American relations, however, only America and the British Empire were involved, and it was thus easier for Gladstone to stiffen the will of his Cabinet at the vital moment.

The problem of the *Alabama* claims involved not only questions immediately arising from damage done to Northern shipping during the American Civil War by the *Alabama* and similar ships, but also the 'indirect claims' (i.e. the claim that the United States should be compensated not only for damage done directly by ships sold to the South during the war by British shipbuilders, but also for the indirect losses suffered—at their most extreme, all the losses caused by the delay in the ending of the war) in settlement of which the United States at one stage suggested the cession of Canada—it had just bought Alaska. The 'claims' also raised the question of security of the Canadian border and the Fenian raids across it, and outstanding Canadian–American disputes on tariffs and fisheries.

Gladstone was also personally involved, in the sense that his notorious Newcastle speech of October 1862, which could be easily and most obviously construed as a recognition of Confederate right to secede, was a severe embarrassment to him and to the government. For most of 1869, following the rejection of arbitration by the Senate in the form proposed in the Johnson–Clarendon treaty of January 1869, Gladstone made little attempt to do more than encourage Clarendon on American questions, sometimes complaining at the 'submissiveness' which the weakness of the Canadian frontier forced upon Britain. The appointment of the historian J. L. Motley as American minister in London severely embarrassed Gladstone personally, for Motley had attacked Gladstone's 1862 speech as a 'consummate work of art', comparable to Mark Antony's burial speech. Gladstone's reaction to Motley's appointment was to demand withdrawal of the phrase; elaborate arbitrations followed, successful only by the time that Motley had lost his own government's confidence.

For Gladstone, unlike Radical pro-Northerners in Britain, did not see the developments leading up to the arbitration at Geneva in 1872 as 'righting a wrong'. He saw the process as exemplifying the means by which two civilized nations could settle differences, without either having to admit being in the wrong. In the autumn of 1869 he began to take a more perceptive view than Clarendon of the highly complex position of Hamilton Fish, the American Secretary of State, to defend Fish against Clarendon's scorn, and to suggest that 'the two countries should set about the consideration of a good prospective system, and should thereafter, in the light of principles thus elucidated, reconsider the matter of arbitration, or any other mode of proceeding in the Alabama case'. Even when Fish revived the demand for the annexation of Canada in exchange for the settlement of the Claims, Gladstone counselled maintaining 'our present composed temper'. The proposal of 'a good prospective system' was embodied in the Treaty of Washington of 1871 whose articles' general significance was in Gladstone's view 'to become rules for international law for the future'.

The successful conclusion of the Washington Treaty seemed to mark the end of the affair, bar the settling of the details. But the American claim, made in their 'Case' of December 1871 prepared for submission to the arbitration tribunal, that the question of the 'indirect claims' was still open, astonished and appalled the British. Gladstone responded with a vigorous denunciation in the Commons of American behaviour, which was both genuinely felt and politically convenient. He then short-circuited the cumbersome channels of communication, by which his own views reached the Americans only via Granville, the Foreign Office, and Thornton, the ambassador in Washington. He proposed to Granville that direct communication between himself and Schenck, the new American minister, should be the first means of negotiation. As Gladstone was already on terms with Schenck, this would give him more personal control and initiative. His first use of this direct access to Schenck was to be the delivering of a vast letter justifying his own record during the Civil War, and replying to the sections of the American 'Case' which seemed to impugn it. In this, he was overruled by the Cabinet, led by Granville. His urge for self-justification was linked to a strong intention to make the negotiation succeed within the terms of the Treaty of Washington and to show that its terms were not ambiguous.

In the extraordinary contortions through which, between March and June 1872, both British and Americans eventually contrived to make the Treaty work, Gladstone's role was to push forward negotiations whenever possible and, when a breaking-point seemed almost to have occurred, to rally his Cabinet, especially Halifax, Kimberley, and Cardwell, the chief dissenters, behind the larger view. 'My determination upon it is now firmly rooted & tested by all the mental effort I can apply.' The strategy prevailed and, greatly assisted by the common sense of Charles Adams, the American arbitrator, the arbitration proceeded without consideration of the 'indirect claims'. Both the Treaty of Washington and the arbitration could be offered to the world as the path for the future. So also, eventually, could Gladstone's self-justification. His vast letter to Schenck —really a political pamphlet—was eventually sent, against Granville's advice, in November 1872 and was published in *Harper's New Monthly Magazine* in the United States in 1876. Gladstone had felt throughout that he and the British position during the Civil War had subsequently been hard done by. He had urged Clarendon to get someone to publish a defence of it.* His letter to Schenck was his version of that defence and marked the start of that assiduous cultivation of American liberal opinion which was to be so marked a characteristic of the rest of his life.

Gladstone's initiatives in some areas of foreign policy thus found him on occasion in disagreement with his Cabinet, and, on the whole, the Cabinet prevailed. Gladstone's concept of an 'ecumenical council' of civilized opinion appealed neither to the Whigs, who preferred the discreet bargains of the closet, nor to the Radicals, who saw in it sinister implications of Continental involvement.

The Colonies, Old and New: free trade, retrenchment, and expansion

Allied to foreign policy, in that it was traditionally a Whig preserve and the subject of routine Cabinet discussion occasioned by the arrival of dispatches, was colonial policy. Of India, the Cabinet heard little. Gladstone's letters to Argyll, the Secretary for India, were largely about British questions. Gladstone's own 'desires' for India's future were that 'nothing may bring about a sudden, violent, or discreditable severance; that we may labour steadily to promote the political training of our fellow-subjects; & that when we go, if we are to go, we may leave a clear bill of accounts behind us'. This vision would have startled many of his contemporaries, but he made no moves to encourage its realization. Indian security was a more immediate problem. On the question of Russian expansion in Turkestan, he followed Granville in a policy of issuing general cautions combined with concessions.

'Colonial policy' for the most part meant the relationship of Britain to her colonies of European descent. Granville's Colonial Secretaryship in 1869 and 1870 was marked by the withdrawal of British troops from New Zealand and preparations for their withdrawal from Canada. This was part of a long-standing and systematic attempt on the one hand to force the colonists to act responsibly, on the other to help to reduce defence costs at home, which accounted for about a third of the British budget. As Colonial Secretary in 1845–6, Gladstone had moved towards self-government in New Zealand as quickly as possible and, as he reminded Granville in 1869, one of his first actions as Peel's colonial secretary had been to instruct the new Canadian Governor-General 'that we did not *impose* British connection upon the Colony, but regarded its goodwill and desire as an essential condition of the connection'.

Even before the 1867 Canada Act, Gladstone had been most reluctant to accept a Vote for Canadian fortifications. As Palmerston's Chancellor, he

---

* Gladstone also felt that his proposal 'early in the war' for rules to govern prospective cases such as the *Alabama* had been neglected, by implication by Russell; but he could make no allusion publicly to this, for Russell was already very touchy on the question of his record as Foreign Secretary.

had played a leading role in the 'Conferences on Canadian Defence' with Canadian politicians which had negotiated the agreement essential to the making of the 1867 Canada Act. Gladstone's readiness to support troop withdrawal was therefore consistent with his position over many years. Considering army reform in 1870, at the height of the Franco-Prussian war, he anticipated getting 'rid of all drafts upon the regular army for Colonial purposes, in ordinary circumstances, except in the four cases of Malta–Gibraltar–Halifax–Bermuda'. But these withdrawals were only to continue in peacetime conditions: where Britain was 'satisfied as to the cause whether Canada were independent of us or not, such [armed] assistance ... would only be limited by our means'. The 'whole power of the Empire' should be used to sustain 'a political connection' as long as Canada wanted one.

Gladstone thus assumed that the 'union of heart and character' would continue as long as it was desired by both sides, and that it would be a union supported by arms if necessary. How little he anticipated unilateral action by colonies is shown by his astonished reaction to the Australian demand for differential tariffs in 1871. 'Do I understand ... that New Zealand (for instance) may admit free shoes made in Sydney and tax at any rate she pleases shoes made in Northampton?' He thought this 'advance ... brings us near the *reductio ad absurdum* of colonial connection, & the people of this country should have an opportunity of passing an opinion on it'. 'Astounding' though this might seem, the British Cabinet was forced to acknowledge there was little they could do about it, despite the fact that it upset all the delicately balanced trade treaties which Britain had concluded with European states in the name of the British Empire as a whole. Reserved powers of commercial treaty-making turned out, to Gladstone's regret more than Kimberley's, to be non-existent, the pass being finally sold by Lord Lisgar, the Governor-General of Canada (formerly known as Young, whose confusions in Ionia Gladstone had been sent out to right in 1858), who without consultation with London gave the Royal Assent to a Canadian Bill establishing differential tea and coffee duties with America.

The movement towards an Empire less formally integrated constitutionally and administratively was thus significant, but it was a movement based on localized fiscal and protectionist priorities, unencouraged and reluctantly conceded by London. The speed with which colonies made use of the legislative freedom which the previous twenty years of imperial policy-making had given them, clearly came as a shock to Gladstone, who seems to have thought that responsible government and support for free trade would go hand in hand. The enthusiasm for colonial development which he had shown in the 1840s was absent; a co-founder of the Canterbury settlement in New Zealand, he gave no encouragement to the various lobbies of similar feeling in the 1870s. Undoubtedly this was a mistake from the point of view of domestic politics: failure to present the positive side of the emotional 'kin beyond the sea' view of colonial relationships and a readiness to rely on an understanding by the electorate of the technical details of long-established policies, made it all the easier for the opposition to link patriotism with Conservatism and claim, as Disraeli did at the Crystal Palace in 1872, that 'there has been no effort so continuous, so subtle, supported by so much energy, and carried on with so much ability and acumen, as the attempts of Liberalism to effect the disintegration of the Empire of England'.

In Cabinet, Gladstone had found himself more cautious than Granville on imperial questions, and differing with Kimberley on the importance of the colonial tariff question. On questions of colonial expansion, he found himself on the defensive. A long rearguard action on the annexation of Fiji, conducted with Gladstone's usual resourcefulness, succeeded in delaying a decision, despite powerful pressures from the anti-slavery lobby, but in the Gold Coast, Gladstone was reluctantly persuaded by the combined action of the Colonial Office and the War Office, to concede the sending of a military force under Sir Garnet Wolseley in the autumn of 1873. He threatened Kimberley with a recall of Parliament, the implied revolt of Bright, the refusal of the Cabinet to defend the expedition in the Session expected in 1874, but it was all to no avail. 'I am not master of the facts', Gladstone told Kimberley, and the War Office saw to it that this remained the case; Gladstone had to rely on newspaper reports for information about the preparation of Wolseley's force, and understandings about Cabinet supervision of the stages of its progress were simply ignored. 'The pressure of the three Departments, with a view to military preparations', Gladstone told Bright, 'has gone beyond what I feel competent to deal with & beyond the mere execution of the orders of the Cabinet.' The Gold Coast question illustrated the weakness both of Gladstone as Prime Minister, and of the office as such. Cardwell and Kimberley effectively prepared and dispatched the expedition on their own authority; the Prime Minister had no constitutional way of stopping them. By the time the Cabinet met, the expedition was on its way. However, the military conduct of the expedition, once launched, on the whole met with Gladstone's approval. It was well organized, cheap and quick, and stood out favourably in all respects in comparison to the Tories' Abyssinian adventure of 1867–8. Gladstone lauded Wolseley's conduct in a flattering letter which may represent, in part, an attempt to repair the generally poor relations between Liberal party and the army.

The discovery of the diamond field at Kimberley in 1869 and the anarchic allegiances of uncontrolled prospectors threatened British informal control of the non-colonized areas of southern Africa. The Cabinet decided in principle to annex the 'Cape Diamond Fields' in May 1871, and the stresses within southern Africa thus provoked prepared the way for the decision to give 'a general encouragement' to 'South African Federation'. However, in the complex maze of southern African relationships and the difficulties of communication with London, the Governor of the Cape, Barkly, on his 'own Act', annexed the Diamond Fields to Cape Colony, regardless of the federation plans—a classic example of action by 'the man on the spot'. Gladstone had warned Kimberley 'that in opening the door to the re-incorporation of the Boer States in the Empire you will (as is your wont) take due precautions against extension of the responsibility of the H[ome] Government'. However, he made no attempt to influence in detail the development of an area which, when he returned to power in 1880, was to prove one of his chief external preoccupations. Neither the Cabinet nor the Prime Minister had any consistent control over imperial expansion, nor, except in the case of Fiji, did Gladstone attempt to intervene decisively in it. 'No objection taken' was the laconic record in the Cabinet minutes of Barkly's initiative.

The Upas Tree: the Irish Church

The second of the chief areas of concern within which it is convenient to discuss Gladstone's Cabinet's preoccupations was its co-ordination and supervision of the form and content of the Government's legislative programme. In Gladstone's first ministry this was a major task, for the programme was exceptionally dense, partly because of the Prime Minister's predilection, partly because of the great volume of bills promoted by the various government departments, and partly, as has been suggested above, because the expectations of the ministry's supporters—to call them a 'party' is to suggest too coherent a description—required that they be kept sweet, or at least supportive, by legislative proposals whether expected to pass or not.

Each legislative proposal must have its own history, its own relationship to government departments and to pressure groups, and will be shaped within the context of a long series of precedents, legal conventions, and departmental preparations. Normally, by the time the proposal reaches the Cabinet, the room for manœuvre is severely constricted. That elaborate and often impenetrable process by which certain measures emerge as the questions of the day can hardly be dealt with in general here. The history of government departments is usually the key to the analysis of this process; but Gladstone had no department, nor did he, except on very rare occasions, deal with departments save through their Cabinet representatives. He did on several occasions, however, act as a one-man department in the sponsorship of legislation, and it will be convenient first to discuss those bills in which he took a particular personal or leading interest.

The Sessions of 1869 and 1870 had Irish legislation as their centre-piece. The Irish Church Bill of 1869 was, and the Irish Land Bill of 1870 became, very much Gladstone's own bill. The Irish Church Bill he prepared himself, in consultation with selected advisers and Thring, the parliamentary draftsman. The Land Bill was prepared in a partnership of varying balance between the Prime Minister and Chichester Fortescue, the Irish Secretary and author of the failed Irish Land Bill of 1866. Not since Peel's Bank Act of 1844 had the Prime Minister been seen as the almost single-handed architect of a major piece of legislation, apart from the unique circumstances of the Reform Bills.

Ireland was for Gladstone a preoccupation, not an interest, an embarrassment, not an intellectual attraction. Clearly, Ireland had not progressed, but Gladstone showed little intellectual curiosity about this anomalous corner of the 'workshop of the world'. His aim in his Irish policy was simply stated: 'our purpose & duty is to endeavour to draw a line between the Fenians & the people of Ireland, & to make the people of Ireland indisposed to cross it'.* Institutional reform (the Irish Church Bill) and social and economic reform (the Land Bill) were intended to have a political effect. Gladstone seems to have believed that if the Irish were shown the Westminster Parliament redressing their grievances by spectacular acts of legislation, then this would encourage their adherence to the existing political structure, both as to institutions and political parties.

The disestablishment of a part of the Anglican Church was, naturally, a formidable political and technical undertaking, an assault on the formal structure of the Establishment as dramatic in principle as anything achieved between 1689 and the present day. Gladstone felt that he had sufficient political impetus to maintain his bill in principle in the Commons despite 'a possible development of *minor* schism in the Liberal body' over details of the Bill affecting Roman Catholics, and indeed this proved correct. In the crisis over the bill in June and July 1869, he was able to use the Liberal majority in the Commons against both the Lords and opponents of his approach in the Cabinet. Almost from the start, he saw the Lords as 'the most formidable stumbling block'.

His bill was predominantly negative in tone: that is, it concentrated on disestablishment, and did not attempt to use the occasion for the more positive incorporating approach which the policy of concurrent endowment implied.† As he told Archbishop Tait, in the Commons 'there is not

* A letter to General C. Grey, the Queen's secretary (and husband of Caroline Farquhar) discussing the release of Fenian prisoners. He admitted, under pressure from Earl Grey, that Fenians in Ireland and England 'have had a very important influence on the question of the time for moving upon great questions of policy for Ireland'.

† i.e. the distribution of the assets of the Anglican Church in Ireland between the three chief Irish denominations, Anglican, Roman Catholic, and Presbyterian; the Roman Catholics and the Presbyterians up to disestablishment received State subsistence through the Maynooth Grant and the Regium Donum respectively. These grants were ended with compensation from the Anglican endowments, though they had been a charge on the Imperial Exchequer, not on the Irish establishment.

that distinction between the question of disestablishment and disendowment which exists in Your Grace's mind', and, he might have added, in the minds of many Erastians, both Conservative and Whig. Concurrent endowment (i.e. the endowment of the Roman Catholic Church in Ireland side by side with the Anglican) went against all Gladstone's principles. If an established church could not represent 'religious nationality', he favoured the opposite extreme of voluntaryism. The notion of the State being involved in the support of various denominations which were doctrinally irreconcilable he profoundly abhorred, and the ending of the Maynooth grant in 1869 was probably one of the most satisfactory consequences of disestablishment for him personally. Gladstone successfully warded off concurrent endowment, favoured by Lord John Russell in his pamphlets of 1868–9, and by some other Whigs, as well as by many Conservatives. It is hardly likely that the Roman Catholic hierarchy would have accepted it if it had been offered.

The bill was rapidly drawn up at Hawarden with the advice of Archdeacon Stopford, and with Granville and Acton in attendance. Gladstone returned to London on 1 February 1869 and by 9 February the Cabinet 'completed the heads of the Irish Church measure to my great satisfaction'. Complex negotiations, 'conclaves', and discussions changed some of the details of the bill, but its substance emerged unscathed, and the bill was given a first reading on 1 March 1869.

Gladstone had made one major change from the plan he drew up in December 1868: originally, the disestablished Church was to have kept its glebe houses, and some of their 'immediately annexed lands'. Under pressure from Roman Catholics, Presbyterians, and John Bright, this continuation of the endowment was drastically reduced. The concession proved fortuitous for, when the clash with the Lords came in July 1869, the dispute centred on three chief questions: concurrent endowment; the glebe lands and other property, and the related question of compensation for curates; and the threat to delay the date of operation of the Act. Gladstone absolutely ruled out any concession on the first, and on 26 June 1869 carried the Cabinet with him: 'Discussion on concurrent Endowment. Govt. do not entertain it.' The Tories might try to keep the issue alive, but, with the Queen wanting a settlement, the issue came down to cash, a bargain to be struck between the two Houses: 'All that remains is to say to the majority of the H. of C. *such and such a sum* is not worth the quarrel and the postponement. This sum must be moderate.' Gladstone's low offer on the glebe lands gave room for manœuvre: Disraeli wanted one sum, Tait a second, Cairns a third and highest.*

Under the strain and excitement of the negotiations, not least for him,

* The glebe (church) lands were sold off by Commissioners, mostly to small proprietors, thus offering an interesting precedent for land purchase schemes in the 1880s.

Gladstone had the first of those short illnesses which often punctuated all his ministries at times of major crisis. Clearly something more than what today would be called a 'diplomatic illness'—nervous exhaustion would seem to have been the cause—it was none the less extremely convenient, for, rather than the slightly frenetic, Tractarian Prime Minister, it left the composed Erastian Granville to conduct the final negotiations, in which the Opposition's hostility swiftly collapsed and a compromise unexpectedly favourable to the Liberals' demands was reached. The favourable issue left Gladstone, upstairs on his sofa, 'almost unmanned, in the reaction from a sharp and stern tension of mind'.

Gladstone believed Ireland had provided the momentum for the party in 1868 and 1869, and his policy of disestablishment without concurrent endowment had satisfied not only himself, but his Roman Catholic and Nonconformist supporters. This policy had been 'the basis on which the late remarkable co-operation of the Liberal majority has been founded ... the question whether any other basis would be abstractedly better is a question, at this moment, for Debating Societies'.

The Upas Tree: Irish Land

On the question of Irish land, Gladstone was at first cautious—'the Church is enough for today'—but, following Bright's outright commitment to a major land bill at the end of April, Gladstone—at least from May 1869—had come to see the pace set by the drafting and passing of the Irish Church Bill as being matched by a Land Bill, although this would involve 'both more difficulty and less support', for 'if we succeed with the Church, & fail with the Land, we shall have done less than half our work'; 'we must lay our first parallel the moment we are out of the Church'. Irish land had little of the mandate which it was hard to deny the electorate had conferred upon Irish disestablishment; within the Liberal party it alarmed the Whigs, not only those with Irish land or connections, like Clarendon, but also great Scottish magnates like the Duke of Argyll; it raised by implication exactly that attack on property generally of which opponents of the household suffrage had warned.

On the other hand, Irish land reform was supported by Irish middle-class opinion represented by the *Freeman's Journal* and Sir John Gray, and by the Irish Liberal MPs in the Commons, opinion which, since the start of Fenianism and the Ribbon Men, had come to be regarded in England as relatively respectable and moderate, limited in its aims to a type of demand which the imperial Parliament might feel itself able to go some way to meeting. The Tenant League, which embodied these demands, already called for the 'Three Fs' (fixity of tenure, freedom of sale, fair rent) which were eventually granted in the 1881 Land Act.

Just as Gladstone had declined to see Irish disestablishment as necessarily implying English, Scottish, or Welsh disestablishment, so he tried to isolate the Irish land question from the general question of British social and economic relationships. A simple change in the law of contract was therefore undesirable, as was the intervention of 'a public authority' to determine prices and consequently rent, for this would be a 'principle essentially imperial', 'no less applicable to England & Scotland, than it is to Ireland'. The solution offered by George Campbell, an ex-Indian judge, had in this context an immediate appeal for Gladstone. Campbell's solution, read by Gladstone on 11 August 1869, was, crudely stated, to use the tradition of the Ulster tenant right—the right to bestow or to sell the right of occupancy—as a way to recognize customary rather than contractual land relationships in Ireland generally. Campbell's solution, if it could be carried through into law, fitted splendidly into Gladstone's political preoccupations. Because its intention was to recognize customary relationships, it could be presented as a conservative measure; because it used a particularly Irish form of customary tenure as its basis, its 'imperial' implications would be much reduced.

It was clearly not the 'Three Fs', but it could be offered to the Irish as reform on indigenous principles, offering both security and compensation to the tenant, ending 'wanton eviction' and, consequently, also ending 'demands for *unjust* augmentations of rent'. The problem was that the simplicity of the 'Three Fs' could not be matched by the bill: 'the circuitous road is really the only one practicable, & is to be much preferred to scaling and descending precipices'. But that depended on how quickly the travellers were determined to reach their destination, particularly if they were not worried about injuries on the way.

For Gladstone as Cabinet coachman, the responsibility was to reach the end of the road; when he tried to take what his passengers saw as the dangerous short cut via the generalization of Ulster tenant right, he was forced to change course. The Whigs led by Fortescue would not stand for so bold a measure, which implied an end of landlord initiative. Fortescue's solution—compensation for disturbance—implied that disturbance, that is, eviction, was to continue, eased by a legislative mechanism. Ironically, this made the question of a precedent for England the more likely. By December 1869 Gladstone found himself faced with the fact that a Land Bill supported by his present Cabinet could not be a tenant-right bill; rather than abandon the bill altogether, he fell back on tenant right for Ulster, compensation for disturbance for the rest.

The Irish Land Act was conceived and passed in the light of what Gladstone saw to be the requirements in Ireland for social and consequently political stability. The plan for some form of State purchase or sponsorship of Irish railways, which he originally intended to accompany the Land Bill to assist in the economic development of this stabilized peasantry, was not pressed. The immediate political objectives of the legislation can be seen in the acute interest Gladstone showed in the reception of the bill in Ireland, and by his attempt to accompany it by the liberation of Fenian prisoners, which the Whigs prevented throughout 1869 until late in 1870, when Gladstone wore down Dublin Castle and obtained 'the very early liberation of all those who can be regarded as purely political offenders'.

The Irish Church Act and the Land Act were intended to stabilize Ireland as it was, not to restructure Ireland for the future. The latter would have involved incorporation of the largely hostile Irish Roman Catholic clergy by concurrent endowment, wholesale evictions, and forced emigration of surplus tenantry, and an agricultural tariff; in other words it would have required the British government to live out of its time, to treat Ireland as the norm and the rest of the United Kingdom as an anomaly.* In the British context, Ireland was an anomaly,† but, in political terms, anomalous treatment could not be taken far; the best that could be done was to hope that marginal social adjustment could produce political tranquillity. 'Right relations' between landlord and tenant might also, in time, encourage economic growth.

Politically, the Land Bill was in trouble from the start. As soon as it was known that a government measure was in the making, expectations and demonstrations rose in Ireland. By November 1869 it was clear that the bill could not meet these expectations. Gladstone attempted to douse them with a letter to Sir John Gray. The Cabinet would not allow the release of Fenian prisoners, and the Prime Minister was unable to avoid having to accompany his Land Bill with a Coercion Bill. In March 1870, Roman Catholic bishops came out for the 'Three Fs', and, in the Irish context, the Land Bill emphasized the inability of the Imperial Parliament to meet Irish demands, rather than the political integration for which Gladstone had initially hoped. Publicly, the Land Bill was marked by alarm among the propertied classes, privately it was one of the two great defeats of Gladstone by the Whigs in Cabinet, the other being the defeat over Alsace-Lorraine a year later.

Irish affairs of Church and land had thus dominated Gladstone's attention in 1869 and early 1870: 'until it is disposed of, it seems to engross and swallow up my whole personal existence', he told Manning, and certainly

---

* Dr Barbara Solow argues that the Act was 'well designed to cure the evils it assumed', i.e. deter evictions and deter landlords from raising rents on tenant improvements, but that it attacked the wrong problems: 'The real problem in Ireland was not the division of a given pie, but the provision of a larger one.' But this is merely to highlight the anomalous position of Ireland in a United Kingdom where growth was spontaneous, considerable, and completely independent of direct government stimulus. B. Solow, *The Land Question, and the Irish Economy, 1870–1903* (1971), 50, 88.

† Bright's demand for simultaneous bills for English and Scottish land, though considered reluctantly by the Cabinet, came to nothing in practice.

no legislative topic, except perhaps the Irish university question, so engaged his attention between 1871 and 1874.

Gladstone had drawn up the Church and Land Bills, and especially the former, as if he were still a department minister. But at the same time, in addition to being First Lord, he was also Leader of the House of Commons. As such, he had responsibility for the details as well as the general strategy of the government's legislative programme, and as such he was expected to be in the Commons to supervise the smooth running of the daily, and nightly, progress of the legislation. It was in this capacity that he was remembered by many backbenchers as responsible in the débâcle of 1865–6, when a large government majority disintegrated over parliamentary reform. Gladstone had, not surprisingly, an acute memory of that crisis in which his political career came near to foundering. The Irish Church Bill held the party together: 'the House has moved like an army', he told Manning, but adding with ominous implication, 'an army where every private is his own general'. The Irish Land Bill passed the Commons, but only after major amendments from Radicals (W. Fowler), and Peelites (Palmer) had been avoided with difficulty, and in the face of the outright opposition of a number of Irish MPs, including Sir John Gray. However, Gladstone's personal authority, and the assumption amongst Liberals outside the Cabinet that the contents of the bill were his, prevented disastrous disruptions on Irish land.

The Upas Tree: Irish education

This was not to be the case with Irish education, 'the redemption of our last Irish *pledge*', to which Gladstone in August 1870 moved after the Land Bill, though without the same insistent urgency as he had moved in 1869 from Church to land. He prodded Fortescue into action without 'violent hurry' and implied to him that he could expect much the same prime ministerial involvement in the preparation of the measure as he had suffered with respect to the Land Bill: 'It seems to me that in the main we *know* what we ought to give them whether they will take it or not.'

The lack of haste and the didacticism were deliberate. The subject was fraught with complexity and possible disaster from the start: 'a difficult & probably a dangerous one for the Government, as there is no more doubtful point in the composition & tendencies of the Liberal party than its disposition to extremes in the matter of unsectarianism as it is called'. A solution could not be reached by negotiation or general discussion. The problem was compounded by events within Ireland, and within Europe. In Ireland, the Keogh judgement of June 1872* infuriated the Roman Catholics, and

---

* Judge Keogh's judgement, in the Galway by-election petition, powerfully condemned clerical excesses in the election campaign.

the O'Keeffe* case seemed to confirm fears of the civic consequences of ultramontanism. In Europe, the 1870 Vatican Council encouraged a general wave of anti-Popery. Added to this was the great debate about science, religion, and the future role of Christianity in schools and universities. As Broad Church empiricism conquered the English universities, many, and not only Roman Catholics, looked to the Irish experiment as a chance for a fresh start through what to others was an anti-intellectual reaction. All these elements worked together to raise the exceptionally intricate details of the Irish university arrangements to the highest level of political significance. Nothing illustrates the tone and central concerns of Victorian politics more clearly than that the government of the British Empire should resign after a narrow defeat on what to the twentieth-century mind might seem, at least at first glance, to be a mere bill about a provincial university.

Some consideration of the details of this complex problem is therefore necessary.

Experience had shown that no plan of general educational reform in Ireland could succeed until disputes about the apex of the system—the university—had been resolved, and it appears to have been assumed from the start by ministers that Irish university legislation would be both first and separate in Irish educational legislation.

Gladstone, through his work on the 1854 Oxford University Bill, was an experienced legislator in such matters, and his view of the question was in part founded on this experience. But an additional precedent for the Irish University Bill was the Scottish Universities Bill of 1858, which he had, though not in office, successfully amended to permit future unification of the various Scottish universities into one national university, the existing universities becoming its colleges. This proposal had not been popular in Scotland, and had cost him the chancellorship of Edinburgh University in 1868.

The problem in Ireland was religious and financial. The Roman Catholics had set up their own, poorly endowed, Catholic university; the Queen's University, with its 'godless' colleges, set up by Peel and Graham in 1845, had been largely ignored by Roman Catholics; Trinity College, Dublin, was well endowed but Anglican. Thus 'the R.C. grievance ... is held to consist in this, that an R.C. educated in a college or place where his religion is taught cannot by virtue of that education obtain a degree in Ireland. ... I think we desire that a portion of the public endowments should be thrown open, under the auspices of a neutral University, to the whole Irish people.' A 'neutral University' was an answer to the Irish demands for

---

* Father Robert O'Keeffe's suspension for taking successful civil action against other Roman Catholic clergy was upheld by the Commissioners of National Education; O'Keeffe then brought a series of civil actions, winning one against Cardinal Cullen.

a separate, concurrently endowed, Roman Catholic university, existing side-by-side with Trinity College. In the circumstances of the day, quite apart from Gladstone's own antipathy to concurrent endowment, it was probably the only solution with a chance of success, even though Hartington, who reluctantly replaced Fortescue as Irish Secretary in December 1870 under the full weight of Gladstone's moral suasion, pushed his hostility to the 'central university' plan almost to the point of resignation. But a 'neutral University' which incorporated colleges with ancient traditions was hard to translate into a statute. Gladstone drew up the bill with Thring much as he had the Irish Church Bill, at Hawarden, in touch with colleagues only by letter, with only scant reference to the Irish officers in his government, advised on the affairs of Protestant Ireland by a Trinity don, J. K. Ingram, who came over for the purpose. The bill was thus as much his own as the Irish Church Bill had been.

Gladstone's solution was characteristically neat and Burkean, in the sense of restorative conservatism. He made a clear distinction between the University of Dublin, which he showed had existed since the fourteenth century, and Trinity College which had existed since the sixteenth century and had since then effectively subsumed the University within the College. Gladstone proposed to restore the University to its original status, and to allow it to have as colleges Trinity College, the Belfast and Cork Colleges of the Queen's University (which would itself be wound up along with its third college of Galway), and such of the 'voluntary' colleges—Newman's Roman Catholic College in Dublin and the Presbyterian Magee College— as wished to join. Many problems sprang from the restrictive details (which had good Colonial precedents) thought necessary to allow the plan a chance to work: no theology, philosophy, or modern history chairs were to be founded, a professor was to 'be punished or reprimanded' for wilfully offending 'the conscientious scruples of those whom he instructs in the exercise of his office', and the legislature was in the early years to exercise much patronage by nominating the members of the University Council.

The comprehensiveness of the plan offered a bold means of solving this vexed question, which was, as Gladstone pointed out, the first stage towards a general plan of Irish education. It was also a frank recognition of sacrifices which would have to be made if partition in education was to be avoided.

Gladstone made it clear in the first sentence of his speech introducing the bill that the proposals were 'vital to the honour and existence of the Government'—that is, it was from its introduction a matter of confidence, a caveat aimed by Gladstone probably more at the 'secularist' English Liberals than at the Irish. That it was a matter of confidence seems to have been largely the result of Gladstone's identification with the bill: Lord Halifax commented dryly, 'Gladstone had to deal with the third branch of the Upas tree, and therefore made a great deal of the University Bill, not in itself a measure of such vital importance.' But once this was the case, clearly the government had to back the second reading absolutely. Thus the ten 'English and Scotch' Liberals, the thirty-five Irish who voted against the bill, and the twenty-two Irish Liberals who abstained, acted in full knowledge of the consequences. Only twelve 'Irishmen' voted with the government, as opposed to sixty-nine against. The government was defeated on 11 March 1873 by three votes and, after considering dissolution in the context of Gladstone's poor health and the generally poor state of the party, resigned, only to be forced back into office by Disraeli in one of the coolest and boldest calculations of British politics—the last occasion on which the Opposition declined to take office when it was offered.

Not for the first time in Irish affairs, the appeal to reason and concilia- tion came to nought. The earlier Irish legislation of the government had not brought Irish trust in the ability of the Westminster Parliament to act in 'Irish interests'. Indeed, the opposite had happened. Since the 1870 Land Act, the Home Rule Association had made rapid strides, and Irish Liberal Members feared for their seats. Thus when Archbishop Cullen denounced the bill, the game was up. The foundations for the maintenance of the Liberal party in Ireland were already eroded. The University Bill stated what the 1874 general election confirmed: Liberal Ireland was soon to be dead and gone.

Despite the run of home rule successes in by-elections, little of this fundamental shift in Irish politics seems to have been perceived by Glad- stone and those around him. During the making of the University Bill, Gladstone had dealt with the Irish hierarchy—as far as he dealt with it at all—through the agency of Manning. Though from the start there had been doubts and caveats, both seem to have expected the bill to pass. Even as late as 1 March, Gladstone assumed that the bishops' Resolutions, which were 'really War to the knife', were the result of mistaken tactics—'how is it possible this should not have been perceived?'—rather than outright hostility. Gladstone saw the defeat first as a stupid rejection of 'boons' offered to the Irish, secondly as a stab in the back by treacherous, ultra- montane bishops: he told Manning, 'Your Irish Brethren have received in the late vote of Parlt. the most extravagant compliment ever paid them. *They* have destroyed the measure; which otherwise was safe enough.'

Gladstone's Irish measures had been conceived in the spirit of Edmund Burke. Irish land and the University Bill had been profoundly conservative in presentation—the first based on the Ulster tenant right, a prescriptive right by definition ('founded on the original grants to the [Ulster] settlers in the seventeenth century'), the second the resurrection of an ancient univer- sity, a prescriptive right in effect. The disestablishment of the Irish Church by the author of *The State in its Relations with the Church* had been the acknowledgement of a pluralism which was self-consciously a second best. 'There is nothing that Ireland has asked and which this country and this Parliament have refused', Gladstone said at Aberdeen in 1871, going on to acknowledge the remaining 'single grievance' of university education. By 1873 the Irish themselves were registering their disagreement with this view at by-elections. English 'boons' were not enough. 'I have looked in vain for the setting forth of any practical scheme of policy which the Imperial Parliament is not equal to deal with, or which it refuses to deal with, and which is to be brought about by Home Rule.' The endowed Catholic university was exactly such a scheme, and its Gladstonian alternative of 1873 provided the occasion for the cutting of what Gladstone had called in 1871 'the silken cords of love', to the weaving of which much of his and his ministry's time had been devoted.

Education in Scotland and England, 1869—1870

The man who disestablished the Irish Church could carry a Land Bill despite the fact that his supporters almost all thought it too little or too much; the essential struggle had been with Cabinet colleagues. The Anglican Tractarian, the former member of the National Society for the Education of the Poor in the Principles of the Established Church, found himself more personally and politically engaged in the great struggle over English education.

The education question had its roots in two royal commissions and two developments of the 1860s; first, the realization that a combination of voluntaryism and the Established Church could no longer realistically aspire to offer an adequate elementary education in the cities; second, the early stirrings of awareness of the achievements of Continental nations in educational and industrial development. It is, of course, a hoary schoolboy myth that the Franco-Prussian war 'caused' the 1870 Education Act—the chronology of 1870 would have to be reversed to allow that—but awareness of the Prussian model certainly existed as a result of Mark Pattison's report for the Duke of Newcastle's Royal Commission in the 1860s. Once the 1870 war began, Gladstone's *Edinburgh Review* article quickly made the connection: 'Undoubtedly the conduct of the campaign, on the German side, has given a marked triumph to the cause of systematic popular education.'

Gladstone had shown little interest in education in the 1850s and 1860s, save for reform of the universities and public schools. In this context, he was personally an unrepentant advocate of the classical curriculum, which many of his essays and books, including *Juventus Mundi* (1869), were intended to justify, and he deplored the fact that the '*low* utilitarian argument . . . for giving it [education] what is termed a practical direction, is so plausible' that it was winning by default. He and the Cabinet declined to give a government grant to Owen's College in Manchester, and Gladstone later used this decision as a precedent for declining aid for the founding of Aberystwyth. Despite the general concern about the strength of technical education in Germany, the Liberal Cabinet, for reasons both of religion and political economy, refused to be drawn into the direct funding of British universities.

Of the Cabinet, Bruce, Forster, and de Grey were well known protagonists of popular education. A bill dealing with England could not fail to be controversial, and the Cabinet dealt first with Scottish education in 1869. Discussion in Scotland on education had progressed further than in England, and in Scotland only two interests, the Established Church and the Free Church, were taken into account—the vast spectrum of denominational concern characteristic of the English debate was absent.* None the less, Argyll's Scottish bill, introduced into the Lords in February 1869, was soon in difficulties. The Lords treated it as a precedent for England, where they already disliked the important Endowed Schools Bill, also of 1869, a measure in whose preparation Gladstone seems to have played no part. The Lords amended the Scottish bill so as to destroy the notion of a 'national system', and leave denominationalism as firmly entrenched as possible. By the time the bill reached the Commons in the summer, it had become enmeshed in the crisis of the Irish Church Bill. Gladstone seems to have given no attention to it outside the Cabinet; concessions were made to keep the bill alive, but there was no real prospect of it passing, and it foundered, eventually succeeding in a revised form in 1872. In October 1869 Gladstone encouraged de Grey and Forster to meet with him 'to lay the foundation stone of our Education measure in England'. This suggests that a vague opinion that there would be an English bill was already forming (Gladstone in early September already assumed the predominance of 'the two large subjects of Irish Land and Education in England'), but Gladstone's letter clearly had a stimulating effect, for no preparations seem to have been made hitherto. Why Gladstone encouraged the question is unclear. Certainly, popular pressure for an English bill was already considerable. Gladstone may have hoped it would prevent Irish land becoming overdominant and contentious. The two issues fed on each other: in Cabinet, land predominated to the extent that education was discussed only once before the full bill was approved in Cabinet on 4 February 1870, without any controversy being noted by Gladstone. In the Commons, Irish land was to some extent subordinated to the great debates on English education.

The Scottish bill had made it clear that the path of a successful English bill would require careful planning: that the route lay through a minefield was not immediately apparent. From Gladstone's point of view, Forster and de Grey's proposals, that the existing system of denominational schools be supplemented where necessary by school boards locally elected, was in

* The interests of Roman Catholics and Episcopalians were virtually ignored in Scotland.

general satisfactory. He was characteristic of his times in showing little interest in the bill's proposals apart from the religious dimension. He never made any attempt to modify the general structure of their plan. This was not surprising as it was the only plan likely to survive the Lords, and it was one which he could, in general, support. Not only Anglican but Roman Catholic interests were at stake, as Gladstone recognized in putting Manning in touch with de Grey at a very early stage.

Following the position that his friend, the High-Churchman Dean Hook, had championed since the late 1830s, Gladstone focused at once on the aspect of the bill which particularly concerned him personally: 'the proposal to found the State schools on the system of the British and Foreign Society would I think hardly do';* he made clear what was to be, with some modification, his consistent preference throughout the ministry: 'Why not adopt frankly the principle that the State or the local community should provide the secular teaching, & either leave the option to the Ratepayer to go beyond this *sine quâ non*, if they think fit, within the limits of the conscience clause, or else simply leave the parties themselves to find Bible & other religious education from voluntary sources.' As he told Bright retrospectively, 'the application of the Rate to be confined by law to secular teaching only' was the only 'solid and stable ground'.

On this issue, Gladstone found he had the Cabinet, the Anglican Church, and the Dissenters against him. If restriction to secular teaching could not be achieved, Gladstone went to the other extreme. In a long memorandum written on 29 May 1870, after meeting several Nonconformist deputations, he made as strong a case as he could against 'the plan that the Bible be read & explained, while formularies are to be forbidden', though admitting that the proposal had some advantages. The absence of formularies (i.e. of an understanding of the dogma, structure, and teaching of the apostolic church) would be a surrender to latitudinarianism and Nonconformity.

However, the absence of formularies was exactly the solution reached through the Cowper–Temple amendment, agreed by the Cabinet on 14 June 1870. As Gladstone's memorandum of 29 May 1870 recognized, 'the concord of opinion' behind this solution was 'due to a great anxiety to maintain a direct connection between religion and popular education', and in practical political terms it was the only way of reconciling the two. The acceptance of this was a major personal blow for Gladstone. It was not exactly a defeat, in that he had not associated himself systematically with the bill and his usual persistence had not been placed behind his own preference. But it was a personal concession which rankled more deeply than any of the many concessions Gladstone made to hold his ministry together.

* The Nonconformist British and Foreign School Society had from 1833 distributed an Exchequer grant and provided non-denominational religious teaching.

The Education Bill was the largest of the government's legislative measures in whose preparation Gladstone did not involve himself intimately at every stage, though, as we have seen, his interventions and encouragement were at certain moments extremely important. It ran side by side with his Land Bill, and once it was in the Commons Gladstone, the most formidable of the Liberal front bench in procedural manipulation, took over much of the responsibility for its safe passage. Together, the Land and Education Bills brought to a dramatic close the Session of 1870—the last occasion until 1911 when two major, highly controversial bills were run together in a single Session.

CHAPTER VIII

The First Government: Distintegration and Downfall

*The Declining Efficiency of Parliament: the legislative log-jam—The Crown and
'the Classes': the Queen, republicanism, army purchase—Patronage, from the
Garter to the Church—The Economy: the working classes and their unions, the
propertied classes and their rates—Fiscal Policy: the Budget, the Estimates, and
the 'scandals'—Chancellor Again: the downfall of the government and
resignation as party leader—Constituencies, Public Speaking, and the Press in the
early 1870s*

1. To engage now [March 1874] is to engage for the term of Opposition,
& the succeeding term of a Liberal Government. These two cannot
probably embrace less than a considerable term of years. (1830–41.
1841–52. 1866–74.)
This is not consistent with my views for the close of my life.
2. Failure of 1866–8.
3. My views on the question of Education in particular are I fear irrecon-
cileable with those of a considerable portion of it. Into any interim
contract I cannot enter.
4. In no case has the head of a Govt. considerable in character &
duration, on receiving what may be called an emphatic dismissal,
become Leader of Opposition.
5. The condition of the Liberal party requires consideration.
    a. It has no present public *cause* upon which it is agreed.
    b. It has serious & conscientious divisions of opinion, which are also
pressing, e.g. on Education.
    c. The habit of making a career by & upon constant active opposition
to the bulk of the party, & its leaders, has acquired a dangerous
predominance among a portion of its members. This habit is not
checked by the action of the great majority, who do not indulge or
approve it: & it has become dangerous to the credit & efficiency of the
party.

The Declining Efficiency of Parliament: the legislative log-jam

The disestablishment of the Irish Church, the Irish Land Act, and the
Education Act of 1870, three of the triumphs of the century, were bought at
a high legislative price. In June 1869 the Cabinet for the first time

considered 'Bills Abandoned', and the midsummer purge of bills proposed but not passed became a distinctive feature of the ministry. The policy of 'filling up the cup', of starting bills which were certain to run into difficulties and then of not allowing enough time for the resolution of those difficulties, might keep the fissiparous elements within the majority occupied, but it would not necessarily keep them happy.* The use of the 'clôture' (or the guillotine as it is called today) was considered, but it was not introduced.

The problem was circular: the bringing forward of legislation was a form of party discipline, but an undisciplined party would not support the means by which such legislation might pass the Commons, namely a readiness to subordinate the interests of particular groups to the success of the government legislative programme. That programme was, of course, impeded by the wrecking tactics of the Lords. But since members of the majority in the Commons were often equally vocal in their hostility to aspects of government bills, the Lords could claim to be doing no more than playing their natural role in the constitution. In fact, government homogeneity barely existed outside the government's early Irish legislation. The whips could never be sure when the spirit of 1866 would arise again, and the large majority obtained at the 1868 election had always been expected to produce problems of management.

Gladstone did not blame Glyn, the chief whip. He thought that 'there is something of a tide in politics. At the Election we had an immense impetus & we came back with more than a natural or nominal majority'; by 1871 he saw the tide as turning, and by 1872 he thought 'that our hold over the Constituencies is weakened, & that the Conservatives may begin soon to think of another advent to power'. Disraeli saw the same pattern. He waited until the 'immense impetus' had spent itself, and in 1872 he pounced. Disraeli's strategy was to let the Liberals discredit themselves. Their vast and unprecedented flood of legislation, whether passed or not, was in itself discrediting; the Conservatives appeared conservative simply by sitting silent on their benches.

Despite his position as First Lord and Leader of the House, there was little Gladstone could do. Several of the proposals were personally repugnant to him; he was reluctant to admit that the preservation of Oxford and Cambridge as national universities required the abolition of religious

---

* Gladstone described the process to his constituents: 'such was the state of public expectation and demand with regard to every one of those subjects [Scottish education, licensing, local taxation, mines regulation in 1871], that it was not in our choice to refuse to place our views before Parliament in the form of a bill laid upon the table; and I believe I am within the mark in saying that if we had attempted to avoid incurring that responsibility, either other members of Parliament would themselves have endeavoured to procure—not legislation upon the subject, but at least the production of measures of their own ...' or resolutions would have been passed demanding government bills.

tests,* and he had little enthusiasm for the ballot, necessary corollary of parliamentary reform though he might admit it to be. The Cabinet did not prove to be a suitable body to redeem the situation. Though it oversaw the details of parliamentary business, it does not seem at all to have acted as a body for developing a coherent party strategy. This may well have been an impossible objective, but Cabinet members do not seem to have thought in terms of a party structure of electoral management. The Cabinet continued to act chiefly as an executive body, distanced and often estranged from the political structure which had placed it in power.

The Crown and 'the Classes': the Queen, republicanism, army purchase

Cabinet members received their seals from the Queen, and relationships with the Court were one of their chief preoccupations. Gladstone's daily journal testifies to the vast amount of time, in letter-writing, visits, and negotiations, that the leader of a government, and especially of a reforming government, had to spend on the monarchy. Both the Queen and the Prince of Wales seemed major problems. In the heady enthusiasm of post-reform Britain, the relationship of the Court and 'the democracy' was very uncertain.

The absenteeism of the Queen and the blatant profligacy of the Prince created the conditions for the only moment in the history of industrial Britain when it seemed as if republicanism might become a serious political issue. Gladstone took the view that the risk was not worth taking, and that the monarchy must be strengthened by positive action on the part of its members and defenders. He believed that to meet republicanism, Bradlaugh and Dilke, by repression 'would tend to establish rather than end the controversy. What is needed is that we should if possible do or cause something to be done of a nature likely to remove the dissatisfaction, of which the absurd republican cry is an external symptom'.

From the first Cabinet of the ministry, he brought forward a plan to associate the monarchy more closely with Ireland, more particularly suggesting that the Irish Office should be reformed, and that the Prince of Wales should become Lord-Lieutenant, presiding as a constitutional monarch in that country. He urged this pertinaciously, especially after the Prince's involvement in the Mordaunt divorce case. From late in 1870 Gladstone pursued his plan with spasmodic assistance from Granville and Halifax. But the Queen was a match for them, and would not give an inch. Gladstone persistently tried to overcome her refusal to appear in public; when she said she would not open a bridge, he demanded she name a substitute. Gladstone's moment came with the Prince's near-fatal illness in

---

* Gladstone hoped for what the Queen's Speech of 1870 called a 'legislative settlement'—i.e. a compromise saving some of the entrenched Anglicanism of Oxford and Cambridge. He worked to head off 'absolute secularisation'.

December 1871. He insisted that the Queen should capitalize on the swelling sympathy for the Prince by a public appearance at a thanksgiving service at St Paul's. He met every argument with a prepared position, and at the crisis of the discussion, when the Queen 'contracted her objection to the length of the service', he trumped her by quoting the '*Annual Register* of 1789 (from which it appears that the Commons set out at 8 a.m., the King and Queen at 10, and their Majesties only returned to the Palace at half past three.)' The Queen gave way, and the service was a great success, especially for Disraeli, who was loudly cheered outside the cathedral.

Gladstone and his Cabinet's battle with the Queen had to be kept a secret within the Establishment. The Cabinet could not say what pains they took to save the Queen from herself and from the Radical wing of their own supporters. What had in bygone years been stock patriotic Whig criticism of the Civil List, now, in the context of post-reform politics, could easily be made by the Tories to seem, and in a few cases actually was, open republicanism. Gladstone himself gave away a trick in trying to win over his constituents at Greenwich by quoting an egalitarian parody of the National Anthem from the *Secularist Hymn Book*, and calling it 'a questionable book [with] verses which I think contain much good sense'. Gurdon, Gladstone's secretary, issued a denial that the book as a whole had his approval, but it was too late. It was to this sort of incident that Disraeli could refer when he accused Gladstone of alternating 'between a menace and a sigh'. The Whigs were of little help, except individually and behind the scenes. Palmerston and Russell had dissipated the legacy of Melbourne, and Gladstone had failed to capitalize on the resemblance of high-principled earnestness between himself and Prince Albert which in the early 1860s had looked as if it could bear substantial fruit.

Undoubtedly Gladstone's overbearing, moralizing manner did no good. We have seen in the case of John Bright that he knew how to flatter; in the case of the Queen, he never took up the trowel. In his persistent advocacy of the Prince of Wales's potential usefulness, and in his meetings with the Prince, there are some signs of a Liberal–Marlborough House alliance being formed, but this would have conflicted too much with Gladstone's plans for the public rehabilitation of Victoria for it to emerge as a serious element in politics.

Personal emollience might have helped, but behind the growing private friction lay great public issues. The abolition of purchase in the army—the ability of army officers to buy promotion rather than, as in the navy, earn it by merit—seemed an assault as brutal as disestablishment on the internal traditions of the landed class and the Court. First raised by Cardwell in Cabinet in March 1870, the question became, for Gladstone, part of a general plan of reconstruction of the mores of that 'vast leisured and wealthy class'. Prompted by the Franco-Prussian war, and particularly by the 'mechanical perfection' of the Prussians, whose 'most consummate army' was 'put into the field with the greatest expedition, and at the smallest cost ever known', Gladstone wanted 'complete and definite' army reform involving India, the Colonies, the militia, and the training of officers by 'making all our young cadets learn a soldier's business in the ranks', and a complete overhaul of the activities of the peacetime army: 'the greatest difficulty of all in truth is this: to redeem the officer's life from idleness in time of peace'. He consistently urged Cardwell to go beyond abolition of the purchase of commissions, but Cardwell's Army Regulation Bill was primarily a purchase abolition and compensation bill, together with the centralization of control of the militia.

The bill appeared therefore as an attack on the privileges of a caste, without offering, as Gladstone had wanted, the prospect of its reconstruction in the national interest. That caste constituted the heart of the most privileged section of Victorian society, and its exclusiveness was emphasized by its leader, the Queen's cousin, the Duke of Cambridge, commander-in-chief and colonel of the Horse Guards. The struggle through the summer of 1871 was long and bitter—much more so than that over Irish land or Church. Back-benchers on both sides of the House defended their interests with a fanatical resolution which the Duke of Cambridge did nothing to moderate. With immense difficulty the Queen, who had in the first instance supported the abolition of purchase, was brought to suggest to her cousin that he should support her government's bill in the House of Lords, but the best he would do was to abstain.

The bill wrecked the government's programme in the Commons and was summarily dismissed in the Lords. Although the proposal was supported in principle by both front benches, the organs of representative government proved unable to abolish the purchase system by legislation. The executive then did what it could have done at any time, effected abolition by Royal Warrant. This was possible because purchase had been made illegal by an Act of 1809, except in those cases in which a Royal Warrant allowed an exception (the 'regulation' price purchase). The Cabinet's Royal Warrant withdrew these exceptions which in fact had spread to cover almost all commissions. This left the officers of the army with the prospect of purchase being ended without the financial compensation which Cardwell's bill provided, and the Lords therefore hastened to pass it. The complexities of the constitutional wrangle about purchase made the government's position difficult to explain popularly. Its use of the Warrant when blocked in Parliament was seen as high-handed, and the fact that a chief need for the bill had been to give compensation to the officers was soon forgotten. To some, Gladstone seemed a bit of a bully. He could equally be seen as resolute and resourceful in a way that few progressive Prime Ministers are.

In Gladstone's view, the defence of purchase represented the failure of the landed class to justify its existence in the modern industrial world. He approved in principle of wealth, the Court, and an hereditary aristocracy. He was cautious about the absorption of the middle class into the aristocracy, despite his own record, telling the citizens of Liverpool in 1872, 'I know not why commerce should not have its old families rejoicing to be connected with commerce from generation to generation. . . . I think it is a subject of sorrow, and almost a scandal, when those families which have either acquired or received station and opulence from commerce turn their backs upon it and seem to be ashamed of it. (Great applause.) It is not so with my brother [Robertson] or with me. (Applause.)' He saw the aristocracy as a separate class with its own duties. His views on army reform centred not on the opening of the army to middle-class entry, but on efficient promotion and training within the traditional military caste. But he wanted Court and County to follow the middle-class values of efficiency, application, and economy. He believed that obsession with wealth was coming to dominate the aristocracy at the expense of duty, especially 'in the Clubs, and in the army'. 'Ploutocracy' he commented in the aftermath of the purchase crisis, produced 'a bastard aristocracy & aristocracy shows too much disposition, in Parliament especially, to join hands with this bastard.'

Gladstone's problems were therefore not confined to the Queen and the Duke of Cambridge; rather, his relationship with the upper echelons of the Court was symptomatic of a general distrust felt for him by landed property, Whigs as well as Tories.

Patronage, from the Garter to the Church

As First Lord, Gladstone was responsible for the exercise of the vast range of Crown patronage, from awarding Garters to filling Regius chairs, bishoprics, deaneries, and rectories. Civil Service reform might have reduced the whips' source of patronage but that of the First Lord was by no means diminished. The response to Gladstone's exercise of patronage strikingly illustrates the extent to which landed society was reluctant to associate itself with his administration.

Offers of honours such as the Garter and posts of influence and significance in the localities, such as lord-lieutenancies, were rejected on political grounds by erstwhile supporters of Whig–Liberal governments. The Garter was declined on political grounds by the Duke of Leinster in 1869 and the Duke of Norfolk in 1870, the latter despite Gladstone's assurance that 'the public would consider your acceptance of the Garter as implying not by any means a permanent pledge but a present inclination *towards* the party & the Govt.: as indeed they may already have thought from so slight a circumstance as your doing me the favour to drive with me on the celebration of the Queen's birthday'. The failure to secure Norfolk, the youthful leader of the English Roman Catholics, was a particular blow, given the lengths to which Gladstone went to solicit that denomination's support. The Lord-Lieutenancy of Staffordshire was offered to Wrottesley, who refused it, to Gladstone's Peelite friend and, in the Oak Farm days, his creditor, Dudley, who refused it, and to Hatherton, who refused it. Wrottesley was eventually persuaded to accept it. Hostility to the ministry and to Gladstone personally was not as marked as it became in the 1880–5 government, but the steady drift of the landed classes away from the Liberal party had clearly begun, as surely as the Court was finding itself the agent of the Tory party.

The exercise of Church patronage the First Lord shared with the Lord Chancellor; Gladstone tried to ease the demand for parish livings, 'which throw me to despair', by informally linking his patronage lists with those of the Lord Chancellor, and he also sent Hatherley a list of those deserving cathedral preferment. Sharp attention was paid to the politics of priests receiving promotion, more so than to their position in the theological spectrum. 'No talents, no learning, no piety, can advance the fortunes of a clergyman whose political opinions are adverse to those of the governing party', wrote Lord John Russell in a dictum generally true of the nineteenth century, and true in some measure of Gladstone's patronage, at least in so far as Liberal bishops could be found.* He asked the ex-Tory MP, Sir William Heathcote, a prominent Tractarian, to report to him on 'eminently good' clergymen, but with the significant proviso that Heathcote should include information about their attitude to Irish disestablishment.

The unexpected recovery of Tait from an illness in 1869 removed the excitement of an archiepiscopal appointment. There was a clutch of appointments of bishops in September 1869—Wilberforce from Oxford to Winchester, Temple to Exeter, Hervey to Bath and Wells, Mackarness to Oxford. These were not appointments of mere ecclesiastical significance— each of them was subsequently circularized by Gladstone with an appeal to vote for the Irish Land Bill in the Lords. He also canvassed episcopal support for the Army Bill abolishing purchase in 1871, and for other measures. Liberalism would certainly seem to be the reason for the appointment of Temple to Exeter. Temple was one of the contributors to *Essays and Reviews* (1860), the modernists' manifesto, and his promotion caused outrage in Tractarian circles. Gladstone re-read Temple's essay after appointing him, finding it 'on reperusal . . . crude and unbalanced, but neither heretical nor sceptical'. The episcopal appointment which caused much the most difficulty was the comparatively minor one of St Asaph, that see whose separate preservation Gladstone had tried to make a condition when first invited to join the Cabinet by Peel in 1843: here Gladstone

---

* Earl Russell, *An essay in the history of the English government and constitution* (1865 edn.), 309.

wished to appoint a Welsh-speaking bishop so as to moderate the appearance of the Anglican Church as an alien element in Welsh culture. Though previously unimpressed by the Welsh language, Gladstone evidently thought that such appointments could affect what he called the 'singularly susceptible population' of the Principality. Joshua Hughes was nominated after a 'very laborious though interesting search'. Gladstone's speech to the Eisteddfod at Mold in 1873 emphasized the seriousness with which he had begun to take Welsh affairs.

The Economy: the working classes and their unions, the propertied classes and their rates

The last of the areas of routine business with which the First Lord and the Cabinet were necessarily involved was government finance and the economy. By the 1870s, 'finance' appeared to have little to do with the state of the economy. It would not be true to say that the Cabinet had no interest in the working of the economy, but it would be true to say that it took no direct responsibility for it. When Daniel Jones, a miner from Newcastle-under-Lyme, wrote to tell him of his unemployment and to complain of low wages, Gladstone made the classic mid-Victorian reply:

The only means which have been placed in my power of 'raising the wages of colliers' has been by endeavouring to beat down all those restrictions upon trade which tend to reduce the price to be obtained for the product of their labour, & to lower as much as may be the taxes on the commodities which they may require for use or for consumption. Beyond this I look to the forethought not yet so widely diffused in this country as in Scotland, & in some foreign lands; & I need not remind you that in order to facilitate its exercise the Government have been empowered by Legislation to become through the Dept. of the P.O. the receivers & guardians of savings.

Gladstone was becoming uneasily aware, as were other perceptive observers of the Victorian economy, that the economy worked with a chronic 'enormous mass of paupers', and that: 'Again, and yet more at large, what is human life, but, in the great majority of cases, a struggle for existence? and if the means of carrying on that struggle are somewhat better than they were, yet the standard of wants rises with the standard of means, and sometimes more rapidly....'* He was moreover aware that 'great vicissitudes mark the industrial condition of society; and we pass rapidly in a series of cycles from periods of great prosperity to periods of sharp distress'. He suggested to Lowe that what would have amounted to a primitive cost of living index should be drawn up, so that the condition of the working

* Budget speech of 1864, in W. E. Gladstone, *Financial Statements* (1864), 519. What exactly Gladstone said on this topic in the 1863 budget is the subject of dispute; see the *résumé* of quotations by Engels in his preface to the fourth German edition of the first volume of *Das Kapital* (1890).

classes in 1832, 1852, and 1872 could be compared, but nothing seems to have come of this. The items Gladstone suggested for the index are an interesting reflection of Victorian priorities: the price of lodging, fuel, clothing, food, travel, books, and newspapers.

Gladstone was fortunate in that, in general terms, his first ministry witnessed the emergence of the nation from a period of 'sharp distress' (the beginnings of which occurred in his later years at the Exchequer in the 1860s) into an upward cycle, largely though not wholly stifling the first widely-based murmurings against free trade since the early 1850s. In 1867 and 1868 during Disraeli's Chancellorship, *per capita* net national income had actually fallen slightly to £21.9, but by 1874 it had reached £27.4 at 1900 prices, or risen from £27.2 to £34.6 at current prices.* Gladstone saw this spectacular rise as a vindication of the fiscal and institutional reforms of the previous twenty years and of the principle that the maximum freedom of the market and the minimum absorption of its funds by the Government was the best guarantee of the creation of wealth.

This dramatic increase in national prosperity was, of course, not necessarily fully apparent to contemporaries, nor did it benefit all groups or classes equally. Its immediate political consequences are uncertain. Gladstone's administration had to deal with two political problems whose origins lay deep in social reactions to economic change: the problem of trade unions and their status, and the problem of the propertied classes' reaction to taxation. It is hard to judge how much the political expression of these problems was occasioned by economic change: first, change in the form of the uncertainties of the 1866 and 1873 disruptions of the money-market; second, in the end of the gradual inflation which had underpinned growth in the 1850s and 1860s, and which gave way at the end of 1873 to the start of the long deflation of the 1870s, 1880s, and 1890s; third, in both downswings and upswings of certain sectors of the economy. A further underlying factor was the political opportunity and alarm which the household suffrage encouraged in the working and propertied classes respectively.

The economic problems of the working classes came before the Cabinet in the form of the trade unions. The Trades Union Congress, which first met in 1868, characterized with a new urgency a problem which had been recognized but not solved in the early 1860s: the legal status of unions and their funds. The Gladstone Cabinet offered the first tentative legislative solution to a series of questions which, a century later, remain contentious. It recognized the legal existence of trade unions and secured their

---

* Feinstein's calculations in B. R. Mitchell and P. Deane, *Abstract of British Historical Statistics* (1962), 367; any such estimates have their difficulties, but all indices for 1868–74 show the same trend; e.g. GNP at constant factor cost (1913 = 100) rose from 43.7 in 1870 to 48.9 in 1874; C. H. Feinstein, *National Income Expenditure and Output of the United Kingdom* (1972), table 7.

property by allowing them to register their rules with the Registrar of Friendly Societies, and sought to ameliorate those areas of the criminal law specifically affecting the actions of trade union members. This legislation took the form of two Acts, both passed in 1871, the Trade Union Act and the Criminal Law Amendment Act. This simple statement disguises a complex narrative in 1869, when a bill introduced by Thomas Hughes and A. J. Mundella was withdrawn in the light of government promises of legislation, and prolonged pressure in 1871 when the government's original single bill finally passed as two separate Acts. The Cabinet's principles were 'to prevent violence; and in all economic matters the law to take no part'. The first phrase revealed the Cabinet's intention to allow peaceful collective bargaining, the second its unwillingness to circumscribe the activities of trade unions on the grounds merely of their alleged violation of the canons of orthodox political economy by combining 'in restraint of trade'.* The bills' drafters, however, underestimated the ingenuity of the bench, for the directions to the jury of Mr Justice Brett in the Gas Stokers' Case of December 1872 revealed that the statute had insufficiently protected trade unionists from the operation of the common law of conspiracy,† whilst local Justices of the Peace tended to interpret the provisions of the Criminal Law Amendment Act affecting picketing in a more restrictive manner than its originators had intended. As a result, the hostility of a labour movement, swelled both in numbers and in confidence by the exceptional prosperity of the early 1870s, was directed towards the Gladstone government.

The TUC campaign for amendment of the labour laws led Robert Lowe, the new Home Secretary, to suggest the possibility of some concession and, on the prompting of Bright, Gladstone encouraged Lowe in September 1873 to bring proposals before the Cabinet following 'some rather careful inquiry'. Under Lowe's guidance the Cabinet, with dissensions from Selborne the Lord Chancellor, moved towards fresh legislation which would restore the position in which the Acts of 1871 had sought to place the unions. The Cabinet in November 1873 seems to have agreed to the heads of a bill which would have done much of what Disraeli's Cabinet eventually did in the Conspiracy and Protection of Property and the Employers and Workmen Acts of 1875.

Gladstone did not set out directly to involve himself in trade union questions, and the legislation seems to have been largely departmental in inspiration. His role in September 1873 was as co-ordinator rather than

---

* Clause 2 of the Trade Union Act 1871 attempted to place unions and their members beyond charges of conspiracy; it was intended that the Criminal Law Amendment Act would do this.

† 'It is clear, therefore, that in 1871 the Legislature was passing a statute regulating all the relations between masters and servants; and by those provisions they practically say that there shall be no other offences as between master and servant but the offences detailed in the preceding part of this section'; Mr Straight's argument defending the Gas Stokers, E. W. Cox, *Reports of cases in criminal law* (1875), xii. 331.

initiator. There is a hint that he played some role in getting the Gas Stokers' sentences reduced. He discouraged the use of troops in the particular case of a farmer who persuaded the army to take over the harvesting to enable him to dismiss unionized labour, but in general Gladstone was characteristic of the ambivalence of the propertied classes towards unions: he recognized their existence and their usefulness in producing order and coherence in industrial relations, but he would not give them the tools they thought they needed to do the job. Thus he encouraged 'the employment of the spare time of soldiers in useful civilian occupations', thinking 'there is always a risk, lest the labouring classes should like other classes be led to exaggerate their own rights in such a matter, so deep does the principle of monopoly lie in human nature'.

As a Flintshire land- and coal-owner he became involved in a bitter controversy over the closed shop, discussed in the next chapter. As Prime Minister, he did not encourage a swift restoration of the intentions of his own government's legislation, and he paid for this politically. The extent of Cabinet agreement in November 1873 was insufficiently wide, or Gladstone was insufficiently interested in the question, for the loss of trust on the part of the unions to be reduced. The snap dissolution of January 1874 occurred during considerable union anger with the Liberals; the election manifesto promised much to the middle classes, but nothing specific to the unions—the plans for restorative union legislation being only hinted at. Not surprisingly some unions and unionists worked for the Tories at the general election, or ran their own candidates.

The reaction of urban ratepayers against government—not necessarily only Liberal governments—was a marked feature of these years. The State in normal circumstances raised its revenue by two quite separate means: national taxation, requested in the budget and granted in the Finance Bill, raising in 1868 £67,800,000, and local taxation, assessed and raised locally mainly from the taxation of owners and occupiers of rateable property, raising in 1868 £19,800,000. But the total expenditure of local authorities (the difference being made up by loans, government subventions, and rents and sales of locally owned property) was £30,140,000—nearly half the figure for the national government's income, a total which Goschen described as 'astounding'.

The difficulties involved were various; in the counties the rates were administered by the non-elected Quarter Sessions, in the towns by the corporations elected on the 1835 local franchise; the Tories had argued since the later 1840s that where local administration had to deal with questions which were essentially national, the cost should be borne by the Exchequer and raised by national not local taxation. This was the line of attack which the Tories returned to in 1869 when at the very start of the first Session Sir Massey Lopes called for a royal commission.

Lopes repeated his demands for an amelioration of the rate-payers' burdens at intervals throughout the government, and with considerable success. G. J. Goschen's two bills of 1871 (which offered an ambitious attempt to consolidate and standardize, 'to make all hereditaments, both corporeal and incorporeal' liable to rates, while at the same time surrendering the house tax to the relief of local rates) were withdrawn virtually without discussion; they were condemned as being overfavourable to urban dwellers. In April 1872, having previously forced the ministry to withdraw by the device of moving the previous question, Lopes defeated in 259:159 a conciliatory amendment moved by the Liberal Sir Thomas Acland and carried his own resolution that 'it is expedient to remedy the injustice of imposing Taxation for National objects on one description of property only'. The Cabinet's decision had been to 'oppose Lopez [*sic*] and stand on things already agreed'.

The problem was that the Cabinet could not agree. Gladstone deplored any concession on the part of the Exchequer: 'my judgment is very hostile to taxing the Exchequer for local purposes. Even Sir R. Peel went too far in that direction.' When the Cabinet tried to agree on legislation following Lopes's resolution, he told Goschen: 'I seem but very little to see my way towards doing the thing that the H. of C. wants us to do.' The Cabinet had a 'much prolonged . . . general conversation introduced by W.E.G. on the question of Local Taxation'. Some agreement was reached on a bill to standardize assessment and valuation, consolidate the rates, and abolish exemptions—that is, to set the existing system on a more regularized basis—but in 1873, despite Tory taunts, no local government bill was introduced, Stansfeld, the new president of the Local Government Board, falling back on a select committee on parish boundaries. The solution that Gladstone had proposed to Goschen in 1869, 'to occupy the ground' by 'a measure for County Boards on the elective principle' was then returned to. At Gladstone's suggestion, Stansfeld drew up plans in November 1873 for county boards; the Cabinet's reaction was uncertain, in general favourable to mixed county boards (i.e. made up partly of elected representatives, partly of JPs), but with ominous reservations from Goschen.

Before the Cabinet could meet to discuss a bill, Gladstone had decided on dissolution. In his election address he pointed out that the government 'have been unable to meet the views of those who appear to have thought that, provided only a large amount of public money could be had in any form to relieve the rates, no great heed need be paid to anything else'. But he recognized the 'very general desire that some new assistance should be afforded to the ratepayers of the country from funds at present under the command of the State', and he promised 'a thorough and comprehensive, not a partial, handling of the question . . . relief coupled with reform of local taxation'; there would be 'relief of rates and other property'.

Gladstone was 'rather uncomfortable' about local taxation, and remained so. He loathed the gradual conflation of imperial and local finance implied by grants-in-aid—'doles' as he called them—but this was a conflation hard to avoid and one which was steadily increasing even before his own government's Education Act gave to grants-in-aid what was in the long run to be their greatest fillip.*

In its dealings with economic questions as manifested by trade unions and the local taxation movement, the Gladstone Cabinet cannot be said to have had much success. Both ran as festering sores throughout the Parliament, and neither was healed by the time of its dissolution.

Fiscal Policy: the Budget, the Estimates, and the 'Scandals'

The Cabinet also dealt with the economy more directly, through the Estimates, the budget, and the Finance Bill, all recurring items with an accepted timetable in the Cabinet's year, the Estimates being drawn up in the autumn, the budget in the spring.

Competence in fiscal management was the long, strong suit which the Liberals had played throughout the 1860s, and it was the card Gladstone's defenders could play when he was accused of erratic behaviour in other areas of policy. It was therefore a major blow to the reputation and self-respect of the government when, in 1871, Lowe's budget had to be withdrawn (following powerful opposition to the Estimates and to his proposals for a match tax balanced by change in the succession duties)—the first time this had happened to an established administration since Wood's budget of 1851.

Gladstone had, on the whole, let Lowe have his head. He had sent him a list of measures which he saw as still outstanding from his long chancellorship, but he had not tried to exercise as close a supervision of the preparation of Lowe's budget as his own experience might have warranted, though the two were, naturally, in very frequent correspondence. Lowe was quite an inventive chancellor, though without raising any major threat to the framework of fiscal behaviour which Gladstone had established. Gladstone only saw the 1871 budget shortly before it was due to be presented to the Commons. The match tax might be thought to have offended against orthodox Gladstonianism, in that it broadened the basis of indirect taxation, but Gladstone does not seem to have objected to it on that score; nor does he seem to have seen soon enough the political dangers involved, though he advised Lowe to discuss the point with Glyn, the Chief Whip. His main reservations were on the political difficulties of reforming the death duties, though even here he showed no real alarm.

Gladstone's 'list of remnants' sent to Lowe at the start of the government

---

* Gladstone supported the proposal of Lowe for the change made mid-way through the Education Bill debates, by which the Exchequer grant to denominational schools was increased.

referred mainly to minor adjustments and improvements to his own work as chancellor; no major constructive measures remained, though many of the adjustments were controversial. Gladstone's remnants were: abolition of remaining corn duty, abolition of tea licences, change in probate duty, abolition of conveyance duties save railways, commutation of fire insurance duty, reduction of income tax, reform of malt duty. In his budget of 1869, Lowe dealt with many of these; he abolished the corn duty, repealed the tea duty, abolished the fire insurance duty altogether, against Gladstone's judgement, reduced conveyance duties, and reduced income tax by a penny. Much more of a problem was the question of retrenchment, without whose continuance the whole carefully balanced compromise which Gladstone reached on taxation in the 1850s and 1860s was likely to collapse. Gladstone found Lowe an ineffective ally in his battles with the spending departments.

The government came into office pledged to further retrenchment, and made much in the electoral campaign of Disraeli's profligacy in his financing of the Abyssinian expedition of 1867–8. Gladstone had spent much of the 1860s in conflict with Palmerston on the question of retrenchment, and especially on the War Office and Admiralty expenditure, which accounted for about a third of government expenditure. Now Prime Minister, with control of appointments, he should have been in a good position to achieve his ends. After the débâcle of Lowe's budget in 1871, and as it became clear that in legislative terms it was going to be very hard to follow the success of the 1869 and 1870 Sessions, he began to look to finance as the unifying element of the domestic programme, as it had been in the 1860s under his own chancellorship. The routine item of the Estimates was seen as central, 'bearing upon the position of the country, the party and the Government'. Gladstone told Cardwell in 1871:

They will be the *key* to our position at the outset of the session. We may announce Bills, but nobody will believe in them (unreasonable as the unbelief will be), except the Ballot; and that is discounted. On the Estimates will depend our chance of a fair start.

Expenditure on defence fell dramatically through retrenchment and reorganization in both army and navy in April 1869 and April 1870, but army expansion following the Franco-Prussian war spoilt the graph, and the abolition of purchase was also expensive, varying from year to year, but around £800,000 per annum. Gladstone hoped to get the figure back as nearly as possible to that of the pre-war Estimates, but, despite considerable savings by Cardwell by the end of 1872, the situation was gloomy: 'we have upon the last Estimates taken back all but some 300,000 of the £2,200,000 saving or thereabouts which in Feb. 71 we had made upon the Estimates of our predecessors'. This was particularly reprehensible in view of the fact that for Gladstone the defeat of France in 1870 had had one great advantage—the disabling by land and sea of 'the only country in Europe that has the power of being formidable to us'.*

Gladstone's view of France had been that she was a potential danger that could be slowly neutralized by commercial ties: her neutralization had now been more decisively achieved by Bismarck. In this sense, the result of the war of 1870 had been a bonus for Britain. The consequence thus ought to be, according to the maxim that 'policy determines expenditure', that naval and military retrenchment should be the easier. But this was not the view of the War Office or the Admiralty, where forces for expansion operated almost independently of the cabinet ministers responsible for those departments, forces to which historians have as yet paid slight attention. 'Policy determines expenditure' seemed to mean to those departments that policy demanded greater expenditure.

The problem of the Estimates was compounded by inflation, which reached its peak at the end of 1873, and was recognized particularly to affect the Navy. But inflation, and the marked rise in national wealth, also benefited the Exchequer: the yield from indirect and direct taxes markedly increased, and splendid surpluses occurred in 1872 and 1873. The opportunity for spectacular budgets was thus created.

In 1873 the major weakening of the government from its resignation and then resumption of office in March was emphasized by further blows to its fiscal record, when irregularities in the use of the Post Office Savings Bank's funds and in the contract for the telegraph to southern Africa were revealed.

The 'scandals' (as Gladstone called them) of the summer of 1873 highlighted a general failing of the administration explicable in part perhaps by Gladstone's absorption in legislation and the legislative process. The falling away of the popularity of the government was in part the result of a dislike for its tone. For all its administrative achievements, especially in the defence departments, it had become associated with departmental mismanagement and even, in the summer of 1873, with a want of probity.

Keen as he was on administrative efficiency in his own department, when he had one, Gladstone rather assumed efficiency in others, and had poor intelligence for gaining early knowledge of when things were going astray. His absence of interest in gossip, written or spoken, and in the small change of politics, perhaps intimidated colleagues and subordinates from keeping him in touch with those small details which signal danger to the acute political eye.† Small incidents that go wrong tend to be as much

---

* This contrasted markedly with Disraeli's conclusion: 'The balance of power has been entirely destroyed, and the country which suffers most, and feels the effect of this great change most, is England.'

† Gladstone's reliance on Granville meant that he was well up on potential crises in foreign policy, but much less so for domestic matters.

remembered as great legislative achievements that go right. An Opposition leader as witty as Disraeli was well placed to exploit this weakness; he waited for the legislative achievements of 1869–71 to run their course and then moved into the attack in 1872, capitalized upon the unpopularity of aspects of the legislation, set the tone for subsequent Toryism by pillorying the patriotism of the government, and, in the government's embarrassment at the 'scandals', reaped the reward for abstaining from accepting office.

By July 1873 Gladstone found himself the leader of a demoralized government which was almost at the point of breakdown. Only the end of the Session offered some respite. In attempting to come to terms with the situation, Gladstone implied that, individual failings and muddle apart, Lowe's suzerainty of the Treasury was too weak: the implication was that he had failed to see that the Permanent Secretary and the Financial Secretary knew the whole business of their department, and it was, of course, the duty of the Treasury to oversee all such financial details throughout the administration. The canons of Victorian public life put the responsibility for 'the scandals' on the head of the department; however much his subordinates had let him down, Lowe was the man responsible for the fiscal probity of the nation. 'Cardwell broke to Lowe the necessity of his changing his office' and he had, in effect, to resign as chancellor, being shifted to the Home Office. After a day off at Chislehurst, and 'a very anxious day of constant conversation and reflection', Gladstone wrote to the Queen on 5 August to submit details of the reshuffle, as a result of which he became Chancellor of the Exchequer: 'he submits this recommendation with extreme reluctance, and greatly in deference to the wish of his most experienced colleagues'.

Chancellor Again: the downfall of the Government and resignation as party leader

Thus it was that on 9 August 1873 Gladstone 'received a third time the Seals of my old office', and became Chancellor of the Exchequer as well as First Lord of the Treasury. He did so with his government in rare and sustained disarray, and by doing so he opened a Pandora's box of constitutional precedents, as to whether he would have to stand at the by-election obligatory to those taking an office of profit under the Crown. He may have accepted the chancellorship with 'extreme reluctance' but he immediately plunged into its work with enthusiasm and apparent forethought. Two days—a Sunday intervening—after taking the seals, he revealed a daring and dramatic plan, and then left for Hawarden:

Saw . . . Mr Cardwell: to whom at the W.O. I told in deep secrecy my ideas of the *possible* finance of next year: based upon abolition of Income Tax & Sugar Duties with partial compensation from Spirits and Death Duties. This *only* might give a chance.

The last sentence of this passage revealed the political motivation which was a central element of the plan—a bold attempt to regain the initiative within his own party and in the country generally. Coupled with the plan outlined to Cardwell, though apparently not mentioned to him, was a substantial relief of local taxation—in the order of £800,000 per annum. This was to be done not through further grants-in-aid, which he so much disliked, but by relieving localities in proportion as they paid national taxes such as the house tax and licensing fees. Gladstone had always looked to the house tax as preferable to the income tax, but in a budget which set out to relieve local taxation, which was largely raised on property, the house tax could hardly be expected to bear all the burden. Gladstone therefore turned also to the death duties in the form of the legacy and succession duties, though these would have constituted something of a 'tit-for-tat' for the local taxation reforms.

The abolition of the income tax was not, of course, a new idea. Gladstone had always disliked the tax as such and when considered purely on its own terms and not in comparison to other taxes. He disliked it first because of the inequities inherent in it; second, because in the 1860s he had come to see it as encouraging rather than discouraging expenditure because of the ease with which it brought in revenue. In the mid-1860s, looking for ways of encouraging retrenchment, he had considered income-tax abolition before deciding that the enfranchisement of artisans would strengthen the retrenching arm of the Commons.

Abolition rather than reduction of the income tax had not been one of the 'remnants' he had left to Lowe, but in the spring of 1873, that is, well before he had resumed the chancellorship, he returned to the subject, when Childers raised it with reference to Lowe's budget preparations: 'The idea of abolishing Income Tax is to me highly attractive, both on other grounds & because it tends to public economy. . . .'

The problem, as it had always been since the 1840s for the Peelites, was that the income tax could not be treated in isolation, or considered on its own terms only. It was, as we have seen, a central feature of the great compromise between direct and indirect taxation which was the distinguished, and in contemporary European terms, distinguishing achievement of mid-nineteenth-century Britain. Before the 1867 Reform Act Gladstone had seen direct taxation as falling upon those with the vote, indirect upon those without it: the direct tax payers had thus been the 'virtual representatives' of the indirect. After 1867 this was changed: the indirect taxpayers, or some proportion of them, now had the vote—the days of virtual representation in the British political system were thought to be ending, save for women and, as yet, farm labourers. 1867 was widely expected to inaugurate a bid for booty from the working classes, but what in fact it marked was a relaxation of the need for responsibility on the part of the propertied classes.

Before 1867, direct taxation had been an act of self-sacrifice on the part of the propertied classes, for they alone paid it and they alone elected the representatives to the Parliament which imposed it. After 1867, however, direct taxation, unless altered, was thought to be the servant of the extended franchise. This alarmed Gladstone just as it alarmed Lord Salisbury, though for different reasons. Gladstone always feared the ease with which the income tax, in particular, raised revenue and consequently encouraged expenditure; Salisbury feared it as a weapon of class vengeance. Abolition of the tax in the new circumstances thus took on a new urgency for Gladstone as a means of maintaining the minimalist State. On the other hand, he retained, as it behoved him as leader of the Liberal party to retain, a strong concern for balance in the incidence of national taxation: income tax might go, but not at the expense of a shifting of the burden on to the non-propertied classes who, despite 1867, could hardly be said to be exerting significant pressure upon the structure of British politics in the 1870s. 'You cannot provide for the means for abolishing Income Tax, either in whole or in part, out of new indirect taxation', he told Childers, and he wanted 'to go a little beyond this & say that when the Inc. Tax is abolished *some part* of the means must be got out of some new impost touching property'. Thus the plan included the reform of and an increase in the death duties, although this was not mentioned in Gladstone's election address.* Death duties might, in Salisbury's terms, wreak great havoc, but they were difficult to use to produce great revenues quickly.

The 1874 budget was intended to ensure retrenchment without upsetting class relationships. But its presentation in Gladstone's election address of January 1874 looked like a bid for the middle-class vote. In the short or even medium term this can be seen as a shrewd enough move, for the battle in British politics in the 1870s and 1880s was a contest for the support of the middle class.

The budget plan was therefore a bold and comprehensive scheme. The 1853 and 1860 budgets had launched great governments; the 1874 plan was intended to end one by crowning it in fiscal triumph. But despite the balancing element of alternative sources of direct taxation, and of some concessions towards the 'Free Breakfast Table' being demanded by the Free Trade League, the 1874 budget plans put their main emphasis on the relief of taxation in the two areas of principal concern to the propertied classes, income tax and local rates: the budget would therefore have lacked the wide social vision which had distinguished the great budgets of 1853 and 1860. In those years, interlocking plans of vast complexity had been presented to the nation as major contributions to the solution of the mid-Victorian problems of political and social integration and order. The 1874

---

* The address reserved the position by mentioning 'judicious adjustments to existing taxes', *The Times*, 24 January 1874, 8.

budget would have been narrower in conception and probably highly divisive within the Liberal party in the country. Moreover, the abolition of income tax would have placed so inelastic a corset around government spending that it would certainly have quickly snapped. Either the income tax would have been swiftly restored, or the Liberal party would have found itself defending a fiscal system in which indirect taxation was given an ever-increasing role, and this would have brought to a much earlier burial its attempt at the creation of a non-class-based popular party.

That those developments were anticipated and that the abolition would have been politically controversial within the party is shown by the reaction of both the Radical *Bee Hive* and Bagehot's *Economist* to Gladstone's election address of January 1874 which outlined his budgetary intentions. The *Bee Hive* argued that the proposal was socially unjust, the *Economist* that it was socially dangerous. James Aytoun in the *Bee Hive* stated that 'To this, as the old consistent advocate of the rights of the working classes we are altogether opposed',* and Bagehot, always a moderate direct taxer, argued in the *Economist* that an intense effort ought to be made by 'the best persons of all parties to retain it', for, in addition to the income tax's valuable elasticity, 'there is . . . much more than mere money in this tax. We want in our taxation not only real equality but apparent equality. . . .'† That tribune of provincial Radicalism, the people's Joseph, retrospectively drove the point home with characteristic, uncompromising hyperbole: Gladstone's proposals in his election address constituted 'the meanest public document that has ever, in like circumstances, proceeded from a statesman of the first rank. His manifesto was simply an appeal to the selfishness of the middle classes.'‡

Reaction on the Tory side tended to express alarm that post-1867 British politics was indeed becoming an auction in which the two parties bid for the prize of democratic support. Lord Carnarvon, an extreme case in the sense that he had resigned with Salisbury in protest at the Derby–Disraeli Reform Bill, but none the less rather typical of High Tory reaction, noted in his diary:

All Engd runs in a state of excitement. In a few days the election will begin. I do not like either Gladstone's or Disraeli's addresses. G. offers a bribe of £5,000,000 in the shape of the remission of taxn & D at once caps it. It is what we said at the passing of the last Reform bill that the constitution wd be put up to auction on each genl election.

But for Gladstone, the plan was the best that could be offered to answer the political problem which had been so clearly defined at the time of the

* *Bee Hive*, 31 January 1874. E. S. Beesly in the same issue argued: 'Mr Gladstone has sacrificed the lower classes, who worshipped him, to the richer classes, who disliked him', but concluded that 'on his past record . . . I do not expect that we shall find him proposing any financial scheme which, as a whole, will amount to relieving the rich at the expense of the poor'.

† *The Economist*, 31 January 1874.

‡ J. Chamberlain, *Fortnightly Review*, xxii. 412 (October 1874).

defeat in March 1873 on the Irish University Bill: 'There is now no *cause*. No great public object on wh. the Liberal party are agreed & combined.' His difficulty was that, despite a surplus of about £5 million, and about £2 million anticipated from 'new sources of revenue', in order to abolish the income tax, relieve local taxation, and make remissions on the sugar duties, he still needed about £600,000 more. He wanted the sum to come from retrenchment in the army and navy estimates, especially the latter. Details of the budget proposals were linked with a general statement on 'the pledges of [18]68', and 'the principles of economy'. But Cardwell and Goschen, the two ministers concerned, could not find the economies. Warning shots were fired in the correspondences of the Recess, inter-mingled with tart exchanges about the purposes and expenses of the Gold Coast expedition. But Gladstone, rightly believing that the long inflation which had lasted since the early 1850s was ended and that prices and there-fore government costs were now falling, saw no immediate reason to bring the issue to a decision, and he suggested that the question of the Estimates be put off until his return to London early in January. He does not seem to have revealed to Cardwell or Goschen the extent of his demand for further retrenchment in the Estimates.

The legislative programme for the Session of 1874 was agreed upon, as was the custom, at the Cabinets before Christmas in 1873. The Cabinet decided '*Not* to take Co. Suffrage, *not* to take Land Laws'. The county franchise, on which Ripon had resigned though without public fuss in the midst of 'the scandals' in July, and to which Gladstone had given, via Forster, general personal approval, was too divisive a topic for the Cabinet to tackle: it threatened a rapid return to the fissures of 1866. Local taxation relief was necessary, but not an adequate basis for party rehabilitation: 'the Tories are completely beforehand with us, secondly they will outbid us if we enter into a competition'.

In Gladstone's view, this left only 'Finance', i.e. the budget, as a focal point round which the party could rally. The November Cabinets thus confirmed the view that Gladstone had held since 'the scandals' of the summer: only the budget could restore the party to something like a coherent and companionable body. He spelt out his arguments in a gloomy letter to Granville on 8 January 1874: he considered the subject of dissolu-tion at this time, in the context of the general weakness of the party and the government, but concluded: 'Dissolution means either immediate death, or at the best Death a little postponed, and the party either way shattered for the time.'

On 16 January 1874 Gladstone returned to London. Cardwell had been sent a copy of the letter to Granville, and the extent of its demands for reduction of the defence estimates had taken him by surprise: 'I have not received from Gladstone any intimation that he considers a further reduction of establishment possible or proper: & I do not see the way of effecting it', he told Granville, with a clear hint of possible resignation. After a conference with Granville and Wolverton, Gladstone found 'the prospects of agreement with the two Depts on Estimates are for the present bad'. Next day, a Sunday, Gladstone returned to thoughts of dissolution:

This day I thought of dissolution. Told Bright of it. In evening at dinner told Granville and Wolverton. All seemed to approve. My first thought of it was as escape from a difficulty. I soon saw on reflection that it was the best thing in itself.

The 'escape from a difficulty' probably meant the Estimates; Gladstone listed the first reason for a dissolution as being 'we gain time, & avoid for the moment a ministerial crisis'; the only other subject for a crisis at that time was the county franchise, on which Gladstone reaffirmed his general and personal support to a deputation on 21 January, but it would have taken some time for a ministerial crisis to have developed on that subject, as the Cabinet had already agreed not to introduce a bill. The large amount of reduction in defence estimates that Gladstone wanted—between £1 million and £600,000—would need much more than marginal adjustments and was bound to produce a major row. Gladstone tried to get Goschen and Cardwell to sign a paper to agree to keep the Estimates question open. The dispute could not be mentioned during the election campaign; but if the government were returned to office Gladstone could bring further pressures of retrenchment and the pledge to abolish income tax to bear upon the Admiralty and the War Office to return to something like the expenditure levels of February 1870. Further, if a dissolution was to be had within the next three months, it was necessary, because of the constraints of the parliamentary timetable for financial questions, that it be done immediately.

The dissolution was therefore essentially a dissolution against the defence departments. Even combining the offices of First Lord and Chancellor of the Exchequer had not allowed Gladstone to prevail against them. First, their expedition to West Africa was on a scale which Gladstone believed was excessive, second, they were behaving, and seemed likely to behave successfully, as if Palmerston had never died. Only an election victory on the general principles of retrenchment, and the specific pledges to remove the most elastic variable of the government's revenue, the income tax, and to make remissions of local taxation by central government help, would suffice to crush them.

The disastrous election bore out Gladstone's earlier forecast of the party 'shattered for the time' rather than the tentative optimism of his notes for the Cabinet: 'I think our victory is as likely in an immediate as in a postponed Dissolution. While we run fewer chances of a crushing defeat.' The long run of by-election losses in 1873 proved no false guide: the 1874 general election ended the pattern of British elections since 1847, that whoever it was that made up the majority in the Commons, it was not the Tories.

Thus ended Gladstone's first administration; he resigned on 17 February 1874 without meeting Parliament. On 19 February he drafted a letter to the chief whip stating 'it is not my intention to assume the functions of leader of a Parliamentary Opposition in the House of Commons to the new Government'. This letter, clearly intended for publication had it been sent, disclaimed difficulties with the party as a reason, but Gladstone's personal views became clearer in a series of notes made in March: the electorate had rejected his view about retrenchment, a significant section of the party differed irreconcilably from him on education; the 'failure of 1866–8' boded ill for his future shadow leadership, especially given the tendency of back-benchers 'of making a career by & upon constant active opposition to the bulk of the party' even when the party was in office. But the first reason was personal: to accept leadership meant to accept the future presumption of office as well, i.e. a Tory Parliament followed by a Liberal Parliament, the two of which could amount to fourteen years: 'this is not consistent with my views for the close of my life'. Pressed by alarmed colleagues, he accepted a compromise, that he should remain as nominal but inactive leader in the Commons, the position to be reconsidered before the start of the Session of 1875.

Gladstone had spent much of his administration in conflict with his colleagues and with groups in his party both 'left' and 'right', but when it came to the point, they could not let him go. The Liberal party aspired to classlessness, but it was riddled with class; it hoped for interdenominationalism but it divided between Erastianism, sectarianism, and secularism; it tried to offer justice to the three kingdoms but it satisfied none. Gladstone stood outside the Cabinet and the party; his class was indefinable, his religion exceptional; he was an extreme Radical on some questions, an unreconstructed Conservative on others; he was at the same time a chief architect of the mid-nineteenth-century settlement and seen as one of the chief threats to its continuation. Disraeli was self-evidently exotic, but viewed from the perspective of any one of the groups that constituted the Liberal party, so was Gladstone.

In the decades after the start of household suffrage, British political parties slowly, surprisingly slowly, and in the case of the Liberals only in part, took on those attributes characteristic of a modern party: bureaucracy and caution. But during the transitional phase, exceptional demands were made of their leaders and especially of the leader of the Liberal party as it struggled to preserve its identity caught between the certainty of a property-based Conservative party and the uncertainty of developments 'to the left'. The position resulting from the defeat of 1874 was, of course, only the start of a long-drawn-out and ultimately unsuccessful attempt by the Liberals to meet the problem of 'the squeeze', but one thing was already clear: no available Whig could successfully appeal over the horizon of his own constituency to the disparate groups beyond. Much as they were coming to fear Gladstone, the Whigs feared isolation more.

Constituencies, Public Speaking, and the Press in the early 1870s

The abrupt dissolution in January 1874 caught the party as well as the country by surprise. Since the abortive resignation of March 1873, dissolution had been, in general terms, a probability, but the speed with which events moved in January and February 1874 was unusual; there had not been a dissolution in the Recess without prior announcement since that of 1780. It found Gladstone in considerable embarrassment with respect to his own seat. His election address was written for 'an unnamed constituency', and the decision to stand again for one of the two Greenwich seats was taken at the last moment. The doubts were justified when he came second to 'Boord the distiller . . . more like a defeat than a victory, though it places me in Parliament again'.

Gladstone's relationship with Greenwich had been neither intimate nor amiable. The constituency was a kaleidoscope of advanced Liberals, Republicans, and naval dockyard workers, many of whom were Tories. Retrenchment by both Tory and Liberal governments had borne heavily on the dockyards, but Gladstone had dealt with the various delegations which waited upon him with homilies on the national need for reduction of government establishments. None of the interest in the unemployed which he had shown in Lancashire in the 1860s was bestowed on the dockyard workers who had lost their jobs. Gladstone's contact with the constituency had been mainly through his colleague as MP, Alderman Salomons, but Salomons had died in 1873, and the Tories captured his seat at the by-election.

Despite the weakness of the local Liberal organization and its obvious need for leadership, Gladstone went to very considerable lengths to avoid speaking in the constituency. 'You cannot treat Birmingham as I am able to treat Greenwich, & you are I believe to address your constituents shortly', observed Gladstone to Bright at the end of 1869. 'No-one had had so little to do with my now being member for Greenwich as I have myself' he told the chief whip, but he did little to remedy this situation.

He spoke, after prolonged stalling, at the great meeting at Blackheath in October 1871,* but even then chiefly because speeches in his son's marginal constituency of Whitby, and in receiving the Freedom of Aberdeen, meant that Greenwich could no longer be ignored. He did not speak there again until the general election, and considered in the meantime other

* For such meetings, see the illustration in this volume.

possibilities for a seat, especially his old constituency of Newark, which he had held between 1832 and 1845.* The rapid dissolution in January 1874 thus found Gladstone almost as much a stranger to his constituents as when he first met them; it allowed no time for a change of seat, and little time for campaigning—only three election speeches were made.

The prototype of a new style of popular executive politician which Gladstone had so carefully developed in the 1860s was thus to some considerable extent set aside. There were no great set-piece addresses other than the few mentioned above. Appearances at the annual Lord Mayor's banquet were resented and resisted when possible. A half-hearted attempt to rally popular support behind the Irish University Bill was made in March 1873, the odd gathering at railway stations or outside the gates of great houses received a few words, but of 'The People's William' there was little sign.

Of course, there were some good reasons for this. After 1870, any speech was likely to be either evasive or divisive, and Gladstone speechifying would license his opponents within the Cabinet to do likewise—the contents of the Blackheath speech were a matter for Cabinet discussion: 'WEG invited contributions, or cautions.' Even so, Gladstone forfeited one of his major assets, and allowed the shades of the Cabinet and the party in the Commons to crowd closely around him; it was strange to see an England with Disraeli as the leading demagogue.

Gladstone's strategy of wooing the votes of the propertied classes— exemplified especially in the relief of local taxation proposals—showed the acuteness of his perception of the real implications of the household suffrage, and it may be that this encouraged him to avoid giving hostages to the Tory press in the form of speeches to great crowds. But the nature of much of the rank-and-file following of the Liberal party was such that deference was no longer enough. Commenting on Gladstone's speech at Whitby attacking the bias of the metropolitan press, Lord Houghton told Gladstone shrewdly: 'there is a Demon not of Demogogism but of Demophilism, that is tempting [you]'. It may be that there was, but Demos personally saw little of it during this government, and was offended.

Gladstone's appearance in the 1860s as a new kind of executive politician had been, as we have seen, buttressed by his shrewd use of the press, and especially of the Liberal *Daily Telegraph*. He retained his press contacts, but used them much less frequently and more formally. His contacts were mainly with editors, whereas previously they had been mainly with reporters. Thornton Hunt, the *Telegraph* reporter whom he had seen sometimes almost daily when at the Exchequer and during the Reform Bill

* He also declined an invitation to stand at a by-election in Kincardineshire, a safe Liberal seat, primarily for 'the family reason'—i.e. his brother Tom's Toryism, Fasque, the family home, being in the constituency; to have resigned his Greenwich seat in mid-Parliament would have been an extraordinary manœuvre. There were various other offers, including Chester.

debates, barely appears in the journal after December 1868; he died in 1873. Contacts with Levy, the owner and editor of the *Telegraph*, were irregular and seem to have been limited to announcements for formal developments, such as the order of government business, the dates of state visits, and the like. Gladstone showed himself willing to use his *Telegraph* contacts to get a 'special' reporter sent to investigate a scandal in Shetland, but he does not seem to have used the *Telegraph*, as he had in 1866, to ventilate his views on Irish policy.

The Times replaced the *Daily Telegraph* as the focus of Gladstone's attentions. Delane, its editor, was kept in touch with the developments of the Irish Church Bill, and to some extent with the preparation of the Irish Land Bill. He was summoned for consultations during the crisis with the Lords in July 1869. When the 1871 Session ran into difficulties, with ballot and army bills being dismembered in the Lords after long struggles in the Commons—both reforms which when passed seemed to general consent both necessary and just—Gladstone singled out the metropolitan press for particular blame in his speech at Whitby in September 1871:

A considerable section of the Metropolitan Press had discussed with greater severity the proceedings of Parliament during the last Session than had been the case with the Provincial Press. He was bound to say that he could find reason for that difference in this fact,—the present Government had not hesitated when it thought the public interest required it to make proposals which had been highly offensive to powerful classes in this country (cheers) . . . the effect of that bias was most felt where wealth was concentrated, as in the metropolis, and where . . . the opinions of the Clubs, rather than the opinion of this great nation, were reflected in a considerable portion of the Metropolitan Press.

In this speech Gladstone indicated the extent to which Liberalism was ceasing, despite its majority in the Commons and its hold over certain sections of the civil service, to be the party of 'the establishment'. Whereas in the 1850s the Tories had found themselves bereft of metropolitan newspaper support, the Liberals in the 1870s found the balance shifting in the other direction. These developments caused the Liberals considerable anxiety. Gladstone suggested to Glyn, the chief whip, that Liberal weakness among the London evening papers might be countered by *The Echo* having a second edition which would serve as an evening edition, but he does not seem to have taken a sustained interest in regaining the initiative for the Liberals. His outburst at Whitby initiated a tradition of complaint within Radical circles which was to prove enduring; that he did little behind the scenes to find a remedy was to be equally characteristic of the Radical leadership.

This indifference may in part have been because the most popular and the most influential of the London papers, the *Daily Telegraph* and *The Times* respectively, remained loyal to Gladstone, if not to the Liberal party.

Both papers supported the return of the government, and especially of Gladstone, at the election of 1874. The *Telegraph* did so in its capacity as still almost a party paper, though already with qualifications; *The Times* with some reservation after an initially very favourable reaction to the financial proposals ('the coloured lights on the stage soon fade'), but none the less quite emphatically:

... there are good chances for a Government which has given proofs of energy and capacity, and has a magnificent programme ready for the Session. After all, no one can do Mr Gladstone's work as well as Mr Gladstone and it is Mr Gladstone's work which the Conservative Party has now proffered itself to do [by agreeing to income tax abolition]. ... On the last occasion the watchword was Gladstone and the disestablishment of the Irish Church; now it is Gladstone alone.

Both papers were soon to be lost not only to the Liberal party but to Gladstone also.

Gladstone did pay attention to publications designed to win the argument at the highest level. His own article on the Franco-Prussian war has been discussed above. In 1872 he encouraged, without success, Cardwell to publish 'in a Pamphlet a full but *popular* account of our army system as it now is ... it would help to stereotype a state of opinion you have well earned'. More successfully, he told Goschen 'I should like to see the whole substance of your Report ... put out in the best form, as a great document upon the subject.' This resulted in Goschen's *Local Taxation* (1872), a work which exemplified the rationalistic approach to public opinion pursued by the Liberals.

Gladstone's first government petered out, never recovering from the abortive resignation of March 1873. In this it followed the Liberal stereotype: every Liberal government between 1830 and 1895 ended by the disintegration of its own support in the Commons; only the Asquith Cabinet bucked the trend. The Liberal Party's strength was its ability to regroup on a basis of compromise and reconciliation during the intervening period of Tory rule. Gladstone felt, as the quotation of March 1874 at the head of this chapter shows, that he had little to offer to that process.

CHAPTER IX

A Prime Minister's Private Life

The Daily Round: fitness, correspondence, the Commons, weekends, and reading—Laura Thistlethwayte: 'duty and evil temptation', 'like a story from the Arabian Nights'—Family Affairs in the Early 1870s—A Public Man and his Money—Religion in Retirement: 'Vaticanism' the end of a career?

Finished my additions to the Article for the Q.R. and the correction of the proof. Read . . . Middlemarch.

On this my 65th birthday I find myself in lieu of the mental repose I had hoped engaged in a controversy, which cannot be mild, & which presses upon both mind & body. But I do not regret anything except my insufficiency: and my unworthiness in this & in all things: yet I would wish that the rest of my life were as worthy as my public life, in its nature & intent, to be made an offering to the Lord Most High.

The Daily Round: fitness, correspondence, the Commons, weekends, and reading

Few politicians in peacetime can have been more fully stretched than Gladstone in his first ministry. The description of the previous two chapters has tried to indicate the main areas of government activity in which he involved himself. Any reader of this survey could not but be puzzled by Lord Houghton's view, that Gladstone had a 'one idea at a time faculty', a view which has had an eminent following since. It may be that Gladstone sometimes presented himself as having one idea at a time, and it is certainly the case that a departmental minister, trying to cope with a line of policy in which the Prime Minister was interesting himself, must have felt that he was Gladstone's sole object of attention. But the first ministry shows Gladstone at the height of political awareness, sensitive to the implications of every phrase in every letter on a vast range of topics. Certainly he was more interested in some topics than in others, and he was completely identified with three of the government's main bills. But even his speeches in the House show the extent of his mastery of the work of the ministry as a whole—indeed he increasingly found himself not merely conducting the orchestra from the piano, but playing most of the other instruments as well.

In a man prone to tension, it is not surprising that this experience was wearing. In January 1874 he had been in office continually since 1859, with the exception of July 1866 to December 1868. The administration was punctuated by Gladstone's illnesses, many of them occurring at moments of crisis. 'Tightness in the chest', fever and diarrhoea removed him from direct political leadership during the crisis over the Irish Church negotiations in 1869, the 'scandals' crisis in July 1873, and the negotiations about the Estimates and dissolution in January 1874. His physician, Andrew Clark, played an important though not quite clearly definable role in the attempted resignation of March 1873. Gladstone also suffered at less politically sensitive moments.

These bouts of illness do not seem, however, to have had any lasting effect. He recovered from them with persistent resilience. His handling of the correspondence of both Chancellor and First Lord in the months at the end of the government certainly does not suggest that he was exhausted either physically or mentally. His walk of thirty-three miles in the rain across the Grampians from Balmoral through Glen Feshie to Drumguish and Kingussie does not suggest a body enfeebled by illness—indeed it recalled his habit as an undergraduate of walking from Oxford to Leamington Spa at the start of the University Vacation. Reviewing himself on his sixty-fourth birthday, Gladstone found it was inward 'strain and tossing of the spirit' which troubled him—outwardly 'a weaker heart, stiffened muscles, thin hairs: other strength still remains in my frame'.

Resilience was one of Gladstone's most notable features as an executive politician. A minor example, though a telling one, was his regular evening entry in the journal. The entries for the first administration are slightly longer than for the earlier years of the 1860s. There may be some link here with Gladstone's decision no longer to write 'political memoranda' recording the course of important events, save for royal interviews and the occasional crisis. Certainly, the recording of the day's activities, however briefly, was important to him: when he left the little volume behind at Hawarden during a visit to Spencer at Althorp, he immediately asked for it to be forwarded, keeping up with the entries on writing-paper and sticking it into the volume once regained.

The journal was preserved partly to record a schedule which was, at the least, exacting. Compared to some Presidents and Prime Ministers in the second half of the twentieth century, Gladstone's level of activity, especially if the Recess is included, was not especially severe. But it must be remembered that a Prime Minister before the First World War prepared all his speeches and answers to questions himself, conducted much of his correspondence personally, and had, comparatively, very little in the way of supporting staff. It was for Gladstone himself to check that Cabinet decisions were carried out, and to complain when returns and tables were not produced as requested.

On top of this was the priority given to the affairs of the House of

Commons. As Prime Minister, Gladstone regularly sat on the Treasury bench in the Commons for seven hours a day, and attendances of over nine hours occur quite frequently. Hours of attendance in the Commons, together with church services, are always recorded in the diary. Gladstone usually began sitting in the Commons about 2.15 p.m. and often sat, with an hour off for dinner, until after midnight. He did not find these long sittings particularly stressful, for, commenting on a rare bout of insomnia prompted by an evening of unsuccessful attempts to persuade John Bright to rejoin the Cabinet, he noted: 'My brain assumes in the evening a feminine susceptibility, and resents any unusual strain: tho' strange to say, it will stand a debate in the House of Commons.' The morning and, sometimes in the Recess, part of the afternoon also, was given over to correspondence, for Gladstone's inclination was always to proceed by written argument, whether his colleague was out of London or on his doorstep. The development of policy by social intercourse was not Gladstone's method: in the whole of his first premiership he does not record entering a political club.*

This personal isolation should not of course be exaggerated. Gladstone saw a very great deal of his colleagues. Political dinners were regularly held at his house in Carlton House Terrace. During the Session, he rarely dined at home. If not entertaining, he dined out, sometimes with members of his government and party, sometimes with old Tractarian friends like Sir Walter James and Sir Robert Phillimore, quite frequently with one of his secretaries (often Algernon West), and quite frequently also with Mrs Thistlethwayte. Gladstone is almost always careful to note in the journal whom his host or hostess was for the dinner, which in the Session was usually an hour long at most. He very rarely notes a political discussion at these dinners. Compared with the Palmerstonian years, Glastone used the country house weekend sparingly, usually visiting aristocratic relatives, such as the Cavendishes at Chislehurst, rather than touring the great Whig houses. Next to Chislehurst and Granville's refuge at Walmer Castle, Lord Salisbury's Hatfield was, surprisingly, his most frequent weekend visiting place.

Gladstone's outpouring of correspondence was huge and his writing methods merit description. When the post was opened, certain letters were set aside to be answered by the private secretaries. These were usually letters about deputations, invitations to speak, begging letters, and the like. Gladstone personally answered the important letters, often at great length. Copies of these letters, save those on family affairs, or to Mrs Thistlethwayte, were then made by the private secretaries. Gladstone indicated on the holograph how the letter was to be recorded—one tick in the bottom left-hand corner meant that it was to be copied into the letter-book, two

* He joined the Reform under strong pressure from Glyn, the chief whip, and resigned in 1874.

ticks that it was to be copied on to a separate sheet of paper and filed separately. This recording process operated, unfortunately, only while Gladstone was in office: systematic recording in the letter-book ceased at the end of February 1874 and on 5 March 1874 Gladstone noted 'tomorrow I encounter my own correspondence single-handed'. While out of office, he had no secretary, though copies of letters were sometimes made for him by his wife or children.

Gladstone thus ran an embryonic 'cabinet office', probably more formally organized and certainly more fully recorded than that of his predecessors. This went some way to compensating for the absence of a Prime Minister's department, but the want of any permanent staff meant that there was no necessary continuity of this practice when a change of office occurred. The records of his premiership are much more systematic than those of any of his predecessors, and the care and attention to recording and filing by both the secretaries and Gladstone himself reflect not only his awareness of the importance of records for the smooth running of business, but also his awareness of his own role as an historical phenomenon. The Peelites were unusually conscious of the use to which private papers might be put—viz. the rapid and unusual printing in 1856 by Cardwell and Stanhope of Peel's memoranda of 1845–6, and of the private printing of Lord Aberdeen's papers by his son, Gladstone's erstwhile secretary, Arthur Gordon, to which endeavour Gladstone as Prime Minister gave very considerable attention. Gladstone's awareness of his own historical role, and the part that his letters were to play in it, was heightened by the death of his close friend of the 1830s and 1840s, James Hope (-Scott) in 1873. A lengthy appraisal of Hope-Scott and a sorting of Gladstone's collected papers followed. Gladstone had reached that stage in his life when his archives were becoming one of the chief sources for British political and religious life from the 1830s onwards. He was soon to reach that strange position—starting perhaps with the biography of Samuel Wilberforce (1879)—of seeing himself as a chief actor in the published biographies of the day, and watching the intimate personal and religious crises of his youth replayed before his own and the public's gaze.

Correspondence was, then, together with sitting in the Commons during the Session, the main business of his day; it was the lifeblood of his ministry and the process by which the Cabinet maintained its identity and the Prime Minister his suzerainty. This was particularly the case given Gladstone's quite frequent absences from London, especially in autumn and winter. In 1872, for example, he was away from London between 5 August and 10 October, and between 16 October and 14 November, as well as for many other short absences. These spells of absence were rarely used for directly political purposes. Attendance at Balmoral was unavoidable, but Gladstone did not otherwise devote much time to political week-ending. As already mentioned, most of his weekends away were spent with Lord Frederick Cavendish and his wife (Catherine Gladstone's niece) at Chislehurst, without a house party. Weekends away were, in fact, for relaxation.

There were of course exceptions. Two visits to Chatsworth were clearly politically important, as were several visits to Lord Salisbury at Hatfield. Salisbury and Gladstone shared a quasi-Tractarian High-Churchmanship and a contempt for Disraeli, but they shared little more. Gladstone felt that these visits, which were not reciprocated, went well ('There are no kinder hosts than here'), and he approved of what he found: 'In few Chapels is all so well and heartily done.' Their shared dislike of Disraeli reflected the intense moral and religious language in which both men expressed their view of politics, but this certainly offered no basis for co-operation, and Salisbury remained one of the ministry's most persistent and effective critics. The two visits to Salisbury's young nephew Arthur Balfour, at his shooting lodge and at his Scottish home, Whittinghame (in 1872 and 1874 respectively), and Balfour's strong friendship—quite how strong is not clear—for Catherine Gladstone's niece, May Lyttelton, had obvious political overtones for both families. But most of Gladstone's visits were to old cronies such as Wolverton, Milnes Gaskell, Edward Ellice, and his undergraduate friend Walter Sneyd. Of course, no act by a Prime Minister is without political implications—Gladstone's visit to the Roman Catholic convert Ambrose Phillipps de Lisle at Garendon had implications well beyond the mere observation of de Lisle's monastery—but it is fair to say that Gladstone did not primarily intend these visits to be political in tone, and that his use of them differed from his rather assiduous use of the political weekend in the 1860s.

This readiness to distance himself physically from his colleagues—especially in the Recess—while remaining in touch with them by letter to the extent that he wished to do so, clearly allowed Gladstone to give himself periods of rest and regeneration which his tendency to nervous illness at times of stress and crisis suggests was essential. Most of his creative work—the three Irish bills, and the budget planned in the autumn of 1873—was done at Hawarden, and he returned to London from the country the more eager and the more resourceful politically.

Although Gladstone was throughout these years an intensely active Prime Minister—much more so than Disraeli in the government which succeeded him—it should not be thought that his energies were wholly devoted to the process and policy-making of government. Gladstone organized his routine in such a way as to permit—in all but exceptional crises—a continuation of his habit of extensive reading in an eclectic range of subjects—from a biography of Schleiermacher, through Trollope, Disraeli, and George Eliot to a vast range of pamphlets, periodicals, and tracts, ecclesiastical, classical, and secular. His very demanding attendance at the Commons naturally reduced his reading during the Session, though even then it is rare for a day to pass without some record of reading outside government papers. But in the Recess and on Sundays, the level of reading differs little from that in earlier decades of the diary. The reading may be said to be rather more practically directed, in that much of it was intended to provide background information to governmental questions—for example, the first three months of 1869 not surprisingly find Gladstone deep in literature and ephemera on the Irish Church. But he also found time in those same months to read, *inter alia*, Bagehot on money, Baxter on taxation, Giffen's essay on his own finance, Matthew Arnold's *Culture and Anarchy*, Cobbett's *Reformation*, Sedgwick's 'charming book on Cowgill Chapel', Coleridge's *Life of Keble*, J. E. Morgan's 'Town life among the poorest', and the Duke of Argyll's *Primeval Man*, as well as various works on the preparations for the Vatican Council. In those months we also find him correcting the proofs of *Juventus Mundi*, a short version of his Homeric views, which was published in August 1869. An important example of Gladstone's reading influencing his views on policy is his study of works on Irish land in 1869, in particular his reading of George Campbell's pamphlet, 'The Irish Land'.

On the whole, Gladstone recalled his reading accurately. The books in his library, now preserved at St Deiniol's Library at Hawarden, show him to have been a careful, if rapid, reader. He annotated his books with lines, ticks, and crosses, and wrote the odd comment in the margin, writing 'ma' (the Italian for 'but') when he disagreed with the author. He often compiled a short index on the back inside cover, books in those days rarely having a printed index.

His parliamentary speeches show a mind hardly ever at a loss for a fact or a reference. Gladstone had nothing of the contemporary trend which he discerned and roundly condemned in a speech at Liverpool College in December 1872—a trend towards 'a scepticism in the public mind, of old as well as young, respecting the value of learning and of culture, and a consequent slackness in seeking their attainment'. This speech, which caused much controversy, including a public exchange with Herbert Spencer, offers an interesting insight into the conclusions Gladstone was drawing from his eclectic gleanings from the contemporary scene, for in it he adumbrated, at a very early stage, what was to become in the hands of others a general critique of Britain's relative economic and cultural decline:

In the ulterior prosecution of almost any branch of inquiry, it is to Germany and to the works of Germans that the British student must look for assistance . . . a far greater number of her educated class are really in earnest about their education; and they have not yet learned, as we, I fear, have learned, to undervalue, or even to despise, in a great measure, simplicity of life.

Gladstone was alarmed at the 'corroding pest of idleness—that special temptation to a wealthy country'. Yet admire German achievement as he did, he deplored its most prominent ideological trend even more, denouncing the materialism of D. F. Strauss's *The old faith and the new* and with it both those in England who promulgated such opinions theologically, and those who—almost all of them in his own party—argued for secularism in education.

His reflections on the spirit of the age thus showed alarm at the corrosive consequences of wealth, and fear that the 'reconciliation between Christianity and the conditions of modern thought, modern life and modern society' which it had been his life's mission to accomplish, might after all be a sham reconciliation dependent on the surrender of traditional Christianity to scientific materialism. Gladstone's hopes for the Christian future rested first on ecumenism between the apostolic churches, Anglicans, Roman Catholics, and Orthodox (with the Nonconformists following in an ill-defined theological relationship)—an ecumenism he worked to promote even when Prime Minister and which he now saw failing—and second, on the refutation of ideas of the Straussian sort through the methodology of Joseph Butler, the eighteenth-century Anglican divine and philosopher, whose '*method of handling* ... is the only one known to me that is fitted to guide life, and thought bearing upon life, in the face of the nineteenth century'. The Vatican Council set the first back by a century, and the onward progress of secular Darwinism rendered victory over the second at best a very long haul.

Laura Thistlethwayte: 'duty and evil temptation', 'like a story from the Arabian Nights'

Correspondence, relaxation, reading, the stress of public life, religion, the conversion of prostitutes, all come together in Gladstone's relationship with Laura Thistlethwayte, the evangelical ex-courtesan whom we have already met and who had, by the time he became Prime Minister, already established a degree of friendship with Gladstone, originally through the Duke of Newcastle.* This friendship consisted of an occasional dinner at her house in Grosvenor Square, and an intermittent correspondence, mostly on religious topics.

However, Gladstone told her in November 1869, 'I have only known you in an inner sense within the last two months.' This was true, for in September 1869, Laura Thistlethwayte made a move towards great intimacy with the Prime Minister, accusing him of misunderstanding and mockery. In response Gladstone wrote describing their relationship since 1864:

In my ragged letter of yesterday, I did not get *through* my answer to your question 'had you knowledge of all this when you came to see me'? Yet it may be short—No!

* See above, pp. 159–60.

I told you some things I did perceive; and I proceed. The modesty (so to call it) struck me, with which, when I rather thrust open your door (I fear) after one friend's death [i.e. the Duke of Newcastle in 1864], you did not hasten to call me in; it struck and pleased me. With regard to myself afterwards, I thought you interpreted me too favourably, and in all things seemed to dress me (so to speak) in colours agreeable to yourself. But I did not dream that, as among your *friends*, I was drawn into any inner circle. I have not a good opinion of myself. And, if I see kindness from any one gushing out upon me, it mainly strikes me what a fund of it they must have, to spend so liberally. Again, you ask did kindness (in, not to, me) draw me to see you? There was enough in what all knew of you, to draw me, without kindness: a sheep, or a lamb rather, that had been astray; (I omit what you do not wish to be mentioned but what, I do not deny, enhances interest—), and that had come back to the Shepherd's Fold, and to the Father's arms. . . . I fretted, as oftentimes I have done, at my want of time and free mind for the cultivation of friendship; but there was no period at which I should not have been very sorry to think I was seeing you for the last time.

Yet I did not then know you as I know you now through your tale, and what accompanies the tale.

The 'tale' referred to was Laura Thistlethwayte's autobiography, now lost, which she sent to the Prime Minister in at least twenty-three batches during September and October 1869. It was accompanied by an outpouring of undated letters written on exotic paper with Eastern symbols in a vast and illegible hand; the scent on the paper still wafts, at least metaphorically, upwards to the reader. The manuscript and letters taken together 'astonished', tantalized, and perhaps titillated Gladstone: 'duty and evil temptation are there before me, on the right and left'. He was clearly deeply attracted to her, and when a joke in one of his letters was taken as a slight, he was mortified and profoundly disturbed until all was set right.

This tiff—almost a lover's tiff—on paper brought the affair to a crisis. Laura Thistlethwayte wrote 'a great, deep, weighty word' which Gladstone in his reply could not bring himself to repeat—apparently 'love'—and she suggested they burn their letters to each other. Gladstone drew back: was she sure the word should be used?—burning letters was 'dangerous. It removes a bridle: it encourages levity in thought.' On the other hand, he admitted she had 'got within my guard'—with Gladstone something achieved perhaps only by his wife and, years before, Arthur Hallam and James Hope.*

In Mrs Thistlethwayte Gladstone had found an ideal object of fascination: educated enough to understand something of his mind, young enough to offer beauty, religious enough to seem redeemed, but exotic enough to

---

* After October 1869, he began his letters to her 'Dear Spirit', though ending 'Ever yours, W.E.G.' He wore a ring she had given him: 'I will have it engraved "L.T. to W.E.G." ' She, with more circumspection, insisted on a mere 'L'. The ring can be seen on Gladstone's right hand in many of his later portraits and photographs.

stand outside the ring of society women with whom he usually corresponded on religion. 'It is like a story from the Arabian Nights, with much
added to it' was his comment on her autobiography.

The dramatic but apparently resolved nature of Mrs Thistlethwayte's
life and religion called forth a response from Gladstone:

There is a *region* beyond that of interest in your tale, beyond bewilderment, beyond
gratitude for an open-hearted confidence: but the first step into that region
prompts me to remember as a sacred trust what is for your peace and weal. If in
speaking thus I seem mysterious and strange it is because I am so. My life is a battle
between inclination and duty. Inclination calls me to repose, duty leads me into
conflict: I have high aspirations, and mean tendencies. But a voice above the din
orders me to study your peace and your weal.

Her bid for attention had come at a timely moment; Gladstone needed the
friendship and attention of a woman outside his family circle. In the 1860s
this role was fulfilled occasionally by Lady Waldegrave, but chiefly by the
dowager Duchess of Sutherland, to whom Gladstone wrote very regularly
when they were apart, letters usually on literature, with some politics
added. The dowager duchess died in October 1868; Gladstone was one of
her pall-bearers.

Mrs Thistlethwayte was hardly the dowager duchess, but Gladstone saw
her in the same context: 'You were never to me simply a common acquaintance. Friendships with women have contributed no small portion of my
existence. I know the meaning of the words "weakness is power": apparent
weakness is real power.' And again: 'what could lead you to tell me I was
made much of by women. I fear only my own declaration, that valued and
precious friendships with women had formed no small part of my life. That
is true. In every principal case they were women older than myself. To be
prized by women in general is in my opinion a great glory, because of their
gift of judging character: but it is a glory I cannot claim and do not deserve.'

The questions her exotic tale raised, the state of her soul, and the relationship between them could only be resolved by a lengthy meeting. This
took place over a weekend at the Thistlethwaytes' house at Boveridge
whither went Gladstone and Arthur Kinnaird, the Whig MP who, with
Newcastle, had introduced the couple. At Boveridge 'Mrs. Th. came to my
rooms aft[ernoon] and at night.'

After this meeting, the affair—for such it must be called—reached a more
balanced state. Letters and meetings, especially the former—sent in
specially marked envelopes to avoid the private secretaries—continued to
be frequent, but without the extreme excitement and intensity of the
months of October to December 1869.

Much of this correspondence reflects the curious ambivalence of the
religious mind. Gladstone's stated urgings were all towards morality. He
accepted Laura Thistlethwayte's protestations of virtue and defended her

against traducers. He urged her towards restoring relations of every sort with her husband, and suggested to her that her 'vocation' should be to 'act upon the bitter wintry frosts which originally cast your wifehood in a mould of ice'. Yet Gladstone's relationship with her was clearly fraught with danger for him, as is shown in his correspondence with her and by his frequent use of 'X' (the sign usually used after a morally dangerous meeting with a prostitute) as a comment on his meetings with her. That willingness to be tempted, to 'court evil' while doing good, which had played so important a part in his early rescue work, that feeling that he must expose his soul and body to spiritual danger, clearly in the case of Laura Thistlethwayte led Gladstone on, for a time, to a point not far short of infatuation.

However, that point *was* short of infatuation. Gladstone did not use 'the weighty word' back to Laura Thistlethwayte, and despite all, he maintained some sort of balance. Though Mrs Thistlethwayte took up much time in letters and meetings, especially in 1869–70, Gladstone never reached the degree of dependence of H. H. Asquith on Venetia Stanley.

The affair was, like Gladstone's work with prostitutes, carried on in the full knowledge of the political élite, amongst whom Laura Thistlethwayte was notorious. It occurred at the height of the Cabinet bargaining about the contents of the Irish Land Bill, and of Tory speculation about the balance of power within the Cabinet. The fifteenth Earl of Derby noted in his journal on 11 December 1869:

Strange story of Gladstone frequenting the company of a Mrs. Thistlethwaite, a kept woman in her youth, who induced a foolish person with a large fortune to marry her. She has since her marriage taken to religion, and preaches or lectures. This, with her beauty, is the attraction to G and it is characteristic of him to be indifferent to scandal. But I can scarcely believe the report that he is going to pass a week with her and her husband at their country house—she not being visited or received in society.*

The episode thus added to Gladstone's reputation amongst leading Whigs and Tories for eccentricity and 'madness'† and contributed to their underestimation of his self-control and resilience.

Generosity and naïvety characterized Gladstone's behaviour. He persistently saw the best—'a sheep or a lamb rather, that had been astray . . . and that had come back to the Shepherd's Fold'‡—where others had seen mere chicanery, and he largely ignored the dangers to himself, both as to

---

* J. Vincent, ed., *Disraeli, Derby and the Conservative Party* (1978), 346.

† Carnarvon had earlier reached this view: 'Gladstone seems to be going out of his mind. Northcote has just told me that Gladstone's last passion is Mrs Thistlethwayte. He goes to dinner with her and she in return in her preachments to her congregation exhorts them to put up their prayers on behalf of Mr G's reform bill.'

‡ Laura Thistlethwayte's feelings are hard to determine from the jumbled state of her letters to Gladstone—several hundred, undated and virtually unsortable—but they seem to be genuine enough: 'Oh how madly I love', she docketed Gladstone's letter of 16 March 1871.

1. Gladstone in 1833. *Oil sketch by George Hayter for the group portrait of the 1833 Parliament*

2. Sir John Gladstone in old age. *Calotype by D. Hill and R. Adamson*

3. Catherine Gladstone. *Watercolour, 1843, by George Richmond*

4. 'The Flight of Daedalus and Icarus! illustrated under a new aspect', by H. B. (John Doyle),
July 1844, with Gladstone seeking the free trade sun even more energetically than Peel

5. Gladstone in 1858, wearing 'Broughams', the checked trousers named after Henry Brougham with whom he became friendly in the 1850s; from Maull and Polyblank's *Photographic Portraits of Living Celebrities*, one of the first such series

6. Tenniel's cartoon 'Critics', captioned: 'MR. G-D-S-T-N-E. *"Hm!—Flippant!"* MR. D-I-R-LI. *"Ha!— Prosy!"* '. *Punch*, 14 May 1870. Unlike Disraeli, Gladstone's features posed problems for cartoonists; this is one of Tenniel's best

7. (a) Agnes
Drawing by G. Richmond

7. (b) Catherine Jessy, died April 1850
Portrait by G. Hayter

7. (c) Mary

7. (d) Herbert John

8. Gladstone's diary of his tour of Lancashire, 13 and 14 October 1864.
Facsimile of the actual size of the volume (pott octavo)

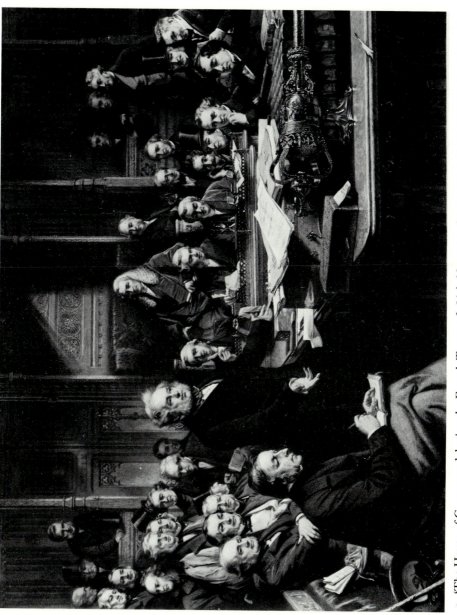

9. 'The House of Commons debating the French Treaty of 1860'. *Mezzotint after the oil painting by J. Phillip. Lewis, Russell and Gladstone are on the front bench, with Palmerston speaking*

10. Gladstone's First Cabinet, by Lowes Dickinson. Seated, clockwise: Lowe, Bright, Argyll, Clarendon, Bruce, Hatherley, Ripon, Granville, Kimberley, Goschen, Gladstone. Standing, left to right: Hartington, Fortescue, Cardwell, Childers

11. (a) Gladstone speaking at Blackheath, 28 October 1871: 'I spoke 1 h. 50 mins.; too long, yet really not long enough for a full development of my points: physically rather an excess of effort'

11. (b) Speech at Blackheath, 28 January 1874, *Illustrated London News*, 7 February 1874. Note the real audience, the press stenographers

12. (a) Two views of Laura Thistlethwayte, as a courtesan (miniature by Girard) and as an evangelical

12. (b) Harriet, Dowager Duchess of Sutherland. *Bust by J. Noble*

12. (c) William and Catherine Gladstone in the 1860s

13. (a) Gladstone in the 1860s

13. (b) Gladstone in Privy Councillor's uniform

13. (c) Sir Stephen Glynne

14. (a) A typical Gladstonian note, ordering books from a catalogue, his handwriting just past its prime but striking by its quasi-italic modernity, with none of the loops and flourishes characteristic of most of his contemporaries

14. (b) A holiday snap at Penmaenmawr in August 1874

15. (a) W. H. and W. E. Gladstone *à la mode*, as imagined by the *Tailor and Cutter*, June 1870: 'Mr. Gladstone, like many other gentlemen who have made themselves a lasting fame, is by no means a "dandy", neither is he ever seen slovenly dressed, but is always neat and gentlemanly in his appearance'

(b) Gladstone (nearest to the camera) at Edgware Road Station on 24 May 1862, the first trial of the Metropolitan railway, in which he was a shareholder

16. Gladstone as Prime Minister. He always wore a glove or a finger-stall to hide the forefinger mutilated in a shooting accident in 1842

the effect all this might have on his relationship with Catherine Gladstone, and as to the public. He several times reassured Laura Thistlethwayte about the security arrangements for safeguarding her letters and manuscript—'Were it to fall into the hands of some rogue'—but he assumed security and confidentiality on her part.

His confidence was justified. Mrs Thistlethwayte seems to have made little attempt to capitalize on her new respectability, save to send Gladstone frequent invitations to dinner, which were quite regularly accepted, and she seems to have had few political ambitions, unlike Olga Novikoff, 'the M.P. for Russia', who emerges in 1873 as something of an alternative to Mrs Thistlethwayte as a female correspondent outside the family, though the intensity of the relationship is in no sense comparable.

'Mrs. Th's' non-political nature may have been part of her appeal (though her Irish origins seem to have played some part in conditioning the tone of Gladstone's expressions about Ireland during the preparation of the Land Act), but her religiosity, constant expressions of suffering and pathetic concern with respectability would seem, in addition to her 'signal soul clad in a beautiful body', to have aroused in Gladstone a powerful fellow-feeling and sympathy. Her youthful sufferings had coincided with his great crisis of 1850–1, his 'saddest' year which 'well nigh tore me to pieces'—the height of his self-flagellation at the time of the Gorham Judgement, the apostasy of Manning and James Hope, and the crisis of his rescue work. With Laura Thistlethwayte in the 1870s he felt he could share, at least in retrospect, something of the crisis of the Victorian soul which his wife's serenity could not begin to comprehend: that Tennysonian mixture of religion, sex, and patriotism, each element both stimulating and moderating the others to produce a soul in great tension but in balance*—a mixture whose balance Gladstone only just maintained, and which conditioned all his public and private actions and thoughts. The pregnant image of his repeated phrase, 'my country is my first wife', was no convenient or casual platitude; it reflected the emotional and in some ways sexual involvement of Gladstone with his nation.

The Thistlethwayte affair seems to have siphoned off a good deal of the nervous energy which usually accompanied Gladstone's work with prostitutes. This certainly continued regularly while he was Prime Minister, and several of his encounters are marked by the sign 'X', denoting temptation on his part. But the sign is also used after some of his meetings with Mrs Thistlethwayte, a fact which in itself testified to the ambiguity of her position in Gladstone's mind. Was she friend, or rescue case? When she left for Egypt on doctor's advice in 1872, he noted in his diary: 'It is well for me that she goes.' She was not away for long, and no rescue case took her place as the focal point of Gladstone's extra-marital fixation.

* Gladstone gave Mrs Thistlethwayte his annotated copy of Tennyson.

Laura Thistlethwayte was not Gladstone's mistress in the physical sense—the reader may here be reminded of Gladstone's solemn declaration in 1896 that he had 'never been guilty of the act which is known as that of infidelity to the marriage bed'. But she fulfilled the other functions of that office.

'It embarrasses' was Gladstone's comment on her 'extraordinary claim for sympathy'; the reader may well feel the same about the correspondence which Gladstone's children, with a commendable sense of responsibility to posterity, decided not to destroy, but to preserve, side-by-side with their father's daily journal.

Not surprisingly, rescue work exposed Gladstone to danger: there is at least one suggestion reaching the stage of discussion with solicitors of what seems to be a paternity suit—'a "plant" as it is called'—though nothing came of it.

Family Affairs in the Early 1870s

What Catherine Gladstone thought of the Thistlethwayte affair, of the rescue work in this period, or of the meeting with the solicitors can only be guessed at. With respect to the 'plant', Gladstone told Freshfield, the solicitor, that his wife 'was wiser than I & said "You are too credulous"'. She may well have thought the same about her husband's relationship with Mrs Thistlethwayte. Self-reliant though Catherine Gladstone was, it is hard to believe that she was not wounded—though she may have become inured.

Certainly the family life of the Gladstones continued happy, though the closeness of the family was necessarily diminished by the dispersal of the children—Henry Neville to India, Herbert to University College, Oxford, and a Third in Mods, Agnes to be married. But Willy worked closely and now more easily with his father politically, and Stephen became rector of Hawarden on the death of Henry Glynne, Catherine Gladstone's brother.

Much the saddest family event of the early 1870s was the death of Sir Stephen Glynne, Catherine's other brother, the shy bachelor whose gentle antiquarianism had charmed away alarm at his financial incompetence. His funeral was a great Hawarden occasion, honoured with a full description in the diary. The mourning was intertwined in classic Gladstonian and Victorian fashion with the resettlement of the estate, as Gladstone gave his children 'a sketch of the romance, for such it is, of the financial history', and Willy entered into an inheritance he can hardly have felt was his own.

Stephen Glynne's death also provoked intense conversation on the future between the diarist and his wife: 'the future seemed to clear a little before her. But how greedy I am—not satisfied with the last 22 years, or the last 35!' Immediately after this, the death of his niece Ida, Sir Thomas Gladstone's daughter, required a visit to Fasque, the family house in

Kincardineshire, and brought about something of a reconciliation between William and his fiercely Tory elder brother. For William Gladstone it was understandably a nostalgic occasion, this visit to his father's house with its 'old and still dear details'. Ida's coffin was placed in the family vault next to that of his cherished daughter Jessy, and Gladstone's thoughts returned, as so often, to the dreadful, shattering year of 1850–1.

A Public Man and his Money

Defeat in the general election in January 1874 and retirement from active leadership of his party placed Gladstone in an unwonted situation. For nearly fifteen years, since 1859, he had been in office or expecting imminently to be in office. Now he was, at his own insistence as well as that of the electorate, responsible largely if not solely to himself. Difficulties at once arose. The first of these was money. 'Expulsion from office' brought to a point of crisis Gladstone's personal finances. The salary of £5000 which he drew as First Lord of the Treasury (he had received the same amount as chancellor from 1859 to 1866) had provided the chief element of the income necessary for his day-to-day living. With this assured, he had been able to make substantial capital purchases while in public office by borrowing, usually from his bankers, S. Scotts. In terms of his total assets, he was a wealthy man. At the end of his period of office, his accounts stood thus:

Class I	Property in Hawarden Parish	153,000
	Seaforth Estate	37,000
	Lease of 11 Carlton House Terrace	23,500
	Mortgage on Trinity College [Glenalmond]	2,500
	Outstanding rents etc.	4,000
		220,000
Class II	£8000 5% Preference Metropolitan District Railway at £62½	5,000
	£57,500 Ordinary Metropolitan District Railway at £30	17,000
	£5000 Philadelphia & Reading Mortgage Bonds	5,000
		247,000
Class III	Furniture, books, porcelain etc.	22,100
		£269,100

Against these assets were to be counted debts of £39,000, which included mortgages on 11 Carlton House Terrace (£4,500), on the 'Chester block' Saltney purchase at Hawarden (£9,000), the Aston estate purchase (£12,000), and the loss by Robertson Gladstone of about £6,000 of his brother William's share of the Seaforth estate near Liverpool. The Aston Hall purchase, which was made in October 1869 for £57,000, contained two collieries, and was a substantial addition to the Hawarden estate, but it only produced £2069. 10s. 1½d. net income in 1873. The net income on Gladstone's Flintshire estates for 1873 was £2695. 8s. 5d. (gross £5703. 18s. 8d.), a return on his assets there of two per cent.

Gladstone's purchases of land in Flintshire were less risky than his holdings of railway stocks and shares. As the above table shows, he was heavily, and in terms of his portfolio, narrowly involved in the Metropolitan District Railway. He had held shares in it for some time, but had increased his holdings at the end of the 1860s, and in 1869, after selling some of its stock, he bought £10,000 more. Unfortunately for him, the company fell into difficulties. Its dividend was passed and its shares fell. It is hard to calculate from Gladstone's records exactly what his losses on this railway were, but they appear to amount to about 50 per cent on about £50,000.

Gladstone's activities in the stock market, both as Chancellor and Prime Minister, were therefore, over a period of a decade, considerable, and known to be so. As mentioned above, he had no qualms about buying Consols when they fell to a favourable 90 when Bismarck invaded France. The *Chester Chronicle* found it necessary to point out that this was not money-making at the public expense and that 'the world of gossip ... ringing with stories of Mr. Gladstone's pecuniary difficulties' was proved wrong.

The *Chronicle*'s report referred to the Aston Hall purchase, but gossip of this sort about Gladstone's share purchases seems to have been quite widely circulated, encouraged, apparently, surprisingly, unjustifiably, and perhaps for personal political ends, by his own stockbroker, James Watson, Lord Provost of Glasgow, whom he knighted in 1874. Lord Derby noted in his diary: 'In singular confirmation of the stories we had heard at Minard, the Lord Provost [i.e. Watson the stockbroker] told Pender, who repeated it to me not an hour afterward, that the Premier had been very active in stock exchange speculations, and had lately employed him (Watson). Very strange—but what motive had he to invent the story if not true?'* This sort of story was a clear exaggeration, and represented that expectation of hyperbole which Gladstone already encouraged among Tories. Gladstone had not been 'very active'; he had made purchases in the Metropolitan District Railway Company over a period of several years which had not paid off. He was at no time in financial difficulty and, with money as cheap as it was in 1869–72, short-term borrowing backed by the sort of assets Gladstone commanded was in no way imprudent.

---

* Watson's implication that his employment by Gladstone was unusual was quite misleading—they had been in regular correspondence and dealings since 1851. Nothing in the summer of 1872 in the Hawarden account books seems to bear out Watson's tale; there were no changes in the MDR holdings; £3,600 Pennsylvanian and Reading stock was bought.

None the less, Gladstone was short of ready cash, and in 1872 he drew the state of affairs to his wife's attention: 'why and how more pinched'. In 1873 he anticipated having to give up his house in Carlton House Terrace 'at or about the expiry of the present Government'. When his salary ended in February 1874, his immediate position became dramatically worse. He calculated in June 1874 that after 'necessary allowances' for his wife and five of his children, and his usual charitable donations, he had only £1000 'for all general expenditure whatsoever'. The death of his brother-in-law Sir Stephen Glynne, the owner of Hawarden, just after these calculations were made, made little difference for by the arrangement of 1865 the Glynne estates went to Willy Gladstone and anyway produced little net income. The way was thus pointed to the sale of 11 Carlton House Terrace and of some of his art collections as the best means of raising his income, and preparations were made in the last months of 1874 for the sales of these assets in 1875.

The second difficulty about the life of 'mental repose' which Gladstone intended for himself was that, still an MP, his activities were necessarily subject to persistent scrutiny. Thus his support for the manager of the Aston Hall Colliery in opposing attempts by the miners to impose a closed shop had national as well as local implications: even the life of the country squire exposed him to national attention and controversy.

The Aston Hall controversy was symptomatic of the sort of class tension which Liberalism could never avoid at the constituency level, however integrative its national ideology aspired to be. But far more dramatically national in implication were to be the religious thoughts which Gladstone retired to Hawarden to contemplate.

Religion in Retirement: 'Vaticanism' the end of a career?

Gladstone's religion had always been a complex and indivisible blend of the national and the personal. Intense personal experience related in his personality intimately and inseparably to intense feeling about 'National Religion'. A similar synchronous purpose pervaded his study of Homer which was always justified in terms of his religious view of world history rather than by antiquarianism. Thus his contemplation in his retirement of things of the spirit necessarily led rapidly to public involvement in ecclesiastical controversy. He found both the Anglican Church and Christian Europe threatened—the first by Archbishop Tait, Disraeli, and the anti-ritualists in both parties, and the second by the Papacy. Partly as a reward to what had been a powerful element in their support in the elections, the Conservatives made ecclesiastical bills—the Public Worship Regulation Bill for England and Wales and the Church Patronage Bill for Scotland—the first chief legislative business for their large majority.

In a manner reminiscent of his opposition to Palmerston's Divorce Bill in 1857, Gladstone moved Resolutions intended to transform the Public Worship Regulation Bill, and had to withdraw them a week later.* His ill-temper shows even through the flatness of the columns of Hansard. But whereas in 1857 he had acted on his own with a few friends to maintain the 'Catholic' position, in 1874 he was still nominally leader of the Liberal party, which contained a significant body of opinion, exemplified by Sir William Harcourt, hostile to 'Puseyism' and in favour of the bill. The isolation of the Tractarian Liberals within the party, evident in the controversy over education during the government, thus became confirmed in opposition.

The problem of the Vatican Council, and the issues of civil liberty and allegiance which it seemed to raise, had, as has been shown earlier, greatly exercised Gladstone's administration, both in its foreign and in its British policy. For Gladstone there was an added element—his longstanding and intense ambivalence about Roman Catholicism. He was drawn by its internationalism and majestic tradition, but repelled by what he saw as its authoritarianism, anti-liberalism, and refusal to acknowledge a distinction between secular, civil allegiance on the one hand, and spiritual obedience on the other. 'Temporal power' was the phrase by which Gladstone summed up these deficiencies; he saw the Vatican Decrees of 1870 as the climax of an attempt by the Papacy to regain by ultramontane authoritarianism what it had lost to nationalism. The apostasy of his sister in 1842 and of several of his friends in 1851 had provoked, as we have seen, the most intense crisis of his married life, a disturbance in the balance between religion, sex, and patriotism causing a reaction in all three elements of his personality. Recollecting this, he told Samuel Wilberforce on the occasion of the apostasy of his brother Robert Wilberforce in 1854:

For could I, with reference to my own precious children, think that one of them might possibly live to strike, though in sincerity and thinking he did God service, such a blow, how far rather would I that he had never been born.

It was not merely prudential politics, important though those certainly were, which caused Gladstone to make, on the occasion of her conversion to Roman Catholicism, a 'termination of any literary relations' between himself and his cousin, Mrs Bennett, his assistant when he translated Farini's *Lo Stato Romano* in the 1850s. Gladstone's public role had involved him in attempts to frustrate the success of the Infallibilists, led by Manning; his private religious contacts had led to links with the Old Catholic movement through his old friend J. J. I. von Döllinger, now excommunicated for his opposition to the decisions of the 1870 Council.

---

* He also powerfully opposed the Scottish Patronage Bill, but in this he had a substantial part of the Liberal party with him.

Just after leaving office, he dropped a hint that public expostulation might be on the way.

Hostility to developments in both Anglicanism and Roman Catholicism were expressed in Gladstone's signed article, 'Ritualism and Ritual', published in the *Contemporary Review*, and begun in August 1874 when the passing of the Public Worship Regulation Bill was completed. Alarmed by the barriers to Catholic ecumenicalism being erected by both sides, disturbed by the conversion to Roman Catholicism of Lord Ripon, his recent Cabinet colleague, moved by Charlotte Yonge's life of the Tractarian bishop J. C. Patteson which he was reviewing, impressed by the arguments and conferences of the Old Catholics, and stimulated by the appeals for help from Döllinger, whom he was visiting in Munich, Gladstone inserted into the proofs of his article on ritualism a fierce denunciation of British Roman Catholics for their supine reaction to the Vatican Decrees. After further consideration of the Old Catholic position, and with initial encouragement from the anti-Infallibilist Lord Acton, Gladstone 'Wrote on the Papal questions', writing which blossomed into his pamphlet *The Vatican Decrees in their bearing on civil allegiance: a political expostulation*, published on 7 November 1874. Acton, Ambrose Phillipps de Lisle, and Arthur Gordon who were at Hawarden during its preparation were alarmed by its intemperance: 'They all show me that I must act mainly for myself.'

Act for himself Gladstone certainly did. The pamphlet was a remarkable blend of political theory, Protestant anti-Popery, and Tractarian *angst*. Beneath the historical and ecclesiastical argument, important in itself and in its political implications, lay a profound sense of anger and betrayal— anger with the 'direct influence' of the Irish Roman Catholic bishops, anger with the Papacy from which much had never been expected, betrayal by Manning who should have known better, and by Newman who should have done more.

The Vatican Decrees showed Gladstone's extraordinary capacity to change direction. He had gone out of office at the start of 1874 after a spirited initiative in national finance; he ended the year as the protagonist of a vast controversy on Church and State whose pamphlets poured as voluminously from presses in America and Europe as they did from those in Britain. But he also confirmed the political direction which he had taken after the defeat of the general election by his informal retirement, for on the last day of 1874 he prepared for transmission his letters to Granville formally resigning as leader of the Liberal party. The Vatican controversy showed Gladstone's inability to leave the world of affairs; his resignation of even the title of party leader showed his refusal to accept that world's conventional limitations.

The day before revising his letters of resignation, Gladstone finished

Middlemarch: 'It is an extraordinary, to me a very jarring book.' 'Every limit is a beginning as well as an ending' remarks George Eliot in her 'Finale', and such a 'limit' was 1874 for Gladstone. What George Eliot called 'the home epic—the gradual conquest or irremediable loss of that complete union which makes the advancing years a climax, and age the harvest of sweet memories in common' was for Gladstone an epic written on a national as well as a domestic scale. From his country, his 'first wife', he found himself estranged, rejected by the political nation, at odds with most of the Protestant element of his own party on Anglican religion and education, and with almost all the Roman Catholic element on the Papacy. Gladstone's career was an extraordinary public epic, and 1874 was an important caesura in it—a break before a further twenty years at the forefront of British public life. That it was not the intended conclusion but a caesura before a long finale was not, and could not be, apparent to Gladstone.

Part Two

Part Two

CHAPTER I

Retirement, Religious Nationality, and the Eastern Question

Gladstone in 1875: Retirement from Politics—Vaticanism and Christian Unity—Nationality, Politics, and the Moral World Order—Disraeli, Gladstone, and the Question of the East, 1876–80—High-Church Nationality, Turkey, and the Concert of Europe—Suzerainty in the Balkans and its Imperial Implications—An Evangelical Campaign—Jingoism and the Move to Midlothian

The year [1875] has been an important one, & not only on account of its great abundance, as usual, in opportunities & in failures. In the great business of unwinding the coil of life & establishing my freedom I have made some progress by resigning the leadership, selling my House (needful for pecuniary reasons) and declining public occasions. But more has yet to be done. To minimise my presence in London is alike needful for growth, for my work, for the great duty & business of solemn recollection & preparation.

I hope my polemical period is over. It has virtually occupied over a twelvemonth: but good has been done, especially in Italy.*

Gladstone in 1875: Retirement from Politics

On 14 January 1875 William Ewart Gladstone met most of the members of the Liberal Cabinet defeated at the general election in February 1874 and told them of his resignation of the Liberal leadership. His announcement was immediately made public in an exchange of letters with Lord Granville being Liberal leader in the House of Lords and Lord Hartington being Liberal leader in the House of Commons. The party of progress was thus led by a peer in each House. This was an awkward basis for its leadership, and one made more awkward by the fact that Gladstone did not resign his Greenwich seat, though he did sell his London house, 11 Carlton House Terrace, in March 1875. He thus anticipated in his domestic arrangements the anti-metropolitanism which was to be an increasingly important theme of the second part of the 1870s.

Gladstone's announcement brought to an end a process begun in a

---

* Diary for 29 Dec. 75.

political sense in February 1874 when, following the election defeat and despite his wife's opposition, Gladstone told the 'ex-Cabinet' that he would no longer act as leader because the party needed time to deal with the religious fissures which had had so harmful an effect on the latter years of the 1868–74 government. But in personal terms the announcement of January 1875 was the achievement of Gladstone's much longer-held intention to rid himself of the day-to-day claims on his time which executive politics and opposition front-bench life implied. He told the 'ex-Cabinet': 'My object is to labour for holding together the Church of England.' And certainly religion was initially to play a central part in the years 1874–80, whether in the form of Gladstone's opposition to the Public Worship Regulation Bill of 1874, his articles and pamphlets of 1874–5 against the Vatican Decrees of 1870, his interest in ecumenism and Orthodox Church affairs, or his involvement from 1876 in the campaign against atrocities on the Christian community in Bulgaria.

Gladstone was just 65 when he announced his retirement from the Liberal leadership. He was fit, spare, and sprightly. A *bon viveur* in the sense of enjoying meal-time conversation, he ate and drank convivially but lightly; he did not smoke. His life-style in London and his regular walking and treefelling at Hawarden kept him in excellent physical condition, as was shown by his stamina during the 1892–4 government and by his ability, even in his early eighties, to undertake without preparation the most demanding Scottish mountain walks.* Standing about 5 feet $10\frac{1}{2}$ inches, and weighing a trim 11 stone 11 pounds, his body was dominated by his unusually large head and by his eyes, which Liberals saw as those of an eagle and Tories those of a crafty hawk. As photographs of him in the 1880s show, he had a tough and on occasion a cocky expression. His voice retained its remarkable capacity to fill vast halls and to lash or cajole the Commons. Like Caruso's, it was probably a tenor voice with the depth and harmonics of a baritone.† Usually wearing a spotted bow tie (of course hand-tied) and a high turned-up collar which in Harry Furniss's cartoons became his trade-mark, Gladstone was conventionally dressed. He shaved his upper lip and his chin to the width of his jaw-bone, but the rest of his face sported occasionally trimmed whiskers. His hair was, in the Victorian fashion, pushed back from his face, but not into what could be called a style. In his later photographs it is almost always untidy, with a loose parting, usually on the left side, a change from his youth and middle-age when his parting (like his party), if identifiable, was usually on the right. His hair thinned at the front, further revealing an always prominent, broad forehead; but he was never bald. Gladstone always wore the ring given him by Laura Thistlethwayte on the third finger of his right hand (it is visible in

* See below, p. 539.
† For the recording of Gladstone's voice, see below, p. 552.

most of his later portraits), and a dark leather fingerstall on his left hand's forefinger which he had accidentally shot off in 1842. He had unusually long fingers. In moments of extreme concentration or irritation, he used to rub his ear up and down with his right forefinger. He was a dapper 65 with the physical resilience of a 30-year-old.

In 1875 he had already been in the Commons for 42 years. He had been Under-Secretary for the Colonies in the 1830s, President of the Board of Trade and Colonial Secretary in the 1840s, Chancellor of the Exchequer in the 1850s and 1860s, and Prime Minister in a famous ministry from 1868 to 1874. He had amply fulfilled the expectations of his school and university friends that he would rise to the very top. If he had died, as Disraeli did, a year after the end of his chief administration, he would have been remembered for a political career as close to classic in its pattern as could be expected in politics. Gladstone had of course changed his party and his ideology, as we saw in Part I, moving from the Coleridgian Idealism of the State–Church theories of the 1830s to being the most effective exponent of the 'minimal state' in the 1860s. But even so, his political career, had it ended in 1875, would have seemed relatively straightforward, with a beginning, a middle, and a Prime-Ministerial climax.

The fact that he died politically only briefly in 1875, and resurrected for a second political career, does not, of course, deny the force of this teleology, but it blurs its focus. It also makes the treatment of this second career uncertain, for Gladstone himself was uncertain, not about its rightness, but about its scope. He himself used the image of death with respect to his formal resignation as party leader in 1875, but the 'better life' that followed was political retirement: 'I seem to feel as one who has passed through a death, but emerged into a better life.' Whereas up to the early 1870s, Gladstone had been self-consciously attempting a 'reconciliation between Christianity and the conditions of modern thought, modern life and modern society', seeing himself as a chief agent in this process and seeing his career as the exemplar of its partial achievement in public affairs, from the mid-1870s onwards his position was more defensive. He found it hard to justify to himself as 'Godly'—as he had since the 1840s—the usual round of public business. As a consequence, his political activity after 1875 took the form of a series of 'campaigns', each with its particular justification. Having retired once and turned away from the party battle, future intervention had to be explained, to himself and to the public, in terms of unusual crises and special causes.

As a younger man, Gladstone had pursued a political career which, if it could hardly be described as typical, was not unusual in its marriage of idealism and ambition. After 1875, Gladstone's emphasis on 'exceptional circumstances' as his political *raison d'être* made the self-admission of ambition in any usual sense impossible. Hence he found himself discovering the politically abnormal, proposing restorative remedies—some of them, such as Home Rule, so radical that contemporaries found it hard to see their restorative dimension—and then orchestrating politics around him as if he were solving the last 'special' crisis and preparing for a final departure. In such an atmosphere, political planning both for himself and for his colleagues became difficult, almost impossible, and the view of politics as a normal process was suspended. By investing politics with something of a millenarian tone, and by turning policy debate within the Liberal party to some extent into the question, 'Will he go?', Gladstone was helping to write the script for his own continuation, for the supposed normality of the 1860s was never restored, and his position as the coping stone of the delicately balanced arch which was the Liberal party meant that he could never simply absent himself, leaving other things and beings equal.

A further difficulty was that it was clear to everyone that, despite his retirement, Gladstone remained an elemental political force. Meeting him in 1877 at Lord Houghton's *soirée*, Henry James, the novelist, observed:

Gladstone is very fascinating—his urbanity extreme—his eye that of a man of genius—and his apparent self-surrender to what he is talking of, without a flaw. He made a great impression on me—greater than any one I have seen here: though 'tis perhaps owing to my naïveté, and unfamiliarity with statesmen.*

There is no suggestion in his daily journal that Gladstone developed the idea of 'exceptional circumstances' as a way of justifying a return which he intended anyway; all the evidence suggests the opposite, that his return to politics was reluctant, was intended to be short, and was unselfconsciously genuine in its motivation. To us, the nature of the 'return' of 1876 may indicate a lack of self-awareness, but there are dangers of anachronism here. The political ethos within which Gladstone worked emphasized Godly calling and service to an extent unknown since the seventeenth century. Faced with conviction of this sort, understanding is probably more fruitful than explaining, for explaining in this sort of case too easily becomes explaining away. A brisk, dusting-down explanation of Gladstone as an ambitious hypocrite or, alternatively, as a self-deceiver, is, at least at first glance, an easy enough exercise; the problem with it is that it leaves the phenomenon curiously unexplained and more mysterious, both as to its interest for historians and its fascination for contemporaries.

The *mentalité* of the Victorian is perhaps more foreign to the twentieth-century mind than any since the Reformation. Gladstone's daily diary, sparsely written for the most part, is a central aid to the understanding not only of its author but of the culture of his times. The diary's relentless mixture of religion, duty, and materialism, as unselfconsciously presented

---

* P. Lubbock, *The letters of Henry James* (1920), i. 53. Gladstone noted in his diary 'Saw . . . Mr James (U.S.)'. James was less approving of Gladstone's policies, attacking his 'almost squalid' view of Egypt in *Lippincott's Magazine*, xx. 603 (November 1877), reprinted in *English Hours* (1905).

as is possible in such a document, helps those who read it to penetrate the hard surface of an age which wished to live by abstract principles but found itself living by experience.

'It has been experience which has altered my politics', Gladstone very truly told Sir Francis Doyle in 1880. This 'experience', which under the influence of Bishop Butler Gladstone elevated to a principle, had from the early 1840s to the early 1870s shifted him, sometimes subconsciously, towards liberal positions in a movement in step with the dominant intellectual tendencies of the age. These tendencies were now beginning to take a different direction.* Much of the interest of the last twenty years of Gladstone's public life comes from the observation of a powerful, dominating, and resourceful personality, increasingly out of temper with its times, struggling to maintain right and order, resorting to means regarded by many contemporaries as revolutionary, in order to sustain the United Kingdom as a Christian, united, free-trading, non-expansionist political community in the comity of nations.

After the self-confident beginning of the early years of the 1868 government, the 1870s turned out to be a decade of fears, alarms, and disappointments, partly redeemed by the domestic success of a great crusade, which was moral and religious as well as political in tone and intention. The Declaration of Infallibility by the Vatican Council of 1870, Gladstone's delayed but explosive public reaction to it, and his consequent estrangement from H. E. Manning, have been dealt with in the previous volume, but the Council's decision continued to cast its shadow, for it raised general questions of the nature of authority, the history of the Church, and the role of Anglicans within it, which could not be quickly or easily answered. Moreover, it caused him intense personal concern about the beliefs of his sister Helen (a convert to Rome) until her death in 1880: had she died a Roman Catholic, or had she seen the light in 1870 and at the least died an Old Catholic?†

If the reasonableness of the European mind had been betrayed by the Papacy, so also did it seem to be assaulted by the brutality and inflexibility of the Ottoman Empire, as a new phase of the 'Eastern Question' was launched in 1875–6, a development which in Gladstone's view was grossly mishandled and misused both internationally and domestically by the Conservative government. The resurgent Conservatism of the 1870s which the Disraeli government of 1874–80 represented coincided with the first

---

* J. P. C. Roach, 'Liberalism and the Victorian intelligentsia', *Cambridge Historical Journal*, xiii. 58.

† Helen Gladstone's death is discussed in Chapter III. The Old Catholics were a group of small national churches—Dutch, German, Austrian, Swiss, and some Slavs—which had at various times separated from Rome. They gained much attention after the Declaration of Infallibility and the Kulturkampf, Döllinger being associated with them after his excommunication and presiding over the Conferences at Bonn in 1874 and 1875 (for which see below, pp. 264–5).

general awareness of the ending of Britain's economic hegemony, and a general crisis in European agriculture which was to encourage the politics of protection and cartelization in most Continental states. Though Gladstone remained optimistic about the future of free trade, his restatement of the concept of the Concert of Europe in the second half of the 1870s had thus to be attempted in the context of economic dislocation and tariff reconstruction rather than that of the free-trade comity which he believed to have been one of the chief advances of the century.

This, then, was the frame of mind—and the complex political context—in which Gladstone retired from the Liberal leadership and from active politics in 1875. 'Retirement' in the nineteenth century did not have the clear-cut meaning of the modern break for males at 65, and the 'retirement' of politicians is, even today, rather different in character from retirement from an ordinary job. Little is known about general social attitudes to retirement in the Victorian period. For the landowner with other than local interests, educated in the rural values of Virgil and Horace, it probably represented a return from public or commercial life to the management of his estates; that is, 'retiring' meant not much more than the absence of appointments 'in town'.

This was not the case with Gladstone, Horatian enthusiast though he always was. In the early months of his retirement, he briefly owned the Hawarden estates when his brother-in-law, Sir Stephen Glynne, died in June 1874. But, in a move very unusual among the landed families of the time, he made over the estates to his son Willy when the latter married in 1875. Gladstone complained when it was generally assumed, as, for example, by G. C. Brodrick in his *English Land and English Landowners* (1881), that he was the owner of the Hawarden estate. Thus, although he continued to play an important role in the estate's development, he passed by the opportunity to play to the full the role of landowner. He was not the master of the estate and never presented himself as such. He did not 'play the squire', except, perhaps, in church. 'I love them not' was his comment as he tried to stop the annual Hawarden bazaar. He never held any local office of the sort to which the considerable size of the Hawarden estates would have entitled him had he been the squire, such as Justice of the Peace or Deputy Lord Lieutenant, though his son Willy was both.* Retirement for Gladstone, therefore, was not simply a matter of a return to country life, and there was always a certain unease about his role at Hawarden, exemplified by the long debate within the family over whether Willy Gladstone should, after his marriage, live in the Castle or build his own house. Gladstone in the mid-1870s addressed the odd local gardening society and the like, but Vickers, the agent, dealt with most of the business of the estate.

---

* Sir Stephen Glynne, Gladstone's brother-in-law, was Lord Lieutenant of Flintshire until his death in 1874; W. H. Gladstone was JP from 1863 and Deputy Lieutenant from 1866.

Gladstone did not now see Hawarden affairs as any more central to his life than they had been; his great effort for the estate had been in the opposition years 1846–52, when he had prevented its bankruptcy. Hawarden's great attraction was that it was literally a 'Temple of Peace', removed from London and, with the exception of the Duke of Westminster's estate nearby, remote from fashion.

Vaticanism and Christian Unity

Retirement, in Gladstone's view, meant retirement from political life to the study, but it was certainly not intended to mean inactivity. Indeed, it cleared the way for the proper pursuit of 'my work'. Politics was always for Gladstone a second-order activity with second-order expectations, in which it was important not to become excessively immersed: one must avoid 'sinking into a party man . . . into a politician, instead of a man in politics'.* Partly to satisfy his wife, Gladstone in March 1875 described a programme of intellectual activity which only 'exceptional circumstances' could suspend:

I endeavoured to lay out before C[atherine] my views about the future & remaining section of my life. In outline they are undefined but in substance definite. The main point is this: that, setting aside exceptional circumstances which would have to provide for themselves, my prospective work is not Parliamentary. My tie will be slight to an Assembly with whose tendencies I am little in harmony at the present time: nor can I flatter myself that what is called the public, out of doors, is more sympathetic. But there is much to be done with the pen, all bearing much on high & sacred ends, for even Homeric study as I view of it [*sic*] is in this very sense of high importance: and what lies beyond this is concerned directly with the great subject of belief. By thought good or evil on these matters the destinies of mankind are at this time affected infinitely more than by the work of any man in Parliament. God has in some measure opened this path to me: may He complete the work.

After completing his short book, *Homeric Synchronism*, in the autumn of 1875 and making some further progress on the often-delayed Homeric Thesaurus, Gladstone turned, as he had intended, to the 'great subject of belief'. The first-order work which he saw as a chief calling of his retirement was the service of the Church, and his actions show that the Church was to be served chiefly by the pen. In considering the activities of his retirement, we therefore plunge with him into the complexities of theological debate.

'Future Retribution. *From this I was called away to write on Bulgaria*': John Morley's memorable quotation of Gladstone's docket at the opening of his chapter on the Bulgarian Atrocities cannot but raise a twentieth-century smile.† Yet 'Future Retribution', 'Eternal Punishment' or, more simply,

---

* See above, p. 60.

† J. Morley, *Life of William Ewart Gladstone*, 3v. (1903) [subsequently: Morley], ii. 548; see 13 Aug. 76.

hell-fire, was a central intellectual concern of the day,* and a frequent talking-point at the weekend houses of the more high-minded of the aristocracy. The unreasonableness of an all-powerful God who condemned his creatures to permanent torment was a formidable argument for the secularists against Christianity—an argument at least as much deployed as evolution—and it was met chiefly by a variety of Broad-Church defences, from 'Universalism' (the doctrine that all free moral creatures will ultimately share in the grace of salvation) to the more moderate position put forward by the Anglican headmaster, F. W. Farrar, in his *Eternal Hope* (1877). Both the arguments of the secularists and the defences of the Broad-Churchmen were instinctively upsetting to Gladstone, whose theological inclinations (if not his eventual intellectual position) were always profoundly conservative.

Gladstone deplored the fact that 'A portion of Divine truth, which even if secondary is so needful, appears to be silently passing out of view, and ... the danger of losing it ought at all costs to be averted.'† None the less, he published nothing in the 1870s directly on the controversy. Gladstone was not at his best on abstract or speculative topics. In religious matters he profoundly mistrusted Broad-Church philosophizing and his instinct (at any rate after his youthful attempt at Idealism in *The State in its Relations with the Church*) was always for the practical and the historical aspects of a subject. He also seems to have thought that the theme of retribution could best be approached in stages.

He thus cleared the way for future work on the subject not by developing the notes written privately on 'Future Retribution' between 1876 and 1879,‡ but by publishing in 1879 the exposition of the views of the eighteenth-century bishop, Joseph Butler, 'Probability as the guide of conduct', which he had written in 1845 during his first period of resignation from politics. The argument from probability, in Gladstone's view, recaptured the initiative for Christianity; 'The maxim that Christianity is a matter not abstract, but referable throughout to human action, is not an important only, but a vital part of the demonstration, that we are bound by the laws of our nature to give a hearing to its claims.'§ 'Human action' meant human co-operation, institutions, local customs and traditions, without an understanding of which both the observer and participant would be without firm

---

* See the *symposia* in *Contemporary Review*, xxxii. 156, 338, 545 (April–June 1878) and *Nineteenth Century*, i. 331 (April 1877).

† W. E. Gladstone, *Studies subsidiary to Bishop Butler* (1896), 199, which uses material from the 1870s; quoted in G. Rowell, *Hell and the Victorians* (1974), 3. See also D. C. Lathbury, *Correspondence on church and religion of W. E. Gladstone*, 2v. (1910) [subsequently: Lathbury], ii. 123 and 20, 23 May 75.

‡ Add MS 44698, ff. 367–491. For his difficulties in dealing with the subject, see the letter to G. W. Potter, 22 October 1878, in Lathbury, ii. 105.

§ W. E. Gladstone, 'Probability as the guide of conduct', *Nineteenth Century* (May 1879), reprinted in *Gleanings of past years*, 7v. (1879) [subsequently: *Gleanings*].

moorings. This 'human action' would be worked out within the concept of 'religious nationality', Gladstone's starting-point as an ecclesiastical thinker. He did not look for complete uniformity of ecclesiastical authority or practice but rather saw an apostolic system based on a degree of variety and a degree of local legitimacy as being natural, necessary, and desirable. The Papacy's increasingly strident absolutist and universalist claims clearly cut straight across this view.

The concept of 'religious nationality', so important to Gladstone in a variety of ways in these years,* reflected a High-Church influence. Commenting on an article on High-Churchmanship by John Morley in the *Pall Mall Gazette*, Gladstone sought to correct Morley on one point: though the Church was universal, it was also 'a fundamental belief' that it was locally national in character and that

Our Saviour through the Apostles founded an institution called in the Creed the Holy Catholic Church, to be locally distributed throughout the earth, that it is [a] matter of duty to abide in this church, and that for England this church is found in the Church of England.

Thus in England and in the Empire the Church of England was the national church, in Eastern Europe the various Orthodox churches represented their nationalities and in Roman Catholic countries the Roman church theirs; but none of these churches had a peculiar claim to universality and universality in the Roman sense was historically and theologically a false claim. We shall see how the concept of religious nationality linked Gladstone's apparently very varied religious interests in the mid-1870s.

Much of Gladstone's contribution to the religious debate of the 1870s therefore took the form first of the anti-Vatican pamphlets of 1874–5, and then of quasi-historical articles designed to analyse the development of Christianity in England since the Reformation, notably 'Is the Church of England worth preserving?' and 'The courses of religious thought'. Even when writing on a more abstract theme, a review of a reprint of the essay 'On the influence of authority in matters of opinion' (1849) by Sir George Lewis, his successor as Chancellor of the Exchequer in 1855, the thrust was the same: Lewis, though right in thinking 'that the acceptance of Christianity is required of us by a scientific application of the principle of authority', had been too narrow and too theoretical: he should have been not merely 'moral and symbolic' but concerned with the 'living and working system not without the most essential features of an unity'.†

It was the notion of unity which emerges as the central theme of Gladstone's religious preoccupations in these years. If the glory of Christianity was the unique representation of Revelation and moral truth in a 'living

* See H. C. G. Matthew, 'Gladstone, Vaticanism and the Question of the East', in D. Baker, ed., *Studies in Church History*, xv (1978).

† *Gleanings*, iii. 151.

and working system', then the harmonious interaction of the different parts of that system must be of central concern to any of its participants.

Gladstone's concern for ecumenism manifested itself at several levels, European, British, occidental and transatlantic, international and local. There were two chief stimuli to ecumenical thinking among Anglicans in the nineteenth century; the *via media* of J. H. Newman, which saw the Church of England as the balancing point, and perhaps the broker between Roman Catholicism and Nonconformity, and the rather more cosmopolitan 'branch church' theory of William Palmer of Worcester College, Oxford, which saw the Apostolic Churches—Roman, Anglican, and Eastern—forming three branches, each with its own legitimacy and traditions, from one central Apostolic trunk.* Rather characteristically, Gladstone made use of both these approaches simultaneously: 'The Church of England appears to be placed in the very centre of all the conflicting forms of Christianity, like the ancient Church between the Arians and the Sabellians.'† This Anglican centrality was to provide the basis for interest and activity in two rather different spheres. First, if a strictly Anglican based 'religious nationality' had ceased to be a practical possibility, then something of its quality might be saved by a broader-based alliance of religious and ethical organizations which could at least agree on second-order principles in the United Kingdom context. Second, the Church of England might play its part in recovering 'the visible unity' of the Church at an international level.

In what may be called domestic religion, Gladstone developed links with prominent Nonconformists such as the Wesleyan J. H. Rigg and the Congregationalists Baldwin Brown and Newman Hall; he attended a number of the Moody–Sankey revivalist meetings in 1875; and when writing about recent religious developments he attempted to stress points of agreement rather than of fault. Thus in 'The course of religious thought', published just before the start of the Bulgarian Atrocities campaign in 1876, in attempting to classify 'multitudes of aimless or erratic forces, crossing and jostling one another',‡ he went out of his way to incorporate 'the Protestant Evangelical' school in a tone not at all characteristic of the 'high Church party' to which he gave the chief place and of which he was in most respects a member. Gladstone even praised Newman Hall's nondenominational Surrey Chapel, and also found some positive points in Unitarianism,§ the

---

* See J. H. Newman, 'Introduction' to *Lectures on the Prophetical Office of the Church* (1837), 8 and W. Palmer, *Treatise on the Church of Christ*, 2v. (1838); Gladstone's interest in Palmer, important at the time of the writing of *The State in its Relations with the Church* in 1838 and its later editions, continued; see his mem. of 1885, Add MS 44769, f. 77; Palmer was in frequent correspondence in 1875, see Add MS 44446. Gladstone played some part in trying to persuade Palmer to produce a second edition of the *Treatise*; see letter to Döllinger, 1 September 1882, in Lathbury ii. 321.

† W. E. Gladstone, *Church Principles considered in their results* (1840), 507.

‡ *Gleanings*, iii. 95.

§ *Gleanings*, iii. 112–21. He had been re-reading Newman's *Arians of the fourth century* in the midst of the Vatican controversy; see 24 Jan. 75 and, for Martineau, 12 Feb. 75.

belief held by his friend, the Belgian economist, de Laveleye. Although in no way conceding his own position, he showed considerable interest in the 'Ramsgate Tracts' series published by Thomas Scott, 'an ardent, unswerving Theist',* and engaged in a good-natured controversy with him about the value of prayer, sending him a series of 'Propositions on Prayer'.

This enthusiasm for integration was given practical effect in Gladstone's quite frequent attendance at the Metaphysical Society, at which he sometimes took the chair. This society, founded by James Knowles of the *Contemporary Review* and the *Nineteenth Century*, brought together leading intellectual figures of the day and for a time provided a remarkable forum for discussion, if not agreement. It was a last attempt at a Coleridgian clerisy, a national intelligentsia—from Manning to Martineau and Huxley—and its disintegration mirrored the gradual waning of Liberal intellectual hegemony, with its eclectic span, best achieved in the 1860s, from Roman Catholic to secularist. In all of this, Gladstone's approach was less like that of a High-Churchman than of a Broad-Churchman, with his stress on areas of agreement. Much though he disliked Broad-Church antidogmatism and much though he held personally to rather rigid doctrinal positions, *in practice* Gladstone owed much more to the Broad-Church tradition than he cared to admit.† He found himself working in ecclesiastical affairs and indeed, as will be shown, in politics also, towards that 'unity of action' despite differences of belief which had been for Thomas Arnold the key to the development of a community.‡

Gladstone's eirenic approach to domestic religion represented an attempt to find an alternative to that youthful ideal of 'religious nationality' whose failure to be realized on High-Church terms had caused such pain in the 1840s. He had never abandoned the ideal in principle, and he continued to believe, perhaps more in the 1870s than in the *dénouement* of the crisis in the later 1840s, in what J. H. Rigg aptly called 'the plastic quasi-secularism—for, after all, Gladstone does not in principle take his stand on secularism proper in any sphere—of his later years'.§

The other great ideal of the youthful Gladstone had been the 'visible unity' of the Church: 'when the mind recurs to that most solemn prayer of the Saviour, at that most solemn hour, for the visible unity of his Church, I feel how impossible it is to wrench away the hope of this (however distant

* Holyoake's description, in G. J. Holyoake, *Sixty years of an agitator's life* (1892), ii, chapter lxxii.

† Though in his handling of the Education Act in 1869–70, Gladstone had followed a clear High-Church line in wanting either full doctrinal teaching, or none at all; see above, vol. i, pp. 201ff.

‡ Thomas Arnold, 'Appendix' to his 'Inaugural Lecture' in *Introductory lectures on modern history* (1845), 39.

§ J. H. Rigg, 'Mr. Gladstone's Ecclesiastical Opinions', *London Quarterly Review*, xliii. 385 (January 1875); a perceptive review both of *A Chapter of Autobiography* and on *Vaticanism*.

and however difficult) achievement from the heart of all true belief in Christ'.* Impracticality and the realities of politics had broken the hope of 'religious nationality'; the Roman Catholic Church increasingly spoiled any immediate prospect of 'visible unity' with a series of developments: the definition of the Immaculate Conception in 1854, the *Syllabus Errorum* in 1864, and the Declaration of Infallibility in 1870. Any possibility of even tentative soundings towards Anglican–Roman union, of the sort proposed in the 1860s by Ambrose Phillipps de Lisle, were hardly worth practical consideration, and the sense of betrayal consequent upon this infused the writing of the second and third Vatican pamphlets written early in 1875.

As an alternative—and here Gladstone worked within an identifiably High-Church group—negotiations were begun with the Bonn Reunion Conferences of 1874 and 1875. These were sponsored by Gladstone's old friend Johann Ignaz von Döllinger, perhaps the only man of his contemporaries whom Gladstone regarded as heroic, whose opposition to the Declaration of Infallibility led to his excommunication. These conferences involved the Old Catholics,† of whom so much was expected and who in the eyes of many High-Churchmen including Gladstone had taken on the mantle of true Continental Catholicism, the Anglican High-Churchmen (particularly H. P. Liddon, Malcolm MacColl, Christopher Wordsworth, and E. S. Talbot, Catherine Gladstone's nephew-by-marriage) and representatives of the Eastern Orthodox Churches, particularly the Greeks. The aim of the conferences, Gladstone believed, was in line with his own preoccupation with the nature of authority; it was that 'of establishing the voice of the individual Church as the legitimate traditional authority'.‡ The conferences were thus simultaneously anti-Vatican and constructive in their own right. Gladstone was asked to attend the 1875 Conference, but declined; he was none the less kept in close touch with developments.

The presence of the Orthodox representatives he found particularly gratifying. Orthodoxy represented the achievement of 'religious nationality' in perhaps its most successful form, an almost complete blending of Church and nation. Gladstone had with some success gone out of his way while Prime Minister to encourage Anglican–Orthodox contacts. Disagreements over the *Filioque* clause of the Creed made progress difficult; on this issue Gladstone, in marked difference with E. B. Pusey and most of the High-Church group, conceded the Eastern Churches' case and hoped that the conferences would lead 'swiftly to the door of *action*'.§ He encour-

---

* *Church Principles*, 507.
† For the Old Catholics, see above, p. 257, n. †.
‡ Letter to Döllinger, 29 August 1875, in Lathbury, ii. 62.
§ Letter to Archbishop Lycurgus, October 1875, Lathbury ii. 63; see 29 Sept., 1 Oct. 75. Gladstone was also in touch with the Greek community in London, especially Mavrogordato, who

aged Döllinger and Lycurgus, Archbishop of Syros and Tenos, whom he had entertained at Hawarden in 1870, to further action. Some hoped for a further round of talks in 1876 or 1877, but the crisis over the rebellion of Serbia and the atrocities committed by the Turks in Bulgaria destroyed these hopes, as the British government watched passively.

The resurgence of the Eastern Question broke these tentative ecumenical roots: the Orthodox Slavs would not attend a conference with Anglicans while the British government was the chief defender of their Turkish persecutors. It also broke the unity of the High-Churchmen: Gladstone, H. P. Liddon, and Malcolm MacColl led the campaign against the atrocities; most Tories would not follow. A conference in 1878 was impossible, Liddon told Döllinger: 'so many good Churchmen (—for instance Mr Beresford Hope—) are political allies of Lord Beaconsfield'.* Beaconsfieldism thus helped to spoil a promising and important ecumenical initiative, just as Pius IX, on a grander scale, had set back Church unity by a century in 1870. The inner force of a Gladstonian pamphlet was always religious, and these failures of ecumenism must be borne in mind as the more political aspects of the Eastern Question are examined.

Gladstone's retirement had thus involved him in a complex series of theological and ecclesiastical debates and discussions, far removed, perhaps, from modern expectations of the retirement interests of a former Liberal Chancellor of the Exchequer and Prime Minister. This disjunction highlights the danger of trying to extrapolate from a fundamentally religious mind those features of Gladstone's opinions, writings, and actions which fit the categories of twentieth-century secularism.

The years 1874–6 form no incidental interval, nor were the issues small-scale or peripheral. The existence of hell and the unity of Christendom were hardly marginal themes: 'By thought good or evil on these matters the destinies of mankind are at this time [1875] affected infinitely more than by the work of any man in Parliament.' Work 'with the pen' in his study in 1875 had brought him to focus considerably, though not uniquely, on the area of Orthodox Christianity which was shortly, for partially though not wholly different reasons, to be the centre of dramatic political controversy. These studies and activities serve as a warning against explaining his subsequent behaviour too much in terms of party or domestic politics. Moreover, interest in the Levant had been further increased by Gladstone's classical studies which, building on his earlier *Studies on Homer*, linked Egypt and Homeric Greece with Hebrew sources and the book of Genesis. The

organized a Greek presence at the Bonn Conference and communicated with Döllinger; Add MS 44447, f. 109.

* Liddon to Döllinger, Trinity Sunday 1878, Liddon MSS, Keble College, Oxford; a conference in 1876 was prevented by disagreements over the *Filioque*, and a conference in 1878 by the Eastern Question; see J. O. Johnston, *Life and letters of H. P. Liddon* (1904), 190.

activities of retirement from political life thus ironically pointed Gladstone in precisely the direction of his political return.

Nationality, Politics, and the Moral World Order

It cannot be said that the Bulgarian Atrocities of 1876 burst upon Britain, or Gladstone, from a clear sky. War and revolution in the Balkans, widely reported in the press from the autumn of 1875, already raised the possibility of the collapse of Turkey-in-Europe and of a consequent partition by the powers. There were two questions, partly but not inseparably joined: the stability of Turkish power, and the lot of the Christian subjects of the Porte, as the Turkish government was technically known. There were also two aspects to the subsequent campaign, its content, and its presentation.

From the autumn of 1875, when at Chatsworth he expressed alarm at 'the amazing news of a purchase outright of the Suez Canal Shares', fearing 'grave consequences' 'if not done in concert with Europe',* Gladstone became increasingly preoccupied with imperial affairs, whether in the form of the Canal share purchase, the Roman overtones of the Queen's new title (eventually announced as 'Empress of India'), the issue of slavery, and the position of Christians in Turkey. Seven of his ten substantial speeches in the Commons in 1876 were on these topics, opening with a brief 'vindication of our concern in the case of the Christian subjects of Turkey'. These interventions were much more critical of the government's Royal Titles Bill and of the Suez Canal purchase than they were of its Turkish policy, though hostility to the purchase partly reflected alarm at a much more direct and uniquely British involvement in Eastern Mediterranean affairs.

During the first six months of 1876, Gladstone's interest in Ottoman affairs certainly increased, with briefings from Stratford de Redcliffe and Lady Strangford and her son,† a reading of Serbian poetry, and assistance to a distressed gentlewoman destitute through the fall of the 1854 Turkish loan stock, but he was also preoccupied with his very important review of Trevelyan's *Macaulay*, and the suicide of his wife's brother-in-law, George Lyttelton. The tone of his speeches on Eastern affairs was as much retrospective as admonitory. He spoke as 'the only person [in the House] who has been officially connected with this great question in its historical character, who is responsible for the proceedings connected with the Crimean War, and not only so, but who says now, in a day when the Crimean War is in a very different state of popularity from that which it enjoyed and elicited a quarter of a century ago, that he does not wish to shrink from that responsibility'.‡

---

* 26 Nov. 75. Gladstone shortly afterwards began a direct personal interest in Egyptian affairs, for he bought £45,000 of Egyptian Tribute Loan at 38, probably in October 1876.

† The Strangfords were involved in organizing relief for Bulgarians.

‡ *Hansard*, 3rd series [subsequently: *H*] 231. 174, 31 July 1876.

None the less, while admitting the difficulties of the government, he asserted the general 'moral right of interference' of the 'European concert', and emphasized the essential need for the government to accept the criterion of joint action apparently abandoned in its unilateral purchase of the Suez Canal shares. He argued first, that Turkish territorial integrity should be, if possible, in principle maintained;* second that Turkey had failed as a governor of Christian peoples ('The principles of civil society as they are understood in Europe are not understood in Turkey, are not embraced in the Ottoman faith'). Consequently 'measures conceived in the spirit and advancing in the direction of self-government' were required: 'if we can get rid of the difficulties of local administration by a Power which is wholly incompetent to conduct it', especially from Constantinople, 'we may attain the very practical object of good government'.† A solution of Turkish suzerainty over devolved local governments, rather than partition or independence for the provinces, was to be Gladstone's preferred position throughout the crisis. Even before the popular agitation had really begun, Gladstone had by the end of July 1876 measured out the ground and the arguments which were, in language much more strident, to be the essence of his position in subsequent years.

Disraeli, Gladstone, and the Question of the East, 1876–1880

The campaign of 1876–80 is one of the great set-pieces of Victorian history, and both Gladstone and Disraeli realized it to be such. That sense of wonder and even of innocence which Victorians brought to their revivalist crusades and to their theatre-going and which Henry Irving, whose performances Gladstone eagerly attended in these years, so astutely played upon, was an essential element of the politics of the time, and in the decaying days of Western representative government it is a quality which is hard to recapture.

Disraeli and Gladstone both played their parts to the full and both had a strong sense of the dramatic. The first, world-weary and ill, rallied his energies to achieve, at the least, the extraordinary personal triumph of the Congress of Berlin, and to set the terms of Conservative imperial rhetoric for almost a century. Recognizing the power of symbol, Disraeli created for the new electorate the myth of the imperial party with its 'patriotic' underpinnings of Queen, Church, and Empire.‡ The corollary of this, the portrayal of the opposing party as unpatriotic, sketched in the 1872

---

* As Prime Minister, Gladstone had pressed Clarendon, his Foreign Secretary, to prevent Egyptian independence from the Porte.

† *H* 231. 186, 198–9.

‡ This is, considering its importance, a curiously understudied phenomenon; the survey in chapter 2 of R. T. McKenzie and A. Silver, *Angels in Marble* (1968) shows the unchanging essence of Conservative propaganda from the late 1870s to the 1950s.

Crystal Palace speech, entered the heart of Conservative electoral methodology in Beaconsfield's 'manifesto' issued during the 1880 general election, significantly for the future uniting constitutional change in Ireland with anti-Imperialism:

There are some who challenge the expediency of the imperial character of this realm. Having attempted, and failed, to enfeeble our colonies by their policy of decomposition, they may perhaps now recognise in the disintegration of the United Kingdom a mode which will not only accomplish but precipitate their purpose.*

Though hardly successful in 1880, this attempt at Conservative pre-emption of patriotism was, appropriately modified to suit the occasion, to have a long and effective life. Disraeli knew it to be a myth in the sense that he knew that his government's policies were not intended to amount to a thorough-going 'Imperialism', but he also seems to have recognized that for certain sections of the electorate quite a wide discrepancy between rhetoric and policy was acceptable and perhaps even expected.

Gladstone brought to bear all his formidable powers of analysis, ethical power, and rhetoric to turn the crisis to encourage a national debate on national objectives, attempting to rally the electorate to the support of a wide range of policy positions. There was, therefore, an implied rationalism about his approach which contrasted markedly with the Conservatives' symbolism. Ironically, he too created a myth, but he differed from Disraeli in not knowing it to be such: the myth that the direction of British imperial policy could be more than marginally affected either by individuals or by popular opinion.

Few stories can be better known, or better documented, than the Eastern Question crisis and its aftermath, and it has called forth a distinguished literature which reflects the kaleidoscopic nature of the crisis, involving as it did foreign and imperial policy, religion, finance, and the form and organization of domestic politics.† Only the Irish Question which replaced it rivalled it for drama, passion, and its capacity to act as a prism for the refraction of national and international attitudes.

This is not the place to offer a detailed account of its very complex

* W. F. Monypenny and G. E. Buckle, *Life of Benjamin Disraeli*, 6 vols. (1910–20) [subsequently: Buckle], vi. 514–16.

† R. W. Seton-Watson, *Disraeli, Gladstone and the Eastern Question* (1935) still holds its place as an outstanding work of research and interpretation, as does B. H. Sumner, *Russia and the Balkans 1870–1880* (1937); the pathology of the first months of the campaign is well analysed in R. T. Shannon, *Gladstone and the Bulgarian Agitation 1876* (1963), with a gem of an introduction by G. Kitson Clark; R. Millman, *Britain and the Eastern Question 1875–1878* (1979) is a detailed survey; W. N. Medlicott, *Bismarck, Gladstone and the Concert of Europe* (1956) deals with the ideology and the negotiations of the late 1870s; 'Gladstonian foreign policy. The contradictions of morality', in A. J. P. Taylor, *The Trouble Makers* (1957) is a sparkling indictment. More sympathetic to the Porte is B. Jelavich, *The Ottoman Empire, the Great Powers, and the Straits Question, 1870–1887* (1973).

narrative.* Viewed retrospectively from Gladstone's point of view, the reader may care to bear in mind that the period 1876–80 fell into three general phases. First, from August 1876 to the spring of 1877, the 'atrocities campaign' attempted to rouse public attention and to force the government and also the Liberal party to respond to the atrocities in Bulgaria. The campaign in its early months was necessarily entirely extra-parliamentary in form, as Parliament did not sit between August 1876 and February 1877. Its focal point was Gladstone's pamphlet, *The Bulgarian Horrors and the Question of the East*, published on 5 September 1876, which led to a series of speeches and other writings, whose details we will examine later. Action was demanded through the Concert of Europe to end acts of atrocities by the Porte and to achieve a resettlement of the relations between the Porte and its Christian provinces. The Conference of Constantinople early in 1877, followed by Turkish rejection of its requirements and by British failure to respond to this rejection, marked the end of this phase.

The second phase was that of the Russo-Turkish war and the sub-sequent settlement at the Congress of Berlin in 1878. It began when Russia cut the knot of inactivity in April 1877 and invaded Turkey on behalf of the

---

* It may be of use to give here a brief *résumé* of some of the main events:

1869 Suez Canal opened

1870 Start of establishment of Bulgarian Exarchate

1871 London conference ratifies changes in the Black Sea clauses of 1856 Paris Peace Treaty

1875 July Insurrection in Bosnia and Herzegovina

 November Britain buys Suez Canal shares

 December Andrassy Note calls for reforms for Bosnia and Herzegovina

1876 April–May Bulgarian insurrection viciously repressed

 May Berlin Memorandum: plan for armistice and pacification of the Balkans not accepted by Britain

 Revolution in Constantinople regains power for the reformers

 June–July Serbia and Montenegro declare war on Turkey

 July Reichstadt agreement between Austria and Russia anticipates Turkish partition

 September 'Bulgarian Horrors' published

 December Constantinople Conference meets

  Midhat Pasha's constitution

1877 January Turkey rejects the Conference's demands

 March Ignatiev's mission to Western capitals

 April Russia declares war on Turkey

 May Gladstone's 'Resolutions' in the Commons

 December Fall of Plevna to Russia

1878 January British fleet despatched to Constantinople, but recalled: Carnarvon resigns

  Turkish–Russian armistice

 February British fleet reaches Constantinople

 March Treaty of San Stephano

  Derby resigns

 April Indian troops brought to Mediterranean

 May–June Secret Anglo-Russian and Anglo-Turkish agreements: Bulgaria reduced and Cyprus British

 June–July Berlin Congress

1879 October German–Austrian alliance

  Russia evacuates Roumania and Bulgaria.

Christian subjects. Gladstone reacted by moving Resolutions in the Commons in early May 1877. These Resolutions were designed to achieve 'a vital or material alteration of the declared policy of Her Majesty's Government', namely, the abandonment of the policy of 'remonstrances and expostulations only' and its replacement by participation in the 'united action of Europe' presently represented by Russia alone.* The failure of the 'Resolutions' and their weak support by the Liberal party in the Commons—the government had a majority of 131 on the only vote—perforce gave way to an attempt to ensure right behaviour by Britain at the peace-making Congress so as to gain a lasting settlement of the problem of the instability in the Turkish Empire and of injustice to its subject peoples. In the third phase, the question of Britain's world role widened. The iniquities of the activities of Beaconsfield and Salisbury in 1878 with respect to Turkish and Mediterranean affairs—'an astounding announcement of the new Asiatic Empire'†—merged with imperial crises in Southern Africa and the North-West frontier of India to produce a general condemnation of 'a whole system of Government'.‡

During the third phase, as the end of the seven-year Parliament neared, Gladstone moved from attempts to influence and redirect government policy to a determination to defeat the government at the coming general election, a determination publicly signalled by his agreement early in 1879 to stand for Midlothian.

It must, of course, be remembered that these phases were hardly apparent at the time. If government policy was uncertain and divided, the task of those in the opposition attempting to influence it was made the more complex and uncertain. However, once his attention was engaged upon Balkan affairs, Gladstone at least had no doubts of the scale of the drama:

My desire for the shade, a true and earnest desire has been since August [1876] rudely baffled: retirement & recollection seem more remote than ever. But [it] is in a noble cause, for the curtain rising in the East seems to open events that bear cardinally on our race.§

This chapter will not attempt to take the reader through the narrative of Gladstone's involvement in the details of the developing crisis in the East and its *dénouement*. Rather, it will offer a discussion of the terms in which he analysed the question and which led him to make a wholesale denunciation of 'Beaconsfieldism' in the Midlothian Campaigns of 1879 and 1880.

Gladstone's behaviour in these years cannot be seen simply in terms of party politics or personal ambition, though these factors no doubt played their part. His approach reflected the theological preoccupations of the

* *H* 234. 404, 416.
† 8 July 78.
‡ W. E. Gladstone, *Political speeches in Scotland* (1879) [subsequently: *Political speeches* (1879)], 50.
§ 29 Dec. 76.

previous eighteen months of retirement: it was High Church in conception, Evangelical in conviction, and Broad Church in presentation. It will be convenient to look at these three aspects of his reaction and contribution very generally in such terms. This analysis will then be set in the context of the party politics of the day, and of the structure of political communication within which politicians were coming to work and which the campaign over the Eastern Question in certain respects dramatically extended.

High-Church Nationality, Turkey, and the Concert of Europe

The High-Church ideology of the Concert of Europe is stated in essence in the opening sentence of the four volumes of *Commentaries upon International Law* written by Sir Robert Phillimore, Gladstone's High-Church friend and confidant: 'The necessity of mutual intercourse is laid in the nature of States, as it is of Individuals, by God, who willed the State and created the Individual.'* The Concert of Europe as it had operated between 1814 and 1871 had rested on the principle of reconciling the interests of the Great Power states through congresses (occasionally), conferences (frequently), and co-ordinated pressure upon deviant members.† Membership of it conferred and confirmed status and in turn expected responsibility, and its members were ready to go to considerable lengths to maintain the framework of Concert and Conference. It thus had a practical and a theoretical justification. It recognized the differing interests of states, it accepted that some states were more powerful than others, and it worked through the existing social structure of Europe, the continuing power of the aristocracy being exemplified in its control of the embassies and chancelleries through which the Concert system was worked.

Of all this, the High-Churchman in Gladstone approved: the Concert could be seen as the Branch Church theory in action. It provided in the affairs of this world a means of co-operation without proselytization between Protestant, Roman Catholic, and Orthodox. Unlike the Pope in 1864 and 1870, it was not inherently anti-national, and the new Italy and the new Germany were assimilable within its structure; 'Religious nationality' of the Gladstonian sort obviously required nations. The Holy Alliance powers of the Concert had, of course, been strongly opposed to the recognition of nationalism as a basis for legitimacy, but Britain and, spasmodically, France, had not been.

In looking to nationalism, Gladstone found himself apparently on common ground with the Liberals, though his nationalism was primarily religious rather than liberal in origin; he had been a nationalist before he had been a liberal. He also shared, to a considerable extent, the Liberal

---

* R. Phillimore, *Commentaries upon International Law* (1854–7), i. v.

† See C. Holbraad, *The Concert of Europe. A study in German and British international theory 1815–1914* (1970).

belief in the benefits of free trade in promoting international harmony, and he saw free trade as the partner of the Concert. When he took the chair on the occasion of the centenary of the publication of *The Wealth of Nations*, he reminded his fellow members of the Political Economy Club and their distinguished guests that 'The operations of commerce are not confined to the material ends; that there is no more powerful agent in consolidating and in knitting together the amity of nations; and that the great moral purpose of the repression of human passions, and those lusts and appetites which are the great cause of war, is in direct relation with the understanding and application of the science which you desire to propagate.'* Free-trade commerce would provide the underlying drive towards amity; the Concert would work at the political level to prevent irresponsible acts by its members. The Concert was, therefore, reactive rather than anticipatory in its actions.† In advocating both free-trade commerce and the Concert as the means towards the avoidance of war, Gladstone stopped short of the classic Liberal position, well stated by F. H. Hinsley: 'The belief that progress was destined to replace inter-government relations by the free-play of enlightened public opinion between societies.'‡ Gladstone's sense of sin was married to his realism and his executive experience in preventing such thoroughgoing optimism.

None the less, Gladstone was optimistic. In advocating a view of international society which had both an economic and a political dimension—free trade the regulator of the one, the Concert of the other—Gladstone at the least offered a wide vision which came to incorporate in British politics both the Manchester radicals, suspicious though they were of external obligation and intervention, and the Whigs, cautious though they were becoming about popular influences on foreign policy. In bringing together Adam Smith and Canning, Gladstone based his position on the precedent and eirenicism of the past, but he also found himself offering, and newly associating with a popular campaign, a vision of international legitimacy and order which, as later developed and institutionalized in the League of Nations and the United Nations, represented the best hope of twentieth-century Liberalism.§ Gladstone was, therefore, a vital part of that process

---

* *Revised Report of the proceedings at the dinner of 31st May 1876 held in celebration of the hundredth year of publication of the 'Wealth of Nations'* (1876), 42–3.

† Thus Gladstone emphasized in his speech on 7 May 1877 that during the 1868–74 Liberal government 'there were no events in Turkey on which we could take our stand. There was, so to speak, no point of departure'; *H* 234. 430.

‡ F. H. Hinsley, *Power and the Pursuit of Peace* (1963), 111. See also Deryck Schreuder, 'Gladstone and the Conscience of the State', in P. Marsh, ed., *The Conscience of the Victorian State* (1979), esp. 96ff.

§ See J. L. Hammond, 'Gladstone and the League of Nations mind', in *Essays in Honour of Gilbert Murray*, ed. J. A. K. Thomson and A. J. Toynbee (1936), 95; see also P. F. Clarke, *Liberals and Social Democrats* (1978), 276ff. Hammond stressed the role of Homer in Gladstone's thoughts about the European comity; classicism offered a bridge between Gladstone and the Murray–Hammond group which crossed the chasm created by his High-Churchmanship.

by which an international order of conservative, monarchic, origin was given a popular base in the era of the extended franchise.

The case of Turkey represented an example of the type of instance with which the Concert, in Gladstone's view, should deal. Since 1856 Turkey had been a member of the Concert, albeit on sufferance; if Turkey had, in the words of Sir Robert Phillimore, 'acquired the Rights, she has also subjected herself to the Duties of a civilised Community'.* These duties on the part of Turkey had in the 1860s and early 1870s been to a considerable extent fulfilled by the Tanzimat movement, with its leaders Ali Pasha and Fuad Pasha. The failure of their programme in 1871–2, and the consequent Islamic reaction, marked the end, at least for the time being, of expectations of a Europeanized Porte.† None the less, the atrocities in Bulgaria in May 1876 occurred within an area now expected to be subject to the usual European conventions and standards of civic behaviour. The scale of the atrocities was thought to be large: 12,000–15,000 killed either by the Turks or by their local agents, the Bashi-Bazouks, was the usual contemporary estimate.‡ But it was not simply the number of dead which was important, large though this was by nineteenth-century standards, but rather that the slaughter had occurred within the boundaries of 'civilization'. Turkey was responsible for ensuring minimum standards of order and justice; thus the Concert was obliged to intervene in her internal affairs if it was shown that these standards had been grossly contravened.§ The Concert had acted in 1854 to prevent Russia behaving irresponsibly towards Turkey; it must now act again to censure Turkey for her proven misbehaviour towards her Christian subjects. The solution, Gladstone thought, must be 'local liberty and practical self-government in the disturbed provinces of Turkey' while at the same time preserving the principle of Turkish sovereignty and thus avoiding partition, 'the imposition upon them of any other Foreign Dominion'. The precedent was the action of the Concert, under Canning's leadership, in the Greek crisis of 1826–7,¶ a precedent publicly recalled by Gladstone (following Earl Russell) at quite an early stage of the campaign.‖

---

* R. Phillimore, *Commentaries upon International Law* (1857), iii. iv.

† See R. H. Davison, *Reform in the Ottoman Empire 1856–1876* (1963), chs. vii and viii. As Prime Minister, Gladstone seems to have taken little interest in the dramatic change of mood in Turkey in 1872–4, although it was well reported by Elliot, the ambassador. In view of his attitude to Turkey from 1876 onwards, it is this absence, rather than his expectations in the 1856–70 period, which is strange.

‡ The actual number of dead remains uncertain; the evidence is surveyed in Millman, op. cit., chapter 10.

§ The bearing of the 1856 Treaty on this issue was a very vexed question; as Phillimore pointed out in 1857, Article ix contains 'the most singular provision, which might almost seem intended at once to recognise and to prohibit the Right of INTERVENTION by the powers of Christendom on behalf of their co-religionists'; *Commentaries upon International Law*, iii. iv.

¶ Gladstone's third and fourth Resolutions of 7 May 1877; only the first Resolution was formally moved but Gladstone made it clear that, despite the reservations of other members of the ex-Cabinet, he stood by all five. ‖ In 'The Hellenic Factor in the Eastern Problem' (1876).

Gladstone's view of the Concert was by no means democratic. The Concert of Europe was essentially monarchic—in 1876 even France had a nominal monarchic majority in the Assembly—and its machinery was that of the overwhelmingly aristocratic structure of European embassies. Gladstone offered no structural proposals to improve or advance upon the Concert's effectiveness. He did not even go as far as those theorists such as J. C. Bluntschli who advocated limited machinery for codifying international law,* though he quoted Bluntschli in his pamphlet 'Lessons in Massacre' to justify intervention and described him as 'the greatest authority on international law of the present day'.† Although Gladstone could certainly point to his own government's use of arbitration in 1872 to settle the 'Alabama claims' of the United States government, to its value in drawing the United States towards the framework of the European Concert, and to its importance as a precedent, he none the less did not personally suggest means of institutionalizing such procedures.

Gladstone's position was thus essentially conservative, in the straightforward meaning of that term, and also in its details rather cautious, though it also pointed, in the long term, towards a restored international order. He represented in international affairs what was fast coming to seem, for a generation, an apparently old-fashioned view of harmony obtainable through Concert and open Conferences, buttressed by free trade, a view soon to be undercut by secret alliances, protectionism, cartelization, and all that Bismarck's *Reich* represented. As with all Gladstone's political initiatives, his conservatism had radical overtones, in this case, as so often, as much in the nature of its presentation as in its content. As applied in the circumstances of the day, it seemed, especially to Conservatives, dangerous and even revolutionary in its implications.

The aim of the Concert was to promote amity, but in its execution this promotion need not necessarily be pacific. The use of arms, though its slaughter was regrettable and its cost undesirable, was a legitimate weapon in the establishment of right. In Gladstone's view, Britain had been right to join other members of the Concert in armed resistance to Russia in 1854, and Russia was right forcibly to impose a solution upon Turkey in 1877–8. Within the context of the Concert, coercion by arms was, in its appropriate context, a proper instrument of policy which would in most cases achieve its result without war. 'Coercion by menace, justly and wisely used, need not lead to war'.‡ Once back in power, Gladstone sent the Concert's fleet

---

* For Bluntschli's realistic recognition of the role of the Great Powers, and for his proposals, see Hinsley, op. cit., 134–5 and Holbraad, op. cit., 66–70.

† Though without naming him directly, in 'The Sclavonic Provinces' (1877), 8. See also, for a similar named tribute, *H* 234. 432 (7 May 1877).

‡ *H* 234. 965 (14 May 1877). The criticism of the government, therefore, was not its use of force to support a political demand, but its willingness to act alone, and in what Gladstone saw as the wrong cause.

to Smyrna in 1880 for a show of force against the Porte with no intellectual embarrassment.

The point of departure of the popular phase of the Eastern Question campaign—the denunciation of Turkish atrocities—should not, therefore, be allowed to give the impression that Gladstone, and most of those involved in the campaign, were pacifists. The difference between types of killing lay in the authority for the action. The Concert had that authority, in Gladstone's view, because it represented the best available institutional representation of Christian morality in international affairs. In 1877, arguing that there was 'an authority that proceeds both from experts and from the race', Gladstone turned naturally to St Augustine's majestic maxim, 'Securus judicat orbis terrarum',* which he had quoted with such force at the height of the Franco-Prussian war in 1870. Just as in the extra-European world the 'prolific British mother . . . with her progeny, may also claim to constitute a kind of Universal Church in politics',† so, in the European context, the Concert linked Gladstone's longing for ecumenicity with his perception of authority in the world of affairs.

This elevated analysis was accompanied by a hard-headed view of Britain's interests. Gladstone wrote three long periodical articles at this time which, taken together, are among the most impressive attempts—in a period of national re-appraisal—to assess what should be Britain's position in the world. They still repay reading today: 'Aggression on Egypt and Freedom in the East', *Nineteenth Century* (August 1877); 'Kin beyond Sea', *North American Review* (September 1878); and 'England's Mission', *Nineteenth Century* (September 1878). In these, he dissented from what was becoming the conventional wisdom of the time, that the route to India must be the defining factor in British policy, and he attacked head on the view that the occupation of Egypt should be 'only a question of time'.‡ India detracted from rather than added to Britain's military strength; it was held only as long as 'the will of the two hundred and forty millions of people who inhabit India' wished it to be held. A world view which placed Indian defence as 'a high doctrine . . . is humiliating and even degrading. . . . The root and pith and substance of the material greatness of our nation lies within the compass of these islands; and is, except in trifling particulars, independent of all and every sort of political dominion beyond them.' Egypt, besides the route through the Canal which was less important than

---

* In his dispute with James Fitzjames Stephen on the nature of authority; *Gleanings*, iii. 211. Augustine's passage in full reads: 'Securus judicat orbis terrarum, bonos non esse qui se dividunt ab orbe terrarum in quacunque parte terrarum' (the calm judgement of the world is that those people cannot be good who, in any part of the world, cut themselves off from the rest of the world).

† 'Kin beyond Sea', *Gleanings*, i. 205.

‡ 'Aggression on Egypt and Freedom in the East', *Nineteenth Century* (August 1877), a dispute with Edward Dicey, mostly reprinted in *Gleanings*, iv. 341, from which quotations in the rest of this paragraph are taken.

made out, was also implicitly dangerous. In a remarkable passage, Gladstone anticipated the events of the next eighty years, but in order to deplore them:

Our first site in Egypt, be it by larceny or be it by emption, will be the almost certain egg of a North African Empire, that will grow and grow until another Victoria and another Albert, titles of the Lake-sources of the White Nile, come within our borders; and till we finally join hands across the Equator with Natal and Cape Town, to say nothing of the Transvaal and the Orange River on the south, or of Abyssinia or Zanzibar to be swallowed by way of *viaticum* on our journey. And then, with a great Empire in each of the four quarters of the world, and with the whole new or fifth quarter to ourselves, we may be territorially content, but less than ever at our ease; for if agitators and alarmists can now find at almost every spot 'British interests' to bewilder and disquiet us, their quest will then be all the wider. . . .

The Eastern Question, reinforced by the subsequent difficulties of the Tory government in Southern Africa and on the Indian frontier, thus brought Gladstone to a bold and prophetic analysis of Britain's possible position in the future world order. He freely and without regret accepted the natural relative decline of Britain's industrial supremacy, and the ending of her unique position, especially through the growth of the U.S.A., which would 'probably become what we are now, the head servant in the great household of the World, the employer of all employed'. While 'we have been advancing with this portentous rapidity, America is passing us by as if at a canter'.* Since Britain's power rested on the strength of her domestic economy, and since that power would in the long run be relatively declining, imperial expansion, justifiable though it might be in particular instances, must be resisted. Otherwise a position would be reached where a relatively declining power sought vainly to defend and control a vast Empire whose new acquisitions would each multiply the points of danger, conflict, and potential crisis. An anxious Edwardian could hardly have put it better.

Gladstone thus held that an independently British policy towards the Straits, separate from the Concert's concern at civilized standards of behaviour in Turkey, was unnecessary, undesirable, and dangerous. There was no unique 'British interest', and there should therefore be no unilateral British action. Indeed, the assertion of a British interest independent of that of Europe played into the hands of Russia, for it left Britain the prisoner of the Turks, while allowing the Russians to appear as the sole champions of Christians in the Balkans, a role which they had, in Gladstone's view, been permitted by the Treaty of Küchük Kainardji (1774), but which they had ceded to the Concert at the end of the Crimean

---

* 'Kin beyond Sea' contains the discussion of the rise of the U.S.A., and continues together with 'England's Mission' the analysis developed in 'Aggression on Egypt'.

War in 1856.* To have allowed the Russians to reclaim, by default, their pre-1854 position, was a further danger. The Conservative Cabinet's policy in 1876 had allowed Russia to 'associate all Europe with her', with the danger of a Russo-Turkish agreement, settling 'matters in such a way as to leave all Europe out of account'.

Gladstone was by no means an out-and-out Russophile. *The Bulgarian Horrors* pamphlet was quickly translated into Russian by K. P. Pobedonostsev, later the famous Procurator of the Holy Synod, and soon sold 20,000 copies,† but its author remained very cautious about Russian intentions. Gladstone recognized Russia's 'special temptations'‡ in the Near East; he had seen Russia disrupt Europe in 1854; he condemned her behaviour in Poland and towards Hungarians; his first government had, at least to his own and Granville's satisfaction, dealt with Russian expansionism towards Afghanistan and her attempt at unilateral disruption of the 1856 Black Sea clauses in 1870 (eventually ratified, but with careful safeguards, by a conference in London in 1871). Moreover, Russia's role in ecclesiastical developments in the Balkans was, at the least, questionable. Gladstone's church contacts with the Balkans in the early 1870s were all with Orthodox Greeks and he had quite extensive links with the Greek community in London. He had already been involved polemically in arguing that the Russian Orthodox Church was in spirit narrower than the Greek Orthodox. The Greeks had reached an accommodation with the Porte by which Greek Orthodox religious supremacy over much of Turkey in Europe, and especially in Bulgaria, was until 1870 supported by the Turkish secular power. Gladstone was reluctant to play 'the game of Russia' to see this situation changed.

Russian influence, through the Panslavist Ignatiev, had encouraged the schism against Greek dominance which led to the Bulgarian Exarchate (separate ecclesiastical province) permitted by the Turkish government's Firman (decree) of 1870. This independence from Greek ecclesiastical authority encouraged Bulgarian nationalism, a development anticipated by the Foreign Office at the time,§ and it was the Turkish reaction to this consequence of their own Firman which developed into the massacres of 1876.

* This was a strongly contested point; see *H* 234. 433, 967 (7, 14 May 1877).

† The translation was arranged 'to redeem British honour' by L. C. Alexander, founder of the Royal Historical Society; Gladstone and Alexander wanted the proceeds to go to Balkan Slavs, but they went instead to Russian Panslavists. See R. F. Byrnes, *Pobedonostsev. His Life and Thought* (1968), 125, 433.

‡ *H* 234. 415 (7 May 1877).

§ H. P. T. Barron, Chargé at Constantinople, to Clarendon, 22 March 1870, Foreign Office Confidential Print 3578: 'The question originated in the Hellenizing tendencies of the Greek clergy, which produced a reaction on the part of the Bulgarians in favour of their national clergy ... it became aggravated by the obstinate resistance of the Patriarch to the originally modest demands of the Bulgarians, and has now become fraught with difficulty ... the part taken by the Government in favour of the Bulgarians must have the effect of alienating the Greeks ... it is very doubtful whether this policy is not playing into the hands of the so-called Panslavist party. ...'

Gladstone regarded the Bulgarians' ecclesiastical action as undesirable, though originally prompted by 'a genuine aspiration of nationality'. The reason was that the Bulgarians, instead of accepting the old Christian principle of 'local distribution', beloved of High-Churchmen, demanded jurisdiction 'wherever there were Bulgarians', thus going against the tradition of the Ante-Nicene Church and making 'a plain violation of the first principles in any religious society'. These reservations about the Bulgarian schism, expressed in 1872 and 1875,* may in part account for Gladstone's delay in August 1876 in involving himself with the rising agitation until the scale of Turkish atrocities became quite certain. Certainly, it is an aspect of Balkan affairs and Gladstone's reaction to them hitherto almost entirely disregarded.

The Bulgarian schism had broken the 'harmony between the Ottoman Porte and the Christian Churches within its dominions', important for 'the peace of the Levant' which Gladstone had encouraged in 1872, as well as being a further blow to ecumenicity. For a man who had looked in the early 1870s to 'a firm union, founded on common interest, between the Porte & its dependent provinces' to switch to regarding the Bulgars and their grievances as the focal point of Balkan affairs required caution and confirmation. This the sheer shock of the atrocities provided. Even when he had made the switch, Gladstone showed himself keen to broaden the question quickly, and he did so in his article 'The Hellenic Factor', written in November 1876, which stressed the importance of remembering 'Greek as well as Slav grievances'.†

---

* See letters to Archbishop Lycurgus of 18 August 1872 and October 1875 in Lathbury, ii. 304, 63; that of 1872 is of especial interest as it anticipates the dangers of a religious dispute leading to Russian exploitation of political crisis. See T. A. Meininger, *Ignatiev and the Establishment of the Bulgarian Exarchate, 1864–1872* (1970) which on the whole bears out Gladstone's reading of the case.

† Gladstone reinforced his position in a letter replying to a request for comment by Negropontis, a Greek merchant in Constantinople (see 9 Jan. 77): 'For me the question of the East is not a question of Christianity against the Porte and the governing Ottomans; because all the grievances of the Mussulman and Jewish subjects—and such, without doubt, there are—ought to disappear in the act of applying an efficacious and well-considered remedy to the grievances of the Christians, who form the mass of the oppressed. I do not, then, recognise any plurality of causes; for me the cause is one only, and I cannot commend either Greeks, who refuse their moral support to the Slavs, or Slavs who refuse it to the Greeks. That efficacious remedy I find in the development cf the local liberties of all such Provinces as are proved to be suffering. . . . The equitable delimitation of Slav and Hellenic Provinces is a question difficult and grave enough; but it is an ulterior question such as cannot, in my opinion, be adjusted in a satisfactory manner unless when Greek and Slav alike shall have imparted to one another, on the basis of a plan of local liberties, the reciprocal sympathy which will be alike generous and wise.' The *Daily Telegraph*, supposedly briefed by Layard, the Ambassador at Constantinople, reported this and a second letter as a call by Gladstone that the Greeks should attack the Turks. A prolonged wrangle between Gladstone, Layard and Levy-Lawson, proprietor of the *Telegraph*, followed, culminating in Ashley's motion in the Commons of 'regret' at Layard's behaviour, which was defeated in 132:206. The correspondence and newspaper reports are mostly printed in *H* 238. 1156 (12 March 1878) and *PP* 1878 lxxxi.

Suzerainty in the Balkans and its Imperial Implications

'Religious nationality' in the Balkans had thus by no means necessarily implied political independence from the Porte and, in advocating the half-way house of suzerainty, Gladstone believed that, at least for the medium term, he was, in contrast to the Conservative government, offering the policy most likely to provide stability in the Near East. As so often in his career, he accepted change to achieve stability. Care must be taken in ascribing to him any full-blown theory of political nationalism. His view of political nationality was not an *a priori* one, but rather the application of 'experience' to situations given by history. Not surprisingly, as the former Colonial Secretary and Prime Minister of the world's most extensive Empire, his point of reference was not the ruled, but the behaviour of the imperial power, whether Turkish, Russian, or British. It was the moral failure of Turkish rule, not the inherent virtue of her 'subject races' or 'subject peoples' (the terms were used interchangeably), which constituted his starting-point.

Gladstone's instinctive interest, outside the sphere of religion, lay in factors preventing amalgamation rather than in those preserving or promoting national identity. In the case of Turkey, generations of rule had not led to that amalgamation of peoples essential to long-term stability, a failure exemplified in the events of 1876–8. In part, the absence of 'an organic union' in Turkey had a 'racial' cause:*

There is, in fact, a great deal of resemblance between the system which prevails in Turkey and the old system of negro slavery. In some respects it is less bad than negro slavery, and in other respects a great deal worse. It is worse in this respect, that in the case of negro slavery, at any rate, it was a race of higher capacities ruling over a race of lower capacities; but in the case of this system, it is unfortunately a race of lower capacities which rules over a race of higher capacities.

More important than this, however, was the failure of the Turks to develop beyond the 'government of force' which they had originally been. Without the influence of law and individual political responsibility, the military genius of the Turks was corrupted and depraved.

The Turks are what circumstances have made them, and depend upon it that if a lot of us were taken and put in their circumstances we, either individually or as a race, would soon cease to do even the limited credit to the Christian name that we now bring to it. They exercise a perfectly unnatural domination over their fellow-creatures; and arbitrary power is the greatest corruptor of the human mind and heart. There is nothing that can withstand it. Human nature requires the restraint

* 'The Sclavonic Provinces of the Ottoman Empire' (1877), 8; further quotations in this paragraph are taken from this lecture. Gladstone read widely in the extensive literature on 'race'; in his journal on 9 September 1877 J. C. Nott and G. R. Gliddon's *Types of Mankind* (1854) is noted as 'Indigenous Races'.

of law. There is, unfortunately, no restraint of law in Turkey, and in the sight of God and man, much as these Christians are to be pitied, perhaps the Turks, who are the victims of that system, are to be pitied still more. The very worst things that men have ever done have been done when they were performing acts of violence in the name of religion. That has been the unfortunate position of the Turks, as a race that not only has conquered, but has conquered in the sacred name of religion. The corruption that results from such a system as that is deep and profound. Mahometans, where they manage their own affairs, and have not got the charge of the destinies of other people, can live in tolerable communities together, and discharge many of the duties of civil and social life. In certain cases, as for instance, in the case of the Moors of Spain, they have exhibited many great and conspicuous merits. It is not the fact that their religion is different from ours which prevents them from discharging civil duties. Do not suppose that for a moment. It is not because they are in themselves so much worse than we are. God forbid that we should judge them. It is that this wretched system under which they live puts into their hands power which human beings ought not to possess, and the consequences are corruption to themselves and misery to those around.

The consequence of this analysis, in many respects classically Liberal in its view of political corruption, was that, although there remained important strategic attractions in Ottoman suzerainty as a solution, a 'clean arrangement' was necessary 'to remove all future occasions of collision and contention between her and the vassal community'.* The Turks had shown their inability to incorporate fully in their Empire 'races of men who were, before the days of Turkish domination, on the same level of civilization as was northern and western Europe, and who carry in them the instincts, and the materials, of freedom and progress'. The self-awareness of the Balkan peoples, chiefly preserved by the Orthodox churches, thus pre-dated the Turkish conquest. The Turks had had their chance and they had failed. Thus, 'let the daily power of the Turk in Bulgaria be destroyed'; even in his advice about the form of the Treaty of San Stephano in 1878 Gladstone stopped short of advocating outright political independence. 'A clean arrangement' did not necessarily mean a clean break. 'Bag and baggage', the catch-phrase of *The Bulgarian Horrors* pamphlet, helped popularize the campaign but it was a misleading distillation of Gladstone's view of a Balkan settlement, which in fact saved as much as it could for the imperial power. 'Bag and baggage' was—like 'the pale of the constitution' in 1864—a phrase whose fame sharpened its author's radical reputation while ignoring the surrounding qualifications.

This appreciation of the difficulties of the process of amalgamation clearly raised rather general questions, going beyond the affairs of the Porte and beyond 'religious nationality'. In a fragment almost certainly written in 1877, Gladstone noted:

* 'The Peace to Come', *Nineteenth Century*, iii. 216 (February 1878).

That no conquest can be legitimate unless it be marked by the introduction of superior laws, institutions, or manners among the conquered. No conquest has been permanent unless followed by amalgamation

Saxons ⎫
Normans ⎬ in England
Franks in France
Lombards in Italy.

The very least that can be expected is that the conquerors should be able to learn civilisation from the conquered as Romans from Greeks.*

If amalgamation was the criterion, how stood the British Empire? England was a splendid example of success—'we have all happily settled down into one homogeneous whole'†—but Ireland and India were obvious subjects of question. Gladstone made glancing remarks about both in his comments on the Balkans, referring to Ireland as 'the far slighter case . . . a vastly milder instance', but none the less admitting an analogy. What was to be compared was Turkey's 'domination', which was 'incurable', with the 'Protestant ascendancy in Ireland', also incurable. Neither case had been in principle hopeless: 'The thing is incurable, but not the men who have to do with the thing. To make them curable, you have to take them out of a position which is false, and leave them in a position which is true, sound and normal.'‡

This the Turks had failed to do, this his own first government's Irish legislation had attempted to achieve, and this must be the motto for the governance of India, where amalgamation in the Saxon/Norman sense was never attempted. The containment and accommodation of 'subject peoples' within an Imperial structure was thus an essential part of the art of government. It might be 'the business of every oppressed people to rise upon every reasonable opportunity against the oppressor'; it might be that 'it was the duty of Bulgaria to rise and to fight';§ but the implication of Gladstone's position was that it was the art of government to see that peoples did not feel themselves to be oppressed and that reasonable policies would remove the 'reasonable opportunity' for a rising. The notion of reasonableness was to prove hard to sustain in the context of late nineteenth-century nationalism.

To draw together the underlying theme of state organization: imperial structures were not inherently unstable or undesirable, but they would become so if local traditions were not accommodated. The notion of suzerainty—an 'infinitely elastic' concept¶—offered a means of allowing

---

* Add MS 44763, f. 96; this paper was used in preparing for 'The Sclavonic Provinces'.
† 'The Sclavonic Provinces', 5.　　‡ 'The Peace to Come', 216, 219.　　§ Ibid., 221.
¶ Described thus in 'The Hellenic Factor', *Gleanings*, iv. 301: 'what it implies is a practical self-management of all those internal affairs on which the condition of daily life depends, such as police and judiciary, with fixed terms of taxation, especially of direct and internal taxation, and with command over the levy of it'.

both local development and the maintenance of large units for the purpose of stability in international relations. If the 1870s saw moves towards both political nationalism and integrative imperialism, Gladstone offered a solution which gave a commitment to neither, and which was to be developed in the context of Southern Africa and Ireland, though events largely superseded it as a solution to the problems of the Ottoman Porte.

The mark of the successful imperial power would be the ability to strike a balance between the requirements of strategic security and the encouragement of local institutions which would preserve local liberties and ventilate local enthusiasm, customs, and traditions. Gladstone did not use the word 'nationalism' in the 1870s—indeed he very rarely used 'ism' as a suffix—and his preferred term, nationality, was applied always in particular cases except when used in conjunction with religion. It would be fair to say, therefore, that Gladstone did not think in terms of nationalism, outside the established nation-states, either as a general phenomenon or as an organizing principle. In keeping with his general anti-metropolitanism in the 1870s, his articles and speeches certainly seemed to reflect important aspects of it, but, as so often, his position was in fact more metropolitan and less 'advanced' than many of his supporters supposed.

An Evangelical Campaign

There lay behind Gladstone's critique of the Eastern Question a coherent argument by no means radical, although coming to seem so in contrast to the strident jingoism of the late 1870s. None the less, the conviction with which he took part in the campaign was exceptional. Between July and September 1876, Gladstone experienced a conversion of Evangelical intensity. The end of his first ministry and the ecclesiastical legislation of 1874 had seen him politically estranged from all but a small group of Liberal High-Churchmen. His resignation as party leader had occurred among a welter of negatives which went well beyond his own wish for an end to political activity: 'out of harmony' was the key-note phrase. However, he had from the first privately reserved his position on a possible return, as he bore in mind 'cases where there is some great public cause for which to contend' which might constrain the immediate reasons for retirement. The Vatican pamphlets of 1874—5 had been an 'expostulation'; they were intended to make a point, and to encourage *others* to action. By the end of 1875 Gladstone hoped 'my polemical period is over'; others had been exhorted, but on the whole they had not acted.* 1876 was to require a different attitude.

As the outcry against the Turkish atrocities developed, especially in the

---

* Ironically, in Ulster Irish disestablishment produced a lowering of sectarianism, so that Orange orators 'did not like to follow Mr. Gladstone and give him any credit for No Popery zeal'; T. Macknight, *Ulster as it is* (1896), i. 331.

North of England, in late July and throughout August, Gladstone was silent. No-one reading the routine entries in his diary between 1 and 27 August would have an inkling that his speech in the Commons on 31 July was to be followed in early September by the most spectacular of all his outbursts. Various reasons for his delay can be offered—uncertainty about the extent of the atrocities, about the Bulgarian position prompted by his views on the religious schism there, unwillingness to embarrass Granville and Hartington, unease about his relationship with the Liberal party, reluctance to commit himself to what was bound to be (on the precedent of 'Vaticanism') at the least a series of highly controversial publications—but no clear conclusion can be drawn.

The reader of Gladstone's diary from 28 August, however, can have no doubt as to the depth and range of his involvement in Balkan affairs. That day he noted: 'Worked on a beginning for a possible pamphlet on the Turkish question.' The entry was accurate as ever: throughout the controversy Gladstone took the actions and responsibilities of imperial Turkey as his starting-point. The crisis was the consequence of an abdication of proper imperial control and responsibility by the Porte.

The 'possible pamphlet' became the most famous of all his publications, *The Bulgarian Horrors and the Question of the East*. The day he began working on it, Gladstone again brought on his lumbago 'by physical exertion', and could not write sitting up: he found 'the back is less strained in bed, where I write against the legs'. The pamphlet, dedicated to Stratford de Redcliffe, was published by John Murray and printed by Clowes, to whom Gladstone began sending copy on 1 September. News of the pamphlet became public and a buzz of excitement rose at every level of the political world. On the night of 3 September Gladstone went to London by overnight train—a mark of his own urgency and excitement—to finish the pamphlet by checking references and quotations in the British Museum. He also that day accepted an invitation to speak on Bulgaria at a meeting in Greenwich: his general involvement in the campaign was thus ensured before the pamphlet was published. The final version of *The Bulgarian Horrors* was discussed on 5 September with Granville on whose recommendation 'various alterations of phrase' were made (i.e. certain passages were softened). At seven p.m. that evening 'complete copies' were received, Gladstone sent them off 'in various directions'—to the press and to friends—and he, Granville, and Hartington went to 'The Heir-at-Law', a farce playing at the Haymarket Theatre.

The rapidity of the publication caught the newspapers on the hop, for publication had not been expected till the next day. This ensured a good sale for Murray, who increased the print-run from 2,000 to 24,000 by 7 September. By the end of the month 200,000 copies of Murray's printing were sold, and it was widely reprinted in newspapers and pirated copies.

Anthony Trollope read it aloud to his family. The publication—on a Tuesday—was complemented on Saturday, 9 September, when Gladstone addressed a huge crowd at Blackheath: he spoke for an hour from three sides of jotted notes to at least 10,000 people. If anyone had missed reports of his pamphlet, he or she could hardly fail to see the page-long reports of the speech in Monday's newspapers or to miss the message that Gladstone was back.

Though the policy prescriptions remained, as has been shown, precise, cautious, and conservative, the passion which urged them was of a new dimension. Reading, correspondence, writing, speaking, all the habitual Gladstonian pursuits bore on a single theme. Moreover, Gladstone recognized he was in for a long haul: the tense used in his retrospect on 29 December 1876, by which time some thought the chief force of the agitation was passed, is significant: 'the curtain rising in the East seems to open events that bear cardinally on our race'. Quite suddenly, in late August 1876, the true nature of Turkish rule had been revealed. As Gladstone put it in his second pamphlet, *Lessons in Massacre* (originally to have been entitled *Who are the Criminals?*), published in March 1877:

The Bulgarian outrages, though they are not the Eastern Question, are a key to the Eastern Question. They exhibit the true genius of the Turkish Government. Externally an isolated though portentous fact, they unlock to us an entire mystery of iniquity. Vast as is their intrinsic importance, they are yet more important for what they indicate, than for what they are. . . . As in individual life, so in the life of Governments, it is the great crisis that searches nature to its depths, and brings out the true spirit of the man.*

As the revelations had been dramatic, so the reaction must be passionate, even if the means of redress be moderate and carefully calculated. This combination of Evangelical enthusiasm and atonement with shrewd and controlled analysis is best seen in Gladstone's article, 'The Paths of Honour and of Shame', written at the height of the crisis in February 1878 as the British Fleet entered the Dardanelles without the permission of the Porte and the Russians halted just short of Constantinople.

The article opens with a classic Evangelical statement—'If this age has pride, and if its pride requires a whipping, the needful discipline is perhaps not far to seek'—and moves on through Bishop Butler to a sharp analysis of what ought to be the policies of Britain at 'the Conference or Congress, be it which it may, that is partly to record, and partly to adjust, the settlement of the great question of the East'.† Evangelicalism involved and implied not only enthusiasm, but a heightened sense of sin and obligation, a commitment to atonement, a crushing of pride, an acute awareness of the

* 'Lessons in Massacre', 73–4. The second pamphlet was originally planned immediately after the first.
† 'The Paths of Honour and Shame', *Nineteenth Century* (March 1878).

penalties for wickedness and, especially among Anglican Evangelicals, an application of these senses to the nation as well as to the individual. Gladstone's refurbished interest in Evangelicalism and its contribution to Anglicanism was reflected in his article of July 1879, which emphasized the close interplay between Evangelicalism and Tractarianism, by which the best features of the former, 'the juice and sap', permeated the latter and thus Anglicanism generally. It did this in part by an 'unseen relation' between the two: 'Causation, in the movements of the human mind, is not a thing single and simple. It is a thing continuous and latent.'*

In a true Evangelical spirit, Gladstone believed himself to have been called 'for a purpose', a call carrying 'the marks of the will of God'. This was a sober analysis of his position. Usually his service to the will of God in politics took the form of the application in particular instances of a general set of beliefs or precepts, carried through with a strong awareness of Godly support. But on this occasion he came to feel that he was the direct recipient of a specific call. Gladstone was conscious of the dangers of such a claim. He was fully aware 'that language such as I have used is often prompted by fanaticism'. He guarded against this 'by tests', that is, he interpreted what he believed to be a Providential calling within a well-established Evangelical context of analysis. The remarkable passage in the diary in which he describes this conviction is of an intensity not experienced since the extraordinary crisis of the 1840s and early 1850s:

Sixty nine years of age! One year only from the limit of ordinary life prolonged to its natural goal! And now these three years last past, instead of unbinding and detaching me, have fetched me back from the larger room which I had laboriously reached and have immersed me almost more than at any former time in cares which are certainly cares of this life.

And this retroactive motion has appeared & yet appears to me to carry the marks of the will of God. For when have I seen so strongly the relation between my public duties and the primary purposes for which God made and Christ redeemed the world? Seen it to be not real only but so close and immediate that the lines of the holy and the unholy were drawn as in fire before my eyes. And why has my health, my strength, been so peculiarly sustained? All this year and more—I think—I have not been confined to bed for a single day. In the great physical and mental effort of speaking, often to large auditories, I have been as it were upheld in an unusual manner and the free effectiveness of voice has been given me to my own astonishment. Was not all this for a purpose: & has it not all come in connection with a process to which I have given myself under clear but most reluctant associations. Most reluctant: for God knoweth how true it is that my heart's desire has been for that rest from conflict & from turmoil which seems almost a necessity for a soul that would be prepared in time to meet its God for eternity.

I am aware that language such as ⟨this is often⟩ I have here used is often

* 'The Evangelical Movement; its parentage, progress and issue', published in the Congregationalist *British Quarterly Review* (July 1879).

prompted by fanaticism. But not always. It is to be tried by tests. I have striven to apply them with all the sobriety I can: and with a full recollection that God sometimes sees fit to employ as his instruments for particular purposes of good those with whom notwithstanding He has yet a sore account to settle.

I am still under the painful sense that my public life is and has the best of me: that it draws off and exhausts from my personal life almost all moral resolution, all capacity for Christian discipline in the personal and private sphere. This it is which makes me anxious for a lawful escape from an honourable struggle, & which but for the clearness of the evidence that it is honourable & is pleasing to God, would make me wretched while it lasts.*

It is, of course, true that Gladstone saw any situation in religious terms, and that, like J. H. Newman and H. E. Manning and other Tractarians and High-Churchmen of Evangelical origin, he continually found the religious experiences of his youth a source of strength in later years when, theologically, he had moved beyond them. None the less, the personal commitment which the Eastern Question called forth from him was self-confessedly of a new order: 'When have I seen so strongly the relation between my public duties and the primary purposes for which God made and Christ redeemed the world?'

It is significant that, despite the intensity of his personal involvement, Gladstone was careful, both in private correspondence and in his journal, to avoid personalizing what is often seen as his dispute with Disraeli. Publicly, Gladstone was on record as stating his view of Beaconsfield's peculiar responsibility for his government's Eastern policy, and his deliberate and persistent efforts to bring him to book. Privately, however, Disraeli was not personally denounced in the strident terms used for the Sultan, 'a bottomless pit of iniquity and fraud' who had a fair chance of defeating Satan in a competition for the fathership of liars. Phillimore noted that 'G. was careful to restrain the expression of his private feelings about Lord B. as he generally is',† and the introspective passages of the journal have the same reticence. There are two substantive comments on Disraeli. On 21 May 1879, Gladstone records: 'Went to afternoon tea with Lady Derby. Found myself face to face with Lord Beaconsfield & this put all right socially between us, to my great satisfaction.' In May 1880, after returning to office, Gladstone closely studied the recently published biography of Beaconsfield by George Brandes, the Danish critic and historian. He commented on it: 'His description of Beaconsfield's mind as metallic & mine as fluid, has merit.' How far this reticence reflects the sort of self-control required by Gladstone's interpretation of Christian behaviour, and how far it suggests that Gladstone may actually have disliked Disraeli's policies rather than his person, cannot now be known.

* 29 Dec. 78.
† Diary of Sir R. Phillimore in Christ Church Library, Oxford [subsequently: Phillimore's Diary], 26 January 1878.

The powerful impulses which brought Gladstone back to the centre of British politics in the autumn of 1876 were to lead, eventually, to his second government in 1880. It took some time, both for Gladstone and for others, before it became clear what was to be the nature of the process which the Bulgarian Atrocities campaign had begun. Privately driven eastwards constantly, Gladstone was reluctant to accept what were to be the full public implications of his position. Two days after the great meeting at Blackheath on 9 September 1876, he records telling Granville 'how pleasant it would be to me if he could publicly lead the present movement', Gladstone seeing his own role, perhaps, as a writer of pamphlets and articles (he began a second pamphlet a few days after his talk with Granville, but converted it, 'I think under a right instinct', into a long letter to the newspapers).

Gladstone was surprised to find a significant section of public opinion, especially non-metropolitan opinion, as anti-Turkish, or more so, as himself. πήγη (spring, fountain) was the docket he wrote on the letter of Alfred Days, secretary of the Workmen's Hyde Park Demonstration Committee in August 1876. On a tour of Northumbria late in September 1876, he found himself pressed to speak wherever he went. Though his visits to villages were 'without notice', 'the same feelings were again manifested as we went along our route'. Even when attending the theatre in Liverpool he found that 'I was never so well received in that town'.

He had good cause to be wary of public opinion. It had thrown him out of South-East Lancashire in 1868; it had rewarded his first government with the first Conservative electoral majority since 1841; it had failed to respond to 'Vaticanism'; it had begun a legal assault on High-Church ritualism. 'The People's William' had certainly had his popular successes, but they had not led to real warmth or popular affection. Gladstone's differences from his followers had always been as obvious as the common ground between them. In the years 1876–80 this was to change. A real empathy seemed to develop among the very different groups which made up the campaign; a genuine fusion seemed to occur between certain sections of the Victorian ruling classes and 'labouring men', as Gladstone called them.

By the end of 1876, Gladstone had become the central figure of the campaign, rather than the valuable extra asset which his *Bulgarian Horrors* pamphlet had made him appear in September. The Resolutions which he moved in the Commons in May 1877 showed him to be not merely the government's most effective opponent on the Eastern Question but also the dominant figure in the opposition, whether formally leader or not. In the initial phase of the campaign, Gladstone had resisted speaking (a speech being regarded by contemporaries as much more directly a political act than a pamphlet), because to make speeches while formally in retirement made him, he felt, 'seem a rogue and imposter'. A 'rogue and imposter' he may well have continued to seem to the embattled Lord Hartington, nominally and, in terms of day-to-day business, actually the leader of the party in the Commons, but to Gladstone it was clear that, at the least, he was back in action for as long as the iniquities of the government continued. The initiative thus lay with the Cabinet and the Prime Minister, as it always must for a government with a comfortable majority,* including the initiative of deciding on the date of the final reckoning, the dissolution. As Gladstone moved again to the centre of the political stage in 1876-7, he could not foresee that to the central errors of 'Turkism' were to be added the buttresses of South Africa and Afghanistan, which taken together, would lead to a general condemnation of 'Beaconsfieldism'.

Since Gladstone did not have the political initiative—a novel experience for a man hardly out of office since 1859—and since it was in no way clear that the Eastern Question Campaign implied an eventual return to office, he continued to try to draw a distinction between 'the part assigned to me in the Eastern Question', and a return to systematic political activity across the board. He described his position in a letter in October 1876 to W. P. Adam, the Liberal chief whip:

I hope you will discourage the idea of any banquet to me in Edinburgh or elsewhere. I am a follower and not a leader in the Liberal party and nothing will induce me to do an act indicative of a desire to change my position. Any such act would be a positive breach of faith on my part towards those whom I importuned as I may say to allow me to retire, and whom I left to undertake a difficult and invidious office. True I have been forced, by obligations growing out of the past, to take a prominent part on the Eastern question; but I postponed it as long as I could, and have done all in my power, perhaps even too much, to keep it apart from the general course of politics & of party connection.†

During 1877 there are some indications that he realized this was beginning to be an untenable position. His reaction to the three large parties of Liberals which visited Hawarden in the summer of 1877 suggests a little movement. The first, a band of Liberal pilgrims from Bolton which collected splinters from the axe as relics, was greeted with some irritation— 'we were nearly killed with kindness'—and Gladstone tried to avoid speaking. But on the third group, from Bacup, he merely comments, 'It is the *reporting* that makes the difficulty in these things.' 'Piracy in Borneo', an article written in the summer of 1877, marked a widening of the area of political controversy towards the imperial dimension. In November 1877

* In Gladstone's previous period of opposition, 1866-8, the initiative had lain almost equally between the government and the opposition, for the government was in a minority should the opposition reunite, as it did over Gladstone's Irish Resolutions and over the abolition of compulsory Church Rates.

† To W. P. Adam, 4 October 1876, Blair Adam MS 4/431 (MS of W. P. Adam in West Register House, Edinburgh).

he decisively defeated Northcote, the Chancellor of the Exchequer, for the Lord Rectorship of Glasgow University, confirming the strength of Liberalism among the youth of Glasgow—the Rectorship campaigns were highly political and very seriously contested. This to some extent also confirmed his own return to popularity among the Scottish university classes— he had been defeated for the Chancellorship of Edinburgh University in 1868. (Not too much should be made of this, however, since, ironically, the Tory Duke of Buccleuch, father of Lord Dalkeith, his opponent in Midlothian in 1880, was elected Chancellor by the Glasgow graduates in 1878.)*

On the one hand, 'quivering hopes' were held in 1877 that a return to sustained work on the Homeric Thesaurus would be possible and a good deal of work on it was done. On the other, no attempt at his usual birthday retrospect was made on 29 December 1877, and only a brief comment was noted in the journal on the 31st—usually both days for introspective writing—and this may indicate an unusual degree of uncertainty about the future.

Too much should not be read into such straws in the wind. It is clear that through 1877 and the first part of 1878, Gladstone was holding back to see what events would bring. His position was consistent, if inconvenient to the Liberal party leadership: he was active in the Eastern Question Campaign, for which the leadership had shown little enthusiasm, and which was unlikely to last in full flood until the dissolution, but otherwise he was an independent force, as he had been in 1875. As the Liberal party had no formal structure, and hardly even informal rules, his behaviour was difficult in party terms either to condemn or to justify.

Gladstone developed 'five reasons' to support his position, describing them for the first time in an important conversation with Sir Robert Phillimore in March 1879, and maintaining them even after the first Midlothian Campaign clearly committed him to some sort of return to office, should the Liberals win. Phillimore noted them down: 'He gave me I think 5 reasons, in regular sequence, why he should not be Premier again. Three of them were 1) his age 2) the immense work of cleansing and repairing there would be to do 3) his pledge to Granville & Hartington.' In 1879 Rosebery noted down the other two, which were 'that he would encounter a more personal and bitter opposition than anyone else' and 'the personal opposition of the Queen to him'.† When Hartington tried to resign as Liberal leader in the Commons in December 1879, Gladstone effectively forced the Whig leaders to continue their party leadership, while maintaining his own

---

* Gladstone declined to stand for the Rectorship of Aberdeen University in 1875. Rectors were elected by the undergraduates, Chancellors by the graduates. Unfortunately, these hard-fought and fascinating contests have as yet no historian.

† Phillimore's diary, 30 March 1879; Rosebery's diary, 28 November 1879.

freedom of action.* There were good political as well as personal reasons for this. Gladstone's campaign worked outwards from what the young H. H. Asquith described as 'the extreme left' of the Liberal party† (the left/right dichotomy was just entering common usage in British political vocabulary), a position now apparently broadened and, in Whiggish eyes, confirmed by his comments on land while in Midlothian: 'compulsory expropriation is a thing which for an adequate public object is in itself admissible and so far sound in principle'.‡ Having Granville and Hartington as leaders to an extent kept on ice awkward questions about Gladstone's relationship with the Whigs on foreign, imperial, and land policy and perhaps also with Nonconformists on English disestablishment and education. As Wolverton, the former Liberal chief whip and Gladstone's envoy in negotiations about the leadership, remarked in 1879: 'many of our weak kneed ones, would feel some alarm if H[artington] went from the front *now*'.§

Jingoism and the Move to Midlothian

'The great sabbath dawning in the East' in February 1878 marked the sharpest point of political conflict since 1876, as Carnarvon resigned from Disraeli's government and the Cabinet backed its sending of the fleet to Constantinople with a Vote of Credit of £6 million for a possible military expedition, and, a little later, by the calling out of the Reserves. Tension mounted in London as well as in Constantinople. The police defended Gladstone's house in Harley Street from a Jingo mob—thought to have been encouraged by the Tory high command—which broke his windows on a Sunday evening:

Between four & six three parties of the populace arrived here the first with cheers, the two others hostile. Windows were broken & much hooting. The last detachment was only kept away by mounted police in line across the street both ways. Saw the Inspector in evg. This is not very sabbatical. There is strange work behind the curtain if one could but get at it. The instigators are those really guilty: no one can wonder at the tools.¶

Soon after this 'the news of the Peace arrived. It seems scarcely to leave openings for future quarrel.' None the less, the Gladstones still could not

* The crisis is described in Morley, ii, ch. vii and J. P. Rossi, 'The transformation of the British Liberal Party', *Transactions of the American Philosophical Society* [subsequently: Rossi, *T.A.P.S.*], lxviii, part 8, 103ff.

† [H. H. Asquith] 'The English Extreme Left', *The Spectator*, 12 August 1876; see *Bulletin of the Institute of Historical Research*, xlix. 150.

‡ *Speeches in Scotland* (1879), 102.

§ Wolverton to Gladstone, 20 December 1879, Add MS 44349, f. 121.

¶ The *Daily News*, 26 February 1878, 5c, noted 'there were ugly symptoms of the worst sort of social decadence in the disturbances of Sunday' and denounced 'organized ruffianism'. T. P. O'Connor claimed Parnell and his sister Anna were in the crowd (*Memoirs of an Old Parliamentarian* (1929), i. 8).

walk to their house, and royalty became notably hostile; the Duke of Cambridge (the Commander in Chief), 'black as thunder, did not even hold out his hand' when he met Gladstone at a Levée.*

In the face of a 'dissolution which might be summary', in March 1878 Gladstone announced the end of his connection with his Greenwich constituency. His relationship with his Greenwich constituents had always been uneasy, and in November 1875 he had told Phillimore: 'Certainly, if it is in my option, I shall not stand again for Greenwich to be hustled between Boords and Liardets [the Tory opponents in the two-member constituency]. But this please mention to *no one*.' In October 1876 he had privately informed Adam, as Liberal chief whip, of his decision: 'I am desirous you should know what may not yet have been directly stated to you that if a Dissolution were to occur nothing would induce me again to stand for Greenwich.' He told Adam this 'because Dissolution is at present among those remote possibilities which a new turn of the wheel *might* any day bring within the realm of the probable'. At that time—shortly after the start of the atrocities campaign—Gladstone was 'in two minds whether if this were disposed of I should incline to stand again *at all* or not: but in any case I am limited to an extremely small number of seats'.† Since the Eastern Question was clearly not 'disposed of', his public announcement in 1878 of his decision not to stand again in Greenwich carefully left open the option of standing elsewhere.

Gladstone's response to San Stephano and the Jingo outburst of the early months of 1878 was thus to open the process of finding another seat, for that was what his announcement to Greenwich implied. Various prospects, including Leeds, quickly presented themselves; these were set aside, rather than rejected outright.‡ Moreover, there is an indication that Gladstone was beginning to see himself as a political tribune of the people—a moral tribune, the Atrocities Campaign had already made him—representing right behaviour against a Court and a Prime Minister seen as increasingly unconstitutional in their behaviour. He comments at this time, after being snubbed by members of the Court, on Prothero's Whiggish account of Simon de Montfort: 'What a giant! and what a noble giant! What has survival of the fittest done towards beating, or towards reaching him?'§ In such a mood, choice of a seat would be an awkward business.

* For accusations of treachery by students of Guy's Hospital, where Gladstone was a Governor, see 25 Feb. 78 and H. L. Eason, 'Students and politics', *Guy's Hospital Gazette* (1936), 547. London was the chief 'Jingoborough'; see Hugh Cunningham, 'Jingoism in 1877–88', *Victorian Studies*, xiv. 429 (June 1971). The rowdyism was reminiscent of Tory anti-popery riots earlier in the century, with the aristocracy cynically exploiting xenophobia; see G. A. Cahill, 'The Protestant Association and the anti-Maynooth agitation of 1845', *Catholic Historical Review*, xliii (October 1957).

† To W. P. Adam, 'Private', 30 October 1876; Blair Adam MS 4/431.

‡ The predominantly Nonconformist tone of Liberal politics in Leeds probably encouraged Gladstone's caution.

§ Gladstone shared the general non-Tory alarm that, first, Disraeli was excessively acting as the

Rosebery, the Narcissus of Scottish Liberalism, and one of the wealthiest men in Whig politics, seems to have taken the initiative together with Adam, the Liberal chief whip and a lowland Scottish MP: 'Lord Rosebery *cum* Mr Adam' waited on Gladstone in London in May 1878 and 'the Midlothian case' was opened, with further discussion in June. The initiative was probably taken by the Scots, encouraged by Gladstone's easy success in the Glasgow Rectorial in 1877, so as to try to strengthen the Liberal cause in the Forth-Clyde valley. Rather characteristically, for all his suspicion of the 'classes', Gladstone talked this over, not with a Whig or a Liberal, but with his own Tractarian crony, Sir Walter James, a Conservative MP in the 1840s. By January 1879, the case was closed: Gladstone was committed to campaign for the seat, and he opened his prosecution with a powerful letter accepting the Liberal nomination from the Midlothian Liberal Association.* He did so as the challenger. The seat had been gained for the Tories in 1874 by the Earl of Dalkeith, son of the Duke of Buccleuch, Gladstone's colleague with Peel in the 1846 Cabinet. Buccleuch had reluctantly accepted the repeal of the Corn Laws, but in other respects he was a ferocious Tory, a dominant and feared landowner in the Lowlands and notorious for turning the screw on his tenants at election time. Gladstone could expect a tough contest. None the less, as we shall shortly see, he had good reasons for confidence about success.

Gladstone thus returned to drive the Tories from representing the area from which the Gladstanes had sprung, and he was to do so in a spectacular, barnstorming campaign which resulted in a triumph for the local Liberals but was of greater importance in its national character and impact. Even so, the move from Greenwich to Midlothian was an admission of weakness: never again would a Liberal Prime Minister represent an English constituency. Gladstone's move from an English borough to a Scottish county reflected a general trend in Liberal politics from the urban to the agrarian and an increasing Liberal reliance on non-English seats. But in personal terms it was to prove a liberation.

Queen's minister, betraying Cabinet colleagues to her, and second, that there were threats to Cabinet control of foreign policy through the intervention of the Court. Carnarvon was the chief inside source for his fears.

* To J. Cowan, in *The Times*, 3 February 1879.

CHAPTER II

The Midlothian Campaign

*The Context of the Campaign: a Broad-Church Popular Front of Moral
Outrage—Dealing in Words: Political Communication and the Platform
Speech—Max Weber and 'Caesarism': Popular Rationalism and the Liberal
Intelligentsia—The Tories' 'loss of moral equilibrium'—The Campaign in Mid-
lothian—The Midlothian Campaign both Charismatic and Rational*

Set out at 8¼: the journey from Liverpool was really more like a triumphal procession. I had to make short speeches at Carlisle Hawick
& Galashiels: very large numbers were assembled & at Edinburgh
where we only arrived at quarter past five, the scene even to the
West end of the City was extraordinary, both from the numbers and
the enthusiasm, here and there a solitary groan or howl. We drove
off to Dalmeny with Ld Rosebery and were received with fireworks
& torches. I have never gone through a more extraordinary day.*

For the last 3½ years I have been passing through a political experience which is I believe without example in our Parliamentary history. I profess it [*sic*] to believe it has been an occasion, when the
battle to be fought was a battle of justice humanity freedom law, all
in their first elements from the very root, and all on a gigantic scale.
The work spoken was a word for millions, and for millions who
themselves cannot speak. If I really believe this then I should regard
my having been morally forced into this work as a great and high
election of God. And certainly I cannot but believe that He has
given me special gifts of strength, on the late occasion especially in
Scotland.†

The Context of the Campaign: a Broad-Church Popular Front of Moral Outrage

The Midlothian Campaign of 1878–80 was the culmination of a political
drama which broadened gradually and sometimes hesitantly from the
relatively limited issue of 'the Bulgarian Horrors' in 1876 to the wholesale
condemnation of innovative Toryism. A former Prime Minister leading a
great popular crusade was a new phenomenon in European politics, and
before examining the substance of the objections to Beaconsfieldism, some
comment on the nature of the campaign is necessary.

* Diary for 24 Nov. 79.
† Diary for 28 Dec. 79.

From the start, Gladstone saw the movement of protest as founded 'on grounds, not of political party, not even of mere English nationality, not of Christian faith, but on the largest and broadest ground of all—the ground of our common humanity'.* At a time when Continental political parties were increasingly narrowly based in terms both of class and doctrine, Gladstone's appeal was for a Broad-Church movement which stressed integration and comprehension. This was to be a Popular Front of moral outrage, a coalition ranging from the Roman Catholic ecumenist Ambrose Phillipps de Lisle to the secularist Charles Bradlaugh, a campaign ranging from the dignified splendour of the St James's Hall meeting in December 1876 (chaired by the Duke of Westminster) to a 'Coffeehouse Company Meeting in Seven Dials' in April 1878.† It was to be a resurgence on a new humanitarian footing of the old Liberal spectrum of the 1860s which had disintegrated over the religious squabbles of 1873–4. Ironically, given the intense religious feeling invested in it by Gladstone personally and by many of its participants, the Midlothian Campaign—with the issue of Scottish disestablishment neatly side-stepped‡—pointed the way towards the secular humanitarianism of twentieth-century Liberalism.§

Hitherto, Gladstone's public career had been in large measure a working out of the consequences of his changing view of the means of achieving 'religious nationality'. The religious 'expostulation' of the Vatican pamphlets seemed anomalous, even anachronistic, to many contemporaries and from the mid-1870s Gladstone came to recognize that his personal religious opinions had to remain personal if he hoped to achieve political results. The acceptance of the Midlothian nomination emphasized this, for Gladstone became a candidate in a country where, as an Episcopalian, he was a nonconformist. Whereas in his years as MP for Oxford University he had represented the heart of the Anglican national establishment, he now aspired to represent constituents most of whose religious views, however ecumenical his tone, he privately regarded as in schism from the Episcopalian Church, which he believed to be the true Church in Scotland. He saw the Church government of the Kirk and the Free Church as deficient in apostolicity. Though he attended afternoon and evening service in Established and Free Churches in Edinburgh, he would have communicated in neither, nor would it even have occurred to him that he might do so.

Gladstone's isolation on religious questions in his own party and his need subsequently to subordinate his own religious priorities, bold though they were, to a political world increasingly secular in tone and language,

* Speech at Blackheath, *The Times*, 11 September 1876.

† 8 Dec. 76, 9 Apr. 78.

‡ Privately, Gladstone had noted: 'Spoke on the Scottish Established Church: which, in that character has not I think another decade of years to live'; 18 June 78.

§ As G. M. Young observed (*Portrait of an Age* (1960 ed.), 166): 'The mind of 1890 would have startled the mind of 1860 by its frank secularism.'

reflected a general losing of the initiative by the Anglican Church. That church's hegemonic political, cultural, and intellectual claims of the 1830s had given way, partly in their political dimension under Gladstone's leadership, to the pluralism of the 1850s and 1860s. But that pluralism had been a pluralism of Christian denominations; paganism had been a regret but not an intrusion. Now, as the 1880s dawned, pluralism linked Anglicans not merely with Scottish Presbyterians, Methodists, Congregationalists, and Roman Catholics, but increasingly with agnostics and secularists, and public language began to assume not merely the latter's existence but their integration.

'I seemed to see the old dream of organic unity surviving where moral unity is lost' wrote Manning in 1865 of the 1840s.* As that dream faded, Gladstone attempted to reconstruct 'moral unity' through the humanitarianism of the party of progress; his religious objectives, once the prescription for the conscience of the nation, became private aims, pursued discreetly by a public figure accepting the religious reserve required for the preservation of 'moral unity' over a wide front—a tacit acceptance of secularism. 'Religious nationality' of the Coleridgian Idealist sort found its replacement in the more explicitly political ideology of a progressive citizenship. None the less, the clerisy which conditioned this political nation, though socially more broadly based, remained surprisingly unchanged, with Gladstone, even at 70, still its rising hope.

Dealing in Words: Political Communication and the Platform Speech

The successes of the Liberals in the 1860s had taken place in the context of the pre-1867 franchise. Could the spectacular result of 1868, when the extended electorate had not had time to form a pattern, be repeated in more settled electoral conditions? By what means could a movement of protest become a parliamentary majority? The extended but still limited electorate in the boroughs greatly exercised politicians generally. The old, 'face-to-face' communitarian politics of the 1832–67 period, supervised by solicitors with generous bribes, were ending. With the secret ballot of 1872, the poll-book—the briber's book of reckoning—was no more. The Liberal party, at least most of it and certainly Gladstone, was committed to introducing household suffrage in the counties in addition to the boroughs, thus prospectively compounding the difficulties.

Politicians' reactions to the problems of political communication and control fell into two categories, organizational and rhetorical. Gorst for the Tories and Chamberlain and others for the Liberals developed the first, through the Conservative Central Office (*ca.* 1870) and the National Liberal Federation (1877) respectively. Bureaucratic developments of this sort were by no means completely welcome to political leaders: political

* H. E. Manning, *The Temporal Mission of the Holy Ghost* (6th ed., 1909), 31.

machines might have a life of their own, and tended, especially in the nine-teenth century, greatly to increase the power and influence of politicians with strong regional bases. Joseph Chamberlain was the most effective of these caucus politicians, but he was by no means unique.

Gladstone became the supreme exponent of the rhetorical alternative, and he is to be seen in the 1870s developing this role both self-consciously and unselfconsciously, both the deliberate developer of a method, and at the same time the unaware prisoner of a media-structure. As a public figure, Gladstone had few assets save his words and his personality expressed in words. He was the epitome of G. C. Brodrick's category of politicians who rose by 'brains and energy'.* The Whigs had money, and they used it; the local and regional politicians sat at the centre of a complex structure of interlocking business, local governmental, and charitable interests. Gladstone hardly spent a penny on elections; his personal patronage extended to two Church of England livings; and he had in opposition no secretary, let alone a political machine. While Whigs and city caucus men dealt in leases, rents, contracts, donations, and votes, Gladstone and those like him dealt in words. When Gladstone did not speak or write, his political force disappeared. 'The word in man is a great instrument of power', Gladstone told a conference on preaching in 1877. Words could be spoken or written or, as was the case with many of Glad-stone's words, they could be simultaneously both spoken and written, the first by the speaker, the second by the shorthand reporter.

Words could be written in pamphlets or periodical articles, the tradi-tional way of making one's point among the educated élite, a method by the 1870s much more personalized as the *Contemporary*, *Fortnightly* and *Nine-teenth Century*, and other periodicals offered signed rather than anonymous articles. Gladstone certainly took full advantage of this medium, writing almost sixty substantial pamphlets, periodical articles and reviews between 1875 and 1880. He was careful to orchestrate the publication of his pamph-lets and articles with releases to the newspapers about their preparation and their contents. The publication of a Gladstone pamphlet was a political event in itself, and Gladstone saw to it that the maximum effect was achieved.

Words could be spoken in the House of Commons, and read in Hansard and the reports in the newspapers. As parliamentary business became more complex and more clogged, this was a less effective and less used means of political communication, though it remained, of course, the most regular forum for political speaking. As early as 1870 Alex Ritchie of the *Leeds Mercury* told the Press Association, the telegraphic agency through which from 1868 the provincial press gained much of its material, that his paper 'would rather not have long Parliamentary reports, except on very special

* G. C. Brodrick, 'Liberals and Whigs', in his *Political Studies* (1879), 249.

occasions, such as that on which Mr Gladstone introduced his Irish Church Bill. It would, as a rule, be a great inconvenience to me to give more than two columns of a [parliamentary] debate. Gentlemen like to peruse their newspaper at breakfast time, and they will not always care to wade through four or five columns of Parliamentary matter.'* Certainly, Gladstone used this means of communication throughout 1875–80, and many of his speeches in the Commons were reprinted as pamphlets.† But the number of occasions, such as the debate on the Resolutions of 7–14 May 1877, when public attention could be easily focused on a parliamentary debate was limited. The rules of procedure in the Commons meant that only rarely could a general question be discussed generally. Gladstone himself condemned debates in the Commons on what he called 'abstract' questions. Moreover, the Resolutions affair showed the limited use of the Commons to Gladstone when he was not in a position to dictate party business: 'This day I took my decision [to move Resolutions]: a severe one, in face of my not having a single approver in the *Upper* official circle.' To avoid humiliation in the vote, he had to agree to move only the first Resolution, a 'nominal' concession, given the way that he treated the debate, but none the less an incident that highlighted what Gladstone felt to be the wide discrepancy of passion between the Liberal leadership and the campaign in the country and one which led to parliamentary manœuvering which obscured the significance of the debate.

The conjunction of pamphlet and extra-parliamentary speech in September 1876 marked the way of the future, though Gladstone was slow to take it. Extra-parliamentary speechmaking by Cabinet-level politicians was not altogether new, though it was still rather unusual. Palmerston had been an effective exponent of it to an extent little recognized by historians.‡ Gladstone had distanced himself from the parliamentary party by his use of it in the 1860s, and shown himself aware of its potentiality, though during his first ministry he had, for several reasons, used the public speech sparingly. Disraeli's famous speeches at the Crystal Palace and in Manchester in 1872 had been an important element in confirming his position in the Tory leadership and in regaining the political initiative for the Conservatives. In the 1870s the number of extra-parliamentary speeches reported in the press markedly increased, because the means of making speeches nationally available through the telegraph networks became

* G. Scott, *Reporter Anonymous. The story of the Press Association* (1968), 41.

† A further disadvantage of the Commons was the lateness of its sittings; speeches after midnight could not be fully reported in next day's papers, as H. W. Lucy explained to Gladstone at the time of the Resolutions debate.

‡ See David Steele, 'Gladstone and Palmerston, 1855–65', in P. J. Jagger, ed., *Gladstone, Politics and Religion* (1985), 117. I have discussed the phenomenon of 'The Platform', as contemporaries called it, in 'Rhetoric and politics in Great Britain, 1860–1950', in P. J. Waller, ed., *Politics and social change in modern Britain: essays presented to A. F. Thompson* (1987).

technically more sophisticated. After the Telegraph Act of 1868, with its clauses favouring the use of the telegraph by newspapers, the Press Association and Exchange Telegraph became the chief agents of political communication in Britain.

A political speech by a major politician now had two audiences; the audience present at the meeting, and the readership of the next day's newspapers. Gladstone's campaigns for the Midlothian seat made excellent use of both, but it was the second that was the more important. When he spoke at the inaugural meeting of the National Liberal Federation in May 1877, he noted: 'A most intelligent orderly appreciative audience: but they were 25000 and the building of no acoustic merits so that the strain was excessive.' This, however, by no means diminished the success of the occasion, for the speech was nationally available next morning, *verbatim* in several columns. Gladstone had discovered—and swiftly in the late 1870s moved to exploit—the central feature of modern political communication: the use of one medium to gain access to another (in this case, the use of a political meeting to gain access to the national debating society made possible by the popular press). Gladstone was not, of course, alone in speaking on 'The Platform'; it was common form by the late 1870s for Ministers and members of the ex-Cabinet. It is hard to say how much others—for example Hartington who spoke publicly in 1880 much more often than Gladstone*—were performing in response to his lead. But it would be true to say that his speeches had that element of danger combined with breadth which gained them pre-eminence in their time.

The dual nature of the audience for the late-Victorian political speech is very well illustrated by the Midlothian Campaign. Early in 1879 Gladstone accepted a requisition to run for Edinburghshire, or Midlothian as it was popularly known. Gladstone did not agree to run until he knew that he could win. He knew that he could win because Midlothian was an old-style county constituency, about as far removed in character from the new, household-suffrage post-1867 borough seats as could be found; only about 15 per cent of the adult males in the constituency were registered to vote, in contrast to the average of about 55 per cent in the boroughs. There were 3,260 registered electors for Edinburghshire, contrasted with 49,000 in Leeds, the other constituency for which Gladstone was returned in 1880.†

J. J. Reid and Ralph Richardson, the Edinburgh lawyers who ran the Midlothian Campaign under Rosebery's superintendence, organized the questioning of each registered voter and precise analyses of the expected vote were produced. Adam confidently and accurately told Gladstone in

---

* In the 1880 campaign, Hartington made twenty-four major speeches, Gladstone fifteen, and W. H. Smith, Bright, and Northcote six each, according to W. Saunders, *The New Parliament, 1880* (1880), 38; see also H. Jephson, *The Platform* (1892), ii. 522.

† See F. W. S. Craig, *British Parliamentary Results 1832–1885* (1977) and H. McCalmont, *The Parliamentary Poll Book of All Elections* (1910).

January 1879: 'the return . . . will shew a Liberal majority of about 200 after giving *all* the doubtfuls (251) to the Conservatives.'* As Granville told Adam, 'I was against Midlothian when Gladstone first mentioned it to me, but was converted by you and Roseberry [*sic*] on the ground of the stimulus it would give to the Scotch Election, and of its being a certainty.'† Gladstone made the same point publicly when accepting the nomination: 'You have . . . been kind enough to supply me with evidence which entirely satisfies my mind that the invitation expresses the desire of the majority of the constituency.' His observation was not an exhortatory hope but a fact. The energetic creation of 'faggot votes'‡ by the Tories, and by the Liberals in response, was the characteristic manœuvre of the traditional pre-1867 political organizer; 'faggots' only worked when the numbers were small and the pledges well-known and reliable.§ On the other hand, it was accepted that these forecasts would only be accurate if the campaign was vigorous. As Gladstone observed when he agreed to be nominated: 'if this thing is to be done at all it must be done thoroughly and you may rely upon it that I will not do it by halves.'¶

The Midlothian Campaign thus had little to do with winning the Edinburghshire seat. It had everything to do with establishing Gladstonianism as the dominant force in Liberal politics and in winning the unknown and unpredictable new electorate in the boroughs. It was essentially a campaign not in or for Midlothian, but from Midlothian. The Campaign used an old-style seat as a base for new-style politics; it was bold, but it was not risky.

The real audience of the campaigns of 1879 and 1880 was the newspaper-reading public, whether Liberal, doubtful, or Tory. With the defection of

* W. P. Adam to Gladstone, 10 January 1879, Add MS 56444, f. 123.

† Granville to W. P. Adam, 17 January 1879, Blair Adam MS 4/431.

‡ A faggot-vote was a vote manufactured for party purposes by the transfer to persons not otherwise qualified of sufficient property to qualify them as electors.

§ Reid told Rosebery (26 January [?1879], Rosebery MSS, National Library of Scotland [subsequently: NLS] 10075, f. 13): 'the chief matter really has been the unbounded creation of faggots, but I really think they have not done *at most* more than 100 in this way, and the largeness of the margin together with the natural increase of the constituency (now that Edinburgh is getting beyond its Parliamentary Boundary) ought to be quite sufficient'. W. P. Adam briefly felt alarmed: 'The Tories have attempted to *garotte* the real constituency by choking them with faggots. What they have been able to do up to the present time does not *really* affect the position, but if the general election be delayed till after next November (which is possible) and they *succeed* in their garotting . . . the Committee will have to consider the propriety of your seat being risked and will have to say whether or not you should withdraw stating fully the reasons. In order to neutralise the present majority *and* the natural Liberal increase of the constituency they will have to create faggots to a disgraceful extent but they are not troubled by scruples of conscience' (Adam to Gladstone, 4 February 1879, Add MS 56444, f. 135). These fears were not realized and the Midlothian Liberals were as confident under the 1880 register as they had been under that of 1879: 'I consider Midlothian is ours till 1 Nov. 1881, & I hear the other side now admit Mr. Gladstone will win' (Richardson to Rosebery, 3 February 1880, NLS 10075, f. 188).

¶ To W. P. Adam, 11 January 1879, Blair Adam MS 4/431.

its flag-ship, the *Daily Telegraph*, in 1876–7,* the Liberal press had begun the slow slide towards Conservatism which in the mid-1880s became an avalanche, but one advantage of the political speech was that it negated the political complexion of the newspaper, for Conservative papers reported the Campaign as energetically as Liberal ones. However stridently a lead-writer might reply, the speech constituted a four-column advertisement in a hostile paper, as well as being a large exhortation in a friendly one.

The speech of a first-rank politician appeared *verbatim* and with little in the way of accompanying report. There was no mediator between the speaker at the meeting and the reader of his words next day in house, railway carriage, public house, or club. The reporter's job was to transcribe the speaker's words accurately, not to interpret to the readers what he thought the speaker had meant. The audience actually present was important for local politics but nationally it could be redundant. Walter Hepburn, known as 'Mr. Gladstone's Fat Reporter'—he was the Press Association reporter with special responsibility for Gladstone's speeches—took down on the moving train a speech intended for a local deputation but not delivered because the train left the station before Gladstone had time to speak.† It is interesting that the young Gladstone, in one of his first pieces of journalism, chose to write 'On Eloquence'; he noted that eloquence was usually discussed in terms of the Senate, the Pulpit, and the Bar; he broadened the discussion to include 'less celebrated kinds of oratory' and among these was 'Advertising ... Eloquence'.‡ A sharp awareness, not merely of the ideological importance of rhetoric, but also of the mechanics of its presentation in the context of nineteenth-century technology, thus characterized Gladstone's approach to public speaking.

At a more mundane level, whether the occasion was a major speech or a brief (i.e. half-an-hour) address to a cookery or gardening society, Gladstone was, at the least, a tremendous old trouper, giving a good performance even when ill. He himself used an acting metaphor to describe how he coped with a major occasion: 'Spoke $2\frac{1}{2}$ hours [on the Congress of Berlin]. I was in body much below par but put on the steam perforce.' It was partly this ability to 'put on the steam' which ensured that he always had a full house, even for a matinée.

The great orations whether on the platform or in the Commons were, like all Gladstone's speeches, delivered from only the briefest notes. The

---

* See S. Koss, *The Rise and Fall of the Political Press in Britain* (1981), i. 211ff. The row over the Negropontis affair (see above, p. 26 n. †) between Gladstone and Levy-Lawson exemplified the split at a personal level.

† G. Scott, *Reporter Anonymous*, 77–8, which also gives an example of Gladstone dictating a speech to Hepburn for telegraphing in advance of its actual delivery: 'the train did not stop as it had been scheduled to do; Gladstone did not make his speech; but the report of it was published just the same'.

‡ [W. E. Gladstone], 'On Eloquence', *The Eton Miscellany*, ii. 110 (1827).

speech was never written out in advance.* In one of the most tumultuous of the debates of these years, the Resolutions debate of May 1877, after 'over two hours ... assaulted from every quarter', a speech of two and a half hours was delivered perforce without a note: 'I could make little use of them from having forgotten my eyeglass' reads the docket on the bundle of redundant speech notes. A rough calculation suggests that one line of speech notes generated about seven or eight minutes of oratory, and on occasion a good deal more. The brevity of the notes did not, however, mean an absence of preparation, indeed perhaps the reverse, as the triumph of the 'forgotten eyeglass' speech suggests. But the condensation of the preparation into a few short headings was deliberately designed so that the speech would exemplify the character of the speaker:

there cannot be too much preparation if it be of the right kind. No doubt it is the preparation of matter; it is the accumulation and thorough digestion of knowledge; it is the forgetfulness of personal and selfish motives; it is the careful consideration of method; it is that a man shall make himself as a man suited to speak to men, rather than that he should make himself as a machine ready to deliver to men certain preconceived words.†

The extemporary speech had always been required in the House of Commons. Gladstone now used it as the basis for the development of a national debate through the columns of the national and provincial press.

The development of the phenomenon of 'The Platform' coincided with the high noon of Victorian religiosity. This was not accidental. The tradition of long sermons, especially in Scotland, had accustomed audiences to expect addresses of at least an hour, and had trained them to concentrate over such a long period. An hour was seen as short-weight and an hour and a half was common. This would have been nothing to those used to Presbyterian sermons. These great addresses thus sprang from and dovetailed into the natural habits and expectations of a churchgoing society. Many of the Midlothian speeches were given in churches, and on one occasion Gladstone spoke from the pulpit.‡ The Midlothian speeches were in a direct sense Gladstone's Bampton Lectures.

Max Weber and 'Caesarism': Popular Rationalism and the Liberal Intelligentsia

The Midlothian Campaign represented the flowering of a new style of politics, long in germination. As politics became more bureaucratized, extra-parliamentary speech-making provided the means for the Liberal

---

* Consequently, the orator relied on the newspaper report to assemble a final version of what was said, if the speech was to be printed as a pamphlet, as most of Gladstone's major speeches were.

† Gladstone's speech on preaching, *The Times*, 23 March 1877.

‡ See W. Saunders, op. cit., 143–4.

intelligentsia to preserve its influence in British political life, and in doing so it linked the intellectual force of Liberal politics to a particular form of media-presentation. The full force of the popularization of the Liberal ethos rose with the political press of the 1860s and died with it in the 1920s. Max Weber, in a justly famous analysis in 1918, argued that Gladstone's campaign represented the arrival of 'a Caesarist plebiscitarian element in politics—the dictator of the battlefield of elections', the natural concomitant to the caucus system which had 'arisen in the Liberal party in connection with Gladstone's ascent to power'.* Certainly Gladstone encouraged the caucuses and the National Liberal Federation in a way alarming to the 'notables' ('Honoratioren') of the party, as Weber called them. Merely to address the N.L.F.'s inaugural meeting was seen by them as a radical act. But this introduced no new element into Gladstone's political position, which, from the 1860s, had always been one of careful distance from party organization. He was equally careful not to be drawn into the affairs of the N.L.F., or of the Marylebone Liberal Association, the caucus which came to run Liberal politics in his area of London, even though as respectable a figure as G. J. Goschen was its first chairman.†

The Midlothian Campaign was more a counterweight to the caucus system than a development from it. As Gladstone had used extra-parliamentary oratory against the 'notables' in the 1860s, so he and his successors used the platform to outflank and to control local organizations rather than to represent them. Weber was right to point to 'the firm belief in the masses in the ethical substance of his policy'—this, we shall see, was exactly what Gladstone believed himself to be appealing to—and to 'their belief in the ethical character of his personality'. Gladstone had been aware since the 1860s of this charismatic element, of his own ability to exploit it, and of its dangers. The phenomenon of being 'Gladstonised' while attending a meeting is well attested.‡ It was to clarify the phenomenon of Midlothian that Weber coined his famous definition of the charismatic political leader. But Weber ignored the means of communication: the huge majority of electors met Gladstone on the column of a newspaper page, in a *verbatim* report of a two-hour speech, remarkably unadorned with ancillary descrip-

---

* 'Politics as a vocation', a lecture given in 1918, translated in H. H. Gerth and C. Wright Mills, *From Max Weber* (1948), 106; the German reads: 'Ein cäsaristisch-plebiszitäres Element in der Politik: der Diktator des Wahlschlachtfeldes, trat auf den Plan' (Max Weber, *Gesammelte Politische Schriften* (1958), 523). Clearly Weber was wrong in his view of the rise of the caucus, which related to Gladstone more through opposition to his Cabinet's Education Bill in 1870 than through concern for his return in 1877.

† He did however referee a dispute between rival candidates there, see the series of letters from Gladstone to S. Chick, its secretary, read to its inaugural meeting: 'I feel it to be my especial duty at the present juncture to avoid taking a prominent part in any demonstrations bearing on politics generally with respect to which I can exercize an option, however sincerely I may wish them well', a position consistent with his statements about the leadership; *St Pancras Guardian*, 26 January 1878, 3a.

‡ For W. L. Watson's account—'I had been Gladstonised'—see Lord Kilbracken, *Reminiscences* (1931), 109–12.

tion of the occasion, and with virtually no comment about the speaker himself. The absence of photographs in the daily newspapers reporting the speech was not compensated for by descriptions of dress or of facial expressions, or even by engravings, which were the prerogative of the weeklies such as *The Graphic* and *The Illustrated London News*, neither of which reached a really·popular audience.

A general impression of enthusiasm was given in the daily papers, but in such brief, dry tones as to be quite non-visceral. For most electors contact with the political leader was made through the rationalistic activity of the reading of his words as printed, without headlines and in small print, in the austere columns of the daily press. For a national leader, only a tiny proportion of the electorate—and that by custom within his own constituency—could have experience of the presence of the speaker personally or of the powerful harmonics of his voice.

The content of these speeches was, Gladstone fairly concluded, 'something like a detailed exposition of a difficult and complicated case'.* Planning the campaign in 1879, Gladstone intended 'to show up' the Tories by dealing with 'some given question in each place'.† Such demagogy as there was in Midlothian was the demagogy of a popular rationalism. No series of speeches intended to fill four columns of a serious newspaper for several days could be demagogic in the German sense: the medium of communication imposed literary and rationalistic standards upon the orator. The Midlothian speeches were popularly presented, but they contained much detailed argument and evidence. They presupposed considerable political knowledge on the part of their hearers and readers, and were addressed to an electorate assumed to be highly politicized. It is interesting that the most emotional section of the speeches—on the plight of the Afghan peasant: 'Remember the rights of the savage, as we call him'—was addressed to a special meeting of women, by definition non-voters (and in Gladstone's view rightly so) who, he told them he believed, had little taste for 'the harder, and sterner, and drier lessons of politics'.‡

The Tories' 'loss of moral equilibrium'

Although Midlothian emphasized a pattern of speeches, if not of meetings, which was to become normative in the 1880s, Gladstone saw the years of the campaign of the late 1870s as, at the time, 'a crisis of an extraordinary character'.§ He believed that Disraeli's government had been 'vexing and alarming' an electorate not usually interested in the details of politics.¶ In an 'age of greater knowledge, man ought to grow more manly; to keep a

---

* *Political Speeches* (1879), 211; Weber called this 'the technique of apparently "letting sober facts speak for themselves"' (Gerth and Mills, 107); the translation softens Weber's perjorative tone ('der ein Techniker des scheinbar nüchternen "Die-Tatsachen-sprechen Lassens" war').

† To W. P. Adam, 14 November 1879, Blair Adam MS 4/431.

‡ *Political Speeches* (1879), 90, 94.　　　　　§ Ibid., 18.　　　　　¶ Ibid., 22.

sterner guard over passion', but the Disraeli Cabinet's policies in the Near East had encouraged 'this want of sobriety, this loss of moral equilibrium', especially in 'large portions of what is termed society'.* 'Strange excesses' required exceptional explanations. Gladstone offered one in the form of an anecdote about Bishop Butler, who

walking in his garden at Bristol . . . asked of his chaplain, Dean Tucker, whether, in the judgement of that noble man, it were possible that there could be in nations or kingdoms a frame of mind analogous to what constitutes madness in individuals? For, said the Bishop, if there cannot, it seems very difficult to account for the major part of the transactions recorded in history. Evidently he had in view the wars and conflicts, of which the blood-stained web of history has been usually woven.†

Only by a belief in such abrogations of reason could a theory of natural law be sustained. It was the duty of 'the leisured classes',‡ whose function was the government of the country, to 'soothe and tranquillize the minds of the people, not to set up false phantoms of glory'.§ Gladstone thus saw the context of his return to sustained politics as being the failure in their duty of 'the classes', and especially those of metropolitan society. Gladstone had come to see certain sections of London society and its press as corrupted by money: 'if it be true that wealth and ease bring with them in a majority of cases an increased growth in the hardening crust of egotism and selfishness, the deduction thereby made from the capacity of right judgment in large and most important questions, may be greater than the addition which leisure, money, and opportunity have allowed'.¶

Corruption by money is a constant theme in these years, most fully described in Gladstone's Address, delivered at the end of the first Midlothian Campaign, as Lord Rector of Glasgow University.‖ Among the wealthy classes, he told the undergraduates, rapid progress—'in itself a good'—had not been balanced by development of 'mental resources or pursuits'. The consequence was an unbalanced moral system among such people: 'disproportioned growth, if in large degree, is in the physical world deformity; in the moral and social world it is derangement that answers to deformity, and partakes of its nature'. These bad qualities, distortions of nature, were most easily seen in 'the growth of a new class—a class unknown to the past, and one whose existence the future will have cause to deplore. It is the class of hybrid or bastard men . . . made up from the

---

* 'Paths of honour and of shame', 8.

† Ibid., 9. This anecdote was related by Josiah Tucker, the political economist, in the context of explaining war expenditure ('And all, alas! for what!!!!'); J. Tucker, *An humble address and earnest appeal . . . [on] a connection with, or a separation from the continental colonies of America* (1775), 20.

‡ 'Postscriptum on the county franchise', *Gleanings*, i. 193.   § *Political Speeches* (1879), 37.

¶ 'Postscriptum on the county franchise', *Gleanings*, i. 200.

‖ The Glasgow rectorial of 5 Dec. 79 is reprinted in *Political speeches* (1879), 229ff. from which quotations in this paragraph are taken.

scattered and less considerate members of all classes', united by 'the bond of gain; not the legitimate produce of toil by hand or brain', a class sustained by the cushion of limited liability, 'not fenced off from rashness, as in former times, by liability to ruinous loss in the event of failure, but to be had without the conditions which alone make pecuniary profits truly honourable'.

This was an analysis similar in conclusion, if not in tone, to Trollope's description of corrupt financial capitalism in *The way we live now* (1875). It was a view of society quite common in the 1870s, shared, ironically—given Gladstone's view of its political consequences—by the Queen. Gladstone did not succeed in showing how this class affected the policies of the Cabinet. He argued that the political system was being subverted and corrupted by the failures of moral education to match the progress of capitalism, but he did not succeed in showing how, or why, this should immediately be reflected in government policy, or why its effect was on the Tory rather than the Liberal party.

The consequence of this analysis was the very non-Liberal view that 'intellectual forces', represented politically through the old property-based franchise and to some extent corrupted, must be counterbalanced by a popular vote which would be moral and ethical rather than intellectual in character: 'As the barbarian, with his undeveloped organs, sees and hears at distances which the senses of the cultured state cannot overpass, and yet is utterly deficient as to fine details of sound and colour, even so it seems that, in judging the great questions of policy which appeal to the primal truths and laws of our nature, those classes may excel who, if they lack the opportunities, yet escape the subtle perils of the wealthy state.'* Here was a curious paradox: Midlothian exemplified the use of rationalist rhetoric in an extended franchise system, yet its stimulus was profoundly conservative, echoing exactly those arguments which had been used by the ultra-Tories in the 1828–30 period to support parliamentary reform—that, for example, enfranchised popular Protestantism would never have permitted Catholic Emancipation.

The paradox is resolved by the self-selection of the electorate through the excluding power of the register. As Gladstone remarked when discussing the political sense and capacity for judgement of 'the masses', 'I have never heard of an attempt, as yet, to register those who sleep under the dry arches of Waterloo Bridge',† i.e. 'the residuum', as those were designated who were excluded from the franchise by the lack of stable residence, by the failure to be male or the head of a household, or by the want of civic competence which pauperism was taken to imply. The 'masses' were in fact sifted so that, in general, it was mainly 'capable citizens' who achieved the

---

* 'Postscriptum on the county franchise', *Gleanings*, i. 199, 201.
† Ibid., i. 197.

status of being placed upon the parliamentary register; in the post-1867 franchise, large though it had relatively become, voting remained a privilege to be earned rather than a right to be claimed.

Though 'intellectual qualifications alone' were insufficient to form a right political judgement, the tone of Gladstone's speeches suggests that they were none the less assumed. Even the Waverley Market speech, addressed to those who 'do not fear to call yourselves the working men of Edinburgh, Leith and the district', though short, made no more concession in vocabulary to the audience than middle-class ministers of religion were wont to do in their sermons.*

The distancing from the caucus and the 'notables' allowed Gladstone—despite the fact that the Campaign was planned by 'notables' such as Rosebery and W. P. Adam—to present himself in 'my Northern Campaign' as a man apart, a peacemaker come from afar, almost as an Aristotelian law-giver. The special train, the journey 'really more like a triumphal procession', the image of physical and moral movement towards a new beginning, the torchlight processions through Edinburgh—'a subject for Turner' with 'no police visible'—would, if not limited and controlled by the means of communication and by the objectives of the campaign, foreshadow disturbing comparisons. In their context, they merely gave that most austere of cities some fun, though not, of course, frivolity.

Ignoring the many family links with Edinburgh which could have allowed his presentation as a home-comer, Gladstone began the campaign by emphasizing his separateness: 'I am come among you as a stranger',† a man called by the requisitioning electors to pacify and to redress. His ally in this process would be a betrayed people, their morals and their prosperity alike defrauded by 'a series of surprises, a series of theatrical expedients, calculated to excite, calculated to alarm':‡

Do not let us suppose this is like the old question between Whig and Tory. It is nothing of the kind. It is not now as if we were disputing about some secondary matter—it is not even as if we were disputing about the Irish Church, which no doubt was a very important affair. What we are disputing about is a whole system of Government, and to make good that proposition that it is a whole system of government will be my great object in any addresses that I may deliver in this country.§

The attack was thus two-pronged: first, exposing 'a catalogue of expedients': second, denouncing 'a new method of government'.¶

It may be noted that Gladstone's personalization of government policy in the 1876–8 period, when Disraeli was held largely responsible, broadens in

* *Political speeches* (1879), 158.
† *Political speeches* (1879), 26. The emphasis on strangeness was premeditated; see the speech-notes reproduced in *The Gladstone Diaries*, ix, plate 3.
‡ Ibid., 36.   § Ibid., 50.   ¶ Ibid., 36. 22.

1878–80 into a more general denunciation, as Salisbury, at first exonerated by his behaviour at the Constantinople Conference, became tarnished by the secret negotiations with Russia and Turkey in 1878, by which Bulgaria and the Armenians were sacrificed and Cyprus obtained.

The content of the Midlothian Campaign was thus by no means that of a simple political raid. It represented, as Gladstone said at its beginning, an indictment made 'many times elsewhere against her Majesty's Government'. It was, in a gathered and comprehensive form, the indictment stated in the vast range of pamphlets, articles, speeches, and letters issued since September 1876.

Building on the basis of the Eastern Question, 'the question out of which almost every other question had grown collaterally',* Gladstone attacked the government's record in an analysis in part geographic—its blunders in Cyprus, Egypt, South Africa, and Afghanistan; in part moral—its abandonment of justice, and liberty and communality as the criteria for British action; and in part financial—its abandonment of the strict canons of Peel–Gladstone budgetary finance and its coquetting with protectionism. This broad denunication still reads formidably. It was carefully orchestrated across six major speeches and the Glasgow rectorial in the first campaign in November 1879, and repeated with variations and extra material supplied particularly by P. W. Clayden's well-researched *England under Lord Beaconsfield* (1880) in fifteen major speeches during the second campaign following the dissolution in March 1880.

Central to Gladstone's position was the argument that moral equilibrium could be swiftly restored by good policies and in his speech on 27 November 1879 he advanced six principles of foreign policy for doing so.† That he thought Beaconsfield's 'Imperialism'—Gladstone first used the word in 1878,‡ though he did not use it often—could be righted in a year or so shows the essentially liberal cast of his thought. Although he believed Disraeli had begun the construction of a new 'system of government', Gladstone also believed a new man with the right morality could dismantle it quite quickly: 'I form a very high estimate of the power still possessed by individuals.' No general critique of Disraelian 'Imperialism' was offered, only the analysis of a series of wrong moral choices. Thus Britain's 'influence is assured by special causes, and can only be destroyed by particular errors of judgment, or by a disposition to domineer, or by an unwise self-seeking: whether these be the result of panic or of pride'.§ The domestic, parliamentary, and financial consequences of these were coherently worked out, and when Gladstone referred to a new 'system' it was

* To H. N. Gladstone, 2 Dec. 81.
† See below, p. 375.
‡ Koebner and Schmidt comment, 'Once the Liberal leader had given the cue, Imperialism became an anti-Disraeli slogan'; R. Koebner and H. D. Schmidt, *Imperialism* (1964), 148.
§ Undated fragment (1878?) in Add MS 44764, f. 44.

usually these internal consequences that he meant. The British, he thought, were inherently imperial—this their history and their character obviously showed: 'It is part of our patrimony: born with our birth, dying only with our death; incorporating itself in the first elements of our knowledge, and interwoven with all our habits of mental action upon public affairs. . . . The dominant passion of England is extended empire.' It was an expansionism that had brought much good, moral and physical, but it was also an expansionism which should and could be limited by will, by 'the exercise of moral control over ambition and cupidity'.* The 1880–5 government was to show in full measure the difficulties of this position.

The breadth of his condemnation enabled Gladstone to broaden the rather narrow base which the initial subject of the Eastern Question had given him. In particular, while many had seen his concern with Turkish iniquities as obsessive, financial and fiscal policy—to which about a third of the first Midlothian Campaign was devoted—allowed him a much more generally acceptable appeal. Gladstone on finance was a call for the restoration of mid-Victorian values in the face of their corruption by profligate, careless, and irregular Tories.

This successfully tweaked a raw Conservative nerve. The Tories' presentation of a policy of prestige and patriotism was, in terms of finance, difficult to combine with the claim to be the heirs of Peel. As the bills came in,† the deficit rose and the political problems increased. When Beaconsfield intervened to prevent a rise in indirect taxation to meet some of the costs, a member of his Cabinet noted, 'the Chief suggested another course [to Northcote's proposal]—not so good financially but almost essential politically'.‡ However much Beaconsfield might privately suspect the competence of his satraps in South Africa and India, publicly he was hoisted on the petard of his own rhetoric. Once he presented himself, however off-handedly, as the proponent of the Roman virtues of '*Imperium et Libertas*',§ the financial costs of '*Imperium*' could not be explained away with a nod of regret as the consequence of separate, local crises of the sort that Gladstone and other contemporaries accepted as inevitable. '*Imperium*' implied metropolitan control, direction, and responsibility.

The new electorate might have its jingo element, but it also had its respectable, cautious citizens, a generation accustomed to Peel–Gladstone finance, with its emphasis on balanced budgets, proper procedures, and minimal expenditure. The large deficit of £8 million, at a time when central government's annual revenue was about £81 million, gave Gladstone an

* 'England's Mission', 569–70.

† Literally in this simple form on one occasion, as an underestimate of £4 million on the cost of the Afghan war was discovered in March 1880; see N. E. Johnson, *The diary of Gathorne Hardy* (1981), 447.

‡ Ibid., 418 (entry for 30 July 1879). Northcote wanted to increase the tea duty.

§ As, e.g., at Guildhall on 10 November 1879, in Buckle, vi. 483.

easy target, given the assumptions of the time. As long as Conservative governments had been minority governments, he told the electors, 'we got on very decently with them', but now, let loose by a majority, 'the extravagance of expenditure ... bubbles up everywhere',* with the consequence that regular, balanced budgets, the centrepiece of Gladstonian finance, had been eclipsed by a series of back-door devices: 'the elementary duty of the Government in the right management of finance has been grossly neglected',† and Northcote's finance was 'truly ignoble'. The exhortation to moral rectitude in government was thus stiffened by a call for a return to fiscal probity, Gladstone, as always, personally seeing the two as inherently related, as was indicated by his taking the Chancellorship of the Exchequer as well as the Premiership in 1880.

Governmental fiscal irregularity and profligacy and the flaunting of wealth by the 'plutocracy' would endanger the social order and disturb the willingness of the poor to accept their lot. As the theme of the Midlothian Campaign was a condemnation of innovations, so Gladstone defended the welfare assumptions of the 1834 Poor Law as the depression of the late 1870s deepened. Midlothian was no call to a new Jerusalem in this world, but its moral rectitude might lead to one in the next. Gladstone's thinking about poverty and the rising concern about what was soon to be called 'unemployment' is well shown in his talk to the 'old folks' of the St Pancras Workhouse in August 1879.‡ Accepting that there were 'dark and gloomy skies that have overspread the land' with the onset of depression, Gladstone none the less reasserted the principle of 'less eligibility' of the 1834 Poor Law, buttressing it with Christian social quietism which, he said, would be 'an act of the basest guilt' unless 'conviction of the truth ... lay at the very root of my understanding and at the very bottom of my heart'. 'Indulgences by rule and under system' were unacceptable:

It is not because the receiving of such indulgences would be dangerous or mischievous to yourselves. It is the effect ... that would be produced upon the community at large if those establishments, which are maintained out of the labour of the community and at its charge, were made establishments of luxury living. It is necessary that the independent labourer of this country should not be solicited ... by thinking he could do better for himself by making a charge upon that community. There is no more subtle poison that could be infused into the nation at large than a system of that kind. ... We live in an age when most of us have forgotten that the Gospel of our Saviour Christ ... was above all the Gospel of the poor ... from His own mouth proceeded the words which showed us in reference to temporal circumstances that a time will come when many of the first shall be last and many of the last first ... blessed are the poor who accept with cheerfulness the limited circumstances and conditions in which they have to pass those few fleeting years.

* *Political speeches* (1879), 136–7.
† Ibid. (1880), 94.
‡ *The Times*, 22 August 1879.

1880 was to be the last general election at which the holding of such opinions by the leader of the party of progress could be regarded as unexceptionable.

The Campaign in Midlothian

In the particular circumstances of the Midlothian constituency, with its tiny, old-style electorate, the manœuvrings of Rosebery and his agents were probably as important as Gladstone's speeches in defeating the Earl of Dalkeith. It was Rosebery, Reid, Richardson, and P. W. Campbell (the Liberal agent) who countered the Buccleuch interest and saw that those who had promised their votes in the canvass were brought to the polling stations. Gladstone addressed a meeting of '40 to 50 convenors' the day before polling began but that was the extent of his involvement in the local details. His duty was to make his public speeches and to be seen. The speeches were partly delivered in Edinburgh and partly in the villages and small towns around the capital, some of them today its suburbs: Corstophine, Balerno, Dalkeith, Penicuik, Mid-Calder, West Calder, Loanhead, Gilmerton, Peebles, and Innerleithen.

As there were fewer than 3,500 voters in Edinburghshire, most of the people in the large crowds must have been unenfranchised. Women attended the meetings in quite large numbers, encouraged by Mrs Gladstone who broke precedent by sitting by her husband in the centre of the platform, rather than in a special 'ladies' section'. The mood at the meetings was fervent, often revivalist in the Moody–Sankey tradition of the 1870s, of which as we have seen Gladstone had had direct experience. Proceedings usually began with Liberal songs, often sung to hymn tunes, to warm up the audience. A brief introduction brought the main speaker to his feet and the speech began. The mood may have been revivalist and the hecklers sometimes boisterous, but the speeches themselves were not out of place in the churches in which they were often delivered. After Gladstone's speech, a vote of thanks would be moved and seconded—an important opportunity for the local politicians—and then the audience and the platform party would process through the town, Gladstone's carriage often being pulled by hand as a mark of special respect.

During his campaigns in November 1879 and March 1880, Gladstone slept in the great houses of the Scottish Liberal aristocracy—Dalmeny (Lord Rosebery),* Taymouth Castle (Lord Breadalbane), and Laidlawstiel (Lord Reay), emphasizing the respectability of his campaign; its novelty was obvious enough. Each day he went by carriage or rail (for the Borders

* When I was a child in Edinburgh, our neighbour, Dr Eason, told me that as a medical student he and his friends had run behind Gladstone's carriage from the West End along the Queensferry Road to Dalmeny, a distance of about seven miles. On arrival at Dalmeny, he told me, the gates closed behind the carriage but Gladstone got out to say a few words to his perspiring supporters. This was probably in fact the 1892 rather than the 1880 campaign.

were then well-connected with Edinburgh by train) to his speaking places, often lunching or dining in the Manse, especially if the meeting was in the Kirk. Scottish ministers were happy to have their churches used—a view inconceivable among Anglicans—for in Scotland 'Church and State' were not seen as antitheses.

Gladstone made his eighteenth and final speech at West Calder—an address of '1h. 25 m, amidst the old enthusiasm'—on 2 April 1880. Next day he felled a Spanish chestnut in Dalmeny Park 'by order'; Rosebery probably planned this by way of enforcing relaxation. It was already clear that the Beaconsfield government would fall. The Midlothian poll closed on Monday, 5 April. Gladstone recorded the moment:

Drove to Edinburgh about 4. . . . At 7.20 Mr Reid brought the figures of the poll G[ladstone] 1579, D[alkeith] 1368: quite satisfactory. Soon after, 15,000 people being gathered in George St. I spoke very shortly from the windows & Rosebery followed, excellently well. Home about ten. Wonderful, & nothing less, has been the disposing guiding hand of God in all this matter.

Gladstone, Rosebery, and the Liberal agents had played their part as well. Midlothian confirmed the results already declared for most of the rest of the United Kingdom: a return to Liberal government was certain, and very probably with Gladstone as Prime Minister.

The Midlothian Campaign both Charismatic and Rational

Taking politics to the electorate as directly as Gladstone did in Midlothian was, in the context of the day, highly controversial. *The Times* gave its verdict on the first Midlothian Campaign:

In a word, everything is overdone. . . . Does it [the country] wish the conduct of public affairs to be at the mercy of excitement, of rhetoric, of the qualities which appeal to a mob rather than to those which command the attention of a Senate?*

Gladstone had anticipated such criticisms in 1877, when replying to Tory objections to the early phase of the Bulgarian Atrocities campaign, which was perforce carried out during the long parliamentary recess:

I suppose it may be said that the House of Commons represents the country; but still it is not the country, and, as people have lately drawn a distinction between the country and the Government, so there might be circumstances in which they might draw a distinction between the country and the House of Commons.†

The restoration of the natural harmony between Commons and electorate had been one of Gladstone's aims since his return in 1876. Such a harmony was represented, in Gladstone's view, by a Liberal majority. The Midlothian Campaign exemplified the drive to achieve it, for while its means were novel, its message was restorative.

* Leader in *The Times*, 29 November 1879, 9a.
† *H* 232. 120 (9 February 1877).

The Midlothian Campaign has its obvious importance in late-Victorian politics. But it has a wider significance also. Various means have been developed through various media to attract the votes of the extended franchises common to the nations of Europe and North America since the 1850s: speeches, pamphlets, organizations, slogans, advertisements, bribes, and intimidations direct or implied. At a constituency level, the Edinburghshire election of 1880 involved all these. At a national level, however, the Midlothian Campaign speeches offered a remarkable solution to the problem of marrying a representative system to a large-scale franchise. Within the context of the given materials—the nature of the franchise and the nature of the media—Gladstone had squared the circle: he had formulated a politics that was both charismatic and rational. The serious discussion of a great national issue can never be simple or easy, but in the conditions of an extended franchise it must at least be widely articulated, and the quality of the articulation will have much to do with the general quality of national political life. Given the difficulties of expounding the complexities of an intricate series of principles, policies, and events, the Midlothian speeches were of international importance in encouraging a new and high standard of political awareness, discussion, and citizenship. The concept of the active citizen, so central to the ethos of Liberalism, was given fresh life and a larger definition by the new means of political discussion and communication.

CHAPTER III

Private Life in Retirement

Houses, Money, and Possessions—Reading, Writing, and Literary Earnings—
Sex and Stability—The Stage—Gladstone, Tennyson, and Ruskin—Friends,
Family, and Deaths

11. Tu.
Ch. 8½ AM. Wrote to Mr Dawson Solr—Mr Pease MP.—W. Taylor—
Mr Leeman MP—Mrs Jane Cross—S. M. Glover. Mr Roden came,
with his remarkable portrait of me. He prosecuted the task while I
worked peaceably at Thesauros Homerikos. (Connection with
Hebrew traditions.) Inquiries on the subject of the Dawson letter.
Felled a cherry tree which is to be sold [blank] a foot over market
price. Read Goldsmith on Owls—Quint. Smyrnaeus—Schl[iemann]
on Mycenae. Conversation with [J. A.] Godley.*

Houses, Money, and Possessions

Gladstone's resignation of the premiership in February 1874 ended his
£5,000 *p.a.* salary and left him with a shortage of ready cash. As we have
seen in an earlier volume, he only had £1,000 *p.a.* 'for all general expenditure whatsoever'. This was by no means poverty, but out of it he was maintaining Hawarden Castle and 11 Carlton House Terrace, a big house in the
smartest area of London, and, as we shall see, most of his children, now all
adults. The announcement in 1875 of formal retirement from politics thus
related to a major change in domestic arrangements, a move from the plush
fashion of the Carlton House area to a—relatively—cheaper and less grand
house in Harley Street. The move was complex. In February 1875, following the announcement of retirement, the lease of 11 Carlton House
Terrace, the Gladstones' house since July 1856, was sold for £35,000 to Sir
Arthur Guinness. William Gladstone then took 23 Carlton House Terrace,
a 'small & rather quaint house just 50 yards from our own' for the season.
From the autumn of 1875, Arthur Balfour's house at 4 Carlton Gardens,
just round the corner from Carlton House Terrace, was used as a London
base. It was not until 8 February 1876 that 73 Harley Street was leased for
thirty years, the assignment being executed on the same day that Gladstone
'spoke briefly in vindication of our concern in the case of the Christian

* Diary for 11 Sept. 77, a characteristic entry.

subjects of Turkey': a secure London base thus ironically being obtained exactly as the start of the long process of political return began, though at the time of the move Gladstone told Phillimore the house was 'for his wife's sake . . . exclusively'.

Gladstone does not seem to have taken much to the Harley Street house. When the family was away, he usually dined and breakfasted with Mrs Birks, his next door neighbour: Mary Gladstone describes her in a Pre-Raphaelite context, at Burne-Jones's house at North End, as having a 'scarlet shawl and gold lockets',* but she also had brewing connections.

The move out of Carlton House Terrace was physically and emotionally exhausting, Gladstone doing much of the donkey work himself. There was a further sorting and destruction of papers, and part of the library appears to have been sold to the omnipresent Lord Wolverton. The considerable art and china collections assembled since the 1830s (and by the 1870s housed partly at Carlton House Terrace and partly at the Brown Museum in Liverpool) were sold by Christie, Manson and Woods in a sale lasting four days in June 1875.

The sale was described by the catalogue as of 'English and foreign pottery and porcelain, bronzes, marbles, decorative furniture, silver-gilt tankards, cups and dishes, Camei, carvings in ivory, jade and wood, water-colour drawings, and pictures of the Italian, Spanish, Dutch and English schools.' It made £9,351. 0s. 6d. The best price was for the last item of the sale, £483 for Bonifazio's 'Virgin',† the next best, £420, for William Dyce's beautiful portrait, 'Lady with the coronet of Jasmin', in fact a portrait of a rescue case, Miss Summerhayes, commissioned by Gladstone in 1859 and reproduced in Volume V of *The Gladstone Diaries*. The large number of Continental paintings and artefacts, so carefully chosen and brought back from the various Continental tours, raised little (£85 for a 'Giorgione',‡ 11 guineas for a 'Murillo'). H. N. Gladstone attempted to reassemble the collection in 1910, but few of the items could be traced.§

The whole business was embarrassing—'two huge Auctioneers' Bills today adorn the doorposts of the portico'—and upsetting: 'Visited my room at No 11 for the last time as the proprietor. . . . The process as a whole has been like a *little* death. . . . I had *grown* to the House, having lived more time in it than in any other since I was borne; and mainly by reason of all that was done in it. Sir A. G[uinness] has the chairs and sofa on which we sat

* Mary Gladstone, *Diaries and letters* (1930), 191.
† The whereabouts of this picture are unknown; it is probably not by Bonifazio and may be by Girolamo da Sta Croce (information from Sir Ellis Waterhouse).
‡ Both the 'Giorgiones' in the Gladstone sale were bought by Agnew's and given in 1926 to the Detroit Institute of Art; they are now ascribed to Palma Vecchio.
§ The St. Deiniol's copy of Christie's catalogue of the sale is marked with the prices and the names of the buyers, mostly dealers. In 1929 H. N. Gladstone docketed a letter from Christie's of 31 August 1910: 'Messrs. Christie found it impossible to trace the collection.'

when we resolved on the disestablishment of the Irish Church in 1868.' As always, Gladstone extracted a moral lesson from unpleasantness: 'I am amazed at the accumulation of objects which have now, as by way of retribution, to be handled, & dispersed, or finally dismissed.' Marx and Engels (the latter lived across the Park from the Gladstones' new house, in Regents Park Road) would have been amused at this Evangelical reaction to commodity-fetishism.

The result of these various sales was the end of the immediate cash crisis which had been worrying Gladstone since 1872, when he began to note concern about being 'pinched'. He was, of course, all-in-all a wealthy man. His 'approximate sketch' of his property in 1878 showed a total value of £280,522, which included £176,032 in land and £92,870 in stocks and shares.* But he was also the father of seven children, most of them, in some degree, still dependent on him. Agnes was married, and the Gladstones enjoyed visits to her and her husband, the headmaster of Wellington College, whose reputation Gladstone successfully defended in the Commons when the school was denounced by J. R. Yorke.† Willy, the oldest son, forty in 1880, at last married, to Gertrude Stuart, daughter of Lord Blantyre, whose wife was a daughter of the Duchess of Sutherland, Gladstone's female confidante in the 1860s.‡

Willy, although technically since 1875 the owner of most of the Hawarden estates, still received an allowance from his father. Stephen, the second son, was prosperously settled in the wealthy rectorship of Hawarden. Harry, the third son, went into the family firm in Calcutta, but his difference with James Wyllie, who ran it, led to a long and bitter wrangle in the 1870s. His spasmodic lack of employment left him from time to time dependent on his father. Mary and Helen, the unmarried daughters, were completely dependent on their father, as was Herbert until he was elected to a lectureship in Modern History at Keble College, Oxford, following his First in the Modern History School in 1876. His entry into politics as MP for Leeds in 1880 (taking the seat won by his father at that election) deprived him of even that modest stipend.

The children therefore still constituted a considerable financial obligation. Only Stephen and Agnes could be described as off the parents' hands. Financial dependence had, of course, from the father's view-point its advantages as well as its obligations. Increasingly the family could be used

* In 'Rough Book B', Gladstone family MSS in St Deiniol's Library, Hawarden [subsequently: Hawn P].

† 'Mr. Gladstone has saved us' was the school's conclusion; see D. Newsome, *A history of Wellington College* (1959), 198 and *H* 245. 149.

‡ At almost the same time Gertrude Glynne married into the ultra-Tory Douglas Pennant family, Barons of Penrhyn, a marriage which soon involved Gladstone in family rows (see 18 Jan. 76).

as a secretariat. Once Helen had gone to Cambridge, first to study, then to teach with Millicent Fawcett at what became Newnham College, Mary found herself manning the post, helped by Herbert when he was at home. Copies of letters in their hands begin to be quite frequent in the late 1870s. Mary's role as her parents' companion—into which she seems to have been drawn unselfconsciously on their part and only partly reluctantly on hers— was beginning to be quite well defined. 'I lost good company in Helen and Herbert; but Mary is all-sufficing in point of society', Gladstone noted in January 1877.

The letters form a major theme and complaint in Gladstone's years of retirement. His involvement in a wide variety of public and private matters generated a huge correspondence. Simply opening and sorting the in-coming mail took a considerable time. In the seventy-one years covered by his diaries, Gladstone mentions over 22,000 different people, and there were few that he met with whom he did not correspond. With many of them, of course, he corresponded almost on a weekly basis. In a typical month in 1877, he wrote—by hand—an average of eleven letters a day. The correspondence drove him near despair: 'It is a terrible oppression.' He made the strategic decision early in his retirement not to employ a secre-tary. Many times in the late 1870s he wondered if this decision had been right, but he did not go back on it, relying instead on his children and, from time to time, J. A. Godley to help out on an unpaid basis.

Pamphlets, speeches, and the campaigns from September 1876 until the return to office in 1880 produced a deluge of mail, a considerable propor-tion of which was from correspondents hitherto unknown to Gladstone. Fifty or so letters a day reached Hawarden or Harley Street, many more at a time of political crisis, and a few days away brought huge accumulations of arrears. Family help in their answering was never regularized: Gladstone did most of the work himself, perfecting the use of the postcard as cheap, polite, but enforcing a convenient word limit. He showed considerable interest in the introduction of the telephone to London, attending several demonstrations of its powers. In 1880 a telephone was apparently installed at Hawarden, probably one of the first political houses to have one. Glad-stone found it 'most unearthly'* and does not seem to have used it, at least in the early 1880s. In any event, and fortunately for the historian, too few of his correspondents would have had a machine for the chore of letter writing to be alleviated.

Burdensome though Gladstone undoubtedly felt his correspondence to be, it enabled him to indulge his passion for order. The same almost physical pleasure that he gained from a neat solution to a difficulty in compiling the national budget is to be seen in his enthusiasm for reducing a confusion of letters or books or trees to an orderly sequence, catalogued—

---

* Probably used in its Glynnese sense of gnomish or nasty.

or, in the case of the trees, distanced between each other—in an intellectually satisfying form. It would be going too far to say that Gladstone was
obsessed with order for its own sake—attacks on 'chaos' were responses to
undeniable problems—but the activity of the bringing of order stemmed
restlessness and justified possession, whether of goods such as letters and
books, or of places such as libraries and estates, or even of the right to existence. The form of the daily diary entry, so remorselessly repeated, reflected
the same preoccupation and offered a similar satisfaction.

Many of the letters were invitations to further political action. Gladstone
resented this, and on one occasion in July 1878 tabled in considerable
irritation the number of invitations (14) turned down that day. His irritation
is perhaps surprising, given the extent to which he was already involving
himself in public activity. It represents, perhaps, the general unawareness
of politicians at this time of that large degree of public exposure which
democratic politics was going to expect of its chief practitioners. Correspondence in these non-governmental years took up as much time as it
had when in office, perhaps even more. Together with Church and meals,
it dictated the rhythm of the day. It allowed Gladstone, sitting in the
Temple of Peace at Hawarden, to maintain contact with the political world
and to agitate its nerves by letters and postcards: such was the efficiency of
the Victorian Post Office* and the attention given to the written word.

The daily routine at Hawarden involved Gladstone in a good deal of
exercise: the early morning walk through the Park to the Church and back
(along a specially built path to ensure privacy), walking in the surrounding
countryside and, of course, silviculture, felling and planting trees. Gladstone always used an axe, and in these years many were presented to him. It
became almost a totem among his admirers. Margaret de Lisle, daughter of
the convert to Roman Catholicism, always wore an axe to indicate loyalty to
Gladstone, until Gordon's death in 1885, when she took it off. Treefelling
kept Gladstone very fit. It was a skill well respected in the countryside and
its employment was a good occasion for bonding with his sons, especially
with Willy with whom his relationship was otherwise sometimes awkward.

Reading, Writing, and Literary Earnings

The rest of the day was often spent in reading or writing. The reader who
wishes to penetrate the mind of the 1870s could do worse than to read
through all the books, pamphlets, and periodical articles which Gladstone
notes in his diary reading in the course of a month. It would be an arduous
but illuminating task, for it would show a curious blend of modernity and
religiosity. In a month taken at random—June 1879—Gladstone read
twenty-eight books and seven periodical articles. The books range from

---

* This efficiency explains how a letter and its reply are often dated the same day, even though
the correspondents may be in different cities.

sustained study of W. E. H. Lecky's *History of England in the Eighteenth Century* (which prompted Gladstone's article on the history of evangelicalism, finished during this month) and of J. R. Green's *A Short History of the English People*, to a number of works on popular science, of which Gladstone in the late 1870s became quite a keen student. Literature is represented by Hannah Swanwick's *Egmont* and the poetry of Coleridge, Goethe, and Tennyson, the classics by a paper on 'Homeric Doubts', and contemporary affairs by L. Kong Meng's *The Chinese Question in Australia* and a number of pamphlets in French, Italian, and English. Sunday reading, spilling over into the rest of the week, was a biography of Alexander Duff, the Scottish missionary, the frequently read Thomas à Kempis, and a number of sermons, tracts, lectures, and addresses.

The selection is a fair representation of Gladstone's reading habits. He liked to have a substantial religious and a substantial secular book 'on the go', and to buttress these with an eclectic bundle of material, increasingly selected from the contributions posted to him by authors and publishers. With a good deal of this latter material he was personally involved, in that the works were often dedicated to him, or attacking him, or requesting by covering letter a public response, quite often given in a letter subsequently released by the recipient to the press. For example, the private remarks he made on the first volume of Duff's biography became the basis of an assessment of Duff quoted in the second volume published later in the year, and his letter approving of Fagan's *Life of Panizzi* was immediately printed in the biography's second edition.

Gladstone's reading was in part a self-education, but even this private act was in fact public, part of the process of 'putting his mind into the common stock'. This was most directly done by the writing which sprang from the reading. There is hardly a month in these years when an article or a pamphlet is not in progress. Between 1875 and 1880, Gladstone wrote almost sixty periodical articles and published two books of new material, *Homeric Synchronism* and *Primer of Homer*, the latter in J. R. Green's popular series for Macmillan (the forerunner of the Home University Library), and 'a treat' rather than a duty. He produced several books of speeches and recently written articles, and he edited his own selected collected articles— 'rather a daring measure'—in seven volumes entitled *Gleanings of Past Years*, published by John Murray in 1879.

In 1879, he noted that his total literary earnings to date were about £10,000 gross; £5,009 was earned between 1876 and 1880.* The largest item was the income from the pamphlets and subsequent book on the Vatican controversy 1874–5 (£2,800), one of the smallest items the £58 received from

* Account book for 1878–94, Hawn P, from which subsequent figures are taken. This book estimates total literary earnings to the end of 1880 as £10,239. If £450 is subtracted for articles from the 1876 total of £1790, this would give £1340 for the 'Bulgarian Horrors' pamphlet in that year.

the Clarendon Press of Oxford University for *Studies on Homer* (1858), the work which undoubtedly cost the most thought and effort.

By the 1870s, Gladstone was, obviously enough, an author much in demand, and able, on the whole, to call his own tune. James Knowles carried articles on classical subjects, such as 'The Slicing of Hector' (£52) in the *Contemporary Review* and later in the *Nineteenth Century* so as to be able to publish great contemporary pieces such as 'England's Mission' (£100). Gladstone's literary work was thus lucrative but not money-directed. He wrote *gratis* for the Congregationalist *British Quarterly Review* and for almost nothing for the Tractarian *Church Quarterly Review*. Had he been writing chiefly for money, he would have written much more for the United States market. His 'Kin beyond Sea', *inter alia* a curious elaboration of Bagehot's *The English Constitution* written for the *North American Review* in 1878, brought a shoal of invitations to write and lecture, all of which were turned down, including in 1878 an invitation from Harvard for a series of lectures on Political Economy for which he was preferred as a speaker to Jevons, Marshall, and Fawcett.

The articles and other writings reflected Gladstone's eclectic interests, covering a vast range of subjects from a cautious introduction to de Laveleye's Weberesque thesis in *Protestantism and Catholicism* (1875), through anonymous and on certain occasions unpublished notices and reviews for Cazenove's new *Church Quarterly Review* to his notable series of comments on affairs of the day in the *Contemporary Review* and the *Nineteenth Century*, for which James Knowles captured him after the latter's row with Strahan, the publisher of the *Contemporary*.

Though all these writings are of interest, and most show Gladstone to be much terser and sharper with the pen than is often thought, there can be little doubt that of the literary pieces the best is his anonymous review in the *Quarterly* of G. O. Trevelyan's *Life and Letters of Macaulay*. In view of the savage attack which Macaulay had made on Gladstone's first book in 1838, it shows generosity as well as understanding. Gladstone's literary output would have made him an important Victorian figure even if his political activities were discounted, but his essay on Macaulay suggests rather more than this. It is a model retrospect, still holding a place on its own merits in the study of Macaulay. Gladstone took a great deal of trouble with the essay, which he began on 13 April 1876 and finished on 12 June, the writing being interrupted by George Lyttelton's suicide and various family illnesses: 'It is a business made difficult by the utter want of continuity in my application to it. And really the subject is beyond the common order.'

From the point of view of our understanding of Gladstone, the essay is interesting for the qualities it praises and condemns: 'As the serious flaw in Macaulay's mind was want of depth, so the central defect . . . is a pervading strain of more or less exaggeration . . . amidst a blaze of glory, there is a want of perspective, of balance, and of breadth.' To demonstrate this effect, Gladstone offered the examples of Macaulay's exaggerated treatment of Milton and Bacon in the *Essays*, and, drawing on Churchill Babbington, of the Restoration clergy in the *History*. But he recognized that to show that Macaulay was 'wrong' was essentially beside the point. What needed recognition was that Macaulay had written an English romance rather than a history: 'his whole method of touch and handling are poetical.' The transcendent quality which redeemed his weaknesses and made Macaulay's works 'a permanent addition to the mental patrimony of the human race' was his nature, best seen in his poems which 'possess the chief merits of his other works, and are free from their faults': the *History* is essentially a poetic romance, 'and greater and better yet than the works themselves are the lofty aims and conceptions, the large heart, the independent, manful mind, the pure and noble career'.*

We can see here how it was that with his low view of his own nature, his persistent self-abasement, Gladstone never completed a major work after his *Studies on Homer* (1858), the product of his earlier years of extended opposition, and how it was that he concentrated on short pieces making limited points. The mass of his scholarly effort went into the Homeric Thesaurus, never published as such though sections of it appeared from time to time in the periodicals. Gladstone had in mind a volume on Olympian religion but, apart from fragments for the periodicals, chips from a Hawarden workshop, little was achieved in the way of a book-length plan.

These short pieces, fervent though many of them are, were always fair. Within the traditions of his age, and certainly compared with any twentieth-century political figure, Gladstone was an erudite, scrupulous commentator and combatant. Even as a politician in retirement, he knew the Blue Books as well as any government spokesman, and his diary continues to testify to the energy of his ephemeral reading. Yet this sort of speaking and writing made him more aware of his weaknesses as an author. Commenting on his letters to Samuel Wilberforce as he re-read them in preparation for their extensive use by Wilberforce's biographers, he observed of them, 'they are curiously illustrative of a peculiar and second-rate nature', and, revising his review of Tennyson's *Maud* for republication in *Gleanings*, he noted: 'The fact is I am wanting in that higher poetical sense which distinguishes the true artist.' The persistent emphasis on control, balance, holding things in check, might not have seemed so obvious to a Tory opponent in this period, but it was of the very essence of Gladstone's character. His nature was poetic, but his character, as he had forged it, was captive.

* Quotations from *Gleanings*, ii. 265 ff.

Sex and Stability

This captivity, not always successfully enforced but always strenuously pursued, was contained by religion, for from regular religious observance, particularly of the Eucharist, Gladstone gained an element of peace, a redress to his restlessness. In terms of his personal life, the later 1870s were relatively tranquil. He was on good terms with his wife and family. Catherine Gladstone differed sharply with him over his retirement in 1875—one of the few occasions on which she intervened politically to disagree—and there were difficulties about the sale of the London house, but these were not long-term differences. Like her husband, Mrs Gladstone ('Cathie' as he often called her in conversation) retained her exuberance and her energy: 'At 64 she has the vigour & freshness of 34.' Quite what this meant in terms of the Gladstones' marriage is not recorded, but Gladstone was always careful when making remarks. Catherine Gladstone continued her work for her charitable homes, and her care for the many members of the Gladstone–Lyttelton connection. She was an important contributor to the management and personal success of the Midlothian Campaign, her regular appearances with her husband on the political platform being widely noticed in the contemporary press.

Gladstone's 'rescue work' with London prostitutes continued in a routine way. An occasional 'X' is placed in his diary entries after his meetings with Laura Thistlethwayte, the evangelical ex-courtesan who had been the focus of the major emotional crisis of 1869–70, but in general his relationship with her seems to have become less charged. The very intense tone of their correspondence of the early 1870s—an intensity surely unsustainable—gives way to a calmer, easier exchange. They were both guests at a house party given by Lord Bathurst at Oakley Park in 1875, but, despite the absence of Catherine Gladstone and three specifically itemized conversations, nothing of the crisis at Boveridge in 1869 was repeated.*

As Frederick Thistlethwayte's financial and sexual life became ever more complex, Gladstone acted as an adviser to Laura, especially when she was summoned to the debtors' court by Henry Padwick, a well-known racehorse owner, gambler, and money-lender. In 1878 Captain Thistlethwayte was in court in dispute with Padwick, and for a time in 1879 it looked as if an action would be brought by Padwick directly involving Laura. The case would have been, at the least, very awkward for Gladstone. Since the late 1860s he had accepted from her gifts 'which in aggregate must have cost hundreds'. He had protested against their receipt and had clearly been embarrassed by them, but he had not put a stop to the practice. When Mrs Thistlethwayte's financial position became serious, in 1878, he attempted without success to return the presents, and he tried again and failed again

---

* For that crisis, see above, p. 241.

in 1879. But the difficulty if the case became public would have gone well beyond the gifts. Padwick's case was that Captain Thistlethwayte refused to honour his wife's debts. Thistlethwayte's defence was that his wife ran them up by entertainment and munificence given without his knowledge. A subpoena was issued to Gladstone to appear as a witness. He was definitely alarmed. The witnesses, he told Laura,

will probably be asked *whom* they met at your table. . . . The witnesses would probably be asked whether they had partaken of your hospitality—I should have to reply yes; especially at luncheons from time to time where I used to meet some greatly esteemed friends. . . . I would probably be asked who were the guests I had met at your table. It would be most offensive to me to detail their names as if charging them with something discreditable. . . . I doubt whether either you or Mr. T. is at all aware of the amount & kind of mischief done by the trial of last year: It was exceedingly great, and rely on it that by any similar trial now repeated it would be aggravated tenfold.

Since 1869, Gladstone had begun his letters to Laura Thistlethwayte, 'Dear Spirit'. As soon as the Padwick action began, he reverted to 'Dear Mrs. Thistlethwayte', clearly fearing the letters might be produced in court.*

Fortunately for Gladstone, for the guests were not all of his usual circle, the case was settled out of court. The Gladstone–Thistlethwayte correspondence for the later 1870s contains the odd political and religious comment, but it consists mostly of arrangements for meals and of family news: Laura Thistlethwayte saw to it that she was well-informed about the doings of the Gladstone children, although her exigency was not always successful. Increasingly, the initiative in the correspondence came from her, with Gladstone responding cordially but often also cautiously, wary of being drawn in further than politeness and his sense of duty required. He felt obliged, even bound to her, as he saw her bravely facing her difficulties, but he also found her importunity on occasion irritating.

One of the guests at the Thistlethwayte table was Olga Novikov, the 'M.P. for Russia'. Several important meetings on Russo-Turkish affairs took place at Mrs Thistlethwayte's house in Grosvenor Square, notably Gladstone's meeting with Shuvalov in December 1876 on the evening of the great St James's Hall meeting on the Bulgarian atrocities. Gladstone saw Olga Novikov as a Russian rather than a woman. The sentimental paternalism characteristic of his letters to women on politics is absent from his correspondence with Madame Novikov. Her views, as an enthusiastic Pan-Slavist, did not fit precisely with Gladstone's, but she was a well-informed source of information about Russian affairs and a useful link for him with the Russian community in London, Paris, and beyond.† He carefully distanced himself from

---

* Gladstone discussed the case with Rosebery, at that time by no means an intimate, in April 1879, which may indicate alarm about its consequences in Midlothian.

† The remnants of the Novikov Papers, now in my possession, unfortunately do not include Gladstone's letters to her; many of these were published by W. T. Stead in The 'M.P. for Russia', 2v. (1909).

her on becoming Prime Minister again in 1880, but maintained a spasmodic correspondence. It may be that Madame Novikov thought she was
using Gladstone, and this was a common view at the time, and indeed later,
but the rumour that she was his mistress is utterly absurd.*

The Stage

Laura Thistlethwayte was also a link with the theatre. It is striking that in
this, one of the most Evangelical periods of his life, Gladstone when in
London became almost a theatrical devotee. He was, in private relaxation,
'enthusiastic' rather than 'earnest'. Phillimore noted, as the Eastern Question reached its climax: 'I was amused to hear him defend plays & the
Theatre—on no subject have his opinions undergone a more complete
revolution.'† He went to one of the first London performances of *Lohengrin*, at Covent Garden,‡ but for the most part his theatre-going was to the
fashionable West End with its comedies and farces, or to Shakespeare in
Irving's productions at the Lyceum. He noted of one production: Irving's
'Hamlet though a work of ability is not good: but how marvellous are the
drama and the character' (he saw Irving's Hamlet five times between 1875
and 1880). Of his Shakespeare productions in the 1870s he also saw *Othello*,
Richard III, *Henry VIII* (a play which fascinated Gladstone), and *The
Merchant of Venice*. Irving's controversial Shylock, a caricature of a Jew and
consequently a comment on Disraeli, then the Prime Minister, was,
Gladstone noted, 'Irving's best, I thought'. Gladstone sampled the increasingly popular Music Hall ('the show was certainly not Athenian' was his
cryptic comment), and the ballet at the Alhambra. He attended a private

* A remarkable letter from R. B. D. Morier to L. Mallet, 20 May 1880 (copy made from the
Wemyss MSS now in Balliol College, Oxford, amongst which this letter is no longer to be found; I
am obliged to Dr Ramm for the copy) reflects this view: 'As regards Gladstone's action it is most
interesting to me from a merely psychological point of view. The real motive powers necessarily
escape the mass because they are to be detected only in a word or a sentence dropped here and
there which only the initiated can comprehend. But if for instance you read his review of that
strumpet Madame Novikoff's book you will see much. The first thing to note is the influence that
woman has over him and the way quite unconsciously to himself, that he sees everything through
her eyes. Now I have often told you that I am convinced no one really understands Gladstone
unless he notes that very much of his ways are the result of what I call suppressed priapism! I maintain that at least one third of human action is determined by the too much or too little of the sexual
intercourse that has fallen to the lot of the actor. Of course in the case of Gladstone it is a case of
too little. I am convinced that he came into the world with the most tremendously virile powers,
that his strongly ascetic religiosity has kept them down—that Mrs G. has been the only flesh he has
ever tasted! consequently that there is even at his time of life a lurking desire within him seeking
unconsciously to himself to be assuaged. Madame N. who is an extremely accomplished whore will
have seized this at a glance. She will have been far too cunning to play on this instrument directly
but she will have known exactly how to utilize her knowledge. . . .' The rest of the letter contains
equally strident anti-Semitic comments about Rosebery's wife and Beaconsfield, Morier being
incensed at rumours of 'outsiders' being appointed to embassies and at Montagu Corry's peerage;
Morier admitted 'I am not just now a perfectly impartial judge.'
  † Phillimore's diary, 26 January 1878.
  ‡ 8 May 75.

performance by Sarah Bernhardt at the house of Mrs Ralli, another of his theatre-going companions, he saw her as Phèdre at the Gaiety ('⅔ full') and with his family he went to the Théâtre Français season in Paris in 1879. His famous appearance at the Haymarket Theatre with Hartington and Granville on the night of the publication of the 'Bulgarian Horrors' on 5 September 1876 was thus by no means idiosyncratic. Unfortunately, it is not now possible to know whether this theatre-going extended Gladstone's range as a speaker. But it is not unreasonable to suppose that his observation of theatrical occasions contributed to his skills in moving an audience, skills which in a large hall required every resource of voice and gesture. An interesting by-product of this theatre-going was his letter to *The Theatre* in 1878 which formed a focal point for one of the early campaigns for a National Theatre.* In this Gladstone touched English life characteristically, for one of the most striking aspects of his long career is the astonishing range of his activities. Rare is the Victorian archive or institution without a Gladstonian dimension.

Gladstone, Tennyson, and Ruskin

Gladstone had always seen Laura Thistlethwayte in a Pre-Raphaelite or Tennysonian light; in the mid-1870s he several times records reading Tennyson to her, notably 'Guinevere' following their visit to the Alhambra ballet. Anything that he tried to see nobly, particularly in women, he saw through the categories of mediaeval chivalry, as softened and made Victorian in Tennyson's poems and plays.† In the later 1870s, Gladstone made considerable contacts with what may be called the respectable elements of Tennysonian Pre-Raphaelitism. These were encouraged by a very different influence from Laura Thistlethwayte, his daughter Mary, who was friendly with the Burne-Jones circle.

In particular, Hawarden was visited by two of the great potentates of Victorian aesthetics: Tennyson and Ruskin.

Tennyson came in October 1876. The visit was not altogether a success, though it was probably more of a success than it might have been if J. H. Newman had accepted Gladstone's invitation also to join the party. Tennyson had finished, but not yet published, his play *Harold* and was nervous about its success. Gladstone noted politely: 'Tennyson read to us his Harold: it took near 2½ hours'; he did not mention that the family thought that he nearly fell asleep, and that his son Willy had a fit of suppressed giggles.‡ The next day Gladstone encouraged conversation on his favourite topic of the time, the decline in the belief in hell. Not surprisingly, although Arthur Hallam had been in a sense the inspirer of

* See *The Theatre*, iii. 103 (13 March 1878).
† See M. Girouard, *The Return to Camelot. Chivalry and the English gentleman* (1981), ch. xii.
‡ See R. B. Martin, *Tennyson. The unquiet heart* (1980), 516.

both, the author of *Church Principles* found himself on different ground from the composer of *In Memoriam*: 'Conversation with Tennyson on Future Retribution, and other matters of theology: he has not thought, I conceive, systematically or thoroughly upon them, but is much alarmed at the prospect of the loss of belief. He left me at one.' Tennyson and Gladstone were to clash with increasing vigour in the 1880s, but their public face in these years was harmonious: Tennyson's sonnet extolling the virtues of the Montenegrins immediately preceded Gladstone's article, 'Montenegro', in the third number of the *Nineteenth Century* in 1877.

Gladstone was always an enthusiast for respectable art, as shown at Agnew's, Colnaghi's, and the Royal Academy exhibition—an enthusiasm marked by his election in 1876, in the room of Connop Thirlwall, as Royal Academy Professor of Ancient History. But he also began visiting the Grosvenor Gallery, the show-place of the avant-garde—immortalized by W. S. Gilbert's lines in *Patience*(1881): 'a greenery-yallery, Grosvenor Gallery, foot-in-the-grave young man!' His correspondence with Oscar Wilde, inaugurated by the latter while an undergraduate, went beyond mere formality: Gladstone made suggestions as to how Wilde should publish a sonnet—inspired by Gladstone's speeches—on the Bulgarian atrocities.

Gladstone to some extent patched up his differences with John Ruskin, the Pre-Raphaelites' patron, who deplored Gladstone's fiscal liberalism, by two successful visits to Hawarden in 1878, though this did not prevent Ruskin, in his campaign to succeed Gladstone as Rector of Glasgow University, observing that he cared no more for Gladstone and Disraeli than he did for two old bagpipes.* With Henry Scott Holland also present at Hawarden, the company had a distinctively Christian Socialist flavour.

On the second visit, in October 1878, Ruskin 'developed his political opinions. They aim at the restoration of the Judaic system, & exhibit a mixture of virtuous absolutism & Christian socialism.' In response, Gladstone delighted Ruskin by declaring 'I am a firm believer in the aristocratic principle—the rule of the best. I am an out-and-out *inequalitarian*.'†

Ruskin charmed Gladstone, but his view of government and political economy can hardly have appealed to him. As to Gladstone's declaration, it is hard at first glance to know whether it is odder that it should have been made by a free-trade Chancellor of the Exchequer, or applauded by a Christian Socialist. At second glance, it can be seen that it is consistent with Gladstone's view that free trade would confirm rather than topple the social order of the nation, and that Ruskin's Christian Socialism was profoundly hierarchic.‡

* For the Glasgow campaign and correspondence, see L. March-Phillipps and B. Christian, *Some Hawarden letters 1878–1913* (1917), 62ff.

† Morley, ii. 582.

‡ See R. Hewison, *John Ruskin* (1976), 182ff. Mary Gladstone noted: 'the experienced Ch. of Ex. and visionary idealist came into conflict'; L. Masterman, *Mary Gladstone* (1930), 142.

Ruskin's visits to Hawarden were followed by one from Edward Burne-Jones, who was active in the Atrocities campaign and who 'left good memories behind him'. Burne-Jones, recovering from an illness, certainly bore the brunt of Gladstonian enthusiasm: 'Read my chapter on Judaism in the "Studies [on Homer]" & inflicted it on Mr Burne Jones' and, next day, 're-read my Chapter [1858] on the Jews and gave it to Mr Burne Jones who approved'. It was Burne-Jones who, after Gladstone's death, carved the beautiful window commemorating him in Hawarden Church.

Friends, Family, and Deaths

A break from the stresses and strains of writing and especially from corresponding was gained by various expeditions, always with a family dimension. A visit to Ireland in 1877 will be discussed later.* There was also a trip with some of the children to the Isle of Man, and a Continental journey in 1879, a break before the first Midlothian Campaign, and the subject of a short separate travel diary. This trip took the Gladstones first to stay with Acton and his wife at Tegernsee in the Bavarian Alps, where Dr Döllinger was also of the party. This visit was of particular importance for Mary Gladstone, for from it sprang her intimacy with Acton.† The Gladstone party then travelled through the Dolomites—at that time an unusual and unfashionable route—to Venice, where Lady Marian Alford acted as hostess, organizing trips and meetings with the members of English society in Venice, such as Robert Browning. Acton rejoined them by a different route.

The stay in Germany and Italy confirmed the rather cautious relationship between Gladstone and Acton, which had been to some extent damaged by the Vatican pamphlet of 1874. Gladstone felt Acton willing to wound, but afraid to strike the Papacy: 'Walk & long conversation with Ld Acton: who seems in opinion to go beyond Döllinger, though in action to stop short of him.'‡ There is not much indication of intimacy, at least on Gladstone's side. The real enjoyment, for him, was the talks with Döllinger, whom the party visited in Munich on the way home. The references to Döllinger in Gladstone's diary are always warm, positive, and enthusiastic, those to Acton, usually neutral. It was during this visit that Lenbach, the Munich artist, painted his first portrait of Gladstone and had the photograph taken which is reproduced in this volume. A few days in Paris completed the holiday, with a Republican dinner organized by de Girardin as a result of which he became particularly interested in the writings of the critic Edmond Scherer, a diplomatic dinner organized by Waddington—

---

* See below, pp. 437–8.
† Described in the fine study by Owen Chadwick, 'Acton and Gladstone' (1976).
‡ 2 Nov. 76. On this occasion, Acton was part of the party to entertain Tennyson; he was also of the party during Ruskin's first visit in 1878.

'He did not open on the Eastern question and I thought it would be bad taste in me'—an incautious interview on British foreign policy with the *Gaulois* newspaper, and shopping, churches, and the theatre.

This was the Gladstones' longest Continental journey since 1866–7. On that previous journey, Gladstone had been well known in certain sections of Continental society. He was now famous. This made the Continental journey much more a public event, a tour of the great, but visits to 'Book & curiosity shops' were still possible.

Not surprisingly for a man who was 70 when he fought the 1880 general election, the death of contemporaries was a quite frequent experience, often producing an optimistic comment in the diary on the probable state of the dead person's soul at the moment of death. Physically, the most immediate was the death of the Duchess of Argyll, who had a seizure while sitting down next to Gladstone at dinner; he attended her funeral in Scotland, finding the Presbyterian burial service more pleasing than in earlier years. Another notable death was that of Antonio Panizzi, architect of the expansion of the library of the British Museum. As Panizzi's health declined, Gladstone tried to ensure that he died in a state of grace. Gladstone recorded the scene as Panizzi lay dying: 'I said to him, as I have done of late: Shall I say our little prayer now before I go? He looked at me and said "What the devil do you mean?" I said: I mean our prayer, the Lord's prayer: that is right, is it not? He said "Yes". (He had asked it shd be in Latin).'* Gladstone assisted in the preparation of Panizzi's biography, and was pleased by the result, commenting on it: 'Panizzi had long acquired a stronghold upon my feelings, and the way in which he has dwelt upon my mind since his death shows me that it was even stronger than I knew of during his life-time.'

A number of family deaths occurred in the 1870s. The most important were those of George Lyttelton, Catherine Gladstone's brother-in-law, of Robertson Gladstone, and of Helen Gladstone. Mentally ill for several years, Lyttelton broke away from his attendant and killed himself by falling into the stair-well in 18 Park Crescent. Gladstone inspected the site in order to be able to contradict to his own satisfaction the view that it was not an accident, but 'intended: intended not by him but by that which possessed him'. He went with his wife 'to observe the fatal stair. Its structure is dangerous; & it confirmed the notion I had previously entertained of the *likelihood* that he [Lyttelton] never meant at all to throw himself over, but fell in a too rapid descent, over the bannisters.'† The whole incident is

---

* 7 Apr. 79; Panizzi died next day.

† 19 Apr., 14 May 76. Lucy Cavendish, Lyttelton's daughter, noted: 'we shall never know if it was in any degree accidental or not, but we *do* know he was as unaccountable as if a lightning stroke had fallen on him'; J. Bailey, ed., *Diary of Lady Frederick Cavendish*, 2v. (1927) [subsequently: *D.L.F.C.*], ii. 196.

Gladstonism in miniature: the implied deductive proposition, inductively demonstrated by probability.

George Lyttelton's death was a shock, but caused little lasting distress. The death of Robertson Gladstone, the third of the four brothers, and the only one with whom William had retained much intimacy, was more disturbing and more difficult, for his slow decline had left his affairs in chaos, and cost his brother William a considerable amount on the family's property at Seaforth. But a searing death, despite their rare meetings since her conversion to Roman Catholicism in 1842, was that of his sister Helen. Her death in the hotel in Cologne where she had lived for many years as 'Mrs. Gladstone' (a conventional Victorianism) was, Gladstone convinced himself, at the least that of a non-Roman Catholic and almost certainly that of an 'Old-Catholic' (i.e. a Döllingerite). Her last painful illness, with suffering possibly compounded by a shortage of her habitual morphia, was watched by her two living brothers, Tom and William, together with Louisa, Tom's wife.

To William Gladstone the death brought back all the memories of the 1840s, the extraordinary 'Self-Examination' of October 1845 occasioned by his bizarre Continental search for his apostasized sister, when sex, religion, and politics intermingled to produce a nervous crisis which all but shook his moral foundations: 'immediately upon the death followed a rush of thoughts & cares'.* Gladstone made 'an examination of all the books of devotion: it was very interesting & set forth the whole history of her mental transition since [the declaration of Infallibility in] 1870. . . . They show she died at one with us as before.'† Gladstone and his brother took the body to the family vault at Fasque, where it was buried according to the rite of the Episcopal Church of Scotland.

Helen Gladstone brought out an otherwise nonexistent trait in her brother: he bullied her. Her attempts at independence, exemplified in her conversion to Rome, seem to have affronted his code of how women should behave, especially when contrasted with the memory of his Evangelical sister Anne, who died in 1829, her birthday still commemorated in the diary in 1878. Apostasy always distressed Gladstone, but apostasy in a sister riled him. Despite his public yearning for ecumenicity, he found it very hard to practise in the family context, as was also seen in the case of his apostate cousin and co-translator, Anne Ramsden Bennett, whom he effectively dropped on her conversion.‡

In his dealings with his sister, Gladstone was not fully in control of himself. Much of his correspondence with her is uncharacteristically harsh, unfeeling and petty, culminating in a brutal letter written in 1878, when Helen Gladstone had failed to repay a loan of £20 and to send a

---

* 16 Jan. 80.   † 18 Jan. 80.   ‡ See 8 June 71.

promised £50 for the Bulgarian refugee fund. The former Prime Minister's letter continues:

A parcel arrived from you a few days ago. It contains I have no doubt a gift or gifts kindly intended by you for me, or for us. *It remains unopened, and at your disposal*; I have paid the charge upon it, but I can have no other concern with it while matters remain as they are. I did not wish to subject you to the further charge upon it for carriage back to you. It is most painful for me to write this letter, which I do without the knowledge of any one, but with a perfectly fixed purpose.*

Usually magnanimous and generous—perhaps particularly so—to those with whom he had differed, Gladstone behaved to his sister as if they were still in the nursery. No biography of this sad woman has yet been written; when it is, one of its major themes will be how her strong-willed brother, usually so careful in control and respect, ground her down and, if he did not 'break' her (the word he used of his own children), at the least exiled her, emotionally and morally as well as physically.

Helen Gladstone's death in January 1880, shortly before the general election which brought him back to power, came at an appropriate time for her brother. With Hope-Scott already dead and Manning hopelessly estranged by the row over Vaticanism, it broke the last links with the emotional Church–State crisis of the 1840s. That crisis had confirmed Gladstone in his move towards fiscal liberalism whose development had taken thirty years and whose *finale* had been, in his view, the government of 1868–74. He had seen his return to political life in 1876 in limited and restorative terms, fighting 'a consecutive battle against ideas & practices neither Liberal nor Conservative'.† But that return had led him to add a much more pronouncedly political liberalism to his fiscal and ecclesiastical beliefs. It had brought him, despite himself, to a new position in British political life, the epitome of a new form of political communication, the harbinger of a revived political liberalism. At an advanced age he had become in politics, that art of the second-best, what he described Macaulay as being in literature, 'a meteor, almost a portent'. Launched upon a second political career, Gladstone concluded the year 1880 with buoyant zest: 'I plunge forward into the New'. He did so reminded 'of the great lesson "onward"'.‡ Indeed, the capacity to move 'onward', to shift a generation as the times change, is one given to very few politicians, and to none completely. Gladstone had already made this shift once. It was not his intention, but it was to be his calling, to do so again.

* To Helen Gladstone, 5 January 1878, Hawn P.
† To Doyle, 10 May 80.
‡ 29–31 Dec. 80.

CHAPTER IV

Gladstone at 70: a Review and a Retrospect

A 'gentler time' but a Need for Action—Gladstonism: an Attempt at Definition and Summary

Let me look a little backward, & around. My position [in December 1883] is a strange one. A strong man in me wrestles for retirement: a stronger one stands at the gate of exit, and forbids. Forbids, I hope only for a time. There is a bar to the continuance of my political life fixed as I hope by the life of the present Parliament, and there is good hope that it may not last so long. But for this, I do not know how my poor flesh & blood, or my poor soul and spirit, could face the prolongations of cares & burdens so much beyond my strength at any age, and at this age so cruelly exclusive of the great work of penitential recollection, and lifting of the heart which has lingered so long. I may indeed say that my political or public life is the best part of my life: it is that part in which I am conscious of the greatest effort to do and to avoid as the Lord Christ would have me do and avoid, nay shall I say for this is the true rule as He would Himself in the like case have done. But although so far itself taken up out of the mire, it exhausts and dries up my other and more personal life, and so to speak reduces its tissue, which should be firm and healthy, to a kind of moral pulp. I want so much more of thought on Divine things, of the eye turned inwards & upwards & forwards, of study to know and discern, to expose and to renounce, my own secret sins. And how can this be done, or begun, or tried, or tasted, while the great stream of public cares is ever rushing on me, & covering my head with its floods of unsatisfied demand.

Yet it is a noble form of life which ministers by individual action to the wants of masses of Gods creatures. Man has one neck, not for the headsman, but for the inflow of good. So I abide, and as I trust obey, until He who knows shall find the way to signify to me that I am at length permitted to depart, whether it be from this world, or as I trust first from the storm and fierceness of it into the shade and coolness and calm where the soul may for a while work in freedom before going hence.*

* 31 Dec. 83.

A 'gentler time' but a Need for Action

Again retirement! The theme that punctuated Gladstone's career from the 1830s and permeated it in the 1870s, cries havoc for the first half of the 1880s. Gladstone was 70 when becoming Prime Minister in April 1880. He formed his second government with clear intentions of quickly retiring from it. But he led it for the almost five years of its existence, one of the most dramatic of British peacetime administrations. The reasons for retirement from the premiership, the detailed phases of which will be discussed below, are clear and natural enough: old age, a spasmodic but fairly frequent sense of failing powers, a well-established intention to escape from a second-order activity to the 'higher' contemplation of religion and scholarship. The decisive attempt was made in 1874–5, in considerable measure successfully, when estrangement from the Liberal party on religious issues was an additional and important factor. Though there were qualifications, Gladstone's political career seemed at an end and one theme of this biography has been that the retirement of 1875 marked the natural conclusion of that first career. Chapters I and II have depicted the start of his second. As was shown in them, this was not seen as a career, in the sense of an extended development, but rather in terms of immediate 'exceptional circumstances'. But the return of 1876 was the start of another eighteen years at the forefront of British political life, often complained of, often regretted, and always explained—explained away some would say—in terms of special causes, fresh crises, new, unforeseen and unavoidable commitments. The commitment to these causes was balanced by the intention of beginning a new, non-political life; as Gladstone put it in 1882: 'What I look to is withdrawal, detachment, recollection. So soon as the special calls that chain me to the oar of public duty are sufficiently relaxed, I look to removal not from office only but from London, & to a new or renewed set of employments wholly different from those I now pursue.'*

Gladstone's career from the 1830s to the 1870s was in its chief features straightforward and anticipated from his youth: establishment as an MP, an effective period as a departmental minister, a noted premiership. Only the change of party was a fundamental surprise to his school friends. But his career after 1875, punctuated though it was by some brilliant moments, was uncertain and tentative in direction. Gladstone was never willing to see himself simply as a political leader. After 1875, the 'great work of penitential recollection' to be undertaken in private was in a series of abatements delayed by political or public activities which formed for Gladstone 'the best part of my life', a part which Christ would, in Gladstone's judgement, 'Himself in the like case have done'. Gladstone had seen political life as a second-order matter, necessary and potentially beneficial but not of

* To Mrs Thistlethwayte, 14 August 1882.

eschatological significance: those excessively enmeshed in it endangered their souls. In the 1860s he had begun to invest certain courses of action with a higher significance, but not one sufficient to bar his retirement at the end of his first government. Now, in the late 1870s and early 1880s, he found political life, rather as he had found it at the start of his public career as a young MP in the 1830s, 'a noble form of life which ministers by individual action to the wants and masses of Gods creatures'. Consequently, two very different dimensions of his personality develop.

On the one hand, he maintained various of the characteristics of retirement and of the 'new employments' he wished to seek: an absence of the full, omnipresent activity of the first government; an insistence at almost all times of a high attention to non-political reading which if not set in the context of this sort of explanation appears at certain moments simply irresponsible; an enthusiasm even at the busiest of political moments for non-political correspondence; an interest in reminiscence, early days, dead friends. Even while Prime Minister, Gladstone sometimes behaved as the differently-employed person he hoped to be: not exactly retired, but resolutely involved in non-political matters. This was not at all the same as the enforced semi-retirement of Beaconsfield in the late 1870s or the apparently low-keyed, disengaged behaviour of the later Salisbury; nor was it seen as a wise distancing from the pressure of events (though this was also sometimes intended), for at other times Gladstone acted with intense and explosive political energy, privately investing his public activities with a powerful sense of calling.*

That 'call' for which fifty years earlier the undergraduate Gladstone had yearned but had not heard now seemed sufficiently clear, in the rather different context of secular causes, to be noted in the diary as a definite summons, though subject to human error (and Gladstone was careful about this point). In this peculiar situation, it was for 'He who knows' to give the sign that the time had come 'to depart'. Gladstone, to be fair, sought earnestly for that sign, but in the 1880s he never saw it, and those whom he consulted almost unanimously told him not to look for it.

We must at this point be rather careful. Though inwardly driven by a powerful sense of calling, Gladstone did not publicly assert it. Labouchere's famous jibe, that he did not object to Gladstone always having the ace of trumps up his sleeve, but only to his pretence that God had put it there, was unfair.† Gladstone often claimed to be right, but he did not publicly claim God's support in the manner of some modern politicians. Indeed, the Anglo-Catholic character of his religious views made unity in

---

* At the same time, Gladstone believed that, apart from these exceptional circumstances delaying his departure, in general 'mankind is not now principally governed from within the walls of Cabinets and Parliaments'; to J. H. Newman, 18 Dec. 81.

† See Labouchere's entry in *D.N.B.*

the Liberal party more rather than less difficult when God was mentioned, and there was much reason for Gladstone not to express himself on religious issues or in religious language. Moreover, the twin fascination with retirement and calls to action encouraged or imposed a balance, and attempts to see Gladstone solving the undoubted awkwardness of his political position by institutionalizing himself into a system of geriatric control, are simply silly.* Gladstone's position was always controlled, carefully and regularly reviewed and discussed with family and friends. As we shall see, his continuing in politics was always strongly encouraged. Indeed, he found that the only Liberal supporter of his retirement was himself. None the less, the dualism of the retired gentleman scholar and the God-summoned statesman was at the least curious, even bizarre, as he himself from time to time sensed. As he wrote to his son Henry in 1886, 'the element of old age, incurable as it is, renders all these matters extremely perplexing'. It was Gladstone's complete absence of self-irony that prevented a permanent sense of embarrassment.

Gladstone took office in 1880 with explicitly restorative objectives: the removal of the excrescences of 'Beaconsfieldism', the restoration of proper financial procedures (exemplified by his holding the Exchequer as well as the premiership), and a general return to the normality of Whig/Liberal government after the restless adventures of Tory jingoism. Unlike the start of his long period at the Exchequer in 1859, and of his first government in 1868, he had in 1880 no personal commitment to innovative legislation. Indeed, the very nature of the campaigns of 1876–80 had tended to direct him away from domestic affairs towards a public debate on Britain's future responsibilities as a world power.

Thus Gladstone in 1880 appears in some respects as a rather conservative figure however radical and even shocking his means, the leader of a popular front of moral outrage at Tory innovations, a front which, in its defence of the mid-century liberal state, to some extent conceded to the Tories on the one hand, and to the Radicals on the other, the role of the initiator. This was a position of some awkwardness for Gladstone, for his earlier strength both as Chancellor of the Exchequer and as Prime Minister had depended first on stymying the Conservatives by pursuing a radical, reforming conservatism which left traditional institutions and status groups stronger and healthier, and second, on outflanking the Radicals by the energetic pursuit of free-trade goals and their accompanying legislation.

Radical conservatism of the Gladstonian sort still had much force, as the Irish question was to show, but free trade had lost its potency to associate Gladstone with radicalism. By the 1880s, the fiscal free-trade programme was completed: the question for the future was not its achievement but its

---

* See A. McIntyre, *Aging and political leadership* (1988), 285.

preservation. Fiscal free-trade had been the great programmatic unifying force of the Whig–Peelite–Liberal–Radical coalition of 1852 which became the Liberal party, and it was to remain the Liberal party's point of fundamental reference until the 1930s. But its achievement necessarily implied a switch from attack to defence by its promulgators. That the defence was so successful for so long does not diminish the fact that the defensive commitment implied that other areas of policy became the advanced front of Liberalism.

Fiscal free-trade meant, of course, much more than simply an absence of protective tariffs. It implied a whole way of conceiving the State as economically neutral with a tax base so small as to give the State no economic responsibility or significance. In the 1860s, little challenge had been offered to this view as both intellectually 'natural' and politically desirable. By the 1880s, however, alternative means of organizing an industrial state were being both widely discussed and, outside the United Kingdom, programmatically achieved. The sharp down-turn in the European economy in the 1870s had produced in most advanced economies save Britain a 'return to protection', marked especially by Bismarck's split with the Liberals, his imposition of protective tariffs in 1879, and the development in the Second Reich of a political economy of cartelization married to harrying the trade unions and suppressing the S.P.D. For those who wished an alternative to the British liberal state, here was one, with all its implications and consequences. Few, of course, advocated out-and-out Germanization, but increasingly Germany was coming to be regarded as the alternative model, the seed-bed for the future. Thus, when the Anglo-French 'Cobden' treaty, due for renewal for the second time in 1880, proved formally unrenewable, Dilke, the minister in charge of the details of negotiations which were spun out until 1882, began to canvass the possibility of 'some day . . . a British Zollverein, raising discriminating duties upon foreign produce as against that of the British Empire'. Such a move would have been not only unacceptable but inconceivable to Gladstone, who showed little interest in the French negotiations, since he regarded the 1860 treaty as 'exceptional and not as being the beginning of a new system of Tariff Treaties'. Gladstone, in other words, embodied the mid-Victorian view that British free trade was economically and morally beneficial regardless of the actions of other states. It was this absence of a sense of comparison—either of comparing relative performance or of discussing alternative fiscal arrangements—that was to prove the most vulnerable point in the free-traders' defences. It explains the rather remarkable absence of any sustained attempt by the British government, and especially the Liberal government of 1880–5, to persuade other major powers of the benefits of maintaining a world free-trade market.

We must be careful not to overstress protectionist feeling in Britain in the 1880s. The Conservatives did not propose tariffs in 1878–80, and as they became an increasingly urban party, so the likelihood of their support for agricultural protection receded. The Redistribution Bill of 1885, by suburbanizing British Conservatism, probably ensured that, for all the noise and for all their majorities in both Houses between 1886 and 1906, the Conservatives never formally proposed a peacetime protectionist duty, tempted though they were by increasing pressure from within their own party. None the less, the sense that free trade was under attack began to be a prominent feature of Gladstone's speeches, and this was in itself a considerable success for the fair trade movement.

But if the now relatively small base of English agriculture limited the extent of protectionist demand, and implied that there were more consumer gainers than producer losers from the world-wide fall in commodity prices in the late 1870s and through the 1880s, this was clearly not the case in Ireland. There the assault on free trade in agriculture revived in the form of a ferocious attack on free-market contract as the basis of land tenure, an attack whose extreme form, as represented by the Land League, was only possible because of the general European crisis of agriculture. Whether the Irish crisis (and the much more narrowly based but in some respects similar crisis in the Scottish Highlands and Islands) could be met without disturbing free trade and free contract was a central preoccupation of British politics through the 1880s, and was a central impediment to Gladstone's attempts to maintain the mid-Victorian minimal and neutral state. While events as much as inclination sucked Gladstone deeper and deeper into the quicksands of the Irish crisis, so its sharp contrasts with the norms of mid-Victorian Britain heightened the anomaly of his position.

The Land League, the Irish National League, and the Home Rule party rejected and set out to frustrate much that the rest of British politics regarded as normative: a free-trade exchequer allied to a centralizing Treasury whose influence increasingly permeated all sections of the British executive; a Parliament at Westminster with two great parties who between them ordered and co-ordinated domestic and imperial policy and legislation by operating within agreed, largely liberal, parameters; a British nation whose admitted pluralism of church, law, and culture was contained within a sense of acceptance, or at least a fairly easy tolerance; an Anglican, largely Oxford and Cambridge ruling élite. That élite had seen off the Chartists; it seemed to have incorporated within its political structure the urban and rural working classes (in so far as the franchises of 1867 and 1884 represented them), and it had by adaptation survived urbanization and industrialization much more successfully than any of its European equivalents. But the 'resources of civilization', except those of coercion and incarceration, were exhausted when it came to the Irish, though the demonstration of this even to the 1880–5 government was to be long delayed. What was clear was that, however Ireland was to be dealt with, it would involve a disturbance of mid-Victorian norms, whether financial, constitutional, or libertarian.

Side by side with a growing awareness that the century-long attempt at Irish incorporation was failing, went a sense of rather uncertain changes in foreign and imperial policy. By definition, the Concert system—which as we have seen it was the aim of Gladstone's campaigns of the late 1870s both to preserve and to justify—required general European agreement if it was to function 'in concert'. The Concert could work to cajole or coerce one or perhaps even two recalcitrant members: but if all except Britain shared in secret alliances against each other, there could obviously be no meaningful or effective Concert. Equally bad would be a Concert whose chief basis of agreement was the extension of imperial responsibilities, for this implied costs, and more costs.

The premises of the mid-Victorian liberal state were thus increasingly questioned both by other powers and by younger British politicians and were also gradually undermined by the behaviour of the economy. The assumption of a natural equilibrium of the economy at the point of full employment and the capacity of voluntary agencies adequately to supply the welfare services of a modern state were both seriously questioned empirically and systematically in the course of the 1880s, the decade which faced both ways, looking back to the high-noon of mid-century minimalism and forwards to collectivism and imperialism. As the chief executive exponent of that minimal state, Gladstone in the 1880s not surprisingly sometimes seemed beleaguered and felt himself to be so even in his own Cabinet. But it would be quite wrong to see him as despondent. It is perhaps the most striking feature of his political personality in this period that he did not share the political, economic, and cultural pessimism which was beginning to infect many Liberals, particularly the Liberal intelligentsia, and one strain of which was elevated in 1881 to the leadership of the Conservative party in the person of Lord Salisbury. 'Disintegration' was Salisbury's negative contribution to the mind of the age. Where Salisbury offered warnings, Gladstone offered hope. He strikingly retained the optimism of the Palmerstonian era, while recognizing the difficulties.* His constant objective was to place the problems of the 1880s in their historical perspective, and the theme of the importance of the history of the nineteenth century was of growing importance in his method of analysis. Looked at in this light, the 1880s demanded thanks rather than regret. In concluding a notable survey of the achievements of the century in the light of 'the Prophet' Tennyson's doom-laden reassess-

* For a general comment, see the fine peroration in R. Robinson and J. Gallagher, *Africa and the Victorians* (1961), 472.

ment, *Locksley Hall, Sixty Years After*, Gladstone echoed Macaulay's epigraph,* that the British

disposition to lay bare public mischiefs and drag them into the light of day, which, though liable to exaggeration, has perhaps been our best distinction among the nations, has become more resolute than ever. The multiplication and better formation of the institutions of benevolence among us are but symptomatic indications of a wider and deeper change: a silent but more extensive and practical acknowledgment of the great second commandment, of the duties of wealth to poverty, of strength to weakness, of knowledge to ignorance, in a word of man to man. And the sum of the matter seems to be that upon the whole, and in a degree, we who lived fifty, sixty, seventy years back, and are living now, have lived into a gentler time; that the public conscience has grown more tender, as indeed was very needful; and that, in matters of practice, at sight of evils formerly regarded with indifference or even connivance, it now not only winces but rebels: that upon the whole the race has been reaping, and not scattering; earning, and not wasting; and that, without its being said that the old Prophet is wrong, it may be said that the young Prophet was unquestionably right.†

That this was no mere show of public bravura is seen by Gladstone's private reaction to the assassination of Lord Frederick Cavendish on 6 May 1882, probably the worst moment of Gladstone's public life, a crushing burden personally, and an apparently shattering blow to the Cabinet's new departure in Irish policy. Dining the next evening with his old Oxford and Tractarian friend, Sir Robert Phillimore, Gladstone though 'quite crushed' remained ebullient:

After the all engrossing topic had been much discussed, G. spoke with a great burst of eloquence upon the subject of the improvements in every department of the State abroad and at home wh. we had witnessed during the last half century.

There was, therefore, the sense of achievement and of the need to preserve that achievement, but also an optimistic sense that, despite the difficulties, the past showed the way to future achievement.

Gladstonism: an Attempt at Definition and Summary

The frame of mind which rejected the timid alarms of fainthearted contemporaries was, of course, highly complex and eclectic, embracing elements both of political Conservatism and of political Liberalism, and certainly offering no simple categorization. An understanding of it is made more difficult by the fact that the Gladstone in this volume is in his seventies and eighties, an age outside the experience of most readers and certainly of the author of this book. The problem of what new pressures old

---

* Macaulay, *The history of England*, conclusion to ch. iii: 'It is pleasing to reflect that the public mind of England has softened while it has ripened, and that we have, in the course of ages become, not only a wiser, but also a kinder people.'

† '"Locksley Hall" and the Jubilee', *Nineteenth Century* (January 1887).

age brings and what allowance to make for them, adds a further dimension to the already tricky task of penetrating a Victorian mind. It is too easy simply to discount Gladstone's age. On the other hand, it is dangerous to offer it as a simple explanation of his behaviour—'an old man in a hurry', the polite expression of the Tory view that Gladstone was in some way 'mad' or senile—and thus discount considerations of ideology and policy. But Gladstone's age is a factor which each reader must bear in mind.

Let us try to see Gladstone as this biography has presented him. What was distinctive about the man who in 1880, aged 70, kissed hands as Prime Minister for the second time? This study has attempted to describe four great themes as distinctively characteristic of Gladstone's political personality and orientation: the adjustment and development of Church–State relations in a pluralist direction; the construction and maintenance of the free-trade, minimal State; flexible, executive *étatism*; and an innovative form of political communication. In none of these, taken singly, was Gladstone unique, except perhaps in the last. In each he came to lead a powerful movement in British society and politics. On various central aspects of mid-Victorian public life Gladstone's views were thus representative and had a wide appeal. But no other figure of the age attempted so all-embracing an expression of them. Gladstone was thus both characteristic and bizarre. Before examining particular aspects of his third and fourth governments, it may be useful to have a *résumé* of these four themes.

First chronologically and probably personally was the religious pluralism developed from the 1840s onwards. To the extent that the nineteenth-century history of England, Wales, and Ireland represented a shift from an Anglican hegemony to a considerable degree of pluralism, Gladstone, in the development of his political beliefs and in the character of his political achievements, epitomized this fundamental change. The need for the promulgation of the truth in religion rather than religion's Erastian utility placed Gladstone, as it did many Tractarians and High-Churchmen, in the Liberal orbit, for it was only such an orbit which permitted the religious pluralism which the Oxford Movement required if it was to survive.* There was an unresolved, probably unresolvable, irony here. Although they supported pluralism, Gladstone and the Tractarian High-Churchmen were far removed from moral or religious relativism. Indeed it was their hostility to relativism which, at bottom, caused their suspicion of an establishment which necessarily implied a considerable degree of latitudinarianism. Looking back in 1886 on 'the actual misdeeds of the Legislature during the last half-century', Gladstone found these to be all religious:

---

* Gladstone's position, as stated to the Unitarian James Martineau (a strong establishmentarian) in the 1860s, is well summarized in Martineau to Bosworth Smith, 23 December 1885: 'He laid down two positions: 1. The Anglican Church is divine and (except in ecclesiastical machinery) unalterable; and 2. the State must bear itself impartially towards all the religions of its subjects'; *R. Bosworth Smith by his daughter* (1909), 208.

the Divorce Act of 1857, the Public Worship Act of 1874, and the Ecclesiastical Titles Act of 1851.* The first encouraged moral relativism, and to avoid it would have needed a continuance of the confessional state as Gladstone had conceived it in the 1830s; the second and third restricted or denied religious pluralism. Thus in the 1880s Gladstone privately regretted Charles Bradlaugh's atheism but permitted his membership of the House of Commons. The pluralistic arguments used in 1851 against the Ecclesiastical Titles Bill could also embrace Bradlaugh, about whose case Gladstone had no intellectual difficulties, developing an argument which was intellectually effective and politically convenient: '*In foro conscientiae* Bradlaugh has committed a gross error by presenting himself to take the oath', but that was not a matter for the House of Commons, which had acted 'beyond its powers. . . . B. has fulfilled the law, or he has not. If he has, he should sit. If he has not, the courts should correct him'; attempts to proceed by 'including Agnostics and Pantheists and yet excluding Atheists' simply endangered sound religion by making it look foolish: 'it is best to recognise frankly that religious differences are not to entail civil disabilities; & in regard to the present controversy that it tends to weaken reverence for religion in the body of the people', a view inherent in Gladstone's position since the 1840s. Gladstone stuck to this position tenaciously, 'obeying the inward voice, but defying almost every outward one!'

With respect to church establishments, however, Gladstone as time passed rather softened the sharply defined principles laid down in the 1840s and early 1850s. Though always able when required to refer to these principles, Gladstone was careful in the late 1870s and early 1880s not to be drawn into support for particular disestablishments. Thus he reached the end of two more Liberal governments neither pledged to Scottish nor Welsh disestablishment, nor committed to preventing it, to the irritation of disestablishmentarians and the scepticism of the establishment lobby.

In principle an acceptor of religious pluralism, in practice Gladstone fought an effective rearguard action on behalf of the Church of England, and in practice his disagreement with politically conservative Anglicans was usually on the wisdom of defending what he regarded as untenable outposts, such as preventing non-Anglicans from using parish churchyards for burials. The last thoroughgoingly Anglican leader of the Liberal party to head a government, his very presence in that position helped to maintain a bipartisan political identity for his Church and in the high noon of political nonconformity to absorb and deflect the central force of attack.

The confessional state envisaged in the 1830s would thus be replaced with a society organized largely through voluntary associations (among which the established church would be important but not unique). These associations would be of various sorts: the religious, social, and educational

* '"Locksley Hall" and the Jubilee', 16–17.

life of the various denominations, the self-sustaining friendly societies and charities, the trade unions and professional organizations, and the vast plethora of other Victorian associational bodies, self-regulating, but with the discreet legal support of the state. Though the central state would thus be minimal and neutral, society was to be not mechanical, but associational, not atomistic and materialistic, but communitarian.

Gladstone was personally active in working such of these institutions as related to his own background, participating energetically in charitable trusts, in the management of various schools, and in a large range of self-help organizations. His support for the Charity Organization Society reflected an awareness that a voluntarist social order needed supervision and co-ordination if it was to achieve equal standards across the nation, but, like the C.O.S. leaders, he certainly did not see the recognition of this as the first step to admitting that voluntarism was in itself generally inadequate. However, in the Elementary Education Act, his first government had denied, in the particular but central area of national schooling, the capacity of a voluntarist society satisfactorily to supply the needs of an industrial nation. But his second government did not directly attempt further replacement of voluntarism by state action.

Pluralism had thus brought Gladstone from a predominantly conservative confessional Anglicanism into what proved to be the main stream of Victorian thought and Victorian activity. In this development he was characteristic of much of his Oxonian generation.

Second, evolving parallel to religious pluralism and in Gladstone's development causally associated with it, was the free-trade, minimal state, its significance re-emphasized by Gladstone's taking the Chancellorship of the Exchequer as well as the premiership in 1880. Religious pluralism took the state out of theology; free trade did the same for the economy. The concept of a 'national economy' with its tariffs, bargains, cartels, and economic pressure groups was alien to Gladstone's mind and was not to be allowed to corrupt British public life. A powerful sense of moralism buttressed the fiscal case for free trade, but in a negative way: as the state should no longer point to a particular church or denomination as true, so it no longer selected particular industries as deserving.

In Gladstone's view, the Budget was a moral as well as a fiscal engine. It should be regular, balanced and minimal, setting a tone for the nation, and Gladstone saw the pressures of the age increasingly threatening each of these. Consequently, invasion of public revenues, however small, was to be resisted, and this led in the 1880s to delayed decisions in imperial affairs, to loss of initiative over land purchase in Ireland, and to a series of petty disputes with individuals over salary reductions and controls. This absence of a sense of a national economy (and of means of measuring it more sophisticated than income tax returns and the like) meant that the costs and economic implications either of governmental activity or of the absence of such activity simply could not be assessed, except for immediate military and naval costs.

This is not anachronistically to blame Gladstone for an absence of a sense of aggregate demand and supply: such concepts were not available to him and his contemporaries. But it is to point out that strategic decisions about the implications of British imperial expansion—in so far as there were strategic decisions—took place in an economic limbo. Gladstone sensed that such expansions were economically damaging, others that they might be beneficial: neither had any means of calculation.

It was, in Gladstone's view, in considerable measure free-trade legislation which had created the circumstances for the great boom in Victorian living standards, and it was certainly that legislation which was *seen* as the basis of prosperity, an argument powerfully restated in an article on free trade, railways, and the growth of commerce written just before the great election victory of 1880.* Thus it was at the end of a paragraph on the economy and 'the condition of England question' that he observed: 'the discord between people and the law is now at an end, and our institutions are again "broad based" upon national conviction and affection'.† Empirically based though his free-trade views originally were, and, in his article of 1880 on free trade and railways, continued to be, Gladstone was certainly not prepared to allow in the 1880s any thoroughgoing reassessment of the case against protective tariffs.

Gladstone had reached his position on both of these subjects—religious pluralism and free-trade minimalism—as a result of the experience of government in the 1840s and, less importantly, of acceptance of dogmatic theory. But both *seemed* to ally him with liberal political and economic theories which pointed to absolute positions. If carried through with stringency, they would have produced on the one hand complete disestablishment and absence of a religious requirement in education, and on the other not only free trade but a sharp reduction of Britain's world responsibilities, and a decline in the size and range of the commitments of the navy and the army (which in the years 1881–5 together accounted for 31.3 per cent of gross central government expenditure), and a rigid hostility to colonial expansion.

Gladstone in principle probably favoured such policies, but in practice his executive *étatism*, the third of our great themes, curtailed him, as it became interwoven with the first two. It worked at several levels to soften and constrain his tendencies. The Liberal–Tory background from which Gladstone sprang and within which much of his governmental practice

* See W. E. Gladstone, 'Free trade, railways, and the growth of commerce', *Nineteenth Century* (February 1880).
† '"Locksley Hall" and the Jubilee', 10.

continued to be conceived was profoundly ambivalent about the British state, seeing it partly in pragmatic, business-like terms, and partly in the much more eschatological language of moral absolutes.* Gladstone through his long executive career reflected this ambiguity: the principles of a mechanistic minimal state were raised but rarely pressed to a conclusion. Indeed executive requirements and particular situations might lead them to quite contrary actions. Gladstone was fully aware of his tendency in this direction. 'In principle', he wrote in 1883, 'perhaps my Coalwhippers Act of 1843 was the most Socialistic measure of the last half century.'†

Gladstone believed that individuals worked with the given data of historical situations, not with the abstracts of *a priori* principles, for Christianity was an historical religion, rooting men and women in particular contexts, in national communities placed at a certain point in the evolution of human society. The politician's observation, judgement, and reason, properly used, though 'faint and dim and mutilated' was 'still the best which our capacities can attain', a vision for his or her time of 'the Divine Will'.‡ Necessarily 'mutilated', this vision could not be complete or perfect. The utopianism of secular liberalism and of an *a priori*, deductivist view of society were thus excluded. The emphasis on time and location gave scope for the politician's art as interpreter, mediator, and leader, however second-best the result of its exercise might be.

In the great divide in the European view of progress, between the deductivist intellectuals and the inductivist practitioners, Gladstone seemed to balance ambivalently, some of his views on pluralism and some of his comments on free trade seeming to place him in the deductivist camp. But his actions and a close scrutiny of his reasoning place him with the inductivists. In the instance of free trade in the 1840s, 'the case was materially altered by events'.§ It was 'events', and the development of a moral view of the neutral state, not the influence of the deductivist case for Ricardian comparative advantage, which conditioned Gladstone's development into a free trader. Probability as assessed by experience was the guide to conduct. In what was clearly a warning to some of his own side, Gladstone observed in introducing the Representation of the People Bill in 1884:

We do not aim at ideal perfection, and I hope Gentlemen will not force us upon that line; it would be the 'Road to Ruin' . . . ideal perfection is not the true basis of English legislation. We look at the attainable; we look at the practicable, and we

* Boyd Hilton, *Corn, cash, commerce. The economic policies of the tory governments 1815–1830* (1977), ch. vi for pragmatism, conclusion for Chalmers and eschatology.

† To E. W. Hamilton, 18 May 83; the 1843 Act foreshadowed Edwardian 'new liberal' attempts to tidy up the dock labour market.

‡ See above, p. 43; the passage was written in 1835, but was characteristic of Gladstone's views throughout his life.

§ Ibid., 78.

have too much of English sense to be drawn away by those sanguine delineations of what might possibly be attained in Utopia, from a path which promises to enable us to effect great good for the people of England.*

At the immediate political level this reflected short-term calculations of prudence and success. But in the context of the various schools of Liberalism, such remarks, made at so important a moment in liberal history, had a more general significance.

They also represented a fundamental view of man's knowledge and ignorance of his world. Gladstone's life-time occurred in a period of vast extension of human knowledge and experience, particularly for the British, yet he saw this as merely emphasizing awareness of ignorance and hence of the sense of imperfectibility: progress made cautions about Utopia more rather than less necessary. He commented thus on Joseph Butler's 'Sermon Upon the Ignorance of Man':

Every extension of our knowledge is an extension, often a far wider extension, of our ignorance. When we knew of only one world we also knew a good deal about its circumstances, its condition, its progress. Now we are surrounded by worlds innumerable, spread over spaces hardly conceivable for their extent; and yet those, who may be rapt in their wonder at the grand discoveries of the spectroscope, may also be the first to admit that as to the condition, purposes, and destinies of all these worlds we are absolutely in the dark. Consider the conditions of our civilization: disease in its multiplied forms is more rife among us than in savage life, while the problems of the social kind seem to gain upon us continually in the multitude of puzzles which they offer to our bewildered minds. Then, in the moral world, we must be still more conscious of our limitations; for, while we are continually required to pass judgement for practical purposes on actions, every right-minded person will incessantly feel that to form any perfect judgement on any action whatever is a task wholly beyond our power. When Butler pronounced his severe sentence on the claims of the Popes, his horror was not the result of theological bigotry, but, without doubt, he was shocked (with his strong, just, and humble sense of our limitations in capacity) at the daring and presumption of the claims set up by some on their behalf. Yet he keenly saw the obligation that knowledge imposes to act when we know, not less than to abstain when we do not.

On this great and critical subject, he seems never to have let fall a faulty word, and of all the topics he has handled there is not one on which we may more safely accept him as a guide.†

The politician therefore retained flexibility and above all cultivated timing, or 'ripeness' as Gladstone sometimes called it, an understanding of the 'golden moments' of history, when political action fused with great, often unseen forces to produce a right and lasting solution. It was the

* _H_ 285. 122–3 (28 February 1884); the chief items thus excluded were proportional representation and women's suffrage; Gladstone perhaps thought universal male suffrage so Utopian as not to require mention in his list of exclusions.

† W. E. Gladstone, _Studies subsidiary to the works of Bishop Butler_ (1896), 106–7.

function of the executive politician both to perceive such moments and to provide the capacity, in the form of legislative preparation and party support, for their realization.* Thus, although flexibility, attainability, and 'experience' suggested caution, trial and perhaps recognition of error, the notion of the ripe, golden moment, properly grasped, suggested both action and permanence. Here lay the centre of the ambivalence of Gladstone's curious blend of settled solutions and flexible *étatism*, and the secret of his appeal to so wide a spectrum of progressive opinion. Gladstone's famous note on political timing was written at the end of his life in this Butlerian intellectual context: the awareness of ignorance and limitation, the use of reason coupled with the affections to reach conviction on certain central matters, so as 'to act when we know', the careful qualification as to complete certainty:

I am by no means sure, upon a calm review, that Providence has endowed me with anything which can be called a striking gift. But if there be such a thing entrusted to me, it has been shown, at certain political junctures, in what may be termed appreciation of the general situation and its result. To make good the idea, this must not be considered as the simple acceptance of public opinion, founded upon the discernment that it has risen to a certain height needful for a given work, like a tide. It is an insight into the facts of particular eras, and their relations one to another, which generates in the mind a conviction that the materials exist for forming a public opinion, and for directing it to a particular end.

There are four occasions of my life with respect to which I think these considerations may be applicable. They were these:

1. The renewal of the income tax in 1853.
2. The proposal of religious equality for Ireland in 1868.
3. The proposal of Home Rule for Ireland in 1886.
4. The desire for a dissolution of Parliament in the beginning of 1894, and the immediate determination of the issue then raised between the two Houses of Parliament.†

Read outside the Butlerian context, the passage might, as Morley noted, be labelled 'with the ill-favoured name of opportunist'.‡ Read within it, it represents a political methodology which reduced rather than encouraged dogmatism.§

* In this process, Gladstone was greatly aided by the likeminded Henry Thring, the parliamentary draftsman who drafted all Gladstone's major legislation from the Finance Bill of 1853 (the first occasion on which financial measures were consolidated into a single bill) to the Government of Ireland Bill of 1886. The first Gladstone government created the post of parliamentary draftsman in 1869; Gladstone knighted Thring in 1873 and made him a peer in 1886.

† Morley, ii. 240 and J. Brooke and M. Sorensen, eds., *The Prime Minister's Papers: W. E. Gladstone*, 4v. (1971–81) [subsequently: *Autobiographica*], i. 136; it is characteristic of Magnus that he turns Gladstone's uncertainty about 'a striking gift' into an unqualified affirmation; see P. Magnus, *Gladstone* (1954) [subsequently: Magnus], 190.

‡ Morley, ii. 241.

§ See Boyd Hilton, *The age of atonement. The influence of evangelicalism on social and economic thought* (1988), ch. 9.

The fourth great theme developed in this study has been Gladstone's integration of the great social forces of his time through the development of a political communication suited to the franchise and media of his day. In part this was a means of control: control of the franchise, influence on the press through the occupation of its columns by great speeches, oratorical leadership of the Liberal party in the constituencies and of the electorate beyond it. By these means, all interrelated, the British Liberal party incorporated within itself Anglicans, Nonconformists, Roman Catholics, and secularists, landowners, manufacturers, merchants, bankers, and trade unionists, to an extent only dreamed of by its Continental equivalents.

Not surprisingly, so extensive and complex a coalition of religion and class was difficult to lead, and the consequence of successful integration was acceptance of a pluralism of policies. Each section of the party, however defined, expected to be disappointed as well as cheered, and the Liberal tradition included political collapse and subsequent reconsolidation almost as much as legislative triumph. At the national level, as we have seen, Gladstone's oratory played a central though not, of course, a unique role in the achieving of the great Liberal successes and in the process of regrouping after the disasters. His oratory and his capacity to represent through rhetoric both the aspirations and the difficulties of his party had been the basis of his return to politics in 1876 and of his curious position with respect to his party in the campaign from 1876 to the 1880 general election. His base for power—it is worth reiterating—was essentially a rhetorical base: if oratory ceased, the party, conceived as a whole, all but ceased also, for it was through the medium of public meetings nationally reported that the party maintained its national self-awareness. Thus, however much the successful resolution of particular political problems and the apparent clearing of the way to Gladstone's retirement might be achieved, the Liberal coalition's political and rhetorical personality paradoxically depended on Gladstone's continuing political leadership. He remained the keystone of the arch of the Liberal coalition's political identity.

Allied to this was the focusing of political change in 'big bills', major statutes the process of whose passing united the party in the Commons with that in the country and with progressive opinion generally. At its most effective, this very public process—for the proceedings of the Commons often occupied half of the content of newspapers—linked the executive and the Commons to public opinion in a dramatic way and on a day-to-day basis. And in so doing it had an integrative effect which was probably a strong countervailing force against class antagonism; it was certainly intended by Gladstone to have this effect. The content of the legislation was thus matched in importance by public involvement in the discussion of that content. The use of major legislation as a means of legitimation of the representative political system (in addition to the direct effect of the bill or budget itself) derived from the Whig governments of the 1830s.* Gladstone adopted it and made heroic legislation and its accompanying debate the diet of progressive government: a technique followed by all governments of progressive parties (and some not so) until the Wilson government of 1964. Such legislation concentrated enthusiasm and by channelling it also circumscribed it. For the handling of the legislation was primarily the duty of Cabinet members and, in a Gladstone government, usually of Gladstone himself. Thus it provided for a union between Gladstone and the progressive political world which he was especially adroit at exploiting, for the bond of that union was oratory.

The reception of oratory, through the physical participation of attending meetings and the mental integration encouraged by the day-to-day reading of the speeches in the newspapers, thus provided the means of party deliberation and harmonization of disagreements. In a wider sense, oratory eased the legitimation of the Victorian State, as voters vicariously shared in the ventilation of political debate on a huge and unprecedented scale. But this was no simple mechanism of social control. The rhetorical *élite*—the cadre of speakers who dominated the speech-reporting of the day—was the product of a new medium and was shaped by the circumstances of the times just as much as it directed and dictated popular opinion. British political leaders were the beneficiaries of a participatory, representative system whose integrative success constantly astonished them. The great mass of the political press with its uniquely large readership, the participation in local, self-sustaining political debating societies, the high turn-out in elections for Oxford- and Cambridge-led political parties, were largely unanticipated boons, and they knew it. 'The strength of the modern state lies in the Representative system', Gladstone remarked in 1884—it is astonishing that such a remark should as late as the 1880s have given such offence—and a healthy representative system was made possible by spontaneous activity on the part of the electorate, the 'capable citizens' which the system was designed to incorporate.† That so many citizens had turned out to be 'capable' was for someone of Gladstone's political origins and generation a matter of constant surprise, delight, and relief. It was also a process to be proud of having shared in; there was no shame in recognizing that his prophecies of doom in the 1830s had been proved wrong.

With this enthusiasm for popular politics rationalistically presented in great speeches and public argument to audiences marked by 'singular intelligence & the practical turn of their understanding' went an increasing distress about its dark obverse: Jingoism and the assertion of class interest.

* See Peter Mandler, *Aristocratic government in the age of reform. Whigs and liberals 1830–1852* (1990), part I.

† *H* 285. 107 (28 February 1884).

The Tories had become the creatures of 'class-preference . . . the central point of what I call the lower & what is now the prevalent, Toryism'.* 'Tory democracy . . . is demagoguism . . . applied in the worst way, to put down the pacific, law-respecting, economic elements which ennobled the old Conservatism.' It depended 'largely on inflaming public passion' and was rootlessly unable to 'resist excessive & dangerous innovation'. As he observed the rising opposition to the Irish settlement in 1886, Gladstone concluded: 'More and more this becomes a battle between the nation and the classes.' 'Am I', he wondered, 'warped by the spirit of anti-class? Perhaps—I cannot tell. My dislike of the class feeling gets slowly more & more accentuated: & my case is particularly hard & irksome, because I am a thoroughgoing inequalitarian.'

This was in the first instance a moral, ethical view of class: 'For the fountainhead of my feelings & opinions in the matter I go back to the Gospels.' But behind this view lay a sense not of a simple division of society into crude classes, but a sense that large and influential groups within society—the army, the established clergy, the agricultural interest—were ready to assert class interests in politics and that these were already privileged groups which, in the Peelite tradition, ought to know better. 'The classes' meant the privileged classes, especially in their metropolitan form, and in Gladstone's view they acted as a class in juxtaposition to an as yet non-class nation. Thus he did not in these years have a sense of the working class as separate or separatist; the success of the integrationalist campaigns and of the Liberal party in 1880 testified to the opposite. It was the growing willingness of already relatively secure groups and institutions—exemplified by the behaviour of the House of Lords—to use political influence immorally and imprudently that was likely to encourage a general sense within the nation of the advantage of asserting separate interests and identities. If the House of Lords gave the example that it did, who could blame other social groups that began to try to use their power to equal effect?

Just as Newman, writing in the centre of a well-established tradition, believed that essential truth is most clearly perceived by the unsophisticated,† so Gladstone believed that while the intellect was important it was not a sufficient guide to right decisions on fundamental questions in politics. Indeed, he believed that intellectual training, while in principle

* Thus the Liberal government's defeat by 8 votes on Chaplin's resolution in July 1883 to restrict foreign cattle importation during a foot-and-mouth outbreak was, Gladstone noted, 'less than we had expected on a class question like this'.

† See J. H. Newman, 'Theory of developments in religious doctrine' (1843), Sermon XV in *Fifteen sermons preached before the University of Oxford* (1872), 312ff. The relationship with Gladstone's position is close, because both he and Newman regarded the arguments of Bp. Butler as offering the method by which this fundamental understanding could be argumentatively developed; ibid., 318. The conclusion of Gladstone's 'Postscriptum on the county franchise' (1878), *Gleanings*, i. 200–2, strongly echoes Newman, though without reference.

encouraging dispassionate judgement, in fact placed the intellectually trained person in a social or professional context in which the self-interest of wealth (intellectual training being a passport to wealth) might well frustrate the exercise of independent judgement: 'the rich too . . . have their mob, as well as their elect and favoured specimens'. Thus, 'the popular judgment on the great achievements of the last half-century, which have made our age (thus far) a praise among the ages, has been more just and true than that of the majority of the higher orders'.* Gladstone's own political career had in part been an escape to just this sort of perception of justice and truth, and its validity was confirmed for him in the rapport he felt with the large popular crowds at his public meetings and progresses. This popular judgement was not, of course, uninformed—to keep it informed was the chief function of the Liberal party in the country—but it was untrammelled by the prejudices encouraged by wealth. This view of popular judgement was first fully stated in Gladstone's dispute with Robert Lowe in 1878 on the franchise and he then, as often later, accompanied it with a litany of reforms passed against the wishes of 'the classes'.†

This view of 'the classes' thus had in Gladstone's analysis a long pedigree. It allowed him to assert his claim to have continued the mapping of the high ground of moral progress for so long shared with the Whigs (and still so with some of them). It reached its fullest statement in his conclusion in Liverpool to his election campaign of 1886, in which in a powerful passage, as influential both in the party of progress and historiographically as anything he ever said, he contrasted what he saw as the growing illiberalism of 'the classes' with the hard-won achievements of the nation, and so by implication associated Home Rule with the litany of nineteenth-century progress. 'It is on the weapon of argument that I rely most', Gladstone told the electors; but against this weapon was opposed 'a different set of means . . . the long purse . . . the imposing display of rank and station . . . the power of political organization, and the command of positions of advantage'. Consequently Liberals

are opposed throughout the country by a compact army, and that army is a combination of the classes against the masses. I am thankful to say that there are among the classes many happy exceptions still. I am thankful to say that there are men wearing coronets on their heads who are as good and as sound and as genuine Liberals as any working man that hears me at this moment. But, as a general rule, it cannot be pretended that we are supported by the dukes, or by the squires, or by the Established clergy, or by the officers of the army, or by a number of other bodies of very respectable people. What I observe is this: wherever a profession is highly privileged, wherever a profession is publicly endowed, it is there that you will find that almost the whole of the class and the profession are against us . . . in

---

* 'Postscriptum on the county franchise' (1878), *Gleanings*, i. 198.
† *Gleanings*, i. 198–9.

the main, gentlemen, this is a question, I am sorry to say, of class against mass, of classes against the nation; and the question for us is, Will the nation show enough of unity and determination to overbear, constitutionally, at the polls, the resistance of the classes? It is very material that we should consider which of them is likely to be right. Do not let us look at our forces alone; let us look at that without which force is worthless, mischievous, and contemptible. Are we likely to be right? Are the classes ever right when they differ from the nation? ('No.') Well, wait a moment. I draw this distinction. I am not about to assert that the masses of the people, who do not and cannot give their leisure to politics, are necessarily, on all subjects, better judges than the leisured men and the instructed men who have great advantages for forming political judgments that the others have not; but this I will venture to say, that upon one great class of subjects, the largest and the most weighty of them all, where the leading and determining considerations that ought to lead to a conclusion are truth, justice, and humanity, there, gentlemen, all the world over, I will back the masses against the classes.

. . . let me apply a little history to this question, and see whether the proposition I have just delivered is an idle dream and the invention of an enthusiastic brain, or whether it is the lesson taught us eminently and indisputably by the history of the last half century. I will read you rapidly a list of ten subjects,—the greatest subjects of the last half century. First, abolition of slavery; second, reform of Parliament, lasting from 1831 to 1885, at intervals; third, abolition of the Corn Laws and abolition of twelve hundred customs and excise duties, which has set your trade free instead of its being enslaved; fourthly, the navigation laws, which we were always solemnly told were the absolute condition of maintaining the strength of this country and of this empire; fifthly, the reform of the most barbarous and shameful criminal code that ever disgraced a civilized country; sixthly, the reform of the laws of combination and contract, which compelled the British workmen to work, as I may say, in chains; seventhly, the change of foreign policy. . . . Mr. Canning, an old representative of Liverpool, . . . emancipated this country from its servitude to the Holy Alliance; and for so doing he was more detested by the upper classes of this country than any man has been during the present century. Eighthly—I take another piece of foreign policy—there was what we call the Jingo policy. That was put down. Who put it down? It was not put down by the classes; it was put down by the hearty response to an appeal made to the people. Ninthly, the abolition of religious distinctions; and tenthly, I take the matter in which I had a hand myself, the disestablishment of the Irish Church. These ten subjects—many of them are really not single subjects, but groups of subjects—are the greatest that have formed the staple employment and food of our political life for the last sixty years. On every one of them, without exception, the masses have been right and the classes have been wrong. Nor will it do, gentlemen, to tell me that I am holding the language of agitation; I am speaking the plain dictates of fact, for nobody can deny that on all these ten subjects the masses were on one side and the classes were on the other, and nobody can deny that the side of the masses, and not the side of the classes, is the one which now the whole nation confesses to have been right.*

* Speech in Liverpool, 28 June 1886, W. E. Gladstone, *Speeches on the Irish question 1886*, (1886), 292. The eight points of the litany in 'Last words on the county franchise' (1878), *Gleanings*, i. 178

Whatever the truth of this analysis of class, this was a risky line for the leader of the Liberal party to take publicly, for it encouraged 'the classes' in the view—with particularly important implications in an era of limited enfranchisement—that they were conservative by temperament and Conservative by party.

These then are the four great themes seen as distinctive in Gladstone's career hitherto: none of them unique to him but, when integrated into a single political personality, extraordinary in their force. It might be objected that the locating of these four compass points of Gladstone's political orientation has omitted discussion of foreign and imperial policies, the very issues which brought him again to form a government in 1880, and of Ireland, the issue which was to form the chief focus of the rest of his political life.

Imperial policy had been his first executive concern, in 1834, and had been a natural preoccupation for anyone with a career at the forefront of Victorian politics. But Gladstone's approach to it was notable in so far as he tried to run together two distinct and sometimes contradictory views. On the one hand, his free trade views encouraged a seemly but none the less determined reduction of direct, metropolitan control, and offered no reason for its extension. On the other, his executive itch, his sense of the immediate, of what seemed to be 'practical', encouraged imperial action, eventually as bold as that of any other Victorian. In foreign policy, his High-Church concept of the Concert of Europe, discussed in Chapter I, represented a continuation and extension of the policies of his youth, and brought him into sharp disagreement with 'the Manchester School'. It was, Gladstone felt, an interest forced upon him by events and, important and distinctive though his contribution was, it was not what he would have seen as a positive interest. Ireland, likewise, was something of an intrusion, an unanticipated ulcer on the body politic to be soothed and with time healed. We see in the course of the early 1880s Gladstone reluctantly concluding that superficial dressings achieved little, and that major surgery was necessary. In the course of that realization, we also see his growing fascination with the problem and history of Ireland.

are exactly the same as the above. On the 'class' question, Gladstone partially exempted lawyers and doctors.

CHAPTER V

The Second Gladstone Government, 1880—1885: Retirement, Cabinet, and Party

Election Victory and Return to Power—An Intention to Retire—Gladstone and the Whigs—The Party and the Commons—The 1880 Cabinet

A reluctant goodbye [at Hawarden] before one. London at 6.30. A secret journey but people gathered at Chester station and Euston. I vaguely feel that this journey is a plunge, out of an atmosphere of peace into an element of disturbance. May He who has of late so wonderfully guided, guide me still in the critical days about to come.*

Election Victory and Return to Power

We have seen how in Midlothian did Gladstone 'hammer with all my little might at the fabric of the present Tory power'. The result of the general election of March and April 1880 was a Liberal majority over the Conservatives of 137, with the Irish Home Rulers winning 65 seats, an even more spectacular victory than the Liberal majority of between 56 and 76 which Gladstone had calculated in November 1878 as likely from the evidence of by-elections.† Elected comfortably, as predicted in Midlothian, and, without visiting the constituency, overwhelmingly in Leeds,‡ Gladstone went secretly from Edinburgh to Hawarden, rejecting plans for a triumphal entry into London—mindful perhaps of his trenchant condemnation of the Roman triumph of Beaconsfield and Salisbury in 1878§—and soon began an article on the Tory *débâcle*. Lord Wolverton (i.e. Glyn, the banker and former Liberal chief whip) arrived at Hawarden and 'threatens a request

---

* Diary for 19 Apr. 80.
† 'Electoral Facts', *Nineteenth Century*, iv. 967 (November 1878).
‡ In 1874, Leeds, a three-member constituency, returned a Liberal and two Conservatives, the other two Liberal candidates not being elected; in 1880, the Liberals ran two candidates only, Gladstone coming top, Barran (a Liberal) second, both with over 23,000 votes, and one of the two Tory candidates third, 10,000 votes behind. Later in 1880, Herbert Gladstone took over the seat his father had won.
§ '. . . the well-organised machinery of an obsequious reception, unexampled, I suppose, in the history of our civilians; and meant, perhaps to recall the pomp of the triumphs which Rome awarded to her most successful generals'; 'England's Mission', *Nineteenth Century*, iv. 560 (September 1878).

from Granville and Hartington. Again I am stunned: but God will provide'. Granville and Hartington were still the nominal leaders of the Liberal party and, of course, much preferred to Gladstone by the Queen as potential Prime Ministers.

Through Wolverton, Gladstone made it clear that in 'the great matter of all' he remained in the position which he had tenaciously held, at least in principle, since his 'retirement' from politics. He was not party leader—he told Wolverton—and '[my] labours as an Individual cannot set me up as a Pretender', but a recognition of the needs of 'public policy' might require suspension of the usual procedures.* He would be seen to be invited back to office by the party leaders who had been so reluctant to support the Campaign especially in its Bulgarian days; his moral and political authority would be seen to be derived from the size of the Liberal majority; his earlier behaviour would be justified.

After cutting down a final sycamore at Hawarden with his son Willy, Gladstone moved to London on 19 April, noting in his diary the apprehensive passage quoted at the head of this chapter. There followed a 'blank day' which Gladstone thought was 'probably due to the Queen's hesitation or reluctance, which the Ministers have to find means of covering'. On 22 April, Hartington was summoned by the Queen.† He came immediately to Gladstone to report on the audience. Gladstone recorded Hartington's description:

She told him [Hartington] that she desired him to form an Administration and pressed upon him strongly his duty to assist her as a responsible leader of the party now in a large majority. . . . Hartington in reply to H.M. made becoming acknowledgements and proceeded to say that he did not think a Government could be satisfactorily formed without me: he had not had any direct communication with me: but he had reason to believe that I would not take any office or post in the Government except that of First Minister. Under these circumstances he advised H.M. to place the matter in my hands.

Hartington thus recognized that Gladstone was indispensable, being 'the chief personage and a most powerful influence in the Liberal Party' and he ceded the political initiative to the former Prime Minister. Granville and Hartington next day jointly advised the Queen to send for Gladstone. The Queen in turn told them to visit Gladstone to ask him to come to Windsor Castle—a most unusual manœuvre, as the Queen's Secretary was the usual agent on such occasions. They came to Gladstone like a pair of attendant

---

* This position was already belied by many small signs; for example, it was Gladstone who on 11 March 1880 answered Northcote's stop-gap budget after the dissolution was announced; H 251. 834. When John Bright visited Hawarden on 16 April he gained the impression that 'it is not likely he will take office in a Government of which he is not the head'.

† Hartington's memoranda in preparation for his audience; two of these are in B. Holland, *Life of Spencer Compton, eighth Duke of Devonshire* (1911), ii. 273ff. and another in Chatsworth House, Chatsworth MSS 340. 940.

Lords and he took full advantage of the moment, putting it to them that 'they had unitedly advised the Sovereign that it was most for the public advantage to send for me. To this they assented.'

When, therefore, Gladstone went to Windsor that evening (23 April 1880) and kissed hands as Prime Minister for the second time, he did so on his own terms both with the Queen and the Whigs. Granville and Hartington's subordinance was explicitly and rather humiliatingly spelt out.

Amiable 'Pussy' Granville and earnest, unimaginative 'Harty Tarty' might each in 1875 have had expectations of the premiership when the Liberals returned to power. Now in 1880 they found themselves 'kowtowing' to the man who had retired. Each was probably rather relieved: neither had the energy or political clout successfully to lead the Liberal party in power. 1880 was the last occasion on which the Whigs were offered a government with a good majority, and their leaders were not strong enough to take it. Granville and Hartington belong to that distinctive, small band of British politicians who have declined the premiership—Granville in 1855, Hartington in 1880 and twice more, in July and December 1887.

It was as much the policy as the political personality which, in Gladstone's view, the Queen and the notables had to recognize. Gladstone may have been 'stunned' by the notion of a return to the premiership, but he played his cards very carefully and shrewdly in April 1880. More was at stake than the acquiring of power: his authority over the party and especially over the Whigs within it needed to be clearly established if his power was to be maintained.

Despite this careful distancing from the party hierarchy, 1880 was the first occasion on which Gladstone had taken office as a 'liberal' (in 1868 he had still been a 'liberal conservative'). This was reflected in a marked shift of tone with respect to the history of his own times. Hitherto, Gladstone had seen progress in the nineteenth century as essentially the achievement of a beneficent governing class: franchise extension had been a necessary process to buttress the legitimacy of the ruling élite, but its cost had been a slowing down of legislative and administrative reform. In some respects he continued to hold this essentially Peelite view, arguing that the pre-1832 Parliament was 'intrinsically more favourable to the public interest than our present system'; early parliamentary reform would have prevented Roman Catholic emancipation in 1829, and had delayed Corn Law Repeal until 1846. On the other hand, 'popular judgment was more often just than that of the higher orders', and the 'instances' of this—abolition of slavery, parliamentary reform, fiscal reform, trade-union reform, a freedom-directed foreign policy, and the others in the litany quoted at the end of the previous chapter—were now regarded as making up 'nearly the whole history of the Country since the peace of 1815'. The election victory of 1880 was seen *a fortiori* as a vindication of this view of popular judgement, giving joy, Gladstone believed, 'to the large majority of the civilised world. The downfall of Beaconsfieldism is like the vanishing of some vast magnificent castle in an Italian romance.'

An Intention to Retire

Gladstone's clearly stated intention of leaving office as soon as he had made sure that the vanished castle was truly gone created widespread unease in his party and in his government. His frequent discussion of imminent retirement did not encourage a consolidation of the Cabinet or the feeling that here was a group working together for at least a Parliament. Appointing himself to the Exchequer meant that two major offices would be vacated by his departure. It also suggested the possibility that 'retirement' might be a two-stage process: first from the Exchequer, then from the Premiership. Despite the large majority in the Commons, there was a sense of the transitory about the Cabinet of 1880–5.

Before discussing the composition of that Cabinet, we will look at Gladstone's various plans for retirement between 1880 and 1885, and at his relations with the Whigs and with the parliamentary party, for the character of the Cabinet was conditioned by each of these. At the start of the government, his intention was to resign after the remnants of Beaconsfieldism—in particular Afghanistan, the Transvaal, and the frontier question in the Balkans—had been tidied up. By 1881 these matters had been largely dealt with and it was hoped that, once the condition of Ireland had been restored to calm, retirement in 1882 would be possible.

In the autumn of 1881 extensive discussions took place, including—always a telling sign in a politician—consideration of the details of new domestic arrangements. Plans for the preliminary step of separating the chancellorship from the premiership were drawn up, but to no immediate effect. Gladstone reviewed the position in December 1881 for his son Harry, who was in India:

As to public affairs, we have the utmost cause to be thankful in regard to the difficult and painful matters which had for some time confronted us before the present Govt. was formed. Montenegro & Greece have got in the main what they were entitled to—Afghanistan is in the main evacuated—the Transvaal is restored. Also we have at home I hope re-established the proper balance between Income & Charge which is the essential condition of all good finance. But two other subjects have sprung up, even more urgent in their character: the condition of Ireland, and the loss of capacity in the House of Commons under its present rules to discharge its legislative duties. I came into office with the view & intention of retiring from it, so soon as the questions I have named were disposed of: that would have been in the autumn of the present year [1881]. But my hopes were dashed.*

* To H. N. Gladstone, 2 Dec. 81.

None the less, Gladstone's close confidant, Sir Robert Phillimore, concluded: 'I think he will retire in May [1882]'. The month could hardly have been chosen with more retrospective irony. Gladstone in what he hoped in March was 'my last Session as Prime Minister', having in April 1882 rented out his London house and thus, as in 1874, planned to have no base but Hawarden, could hardly resign during the Phoenix Park or Egyptian crises.

In the summer of 1882, further plans were adumbrated, and in the autumn of that year, hard on the success of the occupation of Egypt, Gladstone made his most determined effort. Following a visit by Spencer to Hawarden, he sent Spencer a long letter, with copies to Granville and Hartington, setting out the case both political and personal. His return to office had been, as he had always insisted, exceptional; his retirement would 'restore the natural and normal state of things, which existed up to 1880'. Personally, 'it would be of no good to anyone, that I should remain on the stage like a half-exhausted singer, whose notes are flat, & everyone perceives it except himself'. Granville and Hartington both met Gladstone on both counts with clear negatives: no 'young or middle-aged man' exceeded or even equalled him in physical capacity; politically Granville could not 'aid or abet you in striking such a blow on the liberal party'. Hartington was 'convinced that there does not at this moment exist in the party any man possessing a fraction of those mental powers which you consider so necessary to future constructive legislation'; 'as to the effect of your retirement upon the party, I feel bound to state my own clear and distinct opinion. I think the leadership of the House of Commons, in its present temper, an impossibility for any one but yourself.'

A partial solution was reached by a Cabinet reshuffle in December 1882 by which Gladstone ceded the Exchequer to Childers, and Lord Derby, who had refused office in May 1882, joined as colonial secretary. These negotiations and decisions, compounded with the stress of a row about Rosebery's political future, anxiety about an announced visit to Midlothian, and an attack of lumbago, led to a severe bout of insomnia and an extended rest in Cannes.* The new Cabinet arrangements in fact diminished the case for retirement. These changes left Gladstone free from departmental duties and indeed free, should he wish it, from anything other than chairing the Cabinet and answering the First Lord's questions in the Commons. In 1883 this was largely what he did: for the first time since 1869 he was not in the forefront of the legislative programme. By the autumn of 1883, as the party gathered itself for franchise reform, Gladstone, despite the warnings of 1866, found himself again in the legislative van. The constitutional imbroglio of 1884, the need to settle Egyptian finance, and the growing crisis in the Sudan and on the Afghan frontier, which taken together produced from October 1884 an equinoctial flood tide of political

* Insomnia set in by January 1883, but was clearly threatening before that.

crisis, carried him through to the resignation of the Cabinet in June 1885 and the formation of Salisbury's minority Tory government. Following that resignation he wrote 'a Minute for circulation on my retirement' proposing 'a bodily not a moral absence' from the front opposition bench, and anticipating no 'state of facts, which ought to alter my long cherished, and I believe well known, desire and purpose to withdraw, with the expiration of this Parliament, from active participation in politics'. None the less, 'with much difficulty' Gladstone brought himself 'to the conclusion that I ought to offer myself for re-election' as an MP in the autumn of 1885.

It is a curious and exasperating catalogue.* It is easy to be impatient with Gladstone, and to see him using his retirement and his age as a weapon against his colleagues, rather than making a genuine effort to achieve it, and in effect that was what he ended by doing, presenting himself in May 1885, during the quarrel on Irish policy which effectively brought the government to an end, as merely 'an *amicus curiae*'.

The imminence of retirement had advantages. Gladstone could present himself both as a person above party, called back into politics to settle great moral questions, and, on occasion (as with the franchise demonstrations in 1884), as the leader for the time being of the Liberal party, the movement essential to the achievement of those settlements. He thus appealed— peculiarly among executive politicians, but together with John Bright— both to the many Liberals who were sceptical about the legitimacy of party organization and to those who were party activists and came together in the Liberal Hundreds. The convenience of this position became increasingly apparent as the second ministry gave way to the third but it can hardly be offered as an explanation of how Gladstone came to find himself in it; it was the consequence of his views about his retirement, not their cause.

What is striking is not Gladstone's behaviour, which was quite consistent both in the short term and in the general sweep of his career, but the reaction of his colleagues to his various attempts to arrange for his retirement. All the Liberals whom Gladstone consulted—and while the core was the Whig hierarchy they included men as diverse as Bright and Acton— were uniformly appalled. Most Prime Ministers who suggested to close colleagues that the time had come for a successor to emerge would find the proposal rapidly pursued behind the scenes at the same time as being met by an opposition marked by a decorous and cautious formality. But in Gladstone's case there were no plots and few protests. If they thought Gladstone was bluffing, it was a bluff they dared not call. Nobody replied,

---

* An exasperation exacerbated, perhaps, by his pedantic letters and lists on the length of his public life: 'ought my service in the Ionian Islands, unpaid but strictly official, to be reckoned to my credit?'. Various calculations made in 1884 concluded that he was 7th longest-serving Prime Minister out of 31 since the accession of the House of Hanover.

'yes, perhaps the strain is telling, perhaps the party's long-term interest calls for a regrettable change'.*

Gladstone and the Whigs

The fact was that the Whigs could not let him go. They would not let him go in 1874; they tried to stop him going in 1875; they could not do without him in 1885. For all the rows over Irish property, the Whigs looked to Gladstone for defence. Gladstone sent the Duke of Bedford, whose duchess he had failed to prevent resigning as Mistress of the Robes, a copy of Robert Giffen's 'masterly' refutation of 'the well-written but wild book of Mr. George on Progress & Poverty', no doubt with the implicit reminder that the Prime Minister's Irish Land Act was in contrast a limited diversion. The Duke replied that he feared 'disturbance may be at hand. . . . If anyone can save us, it is yourself.' In the fevered atmosphere of the early 1880s, with landowners in a panic unknown since the early 1830s, Gladstone remained the Whigs' last, best hope, unless they were to join the Tories. Kimberley summed up the Whigs' view in 1885:

no one but yourself could steer the party in an even course between our right and left wings, and the future of this country will depend upon the impulse given at the commencement of the new political era.

Kimberley here identifies two of the bases of Gladstone's indispensability: his mediation between the groups that made up the Liberal coalition, and his capacity as an electoral leader. However conservative their policies might be thought to be becoming, the Whigs were not Tories. The possibility of being forced out of the Liberal party with an accommodation with the Tories as their alternative appalled them more than sitting in Cabinet with Chamberlain and Dilke. But increasingly it was only the inertia of constituency complications and political habit that maintained this. Gladstone regretted the 'violent moderation' which seemed more and more the dominant characteristic of the Whigs:

It is high time that the tones of a decided Liberalism should obtain a somewhat more free scope among Peers & Peers sons. I have not the disposition of some Whig Lords to reaction on Conservative as much as on Liberal grounds. For more than two centuries our Liberal movements have been led by Liberal Lords, and I hold this to have been not only an important but a vital point in our history. . . . I keenly desire the continuance of this feature. . . .

* Of course, there were frequent discussions as to what would happen if Gladstone did go; his spasmodic reiteration of intention naturally encouraged these. This is the context of the discussions in January 1885, which Mr Cooke and Professor Vincent in the 'Commentary' in Book One of A. B. Cooke and J. Vincent, *The Governing Passion* (1974), 27, call 'the Liberal plot to rid the party of Gladstone and Gladstonianism'. On that occasion, as on all others, none of those jockeying for speculative positions suggested to Gladstone that he should do what he said he intended to do, and the moment, like the other such moments, passed. Curiously, there is no mention of the 'plot' in the 'Diary' in Book Two of *The Governing Passion*.

The balance of Gladstone's second government had shown how keen this desire was. That balance, and Gladstone's announcement of relative inactivity, gave the Whigs a further chance to determine the scope of a Liberal government, but, as in 1874, they did not take it. The Whigs were ceasing to be a fertile force in British politics and were becoming predominantly reactive. Whigs, like Spencer and Granville on home rule, could follow resolutely, but they could not lead. The intellectual daring and political initiative of the Russell era was being replaced by the grey conventionality of Hartington: moderately competent, politically respectable, but sterile. Outside the field of colonial government and foreign affairs—and even there Granville relied heavily on Gladstone for ideas—it would be hard to name any significant contribution (other than the sounding of the trumpet of caution) for which the Whigs were responsible after 1880. Even their competence in external affairs was called into question in the Sudan, where Gordon was chosen and instructed by the Whigs, whose muddled orders gave Gordon the latitude he needed for his aberrant behaviour. Only Ripon in India, and, fitfully, Rosebery, maintained something of the whiggish heritage of bold political solutions to political questions.

The timidity and caution of the leading Whigs added a further complexity to Gladstone's tactical political position: he could not remove himself and expect the other variables to remain constant, because the nature of the government's character as formed in 1880 was determined by his own peculiar position in it. Hartington and Granville could not 'succeed' Gladstone mid-way through a government, when their own attempt at a moulding of the party had been too fragile and too cautious to avoid being so rudely interrupted in 1876. The party as it existed in the early 1880s was not their party. Gladstone's often expressed regret, that he was keeping Hartington and Granville from what was naturally theirs, was beside the point. It was no longer theirs, and they knew it. Moreover, Gladstone made it clear that if a transfer of the premiership were achieved, he would still retain, as in 1875, a right to and a capacity for ultimate intervention: 'I do not contemplate immediate Parliamentary extinction. A part may yet remain, the part of independent cooperation upon occasion. . . .' The experience of 1876–80 told Granville and Hartington exactly what those sentences meant.

Gladstone was thus boxed in, and so were his colleagues. Derby caught the position exactly in January 1885:

The 'peculiar position' of the Premier, who is always declaring himself to be on the point of retiring, increases the difficulty, for he is very unwilling to do anything that may bind him to stay longer in office, and we cannot act without him.*

---

* Derby's diary, 8 January 1885, quoted in T. A. Jenkins, *Gladstone, Whiggery and the Liberal Party, 1874–1886* (1988), 236.

Gladstone's 'peculiar position' thus unsettled himself and his colleagues. He had formed the Cabinet in 1880 on what he had insisted were clearly seen to be his own terms; yet he had no use for it for the duration of a Parliament.

The Party and the Commons

This necessarily discursive account of Gladstone's political position and of his relationship to his colleagues prepares us for the curious 'stop-go' quality of his second administration. It is full of great dramas and splendid feats of legislation; it is characterized also by delay, prevarication, and incompetence.

The administration depended, of course, on the Liberal party's majority in the House of Commons, an overall majority of about 47 over Tories and Home Rulers, and a majority of about 112 over the Tories alone. The crusading circumstances of the achievement of power in 1880 might suggest that the party in the Commons would be radical, even truculent in tone, but this did not prove to be the case. Rarely can the party of progress have accepted so many changes of direction and of programme with so little protest. Though the majority sometimes dropped, the government was very rarely defeated—much less than in 1868–74—and the party remained firm, if sometimes irritated, until the franchise and redistribution bills had finally gone through in 1885.

Gladstone's practice of keeping the parliamentary party in line by the provision of 'big bills' for which it could vote and through which it could confront Conservatism in the Commons, in the Lords, and in the country generally, was well-established. Though on his return to power in 1880 he had no particular programme of legislation to offer personally, he soon found himself using the Commons' timetable in the old way. He felt, and on the whole the Cabinet felt also, that the most effective way of maintaining party enthusiasm was for him to lead from the front. Since he was not only First Lord of the Treasury, but also Leader of the House and, until December 1882, Chancellor of the Exchequer as well, Gladstone was necessarily very prominent in the Commons in routine business. But he added to this by continuing his practice of personal responsibility for major measures, which might also be seen as his practice of making some measures major by taking personal responsibility for them. His duties as Prime Minister included, as he saw them, 'the supervision, and often the construction, of weighty legislative measures'. Thus in 1881 he saw the Irish Land Bill through the Commons almost single-handedly on the front bench; in 1882 he took responsibility for the Arrears Bill which with the Crimes Bill delayed the intended business, and he worked the new rules for procedure through the Commons during the special autumn sitting; in 1884 he took the chief responsibility for the Representation of the People

Bill and the Redistribution Bill. In addition to this, the Foreign and Colonial Secretaries (Granville, Kimberley, and later Derby) being in the Lords, Gladstone, rather than the relevant undersecretary, often took foremost handling of those subjects in the Commons, particularly at question-time. When, as in 1883, not principally involved in the chief measures planned for the session he reminded Harcourt in May 1883 with respect to the Government of London Bill of the vital connection between legislation and the party: 'The Liberal party as a rule draws its vital breath from great Liberal measures.'

There was, however, a striking difference from the legislation of the first government. Then, the bills on which Gladstone led—with the exception, as it proved, of the Irish Universities Bill—ran with the grain of Liberalism. He led the party against the Conservatives and the Lords. In the second government his lead was needed because several of the bills he sponsored, especially before 1884, frustrated the anticipated Liberal programme and were, though supportable by most Liberals, neither comfortable nor convenient. Gladstone's lead was further needed because his stamina despite his old age could outlast Tory and Irish wreckers, and his 'old parliamentary hand's' resourcefulness could outmanœuvre them. But the effect of this was that Gladstone spent a good deal of his credit with his party on items and issues seen as marginal to the Liberal cause. He himself recognized the danger. 'It so happens that at present we have many good Bills in hand', he told Harcourt in the letter already quoted, 'but they are not understood as distinctively Liberal Bills.' In the 1868–74 parliament, the opposition to coercion in Ireland had come necessarily from within the Liberal party; it had consequently been muted. In 1880–5, opposition to coercion was the constant duty of the Home Rule party that had largely replaced the Liberals as the dominant party in Ireland. Consequently, that opposition was unbridled. Coercion might be necessary, but it was hardly Liberal, and the Liberal party in the Commons now frequently found itself fighting on two fronts: the Tories baying for more, the Home Rulers ignoring gentlemanly convention to show their distinctiveness—and always with the threat of an unholy combination of the two to throw the government out if its own supporters flagged.

Gladstone's chief whip throughout the 1880–5 administration was Lord Richard Grosvenor, MP for Gladstone's own constituency of Flintshire. The appointment of Grosvenor was a clear sign to the Whigs that their interests in party affairs would not be neglected. Despite his only official experience being that of Vice-Chamberlain to the Royal Household in 1872–4, Grosvenor managed the day-to-day business of the government and the party effectively. But he brought to his position no vision beyond that of fixing affairs for the short term. Even there, his usefulness was limited, as his surprising absence from the redistribution discussions in

1884 shows. Gladstone's correspondence with him is rather artificially cheerful, but cautious. For strategic considerations, Gladstone continued to rely on Lord Wolverton, chief whip from 1868 to 1873, and his confidant at all important political moments since. Wolverton, however, also had a very conservative view of the party organization. In terms of structure, the Liberal party, with the exception of the rather fitfully active National Liberal Federation, remained in the 1880s much as it had been in the 1860s, that is, it hardly had one, for the Central Liberal Association was not much more than a post-box and a publisher of speeches and pamphlets. The National Liberal Club and the Eighty Club were interesting attempts to integrate the party with a slightly wider circle of non-Westminster men. The National Liberal Club helped give identity to the growing number of non-Whig Liberals who would have felt uncomfortable at the Reform Club, but it was visited by Gladstone only on the unavoidable official occasion and never socially; if he used a club, it was the older non-party Grillion's or The Club, and those very rarely.* The Eighty Club sponsored oratory, the Gladstonian alternative to organization, and was an important source of speeches cheaply reprinted as pamphlets.

The absence of advance on the organizational front was a striking failure of the Liberal party in this period. Suppose a Liberal party with individual membership, a full structure of organization, constitution, and elections, achieving a universal franchise in place of the 1884 bill, how differently might progressive politics in Britain have developed! Yet such a development was outwith the parameters of Liberal thinking about politics. It would have been regarded as profoundly illiberal. To Liberals, to be a citizen was to be a Liberal: nothing more was essentially needed. Many grass-roots Liberals were extremely reluctant to admit the need for party organization at all, for they saw it as corrupting Liberal individualism, a further means of invasion by the Westminster élite and another example of the dangers of the centralizing State. Even the caucus-men regarded the caucus as a second-best, a regrettable necessity in the circumstances of an extended electorate.

As it was, the Gladstonian method of rhetorical integration increasingly offered a substitution for or alternative to organization at the national level, with Liberal Associations achieving spasmodic success locally through an *ad hoc* caucus system which rarely proved self-sustaining.† As for the franchise, 'a uniform residential, household franchise for the whole country, supplemented by a simple and really effective lodger franchise' was the extent of the demand of Schnadhorst, the doyen of Liberal organizers, to the National Reform Union.‡

* See below, p. 524.
† For the difficulties, see J. Davis, *Reforming London* (1988), 25 ff.
‡ F. Schnadhorst, 'The next Reform Bill', speech to the National Reform Union, 23 November 1881, p. 5.

Gladstone stressed the advantages of variety to the party, and positively discouraged a more organized structure for the parliamentary party:

Liberalism has ever sought to unite freedom of individual thought and action, to which it largely owes its healthy atmosphere, with corporate efficiency. This aim is noble, but it is difficult. For my own part, although it is not the method best adapted to the personal convenience of those who lead, nothing would induce me to exchange it for the regimental discipline which brings the two minorities, each in a well-fused mass, into the voting lobby. For this valued freedom, and this abundance of variety, cherished in the Liberal party, have not disabled it during the last half-century from efficient action. For more than two-thirds of that period the Liberal party has held power, and fully nine-tenths of our useful legislation has been due to its inspiration and its labours. What modern Britain at this moment is, she has become substantially through the agency of the Liberal party.

Such being the facts, it seems natural to ask—why may not the Liberal party of the future be useful, with the same freedom and the same methods, as in the past?*

Striking this balance between 'individual thought' and 'corporate efficiency', gave, Gladstone might have added, a peculiar strength not to the party but to the Cabinet and to his own position as arbitrator, mediator, and key-stone of the Cabinet–Party arch: 'As the Cabinet is the many-sided buffer on which all the currents of will and opinion in the country spend themselves, so within the Cabinet the Prime Minister . . . is charged with the same passive function.' But with Gladstone a passive function, however cautiously exercised, was likely quickly to become active.

He was not, however, active in directly explaining the predicaments of his government to the electors. The great rhetorical crescendo of 1876–80 left an echo and then a silence. Gladstone made no public speeches, apart from the almost unavoidable Mansion House speeches, until the great meetings at Leeds on 7 and 8 October 1881. This visit, several times delayed, was to thank the electors for electing him in 1880, when he had passed on the seat to his son, Herbert. The Leeds visit, a huge political demonstration with several ancillary speeches, was Gladstone's only direct meeting with the electorate until August 1884, when he spoke in his Midlothian constituency—a meeting postponed regularly since 1881—and made a tour of Scotland defending the administration and increasing pressure on the Conservatives and the House of Lords to settle the constitutional imbroglio over the question of franchise and redistribution. Apart from this 'the People's William' was silent outside Parliament until the election of 1885.† 'I have been, I know,' Gladstone told John Cowan, his chairman in Midlothian, 'as scanty in demonstration since the Election of 1880, as I was abundant before it.'

* Political speeches, 1885, 14.
† Of course, there were ad hoc speeches when on holiday etc., an interesting appearance at the Garibaldi commemoration in Stafford House in June 1883, and comments to deputations.

Health, the reason given to Cowan, and, in particular, difficulties with his voice in the mid-1880s and especially in 1885, was part of the problem, and certainly Gladstone found exhausting the combination which these visits necessarily involved, of 'a "progress"' combined with 'a Mass Meeting'. But on the other hand he also found them restorative, enormously enjoying the success of his largely spontaneous Scottish speeches in August and September 1884 when public enthusiasm turned every appearance into a Liberal triumph, from a visit to the Forth Bridge in construction (the workmen presenting him with an axe and he them with a library of 'entertaining and improving' volumes), to a visit to the Liberal aristocracy and tenants at Haddo House. Only Tory Preston on the way south, 'vilely managed as usual', where a 'hissing engine ... effectually silenced me', spoilt the progress.

The limiting of major public appearances had political drawbacks but there were advantages in reticence, not least the avoidance of agitating the Queen and the Whigs. Even without physically appearing, Gladstone was omnipresent, his every action the chief focus of the press. The late 1870s and 1880s saw the full flowering of the Gladstonian icon industry. These were the years in which Liberal households came to display their Gladstone statuettes, jugs, plates, and banners in pride of place on the mantel, the Tory country houses answering with chamber pots with his face looking upwards or inwards (a good example is reproduced in the illustrations in this book). Gladstone's age was beginning to give him, amongst his public, something of the status of a relic and, as he knew from his close observations of the display of relics in Naples, the public processing of relics must be carefully and selectively co-ordinated.

There were therefore prudential arguments for avoiding overexposure, already a constant danger from his very frequent speeches in the Commons, and for consequently extracting the maximum excitement from public speeches and appearances when the moment for them came. This sense of the ripeness of the public moment thus existed side by side with other reasons for not making frequent extra-Parliamentary speeches, such as the alarm they gave the Queen and the Whigs, and the misgivings Gladstone felt about appearing as the people's idol when privately he was trying to resign; anxiety about the presentation of his awkward political position was undoubtedly a factor in the crisis of insomnia of January 1883 which led to the cancellation of the Midlothian meeting and his departure for Cannes.

The absence of public appearances was balanced by a greater use of party meetings than in 1868–74. To some extent, this reflected the anxieties of the party, but it was also a means of explaining particular policies and setting them in a more general context, which was the usual purpose of the mass meetings. There were party meetings on 27 February 1882, 13 July

1882, 10 July 1884, 1 December 1884, and, in the next Parliament, on 27 May 1886. Such meetings were midway between a Commons' speech and a public appearance and to an extent Gladstone used them as substitutes for the latter.

Gladstone had substantial credit with each of the various sections of the party, though each also had substantial reasons for caution about him. Among the radical nonconformists, his opposition to Beaconsfieldism was an impeccable credential, overlaying at least for the time his dispute with them over religious education in the early 1870s. To the Liberal centre, he offered executive competence, a safe pair of financial hands, and a strong urge for legislative achievement. For the Whigs, he represented especially a guarantee against something worse, and an ability to formulate principles of policy in foreign and imperial affairs which Granville, Kimberley, and Hartington, although cautious about Gladstone's prescriptions, found extremely hard to do themselves.

The 1880 Cabinet

As it had done since the 1860s, therefore, Gladstone's gallimaufrous political character boxed the compass of the Liberal party. His Cabinet, however, seemed set upon a predominantly whiggish course, though the notoriety of the second government for whiggish domination is somewhat diminished on close inspection. Of the twenty who served in the Cabinet between 1880 and 1885, nine can be fairly regarded as Whigs or whiggish (the Duke of Argyll and Lords Spencer, Granville, Kimberley, Northbrook, Hartington, Carlingford, Derby, Rosebery); as the term 'whig' was coming by the late nineteenth century to denote more a caste of mind than membership of a particular group of Whig families, it becomes both more flexible and more questionable (Argyll had Peelite origins, Northbrook came from a Liberal banking family (the Barings) and Derby had served in Disraeli's Cabinet as foreign secretary). Gladstone and Lord Selborne were the Peelite remnants. Hugh Childers, J. G. Dodson, George Trevelyan, Sir William Harcourt and W. E. Forster (despite his Radical origins) represented the work-horse, main-stream Liberals, the group which since the 1860s had formed the sturdy ballast of the party, and John Bright (until 1882), Joseph Chamberlain, and Sir Charles Dilke (from 1882) the Radicals (together with, in certain respects, Gladstone himself). All of these were English except Argyll, Rosebery and, depending on definitions, Gladstone, and all were nominally Anglicans except Argyll and Rosebery (Church of Scotland, the latter only when in Scotland), Bright (Quaker), and Chamberlain (Unitarian).* It was striking that the two Nonconformists, Bright and Chamberlain, came from numerically very small sects, and not from

---

* Forster, a former Quaker, as chief secretary regularly attended Anglican services in Dublin.

the great mass of Methodists and Congregationalists.* Despite the fact that most Roman Catholics voted Liberal, the Earl of Ripon was the only Roman Catholic ever to sit in a Liberal Cabinet, and his claims to office in 1886 on his return from India were based on his Cabinet experience before his conversion in 1874.† Apart from Argyll and the two Nonconformists, all had been at Oxford or Cambridge, and most had been either at Christ Church, Oxford or Trinity College, Cambridge (seven each). All of the fourteen members of the Cabinet when it was formed in 1880 had sat in it before, save four: Northbrook, Harcourt, Chamberlain, and Dodson. Of these, Northbrook and, to a lesser extent, Harcourt were experienced men of office, as Viceroy of India and Solicitor General respectively, and Dodson was a long-standing Deputy Speaker.

The Cabinet was thus very clearly a continuation of the previous Liberal administration of 1868–74—rather more so than that had been of the Palmerston/Russell years—and it reflected Gladstone's generally con-solidatory mood in 1880. It was, he noted, 'certainly a strong working Government in almost every department'. Only Chamberlain represented a new tone in 1880; his lack of experience in office was for Gladstone—a man reared in a family where rentier money paid for early entry to the Commons—a bar to his swift entry to the Cabinet. It was the inexperience rather than the tone which at this stage bothered Gladstone: he objected to Rosebery on the same grounds (though the objection was dramatically set aside to accommodate Morley as Irish Secretary in 1886). The consoli-datory character of the Cabinet was further emphasized in its reshuffles. The accessions of Carlingford, Rosebery, and especially Derby implied that the Whig seepage could be stopped and even reversed; in Dilke, Glad-stone recognized a man with some of his own executive capacity, and with Trevelyan and Shaw Lefevre he reassured the Liberal intelligentsia.

'Wonderfully harmonious' had been Kimberley's verdict on the first Gladstone Cabinet; he would hardly have written the same of that of 1880–5. As we have seen, uncertainty about Gladstone's position and the succes-sion prevented the Cabinet ever really settling, and the absence of an agreed major legislative measure—the equivalent of Irish Church dis-establishment in 1869—prevented a parliamentary consolidation of the 1880 election result. Nevertheless, the Cabinet coach rumbled along, few passengers actually leaving it. Nor did many threaten to do so before 1885. Despite the malaise, almost paralysis, which at times seemed to affect the

* Gladstone defended the number of Nonconformists against Henry Richard's complaints in December 1882: 'I may however say that Nonconformity was more largely represented in the two Cabinets it has been my duty to form, than in the Parliaments out of which they were formed'.

† Ripon's conversion caused considerable awkwardness in Gladstone's relationship to him; his appointment as Viceroy of India in May 1880 and not the Cabinet place which he could justly have otherwise claimed allowed a correspondence and intimacy which gained greatly from Ripon's physical remoteness.

Cabinet, despite the drawerful of letters of resignation written in the post-Gordon gloom of the spring of 1885—'Very fair Cabinet today—only three resignations' was Gladstone's laconic note on 16 May 1885*—the resignations in fact came to little. The Duke of Argyll resigned in 1881, as he had threatened to do in 1869, over Irish land. W. E. Forster resigned in May 1882, to a considerable extent driven out by the appointment of Spencer as Irish Viceroy (and still, as Lord President, in the Cabinet) and the Cabinet's 'new departure' in Irish policy.† John Bright resigned in 1882, as he had done in 1870, over foreign policy, in this case the bombardment of Alexandria. It would be neat, but facile, to say that more trouble was in fact caused by the Minister who, contrary to all convention, refused to resign when asked: Lord Carlingford.‡ Facile, because Bright's loss was serious. In the 1870s he had been persuaded to return; in the 1880s he left behind him as the representatives of radicalism Dilke and Chamberlain—both inexperienced and both, in their very different ways, catastrophic for the future of the radical cause. Gladstone's third government in 1886, found him in the same position as in 1880, the most radical Liberal of Cabinet rank. The difference was that the intervening years had led him to a new departure as to radicalism.

Gladstone had good relations with most members of his Cabinet. Although his political *persona* could never be described as whiggish, it is often forgotten how close Gladstone's personal relations with the leading Whigs were. He moved familiarly in Whig society, particularly within the Sutherland and Devonshire connections. Indeed, no one of non-landed origins was more intimately connected with those two great houses. Gladstone was, curiously, much closer socially to the hereditary Whigs than he was to what may be called the professional Whigs, men such as Northbrook. He married into a Whig family; his eldest son consolidated his links with the Sutherland family by marrying the granddaughter of Harriet, Duchess of Sutherland, his political patron in the Palmerstonian years; his closest political confidant, Granville, was a member of that same family; Granville's nephew, George Leveson Gower, was one of his secretaries (Henry Primrose, Rosebery's cousin, was another); his wife's niece, Lucy Lyttelton, whom he had partly brought up, married Lord Frederick Cavendish, Hartington's brother, whose death in the Phoenix Park murders in 1882 was as personal a blow to the Gladstones as it was to the

* That day he also listed the names of nine cabinet ministers, 'A majority', who had 'appeared to consider resignation' within the last month.

† See A. Warren, 'Forster, the Liberals and new directions in Irish policy 1880–2', *Parliamentary History*, vi (1987). The term 'new departure' was used at the time to describe the cabinet initiative in April–May 1882.

‡ A series of letters, of rising exasperation, failed to persuade Carlingford to go quietly in 1884. Nervous about the Whigs, Gladstone stopped short of simply demanding Carlingford's resignation; for the protracted negotiations, see the introduction to A. B. Cooke and J. Vincent, *Lord Carlingford's Journal* (1971).

Devonshires. Gladstone might be keeping Hartington from the premiership, but the latter's prominence in executive politics was due to Gladstone's persistence in bullying him into becoming Irish Secretary in 1870, and he offered him the Exchequer in 1882.* It was Hartington's nerve, not Gladstone's ambition, that limited his promotion.

Chamberlain sat at the opposite point of the Cabinet compass from the Whigs. Gladstone's letter in April 1880 offering the Cabinet adumbrated the differences: 'Your political opinions may on some points go rather beyond what I may call the general measure of the Government', and Chamberlain was cautioned as to Cabinet secrecy. The second proved more of a difficulty than the first. Chamberlain's legislative proposals in the 1880s were the equivalent of Gladstone's in the 1860s; they seemed alarming, but were not out of the question given the usual political game of give, take, and delay. Much more disturbing to the other members of the Cabinet were Radical Joe's leaks. To a body of men accustomed to intimate conversation, to protecting each other's weaknesses, to prevaricating in secret, and to working towards policy decisions sometimes over a period of months, the Radicals' and particularly, it was thought, Chamberlain's use of contacts with the Press seemed to threaten the viability of Cabinet government, to such an extent that a Cabinet committee on 'leakage from Cabinets' was set up in January 1882.† Of course, this was not the first time there had been leaks from Cabinets—indeed, contact with the Press was in no way unusual for Cabinet ministers—but it seems fairly clear that in 1880–5 the formulation and discussion of policy became awkward in a way not found in 1868–74, the leaks making an already difficult Cabinet worse.

Chamberlain and Dilke had a reason: the absence of a party structure and of an agreed programme gave the Cabinet considerable freedom. The party barely had a voice until it was too late: the legislation was drafted and introduced. In that secret process the Radicals often felt excluded and resorted to the leak to embarrass or warn off the Whigs. But this was the consequence of the absence of party structure discussed earlier, not a defect remediable by a method which to some extent spoiled executive government without achieving much in return. Gladstone's practice of avoiding calling Cabinets, and not allowing discussion of certain issues in those called, could be justified as avoiding leaks, and was thus more tolerated than it would otherwise have been. The upshot of the problem of the 'leaks' was their regularization in the form of 'the lobby', that peculiar British institutionalization of the 'leak' which began in 1884.

Though obviously not drawn to Chamberlain, Gladstone certainly had

* On 5 May 1882; the Phoenix Park murders next day made an immediate change impossible, but Hartington could have responded later to the offer.

† The committee curiously recommended an 'additional key' for various persons, the hope presumably being that if there were more keys, the dispatch boxes could be kept closed.

the basis for an understanding with him. As has been suggested, there were aspects of Radical Joe—his willingness to take on the Prime Minister, his use of the platform, his competence in the Commons—reminiscent of Gladstone in his Exchequer days in the 1860s, and Gladstone made the flattering comparison during the 1885 election campaign.* Moreover, Chamberlain was not unlike the Radicals of the Financial Reform Association of which Robertson, Gladstone's brother and Mayor of Liverpool, had been Chairman and which had backed Gladstone strongly in the 1850s. Robertson Gladstone's marriage had brought Unitarianism into the Gladstone family, easing the way for Gladstone's amicable relationship with the crony of his Penmaenmawr holidays, the prominent Unitarian Samuel Darbyshire. But not much was made of this. Gladstone's visit (not a social call) in 1877 to Southbourne, Chamberlain's house in Birmingham, was not reciprocated until he came to Hawarden as one of a string of ex-Cabinet ministers late in 1885. The cheery invitation to stay, quite a common ending to a Gladstonian letter to a colleague, never concluded one to Chamberlain. Gladstone devoted to Chamberlain none of the cossetting he had bestowed on John Bright. He accurately described Chamberlain's 'gifts' to him, 'a strong conviction, a masculine understanding, and a great power of clear expression', but he did not nurture them. Their relationship was businesslike, correct, cool, despite the fact that they were often in agreement on policy. But it was to Rosebery that Gladstone increasingly looked as 'the coming man'.

In the toss of business, and the often rather frenetic atmosphere in which the 1880–5 Cabinet existed, Gladstone found little time to encourage the weaker members of the Cabinet, or those with whom he did not naturally have close ties. Lord Carlingford (the Chichester Fortescue of the 1870 Land Act) is the best example. Brought into office when the 1881 Land Bill was at a vital stage in the Lords, and a considerable asset there, Carlingford was still frequently distraught as a result of the death of his wife, the former Lady Waldegrave. Rather ineffective in business, but quite shrewd on policy, Carlingford was not important but he could be useful. Gladstone seems simply to have lost patience with him. Carlingford's diary shows him to have been well-intentioned towards Gladstone and the Cabinet, though always a little distanced from it. He visited Ireland for some weeks in March 1882 and thus as a former Chief Secretary met the great 'Kilmainham' crisis of April and May exceptionally well-informed. None the less, it was as they entered St George's Chapel for Prince Leopold's wedding that

---

* *Political speeches 1885*, 107 (21 November 1885). Gladstone was a little sensitive when Rosebery returned to the point a few days later: 'Mr G. in great form this mg. taking a favourable view of the election & absorbed in Greville. . . . He talked much of Ld Palmerston & how he plotted against his finance. Speaking of some part of his character I said "Like Chamberlain?" "Ah but" he replied "I never knew that Chamberlain set up for having my character at all in politics"' (Rosebery's diary, Dalmeny House, 25 November 1885).

Gladstone told him of the *fait accompli* of the restructuring of the Irish Offices, including the odd requirement for Carlingford to act as Lord President (*vice* Spencer) without actually being appointed to the office. Carlingford noted: 'This was the first word he had said to me about Irish Govt. or legislation! a characteristic way of acting, wh. is not what I have a right to expect. I said so to Hartington, & he said "I thought you knew everything all along".'* It could be lonely outside the inner group of the Cabinet: Gladstone, Granville, Hartington, Harcourt, and perhaps Kimberley. As so often in his career, Gladstone expected his colleagues to be as resilient as he was. In Carlingford's case, the effect was to make a broken man belligerent. Pushed about, Carlingford dug in; made both Lord President and Lord Privy Seal in 1883, he refused in 1884 to take the important and demanding post of Ambassador in Constantinople to allow Rosebery to enter the Cabinet. The cumulative effect of poor management was to produce later a considerable, if minor, irritation. The neglect of Carlingford was the sillier as he and Gladstone sat next to each other in Cabinet. This was because Gladstone had placed Argyll on his left at the Cabinet table and Carlingford had taken his place. The opportunity for a friendly word thus occurred frequently.

How important the Cabinet's seating was could only be known to those present. We do know that Gladstone took some trouble with the placings, as his planning diagram shows. It is reproduced in the illustrations to this book. He himself sat in the middle of the long side of the Cabinet table. Granville, who chaired the Cabinet in the Prime Minister's absence, sat on Gladstone's right—clearly a key placing for the passing of notes as well as a compliment. Most of Gladstone's surviving notes passed in Cabinet are between him and either Granville or Derby (who sat on Granville's right). Granville thus linked up with a little clutch of Whigs, but Hartington was slightly isolated between Trevelyan and Harcourt. Chamberlain and Dilke sat together opposite Gladstone. This might be seen as an attempt to isolate them or keep an eye on them. But more likely the opposite was the

* Carlingford's diary, 27 April 1882, Add MS 63690. In fact, Carlingford did know a good deal from Spencer from an important talk on 19 April, and Gladstone may have thought this was enough: Spencer 'also told me that Mr G's idea is to make no change in the Cabinet, & for that purpose to leave him, Spencer, President of the Council, although Lord Lt. [of Ireland *vice* Cowper] & to get me to do the work of the Council Office—a strange arrangement wh. I dislike the thought of ... he alluded to other possible shiftings wh. he did not explain. It does not look well for me. Spencer mentioned the names of Kimberley & Dilke as having to do with arrangements wh. were in Gladstone's mind—& also said that it wd be a good thing to move Forster from the Irish Office, on account of the intense hostility to him of the Parnellites, although it could not be done now, as it wd look like sacrificing him & like a change of policy. I think I see what the plan is—to keep the Council Office for Kimberley (who wd have the lead of the H of Lords, or the F.O., or both before his eyes in the future), make F[orster] Colonial Secretary (his great ambition), and Dilke Chief Sec. [for Ireland] in the Cabinet. Nous verrons.' Carlingford's diary is an important source for this Cabinet; it is now in the British Library, save for 1885 (which is largely in print, ed. Cooke and Vincent).

case: they offered Gladstone a ready echo or even amplifications for views with which the Whigs were likely to disagree. The psychological and physical interplay of those long and often discursive Cabinet meetings cannot be recaptured. Gladstone made little attempt to use his diary for such a purpose, and most of the other members of the Cabinet seem to have taken its procedures for granted, though Rosebery noted on attending his second Cabinet: 'I was more accustomed to the abruptness of manner wh surprised me yesterday.'*

The Cabinet usually met weekly on Saturday (or sometimes on Friday) during the Session, i.e. less frequently than Disraeli's Cabinet which usually met twice-weekly in the Session. Gladstone's secretary, E. W. Hamilton, occasionally attended for particular items, but to advise on facts, not to take notes. During the discussions on Commons' procedure and the Bradlaugh affair, the Speaker and Erskine May, the Clerk of the Commons, were sometimes called in. Sir Evelyn Baring once attended to advise on Egypt. Apart from these rare intrusions, the Cabinet met alone. Its proceedings were essentially conversational. In addition to the required formal letter to the Queen, Gladstone maintained his habit of recording its decisions in brief minutes, sometimes written onto an agenda. This 'hasty noting down, scratching rather than writing' of the 'heads of business as it goes on' was done during the Cabinet 'so that I may not have to rely solely on my memory'. The result was admittedly 'slipshod', though it was much more than any other Victorian Prime Minister attempted.

In 1884, at the height of the pressure of events and particularly concerned that decisions about the proposed Gordon expedition be accurately recorded, Gladstone seems to have considered a return to the formal 'Minutes of Cabinet' of the early nineteenth-century, including the possibility of having them signed by the Cabinet Ministers, presumably so as to tie individual Ministers to unpopular decisions and policies. Nothing came of this. For the change to have been more than an occasional formal recording of particularly important decisions would have implied a secretary—either one of the members of Cabinet acting as such, or an additional person. To give the power of minuting to a colleague would have been dangerous; to alter the informality of Cabinet conversation by introducing a clerk, however dignified, was, as yet, unthinkable and never seems even to have been suggested. Thus Gladstone's recording of Cabinet proceedings remained as it had been in his first ministry, whilst his letters to the Queen became, as relations deteriorated, if anything more arch and, on domestic and party politics, more discreet or silent.

Gladstone called an average of fifty Cabinets a year (forty-eight if allowance is not made for those missed during his absence at Cannes in 1883), the same as in his first government. This surprisingly high average is

* Rosebery's diary, 17 February 1885.

sustained by the fact that there were special autumn Sessions in both 1882 (procedure) and 1884 (franchise and redistribution), the Cabinet having to meet to discuss the legislative timetable.

It was a well-established convention that the Cabinet met several times in the autumn and sometimes in January to agree to the chief legislative priorities for the next year.* The Irish Land Bill Cabinets in late 1880 followed almost exactly the pattern for the preparation of the Land Bill in 1869 (though in that year the autumn Cabinets also planned for the Education Bill and a complex structure of other legislation). In 1881, however, only one Cabinet discussed prospective legislation (10 November 1881): a bold plan of 'efficient local Govt. over Ireland & Scotland: London included but not in the van' was adumbrated. But the lack of Prime Ministerial commitment was immediately shown: the plan was remitted to a Cabinet committee of which Gladstone was not a member. Consequently the Cabinet met Parliament in 1882 with its plans confused and its disputes unresolved. In the autumn of 1882, with the special Session on procedure, the Cabinet met quite frequently. But Gladstone's impending retirement, and the Cabinet reshuffle relieving him of the Exchequer, account in part for the fact that no discussion of prospective legislation is recorded. In 1883, autumn planning Cabinets agreed to a County Government Bill for 1884 (again referred to a committee without Gladstone as a member—as we shall see, a sign of lack of political will) and to a Franchise Bill supervised by Gladstone. Whether redistribution was to be included was left for a time as an open question, which gave Hartington time to come round, as he did. This openness caused some confusion, some of the Cabinet thinking, with some justification, that a decision had been taken.† Gladstone's minute of 22 November 1883 is clear enough: 'Redistribution: not to be united with franchise.' The 1884 autumn Cabinets monitored the constitutional crisis but planned nothing of major consequence for 1885. If it was 'big Bills' that kept the Liberal party in good heart, this sad record shows that the successes of the government and the party came despite the planning of the Cabinet.

The composition of the Cabinet was intended largely to reassure, and in doing so it reflected not only the restorative frame of mind in which Gladstone approached his second premiership, but also a more general hiatus in the development of Liberalism. The decade of the 1880s can be seen both

---

* i.e. those that were contentious and required particular Cabinet attention; a regular diet of relatively uncontentious matter went undiscussed, or at any rate unrecorded, at these meetings, its place in the timetable decided mainly by the leader of the House (i.e. Gladstone), the Whigs and the relevant ministers; such bills usually came before Cabinet only at the moment of being dropped at the end of the Session when the timetable became overburdened.

† e.g. Chamberlain; see to Hartington, 7 Dec. 83. The distinction was that if there was a reform bill, redistribution would follow rather than be included in the franchise bill; technically, the Cabinet was not yet committed to a bill, though one was being drawn up.

as the last of the old Liberal party and as the first of the new. It stands poised awkwardly between defending the achievements of the past and building upon those achievements a new structure which would recognize a fresh phase in the evolution of industrial society. The 1880s were, there-fore, an awkward moment for the party of progress. The ambivalence of the party's and the government's direction opened both to domination by crises. Any government is, of course, likely suddenly to be affected by an unexpected crisis, but a government, and especially a progressive govern-ment, which is uncertain about its own direction is likely to find such crises particularly difficult.

Moreover, we now know that the crises of the 1880s in Ireland, in foreign and imperial affairs, and to some extent in domestic politics also, were in considerable measure affected by a common stimulus whose very existence the Liberals denied: the recession in the world economy. Orthodox politi-cal economy could not admit more than a temporary dislocation to the balance of equilibrium, and they believed that the re-establishment of that balance needed only the corrective forces of the free market. Consequently, the Liberal ex-Cabinet refused to sit on the Royal Commission on the Depression of Trade set up by Salisbury in 1885, because to do so would admit the possibility that such a depression could exist and would associate Liberals with an inquiry which would at the least consider protectionist solutions. Because in terms of orthodox Liberal political economy no long-term depression could or did exist, no general explanation of the phe-nomena of the 1880s could be offered by Liberals. The various crises were thus seen as having discrete and usually political causes. Crises thus reared up unanticipated and to a large extent unexplained,* being dealt with in their overt terms. Though developments in imperial policy sometimes reached simultaneous pitches of intensity—Ireland and the Transvaal in December 1881 and the spring of 1882—what is striking is the extent to which, for members of the Cabinet, regional policies remained regional. Though there were obvious similarities between Ireland and the Trans-vaal, only the odd comment suggests a recognition of this; indeed, in Glad-stone's mind and writings, much less so than his analysis of 'conquest' and subsequent 'amalgamation' made in the late 1870s would lead us to expect.

It would not be hard to present the first half of the 1880s simply as a series of events and crises buffetting the Cabinet and the government. But this would be misleading. Crises there certainly were. But Gladstone and his colleagues had a clear sense of the categories within which they under-

* Thus Sir Hercules Robinson, the liberal and perceptive colonial governor, wrote in January 1884: 'How strange it is that the Government which came in on the platform of curtailing Imperial responsibilities should be likely to add more to them than any previous Ministry in the present century—New Guinea, the South Pacific, South Africa—and last but not least Egypt, in which we are drifting into a protectorate. It is surely the irony of fate'; *Correspondence of J. X. Merriman*, ed. P. Lewsen (1960), 155.

stood and analysed the various crises with which they had to deal. To analyse the pattern of events and to discuss the peculiar contribution which Gladstone made to his second government, it will be convenient to retain these discrete categories and to examine them in the following order: colonial, foreign, and defence policy; the domestic legislative programme and the economy; Ireland.

Some have seen Gladstone as governed merely by expediency. He, even in a government of which his membership was intended to be temporary, saw himself primarily as an executant, a defender and, as circumstances required, an originator of policy. Detailed scrutiny reveals a much more coherent and consistent approach to policy than the *ad hoc* character of the second and third Gladstone governments which is suggested by a first glance.

CHAPTER VI

Colonial, Foreign, and Defence Policy, 1880–1885

*Six Principles—India, Islam, and Central Asia—'Egypt for the Egyptians'?—
Gladstone as Bondholder—Liberals as Imperialists: the Bombardment, Occupation, and Settlement of Egypt—Gordon at Khartoum: the Mahdists 'struggling
rightly to be free'—African Scramble: Central, East, and South—Foreign Policy
and the Navy Scare, 1884*

Cabinet, Monday Jul. 31. 82. 2 PM...
3. Instructions to Wolseley; Put down Arabi & establish Khedive's
power. Alison to pass under Wolseley's authority when he arrives. &
other points.*

Conclave on Egypt $12\frac{1}{2}$–$2\frac{1}{2}$. Another flood of good news. No more
blood I hope. Wolseley in Cairo: Arabi a prisoner: God be praised.†

After 11 AM I heard the sad news of the fall or betrayal of Khartoum: H. & I, with C. went off by the first train & reached D. St
soon after 8.15. The circumstances are sad & trying: it is one of the
least points about them, that they may put an end to this Govt.‡

H. of C. $4\frac{3}{4}$–8 and $10\frac{1}{2}$–2. The pressure of affairs, especially Soudan,
Egypt, & Afghan, is now from day to day extreme.§

Six Principles

Colonial or, as it was increasingly called, Imperial policy and foreign policy
were the chief areas in which Gladstone intended to restore right conduct
and right principles after the disasters of Beaconsfieldism. Gladstone had
seen these disasters as caused by individual failures of 'panic or pride'
within what he saw as a systematic perversion of good government: good
men with right principles—'the exercise of moral control over ambition
and cupidity'—could restore proper conduct and right relations. Though
recognizing Britain's inherent capacity for Empire, he explicitly declined
to accept that there was any underlying or determinist pattern of causation

---

* Cabinet minutes for 31 July 1882.
† Diary for 15 Sept. 82.
‡ Diary for 5 Feb. 85.
§ Diary for 16 Mar. 85.

in recent accessions. On the other hand, he did recognize that certain regional policies, once put in train, were difficult to stop, and he was careful in his criticisms in Midlothian in 1879 and 1880 to avoid absolute commitments and to decline to disavow agreements entered into by the Conservative government. Consequently, despite the apparent differences, British policy in this period was much less oscillating than the French, whose internal political instability was reflected in violent swings in Imperial policy.

In Midlothian in 1879 Gladstone told the electors 'what I think to be the right principles of foreign policy'. These were 1. good government at home, 2. the preservation to the nations of the world, and 'especially to the Christian nations of the world', of the blessings of peace, 3. the cultivation and maintenance of the Concert of Europe, 4. the avoidance of needless and entangling engagements, 5. to acknowledge the equal rights of all nations, 6. the foreign policy of England [sic] should always be inspired by the love of freedom.*

These famous 'six principles' were cautiously qualified ('avoid needless and entangling engagements') at the same time as bold. But on the fifth principle, the acknowledgement of 'the equal rights of all nations', Gladstone was unequivocal: this was the principle to which he attached the 'greatest value' and to which he returned in his peroration:

Christendom is formed of a band of nations who are united to one another in the bond of right; ... they are without distinction of great and small; there is an absolute equality between them ... he who by act or word brings that principle into peril or disparagement, however honest his intentions may be, places himself in the position of one inflicting ... injury upon his own country, and endangering the peace and all the most fundamental interests of Christian society.†

This passage seemed of world-wide application, but in its context it applied to Europe. The ambivalence haunted Gladstone through the imperial crises of his second government.

Moreover, it is important again to recall that Gladstone was, outside free trade, no Cobdenite. He saw intervention as a natural part of the maintenance of the civilized order of the world. He used military and naval force coolly and without embarrassment. Every Cabinet that he had sat in since 1843 had dispatched a military expedition. He willingly led the Concert of Europe in sending a fleet against the Sultan in the autumn of 1880 to force a solution of the dispute over the frontier of Montenegro. On 12 July 1882, the day after the bombardment of Alexandria, Sir Wilfrid Lawson jibed that if a Tory government had been in office Gladstone would have

---

* *Political Speeches* (1879), 115ff. (third Midlothian speech, 27 November 1879).
† Ibid., 129.

stopped his train at every station to proclaim non-intervention as the duty of the government. Lawson's jibe produced this angry retort:

He seems to think that I am a general apostle of non-intervention. I do not, however, see why he should say so; he has quoted nothing that bears out that view. On the contrary, if he will take the trouble to recollect, all my objections to the conduct of the late Government for a certain time—in the year 1876 and the year 1877—were, he will find, expressly founded on the charge that we had not had intervention enough.[*]

It was where to intervene, and where not to be drawn into intervention, and for what reasons, that concerned Gladstone. And that was a question of policy and balance of advantage.[†] A reconciliation between the 'equal rights of all nations' and the requirements of international order was a highly problematic duty for the Liberal Prime Minister of an imperial power.

Gladstone sought no expansion of British imperial responsibilities. He was consequently ready to concede that other powers might expand if they wished to. He was certainly not, as some Liberals were, hostile to colonization *per se*, but accepted it, subject to certain provisos, as entirely natural if the relevant European nation judged it to be in her interest. Thus he twice publicly welcomed German colonial expansion, while sceptical as to whether it was really in Germany's interest:

if Germany has the means of expanding herself and sending her children to unoccupied places of the earth, with due regard to the previous rights of other nations, and with due regard to the rights of the aboriginal inhabitants—subject to those two reserves, gentlemen, I tell you I look with satisfaction, sympathy, and joy upon the expansion of Germany in these desert places of the earth, upon the extension of civilization, and upon the blessing to these waste places by the presence of an intelligent, industrious community, which will bring forth from the bosom of the land new resources for the comfort, advantage, and happiness of mankind. Do not suppose for a moment that it is anything but the utmost meanness for us to be jealous of Germany. Germany cannot rob this country, even if she desired it, of her colonizing character. It is evident—no man can deny it—that it is among the most patent and palpable facts of the condition of the world, that God Almighty has given to the people who inhabit these islands a great function and a great duty of colonization. And that duty has been fulfilled by a pretty liberal appropriation of the country which had not been occupied. Come what may, let every other country

---

[*] *H* 272. 174.

[†] Confronted by A. I. Myers, proprietor of the *Jewish Chronicle*, with information about the Russian pogrom of 1881, Gladstone asked Olga Novikov if there was any satisfactory reply that could be made to the appalling charges. Novikov dismissed the reports as mere Jewish 'agitation'. Gladstone fell back on the argument that in 1851 (Naples) and in 1876 (Bulgaria) he had been a private citizen urging the government to action; it was now for others to do the same—a very weak argument as the object of his previous actions had been a change in government policy, the sort of change he was now in a position to make. He also argued that 'the interference of foreign governments in such cases is more likely to do harm than good'.

do what it will,—it is for them to consider how far their political strength will be increased by it. Into that question I do not enter.*

Gladstone looked to balance and stability in the Empire. The essential strength of the Empire sprang, he believed, from the power of the British economy. Anything that diminished that power, such as increased taxation, was undesirable. He was thus a leading exponent of that school which has criticized the extent of Britain's world-wide defence commitment as an important economic incubus and, as the imperial epoch in British history recedes, his views have received increasingly powerful historiographical support.† During his first government a determined effort was made to force local defence costs on to colonies with responsible government, and the criticism of over-extension was, as we have seen, central to his attack on Beaconsfieldism. If there had to be Protectorates, he looked to Selborne's minimalist, and cheap, definition of British responsibility in them.‡ He showed little interest in the anti-slavery cause which made imperial expansion and intervention acceptable to many Liberals.

Gladstone's imperial interest had been largely in the areas of significant European settlement. In those, 'progress' would occur through responsible government and the development of suitably adapted British-style ways of behaving. He remained an active trustee of the Colonial Bishoprics Fund. But 'progress' in the areas of imperial acquisition which were not suitable for European settlement produced a paradox: it depended on a much greater element of governmental intervention (ultimately a matter of metropolitan decision) than free-trade and minimal-state supporters such as Gladstone were easy with. He showed no interest whatever in Dilke–Chamberlain notions of pro-active imperial government. The sort of government introduced in much of Africa as a result of what were predominantly Liberal acquisitions consequently embalmed rather than galvanized the occupied localities. It is hard to judge whether this was advantageous to them or not; but it was a strange consequence of Liberal imperialism.

India, Islam, and Central Asia

Strategic concern about the 'route to India' was not one of Gladstone's principles of foreign policy, and he was 'one of those who think that to the actual, as distinguished from the reported, strength of the Empire, India

* In Edinburgh, 1 September 1884, in *Speeches in Scotland, 1884*, 78.

† See L. E. Davis and R. A. Huttenback, *Mammon and the pursuit of Empire. The political economy of British imperialism 1860–1912* (1986) and P. K. O'Brien, 'The costs and benefits of British imperialism 1846–1914', *Past and Present*, 120 (1988).

‡ See Selborne's memorandum on the different responsibilities involved in annexation (normally leading to a 'colony') and in declaring a protectorate (PRO FO 84/1819) and W. R. Louis, 'The Berlin Congo Conference', in P. Gifford and W. R. Louis, *France and Britain in Africa* (1971), 209–13.

adds nothing. She immensely adds to the responsibility of Government. . . .' On the other hand, he continued, recognizing the imprisonment of his world vision in the cage of history, 'none of this is to the purpose. We have undertaken a most arduous but a most noble duty. We are pledged to India, I may say to mankind, for its performance and we have no choice. . . .'*

This was the position in which Gladstone constantly found himself with respect to Imperial affairs. His executive role countervailed his inclinations and ultimate anticipations. From the failure to hold in balance these two forces sprang many of his difficulties. But the existence of both these forces, and his spasmodic skill in employing them, allowed him considerable manœuvre in Cabinet, in the Commons, and in his appeal to public support.

The Midlothian Campaign and victory at the polls in 1880 had an important effect in India: a significant change of tone on the part of the Imperial government and a sense among some Indians that the dismantling of 'Beaconsfieldism' could have long-term benefits for India. It cannot be said that Gladstone gave frequent attention to Indian affairs, but he undoubtedly sensed the character of the change that was occurring. On the whole he welcomed it. When he did intervene it was to stiffen the resolution of Lord Ripon, the Viceroy he appointed almost immediately on the formation of the 1880 government; Gladstone saw Ripon's job as being to end what they both saw as the eccentricities of the Tory government in its Indian policy. But the restoration of normality in itself involved change. Repealing 'that disgraceful [Vernacular] Press Act . . . one of the last steps in the great undoing process which the late Government bequeathed to us' was an encouragement to Indian opinion and provided the context for the violent reaction of the British community to Ilbert's Criminal Procedure Amendment Bill which allowed certain Indians jurisdiction over Europeans. It was also the context within which the first National Conference was convened in Calcutta (in December 1883) from which developed the Indian National Congress, founded in 1885. Advised by his son Harry (in Calcutta with the family firm of Ogilvy, Gillanders), Gladstone at each stage in the extended negotiations about the bill in 1883 and 1884 encouraged Ripon not to back down in the face of the hostility of the British merchant community. He certainly saw the question as establishing the general direction of power in India:

There is a question to be answered; where, in a country like India, lies the ultimate power, and if it lies for the present on one side but for the future on the other, a problem has to be solved as to preparation for that future, and it may become right and needful to chasten the saucy pride so apt to grow in the English mind towards

* To Ripon, 4 Nov. 81.

foreigners, and especially towards foreigners whose position has been subordinate. The uprising of native opinion on your side is a circumstance full of interest.*

The row over the Ilbert Bill was more over symbol than over a substantial shift of balance of power within India. But in a country where British rule was, more than anywhere in the Empire, an artful show of flummery backed by an army, symbol was of peculiar importance. The repeal of the Press Act and the enactment of the Ilbert Bill suggested much. 'Great interests of the future seem to me to be at stake,' Gladstone told Ripon.† But the direction of that future he left largely to take its own course. The importance of the Ripon–Gladstone period in India was marked in British as well as Indian politics. Immediately after helping to form the Indian National Congress in 1885, Dababhai Naoroji stood (unsuccessfully) as Liberal candidate for Holborn. He was elected for Finsbury Central in 1892. By the end of the 1880–5 government, the association of Liberalism with the first modern nationalist movement outside these islands was explicit. That part of Gladstone's policy that looked beyond the immediate context of imperial security was, as usual with him, powerfully effective in emphasizing the comprehensiveness of the Liberal party.

Imperial security in the East was, however, the immediate concern of the 1880 government. The Cabinet faced acute instability at either end of the Islamic area: in Afghanistan, and in Egypt and its satellite, the Sudan. The Conservative government had bought the nest egg of the Suez Canal shares; it had declared, as Gladstone saw it, a 'new Asiatic Empire' through the Anglo-Turkish Convention of June 1878; and it had embarked on a forward policy in central Asia which led to punitive expeditions, the imposition of a new ruler, Abdur Rahman, in Afghanistan, and the possibility of a military presence there for the foreseeable future. This was, in Gladstone's view, primarily inexpedient and imprudent; it was morally wrong only in the execution of the policy.

The British government seemed to extricate itself from Afghanistan, but found itself doing in Egypt what it avoided on the North West frontier of India, and on a far more lavish scale. Militarily overstretched, the government ended with a crisis in each area as the Russians took advantage of the disaster in the Sudan and the consequent instability of the Gladstone government to push forward against the Afghan frontier.

In Central Asia, the subject of the first cabinet of the ministry on 3 May 1880, Gladstone had his way. Ripon was appointed Viceroy, leaving on

* To Ripon, 17 Apr. 83.

† To Ripon, 1 June 83. A more traditional aspect of Gladstone's treatment of India was his energetic assertion of Britain's right to extract a substantial contribution from India to help pay for the Egyptian expedition of 1882. It was eventually agreed that India should pay all of the cost, £1,297,000, minus a British grant of £500,000. This was despite Ripon's (equally traditional) objections on behalf of the Indian government that there had been insufficient consultation with India and that Indian interest in Egyptian security had been greatly exaggerated by London.

14 May 1880, after Gladstone had worked out for Granville, almost immediately on taking office, the bones of a policy. Salisbury's negotiation with
Persia to partition Afghanistan (by Persia's absorbing Herat) was immediately broken off.* Gladstone led the Cabinet in the withdrawal from most
of Afghanistan, achieved by the spring of 1881, against the advice of the
Queen and many others. But the evacuation of troops from Afghanistan
was by no means an abandonment of the area, merely an abandonment of
the 'forward policy' method of safeguarding it. A stable *régime* in Afghanistan was a better safeguard than an imposed one, especially if it could give
effective British control without direct responsibility. Thus the way continued through 1880 until the defeat at Maiwand was exceeded by the
victory at Mazra. Abdur Rahman emerged the victor in the fratricidal
struggle for power, his *régime* backed by a British guarantee against un-
provoked aggression, in return for British control of Afghanistan's external
relations,† a guarantee confirmed and extended by Hartington in August
1881 following further Russian activity. Prompted by the Indian government, and strongly supported by Northbrook, the former Viceroy,‡
Hartington, the Secretary for India, then proposed a treaty between Britain
and Russia, confirming the Afghan frontier in exchange for tacit acceptance of Russian expansion up to it. This was too bold for Granville, who
fell back on the agreement of 1873 and the internal strengthening of
Afghanistan. Hartington's enthusiasm for a treaty waned, and Northbrook
was subsequently unable to gain Cabinet attention for the proposal.§

Gladstone seems to have shown no interest in the idea of a treaty. But
Russia was expanding naturally under her own momentum, there being
never a serious proposal of a double buffer: a Turkestan buffer to protect
the Afghan buffer. When in 1883 Russia demanded from Persia territory
which would 'place Russia in contact with Afghan frontier', Gladstone
noted 'There can be no objection.' The chance of bargaining an agreed
frontier against Russian expansion into Turkestan passed, and Russia, in a
British-style manœuvre, accepted the invitation of the local elders in

---

* See F. Kazemzadeh, *Russia and Britain in Persia 1864–1914* (1968), 72.

† See C. Howard, *Britain and the* Casus Belli *1822–1902* (1974), 116. Abdur Rahman was Lytton's
choice as a stable ruler, despite his extensive exile in Russia; he was subsequently backed by Ripon
despite the hostility of Stewart, whom the Cabinet had made political adviser as well as military
commander at Kabul.

‡ Northbrook to Ripon, 19 May 1882, Add MS 43572: 'The question of a Treaty with Russia
unluckily came before the Cabinet at the only cabinet since the Govt. was formed at which I was
not present, having been at Balmoral. I believe the opinion was adverse to taking any steps towards
a treaty . . .'; on 9 July 1882, ibid., f. 47: 'You and I are in a minority on the Treaty question.' Northbrook observed Russia's move to Merv with equanimity: 'If we have a conciliatory answer from
Russia, we propose to enter into negotiations for laying down the N. Western boundary of
Afghanistan by Russian and English officers, and I hope to have this embodied in a Treaty. This is
what you & I have long wished for' (Northbrook to Ripon, 22 February 1884, ibid., f. 96).

§ See Northbrook to Ripon, 11 March, 19 May, 9 July 1882, Add MS 43572, ff. 6, 31, 47.

February 1885 to control of the ancient city of Merv.* The moment expected for twenty years had come: Russia was effectively on the Afghan frontier. The logical boundary commission followed, the building of the railway to Quetta was again recommended, and Russian brinkmanship† at Pendjeh in March–May 1885 was resolutely blocked.

The sturdy resistance of Gladstone and his Cabinet is sometimes thought of as a ploy to extricate them from the Sudan in the early months of 1885.‡ But it was in fact wholly in line with their Afghan policy: a friendly, nominally independent and therefore static Afghan state clearly and boldly defended, and with no attempt to meddle with Russia beyond that. What had changed was the need to give precise definition to the frontier. This became necessary once Russia was at Merv; the 'masterly inactivity' school, particularly represented in Cabinet by Northbrook, felt it undesirable to define it earlier. Definition would merely encourage Russia and might force a greater British involvement in Afghanistan's internal affairs. This squared with Gladstone's view: Russian expansion in Central Asia was natural and, with respect to India, benign. There was, in his view, no Russian plan or intention to invade British India; an independent, unified, and guaranteed Afghanistan was therefore a quite sufficient bastion.

Despite constant Conservative charges of negligence and weakness, the Afghan policy was a notable success. In the spring of 1885, without annexation, the Russians were firmly halted at a viable frontier. For the rest of the Imperial period, they never crossed it. 'Surely it must set for a *few* hours' was the apprehensive question of the Bokharan gentry to the traveller Henry Lansdell§ when he told them in the early 1880s that on the Queen's Empire the sun was unceasingly shining: at least in Central Asia the Liberal Cabinet ensured that there was no British protectorate for Tommy Atkins to defend in the noon-day glare.

Gladstone began and ended his second government resolutely involved in Central Asian affairs. He was not much otherwise directly engaged in the subject because he did not have to be. There was a depth of experience and competence on the Liberal side, deepened by the bonus of Northbrook's presence in the Cabinet. Moreover, there was a general agreement that 'Mervousness' as Argyll dubbed it—panic that Russian extension to the Afghan border implied Russian plans to invade India—was wholly

---

* See R. L. Greaves, *Persia and the defence of India 1884–1892* (1959), ch. iv.

† That it was such can be seen from D. Geyer, *Russian Imperialism. The interaction of domestic and foreign policy 1860–1914* (1987), 114.

‡ Holland, ii. 31. For a useful comment on this see *In relief of Gordon. Lord Wolseley's campaign journal of the Khartoum relief expedition 1884–5*, ed. A. Preston (1870) [subsequently: *Relief of Gordon*], xliii.

§ H. Lansdell, *Through Central Asia* (1887), 352, quoted in A. P. Thornton, 'Essay and reflection: third thoughts on Empire', *Int. Hist. Rev.*, x. 592 (1988); Lansdell has a useful map and Appendix on the 1885–6 border dispute.

unnecessary. Though the command structure for dealing with the area was complex, involving the Prime Minister, the Foreign Secretary, the Indian Secretary and his Council in London, the Viceroy and his Council in India, the exercise of authority within it was containable and worked well. It was clear what the policy, once established, was, and it was clearly executed. The effectiveness of the structure was well illustrated by the majestic display in the spring of 1885 as the Executive, Parliament, and the Empire in the East were swiftly and easily placed on a war footing backed by an £11 million Vote of Credit (i.e. 10 per cent of the annual budget).

'Egypt for the Egyptians'?

Authority with respect to Egypt was, by contrast, at every turn confused and oblique. If Ireland was the great deflector in domestic policy, so was Egypt in foreign and imperial. The Ottoman Empire nominally ruled North Africa. In Egypt the Sultan's authority was rarely effective, though he retained his position as a religious leader and even reformers claimed to act in his service as representative of the realm of Islam.* European authority was already asserted by the Anglo-French Dual Control of 1876 and 1879, and de Lesseps retained the 'Concession' of the Canal. Disraeli's purchase of the Suez Canal shares in 1875 had exemplified the extent to which the general interest of safeguarding an international waterway was also a particular British imperial and now also financial interest.

Gladstone's campaigns of the 1870s had given a general impression of hostility to the Ottoman Empire, and the Sultan cannot have welcomed the start of Gladstone's second political career. In fact, however, Gladstone had seen Turkish suzerainty over locally autonomous Christian states as the best way of maintaining stability in the Balkans, and had disliked independence and partition.† But his public and private views had hardly been flattering to the Sultan, and in the early months of the government he energetically pursued the Balkan boundary question, being prepared to use British force to coerce the Porte if the Concert failed to act. In 1881 the Sultan lost Tunis to the French. There was never any serious question of British opposition to this move, effectively an extension of Algeria. Gladstone covered the Liberals' position by publishing some of the dispatches on Salisbury's promises in 1878 which seemed to recognize the naturalness of France's expansion, and which had, in Gladstone's view

---

* A. Schölch, *Egypt for the Egyptians! The socio-political crisis in Egypt 1878–82* (1981), 284, a remarkable, original book. See also J. S. Galbraith and Afaf Lufti al-Sayyid-Marsot, 'The British occupation of Egypt. Another view', *International Journal of Middle East Studies*, ix (1978).

† See above, Ch. I; Gladstone's view was similar to his policy in the 1860s on compulsory church rates: pruning the rotten bough to maintain the tree.

(conveniently?), 'cut away the ground (Italy being out of the question) from under our feet'. This worked for domestic politics; it did not improve British influence with the Sultan. The consequence of all this was that the Liberal government had no capital to draw on as it looked to Constantinople to maintain order in Egypt.

The autochthonous Egyptian reform movement led by Arabi Pasha, prompted in part by the British/French attempt to rule Egypt through the imposed Khedive Tewfik (equally disliked by the Sultan)· and through the treasury in the form of the Dual Control of 1879 and in part also by the French occupation of Tunis, was at first reported not altogether unsympathetically by Colvin, the British controller of finance, and by Malet, the British consul.* Gladstone's reaction to it was to see it sympathetically through the eyes of Wilfrid Scawen Blunt in the sort of terms he had used for Balkan nationalism, a form of analysis which in 1882 he notably did not use with respect to Ireland:

I suppose we are entitled to hold the present position so far as it is necessary to guarantee the pecuniary interests on behalf of which we have in this somewhat exceptional case been acting in Turkey.

But I should regard with the utmost apprehension a conflict between the 'Controul' and any sentiment truly national, with a persuasion that one way or other we should come to grief in it.

I am not by any means pained, but I am much surprised at this rapid development of a national sentiment and party in Egypt. The very ideas of such a sentiment and the Egyptian people seemed quite incompatible. How it has come up I do not know: most of all is the case strange if the standing army be the nest that has reared it. There however it seems to be, & to claim the respect due to it as a fact, and due also to the capabilities that may be latent in it for the future. 'Egypt for the Egyptians' is the sentiment to which I should wish to give scope: and could it prevail it would I think be the best, the only good solution of the 'Egyptian question'.†

When Wilfrid Blunt in December 1881 sent the 'Programme of the National Party of Egypt' written by Arabi and himself, Gladstone felt 'quite sure that unless there be a sad failure of good sense on one or both or as I should say on all sides, we shall be enabled to bring this question to a favourable issue'.‡ But, partly at Granville's urging, Gladstone backed away from this contact.§

* Schölch, op. cit., 185–6.

† To Granville, 4 January 1882, in Agatha Ramm, *Political correspondence of Mr. Gladstone and Lord Granville 1876–1886*, 2v. (1962) [subsequently: Ramm II], i. 326.

‡ To Blunt, 20 Jan. 82; see also W. S. Blunt, *Secret history of the English occupation of Egypt* (1907) [subsequently: Blunt, *Secret history*], 202, 559. After the occupation Gladstone, perhaps not surprisingly, found Blunt 'intolerable' but retained some sense—more than Granville—of the possible force of his criticisms; see Ramm II, ii. 97, 101, 104 and *Modern Egypt by the Earl of Cromer*, 2v. (1908) [subsequently: Cromer], i. 279–80.

§ Blunt's subsequent letters were dealt with by E. W. Hamilton; from them Hamilton—already a friend of Blunt—gained the view of a moderate, non-belligerent Arabi now largely held by

Blunt was to be no Mrs O'Shea, and Gladstone's knowledge of Egyptian developments depended subsequently on official reports. The reports of Colvin and Malet from February 1882, increasingly hostile to the reform party and Arabi, prepared the way for European occupation: 'it would . . . be necessary, if it be determined that the present state of things cannot be allowed to continue, that an occupation of the country should precede its reorganization, but it would be wise to allow the experiment to prove itself clearly impracticable before such a measure is resorted to. For very clear grounds can alone justify the suppression by arms of the effort of a country to govern itself.'* Moreover, there was always a difficulty for Liberals in seeing constitutional nationalism as worthily embodied in an army, and, however broadly based Arabi's movement may have been, its prospects of success always depended on the army.

As during 1882 the situation in Egypt developed (or deteriorated in the view of many Europeans), the following points need to be borne in mind about Gladstone's position. He was not in principle hostile to intervention for the preservation of order, but this had to be balanced by the claims of local autonomous powers. It was hard for anyone dependent on the information about Egypt being supplied by Malet and Colvin in the spring and summer of 1882 to believe other than that the Arabi movement represented disorder promoted by a small military clique, and not as Gladstone had thought in January 1882, though with some uncertainty, a 'sentiment truly national'.† Thus when he told Bright that 'the general situation in Egypt had latterly become one in which everything was governed by sheer military violence and a situation of *force* had been created, which could only be met by force', he expressed what was by July 1882 a very generally held orthodoxy.‡ Gladstone had publicly and stridently warned since 1876 that Britain's acts were entangling, and that British policy had no prudential basis. But he certainly never held that by 1880 Britain was exempt from involvement in some form. The ends of British policy had been, he told the Commons, 'most distinctly and repeatedly stated . . . they are well known to consist in the general maintenance of all established rights in Egypt,

historians (see Schölch, *passim* and A. G. Hopkins, 'The Victorians and Africa: a reconsideration of the occupation of Egypt, 1882', *Journal of African History*, xxvii. 353 (1986)). But by May 1882 Hamilton had been converted by Malet and Rivers Wilson: 'I am afraid Wilfrid Blunt and all his enthusiasm for the "National" party in Egypt has been shown up'; Bahlman, *Hamilton*, 21 May 1882; none the less he remained in touch with Blunt (see Blunt, *Secret history*, 339).

   * Malet's despatch of 27 February 1882, PRO FO 78/3435, in Schölch, 220. See also A. Schölch, 'The "Men on the Spot" and the English occupation of Egypt in 1882', *Historical Journal*, xix. 773 (1976).
   † To Granville, 4 January 1882, Ramm II, i. 326.
   ‡ To Bright, 14 July 82. *The Economist*, 1 July 1882, 802, strongly defending British policy, took just this view: 'the contingency of anarchy in Egypt, in which event Lord Granville has throughout stipulated for perfect freedom of action, has arrived. Those who were credulous enough to imagine that Arabi was the sincere exponent of a genuine and innocent popular movement must be rudely deceived by the facts disclosed in the papers recently presented to Parliament.'

whether they be those of the Sultan, those of the Khedive, those of the people of Egypt, or those of the foreign bondholders'.* The Egyptians could work out their destiny only within a tightly defined and controlled framework, externally supervised and consequently, by implication, externally policed.

Hoping that the preferred solution of 'Egypt for the Egyptians'—but with, of course, their finances still under international direction—would be shown by events to be a solution which could prevail, Gladstone kept the Cabinet away from the question as much as possible, and in the spring and summer of 1882, Ireland by itself supplied a full budget of business. When the Sultan offered Egypt to the British, reserving only his own suzerainty, Gladstone and Granville turned him down without consulting the Cabinet.† This absence of Cabinet discussion paid a high price, for it encouraged and indeed legitimized independent action and planning by the Admiralty, the India Office, and the War Office.

As the weight of opinion in London turned against seeing 'Egypt for the Egyptians' as compatible with 'order', the hope—irony of ironies for Gladstone—was for action by the Porte: 'our first object should be to have the Sultan committed visibly in Egypt against the unruly'.‡ This failing, and with 'stiff and difficult' opposition from Hartington, Gladstone and Granville persuaded the Cabinet on 31 May 1882 to accept the French proposal for a Conference at Constantinople. With the Porte still prevaricating, the French doubtful (though by now present with the British fleet in the harbour at Alexandria), and the absence of 'order' apparently confirmed by the riots in Alexandria on 11 June,§ contingency plans for a separate British expedition were authorized on 15 June at a 'Quasi Cabinet' (i.e. a semi-formal meeting). The difference between Hartington and the rest of the Cabinet was merely that a public announcement of this at the Conference would be 'premature'. By 21 June Gladstone had drawn up the sequence for military involvement. It was clear that troops were to go: the only question was, whose? The answer was 'to ask the Powers to provide for or sanction a military intervention other than Turkish under their authority'.¶ Given the preponderance of British interest and influence in Egypt, this was all but a British, or an Anglo-French force. When the French suggested negotiation with Arabi, they were quickly reprimanded. Thus Arabi's strengthening of the forts of Alexandria—the occasion for the bombardment by the British navy on 11 July—was merely an incident after the strategic decisions had been taken.

* *H* 270. 1146 (14 June 1882).   † Exchange of letters on 25 June 1882, Ramm II, i. 381–2.
‡ To Granville, 29 May 1882, Ramm II, i. 376.
§ For these and the Cabinet's misunderstanding of their nature, see M. E. Chamberlain, 'The Alexandrian massacre of 11 June 1882 and the British occupation of Egypt', *Middle Eastern Studies*, xiii (1977).
¶ At this meeting, the security of the Canal came to the fore, as a rather late concern.

Certainly Gladstone was very sceptical about aspects of those decisions. He did not associate himself with the India Office argument about the security of the route to India, a factor in play in Cabinet from 21 June. He very strongly opposed independent British seizure of the Canal—proposed by Hartington, the Secretary for India—as Arabi was unlikely to tamper with it unless provoked and as 'an act full of menace to the future peace of the world', supplying 'dangerous arguments' which might be used against Britain in Panama, the Dardanelles and the Bosphorus.* His article, 'Aggression on Egypt and Freedom in the East', written in 1877, had spelt out his general objections. He referred Blunt to this article in 1882, as containing his 'opinions about Egypt . . . I am not aware as yet of having seen any reasons to change them'. In 1884 he republished the article as a pamphlet, almost unchanged (and clearly intended as a warning, to some of his colleagues as well as the public, of the dangers of further involvement in the Sudan). His concern was for order, engineered, he hoped, through the Concert. He told his son Harry, then in India: 'In Egypt the embarrassments have been extreme. But the Conference has gone to work and this is of itself a considerable fact; a bulwark against precipitate follies.'†

But if, for Gladstone, strategic arguments were not convincing and indeed were even dangerous, what was it that made 'order' in Egypt a question on which Britain was to act singlehandedly, in the face of the reluctance of France (her most likely partner) and of the Conference sitting in Constantinople? Why was Gladstone ready, however reluctantly, to agree, despite his better judgement, to the demand of the India Office, the War Office, and the Admiralty for a decision to which he could be 'no party'?‡ There was no doubt about the significance of the moment. The bombardment of Alexandria in 1882 matched the bombardment of Canton in 1857 as an assertion of British strength against a non-European power; but a bombardment was a 'lesson' whose teacher came and went at will by sea. Actual invasion of Egypt was of a different order: a return to the imperial military expeditions of the eighteenth century, and with consequences hard to assess, forecast or control.

The most obvious reason was that, by the end of June 1882, Gladstone was simply outnumbered and outflanked in his Cabinet and was anyway physically and mentally exhausted by his constant work in the Commons on the Irish Crimes and Arrears Bills: on 1 July, he wrote in his diary: 'My share of the sitting I take at nineteen hours. Anxious Cabinet on Egypt behind the [Speaker's] Chair 4–5'; by 5 July, 'My brain is *very* weary.' But Gladstone did not take, even in principle, John Bright's view of intervention as simply wrong. As we have seen, he was not a non-interventionist in

* Mem. for Granville, 5 July 1882, in Ramm II, i. 385.
† To H. N. Gladstone, 23 June 82.
‡ To Granville, 4 July 1882, Ramm II, i. 384.

international affairs. 'Disorder' in Egypt threatened various interests and raised several spectres. One of them was the question of the Egyptian debt and the possibility of the failure of the Dual Control to extract payments and of the Khedive being prevented from paying the annual Egyptian Tribute to the Porte. In 1880, no less than 66 per cent of the revenue of Egypt went to servicing the debt and the Tribute:* was it likely that a government representing 'Egypt for the Egyptians' could honour so enormous an obligation? 'Order' meant civilian and strategic order, but it also meant financial security. Money was tied in with power and imperial strategy in an unusually direct and explicit form in Egypt, however careful the attempts to keep the foreign bondholders a legally separate international entity, different from the interests of their respective national governments.

Gladstone as Bondholder

The interest of the bondholders was real, and the Prime Minister was in a sense one of them—a bondholder at second hand. He was a substantial holder of the two Egyptian Tribute Loans, Turkish loans guaranteed by the Egyptian Tribute paid annually to the Porte by the Khedive out of Egyptian revenues. In December 1875 Gladstone owned £25,000 of the 1871 Tribute Loan at 42, worth £10,500; by 1878 this had risen to £30,000, worth £15,900; in 1879 he added £15,000 of the 1854 loan, worth £12,000. Thus by December 1881, as the Egyptian crisis began to break, Gladstone owned in all £51,500 of Egyptian Tribute Loan Stock, worth £40,567. The Egyptian Tribute Loan Stock 1871, bought at 42, was worth 62 in 1881 and had fallen to 57 in the summer of 1882; but by December 1882 it was worth 82.† That is, Gladstone's 1871 stock was worth £17,100 before the invasion of Egypt and £24,600 soon after it. At his annual reckoning of his assets in December 1882 (drawn up, as always, in his own hand), Gladstone's holdings of

* A. Milner, *England in Egypt* (1894 ed.), vii.

† Figures taken from the 'Approximate Annual Sketch of Property' prepared by Gladstone at the end of each calendar year; Hawn P. What Gladstone noted in his accounts as 'Egyptian Loans' were in fact the Turkish government loans of 1854 and 1871 raised on the international market by Messrs. Dent, Palmer & Co.; the loans were guaranteed by the 'Egyptian Tribute' paid to the Sultan by the Khedive as the first call on Egyptian revenues not assigned to the debt. *The Times*, 5 September 1871, 5a, explained their working: 'The first hypothecation of the Egyptian tribute was to its entire extent of £282,872, but in 1866 the sum payable by the Khedive was raised to £705,000 and it is this extra amount of £422,128 that is now pledged, and of which His Highness has engaged to remit direct to the Bank of England the sum of £399,000 per annum.' When the 1871 loan was launched, *The Economist* (9 September 1871, 1089) warned: 'the security of the tribute is not a firm one—no firmer than the credit of Egypt, which is better than Turkish, but is not of the best'; after 1876 Egyptian credit was, of course, much less secure than Turkish. The price of the Tribute Loan stock rose not on the bombardment of Alexandria, but on Wolseley's expedition in August with its implication of at least a short-run occupation; *T.T.*, 21 August 1882, 8a, noted 'There was a strong demand for those Turkish loans which are secured on the Egyptian loan' and on 16 September 1882 *The Economist*, 1157, recorded 'the fresh great rise in Egyptian and in the Turkish Tribute Loans'. The Egyptian Tribute Loan was not part of the Egyptian debt subject to the Law of Liquidation and to the International Conference which met in 1884.

Egyptian Tribute Loan accounted for about 37 per cent of his portfolio, a really remarkably high proportion. To have over a third of his portfolio invested in stock dependent on the credit of a *régime* whose deceit, untrustworthiness, and immorality he had so frequently denounced was hardly rational, unless he presupposed that external action would in the last resort require the Sultan and the Khedive (or whoever was ruling Egypt) to honour the loan.

Gladstone clearly saw no conflict of interest in his holding of this stock, nor was there a code of practice or even a convention to which he might have referred. It would no doubt be crude and simplistic to infer any personal corruption, or even a conscious awareness of an association between personal investments and 'order' in Egypt. Certainly there is no evidence of such an awareness. But the absence of any sense of peculiarity or incongruity simply heightens the naturalness of the British occupation and of the inherent, almost unselfconscious relationship of capital and imperial policy. Almost unselfconscious, because, as we have seen, before occupation was decided upon Gladstone mentioned the rights 'of the foreign bondholders' as on a par with those of the Sultan, the Khedive, and the people of Egypt. After the bombardment he told the Commons 'that undoubtedly it is not for the exclusive or special interest of the bondholders of Egypt—and indeed it is almost wholly without reference to them—that the proceeding of yesterday was taken'.* In the context of the bombardment, this was true. But the careful Gladstonian qualifications are revealing: if not in the 'exclusive or special' interest of the bondholders, it was in their general interest as part of the clutch of 'established rights' in Egypt which Gladstone had earlier defined as subject to the British government's guardianship and which it was now moving to guard directly. The means had changed, not the end.

It can now only be a matter of speculation as to what part, if any, the Prime Minister's personal stake in the stability of Egyptian affairs played in his eventual agreement to go along with the change from indirect to armed intervention in Egypt by Britain alone.† His behaviour suggests that it was at most an underlying factor encouraging private accommodation: Gladstone certainly cannot be presented as a proponent of the invasion nor was he, once their major objective of a European presence had been gained, a friend of the bondholders of the Egyptian debt in the long negotiations

---

* *H* 272. 173; 12 July 1882.

† It should be noted that Arabi's movement was loyal to the Sultan (and may actually have been in league with him against the Khedive), and was therefore less likely to forswear the Tribute than to repudiate the debt; it should also be noted that the constitutionalists' stated aim was only to control that part of the budget not needed for servicing the debt and the Tribute (Schölch, op. cit., 203, 213, 246, 310–13). On the other hand, Gladstone's complete discounting of Arabi's stated constitutional objectives would imply a discounting of this assurance also.

after 1882. When trying to settle this question in 1884, he was ready to leave the bondholders exposed and almost defenceless, by reducing the rate of interest on all Egyptian debts.

Gladstone's candid preservation of his financial archives, and their unusual public availability, gives a peculiar insight into the financial interests of a man of power. His holdings were probably not unusual for a person of his class and scale of assets; almost anyone with a substantial portfolio would have held one or other issue of 'Egyptians' (though few would have been likely to have had so high a proportion of their investments dependent on the Sultan and the Khedive).* Indeed, it was probably in his reluctance to invade Egypt that Gladstone was unusual. Even so, his holding of Egyptian Tribute Loan is a fact that, once known, is hard to forget.

Liberals as Imperialists: the Bombardment, Occupation, and Settlement of Egypt

Though Gladstone 'did not feel the necessity', he agreed to the bombardment of Alexandria on 11 July 1882 with no comment on its morality and without an expression of regret as Britain began the imposition of 'order' on behalf of the international community. When John Bright resigned, Gladstone rightly placed the Alexandrian forts and the bombardment as a 'bye-question' to the general issue of order. He told Musurus, the Sultan's ambassador, that the bombardment 'was a supreme moment for the Ottoman Empire', but when the Porte refused to act, he planned Sir Garnet Wolseley's expedition with enthusiasm. No expression of regret or reluctance qualified Gladstone's determination that once the decision to intervene militarily in Egypt was taken it should be done comprehensively. The Cabinet minute of 31 July was decisive, brutal and brief: 'Instructions to Wolseley; Put down Arabi & establish Khedive's power.' Wolseley departed for Egypt, and Gladstone for a short holiday. On 15 September 1882 the relevant ministers met in London to hear the news: 'Conclave on Egypt $12\frac{1}{2}$–$2\frac{1}{2}$. Another flood of good news. No more blood I hope. Wolseley in Cairo: Arabi a prisoner: God be praised.' Gladstone asked the Archbishop of York and the Bishop of London (the Archbishop of Canterbury being ill) to have the church bells rung and the Secretary for War to have the guns fired in the London parks to mark the triumph: 'I hope the guns will crash all the windows.' These were no mere public gestures, though they were that also: a decisive answer to the long years of Tory baiting.

* When in 1884 Gladstone had time to survey his portfolio, he made no comment on his 'Egyptians', concentrating on his 'one heavy mistake', his Metropolitan District Railway holdings (see 3 Oct. 84). However, in 1884, though it certainly could not be regarded as a mistake, he sold his Egyptian Tribute Loan (1854) stock and invested the money in New Zealand 4%s and in Canadian and Scottish railways stocks, thus reducing the 'Egyptians' to about 22% of his portfolio, clearly a much more prudent distribution. He retained the 1871 Egyptian Tribute Loan stock until the late 1880s.

Gladstone read Macaulay's patriotic *Lays of Ancient Rome* and Campbell's *Battle of the Baltic* during the crisis and he welcomed the troops home with obvious enthusiasm. The Liberal, Cardwellian army had performed with efficiency: 'We certainly ought to be in good humour, for we are pleased with our army, our navy, our admirals, our Generals, and our organization. Matters were not so conducted in the days of the Crimea. . . .' Moreover, unlike the Crimea, a good proportion of the military expenses were charged to the Indian government, even though it had not been consulted about the expedition. Gladstone was even able to score a point off the Queen who could hardly refuse to Wolseley the peerage she had for the two years previously so energetically prevented.

If there was to be an expedition, it could hardly have gone better. On 10th July 1882, Britain's involvement in Egypt had been oblique and without immediate responsibility. By 14 September she was the effective power in the land. It was a spectacular exhibition of British supremacy, and a marked contrast with the earlier French imbroglio in Algeria. It was also, however unintended, the chief step towards the fulfilment of the prophecy issued by Gladstone himself in 1877 like a latter-day Isaiah (the prophet who warned against foreign entanglements):

our first site in Egypt, be it by larceny or be it by emption, will be the almost certain egg of a North African Empire, that will grow and grow until another Victoria and another Albert, titles of the Lake-sources of the White Nile, come within our borders; and till we finally join hands across the Equator with Natal and Cape Town, to say nothing of the Transvaal and the Orange River on the south, or of Abyssinia or Zanzibar to be swallowed by way of *viaticum* on our journey.*

In 1877, the prophecy was intended as a warning against taking that first 'site'. In 1882, the prophet himself ordered the church bells to be rung. The hope was for a limited stay and a swift restoration of 'order', but the prophecy suggested otherwise; moreover, it had continued with respect to Egypt: 'it is vain to disguise that we shall have the entire responsibility of the government, if we have any of it at all'.

The Cabinet was no more agreed as to what to do with Egypt than it would have been if the Canal had been captured when Eden attempted invasion in 1956. But the range of options was, unlike 1956, considerable, from withdrawal through protectorate to annexation. India offered many precedents of informal advice backed by force. The day Wolseley entered Cairo, Gladstone tried to narrow the possibilities by writing a long memorandum for the Cabinet, 'The settlement of Egypt', emphasizing the need for neutrality, the support of the Khedive by a minimum force, and the effective ending of Turkish authority in Egypt, using the model of 'the Balkan and Rouman Suzerainties' (though Gladstone was careful to retain

---

* 'Aggression on Egypt', *Nineteenth Century*, ii. 149 (August 1877); *Gleanings*, iv. 358.

for the Sultan 'the continuance of the tribute', by which the Turkish Egyptian loans were guaranteed). He looked in fact for the sort of solution he had advocated for the Balkans in the 1870s. He gained support for much of this in Cabinet. The first of what were to be at least sixty-six protestations of the temporary nature of the British presence in Egypt were made,* and Gladstone was sufficiently confident of calm in Egypt to make in October 1882 the most determined of his efforts at retirement.

There were two difficulties. Withdrawal of the army was to be 'regulated exclusively and from point to point, by the consideration of security for life and property', which included the Canal. But the Canal would never be as secure without British troops as with them, and thus a presence would be needed as long as Britain held India. The Indian argument may not have weighed much with Gladstone, but it certainly did with others.† Second, political settlement depended, in Gladstone's view, on replacing Turkish sovereignty with a Khedive supported by a law of succession and 'the reasonable development of self-governing institutions'. But Wolseley's army had smashed the Egyptian constitutional movement, the only possible basis for such institutions, and Gladstone, influenced by his Tractarian friend Phillimore, at first backed the execution of Arabi, its leader.‡ As Gladstone pointed out, the 're-establishment of orderly Government . . . has been accomplished not by the Proclamation of the Sultan but by the victory at Tel-el-Kebir'. As in India, 'order' in Egypt now rested ultimately on British force. That force might be small and 'fixed as a minimum' and Gladstone might be successful in combating the Queen's arguments, 'almost as unconstitutional as they are irrational', that it should be large. But a force it had to be. Egypt had become like the income tax, disliked, 'temporary', but indispensable.

On the other hand, even if desirable (and it is unlikely that even a Tory cabinet would have found it so in 1882), formal rule—a Protectorate or annexation—would have been diplomatically explosive; it would also have been financially expensive as Britain would have taken over direct responsibility for Egyptian affairs, and an even more dramatic blow to the stability of the Ottoman Empire than 'temporary' military occupation. Thus it came about that Britain as the representative of the international interest maintained local 'order', but by disclaiming sole responsibility left open the door to other members of the Concert to exercise theirs. From

* See Hopkins, art. cit., 388.

† Northbrook told Ripon, who had doubts at least about the bombardment: 'my own opinion is that India might fairly be asked to pay the whole cost of the contingent, for the interest she has in the canal . . . is undoubtedly great—greater indeed than England's—for if we had not India why should we be meddling in Egypt at all?' (25 August 1882, Add MS 43572, f. 70); Kimberley told him the same: 'But for India, I feel certain that no Egyptian expedition would ever have taken place' (11 January 1883, Add MS 43523, f. 12).

‡ To Granville, 22 September 1882; Ramm II, i. 429. Arabi was made to plead guilty, and was then imprisoned in Ceylon.

this sprang long and complex series of negotiations on the succession to the Dual Control and the settlement of Egyptian finances. It was one of the many ironies of the Egyptian diplomatic imbroglio that it was the Liberals, for so long the party of non-entanglement, who should, by the occupation of Egypt and the consequent management of Egyptian finances, give the Continental powers and especially Germany the general lever of purchase on British diplomacy which they had for so long lacked. That same imbroglio, as Gladstone had foreseen in 1877, brought to an end the *rapprochement* with France which the Gladstone/Cobden Treaty of 1860 had exemplified a generation earlier.

Regularization of Egyptian affairs, the situation complicated by Lesseps' concession, went on through 1883 into 1884. A second canal, getting round the difficulty of the concession and of the narrowness of the original, and backed by a British government loan of £8,000,000, was negotiated with Lesseps in 1883 only to be shouted down by the British shipping interest as too favourable to the Canal Company.* The financial settlement of Egypt was highly contentious, for it involved some definition of Britain's governmental relationship to the area which with the defeat of Hicks Pasha in the Sudan had from November 1883 a further strategic dimension which will be examined shortly.

Gladstone saw the resolution of the confusions of Egyptian finances as the essential preliminary to British withdrawal. It was, he thought, a 'holy subject'. It was also politically a very dangerous subject, for even his own Cabinet included the spectrum from immediate withdrawal and a declaration of Egyptian bankruptcy to long-term, sole British occupation. With considerable labour, a Conference of the Powers was convened in London in June 1884 to settle the finances of Egypt and the position of the bondholders. Gladstone was

much oppressed beforehand with the responsibility of my statement upon Egypt: but much pleased with the reception of it. . . . God is good: & I feel strong in the belief that we have the interests of justice, peace, & freedom in our hands.

As the pressure mounted in Cabinet in 1884 for a Sudan expedition to rescue Gordon and as the Lords prepared to reject the Franchise Bill, the Conference failed to agree. The British proposals were rejected by France, despite an advance private agreement, and the Conference was abandoned in early August 1884. Gladstone wrote later that 'we broke up the Conference because it would not consent to dock the dividends [of the bondholders]'. This was partly true, but the financial details were only one aspect of the question. France, encouraged by Germany, had Britain on the rack and energetically exploited the opportunity. Britain's dependence on international agreement opened a door at which Bismarck pushed. The

* D. A. Farnie, *East and West of Suez* (1969), ch. xvii.

Egyptian negotiations involved Britian in the complex balance of French domestic politics and of Franco-German relations: when that balance altered, as it did at the end of 1884, the way for a negotiated solution quickly appeared.

The failure of the Conference was a major setback for Gladstone: withdrawal from Egypt moved into the middle distance at best and at home the failure implied a further bruising series of Cabinet and parliamentary struggles. 'Egypt. Egypt. Egypt. Egypt.' read the heads of one Cabinet's agenda on 16 July 1884. For the next ten months Egypt in its various manifestations threatened to break up the Cabinet and bring about the fall of the government. 'The Egyptian flood comes on us again and again, like the sea on the host of Pharaoh, which had just as much business to pursue the Israelites as we have to meddle in Egypt,' Gladstone wrote in January 1885. Still, meddling they were, and with more effect than the host of Pharaoh had had on the Israelites.

Faced with the failure of the Conference in July 1884, Gladstone and Granville led the Cabinet—with a rapidity which they perhaps later came to regret—quickly to persuade Northbrook to go on a mission to Cairo to report and to advise. His appointment was announced on 5 August 1884, moments before Gladstone moved the Vote of Credit for the Gordon relief expedition. Northbrook's instructions were as hurriedly drawn up as Gordon's had been and led to a rather similar difficulty. Northbrook's report in November 1884 proposed sole British financial control and a more favourable treatment of the bondholders; it simply discounted the objections of other Powers. The report was a considerable victory for the Hartington wing of the Cabinet and was quite unacceptable to Gladstone* and many Liberals. A '*réchauffée* of the proposals put before the Conference'† was quickly prepared as an alternative. But Northbrook (a Baring and a relative of Evelyn Baring, the British agent and consul-general in Egypt) represented powerful interests: the government faced dangers from the radical wing of the party and other Liberals for going too far and from a potential Tory–Liberal/Whig combination for not going far enough. On 20 January 1885 the Cabinet voted 8:4 to accept that 'French proposals form a reasonable basis for friendly communications with a view to a settlement of Egyptian finances'. On the basis of these proposals, with Northbrook and Hartington just kept in tow (the Gordon crisis may have helped here), a

* 15, 19, 20 Nov. 84; see also *The diary of Sir Edward Walter Hamilton 1880–1885*, ed. Dudley W. R. Bahlman, 2v. (1972) [subsequently: Bahlman, *Hamilton*], ii. 729, 735. Northbrook, the First Lord of the Admiralty, returned from Egypt to find the navy crisis at its height; his position in Cabinet to press for his report was thus much weakened and the Gordon crisis, with troops in action, made it very difficult for Hartington, the war secretary, to resign. Sir James Carmichael was sent to Egypt to make further inquiries about increasing Egyptian revenues. He recommended extra taxation on the rich, a course which Gladstone thought 'more equitable' than taxing the bondholders or placing the burden 'on the shoulders of the British people', but Northbrook thought this impracticable.

† Hamilton's phrase, 20 November 1884; Bahlman, *Hamilton*, ii. 737.

settlement was reached in March 1885 expressed in a Declaration, a Convention, and a Decree by the Egyptian government, agreed to by the Powers and by the Porte, the latter under threat of losing Egypt altogether. The settlement included a two-year breathing space for Egypt to put her finances into order and decide whether or not taxation levels could reasonably support the whole of the payments to the bondholders who in the *interim* would suffer a half per cent reduction on their receipts. The settlement was backed by an internationally guaranteed loan of £9 millions. After the two years there would be, if necessary, an International Commission of inquiry.

An international dimension was thus maintained, as Gladstone wished, but, as he also wished, it was not an international control.* The ending of all control in Egypt remained his objective and there was, he argued, even after 1882 no *de jure* interference in the government of Egypt: even Britain had 'no determinate or legal right of interference'. But there were, however, 'rights which are indeterminate, that are frequently as real as those which are more defined, and there are moral rights', and these Britain did have. Moreover, Britain had the function of the 'natural adviser': 'In the present circumstances, and especially until some more permanent arrangement can be made by general consent, we are the natural advisers of the Egyptian Government for the time.'†

Like the Princely states of India—though Gladstone did not make an analogy which would have suggested a long-term stay—Egypt was to enjoy the advice of the British government and to have the privilege of paying for an army of occupation. The position of Egypt was thus regularized by the Gladstone government, shortly before its resignation, but with options remaining open: no permanent, direct imperial responsibility had been accepted and the possibility, indeed the stated intention of withdrawal remained. On the other hand, the Hartingtonians knew that the longer *de facto* occupation continued, the more entrenched British control of Egypt became, whatever the legal fiction. What Alfred Milner called 'the veiled Protectorate' was firmly in place.‡

Gordon at Khartoum: the Mahdists 'struggling rightly to be free'

The settlement within Egypt was hardly what Gladstone had intended in 1882, though it was what he had feared: the 'nest egg' was hatching. Would it prove to be a double-yolker? What was to be the fate of the Sudan, that territory to the south whose order was the responsibility of the Khedive acting for the Sultan?§

Gladstone showed little interest in the impact of his Cabinet's actions on

---

* *H* 296. 687 (26 March 1885).   † Ibid., 688.
‡ A. Milner, *England in Egypt* (1894 ed.), title of ch. iii.
§ For a map of the Sudan, see p. 401.

North Africa generally. He did, however, note in his memorandum on settlement in September 1882 that the defence of 'the territory especially in the direction of the Soudan' was a prime military responsibility. But while advice backed by British force worked conveniently within Egypt, it was an extremely complex device when applied to Egypt's peripheral territories. In these, the Porte and the Khedive both exercised responsibility; moreover, there was great reluctance to commit British troops to the extreme conditions and extended lines of supply of the upper Nile. The Cabinet decided to have the 'Southern Army separate, paid from Soudan revenues'. The control of this army was left to the Khedive who took full advantage of the chief sphere of activity left to him by the British. He determined on an Egyptian reconquest of the Sudan, where Egypt's usual authority had been challenged by a religious uprising led by the Mahdi. Thus it was that in September 1883 William Hicks (in the Khedive's employment) led the southern Egyptian army into the Sudan to suppress the Mahdi, who had been declared a 'False Prophet' by orthodox Islamists but who represented in an extreme form that militancy which Britain thought she had seen in Arabi.

As with Arabi and his movement, Gladstone initially had considerable sympathy for the Mahdists; it was of them that he coined one of his most famous phrases: 'Yes; these people are struggling to be free; and they are struggling rightly to be free.'* Moreover, unlike Egypt, the Sudan in the early 1880s was not thought of immediate importance by even the most ardent imperialist.

The first miscalculation was a lack of understanding of Egypt's interest in the area, of the tensions within different schools of Mohammetanism, and of Egypt's willingness to take risks. Though successful earlier in the year at Berber, Hicks was killed and the Khedive's army ambushed in November 1883 just as the Cabinet was preparing the further reduction of the Egyptian garrison and its withdrawal from Cairo to Alexandria. The failure to prevent the Khedive's sending of Hicks into the Sudan was, Cromer later thought, 'the sum total of the charge which can be brought against Mr. Gladstone's Government'.†

The Cabinet heard the news of the Hicks disaster in November 1883, but no further Cabinets were held that year so as to prevent the issue of redistribution of parliamentary seats causing Hartington's resignation. That tactic was successful, but meant that Sudanese policy was arranged by letter. Even so, agreement was reached: the Sudan was to be evacuated, a decision confirmed at the Cabinet of 3 January 1884. The consequent resignation of the Egyptian ministry was successfully surmounted. Gladstone returned to Hawarden and left the small print to the relevant ministries, run by the Whigs.

* H 288. 55 (12 May 1884).   † Cromer, i. 385.

In retrospect, this seems casual. At the time, it was not an unusual pro-ceeding, though Gladstone must often have regretted it later. Granville, Hartington, and Northbrook (respectively the Foreign and War Offices and the Admiralty) were hardly inexperienced and the agreed policy was a simple withdrawal: a policy of occupation would have warranted greater Prime-Ministerial superintendence. To Northbrook, accustomed as a retired Viceroy of India to rapid and complete obedience, the operation seemed straightforward:

I have been spending a good part of the day in arranging for the mission of Chinese Gordon to Suakin [on the Red Sea] to arrange for the evacuation of the Soudan.* I was very glad to find that he readily & even cordially accepted our policy that the Egyptians should give up the administration only holding to the sea coast. He is not at all alarmed at the situation; & does not believe in the immense power some think this Mahdi has, either spiritual or physical.†

Of course, it was not so simple. Gladstone had an acute sense of political trouble which operated well with respect to others, less effectively with himself. Perhaps remembering his own restless activity as High Commis-sioner in the Ionian Islands 1858–9, he warned Granville about Gordon when his appointment was in the air but not settled, that 'while his opinion on the Soudan may be of great value, must we not be very careful . . . that he does not shift the centre of gravity as to political and military responsibility for that country'.‡ However, Gladstone did not countervail an appoint-ment he knew was about to be made. Thus the Prime Minister and Baring, the 'man on the spot', were both sceptical:§ but it was left to the ministries. These, undoubtedly, failed in their technical assessment of the situation. 'Withdrawal' was not a simple matter: many civilians were involved, Egyp-tian troops were scattered in pockets about the Sudan, the logistics of movement were complex, some sort of alternative authority was needed, Gordon was in the employment of the Khedive, not of the British govern-ment (this, indeed, had been part of the attractiveness of sending him, for

---

* Even here, there is muddle: Gordon was to *report* on the means of evacuation, not to 'arrange' for it.

† Northbrook to Ripon, 18 January 1884, Add MS 43572, f. 72; Northbrook gave a slightly differ-ent account to Baring (Cromer i. 429); he told Ripon, 25 January 1884, Add MS 43572, f. 78: 'Gordon has gone out heartily to carry out our policy of withdrawal from the Soudan. He is quite against reconquering it for Egypt.' Charles George Gordon (1833–85) had served in the Crimea and taken part in the invasion of China in 1860; he had then worked for the Chinese government and then for the Khedive in the Sudan, each time dramatically imposing order on chaotic and rebellious peoples.

‡ To Granville, 16 January 1884, Ramm II, ii. 150.

§ See Cromer, i. 423–6. Gordon's appointment was urged from 1882; the campaign led by the *Pall Mall Gazette* and the *Morning Advertiser* merely gave the last push to a move widely welcomed by the army. Stephenson, the commander in Egypt, wrote on 21 January 1884: 'Gordon . . . is, I think, by far the best man the Government really could have sent out, and if anyone can get the Egyptian Government out of their Soudan difficulties, he will'; F. C. A. Stephenson, *At home and on the battlefield* (1915), 313. See also M. Shibeika, *British policy in the Sudan 1882–1902* (1952), 146–60.

he had held similar employment before in the Sudan, with conspicuous success). No-one in Britain was directly responsible for assessing the situation militarily: the Foreign Office got information from Evelyn Baring in Cairo, the Admiralty from the Red Sea ports, the War Office rather indirectly from British officers trapped in the Sudan. As Gladstone noted on the plans for the Nile route for rescue, 'although this may not properly be Admiralty business, it is I suppose still less within the view of the War Office'.

Gladstone appreciated that the problems of ignorance in London about the details of the situation in the Sudan implied giving Gordon what amounted to a free hand. Thus he did not require, nor did his departmental ministers offer, categorical advice. His political instincts told him things might go wrong; his rather legalistic sense of 'rightness' told him that it was not the government's fault. Nor was it technically, for Gordon effectively disobeyed the orders which he had been given in London and which had been reinforced in Cairo by Baring, though also crucially restated. But the popular excitement which had been a part of Gordon's appointment, the penetration of the telegraph a good way up the Nile and the consequent frequent bulletins in the London press, either from Gordon or, after his isolation, from the advancing rescue force, meant that the Gordon drama was played out morning by morning at the breakfast tables of Britain. Even after March 1884 when he was out of direct telegraphic contact (the government suspected deliberately), he continued to be heard from indirectly 'in so many odd ways', as Gladstone complained in August 1884. Gordon had as instinctive a sense of how to play the 'media' as Gladstone himself.

David Livingstone had disappeared in Africa for years at a time; Charles Gordon's was a death almost on stage. And since the flow of information was largely one way—from North Africa outwards, whether from Gordon or Wolseley—it was a flow that they could control, and which they did control with skill. The Sudanese journals of Gordon and Wolseley vie with each other in contempt for their governmental superiors, Wolseley's also reflecting an almost pathological hatred of representative government which would have amazed and appalled the Liberal politicians whose patronage he apparently so gratefully received.* It is curious that Gladstone, of all the Victorians usually the most hypersensitively aware of the possibilities of political presentation, seems to have failed to sense this central dimension of the Gordon mission.

It was Gordon as symbol, as an icon of his age, that was important, a point grasped by Gordon himself and by W. T. Stead, the leading liberal journalist of the day. Stead's championing of the appointment of Gordon was partly intended to show that the patriotic card was one that Liberals could play: Palmerstonianism was not necessarily lost to the Tories.

* See *Relief of Gordon, passim.*

Whatever the details of the rights and wrongs of the Gordon affair, the Cabinet bungled this hand. They did so partly because they, and Gladstone in particular, refused to look beyond the complexities of Egyptian and Sudanese policy. They took their stand on details, and on these they had a much better case than is often allowed, when what was really at issue was presentation and image.

Once off the leash and officially the employee of the Khedive and made Governor General of the Sudan by him, Gordon acted as Gladstone had warned. His position as Governor General and the restatement of his orders approved by Baring when he was in Cairo suggested an executive role markedly different from his original instruction to 'report' on withdrawal from the Sudan.* Quickly, these executive functions predominated. By the start of February 1884 the Cabinet realized the 'Soudan business' was adrift, and began the long series of meetings that continued almost to the end of the ministry; Gladstone was incensed to find Gordon had effectively rewritten his orders: 'the times are stiff & try the mettle of men. What shd *we* have done, with the Mutiny at the Nore.' Gordon was not exactly a mutineer, but he was in that position that always alarmed Whitehall, regardless of party: he was an imperialist on the loose.

By the middle of February 1884, the possibility of having to 'rescue' Gordon—or in effect to arrest him—was becoming a possibility, perhaps a necessity. But with Gordon in post and on the Upper Nile, the hope was still that all would be well. Once on the Nile at Khartoum, Gordon was never given a simple, direct instruction by the government to withdraw with his immediate force to Cairo, or even to Berber.† Gladstone and Granville considered such an instruction in September 1884, but did not nerve themselves to send it. Gladstone supported Gordon's request that Zobeir, the notorious slaver, be made Governor of Khartoum as the most effective person to maintain order, but the Cabinet took fright at the anti-slavery lobby (which wanted, moreover, occupation rather than withdrawal from the Sudan).

The spring and summer of 1884 were spent debating various possibilities: whether to relieve at all, a large *versus* a small force, the Nile route *versus* the route west from the Red Sea port of Suakin, a relatively short distance but across very difficult terrain partly held by the Mahdists. Even a rescue via the south (i.e. Uganda and down the Nile) was considered, a solution that would have had spectacular consequences for East Africa. Gladstone dreaded that the rescue expedition would—as it nearly did—become effectually an occupation. Thus he especially disliked a railway from Suakin, with its implication of permanence, 'the substitution of an Egyptian domination there of an English domination over the whole or a part', and he therefore favoured a small, fleeting force, 'leaving no trace

* Cromer, i. 440–52.   † Ramm II, ii. 259–62.

behind it'. The military advice was self-contradictory. Costs were drawn up anticipating a Red Sea expedition, but 'nothing to be done now beyond preliminary proceedings'. By 16 July 1884 when the Cabinet agenda read 'Egypt. Egypt. Egypt. Egypt', two of those 'Egypts' meant the Sudan. Slowly the balance, pushed energetically by the Whigs, tilted towards action and a Vote of Credit, and in September 1884 Garnet Wolseley was on his way up the Nile. The route was chosen chiefly by Wolseley on the basis of his Red River experience in Canada a generation earlier, (when he had efficiently suppressed a much smaller rebellion, partly by moving soldiers up-river at speed using whaling boats) and forced through by the 'Wolseley Ring' in flagrant disregard of the warnings about its difficulties offered by the Admiralty and Sir Frederick Stephenson, whom Wolseley replaced as commander at the last moment.

The news came on 5 February 1885 when Gladstone was staying at Holker Hall with Hartington:

After 11 AM I heard the sad news of the fall or betrayal of Khartoum: H. & I, with C. went off by the first train and reached D. Street soon after 8.15. The circumstances are sad & trying: it is one of the least points about them, that they may put an end to this Govt.

Gordon probably dead, though it was briefly hoped that he might not be,* the Cabinet moved with a rapidity and apparent decision it had never shown when he was alive: within two days it had instructed Wolseley to crush the power of the Mahdi at Khartoum (probably in the autumn), had begun the railway inland to Berber from the Red Sea, and prepared to crush the revolt of Osman Digna in the eastern Sudan with a substantial body of force.† This might be thought to imply a dramatic reversal in the government's Sudanese policy which if it had been capped—as it very nearly was—by the appointment of Wolseley as Governor-General would have amounted to accepting for the Sudan at least the same responsibility as Britain now had in Egypt. Gladstone told the Sultan's envoys on 10 February 1885 that the 'original policy ... has undergone no change ... the recent decisions are military decisions'. Technically this was true: the Governor Generalship, though approved in draft, was withheld.

Was this a change of policy, or merely the armoury necessary for the

---

* Wolseley's telegrams encouraged the view that Gordon had been captured. His body was never found.

† Gladstone offered no explanation to the Queen for this, but merely referred her to an enclosed telegram; P. Guedalla, *The Queen and Mr. Gladstone*, 2v. (1933) [subsequently: Guedalla, *Q*], ii. 330. He told Hamilton, who protested mildly at the change, that 'the decision had been determined by the regard which they felt bound to have for the effect which the triumph of the Mahdi might have on our Mahometan subjects'; Bahlman, *Hamilton*, ii. 790. Wolseley's diary shows that Gordon was not the only British military commander of bizarre views in the Sudan; Wolseley noted: 'I earnestly pray he [Gordon] may have been killed.... If anything can kill old Gladstone this news ought to ...' (*Relief of Gordon*. 134–6).

survival of the government? The instruction that the 'power of the Mahdi at Khartoum must be overthrown' maintained a degree of ambivalence (what did 'at Khartoum' imply?), and Gladstone avoided an immediate Vote of Credit for a Sudan war.* Certainly, nothing could happen quickly, except perhaps a further disaster: the loss of Wolseley's army, for, Khartoum fallen, Wolseley was in an extremely exposed position and had consistently underrated his opponent's strength.† The death of Gordon was a blow in terms of policy and prestige but, like Majuba, was militarily insignificant. The defeat of Wolseley, representing, as he was seen to do, the liberal ideal of merit, reform, and efficiency, would have been a real disaster. The Mahdi sat tight in Khartoum and by so doing let Wolseley and the government off the hook. The Cabinet, whose discussions after the death of Gordon were 'difficult but harmonious', was afforced in the Lords by Rosebery (who at last, after many refusals, agreed to join the government for reasons of 'patriotism'), and it just survived, by 14 votes, the vote of censure in the Commons. Gladstone lobbied Bright, who voted with the government, and Goschen, who voted for the censure motion. It was, Gladstone noted, 'an extreme case of the irony of Fortune' that he should receive 'a telegram from the Sultan expressly to congratulate the Govt. & me personally on the defeat of the Opposition & on our continuance in office'.

Gladstone's reaction to the events of February 1885 did not at first display his usual resource. Despite his secretary's advice, he greatly and wilfully offended by going in the Dalhousies' party to 'The Candidate' at the Criterion Theatre ('capitally acted') on the night Gordon's death was confirmed. The crisis made him physically ill, and he took to his bed, 'the disturbance, wh has had so many forms, having at last taken the form of overaction of the bowels', and anxiety produced a skin disease on his hands. His initial Commons statement was brusque. Gladstone admitted to himself his 'reception could not be warm', but he went out of his way to make it cold, deliberately omitting any compliment to Gordon, the troops or the colonies for their offers of help.‡ It was, as he said, 'a serious crisis in the face of the world'.§ Rarely can a Prime Minister have faced the Commons in more embarrassing circumstances—embarrassing, because the Gordon affair handed to the Tories a jack (G.O.M. = M.O.G.: Grand Old Man = Murderer of Gordon), if not an ace, to be played at convenience for

* To Childers, 16 Feb. 85. The suggestion in *The Governing Passion*, op. cit., 196–7, that Gladstone hoped for an 'innocuous and early success on the Suakin front' which he could trade against Wolseley's autumn campaign is intriguing, but it is unlikely that in the hot season a successful assault on Osman Digna could have been quickly enough mounted to have such an effect. It is more likely that Gladstone's concern over the command of the Suakin expedition was one further round in the battle with the Court.

† *Relief of Gordon*, 137–40.

‡ Bahlman, *Hamilton*, ii. 798.

§ H 294. 1099.

the rest of Gladstone's career and beyond.* When Northcote loyally did not play this card in opening the censure debate, Tory contempt for him reached its height. Gladstone was clearly within a whisker of resigning. He discussed Commons' contingencies 'on the possible resignations' with the Speaker. When the government's majority fell to 14 on the censure motion on 27 February, he noted: 'the final decision in my mind turned the scale, so nicely was it balanced'. Next day, he persuaded the Cabinet to continue; within a week, he felt 'wonderfully better'. The Queen's notorious telegram *en clair*† sent to Granville, Hartington, and Gladstone as a public rebuke on the day the news of the fall of Khartoum reached London was the most personal of several reasons which made a resignation dishonourable (a dissolution with the Redistribution Bill not yet passed was impossible).

The same day as deciding to carry on—28 February—the Cabinet considered developments on the Afghan frontier, where, as we have seen, the long wave of Russian expansion was finally breaking on the Penjdeh breakwater. Two Cabinets later, Wolseley was warned that because of the military dangers in Central Asia 'we are unwilling to take any step in the nature of a further general declaration of policy'. The government thus faced simultaneous crises in Egyptian finance, as the negotiations reached their final phases, the Sudan, and Afghanistan. Estimates for a Vote of Credit went quickly from £7½ millions to £11 millions: 'The pressure of affairs, especially Soudan, Egypt, & Afghan, is now from day to day extreme', Gladstone noted on 16 March. The Vote of Credit for £11 millions was the largest ever raised for military purposes. Moved on 21 April, it studiously did not distinguish between Central Asian and North African needs, being for Egypt and the Sudan and for 'special naval and military preparation'. By May, with the financial affairs of Egypt at last internationally agreed,‡ the evacuation policy for the Sudan was confirmed. The Cabinet of 7 May decided to withdraw, despite Wolseley's continued request to be allowed to 'break Mahdism'. The Sudan was put on ice—a return to what had been the Cabinet's consistent policy save for the flurry in February 1885. Wolseley withdrew and, for all the noise, the Tories did not send him back. The Liberal policy had been sensible: unless another European power threatened occupation, Britain had no interest in the Sudan. It was a simple enough policy which had not been simply enough stated or pursued.

---

* Giving talks in the 1970s and 1980s on Gladstone to non-historians, I have been struck by the fact that Gladstone's part in the death of Gordon was almost always raised by a questioner.

† i.e. the Queen's complaint at the government's handling of the Gordon affair was not sent in cypher; it was consequently immediately leaked and published in the press.

‡ The London Convention was signed on 17 March 1885.

African Scramble: Central, East, and South

North Africa was thus within three years the scene of the most successful of all the Victorian military expeditions and, in political terms, of the greatest fiasco before the 1899 South African War. But it was the 1882 success in Egypt which set the tone. In the 'grab' for colonial possessions which followed, others would niggle at but would not directly confront British power. On the other hand, the Gladstone Cabinet showed little interest in exploiting this advantage, for the existing difficulties in North and South Africa sufficiently absorbed its energies, and even these fought often unsuccessfully for Cabinet time with Ireland and domestic legislation. Although it was clear that the Cabinet was overburdened, little was done to make it a more effective institution and few lessons about the co-ordination of policy seem to have been learned. From time to time a Cabinet committee was used, as with considerable effect in the case of West Africa,* a committee renewed when the Cabinet agreed to the West African Berlin Conference on 8 October 1884, but there was no system of Standing Committees of Cabinet even for problems such as Egyptian finance which were obviously enduring, nor does one ever seem to have been considered: it would no doubt have been thought inimicable to Cabinet solidarity. It would also have been regarded by Gladstone as likely to produce activist and therefore expensive policies. Thus it was that there was little overall superintendence or co-ordination of policy save at the highest level and, in so far as this was possible, within individual ministries.

At the highest level, Gladstone's attention to foreign and imperial affairs in all their dimensions was, as we have seen, spasmodic. Granville's decline—his gout was distractingly painful—made the situation worse; his colleagues were agreed in 1885 not to allow him back to the Foreign Office. Derby at the Colonial Office had a reputation for a lacadaisical attention to policy and at first glance it would seem that Cabinet decisions on the New Guinea protectorate were simply not implemented. A second glance shows, however, that the maintenance of a coherent policy on New Guinea was extremely difficult, for it was at the centre of the awkward attempts of the British government to come to terms with German colonial aspirations.†

The difficulties of both Granville and Derby were not merely personal. They were caught in the centre of a Cabinet which represented most, if not all, of the various British political responses to the imperial tide. Thus, as other European nations capitalized on Britain's bondage in Egypt and the Sudan to increase colonial activity in 1883 and 1884, Britain was particularly awkwardly placed to respond. The alienation of France, the contempt

* 25 Oct., 22 Nov. 83.
† See 6, 9 Aug., 6 Oct. 84, 21 Jan. 85.

of Bismarck for Gladstone and the British Cabinet generally, the absence of agreement in the government about an overall policy for Africa, and the need for foreign support to achieve a financial settlement in Egypt all encouraged other Powers to action, not in the form of a major assault on a central British interest, but in the form of a series of initiatives in places of apparently marginal significance.

A flurry of darts blew from Continental blow-pipes: West Africa, Madagascar, Angra Pequeña (in what became German South West Africa), Zanzibar and East Africa, New Guinea, islands in the Pacific. Each had its complex case history involving local interests and, in the British case, the sub-imperial interests of the various white colonies, but each also related to the other in the sense that the decisive agents were Britain, France, and, *tertius gaudens*, Germany. By pressing forward these questions in 1884–5, the Continental Powers forced Britain towards a coherent, active imperial policy in response. This, Gladstone was determined to avoid.

Gladstone's view was that while Britain had certain historic interests, she had no manifest destiny in tropical Africa and that local accommodations would be sufficient: Britain could hardly expect to exclude other major powers should they be determined on activity. Thus in his view no plan co-ordinated Zanzibar with Nigeria, Egypt with Angra Pequeña: Britain had no unique and not many particular interests. Distinctively among British statesmen confronted imperially by Germany, Gladstone's policy was not the maintenance of the *status quo* (i.e. a British hegemony either formal or informal which excluded Germany), but rather an accommodation of German ambitions. As he wrote in 1884 to Derby on German activity on the East African coast: 'Is it dignified, or is it required by any real interest, to make extensions of British authority without any view of occupying but simply to keep them out?'[*]

Gladstone recognized that in the temper of the 1880s this was an 'old fashioned' view.[†] 'Colonial alarmism',[‡] as he called it in 1884, was making the running and was hard to prevent. Yet from the perspective of the 1990s his view has a curiously modern ring, certainly more so than the Cape-to-Cairo enthusiasms of the Imperial Federation League, also of 1884, so quickly has the British experience in tropical Africa begun to seem remote, strange, and, from the British point of view, almost comic in its presumption.

The incorporation of Germany in the imperial brethren was simply done. Bismarck, assuming British deviousness to equal his own and supposing the British Cabinet to regard all deserts with maximum jealousy,

[*] To Derby, 30 Dec. 84.   [†] Ibid.
[‡] To Derby, 24 Dec. 84. John Bramston, assistant under-secretary at the Colonial Office, told Robert Meade, the C.O.'s representative at the Berlin Conference, 'clearly the G.O.M. alone stops the way' (this with respect to securing the whole S.E. African coast); 31 December 1884, Public Record Office of Northern Ireland, Clanwilliam/Meade MSS D.3044/J/17/54.

involved himself in extraordinary contortions with respect to Angra Pequeña (on the S.W. African coast), not revealing his own plans and dispatches to Münster, his ambassador in London, or, consequently, to Granville. But once it was clear what Bismarck wanted, he got it immediately. The Cabinet of 14 June 1884, baffled by a rising German antagonism whose basis was, to the British Cabinet, quite obscure, agreed to ask *via* the Chancellor's son, Herbert Bismarck, then in London, 'what it is the German Govt. want'. The Cabinet of 21 June ('Important') gave it to him: 'Angra Pequeña: No objection could be taken to the claim, or intention, of the German Government to provide means of protection for German subjects.'

Not only this: a German presence in Southern Africa and in the Pacific could in Gladstone's view be a useful device for keeping the increasingly truculent white colonies in order. The first Gladstone government had been alarmed to find that responsible government led to irresponsible tariff policies by Canada and Australia.* The second found a complex international situation further confused by 'sub-imperialism' (expansionist policies urged on Britain by her colonies, or even carried out by them—particularly Australian expansionism in the Pacific).

Gladstone was in 'absolute sympathy' with Derby in regarding the proposals of the Australian Convention for a 'Monroe doctrine laid down for the whole South Pacific' as 'mere raving'; he went further than Derby in also proposing again to reject Australian claims for a protectorate in New Guinea (already once refused),† but he went out of his way to accommodate Germany's claims there, conceding Bismarck's case while disliking his tone and method. The advantage was clear: 'German colonisation will strengthen and not weaken our hold upon our Colonies: and will make it very difficult for them to maintain the domineering tone to which their public organs are too much inclined.'‡

The same was the case in Southern Africa: 'I should be extremely glad to see the Germans become our neighbours in South Africa, or even the neighbours of the Transvaal. We have to remember Chatham's conquest of Canada, so infinitely lauded, which killed dead as mutton our best security for keeping the British Provinces.'§ Far from being a threat, therefore, Germany could be seen as a means both of reducing the amount of vacant territory into which Britain might be drawn, and of bringing the existing

---

* See above, p. 191.
† To Derby, 8 Dec. 83. See 13 June 83 for the rejection of the 'so-called annexation'.
‡ To Granville, 29 January 1885, Ramm II, ii. 329.
§ i.e. by eliminating France as a threat; to Derby, 21 Dec. 84. This letter was widely circulated in the Colonial Office; Fairfield, the clerk with particular responsibility for Southern African affairs, told Robert Meade, hard pressed at the Berlin Conference: 'We have been plying Lord Derby with annexation pills, but it is no good up to now, as the G.O.M. objects' (Fairfield to Meade, 31 December 1884, Clanwilliam/Meade MSS D. 3044/J/17/47).

colonies to heel. This view implied a sense of Germany as a rival in that region, with an implication of future local defence costs which Gladstone does not seem to have anticipated, or which perhaps he thought would be borne by the colonists; but it also recognized the extent to which German colonization unsupported by a fleet was always ultimately subject to British permission. The further corollary, that encouraging German colonialism would ultimately encourage such a fleet, was not considered.

The notion of Germany as a *deus ex machina* in South Africa showed the extent to which the difficulties in that area remained intractable: 'To piece together *anything* in South Africa is an attractive prospect rather than otherwise.'* The high-profile problem was the Transvaal, but the long-running difficulty was Zululand. At the start of the ministry, the Cabinet, despite the expectations raised by Gladstone's Midlothian speeches, returned to the policy of voluntary confederation which it had introduced in 1871 and an attempt was made to soldier on along the Beaconsfield–Carnarvon road to confederation taken in the late 1870s by the Tory government with Sir Bartle Frere (Governor of the Cape and High Commissioner of South Africa) the 'man on the spot'.

Gladstone operated from an unusually narrow base with respect to South African policy. Against his usual custom, he seems to have had no private information with which to balance the departmental view. His reading shows little interest in Southern African works, though he did read some, such as J. W. Akerman's 'Native government in Natal' (1877) and J. W. Winter's *'Gigantic inhumanity' . . . note on women slavery confederation* (1877) (read twice). He knew a great deal about the war-like characteristics of the Montenegrins, but little of the Boers. Donald Currie, chairman of the Castle shipping line (later Union-Castle), who sponsored Kruger on his visits to London in 1877 and 1878 and who took Gladstone on cruises on his steamers in 1878 and 1880, might have filled the role of confidant, especially during the convalescent voyage in August 1880, but does not seem to have done so. The links with Sir Garnet Wolseley, in 1880 in charge of South African forces, which had been quite close in the later years of the 1868–74 government, were not maintained. Wolseley would have alerted Gladstone to the complexities and dangers of the Transvaal situation.† The 'official mind'—such as it was—of the Colonial Office thus had exceptional authority and, very unusually—probably without precedent in Gladstone's premierships—drafted a vital letter for him, the letter to Kruger and Joubert on the future of the Transvaal of 15 June 1880. Gladstone slightly amended the draft, whose final version stated that

* To Derby, 2 Sept. 83. The Transvaal had been annexed in 1877.

† D. M. Schreuder, *Gladstone and Kruger. Liberal government and colonial 'Home Rule' 1880–85* (1969), 62.

Looking to all the circumstances both of the Transvaal and the rest of South Africa, and to the necessity of preventing a renewal of disorders which might lead to disastrous consequences not only to the Transvaal but to the whole of South Africa, our judgment is that the Queen cannot be advised to relinquish her sovereignty over the Transvaal; but, consistently with the maintenance of that sovereignty, we desire that the white inhabitants of the Transvaal should without prejudice to the rest of the population enjoy the fullest liberty to manage their local affairs; we believe that this liberty may be most easily and promptly conceded to the Transvaal as a member of a South African confederation.

In 1880, therefore, as in the early 1870s, the hope was that the Cape would relieve Britain of her direct South African responsibilities by leading, as Ontario had done in Canada, an autochthonous movement for confederation; hence for the time being, the Transvaal and Sir Bartle Frere must be retained.* In June 1880 the Cape declined to act; confederation was dead; Frere was recalled; but no solution to the position of the Transvaal was found. The Transvaal ignored Gladstone's offer of 15 June. On 19 December 1880 the news came that the Transvaal had proclaimed its own solution, an armed rebellion. On 20 December at Bronkhorstspruit occurred the first of several Boer victories in small skirmishes and the Gladstone government seemed committed to armed resistance. The series of skirmishes culminated in the death of Colley and ninety-two British soldiers on Majuba Hill on 27 February 1881, news of which reached Downing Street by telegraph within a few hours: 'Sad Sad news from South Africa: is it the Hand of Judgment?'†

The news found Gladstone wounded ('slipt off my heels in the powdered snow by the garden door, fell backwards, & struck my head most violently . . .' 'with very uncomfortable feelings *inside* the skull'),‡ battling with the Queen over a peerage for Wolseley, and in the final stages of preparation of the Irish Land Bill. None the less, he handled the crisis consummately. Majuba sprang largely from a failure of commonsense and co-ordination on the veldt. The Cabinet had already offered a Royal Commission to the Boers which was almost certain to recommend an end to annexation. Colley both bungled the timing for the acceptance of an armistice (Kruger being out of touch), and had unnecessarily brought his troops forward to Majuba. Gladstone protected Kimberley, the colonial secretary, from both Whigs and Radicals, gained time for the details of the muddle on the veldt to clarify themselves, and maintained the existing policy of conciliation of the Transvaal and an agreed solution with the Boers.§ This could only mean an ending of annexation and some recognition by the Boers of

---

* See the excellent analysis in C. F. Goodfellow, *Great Britain and South African Confederation 1870–1881* (1966), 188–9.

† 28 Feb. 81.   ‡ 23 Feb. 81.

§ See cabinet and letters to Kimberley, 27 Feb.–8 Mar. 81 and Schreuder, op. cit., 134–46.

Britain's general supremacy in the area. The negotiations were handled with considerable good sense by Colley's successor, Sir Evelyn Wood, and the settlement was set down in the Convention of Pretoria, signed on 3 August 1881. It was, Gladstone recalled, 'the best, perhaps the only feasible, expedient in a critical situation'.* The 'native' interest was safeguarded by a British Resident at Pretoria, the imperial interest by the Transvaal's acceptance of 'suzerainty' and British control of foreign policy. 'Suzerainty' was the solution Gladstone had advocated for an Ottoman Empire unable to retain control in the Christian Balkans. It was used, therefore, in the context of weakness.† Gladstone's advocacy of it for South Africa represented an acknowledgement that any long-term solution must recognize Dutch obduracy, the cost of permanent military subjugation of the Transvaal and perhaps the Orange Free State, and the danger of Dutch revolt at the Cape. Moreover, had not the South African Dutch done what the British had wanted, and that rather well?

Is it unreasonable to think that as the Dutch have Africa for their country, as they went out from the Cape greatly to our relief, as they have solved the native question within their own borders, they are perhaps better qualified to solve the Zulu question outside the Reserve, than we can in dealing with it from Downing Street?‡

This regard for the Dutch character allied to a general irritation with the various parties in Southern Africa and a feeling that British interests there were already adequately safeguarded, allowed Gladstone to watch without dismay the Transvaal's demands of 1883 for a renegotiation of the Pretoria Convention. He did not discourage the renegotiation, which implied the dismantling of the Convention, but he did dislike this being done by a Transvaal deputation in London.§ Even an accommodation between the deposed Zulu chief, Cetewayo, and the Transvaalers—one of the great nightmares of the Cape politicians and of the Colonial Office—did not alarm him: 'It does not appear to me certain that it would be a very bad thing if he [Cetewayo] and the Boers were, in the old phrase, to put their horses together.'¶

Gladstone set up the Cabinet discussion on the renegotiation with a series of questions to Derby which implied regarding the Transvaal as being in the same relationship to Britain as the Orange Free State. Consequently, in Cabinet the suggestion, 'shall we reserve a *veto* over any engagements they may make with foreign countries', and the answer

* To Derby, 25 Apr. 83.
  † As a legal title for intervention, the word was vague; Kimberley prepared a memorandum on its meaning, using quotations supplied by James Murray, the lexicographer, who had recently become friendly with Gladstone; Murray's quotations included several from Gladstone's classical articles, but none from his articles on the Balkans; 29 April 1881, Add MS 44627, f. 1.
  ‡ To Derby, 11 June 84.   § To Derby, 20 June 83.
  ¶ To Derby, 2 Sept. 83. Gladstone offered his Harley Street house for Cetewayo when he came to London to negotiate.

'Cabinet inclined to make this demand', seemed like a positive move from no safeguards to limited safeguards, rather than the dilution of the 1881 Pretoria Convention that in fact it was. Probably the minimalist retention of control of treaties in the 1884 London Convention represented what Gladstone had wanted all along. Even the 'native' question did not bother him, as he argued that the popularity of 'native' immigration into the Transvaal showed there was no need 'for retaining any power of interference within their frontier'. His reading of Olive Schreiner's *Story of an African Farm* (1883) in 1885, 'a most remarkable, painful, book', came too late to affect this view. Nor did he show concern when the Transvaal immediately broke the new convention by expanding across the agreed frontier into Bechuanaland. Given all this—the readiness to accept Germany, the satisfaction with the Transvaal, the absence of strategic concern—the Cabinet's decision in November 1884 to send Sir Charles Warren to declare a Protectorate over Bechuanaland* (in effect restricting German expansion inland eastwards and Transvaal expansion westwards) was a considerable defeat for Gladstone, though he does not seem to have fought very hard against it. Probably he recognized that the combination of the 'forward' group in the Cabinet with the demands for protection by the Cape politicians would be too strong to defeat. When Warren wrote of the danger of German interference in the Transvaal, Gladstone commented, 'such a letter makes me as much afraid, at least, of Sir C. Warren as of the Germans'.†

Gladstone had his best success in East Africa, the only area where in this administration he successfully stopped the expansionists. German activity in the Zanzibar hinterland increased in 1884 as it did in South West Africa; the British countered by reasserting their traditional influence over the Sultan of Zanzibar. Early in December 1884 Gladstone spotted in the papers circulating in the despatch boxes a plan for a forward policy in the East African hinterland. He expostulated memorably to Dilke, one of a group of Cabinet ministers advocating, successfully in the Bechuana instance, sustained blocking or prevention of German colonial expansion:

Terribly have I been puzzled & perplexed on finding a group of the soberest men among us to have concocted a scheme as that touching the mountain country behind Zanzibar with an unrememberable name [i.e. Kilimanjaro]. There *must* somewhere or other be reasons for it, which have not come before me. I have asked Granville whether it may not stand over for a while.‡

Stand over it did until the end of the government. The 'forward' group on the East African question had no equivalent of the Cape ministry with which to coalesce against the Prime Minister. The key was Egypt. There,

---

* Discussed since 1882 *pari passu* with the Transvaal question and hitherto avoided.
† To Derby, 17 Nov. 84.
‡ To Dilke, 14 Dec. 84.

with the break-up of the Conference on finance, the need for the approval of the powers for British proposals for resolving the financial deadlock, and the Wolseley expedition heading for the Sudan, German help against France seemed essential. Gladstone told Derby a week after challenging the East African initiative:

No doubt we must be most cautious here as to Colonial alarmism: but any language at Berlin [i.e. at the West African Conference] appearing to convey sympathy with it might at this moment do extraordinary mischief to us at our one really vulnerable point, Egypt.*

If this was so with respect to West Africa, where Britain already had significant commercial interests, it was *a fortiori* the case in East Africa where she had none of much importance. Thus Gladstone successfully avoided balancing concessions to Germany in West and South West Africa by resistance in East Africa. The German protectorate of Tanganyika was declared in March 1885, and it lay as a *bloc* across the Cape to Cairo route, preventing in the twentieth century the consolidation of a settler-dominated British Empire in Central Africa.† Gladstone's view that German colonies would act to curb the wilder excesses of British colonialism received a powerful posthumous vindication.

This survey of Gladstone's involvement in imperial affairs in his second administration has necessarily focused on those subjects with which he allowed himself to be particularly associated. With some, for example the Berlin Conference of 1884–5, he was hardly involved, despite the interest he might have been expected to take in one of the chief constructs of the Concert in that decade.‡ His interests bear out his own view that he was carried forward in office by difficulties. The means of squaring the circle between local nationalism and European expansionism had not been

---

* To Derby, 24 Dec. 84. Meade, negotiating with Bismarck and Busch in Berlin, and caught in the difficult position of both making concessions to the Germans and resisting them, considered (ironically?) the full implications of Gladstone's position, though without referring to East Africa: 'If however the Government really share Mr. Gladstone's view that he "should be extremely glad to see the Germans become our neighbours in South Africa, or even the neighbours of the Transvaal", why do we annex the Kalahari desert in order to cut the Germans off from reaching Bechuanaland and the Transvaal from Angra Pequeña on the west, and why hoist the flag at St. Lucia Bay to cut them off on the south east? Surely it would be better to go to the Germans with such an offer, which would enable us to make almost any terms we pleased about Egypt, New Guinea and the South Seas. . . . But, I submit, it is bad policy to do neither one thing nor the other. We are now neither making terms with Germany nor stopping the gap' (Meade to Herbert, 3 January 1885, Clanwilliam/Meade MSS D.3044/J/17/56).

† Even once in British hands, after 1918, Tanganyika, as a League of Nations Mandate, could not be part of Sidney Webb's dream (as Colonial Secretary) of a single white-settler colonial unit stretching from Kenya to the South African border; fulfilment of this would surely have given Britain the Algerian imbroglio only just avoided in Southern Rhodesia in the 1960s and 1970s.

‡ It is interesting, in view of the recent stress placed on the limited objectives of the Conference, to note that Gladstone records it in Cabinet as 'a conference on colonising Africa & application of principles of Treaty of Vienna to Congo & Niger' (8 Oct. 84).

found, nor in certain cases, as the Egyptian instance showed, could it be. Gladstone's case was not that such expansionism was wrong, indeed he saw it as natural, but that in the British case it was imprudent, particularly as exemplified by cost, actual and prospective. Unfortunately for him, prudence, a reasonably effective criterion in his first administration, was hardly such in his second. With Bright gone and the Cabinet Radicals Chamberlain and Dilke fast turning into Radical Imperialists, Gladstone increasingly fought his corner alone. That corner was not anti-Empire, but it was anti-imperialist. Unfortunately for Gladstone, the distinction was by the 1880s becoming politically unsustainable. Peel's colonial secretary had no difficulty with the Empire as such, but he disliked its marginal expansion, and in the 1880s the margins were becoming very wide.

Foreign Policy and the Navy Scare, 1884

These extra-European developments were the context for Britain's relations with foreign states during the second Gladstone government. This was a dramatic change from the first government, which was dominated by the Eurocentric Franco-Prussian war and its aftermath. As Bismarck used his new German Empire to develop a series of entangling alliances, fundamentally ruinous to Gladstone's concept of the Concert of Europe, there was little that the Liberal government could do. Though it was common ground (to all but Bright) that Britain might intervene in some major crisis, such as an imminent occupation of Belgium, and that she might intervene *via* the Concert on behalf of worthy causes, it was inconceivable to the Cabinet that she should become involved on a regular basis in an alliance with a European power of Concert-level, a point recognized by Bismarck, who did not continue with the Liberal government the suggestion of an Anglo-German alliance made with some success to Disraeli.* Moreover, the considerable number of Conferences in these years, dealing with Turkish, Egyptian, and imperial questions, disguised the extent to which the alliance system would in the long-run undermine the concept of the Concert.

The transition of the Concert system from the club of monarchies which it had been since the eighteenth century to a wider base of popular legitimacy of the sort attempted by Gladstone in the campaigns of the 1870s was given no further encouragement. The moderate interventionism of the Gladstonian liberals in fact took for granted a good deal of Cobdenite international harmony promoted by international trade. The rapid introduction of protection in many countries in the late 1870s might have suggested that as the Cobdenite basis eroded, so the Concert system needed codification and institutionalization, but Gladstone was entirely at one with those who thought like him in making no effort to counter protec-

* See P. Kennedy, *The rise of the Anglo-German antagonism 1860–1914* (1980), 34–6.

tionism and the Continental system of secret alliances by the advocacy of a refurbished, modernized Concert system. The old system limped on in decline, but there was little attempt at invigorating or strengthening it until the First World War had shown its impotence.

As the Cabinet simply took for granted the efficient working of the British economy, so it presupposed an harmonious international order. In this sense, the second Gladstone government in general, and Gladstone in particular, remained thoroughly mid-Victorian, the last ministry and the last Prime Minister to be so.* There would always be minor dislocations to be corrected, but fundamentally Britain had no enemies and sought no enemies. Bismarck's wild rages against Gladstonian Liberalism were met with an indifference,† wrongly interpreted by Bismarck as contempt, which made him wilder still. Bismarck's duplicity which broadened from muddle about the disclosure of his aims in 1884 to open contempt for agreed procedures in 1885, did not `deflect Gladstone. As he told the Queen, 'there is no great objection to the acts of Germany in themselves, but only to the careless impropriety, which attaches to the manner of them'.‡ The chief difficulty in foreign policy was the fluctuation of French politics and policies, especially in 1882; but this was an imperial difficulty with no real European consequences. France might seem a rival, but it was still a country where the British Prime Minister would, quite naturally, spend weeks by the sea-side convalescing.

Behind this sense of security lay the fleet: the strength of Britain was 'not to be found in alliances with great military powers, but is to be found henceforth, in the sufficiency and supremacy of her navy—a navy as powerful now as the navies of all Europe'. The 1868–74 government had devoted considerable effort to a reconstruction of the army, Gladstone being only partially successful in achieving the full scope of his plans. Apart from the final abolition of flogging and minor adjustments to the Cardwellian system, there was little military reform in 1880–5. Despite the implications of increased colonial rivalry in the 1880s, the Admiralty was left to itself to expand and refurbish the fleet. When, after eighteen months of work, Northbrook sent his memorandum comparing the deficiencies of the British fleet, as left by the Disraeli government, with the condition of the French, Gladstone sent the briefest of notes, accepting it 'freely'.§ The

* Hamilton caught the mood well: 'Stead taunted me with our having no allies. . . . He was a little surprised when I held that we did not want to make allies'; Bahlman, *Hamilton*, ii. 763.

† See Kennedy, op. cit., 157ff. for Bismarck's 'Ideological war against Gladstonism', a war of which Gladstone seems to have been oblivious.

‡ To the Queen, 5 January 1885, in A. C. Benson, Lord Esher and G. E. Buckle, *Letters of Queen Victoria*, 9v. (1907–32) [subsequently *L.Q.V.*], 2nd series, iii. 592.

§ Gladstone to Northbrook, 27 January 1882, Add MS 44545, f. 96. There was a real substance to Northbrook's concern; to make adequate dispositions for the bombardment of Alexandria, the Admiralty was forced to assemble almost all its effective ships; see C. S. White, 'The bombardment of Alexandria 1882', *The Mariner's Mirror*, lxvi. 35 (1980).

secret Royal Commission on Colonial Defences, set up by the Disraeli government under Carnarvon's chairmanship, received even less attention. To Carnarvon's fury, its report, which had important recommendations on coaling stations and the navy, was effectively shelved.*

None the less, as with the foreign policy which it buttressed, the ability of the mid-Victorian fleet to defend British interests was being questioned. The bluff of 'a gigantic deception, perpetrated by all and believed by all'† was being called, and the first really loud shout was in 1884. Carnarvon then had his revenge. As the Egyptian and Sudanese crisis worsened, he supplied W. T. Stead with encouragement and information for the *Pall Mall Gazette*'s 'navy scare' in September 1884,‡ which broke just after Northbrook, the First Lord of the Admiralty, had been appointed to go on his special mission to Egypt to report on the financial deadlock.

The moment was well-chosen: Gladstone was caught in a pincer-movement of Tories, Whigs, and 'blue-water' Radicals§ (the same combination as had convinced the Cabinet that to go forward with plans for a Channel tunnel was pointless).¶ He did not try to escape, but, after deferring the expected statement, succeeded on 2 December at the last minute—the statement in the Commons being due that day—in persuading the Cabinet to reduce the extra sum for naval expenditure from £10,725,000 to £5,525,000. He declined to be seen supporting the programme, telling his Cabinet colleagues: 'As one resolved on retirement when the "situation" is cleared, I do not feel justified in using pressure with reference to a prospective plan reaching over a term of years, although it has not my sympathy.'‖ Coming on top of extra estimates from the Sudan and Bechuanaland less than a month earlier, with a penny on income tax to pay for them, it was an important moment in the gradual crumbling of the edifice of Gladstonian finance, and, as we shall see, played an important part in the fall of the government five months later. The naval 'scare' also marked an alliance repeated in each subsequent Liberal government, which each of those governments, like that of 1884,

* See to Kimberley, 12 June 80 and n.; Sir A. Hardinge, *Carnarvon* (1925), iii. 38ff.; *H* 278. 1831 (4 May 1883).

† The view of N. A. M. Rodger in 'The dark ages of the Admiralty, 1869–85', *The Mariner's Mirror*, lxi–lxiii (1975–7).

‡ See Stead–Carnarvon correspondence, July–September 1884, in Carnarvon MSS, Add MS 60777. It would be wrong to see Carnarvon as instigator of the scare; Stead later credited this role to H. O. Arnold-Forster; see F. Whyte, *Life of W. T. Stead* (1925), i. 146ff.

§ Radical support was thought to be quite extensive; see Bahlman, *Hamilton* ii. 687, 690, 699.

¶ A further attempt was made in the third government. Gladstone visited the exploratory works for the tunnel, about which he was enthusiastic, in March 1882.

‖ 2 Dec. 84. The episode remains rather obscure: were there expansionists in the Admiralty keen to take advantage of Northbrook's absence?

found irresistible. Never was the Admiralty happier, than with the Liberals in office and the Tories free to combine with 'blue water' Liberals to agitate for the fleets they found too expensive to build when themselves in office.

CHAPTER VII

Domestic Policy in the 1880s

A Self-Regulating Economy—Taxation and Retrenchment—Reform of Government, Local and National—The 'Third Reform Act': Franchise Reform and Redistribution

During the last half-century, the whole course of our legislation in great matters, has been directed by the Liberal party; though, in some cases, the work has not finally been finished in its hands. But every great question, once adopted into its creed, has marched onwards, with real and effectual if not always uniform progress, to a triumphant consumation.

It may suffice to name Repeal of the Test Act, Roman Catholic Emancipation, Parliamentary Reform, Repeal of the Corn Law, Repeal of the Navigation Law, Reform of the Tariff, the Abolition of Church Rate, the Reform of the Universities, the abolition of Tests in them and elsewhere, the Disestablishment of the Irish Church, Municipal Reform, important changes in the Land Laws, Secret Voting, and National Education.

It seems difficult in reviewing this list, which might be greatly extended, to deny that we seem to have hold of something like a political axiom when we say that the adoption of a legislative project into the Creed of the Liberal party at large is the sure prelude to its accomplishment.*

A Self-Regulating Economy

Gladstone supervised the domestic and legislative policy of his second government from four perspectives. As Prime Minister he had an overall responsibility for balance and content. As Chancellor of the Exchequer (until December 1882) he was responsible, at the least, for raising revenue and controlling expenditure. As Leader of the House of Commons, he was in charge of the strategic and tactical conduct of the legislative programme and of the proper working of the Commons, involving daily and usually lengthy attendance there. Lastly, as the chief force behind several of the Government's major bills, he was responsible for arguing their case at second reading and for seeing them through the Committee stage. Any one of these responsibilities would normally be regarded as an adequate load.

* Memorandum of 19 Aug. 84.

Taken together, with foreign and imperial affairs added, it is surprising that Gladstone, in his early seventies, was not more often ill and out of action.

It was, in fact, an extraordinary, excessive burden, which overpersonalized the government, held back able men, and encouraged attention to the particular rather than the general. Yet it was a load which did not break its bearer's back and which remained more or less in balance until towards the end of the government. It was inherent in the antecedents to the government's formation that Gladstone should bear a load of this sort. It was exactly the range of responsibilities he had had in the last months of his first government and it was, as we have seen, his intention to shed all of it after a year or so by resigning from political office. As we know, only the Chancellorship was discarded.

Gladstone took the Exchequer personally in 1880 to mark a return to proper financial procedures. The maxim of the Midlothian Campaign—taken from Cobden and echoing Adam Smith—was that 'public economy was public virtue'. This was not merely negative cheese-paring. Allied to the ending of Beaconsfieldian profligacy was the restoration of the creative side of Gladstonian finance. Using the traditional Peelite method of a short-term increase in income-tax to cover a temporary deficit caused by a beneficial commercial reform, he commuted the malt tax into a beer duty in 1880; and in 1881 he carried further and reformulated Northcote's reforms of the various death duties* in order, in part, as we shall see, to prepare the way for a reform of local government finance. Both of these were quite formidable technical achievements, the first an objective of Chancellors for half a century, and they were accompanied by declarations of superlatives: they were questions, he said, which were 'the largest and most difficult still remaining to be effectively dealt with by Parliament'.

Gladstone deliberately set out by such hyperbole to maintain the narrow horizon of expectations of the Exchequer. For him, the government's relationship to the British (perhaps not the Irish) economy was what it had been since the days of Peel: minimal. The Cabinet had no view of 'the economy' as such: economic policy simply did not exist as an item on its agenda. Whereas it had extensive data on the performance of the Egyptian economy and the productivity of the fellaheen, the Cabinet had none on the British economy, save the odd comment on the buoyancy or otherwise of indirect taxes. The 'Great Depression', so prominent a feature of the literature of and on the period, went unrecognized.

The Cabinet never, between 1880 and 1885, discussed the consequence for Britain of the sharp rise in the price of gold nor did it discuss 'unemployment', the intellectual discovery of the decade. It was, of course, to

---

* A useful consequence of Gladstone's 1881 reform was that probate grants now gave the exact value of the estate (hitherto a tax-band had been given).

be a long time before Cabinets could usefully discuss macro-economic prescriptions for 'unemployment', but it is remarkable, in the light of the exceptional dependence of the British economy on overseas trade and on world banking—both backed by the gold standard—that no attention at all should have been given by the Cabinet to the problem of gold supply and the implications of changes in the price of gold.*

It was not, of course, that individual Cabinet members were ignorant of either industry or banking. Though few were still involved directly in firms or banks, most were men of affairs with extensive financial interests especially in agriculture, railways, banks, and the debts of various governments. Land owners such as Gladstone and Granville were also coal mine owners. None knew better than Gladstone the personal consequences of a fiscal crisis for local industry and estate finances, the long-term consequences for the Glynne family finances resulting from the Oak Farm bankruptcy occasioned by the 1847 crash and the shorter-term (but related) difficulties of the Hawarden estate in the early 1880s bore on him almost daily.† He also had a general sense of the direction of the economy and was aware of its difficulties, but he never in these years either as Chancellor or as Prime Minister suggested that the Cabinet should discuss these. The absence of such discussion showed how the mid-century view of government as parallel to and completely distinct from economic activity was, for a Liberal Cabinet, now thoroughly entrenched and instinctive.

When the minority Salisbury government of 1885 set up a Royal Commission on depression of trade and industry under the chairmanship of Northcote (by then Iddesleigh), thus effectively guaranteeing a majority free-trade report despite the nod to fair trade that the appointment of the Commission represented, the Gladstonians refused to nominate any members of it. They felt that the Commission would not only give a platform to anti-free traders, but that it dignified a nonsense: 'depression of trade', other than short-term dislocation which was self-corrective, was intellectually and practicably impossible. When in 1882, in his last Budget Speech (rather skimpily prepared in the midst of the 'Kilmainham' discussions) Gladstone considered this question he looked in classic Peelite terms to a 'natural' return to equilibrium disturbed by 'unhealthy' fiscal dislocation. There was no significant comment to be made on wider questions:

* The Cabinet once (25 June 1881) discussed bimetallism, surprisingly not with complete hostility: 'WEG stated his willingness to apply to the Bank on cause shown, but not to take the initiative'; this may simply have been a ploy: when Hartington tried to take the matter further, Gladstone sent his letter on to the Treasury Secretary (i.e. Cavendish, Hartington's brother) and nothing further came of the matter, the Treasury being systematically opposed to bimetallism; see to Hartington, 27 June 81 and, for the Treasury, E. H. H. Green, 'Rentiers versus Producers? The political economy of the bimetallic controversy c.1880–1898', E.H.R., ciii. 611 (1988).

† W. H. Gladstone did not stand for re-election in 1885 partly to have more time for the Hawarden estate which was, Gladstone told Grosvenor, the chief whip, 'to a certain extent checked by the double pressure of corn and coal distress, those being its two props'.

the position of the Expenditure is that it is a somewhat growing Expenditure, and with respect to the Revenue is that it is a sluggish Revenue. . . . It is very remarkable that although employment is generally active, and although the condition of trade cannot be said to be generally unsatisfactory, yet the recovery of the country from the point of extreme depression has been a slow and languid recovery, especially as regards the action of that recovery upon the Revenue of the country. No doubt, there is a natural explanation of the circumstances in the extreme excitement—the unnatural and the unhealthy excitement—of prices which existed during the period of prosperity which preceded the time of depression; and it is to that cause that we must look for the slackness of the recovery to which I have referred, and not to any diminution whatsoever in the resources of the country, or any deterioration in its industrial prospects.*

The consequences of the heavy-handed corrective mechanism of the market were very much with the government, but they were dealt with departmentally. For example, Chamberlain's famous Board of Trade circular on public works in 1886 was not discussed by the Cabinet and went unmentioned by the Prime Minister. As we have seen, fiscal unorthodoxy was very occasionally mentioned in Cabinet but apart from the subject of non-protectionist commercial treaties there was never any recorded discussion either of Britain's trade deficit or of her enormous export of capital in this period. There was no attempt to gather information on such subjects. Nor was there any attempt in the Treasury at a general appraisal of the costs and economic benefits of imperial expansion. Since the Treasury did not think in terms of the 'economy' as such, but only of the revenue potential of sections of it, an appraisal of that sort was intellectually inconceivable. Any reform which implied the recognition of a national economy and consequently of some governmental responsibility for it was strongly resisted. Thus Gladstone rejected Chamberlain's suggestion of a Ministry of Commerce and downgraded the equivalent proposal for a Ministry of Agriculture, ensuring that it took the form of a Committee of Council, a mechanism already known for ineffectiveness from the example of the education committee. Moreover, by putting Carlingford in charge of the committee, he made inaction certain.

After the Trafalgar Square 'riots' of February 1886, Gladstone pointed out that the fall in commodity prices had made the 'bulk of the working classes . . . (comparatively) not ill but better off' and that it was 'dangerous in principle' to make 'the State minister to the poor of London at the expence of the nation'.† In recognizing the untypicality of the London labour market as a basis for generalization about national conditions, he was well ahead of most of the social commentators and his observations on living standards were correct with respect to most of those in employment,

* *H* 268. 1273–4; 24 Apr. 82.
† To Ponsonby, 16 Feb. 86.

but he used his denial of the 'great depression' and of the primacy of London as a reason for a mere reliance on existing voluntarist and poor law mechanisms.

Taxation and Retrenchment

Gladstone resisted new ministries which might be active, but he hankered, as he had since the 1850s, after a Ministry of Finance, which would be negative in its influence, keeping down government expenditure by further extending Treasury control over other government departments and generally preserving the minimal State. Rising expenditure was often thought of as a chief and growing concern, and Gladstone often presented it as such. The Budget of 1873 had estimated expenditure of £73 millions; that of 1881, of nearly £85 millions, prices in the interval having fallen significantly. Gladstone declared that he had 'great doubts' as to whether the system by which the estimates were prepared 'upon the exclusive responsibility of the Government' was a good system: the Commons ought to be involved also.* This was a return to the view expressed in 1862, that posthumous scrutiny by the Public Accounts Committee was insufficient,† but, as in the 1860s, he was unwilling to make proposals which significantly diminished the executive's freedom and flexibility. The furthest he would go was the suggestion—not in fact carried out—that there be a Select Committee on Expenditure to scrutinize the estimates, and expenditure generally.‡

Executive prerogative was one reason for inaction. Another was that, despite Gladstone's lamentations that the era of economic reform was passed, and despite his complaints about the costs of military expeditions and the 'contagion' of foreign countries which 'necessarily affects us',§ in fact central government expenditure remained remarkably low in relationship to the size of the economy, given that Britain found herself still the only world power. The increases of the 1870s and the first £100 million Budget in 1885 seemed large, but in that year central government expenditure bore the same relationship to G.N.P. as in 1865: 7.9 per cent.¶ When the Radicals in 1883 moved a Resolution to reduce government expenditure consistent with the efficiency of the public service, Gladstone, speaking for the government, was rather caught. He accepted the Resolution, partly on the grounds that there were no significant reductions to be made. He calculated that if grants-in-aid and payments to reduce the debt were taken out of the figures, a central government expenditure of £47 million in 1840 had only risen to £62 million in 1882—an increase of about 34 per cent, in a period when the

---

* H 268. 1297–8.
† See above, p. 117.
‡ Speech on Rylands' motion on national expenditure, 6 April 1883; H 277. 1669–70.
§ H 268. 1298.
¶ See table above, p. 115. In the 1980s the equivalent figure was *ca.* 38 per cent.

population had increased by 65 per cent and the taxable revenue of the country (the nearest contemporary concept to G.N.P.) by 115 per cent,* a remarkable absence of government growth and an exceptional success for Peel–Gladstone finance, though with serious if unrecognized consequences for the 'national economy' which existed despite the attempt of Cabinet and the Treasury to assume that it did not.

The household suffrage in the towns had not led to the surge of expenditure financed by direct taxation feared by its opponents. Indeed what is striking in the 1880s is the absence of sustained or systematic political challenge to the Gladstonian minimal central state. Of course there were individual claims from particular interest groups—more money for education, for the navy, for imperial ventures—but there was no general argument for the government to answer for a positive move away from the minimal state to a new plateau of public expenditure. Though Imperialists, New Liberals, and Socialists were in the 1880s each in their different ways challenging the presuppositions of the mid-nineteenth century minimal state, their challenges were surprisingly slow to take on a programmatic form. Only in Ireland was there significant demand for central government money for social purposes, and land purchase was as much a cry of the landed class as it was of the peasantry (which as yet of course had no vote).

Expenditure was thus low. Marginal increases, or potential increases, were to be sternly resisted so as to keep it low. Gladstone fought these at every level. The difficulty was the classic one. Large expenditures tended to go relatively unsupervised. To gain a policy objective once agreed upon, Gladstone was ready to allocate whatever sum was necessary; hence his combativeness up to the point of decision. Thus expeditions were well-financed and well-manned. To gain the objective of an effective second Suez Canal, the Cabinet was ready to give Lesseps an £8 million loan at minimal interest, in effect, Gladstone told the Commons, 'a great pecuniary gift to the Canal Company'.† On the other hand, small expenditures were curtailed in ways that sometimes seemed petty and vindictive. This was particularly so in the area of official salaries, where Gladstone hoped to save money by abolishing the Privy Seal‡ and by a series of minor money-saving measures, the most notorious of which was his attempt to reduce by £300 the salaries of Jesse Collings and Henry Broadhurst when they took office in 1886.

Large, exceptional items of expenditure such as naval expansion and the 1884–5 Votes of Credit drove budgetary planning into a corner. By 1885 the Cabinet faced the need to raise revenue to cover expenditure of over

* H 277. 1673–4. † H 282. 145.

‡ This controversial suggestion was discussed throughout the 1880–5 ministry; in 1886, Gladstone took the post himself (Disraeli had done the same in 1876–8), getting Cabinet agreement to its being merged with the First Lordship; but Salisbury revived it as a separate office. Gladstone again held it with the First Lordship in 1892–4.

£100,000,000 if all of the Vote of Credit for the Sudan and Russia were spent, and this in the face of an imminent General Election on the new franchise. Even before the need for the Vote of Credit, Gladstone had been alarmed that some increase in indirect as well as direct taxation would be necessary, and 'such a proceeding, esp. in the last year of a Parlt., would raise a political question of the first order'. With the Vote of Credit adding an extra £11,000,000, some increase in indirect taxation was hardly avoidable. The Budget in its first form, presented on 30 April 1885, largely met a deficit of £15,000,000 by increasing income tax from 5d. to 8d. (producing £5,400,000 extra), by increasing indirect taxes on drink (producing £1,650,000), by extra succession duties, and by adjustments to the debt. Despite the fact that direct taxation bore much the larger share of the increase, and indeed reminded voters that the Liberals were the party of direct taxation, Chamberlain and Dilke made a strong pitch, almost to the point of resigning, against the increase in indirect taxation.

A revised version of the indirect tax proposals was prepared—embarrassing in itself given Gladstone's complaints in the late 1870s about irregular Tory budgeting—but on this occasion the revisions were downwards as £2,000,000 of the Vote of Credit were not needed (that £9,000,000 were needed was odd in view of the fact that neither the new phase of the Sudanese campaign nor the Russian war, for which the Vote had been jointly raised, had occurred). The revisions were announced on 5 June. On 8 June Beach's amendment on indirect taxation was the occasion of the defeat and resignation of the government, the victorious majority being, in Gladstone's view, wholly unprincipled, made up of '1. The Irish who are opposed to indirect taxation generally: 2. The Tories who are even more friendly to it than we are.' In the light of the financial and 'economical' elements of the attack on 'Beaconsfieldism' in the Midlothian Campaigns of 1879 and 1880, it was a striking irony that it was on finance that the Liberal majority of 1880 withered away in 1885. This was a posthumous revenge for Disraeli, the more so as 1852 was the previous occasion on which a defeat on its budget had led to the resignation of the government.

Reform of Government, Local and National

Gladstone's argument in 1883 that government expenditure had not relatively increased greatly depended in part on deducting grants-in-aid—the 'doles', as he called them—paid by central to local government. Awareness of the importance of this deduction in fact lay behind what was intended to be one of the chief legislative achievements of the Liberal government: the creation of a nation-wide series of elected county and district councils to supplement the limited system of elected municipal corporations. Related to this was to be the long-demanded reform of the rates, by early 1881 threatening to be as much of a nuisance as it had been 1868–74.

Gladstone had sketched his position in January 1874, and he returned to it in 1881 as the ministry worked towards a County Government Bill. His position was this: elected local authorities should take over 'certain taxes or parts of taxes' allocated to local authorities by central government, thus abolishing grants-in-aid and decentralizing powers presently exercised by the Local Government Board; these local authorities would be subject to 'general rules and conditions to limit their discretion where necessary', though it was hoped such control would be minimal; there would thus be 'not only a great Local Government Bill, but a great decentralisation Bill' in which local initiative would be linked to local financial responsibility, though education would have to continue to be centrally supervised. Much of the money to replace the grants-in-aid (which Gladstone saw as being unfairly paid by 'a fund of which one half (more or less) is contributed by labour') and to reduce the rates, would come from taxes on personalty, in particular 'the abolition or diminution of the remarkable preferences now allowed to land under the Death-duties'. Gladstone's idea was thus to end the oblique method of grants-in-aid and replace it by taxation which local electors would relate directly to local expenditure, and register their approval or disapproval through local elections. This was too bold for Dodson, despite a reminder. His draft bill was, in the view of Sir Henry Thring, the parliamentary draftsman, 'in no respect a decentralising Bill';* its proposals were based on the continuance of the existing county rate with some reform, plus grants-in-aid.†

Gladstone's financial interest in county government associated him with a much wider movement in the Liberal party which favoured a plurality of representation at every level, exemplified by the fact that the draft County Boards Bill of December 1881 became the draft County Council Bill of 1882 which, under Dilke, became a draft Local Government Bill (i.e. County and District Councils) for 1884.‡ Yet the government failed to pass a single one of the various English, Scottish, and Irish county and local government bills discussed and in some cases introduced in the 1880–5 Parliament. The County Government and the London Government Bills planned for 1882 and the Provincial Councils (Ireland Bill) drafted by

---

* See Thring's mem., 17 November 1882, Monk Bretton MSS, Bodleian Library, 55.

† Dodson's mem., for Cabinet of November 1881, allowed for 'the levying of some local tax or taxes other than rates' but this is not explicitly mentioned in his drafts of a County Council Bill, January and March 1882 (Monk Bretton 55); the Queen's Speech for 1882 promised 'financial changes' and Gladstone, when announcing no bill could be introduced in 1882, mentioned that 'an important financial re-adjustment' would have accompanied it; *H* 268. 1301 (see also *H* 266. 1307); Thring's mem. of 17 November 1882, looking to a bill in 1883, stated 'it is important to recollect that the Government associate with the scheme of county government a proposal to pay to the county authority, in a lump, the large subventions now contributed by the Treasury for local purposes and to entrust the expenditure of those sums to the County Council, free from all central control'; but he made no mention of a tax or rate reform; Monk Bretton 55.

‡ See Dilke's draft bill, 21 November 1883; Monk Bretton 55.

Gladstone in April 1882 came to nothing in that year, nor again in 1883; in 1884 there was an attempt to give a London Government Bill a run, but it did not get beyond Second Reading; in 1885 Irish local government brought the Cabinet to the edge of disintegration. The resignation of June 1885 was the consequence of these two elements coming together. The rift in the Cabinet over Chamberlain's Central Board proposal for Ireland was almost irreconcilable; the failure to reform the rates despite all the attempts in the first government and between 1880 and 1885 was an important ingredient in the success of Hicks Beach's amendment to the Budget in 1885, the occasion of the resignation.

Undoubtedly, the clogged parliamentary timetable was partly to blame for the failure to pass a bill: local government needed to be the priority bill of the session. It had its best chance in 1882, but this was spoilt by the unforeseeable crisis in Ireland, as the 1881 Land Act turned out to be the first step, not, as Gladstone had hoped, the last. Moreover, Dodson, the minister responsible, was a man of worth but not of power, unable to provide the force needed to drive a bill of this sort through (Gladstone recognized this in pushing him aside in the 1882 reshuffle). As early as March 1882, Gladstone told him that, as the result of 'the obstructionists of the two Oppositions', 'no confident expectations can be formed as to any Bill of magnitude & complexity like this until we see our way in some degree as to Procedure & Devolution to which we must give all our disposable energies'.

An important dimension of the Home Rule Bill of 1886 was its attempt to bypass this deadlock by removing Irish business and all or most of the Irish MPs from Westminster. But the difficulties went beyond obstruction and the timetable. The Liberals had not brought local government into coherence. Like Egypt in foreign affairs, it was the concern of a variety of ministries: the Local Government Board, the Home Office, Dublin Castle, the Lord Advocate, or the Scottish Office (if the Government could agree to have one: a bill establishing administrative devolution for Scotland was one of the various measures introduced each year too late in the Session to be passed, the Tories putting it through in 1885). Thus Dodson and Dilke at the Local Government Board with their County and Local Government Bills jockeyed with Harcourt at the Home Office with his London Government Bills. Gladstone moved in and out of the question, directing Dodson on finance, trying and failing to persuade Harcourt that the police in London should be subject to the elected body, spasmodically encouraging Forster and then Spencer to action on local government in Ireland, and himself drafting a Provincial Councils (Ireland) Bill to go with land purchase in 1882. Sidetracked by Bradlaugh, Ireland, and the aftermath of the murders in 1882, exhausted and absent from the planning cabinets in 1883, Gladstone failed to assert a strategic command over the plurality of local government measures considered by his Cabinet.

Beyond this hung the difficulty that the question of the county franchise had not been resolved: by the 1880s, it seemed odd to give voters a local while denying them a parliamentary vote, and, alternatively, the achievement of local government might be used as an effective argument against resolving the parliamentary franchise question. Yet here was a paradox: conventionally, a new parliamentary franchise led quickly to a general election. If the county franchise were to enable new voters to shape local government, the achievement of the first might put at risk the Liberal Parliament which would deal with the second. Moreover, the exercise of that parliamentary franchise would very probably result in Irish local government—in whatever form—becoming a very strongly asserted priority. If the Liberals got local government and franchise reform the wrong way round, there were strong reasons why that was the case.

To two of the questions related to local government reform, Gladstone did however give full attention: 'Procedure and Devolution', and parliamentary reform.

'Procedure and Devolution' meant devolving Commons' business to Grand Committees and introducing the mechanism of the closure to enable government business to be expedited. 'Devolution' in minutes and correspondence in the early 1880s thus usually has this technical meaning, rather than the usual one of Home Rule or extensive local government. As Leader of the House, Gladstone necessarily played a central part in formulating and carrying the various measures. The clogged parliamentary timetable was a long-standing problem, especially for Liberal governments with their habit of starting government bills in the knowledge that many of them would have to be axed by the July Cabinets. The introduction of *clôture* (the term emphasized the foreignness of the concept to the habits of the Commons) was considered in the first government but never to the point of a proposal. The general context for a change in the Commons' Standing Orders thus existed as the large majority of 1880 made slow progress with its legislation, but the particular context for change was created by the Irish crisis of the early 1880s.

Irish 'obstruction' took two forms: first, out-and-out filibustering, points-of-order, motions that Gladstone be not heard, etc.; second, and much more common, there was what to non-Irish MPs seemed an over-conscientious attention by Home Rule MPs to the improvement of proposed legislation, usually that affecting Ireland, of which there was, between 1880 and 1882, a vast amount. The first form, already tried in the latter phases of the Beaconsfield government, was rare, but it reached its culmination in the famous $41\frac{1}{2}$ hours sitting of 31 January to 2 February 1881, when Speaker Brand, 'worthy of his place' in Gladstone's view, adjourned the House on his own responsibility. The Cabinet plans for *clôture* were already in preparation but Northcote, 'weaker than water' (Gladstone thought), withdrew his support. On 3 February there was

> An extraordinary evening. The crass infatuation of the Parnell members caused the House to be cleared of them before nine. I then proposed my Resolution for a quasi Dictatorship. Before two it was adjusted in all points, and carried without division.

Next day, on the Protection of Property Bill, 'What a change!'

In the sense of provoking the House to the extent of passing the 'urgency' Standing Order, Parnell had blundered, and the Protection Bill passed under its aegis. But, of course, in the sense of promoting his own position in Ireland and of making a draconian Bill be seen to be being passed draconianly, Parnell had lost nothing. This was the difficulty for a Liberal Cabinet: the Irish crisis might be responsible for corrupting the conventions of the Commons, but the result was a considerable increase in the power of the executive, however much it might be disguised by making it the Speaker's job to superintend business during the period of 'urgency'. This was confirmed when the Speaker laid on the Table a further sixteen rules to apply during 'urgency', one of which was the *clôture* agreed with the Cabinet before the Irish *fracas*, and another what became the *guillotine*.

The 'quasi Dictatorship' of 'urgency' was unpopular and undignified: it suggested panic in the heart of the Mother of Parliaments. Moreover, the constructive, devolutionary dimension was lost, as indeed it had been on a greater scale in 1880 when Gladstone's ambitious 'Obstruction and Devolution' proposals were pushed aside by the Irish emergency. In 1882, therefore, the Cabinet with the Speaker and Erskine May, the Clerk of the Commons, in attendance tried to normalize procedures by expediting business without a declaration of 'urgency', and by creating Grand Committees for Law and Trade to relieve the Commons' timetable. Ireland and Egypt and the Cabinet's indecision about the Conservatives' amendment that a two-thirds majority for closure be needed, meant deferral of 'procedure and devolution' to a special Session in the autumn of 1882 when, with the '2/3 amendment' defeated by 84 votes, the new Standing Orders passed after 34 nights of debate: 'A great day, as I think, for the House of Commons itself.'

So might Gladstone think, but it was really a great day for executive government. Many Liberals were uneasy. Despite the success of the Grand Committee in dealing with Chamberlain's Bankruptcy Bill in 1883, the devolutionary side of the system lapsed at the end of 1883 and was not renewed.* The details of the Standing Orders were unpopular and not

---

* The Standing Orders for Grand Committees were for 1883 only; the failure to continue them is something of a mystery; asked about them on 31 July 1883, Gladstone replied that despite their 'increased importance' the government did not 'think the time or the circumstances convenient for making a proposal'; *H* 282. 1156.

brought into play.* Despite all the time spent on procedure and devolution, little more progress was in practice made than was made legislatively on local government. And as with local government, the solution pointed one way: remove the Irish from the House.

The 'Third Reform Act': Franchise Reform and Redistribution

Parliamentary reform was the great Liberal legislative triumph of Gladstone's second ministry, going far to redeem the promise of the majority of 1880 and to obliterate for many Liberals the disappointments and failures of the government. 1831–2 and 1866–7 had created a pattern and a warning: 'reform' meant a clutch of related measures and a political crisis. There was no such thing as a straightforward reform bill, for it involved that most complex of all political manœuvres: a political system transforming its nature by changing its own rules. The new dispensation of franchise and redistributed constituency boundaries had to be constituted by the members of Parliament (in both Houses) who owed their power and presence to the old. Gladstone's aim was to simplify the clutch of measures and thus, he hoped, contain the crisis. This would be achieved by keeping franchise and redistribution separate, with various other measures, such as a new registration bill for each country, to follow. It would also permit Gladstone to pass a simple franchise bill and then retire, leaving the details of redistribution to his successors.

Gladstone was committed to franchise reform by his pledge of 1873 that he believed 'the extension of the Household Suffrage to counties to be one which is just and politic in itself, & which cannot long be avoided'.† The reform of the county franchise—despite Gladstone's wishes—linked parliamentary reform to the land campaign in Britain as well as in Ireland and was urged in Cabinet by Chamberlain from an early stage in 1880. Chamberlain ran up against Gladstone's argument that 'this subject, entailing as it would a new dissolution, ought to be deferred till towards the close of the new Parliament just elected',‡ i.e. deferred till 1884 or 1885, the latter being probably the latest year for a bill or bills on which a dissolution on a new register and with new boundaries could be held in early 1887 (the latest time allowed by the Septennial Act and the financial timetable of the year). It was most unusual for a Parliament to run its full course, and thus

* J. Redlich, *The procedure of the House of Commons*, 3v. (1908), i. 174–5: 'the House tacitly abandoned many parts of the new procedure and it never was really put into force'. It seems the closure was never used in 1882–5, for in the one case noted by Redlich, i. 177n., that of 20 February 1885, the Resolution for precedence for the Redistribution Bill was not in fact moved under the Standing Order and was not a closure but a precedence motion, of a sort that could have been moved at any time. † See 23 July 73.

‡ J. Chamberlain, *A political memoir 1880–92*, ed. C. H. D. Howard (1953), 4 and A. Jones, *The politics of reform 1884*, (1972), 3; Gladstone did not record Chamberlain's proposal. Chamberlain raised the question again in 1881, proposing the sequence followed by Gladstone in 1883, a franchise bill alone, with redistribution 'postponed'.

the Cabinet's move in the autumn of 1883 to plan a bill or bills for 1884 was a choice for the earlier of the two options. In that sense it reflected the disappointment of the Liberal party in the absence of achievement by its majority in 1880–3, but not too much should be made of this. Indeed, in 1882 Gladstone had seen the Session of 1884 as the latest year in which to tackle the question, keeping 'a year to spare in case of accidents'—as it turned out, a very prudent safeguard. The Cabinet's movement towards parliamentary reform in the autumn of 1883 was thus anticipated and was not haphazard.

Gladstone initiated matters on his return from a cruise to Scandinavia with Tennyson by asking Sir Henry James, the Attorney General, to consider the possibility of drafting a single Bill for all three 'Kingdoms' (Scotland, Ireland, England-and-Wales); hitherto there had been a separate bill for each, the Irish franchises being almost unrelated in character or chronology to those of the mainland. Thus Gladstone's strategy was clear from the start. Remembering the disastrous set-back of 1866, when the Gladstone/Russell bill led to the fall of the ministry—though ignoring the importance of the absence of a redistribution proposal in causing that set-back—he was determined to keep the legislation as simple as possible: 'form is of the utmost political importance. And by form I mean brevity. . . . Every needless word will be a new danger', because 'the endeavour will be to beat us by and upon entangling details'.* A single bill for the three Kingdoms would trump the opposition to franchise extension in Ireland, assuming Ireland were to be included at all, as well as shortening the amount of parliamentary time needed. With luck, only half a Session would be needed, leaving room for a local government bill.† Ireland, in Gladstone's view, had to be included in both the franchise and the redistribution bills: 'It would I think be impolitic and inequitable to exclude Ireland from both [*sc.* either of] these great subjects: I believe too that the exclusion would ensure failure.'‡

In Gladstone's mind, therefore, the question was not whether to include Ireland, but on what basis: a harmonization of the existing Irish borough and county franchises on the £4 borough standard, or, what might be in fact though not in appearance 'more conservative', the assimilation of the Irish franchise with 'the pure British franchise', i.e. a household suffrage for the three kingdoms.§ The view of Dublin Castle, as expressed by G. O. Trevelyan, the Irish Secretary, was that it was 'impossible to propose a different franchise for Great Britain and Ireland' and that household suffrage, in reducing the influence of farmers, would encourage in the latter

* To James, 5 Nov. 83.
† To Hartington, 22 Oct. 83.
‡ Ibid.
§ To Trevelyan, 23 Oct. 83.

'some sense of political responsibility'.* By early November 1883, a harmonization of the United Kingdom's franchises, on the basis of household suffrage in the boroughs and counties of the three kingdoms, was the basis of the bill, if there were to be one. Gladstone coaxed the bill through the autumn Cabinets with considerable skill: its 'provisional' nature technically allowing dissidents to hang back; *if* there were to be a bill 'it shall be with the franchise *alone*',† i.e. redistribution to be taken separately. This was partly a means of keeping open the possibility of retirement in the foreseeable future: Gladstone argued that he could manage a franchise bill but not a redistribution bill. But there were wider considerations also. The chief whip thought the Cabinet 'never made a more sensible decision' than 'the Franchise *alone*'.‡ This way of proceeding Gladstone required as part of his strategy of ensuring safe passage through the Commons, despite the precedent of 1866 when the failure to deal with redistribution had been a chief cause of disaster.

In one way this was a fair point: the attempt to deal with franchise reform in one bill only was a novelty and, given the history of legislation in 1880–3, the assumption of delays and difficulties was not unreasonable. But the separation of franchise and redistribution admitted another point: the Liberals generally agreed, as with local government, that reform was a natural use of their large majority, but also, again as with local government, there was little agreement about how the redistribution should be carried out, and there was no mechanism for arriving at a party view on the matter. The distinction between town and country, so carefully preserved in 1832 and 1867, the accommodation of extensive demographic changes, the possibility of proportional representation: all these were disputed areas which could reasonably be seen as jeopardizing the harmony of Liberal agreement on a simple franchise extension, if they were dealt with in the same bill. Moreover, there was the obvious point, characteristically not made in the rather decorous style of Liberal letter-writing, that redistribution in 1885 would keep the government's supporters (who on this issue included, unusually, the Parnellites) in line for another Session, thus delaying the dissolution which would naturally follow the passing of the various reform bills. This indeed proved to be the case, though not in the circumstances Gladstone had expected.

Gladstone carried his approach; Hartington's price for agreeing to it was that Gladstone should therefore be seen to be responsible by taking charge of the Bills in the Commons (including redistribution), an arrangement patched up in a flurry of letters and meetings in the week after Christmas 1883. Gladstone carried the Franchise Bill in the Commons by the end of

* To Trevelyan, 23 Oct. 83.
† 22 Nov. 83 and to Grosvenor, 23 Nov. 83.
‡ To Grosvenor, 23 Nov. 83n.

June 1884, largely through the self-restraint of the Liberal party which on the whole obeyed Gladstone's entreaty to his supporters 'not to endanger the Bill by additions',* and of the Home Rule MPs who sensed from the start the advantage they would gain from the bill.

Conceptually, the 'Bill to amend the Law relating to the Representation of the People in the United Kingdom', whose motion for introduction Gladstone moved on 28 February 1884 was, as we would expect from him, extremely conservative. In this, belief merged happily with prudence. Radical issues such as proportional representation and the enfranchisement of women were ruthlessly thrust aside. The bill followed the 1832 and 1867 models in adding to the existing franchises a household franchise for county voters, together with two 'enlargements' of the household franchise, the lodger and service franchises. There was no attempt at 'reform upon a system', and the vote was no more a right than it had ever been: it was a privilege granted by statute to certain adult men.† The purpose of the bill was 'the enfranchisement of capable citizens', and the criterion of capability had become, through weight of numbers and the absence of the expansion of other forms of franchise, the occupation of property: 'occupation will inevitably be, under the new system, the ground and main foundation of our electoral system'.‡ The man who did not occupy property, as a householder, as a lodger (narrowly defined and hard to register),§ or as the living-in servant of a householder or as owner of business premises, could not expect a vote. Gladstone admitted no category of persons as deserving but still excluded from the franchise,¶ with the possible exception of women. Gladstone argued with respect to female suffrage that concern for the passing of the bill meant that 'to nail onto the Extension of the Franchise, founded on principles already known & in use, a vast social question, which is surely entitled to be considered as such, appears to me in principle very doubtful'; if passed in the Commons, a women's suffrage amendment

---

* H 285. 132.

† Ideas of abolishing ancient right franchises were dropped: 'we leave the "ancient right" franchise alone' (H 285. 120); the Bill did abolish the £50 Chandos clause of 1832, as no longer necessary; ibid., 113.

‡ H 285. 116. E. Gibson, the Irish Tory, though strongly opposed to the bill, sharply picked up Gladstone's skilful elision of the criteria of capability and occupation: 'The argument of the Prime Minister prove[d] infinitely too much. It proved that it was right to give the franchise to every man with a house; but every man without a house, although fully qualified in other respects, was not said to be capable of the franchise'; H 285. 152.

§ Gladstone maintained the especial restrictiveness of the register with respect to lodgers (whose small representation on the register he had correctly and approvingly anticipated in 1867) by suggesting to Lambert of the Local Government Board that it would continue to be desirable that 'lodger-votes, and property votes of all kinds, must come there by claim', i.e. must be claimed in person each year; to Lambert, 22 Dec. 83.

¶ Of the various other possible changes (chiefly reducing existing property franchises) mentioned by Gladstone as necessarily omitted—'we are determined . . . not to deck-load our Franchise Bill'—only the enfranchisement of women would have extended the franchise to those without it; H 285. 123.

would give the Lords just the excuse they sought to reject the bill.* Gladstone's own position on whether women were admittable to the franchise thus remained studiously undisclosed.

Retrospectively, the 1884 bill seems conservative, an important step in the long process by which the British ruling class created the illusion of democracy while carefully limiting its reality. To contemporaries, however, the bill seemed dramatic and, in the context of the politics of the 1880s, several of its consequences were so. The bill seemed to enfranchise both the Liberal land campaign and the residue of the Land League. The distinction drawn between a Franchise Bill in 1884 and a Redistribution Bill in the near but unspecified future opened, despite Liberal disclaimers, the possibility of a dissolution on the new franchise but on the old distribution of seats.

In 1866 the bill had failed in the Commons largely because of the re-distribution question; in 1884 it passed the Commons despite it. Accordingly, on 8 July the Lords rejected the Second Reading of the bill by 205 votes to 146: 'What a suicidal act of the Lords!', Gladstone noted, as Salisbury played the first card of a long-drawn out poker game. It was a game Gladstone manifestly enjoyed. In the short term, Salisbury seemed to have given him a considerable advantage. That the Lords would reject the bill (except, *via* Cairns' amendment, as part of 'an entire scheme') was certainly not part of Gladstone's initial calculations. As the possibility arose, he went to considerable lengths to mobilize the bishops and peers of Liberal appointment or creation, including Tennyson.

Gladstone was certainly seen to have tried to get the bill through the House of Lords, but failure to have done so was not necessarily a tactical disadvantage. Privately, Gladstone could point out to the Queen the folly, irresponsibility, and riskiness to the monarchy of the Tories' position in making 'organic change in the House of Lords' an issue which, if the Franchise Bill were not passed, the Liberal Party, however reluctantly, would be bound to take up, an issue which, once taken up, would eventually be taken to a conclusion. With the Queen, it was for once Gladstone who was the calming man of caution, and he encouraged her mediation with a long, skilfully-angled memorandum pointing out the dangers to the hereditary principle (and consequently to the monarchy) if the Tory peers were not brought to reason.† Publicly, Gladstone could reap the advantage of the Lords' action by the hugely enthusiastic reception he was given during his tour of the agricultural constituencies of central and east

---

* To Dilke, 13 May 84; see also to Woodall (who moved the women's suffrage amendment on 11 June 1884), 10 June 84. On Mason's motion on women's suffrage in 1883, Hamilton noted: 'Mr. G. and the preponderance of the Government did not support it. The balance of his mind seems to be against such a proposal, but he would not equally object to the extension of the franchise to women on the Italian plan which is, I believe, that they vote by male proxy'; Bahlman, *Hamilton*, ii. 458.

† 19 and 25 Aug. 84.

Scotland in the late summer of 1884, 'a tour of utmost interest: which grew into an importance far beyond anything I had dreamt of'.* The party of progress was given the opportunity for a really hearty cheer, its last for almost twenty years. Gladstone denounced the specific action of the Lords, while defending the principle of an hereditary second chamber. This tour, which generated vast processions and demonstrations in the cities, towns and villages of Scotland, represented a peak of enthusiasm for the franchise and for participation in the parliamentary process by the ability to exercise it. Never before or since was a Prime Minister given the opportunity of leading so popular a constitutional crusade. The Scots enjoyed this climax to traditional liberalism.

But if the Lords' action posed problems for the Conservatives in their appeal to the new democracy, it also created considerable difficulties for the Liberals. Gladstone needed the bill: he it was who had persuaded the Cabinet and the Commons that a Franchise Bill first, with redistribution second, would expedite and simplify. The Cabinet had already lost the business of one Session; it could not be seen to be subservient to the dictates of the Lords. Although Gladstone 'considered the points of a Manifesto speech', he persuaded the Cabinet not to dissolve on the Franchise Bill, but instead to hold an autumn Session: 'To allow Lords to force a dissolution would be precedent worse than anything since beginning of the reign of Geo. III.'† Moreover, the crises over Egyptian finance and over the rescue of Gordon in themselves made a dissolution in July 1884 almost impossible: 'This day [2 August 1884] for the first time in my recollection there were *three* crises for us running high tide at once: Egypt, Gordon, & franchise.' The creation of peers as a means of curtailing the Lords would have gone against all Gladstone's personal constitutional instincts, and would anyway have been unacceptable to the considerable Whig/Liberal group led by Hartington which had argued all along that the bill should deal with redistribution and franchise together. Even less would it have been acceptable to the Queen.

A coming to terms was thus called for: the issue was, on what terms and on whose? By his cool playing of the Lords' card, Salisbury had gained a considerable advantage: he had blocked the Liberal majority in the Commons and, since the Liberals had continued to play within the existing constitutional conventions (while complaining that Salisbury was flouting them), he had gained the point that the Tory majority in the Lords counted. Put crudely, the Liberals were to gain on the franchise, the Tories on the redistribution. This was the effect of the agreement by which Gladstone, Dilke, and Hartington met Salisbury and Northcote as 'Legates of the

---

* 26 Sept. 84.
† Monk Bretton's note of Gladstone's remarks; 9 July 84n.

opposite party' in a series of secret meetings in November 1884* which settled the political geography of the United Kingdom until 1918.

The Cabinet had moved towards preparation for an accommodation of some sort by appointing a Committee, of which Gladstone was not a member, on 9 August 1884 'to prepare materials for Redistribution and give directions as to Boundaries'.† Gladstone had laid out his own position during the initial arguments the previous winter:

While looking to a comparatively large arrangement, I am not friendly to Electoral districts, am ready to consider some limitation on the representation of the largest town populations, & am desirous to keep alive within fair limits the individuality of towns with moderate population.‡

He had little enthusiasm for Hartington's demand for the representation of 'minorities' (i.e. Protestants) in Ireland, and insisted that if there were to be such representation it would have to be accepted that 'we cannot have a minority plan *for Ireland only*'. Apart from the question of minorities— brushed aside in the rush in November 1884—Gladstone found himself on the defensive. The energetic radicalism of Dilke, who effectively controlled the Cabinet committee, and the—as Gladstone saw it—thoroughgoingly unconservative opportunism of Salisbury left little space for Gladstone's Peelite notion of the continued harmony of town and country separately represented according to the criteria of communities rather than that of numbers. A rearguard action to keep seats for boroughs of 10,000 popula- tion yielded to Dilke's 15,000 (Dilke and Gladstone subsequently success- fully defending this against Salisbury's demand for 20,000), as did the attempt to confine single-member seats to the boroughs. But Gladstone did not press his views very hard. Surrounded by difficulties in foreign and imperial affairs, he was relieved to find in Dilke an energy and competence as to detail rare in his ministry, and was consequently willing to make concessions 'if we could thereby effectually promote peace & get the Franchise Bill passed'. Gladstone was an effective broker with the Tories partly because of his innate command of the sort of detail which redistribu- tion required, and partly because he was working to the Cabinet's brief, not his own. Thus was the bargain struck: the Franchise Bill was 'to pass forthwith' in exchange for a radical redistribution, the ending of double- member constituencies save in cities between 50,000 and 150,000 and the

* Gladstone had hoped to get away with a compromise which did not involve bargaining with the Tories, by meeting Northcote (once his private secretary) in Algernon West's house, but Salis- bury would have none of it.

† As it was agreed that redistribution would follow franchise reform, it is perhaps surprising that the Cabinet had not made this move earlier; this was probably because the disagreements in Cabinet on redistribution were likely to be much sharper than those on the franchise. According to Dilke, he and Gladstone had already 'hatched the Bill' in July; see 14 July 84n.

‡ To Hartington, 29 Dec. 83.

absorption of existing borough seats of under 15,000 into the surrounding counties.

This was not perceived as a bad bargain. In that it dismantled a distribution of seats in which the Liberals usually won, it was clearly risky. But Liberals do not seem to have seen the extent of the advantage to the Tories of single member constituencies and absorption of small borough seats into the counties. Liberals counted on their gains in the rural seats through the enfranchisement of the agricultural labourers at least balancing Tory advantages in the redistribution. Dilke, generally acknowledged as an expert, at one point contemplated a much more widespread absorption of boroughs into the counties.* Gladstone's attempt to defend the small borough seats was not based on Liberal advantage but on historic principles and a communitarian theory of representative government, 'a tenderness for individuality of communities in boroughs & counties' rather than their disintegration into areas of class or sectional interest.† Indeed, the absence of party calculation by the Liberals on the redistribution question is rather striking. They relied too simply on the advantage of franchise extension, and even there what calculation there was spelt difficulty: the assumption was that the 'so-called National Party in Ireland' would increase its number of MPs from 'a little over forty to near eighty', about twenty-five of these being taken from the Liberals.‡ Despite this acceptance of the disappearance of Liberalism in Ireland, a reduction of the number of seats in over-represented Ireland was strongly resisted. The chief consequence of the Reform Acts for the mainland—the enabling of villa Tory suburban voters to escape to single member seats, 'high and dry on islands§ of their own', and thus found the modern Conservative party§— was far less anticipated by Liberals than it was by Tories. The Liberals rightly anticipated gains in the counties; they did not anticipate that they would soon in England be predominantly a party of the countryside.

For Liberals generally, this was because they did not have and could not have a developed sense of class—to do so would cut straight across the nature of the Liberal mind—and the view that votes were won by policies, not contained by class-affiliation. In Gladstone's case, though he shared that view, there was a further reason. In the long haul of the reform process—from September 1883 to the passing of the final bills in the summer of 1885—Gladstone conducted himself effectively, and in marked contrast to his impassioned behaviour in 1866–7. The 'smash without example' was not repeated. But in 1866–7 Gladstone was so impassioned because his reform proposals had a close, direct, and organic relationship

* S. Gwynn and G. Tuckwell, *Life of Sir Charles Dilke, Bart.*, 2v. (1917), ii. 67.
† To Dilke, 29 Sept. 84.
‡ 19 Aug. 84.
§ J. Cornford, 'The transformation of conservatism in the late nineteenth century', *Victorian Studies*, vii. 58 (1963).

to his more general plan of public finance and political economy. His deliberately limited proposals of 1866 had precise intentions, and the household suffrage of 1867, the creation of the curious alliance of Radicalism and what Gladstone regarded as Conservative opportunism, had created a political world not of his making.* Ironically, he and Salisbury, who had resigned over household suffrage in 1867, both danced in 1884 to the dead Disraeli's tune. They both, however, danced happily. Salisbury was able to exploit any advantage which the system gave him: if that system had little legitimacy, so then was his activity liberated and Conservatism was free to take what it could. Gladstone had found the household suffrage in fact enfranchising very much the sort of electorate for which he had been seeking in 1866: the campaigns of the 1870s had shown its capacity for capable citizenship. Even so, there is a certain sense of distance between Gladstone and the reform measures in 1883–5. He saw his role in them as an executive rather than a creator, and with respect to them his tactics were as sharp as his strategy was disastrous.

The Redistribution Bill cleared the Commons on 11 May 1885, and the three Registration Bills received Royal Assent on 21 May 1885; the new dispensation was all but in place, and the need for extreme self-control in the Commons by the Liberals ended, and so did the need for Parnellite support for their reform measures: the doubling of the Home Rule party now lay before it. On 8 June a combination of Tories and Parnellites carried Hicks Beach's amendment to the budget with many Liberal MPs absent: 'Beaten by 264:252. Adjourned the House. This is a considerable event.'†

The defeat of the Budget in 1885 conformed to type: in every Liberal government between Grey in 1832 and Campbell-Bannerman in 1905 the parliamentary majority eventually disintegrated and led to a dissolution or, more usually, a minority Tory government. In 1885 dissolution was impossible, the Redistribution Bill being still in the Lords and the registers of the new constituencies and new voters not yet drawn up. Gladstone therefore did as he had done in 1873 on the Irish University Bill and resigned, on this occasion with the positive encouragement of a Cabinet exhausted by crisis and crushed yet again in the Irish forceps of coercion and conciliation. Salisbury then followed precedent (Peel in 1834, Derby in 1852, 1858, and 1866) and, ignoring Disraeli's reticence in 1873, accepted office after considerable haggling. Thus one Christ Church man ceded the premiership to another, so small in one sense was the nexus of the Victorian ruling class.‡ Salisbury's behaviour during the haggling moved Gladstone to a rare note of personal criticism in his diary: 'He has been ill to deal with,

---

* See above, Part I, ch. 5.
† 8 June 85. See also p. 461.
‡ Christ Church held the premiership from 1880 to 1902.

requiring incessant watching.'* So the second ministry ended: 'At 11.45 cleared out of my official room & had a moment to fall down and give thanks for the labours done & the strength vouchsafed me there: and to pray for the Christlike mind.'†

If precedent were to be followed, the Liberals would regroup and return to office invigorated by a spell in opposition and reunited in some fresh cause: 'It is in opposition, & not in Govt., that the Liberal party tends to draw together.'‡ It was clear from the circumstances of the resignation of the Cabinet that effective reunion would in large measure depend on Irish policy, either by replacing the dispute on Ireland by some quite different issue, or by resolving it in favour of an agreed initiative.

It is therefore time to turn to the second ministry's handling of Irish affairs, of all the travails of the government the least rewarding and still today the most contentious.

* 24 June 85.
† 25 June 85.
‡ 12 July 86.

CHAPTER VIII

Gladstone and Ireland 1875–1885

Ireland in Perspective—Gladstone's Irish Visit, 1887—The Land League and the Liberal Response—Property and the 'Three Fs': 'breaking the Land League'—The Land League on the run—Home Rule under Consideration—The 'Kilmainham Treaty' and the Phoenix Park Murders—Irish Local Government and Franchise Reform 1883–1885—Defeat, Resignation, and the Future of Ireland

$11\frac{1}{2}$–$1\frac{1}{2}$. Visit to Maynooth College. It produced upon the whole a saddening impression: what havock have we made of the vineyard of the Lord! Hard work, of its kind, & economy pervaded the whole: but they are honourably beginning a rich Chapel.

In aft. drove in the Park, through the curiously denuded valley: & our most kind hosts saw us off from the Station. In Dublin we walked to the Archbishops. We were concerned to find this excellent man worse & still suffering: in an entourage I fear little worthy of him.*

Conversation with H.J.G. on 'Home Rule' & my speech: for the subject has probably a future.†

Dined at Austrian Ambassador's: walked home: met by the frightful news from Dublin of the assassination of dear F. Cavendish and Burke. We went over to see Lucy, already informed by Lady L. Egerton. It was an awful scene but enlightened by her faith and love. We saw likewise Granville and Hartington: and we got to bed before two, Meriel staying with her sister.‡

Ireland in Perspective

In 1921 the British government, sustained by a Conservative-dominated coalition, signed a treaty with the Irish Free State, already a *de facto* republic, thus effectively admitting the end of union between the United Kingdom and most of Ireland. Such an outcome would have been regarded by any member of any British Cabinet of the 1880s, and certainly by Gladstone, as an utter failure for British policy. That this was less than forty

---

* Diary for 5 Nov. 77: Gladstone's visit to Ireland.
† Diary for 10 Feb. 82.
‡ Diary for 6 May 82: the Phoenix Park murders.

years after the 'Kilmainham Treaty' and that one participant in the events of the 1880s, A. J. Balfour, was still in the Cabinet and another, T. M. Healy, was the first Governor-General of the Irish Free State, are reminders of how misleading it is to dissociate the developments of the 1880s from their results, by setting them merely in a short-term, tactical context. For those concerned to maintain the United Kingdom as an entity, it is also a reminder of a lesson learnt too late. 'What fools we were,' George V told Ramsay MacDonald in 1930, 'not to have accepted Gladstone's Home Rule Bill. The Empire now would not have had the Irish Free State giving us so much trouble and pulling us to pieces.'*

In his first government, Gladstone had set out to show the Irish that 'there is nothing that Ireland has asked and which this country and this Parliament have refused. . . . I have looked in vain for the setting forth of any practical scheme of policy which the Imperial Parliament is not equal to deal with, or which it refuses to deal with, and which is to be brought about by Home Rule.'† Disestablishment of the Irish Church in 1869 and the Land Act in 1870 sought to demonstrate this point and hence to encourage constitutionalism as against Fenianism, as did, less probably, the abortive Irish University Bill of 1873, a bill which, however, seemed to show that Gladstone's notion of the virtual representation of Home Rule interests by the Westminster Parliament was increasingly difficult to sustain.

His position, self-evidently, implied that if the Westminster Parliament could not by its various 'boons' give the Irish what they believed they needed then some form of 'Home Rule' or more would, eventually, be the natural consequence. The objective of the first government, of attempting to remove the Protestant ascendancy, would, if achieved, pacify Ireland by leaving no major grievance. The problem of this strategy was that its measures, dramatic though they seemed at the time, were too modest and too slow. They did not prevent and perhaps even encouraged the emergence of a more organized Home Rule movement in the mid-1870s. To Gladstone's surprise, Irish questions were the chief parliamentary business of his administrations in the 1880s.

In the 1860s, Gladstone had hoped to make the Irish choose between constitutionalism and Fenianism and to express their choice by support for the Liberal party which then held most of the Irish seats. Now, by 1880, Liberal seats were turning into Home Rule seats and the choice was between liberal constitutionalism and a rapidly growing Home Rule movement, constitutional in objective but linked, through the Land

---

* MacDonald's diary, 6 July 1930, quoted in K. Rose, *George V* (1983), 240. George V was 21 in 1886, so the events of that year were part of his adult political experience. In August 1882, the Prince of Wales had taken him and his brother on a visit to Gladstone in Downing Street.

† See above, p. 203.

League, to aspects of Fenianism. Quite quickly, Ireland had become from the metropolitan point of view much more problematic. Irish demands were becoming systematized in a call for constitutional reform and institutionalized in a Home Rule party which was assimilable within the ideology of British politics. Indeed, like the Indian National Congress founded in 1885, they appealed to what was best in the British liberal tradition. British politics had been bound to reject Fenianism in the same way that it had rejected Chartism: the demands made were simply not compatible with other assumptions about the nature of the political system. But an effective Home Rule party was bound to put the Liberals on the spot. Home Rule was the equivalent of the Reform League for franchise reform in the 1860s: the demands might be disliked but they were not instantly incompatible with the assumptions of contemporary policy makers, unless, that is, 'Home Rule' came to be seen as an aspect of Fenianism rather than as the means to its defeat. Judgement of this balance was to be a central question for the 1880s. In its Land League phase, constitutionalism was, at least superficially, severely compromised.

Gladstone's Irish Visit, 1877

Gladstone's handling of Irish policy on his return to office in 1880 was tentative. He was, of course, by no means ignorant of Irish affairs generally, or of its agricultural problems. By the end of December 1880, he noted 'The state of Ireland in particular' as the chief concern of the year. Yet the view that Ireland came to Gladstone like a cloud from the west unheralded is well supported. Gladstone came to see Ireland as he had seen its famine in 1845, as a divine retribution, 'a judgment for our heavy sins as a nation'.* But the revelation of the punishment was sudden, certainly not anticipated during his visit to Ireland in the autumn of 1877, when he spent almost a month in County Wicklow and Dublin. This visit turned out, against his intentions, for the most part to be a holiday; for political reasons plans to extend it to Ulster and perhaps Killarney were abandoned. What seems to have been designed as a wide-ranging visit became more limited: 'the larger parts of my project gradually fade from view, & my movements must be in a small[er] circle'. As Gladstone noted, he was in 'the least Irish part of Ireland'.

This was true, for the Fitzwilliam estates at Coollattin, where Gladstone stayed, were a model of high capitalization and benificence, generous treatment of tenants and a low rate of return to the landlord (about 1%). Finlay Dun, *The Times* journalist who discussed Irish land with Gladstone at Hawarden at an important moment of the discussions in December 1880, described the Fitzwilliam estates as exceptional: 'prosperity, peace and

* 31 Dec. 80; there are several echoes of the famous 'cloud in the west' letter of 1845 (A. Tilney Bassett, *Gladstone to his wife* (1936), 64) in 1880.

progress, spread through a wide area'.* It would be wrong to see this visit as simply a tour of great houses. Gladstone was diligent about visiting 'farms, cottages, & people' and holding conversations, 'turning my small opportunities to account as well as I could'. Undoubtedly there were diffi- culties about doing this, and Gladstone shows some irritation at a day spent with the potentates of the English establishment in Dublin: 'not enough of *Ireland*'. He did, however, succeed in visiting a number of farms, including one on Parnell's estate. The tour included a visit, on Guy Fawkes Day, to Maynooth College, the Roman Catholic seminary whose extended grant had been the cause of his resignation from Peel's Cabinet in 1845: 'It produced on the whole a saddening impression: what havock have we made of the vineyard of the Lord?'†

Such might be Maynooth, but this was not the general impression of Ireland in 1877 on Gladstone. The burgeoning Home Rule movement he was well aware of, and on receiving the Freedom of Dublin on 7 November, 'treading on eggs the whole time', he could not 'be too thankful for having got through today as I hope without trick & without offence'. His com- ments in Dublin on local government anticipated the paper on 'Devolu- tion' which he presented to the Cabinet in 1880, but they were not offered with any great urgency. Ireland generally, such as he was able to see of it, did not disturb him. This was not surprising, for Ireland was not yet disturbed; 1877 was the lowest year of the decade for evictions.‡ What is surprising, is that Gladstone does not appear to have anticipated the effect on Ireland of the agricultural crisis of the late 1870s. He was well aware of its causes, both long-term, through the Ricardian comparative advantage effects of the expansion of the American and Canadian wheat lands,§ and immediate, through the disastrously wet summer of 1879, carefully observed in his diary. Hawarden estate rents were reduced by 15% in 1879 ('It is to be 15% and as a rule in kind') and by the same again in 1880 to meet the emergency. However, what was a crisis in English and Welsh agri- culture could hardly be less than a catastrophe for Ireland and Scotland, even allowing for their smaller proportion of cereal production.

The Land League and the Liberal Response

On the other hand, the founding of the Land League in October 1879 did not in itself make its success nor the scale of its ultimate demands inevit- able. When the Liberal government took office, the Land League was still 'basically a Connaught phenomenon', and its programme still uncertain. In April 1880, Parnell was still thinking in terms of a mere revival of Butt's

* Chapter iv of Finlay Dun, *Landlords and tenants in Ireland* (1881), a reprint of earlier reports for *The Times*, describes the Fitzwilliam estates.
† For his Irish visit, see his diary, 17 Oct.–12 Nov. 77.
‡ See the table in P. Bew, *Land and the national question in Ireland 1858–82* (1978), 36.
§ See *Political Speeches* (1879), 95ff. and 'Kin beyond Sea', *Gleanings*, i. 203.

limited Bill of 1876.* The new Liberal government was faced with suffering and confusion in Ireland, but not yet with systematized disorder. Initially the Cabinet moved quickly, though without Gladstone playing more than a co-ordinating role. The early Cabinets of the administration discussed both 'Peace Preservation' and an extension of the Bright Land Purchase clauses of the 1870 Land Act. The Cabinet's assessment was that it was not necessary to renew coercion, in the form of the Peace Preservation Act, due to expire on 1 June, 'but general duty to be recognized'† (so little impact had the Land League as yet made), and that, the 1880 Session being short, amendment of the Land Act by extending the Bright clauses was 'too complex' for that year. Consideration of the Bright clauses referred to the long-term pattern of land tenure in Ireland: 'We never considered the question of ejectments connected with the present distress in Ireland.'‡ By June 1880, the question of these had been forced upon Gladstone and his Cabinet: 'I *was* under the impression that ejectments were diminishing, but I now find from figures first seen on Saturday [12 June] that they seem rather to increase.' Hence 'the duty of enquiring, where I had not previously known there was urgent cause to inquire'.§

The consequences were twofold. First, the Bessborough Royal Commission on the working of the 1870 Land Act was set up in June 1880 parallel to the Royal Commission on agricultural distress earlier set up by the Tories for the United Kingdom as a whole. The Bessborough Commission could hardly take evidence and report before January 1881 at the earliest, and clearly looked to some general development of the 1870 settlement. Second, the immediate crisis was to be met by taking over the private member bill of the Parnellite O'Connor Power and replacing it by a government-sponsored Compensation for Disturbance Bill. This was eventually lost in the Lords in August 1880, its legitimacy destroyed by the government's uncertainty about its own statistics. As a consequence of the landowning interests's bitter opposition to even this rather modest initiative, the first resignations from the government had to be accepted: alarm set in among the Whig court officials, Lords Listowel and Zetland resigning, with Gladstone admitting that 'many sound & attached Liberals shared your scruples'.

'Is the non-payment [of rents] due to *distress or to conspiracy?*' The Compensation for Disturbance Bill assumed it was '*distress*': the dénouement, as the Land League gained support and confidence in the second half of 1880, suggested to Gladstone that it was both. '*Conspiracy*' was to be met by the

* See Bew, op. cit., chapters 5 and 6.
† The position respecting the Act (a watered-down version of the liberal Acts of 1870 and 1871) was complex because of the timetable in the Commons and the Tory Cabinet's failure to renew the Act before dissolving. The act, as it stood, would have been of little use against the Land League, but the failure to renew made the Irish landlord class feel the more isolated.
‡ To Argyll, 14 June 80.   § Ibid.

prosecution of Parnell, Dillon, Biggar, and other Home Rule MPs. This was agreed in principle at the Cabinet of 30 September 1880 subject to the Law Officers' advice, with the hope of showing that the Land League's policy of combination to encourage breach of contract was illegal, and, if it was not, opening the way for an Act that would make it so. Gladstone hoped for much in the way of 'moral effect' from the trials. He also hoped they would make a suspension of Habeas Corpus unnecessary, for he regarded such a measure as futile, since 'Parnell Biggar & Co' were not intending to commit crimes, but to incite others 'by speech': if prosecution could not 'enforce silence', no more could Habeas Corpus suspension.

The prosecutions announced on 2 November 1880 failed in January 1881 because the jury in Dublin could not agree. Gladstone had personally intervened to ensure a fair trial, and the probability of a stalemate does not seem to have occurred to him, only the possibility that the law might not be sufficiently extensive. The prosecutions at least gained enough time to make impossible an emergency pre-Christmas Session for Habeas Corpus suspension.

'*Distress*', in the rising tension following the Lords' rejection of the Compensation for Disturbance Bill, would have to be met by 'remedial legislation' to balance the demand for coercion which by late autumn was becoming hard to resist. By 'remedial legislation' Gladstone did not mean merely a Land Bill, and, until a late date in 1880, perhaps not a Land Bill at all. Only with extreme reluctance did he come to accept the need for another Land Bill. He saw the problem in much wider terms. After reading various works on the 'closure' and after studying the speeches of Grattan and Pitt on the Irish Union, he wrote a long paper on 'Obstruction and Devolution', completed on 23 October. This paper met what Gladstone saw as the long-term corruption of the British legislature, clogged with detail and arrears even before the Irish and others began 'obstructing'.

This corruption, unworthy of a great Empire and possibly fatal to it, had been a major theme of his articles and speeches in the late 1870s, re-inforcing views expressed since the 1850s, and had Gladstone anticipated being Prime Minister for a full term, he might well have worked more on his plan before the ministry began, and presented it to his Cabinet in more normal circumstances. As it was, one of the chief legislative corollaries to the Midlothian Campaign came before the Cabinet in the context of the Irish emergency. Devolution would restore the capacity of Parliament, and in the Irish context it would have a direct political advantage:

I must add that besides the defeat of obstruction, and the improvement of our attitude for dealing with arrear, I conceive that Devolution may supply the means of partially meeting and satisfying, at least so far as it is legitimate, another call. I refer to the call for what is called (*in bonam partem*) Local Government and (*in malam*) Home Rule.

Circulated among ministers, and discussed without enthusiasm in Cabinet—only Chamberlain and Bright showing strong interest—the scheme was, for the time being, largely lost in the exigencies of the 'sheer panic' in Ireland though it was still on the agenda, as 'measures of self-government', bracketed with Irish land, at the extraordinary Cabinet held on 31 December 1880. It showed, none the less, the natural tendency of Gladstone's mind towards a political and constitutional initiative and solution.

Even with this constitutional initiative effectively frustrated, Gladstone was unwilling to be launched on a new Land Bill, preferring instead a new bill to defend contracts between landlord and tenant. He looked to the Tories' Royal Commission on agricultural distress to countervail the unexpectedly radical proposals of the Liberals' Bessborough Commission whose report, known to the government by December 1880, was to Gladstone's alarm tantamount to endorsing the 'three Fs' of fair rents, fixity of tenure, and free sale. Angry at what he saw as the 'unmanliness', the 'astounding helplessness' of the landlord class in failing to resist the Land League, and at the 'cupidity' in assisting the League which he ascribed to various institutions and individuals, he moved towards a Land Bill only when it became clear that coercion was becoming politically unavoidable and that a positive political act would be needed to balance it. Even then, Gladstone was 'very desirous to keep if possible on the lines & basis of the [1870] Land Act'. 'The three Fs . . . in their popular meaning . . . will I fear break the Cabinet without conciliating the Leaguers', he told Forster, the Irish Secretary.* Yet it had to be recognized that support for the three Fs was strong: 'evidence comes in, rather more than I should have expected, of a desire for a measure such as the brewers call treble X'.† The final Cabinet of 1880, on 31 December, left the situation open-ended: 'Irish Land 1. To stand on the principles of the Land Act of 1870. 2. To propose measures of self-government.' Forster passed a note across the Cabinet table: 'To what does this conversation pledge us?'; Gladstone replied, 'We are pledged to take Land Act for starting point and develop it. Each man his own interpreter.'‡

Gladstone's 'development' in 1881 was, in the light of his comments and correspondence in 1880, to be startling. There is, to posterity, a striking feature about these comments and letters. At this stage Gladstone made no analogy between the Montenegrins and the Land League. That crisis of Balkan nationalism which had subsumed his energies and his sympathies in the mid-1870s and which had led as has been shown to some Irish analogies, seems to have offered him, despite a conscientious reading of Gavan Duffy's *Young Ireland*,§ no insight into the phenomenon with which

---

* To Forster, 3 Dec. 80.   † To Forster, 4 Dec. 80.
‡ 31 Dec. 80.   § Read throughout November 1880.

he now had to deal. His reading gave him information about Irish land reform proposals, but his opinion of Parnell's intentions ('curious, perhaps hopeful')* came from the newspapers.

Gladstone was less well informed about the objectives of the Land League leaders than he was about Balkan nationalism. He was already cautiously in touch with Captain O'Shea; he was supplied with the views of the Ulster Liberals, and with those of some of the older tenant-right campaigners, but he was unable to support his opposition to Habeas Corpus suspension with any inside information save that supplied, usually late and inadequately, by Dublin Castle and various members of the Irish aristocracy.

In 1880 Gladstone regarded the Land League simply as a criminal conspiracy, 'a fit object for permanent and effective prohibition'.† But, at the least, 'Parnell & Co.' had upset the reasonableness of British politics. The two measures, 'both most reasonable',‡ which in the summer of 1880 had seemed sensible within the usual practices of Cabinet government—the application and testing of the existing law, and a Royal Commission to inquire into possible changes—had led the government not only into a timetable trap, though one which Gladstone manipulated in the November Cabinets very adroitly to play for delay, but had made its response, looked at from any angle, seem inadequate, unimaginative, and feeble.

As with the household suffrage in 1866–7, Gladstone held out in 1880 against a 'radical' solution until it became irresistible. When it became so, all his resourcefulness, his speed of movement, and his control of detail were to enable him in the early months of 1881 very swiftly to regain the initiative, take the lead, and drive towards a legislative triumph.

The Land League's campaign was as near a revolutionary movement as anything seen in the United Kingdom between 1800 and 1914. Though having important regional variations in its support and in its techniques, the Land League was, none the less, in the circumstances, a fairly cohesive organization in the sense of having an institutional presence in most of Ireland.§ But its thrust came not from its structure or from its central committee, but from the tenant farmers who were its motor, afforced by agricultural labourers and small-town shop-keepers.¶ Innovative on the British political scene though the Land League was, the essentially conservative objectives of its tenant farmer supporters gave the government the opportunity to leave its more politically motivated high command stranded. Making this distinction between the motives of the supporters of

* To Forster, 11 Nov. 80.

† To Bright, 23 Dec. 80. See K. T. Hoppen, *Elections, Politics, and Society in Ireland 1832–1885* (1984), 473ff. for the League's success in achieving a farmer–agricultural labourer alliance.

‡ To Forster, 3 Dec. 80.

§ S. Clark, *Social origins of the Irish land war* (1979), ch. 8.

¶ Ibid. and K. T. Hoppen, op. cit., pp. 473ff.

the Land League and those of its leadership, and, even more, acting on it, required at the time considerable boldness on the part of Liberal Cabinet members.

The Land League had no ideology of modernization or efficiency; it faced the government with no call for a fundamental recasting of the Irish economy. For its primary objective it did not look beyond the consolidation of the position of the tenant farmer as less of a tenant and more of a proprietor, a fixed figure on the social scene absolved from the obligations of a tenant but without the fixed-cost burdens of the landowner. Some, notably Davitt, saw that this could only be a short-term settlement, and that the success of the rent-strike and of the legal recognition of 'fair rent' must imply the end of the landowning classes.*

The debate within the Liberal Cabinet in 1880–1 took place largely on these terms: however violent some of its methods, the Land League called for stability in the Irish countryside: how should the Cabinet answer this call? Its first response, as we have seen, was to attempt the destruction of the League's organization through coercion and the prevention, as far as possible, of physical violence in the localities (the Protection of Person and Property Bill and the Peace Preservation Bill, a savage measure of coercion, permitting the gaoling of 'suspects' for long periods without evidence having to be brought against them). These dealt with the methods of the League: its aims would be dealt with by a land bill which would consolidate order in the Irish countryside. The Land Act of 1870—dictated by similar political considerations of stability and order—had contained two approaches: a strengthening of the tenant's position, and, through the clause introduced by John Bright, a very limited provision for tenants to turn themselves into owners by purchasing their farms with a government grant.

The Land League was predominantly a tenant-right organization, though a peasant proprietary was the objective of the more politically conscious central committee.† Tenant-right implied a legal readjustment of social and financial relationships: no State money was involved. It also meant that tenants continued to be tenants, however secure; thus landlordism continued also, however weak. The alternative solution, peasant proprietorship, through the wholesale removal of the landowning class and the creation through a land purchase scheme—financed directly or indirectly by the State—of a large class of small landowners in hock to the government for their properties, raised very large questions of finance and, Gladstone always argued, of the creation of a representative local government structure of some sort to make it work. All Gladstone's notions of social hierarchy, finance, and debt predisposed him to the first of these,

---

* See B. L. Solow, *The land question and the Irish economy 1870—1903* (1971), 166–7.
† Clark, op. cit., 302–3.

though he had always, even in moving his Irish Church Resolutions in 1868, recognized the potential importance of the second.*

The absence of a significant scheme of land purchase had important consequences.† It implied a sequence of governmental involvement: the continuance of the overwhelmingly Protestant landowning class meant that there would be more land agitation, which in turn would mean more coercion. The landowning class was, in Gladstone's view, maintained so as to keep order in Ireland, but the opposite was really the case: it was the landowners that were the cause of the disorder. The landowner was, Gladstone came to see in 1886, 'the salient point of friction'.‡ Maintenance of the landowner simply intensified metropolitan rule through coercion bills passed against the votes of an ever-increasing body of Irish Home Rule MPs. Maintaining coercion so as to maintain the landowner guaranteed the demise of Liberalism in Ireland. This was the treadmill on which the Liberal party ran from 1880 to 1885.

Property and the 'Three Fs': 'breaking the Land League'

In the novel context of quasi-revolutionary Irish politics the 'Three F.s'— fixity of tenure, fair rent, freedom of sale—once so bold a demand, quickly became a modest request advocated not only by the Land League but by Dublin Castle, by the Bessborough Royal Commission, appointed by the Liberals, and by the Liberals' minority report to the Richmond Royal Commission, appointed by the Conservatives. To both of these Commissions Gladstone had looked for caution: 'Read Reports of Commn—(Confusion worse confounded).'§ Gladstone only reluctantly agreed with W. E. Forster, the Irish Secretary, 'that the Cabinet ought to understand that while there is a great body of Irish opinion for something called the 3 F.s, & another body as I suppose for Parnell's plan & that of the Land League, there is no such body in favour of anything short of these, though intelligent & weighty *individuals* may be cited in some strength who are for amending the [1870] Land Act'.¶ Gladstone's position of 1880, that all that was needed was a modest amendment of the 1870 Act, was thus admitted by January 1881 to be quite insubstantial: if he tried to sustain it he would find himself cornered with Whigs such as Argyll.

There was therefore a strong prudential element in Gladstone's thinking as in December 1880 and January 1881 he came to terms with the scale of change which would be necessary if the land bill was to balance the various measures of coercion. What was needed from Forster was an assessment of exactly at what point on the scale of Irish demands 'a definitive settlement'‖

---

* See H. Shearman, 'State-aided land purchase under the disestablishment act of 1869', *Irish Historical Studies*, iv. 58 (1944).

† There were spasmodic but never very determined attempts at a government scheme; see, e.g., 28 Apr. 84.   ‡ 23 Mar. 86.

§ 11 Jan. 81.   ¶ To Forster, 10 Jan. 81.   ‖ Ibid.

of the land question could be made. This shows the extent to which the Bill of 1881 was a political operation. Only in its emigration clauses was the wider question of the creation of a more prosperous Irish economy directly touched, and then only negatively.

Gladstone's attitude to the various options was complex. Ultimately, he saw the occupation of property as a fulfilment of a God-given privilege, property having duties attached to it, but no absolute rights. The land-owner or occupier was thus the executor of 'a kind of sacred trust', and of course it was, and is, the case that there is no absolute ownership of land in the United Kingdom save by the Crown. However, in his acceptance in the 1840s and 1850s of much of the intellectual framework of liberal political economy as the most suitable available mechanism for the proper organ-ization of a modern society, Gladstone had placed himself, particularly in his view of the fiscal state, in the camp of political economists for whom fiscal, and consequently social, relationships were essentially a-temporal, predicated on general, universal rules and not on inductive enquiry into particular historical traditions.

It would, however, be wrong to see Gladstone as in every respect a supporter of that view. His sense of the fiscal state did have that a-temporal dimension; but his understanding of community and particularly of religious communities and national churches as being particularist, local examples, each with subtle variations, of the 'institution called in the Creed the Holy Catholic Church',* also gave him a historical and localist per-spective. As this religious analysis was the starting-point for Gladstone's analysis of any society, there was therefore an inherent historical dimen-sion to his approach which cut across his political–economic universalism.

In the Irish case, Gladstone had doubly incorporated this historical dimension: disestablishment in 1869, and his proposal in 1869 that the Land Bill be built on a generalization of Ulster tenant right, a proposal limited by the Cabinet to tenant-right in Ulster, compensation for dis-turbance for the rest. The tenant-right solution had several attractions, not least that as it could be presented as thoroughly Irish it could not obviously be used as a precedent for England† nor, probably, for Scotland (though the historicist argument would have more force there). Compensation for disturbance could, however, be so used, and so could several aspects of the 'Three F.s'.

Gladstone's initial view of Irish land in 1880–1 was to keep reform as much as possible within the precepts of the free market. Thus, if there had, for political reasons, to be fixity of tenure, could there not be a provision for

---

* To Morley, 27 Oct. 80. This seems to me an important further dimension to the interesting approach in C. Dewey, 'Celtic agrarian legislation and the Celtic Revival: historicist implications of Gladstone's Irish and Scottish Land Acts 1870–1886', *Past and Present*, no. 64 (1974).

† See above, pp. 196–8.

'a future return to free contract'?* Explaining the bill to Carlingford, his colleague in drafting the 1870 Act, Gladstone 'seemed very averse to interference with "freedom of contract"'.† As the coercion bills were forced through between January and March 1881, Gladstone sought to keep this in the forefront of the drafting of the Land Bill. The consequence was that the bill only equivocally granted the 'Three F.s' and, so as to incorporate this equivocation, was in its drafting tortuous, wordy, and sometimes obscure. Gladstone's position was reflected in the distinction the bill made between 'present tenancies' and 'future tenancies' (those created after 1 January 1883), to which the Act would not apply. For 'present tenants' the Act would apply for a period of fifteen years, renewable after review by the Court.‡

The consequence of all this was not only an opaquely drafted bill but the loss of the Duke of Argyll, who resigned as Lord Privy Seal on 31 March. Argyll was one of Gladstone's oldest political friends and they hugely enjoyed their many political and theological rows, usually carried on in extensive correspondence between Hawarden and Inveraray Castle. Gladstone maintained this after Argyll's resignation; for other Whigs, resignation led to silence from Gladstone. Argyll's resignation did not precipitate the more general Whiggish exodus expected by some. He was too maverick and was probably too Scottish in his viewpoint to act as a focus for disgruntled English and Irish Whigs.

In introducing the Bill on 7 April 1881, Gladstone's ambivalence between historicism and economic deductivism was clearly stated. On the one hand, 'the old law of the country, corresponding, I believe, with the general law of Europe, recognizes the tenant right, and therefore recognizes, if you choose to call it, joint proprietorship'. On the other hand, 'there is no country in the world which, when her social relations come to permit of it, will derive more benefit than Ireland from perfect freedom of contract in land. Unhappily she is not in a state to permit of it; but I will not abandon the hope that the period may arrive.'§ Not surprisingly, therefore, given the discrepancy of the economic need for larger farms as against the

* To Forster, 10 Jan. 81, repeated to him, 5 Mar. 81.

† Lord Carlingford's diary, 25 March 1881, Add MS 63689; 25 Mar. 81n. In 1870 he had been known as Chichester Fortescue.

‡ Leaseholders and tenants in arrears were excluded from the Act, though there was provision for arrears to be wiped out by a loan from the Land Commission financed by money from the Church Temporalities Commissioners. For the Act and a detailed commentary, see R. R. Cherry, *The Irish Land Law and Land Purchase Acts 1860 to 1901* (3rd ed. 1903). On the making of the Act and its political consequences, see A. Warren, 'Forster, the Liberals and new directions in Irish policy 1880–1882', *Parliamentary History*, vi (1987) and, for the general context of Gladstone's views on Irish land, his 'Gladstone, land and social reconstruction in Ireland 1881–87', *Parliamentary History*, ii (1983) which forcefully demonstrates Gladstone's insistence that land purchase must be linked to Irish local government of some sort and also shows the significant relationship of the events and decisions of 1882 to those of 1885–6.

§ *H* 260. 902.

bill's consolidation of the division of Irish land into smallholdings, Gladstone told the Commons 'I decline to enter into the economical part of the subject'.*

The immediate context of the bill was the Land League Campaign, and the nature of the bill was squarely in line with the Gladstonian tradition of a big bill and a long passage in the Commons to enable its public, political effect to be established and dramatized. Thus: 'Again worked hard on Irish Land: and introduced the big Bill (for such it is in purpose more than bulk) $5\frac{1}{4}$–8.'† The bill was intended to castrate the Land League by attracting the Irish tenants into Courts and a Land Commission appointed by the Westminster Parliament, local agencies of the State to which the Irish tenantry would voluntarily apply and which would reduce their rents. Thus the Irish tenantry would voluntarily associate itself with a mechanism provided by Westminster for the creation of social order in the Irish countryside. The metropolitan Parliament would thus be seen to be offering a boon which the Land League could not match. Thus the Land Bill (and not Forster's Coercion Bills) 'seems to constitute nearly the whole of our substantial resources for confronting & breaking the Land League'.‡ Hence for Gladstone it was the provision of the Land Court which was 'the salient point and the cardinal principle of the Bill'—a legal authority, voluntarily used, reaching into the far recesses of the confusions of Irish social relationships, an orderly presence creating stability and reconciliation in exactly those places which state coercion could never reach. This was a 'right and needful measure', but it was one that admitted existing chaos, for it was a 'form of centralization, referring to public authority what ought to be transacted by a private individual'; Gladstone advised the Irish not to 'stereotype and stamp [it] with the seal of perpetuity',§ but he made no provision for its review.

Presenting the bill both as a 'definitive solution' and as containing an ultimate escape back to free contract, Gladstone was able to offer it, ultimately unsuccessfully, to Argyll as the latter,¶ and to the Irish as the former. In this sense, it has the ambivalence of all the great Gladstonian initiatives from the 1853 budget onwards. Because of it, Gladstone never admitted that the bill granted 'the Three F.s', but he was certainly not going publicly to deny that it did: 'the controversy as to whether or not the "three F's." are in this Bill is one into which I have not entered', he told the Commons, continuing in a passage of classic obscurity: 'the "three F's"

---

* *H* 260. 918.   † 7 Apr. 81.

‡ To Lorne (Argyll's son), 1 June 81. Given this objective, Gladstone could hardly have consulted Parnell, the leader of the Land League, on the drafting of the bill, as Hammond, 220, thought he should have done. Dillon's remark on 13 April 1881 was fair enough: 'I very much fear that this Act was drawn by a man who was set to study the whole history of our organisation and was told to draw an Act that would kill the Land League'; F. S. L. Lyons, *John Dillon* (1968), 49.

§ *H* 260. 908.   ¶ To Argyll, 9 Mar. 81.

I have always seen printed have been three capital F's; but the "three F's" in this Bill, if they are there at all, are three little f's.'*

The long battle over the bill in Committee through the summer of 1881 was a formidable physical effort for Gladstone, and he found it absorbing to the point of difficulty: 'Spoke on Transvaal & voted in 314:205. But I am too full of Ireland to be *free* in anything else.'† But the prolonged debate had political advantages. It worked the Liberal majority towards a positive end approved of by much of the party, and it split the Land League. As Gladstone intended, the introduction of the bill recaptured the initiative from the League, already putatively split over the abstention *versus* constitutionalist debate about the proper reaction to the suspension of Irish members following their obstruction of the Protection Bill.‡ The League was confronted with an Irish agricultural community eager to take advantage of the new Court and Commission and it thus faced a dilemma. To obstruct the Bill in the Commons and the Act in the countryside was to do down its own supporters; to make the bill better by amendment and to encourage the use of the Court and the Commission was to prove the Government's point that Westminster legislation could still give Ireland valued boons.

The Land League on the run

Gladstone ruthlessly drove home his advantage against the League. On 29 April his casting vote in Cabinet (having already voted once in the tie) imprisoned John Dillon despite his ill health, one of the most intransigent opponents of the bill. In October, prompted by Forster, he goaded Parnell into attacking him. Gladstone believed Parnell to be weak, vulnerable, and dangerous. Parnell was 'by his *acts* (not motives) . . . an enemy of the Empire'.§ Gladstone drew a distinction between the twelve or so MPs who with Parnell adhered to the League, and whom he regarded as intent on wrecking the Act, and the wider movement of the League in the localities, largely intent on using it. It was for the latter that the attraction of the voluntary use of the Court was provided by the Westminster Parliament. He thus had to maintain an awkward balance between defusing the passion of the Land League's rank and file through the release of some suspects, while at the same time preparing to break up its leadership by incarceration. Gladstone attached a quite misguided importance to a speech by Dillon (released from gaol in August 1881) which seemed to advocate a free run for the Land Act, and he contrasted it with 'the almost frantic denunciations of Parnell (not to mention Miss Anna [Parnell's sister]) the

---

* *H* 263. 1419; 20 July 81. The concept of a 'fair rent' which the bill attempted to define proved legislatively, if not practically, extremely perplexing, and was unresolved well after the bill was already in Committee.   † 25 July 81.
‡ See Lyons, *Dillon*, op. cit., 44ff.   § To Forster, 21 Sept. 81.

violence of which I take to be the measure of his apprehensions lest the Land Act should take the bread out of his mouth, as a speculator on public confusion, by tranquillising the mind of the Irish people'.*

Liberal success in the Tyrone by-election—'a great event as a defeat of Toryism in a strong hold but far greater as a defeat of Parnell'—encouraged the tactic of splitting the League further by releasing suspects such as Father Sheehy, the Land League priest. Dublin Castle counselled waiting until after the Land League conference of 16 September. Forster was at Hawarden that day, and a programme for the release of suspects seems to have been agreed upon. Gladstone determined at the same time on preventing 'Parnell & Co', whom he thought had gained a monopoly of speaking in Ireland, from making further headway. He was especially angered by Parnell's proposal to arrange test cases for the Land Act, and in interpreting this as a hostile approach he was influenced by Forster, and probably also by Cowper, the Irish Viceroy, who was also visiting Hawarden: 'It is quite clear as you said that P. means to present cases which the commission must refuse, and then to treat their refusal as showing that they cannot be trusted, & that the Bill has failed.'† Of course, if that were the outcome, the whole spring and summer of 1881 would have been squandered.

In his speech at the great meeting at Leeds on 7 October 1881, Gladstone repeated the contrast already drawn privately between Dillon (by now 'an opponent whom I am glad to honour') and the malicious Parnell in what has been called 'a classic instance of English incomprehension of Irish realities'.‡ In one of three speeches made that day, Gladstone publicly addressed Parnell with an appeal which was also a provocation and a threat, as well as containing one of his most famous phrases:

if the law, purged from defeat and from any taint of injustice, is still to be refused and the first condition of political society to remain unfulfilled, then I say, gentlemen, that the resources of civilization are not yet exhausted.

Gladstone estimated the torchlight procession which followed the speech as attended by over a quarter of a million people. He wrote that evening in his diary: 'Voice lasted well. It was a great relief when the anxious effort

* To Portarlington, 2 Sept. 81.

† To Forster, 21 Sept. 81. Gladstone later said that 'the Land Act . . . created the crisis [in October 1881] by compelling the promoters of the Land League to take choice between a good course and a bad one. It compelled them either to advance or recede, and they chose to advance; but by that advance they created for us a completely new state of circumstances. That new state of circumstances led to the arrests . . .'; he then explained that the demand for lower rent was 'an important factor' and that the series of test cases was 'an important fact in the history of the whole transaction', but that the arrests under the P.P.P. Act were for reasonable suspicion of some crime punishable by law; 'we did not believe, up to that time, that we could allege any case to Parliament that we had this suspicion of such persons individually. We then had belief, and upon that belief we have acted'; H 266. 874, 16 February 1882.

‡ Lyons, Dillon, op. cit., 56.

about Ireland had been made.' Parnell gave no ground and was consequently incarcerated in Kilmainham Gaol in Dublin in the first of a series of arrests approved by the Cabinet, on Forster's recommendation, on 12 October: 'arrests to be made also in the provinces progressively for speeches pointing to ⟨an Irish Republic⟩ treason or treasonable practice ... Land League meetings to be prohibited when dangerous to the public peace or tending to intimidation'.* On 20 October, after declaring an ineffective 'No Rent' strike in response to Parnell's arrest, the Land League was proscribed.

Gladstone may have misunderstood Irish realities. Parnell may not have been trying to bring down the Land Act, Dillon was certainly not trying to give it a fair chance. But Gladstone was right in his central perception. The Land Act had had the intended effect. He had the Land League on the run. Usually cautious about coercion, and particularly indiscriminate coercion, Gladstone was as ruthless a wielder of power as any contemporary when he saw a necessity or a benefit, as Parnell found in 1881, and Arabi in Egypt in a more violent form in 1882. The benefit was the working of the Land Act and the weakening of the League, and in this Gladstone was successful: as Parnell wrote to Mrs O'Shea on the day of his arrest, 'the movement is breaking fast'.† By December 1881, Gladstone told his son, 'the difficulty is now that we cannot open [Land] Courts enough for them' and the Land League was broken. Whether the arrest of Parnell was necessary for this is not-proven. The arrest or flight abroad of the other members of the League's high-command probably did prevent its capitalizing further on the continuing agrarian crisis and thus preserving its formal structure; it would have been odd to exempt Parnell from a programme of mass-arrests (and, incidentally, disastrous to Parnell's own standing in Ireland). Parnell's imprisonment was advantageous to him (though he never forgave Gladstone for it),‡ and his arrest encouraged the constitutionalist 'new departure' of 1882.

Home Rule under Consideration

The Land Act and its *démarche* was a high-risk strategy which had considerable political success in the medium-term.§ It was perhaps Gladstone's most successful use of the combination of legislative example and executive action which he especially prized. But it opened a number of

---

* 12 Oct. 81. Words in ⟨ ⟩ were deleted by Gladstone.

† Katharine O'Shea, *Charles Stewart Parnell. His love story and political life*, 2v. (1914) [subsequently: O'Shea, *Parnell*], i. 207.

‡ See Lyons, *Dillon*, 55-6.

§ Historians of Ireland are unwontedly harmonious in their agreement that the Land Act combined with arrests successfully undercut the Land League; see Clark, op. cit., 334ff., Bew, op. cit., chs. 8 and 9, R. Barry O'Brien, *Life of C. S. Parnell, 1848-1891*, 2v. (1898), 65ff., J. S. Donnelly, *The land and the people of nineteenth-century Cork* (1975), 288ff.

awkward questions. The Act was explicitly a Liberal assessment of Irish needs, a further 'boon' bestowed. For all Gladstone's qualifications and expressions of hope for a return to free contract, it went a considerable distance towards social immobility, while simultaneously declining to give the Irish MPs who tried to amend it what they wanted, that is, at the least, an explicit recognition of the 'Three Fs'.* It left the Irish landowning class with a diminished role, and diminished expectations. Gladstone frequently complained of the failure of the landlords to act effectively against the League. He no longer looked to them as a reliable support for the government; the Land Act presaged their economic eclipse while retaining their nominal presence. To whom, then, was the government to turn in Ireland? Would it be possible to build a stable political society in collaboration with a political movement whose objective was Home Rule, without admitting the validity of that objective? This was, of course, an even more awkward question for the Conservatives, as in 1881–2 they began to advocate land purchase (i.e. buying out the landlord class) as the next necessary step in Ireland.

In the winter of 1881–2, Gladstone began to consider these questions. The ability of the landlords to act effectively as a separate class was gone but he hoped that they would reassert their influence through an alliance with the tenantry, 'call meetings of their tenants, propose to them united action on behalf of law & personal freedom'. If some such union of property was not developed, then the options offered by the existing constitution were exhausted:

If Ireland is still divided between Orangemen & law-haters, then our task is hopeless: but our belief & contention always is that a more intelligent & less impassioned body has gradually come to exist in Ireland. It is on this body, its precepts & examples, that our hopes depend, for if we are at war with a nation we cannot win.†

Such a body would have to be able to express itself not merely by its orderly presence at the local level, but institutionally. What form that institutional representation should take was a central preoccupation of British politics until the mass of Ireland was lost in 1921. In the autumn of 1881, Gladstone toyed with the Home Rule solution, telling Granville: 'I am rather advanced as to Home or local rule, not wishing to stipulate excepting for the supremacy of Parliament, and for not excluding Scotland in principle from anything offered or done for Ireland',‡ and he continued to think along these lines through the winter.

When P. J. Smyth moved a home rule amendment to the Queen's Speech in February 1882, Gladstone's reply concentrated, after a statement on the

---

* See e.g. Healy: 'The Prime Minister said that the measure did not give all three "F's", and that was certainly true. The tenants of Ireland could not exercize free sale . . .'; H 261. 1469; 27 May 1881.

† To Forster, 13 Oct. 81.   ‡ To Granville, 13 September 1881, in Ramm II, i. 291.

need to maintain ultimate Imperial authority, on the difficulty of defining the distinction between Imperial and Irish affairs. He told those who wished for change that 'they cannot take the first, the most preliminary step, until they have produced a plan and set forth the machinery by which they mean to decide between Imperial and local questions'.* As we shall see, this call for the Irish to offer a plan took on considerable importance for Gladstone in 1885. The day after his speech on Smyth's amendment, Gladstone noted a talk with his son Herbert: 'Conversation with H.J.G. on "Home Rule" & my speech: for the subject has probably a future.'† But Gladstone in the winter of 1881–2 was also planning retirement. An Irish local government bill was thus a more practicable objective, which, 1881 having been largely devoted to Irish affairs, would follow the English and Scottish local government bills intended for 1882. Irish local government might be risky, but it was an important means of consolidating the success of the Land Act:

[If] your [Forster's] excellent plans for obtaining local aid towards the execution of the law break down, it will be on account of this miserable & almost total want of the sense of responsibility for the public good & public peace in Ireland; & this responsibility we cannot create except through local self government.

If we say we must postpone the question till the state of the country is more fit for it, I should answer that the least danger is in going forward at once. It is liberty alone, which fits men for liberty. This proposition like every other in politics has its bounds; but it is far safer than the counter-doctrine, wait till they are fit.

In truth I should say (differing perhaps from many) that, for the Ireland of today, the first question is the rectification of the relations between landlord & tenant, which happily is going on; the next is to relieve Great Britain from the enormous weight of the Government of Ireland unaided by the people, & from the hopeless contradiction in which we stand while we give a Parliamentary representation hardly effective for anything but mischief, without the local institutions of self-government which it presupposes, & on which alone it can have a sound & healthy basis.‡

This classic statement of the primacy of politics and political institutions melded with several very different preoccupations: the Conservative plan for a land purchase bill, supported by Irish MPs generally, including Home Rulers; the apparent acceptance of the Land Act by those Home Rule MPs not in gaol, in the form of a bill to amend it; the renewal, partial renewal or nonrenewal, of coercion in Ireland as the bills of 1881 expired, and the replacement of Cowper, the Viceroy, probably by Spencer, a move 'long delayed'.§ The land purchase plans (combined with a call for the release of Parnell) of W. H. Smith, the Tory MP, were known to Gladstone

* *H* 276. 260; 9 Feb. 82. See also to Roundell, 26 Oct. 83.
† 10 Feb. 82.
‡ To Forster, 12 Apr. 82.
§ See Warren, loc. cit., 112–16 and to Spencer, 3 Apr. 82.

from an early stage because they were, most unusually, prepared with the help of the Treasury.* In response, Lord Frederick Cavendish and Childers prepared a Liberal scheme.† Gladstone was not enthusiastic about land purchase, but he met it not by a negative but by raising questions about the difficulty of its integration into the political process, and the need for its proponents to accompany it with Irish local government, which, as we have seen, he already favoured on other grounds. It was to a Provincial Councils Bill, which would provide the local framework which Gladstone believed essential to land purchase, that he gave attention, drafting a bill in early April 1882, the effort relieved by an entertaining meeting afterwards with Lillie Langtry, about whom he noted: 'I hardly know what estimate to form of her. Her manners are very pleasing, & she has a working spirit in her.' She had, Gladstone may have thought, more of a 'working spirit' than his Cabinet when dealing with local government.‡ Certainly, it was already common ground for all parties in early 1882 that the 1881 Land Act did not represent a 'definitive settlement'. The development of its limited land purchase clauses, or of its arrears clause, or both, was widely canvassed. When Gladstone introduced the Arrears Bill (a bill relieving those who had not paid their rents) in May 1882, he was able to offer it as a limited, rather restricted measure compared with other land reforms in the air.

The 'Kilmainham Treaty' and the Phoenix Park Murders

The events of 1881 thus led, on several simultaneous fronts, to the developments of 1882. With the breaking of the Land League, the use of the Protection of Person and Property Act became less necessary, and Herbert Gladstone's view that outrages were now 'committed to prove the government wrong in coercing' received a sympathetic hearing from his father, who favoured replacing direct coercion with a supplementing of the ordinary law.§ Forster's advocacy of further coercion through a renewal of the full-blooded P.P.P. Act for a year came as a shock.¶ It seemed to suggest that all the travails of 1881 had been to no effect. Gladstone reminded Forster of his plan in 1880 for an alternative to the P.P.P. Bill, namely, proscription of named societies in the United Kingdom as a whole, thus avoiding particularist legislation for Ireland and indiscriminate coercion there.‖ He admitted that the P.P.P. Act 'has served a most important purpose during a great crisis, which without it we should not have had the

---

* To Welby, 17, 27 Mar. 82. † To Cavendish, 12 Apr. 82.
‡ 3 Apr. 82 and J. L. Hammond, *Gladstone and the Irish Nation* (1938) [subsequently: Hammond], 259.
§ Herbert Gladstone's diary, 23 March, 6 April 1882, ed. A. B. Cooke and J. Vincent, *Irish Historical Studies*, xviii. 75, 77 (1973).
¶ Bew, op. cit., 201ff.
‖ See Carlingford's diary of his Dublin visit, Add MS 63690.

means of adequately meeting'.* But that great crisis was now over. Gladstone's approach was to build on what he saw to be the constitutionalism inherent in the Healy/Redmond bill to bring tenants in arrears and some leaseholders within the scope of the 1881 Act.

It was in this context that the various discussions at second-hand with the imprisoned Parnell (already let out on parole for his nephew's funeral by Forster and Cowper) began in late April 1882, some conducted by Herbert Gladstone with F. H. O'Donnell, but mostly, and more famously, by Joseph Chamberlain with Captain O'Shea with Cabinet knowledge and approval. It was these discussions which led to what quickly became known as the 'Kilmainham Treaty', a tacit understanding that a released Parnell would encourage constitutional behaviour in Ireland, with the government relieving the social crisis in Irish agriculture by proposing a thoroughgoing Arrears Bill. The decision for the release of Parnell, Dillon, and O'Kelly was finally made on 2 May 1882, that for Davitt on 4 May.

Gladstone was very careful to keep his hands clean. Commenting on Chamberlain's report to the Cabinet on 1 May 1882, he noted, *inter alia* in his Cabinet minutes, his own position:

W.E.G. Not for arrangement or for compromise or for referring to the present assurances. There has been *no* negotiation. But we have obtained information. The moment is golden.

The 'information' was that Parnell and his immediate colleagues intended to promote law and order *via* the land legislation: 'Arrest was for intentions wh. placed us in the midst of a social revolution. We believe the intentions now are to promote law & order. . . . *Had Parnell (the No Rent Party) declared in October what they declare now, we could not have imprisoned him.*'†

This was quite true. The release of Parnell and the other 'suspects' (under the P.P.P. Act they had not had to be indicted) reflected strength rather than weakness on the part of the government. Parnell's position, as understood through Captain O'Shea, represented an admission that the quasi-revolutionary phase of Irish politics had passed. The League in disarray, local government in the offing, the support of Parnellite MPs for the Land Act acknowledged through an Arrears Bill which would greatly increase the number of tenants who could be incorporated in the Act: Gladstone saw in this 'golden moment' a chance worth taking: 'Prevention, not punishment. The future, not the past'.‡ Spencer had already replaced Cowper as Viceroy,§ Cowper having proved both negative and rather feeble, and the resignation of Forster as Irish Secretary on the day of the Cabinet's decision to release Parnell allowed a second fresh appointment:

---

* 30 Apr. 82.   † Gladstone's italics; 4 May 82.   ‡ 4 May 82.
§ At least in principle; Cowper was still technically Viceroy, and thus had to sign the papers for Parnell's release; see to Cowper, 2 May 82.

Lord Frederick Cavendish, the brother of Hartington (and a member of one of the largest of the Irish landowning families), a man closely associated with the movement within the Liberal party for land purchase (Cavendish was offered the post after the Ulsterman, Andrew Porter, turned it down). Had Cavendish lived, it is hard to believe that a development of the 1881 land purchase clauses would not have been an important part of the legislative programme for 1883 or that the land purchase plan of 1884—the nearest the government got to a serious proposal—would not have been more thoroughly prepared and supported by a stronger political will.

Two days after Parnell's release, Gladstone had a long interview with Captain O'Shea, who reported Parnell's confidence that 'the state of Ireland will have greatly improved in a short time' and gave details of Parnell's renunciation of the 'lawlessness' which he had been willing to use for his own ends. Parnell's renunciation exposed him politically: 'he feels himself in some danger of being supplanted by more violent men'. Such, indeed, was the superficial reading of the events in Dublin almost immediately after this; either that, or deliberate duplicity on Parnell's part. In fact, the success of the government in breaking the Land League's central control was about to be dramatically and horrendously demonstrated.

The murder of Cavendish and Burke in Phoenix Park, Dublin, by a group of mavericks on 6 May 1882 was the Cabinet's Majuba in Irish policy: a disaster, but one essentially irrelevant to the flow of policy. Gladstone was, naturally, severely shaken by Cavendish's murder. Lord Frederick had been his Financial Secretary at the Treasury and was married to Lucy Lyttelton, Catherine Gladstone's niece. Gladstone had helped him make the sort of political career which he had hoped his own son, Willy, might have followed. Not surprisingly, 'grief lay heavy & stunning upon us'. Moreover, the political timing could hardly have looked worse for the 'new departure', the tacit co-operation with a constitutionally-minded Home Rule leadership. Cavendish's murder stood out in brutal contrast to the open character of public life on the mainland, where politicians walked at will and unguarded through the streets without a thought for their security. But Gladstone was not politically deflected, and the Arrears Bill was introduced on 15 May, outstripping in significance the Crimes Bill into which the coercion measures, already in preparation though not yet agreed, necessarily developed. He was both confident and unrepentant about his position with respect to the discussions with Parnell, and refused ever to admit that there had been a 'Kilmainham Treaty'. It was only with difficulty that the Cabinet dissuaded him from deciding to second Northcote's motion for a select committee of inquiry into the Kilmainham negotiations, and from offering to appear before such a Committee. That the Arrears Bill followed almost exactly what Carlingford noted as the Irish 'condition' (in the sense of requirement), Gladstone of course did not allude to.*

There was some elision of view in all this. If Parnell now represented the encouragement of legality and constitutionalism, then there was no more objection to an arrangement with him than to any other political pact. If he did not represent these forces, then he might be released in due course through an absence of any reason to restrain him, but not on the ground of positive advantage. Of course, nothing was so clear cut. The simple juxta-position of moral force and physical force in Ireland was always a gross oversimplification.† What is curious and important about Gladstone's attitude to Parnell at this time was the Prime Minister's transformation of the rather isolated leader with his little band of twelve or so MPs—Glad-stone's view of him in the autumn of 1881—into the central figure in the calculations about the future of Irish politics. If the Land League was broken, why bother about Parnell, who was hardly in any position to make 'conditions'? No comment by Gladstone on this in early 1882 seems to have survived. The answer is probably to be found at least in part in the absence of alternatives. There was something of an attempt in March 1882 to revive William Shaw, the previous Irish leader who had seceded from the Home Rule group in January 1881, as a significant political figure, but Shaw came to nothing. Further, the prospects for a Liberal revival in Ireland were quite unrealistic. If Irish politics were to remain incorporated within British politics, the Parnellite position was unavoidable. That position, of course, sought to use British politics to achieve 'Home Rule'. Given the Liberals' decline in Ireland, seeing Parnell as the focal point of Irish political development was only undesirable to the extent that Home Rule was undesirable. Such was the implication of Gladstone's position in the summer of 1882, and also, it might be thought, of Joseph Chamberlain's, the chief negotiator with Parnell *via* Captain O'Shea and also the chief

---

* If he had, his explanation would doubtless have been that the making of the Arrears Bill, which gave a gift to tenants-in-arrears from the Consolidated Fund Commissioners *via* the Church Temporalities Commissioners, was a good deal more complex than a simple recognition of Parnellite expectations or 'conditions'; for Gladstone's statement on the Healy/Redmond Bill, and the content of the Arrears Bill, significantly narrowed the area of further land reform by cutting out land purchase which, according to Carlingford, was in the early stages of Cabinet discussion of Healy's bill very much in play: 'the idea of a Bill was dropped, *except as to Arrears & Purchase*' (22 April 1882, Add MS 63690). On 5 April Hamilton had noted: coercion of some sort, plus measures 'to extend the purchase clauses of the Land Act and to deal with arrears (both of which questions must be taken in hand) will absorb all the remaining legislative time of the session'; Bahlman, *Hamilton*, i. 250. There were certainly many more forces in play in April/May 1882 than Parnell. In this sense the Arrears Bill, meeting the most immediate but also the most short-term of Parnell's conditions, was an opportunity for Gladstone to set aside an embryonic Tory–Whig–Irish collaboration on land purchase.

† See, e.g. Bew, op. cit., 121–6 on the sophisticated ambivalence of the 'rent at the point of the bayonet' tactic.

proponent in the Cabinet of the franchise reform which would turn Parnell's influence in Ireland into seats at Westminster.

Gladstone was coming to recognize what the Tories refused to recognize, that if Ireland was to be pacified, the leaders of constitutional opinion in Ireland would have to be accommodated constitutionally within the general framework of the United Kingdom: it was therefore vital that the terms being set by those leaders should be terms which the United Kingdom as a whole could reasonably accept. The enigmatic personality of Charles Stewart Parnell, landowner, Protestant, and former Cambridge undergraduate, as well as Irish Nationalist, seemed the best, if risky, hope for a future better than rural violence in Ireland and bombing in Britain.

Immediately after the Phoenix Park murders, Parnell got Captain O'Shea to tell Gladstone secretly that if the latter felt it needful, he, Parnell, was ready immediately to resign his seat in the Commons. Gladstone at once rejected the offer, with a reference to Parnell's 'honourable motives'. A fortnight later began the long series of letters between Gladstone and Katharine O'Shea, Parnell's mistress. Mrs O'Shea, presumably writing at Parnell's suggestion, instigated the correspondence by offering to arrange a meeting between Gladstone and Parnell. She had written without telling her husband. From that moment she became a secret and highly effective go-between, and, as we shall see, was the link at the vital moment in the move towards Home Rule in the autumn of 1885.*

'Kitty O'Shea' has the smack of a colleen, but she was in fact a very suitable person for her role. She was the daughter of the Revd Sir John Page Wood, an Anglican clergyman, and the niece of Lord Hatherley, Lord Chancellor in Gladstone's first government. Moreover, she was the sister of Sir Evelyn Wood who had so sensibly led the negotiations with the Boers after Majuba, a year before the Gladstone–Mrs O'Shea correspondence began. Katharine O'Shea was thus a member of a distinguished Liberal family. In marrying O'Shea she had married beneath herself politically and financially. Gladstone had some sympathy for her and her husband and tried, perhaps inadvisedly, to help him to a post in Dublin Castle later in 1882. Grosvenor, the chief whip, replied with the retort that '*every* Irishman, without exception always jobs' and the attempt came to nothing.

Mrs O'Shea was an unexpected bonus. She played her part confidentially and with some skill. Gladstone and Parnell were enabled to establish a fairly close, vicarious relationship which, had it been direct, would have been very impolitic, probably indeed impossible, on both sides. On the

---

* Herbert Gladstone went to considerable pains to discredit parts of O'Shea, *Parnell* (see *After thirty years*, 295ff.); curiously, he does not mention Mrs. O'Shea's error in dating Parnell's 'proposed Constitution for Ireland' as having been written and sent early in 1884; her book is an odd mixture of exaggeration and accuracy; though written *ca.* 1913, the dates of her meetings with Gladstone in 1882 are correct, as are various other details checked against Gladstone's diary; clearly, when she wrote, she had quite an extensive archive available to her.

Liberal side there was no secrecy in the sense that the letters were all shown to the chief whip and usually to the Irish ministers. Undoubtedly, the Katharine O'Shea connection carried matters forward. It was an important factor in encouraging Gladstone to conclude in 1883: 'though Parnell is a Sphinx, the most probable reading of him is that he works for & with the law as far as he dare. I have even doubt whether he hates the Government.'* There is no record of what Gladstone knew or thought at the time of the private relationship between Mrs O'Shea and Parnell. Probably he felt that the less known, the better.† He paid Katharine O'Shea, as he did Olga Novikov, the rather modern compliment of treating her as a political figure rather than a woman.

Irish Local Government and Franchise Reform, 1883–1885

In 1883 Gladstone agreed, at the request of Hartington, to delay his retirement so as to see through the franchise and redistribution bills, a process uncompleted by the fall of the government in 1885. The intention was that the Franchise Bill would be immediately followed by 'a heap of Local Government', and thus both the representative and the constitutional structures of the United Kingdom would have received legislative completion. Gladstone, however, expected to play no part in the second part of this process: 'I am glad the time has not come when new points of departure in Irish legislation have to be considered, and that good old Time ... will probably plant me before that day comes outside "the range of practical politics".'‡ In the winter of 1883–4 imperial policy and parliamentary reform thus formed his horizon of personal commitment.

Parliamentary reform was likely considerably to increase Irish difficulties. As we have seen, household franchise in Ireland might be construed as more 'conservative' than a lesser extension, but the likelihood was never strong that the Irish National League which succeeded the Land League could be stranded as a tenant movement with a limited electoral base. Gladstone might assure Hartington in December 1883 that 'according to all the authorities you greatly overestimate the effect of an altered franchise in augmenting the power of Parnellism',§ but he told the Queen in 1884 that the Liberals would lose about twenty-five seats in Ireland, with the Home Rulers returning nearly eighty MPs.¶ The essential Cabinet decision had been whether to allow the situation in Ireland to

---

* To Spencer, 29 June 83.

† According to Dilke's 'Memoir' (Gwynn, i. 445), Harcourt told the cabinet on 17 May 1882 that 'Captain O'Shea [was] "the husband of Parnell's mistress"'. But there was no cabinet that day; it seems likely, however, that Harcourt made an announcement of that sort during the post-Kilmainham cabinets. See also Sir R. Ensor, *England, 1870–1914* (1936), Appendix B.

‡ To Harcourt, 29 Dec. 83.

§ To Hartington, 29 Dec. 83.

¶ 19 Aug. 84.

frustrate franchise reform generally. The decision had been, to take the consequences.

Those consequences were considerable, but they became fully apparent only in a context of increasing and unanticipated complexity. The absence of Liberal agreement about the form of local government applied *a fortiori* in Ireland, where the question was compounded by complications of order and imperial power. In early 1885 all the factors were still in play: land reform (in the form of land purchase, already an abortive government proposal in 1884), local government, and coercion (the Crimes Act of 1882 expired in September 1885). Over this hung the question of the accommodation of the Irish representatives after the elections to be held once the reform bills were all passed. As dispute within the Cabinet rose to a point of irreconcilability far greater than any reached hitherto on Ireland and as the Sudan and Afghan questions reached at least partial solution, Gladstone made a further effort at retiring in the spring of 1885.

The new element in early 1885 was the Chamberlain–Dilke attempt at an Irish settlement based on a 'Central Board' solution (i.e. elected County Councils sending representatives to a central board which would have control of various Irish government departments). Not surprisingly, Dublin Castle, accustomed to an almost Indian-style autocracy, had reservations about the viability of such an arrangement which, if seen as a settlement of the constitutional future of Ireland, still left the role of the Irish MPs uncertain. Parnell promoted the idea *via* Captain O'Shea to Chamberlain because it would give Ireland greater domestic control without harming the case for an Irish legislature; Chamberlain saw it as a solution which would remove the case for such a legislature. Misunderstandings led to ructions between Chamberlain and Parnell. The Radicals built up the case for a central board in the Cabinet until on 9 May 1885 it was narrowly rejected.

Gladstone's position with respect to the proposal and to the negotiations was oblique: he was associated with the central board scheme, but not fully committed to it. Partly this was because the Gordon crisis in the Sudan, the solution of the Afghan frontier crisis, and the complexities of the Redistribution Bill, coincided with the Chamberlain–Dilke initiative: 'The pressure of affairs, especially Soudan, Egypt, & Afghan, is now from day to day extreme.'* There was no agreed plan of legislation beyond the Franchise Bill and, since December 1884, the Redistribution Bill: the Queen's Speech which began the Session lasting through the summer of 1885 was that of August 1884, mentioning only the Franchise Bill.† This absence of even a nominal framework of legislation beyond a Franchise Bill reflected

---

* 16 Mar. 85.
† This was because the autumn Session in 1884 was intended—at least in theory—to be short, with the Franchise Bill being passed in both houses.

the extent to which imperial affairs and the reform crisis dominated politics. It also perhaps reflected Gladstone's intention not to be shackled to some further round of legislation which would again prevent his retirement. As it became clear that the special autumn Session of 1884 was in fact likely to last through to the summer of 1885, so the need for legislation other than redistribution, registration, etc. became clear. There was an understanding that local government would be prominent, but there was no attempt to draw up a programme.

It was in this rather vacuous context that Chamberlain and Dilke made their moves. Without Gladstone's close involvement, there was never much likelihood of the Radical plan succeeding. The Chamberlain–Dilke base in Cabinet was too narrow to take on Spencer, Campbell-Bannerman (by now Irish Secretary), and Dublin Castle on such a central question of Irish politics. An Irish local government measure would have to come publicly either from the Prime Minister or from the Irish ministers. Gladstone gave the central board plan a general support, but there was none of the curiosity about detail, the craftiness of Cabinet presentation, the gradual build-up of correspondence and the careful integration of potential Cabinet opponents, which were the hallmarks of a serious Gladstonian initiative.

The absence of interest in detail is reflected in Gladstone's diary and in the Cabinet minutes. Several of the meetings with Chamberlain and Dilke are not recorded by Gladstone. It is curious that one noted by Chamberlain as having taken place on 18 January*—his initial report of his meeting with O'Shea and Gladstone's encouragement to continue the communications—could not have taken place that day, Gladstone then being at Hawarden and Chamberlain not being a visitor there. When Cardinal Manning intervened to support the Central Board plan, Gladstone left contact with him entirely to Chamberlain; Gladstone's poor personal relations with Manning in the aftermath of the *Vatican Decrees* no doubt largely accounts for this, but if he had been fully committed to seeing the Central Board solution as a successful bill, he would have found a way round.† Gladstone's behaviour over the Central Board affair testifies to the genuineness of the attempt at retirement which was then his objective.

When the Central Board plan was narrowly defeated in Cabinet, Gladstone declared it 'dead as mutton for the present, though as I believe for the present only. It will quickly rise again & as I think perhaps in larger dimensions.'‡ Gladstone had, humiliatingly, to announce that despite expectations, no measure of local government for Ireland could be pro-

* Chamberlain, *Political memoir*, 141.
† For the Central Board episode, see C. H. D. Howard, 'Joseph Chamberlain, Parnell and the Irish "Central Board" scheme, 1884–5', *I.H.S.*, viii. 324 (1953).
‡ To Spencer, 9 May 85.

posed that Session. Privately, he mixed warnings about the future of Ireland with statements about his own imminent retirement. His self-presentation as only an *'amicus curiae'* in Cabinet—his work on re-distribution nearly completed, and the Sudan and Afghan frontier no longer points of immediate conflict—contributed to the Cabinet's malaise.

Defeat, Resignation, and the Future of Ireland

On 8 June 1885, Gladstone began the Cabinet by announcing that defeat on the Budget that evening was a possibility.* Thus defeat was not, as is some-times thought, a surprise or a bolt from the blue. The Cabinet that day continued to be deadlocked on the renewal of coercion. That evening the government was defeated on Hicks Beach's amendment to the Budget on indirect taxation by 264 to 252 votes. This was, then, a substantial house. It was not a surprise defeat in a small house, like the Rosebery government's fall on the 'cordite vote' in 1895. Much was made then and since of the Tory–Irish alliance which contributed to the defeat of the government. But the government could only lose its overall majority through abstention or absence on its own side. Despite a speech on the amendment by Glad-stone, seventy Liberals were unpaired and absent from the lobby. It is hard to avoid the conclusion that Grosvenor, the chief whip, had given up. Gladstone noted that there was no Tory–Irish harmony on the immediate issue of indirect/direct taxation, the Liberals being a buffer between the Irish 'opposed to indirect taxation generally' and the Tories 'even more friendly to it than we are'.† Next day ministers agreed to offer their resig-nations; and, after declining a peerage, Gladstone on 24 June 1885 kissed hands to mark the end of his second premiership.

The end of the government thus left Gladstone curiously uncommitted as to the future of Ireland. He was associated with the Central Board plan, a 'posthumous bequest' he told the Queen's secretary,‡ but not as its protagonist. He had announced, separately, both a modest renewal of the Crimes Act and a land purchase bill, but viewed neither with enthusiasm. The end of the government also imposed upon Gladstone the release so often claimed. Surely at last the moment had come? But even before the government was defeated, the usual forces for retention were operating. Gladstone had openly talked of retirement in May 1885§ and discussed it with his son at Hawarden.¶ Predictably, Wolverton appeared, as he had at most moments of importance since his days as chief whip in Gladstone's first government. His previous interventions had all been against retire-ment, and it therefore seems likely that, when Gladstone and Wolverton

---

* Rosebery's diary, 8 June 1885, Dalmeny MSS: 'Mr. G. opened by saying that there was some chance of our being beaten on budget tonight.'

† To Hartington, 10 June 85.   ‡ To Ponsonby, 29 May 85.

§ See, e.g., to Chamberlain, 6 May 85, to Spencer, 9 May 85.   ¶ 25 May 85.

'opened rather a new view as to my retirement' on 30 May, it involved some arrangement for further delay. Wolverton remained on the scene during the aftermath of the Cabinet's resignation and on 16 June Gladstone circularized his ex-Cabinet colleagues with a minute stating that he would take his seat 'in the usual manner on the front Opposition Bench' but because of his loss of voice would take 'the first proper opportunity . . . of absenting myself from actual attendance . . . a bodily not a moral absence'. He did not 'perceive, or confidently anticipate, any state of facts' to prevent his withdrawal from active participation at the end of the Parliament.* Elsewhere, though not in this minute, the usual qualifications about future usefulness and need were made.†

Gladstone's second government ended in a flurry of activity: the Vote of Credit for the Sudan and Central Asia, the failed budget, the fag-end of the bills which made up the reform package, local government generally and Irish government particularly. Defeat and the breathing space of a Tory minority ministry dependent on Irish Home Rule votes solved few of these questions and in some respects made them more complicated for the Liberals. There was an understanding that the Tories would soon dissolve for a general election on the new franchise and distribution of constituencies. That election could hardly do other than confirm the strength of the Home Rule party in Ireland, a fact of which both British political parties were well aware.

Gladstone ended the government energetically, despite his sore throat and impaired voice, which as we shall see, had political as well as personal consequences as the summer of 1885 progressed. He was 75 when he resigned and, as Chamberlain and Dilke had cause to know, was as capable of political manœuvre as ever he had been. The government's fall and the subsequent pattern of politics in fact ended rather than enabled the political retirement discussed in May and June. Gladstone moved straight into the business of opposition. There was little doubt that it was the Liberals' unresolved dispute about the future government of Ireland that was the most problematic of the remnants of the 1880–5 administration. Moving restlessly from the Aberdeens' house at Dollis Hill in north London to the Talbots at Keble College, Oxford, then to the Rothschilds at Waddesdon, and then back to Dollis Hill, Gladstone tossed the Irish question about in conversations and letters. The minority Salisbury government gave time for reflection and consultation, but it was borrowed time on a clock which seemed to speed up.

---

* 16 June 85.   † To Sir T. Gladstone, 19 June 85.

CHAPTER IX

Towards Home Rule

The History of an Idea: 'Ireland is inhabited by Irishmen'—Ireland and the Constitution: Home Rule and Pluralism—The 'Irish Trilogy' of Order, Land Settlement, and Autonomy—Parnell, Gladstone, and the Events of 1885—Parnell's 'Proposed Constitution' and Gladstone's Sketch of a Home Rule Bill, November 1885—A Tory Home Rule Bill?—The 'Hawarden Kite' and the Tory Government's Resignation—Gladstone's Third Government and the Chances of an Irish Settlement—The Liberal Party unprepared for Home Rule

I have long suspected the Union of 1880. There was a case for doing something: but this was like Pitt's Revolutionary war, a gigantic though excusable mistake.*

Secret No. 1.

1. Irish Chamber for Irish affairs.
2. Irish representation to remain as now for Imperial affairs.
3. Equitable division of Imperial charges by fixed proportions.
4. Protection of minority.
5. Suspension of Imperial authority for all civil purposes whatsoever. Nov. 14. 85.†

The History of an Idea: 'Ireland is inhabited by Irishmen'

Within thirteen months of the fall of his second government in June 1885, Gladstone had fought two elections, had proposed a gigantic settlement of the Irish question which dominated Liberal politics for the rest of their significant existence, and had split his party. We now, therefore, turn our attention to that 'mighty heave in the body politic', 'the idea of constituting a Legislature for Ireland'.‡ *History of an Idea* was the title of the first half of the apologia on Home Rule which Gladstone wrote in 1886 after his electoral defeat.§ The phraseology and the format of a public, historical explanation take us back to *A Chapter of Autobiography* (1868), Gladstone's other public apologia. There are obvious parallels between his handling of Irish disestablishment and Home Rule. But it is important to note that

---

* Diary for 19 Sept. 85.   † Gladstone's 'Sketch' of a Home Rule Bill, 14 November 1885.
‡ To Rosebery, 13 Nov. 85.
§ *The Irish Question. I.—History of an Idea. II.—Lessons of the Election* (1886) [subsequently: *The Irish Question*]; see 26 July 86.

Gladstone denied that Home Rule involved a change of mind, even as it is often phrased a 'conversion', of the sort that undoubtedly did occur over disestablishment. In the case of the Irish Church, 'change of opinion' had required public explanation; in the case of Home Rule, 'I have no such change to vindicate'.*

Gladstone's diary bears this out, albeit in a negative way. In the 1840s, Gladstone went to great lengths to chronicle for himself and for posterity the process by which his view of the confessional state came to be seen as practically untenable. The reason for his careful records of the public and private crises of the 1840s is clear enough; the process of change, and Gladstone's need to understand it, was fundamental to his ecclesiastical and political identity. In the 1880s, the path to Home Rule receives only glancing mentions. This may irritate the historian, but it reflects two important aspects of the process by which the Home Rule policy evolved.

First, the evolution involved for Gladstone no inward struggle, no resolution of contending tensions. Second, he saw the policy as political in the narrow sense of the word, evolving not from an inference from some cosmic, *a priori* interpretation of the nature of man and his world, but from the experience of government and the consideration of alternatives. He had stated his view of the ideal state in *The State in its Relations with the Church*, and he had been forced from it by experience and by a painful public and private process to a liberal, pluralistic view of citizenship. But this was always a second order principle. The secular state and political life were matters of temporary arrangements not of eternal verities. Gladstone did not share that potent Imperial-State worship which for many Unionists in the late-Victorian period became a substitute for the Church-and-State Toryism of the past, and his underestimation of its strength was probably of considerable importance in 1886. He realized Home Rule was a 'mighty heave'; but he probably did not realize quite how mighty a heave it would in fact turn out to be.

The process of evolution of Home Rule for Gladstone was thus similar to the process of the gradual disclosure of his disestablishmentarianism in the years 1845–68, an assessment of opportunity and 'ripeness', but it lacked the public and private crises of the 1840s and also 'the ideal' from whose abandonment those crises sprang. Rather, it was a further development or consequence of the crises and reappraisals which had led to the 'conversion' to disestablishmentarianism and the abandonment of the notion of Ireland as part of a British confessional state. In 1839, Gladstone had been struck 'ineffaceably' by a remark in the House of Commons by Lord John Russell, then his political opponent. Gladstone recalled it to Russell during the Irish land debates in 1870 and he recalled it to the

* *The Irish Question*, 3–4.

House of Commons during the Home Rule debate in 1886:* 'You said, "The true key to our Irish debates was this: that it was not properly borne in mind that as England is inhabited by Englishmen, and Scotland by Scotchmen, so Ireland is inhabited by Irishmen".'† In the sense that the Government of Ireland Bill was Gladstone's ultimate comment on the implications of this simple nostrum, there was a clear relationship to his youthful political reorientation. But it was a relationship mediated through the attempt in the 1868–74 government to end the Protestant ascendancy by disestablishment, the land bill, and the university bill. Whether that ascendancy could be ended without the process of ending it in itself promoting Home Rule or something like it, was an obvious question which faced Gladstone in the 1870s and early 1880s, and whose answer was never clearly stated.

The context of Gladstone's way of thinking was thus in 1885 very different from that of those who were by then his contemporaries and for whom his curious political odyssey since the 1830s, by which whiggish political positions were reached by non-whiggish paths, was part of a history of which they had perhaps read but had not shared. This in part explains Gladstone's isolation.

Home Rule also related closely to Gladstone's theoretical disestablishmentarianism in another way. Disestablishment, especially in Scotland, was a major cry in 1885, and had been for some time. Unlike several of the ingredients of the 'Radical Programme' of that year, it was in principle clearly acceptable to Gladstone and we know that privately he did not expect the Church of Scotland to remain established for long. Though during his second government he dampened down Free Church enthusiasm on the grounds of the already clogged legislative timetable,‡ the position he took was of considerable importance for Home Rule for it set up a framework of proof: Disestablishment in Scotland on fair terms was not impossible: 'It is a Scotch question and ought to be decided by the people of Scotland, i.e. Parliament ought to accept their sense.'§ The Scots would have to show that the proposal was 'the genuine offspring of Scottish sentiment and Scottish conviction'.¶ Thus, if Scotland spoke clearly and specifically, in terms not of an abstract resolution but of a viable legislative

---

* W. E. Gladstone, *Speeches on the Irish question in 1886*, (1886), 63–4 (13 April 1886).

† To Russell, 12 Apr. 70; see above, vol. i, p. 44. It was a curious feature of Unionism that it never found a word to describe all the inhabitants of the Union it argued was indissoluble; 'English' was commonly used for all on the British mainland (Gladstone so used it in Midlothian in 1879), but, especially after the 1870s, became offensive to the Scots and the Welsh; 'British' was taken by mainlanders to mean the inhabitants of these islands, but it was never accepted by the Irish as applying to them, and, of course, Ireland is not part of Great Britain; not surprisingly, United Kingdomer never gained any ground.

‡ In late 1881 and again in August 1884.

§ To G. C. Hutton, 28 July 85; the letter was released to the press, as Gladstone must have expected.   ¶ *Political speeches (1885)*, 66.

proposal, there could be no reason in principle to decline her case. Gladstone was not personally prepared to play any part in enabling Scottish opinion to express itself. He did not see himself as the progenitor of a bill and he was cautious about involving himself with the Free Church Liberals. During the 1885 election campaign, in a speech intended, for tactical reasons of Liberal party unity, to play down the disestablishment question both in Scotland and England—a speech clearly delivered with considerable private embarrassment on Gladstone's part*—he told the Scots that, following his usual practice, he would not vote for an abstract resolution on Scottish disestablishment: it would have to be seen 'in a long vista', that is, not in the next Parliament.† Even so, Gladstone had set the Scots a target on a question of organic constitutional and national importance.

In the second half of 1885, therefore, Gladstone approached the differing sorts of claims from Scotland and Ireland in a rather similar manner. The difference was that he knew that the Scots, whom he publicly instructed on the means to success, would not speak with sufficient unanimity, whereas the great majority of the Irish, to whom he refrained from giving quite such explicit instruction, would. In both cases, the one public, the other largely private, there was a willingness, unprecedented and rarely repeated, to make metropolitan politics available to the claims of the numerically inferior constituent nationalities of the United Kingdom. In this sense, the Scots had played an important though clearly subordinate part through their disestablishment campaign since the 1870s in setting up the context for Home Rule.

The idea of 'Home Rule' did not, of course, spring up fully formed in an instant, nor was there a single moment of decision. Since it was for Gladstone not a deductive construct resulting from a general constitutional hypothesis, but rather the product of experience and the recognition of particular contingencies, its emergence was a complex process integrating long-, medium-, and short-term influences. In attempting to understand Gladstone's mind in 1885 and 1886, a wide variety of factors must therefore be taken into consideration which may for convenience be discussed as the general context of nineteenth-century liberalism, the immediate context of the mid-1880s, the process of 1885–6, and the policy. As Gladstone saw the

* On 11 November 1885 in the Free Church Hall in Edinburgh, noted as 'a difficult subject'. For this speech and the tactical context see A. Simon, 'Church disestablishment as a factor in the general election of 1885', *Historical Journal*, xviii. 791 (1975). The tactical difficulty was well stated to Rainy, the Free Church leader, on 3 November 1885: '. . . the one case is the inverse of the other. In Scotland Disestablishment is I believe pressed largely as a test by the Liberals. In England Establishment is keenly pressed as a test by the Tories: & the request is coolly made that no Liberal shall vote for a candidate favourable to disestablishment. This we entirely resist, but the resistance appears to be incompatible with a forward movement in Scotland.'

† *Political speeches* (*1885*), 70. He consequently spoke but did not vote on Cameron's disestablishment and disendowment motion (or on Currie's amendment) on 30 March 1886.

17. Catherine Gladstone (*photograph by Miss Sarah Acland, Oxford, 25 October 1892*)

18. Gladstone and his secretaries *ca.* 1883 (left to right: Horace Seymour, Spencer Lyttelton, George Leveson Gower, Edward Hamilton)

19. Gladstone in the 'Temple of Peace' at Hawarden, photographed as the Royal Academy's Professor of Ancient History on 6 June 1884 by J. P. Mayall for *Artists at Home*

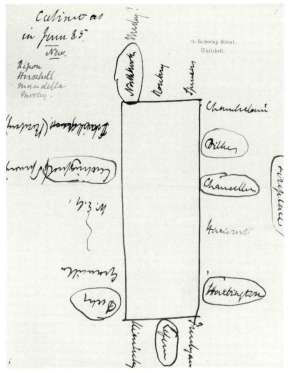

20(a). Gladstone's plan of Cabinet seating, June
1885, revised 1886

20(b). The Cabinet in July 1883

21(a). Electioneering at Warrington, 28 November 1885

21(c). A Unionist chamberpot

SERIOUS ANNOUNCEMENT.

Mr. Gladstone's Collars are worn out.
No more after to-day. Last appearance !

21(b). 'Mr Gladstone's Collars' (*Harry
Furniss' cartoon in* Punch)

22(b). Millais's portrait of Gladstone, 1885, for Christ Church, Oxford

22(a). Studio photograph by Rupert Potter, 28 July 1884

23. The Gladstones planting a tree at Newnham College, Cambridge, 31 January 1887

24(a). 'Enemies on his flank' (*cartoon by F. Carruthers Gould*)

24(b). 'Sitting out a debate' (*cartoon of Lord Salisbury by F. Carruthers Gould*)

Lord Granville

Lord Spencer

Lord Frederick Cavendish

Lord Hartington

25. Whigs all: Granville, Spencer, Lord Frederick Cavendish, Lord Hartington (*photographs in G. Barnett Smith*, Life and times of . . . Gladstone (*illustrated edition, n.d.*))

26(a). 'Salisbury, Gladstone and Chamberlain'
(*cartoon by F. Carruthers Gould*)

26(b). 'Over the hills and far away' (*Tenniel's cartoon of Gladstone in the Highlands, September 1893, in* Punch)

27. Gladstone, W.H. Gladstone and the family tree-felling at Hawarden in the 1880s

28(b). Herbert Gladstone

28(a). Gladstone in Munich, 13 October 1879 (*photograph by F. von Lenbach*)

29(a). Gladstone and Döllinger, September 1886 (*unfinished portrait by F. von Lenbach*)

29(b). Gladstone, Döllinger, Acton, and others at Tegernsee, 1886

30(a). Gladstone reading (*drawing by George Howard, M.P., 5 June 1879*)

30(b). W.B. Richmond's drawing of Gladstone dead, 21 May 1898

30(c). The Gladstones' visit to J.J. Colman in Norfolk, 19 May 1890

31. Last entry in Gladstone's diary, 29 December 1896

32. Gladstone, dead, laid out in his doctoral robes in the 'Temple of Peace', Hawarden Castle policy as inherently related to the process, a consequence of evolution by 'stages', the reader will find that discussion of the process merges seamlessly into the discussion of the policy. Let us, therefore, discuss further the intellectual assumptions through which Gladstone saw Home Rule. We will then consider the complicated political process which in 1885–6 shaped the emergence of Home Rule as an objective of policy, and finally the details of the policy itself as it took the form of a Government of Ireland Bill allied to a Land Bill.

Liberalism in the nineteenth century had sought and seen the achievement of the grouping of small, often princely, states into large units roughly defined by nationality. Gladstone had, with reservations, favoured this development in both Italy and Germany. But liberalism with its stress on representation and minimum central government had also favoured decentralization within these large units in the form of various types of local government to counteract the centralization inherent in its imposition of national standards. The *Essai sur les formes de gouvernement dans les sociétés modernes* (1872) by Gladstone's friend Emile de Laveleye is a good statement of this sort of constitutional modernization.

Liberalism thus tried to incorporate both nationalism and efficient devolved government. The interests of nationalism and of lower tiers of government—whether at the regional or the local level—did not necessarily coincide. Indeed, in the United Kingdom they conflicted, for nationalism saw England, Scotland, Wales and Ireland as the units, and to divide the United Kingdom into four such units for purposes of devolved government would produce an obviously lop-sided result. In Britain, the tension between nationalism and regionalism was never resolved: the size of England always unbalanced plans for devolution to the constituent nations of the United Kingdom ('Home-Rule-all-round' as it came to be known), but the strength of local nationalism, including that of England, prevented serious support for regional devolution. To put the point another way: Scotland, Wales and Ireland were rather good-sized units where national and regional criteria fitted together quite well; it was England that was the problem. The extent to which Home Rule was primarily an English problem—in the sense of raising questions about English identity—has been underestimated.

As we have seen, the state of Parliamentary business in the 1870s and early 1880s suggested that the single level of government for the whole of the United Kingdom created by the Act of Union of 1800 was becoming seriously overburdened. A development of the Whigs' Municipal Corporations Act of 1835 into a general system of local government had been several times attempted by the second Gladstone government without legislative success, though ironically Ripon achieved by Resolution in India in 1882[*]

[*] See S. R. Mehrotra, *The emergence of the Indian National Congress* (1971), ch. 6.

what the Liberal Cabinet failed to achieve for Britain by legislation. At the larger level of imperial affairs British policy had, since the 1830s, been one of general devolution whenever possible, with the British North America Act of 1867, passed by a Conservative government but largely prepared by the Liberals with Gladstone handling the financial settlement, as the chief triumph. It is important to remember that, for a man of Gladstone's generation, this was the main direction of imperial development, not the creation of the autocratic structure of district officers on the Indian model which was the consequence of the tropical acquisitions of the 1870s and 1880s. Devolution of power was the way to achieve both order and loyalty and consequently, from the metropolitan point of view, strategic safety. Advocacy of responsible and representative government in the settled colonies, with particular attention to the demarcation between Imperial and colonial responsibility, had been an important aspect of Gladstone's developing liberalism in the late 1840s and early 1850s.*

Ireland and the Constitution: Home Rule and Pluralism

It is, therefore, not surprising that as Gladstone began to turn 'Home Rule' into a legislative proposal in the autumn of 1885, he asked Grosvenor, the chief whip, to send him copies of 'the Canada Union & Government Act *1840* ⟨or *close* to that year⟩ and Canada Government (Dominion) Act 1867'.† Clause 2 of the Government of Ireland Bill empowered the Queen 'by and with the advice of the Irish Legislative Body, to make laws for the peace, order and good government of Ireland'; Gladstone noted next to these words in his early draft for the Cabinet 'The words proceeding are *mutatis mutandis* from "The British North America Act, 1867".'‡ Representative decentralization was thus a common policy for the United Kingdom and its overseas possessions and it is in this rather than in European precedents that the groundings of 'Home Rule' are to be found.

Ireland, with her peculiar combination of MPs at Westminster and Viceroy in Dublin Castle, fitted neither the colonial nor the simply localist model exactly. As Grattan's famous metaphor ran, quoted by Gladstone when introducing the Government of Ireland Bill:§ Ireland 'hears the ocean protesting against separation, but she hears the sea protesting against union. She follows therefore her physical destination when she protests against the two situations, both equally unnatural, separation and union.'¶ Grattan used this metaphor to argue that the union of the Parliaments was

---

* See above pp. 73 ff.

† To Grosvenor, 9 Oct. 85; i.e. before the dissolution was announced. It was a little unusual to ask Grosvenor for documents of this sort, and was probably also intended as a hint.

‡ Add MS 44632, f. 194; 31 March 1886.

§ Gladstone quoted it in the form 'The Channel forbids union, the ocean forbids separation'; *Speeches on the Irish question 1886*, 50.

¶ S. Gwynn, *Henry Grattan and his times* (1939), 337.

unnecessary as Britain and Ireland were thus inherently related. Gladstone regarded the Act of Union of 1800 as a gigantic, though excusable, mistake, the product of the war against France which he regarded as an even greater mistake, but he never seems to have seriously considered its repeal, partly because he saw no serious demand for it, and partly because the Irish Parliament in its historic form had not existed for eighty-five years.

Self-evidently, any settlement of the Irish question short of Irish independence was bound to reflect the complications of Ireland's curious relationship to the rest of the United Kingdom. Even those who advocated the *status quo* advocated what was already a form of pluralist constitution created by the process of historical change, a pluralism that existed despite, and parallel to, the 'absolute supremacy of Parliament' identified by A. V. Dicey in his *Law of the Constitution*, a book read and strongly approved by Gladstone as the decision to commit himself publicly to Home Rule evolved in November and December 1885.*

In those months, Gladstone reminded himself of Edmund Burke's historicist and prudential case for magnanimity and an empire whose cohesion came from decentralized power. This gave him a distinguished pedigree of conservative whiggery which he might have more acutely exploited against the dissentient Whigs in 1886. At the same time, Dicey's analysis had a strong appeal for Gladstone, whose instinct was always to think in terms of executive action and progress through statute; he never showed much interest in common law, the bar to Dicey's universal sovereign.

Gladstone strikingly quoted Dicey when introducing the Government of Ireland Bill:

No work that I have ever read brings out in a more distinct and emphatic manner the peculiarity of the British Constitution in one point to which, perhaps, we seldom have occasion to refer, namely, the absolute supremacy of Parliament. We have a Parliament to the power of which there are no limits whatever, except such as human nature, in a Divinely-ordained condition of things, imposes. We are faced by no co-ordinate legislatures, and are bound by no statutory conditions. There is nothing that controls us, except our convictions of law, of right, and of justice.†

Here in fact lay the intellectual key to Gladstonian Home Rule: the creation of a new form of pluralism, recognizing historical forces and traditions, but contained within the a-temporal casket of Dicey's parliamentary absolutism: a combination of historicism and deductivism

---

* Begun 2 November 1885, resumed 3 December, finished 29 December 1885. Gladstone had thus started to take Dicey on board—and the central theme of the book is immediately obvious to the reader—before the sketch of the Government of Ireland Bill made on 14 November 1885; his rereading of Burke followed on from this.

† *Speeches on the Irish question 1886*, 13–14.

which would reflect the peculiarities of the British and Irish predicaments. Common-sense and self-interest would harmonize to create a natural balance. Gladstone criticized Dicey in 1886 for his absence of historical awareness* and, certainly, Dicey's argument in *England's case against Home Rule* (1886) was deliberately abstract, a theoretical dissection of the inconsistencies of the Government of Ireland Bill. But as every British statesman knew, the constitution was already riddled with inconsistencies: the function of statesmanship was to make it work and adapt by observing custom, convention, and compromise. Within this context of living by experience rather than by abstract principles, the Home Rulers argued, Home Rule could be accommodated. On the other hand, Gladstone relied on Dicey's systematic and deliberately non-historical formulation of the absolute supremacy of the Crown in Parliament for part of the intellectual force of his argument that Home Rule in no wise impaired, but rather strengthened, 'the supreme statutory authority of the Imperial Parliament'.† With Dicey on the reference shelf, the imperial veto was secure. Dicey was turned against himself. The Unionists' most famous apologist had shown the essential intellectual harmlessness of Home Rule,‡ because a Government of Ireland Act could always be repealed by the same process as created it, the Crown in Parliament. In practical terms, however, this was something of a legal fiction and experience was the guide: 'The case of the Veto cannot be solved by any theory, but has been practically solved by a Colonial policy now nearly half a century old which combines the judicious use of it with the free action of responsible Government.'§

The 'Irish Trilogy' of Order, Land Settlement, and Autonomy

A further dimension and one closely associated with Liberal enthusiasm for decentralization, was the corruption of the British liberal state which the constant presence of the Irish question in British politics involved: the normal processes of the 1880–5 Parliament had been perverted by the introduction of closure and guillotine (needed in turn to impose coercion and to give yet more power to a Viceroy responsible only to the executive); a Liberal Cabinet had found itself returning to the *ancien régime* in the use of secret service money for surveillance and the establishment of what became the Special Branch; the Prime Minister needed an armed bodyguard for the first time since the 1840s or earlier. Gladstone hated all of these, and saw them as examples of the gradual corrosion of a liberal society. He left the Cabinet room rather than attend a discussion of the use of secret service money, and he gave his police bodyguard the slip when-

---

* To Dicey, 12 Nov. 86. Gladstone criticized Dicey on this from the first; see to MacColl, 4 June 83.
† *Speeches on the Irish question 1886*, 15.
‡ See to Stead, 18 Dec. 85.
§ To R. W. Dale, 29 Apr. 86.

ever possible, complaining of its imposition and its cost. The Fenian bombing campaign in Britain (especially London), at its height in 1883–5, corroded the liberalism of domestic legislation, with the Home Office's reluctance to allow local control of the Metropolitan police scuppering the London Local Government Bill.*

Gladstone was prepared, reluctantly, to meet violent disorder in Ireland with coercion, but the more he had to do so, the more he sought a long-term political solution which would pacify the Irish, achieve social order, and restore the norms of liberal civil society. Pacification and the absence of the forces which made coercion necessary were the goals Gladstone sought through the 'Trilogy' of social order, a complete land settlement, and Irish autonomy in Irish affairs which made up the proposed Irish settlement of 1886: land and the Irish legislature were the means, 'social order' was the goal. Only with the achievement of this 'Trilogy' would there exist the prerequisite for liberty for the Irish, peace for the Empire and the clearing of the way at Westminster. Gladstone never thought, as many Victorians did think, that the Irish were inherently violent or that violence there was chronic and endemic; he always believed that a proper social and political relationship between Britain and Ireland would rather quickly lead to pacification. Political action and, particularly, dramatic legislation could therefore be quickly and directly effective. Thus the 'Trilogy' of 1886 replaced the 'Upas Tree' of 1868: the means had changed but the mission of pacification, and the assumptions about the way of achieving it, remained.

Parnell, Gladstone, and the Events of 1885

In the development of Gladstone's views on Ireland, the precise context of 1885 and early 1886 was also of great importance. Though he did not attempt, in his diary or elsewhere, to maintain a self-justifying record, this immediate context is fairly well defined. There was a clear deadlock on Ireland in Cabinet in the spring of 1885. The government's timetable in 1880, 1881, and 1882 had been ruined by unexpected Irish legislation. If the usual pattern of Liberal consolidation during a Tory minority government was followed by the accustomed Liberal victory at the polls—a generally expected result—the next Liberal government would find on taking office that little had changed. As in 1868–70 and 1880–2, it would spend its early years attempting to pacify Ireland, with the additional difficulty that with each round of quasi-pacification, the Liberal Cabinet found it more difficult to agree on measures, as 1885 had shown. Unless there was an alternative initiative, coercion, eschewed by the Tory minority government but by the end of 1885 felt to be unavoidable, would be the first business of

* B. Porter, *The origins of the vigilant state* (1987), 36 and *passim* for an interesting discussion of this subject.

the session. Directly related to this, there would be the additional difficulty of a greatly increased number of Home Rule MPs, an obvious development since 1884, but one focused upon particularly by Gladstone after the fall of his government in June 1885:

The greatest incident of the coming election is to be the Parnell or Nationalist majority. And such a majority is a very great fact indeed. It will at once shift the centre of gravity in the relations between the two countries.*

These two factors—Liberal fissiparousness and Irish Home-Rulers' imminent strength—especially conditioned Gladstone's views in the summer of 1885. Not surprisingly, therefore, as he considered future Liberal policy for Ireland, Gladstone started from a rather negative position: as Derby noted after a visit, 'One thing he saw plainly, that parliament could not go on as it had done.'† From the liberal point of view, all the alternatives had been tried and had produced neither lasting social order nor an Ireland politically integrated into the United Kingdom: despite all efforts the integration was the other way, towards an Ireland largely integrated by a demand for Home Rule. This tone continued through to the introduction of the Government of Ireland Bill on 8 April 1886. Concluding his speech, Gladstone observed, 'Well, sir, I have argued the matter as if it were a choice of evils'; even when he then came towards his peroration, the mood was significant: 'I cherish the hope that this is not merely the choice of the lesser evil, but may prove to be rather a good in itself.'‡

The process of working through the choice of evils to the point of regarding as the least of them the settlement publicly proposed in April 1886 was complex. It began during the hiatus following the Liberal Cabinet's resignation in June 1885: 'Prepared a sketch on Irish Contingency', Gladstone recorded on 12 June 1885.'§ This sketch has unfortunately not been found, one of the very few significant records of Gladstone's life which has not survived but is known to have existed. It must partly have involved the considerable possibility that Salisbury would decline or be unable to take office at that time, leaving the Liberals again immediately face to face with coercion, land purchase, and the Central Board; but it may also have reflected conversations with Wolverton, whose comments on Gladstone's secret circular of qualified resignation (sent round on 16–17 June 1885) referred to 'your proposed Irish policy', and to Wolverton's hope that 'reading between the lines of your memorandum, I see your patriotic inclination upon a defined and great policy to forgo for the sake of all, your strong claim for immediate release'.¶ Wolverton had thus

* To Spencer, 30 June 85.   † *Derby*, 32 (1 October 1885).
‡ *Speeches on the Irish question 1886*, 51.
§ The circular of 16 June 85 was probably a reduced version of this; Gladstone told Granville that the mem. circulated was an 'amended' version 'in the mildest form available' (Ramm II, ii. 386).
¶ T. A. Jenkins, *Gladstone, whiggery and the Liberal Party 1874–1886* (1988), 241. Gladstone's letter

extracted from Gladstone an agreement which confirmed his by now well-established position, that is, as Gladstone put it to his brother Tom: 'My profound desire is retirement, and nothing has prevented or will prevent my giving effect to that desire, unless there should appear to be something in which there may be a prospect of my doing what could not be as well done without me.'*

Gladstone at once combined this 'doing' with the Irish consequences of the 1884 Franchise Bill:

Nothing can withhold or suspend my retirement except the presentation of some great and critical problem in the national life, and the hope, if such a hope shall be, of making some special contribution towards a solution of it.

No one I think can doubt that, according to all present appearances, the greatest incident of the coming election is to be the Parnell or Nationalist majority. And such a majority is a very great fact indeed. It will at once shift the centre of gravity in the relations between the two countries.

How is it and how are its probable proposals, to be met?

If the heads of the Liberal party shall be prepared to unite in rendering an *adequate* answer to this question, and if they unitedly desire me to keep my present place for the purpose of giving to that answer legislative effect, such a state of things may impose upon me a formidable obligation for the time of the crisis. I cannot conceive any other form in which my resolution could be unsettled.†

This position therefore involved Gladstone in two very different and perhaps conflicting activities: helping the Liberal party and solving the Irish crisis. 'An Irish crisis, a solid party': these meant, John Morley thought when writing his *Life of Gladstone*, a course between 'two impossibilities'.‡

The first step, as Gladstone saw it, was to establish what the 'Parnell or Nationalist majority' would want. 'Home Rule' was their demand, so they must state what they meant by it. Thus immediately after his formal resignation and the day after moving out of Downing Street, he asked for Parnell's paper of January 1885 on the central board which Gladstone had on receipt sent on to Spencer, 'that I may (for the first time) peruse it'§ (even given the press of events in January 1885, it is astonishing that the Prime Minister should not have found time to read such a proposal from such a source). Having got the paper, he asked Grosvenor to discover through Mrs. O'Shea if the proposal 'stands good as when it was written'.¶ Parnell made no definite answer. Thus, though there was a presumption that the Central Board scheme was dead, by the start of August 1885 Gladstone had

to Wolverton (see 17 June 85) clearly establishes that the circular of 16 June is the 'secret draft' to which Wolverton's letter refers. The 'sketch' of 12 June does not seem to have been sent to anyone, and is not referred to by Hamilton, Gladstone's secretary and a conscientious diarist.

* To Sir T. Gladstone, 19 June 85.   † To Spencer, 30 June 85; see Hammond, 390.
‡ Morley, iii. 220.   § To Spencer, 27 June 85.
¶ To Grosvenor, 6 July 85.

'entirely failed to extract any independent information on the question whether the Central Board scheme is dead or not'.*

In the meantime, 'the high biddings of Lord Randolph'† and the unprecedented attacks by the Tory ministers on Spencer's record as Viceroy in his handling of the Maamtrasna murder case made it likely that Parnell's confidence would grow as the increase of his parliamentary party became imminent. On the Liberal side, Chamberlain and the Radicals proposed a plan of national councils and Gladstone, vocally out of action, failed to persuade Childers, in his role as ex-Chancellor, to oppose Ashbourne's land purchase bill, which was, in Gladstone's view, 'a real subsidy to the Irish landlords'.‡

Gladstone then wrote directly to Mrs O'Shea on 4 August about the absence of a definite reply on the Central Board question. This letter was written—unbeknown at the time to Gladstone—just after the bizarre, secret meeting of Parnell with Carnarvon, the Irish Viceroy, which led the Irish leader to believe that a Tory Home Rule Bill was not an impossibility. Parnell's belief that he might get something substantial from the Tories must have affected his dealings with the Liberals in August–December 1885. He was not to know that Salisbury said nothing to his Cabinet about his Viceroy's initiative. Mrs O'Shea replied to Gladstone that the approach *via* the development of county councils would be 'putting the cart before the horse ... it is now felt that leaders of English opinion may fairly be asked to consider the question of granting to Ireland a Constitution of similar nature to that of one of the larger Colonies', while taking account of 'guarantees for the Crown, for landowners, and for freedom of conscience and fair treatment of the minority'. 'Mr Parnell', wrote Mrs O'Shea, 'would like me to send you a draft of detailed propositions.' But Parnell's 'Proposed Constitution for Ireland' was not sent to Gladstone until early November. Mrs O'Shea's letter of 5 August had been written just after Parnell's secret meeting with Carnarvon, and it may well be that the delay was caused by the need to see the fruits of that remarkable discussion. In early August, therefore, Gladstone knew that Irish expectations as expressed through the Home Rule party were moving well beyond the Central Board proposal regarded by it in the early months of 1885 as the immediate goal. The cart and the horse had changed positions.

At the same time as exploring Parnellite intentions, Gladstone had been involved in a series of discussions on Ireland with members of the inner circle of his party. A special dinner had been set up with the ultra-cautious Goschen, but it had not been a success. Despite a doctor's embargo on using his voice, Gladstone 'had to speak more than was desirable: the

---

* To Chamberlain, 1 Aug. 85.
† To Derby, 17 July 85.
‡ To Chamberlain, 1 Aug. 85 and to Carmichael, 23 Apr. 86.

occasion was important; it was the coming Irish question'.* After disagree-
ing with Goschen, who objected to the idea of a National Council because
it was '*elective*', Gladstone spoke to Sir Thomas Acland, the only one of his
undergraduate friends still in politics. Acland noted: 'he beckoned me to sit
on the sofa by him—& said the Lib. party wd. break up—he should have no
more to do with leading still less with combinations of moderate Lib's &
conservs. The only thing that would call him out wd. be the need of seeing
some great ansr[?] to the Council question.'† Conversations such as these
showed Gladstone that his view that 'there *is* an emergency at hand'‡ might
be shared, but that there was little agreement about the means of dealing
with it.

It might be thought that during the summer of 1885 Gladstone dragged
his feet. But it must be remembered that a serious throat condition
prevented him from any public and most private speaking, and that he was
going through an arduous series of twenty-one daily treatments. We will
look later at the medical details of this episode. Politically, it was an interruption at an important moment. Even more significant was the convalescence. Good progress in the treatment seems to have been made, and
on 8 August Gladstone left for a voyage to the Norwegian fiords on Thomas
Brassey's yacht *Sunbeam*. He was away until 1 September. Before leaving
he brought together the Irish and the party elements of his thoughts and
conversations since the fall of his government by a conversation with
Hartington, at which Gladstone read a memorandum, in fact the basis for
his election address. This reviewed the spectrum of Liberal problems and
possibilities with a view to the general election, but it was Ireland that
Gladstone particularly emphasized ('Ireland. An epoch: possibly a crisis
. . .'). He does not seem to have told Hartington of his recent sounding of
Parnell *via* Mrs O'Shea,§ but he made it clear that the basis for agreement
on a limited 'Central Board scheme' had gone. Gladstone remained
puzzled both as to his personal position and as to an appropriate Irish
policy: 'What to say publicly' about the 'considerable changes' that may be
desired 'must be most carefully considered on my return'.¶

On board the *Sunbeam* Gladstone developed the memorandum into a
draft address, to take the form of a 'small pamphlet'; its unusual length
partly reflected the fact that it was not yet clear that he would be able to
resume public speaking. It attempted to bridge the gap between the 'left' and
the 'right' Liberals by emphasizing four topics on which the party was agreed
for action: parliamentary procedure, land reform, electoral registration

* 14 July 85.
† See *The Gladstone Diaries*, Vol. X, Appendix I.
‡ To Goschen, 11 July 85.
§ He had told Granville 'It would not surprise me if he [Parnell] were to formulate something
on the subject' (6 August 1885, Ramm II, ii. 390).
¶ 7 Aug. 85.

reform, and 'local govt (liquor laws)'. On his return, he solicited and received general support for his continued leadership which was to be based on his role as consolidator and co-ordinator and which was to be pursued by consulting Hartington and Chamberlain 'who may be considered to be our two poles', only Hartington's unsuccessful request for a meeting of the ex-Cabinet indicating unease. At the same time Gladstone let it be known that he remained 'perplexed' about Ireland. Meanwhile, Hartington's speeches in reply to Parnell's demands showed how difficult it was to move Hartington and 'our friends' towards what Gladstone regarded as a recognition of the consequences of the development of British and Irish history since the 1830s.

The position was made more complex by uncertainty about Parnell. The document which Mrs O'Shea had promised in early August was still not available. Gladstone, while on ship, had asked Grosvenor to enquire further about it so that the Irish section of the Address could take it into account, but the Address was written without Parnell having replied. As published, that section, placed at the end, could be read as offering either the maximum or the minimum. It was a masterpiece of short-term political integration. This was deliberate. Parnell's recent declarations oscillated between demands for 'national independence' and for Ireland being treated like 'one of the larger colonies'. Gladstone was 'astonished at the rather virulent badness of what he [Parnell] has uttered with respect to Irish Government'.* Because any successful settlement had to involve, in Gladstone's view, some accommodation with the Home Rule party, no step could be taken until Gladstone could be reasonably satisfied that demands for 'Home Rule' were exactly that: Irish control of their domestic government.

This then was Gladstone's position by the end of September 1885: his address, the 'small pamphlet' drafted on the *Sunbeam* and now carefully entitled 'On the Liberal Party', was published, offering a programme of the lowest common denominator, designed to maintain the moderates within the party at the risk of estranging Radicals who had nowhere else to go. The intention in issuing so extensive an address well before the date of the dissolution was known was clearly to try to give the Liberal party a unifying reference point in the face of the Radical Programme, the disestablishment issue, and the Irish question. The address thus admitted policy weakness and called for the party to fall back on its inherent strength in the mainland constituencies. It was thus the obverse of Gladstone's calls to legislative action during the previous period of Liberal regrouping during a Tory minority government when in 1868 Irish disestablishment had provided a rallying point of spectacular constitutional innovation. The address of September 1885 was the only moment in Gladstone's career when he acted

* To Dilke, 18 Sept. 85.

as a party leader in the normal modern mould, integrative, cautious, holding the centre ground.

Privately, encouragement was given in various directions to think of the consequences of an eighty-strong Home Rule party and of the need to see the Irish question in other than a short-term perspective. Here lay the paradox of Gladstone's position. On the one hand, he shortened the political horizon, seeing no further than ensuring a reasonably united party at the time of the dissolution: Hartington and Chamberlain were wrong to 'write as if they were fixing the platform of a new Liberal Government, whereas I am solely endeavouring to help, not to embarrass, Liberal candidates for the Election. The question of a Government may have its place later on, not now.'* On the other hand, he anticipated an Irish crisis 'open, after the Dissolution, like a chasm under our feet' in which a brief moment, ripe for action, would embody the consequences of great historical forces and changes: Pitt's Act of Union, Gladstone concluded in mid-September, had been 'a gigantic though excusable mistake'.† But out of this situation he still could not 'pretend to see my way'.‡

During October 1885, Gladstone read and reread works on Ireland in the eighteenth and nineteenth centuries and began thinking of a measure based on the Canada Acts of 1840 and 1867.§ His main reading and writing, however, was for his article 'Dawn of creation and of worship'¶ (whose long perspective doubtless helped set the Irish question in context) and an extensive reading of the French religious sociologist, Le Play. He also, on 11 October, drafted for Herbert Gladstone, whose Home Rule views were pronounced and well-known, a letter for Herbert to send to Henry Labouchere, who was in touch with Parnell. This was indeed an oblique way of communicating with Parnell. The letter Gladstone drafted explained 'my own [i.e. Herbert Gladstone's] impressions as to my Father's view', namely that he stood by his Address on Ireland, and that 'he, as I think, in no way disapproves of the efforts of the nationalists to get the Tory party to take up their question . . . it might be the shortest way to a settlement'; Gladstone regarded the launching of a specific plan as 'gratuitous': Ireland must speak through her representatives 'plainly and publicly'. This was to be his position through the general election: no plan should be announced pending Ireland's statement through the ballot box, with the hope that the Tories would take the lead in legislating for a settlement.

---

* To Harcourt, 12 Sept. 85.
† 19 Sept. 85; for the full quotation, see the heading of this chapter.
‡ To Spencer, 15 Sept. 85.
§ To Grosvenor, 9 Oct. 85. For his reading, see below p. 546.
¶ See 6 Oct. 85.

At the same time, reading and reflection were producing consolidation of view:

I am trying to familiarise my mind with the subject and to look at it all round, but it still requires a good deal more looking at before I could ask myself to adhere to anything I had conceived. I adhere however to this one belief that there is great advantage in a constructive measure (which would be subject to change or recall) as compared with the repeal of the Union.*

The spectrum was thus between 'a constructive measure' and repeal of the Union, the former being preferred since the continuing supremacy of the Westminster Parliament—this was the period of Gladstone's study of Dicey—could always, in the last resort, 'change or recall'.

Parnell's 'Proposed Constitution' and Gladstone's Sketch of a Home Rule Bill, November 1885

But what was 'a constructive measure'? On 1 November, Gladstone at last received Parnell's 'proposed Constitution for Ireland'.† This gave Gladstone just what he needed: a short statement, impeccably constitutional, of what 'Home Rule' would involve. If this had been sent in August, when it, or something like it, was first mentioned by Mrs O'Shea, the effects on Gladstone's election Address might have been dramatic. As it was, the process was under way and the narrow, unifying terms for the Liberal party were set for the general election. Gladstone refused to be drawn by Parnell into a public auction for the Irish vote, and his reply, sent in the name of Grosvenor, was non-committal. Gladstone drafted a much more elaborate reply to Mrs O'Shea (i.e. to Parnell) which set out his thinking at some length, repeating the message sent to Labouchere and emphasizing the importance of Conservative settlements of 'sharply controverted matters' in 1829, 1845, 1846, and 1867.‡ But it was thought impolitic to send it.

Publicly, therefore, as the election campaign in November proceeded, Parnell probed and Gladstone parried. Privately Parnell believed he knew that he had a degree of Tory support for Home Rule. He did not know that, whereas the various Liberal ministers who had conducted discussions with him in 1885 had kept their Cabinet informed of details, his conversation with Carnarvon on Home Rule was not reported to the Tory Cabinet by Salisbury. In November and December 1885 both Gladstone and Parnell underestimated the narrow cynicism of Salisbury, the leader of the 'patriotic' party whose conception of the national interest was to equate it with the short-term advantage of the Conservatives.§ Gladstone hoped Salisbury would be a Peel, but he turned out a Castlereagh, though longer-lived.

* To Granville, 22 October 1885, Ramm II, ii. 411.
† See O'Shea, *Parnell*, ii. 18, Hammond, 422 and above, p. 205n.
‡ To Mrs O'Shea, 3 Nov. 85.
§ For Salisbury's single-minded pursuit of party advantage in 1885–6, see P. T. Marsh, *The discipline of popular government. Lord Salisbury's domestic statecraft 1881–1902* (1978), ch. 3.

Parnell's 'proposed Constitution' must have pleased Gladstone for it showed Parnell, and committed him on paper, as a rather moderate constitutionalist, flexible as to detail (Irish MPs at Westminster might be in or out) and well within the framework of colonial precedent which Gladstone was looking at in the Canada Act of 1867. At Dalmeny for the Midlothian election campaign, Gladstone was asked by Rosebery why he did not respond specifically to Parnell's public request for a Liberal plan. He explained his reasons to Rosebery in a letter on 13 November (even though they were staying in the same house) in a series of points drawing together those made in the previous weeks, with the 'final and paramount reason . . . that the production of a plan by me would not only be injurious, but would destroy all reasonable hope of its adoption'. Abstinence from stating a plan presupposed that 'such a plan can be framed'. As yet there was no such plan. Thus the next day Gladstone 'wrote on Ireland', jotting down the headings of a Home Rule measure and telling his son Herbert the gist of them in a letter. These headings related to Parnell's 'proposed Constitution' quite closely. The private need for knowledge of Irish intentions having been satisfied by Parnell, the sketch of Gladstone's measure followed quickly and naturally.

Gladstone in fact wrote three papers on 14 November 1885, the first two on the 'Bases', the third a 'Sketch' giving substance to the stark points of the first two papers. From them derive all British legislative attempts at Home Rule, whether for Ireland, Scotland, or Wales. They are printed in *The Gladstone Diaries* and 'No. 1' is the heading of this chapter, but it may be helpful here to give Gladstone's 'Sketch':

Secret. No. 3.

Establish an Irish Chamber to deal with all Irish, as distinct from Imperial questions.

To sit for [   ] years.

Subject to the same prerogatives of the Crown, as the Imperial Parliament.

Provisions for securing to minority a proportionate representation.

Provision for Imperial Charges to be made by appointing a due fixed proportion thereof to be the first charge on Irish Consolidated Fund.

Imperial charges to be set out in Schedule: Royalty, The Debt, Army & Navy, the chief.

One third of House to be named in Act: two thirds to be the present representation duplicated: except Dublin University to remain as now, Royal Univ. to have two members.

Nominated members to sit until Parliament otherwise provide, (vacancies to be filled by the Crown?)

Officers of State & civil functionaries in Ireland to cease to be subject to any British authority, except as herein provided, to be suspended in Ireland so long as the conditions of this Act are fulfilled.

Matters of defence remain under Imperial authority as now.

Crown property held for civil purposes to be at the disposal of the Chamber.

Irish representation in both Houses of the Imperial Parliament to remain as now, for Imperial subjects only.

If speech or vote be challenged question to be decided by the House or the Speaker thereof.

Schedule of subjects withdrawn as Imperial from the Irish Chamber.

Irish representatives to share in all questions of grievance & ministerial responsibility which touch the reserved subjects only.

Specify parts of Act alterable by Chamber, including particulars of representation, except such as secure proportionate representation of minority.

With regard to all civil establishments whatever it is presumed that Irish Officers of State will be under the sole control of the Chamber and advise the Crown for Irish purposes (as e.g. in Canada Canadian Officers of State).

A seat in the Imperial Parlt. not to disqualify for sitting in the Irish Chamber.

Seat in Irish Chamber not to disqualify for holding office in Great Britain.

Auxiliary forces to be charged on Ireland & only raised by authority of Chamber but when raised to be under controul of the Crown. Nov. 14. 85.

Several limitations like those on the State Governments in America ought to be inserted in any plan.

This is the point at which we may say that the process of considering various possible policies and of taking into account the complex changes of British politics hardened into a policy. Gladstone's 'Sir Robert Peelian horror of *abstract* resolutions' and his training in the practical, down-to-earth school of the British Cabinet made him suspicious of propositions in politics (however attractive they might be in principle) until he could see his way to a legislative enactment, that is, the statement of concepts and aspirations in the clear, hard clauses of a bill which could be put to Parliament. Moreover, as the point of 'Home Rule' was in part to meet Irish demands, the development of a policy had to be in part a response to a clear and in Gladstone's view practical statement of those demands. This he now had.

Gladstone's commitment to Home Rule involved the Peelite view that government should, through legislation, redress an established grievance, and he saw the 1885 election as the moment at which that establishment of grievance would be publicly confirmed. But 'Home Rule' was a notoriously empty casket, as Gladstone himself had several times remarked. As soon as it began to be filled by Parnell's 'proposed Constitution', Gladstone conceived a measure to which the Irish would necessarily be attached in detail as well as in principle. In this sense, he began a process of imposing Home Rule upon the Irish, turning a slogan into the fine print of legislation bold in conception but regarded by its framer as essentially within the confines of the Imperial constitution. There was also, in the accompanying proposals for a land settlement, an element of retribution, as the Home Rule party was put in charge of rent and repayment collection in Ireland.

Gladstone cannot but have enjoyed the thought of the ex-Land Leaguers running the government in Ireland which would collect the monies for the Receiver General.

Gladstone does not seem to have shown Rosebery, his host in Mid-lothian, either Parnell's 'proposed Constitution' or his own sketch despite their frequent conversations on Ireland during the campaign.* But from this point, his argument to his close colleagues was that no plan should be publicly produced, not, as hitherto, that he did not have one.

A Tory Home Rule Bill?

The argument that a settlement should be introduced by the Salisbury government was thus formulated before the general election. As it was associated with expectations of a political crisis in three months' time, that is, at the start of the Session, it suggests that Gladstone may have been less confident about a Liberal majority than many others. It would have been an extraordinary manœuvre that a Tory government should, whatever the grounds, remain in office if the Liberals had a working majority over them and the Irish (that is, if there was a repeat of the 1880 result in 1885, as many Liberals at first expected).

The Irish National League issued a directive published on 21 November calling on Irish voters in mainland constituencies to vote against the Liberal party, since it was 'perfidious, treacherous and incompetent', and Parnell made a speech in support. The Home Rulers could not have asserted more ruthlessly their independence of the two main British parties. The view that Home Rule had an equal chance from both parties can hardly be seen as other than quixotic—only Disraeli in his heyday might have risked it—but the view that a Tory measure of Home Rule—or something like it—was the most straightforward way out of a potential stale-mate was, as we have seen, one which Gladstone shared. The general election result of Liberals 333, Tories 251, and Home Rulers 86, suggested either a clear, large majority for a Liberal–Irish alliance, or a dead heat if the Tory–Home Rule alliance of the summer was maintained, with the possibility of some other permutation if either the Tories or the Liberals temporarily or permanently split. The position after the election thus intensified the case for Gladstone's view that all must wait until govern-ment policy was clarified. Thus during December 1885 he made no sig-nificant change to his position. He began to codify the tests needed for judging action, and to encourage his senior colleagues to accept 'a healthful slow fermentation in many minds, working towards the final product',

---

* Rosebery would surely have recorded in his diary sight of so historic a document; he does record receiving Gladstone's letter 'composed yesterday' as to 'why (rightly) he will not put a plan before the public. We talked over this letter after luncheon' (Rosebery's diary, 14 November 1885, Dalmeny MSS).

while at the same time discussing the situation with visits to Hawarden from Granville ('we are already in promising harmony'), Spencer (the key man if a Home Rule policy was to be seriously advanced), Rosebery, Wolverton, Chamberlain, and Sir Thomas Acland.   There were two main difficulties about this position. Gladstone wanted to give the Conservatives a chance at a Home Rule bill, and he was no doubt correct in thinking that support, or at least lack of fundamental opposition, on the part of the political right was, if not an essential, at the least a highly desirable part of a Home-Rule settlement. Yet his contempt for the Conservative party, which 'leans now upon its lame leg, the leg of Class interest',* grew by the month. Gladstone knew by December of the strong Home-Rule influence among the senior civil servants in Dublin Castle, and believed 'Salisbury & Carnarvon are rather with Randolph [Churchill]' (then thought to be canvassing a Home-Rule solution), though they 'are afraid of their colleagues and their party'. He approved more of Salisbury than he had in the summer, no doubt recalling the spirit of 'equity and candour' which Salisbury had shown in the redistribution conferences in 1884, the best recent precedent, though clearly only a partial one, for the sort of agreed settlement which Gladstone sought. He had mitigated his anger at Balfour whose 'almost raving licence of an unbridled tongue' in 1882 had grieved Gladstone to the point of a vicarious rebuke.† Yet he despaired of the party which would be their instrument.

The second difficulty was that Gladstone's desire to encourage discussion, reading and thought on Ireland could only be done privately and without a clear public lead from him. He had devised a public position which protected his party from division and the Irish question from partisanship, but at the price of putting public discussion of Liberal Irish policy on ice. The election result lowered the temperature even further, with Gladstone even more determined not to be seen bidding for the Irish vote and not to make any move until the Irish had publicly ended their alliance with the Tories. Without this, any move would look like a bid or a bribe. Thus the fruit of party support for Home Rule had to ripen without the attentions of the chief gardener.

Gladstone made a move implicit in his position since early October: on 15 December at Eaton Hall, the Westminsters' house in Cheshire, he 'saw . . . A. Balfour to whom I said what he will probably repeat in London'. Next day, a 'day of anxious & very important correspondence', he drafted a letter to Balfour confirming the 'urgency of the matter' and going further by emphasizing the 'public calamity if this great subject should fall into the lines of party conflict', and promising his support if a Tory government

* 10 Dec. 85.
† To Hartington, 15 Dec. 85 and to Helen Gladstone, 17 May 82.

proposed a complete settlement. But the letter was not sent until 20 December. Meanwhile:

Matters .of today required meditation. After dealing with the knottiest point, I resumed Huxley. We felled a good ash. Read Burke, Dicey. Suspended the Balfour letter.*

Gladstone's initative, curiously half-hearted and delayed considering its importance to his position—he told Granville later that he had met Balfour 'accidentally'—was too late in every sense. The Cabinets on 14 and 15 December had decided that the Conservative government had no Irish policy. Carnarvon, the Viceroy, who had tried to move the ministry towards some sort of Home Rule solution and whose resignation was being held back at Salisbury's request, noted in his diary:

14 December ... discussion on Ireland—the result of wh. was that the Cabinet would do nothing & announce no policy—but they wd. not debar themselves from proceeding later by Committee if circumstances sd. favour this.
  15 December. A long talk again on Ireland. The Cabinet will do nothing & they only say that if & when a gt. change comes it must be done by other hands.†

The 'Hawarden Kite' and the Tory Government's Resignation

The delay meant that the letter to Balfour was not sent until after Herbert Gladstone had inadvertently flown the 'Hawarden Kite', the culmination of a series of newspaper speculations and supposed disclosures. Herbert, a pronounced Home Ruler, was privy to his father's views in general, and, having had considerable experience in Ireland, probably influenced their development. He also knew a good deal about the particulars. He had made a copy of Gladstone's note of 12 December that amounted to a brief restatement of his Home Rule sketch of 14 November (of which Herbert had been sent the gist), and he had at the time of the drafting of that sketch unsuccessfully encouraged his father to a public declaration. Gladstone had spoken through him before, but there is no evidence that he incited or encouraged Herbert's visit to London on 14 December. Given that that was the day before the private initiative to Balfour (of which Herbert could not have known as it occurred 'accidentally'), it was exactly the wrong moment for what was widely interpreted as a public bid for Irish support. Herbert Gladstone went to London because he had been told by Wemyss Reid, the Liberal journalist, that there was 'a regular plot on foot among a section of the party to shelve the Irish Question, to keep the Tories in office, and to prevent under *any* circumstances my Father from forming a Government'.

---

  * 16 Dec. 85. For the Balfour letters, see 20, 23 Dec. 85; Balfour's report to his uncle was wholly tactical and showed no interest in the general 'grounds of public policy' which Gladstone tried to draw to his attention; see Balfour to Salisbury, 23 December 1885 in *The Salisbury—Balfour correspondence 1869—1892*, ed. R. Harcourt Williams (1988), 127.
  † Add MS 60925.

Herbert saw Henry Labouchere, Wemyss Reid, and Dawson Rogers of the National Press Agency. The talks were 'supposed to be confidential' but Herbert was an experienced enough politician to know what in the circumstances would happen. *The Standard* published on 17 December 1885 what it called the 'Authentic Plan' of Mr Gladstone, *The Pall Mall Gazette* an article headed 'HOME RULE. Mr. Gladstone's scheme', and the National Press Agency also fed its newspapers with copy that day. Herbert's diary records the view that the articles were 'an accurate report of my "private" interview'.* His father's response was calm and and unalarmed: 'Wrote . . . Telegrams to Press Assn., C. News & other quarters on the Irish rumours about me.'† Herbert noted in his diary the same day, 'Father quite *compos*.'

The 'Kite' lessened the likelihood of a Tory-led, nonpartisan settlement, and it coincided with a gathering awareness that it would be the Liberals who would have to face up to home rule: such indeed was the immediate reaction to the 'Kite' in the metropolitan Liberal newspapers, the *Daily News* and *The Pall Mall Gazette*. Gladstone maintained his position that only a government was equipped to prepare a plan, but in December he also toyed with the tactic of 1868 of proceeding by resolution as a preliminary to removing the Tory government.‡ Though renewing contact with Parnell through Mrs O'Shea, he was extremely careful to make no commitment while making clear the general drift of his thinking: 'My fear is that to open myself on this subject before the Govt. have answered or had full opportunity of answering, would probably be fatal to any attempt to carry with me the Liberal party.'§ The notion of 'carrying' the Liberal party could only suggest to Parnell one direction of movement.

During the course of December 1885, Gladstone was coming to see the Liberal party in some sort of association with the Home Rulers as the providers of a settlement for Ireland. This represented a shift of view. Before the election, he had thought: 'Nothing but a sheer and clear majority in Parlt. could enable Liberals in Government to carry a plan. Personally I shake myself free of any other idea.'¶ But Gladstone did not shake himself free of other ideas, nor could he, given the electoral arithmetic. If Home Rule was workable, as he knew it was, if it was acceptable to the Irish MPs, as he knew it was, and if it was not acceptable to the Tory government, as he was almost certain by the end of December it was not, then only one course was open to him.

The general constitutional crisis of Ireland, under consideration at least since July 1885, took on a particular urgency. Gladstone knew in December

* Herbert Gladstone's diary and correspondence on the 'Kite' are published in Appendix I D of Vol. XI of *The Gladstone Diaries*.
　† See 17 Dec. 85.
　‡ See Rosebery's note of his visit to Hawarden, 8 Dec. 85n.
　§ To Mrs O'Shea, 19 Dec. 85.
　¶ To H. J. Gladstone, 18 Oct. 85.

from men as various as James Bryce, Sir Robert Hamilton of Dublin Castle and E. G. Jenkinson, head of the Special Branch in Ireland, that the political and social calm there was very fragile, and in the view of all three that the fragility pointed to a Home Rule initiative to defuse a further rent crisis and to incorporate the Parnellite MPs in the Westminster process. Otherwise there was thought to be a real chance of their withdrawing to Dublin and setting up their own Assembly.* This would make an orderly Liberal compromise on devolution impossible. The Gladstonian case rested on an Irish legislature being inaugurated by the Westminster Parliament, as a result of a legislative proposal from a British government responding to a respectably stated case. Though intended to deal with an abnormal situation, a political settlement of Ireland would have to be seen to be done by the book.

Given his premises, Gladstone played his cards well in December 1885 and January 1886. He gave the Tories the maximum chance to take the initiative, and they stood aside. He flushed them out as the party of coercion, the policy which they had rejected in June 1885 as the price of removing his previous government. He avoided any public or private pledges to the Home Rulers and he sought no assurances from them. He insisted on waiting until it was publicly established that the Tory–Irish alliance was at an end. He bided his time during a series of tactical discussions about how the government might be removed without the Liberals being compromised on Home Rule, and he took the opportunity of Jesse Collings' amendment on English agricultural policy for the felling of the Tories, thus defeating the government before the item on Ireland in the Address to the Queen was reached (it was the item next after agriculture) and avoiding public display of the variety of Liberal views on Ireland.† 'I spoke on J. Collings's motion & we were driven by events to act at once. We beat the Government, I think wisely, by 329:250 so the crisis is come. . . .'‡ Salisbury's resignation was announced to the Commons on 28 January and effectively only the Queen stood in the way of a third Gladstonian premiership.

Gladstone's Third Government and the Chances of an Irish Settlement

Gladstone was thus in a position to form his third government without publicly going further than the pre-election Address which had been designed to hold the Liberal party together. The outline of his approach given to John Morley in January 1886 was consistent with his behaviour generally: 'He had "expressed opinion, but not plans or intention". We

---

* To Grosvenor, 7 Jan. 86. This is Gladstone's only known reference to this possibility; it seems to me to be an important but not a determining factor.

† Not to have put Ireland earlier in the Speech and the consequent Address was clearly a tactical error on the part of the Conservative Cabinet.

‡ 26 Jan. 86.

must advance by stages: consider each stage as it arises: next stage is the Address [on the Queen's Speech].'* This approach continued after the formation of the Cabinet. The first step to be taken by the Cabinet with respect to Ireland—and the basis on which its members were invited to join it—would be an examination of the practicability of 'the establishment, by Statute, of a Legislative body, to sit in Dublin'.†

In this sense he followed a thoroughly Peelite interpretation of the right and duty of government to propose legislation and policy unencumbered by mandate. With its many echoes of Peel's handling of protection in 1840–6—and with its similar *dénouement*—Gladstone's handling of Home Rule in 1885–6 was a return to the constitutional orthodoxy of his youth and a marked contrast to the prophetic Irish programme endorsed by the 1868 general election. This is yet another example of the way in which Gladstone saw Home Rule as essentially a conservative rather than a radical measure.

So ended the process of opposition. Gladstone had aimed at consistency and sequence, and on the whole he had found both. Not asking to see the distant scene, he found 'one step enough for me'. It is interesting that, at the same time, Gladstone was involved in a controversy on evolution and Genesis, in which he defended the tradition of Christian evolutionism. He linked it to that sense of a 'series' which had since the 1840s formed so important a part of his Butlerian conception of politics:

Evolution is, to me, series with development. And like series in mathematics, whether arithmetical or geometrical, it establishes in things an unbroken progression; it places each thing (if only it stand the test of ability to live) in a distinct relation to every other thing, and makes each a witness to all that preceded it, a prophecy of all that are to follow it.‡

He hoped 'to make a Butlerian argument upon a general and probable correspondence'.

In hindsight, what is perhaps most striking about this process are the lacunae: the House of Lords, the problem of Ulster, and the problem of the Liberal party. The Lords, thought Gladstone, simply 'would not dare': presupposing a land purchase settlement, the Lords would back down on a plan 'carried by a sheer Liberal majority', though it might take a governmental resignation to achieve this.§ It is important to note that Gladstone formed this view in October 1885; he does not seem to have considered the implications for the Lords of a bill carried in the Commons by Irish as well as British votes. It was Gladstone's view throughout that the Irish representatives were exactly that: representatives of Irish opinion whose views

* Morley's diary, 15 January 1886.   † 30 Jan. 86.
  ‡ 'Proem to Genesis', W. E. Gladstone, *Later gleanings. A new series of Gleanings of Past Years* (2nd ed. 1898) [subsequently: *Later gleanings*], 69–70.
  § To Rosebery, 13 Nov. 85, to H. J. Gladstone, 18 Oct. 85.

had to be taken at face value and that what they valued was 'Home Rule'. He paid Parnell the compliment of treating him like any other party leader and treating his 'proposed Constitution' as the objective of those MPs who followed him. Sir Thomas Acland noted after an important conversation with Gladstone in December 1885: 'any ideas of going behind the constitutional voice of the present Irish MPs is brushed aside as out of the question'.*

These two presuppositions, that parliamentary representation and its expression through votes on legislative measures was the determining feature of the British constitution, and that the Home Rulers were not separatists, were the two 'essentially contested concepts't of the next generation of British politics, and therefore, by definition, the dispute admits of no resolution.‡ Gladstone did not anticipate, perhaps understandably, the development of the Unionist view that Irish votes did not count and that though Unionism by definition regarded the United Kingdom as requiring a single representative assembly, within that assembly only English votes counted on questions of organic change.

Gladstone paid little heed to Ulster. He had attempted to allow the Province an important voice in Irish government on Forster's resignation of the Irish Secretaryship in 1882 by offering it to Andrew Porter, MP for Londonderry and a Presbyterian, but Porter declined it.§ In 1883 he considered the electoral chances of the Ulster Liberal MPs to be poor, and seems to have discounted them. When planning Home Rule in November 1885 it was the position of landowners not of Protestants in Ulster that he thought needed particular attention: 'I do not quite see what protection the Protestants of Ulster want, apart from the Land of the four provinces.'¶ The collapse of the Liberal party in Ulster might even be seen as an advantage: 'Perhaps had we large and cordial Ulster support, it might have abridged our freedom more than it would have enlarged our Votes.'‖ He included provision for 'the minority' in his early plans, and his Government of Ireland Bill speech in April 1886 seemed to encourage amendment of the bill on this point. But in general his view was that Ulster could not be

* See Acland's notes of 12–20 December 1885, Appendix I B, *The Gladstone Diaries*, Vol. XI.

† W. B. Gallie, 'Essentially contested concepts', *Proceedings of the Aristotelian Society* (1955–6); 'Home Rule' is an exceptionally good example of such a concept.

‡ The contemporary Unionist concern was that 'Home Rule' was not a settlement but a significant and irreversible step towards Irish separation; the Unionist fear was that the Parnellites meant more than they said. Recently, it has been argued that they meant less, and were not really serious or committed to home rule; see A. O'Day, *The English face of Irish nationalism: Parnellite involvement in British politics, 1880–86* (1977). K. T. Hoppen, *Elections, politics, and society in Ireland 1832–1885* (1984) sees Irish politics as characteristically localist, but punctuated by periodic 'peculiar moments' of nationalism.

§ 3 May 82.

¶ To Hartington, 18 Nov. 85; a consistently held view, see to Childers, 28 Sept. 85, to H. J. Gladstone, 18 Oct. 85.

‖ To Bryce, 2 Dec. 85.

allowed to dictate the future of Ireland: 'I cannot allow it to be said that a Protestant minority in Ulster, or elsewhere, is to rule the question at large for Ireland.'*

On both these questions—the Lords and Ulster—Gladstone's view was that a quick, clean passing of a definitive settlement would avoid constitutional blocking and would not be seriously challenged within Ireland.†

The Liberal party was a much more immediate difficulty.

It will be as difficult to carry the Liberal party, and the two British nations, in favour of a legislature for Ireland, as it was easy to carry them in the case of Irish Disestablishment: I think it can be done but only by the full use of a great leverage. That leverage can only be found in the equitable and mature consideration of what is due to the fixed desire of a nation, clearly and constitutionally expressed.‡

But a lever requires an operator to pull it. Gladstone's tactics, successful though they were in bringing about his third government, themselves frustrated his role as operator and educator. And his position once in government, of preparing his Irish settlement in much the sort of purdah in which he was accustomed to prepare his budgets—the Irish bills of 1886 received far less Cabinet discussion than any of his previous Irish measures—compounded party confusion.

The tactics were clear enough. The Cabinet, formed on a tentative basis to 'examine', was never given an opportunity thoroughly to do so. Gladstone hoped to trump Cabinet doubts and party unease by the production of a great bill. This, surely, is the chief explanation of the pace of preparation in the spring of 1886. 'Action at a stroke', Gladstone told Hartington before the elections in November 1885, 'will be more honourable, less unsafe, less uneasy, than the jolting process of a series of partial measures.'§

The Liberal Party unprepared for Home Rule

Such a proceeding was completely in line with Gladstone's usual approach to the handling of the party in the Commons. There was considerable force behind his view that the preparation of a measure was quite different from its discussion in opposition, that many centrifugal forces operate on those in office and on those sustaining a government from the backbenches which a skilled operator could manipulate. Gladstone's experience in

---

* The secret draft on Irish government of 20 March 1886 provided for the consideration during the progress of the bill of the exception from it of 'any particular portion of Ireland' (Gladstone noting that if Ulster was omitted, it was hard to see how she could enjoy the benefits of the land purchase bill); his speech on 8 April 1886 adumbrated this possibility; *Speeches on the Irish question, 1886*, 19–20.

† i.e. seriously in the sense of rebellious resistance; see J. Loughlin, *Gladstone, home rule and the Ulster question 1882–93* (1986) for the view that 'while Ulster Protestant opposition to Home Rule was certainly intense, there is nevertheless little evidence to support the view—still widespread—that they were prepared to resist violently the implementation of Home Rule in this period'.

‡ To Rosebery, 13 Nov. 85.   § To Hartington, 10 Nov. 85.

preventing resignations, however often threatened, during the 1880-5 government had shown how effective could be the 'one step at a time' tactic with its series of reasons for remaining in office. No one should resign on a possibility: wait until a formal proposal is made: once the proposal is made, then the intending resigner is responsible in part for the Cabinet that has made it: even then, wait until the Commons votes upon it, there being no point in resigning unnecessarily: once the Commons has approved the principle on the Second Reading, there is always the possibility of amending unsatisfactory details.... Many a member of a Gladstone Cabinet, however stern his intentions at the start, had found himself sucked in by these arguments and carried, as by a rip-tide, almost unawares into voting for a Third Reading.

Gladstone's step-by-step handling of Ireland since June 1885 was intended to facilitate just such a series of developments, and Hartington, caught so often before, was equally intent on avoiding the trap. It was sprung with full force on Chamberlain and Trevelyan and various courtiers in March 1886 but with limited success, at least briefly achieving the postponement of the Chamberlain–Trevelyan resignation. This sensitivity to the process of politics, this Machiavellian awareness of the eventual primacy of *virtù* in the context of an acute sense of timing, of 'ripeness' and of political control, had its limitations. With the resignations of Chamberlain and Trevelyan already in but deferred, Gladstone tried a last twist, and switched to a general Resolution which might get round or diminish the importance attached to the difficulties of the details and refocus Cabinet attention on the general problem of Irish government. But this came to nothing and Chamberlain and Trevelyan's resignations became public.

The greatest limitation to this method of proceeding by stages and 'series' had, as we have seen, already been stated by Gladstone himself. The Cabinet, or most of it, might be drawn into the process, but the party was not.

The sensational production of the Government of Ireland Bill on 8 April 1886, the greatest of all the Gladstonian 'big bills', was also, self-evidently, the riskiest: the lever was to be pulled in one stroke. Consequently, the education of the party could not begin until the examination was almost at hand and it was necessarily unaccompanied by any Gladstonian extra-parliamentary speechmaking.

Gladstone had sensed this difficulty all along, and had been alarmed in the autumn of 1885 that close colleagues did not view what seemed to him to be a self-evidently grave situation with the same alarm or historical perspective. He had, as early as August 1885, encouraged discussion of the future of Ireland in Knowles' *Nineteenth Century*; from this sprang Barry O'Brien's notable series of articles. This was quite in line with the usual liberal expectation of the primacy of rationality and exposition, but it hardly amounted to an adequate public discussion. Gladstone's own publications in these months were articles defending, from a moderate evolutionist position, Genesis against Réville and Huxley.* These to some extent recovered the ground that he had lost during the election, when his ambivalent handling of the disestablishment question had left the party just united but his own position defensive. His Christian evolutionism was well and widely received,† but it was, even so, a strange production on which to spend considerable time when personal and public education on Irish history was essential. The real drive to win the argument through pamphlet warfare did not come until *after* the defeat of the Government of Ireland Bill, when, using the secret service money as part of the finance, Gladstone, as we shall see, encouraged a series of publications. Neat though was the paradox of the secret service money funding liberal rationalism, it was a classic case of bolting the stable door with the horse already gone. The Liberal party faced Home Rule with remarkably few intellectual points of reference. 'The people do not *know* the case'; this was an appalling admission (in July 1886) for the leading exponent of government by argument to have to make.‡

* See above, p. 486 and 6 Oct., 8 and 26 Dec. 85.
† See, e.g., *The Christian Million*, 7 Jan. 1886, 172.
‡ To Bryce, 8 July 86.

CHAPTER X

Home Rule, Land, and the Proposed Pacification of Ireland 1886

The Government of 1886—Drafting the Irish Settlement—The Pacification of Ireland: Gladstone's Third Land Bill—The Pacification of Ireland: Gladstone's First Government of Ireland Bill—The Financial Clauses: a Boon for Ireland— The Irish MPs: in, partly in, or out?—Commonsense and the Constitution— Defeat and Resignation—A 'golden moment' turned to lead

I propose to examine whether it is or is not practicable to comply with the desire widely prevalent in Ireland, and testified by the return of 85 out of her 103 representatives, for the establishment, by Statute, of a Legislative body, to sit in Dublin, and to deal with Irish as distinguished from Imperial affairs; in such a manner, as would be just to each of the three Kingdoms, equitable with reference to every class of the people of Ireland, conducive to the social order and harmony of that country, and calculated to support and consolidate the unity of the Empire on the combined basis of Imperial authority and mutual attachment. W.E.G.*

H of C. $4\frac{3}{4}$–$8\frac{1}{2}$ and $9\frac{3}{4}$–$2\frac{1}{4}$. We were heavily beaten on the 2d Reading, by 341 to 311. A scene of some excitement followed the declaration of the numbers: one or two Irishmen lost their balance. Upon the whole we have more ground to be satisfied with the progress made, than to be disappointed at the failure. But it is a serious mischief. Spoke very long: my poor voice came in a wonderful manner.†

The Government of 1886

The Queen's commission to form a government arrived at a quarter past midnight on the morning of Saturday, 30 January 1886, brought by her Secretary, Sir Henry Ponsonby, just as Gladstone was going to bed: 'in came Sir H. Ponsonby with verbal communication from H.M. which I at once accepted'. Ponsonby was late because G. J. Goschen, whom he had been told to sound out about the possibility of a coalition government of Whigs and Tories, had been out till midnight. Goschen advised Ponsonby to go at once to Gladstone; the verbal commission was thus, it would seem,

---

* Gladstone's memorandum of 30 January 1886, read to those being invited to join the Cabinet.
† Diary for 7 June 86: defeat in the Commons of the first Government of Ireland Bill.

made on Ponsonby's initiative, at least as to its timing. For Victoria, in 'an almost incoherent outpouring of protest and dismay' (as Lady Gwendolen Cecil later put it), had refused to accept Salisbury's resignation, had wanted another dissolution—anything to avoid what she called 'this half-crazy & really in many ways ridiculous old man'.* Ponsonby made it clear that the Queen's offer was on the preliminary understanding that Rosebery would be Foreign Secretary.

Saturday was spent in intense politicing. On the Sunday night, after a Sabbath interrupted by constant business except for a moment to attend church, Gladstone could not sleep. As always, he derived an encouraging lesson from discomfort: 'for the soul it was profitable driving me to the hope that the strength of God might be made manifest in my weakness'. Early on the Monday a telegram arrived summoning him to Osborne House on the Isle of Wight for the formal audiences with the Queen who, following her custom, did not alter her own arrangements to suit the convenience of her politicians. Annoying though they often seemed to ministers, rail journeys to Osborne in fact often gave time for rest and reflection.

Gladstone felt the audiences went well even though Ireland was openly discussed—perhaps because she disagreed so violently with Gladstone on so many points it was unusual for Victoria to raise a substantial point of policy face to face with him. The journey and the Osborne visit took nearly twelve hours. He noted in his diary: 'I kissed hands and am thereby Prime Minister for the third time. But as I trust for a brief tenure only. Slept Well, D[ei] G[ratia].'

Next day he attended his daughter Mary's wedding to Harry Drew and gave her away. The same day—Tuesday—he continued the complex series of personal negotiations needed to form a Cabinet. Gladstone had begun to see potential ministers the morning after Ponsonby's late-night visit. His procedure for the formation of this government was unusual and perhaps unprecedented: each of those being invited to join the Cabinet was read the memorandum printed at the opening of this chapter, so that he accepted office having accepted the specific policy of enquiry into the practicability of Home Rule. This memorandum, effectively a quasi-commitment to Home Rule, successfully bought time, for the test of practicability would be the drafting of relevant bills. Thus the stage of testing would also be the stage of the preparation of the bills, and so the test would end when the

---

* Lady Gwendolen's explanation of the Queen's conduct is revealing as an insight into the mind of the Hotel Cecil, grotesque though it is as an account of Victoria's views on domestic politics; the Queen's 'burst of distress' at an imminent Gladstone premiership, Lady Gwendolen explains in her life of her father, 'was largely an indirect outcome of her long training in constitutionalism. To a degree remarkable in a person of her mental activity, she had accommodated herself to a convention which forbids the Sovereign to have opinions on home politics. The result had been to destroy her interest in them and to concentrate it almost wholly upon questions of external and national policy. Thus the personal aspect of the present crisis, as it reacted on these, obscured all others in her eyes'; *Life of Salisbury*, iii. 289.

Cabinet was presented with proposed legislation. Gladstone thus effectively put discussion of 'Home Rule' on ice while he worked up his settlement of the Irish question. He clearly felt that Cabinet discussion of the principle of Home Rule would lead to disintegration but hoped that the Cabinet would hold together if presented with the details of a bold and comprehensive settlement.

As always, Granville played a smoothing role in the making of the administration even though his position in the government was to be much less important, since for the first time he was not Gladstone's Foreign Secretary (Spencer was given the awkward job of persuading him not to assert his claim). That office was, as required by the Queen, offered to Rosebery who, for the only time in his official life, made up his mind almost without dithering. Lord Spencer, a staunch Home Ruler, was made President of the Council, rather than Irish Viceroy, so that Gladstone would have him in London during what was certain to be a tough political struggle. The new Chancellor of the Exchequer (after Gladstone had set aside Wolverton's suggestion that he should again take the post himself) was Sir William Harcourt, and the new Irish Secretary (in the circumstances the next most important post) was John Morley. Morley's appointment was agreed before Gladstone saw the Queen. It contravened all Gladstone's maxims about the Cabinet only being open to those with proven executive competence. It indicated that Gladstone would run much of Irish policy himself, for Morley's inexperience was bound to leave him subservient to Gladstone on the details of a Home Rule settlement: Lord Aberdeen, the Viceroy, was equally inexperienced. Gladstone offered executive expertise and a lifetime's experience of detail and drafting; Morley brought a supple and, on the whole, sympathetic intellect, and a wide range of contacts, radical, Irish, and journalistic. One of his closest political friendships was with Joseph Chamberlain, and Gladstone may have hoped Morley could keep Joe on ship.

Rosebery, Harcourt, and Morley were quickly in place. Gladstone's appointments to the key executive positions of his government were thus those people who, together with Lord Spencer, were to be the dominant forces in the Liberal leadership until the end of the century. Lord Hartington had already—before Gladstone saw the Queen—made it clear he would not join the Government: a vital moment for the main body of the Whigs which thus disassociated itself from active support of the party of progress. The last of the active Peelites—with Gladstone—was Lord Selborne (Roundell Palmer), Lord Chancellor in 1880–5. He had been involved in a bitter row with Gladstone during the general election over disestablishment. To be politic, Gladstone cast a fly over him: he 'nibbled', but Gladstone deliberately made little attempt to hook him, for he would have been an almost certain early resignation.

Chamberlain, his 'Unauthorised Programme' rather sidelined by the 'Hawarden Kite', declined the Admiralty and rather sceptically accepted the Presidency of the Local Government Board, his awkward relationship with Gladstone further complicated by the latter's attempt to reduce the salaries of Jessie Collings and Henry Broadhurst by £300 as an economy measure (Collings was Chamberlain's friend and deputy at the L.G.B. and Broadhurst especially needed the money). Gladstone was willing to give way if Chamberlain insisted, for he was, he told Chamberlain, 'in these matters ... like Lot's wife, solitary and pickled on the plains of Sodom'. Other prominent members of the Cabinet were Kimberley as Indian Secretary (Gladstone's original choice as Foreign Secretary but dropped when the Queen wanted Rosebery), Ripon at the Admiralty (the first and only Roman Catholic to sit in a Liberal Cabinet), and G. O. Trevelyan at the Scottish Office (the first Liberal Secretary of State for Scotland). Old stagers declining to serve allowed some new appointments in addition to Morley: Herschell as Lord Chancellor, Henry Campbell-Bannerman as War Secretary, A. J. Mundella at the Board of Trade. The Cabinet of February 1886 thus differed markedly from that which had resigned in 1885.

To a significant extent, the Cabinet formed in February 1886 already reflected the party split which occurred in the summer of that year. Of the previous Cabinet, many who could have served again did not. Not only Hartington and Selborne, but Derby, Northbrook, and Bright declined; Gladstone felt Carlingford too uncertain on Ireland to be worth chasing (he was on the Riviera and hard to reach). Goschen (a member of the 1868 government but not of that of 1880) was sounded out but declined; he was an important indicator of City opinion. It was Bright's absence which pointed to the most surprising development of Liberal politics in 1886: the loss of a significant section of Birmingham radicalism. That the 'Unauthorised Programme' of 1885 was put forward by the same person as established the basis in 1886 for what eventually became a single Unionist party, was a development perhaps even more surprising to Joseph Chamberlain than it was to Gladstone.

Drafting the Irish Settlement

Even before the exhausting work of forming the ministry was completed, Gladstone withdrew to Mentmore, Rosebery's vast house in Buckinghamshire, and 'worked for some hours in drawing my ideas on Ireland into the form of a plan'.* Thus at the earliest moment, Gladstone as Prime Minister began his work on the 'definitive settlement' of Ireland, and his diary shows him working daily on Ireland through February and early March 1886, particularly assisted by Welby and Hamilton of the Treasury and Sir Robert

* 8 Feb. 86.

Hamilton, the Permanent Under-Secretary at Dublin Castle, who had urged on Carnarvon the need for Home Rule.

During this period, the Cabinet was in as much difficulty over finance as it had been at the same time in 1885, Gladstone placing Harcourt in the embarrassing position of having Childers, the previous Chancellor, brought in to supervise his work at the Exchequer on the army and navy estimates. Time for the preparation of the Irish bills was gained by introducing the Crofters Bill, which also had the advantage of working the Liberal MPs together on a 'Celtic fringe' question. Gladstone had been initially as cautious about the bold recommendations of the Napier report in 1884 on the condition of crofters and cottars in the Highlands and Islands as he had been about those of the Bessborough report in 1881 on Irish land. In 1884–5 he had worked hard on Harcourt, then Home Secretary, to limit the terms of the Crofters Bill which followed from the Napier report. But having established that the bill would apply to the Highlands and Islands only and would have no general implications, Gladstone showed himself a powerful historicist. Initially, his solution had been 'compensation for disturbance' on the model of the 1870 Irish Land Act, that is a solution generally applicable to any case of social tension caused by land.* By 1885 he was arguing in a classically historicist way:

no one intends to change at this moment the Land Law in general for the sake of the Crofter parishes . . . the new law should take effect in Parishes where it should have been proved to the satisfaction of some proper judicial authority . . . that within the last hundred years the hill lands of the parish . . . had been held and used in common pasturage? For it is, after all, this historical fact that constitutes the Crofters' title to demand the interference of Parliament. It is not because they are poor, or because there are too many of them, or because they want more land to support their families; but because those whom they represent had rights of which they have been surreptitiously deprived to the injury of the community.†

The Crofters Bill thus went further than either of Gladstone's Irish Land Acts in an explicit acceptance of historicist criteria. It squeezed through in June 1886, just before the dissolution.

On 13 March, the land purchase part of the Irish settlement plan was explained to the Cabinet. Members of the Cabinet, particularly Chamberlain and Kimberley, then 'opened the subject of Home Rule', that is, were reluctant to discuss the land purchase proposals without knowledge of the political settlement of which land purchase was the corollary.

Gladstone consequently 'stated his view that there be an Irish authority one & legislative'. Next day he prepared a circular stating that in view of the

* The 1885 bill was effectively lost by the government's resignation.

† To Harcourt, 19 Jan. 85. This was despite critical comments on J. Stuart Blackie's strongly historicist *The Scottish Highlanders and the land laws* (1885). See also C. Dewey, 'Celtic agrarian legislation and the Celtic Revival: historicist implications of Gladstone's Irish and Scottish Land Acts 1870–1886', *Past and Present* (1974).

'closeness of the connections between the two subjects of Irish Land and Irish Government, which the Cabinet have justly felt', he would press forward 'the drawing into a Bill of the first option [i.e. land purchase]' while at the same time endeavouring 'to set into better shape materials which I have prepared on the subject of Irish Government' (presumably the notes on an Irish legislature prepared on 14 November 1885 and subsequent memoranda) so that the Cabinet would then 'have the whole matter in view at once'.*

Let us turn then to what Gladstone regarded as the constituent elements of 'the whole matter'. These were, he told the public on seeking re-election for Midlothian on becoming First Lord, 'social order, the settlement of the land question, and a widely prevalent desire for self-government'. The problem of social order was to be solved by the resolution of the other two issues.

The Pacification of Ireland: Gladstone's Third Land Bill

Gladstone had been consistently cautious about land purchase, but, from disestablishment in 1869 onwards, he had never excluded it. The idea of a peasant proprietary, especially favoured by Bright, had run as a quiet counterpoint to the dominant theme in 1870 and 1881 of tenants' security. From 1882, Gladstone had begun to accept the future primacy of purchase, but he strongly disliked the expensive form of the Conservatives' Ashbourne Act of 1885. None the less, he saw land purchase, from the start of serious consideration of Home Rule in 1885, as an essential element of a settlement, but only within the context of a general settlement.† There were two reasons for this: the strategic argument that an orderly Ireland now could not be so without a considerable degree of peasant proprietary, and the tactical argument that without the opportunity for escape which land purchase gave to the landlord class, a home rule bill would have no chance of passing.

Both reasons presupposed that a political settlement was not achievable without a large measure of social engineering—the British solution to the settler problem from the West Indies in the 1830s to the Kenyan highlands in the 1960s. The euthanasia of the landlord through his transfiguration into a rentier was the price paid for decolonization by governments across the political spectrum, but it was not a price Joseph Chamberlain was willing to pay in 1886. Though largely forgotten as an aspect of the legislation proposed in 1886, land purchase preparation took up much more time

---

* 14 Mar. 86; Granville and Spencer advised against disclosing 'our whole plan' to Chamberlain in this circular, but the version finally sent was more assertive ('I cannot see my own way to any satisfactory measure except . . . a Statutory Legislative Chamber in Dublin'; ibid.).

† The land settlement was at first referred to in the context of the 'protection of the minority'; it is explicitly referred to as 'Land Purchase' in the memorandum at 23 Dec. 85, though with reluctance.

than the political settlement. The Land Purchase Bill was to have been the third of Gladstone's Irish Land Acts, but, in contrast to the others, it was integrally linked to a political settlement. The Acts of 1870 and 1881 had been alternatives to political change; that of 1886 was intended to facilitate it.

Unlike the first two Land Acts, which had sought to alter legal relationships, the 1886 bill was based on the employment of the credit of the British state. Gladstone told his Chancellor of the Exchequer:

I am the last to desire any unnecessary extension of demands on our financial strength. But I am morally certain that it is only by exerting *to the uttermost* our financial strength (not mainly by expenditure but as credit) on behalf of Ireland, that we can hope to sustain the burden of an adequate Land measure; while, without an adequate Land measure, we cannot either establish social order, or face the question of Irish Government.*

The detail of such a scheme was extremely complex, and it therefore took priority of preparation: 'I have framed a plan for the land and for the finance of what must be a very large transaction. It is necessary to see our way a little in these at the outset, for, unless these portions of any thing we attempt are sound and well constructed, we cannot hope to succeed.'†

The precedent was the buying out of the black apprentices from their owners in the West Indies in the 1830s,‡ the settlement in which Gladstone had effectively been the spokesman for the owners in their negotiations with the Whig government. The precedent, with its implication that some Irish landlords were little better than slave-owners, was a nice reply to Salisbury's much more explicit implication that the Irish were like Hottentots.§ The land purchase scheme, unlike the West Indies settlement, was to be voluntary, that is, landowners did not have to sell unless they wished to. Gladstone personally still hoped landowners would stay on in Ireland. He recognized that 'there is something most grave in the idea of bringing about a wholesale emigration of the resident proprietors and depriving society of those who should be its natural heads and leaders'.¶ But the 'object of this bill is to give all Irish landowners the option of being bought out'.‖ The bill was thus a cushion for a nervous class, in England as well as in Ireland. The Irish would have to pay a double price. First, to ensure the escape of landowners unwilling to live with an Irish legislature, the tenants of a landowner wishing to sell would be compelled to buy (with the exception of very small tenants). Second, the security of the Imperial

* To Harcourt, 12 Feb. 86.
† To H. N. Gladstone, 12 Feb. 86.
‡ *Speeches on the Irish question 1886*, 76: 16 April 1886.
§ The precedent was to the fore in both the 1881 and 1886 land bills, in 1886 for its financial dimension, in 1881 as an interference in contract; in the 1881 instance Gladstone was more careful than in 1886 to deny the correlation of Irish landowners and the slave owners; *H* 290. 893–4 (7 April 1881). ¶ Memorandum of 23 Dec. 85.
‖ *Speeches on the Irish question 1886*, 101.

loan would be that all the 'rents and other Irish revenues whatsoever' must go in the first instance to a Receiver General under British authority, though he would not be responsible for levying or assessing.

This raised two obvious difficulties: first, the whole point of the agrarian crisis in Ireland was that many tenants could not pay their rents; second, that, even if the rents were paid, Gladstone calculated privately, 'for a time, seventy or 60 per cent, in round numbers, of the gross revenues & (public) rents of Ireland may be due to us', chiefly in the form of payments through the Receiver General on the credit advanced for land purchase. The political tensions in such a situation were obvious, and widely expressed. Gladstone's reply was that 'a measure quite out of the common way' necessitated this, and, less moralistically, that the Irish would be anxious to build up a credit market of their own. In the circumstances of world financial markets, this would effectively mean raising money in London. Thus 'Ireland, towards us, must be Caesar's wife',* that is, her reputation for creditworthiness must be above suspicion.

Because the scheme was voluntary, it was difficult to cost. The first settled estimate was that an issue of £120 millions of three per cent stock would be needed for purchase to be available until 1890. Faced with the objection of Chamberlain and others that this was an 'enormous and unprecedented use of British credit',† Gladstone reduced this to £60 millions on 20 March and to £50 millions in the bill, while privately noting, for a meeting with his Irish ministers and Harcourt as Chancellor, that the reasons for this were presentational, and that, if the Act worked well, Parliament could enlarge the sum, a point made publicly though briefly by Gladstone in his speech introducing the bill.‡ Privately, Gladstone continued to anticipate '2 or 3 years hence, another 50ᘌ may be required' (ᘌ was his shorthand sign for million).

There was a curious ambivalence about the land purchase proposal, reflected in the fact that it was strongly pressed on Gladstone by both Spencer and Parnell. In one sense it sought to allay the fears of the propertied classes in Ireland and in the United Kingdom. But its financing alarmed the monied as much as its social objective pacified the landowners. In another sense, it sought to respond to the Irish National League's call for a peasant proprietary to ease the question of social order in Ireland for the Home-Rule dispensation.§ Yet it expected a high level of

* To Morley, 19 Apr. 86 and *Speeches on the Irish question 1886*, 104.

† Chamberlain's letter, 15 March 1886, J. L. Garvin, *Life of Joseph Chamberlain*, 3v. (1932–4) [subsequently: Garvin], ii. 187.

‡ *Speeches on the Irish question 1886*, 101.

§ Rhetorically, Gladstone tried to square his circle by calling as his chief witness J. A. Froude, a man by this time notoriously hostile to him and particularly to his Irish policy; see *H* 304. 1782ff. and 25 Mar. 86. It should be noted that Gladstone's re-reading of Froude occurred well after the main decisions on the Land Bill of 1886 had been taken.

economic performance and political steadfastness from these peasants. The large tenant farmers would no doubt respond to calls for the need for Irish creditworthiness but the small tenant turned peasant proprietor might well have more immediate and personal criteria. In both cases, Gladstone probably underestimated the cross-currents within classes and probably overestimated the integrative effect of his two huge bills.

For Gladstone, it is clear that it was the first of these—the convenience of the landowners to go or to stay—that was foremost: 'the great object of the measure is not to dispose of the entire subject of Irish land, but to afford to the Irish landlord refuge and defence from a possible mode of government in Ireland which he regards as fatal to him'.* The land bill was regarded by some, Gladstone noted after the election in *The Irish Question*, as a 'gigantic bribe' to the landowners and he did not disavow this. The bill was a 'daring attempt we made to carry to the very uttermost our service to the men whom we knew to be as a class the bitterest and most implacable of our political adversaries'.†

Certainly the sums involved were large, but they need to be kept in perspective, and they were very much less than would have been the case if the Ashbourne Act of 1885 had been expanded and used as the mechanism for the 1886 proposal. If we presuppose the maximum, that the measure had been very popular with the tenants and the £50 millions had to be extended to £120 millions over the period 1886–90, the issue of stock would have meant an increase of about 4.5 per cent in the national debt in each of its four years (1.9 per cent if the £50 millions in the Bill were not increased). The interest on the money advanced for land puchase was to be the first charge to be paid out of the receipts to the Irish Receiver General, and would thus cost the British taxpayer virtually nothing. Even if those receipts were zero, that is, even if the Irish legislature completely reneged on all its financial obligations under the Land Purchase Bill and was permitted to do so by the Imperial government and Parliament—an extremely improbable outcome—the increment to the British budget would be about 4.0 per cent (1.7 per cent if the £50 millions were not increased). The export of British capital was reaching its height in the later 1880s, with interest rates remaining low and the price of Consols rising. It could hardly be argued that the stock to finance the land purchase scheme would have been difficult to issue, expensive, or prejudicial to the British economy. Indeed, by retaining the capital within the United Kingdom's economy, albeit for a rather unproductive purpose, it could have been beneficial both in itself and as a precedent.

This guarantee for the propertied class in Ireland was incorporated into the Government of Ireland Bill. Similarly, the Land Purchase Bill could

* Paper for cabinet, 10 March 1886, Add MS 44632, f. 165.
† *The Irish question*, 44.

not become an Act without the passing of the Government of Ireland Bill. There was, therefore, a 'Siamese twinship' of the bills, as Gladstone put it. It may well be that the greatest tactical error of 1886 was not to include both purchase and government in a single bill. This was Lloyd George's successful solution in 1911 to outflanking the various opponents of unemployment and health insurance. Certainly the political formula for mutual self-contradiction was there: the landowning classes disliked Home Rule: many Home Rulers in England, Wales, and Scotland, disliked land purchase.

At first, work on land and on the 'Irish Authority' proceeded *pari passu*, papers on them being circulated to some Cabinet members as 'different Chapters'. Early in March, partly for manageability and partly for tactical reasons, separate bills were envisaged. But considerable movement of content between the bills seems to have existed up to almost the last moment in early April. 'The question of precedence between the two plans seems to be one of policy', Gladstone told Spencer.*

The need to lead with Home Rule was the need to set the Liberal Party behind it, Gladstone never having much doubt that the landowners would swallow the land purchase bribe. But to alarm the Liberals with land purchase first, when they were already uncertain about Home Rule— anxieties confirmed by the resignations of Chamberlain and Trevelyan— would be obviously foolish. Delaying land until after Home Rule also to some extent silenced Chamberlain, who knew most of the details of the land purchase proposals but was not allowed to mention them until the bill was introduced, whereas he had resigned from the Cabinet before the Home Rule details were disclosed.†

The Pacification of Ireland: Gladstone's First Government of Ireland Bill

The second 'Chapter' or 'plan', but the first to be introduced to Parliament, was the Government of Ireland Bill. Sketched earlier, but finalized later than land purchase, the Irish Government Bill was less problematic than land. Initially, it was, like Gladstone's great budgets, almost literally sketched on the back of an envelope, when on 14 November 1885 he jotted down the 'sketch' of a Home Rule Bill on a small sheet of Dalmeny Park writing paper. The relative simplicity of Victorian central government and the bold decisiveness of the Victorian statesman made this possible. Though land purchase was unavoidable, it was the Irish Government Bill

---

* To Spencer, 18 Mar. 86.

† See to Chamberlain, 4, 11 Apr. 86. The text below for February to April 1886 certainly supports Loughlin's view, op. cit., 8off., that throughout this period Gladstone saw Irish government and land purchase as linked and with a combined priority. For a different view, see J. Vincent, 'Gladstone and Ireland', *Proc. Brit. Acad.*, lxiii. 226 (1977), and *The Governing Passion*, 52, 55; but the 'Diary' in Part 3 of *The Governing Passion* (especially 377ff.) gives a very useful narrative of these events.

which was essential. The object of the bill was 'social order',* and it was thus the constitutional culmination of that long series of measures proposed by Gladstone since 1868 to solve the Irish question. His mission was still to pacify Ireland, not to liberate it.

In this sense, the bill was a great metropolitan, imperial measure. Pacification meant social, political, and civil order, and consequently, as with Canada, imperial security. Gladstone's experience had eventually taught him that only through liberation could pacification be achieved, but the latter remained the objective. Hence there was no recognition of Irish nationalism in any absolute sense, but only in so far as the Irish were perceived as a distinct but component part of the United Kingdom. Nothing could be done for Ireland that could not also be done for Scotland: this was one of the earliest tests devised by Gladstone for any political settlement. That was why, when returning from his convalescent cruise to Norway early in September 1885, he was 'embarrassed' to find Parnell claiming the Scots had lost their nationality. This view of Irish nationality as, at bottom, centrifugal rather than centripetal, or as at least neutral as between those forces, was fundamental to the central concept of the bill.

The Government of Ireland Bill set out to devolve the authority of the Westminster Parliament to what in the first instance was called 'An Irish Chamber for Irish affairs', then an 'Irish Authority', then 'a Legislative Chamber or Parliament', then, in the bill itself, 'a Legislative Body'. Much was in a name, because it mirrored the conceptual difficulty. The British constitution—a series of acts historically cumulative recognizing conquests and bargains, ancient pre-parliamentary Crown powers balanced by the common law, vital institutions such as the Cabinet and political parties unmentioned in law—worked by convention. Attempts at codification had always been resisted. Thus its only abstract definition was likely to be of the sort that Dicey advanced in his *Law of the Constitution*. Any attempt at devolution was therefore bound to be a messy business, for it was very hard to devise an intellectually systematic plan when the constitution whose powers were to be devolved was not systematically stated in law.

Gladstone's solution raised all the problems which still face devolution a hundred years later. There were two possible models, once the idea of a 'co-ordinate Legislature' (i.e. a return to a separate Irish Parliament) had been set aside—and that possibility never seems to have been seriously canvassed in 1885–6. Gladstone examined the Norway/Sweden parallel legislatures during his cruise in August 1885, but those, and the rather similar dual monarchy in the despised Hapsburg Empire, were merely used as an end of a spectrum which highlighted the Irish Government Bill's moderation.

* See the opening of his speech introducing the bill on 8 April; *Speeches on the Irish question 1886*, 1.

The real models were the Canadian* and the federal. The Canadian was clearly dominant. Intellectually, it had the merit of simplicity and precedence. Gladstone's first paper for the Cabinet on Irish government followed it in devolving to the Irish Body legislative powers, except in certain reserved areas, most importantly, defence, foreign and colonial relations, and trade and navigation to the extent of preventing protectionist duties (a characteristic touch, recalling Gladstone's irritation at Canadian and Australian protectionism) but not non-protective indirect taxes. This at once highlighted the difficulty. Ireland was to remain part of the United Kingdom fiscal system, her defence was to be integrated, and she was to pay an annual sum. Thus Canada was the precedent at first glance, but not in the details.

The alternative, federal solution, was hinted at in 1886 in Gladstone's criterion that nothing be done for Ireland that could not be done for Scotland. But it was no more than hinted at, for there was no basis of support for federalism in England, and very little in Scotland, where the cry, led by Rosebery, was, until the Government of Ireland Bill, for administrative not legislative devolution. Wales, Gladstone simply ignored. The Government of Ireland Bill, if passed unamended, would in fact have made a subsequent federal solution very awkward, since it proposed there be no Irish MPs at Westminster. Such a provision would also have made subsequent Scottish devolution on the Irish precedent almost impossible, because the two devolutions would have had the effect of leaving an 'Imperial Parliament' composed of English and Welsh MPs only.

What was offered, therefore, was a diluted version of the Canadian precedent, designed for the peculiarities of the Irish case. The dilution strapped the Irish firmly to the United Kingdom, as did the complex composition of the Legislative Body. Gladstone seems at first to have thought of simply constituting it from the 103 Irish MPs plus another 103 elected by the same constituencies.† But this was thought too simple with respect to minorities and too open to control by a 'single influence'.‡ So it was to include two 'Orders' normally debating and voting together, but with each able to call for a separate vote, thus giving each 'Order' a veto (though only for a limited time). The 'First Order' would be made up of twenty-eight Irish Peers (Gladstone hoped that most of the Irish Representative Peers at Westminster would sit) plus seventy-five members elected for a ten year term on a £25 occupier franchise, with candidates having to be men of

---

* Used in the sense of power devolved from the Westminster Parliament to another legislature; the constitution devolved to Canada was, of course, federal in form in the way that it worked in Canada, but this is irrelevant to the concept of devolution from Westminster.

† See mem. at 28 Dec. 85; this explains the passage introducing the 'Legislative Body' in his speech on 8 April 1886 (*Speeches on the Irish question 1886*, 32); but his mem. of 28 Dec. 86 may also imply a second chamber.

‡ *Speeches on the Irish question 1886*, 32; see ibid. and pp. 317–19 for the following details.

substantial property. The 'Second Order' was to consist of 202 county and borough members, 101 of whom would in the first instance be the existing Irish MPs (plus two seats for Dublin University and provision for two for the Royal University). These would stand for election at least every five years. From the two 'Orders' an executive would gradually emerge *via* Privy Councillors as the Viceroy became like the Canadian Governor-General. The narrow franchise and slow turn-over of the 'First Order', and the provision for a veto for each 'Order', made this body powerfully conservative in constitution. Though allowing the unpromising parallel with the States General in 1789, Gladstone did not think there would be a deadlock through the First Order being simply Tories and the Second, simply Home Rulers.

The Financial Clauses: a Boon for Ireland

As Gladstone had anticipated from the moment he received Parnell's 'proposed Constitution for Ireland',* it was the financial arrangements that posed the chief difficulty between the government and the Home Rule MPs. Under pressure from the Cabinet, which thought the Irish would pay too little, and from Parnell who thought they would pay too much, Gladstone began negotiating. The negotiations revolved round the financial settlement, but also raised the question of the future place of the Irish MPs. The bargain struck was this: all customs and excise duties would be managed by Westminster, and the Irish would only have to pay one-fifteenth of Imperial costs rather than one-fourteenth as hitherto envisaged (or one-thirteenth in the first Cabinet paper).† So keen to gain this reduction was Parnell that he agreed to Westminster control of indirect taxation without Irish MPs in the Commons, that is, he agreed to taxation without representation.

Though the size of the Irish contribution was calculated during the discussions as a proportion and has been erroneously discussed as such by historians ever since, in the bill it was expressed as a fixed sum of money, unalterable (except downwards) for thirty years: £4,236,000 *per annum*, plus £360,000 *per annum* to service the Irish share of the national debt. This showed a touching faith in the stability of money values not uncharacteristic of the Victorians, though Gladstone knew well enough how inflation had after 1832 eroded the excluding force of the £10 criterion for the householder vote. In the 1880s the value of gold rose and the Irish would thus have paid rather more than they had expected, but from the later 1890s deflation turned to inflation and thus the Irish in the later part of the thirty years would have had an extraordinary bargain, even supposing British defence costs remained constant. That the Treasury, in the person of

---

* See the first draft (not sent) of reply to Mrs O'Shea, 3 Nov. 85.
† Initially (see mem. at 28 Dec. 85) Gladstone had considered the much larger proportion of $\frac{1}{8}$.

Harcourt, should have agreed to a money rather than a proportionately expressed contribution is perhaps the most remarkable of all the Cabinet's concessions to Gladstone. For it reflected a view of the minimalism of the British fiscal state which Gladstone wished was true, but which the experience of recent decades of British finance overall hardly warranted.

Gladstone's argument was that though overall central government expenditure had risen (£71.8 millions in 1868, £92.2 millions in 1886), none the less on the two chief items of the Irish contribution—the national debt and defence—costs had not risen much over the previous fifteen years. Gladstone required the Irish to be provident in domestic government costs in a way that the British were failing to be and in which he thought the Irish administrations of the past had been particularly profligate. It would also be the case that if Home Rule was successful in ending Irish disorder, the traditionally high expenditure on the Irish police would fall. In requiring Home Rule Ireland to be, like Britain, both low-spending and non-protectionist, Gladstone was discounting the peculiar character of the Irish economy *vis-à-vis* the British, exactly that factor which had been one of the chief stimulants to the Irish sense of distinctiveness.

But if we look at the way the settlement would have worked over its first thirty years, we shall see a spectacular boon to the Irish. On the debt charges, they would have been entitled to a small rebate, as provided by the bill (debt charges falling from £23.5 millions in 1886 to £20.8 millions in 1910). But on defence, the Irish contribution would have fallen from one-fifteenth to one-thirtyfourth by 1910.[*] Overall—the exact figures are uncertain because of definitions of Imperial civil charges—the Irish contribution, because it was expressed in fixed money terms, would by 1910 have fallen from one-fifteenth to about one-twentyfifth: the Irish contribution of £4.6 millions would have remained the same, but the Imperial expenditure to which it contributed would have gone up from £92.2 millions to £156 millions (1910). The financial clauses of the 1886 bill are sometimes seen as a source of subsequent friction because of Irish difficulty in paying the contribution. More likely, had the bill become an Act, would have been a British demand for an amendment to the 'thirty year rule'. It would have been a further irony of Irish history if 1916 (the year for review) had in fact been the occasion of a desperate attempt by an Irish Legislative Body to preserve the financial bargain struck in 1886. Unsatisfactory to Britain though Gladstone's settlement would have been in its financial terms, they could have turned out to be the most powerful of all reasons for Irish enthusiasm against separation and for the settlement. It is

* The bill provided for a rebate if United Kingdom expenditure fell, but expressly forbade an increase, except in time of war 'for the prosecution of the war and defence of the realm'. By excluding 'what strictly ought to be called war charges', i.e. votes of credit for imperial campaigns of the sort the Parnellites usually opposed, the bill avoided a potentially very serious irritant; British imperialism was to be financed from British taxation; *Speeches on the Irish question 1886*, 43.

obvious that the financial settlement would not have been definitive, but it is unlikely it would have produced more than the sort of second-order revisions with which we have been familiar in the European Economic Community since 1972.

The Irish MPs: in, partly in, or out?

The inclusion or exclusion of the MPs of the devolved area has been a central point of controversy in all attempts at devolution in Britain. In his 'proposed Constitution', Parnell was unemphatic: the Irish MPs 'might be retained or might be given up'; if retained, the Speaker could rule on what were the Imperial questions in which they should take part.* Gladstone's sketch of 14 November 1885 kept them in, 'question to be decided by the House or the Speaker', with a 'Schedule' of Imperial questions as a guide, and Irish MPs to be involved in votes on 'Ministerial responsibility which touch the reserved subjects only'. This was a position difficult to sustain, for such votes also affected the continuance or fall of the ministry, with many implications for non-Irish affairs. By the time of the introduction of the Government of Ireland Bill, and as a result of pressure especially from John Morley, the Irish Secretary, the Irish MPs were to be out altogether, a provision widely felt to encourage subsequent separatism.

This uncertainty on such a central question reflected the English stranglehold on the United Kingdom constitution. The English would not alter the Imperial parliament, because it was their domestic parliament also: the Acts of Union of 1707 and 1800 had simply brought Scottish and Irish MPs to Westminster. But the unitary parliament offered non-unitary legislation, thus maintaining legal as well as sentimental nationalism within the United Kingdom. When such nationalism wished to regain, short of repeal of the Union, some control of the legislation lost, effectively to England, by the Act of Union, then the absence of a genuinely Imperial parliament, to which all such areas (including England) could relate was bound to produce an intellectually untidy result with respect to the constitution of the Parliament at Westminster. Such untidy results could of course be lived with: from 1920 to 1972 there was a devolved parliament in Ulster with Ulster MPs at Westminster. Probably the solution envisaged by both Parnell and Gladstone in November 1885—a Speaker's ruling on Irish inclusion—offered the characteristically British way out, as it did to the question of finance bills and the House of Lords a generation later.

Commonsense and the Constitution

The Irish settlement proposed in 1886 would have required tolerance on both sides for it to work: 'the determining condition will I think be found to

---

* O'Shea, *Parnell*, ii. 20.

be the temper in which men approach the question'.* This was no more than the Westminster constitution already required of the political class to keep its bizarre balance of Crown, Lords, and Commons in equilibrium. Gladstone's calculation was that the Home Rule party which would take power in Ireland would act as men of 'common sense', anxious to gain credit in the financial markets, and with no reason to distance themselves further from the United Kingdom. Indeed, the opposite would be the case: 'Home Rule is . . . a source not of danger but of strength—the danger, if any, lies in refusing it.'† The Dissentient Liberals were the real 'Separatists'.‡ Gladstone's 'work and purpose' was, he said, 'in the highest sense Conservative'.§ The proposed settlement of 1886 thus fitted exactly into the approach to Ireland pursued since 1868 even, perhaps, since the *bouleversement* on Maynooth in 1845. It was the boldest of all possible attempts to save Ireland for constitutionalism and from Fenianism.

Defeat and Resignation

Gladstone had, since the autumn of 1885, recognized the likelihood of failure in the Commons. Characteristically, he had not done much to prevent it. As in 1866, during the Reform Bill *débâcle*, there was an off-hand, 'take-it-or-leave-it' quality about his approach, which relied largely on public rhetoric for its success. Even press contacts, so assiduously nurtured in 1866, were not exploited. The Liberal party, perceived from the start as the weak link, was only reluctantly courted. Gladstone tried to use the Irish government and land purchase bills as measures so large and so important that, like the Lords, the Liberal party 'would not dare'. Proposed legislation could, perhaps would, integrate in a way that generalized resolutions could not do.¶

It was clear that the Liberal party was at best only likely to be sufficiently integrated for a bare pass on second reading. Various possibilities were considered—the Irish MPs back in, the financial settlement rearranged— but Gladstone refused any basic change either in the bill or in the parliamentary strategy. When he spoke on the 10 May on Second Reading of the Government of Ireland Bill, he privately felt 'the reception decidedly inferior to that of the Introduction'. Next day, 'Prospects much clouded

* To R. W. Dale, 29 Apr. 86.
† Public letter to *Daily Chronicle*, 24 Apr. 86.
‡ To Argyll, 20 Apr. 86; 'Separatist' is here used punningly, the dissentient liberals being separatists from their party and also promoting Irish separation by opposing Home Rule.
§ To Tennyson, 26 Apr. 86.
¶ The suggestion of proceeding by resolution, considered in December 1885, fell away, to be revived by Pease when the bill was in serious danger (see to Pease, 15, 21 May 86). No comment by Gladstone on this switch has been found. The precedent of the 1868 Irish Church Resolutions, it is sometimes forgotten, was a precedent of resolutions moved in opposition; between July 1885 and Salisbury's resignation in January 1886 there was only the opportunity of the Queen's Speech, and by then Gladstone was committed to his tactic that only the government was in a position to judge.

for 2 R'. In the face of this, he agreed to tell the party that if the bill was given a second reading, it would be withdrawn, the clauses on Irish representation reconstructed (largely in fact in line with Gladstone's original plan of November 1885), and the bill reintroduced at an autumn Session. On 31 May there was 'great dismay in our camp on the report of Chamberlain's meeting', i.e. the decision, on John Bright's lead, to vote against the second reading of the bill rather than abstain.

Barring a spectacular last-minute shift of opinion among Liberal MPs, defeat was probable. But Gladstone, whatever situation he found himself in politically, always believed he could win. Never was there a less pessimistic political tactician. Only an astonishingly bold, robust, and self-confident politician could have forced the pace the way Gladstone did between January and June 1886. What others saw as wilfulness was Gladstone's armour: the obverse of self-confidence was the absence of self-doubt.

The vote on the second reading was taken on 7 June 1886:

Worked on Irish question & speech through the forenoon at Dollis [Hill] in quiet ... H. of C. 4–8$\frac{1}{2}$ and 9–2$\frac{1}{4}$. We were heavily beaten on the 2d Reading, by 341 to 311. A scene of some excitement followed the declaration of the numbers: one or two Irishmen lost their balance. Upon the whole we have more ground to be satisfied with the progress made, than to be disappointed at the failure. But it is a serious mischief. Spoke very long: my poor voice came in a wonderful manner.

Next day (as always in such circumstances) taking the advice of Lord Wolverton, Gladstone drove through an uncertain Cabinet the decision for an almost immediate dissolution of Parliament. He gave the Cabinet twelve reasons for his view, the culminating being: 'a Dissolution is formidable but resignation would mean, for the present juncture, abandonment of *the cause*'. Though he carried the National Liberal Federation with him, this was insufficient to organize an election campaign. Divided and confused, the Liberals left many seats uncontested. Returned unopposed in Midlothian and Leith Burghs (where his last-moment nomination caused the withdrawal of a person thought to be a Liberal Unionist) Gladstone tried to focus attention on '*the cause*' by an unprecedented outpouring of letters and telegrams to constituencies in addition to his usual speeches. His son Willy's decision not to stand as a candidate was an ominous and telling sign. 'Whenever I come to consider the matter', Willy told his father, 'I found that there remained in my mind the fixed opinion that Home Rule was not the thing Ireland required & was not necessary for clearing the honour of England.'

The election result was in one respect less disastrous than might have been the case: no party had an overall majority. But the Liberals fell from 333 to 196 and the Tories rose from 251 to 316: the political balance had shifted to a majority for Unionism of over 100 (316 Tories plus 74 Liberal

Unionists against 196 Liberals and 86 Home Rulers). 'The defeat is a smash', Gladstone noted accurately enough in his diary. But, characteristically, he also saw it as welcome retribution and relief: 'I accept the will of God for cessation of my painful relations with the Queen, who will have a like feeling.' After some discussion of holding on to meet Parliament and be voted out of office, the Cabinet of 20 July 1886 decided on immediate resignation. Rosebery observed that 'all applauded' when Gladstone stated his willingness 'to retain the responsibility of leadership' of the Liberal party. Gladstone could now hardly do otherwise: the making of the policy and its political presentation had linked a single personality with a great cause, and its presentation had linked a great political party to a single personality to an extent quite exceptional in British politics. Gladstone responded aggressively, moving as quickly as possible to recapture the initiative. He re-read his *Chapter of Autobiography*, his earlier political *apologia*, and by the time of his closing audience with the Queen was well into the writing of *The Irish Question. I. History of an Idea. II. Lessons of the Election*, published in August 1886.

A 'golden moment' turned to lead

Gladstone commended his Government of Ireland Bill to the House of Commons in words which still haunt Anglo-Irish relations:

This, if I understand it, is one of those golden moments of our history; one of those opportunities which may come and may go, but which rarely return, or, if they return, return at long intervals, and under circumstances which no man can forecast.*

This was the second 'golden moment'; the first had been the start of the confirmation of constitutionalism through the release of Parnell in 1882.†
Whether the settlement would have worked, of course we cannot know. As the Kilbrandon Royal Commission on the Constitution remarked in 1973, the 1920 Act was the only Home Rule bill 'that ever came into effect, and then in the one part of Ireland that had said it would fight rather than accept home rule. Northern Ireland, by one of history's choicest ironies, is the one place where liberal home rule ideas were ever put into practice—and by a solidly Unionist government. It can be truly said to have been given a constitution that it did not want and that was designed for another place.'‡
    The Irish settlement of 1886 was forged, as were all the great initiatives of Victorian Britain, by a politician working with the given circumstances of the moment. Like those other initiatives, it was not an *a priori*, systematic

---

* *Speeches on the Irish question 1886*, 165.
† 1 May 82.
‡ *Royal Commission on the Constitution* (1973), i. 376.

dispensation drafted, as a Utilitarian would have liked, by politically neutral experts, but a proposal hammered out in the heat of the political sun. It was not 'reform upon a system', in Lord John Russell's phrase, but reform within the conventions of British political behaviour. A majority of MPs felt Gladstone was trying to stretch those conventions too far and too quickly.*

Gladstone asserted the individual's capacity to change the political climate at a stroke with a dramatic innovation larger in scope than any of the other participants in political life had anticipated. In this he fulfilled just the sort of Liberal role which men such as Acton expected of him, while also satisfying his own criteria of continuity, development, and growth. He worked thoroughly within the British political tradition by advancing the view that the British constitution already contained all the necessary ingredients of a just political society, needing only a little modification and assistance to achieve a new balance. Gladstone was never a Whig in a party political sense, close though his ties with leading Whigs were, but never was there conceived a more classically whiggish measure than Home Rule.

1884–6—the parliamentary reform settlement and the consequential Irish settlement—was the last great Victorian political initiative. It represented a belief in the primacy of constitutionalism, both as the chief activity of Parliament and as the ultimate means of solution to questions of social, economic, and political order. The first part of the settlement passed with difficulty. The second was rejected on principle. The way was not, however, clear for a simple switch from the politics of constitutionalism to those of welfare, for the cause of the delay in 1884 (the House of Lords) and a cause of the promotion of the Irish settlement (the 85 home-rule MPs) were each by the experience of these years both emboldened and entrenched. It was to take Britain a generation to pass those two issues through her political digestion†—exactly that generation when a bold new form of the British State was, by the development of relative economic decline, most needed.

The delay was, from the viewpoint of the twentieth century, disastrous. The chief irony is that of all those involved in the crisis of 1884–6, Gladstone most dreaded the onset of the politics of welfare, that 'leaning of both parties to Socialism which I radically disapprove'.‡ Yet it was his failure, not his success, that delayed the advent of such politics. The settlement of Ireland in 1886, if achieved, would have both shown that the Lords 'did not

---

* For the view that MPs voted on the Government of Ireland Bill on the basis of policy (rather than class), see W. C. Lubenow, *Parliamentary politics and the home rule crisis* (1988), especially ch. 6.

† The metaphor is Gladstone's; he thought Ireland brought into political life 'what I may perhaps call constipation'; to McLaren, 22 Dec. 81.

‡ To Argyll, 30 Sept. 85; see also to Southesk, 27 Oct. 85 and to Acton, 11 Feb. 85.

dare', and would have cleared the way for the development of the Liberal party as a party of positive social welfare. The defeat of the Irish settlement in 1886 meant that the political parties of Great Britain were tied into an extraordinary knot. The Unionist coalition, supposedly dedicated to the burial of Home Rule, had no greater political interest than that Home Rule should continue to be the leading question of the day. Nothing cheered the Unionists more than another Home Rule speech by Gladstone. The Liberals, dedicated to clearing the way, found themselves unable, save in 1905–10, again to form a government without the support of the Irish they wished to remove. Thus both British parties found themselves still sweating on the Irish treadmill, the Unionists fearing the disappearance of Home Rule, the Liberals toiling for a success whose achievement would mean their political eclipse. The gold of the moment of 1886 indeed turned to lead.

CHAPTER XI

The Daily Round: Court, Patronage, and the Commons

The Queen—Patronage and the Peerage—Patronage, Painters, and Portraits—Church and Scholarship—Leader of the House

Pol[itics].

Causes tending to help the Conservative party & give it at least an occasional preponderance though a minority of the nation.

1. Greater wealth available for the expences of elections.
2. Greater unity from the comparative scantiness of such explosive matter within the party, as is supplied by the activity of thought and opinion in the Liberal party, not always sufficiently balanced: with which activity self-seeking is apt to mix.
3. The existence of powerful professional classes more or less sustained by privilege or by artfully constructed monopoly: the Army, the Law, the Clergy.
4. The powerful influence attached to the possession of land, & its distribution in few hands not merely from legal arrangements but from economic causes.
5. The impossibility of keeping the *public* in mind always lively and intent upon great national interests, while the opposite sentiment of class never slumbers.
6. The concentration of the higher and social influences, thus associated with Toryism, at the fixed seat of government, and their ready & immediate influence from day to day on the action of the legislature through the different forms of social organisation used by the wealthy & leisured class.*

The Queen

We have thus far looked at the high-ground occupied by Gladstone in this period, a ground marked out by the 'special causes' which retained him in political life. His own view was that those special causes were external to himself, causes objectively given by the process of politics. Yet in the 1880s that process was so dominated by his own political personality and so shaped by his distinctive style of rhetorical leadership that it is hard and

---

* Memorandum on politics, 14 August 1882.

probably unhistorical to try to separate the personality and the process. Gladstone seems to have underrated the extent to which the force of his political personality in itself shaped those causes, and it is in that under-estimation that we find the key to what otherwise can seem like a dis-ingenuous series of excuses for not keeping his word about retiring.

We must be careful here: parliamentary and local government reform, Ireland, a correct financial, imperial, and foreign policy, these would have been obvious Liberal concerns in the 1880s even if Gladstone had died before the 1880 general election. Yet each of them as actually shaped by the British government in the 1880s bears a distinct Gladstonian stamp. Though 'counterfactuals' stimulate the historical imagination and are a natural consequence of the advantage that hindsight gives the historian, they are particularly difficult to apply to questions of political judgement: political leadership is the most unquantifiable of phenomena. So the answer to the question, what form would British handling of the Irish question in the 1880s have taken without Gladstone? can hardly rise above speculation. But equally tricky, then, is the distribution of blame. The historian can point to failure or inconsistency within the terms and goals set by his or her subject. We have seen that there is such in Gladstone's handling of Egypt and of Ireland, particularly in his estimations of the parliamentary success of Home Rule. Yet complaint and blame over details are not to much constructive purpose: the fascination of the period lies in the understanding of a remarkable, and in some ways remarkably distant, liberal mind and its consequential actions. The consequences can be assessed, but there is not much point in expecting Gladstone to have been different from what he was.

Gladstone's extended political career, though dedicated to 'special causes', led also to his involvement as Prime Minister, as Leader of the Commons (and as *de facto* Leader of the Liberal party though the fiction of a mere temporary *hiatus* was maintained) in a wide range of more ordinary activities. Even these, partly because of Gladstone's involvement in them, sometimes took on extraordinary dimensions. Let us now look at these more routine aspects of his premierships in the 1880s.

As Prime Minister, Gladstone spent more time dealing with the Queen than with any other person. Victoria was not a model Bagehotian consti-tutional monarch; indeed she did not see her role in Bagehot's terms. The history of Liberal governments in late Victorian Britain does not suggest the successful evolution of a non-executive constitutional monarchy with its prerogative powers in commission to the Cabinet. Victoria saw herself as an integral part of the making of policy, with the right to instruct, to abuse, and to hector. She corresponded about Liberal government policy and the content of the Queen's Speech with Conservative opposition leaders (but not *vice versa*); she continued to exclude certain Liberal MPs from Cabinet, and to object to lower-level appointments on grounds of policy; she expected revenge for Majuba; she opposed the Cabinet's with-drawal or reduction of British troops from Afghanistan and Egypt; she abused her ministers privately and, in the notorious episode of the '*en clair* telegram', publicly over their handling of Sudanese policy; she objected to Cabinet ministers' speeches; she offered to help Salisbury dissolve at the most propitious moment in 1885; she opposed Home Rule; and she did all these in her official capacity as Queen and Empress.*

As in his first government, Gladstone shielded the Queen from the consequences of her actions.† As far as possible, her railings were kept from the Radical and even the Liberal members of the Cabinet. Gladstone and Granville, especially the former, bore the brunt of the royal onslaught with discretion and, on the whole, remarkable patience. Gladstone person-ally wrote to the Queen after each Cabinet and, as Leader of the House, each evening when the Commons was sitting, reporting its proceedings. These were routine letters, expected of any Prime Minister who was in the Commons (though Gladstone was the only such in Victoria's reign after 1878). But there were many extra letters to be written as replies to the Queen's frequent letters and telegrams, particularly at times of political crisis. Sometimes these amounted to six in a day.

Gladstone was painstaking about these replies, and about his handling of the Court generally. The conservative side of his political personality gave a high religious and constitutional role to monarchy. In his conception of

* The Court tried to have it both ways, letting the Queen have her head when alive, but once dead not being ready to accept responsibility for her actions while at the same time trying to prevent some of these from being disclosed. There was little discernible attempt to moderate the Queen's partisan behaviour during her life-time. Between 1926 and 1932 there appeared G. E. Buckle's edition of the second and third series of the *Letters of Queen Victoria*, designed to show, in Buckle's words (themselves highlighting the ambivalence) that 'the approach of old age did not lessen her steady, day-by-day application to her duties as a Constitutional Monarch; while the maturity of her judgment and the wider range of her experience gave increased weight and author-ity to her *decisions*' (my italics). In *After Thirty Years* (1928) Herbert Gladstone tried, by disputing particular incidents, to contest what he saw as Buckle's 'definite scheme of attack on Mr. Glad-stone'. This approach was not very effective. The Gladstone family then decided rather shrewdly that the best way to correct the record and answer Buckle was simply to publish the Gladstone–Victoria correspondence. H. N. Gladstone commissioned Philip Guedalla to edit an extensive selection from it. When Guedalla in 1933 sent George V the proofs of his edition of *The Queen and Mr. Gladstone*—an edition prepared not under the scrutiny of Windsor Castle but from the Queen's letters to Gladstone (many of which were sent without copies being made) and Gladstone's copies of his letters to her—the Court was clearly alarmed to find just how immoderate her behaviour had been. Letters written in the authority of the Crown (including comments on South Africa and an attempt to exclude L. H. Courtney from appointment as colonial undersecretary) were proposed for excision (including some already printed in Buckle's *Letters of Queen Victoria*!). Clive Wigram, George V's secretary, concluded one letter: 'one feels that, as it were, she needs a little "protection from herself". I am sure you will know what I mean' (Wigram to Guedalla, 30 August 1933, Bodleian Library, Guedalla MSS Box 3). Guedalla probably did know what was meant (i.e. that he should play the Court's game) but he ignored Wigram's attempt at suppression.

† Whether the Queen was 'right' in some of her demands is irrelevant to the fact of their existence.

hierarchy and order, the monarchy was a natural point of focus. Nor does he seem to have been hostile to the notion of the monarchy as a functioning part of the constitution. His objection to Victoria's behaviour was to its tone, its omnipresence, and its partiality, not to its reasonable activity. He saw, probably correctly, Victoria's behaviour as *sui generis*, unlikely to be repeated. His friendship with the Prince of Wales, marked in the 1880s by frequent meetings of an amiable sort, told him that the Crown would pass, eventually, to a much more liberal spirit, who had to be restrained from voting in the House of Lords for the Franchise Bill in 1884.*

There was also a prudential consideration to Gladstone's reticence about the Queen's behaviour. The monarchy and the House of Lords stood together at the apex of the constitution, an extraordinary hierarchical *bloc* in an increasingly egalitarian political culture. Each knew that they might also fall together, or, at least, that each was unsustainable without the other. Any criticism of the monarchy within the Liberal party instantly raised whiggish alarms, for as the Whigs felt increasingly threatened so their whiggery became less whiggish in the traditional sense,† more defensive and less cautious about the Court. Gladstone could in 1884 use this to advantage. His long memoranda to the Queen argued that the Lords' action in rejecting the Franchise Bill raised the question of 'organic change' in the constitution; that if the Liberal Party were forced to make that change a political objective it would, like all other major Liberal reforms, eventually be carried; that 'organic change of this kind in the House of Lords may strip and lay bare, and in laying bare may weaken, the foundations even of the Throne'. But, for Gladstone, this was an unusual position of strength.

The Queen, in the end, rarely got her way directly, though she did sometimes (for example, in 1882 preventing Derby from becoming Secretary of State for India and Dilke from becoming Chancellor of the Duchy of Lancaster, thus affecting the Cabinet reshuffle generally). It would not be possible to argue that she imposed a royal imperial policy, much though she would like to have in 1880–5. But if her aim was to drive Gladstone from office by attrition, she had some success: 'Position relatively to the Queen' was high on his list of reasons for trying to leave.‡ More generally, she was undoubtedly successful in contributing to the creation of what was for Liberals an atmosphere of caution and restriction, with the telegram from Windsor, and the wearisome explanations it required, being the first consequence of the expression of many a political intention.

These telegrams, letters, and visits from Sir Henry Ponsonby, Victoria's

---

* P. Magnus, *Edward VII*, (1964), 182.
† Traditional whiggery had had something of a final fling in the opposition to the Royal Titles Bill in 1876.
‡ To Bright, 29 Sept. 81.

secretary, could not be set aside. They related, and were known to relate, to a body of opinion of considerable importance, particularly in the army where royal obstruction supported what Gladstone called, in the context of the Wolseley peerage dispute, 'the great conspiracy against the nation, in respect both to change and to reforms, which lives and moves among the heads of the military class, and which enjoys in the House of Lords its chief arena for development and exercise',* a view interestingly echoed by Sir William Butler, one of the Wolseley 'ring' but a much more committed Liberal than his chief. Butler accounted for the Gordon imbroglio, in which he was involved, not only by emphasizing the extent of opposition to evacuation of the Sudan by 'the official world of Cairo—English and Egyptian', but also by distinguishing between the 'permanent' government of Britain which was conservative and entrenched in the army and the navy, and 'the passing Liberal Executive Administration' which was thus doomed to frustration.†

Gladstone's championing of Wolseley's peerage—'a nasty pill for Her' he told his secretary, Edward Hamilton‡—was a deliberate assault on this sort of royal obstruction. The Court view related also to opinion in parts of the foreign and colonial services, certainly in the Tory party and in parts of the Liberal party. The Court was by no means a negligible force in the development of the climate of imperial expansion which was, however reluctant in tone, such a central feature of the political culture of the governing class in the 1880s. Indeed, to some extent the Queen did the Whigs' work for them. She was able to disagree with the Prime Minister with a stridency and tenacity which in a Cabinet minister would have implied resignation.

'It is innocence itself' was Gladstone's comment on reading *More Leaves from the Journal of a Life in the Highlands*. But the innocence in this instance was his. The Queen's second book was an important and shrewdly judged stimulus to the public perception of her as a non-political person, interested chiefly in worthy rural pursuits.§ It confirmed exactly that view of the monarchy which made Liberal protests against her political partisanship impossible unless they were to be part of a planned attempt at a reconstruction of the monarchy.

Gladstone's position was particularly awkward, for in shielding the Queen from the Liberals and Radicals in his Cabinet, he isolated himself

---

* To Hartington, 21 May 81.
† Sir W. F Butler, *Charles George Gordon* (1889), 213–14.
‡ Bahlman, *Hamilton*, i. 112.
§ See e.g. Max O'Rell [L. P. Blouett], *John Bull's Womankind* (n.d. [1884]), 113: 'In the second volume of the Queen's *Life in the Highlands* ... you will look in vain for the slightest allusion to politics; it is the journal of a country gentleman's wife, who takes but small interest in anything outside the family circle. It is the diary of a queen that gives her people but one subject of complaint, which is that they do not see enough of her.'

from those who were on many issues his natural Cabinet allies against the Court. His discretion meant that there was no basis for public comment, and his discretion was necessary unless he was prepared to lead a crusade which would be immensely divisive for his party, which would play into the hands of the 'patriotic' lobby in the Conservative party—always on the look-out for a closer identification of Crown, Church, and Party—and which would go against all his instincts. There was little Gladstone could do but write the letters and remain polite. It was a considerable strain. A characteristic entry in his diary is that for 30 November 1881: 'Off at $11\frac{3}{4}$ for Windsor. Received with much civility, & had a long audience: but I am always outside an iron ring: and without any desire, had I the power, to break it through.' The absence of such a desire on Gladstone's part no doubt made a bad situation worse, but the reason for the absence was a partisanship on the part of the monarch which by 1881 had on her part become instinctive. Very different was a meeting with the Queen's daughter and her husband, heir to the German throne: 'He was as always delightful: she talked abundant Liberalism of a deep-rooted kind.'*

Patronage and the Peerage

Closely related to dealings with the Crown was Prime-Ministerial patronage. Despite the increasingly partisan character of the House of Lords, and Gladstone's perception of it as a major political problem, his creation of peers remained orthodox. That is to say, he accepted the usual criteria of land, wealth, and status, and appointed peers within those lines of guidance. Gladstone was quite aware of the increasing tendency of property and privilege to fuse with Conservatism. In analysing in August 1882 the 'causes tending to help the Conservative party' he included 'the concentration of the higher and social influences . . . and their ready & immediate influence from day to day on the action of the legislature through the different forms of social organization used by the wealthy & leisure class'. Of these forms, the peerage was obviously the political and institutional seal. Yet Gladstone, despite this analysis, made no attempt to break that seal. Indeed his approach, if anything, set it more firmly. He did not try to refurbish the peerage. Indeed, as his table, drawn up in 1892, shows, he was in the 1880s a good deal less lavish with his use of honours than Lord Salisbury, who fulsomely rewarded his supporters, especially during his minority government of 1885–6, with a shower of every sort of status promotion. Though the Liberals were in a clear minority in the Lords, considerably fewer Liberal peers (84) were created in the eleven years of Liberal governments between 1868 and 1892 than were Conservative peers (101) in the twelve years of Conservative rule between 1874 and 1892.

---

* 16 July 81.

Salisbury ensured that the House of Lords was not only packed but crammed with Tory peers.

	Peers	Privy Councillors	Baronets	Knights*
Gladstone 1868–74	42	56	31	117
Disraeli 1874–80	37	56	32	82
Gladstone 1880–5	33	39	34	97
Salisbury 1885–6	14	25	16	24
Gladstone 1886	9	17	4	25
Salisbury 1886–92	50	54	63	193

Gladstone, always a stickler for form, was cautious in these matters and would not create peers except when a peerage was clearly deserved and strongly supported. Acton in 1869 was perhaps his only idiosyncratic creation. Even the eighty-four creations are a little misleading, for of the thirty-three peers created in 1880–5, twelve were promotions within the peerage and one was a royal duke. But there were, of course, restrictions of a less personal character. Since Gladstone accepted that the conventions were not to be set aside, there were by the mid-1880s fewer suitable Liberal candidates than Conservatives for these positions. It was difficult to find Liberals for the peerage who passed the usual tests and who would remain loyal Liberals, and whose children were likely to be loyal Liberals: there was no point in increasing the Tory peerage a generation into the future. It was the job of J. A. Godley and Edward Hamilton, Gladstone's private secretaries, to make discreet inquiries about such matters. Moreover, the dignity of the peerage and the absorption of the new Peer into a political culture suffused if not dominated by what was now on most issues an intensely partisan Court at Windsor, if not at Sandringham, encouraged conservatism in newly created Liberal peers. The Lords did not have to vote on the Government of Ireland Bill of 1886, but the split in the Liberal party in that House was at least as serious as that in the Commons.

This failure to build a Liberal peerage was exemplified in an angry public exchange in July 1886 between Gladstone and Westminster, whom he had created a duke in 1874 and who campaigned energetically against the Liberal government in 1886.† The Duke of Westminster was not aberrant. Of the thirty-three peers created during the government of 1880–5, at least 20 were Unionists after 1886 (and four others were dead). Of those 33, at most eight were active Liberals after 1886. Whereas for a Conservative a

---

* Secretary's tables made in 1892, at Add MS 44775, f. 278.

† Westminster had been annoyed in 1881 at not being made volunteer *aide de camp* at Court; Rosebery noted: 'he has been made a Duke, a K.G., & Ld. Lieut & his brother patronage secretary for no service that I can make out except the one for leading the other for whipping the party that turned WEG out in 1866. The fact is that Westminster is a very good noble fellow, but a spoilt child' (Rosebery's diary, 28 June 1881).

peerage was an additional bond with his party, for many a Liberal it was a solvent.

Two of Gladstone's creations in the 1880s rose above the usual routine of political worth, and both of them were his holiday companions on sea voyages to Scandinavia. Thomas Brassey, son of the railway magnate, and founder of the *Naval Annual* and a social commentator, took Gladstone on a cruise to Norway on his famous yacht, *Sunbeam*, in 1885. In 1886, though he had not risen above the rank of parliamentary undersecretary, he was created baron, his wealth, increasingly deployed in land and leisure, enabling him to leap-frog most of his official colleagues.

The Brassey voyage, during which Gladstone wrote his manifesto for the 1885 election, was less dramatic than the Tennyson voyage two years earlier. In September 1883 Tennyson was part of the company on the cruise to Norway on Donald Currie's *Pembroke Castle*. Indeed Tennyson got Gladstone into a 'scrape' with the Queen, for it was at the former's request that the steamer made an unplanned visit to Copenhagen, pitching Gladstone, without permission from the Queen, into a huge gathering of Eastern European royalty. Angry rebukes from Windsor followed. In the course of the voyage, Tennyson raised the question of the baronetcy which he had previously declined, indicating that this time he would accept. Alerted to this by Arthur Gordon, Gladstone was agreeable. Gordon recorded

I then asked him whether he did not think he might go a step further and offer Mr. Tennyson a peerage. His first answer was characteristic: 'Ah! Could I be accessory to introducing *that hat* into the House of Lords?'[*]

Enquiries were made about Tennyson's financial position and as to whether he would vote in the Lords 'if an urgent question of state-policy required it'; the offer of a barony was formally made and accepted with protestations of reluctance.[†] Some delay of the announcement was felt suitable 'to dissociate the peerage from the trip'. In a letter characteristically analysing the precedents, Gladstone arranged with the Treasury for Tennyson's patent fee, about £500, to be waived: 'I propose to let Tennyson off. Macaulay appears to have paid; but he was a confirmed bachelor & there was no succession.'[‡] Gladstone discreetly forbore to mention that Macaulay had made so much money from his *History* that £500 was of no account, whereas Tennyson's profitable earnings—never very large—were in 1883 long in the past, a point on which Tennyson almost morbidly dwelt. Despite attempts to link Tennyson to Liberalism, he sat on the cross-benches and during the autumn session of 1884 on the Franchise Bill

[*] *The Gladstone Papers* (1930), 80–1.
[†] See R. B. Martin, *Tennyson. The unquiet heart* (1980), 539ff.
[‡] To Childers, 25 Sept. 83.

issued his sonnet, 'Compromise', with its admonitory opening, 'Steersman, be not precipitate in thine act'—lines, Gladstone may have felt, better addressed to the House of Lords than to himself.

Patronage, Painters, and Portraits

Gladstone also wished to reward the pre-Raphaelite artists, a school with which he had been associated since the 1850s, and with which additional links, particularly with Burne-Jones, were made by his daughter Mary. A crop of artists, their lack of respectability now sufficiently in the past to be ignored, was to be given baronetcies (Ellen Terry, Watts's divorced wife, was an interesting link to the Irving set). This plan led to considerable rancour. Gladstone wanted to baronet G. F. Watts (who had painted him three times, the third time, as we shall shortly see, unsuccessfully), J. E. Millais (whose second portrait was then in the process of being painted), and Frederic Leighton. Gladstone tentatively mentioned the three names, while feeling that the Queen 'would (*justly*) think the number too large'. She did. Leighton was dropped, to the Queen's irritation. So two baronetcies were offered, to Watts and Millais. Despite prior indication that he would accept, Watts declined. Leighton already knew of the offers to the other two and in such circumstances could not be offered the title which Watts had declined. Gladstone anyway had ceased to be Prime Minister and was thus 'out of court'. Robert Browning interceded on Leighton's behalf; Gladstone told Ponsonby of the muddle, and Leighton got a baronetcy in February 1886.

Millais was delighted with his baronetcy, the more so, perhaps, as his behaviour towards Gladstone had been rather odd. So also, in a very different way, had been that of Watts. The episode of a Gladstone portrait for his old college of Christ Church, Oxford, merits a short detour, for it involved both artists. The college—a predominantly Liberal one under Dean Liddell—wanted a portrait of its distinguished member and in 1874 commissioned one from G. F. Watts (who had painted two earlier portraits of Gladstone from sittings beginning in 1859). Watts began his third portrait in May 1874 and there were various sittings between then and 1879. In 1876 Gladstone noted of them: 'Delightful conversation, but little progress on the picture' and in 1878: 'Sat to Watts from 12 to 4. He would but for courtesy willingly have had more. This length of time is really a vice in English artists.' At last the picture was hung in Christ Church Hall, but opinion at the annual Gaudy feast—not the best moment for aesthetic judgement—rejected it. The canvas was returned to Watts in 1879 who 'partially defaced it in the hope of making a more satisfactory likeness'. Eventually, in 1881, after further sittings proved difficult to arrange, Watts returned his fee to the College and kept the picture.* The next attempt was

---

* There is a small photograph of the portrait in the Watts Museum near Guildford. Mary Gladstone noted: 'To see the Watts picture of Papa, couldn't bear it—a weak, peevish old man; quite

by William Blake Richmond, son of George Richmond whose beautiful portraits of William and Catherine Gladstone are reproduced in the first volume of this biographical study. W. B. Richmond had painted Gladstone in 1867 but his effort in 1882 was not a success. It was 'shewn in [the] Grosvenor Gallery, and condemned'.* The college tried again, commissioning Millais in 1884. Millais had painted Gladstone in 1878 in a three-quarter length portrait, a pair with one of Disraeli painted at about the same time. On that occasion the initiative had been Millais'. He had told Gladstone, 'I have often wished to paint your portrait . . . one hour at a time is all I would wish.' In fact the sittings for that first portrait were sometimes two hours, but the picture was finished in under a month in five sittings. Gladstone noted during the sittings that Millais' 'ardour & energy about his picture inspire a strong sympathy'. The portrait is now in the National Portrait Gallery with its Disraeli pair. Fine as an image, it gives little sense of power and presents Gladstone in a passive attitude, looking elegant if a little effeminate, echoing the Tractarian quality of George Richmond's earlier drawing (which Millais would have known, as it was one of a published series done of members of Grillion's Club). Very different were the two portraits of Gladstone painted by Millais in 1884–5, the second eventually fulfilling Christ Church's commission. Sittings began in July 1884, the day before the Lords threw out the Franchise Bill. A reference photograph was taken by Rupert Potter, father of Beatrix Potter the writer and illustrator, so that Millais could reduce the number of sittings. Millais was excited: 'Only a moment to write, so hard at work. I have Gladstone better than the first time . . . I never did so fine a portrait.'† All was thus set fair for a triumph for Christ Church and a great satisfaction for Gladstone, devoted as he was to Oxford and to art. However, a most curious intervention then took place. Lord Rosebery visited Millais' studio to see the portrait of his daughter, in preparation alongside that of Gladstone. Rosebery noted in his diary:

To Millais' studio where Peggy's portrait finished. Gladstone's half finished. M. very pleased & straightforward. Peggy will cost 2000£—he will paint a kitcat for Ch.Ch. of Gladstone & let me have this for 1000£.‡

Rosebery, in other words, was to have Millais' finest portrait, while the body that commissioned it was to have a half-length copy. In fact, all turned

wretched over it'; *Mary Gladstone (Mrs. Drew). Her diaries and letters*, ed. Lucy Masterman (1930) [subsequently: *Mary Gladstone*], 143.

* See Christ Church Governing Body Minutes, i. 298, 301. The chronology in A. M. W. Stirling, *The Richmond Papers* (1926), 236, is hopelessly muddled, confusing W. B. Richmond's portraits of 1867 and 1882.   † J. G. Millais, *Life and Letters of Sir J. E. Millais* (1899), ii. 166.

‡ Rosebery's diary, 14 November 1884. See also Christ Church Governing Body Index to Minutes (Po): 'Millais undertook to paint Mr. Gladstone's Portrait for Ch. Ch. This portrait Millais sold to Lord Rosebery for (on dit) 1000£ & was then going to send us a Replica; but Mr. Gladstone sat again, & the result is the Portrait now in Hall.'

out well in the end. Rosebery bought the 1884 Millais (it is now in Eton College), but Gladstone, hearing of the strange transaction, refused to let Christ Church be fobbed off with a copy and offered to sit again. In the summer of 1885 there were three more sittings, just as Gladstone was resigning as Prime Minister. The portrait now in Christ Church (and reproduced in this volume) was hung in the Hall in October 1885, a much better picture than the one now in Eton, for in the 1885 version Millais captured magnificently the angry glare of Gladstone at bay. Thus ended the long saga of the portrait for Christ Church. Rosebery, another Christ Church man, may not have known that the picture was commissioned by the college. Millais obviously did know and his treatment both of his patron and of his subject made his baronetcy the more generous.

Church and Scholarship

Church patronage was equally problematic, but overall rather more satisfactory, even though it involved a further series of tussles with the Queen. By the 1880s, Gladstone saw the clergy, together with the army and the law, as part of the 'existence of powerful professional classes more or less sustained by privilege or by artfully constructed monopoly';* these classes he saw as increasingly deliberate buttresses of the Conservative Party: an 'Established Clergy will always be a tory Corps d'Armée'.† He deplored 'the unmitigated Toryism of the bulk of the clerical body'.‡ This view of the clergy encouraged him to make Liberal appointments, *ceteris paribus*. He was distanced from the Queen in this area by G. V. Wellesley, Dean of Windsor, who had the confidence of both and acted as mediator. Even so, on A. P. Stanley's death in 1881, Gladstone lost the filling of the Deanery of Westminster, the Queen's candidate, G. G. Bradley, being appointed. This was a difference about personalities rather than politics, for Bradley was a Liberal. 'Does she really think the two positions of Sovereign & Minister are to be inverted?' Gladstone expostulated to Wellesley. In the Westminster case, they were.

Wellesley's death in September 1882 seemed a sharp blow to Gladstone as it removed a buffer between the Queen and himself on what was—at least for him—the tenderest of subjects: 'with few of my colleagues have I taken as much personal counsel as with him [Wellesley] during the last 14 years. . . . I reckoned his life the most precious in the Church of England',§

---

* 14 Aug. 82. † To Harcourt, 3 July 85.
‡ To Bp. Goodwin, 8 Sept. 81.
§ To Anson, 19 Sept. 82; and see 18 Sept. 82. Wellesley's death in the middle of Tait's fatal illness made the filling of the archbishopric of Canterbury, eventually by Benson against the Queen's wishes, even more problematic. After recommending Benson, Gladstone thought he might not prevail and covered himself by consulting Jacobson, bishop of Chester, about Benson and E. H. Browne (Gladstone's original preference). The dispute about Benson coincided with the Queen's obstruction of aspects of the government reshuffle.

a noteworthy assessment made two days after the death of E. B. Pusey. As it happened, after the difficulty of appointing E. W. Benson to Canterbury was got round—Gladstone prevailing over the Queen with a candidate about whom he had some reservations—there were few contentious church appointments until a flurry of sees early in 1885. In the meantime Benson, an underestimated figure, gave what was in the circumstances rather a brave support to the Liberal government over the reform crisis in 1884 and provided something of a balance to the disciplinarian, conservative ethos of Tait's last years.*

Political allegiance in clerical appointments was thus of importance, but it should not be overstressed. Gladstone was probably more exercised over the church party affiliation of candidates for preferment. Challenged by the Queen for appointing too many High-Churchmen, he made a devastating statistical response: only eleven out of thirty places had gone to High-Churchmen in the early years of his second administration; his main fault was that, of the residue, the Broad Church was disproportionately higher in representation than the Low. Suitable Evangelical candidates for bishoprics were hard to find with 'the Evang. party now so barren'. Gladstone rose at 5.00 a.m. one morning at Hawarden to telegraph Ponsonby not to put to the Queen his recommendation of James Moorhouse for the see of Southwell; he had been troubled in the night by thinking about a report that Moorhouse had allowed a presbyterian to preach in his cathedral in Melbourne.†

Gladstone spent a great deal of time over these appointments aided by E. W. Hamilton, his secretary and the son of a bishop, and his daughter Mary. The Prime Minister's peculiar position as the fulcrum of clerical patronage made him central to the effective discharge of what Gladstone called 'the working energy of the Church'.‡ The search for suitable appointees had a peculiar fascination for Gladstone. He enjoyed mentally filing away potential candidates and could recall strengths and weaknesses years after hearing a sermon. His ingenuity was always stretched by Welsh sees. He was particularly concerned to show the Welshness of the Anglican Church in Wales, as he believed Nonconformity was a recent deviation, Wales during the Civil War having been 'a great stronghold of the Church: so says Mr Hallam.... Puritanism struck there but small and feeble roots.'§

* Gladstone tried to secure the release of S. F. Green, the rector of Miles Platting imprisoned for ritualism under the Public Worship Regulation Act, whose passing in 1874 Gladstone had vigorously opposed; his tactic was to release Green for ill-health; Harcourt, the Home Secretary and a strong supporter of the Act, disliked this, as did Green, who did not want release on a compromise. On the other hand, having failed to secure a compromise, Gladstone was careful not to be drawn into the agitation for the release of Green, treating his case with a certain caution ('Ecce aeternum Greene').

† 15 Jan. 84; see also to Benson, 20 Apr. 84.

‡ To Ponsonby, 14 June 83.   § To Bevan, 13 May 83.

A vacancy in a Welsh see costs me more trouble than six English vacancies. I feel it my duty to ascertain if possible by a process of exhaustion whether there is any completely fit person to be had among men of Welsh mother tongue. In the main it is a business of constantly examining likely or plausible cases & finding they break down. The Welsh are to be got at through the pulpit: & yet here is a special danger, for among the more stirring Welsh clergy there is as much wordy & windy preaching as among the Irish.*

In the case of the see of Llandaff, the process was literally exhausting, as it contributed to the insomnia which drove Gladstone to recuperate in Cannes in January 1883.

Less arduous, indeed almost off-hand, was Gladstone's treatment of the vacancy in the Regius Chair of Modern History at Oxford which he created by sending William Stubbs to the see of Chester in 1884. As was his usual practice with Oxford appointments, Gladstone wrote for advice to H. G. Liddell, the moderately Liberal Dean of Christ Church. Gladstone mentioned S. R. Gardiner and Mandell Creighton as possibilities, but thought E. A. Freeman, the medievalist and Liberal campaigner, as 'the first Oxford man by far', perhaps even unjustly treated when Stubbs was appointed in 1866: a remarkable judgement. Gladstone noted that Freeman 'is a strong Liberal. I fear he makes enemies and I am told he is little versed in manuscripts . . . [but] he would give a powerful impulsion to historical study at Oxford.'† How the Dean responded to this is unknown, but his reply, if made, was probably redundant. The same day, Freeman wrote to the Prime Minister proposing himself for the chair, very possibly the only occasion on which a Regius Chair has been applied for. Gladstone told Freeman next day that he had submitted his name to the Queen, and concluded: 'I anticipate with lively satisfaction the introduction into academical life of a fresh and solid piece of not less stout than healthy Liberalism, as well as the great impulse which your depth, range and vigour will impart, in our beloved Oxford, to a study so vital to all the best interests of man.'‡ It is unlikely that Gladstone would have used so political a tone in his first government; it reflects the stronger concern for a liberal historicism which he had developed during the campaigns of the late 1870s, as well as the increasingly partisan temper of the times.

A more successful use of patronage in academic matters was the award of a Civil List pension to James Murray to aid him in his work on his dictionary.§ The pension meant that the State effectively bore a third of the editor's salary and also encouraged Oxford University in its support for that remarkable work. The pension for Murray was an exception to

---

* To Lightfoot, 28 Dec. 82.
† To Liddell, 13 Feb. 84.
‡ To Freeman, 14 Feb. 84.
§ 1 Oct. 81 and K. M. E. Murray, *Caught in the web of words* (1977), 236.

Gladstone's usual rule, that the ancient universities had large endowments to enable them rather than the State to fund institutions such as the new British School in Athens. Gladstone was happy to speak as a private person in support of the School, but he refused a request for government money for it.* In the case of the dictionary, he had a high opinion of Murray, whom he first met in 1879 and with whom he corresponded on lexicography, and he probably recognized the unique importance of the dictionary. He was also, in Murray's case, supporting an individual rather than an institution.

Leader of the House

Leadership of the House of Commons was another routine call on Prime-Ministerial time, and a very considerable call it was. As with church services, Gladstone always noted in his diary his attendance at the Commons and the time spent there. When he was piloting a bill as well as leading the House, this could be lengthy. In July 1882—the month of the Egyptian crisis—he spent 148 hours on the Treasury bench, an average of nearly seven hours per day and night (he frequently sat on the bench until after 1.00 a.m.). In that month, he was not only answering frequent questions and guiding the passage of the Arrears Bill, but he had to take over the Egyptian Vote of Credit as well: 'spoke (40m) in winding up at Hartington's request, who was to have done the work'. In a very easy month, and leading on no bill, as, for example, June 1883, he still attended the House every day it sat except four, and averaged almost six hours on those days that he attended.

Gladstone usually broke from the Commons for dinner at 8.15 for about an hour. Sometimes he dined at home at Downing Street, sometimes with one of his secretaries, sometimes with a friend (almost always one like Sir Charles Forster, not of the first or even of the second political rank: rarely with another Cabinet minister), occasionally at The Club or Grillion's, and only very occasionally at a political club as a guest. At Grillion's he once dined alone, noting in the club's minute book this couplet from *Paradise Lost*:

> The mind is its own place, and in itself
> Can make a heaven of hell, a hell of heaven.†

This solitary occasion in 1885 was commemorated by Lord Houghton (formerly Monckton Milnes), Poet Laureate to the club, in some sharp verses:

> Trace we the workings of that wondrous brain,
> Warmed by one bottle of our dry champagne;
> Guess down what streams those active fancies wander,
> Nile or Ilissus? Oxus or Scamander?

---

* To Jebb, 6 Feb. 83 and 18 May, 25 June 83.
† *Grillion's Club. A chronicle 1812—1913* (1914), 96.

Sees he, as lonely knife and fork he plies,
Muscovite lances—Arab assegais?
Or patient till the food and feuds shall cease,
Waits his des(s)ert—the blessed fruits of peace?
Yes, for while penning this impetuous verse,
We know that when (as mortals must) he errs,
'Tis not from motive of imperious mind,
But from a nature which will last till death,
Of love-born faith that grows to over-faith,
Till reason and experience both grow blind
To th'evil and unreason of mankind.*

Houghton's tone, moving from the genial to the acerbic, shows why it was that during the sessions of the 1880s Gladstone was rather careful about the extent to which he offered himself to a London society which he regarded as increasingly illiberal, corrupt, 'ploutocratic', and isolated from the Liberalism of non-metropolitan Britain. But beyond this, Gladstone probably had enough of exclusively male political society in the House of Commons. He enjoyed the company of women. Having resigned from the Reform Club on resigning as Prime Minister in 1874 (he had only joined on the chief whip's insistence), he did not rejoin in 1880; though President of the new National Liberal Club, he did not use it as a club and only went there when required to make a speech.

The great procedural reforms of 1882 did not lead to a reform of Gladstone's parliamentary habits. He reduced the burden in one minor but significant way: questions to the Prime Minister, hitherto indiscriminately intermingled with the other questions, themselves in no particular order, were on Gladstone's suggestion to the Speaker† gathered into batches as were those of other ministers, thus beginning what later became 'Prime Minister's Question Time'.

There was little complaint about these hours spent listening and speaking. Gladstone enjoyed the House and enjoyed being an 'old Parliamentary hand'. 'Peel', he recalled, 'once said to me when I was going to speak officially "don't be short".'‡ Gladstone could certainly never be accused of neglecting that advice. He relished the procedures of the House and their manipulation, and he respected those who used them as resourcefully as himself. Apart from their spasms of obvious obstruction, he admired the way the Home Rulers used the House in Committee: their mastery of the details of legislation and of procedure. He saw in this the essential constitutionality of their politics, a broadminded view considering that it was

* Ibid.
† See to Brand, 3 July 81; Gladstone at the same time suggested that his questions should come last, but this did not happen.
‡ To Kimberley, 8 May 83.

often at him that their tactics were directed. Gladstone disliked the tone of the 'Fourth Party', complaining to his daughter that Balfour's comments on Kilmainham were 'the almost raving licence of an unbridled tongue'* (he especially resented the violent personal comments of Balfour, a friend and a frequent guest), and noting on reading Churchill's anonymous article 'Elijah's Mantle': 'very cleverly *written*, but a sad moral bathos'.† But he respected the 'Fourth Party's' toughness and resource, and was easily drawn into verbal scrapping with its members. Despite his complaints about Balfour, the latter continued to be a family friend and a visitor to Hawarden. It was Stafford Northcote's supposed lack of back-bone in his role as Leader of the Opposition that Gladstone despised: 'really weaker than water' was his repeated dismissal of his former private secretary.

This brief survey of areas of routine Prime-Ministerial activity shows that, while great causes were the stated reason for Gladstone's continuation in office and while on occasion he might act the part of a retired person, he was certainly not idle in routine matters. Indeed, his attention to Court and parliamentary detail was, if anything, overdone. For a man in his seventies, his vigour was exceptional. Even so, it is hardly surprising that the pace of the 1880 government caused strains and breakdowns. We now turn, therefore, to the private Gladstone.

* To Helen Gladstone, 17 May 82.
† 14 May 83.

CHAPTER XII

Behind the Scenes

*Relaxation: Reading and the Stage—Always on show—Propping up the
'G.O.M.'—The Private Secretariat in the 1880s—Ill-health and Insomnia—
Houses and Weekending in the 1880s—Rescue Work: Warnings and a Promise—
Laura Thistlethwayte in the early 1880s—Gladstone and the
Spiritualists—Gladstone's Diary and Ireland—Looking forward from 1886*

16. [October 1884] Th.
Ch. 8½ A.M. Wrote to The Queen l.l.l.—Mr Downing—Ld
Spencer—Mr Trevelyan—Mr H. Tracy—Mr C. Bannerman—Ld
Derby—Mr Hamilton. 1–5¾. To Birkenhead for Railway function.
Two speeches: great enthusiasm. 100,000 people out: or nearly. Read
Caroline Bauer—Reid's Sydney Smith.

17 Fr.
Ch. 8½ A.M. Wrote to Bp of St Asaph—The Queen l.l.—Watsons—
Ld Granville—Ld Spencer—Ld Winmarleigh—Mr Hamilton—&
minutes. Our friends went. We began to cut the obnoxious tall Elm
by the keep. Commenced a long letter to Bp of St Asaph. Read
Karoline Bauer and Reid's Life of S. Smith.

18. Sat. St Luke.
Agnes's birthday. Ch. 8½ AM & H.C. Wrote to Ld Granville Tel.
l.l.—Mr. Childers Tel.—Att. General—Messrs Robertson—Sir E.
Watkin—Mr Hamilton Tel.—Ld Spencer Tel.—and minutes. Began
l. to Bp of St A. Read Life of Sydney Smith. Finished the astonishing Memoirs of Karoline Bauer. A party of 40 or 50 came to tea: &
we had the fall of a great Elm by the keep for them.*

Relaxation: Reading and the Stage

Gladstone rather haphazardly protected himself from the consequences of
old age and overstrain and was in his turn rather more systematically
protected by the Gladstonian circle, by the 1880s a well-defined body.

First, his relaxation. Gladstone read prolifically. Though he kept very
well up to date with the questions of the day, as a glance at the diary will
show, his reading is, taken as a whole, less policy-orientated in his second
and third governments than in his first. He particularly enjoyed memoirs of

---

* Diary for 16–18 Oct. 84; characteristic entries during the parliamentary recess.

court life and read extensively on the French eighteenth-century court, for example Touchard-Lafosse's *Chronique de l'oeil-de boeuf*, a large work on the *petits apartements* of the Louvre. The records of the French monarchy of the *ancien régime* may have encouraged him in his tussles with the Queen. He read the novels of the day, Shorthouse's *John Inglesant* being of particular interest to him, with Henry James's *Madonna of the Future* and *Daisy Miller*, Olive Schreiner's *The Story of an African Farm*, and many lesser works which made an impact in their time, such as Annie S. Swan's *Aldersyde* and General Wallace's *Ben-Hur*. He reread much of Cervantes, Defoe, Dickens, George Eliot, and, as always, Walter Scott, and partially caught up with Disraeli, reading *Sybil* for the first time in February 1884. He made no comment on the latter, but sometimes his telegraphic diary notation of his reading conveys a paragraph in a phrase: 'Silas Marner, finished—noble, though with spots'; 'Finished S. African Farm. A most remarkable, painful, book'; 'Read through Kidnapped [at a sitting]: a book to be recommended.'* Outside fiction, he ranged eclectically from 'Muggletonian Hymns!!'† through Olga Janina's *Souvenirs d'un Pianiste*, 'an almost incredible book', to the *Kama Sutra*, no comment recorded. He was also capable of letters of a high order of literary criticism, as for example his observations on Mary Wollstonecraft in whom he became considerably interested. The reader who follows Gladstone's non-political reading and writing through these years of office would think he or she was pursuing a rather well-occupied *littérateur*.

A particular pleasure was helping in the preparation of biographies of his former contemporaries in many of which he was a principal character. He continued to supply letters for and read the proofs of the *Life of Samuel Wilberforce*; he prepared materials, helped with research, and read all the proofs of the *Life of James Hope-Scott*, and he much enjoyed reading Milnes Gaskell's *Records of an Eton schoolboy* (1883). He had a high estimate of John Morley's *Life of Cobden*—'it is one more added to the not very long list of our real biographies'—in whose preparation he had, as a correspondent and as a trustee of Cobden's MSS, been considerably involved. Out of office, he made papers and his library available to C. S. Parker, the Liberal MP, for the preparation of his *Papers of Sir Robert Peel*. He read enthusiastically about his own past in these and various other works, complaining to John Murray in December 1884 about the index to the *Croker Papers*: 'the Index is rather *thin*. I find in it two references following my own name. I have

---

* 30 July 86 (out of office); he also read Stevenson's *Dr Jekyll and Mr Hyde*, *Treasure Island*, and *The New Arabian Nights*, the last two perhaps at the suggestion of Henry James, the novelist, whom he met at Rosebery's house, The Durdans, in April 1884 (see p. 539).

† 13 Dec. 81. He followed this up, trying to buy a Muggletonian hymnbook ('uncut') from a bookseller's catalogue. This interest is an unusual confirmation of the continued presence in the public mind of the seventeenth-century sect; see W. Lamont, 'The Muggletonians 1652–1979: a "vertical" approach', *Past and Present*, xcix. 739 (1983).

noted in the text at least twelve. What is more important, such a point as the authorship of the Waverley Novels p. 351 is not noticed except under Croker, where it might not be looked for.' He also read widely in the other biographies of the day, taking a particular interest in the 'Life of Miss Evans' (as he archly called J. W. Cross's life of George Eliot (often spelt 'Elliot' by Gladstone)); he found time in the midst of the Gordon crisis to regret that his daughter Mary and Acton had 'lifted her above Walter Scott . . . yet I freely own she was a great woman. I have not yet got to the bottom of her ethical history.'*

Gladstone was also quite a regular theatre-goer, and moved enthusiastically among the Irving–Terry set as well as frequently visiting performances of drawing-room comedies and dramas. He continued to visit Henry Irving's notable series of Shakespeare productions at the Lyceum, often going backstage after the performance: 'Saw Miss Terry behind' as he unfortunately put it. Gladstone hoped to get a knighthood for Irving, but the actor's lack of respectability—his estrangement from his wife and his friendship for Ellen Terry—prevented this plan from going forward. Gladstone's view of the objections raised to a knighthood may be judged from his subsequent invitation to Irving to visit Hawarden; unfortunately, the dates were not convenient, but they met instead in October 1883 at Derby's house, Knowsley—a notable promotion for the profession of the stage. Friendship with Irving was the context of Gladstone's well-blazoned friendship with Lillie Langtry, whom he first notes meeting in January 1882, soon afterwards going to see her in Robinson's 'Ours' at the Haymarket. The friendship, from Gladstone's point of view, was much less important than contemporary rumour suggested, though such rumours were not surprising, given Lillie Langtry's reputation and the gossip about Gladstone's nocturnal activities circulating in the clubs. He noted: 'I hardly know what estimate to make of her. Her manners are very pleasing, & she has a working spirit in her.'† In February 1885 he noted: 'saw Mrs Langtry: probably for the last time'.‡

Gladstone took a considerable interest in foreigners playing in London. He attended a performance of 'The Winter's Tale' in German, presented by the visiting Saxe-Meiningen Court Theatre; when the American actress Mary Anderson played Juliet at the Lyceum he saw the performance and later arranged a large breakfast at 10 Downing Street, a notable recognition of a famous production but also an important step in the growing respectability of the theatre.§ A very different American import was Buffalo Bill Cody's Wild West Show: Gladstone enjoyed the 'marvellous equitation',

* To Acton, 11 Feb. 85.
† 3 Apr. 82. ‡ 16 Feb. 85.
§ 8 Nov. 84, 23 Apr. 85 (on which day he also saw her in a double bill at The Lyceum, 'Pygmalion' and 'Comedy and Tragedy').

had a 'sumptuous luncheon', chatted to 'Red Shirt' (a Sioux chief) and spoke on Anglo-American cordiality, 'an easy subject'.*

A new development for Gladstone was an interest in operas and musicals: he may have been encouraged in this by E. W. Hamilton, a knowledgeable and regular opera-goer. Gladstone went to 'The Phantom of the Ship of Wagner' and was seen clapping enthusiastically;† he saw MacKenzie's 'Colomba' and the Carl Rosa Company in 'Carmen'. He went with Granville—rather a suitable choice—to 'Iolanthe'; he later, out of office, went to 'The Mikado', and heard George Grossmith, the D'Oyly Carte's patter-singer, at a private cabaret ('very entertaining but less than on the stage').‡

Always on show

For all the cares of office and of the Commons, Gladstone had rather a jovial time in the 1880s; his general boisterousness is confirmed by the various accounts of his dancing with his wife and frequently singing songs at dinner such as 'My 'art is true to Poll'.§ This persistent good cheer, most frequently exemplified by a stream of miscellaneous but erudite conversation, at first almost always charmed. It reflected the natural confidence, curiosity, and ebullience of his character. But it probably had a purpose also. Gladstone knew the significance of the actor's craft, directly comparing his own with it,¶ and he knew, as he said with respect to public speaking, how to 'put on the steam'.‖ In this period, he knew that even every private dinner party was a performance for the record: it was almost certain that one of the guests would note his conversation and mood in a letter or diary. He knew that between E. W. Hamilton and his daughter Mary most of what he did or said, and particularly every sign of frailty, went into their diaries. When he went to Norway on the *Sunbeam* in August 1885, at least four of the company were keeping diaries; that of his hostess, Lady Brassey, was immediately published in the *Contemporary Review*. He must have been when in company as constantly on his guard as an actor on the stage.

Margot Tennant, later Asquith, who became a friend of the family in these years, thought Gladstone had 'a tiger smile'.** Derby, when exposed at some length to Gladstone's conversation when he stayed at Knowsley, was at first captivated, but then had second thoughts: 'For the first time, a suspicion crossed my mind that there is something beyond what is quite healthy in this perpetual flow of words—a beginning perhaps of old age.'††

* 28 Apr. 87.   † 10 Mar. 82.
‡ 4 Dec. 82; 29 July 85; 10 Aug. 86.   § *Mary Gladstone*, 313 (1 May 1884).
¶ See to Mrs Tennyson, 14 Nov. 82.
‖ A recurring metaphor, see 30 July 78, 3 Apr. 84.
** Countess of Oxford and Asquith, *Off the Record* (1943), 47.
†† Derby's account of Gladstone's visit to Knowsley, October 1883, quoted in *The Gladstone Diaries*, Vol. XI, Appendix I.

It is more likely that it was not old age in the sense of senility or loss of grip but a calculated attempt to keep old age at bay which in the case of the Knowsley visit was taken too far. The flow of words produced entertainment and offered flattery; it suggested intimacy across the generations while at the same time preserving distance. For a man whose close friends were all dead—Sir Robert Phillimore, the last friend who was an old crony rather than being in some way politically involved or obliged, died in 1885*—such an emphasis on this aspect of his personality was advantageous. It allowed Gladstone to present himself in an engaging character, which by its nature allowed him to keep a little apart from those who were now his contemporaries. Much is made of Gladstone's lack of self-consciousness. But Margot Tennant thought that 'this curious lack of self-consciousness, though flattering, was deceptive'.† It may well be that, by the 1880s, Gladstone's lack of self-consciousness was being consciously cultivated.

Propping up the 'G.O.M.'

Gladstone began his second government aged 70; he was 76 when he introduced the Government of Ireland Bill. A generation, or two generations, older than many of his colleagues, the 'Grand Old Man', as Labouchere dubbed him, needed carefully orchestrated support behind the scenes to a much greater extent than in his first government. The family circle and the 'Private Secretariat'—the two quite often tending to merge—were thus additional and increasingly important props. The Gladstone family was an integral part of a Gladstone administration. Catherine Gladstone always opposed her husband's attempts to resign. In October 1885, on the question of whether Gladstone should attempt to form another government after the election, Rosebery noted: 'his family has settled the question for him'.‡ Though Mrs Gladstone continued her charitable work and her assistance to sick relatives, her attention was much more than hitherto focused on her husband, and she was much less away from him than in his previous periods of office. She even helped at critical moments as secretary, her arthritic hand painfully adorning the copies of the letters, and she undertook a political mission to Rosebery, though without success, during the confusions about his position in January 1883. Gladstone took her support for granted, though from time to time he gave her an admiring mention in his diary. When apart, Gladstone wrote a short note or letter to her each day; the tone of these shows the extent to which a considerable level of political discussion was a part of their life when together. The letters almost

---

* Gladstone baronetted him in 1881; Phillimore was '"over the moon" with a most innocent delight'; Phillimore was perhaps the only confidant to encourage Gladstone to retire; see 10 Dec. 82.

† Countess of Oxford and Asquith, op. cit., 46.   ‡ 27 Oct. 85n.

always begin 'My own C.' and usually conclude 'Ever your afft. WEG' (occasionally 'Your most afft. WEG'). They show a Gladstonian style much more relaxed than the rather rigid correctness of most of his correspondence. Added to the rather formal subscription he used for letters to his wife, the effect is sometimes curious: 'I must however knock off, & am your ever afft. WEG'.

When the Gladstones were at Hawarden, the two oldest sons, Willy and Stephen, now respectively the squire and the rector (and aged 43 and 39 in 1883), helped out, putting up the parents, helping the tree-cutting, ferrying the guests. The strain told. Willy's political career languished. He did not stand in the 1885 election, partly because of the need to tend the Hawarden estates, and he opposed his father on Home Rule. He was with difficulty encouraged into editing the 1886 Irish speeches. He may well already have been affected by the brain tumour which killed him in 1891. The birth of his three children, Evelyn in 1882, Constance in 1883, and William Glynne Charles Gladstone, heir to Hawarden and killed in action in 1915, cheered his rather forlorn life as he worked to mitigate the consequences of the agricultural depression on the Hawarden estates. Stephen suffered a crisis of self-confidence as a result of holding the family rectory, one of the wealthiest in the land. He wished to go to India as a missionary because of a failed engagement and because at Hawarden he felt, as Rector, 'too closely related to what may be called the "temporal power" or the ruling family of the place'. Nothing came of this and he was, after his marriage in January 1885, much more settled at the Rectory.

Henry, the businessman, was in India for much of this time, the recipient of some of his father's most interesting letters. When at home he helped secretarially. He gradually established himself as the determining future influence on the family's fortunes and, within the family, as the most effective guardian of his father's reputation. Herbert was given the seat his father won in Leeds in 1880 and began to make his own political career in the form of an advanced version of aspects of his father's. Several visits to Ireland—he was unsuccessfully urged on Spencer as an assistant by the Prime Minister after the Phoenix Park murders—made him an important conduit of Home Rule opinion into the household. He, like the others, helped as secretary and as an important link with the party. He managed with considerable tact both to work with his father and to develop his own position—though the attempt to do both simultaneously broke down spectacularly in December 1885 with the 'Hawarden Kite'.

More important in the household than any of the sons was the second living daughter, Mary—known as 'Von Moltke' outside the circle. Much of the day-to-day organization of her parents—by the 1885 election aged 75 and 73—fell to her, especially out of Session. She discreetly organized the household at Hawarden and her obvious intelligence placed her on something like a par with visitors such as Acton. There is some indication that she screened Gladstone's fiction for him but probably not too much should be made of this. In February 1886 she married Harry Drew; as he was curate at Hawarden this marriage made much less difference to the working of the Gladstonian *ménage* than had that of the first daughter, Agnes, whose marriage in 1873 had taken her outside immediate contact with her parents. Helen, the youngest daughter, was outside such contact in term-time because of her Fellowship at Newnham, Cambridge. She turned down the offer of the headship of Royal Holloway College in 1886 as, unlike Newnham, it would prevent her being at Hawarden in the vacations to assist and sometimes relieve Mary's secretarial work.* On the fringes of the family circle was the tragic figure of Lucy Cavendish, Mrs Gladstone's niece, widow of the murdered Lord Frederick Cavendish whom Gladstone had from an early stage groomed for high office, much more than he had his sons. Lucy Cavendish—'altogether one of us'—was often at Hawarden; she was politically shrewd, was a committed Liberal, and acted as an additional link on a number of occasions with her brother-in-law Hartington. The Gladstones stayed with her at 21 Carlton House Terrace in January and February 1886, while the Home Rule Cabinet was being formed, and again after the defeat of the government.

With the partial exception of Willy, the Gladstone children were all strong political supporters of their father. Taken together, they offered a powerful political and domestic support to their parents, who expected one or other of them to be on hand as needed. With the exception of Agnes and her children at Wellington College, and H. N. Gladstone when in India, the Gladstones remained a very locally based family with the parents, whether in Downing Street or at one of the various houses at Hawarden, very much the focal point, an arrangement which seems to have been regarded as natural on both sides. Willy, Stephen, Herbert, Mary and, in the vacations, Helen, were each in their different ways powerful buttresses of a Gladstonian premiership, and Catherine Gladstone was its emotional and physical bedrock.

The Private Secretariat in the 1880s

The secretariat overlapped with this. As we have seen, several of the family helped with the secretarial work, even at the most confidential level. One of the official secretaries, Spencer Lyttelton, was Mrs Gladstone's nephew. The other secretaries also had close connections with Gladstone or other members of the Cabinet. Horace Seymour was Lord Spencer's brother-in-law; Henry Primrose, later the most dogmatic Gladstonian in the Edwardian Treasury, was Rosebery's cousin; George Leveson-Gower was

* It was characteristic of her relationship with her father that she only took charge of North Hall of Newnham College after he 'freely assented' to her so doing; 13 Jan. 82.

Granville's nephew. J. A. Godley was the son of J. R. Godley, the colonial reformer with whom Gladstone had worked in the 1850s on the Canterbury Association for settlement in New Zealand; Godley further related to the Gladstonian past by marrying the daughter of W. C. James, Lord Northbourne, once a Peelite MP and now one of Gladstone's oldest political friends. E. W. Hamilton, who succeeded Godley as principal private secretary in August 1882, was the son of W. K. Hamilton, one of Gladstone's closest undergraduate friends and with him at one of the most important moments of his life, the vocational crisis of 1830; Gladstone had helped to secure his bishopric against Broad and Low Church opposition. Sir James Carmichael, bart., on the secretarial staff in 1885 and again in 1886, had been Childers' secretary and was an authority on Egyptian land and finance; as such he was useful on Ireland in 1886. Unusually among Gladstone's Prime-Ministerial secretaries, he went on to a political rather than a civil service career.

Many of the functions of the secretaries were routine. Gladstone continued to write all important and many less important letters in his own hand. The secretaries copied these into the letter book when Gladstone marked the letter ✓ in the bottom left-hand corner, or, when he marked it ✓✓, onto a separate piece of paper.* They answered low-level non-official correspondence in his name and as these letters were often immediately published in the press considerable tact was required. Gladstone's confidence in them was well-justified. The secretaries also had a more complex role, liaising with the Queen's secretary, with Cabinet ministers and with MPs on points of policy. Here the emollient and cheerful Godley and Hamilton were rather effective, compensating to some extent for Gladstone's notorious absence from the lobbies and the tea-room, an absence the more remarkable considering the amount of time we have seen him spending in the House but on the front bench. Most of the secretaries—Seymour was the exception—formed strong personal bonds with Gladstone, who in most cases saw that they went on to influential posts in the civil service. But their relationships to the Cabinet Whigs meant that they also represented something of a watching brief for the whiggish section of the Cabinet on the innermost activities of the Premier.

The secretaries also delayed business or restrained Gladstone when they—particularly Hamilton—thought he was acting precipitately. Because

---

* When combined, these copies almost always provided a fuller record of Gladstone's outgoing correspondence (when in office) than the collection of holograph letters kept by the recipient; this may be in part because ministers often forwarded his letters to colleagues or civil servants for comment and they were not returned. Gladstone's own papers have curious gaps in the incoming correspondence—a surprisingly high number of his letters have no recorded reply, even when one was obviously called for. This may be because the reply was forwarded and not returned or because the reply was given verbally: not all ministers had Gladstone's appetite for writing or his enthusiasm for being 'on the record'.

they read the papers and letters going in and out, they were very well-informed. But the creative side of Downing Street policy-making came from Gladstone. The secretaries were not a *cabinet* in the sense of generating policy proposals or position papers. Hamilton played something of such a role in the preparation of the Irish land legislation in 1886, but by that time he was seconded by the Treasury and was not part of the Downing Street staff. To a remarkable extent, Downing Street's influence on politics was Gladstone's own. For all the support of family and secretaries, Gladstone remained, as he always had been, a rather solitary figure, usually at least one step ahead of those around him.

Ill-health and Insomnia

A government which depended so much on the Prime Minister's leadership also much depended on his health. Gladstone suffered from bad eyesight, bouts of diarrhoea, of lumbago, and of neuralgia in his face, chronically poor teeth, spells of insomnia and, in 1885, a loss of voice. His oculist, T. Henri, was not successful in preventing a marked decline in his eyesight; it may be that the '"Pure Periscopic" pebbles' which he fitted to Gladstone's pince-nez were not quite what was required. His doctor, Andrew Clark, and his dentist, Edwin Saunders, whom he respectively baronetted and knighted in 1883, kept him on the whole up to the mark with the assistance of Catherine Gladstone, who sent him to bed early when possible, administered quinine and chloroform and prepared the small bottles of sherry and egg to go by the despatch box in the Commons—one for an important speech, two for an exceptionally long one, such as the introduction of the Government of Ireland Bill. The Commons thus knew what to expect by the number of bottles on the table.

Despite their efforts, Gladstone was from time to time unwell, sometimes missing Cabinets at important moments, such as the wrangle over Gordon's request for the help of the slaver Zobeir Pasha.* Under the strain of Irish business in 1880, Gladstone's health gave way at the end of July. This was not the brief 'diplomatic' sort of illness quite often seen in the first government, but a real crisis. For the first time in half a century, death seemed possible, though not imminent: 'On Sunday I thought of the end—in case the movement [of temperature] had continued—coming nearer to it by a little than I had done before: but not as in expectation of it. C. read the service.' The possibility of resignation and the subsequent succession was discussed. Convalescence took the form of a speedy round-Britain cruise on Donald Currie's *Grantully Castle*, during which a brief stop was made, amongst other places, at Dublin, 'in time to land suddenly

---

* 9–18 Mar. 84; a heavy cold affecting the chest, larynx, and voice. The Cabinet met at Coombe Warren (Bertram Currie's house) where Gladstone was convalescing, but only after the decision to appoint Zobeir had been reversed; 29 Mar. 84.

& go to Christ Church [Cathedral]'. Thus almost the only visit to Ireland by a Prime Minister in office between the Act of Union and 1914 was to attend an Anglican church service as a result of ill-health.

Sometimes he was ill simply from nervous strain, as in the stress he felt as a result of the death of Beaconsfield in April 1881:

> At 8 a.m. I was much shocked on opening a Telegram to find it announced the death of Ld Beaconsfield, $3\frac{1}{2}$ hours before. The accounts 24 hours ago were so good. It is a telling, touching event. There is no more extraordinary man surviving him in England, perhaps none in Europe. I must not say much, in presence as it were of his Urn.
>
> I immediately sent to tender a public funeral. The event will entail on me *one* great difficulty; but God who sends all, sends this also.

This '*one* great difficulty' was that it fell to Gladstone, both as Prime Minister and as Leader of the House, to propose in the Commons a public memorial to the man whose premiership he believed had been a moral and a practical disgrace. The offer of the public funeral was declined; Gladstone was invited to the private one at Hughenden but told Rothschild that heavy engagements would prevent his attending. The next piece of Disraeliana was the Royal Academy dinner: 'Made my speech: this year especially difficult.'* This was because in the ante-room to the dining hall was prominently placed Millais' portrait of Beaconsfield—the pair to his portrait of 1878 of Gladstone. Comparison and comment was thus unavoidable; Gladstone turned the moment with a classical quotation. Next day he became ill with diarrhoea and remained inconvenienced or worse until the speech proposing the public monument was made six days later. As usually happens with such situations, the contemplation was worse than the action: 'Meditated over my very difficult task a little before the House; & I commit myself to God, who has ever helped me. . . . As to the Monument all went better than I could have hoped. . . .'† This was, obviously, a unique moment, the death of the only person in British politics with whom Gladstone had been able to strike no personal *rapport*. Gladstone comforted himself that there was at least a bond in their respective devotion to their wives.

Two longer illnesses are of particular note. December 1882 started badly with diarrhoea spoiling the end of the procedure debates. By the end of the month Gladstone—usually a sturdy sleeper even before a big parliamentary occasion—began to suffer from severe insomnia,‡ that most curious of conditions, which the exercise of the will compounds rather than alleviates. There was a clutch of causes: his wife's insomnia, a problem since the summer; the failure of his plans to resign; the anxieties and arguments with

---

* 30 Apr. 81.
† 9 May 81.
‡ First noted on 2 Jan. 83, but clearly earlier ('my sleep was further cut down . . .').

colleagues and with the Queen over the reshuffle; concern about the see of Llandaff; irritation at Rosebery's refusal to come easily into line; and anxiety about what to say at the meeting arranged for January 1883 in Midlothian. In these fraught circumstances, the husband's insomnia encouraged the wife's, and *vice versa*. Clark, summoned to Hawarden, prescribed rest, and Wolverton, intervening discreetly as always at a time of crisis, arranged for the Gladstones to stay at Château Scott, his villa in Cannes, a stay that was extended until after the session had begun in London. The Gladstones were thus away from 18 January to 26 February 1883. Gladstone's sleeping quickly revived but Catherine Gladstone's insomnia, deeper seated than her husband's, was much slower to improve. She kept a little diary of the visit, a rather desolate document with a hint of desperation in the scrawled hand. She noted the sleeping each night, usually referring to William Gladstone as 'he' or 'Husband': 'Not a good night but Husband sleeps very well *every night*!!!'*

Gladstone missed Westminster: 'I feel dual—I am at Cannes & in D. St at my [eve of session] dinner.' But he revelled in the break, enjoyed long walks and conversations with Acton, 'a most satisfactory mind', meeting the young Clemenceau—the conversation was overheard and reported in the *Daily News*—having lunch with the Comte de Paris, and inspecting the French ironclads. He commented on two old men whom he saw: 'Count Pahlen: aged 93. Suggestive of many thoughts' and Edward Cardwell, now senile, 'a sad spectacle, monitory of our lot'.†

The insomnia episode was a warning. Gladstone got over it quickly, and the relative inactivity of the 1883 session (partly the result of his absence from the January cabinets which effectively ducked the issue of Irish local government) helped to settle and relax him. There was a recurrence of insomnia in December 1884–January 1885, following the Seats Bill negotiations and a painful dispute within the Cabinet on Egyptian finance and, with sleep on one night down to an hour and a half, there was again talk of a retreat to Cannes. This time, however, the lack of sleep did not become chronic and rest at Hawarden proved a sufficient cure. Sometimes he read Walter Scott in bed to compose himself for sleep, and sometimes he 'took up a good supply of strawberries'.‡

Loss of voice in 1885 was the second of Gladstone's illnesses which seriously affected the pattern of his political behaviour. By the time of the resignation of the government in June 1885 he was seriously concerned about his speaking powers, referring in his memorandum on his future

* Catherine Gladstone's diary, written on loose sheets of paper, is in Mary Gladstone's papers, Add MS 46269, ff. 1–14.
† 23 Jan., 22 Feb. 83.
‡ To Mrs Gladstone, 1 July 86.

position to his need to restore them 'to something like a natural condition'.* Obviously enough, a Gladstone silenced would be a Samson shorn.
In early July he visited Oxford, staying with the Talbots at Keble College.
As usual there was a round of visits to town and gown—Christ Church,
New College, a tour of Headington, a visit to 'the "Puseum" so called [an
early version of Pusey House, commemorating E. B. Pusey]: disappointed:
in the House and Library'. Something, perhaps the dampness of the air in
that city of sore throats, markedly worsened his condition and medical
assistance was summoned. Next day he foolishly spoke for nearly an hour
in the Commons despite having seen Saunders, his dentist and throat
specialist, in the morning. Once a proper examination was made by
Saunders and Clark, 'silence rather rigidly enjoined [as] a condition of
fairly probable recovery. No House of Commons.'† Soon after, 'immediate
"treatment" of the throat decided on'. Mr Thistlethwayte presented him
with an 'aureoniophone'—presumably an amplification device of some
sort, possibly a hearing trumpet used as a loud speaker—but Gladstone
told Mrs Thistlethwayte that his needs went much beyond its powers.

Gladstone was suffering from acute vocal strain, nowadays called
'myaesthenia laryngis', a condition common enough among elderly actors,
less so today among politicians as their calling no longer requires such
prodigious or regular feats of vocal projection. Felix Semon, to whom
Saunders and Clark referred their patient, was the leading expert of the day
on cancer of the larynx. He diagnosed Gladstone's condition as 'chronic
laryngeal catarrh'.‡ In a series of twenty-one daily treatments between 18
July and 8 August 1885, Semon applied 'daily treatment by medicine & by
interior applications to the vocal chords as well as by galvanism outside'. It
may be that this treatment included cauterization of the polyps which are
sometimes part of this condition. Whether it was Semon's treatment or
simply rest which caused improvement cannot now be known. Gladstone
was uncertain whether the voyage to Norway in August 1885 on the
Brasseys' yacht *Sunbeam*, planned from the start as a part of the treatment,
was in fact beneficial, for the 'soft air is against my throat'. Clark accompanied him on the cruise and continued 'applications'. However, during
the Midlothian Campaign of November 1885 Gladstone was able to make a
series of speeches of over an hour each. Clearly he was not up to full power
and his performance on 28 November disheartened Rosebery and Hamilton.§ But to manage six major speeches, several of them to audiences of
over 2,000 without, of course, any form of amplification, was in the circumstances at the least satisfactory. There was a return of the condition just

---

* 16 June 85. The condition was noticed in 1881; to Kitson, 2 Oct. 81. For a previous period of
enforced silence (occasioned by a cough), see 18–22 Apr. 82.

† 14 July 85.

‡ 20 July 85.

§ See 28 Nov. 85.

before the speech introducing the Government of Ireland Bill in 1886, but Clark was able to maintain the voice by administering three 'inhalations'.

The recovery was characteristic. It reminds us of the underlying toughness and resilience of Gladstone's physique and of the danger of generalizing from a particular episode. Clearly his health in his seventies needed watching and could obtrude, and on occasion could be used to obtrude, dislocating political life. It contributed to his uncertainty about his political future, his doctor, Clark, often being consulted when retirement was in the air. But Gladstone remained fit and hard, the illnesses usually being understandable reactions after periods of intense strain. During such periods he mostly performed as well or better than his colleagues, still on his feet in the Commons when men half his age had collapsed. Staying at Balmoral in 1884, he climbed Ben Macdhui, the highest point in the Grampians, in a walk from Derry Lodge of 20 miles in 7 hours and 40 minutes 'with some effort' on what is even today a little used route.* He compared it with his previous ascent by a longer route in September 1836 and noticed 'A change!'† But it was by any standards a creditable performance and rather more than that for someone aged 74.

Houses and Weekending in the 1880s

Weekending was an important part of Gladstone's relaxation throughout the 1880–5 government. Hawarden was too far from London to be convenient for a weekend and was only used out of session or during the Easter and Whitsun breaks. There was no 'Chequers' in those days and the Gladstones were thus always guests for their weekend breaks. Even with the most amiable of hosts this must have been less relaxing than if they had been in their own house. Rosebery provided in The Durdans at Epsom (just off the race course) a house which was convenient and an atmosphere which was congenial: bookish but not demanding, though some of the guests, for example the novelist, Henry James, sometimes were so.‡ James was left by Rosebery to look after the Gladstone party. Not surprisingly, as he told Rosebery, he felt 'nervous about dinner this evening and should like to read up beforehand'.§ Gladstone also prepared for the occasion, reading James's *Daisy Miller* during the day. At the dinner, Gladstone was in eloquent form, discussing bookbinding, 'the vulgarity of the son of a Tory Duke', the Bible, and the Hebrew Chair at Oxford. But the stringency of a dinner with Henry James was not characteristic of the usual tone of The Durdans. It was usually like Freddy Leveson-Gower's house, Holmbury (near Guildford)—a comfortable bolt-hole. Some of the misunderstanding

* 11 Sept. 84.
† 9 Sept. 36, 26 Sept. 84.
‡ 14–15 Apr. 84.
§ See L. Edel, *Henry James Letters* (1980), iii. 38.

about Rosebery's expectations about his political promotion may have arisen from a confusion of roles. As Gladstone's frequent host, Rosebery—also of course his patron in Midlothian—gained a familiarity which he expected to see reflected in a rapid rise to the Cabinet. Gladstone was perhaps unwise to allow the confusion of roles to develop.

The other houses were those of persons often with political interests but without strong political ambitions. Dollis Hill, the Aberdeens' Villa then north of London, was an attractive and very close refuge, much used from 1882; Gladstone's connection with the area was commemorated when the exchange system of telephone numbers was introduced, the exchange for that area being GLAdstone, and is still marked by Gladstone Park. Little-burys at Mill Hill, also Lord Aberdeen's, was a similar sort of place; Gladstone became fascinated by its connection with Nell Gwyn, and it was when staying there that he struck up a friendship with James Murray, a pronounced Liberal, then beginning his dictionary while teaching at the nearby school. The other houses generally used were Wolverton's Combe Warren and Combe Hurst, owned by Mrs Vyner, a distant relation of Lord Ripon whom he met at Cannes.

These were all secluded retreats. The Gladstones' company was also sought by less reticent hosts. Gladstone was sometimes displayed as an icon or more often paraded as a 'turn' and held up as a 'catch' by one of the predators hovering on the fringe of the Gladstonian court, such as Sir Donald Currie (knighted in 1881) whose shares stood to benefit at least as much as Gladstone's health from one of his trips on the Castle Line steamers.* A cruise on one of Currie's steamers was as public a holiday as a trip to Brighton.

The usual out-of-session break was, as in the first government, a long spell at Hawarden: sometimes staying in the Castle with Willy and his family (until his house in the Park was finished), sometimes with Stephen at the Rectory, sometimes moving from one to the other in the hope of better sleep. Even at Hawarden, therefore, there was a degree to which the Gladstones were guests. Their own home, 73 Harley Street, was rented out from 1882, an emblem, not willingly shared by his wife, of William Gladstone's intention to retire and leave the London scene. The Glad-stones' curiously nomadic life, with a series of borrowed houses in 1885 and 1886 and no house of their own in London, reflected the uncertainty of his political position.† Undoubtedly, Gladstone felt most at home in

---

* Currie's K.C.M.G. was described by *Vanity Fair* as 'Knight of the Cruise of Mr. Gladstone'; for this, and for the value to Currie of the Gladstonian connection, see A. Porter, *Victorian shipping, business and Imperial policy* (1986), 76, 108, 226.

† On moving out of Downing Street in June 1885, the Gladstones camped with Bertram Currie, a partner in Glyn's bank and thus a further dimension of the Wolverton connection. In July 1885, they stayed with the Aberdeens at Dollis Hill, leaving their possessions with Currie; in 1886, before and after the third government, they stayed with Lucy Cavendish.

Hawarden Castle, sorting his books in his study, 'the Temple of Peace', or chopping trees in the Park with one of his sons. This book contains a fine photograph of him among his books in the 'Temple of Peace' taken by J. P. Mayall for his series *Artists at Home*. Gladstone qualified for the series on the rather curious grounds that he was Professor of Ancient History at the Royal Academy throughout this period, though he never lectured.

There were political gatherings at Hawarden, but not often. The flurry of visits in the autumn of 1885—Bright, Chamberlain, Granville, Rosebery, Spencer*—was distinctly unusual (as was the Gladstones' stay at Chatsworth in February 1885 and his two visits to Derby at Knowsley in October 1881 and October 1883). For a good deal of the parliamentary vacation, Gladstone's links with his Cabinet colleagues were by letter. This allowed him to some extent to control the speed and distribution of his views. Gladstone's absences from London helped his own and his colleagues' recuperation from what were usually very tiring sessions, but they had the result that there was often an absence of force behind the build-up to the pre-Christmas planning Cabinets, and, as we have seen earlier, this lack of force had a high cost in the absence of a coherent plan for the various initiatives in local government legislation which constituted both the chief ambition and the chief failure of the ministry.

Rescue Work: Warnings and a Promise

Very different from the family evenings and early-to-bed life at Hawarden, though in its own way also a relaxation from the strain of politics, was the 'rescue work' which Gladstone pursued when in London. Though not as intense an experience as it had been in his early middle age, it remained regular. Quite often on two evenings a week during the session he would record a conversation with a prostitute (often with more comment than he would make on political conversations). Few of the encounters were highly charged, though Mrs Bolton, eventually saved from prostitution and herself involved in rescue activity, encouraged something of the fascination he had experienced with other cases in earlier times, and in an encounter with 'Cooper (& another) [Gladstone] was carried into dreamland, with disappointment X'. He encountered prostitutes of all ages, including 'Hunter (12)', but this did not encourage him to a favourable view of W. T. Stead's 'Maiden Tribute' campaign in the *Pall Mall Gazette* against child prostitution. At Mrs Meynell Ingram's request he read 'the first of the too famous P.M.G.s. Am not well satisfied with the mode in which this mass of horrors has been collected, or as to the moral effect of its general dispersion

* These visitors were: Chamberlain (7 Oct. 85), Bright (15 Oct. 85), Harcourt, Whitbread (22 Oct. 85), Rosebery (27 Oct., 8 Dec. 85), A. Morley (28 Oct. 85), Granville (31 Oct., 5 Dec. 85), Spencer (8 Dec. 85), T. Acland and Wolverton (10 Dec. 85), and several visits from Grosvenor who lived nearby. Henry James, the attorney-general, was summoned for an important discussion on franchise; see 19 Oct. 83.

by sale in the streets.'* 'Rescue work' for Gladstone had always been a private matter coming under the Tractarian doctrine of 'reserve'. He disliked sensationalism and also the politicization of the question whether in the form of the campaign against the Contagious Diseases Acts or for the raising of the age of consent and he remained as apart as he could from pressure groups.

The absence of interest in the role of the State in such matters may have reflected political prudence, but this is unlikely, for Gladstone's behaviour night by night was not prudent. On at least four occasions he was warned about the supposed political dangers, first by Rosebery (after nervously losing the toss of a coin to Granville) in February 1882, and three times by E. W. Hamilton in May 1882, February 1884, and July 1886. On each occasion Gladstone noted the conversation but without comment. Rescue work by this time seemed an inherent part of his London life, nor was Rosebery quite the sort of person to persuade him to give it up. Hamilton had a much better chance. In February 1884 he warned that the reticence of the policemen responsible for guarding Gladstone could not be relied on: 'For the simple affidavit of one of them there are many malicious and unscrupulous persons who would give large sums. There is no saying to what account these persons might not turn such information.'†

Gladstone ignored this warning. In July 1886, at the height of the divorce scandal involving Sir Charles Dilke, Hamilton tried again. This time, responding to warnings from Canon MacColl and Stead, he emphasized the effect which rumours were already having in the metropolitan constituencies and the extent to which Liberal friends were bewildered as to what they should say when challenged with stories of Gladstone's activities. He told Gladstone that there was 'a conspiracy on foot . . . to set spies on you to watch your movements'.‡ The implication that 'rescue work' endangered victory in the Home Rule campaign did the trick. Gladstone replied to Hamilton: 'As I fear there *does* exist in the world the baseness you describe, I believe on the whole that what you say is true and wise, and I give you my promise accordingly.'§ For the rest of 1886 and for all of 1887, though considerable time was spent in London, rescue work ceased—a remarkable achievement for Hamilton.

Soon after this Gladstone burned the letters of one of the most striking of the courtesans with whom he had had dealings in the 1850s:

Today I burned a number of old letters, kept apart, which might in parts have suggested doubt & uneasiness: two of the writers were Mrs Dale and Mrs

* 15 July 85.
† Hamilton to Gladstone, 6 February 1884, Lambeth MS 2760, f. 188.
‡ Hamilton to Gladstone, 14 July 1886, Lambeth MS 2760, f. 192 and 26 July 86n.
§ To Hamilton, 26 July 86.

Davidson: cases of great interest, in qualities as well as attractions certainly belonging to the flower of their sex. I am concerned to have lost sight of them.*

Mrs Dale was the courtesan, first met in 1859, whose portrait Gladstone had commissioned from William Dyce.† It is very unlikely that the destruction of these letters was the elimination of a political risk, for the letters kept in the 'Octagon' at Hawarden were completely safe. It is more probable that this was part of that preparation for death and for posterity which culminated in the declaration about his rescue work made in 1896 to his son Stephen. Gladstone was well aware that his diary and his papers contained material that would astonish his children and perhaps even his wife.

Laura Thistlethwayte in the 1880s

Mrs Thistlethwayte was not a political risk: her salon in Grosvenor Square was by the 1880s quite respectable, more regularly attended by various political figures such as C. P. Villiers, the veteran MP for Wolverhampton, than by Gladstone. 'Mrs. Th.' was by now no longer a temptation and had in fact become something of a burden: her frequent little gifts and invitations to lunch, tea, or dinner needed acknowledgements (quite how her letters were to be processed in the office led to irritating muddles); Gladstone quite often accepted invitations only to cancel at the last minute. Even allowing for the calls on his time in these years, duty rather than pleasure seems to predominate in his visits. On the other hand, in 1883, while Catherine Gladstone was at Hawarden, he visited her two days running, and he visited her in her cottage in Hampstead immediately after the resignation Cabinet on 20 July 1886. Mrs Thistlethwayte's financial rows with her husband—leading in 1882 to a new law case reported in the newspapers—occasioned his sympathy and support. He was also grateful for her help to the wretched Lady Susan Opdebeck (divorced widow of his former colleague the Duke of Newcastle) now almost penniless.

It was through Newcastle in the mid-1860s that Gladstone had first come in contact with Laura Thistlethwayte, then a notorious and only recently, perhaps only partly, retired courtesan. Gladstone delayed his retirement in 1881 as a Trustee of the Newcastle Estates so as to try to obtain a better settlement for Lady Susan which, with Mrs Thistlethwayte mediating with the Newcastle children, he seems to have succeeded in doing. The episode must have brought back both the high noon of his relationship with Laura Thistlethwayte and his bizarre expedition to Italy in 1849 shadowing the beautiful Lady Susan, 'once the dream of dreams', and her lover: 'I cannot dismiss the recollection of her as she was 50 years back one of the brightest among stars of youthful grace & beauty.'‡

* 16 Oct. 86.
† She was also called 'Summerhayes'. For her, see above, pp. 158–9 and p. 314.
‡ To Mrs Thistlethwayte, 3 August 1885; a further attempt at raising money for Lady Susan.

Gladstone and the Spiritualists

Gladstone did not visit Laura Thistlethwayte often but he found her *salon*, if not Laura herself, attractive when he did. It was perhaps at dinner in her house in Grosvenor Square on 8 October 1884 that he became drawn into the spiritualist movement, then fashionable in certain sections of society* (though in June 1884 he had, together with some fifty other MPs, attended a 'Thought-reading' at the House of Commons). Certainly, Laura Thistlethwayte's religion—deistic post-evangelicalism—was a common feature of the spiritualists of the 1880s.

Whether or not Laura Thistlethwayte was the link, Gladstone attended a *séance* on 29 October 1884 at 34 Grosvenor Square, a house rented by Mrs Emma Hartmann, no doubt the wife of Eduard von Hartmann, a well-known writer on spiritualism. The *séance* was conducted by William Eglinton and mainly took the form of 'slate writing', Gladstone participating by writing two questions, first: 'Which year do you remember to have been more dry than the present one'; second, 'Is the Pope well or ill', to which the medium replied (supposedly without seeing the questions): 'In the year 1857' and 'He is ill in mind, not in body'.† In reply to another question, the medium was unwilling to tip the winner of the Cesarewitch.

Gladstone was intrigued but cautious: 'For the first time I was present at his operations of spiritualism: quite inexplicable: not the smallest sign of imposture.'‡ He was unfortunate in the choice of medium. Eglinton was, in the view of a number of spiritualists, a society fraud. He was denounced as such by Mrs Sidgwick, A. J. Balfour's sister and Helen Gladstone's superior at Newnham College, Cambridge, in what became a bitter controversy in the pages of the *Journal of the Society for Psychical Research* in 1886.§ Shortly after the *séance*, mention of it appeared in the London evening papers. Eglinton blamed one of Mrs Hartmann's servants and promised a 'correct version of the whole affair in next week's *Light*',¶ an account also printed in the *Morning Post* of 7 November 1884, in the midst of the parliamentary crisis over the reintroduced Franchise Bill. Recourse to blaming the servants was the last refuge of many a Victorian scoundrel and, given his record elsewhere, the likelihood must be that Eglinton could not resist creating the excuse to write a public account of the proceedings (in

---

* Mrs Thistlethwayte's agency is my supposition; spiritualism is not discussed in Gladstone's letters to her. However, it is clear that she was acquainted with Lady Sandhurst who organized the second *séance* attended by Gladstone.

† *Morning Post*, 7 November 1884, 3 f.

‡ 29 Oct. 84.

§ *Journal of the Society for Psychical Research*, ii. 282 (June 1886). For the Sidgwicks' successful visit to Hawarden, see 24–5 Sept. 85.

¶ See Eglinton to Mrs Hartmann and Mrs Hartmann to Gladstone, neither dated, the latter docketed 1 November 1884, Add MS 44488, f. 4.

the *Morning Post* report, Gladstone and Eglinton were the only named members of the company).

Despite this publicity, Gladstone tried again, attending a *séance*, this time with guaranteed privacy, at Lady Sandhurst's on 18 November, the day before the first conference with Salisbury on redistribution. The medium, Mrs Duncan, was clearly much more satisfactory, falling into a trance and offering religious and moral exhortation, as well as advice about his throat. Gladstone did not contribute actively to the proceedings: 'I declined all active part hearing & noting it *ad referendum*. To mix myself in these things would baffle & perplex: but good advice is to be remembered come how it may.'*

Such were Gladstone's direct dealings with the spiritualists, though he agreed to be elected as an honorary member of the Society for Psychical Research in 1885† and occasionally read its journal. In general terms, involvement with spiritualism in the 1880s was common enough in the professional classes and the aristocracy. As traditional beliefs about heaven, hell, and sacramental religion declined among the intelligentsia and 'agnostic' became a common self-description, attempts to communicate beyond immediate consciousness were seen as a natural form of progress, rather as the eugenics movement a little later sought for physical progress. This may explain why the detailed report in the *Morning Post*, irritating though it was for the Prime Minister, seems to have had little ongoing effect in the press. The Society for Psychical Research, led by Cambridge intellectuals such as the Sidgwicks and F. W. H. Myers, Fellow of Trinity, had several clergy on its Council including two bishops: Goodwin of Carlisle and Boyd Carpenter of Ripon, both Gladstonian appointments.‡ The Society offered a meeting ground for Christians and agnostics.

Even so, it is surprising to find Gladstone involved in this circle. In most respects he was an orthodox sacramentalist with what was by the 1880s an old-fashioned view of heaven; an Anglo-Catholic was the least likely sort of Anglican to be drawn to the Society. The lingering Evangelicalism of his youth was certainly not of the post-Christian, 'other world' character of some of the members of the Society for Psychical Research. On the other hand, Gladstone was always curious and we have often seen the extent to which he was, rather despite himself, attracted to certain Broad-Church views, as when he defended Seeley's *Ecce Homo*.§ He believed that all phenomena were explicable within the Christian experience. Thus, if

* 18 Nov. 84.

† *Journal of the Society for Psychical Research*, ii. 449 (July 1885).

‡ For the movement, see J. Oppenheim, *The other world. Spiritualism and psychical research in England, 1850–1914* (1985), especially ch. 3, 'Spiritualism and Christianity'. Lady Sandhurst told Gladstone that 'the spirit and purpose' of her *séance* was 'wholly Christian and biblical'; 18 Nov. 84.

§ See above, pp. 156–7.

contact with the 'other world' existed, it would be so explained. He attended the *séances* in this spirit of investigation. Annoyed by Eglinton and fundamentally unimpressed by Mrs Duncan, he seems to have taken no further active part in psychical research.

Gladstone's Diary and Ireland

This brief survey of some aspects of the private Gladstone indicates the richness and variety of his life beyond politics. The daily diary gives a spine to this material and those who seek a narrative account of his life will find if they read it that his diary gives them one. Individual entries remain uninviting. Gladstone did not find writing his diary a literary relaxation, nor did he use it as a means of scoring points in the debates of posterity. The alternative model of Greville came before him in 1883 in Lady Enfield's edition (part of which he reviewed) but he made no change of format even when out of office. For the most part, the diary continues to be an accumulation of recorded facts, of letters written, church services and political debates attended, books, pamphlets, and articles read. Used for individual entries, it will disappoint; used cumulatively it will illuminate. It yields little at a skim. But the more the reader reads, and enters the complex connections of Gladstone's world, the more apparent becomes the extraordinary inter-relatedness of his activities and the more arresting the pithiness of his occasional judgements.

A good example and one of central interest to this period is the diary's record of Gladstone's Irish reading (and its relationship to his correspondence). His reading on Ireland was always thorough. It shows that there were few works of substance that did not catch his eye. He was particularly interested in all aspects of Irish history and read at a variety of levels. He twice read O'Connor's *Chronicles of Eri*,* he had read J. A. Froude, Lecky,† and the various works of Barry O'Brien as they came out.‡ He read extensively in the seventeenth-century history of Ireland especially through the large pamphlet collection made by J. T. Gilbert in his *History of the Irish Confederation and the War in Ireland*, the chief research collection for Irish history published in these years.§ Not surprisingly, there was a particular emphasis on eighteenth- and nineteenth-century Ireland and the constitutional developments of the Pitt–Grattan years. However, it is important to note that though this reading intensified in the autumn of 1885, especially at the time of the important entry on the Union ('I have always suspected the Union of 1800 . . .'),¶ this was mostly a checking of well-known sources.‖

---

* 15 Jan. 83, 20 Apr. 86.

† See e.g. for Lecky, 6 Feb. 72; for Froude, 25 Nov. 72, 25 Mar. 86.

‡ For R. Barry O'Brien's *Parliamentary history* (1880), see 4 Nov. 80; *Irish land question* (1881), 11 May 81; *Fifty years of concessions* (1883–5), 9 Oct. 83, 12 Oct. 85.

§ 11 Jan. 82 etc.   ¶ See 19 Sept. 85.

‖ See, e.g. 18 Oct. 80 for Grattan's *Speeches . . . comprising a brief review of the most important political*

What was systematically engaging Gladstone's attention at the time was P. G. F. Le Play's *La réforme sociale en France*, 2v. (1864) (an important work of conservative religious sociology emphasizing the need for paternal authority in the factory as well as the home)* and, a little later, his controversy with Huxley. Gladstone was a life-long student of Burke and he turned again to that 'magazine of wisdom' in December 1885 as Home Rule became a political probability. Thus Burke on America and Dicey on *The Law of the Constitution* constituted a neat pairing—the old historicism and the new deductivism—for systematic study in the important months of November and December 1885. Gladstone had always had a general interest in Irish history and he continued, as always, to read the literature, including many pamphlets and articles, as it was published. But what is striking about Gladstone's historicist reading is that the period of really intense reading on Ireland *per se*—general interest there had always been— was after the strategic decisions for Home Rule had been taken. It is in the spring and summer of 1886 (from March 1886 onwards) that we find the full emphasis on the need for historical understanding; the extensive 'inquiry' and note-taking† date mainly from that time.

Just as organization of propaganda paradoxically followed the Home Rule defeat, so detailed work on the history of the Union followed rather than anticipated the decision for Home Rule. The second paradox is not as great as the first: as we have seen, Gladstone was well-informed, at least *via* the medium of reading, about Irish history and Irish affairs, and that general understanding was clearly important to him in his sensing in 1885 that a turning point had been reached. Even so, the relative absence of Irish historical reading in the summer and autumn of 1885 and the relative dominance of it in 1886 are striking.

Looking forward from 1886

The domination of Ireland increased as Gladstone's ability to control events decreased. The frenetic election campaign of June–July 1886 saw Gladstone at bay, attempting to hold the Home Rule line and to defend Home Rule candidates with a flurry of endorsing and sometimes injudicious letters and telegrams. The absence of a proper party structure, despite the securing of the National Liberal Federation for the Gladstonian cause, was never more marked.

A mood of stoic optimism followed the election defeat. Having written *The Irish question*, Gladstone, with Acton, visited Döllinger in Bavaria in

events in the history of Ireland (1811), and Pitt's speeches on the Union; 10 Apr. 82 for consultation of the *Annual Register*'s recording of the Union debates.

   * Read 29 July 85–19 Sept. 85; the book was sent to him by Olga Novikov; see 1 July 85. On 20 Sept. 85 Gladstone began Le Play's *La constitution de l'Angleterre*, 2v. (1875).

   † See Add MS 44770 for Gladstone's extensive notes on his Irish reading.

August: Döllinger 'gratified me much by his view of my pamphlet'. He restarted work on the Olympian religion, the work planned in the 1860s as the successor to *Studies on Homer and the Homeric Age*, 3 vols. (1858). But he found it hard to concentrate. In bed with a cold, he noted

There is a disposition to grudge as wasted these days. But they afford great opportunities of review. Especially as to politics, and my politics are now summed up in the word Ireland, for probing inwardly the intention, to see whether all is truly given over to the Divine will.*

For all the difficulties, Gladstone was fundamentally optimistic. At home he planned for the future, discussing the 'meditated Nucleus-Building' and making the first steps towards what became St Deiniol's Library, the residential library at Hawarden that is his national memorial. At large, he wrote the defence of nineteenth-century optimism, '"Locksley Hall" and the Jubilee', with which we began this discussion of his two governments of the 1880s;† he looked with delight at the 'varied and far-reaching consequences'—the possible disintegration of the Salisbury administration—which he anticipated from Randolph Churchill's resignation in December 1886; he looked with caution at the implications of a return of Chamberlain and the 'dissentient Liberals'; and he found in his own political position a cause for fundamental calm and reassurance which set the tone for the remainder of his life:

O for a birthday of recollections! It is long since I have had one. There is so much to say on the soul's history: but *bracing* is necessary to say it, as it is for reading Dante. It has been a year of shock and strain: I think a year of some progress: but of greater absorption in interests which though profoundly human are quite off the line of an old man's direct preparation for passing the River of Death. I have not had a chance given me of escaping from this whirlpool, for I cannot abandon a cause which is so evidently that of my fellowmen *and* in which a particular part seems to be assigned to me. Therefore am I not disturbed 'Though the hills be carried into the midst of the sea'.‡

---

* 12 Oct. 86.   † See above, p. 85.   ‡ 29 Dec. 86.

CHAPTER XIII

An Energetic Octogenarian

Ireland still to the fore—A Totemic Presence through voice and pen—An Oratorical Sage

This has been a period of inner education, and disclosure of special wants: the spirit of faith: the spirit of prayer: the spirit of dependence: the spirit of manhood: the spirit of love. The weight on me [in August 1892] is great and presses at many points: but how trifling when compared with the trials of great Christians.*

Eighty three birthdays! What responsibilities have old men as such for prolonged and multiplied opportunity. And what have I, as among old men. What openings, what cares, what blessings, and what sins.†

Ireland still to the fore

The seventh decade of Gladstone's public life was dominated, as had been most of the others, by Ireland. In the age of industrialism, the British had expected that class—whether the middle or the working class—would disrupt the political system. But it was the national question, not the class question, which the British political establishment failed to solve. In 1886, Gladstone had offered a bold answer, an answer which recognized national distinctiveness and at the same time pacified it within the Union. His answer was rejected by the Commons in 1886—a decision on the whole confirmed by the electorate later that year—and by the Lords in 1893. None the less, it was an answer so compelling that it was eventually adopted by the Unionists—too little, too late—in 1920, and it provided the framework within which all subsequent legislative attempts at modification of the constitution of the United Kingdom at the parliamentary level have been made. Over a century later, and with six governmental Home Rule initiatives having failed (with the ironic exception of their implementation by the Unionists in Ulster), Gladstone's proposals of 1886 still hold the field as the means of constitutional reorganization of the United Kingdom. If there was to be constitutional change, it would be by some form of devolved Home Rule: Chamberlain's federal alternative has never, as yet, received serious consideration by a British Cabinet.

* 9 Aug. 92.   † 29 Dec. 92.

Gladstone sensed in 1886 that he had taken the first step down what was to be a long trail. He had linked the Liberal party and the Home Rule party in Ireland in the boldest way. He had done so not as a crude political bargain, but as a recognition of a just demand fairly stated and as a conservative means of maintaining for its most important purposes the unity of the State. Gladstone termed 'the measure Conservative in exactly the same sense as he would term the repeal of the Corn Laws conservative, through its promoting the union of classes and giving a just contentment to the people'. Failure to so act would eventually endanger the State: 'There is but one end to that matter', he wrote after the defeat of the first attempt to give Ireland 'Home Rule'; 'if what we ask is refused, more will have to be given'.

The failure of the plan of 1886 in the context of the disruption of the Liberal party and an exceptional level of political vituperation encouraged in Gladstone and in some of his followers a Mosaic view of political life, with Gladstone leading a purged party through the wilderness. Biblical comparisons in the political language of the day—a sharp shift from the coolness of traditional classicism—reflected the intensity of political feeling, especially at the Westminster level. As the quotations at the start of this chapter show, Gladstone was aware of the comparisons. Yet they also show his sense of balance and of obligation: his mention of the 'trials of great Christians' reflects the level of comparison commonly made at the time in Liberal circles, but he mentions it in order to present his role as, relatively speaking, 'trifling'. 'Self-glorifying' was to be avoided; but, of course, the mention of it acknowledged at least the danger and perhaps the fact.

A Totemic Presence through voice and pen

Gladstone was 82 when he became Prime Minister for the fourth time on 15 August 1892. His age is, consequently, a dominating theme of his last public years, both for him and for others. It is significant in several different respects.

First, it gave him a totemic role in progressive politics. To see a man in his eighties successfully addressing full-scale speeches to large meetings without any mechanical means of amplification was to see what was clearly a remarkable phenomenon. These were often extraordinary occasions. The physical and mental power required from the orator seemed to emphasize the heroic individualism which was so central a feature of late-Victorian politics, and especially liberal politics. The leader's speech was both a rationalistic transfer of opinion and the focal moment of an emotional rally. In so being, it captured the essence of liberal political consciousness in an extended electorate, by being both rationalistic and popular. It had to contain content interesting to the readers of its report in the next day's newspapers and it had to move the audience actually present. This mode of political communication fitted Gladstone perfectly. His physical qualities, even in advanced age, enabled him to control the largest of audiences; the content of his speeches retained to the end the element of unpredictability which had made him throughout his long oratorical career so mesmeric a figure. After addressing the N.L.F. in Birmingham in 1888 he noted: 'To the great meeting at Bingley Hall, 18,000 to 20,000 persons. I believe all heard me. I was at once conscious of a great strain upon the chest: yet strength & voice were given me for a speech of 1¾ hours. . . .'

Despite his age, Gladstone maintained the breadth of his appeal. He retained his curiosity and his enthusiasm, and the range of his speeches reflected this. He addressed vast meetings in—amongst numerous others—Swansea and Cardiff in 1887, at the Eisteddfod in 1888, in Plymouth in 1889, in Midlothian and in Dundee in 1890, on Clapham Common in 1892, in London, Glasgow and Midlothian in his last but demanding election campaign in 1892. After a short tour of the West Country in 1889, he noted: '18 sp[eeches] in all'. He led a great crowd up the slopes of Snowdon in September 1892 and spoke to them from what became known as 'Gladstone's Rock'. He addressed the annual meetings of the National Liberal Federation in 1887 (Nottingham), 1888 (Birmingham), 1889 (Manchester), and 1891 (Newcastle), large and important meetings, vital for the maintenance of party enthusiasm. He was the first party leader regularly to attend and address an annual conference.* He could turn his hand apparently to any topic, from an attractive little speech at the Port Sunlight gallery to addressing a 'labourers' conference' in the Holborn Restaurant in London a few days later.

Gladstone also remained able to lecture extensively and successfully to academic audiences, in French—'after doubting to the last moment'—to the Paris Society of Political Economy (one of several speeches during the celebrations of the centenary of the Revolution), on Homeric subjects at Eton and at the Oxford Union, and on 24 October 1892 in the Sheldonian Theatre in Oxford on medieval universities—the first Romanes Lecture and a major academic occasion.

In the House of Commons, Gladstone was still in the 1890s a compelling figure, pushing the Government of Ireland Bill through its various stages over 82 days in the face of intense Unionist hostility: any slip or momentary absence of concentration would have been immediately and viciously exposed. Gladstone's energy held out to the end: the muddles over the bill—as we shall see—were in its planning and drafting, not in its defence.

Gladstone was not only known through his words, but directly by his voice (or a rendering of it). He was the first European politician whose voice was heard across the English-speaking world, through the new

---

* He avoided the 1890 Conference, held in the midst of the Parnell divorce hearings.

medium of the phonograph. Colonel Gouraud, Thomas Edison's European agent, made several phonographic recordings of Gladstone which were played at public meetings in Britain and America.* Gladstone's recording on 8 March 1890 for Lord Carrington, Governor General of New South Wales, was the first ever sent from England to Australia. What appears to be the original Edison recording is in the possession of the BBC.† Gladstone made a note of the occasion:

I dined with Mr. Knowles & afterwards witnessed the astonishing performance of Mr Eddison's [*sic*] phonograph, and by desire made a brief address to him which is to pass vocally across the Atlantic.‡

Its powerful harmonics, strong vocal range, and slight North Welsh accent attest to its authenticity,§ as does the confidence and vitality of the voice: the hearer can readily imagine it filling the Manchester Free Trade Hall. As Gladstone had in the 1860s grasped so quickly the opportunities of the extra-parliamentary speech nationally reported, so in the 1880s he quickly associated himself with what was to be the political weapon of the future: the politician's recorded voice. It awaited only broadcasting to make the full transition to the modern age.¶

Gladstone paralleled this persistence of oratorical energy with a remarkable demonstration of literary productivity. In the years between the first Home Rule Bill and his death, he wrote six books, sixty-eight articles and

* See 22 Nov. 88, 7 Mar. 90, 24 July 90. Gladstone had attended an early demonstration of the phonograph, see 18 Mar. 78. For an example of a public playing of the recording in the U.S.A., see Colonel Gouraud's letter in *Scottish Leader*, 5 April 1890, 6e: 'the golden words you spoke have been communicated in your matchless voice to delegates representing over 5000 associations ...'. Recordings of his voice were played at fair-ground stalls, e.g. at Witney in Oxfordshire (a small town with a Nonconformist tradition in a Tory county); at the 1893 fair, 'Mr. Gladstone's Speech' was played in repertoire with 'The Charge of the Light Brigade' and 'Daddy wouldn't buy me a bow-wow'; *Witney Gazette*, 16 September 1893. I am obliged to Christine Bloxham for this reference.

† BBC Sound Archives. As the wax cylinders on which the voice was preserved could not be duplicated, actors made copies by rendering the original voice as accurately as they could. The BBC recording certainly has an authentic quality.

‡ 22 Nov. 88. The BBC recording's content is quite different from the *verbatim* report of another recording (also dated 1888) in the Edison archives, printed in F. A. Jones, *Thomas Alva Edison. Sixty years of an inventor's life* (1908), 161. As both versions address the absent Edison, they may have been recorded at the same time. This is the more likely given Rowland Prothero's story, that the listeners were so absorbed by Gladstone's voice that they failed to notice that space on the cylinder had expired! This would account for the rather inconclusive end of the BBC recording and the more finished version in Jones's book. However, it is not clear to which recording session Prothero's account refers; for it, see Lord Ernle, *Whippingham to Westminster* (1938), 140.

§ It is sometimes said that Gladstone retained a slight Liverpudlian accent. This is probably not incompatible with the accent on the recording, though today that would be regarded as North Welsh rather than Liverpudlian; the two cultures are of course closely intertwined. Gladstone cemented his links with Liverpool by purchasing the advowson of the city for £7,200 in 1889 (see 23, 31 Dec. 89); he then appointed its clergymen.

¶ His is the earliest recording of a statesman that survives. The earliest surviving recordings of a President are, surprisingly, those of Taft (1908) and Roosevelt (1912); earlier recordings were made but were lost; see A. Koenigsberg, *Edison Cylinder Records, 1889–1912* (1969), xxiv.

book reviews—many of them substantial—and edited a further volume of collected articles in *Later Gleanings*. In 1890 he was still able to earn £1,915 8s. 7d. from articles and reviews. An attempt at his collected speeches was begun, edited by A. W. Hutton and H. J. Cohen. Only two volumes were published: if Gladstone had been his own editor, the series would doubtless have been completed!* He finished his long-planned edition of Bishop Butler, with a volume of commentary. Of his major projects only his work on 'Olympian Religion' was left partially finished. His sole half-hearted effort was his autobiography, spasmodically started under pressure from friends and publishers and never gaining his full involvement.

In addition to this, he planned what he saw as his memorial, the future St Deiniol's Library at Hawarden (briefly named 'Monad' (the first number, ultimate unity) but named 'St Deiniol's'—a Welsh saint—in December 1889 when the first transfer of books from the Castle began).† He drew up a detailed memorandum on its purposes, and spent much energy surveying and pegging out various possible sites, moving books from the Castle into a temporary iron building, spending hours humping the books out of boxes and onto shelves. When at Hawarden, work in the library at St Deiniol's took the place of treefelling—or 'axe-work' as he described it with characteristic precision when he ceased to be able to topple a tree—which from December 1891 he could no longer physically undertake. He last recorded felling a tree on 2 December 1891.

Even in his eighties, Gladstone retained undiminished the restless drive for self-improvement, the *leitmotiv* of his diaries and of the epoch they chronicled. The struggle for self-knowledge, the urge not only to understand but to act on that understanding, the need to justify through a demonstration of time well-spent, and the sense that he could do better, drove Gladstone forward. A true representative of his age, he sought repose through achievement but knew that he had not found it: 'May God at the length give me a true self-knowledge. I have it not yet' was his note to himself on his eighty-second birthday.

An Oratorical Sage

All this represented the reality, not merely the appearance, of an exceptionally energetic octogenarian,‡ able to maintain his position as the dominant

---

* Gladstone checked the list of speeches proposed for the volumes which were published (covering 1886–91)

† It is not quite clear in which precise sense Gladstone used the term 'Monad'; in Pythagoras it means an arithmetical unit; *O.E.D.* gives several definitions, including its use as a definition of the Supreme Being, quoting Newman's *Grammar of Assent*, i, iv. 49 (which Gladstone had read and annotated): 'But of the Supreme Being it is safer to use the word "monad" than unit.' See also below, pp. 618 ff.

‡ He was fit enough, when knocked down by a cab at the age of 79, to pursue it, though badly shaken, to apprehend the driver, and to stay with him until the arrival of the police, without revealing his identity.

political personality of his time. Gladstone himself sensed the extent to which work towards an achievable end sustained his constitution: the Irish crusade, and confidence in its accomplishment, retarded the natural process of bodily and mental decline. He noted on his eightieth birthday:

My physical conservation is indeed noteworthy. In the senses of sight and hearing and in power of locomotion there is decline, and memory is not quite consistent. But the trunk of the body is in all its ordinary vital operations, as far as I can see, what it was ten years back: it seems to be sustained and upheld for the accomplishment of a work.

This vigour, carefully guarded, underpinned the continued projection of Gladstone's public personality and the constant promotion of his Irish policy. Public prominence, maintained by speeches and periodical articles was, as ever, vital to his success.

The press, predominantly Liberal before 1885, swung to Unionism more decisively than the electorate. From 1886 and for at least a century, the press was to be chiefly Unionist and hostile to the parties of progress. For the Liberals, this was the reversal of a quarter-century of Liberal press-predominance and with their rationalist approach to politics this was a clear disadvantage. Gladstone's position in politics and his capacity to mesmerize Unionists even while they hated him was a powerful counter-vailing force to the Liberals' loss of press control. His speeches were reported *verbatim* in the Unionist press—the only Liberal leader consistently thus reported in these years—and he therefore constituted in effect a regular free page of advertisement for Liberalism in the Unionist press. His centrality to the Liberal campaign thus intensified in his later years, and his vigour became the focus of constant interest on both sides. A fall, a cold, even his insomnia, received detailed coverage in the newspapers.

This ability to convey a genuine sense of vigour was sustained on less public occasions also. Charles Oman, a strong Tory, recalled of Gladstone's visit to All Souls early in 1890, when he spent eight days in the College:

I was beginning to regard him as past mischief. . . . Rather a pathetic picture of fallen greatness was the way in which I summed him up. . . . I was far from suspecting, till I had seen him close, what vigour there still was in the old man.*

Gladstone charmed the Fellows with his vigorous conversation, skilfully avoiding recent political controversy. What Oman and C. R. L. Fletcher— both of whom left memoirs of the visit—failed to realize was that they were seeing only one side of Gladstone's Oxford visit. In addition to cultivating the Fellows of All Souls with classical and literary high-table chat and giving them the impression of his single-minded attention, he was also conducting a complex series of political negotiations with the Oxford

---

* Sir Charles Oman, *Things I have seen* (1933), 77.

Liberals, who wanted a more obvious political presence in the city from their leader. On this occasion, Gladstone worked to exclude politics as much as possible from his visit; he could do so because he still had the capacity to work several different interests simultaneously.*

The vigorous literary *persona* which he presented in All Souls reflected an important aspect of his character, especially in his last years. Gladstone was the oratorical equivalent of the Victorian literary sage. Victorian sages were defined as being writers who talked; Gladstone was a talker who wrote. His conversation was recorded by diarists and memorialists, who were not necessarily political admirers. His age linked the generation of the 1890s to an epoch by now almost mythical: the epoch of the 1830s, a golden age of whiggery; of the start of Tractarianism; of the pre-railway, localized political system with its Eatanswill hustings; of Scott, Wordsworth and Coleridge. Yet the Prime Minister of the 1890s had been in office, as a Treasury whip and an undersecretary for war and the colonies, in those days of William IV. He could even recall the defining years of nineteenth-century Britain, for, as a four-year-old, he had heard the guns of Edinburgh Castle rattling the windows as they announced the abdication of Napoleon.† To be cogently pre-Victorian in the 1890s was a triumph in itself: '14 to dinner. I had to tell many old stories of politics.'

Gladstone as an historical repository was a subject in itself. He wrote the history of his time in a variety of ways: through his huge output of articles on contemporary subjects; through his autobiography, begun in July 1892 and never completed; through various memoirs of his friends and colleagues, written as obituaries or reminiscences, or as prefaces to biographies or reviews of them; and behind the scenes through the availability (or sometimes unavailability) of his vast collection of private papers in the Octagon which he built to house them at Hawarden—he was probably the first Prime Minister to have a catalogued collection of private papers being used by researchers during his own lifetime‡—and more discreetly by the

---

* For Fletcher's patronizing recollections, see C. R. L. F[letcher], *Mr Gladstone at Oxford 1890* (1908). The Fellows of All Souls evidently seem to have thought they were being generous in allowing Gladstone, an Honorary Fellow of the College since 1858, to exercise his rights. Fletcher was, in fact, a Fellow of Magdalen College at the time of Gladstone's visit; but his tone is throughout proprietary.

† *Autobiographica*, i. 14. Characteristically, Gladstone checked with D. Macgregor, the proprietor of the Royal Hotel in Princes Street, that his recollection was correct that there were five windows in the room.

‡ In these years he was especially involved in the making of C. S. Parker's *Peel*, Wemyss Reid's *W. E. Forster* and *Monckton Milnes* (Houghton), Lane Poole's *Stratford de Redcliffe*, Davidson's *Tait*, Gordon's *Sidney Herbert*, Hallam Tennyson's biography of his father, and Purcell's *Manning*. In the case of Tennyson, Gladstone was unable easily to extract the letters, for they were filed by date rather than person. Gladstone's letters were also in the auction rooms. He was able to prevent the sale of his Eton letters to W. W. Farr.

Gladstone was accommodating but careful: in March 1893 he refused permission to publish in Ricasoli's papers his account of his conversation with Pius IX in 1866.

He assisted Kotaro Mochizuki with his translation of a life of Gladstone into Japanese; see advice and interviews he gave to biographers of his friends, most notably in the case of E. S. Purcell's preparation of his *Life of Manning*, in which Gladstone played a central role.* He was a prompt and assiduous contributor to the *Dictionary of National Biography*, writing a good deal of the content of the articles on E. C. Hawtrey, Sir Stephen Glynne, George Lyttelton, and his father, though his name does not appear as a contributor.

We must beware of seeing Gladstone too much in his role of Victorian cultural remnant. It was certainly an important aspect of his activities in these years, and a side of his character that he carefully developed: his beguiling of the Fellows of All Souls shows it at its most effective. His journal records the time and enthusiasm he spent in this way. He himself was aware that the 'excitement' that his presence often occasioned 'is capable of explanation on grounds less flattering than self love would suggest. For a very old man is in some sense like a commodity walking out of a Museum or menagerie into the haunts of men.' But we must not allow this to distract us from the fact that Gladstone remained an extremely effective politician. He sometimes liked to give the impression that he was in some way removed from politics: but the years after 1886 were very different from those of the opposition years after 1874. Then he had talked of political retirement to literary and theological pursuits even when effectively leader of the opposition: now he was clearly committed to winning an election in order to lead another government. Amiable talk of literature might charm the literary classes—now in the main Unionist—but Gladstone's essential relationship was by this time with 'the masses'.

It was at this time that a mythic Gladstone gained a firm place in the public mind, lasting well into the twentieth century. Children learned to sing 'Let us with a Gladstone mind' and to emulate the great statesman by chewing each mouthful 32 times. The unique use of 'Mr.' as an invariable prefix was still common in the 1960s among ordinary people for whom the nineteenth century meant the Queen and Mr. Gladstone.

In all Gladstone's outpouring of activity, there was an element of Dr Johnson's female preacher: what was remarkable was not that it was done well, but that it was done at all. Much of it was done well, and especially in chosen areas of political action Gladstone still acted effectively and powerfully. Yet he knew that his physical system was maintained by will, and that

21 Apr. 91n.

He does not seem to have been asked for help by A. F. Robbins whose careful study, *The early public life of William Ewart Gladstone* was published in 1894; it is based on published sources and there is no suggestion in the preface that Robbins had asked Gladstone for information.

* Gladstone's conversations with Purcell were an important influence on this controversial biography, as Purcell's preface makes clear (though Purcell exaggerates the amount of attention Gladstone gave to him). Gladstone regarded Manning as a lost 'gem' of the Church of England and especially deplored his Ultramontanism. His copy of Purcell's *Life* (presently in my keeping) is one of the most heavily annotated of all Gladstone's books and has many *marginalia* rebuking Manning and correcting what Gladstone saw as his inaccuracies.

his body was failing faster than his mind. Poor eyesight made him increasingly reliant on secretaries; neuralgia in his face—perhaps an early symptom of the cancer of the cheek which killed him—affected him and his sleeping from 1889. Colds and influenza were serious setbacks. Deafness led to an end of regular theatre-going, such a feature of the 1870s and early 1880s: when he did go, he sat on the stage, but even then 'heard but ill'.* His memory, remarkably accurate with respect to the long-term past, began to fail him in the short-term. In 1887 he began to forget some of the names of his correspondents for the daily lists which form one of the standard components of the diary. At the same time, he prepared for a political speech to Yorkshire MPs and Liberals: 'Thought over what to say tonight. I wrote even three sets of notes: but forgot to take any of them.'

As long as the drive towards success in Irish policy was uninterrupted, bodily vigour was sufficiently sustained, and such difficulties were inconvenient but not seriously intrusive. Such an interruption came with the Parnell *débâcle* in 1890, and it aged Gladstone by the decade he thought he had saved.

In July 1892, in the face of his fourth premiership, he candidly noted this remarkable judgement:

Frankly: for the condition (*now*) of my senses, I am no longer fit for public life: yet bidden to walk in it. 'Lead thou me on'.†

The bidding was the bidding of God, and the call was still 'Ireland, Ireland, Ireland'.

* 11 May 92 (Irving and Terry in *Henry VIII*).   † 15 July 92.

CHAPTER XIV

Leading the Liberal Party, 1887–1892

The Primacy of Home Rule—Conversations with Parnell—'The sin of Tristram with Isault': Parnell and Mrs O'Shea—Liberalism, Free Trade, and Internationalism—Liberals and Labour and Women

On this great [Easter] day [of 1887] what are my special prayers? They are three

1. For the speedy concession to Ireland of what she most justly desires.

2. That the concession may be so timed and shaped as to be entirely severed from all temptation to self-glorifying so far as I am concerned.

3. That thereafter the tie between me and the contentious life may at once be snapped. But now one prayer absorbs all others: Ireland, Ireland, Ireland.*

The Primacy of Home Rule

The dominance of 'Ireland' in this period of Gladstone's life. is obvious enough. The circumstances of 1886 gave Gladstone, as he saw it, a clear role: the duty of leading a Liberal majority to pass a second and successful Government of Ireland Bill. The Home Rulers would show the genuineness of their commitment to a devolved Assembly, their moderation the more remarkable under the provocation of Unionist coercion; the purged Liberal party would win the next general election outright with a significant majority, and would pass a Government of Ireland Bill (with the Home Rulers in support but at a distance) which the Lords would not dare reject; Gladstone would then retire. He underestimated the skill of Salisbury in forging the various groups of Unionists into what the Liberals liked after 1886 to refer to as the 'Unionist coalition' but what was by 1892 not far short of a Unionist party ('Toryism ... now includes what was once Liberalism, for shortness I call it all Toryism—there is no use beating about the bush in these matters and wasting time')† and he overestimated the capacity of Parnell as a political leader in the round.

---

* Diary for 10 Apr. 87.

† A. W. Hutton and H. J. Cohen, *The Speeches . . . of W. E. Gladstone*, vol. x (1892) [subsequently: Hutton and Cohen, *Speeches*], 408 (to conference of agricultural labourers, 11 December 1891).

'The speedy concession to Ireland of what she most justly desires' was thus the objective of his prayers, and the statement of what was desired was that of the elected Home Rule party. If the Liberal party could be reunited to achieve this goal quickly, so much the better. Gladstone was happy to go along with the Round Table talks about Liberal reunion in the early months of 1887, because they accorded well with his concept of politics as a process, so often deployed with Hartington and Chamberlain in the years 1880–6.* In 1886 he had succeeded at least in attracting Chamberlain and G. O. Trevelyan into his Cabinet. In 1887, a carefully arranged meeting over dinner with Gladstone provided the means of Trevelyan's return. In so returning, Trevelyan admitted the principle of Home Rule (the concession was on the question of the inclusion of the Irish MPs at Westminster). It was clear enough that an admission of this principle was the context within which Gladstone was working, as his speeches and literary productions showed. In this sense the process was teleological, not open-ended, and in this sense it differed basically from the early months of 1886, when the process was one of exploration of the *possibility* of Home Rule. After 1886, the principle of Home Rule gave Gladstonianism a political rigidity matching the fiscal rigidity of free trade.

Was Joseph Chamberlain seriously considering what was in fact a required capitulation on this basic point? His behaviour was, as ever, erratic, with none of the sinuously developed fall-back positions of Gladstone in his pre-Home Rule days. Chamberlain's scathing public attack on the primacy of Home Rule in the Liberal programme, made in the midst of the private negotiations, seemed to deny any serious intention of reunion.† Gladstone appeared to have nothing to lose: he half-turned his cheek and met Chamberlain twice at dinner. Both occasions went well, with 'Easy *general* conversation with Chamberlain' (easiness was not a usual feature of their always stiff relationship) at the first and 'very free conversation on the closure' at the second. A few days later, on 5 April 1887, they met *tête à tête*: 'ambiguous result but some ground made'. Gladstone tried to secure agreement on coercion, presumably as a first step, but nothing came of this. Chamberlain and his group of radical Unionists—Hartington kept well clear of Gladstone at this time—went their own way.

The talks of 1887 confirmed the split of 1886 with respect to most of the

---

* It cannot be said that Gladstone made strenuous efforts personally to achieve a negotiated return of the radical Unionists as a group, though he worked willingly enough to complete negotiations set up by others. He probably felt, as his own behaviour suggests, that personal contact with particular individuals was the more fruitful route. He seems to have worried more about the defection of old cronies, such as C. P. Villiers (his dining companion at Mrs Thistlethwayte's and his former foreign secretary's brother) than that of the Chamberlain clique.

† See 26 Feb. 87 and M. Hurst, *Joseph Chamberlain and Liberal Reunion. The Round Table Conference of 1887* (1967), ch. vii.

Liberal Unionists: 1846 more than 1866 was the precedent.* This applied to the Liberal party as much as to those who had left it. At least under Gladstone's leadership, and probably well beyond it given the political arrangements that that leadership implied, the Liberal party was a party of Home Rule. Those who left it recognized this by their continued absence; those who stayed in, however much they might, like Sir William Harcourt, dislike Home Rule, recognized this by their presence.† This 'Home Rule' was therefore essentially that defined by the Government of Ireland Bill of 1886, in so far as it met the requirements of the Irish.

As Gladstone reminded the National Liberal Federation at the famous Newcastle meeting in 1891, whatever there was to be said about the various other items of policy with which a Liberal government would wish to deal, there was no doubt about the priority of Home Rule:

As to the title of Ireland to the precedence, there is no question at all about it—it is a matter fixed and settled and determined long ago, upon reasons which in my opinion—and what is much more, in the opinion of the people—cannot be refuted, cannot even be contested.‡

There were therefore two elements to the case Gladstone so painstakingly elaborated after 1886: first, that Ireland had a legitimated and established grievance of such force as to demand priority; second, that 'Home Rule' was the natural constitutional development for the United Kingdom, a natural pluralistic evolution of the unitary constitution.

The background to the grievances and requirements of the Irish Gladstone investigated laboriously in his private reading. He reappraised his view of Daniel O'Connell (his first Cabinet meetings in 1843 had committed the Peel government to the prosecution of O'Connell for treason): O'Connell had been 'the missionary of an idea. The idea was the restoration of the public life of his country.'§ Gladstone repented of his youthful views: 'In early life I shared the prejudices against him, which were established in me not by conviction, but by tradition and education'. Now, 'there cannot but be many, in whose eyes O'Connell stands clearly as the greatest Irishman that ever lived. . . . By the force of his own personality he led Ireland to Saint Stephen's, almost as much as Moses led the children of

---

* The 1846 analogy was not absolute, for many more of those who opposed Home Rule in 1886 returned to the Liberal party than those who went with Peel in 1846 returned to the Conservatives.

† Hurst, op. cit., 3, 58, rightly points out that, in the immediate context at least, Harcourt and the 'goodwill' Liberals were the real losers from the failure of the Round Table negotiations.

‡ Hutton and Cohen, *Speeches*, 382 (2 October 1891).

§ 'Daniel O'Connell', a review of Fitzpatrick's 2v. edition of O'Connell's correspondence (1888), reprinted in W. E. Gladstone, *Special Aspects of the Irish Question* (1892), 263ff. Gladstone's reappraisal of O'Connell had begun as a result of a meeting with Revd John O'Rourke during his visit to Maynooth in 1877, which led to Gladstone's memorandum of a conversation with O'Connell in 1834 being published in the 3rd ed. of O'Rourke's *Centenary life of O'Connell* (1877), see 4, 17 Nov. 77.

Israel to Mount Sinai.' O'Connell did this with support 'in the narrower rather than in the wider sense, [of] the masses only, not the masses with the classes'—a clear terminological analogy between Gladstone's view of O'Connell and Gladstone's view of himself. Gladstone's repentance must become a national repentance. The policy of Home Rule was in part a recognition of an historical and therefore an empirically demonstrable grievance, not a deductivist case dependent upon abstract argument about a perfectible constitution. Winning this historical argument was therefore essential to the struggle. Unionist authors must be combated—and this involved Gladstone in sharp disputes with W. E. H. Lecky, J. Dunbar Ingram and others, and, more constructively, in his own essay on Irish history in the eighteenth century, published in James Bryce's *Handbook of Home Rule* (1887).

Winning this argument was important in part because to do so established the naturalness of Home Rule. The case against Home Rule in 1886 had been in part that it was unnatural—sudden, arbitrary, a break with the constitution—consequently leaving the British party which supported it as in some sense deviant and exotic. Gladstone, as we have seen in Chapter IX, insufficiently educated his party by public debate in 1885–6 on this point, and was aware of it. Recognizing that 'the political education of a people is not to be effected in a moment, in a day, or in a year',[*] he set out to provide such an education. Home Rule was the established policy for the colonies:

Sixty years ago we governed our own British Colonies from Downing Street. The result was controversy, discontent, sometimes rebellion. We gave them Home Rule, with the same reconciling results as have followed elsewhere; and with this result in particular, that what was denounced here beforehand as separation has produced an Union of hearts between us and the Colonies such as had never been known before.

The Imperial argument thus supported the policy, as did the military: 'we might at some period be involved in a great war', and the precedent of the French wars was that 140,000 men had been required in Ireland to subordinate the population: 'such, with an anti-Home-Rule policy, was the frightful demand of Ireland upon our military resources. . . . We must not then maintain, but alter the present state of things, if we wish to have our full strength available in war.'

Home Rule, far from being a sudden invention of 1886, was a well-established European policy. States that declined it had done so at their peril: Holland had lost Belgium, Denmark Schleswig-Holstein, Turkey

---

[*] 'Home Rule for Ireland. An appeal to the Tory Householder' (1890), reprinted in W. E. Gladstone, *Special Aspects of the Irish question* (1892) [subsequently: *Special aspects*], from which subsequent quotations are taken. This article presents the same arguments as those used by Gladstone in his speech on the second reading of the Government of Ireland Bill, 1893.

her European provinces: 'such, with respect to the denial of Home Rule, are the teachings of experience'. Moreover, 'as the denial has in no case been attended with success, so the concession has in no case been attended with failure'. Norway and Sweden, Denmark and Iceland, Austria and Hungary, Turkey and Lebanon, all had improved and settled relations as a result of the same essential policy:

Home Rule has everywhere appeared as in the nature of a cure, and the denial of it as a loss or a disgrace. It may be said, and said with truth, that in all those cases there are circumstantial differences from our case; but the essence has everywhere been the same.

Home Rule was thus neither strange nor unnatural, but commonsensical and successful, and especially so in the peculiar case of the British Empire. It was thus those who opposed it who should be seen as dangerous. The Unionists were the danger to the constitution, not those who agreed with the Irish in making a 'modest and temperate demand for a self-government complete indeed but purely local'. Gladstone made only 'one very simple' demand on the Tory householder: 'We only ask him to *think*.' If he did think, he would see the naturalness of the Home Rule solution; if he did not, the United Kingdom might go the way of the rest.[*]

Conversations with Parnell

As an essay in prudential conservatism radically applied this view was characteristically Gladstonian. Essential to it, of course, was the assumption that Home Rule would be consolidatory not separatist, the last step not the first. Gladstone believed this would be the case. His first draft of a Home Rule Bill had followed the receipt of Parnell's 'Proposed Constitution for Ireland' and had followed it quite closely. The behaviour of the Home Rule party after the disappointment of 1886 confirmed his view. The revival of the land movement in the form of the Plan of Campaign, from October 1886 on, deliberately avoided the criminal aspects of the land war of 1880–2. Parnell went out of his way to distance himself even from the Plan. It was the Unionists and the Unionist press which practised dishonesty, defending forgery and unnecessary coercion. In the testing period of the Crimes Act, the Special Commission, and the Michelstown shootings, Parnell and his party confirmed the view Gladstone had formed of them in the period after the arrests of 1881: they were essentially sturdy constitutionalists. The difficulties were about details, not principles, and those details would be a re-run of the points of dispute in 1886: precise

* Even the 1893 Home Rule Bill can be seen as too late; see Emmet Larkin's view: 'the reality of British power in Ireland had been rendered marginal by 1890, and it became increasingly marginal until 1921, when it was finally liquidated'; *The Roman Catholic Church and the fall of Parnell 1888–91* (1979), 297.

demarcation of powers, the financial bargain, and the role of Irish MPs (if any) at Westminster.

Gladstone discussed these matters at two meetings with Parnell, on 8 March 1888 in London and at Hawarden on 18–19 December 1889 (i.e. five days before Captain O'Shea petitioned for divorce). On each occasion Parnell's demands were entirely within the accepted parameters of liberal thinking. After the first conversation, Gladstone noted: 'Undoubtedly his tone was very conservative'* and after the second, 'He is certainly one of the best people to deal with that I have ever known.'† The purpose of these meetings was partly tactical—at the first Gladstone characteristically urged keeping the working of the Crimes Act 'before the eye of the country, and of Parliament by speeches, and by statistics'—and partly prospective, agreeing the terms of the future Government of Ireland Bill.

To the modern eye, the most curious feature of this period of Liberal opposition is the absence of systematic 'forward-planning' on this bill. It was clear there was to be a bill, and that it would be the chief immediate business of the next Liberal government in its first full Session. It was also clear from the experience of 1886 that there were many complex points of detail about such a measure, some of them involving major constitutional matters. Yet the Liberals re-entered government in 1892 with many of these points undecided or unconsidered.

Gladstone's talks with Parnell in December 1889 were clearly intended to make a start on such matters. For the second meeting, Gladstone prepared an elaborate memorandum setting out 'all the points of possible amendment or change in the Plan of Irish Government'. It pointed to a Government of Ireland Bill somewhat more confined than that of 1886, and, in its major departure from that bill, it retained 'an Irish representation at Westminster . . . in *some* form—if the public opinion, at the proper time, shall require it'. Gladstone had already, at Swansea in 1887, raised this probability.‡ It was not for him a major change, for in his initial draft of a Home Rule bill in November 1885, the Irish MPs had been 'in', and Parnell at that time had also taken an easy view of the matter. The memorandum also took up the question of the financial bargain (of the importance of which Gladstone had reminded Parnell at their earlier meeting), and suggested a clause explicitly 'reserving the supremacy of Parliament over Ireland in common with the rest of the Empire'; it also dealt with some details of a land settlement, safeguards for contracts, and an imperial veto for seven or ten years on judicial matters.

After the first meeting, Gladstone noted: 'we had 2 hours of satisfactory

---

* 8 Mar. 88.

† 19 Dec. 89. See also 30 Apr. 88, a meeting at Armitstead's dinner table 'to meet Mr. Parnell. His coolness of head appeared at every turn.'

‡ Speech on 4 June 1887.

conversation but he put off the *gros* of it'. The next day, there were two hours more of conversation *tête-à-tête*, following which Gladstone sent a memorandum round the members of the ex-Cabinet: he sensed no real difficulties: 'Nothing could be more satisfactory than his conversation; full as I thought of great sense from beginning to end . . . nothing like a crochet, or an irrational demand, from his side, was likely to interfere with the proper freedom of our deliberations when the proper time comes for practical steps.' The problematic area remained the Irish MPs at Westminster, but here Parnell had expressed 'no absolute or foregone conclusion'. Gladstone reported the conversations to the ex-Cabinet in more detail when it met: 'At 2.30 to 4.30 political meeting. I related my interview with Parnell. Sir W. H[arcourt] ran restive: but alone.'

Parnell's conduct at these meetings thus suggested to Gladstone that, just as he had seen a Government of Ireland Bill in 1886 imposing responsibility on the Irish as well as satisfying their demands, so association with the Liberal party in the preparation of the next bill brought out the best qualities of Irish constitutionalism. The 'public life' of Ireland was being restored through unity of action on the Home Rule question. If the matters which Gladstone put to Parnell for discussion in 1889 amounted, as Parnell in the crisis of 1890 claimed, 'to a compromise of our [i.e. Irish] national rights by the acceptance of a measure which would not realise the aspirations of our race',* then Parnell certainly did not say so when they were put to him, either at the time or in subsequent months.†

It may be that Gladstone felt that the work done on the 1886 bills, and in these conversations with Parnell, was sufficient preparation and that to attempt detailed decisions played into the hands of the Unionists. Certainly, it was wholly within the tradition of British government not to work out details of legislation before entering office. Yet the question of whether Irish MPs would be 'in' or 'out' of the House of Commons went to the heart of the difficulties raised about the 1886 bill, and had important bearings on the 'home-rule-all-around' question. Gladstone several times in these years, including in his first conversation with Parnell, raised the question of

---

* The concluding sentence of Parnell's manifesto 'To the Irish People', published on 29 November 1890; printed in O'Shea, *Parnell*, ii. 166.

† A point Gladstone made in his public response to Parnell's manifesto 'To the Irish People' in November 1890. As always in Parnell's dealings with British political leaders, there are no records on his side of these conversations. It may be said that Gladstone's denial of Parnell's statements— e.g. that he [Gladstone] made no statements whatever about County Court judges and resident magistrates (as opposed to judges)—seems entirely consistent with his memoranda preparing himself for the conversations: 'every suggestion made by me was from written memoranda' etc. Gladstone was of course exceptionally experienced at recalling the specific details of official discussions (in which category he clearly placed these) and in general his memory was accurate. Moreover, he had no reason to misrepresent the conversations of December 1889 to his ex-Cabinet colleagues. In those conversations he was recognizing Parnell as an equal, in the sense of party leader and Prime Minister of Ireland-in-waiting, and he presumed he would behave with the appropriate stiffness of honour he expected from such persons.

whether the 'American Union' was 'a practical point of departure'. In seeming not to see the qualitative differences between devolution of power (which, as he frequently made plain, was a boon bestowed by Westminster and removable by it) and a federal system—in effect a new constitution—he seemed to share a common contemporary confusion;* but it was a serious confusion none the less.

There was, of course, an element of menace in the Irish MPs' position: that was inherent in their presence at Westminster as a party whose fundamental objective was to require the Crown in Parliament to pass a Government of Ireland Act. Gladstone recognized that the Irish should take what they could get, and if what they wanted could be got from the Tories, so much the better. He continued to think, privately and publicly, that Home Rule would be best settled by a Tory government.† But in the years after 1886 this could be no more than a fancy. The menacing, disruptive edge of the Irish party could for the time being only cut the Liberals. That was why the securing of Parnell to the lines of discussion about the future bill was so important. By the late 1880s a natural progress towards a fairly decisive Home Rule majority in each of the Kingdoms seemed a clear probability and Gladstone's goal since 1886 seemed within grasp. Indeed the conversion of the minority into a large majority seemed in the autumn of 1890 as certain as anything in politics could be certain. But the cutting edge of Irish disruption sliced dramatically through the 'silken cords' at the end of 1890, when the O'Shea divorce case caused a political disruption greater than any achieved by a Fenian bomb.

'The sin of Tristram with Isault': Parnell and Mrs O'Shea

On 17 November 1890 Katharine O'Shea did not appear in court, despite the pleadings of her counsel, Frank Lockwood (Liberal MP and soon to be Solicitor-General), and a decree *nisi* was given to Captain O'Shea, with Parnell as the co-respondent. Gladstone, at Hawarden, pursued his usual activities. On 20 November he held 'family conversations on the awful matter of Parnell'. Next day, with 'a bundle of letters daily about Parnell: all one way', he spent the morning 'drawing out my own view of the case', and writing it down. His conclusion was:

I agree with a newspaper, supposed to convey the opinion of Davitt (*The Labour World*) that the dominant question, now properly before Mr. Parnell for his

---

* Gladstone's idea that the 'American system' might 'in case of need supply at least a phrase to cover them [opponents of Home Rule] in point of consistency' greatly underestimated the implications; 8 Mar. 88. For an interesting discussion of the contemporary debate about federation, see John Kendle, *Ireland and the federal solution. The debate over the United Kingdom constitution, 1870–1921* (1989).

† See point 2 of his notes for conversation with Parnell, 8 Mar. 88, and *Special aspects*, 344: 'I for one have always declared my wish that this great measure should be carried by the Tories; because they can do it with our help (which they know they would have), more easily and rapidly than we can.'

consideration, is what is the best course for him to adopt with a view to the further-ance of the interests of Home Rule in Great Britain. And with deep pain but with-out any doubt, I judge that those interests require his retirement at the present time from his leadership. For the reason indicated at the outset [i.e. that the decision rests in the first place with the Irish Parliamentary party and the Irish constituents generally], I have no right spontaneously to pronounce this opinion. But I should certainly give it if called upon from a quarter entitled to make the demand.

This was a reasoned restatement of his letter to Morley, two days earlier, that, whatever the qualifications and allowances to be made, 'I again and again say to myself, I say I mean in the interior and silent forum, "It'll na dee".' As his notes show, Gladstone at least half wished to say this in the public forum: that is, he wished to bring direct pressure to bear upon Parnell and his party, whose eve-of-session meeting was to be held on 25 November. Next day (a Sunday) after another 'cloud of letters', he decided 'I think the time has come'. He travelled to London on the Monday, held a conclave with Granville, Harcourt, John Morley and Arnold Morley, the chief whip. Following this, he 'saw Mr. MacCarthy'. This was Justin McCarthy, the Home Rule MP and journalist, with whom Gladstone had had various earlier dealings. His account of this meeting was stated in a letter to John Morley, the gist of which was that, if Parnell looked like persisting with his leadership at the meeting of the Irish party on 25 November, McCarthy should disclose to the meeting that Gladstone's view was that Parnell's 'continuance at the present moment in the leader-ship would be productive of consequences disastrous in the highest degree to the cause of Ireland'. McCarthy probably did not know of a further point, added into the letter at John Morley's prompting, that this would 'render my [Gladstone's] retention of the leadership of the Liberal party . . . almost a nullity'.

Parnell, rather than McCarthy, was the objective of all this. Gladstone's face-to-face interviews with Parnell in 1886, 1888, and 1889, had been aber-rant. His normal means of communication with him was indirect: by letter and usually *via* Mrs. O'Shea. She could hardly be asked to play a part on this occasion, so the alternative indirectness of a letter to Morley was used. The strength of the O'Shea link in the 1882–6 period was that it was indirect but immediately efficient. Carefully avoiding inquiry into the details of Katharine O'Shea's domestic arrangements, Gladstone none the less knew that a letter to her was effectively a letter to Parnell which would immediately reach that notoriously elusive character. But on 24 November 1890 Morley, like many a Liberal in the past, could not find Parnell to show him Gladstone's letter. Justin McCarthy, chosen presumably because of his journalistic connections with Gladstone, told Parnell of his interview with Gladstone, but when Parnell pressed ahead, did not tell the party meeting of Gladstone's letter, and Parnell was re-elected chairman. Gladstone published the letter two days later in the press, with sensational impact on Irish MPs and public opinion generally.

As is well known, Parnell then published his manifesto 'To the Irish People' on 29 November, unprofessionally misrepresenting the conversations of 1889 on several points which Gladstone could and did correct from his memoranda; Gladstone rejected requests to make specific assurances to the Irish party on particular points about a Home Rule bill; and the party meeting of Home Rule MPs in Committee Room 15 disrupted on 5 December, McCarthy leading 45 MPs from the room leaving Parnell with 28.

As his birthday retrospect for 1890, Gladstone uniquely wrote a memorandum rather than an extended entry in his journal. It was, in personal terms, the most disappointing moment of his political career since the 1840s, as the 'master-violence of politics' tightened a grip which Gladstone had believed was shortly to be released. He recorded the full extent of the *débâcle*, triggered by what he called 'the sin of Tristram with Isault'—an interesting nod towards the Celtic revival (though one which was in the case of Parnell wildly inappropriate). But in that analogy he caught as well as any the mythic element of Parnell's tragedy and its private and public dimensions and, perhaps, his own forlorn and betrayed position as King Mark.

The task had been clear:

In Ireland the Nationalists were to hold their ground; in Great Britain we were to convert on the first Dissolution our minority into a large majority and in the Autumn of 1890 we had established the certainty of that result so far as an event yet contingent could be capable of ascertainment.

The case was 'not hopeless', but 'the probable result of so scandalous an exhibition will be confusion and perplexity in the weaker minds, and doubt whether while this conflict continues Ireland can be considered to have reached a state capable of beneficial self-government' (thus wrote the former Colonial Secretary). The result was to

introduce into our position a dangerous uncertainty . . . Home Rule *may* be postponed for another period of five or six years. The struggle in that case must survive me, cannot be survived by me. The dread life of Parliamentary contention reaches outwards to the grave.

Not surprisingly, 'this change of prospect hits me hard'. Gladstone's optimism had been 'based on pride and on blindness: He who sees all sees fit to quench it.' His duty was 'of course to preserve the brightness and freshness of our hopes as they stood a couple of months back'.

Gladstone, despite his considerable public crusade at this time against divorce and in favour of marital fidelity, did not blame Parnell or Mrs O'Shea. Though he never refers to it, he must have suspected that a liaison as close as theirs and one which he himself knew to be so established might have a sexual dimension. The affair was public from the day O'Shea filed his petition for divorce on 24 December 1889 (just after Parnell's visit to Hawarden). There was therefore almost a year to come to terms with its possible consequences (longer than initially expected).* The possibility that the case would require Parnell's withdrawal from public life had of course occurred both to Parnell and to Gladstone and the Liberal leadership. In March 1890, Gladstone's view had been that such a withdrawal would be 'a public calamity' and he seems to have thought it an avoidable calamity. But he took no steps to avoid it. There were no meetings with Nonconformist or Roman Catholic leaders to limit the potential damage. Nor was there any discussion with Parnell as to how either of them might handle the political aspects of the case. The latter would have been a contradiction of the view that Parnell was a competent party and national leader.

It was not Parnell's morality that Gladstone deplored—he no doubt thought it no worse than Hartington's long-standing liaison with the Duchess of Manchester—but his inept management of its public consequences. It was Parnell's public handling of his position that he condemned, and his public handling of private political conversations which took place within very clearly accepted canons of political life. These showed Parnell to be less than the man Gladstone had taken him for.

Gladstone soon put Parnell behind him: he never had the nagging status of Disraeli. The journal entry on the receipt of the news of Parnell's death in 1891 has a cool edge to it:

In 18 hours from six P.M. yesterday I have by telegram the deaths of Mr. W. H. Smith, Mr. Parnell—& Sir J. Pope Hennessy (not an inconsiderable man). So the Almighty bares his arm when he sees it meet: & there is here matter for thought, and in the very sad case of Mr. P. matter also of much public importance.†

Liberalism, Free Trade, and Internationalism

Gladstone's years as leader of the Liberal Party in opposition—and the period 1886–1892 was the only sustained period when he was the opposition leader—were by no means solely concerned with the Irish question, important though the maintenance of its prominence was to him. Though he was an opposition leader in Britain, in many countries he was regarded as the prime British politician. This almost reached the level of actuality when he attended the centenary celebrations of the French Revolution in February 1889, celebrations that Salisbury's government declined to recognize officially. Fêted all over Paris, Gladstone ascended the Eiffel Tower ('I was persuaded to go up the tower & propose his [Eiffel's] health in a French oratiuncle [brief speech]'), visited the exhibitions, and made the

* In December 1889, it was expected that the case would be heard in June 1890.
† 7 Oct. 91.

speeches. When he entered the Paris Hippodrome, 'the performance was arrested and God save the Queen played'; when he attended the Opera, he sat in the President's box.

If he had accepted any of the various invitations to visit the United States, his reception would have been even more lavish, despite the success of American protectionism. As Gladstone knew well, his Home Rule policy had gained him a world-wide reputation and, he believed, a consensus of support far greater than in England. In the areas of Irish-American settlement in this period the name of Gladstone rivalled that of Lincoln.

Gladstone throughout his life was well read on the United States. In his later years, he followed American politics and theological debate—obvious subjects for a Briton in public life—but he was also fascinated by the Shakers and he read on publication Jacob Riis's trail-blazing work on poverty in New York, *How the other half lives: studies among the poor* (1890). It was a report of the state of marriage in the U.S.A. that prompted him to declare that, were he not so old, he would launch a Bulgarian-style campaign against birth-control. His association with W. H. Rideing of the *North American Review* resembled to a lesser degree that with James Knowles of the *Nineteenth Century* and *Fortnightly Review*. His friendship with Andrew Carnegie, the greatest industrialist of the age, reflected—as did Carnegie's enthusiasm for his Scottish roots—the *rapprochement* taking place between the British governing class and East Coast wealth and politics. Gladstone energetically encouraged such links.

He enthusiastically welcomed the economic prominence of the American economy. He seems to have been unconcerned at the course of American 'boss' politics in this period, which so preoccupied most Tories and Liberals at this time. He saw it merely as a symptom of American protectionism, whose follies he went to some lengths to demonstrate in articles in the *North American Review*. His argument—in perhaps the most deductivist account of the free-trade case that he ever made—was the universalism of free trade and of its benefits: what had benefited Britain in her economic prime would benefit America in hers. All protection was monopolistic and corrupting: 'all protection is morally as well as economically bad'.* Gladstone's appeal to American universalism, as opposed to James Blaine's localist reply, anticipated the twentieth-century dominance of the United States and sought to harness it for the cause of progress and international harmony based on free trade. In anticipating the danger of an America whose political arrangements were locally

* 'Free Trade', *North American Review*, cl. 1 (January 1890), 25; the article was planned over an extended period, being delayed in publication so as not to interfere with the American election (another example of Gladstone's quasi-Prime-Ministerial position abroad).

defined while her economic strength was hegemonic, Gladstone anticipated a vital failure of the world liberal system in the early decades of the
twentieth century:

How will the majestic figure, about to become the largest and most powerful on the
stage of the world's history, make use of his power? Will it be instinct with moral
life in proportion to its material strength? Will he uphold and propagate the Christian tradition with that surpassing energy which marks him in all the ordinary
pursuits of life. . . . May Heaven avert every darker omen, and grant that the latest
and largest of the great Christian civilization shall also be the brightest and the
best!*

This cosmopolitanism and Gladstone's defence of it was important in a
world moving quickly into nationalistic protectionism. From the Liberal
point of view, the cause of Irish nationalism in the form of Home Rule was
a contribution to the maintenance of international right, because it recognized constitutional change in a free-trade context: Home Rule was
intended to show that recognition of national identity need not mean
protection and cartelization.

By the time of the election of 1892, Gladstone stood as the world leader
of a free-trade movement clearly in retreat, but still able to offer the world
the best model of international harmony. It was an important consequence
of the Home Rule preoccupation that British Liberalism did not in these
years play a more active role in advancing the sort of institutional development of internationalism implicit in Gladstone's campaigns during his
previous if unofficial opposition years in the 1870s. When Gladstone came
to challenge British armament expansion, as he did in 1892–4, he was able
to do so in the context of national politics only: the liberal movement had
neither associated itself with the Second International (formed in 1889),
nor provided an alternative international institutional structure. As the
leader of world Liberalism in its political form, this failure was a perhaps
surprising blot on the British liberal record between the 1880s and 1914.

Free trade was to Liberalism what class was to the International.
Though 'free trade' was by definition an absence of impediments, it was
not impossible to institutionalize it by treaty and international organization, though it would have seemed odd to most nineteenth-century
Liberals to try to do so. By the 1890s it was a fiscal system clearly on the
defensive: time was no longer on Liberalism's side. What is curious is that
British Liberals made no attempt to co-ordinate its international defence
by co-operation with Liberals in other countries (except in a mild way in
the Empire and through trade-treaty negotiations with individual states).
The generation of British Liberals which played so prominent a part in the
founding of the League of Nations was, for Liberalism, really a generation

* *North American Review*, cl. 1, 26–7.

or perhaps two generations too late. In his old age, we have seen Gladstone contemplate a campaign in the Bulgarian atrocities style against birth control, which he saw as an attack on moral values in the private sphere. But the defence of free trade—the ordering principle of liberal internationalism—was seen in terms of articles for the *North American Review*.

Liberals and Labour and Women

The suggestion of a liberal association with the Second International is, in the context of European politics and ideologies, no doubt to point up its impossibility. Yet in domestic politics this was just what Gladstone achieved. Keir Hardie lost the by-election at Mid-Lanark in 1888 to a Liberal, but his slogan was: 'a vote for Hardie is a vote for Gladstone'.* Although Home Rule could be seen as demoting 'labour questions' in the order of precedence, it was also a question on which the parties of progress could unite, specially at a time when class questions were becoming more acute. All groups within the developing labour movement were enthusiastic Home Rulers, supporting the policy on the very Gladstonian argument that it was both right in itself, and an important means of clearing the legislative path in the Commons, and perhaps achieving reform of the Lords *en route*. It also associated the Gladstonian Liberals with an even wider argument. Gladstone argued that the Union was legal technically but not morally, because 'no law can possess moral authority in Great Britain, can be invested with that real sacredness which ought to attach to all law, except by the will of the community'.† This appeal to fairness and moral authority rather than to law made by a process of government, fitted well with Gladstone's rhetoric of 'the masses against the classes', and also with the sort of arguments that the labour movement was developing as it moved into a phase of parliamentary activity. Home Rule and the constitutional question thus probably aided the Liberals in their attempt to continue as the hegemonic party of the left more than it disadvantaged them, at least in the short to medium term.

A plethora of political argument was seen by many Liberals as desirable in itself. For Gladstone, public discussion of issues was the life-blood of a healthy polity. He recognized that Christianity had, by its assertion of individualism, dethroned the Aristotelian ideal of an organic civil society. He also recognized that 'the modern movement of political ideas and forces' had afforced this Christian individualism, lowering 'in rank the political art by substituting in a considerable measure for the elaborated thought of the professional statesman the simple thought of the public into which emotion or affection enter more and computation less'.‡ How then

---

* Henry Pelling, *The Origins of the Labour Party* (1965), 65.
† 'Plain speaking on the Irish Union', *Special aspects*, 311.
‡ 11 June 88.

were the desirable aspects of Greek civic life to be maintained in a society in which both Christian individualism and demotic emotion seemed to contrast with the concept of a good polity? The task of Liberalism as the party of progress was to square this circle, to show that public debate could be adequately conducted within the enlarged franchise, that 'elaborated thought' could be understood by an extended electorate, and that individualism was not simply the assertion of an interest, through its participation in the rhetoric of self-government, but the basis of an organic society.

This implied a complex party ideology. Free trade and Home Rule (a settled fiscal and political constitution) might be its first-order determinants, but around them would cluster many related if lesser causes. Gladstone had always been good at developing second-order principles which groups within the Liberal party might agree on for fundamentally different reasons. Irish disestablishment in the 1860s had been for Liberal Anglicans the pruning of the rotten branch, for Nonconformists the first step to a secular state. Home Rule in the late 1880s could be either the means of purifying the constitutional system and consequently leaving the British state with its natural harmony restored—as Gladstone saw it—or as the first, just step to a new system—as many labour leaders saw it. As he pointed out to the Queen, Home Rule might be in essence conservative, but the delay in implementing it might cause it to 'become very far from conservative' in a variety of directions, both Irish and British: 'the longer the struggle is continued, the more the Liberal Party will verge towards democratic opinion . . . indeed in the mouths of many the word democratic has already become a synonym and a substitute for the word Liberal'.[*]

Gladstone worked this vein carefully. During the opposition period, meetings were arranged, usually by a member of the Gladstone political circle such as Stuart Rendel or George Armitstead, with most of the groups that made up the Liberal party—the Scottish and Welsh MPs, the Wesleyans and others—and these included the 'Labour M.P.s'. Thus, 'dined with Mr. Armitstead to meet the Labour MPs—There was speaking'; and, 'to Greenwich with Rosebery: he entertained the Labour members, & a good lot they are'.[†] Two days later Gladstone 'devised a scheme for payment of members'[‡] (the absence of which was held to be one major difficulty preventing an increase in the number of working-class MPs). Such meetings had a paternal element to them, but they would have been inconceivable in Germany.

At the Newcastle N.L.F. meeting in 1891, Gladstone included various

---

* 28 Oct. 92.   † 26 Apr. 87, 30 June 88.

‡ 2 July 88. Andrew Carnegie followed this up with a remarkable offer: 'Mr. Cecil Rhodes gave Parnell ten-thousand pounds to secure one point in Home Rule [the inclusion of Irish M.P.s at Westminster] which he thought vital to the unity of the Empire. I should like to give ten-thousand pounds for a bill paying members three-hundred pounds per annum; but we should talk this matter all over'; Carnegie to Gladstone, 28 March 1892, Add MS 44514, f. 156.

items affecting 'labour' representation (amendment of registration, the lodger franchise, election expenses, payment of MPs) in the list, and he seemed to give them high priority: 'there ought to be a great effort of the Liberal party to extend the labour representation in Parliament'.* But the Liberal Party was not as an institution capable of enforcing this intention. When it came to the point, with the Liberals in power in 1893, it was decided that Gladstone should not speak on the matter, and nothing happened. It was a clear chance lost. Notoriously—as Gladstone's son Herbert found when, as chief whip after his father's death, he attempted a systematic improvement in labour representation—the local Liberal associations would only very rarely select working-class candidates and then usually in the few remaining two-member seats where a Liberal could run in tandem with a Labour candidate. Gladstone met the problem in principle, and the attention he paid to it was important in holding 'the party of progress' together. But it was attention that Gladstone provided, not a practical solution.

On fundamental questions of political economy, Gladstone remained, hardly surprisingly, a mid-century free-trade retrencher. The role of the State was that of an enabling agent in a society self-regulated by thrift, on the model of the Post Office Savings Bank he had set up in 1861:

I rejoice to say that it has been in the power of the State to affect this [practice of thrift] by judicious legislation—not by what is called 'grandmotherly legislation' of which I for one have a great deal of suspicion—but by legislation thoroughly sound in principle, namely that legislation which, like your savings bank, helps the people by enabling the people to help themselves.†

The 'Newcastle Programme' contained no proposals, beyond an opaque passage on the 'eight hours' question, for any alterations to the mid-Victorian fiscal state in whose creation and definition Gladstone had played so large a part. On the other hand, Gladstone recognized that opinion was moving away (though perhaps less swiftly than is often thought) from a rigid distinction between politics and the economy, and his own view of the state had always recognized categories of 'interference',‡ including 'positive regulations . . . for the sake of obviating social, moral or political evils'.§ The identification of those evils came through the working of the representative system, and it was therefore for supporters of causes—whether political, religious, or economic—to work that system for the promotion of their cause. For Gladstone, injustice to Ireland was an 'evil' which required his prime attention in part because the Home Rule MPs represented that it was so. But he recognized that others of a different

* Hutton and Cohen, *Speeches*, 382 ff.
† Speech to railway savings bank depositors, *T.T.*, 19 June 1890, 6e.
‡ See above, p. 119.
§ Ibid.

generation (or several generations) from himself would identify other such evils, and there was always a wishful, elegiac quality in his references to his own position in the traditional cause of retrenchment: economy was 'like an echo from the distant period of my youth';* Gladstone was in this area 'a dead man, one fundamentally a Peel-Cobden man'.† Hints might be given, but once again in office Gladstone's position—though not that of all other members of his Cabinet—was in principle clear enough. Questioned on the unemployed by John Burns, one of those Labour MPs so carefully incorporated, Gladstone replied:

questions of this kind, whatever be the intention of the questioner, have a tendency to produce in the minds of people, or to suggest to the people, that these fluctuations can be corrected by the action of Executive Government. Anything that contributes to such an impression inflicts an injury upon the labouring population.‡

The association of Gladstone and the organized labour movement was based on a policy for constitutional change, on co-operative action on a wide front to achieve that change, and on an attempt to secure for labour a greater representation. On the underlying question of the future of the economy, Gladstone saw no need for significant change.

The case for constitutional development occurred, Gladstone believed, in a curious context. The nineteenth century had been one of substantial progress for 'the labouring man': 'instead of being controlled by others, he now principally, and from year to year increasingly, controls himself' and in so doing offered an example to the world.§ Yet the political system within which this 'peaceful and happy, if not wholly fulfilled, revolution on behalf of the working man' was occurring was bizarre:

the spectacle presented by this country at the present time is a remarkable one. The ultimate power resides in the hands of those who constitute our democracy. And yet, our institutions are not democratic. Their basis is popular; but upon that basis is built a hierarchy of classes and of establishments savouring in part of feudal times and principles; and this, not in despite of the democratic majority, but on the whole with their assent. I do not know whether history, or whether the present face of the world presents a similar case of the old resting on the new, of non-popular institutions sustained by popular free-will.¶

The labouring class within this system, 'if they acted in union and with the same political efficiency as the classes above them', could 'uniformly be the prevailing sense of the country'. Yet the technicalities of politics and

---

* Hutton and Cohen, *Speeches*, 377 (2 Oct. 91).

† Gladstone to Bryce, 5 December 1896, Bryce Papers 10, f. 167; see H. C. G. Matthew, *The Liberal Imperialists* (1973), vii.

‡ 4*H* 16. 1734 (1 Sept. 1893).

§ W. E. Gladstone, 'The rights and responsibilities of labour', *Lloyd's Weekly Newspaper*, 4 May 1890, 8–9; see 28 Mar. 90 (this important article had not been hitherto noticed).

¶ Ibid.

the lack on the part of working men of 'the means of constantly focusing current and fugitive opinion, such as are supplied by clubs and by social intercourse to the upper class, especially in the metropolis', left day-to-day political life in the hands of the wealthy. Acceptance of this situation presupposed agreement on fundamentals and the capacity of the political class to respond to changes 'on great and engrossing subjects', on which, once roused, 'the nation is omnipotent'.

The public articulation of such 'great and engrossing subjects' was, in Gladstone's view, the distinctive and pivotal role of the Liberal party, the lens through which general objectives could be focused into political propositions and actions. The Liberal party was thus the agent of political integration. That another party, with labour representation as its primary aim, could develop within the political system was not excluded from his analysis. But the difficulties would be formidable: 'notwithstanding his wide franchise, and though he were to widen it as he pleased, he [the working man] bears only a divided rule: and perhaps his share is the smaller one. It would be a great error, were he to overrate his strength through omitting to notice the causes which detract from it.' Consequently, Gladstone's message throughout his later years ran, the labouring man had a prudential as well as a principled interest in continuing to support the Liberal party; once Home Rule—in itself a good—was achieved, the 'secret garden' of delights could be unlocked. It was a teasing prospect, whose realization depended on not losing the home-rule key.

Liberalism thus had a central role to play in the process of integration and representation. But it played it in the knowledge that virtual representation in a political system which claimed direct representation meant a constant squaring of a circle, and that required constant vigilance and ingenuity on the part of the Liberal leadership of the sort Gladstone was so adept at providing. Class was acknowledged but could be contained.

This drive towards an increase of labour representation was intended to broaden yet further the still broad base of the Liberal party. Many Whigs, some radical businessmen, a significant proportion of the press and of the intelligentsia might have left the party—some permanently, some temporarily—but the Gladstonian Liberal party appeared to retain—uniquely among the forces for progress in Europe—the capacity for class and national integration. The breakup of such a spectrum of progressive forces as the Liberal party represented was a dangerous and formidable step, as the tentative founders of the various groups which eventually made up the Labour party realized. But the very existence of those groups showed that the Gladstonian solution of constitutional change as the focal point of integration was not enough, however much one of its implications was a cleared road for labour legislation, if that was what the party of progress in the post-Home Rule period might wish to pursue.

The Gladstonian argument on grievance was widely applied. It was for the Scottish and the Welsh MPs to show that they represented significant demands for disestablishment: if they could, then disestablishment would take its place in the Liberal programme. Since there was no party mechanism outside the limited forum of the N.L.F., the character of this process was uncertain and often irritating for those taking part in it. It set up an open competition within the Liberal party as well as between the Liberal party and its opponents. Clearly it seemed to leave a decisive role for Gladstone and the Cabinet. However, this should not be overestimated. It is clear that Gladstone personally regarded Scottish disestablishment as a natural development which would in time ripen: his correspondence with Scottish disestablishers from 1885 is couched in these terms. Welsh disestablishment he regarded as much less natural. The strength of the Church of England in Wales before the eighteenth century was a favourite theme (with Gladstone unsettling the young Lloyd George with a question on this point):* Gladstone saw Welsh Nonconformity as a late and perhaps transitory phenomenon. None the less it was Welsh and not Scottish disestablishment which the 1892–4 government put forward as a bill.

One subject not included in the 'Newcastle Programme's' list of points for discussion was that of the position of women in public life. Gladstone's private uncompromising hostility to birth control—'the most saddening and sickening of subjects'†—was not altogether characteristic of his view of the changes in the position of women at the end of his life. Undoubtedly, he was very cautious about 'votes for women', but he was careful not to be drawn into public opposition in principle.‡ He had not been personally involved in the detailed preparation of reforms which particularly affected women, but his governments had passed the Married Women's Property Acts and introduced an important principle by giving certain women the vote in elections for local government. His argument in 1884—that to include the female franchise in the Representation of the People Bill would be to 'nail on to the Extension of Franchise, founded on principles already known and in use, a vast social question' which would endanger the whole franchise measure§—was one no doubt convenient from the view-point of his personal inclinations. But it was also true. Once the 1884 Act was in place, however, he made no direct effort to encourage his party even to discussion of the question.

* See 29 May 90 and B. B. Gilbert, *David Lloyd-George*, i. 79–80 (1987).

† 28 Oct. 88.

‡ See Ann Robson, 'A bird's eye view of Gladstone' in B. L. Kinzer, ed., *The Gladstonian turn of mind* (1985). See also Gladstone's letter of 3 October 1892 to Adele Crepaz, printed as a preface to the English translation of her influential conservative essay, *The emancipation of women* (1893): 'In such a region it is far better, as between opposite risks, to postpone a right measure than to commit ourselves to a wrong one.... For this as for other subjects, I deeply regret the death of J. S. Mill: he had perhaps the most *open* mind of his generation.'

§ To Dilke, 13 May 84.

It was not one of those matters which he identified as needing discussion within the party so that a view of its 'rightness' could be arrived at. Gladstone probably saw 'votes for women' as one of those changes which, like the secret ballot, could not ultimately be avoided but which he personally declined to encourage. His careful public pronouncements—always casting doubt but avoiding closing the Liberal door—were subtly crafted; they could be seen either as clever evasions or as the prudent cautions needed from a leader differing from a small but energetic group within his party. It had always been his task to accommodate some views with which he was not personally in full agreement. But in the case of the 'women question' one senses that this was a matter Gladstone was glad to see deferred until he was no longer responsible for the party.

'Votes for women' was like the repeal of the Corn Laws: it focused a complex change on to a single, stark question. Gladstone had disliked the Anti-Corn Law League's 'single issue' approach to the ending of protection and he equally disliked the focusing of the general question of the position of women in society and in public life on to the gaining of the national franchise. He agreed, however, with the female suffragists that the gaining of the parliamentary vote was an emblem of 'a fundamental change in the whole social function of women'. In his most extensive discussion of it—his published letter of 11 April 1892 to Samuel Smith*—he opposed Smith's bill on the grounds of its narrowness: it excluded married women, who, Gladstone thought, 'are not less reflective, intelligent, and virtuous than their unmarried sisters, and who must . . . be superior in another great element of fitness, namely the lifelong habit of responsible action'. He then discussed the question generally, in terms of the absence of national discussion and of lack of a clear demand for the franchise from women: 'there never has within my knowledge been a case in which the franchise has been extended to a large body of persons generally indifferent about receiving it'. There was, Gladstone believed, 'a permanent and vast difference of type . . . impressed upon women and men by the Maker of both'. These 'differences of social office' rested on 'causes, not flexible and elastic like most mental qualities, but physical and in their nature unchangeable'. It was not impossible for women competently to fulfil political duties, including holding office, hitherto regarded as the province of males, but this would involve, he argued, a major change in public and family relationships, and he clearly personally disliked the implication of that change for women: 'As this is not a party question, or a class question, so neither is it a sex question. I have no fear lest the woman should encroach upon the power of the man. The fear I have is, lest we should invite her unwittingly to trespass upon the delicacy, the purity, the refinement, the elevation of her own nature, which are the present sources of its power.' He consequently, on 27

* See Samuel Smith, *My life-work* (1902), Appendix XI, from which these quotations are taken.

April 1892, 'voted against the Women's Suffrage Bill in an uncomfortably small majority of 23'.*

At other levels, he was, by his practice, modestly pro-active. His daughters were given important positions in the Prime-Ministerial secretariat, performing from time to time all the duties of the private secretary. He encouraged the development of organizations within the Church of England run by women, such as the Houses of Mercy. He encouraged his wife in her various charitable initiatives and he supported the Women's National Liberal Federation with Catherine Gladstone as its President. The extent to which Mrs Gladstone was seen as his partner in public life was a marked novelty. It would be silly to try to portray Gladstone as in the van on such matters, but it is too easy to use his opinions on sex, marriage, and divorce (on which he was undoubtedly conservative) to present him as, in general, a reactionary with respect to women. In his careful and cautious ambivalence on this matter, he can fairly be seen as rather characteristic of much of Liberal opinion. It was, of course, a major disappointment for female suffragists (though it can hardly have been a surprise) that Gladstone did not join them in promoting their cause. But they could not have argued that he was singlehandedly preventing progress. In not bringing 'votes for women' to the fore in Liberal discussion about priorities he set a trend which all subsequent Liberal leaders, men much more likely to be favourable to the change, found it prudent to follow. It was an uneasy position for the 'party of progress' to hold but it was undoubtedly a convenient one for Gladstone.

Gladstone's leadership of the Liberal party between 1886 and 1892 was thus arranged on terms suitable to him, though the consequences might not always be agreeable. His leadership and the primacy of Home Rule and free trade were the fixed points. All other aspects of domestic policy were open to competition and proof of support. This leadership then, despite the immediate block of Home Rule, encouraged a form of party debate which to many outside the party and some within it seemed factious and 'faddist' (the pejorative adjective of the day). However, in the complex nether-land of British progressive politics in the period of the waning of the *laissez-faire* state, this pluralistic approach permitted a reformation of Liberalism without serious schism and with eventual success.

---

* 27 Apr. 92. Gladstone's Cabinet agreed on 21 Nov. 93 to put married women on the same basis as single women for all local franchises (municipal, county, poor law guardians and school boards), but to resist a proposal 'to enfranchise locally all women who cd. vote if they were men'.

CHAPTER XV

The Fourth Gladstone Government, 1892–1894

*A Disappointing General Election—Physical Setbacks—The Primacy of Home
Rule in doubt, but confirmed—The Cabinet of 1892—The Second Home Rule
Bill—Thoughts of Retirement—Minor Aspects of the Premiership—Africa and
Egypt: a Prophecy reluctantly fulfilled—The Navy Scare of 1893–1894 and the
Prelude to Resignation—'Final Cabinet' and Last Speech in the Commons*

Wrote to Sir C. Dilke–Author Life of Abp Laud–Sir Horace Far-
quhar–The Queen l.l. Saw Sir A.W.–Mr Marj.–Sir W. Harcourt–Mr
Morley.
Dined at Ld Rosebery's.
Final Cabinet 12–1¾. A really moving scene.
H. of C. 3¼–5. 'His last speech['']. I tried to follow the wish of the
Cabinet: with a good conscience. The House showed feeling: but of
course I made no outward sign.
Worked on [Horace's] Odes.*

A Disappointing General Election

On 15 August 1892, Gladstone went to Osborne House to receive the
Queen's commission to form a government: the only one of the four times
on which she did not seriously attempt to find an alternative.† She did not
need to: Gladstone's party position was unassailable, but his political position was broken by the results of the general election. Early results at the
start of July were 'even too rosy', but a gain of 80 British seats at least was
expected. Soon this was seen to be clearly over-optimistic: 'The burden on
me personally is serious: a small Liberal majority being the heaviest weight
I can well be called to bear' . . . 'an actual minority, while a personal relief
to me would have been worse in a public view'.‡

Not surprisingly, the result was an improvement on the catastrophe of
1886, when in England 105 Unionists were returned unopposed and the

---

* Diary for 1 Mar. 94.
† She wished to send for Rosebery as a gesture, while recognizing that 'she will have that
dangerous old fanatic thrust down her throat' eventually; in 1880 she had sent 'for Ld Hartington &
Ld Granville. Why not [in 1892] send for Ld Rosebery or some other person? She will resist taking
him [Gladstone] to the *last*'; Ponsonby dissuaded her from this course; A. Ponsonby, *Henry
Ponsonby, Queen Victoria's Private Secretary* (1942), 216–17.
‡ 6, 9 July 92.

Liberals only won 47.2 per cent of the votes: a wretched performance for a party accustomed to winning clear majorities and to regarding 1874 as an aberration. The Liberals increased their vote in England from 1,087,065 (1886) to 1,685,283 (1892), but this was largely a measure of the increase of contested seats: the Liberal share of the vote in England in 1892 was 48 per cent—just short of the level necessary to make dramatic inroads on the Unionists (in the glory year of 1906 the Liberals won 49 per cent of the English votes, which puts the Liberal effort of 1892 in a more favourable light than it is often seen). In Wales in 1892 the Liberals won 62.8 per cent of the vote and in Scotland 53.9 per cent. In Ireland the Unionists fielded many more candidates than in 1886, but there was no sign whatever that Home Rule had been killed by kindness: the Home Rulers, for all their problems over Parnell, took 78.1 per cent of the votes and 80 out of 103 seats. The effect of all this was to make the Liberals the largest party with 272 MPs, followed by the Conservatives with 268 (which with the 46 Liberal Unionists made 314) and the Home Rulers with 81: effectively a minority Liberal government sustained by Irish votes.

In view of the expectations at the start of the campaign of a clear Liberal majority this was a poor result.* It was, Gladstone reflected six months later, 'for me in some ways a tremendous year. A too bright vision dispelled. An increasing responsibility undertaken with diminished means.' The general sense of failure was compounded by a sharp fall in Gladstone's majority in Midlothian, where the poll was taken after the Liberals' setback in England was known: 'The "Church" has pulled down my majority much beyond expectation.'†

Physical Setbacks

This political blow was reinforced by two serious physical accidents and the appearance of one symptom of decline. First, on 25 June Gladstone had been hit in Chester on 'the left & only serviceable eye' by a 'hardbaked little gingerbread say $1\frac{1}{2}$ inch across' flung by 'a middle aged bony woman ... with great force and skill about two yards off me'. This required four days in bed, impeded his electioneering, and severely affected his reading powers for several weeks. After making his first speech in Midlothian, a week after the accident, Gladstone realized there was 'a fluffy object floating in the fluid of my servicable eye', i.e. that just recovering from the gingerbread attack. These developments marked the end of his ability to rely on his eyesight: though there was some recovery in October 1892, writing and especially reading were increasingly burdensome and by 1893

* Even so, the percentage of votes won by the Liberals in England was the third best of the eight general elections between 1885 and 1914.
† He only beat Wauchope, his Tory opponent, by 690 votes.

he saw the world through a 'fog'. Next, while still recovering and having just become Prime Minister, he

walked and came unaware in the quietest corner of the park [at Hawarden] on a dangerous cow which knocked me down and might have done serious damage. I walked home with little difficulty & have to thank the Almighty.*

In fact, Gladstone was affected by the attack for about three weeks. Both these incidents were reminders that a frail majority was to be led by a frail 82-year old. As always, however, we must be careful about the extent of that physical frailty. Unable to read, Gladstone instead wrote: 'I made today [8 July 1892] an actual beginning of that quasi Autobiography which Acton has so strongly urged upon me.' It was also perhaps, for Gladstone began at the beginning, a deflection from the disappointments of 1892. He also began work on his translation of Horace's *Odes*, wrote an article for the *North American Review* attacking Argyll's views of Home Rule, and a little later began work on a paper for the Oriental Congress and on his Romanes Lecture, due to be delivered in Oxford in the autumn. Of these, only the Romanes was a commitment hard to avoid. In the gloom of the post-election period, Gladstone seemed driven to remind himself and others that he was, as he always claimed, 'a man in politics', not a mere politician. In politics he certainly was and moreover, he was by choice (most would say) or by God's calling (he felt) leader of a party with a mission, but now a mission almost impossible of fulfilment in the coming Parliament. While at Dalmeny, on the day after he began his autobiography, he 'also sketched a provisional plan of policy for the future'.

Gladstone recognized that the small majority of about 40 (353 Liberals and Home Rulers combined over 314 Conservatives and Liberal Union-ists) 'much reduces the scale of our immediate powers, as compared with our hopes ten days ago'. It also threw the primacy of Ireland into question: 'if we had thrown British questions into the shade we should have had no majority at all'. With a brutal realism, given all his hopes and claims since 1886, his first plan of action for the 1893 session accordingly demoted Ireland.

The Primacy of Home Rule in doubt, but confirmed

The context of the formation of the government perhaps in part justified Gladstone's view that it was unwise to plan far ahead, and better to wait for 'the crisis' to act as a formative context for decision-making. For the con-text of Irish legislation could not but be gloomy. Gladstone aimed 'at obtaining a judgment upon the great Irish question without spending the bulk of the session upon its particulars (viewing the unlikelihood as far as can now be seen of their at once passing into law: and obtaining a good or

* 29 Aug. 92; the heifer was shot; its head can be seen in the Glynne Arms, Hawarden.

fair sessional result for the various portions of the country) ...'. He structured the various elements of Liberal intentions into three (later four) categories: government bills, bills initiated by private members and supported by the government, bills worked through Grand Committees, and reforms achievable by administrative action. It was the most systematic plan made for any of his four ministries. The main points of the 'Newcastle Programme' with respect to England, Scotland and Wales were to be translated into legislation.

In Gladstone's initial plan, Ireland was to be dealt with by Resolution—a return to a suggestion considered in 1885–6—which would have involved only a small amount either of preparation or of parliamentary time, and also by the repeal of coercion and various minor measures. But 'stiff conversation' with Spencer and John Morley followed, with a long meeting on 28 July 'on the course to be pursued as to Home Rule'.* As a result, in the second version of the 'provisional outline of work' for the 1893 Session, Ireland came first in the form of a 'Bill for the Government of Ireland'.† This was a dramatic change. Gladstone had committed himself to the major task of drawing up the bill and to doing much of the work for it in the Commons, for the Viceroy would be in the Lords or in Dublin and the Chief Secretary often in Dublin also. The price of Irish support for the minority Liberal government was a full-scale Home Rule bill.

This decision predicated much of Gladstone's work for the next eighteen months. It was a decision encouraged by most of the senior members of the incoming Cabinet except Harcourt, and, as we have seen, one taken against Gladstone's own preference which was, ironically, much the same as Harcourt's: both had initially felt that the election result implied giving priority to British bills. It was not surprising that as the Cabinet gathered in London Harcourt made a fuss. Gladstone archly noted on 14 August: 'I am sorry to record that Harcourt has used me in such a way since my return to town that the addition of another Harcourt would have gone far to make my task impossible.'‡ Harcourt's manner was over-truculent, but his basic demand was only that Gladstone should remain true to his own best judgement.

The Cabinet of 1892

Gladstone's fourth Cabinet contained four members of Palmerston's last administration, six who would be members of the 1905 government, and

---

* Spencer was sent the first version and replied that he was 'doubtful as to dealing with the Irish question next Session by Resolution'; the Liberals would 'be regarded as "faint-hearted", if we did not bring in a Bill, and send it up to the H. of Lords. We do not moreover know what the Irish will say'; *The Red Earl. The papers of the 5th Earl Spencer 1835–1910*, ed. P. Gordon, 2v. (1981–6) [subsequently: *Spencer*], ii. 211.

† 1 Aug. 92.

‡ 14 Aug. 92.

two who would be active in Liberal politics after the First World War. It thus spanned the office-holding epoch of the British Liberal party. Gladstone diminished the proportion of peers in the Cabinet (5 out of 17 as opposed to 6 out of 14 in 1880 and in 1886) and increased the number of non-Anglicans to 7, as opposed to 5 in 1886 and 4 in 1880. In certain respects, therefore, Gladstone's Cabinet represented a changing party. In other respects, it represented the continued dominance of Oxford and Cambridge in progressive politics. All its members had been educated at Oxford or Cambridge* except one who had been at London University (Herschell), one who had been educated privately (Ripon), and two who had not been to university (Mundella and Fowler). Its largest profession was writing—it was probably the most literary Cabinet ever—with six of its members well-established and substantial authors in the area of history and allied subjects (Rosebery, John Morley, G. O. Trevelyan, Bryce, Shaw-Lefevre, Gladstone) and two more who had earned their early keep as journalists (Harcourt and Asquith). Several of the Cabinet had significant business interests on their estates, but only one, Mundella, had manufacturing experience. For all his years, Gladstone had much in common with the younger members of his Cabinet. Indeed, H. H. Asquith and A. H. D. Acland represented exactly the progressive, public-spirited generalists which his Oxford University Act of 1854 had been designed to nurture.† Gladstone had clearly identified Asquith's potential: 'He will rise', he noted in a comment rare of its sort in his diary.‡

Important to Gladstone both personally and politically was John Morley. After a few months of office, Gladstone remarked of Morley: 'He is on the whole from great readiness, joined with other qualities, about the best stay I have'§—a slightly guarded encomium, but a strong one none the less. In dealing with Gladstone, Morley in fact kept himself on a tight rein. He sometimes found the old man with his 'monstrous glasses' physically repellent. He was put off by Gladstone's habit of putting his hand before his mouth when speaking and, recording Gladstone's conversation at Dalmeny, he 'felt something horrible and gruesome about it'. There was 'a horrid ⟨black⟩ pall of physical decline hanging over all, slowly immersing the scene and its great actor in ⟨dismal⟩ dreary night'.¶ Morley saw

---

* Trinity College, Cambridge led with 6, Christ Church, Oxford came second with 4.

† A. H. D. Acland was the son of T. D. Acland, Gladstone's Christ Church contemporary who had taken the same path to High-Church Liberalism; A. H. D. Acland had been Steward of Christ Church in the 1880s and had greatly improved Oxford's extra-mural activities—a particular interest of Gladstone in the 1840s and 1850s.

‡ Comment noted during Asquith's visit to Hawarden—also a very rare accolade for a young member of a Gladstonian Cabinet; 28 Oct. 93. Asquith had first come to Gladstone's notice to the extent of mentions in his diary in April 1887; see 2, 16, 19 Apr. 87.　　§ 6 Nov. 92.

¶ See the description of the scene at Dalmeny in July 1892, taken from Morley's diary and printed in *The Gladstone Diaries*, Vol. XIII, Appendix I, as are the other quotations in this paragraph.

Gladstone at the most wretched political moments of his later years. He disliked Gladstone's political devices, referring in his description of his final Cabinet to 'that sham theatric accent of his'. His descriptions in his diary of Gladstone in the waning months of his last premiership reflect impatience and horror as well as pity and admiration; they are far from the depiction of simple nobility found in the third volume of his biography.

A notable missing minister was Lord Granville, who had sat in Cabinet with Gladstone since 1852. Granville died in 1891, his finances in as disastrous a state as those of the Duke of Newcastle twenty-seven years earlier. Gladstone had toiled to straighten out the Clintons' affairs: now he spent part of the early weeks of his government raising money among the aristocracy to prevent the Granvilles going bankrupt. Rosebery and Hartington (now the Duke of Devonshire) especially stumped up: the Duke of Westminster would not help. Gladstone paid the balance himself and public embarrassment was avoided.* He thus benefited the family twice over, for he had already helped to save the library of Granville's stepson, the historian Lord Acton, by similar behind-the-scenes arrangements, in Acton's case *via* Andrew Carnegie.†

Gladstone missed Granville for his political skills: an 'infinite loss', he felt. In Rosebery he had a Whig successor with a sharper edge but a political personality which both beguiled and infuriated. Gladstone went to greater lengths than he had with any colleague to persuade Rosebery into his Cabinet in 1892—partly because he needed him to assuage the Queen and her circle and partly because he had seen him as a possible successor and apparently still did. In his efforts to hook Rosebery, he cast the fly of the premiership over him by 'glancing at the leadership'. He soon regretted his persistence.

It would be wrong to go so far as to say Gladstone had planned the party's future leadership and, with the exception of his energetic efforts to get Rosebery into office in 1892, he so carefully avoided identifying his successor that when he resigned and the Queen, as we shall see, did not consult him, there was no person obviously supported by Gladstone and set aside by the Queen. But, helped by the exodus of 1886, he had given some younger, fresher Liberals their heads.

Gladstone thus led a Cabinet of sturdy Liberals, some ending their days in politics, some in mid-career and anxious, some with the knowledge that they were being given the best chance of their generation for the future. Their Liberalism was controlled and determined, with a certain ambivalence about the metropolis. It was not clear whether the Liberalism they

---

* A loan of about £60,000 was needed to stave off bankruptcy. B. W. Currie vetoed the first plan, initiated by Devonshire; after the election F. Leveson-Gower visited Gladstone at Hawarden and it fell to the latter to co-ordinate arrangements, which he did successfully at what was a highly inconvenient moment. He must have felt a certain piquancy in co-ordinating the politically divided Whigs in their rescue operation. † See 14 May, 9 June 90.

represented was still that of the governing classes, or whether they were an incursion of anti-metropolitanism into what had become a Unionist-dominated political culture. It had been an important objective of Salisbury's leadership since 1885 to establish conservative unionism as the normative reference point of British politics, with the Liberals seen as a dangerous and unpatriotic faction. It was an important part of Gladstone's leadership of the Cabinet and of the party that he presented himself as both the best product of the Christ Church tradition, working self-consciously in the main-stream channelled by Canning and Peel, and as the representative of 'the masses' against 'the classes' which constituted a political establishment corrupted by imperialism and self-seeking Unionism.

As in his previous governments, he was Leader of the House as well as First Lord,* a duty which involved him staying to the end of each day's sitting—often in the early hours of the next morning—and writing the daily report to the Queen. In 1893, Harcourt took on the late-hours watch on non-Irish nights (a minority). Despite Gladstone's age, leading the House was a sensible tactical precaution as well as a characteristic maintenance of the tradition that the First Lord should lead the House if a member of it.

Gladstone still led the Cabinet, as he had done since 1868, as its most effective parliamentary fighter. Even in his eighties he was always ready with an authoritative reply to a Tory attack, almost always able to rally his forces in the Commons and give them cheer. In a government whose Commons' majority was made up from two parties, this was a vital attribute of his leadership, and one which his colleagues knew was very hard to replace. He retained the ability to command the attention of the Commons by a skilful combination of the general and the particular, the humorous aside, and the well-turned impromptu peroration. He could also, in this last Parliament, bring adequately to heel what H. W. Lucy called 'the malcontents in his own camp'† and maintain the loyalty of the Irish. Despite the awkward character of his government's majority, it lost no important divisions.

As the Cabinet huddled together in the sharp Unionist wind, Gladstone gave its members a degree of confidence and even enthusiasm. He protected them from both their enemies and their supporters. Even in the very last meeting of his Cabinet, he found himself, as we shall see, sent out to round an awkward corner, taking on both the Lords and the Radicals.

Gladstone linked the 1892 Cabinet with the great days of hegemonic Liberalism, and he did so not sentimentally or nostalgically but positively and optimistically. In a political situation in which the Liberals could at best peg out claims for posterity, and at worst face considerable embarrassment if their majority fell apart, Gladstone offered dignity, resourcefulness,

---

* He was also Lord Privy Seal—effectively a frozen post.
† H. W. Lucy, *A diary of the Home Rule Parliament 1892–1895* (1896), 312.

resilience, and a determination to see his party through. In the history of the party of progress, now so scorned by a Unionism confident even in the face of electoral defeat, these were happy qualities. The government of 1892 was a disappointment. But it could have been a great deal worse.

In the difficult political circumstances created by the 1892 election, Gladstone avoided risk in forming his Cabinet. He did not countenance Dilke,* and he saw off Labouchere. A Home Rule Bill would not have failed until the Lords had actually rejected it; Gladstone went to considerable lengths to keep the Court as sweet as possible in the circumstances. Insulted by the Queen's extraordinary public announcement that she accepted Salisbury's resignation 'with regret', Gladstone accepted all the lectures and reprimands (fortunately for the Queen, Ponsonby's discretion prevented her most grotesque language reaching the Prime Minister). He had incurred the irritation of much of his party (led by Labouchere) by his bipartisan approach to the Royal Grants question in 1889,† and he declined to press Labouchere on an unwilling Victoria.‡

The fourth Gladstone Cabinet was thus chosen to reflect stability and continuity, with a nod to the future. As Gladstone liked to remind his colleagues, Melbourne's similarly placed government had lasted from 1835 to 1841. By continuity, Gladstone understood continuity in the preoccupations of the 1886 Cabinet: the 1892 Cabinet was formed after the strategic decision to press forward with a full-scale Home Rule bill had been taken.

Given the difficulties of its political position, and the complications

---

* Gladstone was not initially hostile to finding a way to bring Dilke back to political respectability after the Crawford divorce case; various discussions occurred and a meeting was arranged which Dilke failed to attend (see 1 July 89). In the post-Parnell atmosphere of 1891, Gladstone wrote a memorandum distinguishing between the implications of the Parnell and Dilke scandals but concluding that, for the time being, the adoption of Dilke as a candidate would have 'a most prejudicial influence' because it would weaken the position of the anti-Parnellite Irish Parliamentary party. In 1892, Gladstone was irritated by Dilke's implication in 'a plaguy speech' that Gladstone supported his candidacy for the Forest of Dean seat; Gladstone took the high ground 'on the great subject of conjugal life' in a letter to W. T. Stead: 'You are right in supposing that my lately published letter is meant to show my entire and absolute disconnection from all matters associated with the Candidature of Sir Charles Dilke'; see 13 Mar. 91, 4 May 92.

† See 9–25 July 92 and M. Barker, *Gladstone and Radicalism* (1975), 171ff.

‡ Of course, Labouchere had little of the substance of Dilke or Chamberlain, whose appointments Gladstone had insisted on and energetically defended in the 1880s; see Barker, op. cit., 173–4. It is unclear how seriously Gladstone took the campaign for the Cabinet of 'Mr Labbi M.P.'. It proved a major talking point from 3 July 92 onwards. Gladstone went through the motions, but without much drive. He must have known that the Queen would—as she did—object. When Labouchere published the correspondence between himself and Gladstone he referred to Gladstone's 'chivalry in covering the Royal action by assuming the constitutional responsibility of a proceeding', but the opposite may just as well have been the case: the Queen (for once) useful to Gladstone. It was important, with respect to keeping the Radicals in line for 1893, that Gladstone be seen to have tried and the Queen to have behaved prejudicially.

After an amazed initial reaction, Gladstone viewed more open-mindedly than might have been expected Labouchere's next request, for the Washington embassy: 'I am not at all sure that Labouchere would do the work of a mission badly. I had no idea he was so young at 60' (to Morley, 17 Oct. 92; see also 11 Nov. 92).

surrounding the negotiations which got Rosebery in and kept Labouchere out, the Cabinet worked better than might have been expected. It was an odd staging post in the history of the Liberal party, and its members knew it. Everything about it was transitory: its leader, its majority, many of its legislative proposals.

It was primarily an emblem. Liberalism could still form a government, and govern well within the limits permitted by its majority. Home Rule could be passed by the House of Commons, and the Home Rule MPs consequently had a prospect of eventual success. The Unionists could be shown up as relying ultimately on an hereditary class to defend their interests regardless of the wishes of the majority of the representatives of the United Kingdom taken as a whole, and their willingness to corrupt the natural evolution of the constitution could be seen not merely on Home Rule but on other questions also. The self-contradiction of a Unionism which gave England a veto on constitutional questions could be exposed. Of course, this was a limited ground: it admitted the extent to which the Liberal party, once the natural party of government, had become a party dispossessed. But the government of 1892 was a government for all that: if the Unionists cared to use the Lords to frustrate the Commons, then they would be seen in their true light.

The extent to which Salisbury would use the Peers was not apparent in August 1892. The Government of Ireland Bill was in question, but not the rest of the programme. Moreover, on all the previous major clashes with the Lords, the Commons had, rather quickly, triumphed. The Cabinet thus met for the first time on 19 August for 'an initiatory Cabinet', not seated formally by portfolio, but 'in looser order' for an informal discussion of priorities: 'To contemplate by preference (except Home Rule) subjects capable of the most concise treatment.' The 1893 Session was to have a 'twin purpose': Ireland and British business.* The burden of Ireland was to fall to the Prime Minister. Gladstone's last premiership was to be no dignified autumnal parade, like that of Churchill in 1951, but a full-scale battle with the Prime Minister at the head of his forces.

The Second Home Rule Bill

The Government of Ireland Bill 1893 was the last great statute prepared by Gladstone. It reflected all the strengths and weaknesses of the 1886 bill and, unlike the 1886 bill, it stood alone. The Land Bill, central and integral to the 1886 plan, was not repeated. Land legislation was mentioned in the conversations with Parnell before 1890, and a bill on evicted tenants was to be started from the backbenches, but of the bill which had occasioned Chamberlain and Trevelyan's exit from the Cabinet in 1886 there was no sign. That bill had had two objectives: to assist in the creation of a loyal

* 19 Aug. 92.

peasant proprietorship, and to offer a way out of Ireland for the Anglo-Irish landowners. Unionist land purchase was doing the second, albeit in a form Gladstone had disliked. The proposal of Home Rule and the Liberal party's steady adherence to it had already secured the Home-Rule movement for constitutionalism and consequently the social prudentialism of 1885–6 had to a significant extent become unnecessary.

The 1893 bill was thus more limited in conception than that of the 1886 twin-bill plan: it was a straightforward proposal for constitutional amendment. The bill established as its central feature an Irish legislature with two houses and a British-style executive dependent upon it. Ireland would enter gradually into her full powers, with legislation on land, the judiciary, the police, and finance only permitted after a variety of intervals. There was, therefore, a deliberate element of the provisional about the initial character and powers of the Irish legislature. Since Irish representative government and politics would be starting from scratch, establishing its executive, its offices, its buildings and its parties, this was a common-sense approach, accepted as such by most of the Irish MPs and especially disliked by the Liberal Unionists because it was premised on the natural development of institutions rather than on the sort of schematic rigidity which Chamberlain favoured. It was also more limited in another sense. The 1886 bill had been seen as the precursor to a general restructuring of the constitution of the United Kingdom—much of the debate on the exclusion or inclusion of the Irish MPs had focused on this point. For if they were excluded, it could hardly be a precedent for extension of further measures for Home Rule (as Westminster would end up with no MPs at all). Save for the accompanying Parish Councils Bill, the 1893 bill made no response to the 'home-rule-all-round' cry which the 1886 bill had encouraged, and Gladstone attached to the preparation of the bill—through the device of a Cabinet committee—those of his Cabinet especially committed to a simple Irish bill.* Terms of reference were discussed, but the Cabinet gave its committee no very clear direction.

Gladstone now paid the penalty for his reluctance to get an agreed party position on the central problems. The Cabinet accepted the committee's recommendation that 80 Irish MPs be included at Westminster, but only for certain purposes: Irish and Imperial but not British questions. This was a distinction which for second-order matters could be drawn by compromise and experience. But on fundamental questions of power certainty was needed. The traditional means of forcing the expulsion of a ministry was a 'no confidence' motion in the Commons. As Gladstone himself

---

* Its members were Gladstone, Spencer, Herschell, John Morley, Bryce, and Campbell-Bannerman. See 21 Nov. 92. Gladstone considered including Asquith, who saw Home Rule in the context of the development of an Imperial constitution, but Spencer in a note preferred Campbell-Bannerman; ibid. See also J. Kendle, *Ireland and the federal solution* (1989), 74ff. for the 'home-rule-all-round' movement and the bill.

pointed out, such motions would not mention details. Would the Irish vote on them, or not? This was the basic problem raised by keeping the Irish MPs 'in', even if in a reduced number. As in 1886, dispute about this point led to a government amendment to the clause (clause 9) during the Committee stage in 1893 (Irish MPs were to attend the Commons at Westminster without any restrictions). Unlike 1886, however, the change was made without the bill's majority being lost.

An agreement before the 'time of crisis' might have been reached in such a way as to tie the party to it, and it may have been Gladstone's intention to build on his conversations with Parnell in 1889, when this point was discussed, to achieve a quasi-public agreement. The split in the Irish party and its absence of an agreed leader made this impossible, from a Liberal point of view, after 1890.

Less easy to settle in advance was the question of finance. Gladstone had come to realize that the settlement proposed with Irish concurrence in 1886—a fixed cash contribution by Ireland to the Imperial exchequer, to be reviewed in 1916—took no account of inflation or deflation of the currency.* The conversation with Parnell in 1889 pointed to Ireland paying 'a fixed percentage of the total *Imperial* charge, varying in amount only with the variation of that charge', but this was not the proposal made in 1893. This was to retain some element of the notion of a fixed sum, but not in a cash form. A financial settlement was approved by the Cabinet, but with a number of important questions left open for decision during the Committee stage and with Harcourt (as Chancellor of the Exchequer) trying to introduce major modifications after the bill had been introduced and on the evening before its publication.† The British exchequer was to be credited with Ireland's customs duties (levied by Westminster) as her contribution, an arrangement to be reviewed after 15 years. The balance between that sum and the present Irish revenue would be the Irish government's income (which as it would control all taxes except customs and excise it could increase or decrease if it wished). The adequacy of this balance and the fairness of the solution rested on the financial expertise of the Treasury (Welby and the young Alfred Milner) and Dublin Castle in providing the figures. When they did provide them, they were wrong: the amount raised from excise duties in Ireland was badly exaggerated by a faulty calculation. Nobody spotted the mistake until after the bill had been introduced.‡

* See memorandum at 18 Dec. 89. Parnell's manifesto 'To the People of Ireland' of November 1890 did not mention the financial settlement as one of the topics about which the 1889 meeting had disquieted him.

† Harcourt's objective was to retain strategic financial control by the Treasury; his various proposals thus had the implication of sharply limiting the area of Irish financial autonomy.

‡ The effect of the miscalculation in Excise receipts was to reduce the amount for government in Ireland by over £200,000 to a clearly inadequate level. Hamilton laid the blame for 'the blunder'

A complete restructuring of the financial clauses thus became necessary when the bill was in Committee. The bill was changed so that all Irish taxation would be aggregated as Irish revenue (instead of the Customs being transferred to the Imperial exchequer). Ireland would then contribute to the Imperial exchequer 'one third part of the general revenue of Ireland'. That is, there would be a calculation of what the general revenue of Ireland was—a highly contentious procedure; of this, one third would go to the Imperial exchequer as Ireland's payment for defence and all the governmental activities not devolved, and two-thirds would be available for expenditure on activities devolved to Ireland. Consequently, if the Irish revenue increased (through a higher yield from greater consumption or through higher taxes), one-third would go to the Imperial exchequer. Unlike the proposals of 1886, which as we have seen would have been highly favourable to the Irish, and the initial proposals of 1893, this hastily produced recommendation would have been a serious political irritant, especially during the transitional period of six years.

The error and the consequent amendments were humiliating for Gladstone: 'a very anxious & *rather* barren morning on Irish Finance. My present position as a whole certainly seems peculiar: but of this it is unheroic either to speak or think.'* The confusion compounded the Cabinet's change of front on the question of how far the Irish MPs should be 'in' at Westminster. In 1886, the bill had been forged in the heat of a great political crisis. That of 1893 had been in the offing for seven years, yet there was still disagreement and muddle about the two central clauses of the bill. To say that this simply reflected the inherent ambivalence of 'Home Rule' simply further reflected the short-term strength of the Unionists' case.

Despite this, the passing of the 1893 Government of Ireland Bill in the Commons was a remarkable exercise in representative politics. The Unionists appeared to take the bill at face value and fought it clause by clause, making most of the speeches. Backbench Liberals and most of the Irish were almost silent, by the self-denying ordinance agreed at the 'excellent: most opportune' Liberal party meeting on 27 March. Only on 27 July as the guillotine fell on the Committee stage after sixty-three days did the mask slip. Chamberlain told the Liberals that never since the days of Herod had there been such slaves to a dictator: he was answered by shouts

---

clearly on Milner; Gladstone was less willing to apportion it. The explanation of how the mistake in calculation occurred was given by Milner and Lacy Robinson in a letter published in *Parliamentary Papers* 1893–4 l. 345. They remarked: 'On the basis of the revised figures, the contribution for Ireland for the year 1892–3 is £2,240,351, not £2,605,000, as estimated by Mr. Gladstone (relying upon the amount for the previous year given in the "Financial Relations" papers of 1891 and 1893) in his speech on the First Reading of the Home Rule Bill. We can only express our great regret for the occurrence of an error of such magnitude. . . .'

* 30 May 93.

of 'Judas'. In 'the sad scene never to be forgotten', fighting broke out on the floor of the House when the Unionists refused to clear for the division.

The time-saving reticence of the Liberal-Irish backbenchers during the summer highlighted Gladstone's role on the Front Bench as he worked the bill seemingly single-handed and through a heatwave. He was from time to time garrulous and the Unionists knew how to lead him on. He felt himself supported by some external force: 'It is fanatical to say I seemed to be held up by a strength not my own. . . .' 'Never have my needs been so heavy: but it seems as if God were lovingly minded to supply them only from day to day. "The fellowship of the Holy Ghost" is the continuing boon which seems the boon for me.' Beginning a new volume of his daily journal, he made a list of biblical 'Texts for the present stress.'

Gladstone was supported not only by such thoughts but also by the sense that the bill of 1893 was not the end of the matter. Once decided upon it—and as we have seen he was, in the light of the arithmetic of the election result, sceptical about going ahead—he saw it as a first step. The Lords would of course throw it out, but would they dare to do so again in 1894 if the bill—or a Resolution on it—again passed the Commons. There must come a point when the Lords 'would not dare' (as he had put it in 1885). In thinking this, Gladstone probably underestimated Salisbury's resolute combination of short-term pragmatism and long-term constitutional sterility.

'This is a great step', Gladstone noted on the passing of the Third Reading by a majority of 34 on 1 September 1893 after eighty-two sittings and an extended Session. If he meant that it was a step to be followed by another great step, he soon found himself to be wrong. The Government of Ireland Bill of 1893 showed that a Home Rule bill could pass the Commons, but it had not shown that it could do so conclusively.

This was a serious weakness, for it spoilt the thrust of Gladstone's second position, a dissolution on the House of Lords. If there was to be a dissolution on the wrecking powers of the Lords, it would have to be on a clear misuse of those powers. The events of the summer of 1893 played into the Unionists' hands. There was no overwhelming case for a dissolution on the Lords' rejection of the bill. On the day of their vote, 8 September, when the bill was rejected after a brief debate by 419 to 41, Gladstone was driving 'to the pass over Pitlochrie' and was translating Horace's *Odes* in the Scottish Highlands. He made no comment on the Lords' actions in his journal. In the autumn he floated the idea of a return to Home Rule in 1894—perhaps by a bill or a Resolution—but his colleagues would not follow. There was no Cabinet meeting to discuss the fate of the bill, and Gladstone did not return to London until 1 November. When the Cabinet did meet, the Lords were not on the agenda, and neither was Ireland except for the position of the Evicted Tenants Bill in the usual Commons' log-jam.

The great drive for the second Home Rule bill which had begun in the aftermath of the election defeat in 1886 and which had reached a point of genuine optimism in the late 1880s, had ended with a stand-off. The Commons had passed a bill and the Lords had rejected it. The Liberal-Irish partnership was not strong enough to dissolve upon the Lords' actions. The 'cause' was not dead but it lacked the vitality and the urgency to take on and defeat Unionism. Such remained the case for the rest of Ireland's presence within the Union. Outrageous though the Lords' actions might be, Ireland by herself was not a sufficient battering ram to break them.

Thoughts of Retirement

The failure of the Government of Ireland Bill brought Gladstone close to a final reckoning with political life. His political presence since 1874 had been self-admittedly abnormal. He was in politics for the furtherance of specific causes, not for a political career of the usual sort. The last of those causes continued, but hardly in a way in which he could hope to assist: any further Irish initiative by the Liberals would require a fresh majority in the Commons, and Gladstone's hopes for a new Government of Ireland Bill in 1894 were, as we have seen, ignored by his colleagues.

Yet the resignation of a Prime Minister, however much it might be natural and expected, can never be a simple matter, and the sinuous complexities of Gladstone's life in politics would lead us to expect ambivalence. There were factors beyond his own preferences. He had spent 1893 largely absorbed in the Irish bill, but his colleagues had not been similarly absorbed, as their absence from the government bench during its committee stage had made rather clear. The government was pursuing as full a legislative programme as the 82 days taken by the Irish bill permitted. It became clear that the willingness of the Lords to amend Liberal bills was not confined to Ireland: here was a possible opportunity for the furtherance of the Irish cause within a more general context. Instead of being seen as the impediment which blocked the way, Ireland might be linked to British measures obstructed by the Lords and thus the difficulty of the 'English' majority against Home Rule side-stepped. The House of Lords and all it represented would become the chief focus of Liberal attention, with Irish Home Rule one aspect of it. Even on his own terms, therefore, there were reasons for Gladstone continuing in office, perhaps even fighting a final election on the basis of the Lords' disturbance of the balance of the constitution.

In addition to the question of the Lords, two other factors affected Gladstone's thinking about his retirement: his personal condition and the 'mad and mischievous' matter of the defence estimates, to which we shall return.

Gladstone ended the Irish marathon in fair shape. On his 84th birthday he noted:

I record my 84th birthday with thanks and humiliation. My strength has been wonderfully maintained but digestive organs are I think beginning to fail: deafness is (at present) a greater difficulty, and sight the greatest.

His eyesight recovered up to a point from the 'gingerbread' incident in Chester in 1892, but the cataract in his eye increasingly impeded sight. Colleagues tried to help by having their letters to him typed, but he found this worse than their handwriting. Moreover, the cataract was 'of the kind obstinately slow', so an operation to remove it was not yet possible. His eyesight was thus a reason for retiring, but it was not sufficiently bad to make retirement imperative.

Gladstone's worries about his health were increased by the death of his physician, Andrew Clark, on whom he had often relied at important political moments for advice as to how far his various illnesses and physical difficulties should determine his actions. Clark, with Mrs Gladstone, had always encouraged continuing in politics. The domestic importance of Clark's death was compounded by the suicide of Zadok Outram, Gladstone's valet, whose alcoholism had been an increasing concern of the household. He had been replaced as valet in October 1892 'after what a course of years!', subsequently disappearing and being found drowned in the Thames. Gladstone wanted 'to attend the Inquest, but at any rate I gave particular testimony by a letter'. The episode considerably disquieted him. He noted after Zadok's disappearance:

Outram's absconding really afflicts & somewhat alarms me. Ever since I began to feel I was growing old I have been his daily care & he has served me with daily intelligence and daily affection.*

The deaths of Clark and Outram were important disturbances in a routine of life in which Gladstone was, hardly surprisingly, increasingly dependent on his immediate circle:

I have had a heavy loss in Sir A. Clark: & a touching one in Zadok Outram. The love & service of C[atherine] remains wonderful: that of all my children hardly less so.†

Minor Aspects of the Premiership

Personal difficulties such as these encouraged a review already required by the more general political situation. Moreover, Gladstone's handling of business began to show a want of proportion. Small items of business engaged his attention at the expense of more major matters. The career of West Ridgeway (a Unionist civil servant), the question of a dukedom for

* 3 Dec. 93.   † 29 Dec. 93.

the Marquis of Lansdowne on his retirement as Viceroy of India, and the financial settlement for the Duke of Edinburgh on succeeding as Duke of Saxe-Coburg and Gotha generated a considerable correspondence. But the Cabinet's move towards direct involvement in labour relations by appointing Rosebery as conciliator in the major mining lockout in the autumn of 1893—a vital moment in the history of British corporatism—seemed hardly to engage Gladstone's attention at all, despite its implications for his view of political economy.

It was not that in earlier governments Gladstone would have fought the Queen any less stoutly over Lansdowne's title—Lansdowne would have been Gladstone's second duke and an important Liberal creation: the Queen was determined to block him—but that in earlier governments the Lansdowne affair would have been one item among a hundred. In 1893–4 the affair seemed to show Gladstone crotchety.

If the miners' settlement flitted by, the vacancy in the Poet Laureateship consequent on the death of Tennyson in October 1892 did not. This was a parlour game which all could play, including, of course, the Queen. Tennyson died on 6 October, babbling of Gladstone and trees. Gladstone was at Hawarden and felt himself too busy with Uganda and the writing of his Romanes lecture to accept Hallam Tennyson's invitation to act as a pall-bearer at the funeral, despite the significance of the Tennysonian link to the closest friend of his youth, Arthur Hallam. None the less, Gladstone was immediately in correspondence about a new Laureate, which he was keen to keep 'on the high moral plane where Wordsworth and Tennyson left it'.* His preferred solution was John Ruskin—a poet in prose—suggested by Acton. The appointment of Ruskin would have certainly represented the incarnation of the sage. The thought was magnanimous, for Gladstone had been denounced by Ruskin almost as vehemently as he had been by Tennyson, whose peerage he had secured: he had enjoyed with both an ambivalent *rapprochement* in old age. Henry Acland reported that Ruskin's mental illness ruled him out. Swinburne and William Morris were inquired into, Gladstone being quite sympathetic to each (Morris had of course been a strong supporter of the Bulgarian atrocities campaign). He was already fairly well read in their works, more so in Swinburne than in Morris. When he had read Swinburne's *Marino Faliero* in 1885 (at Laura Thistlethwayte's suggestion) he had thought it 'a work of great power: dramatic power, power of thought, and wonderful mastery over the English language'. But both Swinburne and Morris were impossible candidates to propose to the Queen, Swinburne for his 'licentiousness', Morris for his

* To H. W. Acland, 10 Oct. 92. For the Laureateship, see also Alan Bell, 'Gladstone looks for a Poet Laureate', *Times Literary Supplement*, 21 July 1972, p. 847.

'Socialism'.* Others were looked at—William Watson, Lewis Morris, Robert Bridges, Fred Henderson the I.L.P. poet, Alfred Austin the jingo versifier—but none was felt appointable. With no candidate strong enough to be an adequate replacement for Wordsworth and Tennyson or to be worth a row with the Court, and with the detailed work on the Government of Ireland Bill predominating, Gladstone rather lost heart. The Laureate-ship was discussed at an audience with the Queen on 25 November 1892 and it was agreed to leave it in abeyance. After Kipling declined in 1895, Salisbury in 1896 successfully recommended Alfred Austin, the worst poet to hold the post in modern times, an appointment which emphasized the bathetic character of the 1890s and one which vindicated Gladstone's view (rather unusual for him) that it was sometimes best to do nothing.†

Africa and Egypt: a Prophecy reluctantly fulfilled

On the whole, ministers had a free run in the fourth Gladstone Cabinet. That overarching involvement of the Prime Minister in almost all his government's affairs had, hardly surprisingly, been lacking in the 1892 administration. Also hardly surprisingly, when Gladstone did attempt to assert his authority in a major way outside the area of Irish policy, it was in that other area of unsettled business of the 1880 government, Imperial policy. His fourth government began with a row about the extent of imperial commitments, and it and his premiership ended with one. On both questions, Gladstone was on the losing side. In the initial months of the government he led a majority of the Cabinet against Rosebery and the Foreign Office on the question of Uganda (which because there was no question of a formal colony came under the Foreign rather than the Colonial Office).

East Africa had been the single area of Africa where Gladstone had been able in the 1880–5 government to frustrate the 'forward movement'. The Salisbury government in 1890 signed the Anglo-German Agreement by which the German government ceded British control of the areas later called Uganda and Kenya and recognized a British protectorate over Zanzibar in exchange for Heligoland. The Salisbury government had had recourse to imperialism by the back door in the area north and west of Lake Victoria, *via* the device of the Chartered Company, that curious but con-venient half-way-house where venture capitalism and the British govern-ment could each have its separate room under the same roof. But when the roof began to fall down, the tenancy agreement was always found to be poorly drawn. Like other Chartered Companies, but quicker than most, the

---

* Either would probably have produced a view of the Queen more recognizable to Gladstone than that found in Tennyson's 'On the Jubilee of Queen Victoria': 'She beloved for a kindliness Rare in Fable or History . . . All is gracious, gentle, great and Queenly.'

† It was said that Salisbury justified the appointment by saying he had made it for the best reason in the world: Austin wanted it.

East African Company collapsed, leaving the Imperial government with undefined but implied residual responsibility. This responsibility was admitted by the Salisbury government only to the extent of making preparations for the building of what became the Mombasa–Kampala railway. But there can be little doubt that Salisbury would have done whatever was necessary to maintain British control of the headwaters of the Nile against the French and the Belgians.

Somewhat to his surprise, almost immediately after persuading Rosebery to be Foreign Secretary, Gladstone found himself involved in a major row with the Secretary and the Foreign Office, which he saw as withholding information and misleading the Cabinet. As always in Imperial matters, disagreements about general principles were impossible to disentangle from the complex details of the historically given position. Thus Rosebery could argue with only partial disingenuity that what was at issue 'is not now the expediency of an East African Empire' but the fact that a Company 'has been allowed to interfere, with a royal charter granted by the Executive for that purpose' and that if the Company could no longer administer the area, the British government had effective responsibility for the fate of 'the territory, the inhabitants and the missionaries'.* In addition to his usual objections to Imperial expansion—that 'prevailing earth-hunger'—Gladstone not implausibly feared a repeat of the Gordon *débâcle*. There were several common elements: the Company not the Cabinet was nominally in control; it would be difficult simply to retreat; communications made it almost impossible for the Cabinet to direct policy. On the other hand— unlike the case of the Sudan—there were missionaries of various denominations already in the area and there had already been deaths. An evacuation which did not include the missionaries could lead to a disaster, as Rosebery pointed out.

Gladstone cunningly argued for a continuation of Salisbury's policy, by which, he told Rosebery, 'I saw clearly that they accepted the evacuation'. This attempt to cast Rosebery as the radical disturber was only partly successful. Gladstone mounted the last of his full-scale campaigns, a blitz of letters and memoranda in September and October 1892 by which he hoped to close down Rosebery. Much of the Cabinet was with him, or ahead of him. Gladstone rather assumed that having the Cabinet with him meant the success of his views. The object of much of his correspondence was to avoid defeating Rosebery in such a way as to provoke the latter's resignation.† But the steady drip-drip of Imperial expansion wore the Prime Minister down. The Foreign Office craftily encouraged the mis-

---

* Rosebery to Gladstone, 29 September 1892; see 27 Sept. 92n.

† This was why he worked so hard—ultimately without success—to prevent Uganda coming to the Cabinet: he thought a Cabinet meeting would mean a public humiliation for Rosebery (for news of a defeat for Rosebery would immediately be leaked by the Court).

sionary societies to agitate for a protectorate by petitions, letters to the press, and public meetings. These had a powerful effect. Rosebery secured a Cabinet discussion—against Gladstone's will—and extracted a delay: the Cabinets in November 1892 agreed to an inquiry, conducted by a Commissioner who would report 'on the actual state of affairs in Uganda, and the best means of dealing with the country'. The possibility of indirect rule *via* a Zanzibari protectorate (a protectorate governed by a protectorate) was thrown in as a further softening of the pill.

Gerald Portal, the appointed Commissioner, was an old Cairo hand, formerly Cromer's secretary, and was already consul-general for British East Africa. He was a skilful propagandist, infuriating Gladstone with his public pronouncements.* In his report he did his duty.†

The remote town in Uganda named Fort Portal is placed at the meeting of the Ruwenzori Mountains and Lake Albert, which by the 1890s was the most vulnerable of the sources of the Nile to non-British European control. It symbolizes therefore the extent to which the question of Uganda was but an aspect of the larger dispute about Britain's role in the Near East. Gladstone had discussed precisely this region with Sir William McKinnon and H. M. Stanley, the explorer, at the time of the 1890 Heligoland–East Africa Agreement. The meeting was arranged by Dorothy Tennant, Stanley's *fiancée*, who advised Gladstone on aspects of his reading. Stanley produced a map of East Africa, hoping for an imperialistic discussion of its developmental potential, but Gladstone turned the conversation into a lecture on the folly of giving modern names to Crophi and Mophi, Herodotus's names for the highest peaks in the Ruwenzori Mountains. It is hard to tell which side of the conversation was the more surreal: Stanley's view that Uganda was the answer to the problems of the South Wales coalfield, or Gladstone's pedantic classicism. The latter, at least, was probably a political ploy.

Uganda, because of its remoteness, was one of the last pieces in what was now a largely complete imperialist jigsaw puzzle. Its shape thus related to the general pattern of African demarcation. The row about Uganda consequently became interwoven with discussions with the French about Egypt.

All the old ambivalence continued. The British presence in Egypt was temporary, but how temporary? Could the collaboration of the early 1880s with the French on Egyptian policy be restored? Any progress towards developing a context within which a Liberal Cabinet might attempt a

---

* Portal died of fever soon after his return to London in November 1893, but he had time to write an account for publication of his mission (*The British mission to Uganda* (1894)) which provided a useful base for protest should the government have rejected the report.

† The policy of withdrawal from Uganda was officially abandoned in March 1894 immediately after Gladstone's retiral and a protectorate was declared on 19 June 1894; see K. Ingham, *The making of modern Uganda* (1958), 60–2.

withdrawal was halted by the Egyptians themselves. In January 1893 the new Khedive, Abbas II, dismissed his Prime Minister, Cromer's puppet. Cromer demanded action from London in the form of extra troops and what Gladstone understood to be 'the putting down of treaty rights (such I believe they are) of the Khedive by British forces; the threat of it is the same thing'. Sufficient troops were redirected to Egypt to assuage the Egyptian lobby and the immediate crisis passed.

The Gladstonian occupation of Egypt in 1882 had had the objective of securing order, and order was understood to mean order on European terms. Only through demonstrated order could a context for withdrawal be achieved. But since this sort of order meant a harmony of European/Egyptian interests, with the Khedive's ministers effectively in the same position as the Residents at the courts of the legally independent Indian Princes, a context for withdrawal could by definition never be achieved. The only likely change was a calling in of the European Powers. The Cabinet recognized this, however unwillingly:

the general sentiment was that if the severance in spirit of Native and British Govt. became chronic, the situation in Egypt would be fundamentally changed, & the Powers would have to be called in.

'Egypt for the Egyptians' was further off than it had been in the aftermath of the occupation of 1882.

This was the basic weakness of the Gladstonians' attempt to avoid involvement in Uganda. The complex forces of capital investment, geography, and British strategic interest which had sucked the Gladstone government into Egypt in 1882 made British occupation of the rest of the Nile hard to avoid. To repeat Gladstone's prophecy of 1877:

our first site in Egypt, be it by larceny or be it by emption, will be the almost certain egg of a North African Empire, that will grow and grow until another Victoria and another Albert, titles of the Lake-sources of the White Nile, come within our borders.*

That Gladstone's 1880–5 government had taken the first two steps, in Egypt and the Sudan, had been ironic enough. That his last government had had to take the third showed how far beyond the control of individuals, however powerful, the forces behind imperial expansion lay.

Gladstone had resisted almost all of the many Imperial acquisitions of the Cabinets in which he had sat since 1843, but he had failed with almost all of them. His vision of a world economy progressing through free trade was frustrated by the territorial ambitions of some of his colleagues, the exigencies of the great departments of state and the historical forces of venture-capital expansion and strategic interest which conditioned the actions of British governments in the second half of the nineteenth century.

* See above, p. 276.

Like the Liberal Imperialists, Gladstone had had no answer to the question: by what agency, if not European authority, was an infrastructure to be provided when venture-capitalism—the spearhead of that free trade which was the natural consequence of progress—spread to areas of the world hitherto outside the Atlantic economy and lacking a political structure which could maintain itself in the face of 'progress'?

The question was brutally posed by the actions of the British South Africa Company in Mashonaland and Matabeleland in 1893, as a manufactured war made those territories into Southern Rhodesia. Lost in the complexities of an administrative and legal structure obscure even by the standards of Chartered Companies, absorbed by the Government of Ireland Bill's passage in the Commons, obsessed and absented by the trivial case of the Duke of Edinburgh's settlement on accession to the dukedom of Coburg,* Gladstone, somewhat alarmed but disconnected, failed to stiffen Ripon, the Colonial Secretary, in his attempts to maintain Imperial control in the summer and autumn of 1893. Gladstone focused on the allocation of costs and the distribution of responsibility rather than on consequences. 'Rhodes wants nothing' read Gladstone's note jotted down during the Cabinet on 31 August 1893—one of the most erroneous observations in the history of British imperialism—and Rhodes was effectively given a free hand. This was not altogether surprising. Rhodes had contributed to Liberal party funds and had energetically courted the party leadership. Meetings and dinners had shown him to be a good fellow: 'A notable man', Gladstone recorded on dining with him on 19 February 1891. Morley—hardly a politician prone to imperial expansionism—thought Rhodes 'Evidently a man capable of wide imperial outlook and daring and decided views. I found nothing to dislike in him.'† Thus Gladstone's defence of Rhodes in the Commons—'that very able man'—and of the Company fitted an established context. Moreover, Gladstone thought race relations best sorted out locally between a responsible colonial government and the indigenous population, the Imperial factor being as likely to cause complications as to do good.‡ Though he recognized that the Company could not be regarded as a responsible colonial government, he effectively treated it as such.

Thus, Gladstone's last administration continued the process of mopping

---

* The Coburg affair was symbolic of the extent to which Gladstone had become mesmerized by the Court. It took precedence over Matabeleland at the Cabinet of 4 Nov. 1893, and Ripon complained at the 'brief and unsatisfactory' discussion of the latter. After the Cabinet, Gladstone took the Coburg affair further in great detail but appears to have made little effort to meet his promise to Ripon for a thorough subsequent discussion about Matabeleland.

† Morley's diary, 19 Feb. 1891, reporting a dinner with Rhodes hosted by Rendel at which Gladstone was also present. Though Rhodes sat between Gladstone and Morley, his chief conversation was with the latter, for Morley noted: 'The African has a fine head; a bold full eye, and a strong chin. He talked to me during the whole of dinner, in favour of imperial customs union. . . .'

‡ 4H 18. 595 ff.

up what was left of sub-Saharan Africa. It did so in the face of Gladstone's own warnings about strategic and political involvements overstretching Britain's economic base, and it did so with no corporate commitment. None the less, act it did. For all the absence of real Imperial enthusiasm in the Colonial and Foreign Offices and for all the supposed power of the Prime Minister, Gladstone's will was frustrated. Uganda was an undoubted and obvious humiliation for Gladstone, and it turned him against Rosebery for the premiership. It was ironic that Uganda, an area of significance to only the most determined Imperialist, was the focus of a major row and a powerful defeat for Gladstone and the anti-Imperialists, while, with Rhodes benefiting from Rosebery's victory over Uganda, Southern Rhodesia—eventually to come within an ace of being Britain's Algeria—was acquired in what was, as far as Gladstone was concerned, very nearly 'a fit of absence of mind'.

The Navy Scare of 1893–1894 and the Prelude to Resignation

In what turned out to be the final months of his fourth government, Gladstone found himself more isolated and even impotent on another Imperial question: the size of the navy. He was more isolated because a strong navy was the centrepiece of the 'blue water school' of strategic thought, of which almost all Liberals were members. The increase of the French and Russian fleets and the *rapprochement* between those two nations (shortly to become an alliance), the pace of technical advance in shipbuilding, the questionable competence of the British fleet exemplified by the *Camperdown-Victoria* collision in June 1893 and the early stirrings of the Kaiser's navy programme, all pointed to increased expenditure on the navy. The question was linked to Egypt and to Imperial strategy by the fact that the immediate area of concern was not the strength of the home fleet but of that in the Mediterranean. This was precisely that area where the events of the government hitherto suggested that even Gladstone with Cabinet backing would find it difficult to stop the Imperial departments of state, and particularly the Foreign Office and the Admiralty, adept as they were at co-ordinating their tactics and at using the Queen and even the opposition as auxiliaries.

From the summer of 1893, Spencer, the First Lord of the Admiralty, accepted strong advice from his Sea Lords and laid plans, keeping Rosebery and the Foreign Office informed.* Energetically working the Irish bill, then out of London, then preoccupied by the deaths of Clark and Outram, Gladstone seems to have been unaware of the dramatic plan that was to be put to the Cabinet by the Admiralty when the estimates were first considered in December 1893. His mind was focused on the matter by the Queen, who in a manœuvre constitutionally extraordinary even by her

* See *Spencer*, ii. 223, 225ff.

standards instructed him to read to the Cabinet her letter on the condition of the navy—which he did on 14 December—and by Lord George Hamilton (Salisbury's First Lord in the 1886–92 government) who moved a motion on the navy in the Commons.

Gladstone persuaded the Cabinet to treat Hamilton's motion (intended to appear bipartisan while in fact embarrassing the government) as a motion of no confidence. Gladstone moved an amendment to it on 19 December:

Moved my amendment. Majority 36. The situation almost hopeless when a large minority allows itself in panic and joining hands with the professional elements works on the susceptibilities of a portion of the people to alarm.

He then went on to make the navy estimates a matter of the Cabinet's confidence in him. Twenty years earlier he had dealt with an analogous situation, then to do with Cardwell's army estimates. The 1874 dissolution of Parliament had been, unbeknown to the public, a dissolution by Gladstone against the army expenditure of his own first government. In 1894 he threatened a resignation against the Liberal Cabinet which would be disastrous for it at the general election, whenever that came. The Admiralty's press campaign, accompanied by well-leaked threats of the Sea Lords' readiness to resign and Hamilton's motion, had made open a question which would not normally have been before the public at that stage. The difficulty which had in the past sometimes affected Gladstone's plans for a resignation of protest—that the matter was not one of public discussion—had thus been removed by his opponents. But as so often before, the Whigs would not let him go.

Spencer was as well-placed as anyone could be to keep the old man on ship. Though he was First Lord of the Admiralty he was also, beside Gladstone himself, much the most effective and perhaps the most committed of the Home Rulers. Despite the row over the navy estimates, he was to be Gladstone's preference as his successor. They met, cordially, but made no progress. But 'we agreed that in any case I ought to wind up the present Session' (then due to end in mid-February 1894).* Spencer may not have picked up the significance of this remark, which Gladstone probably expected would be passed on to other Cabinet colleagues.

Gladstone felt a rage of impotence against his failing powers and his weakening political position. John Morley saw him at the nadir, on 8 January 1894, when Gladstone returned from Brighton on a foggy day feeling 'haunted by the Spectre in front'. Morley 'roused him from a doze' and the old man rambled in his fury, as Morley recorded in his diary:

not exactly an incoherent conversation, but there was no *suite* or continuity to it . . . [Gladstone told him] 'It is not a question of a million here or a million there. It is a

* 3 Jan. 94.

question of a man resisting something wh. is a total denegation of his whole past self. More than that', he sd. with suppressed passion, 'I seem to hear, if I may say so, I seem to hear voices from the dead encouraging me.' With a gesture pointing to a distant corner of the darkened room. He soon came to what was, I verily believe, the real root of his vehemence, anger and exaltation. 'The fact is', he sd., 'I'm rapidly travelling the road that leads to total blindness. You are all complaining of fog. I live in fog that never lifts. . . .'

This was perhaps the most painful thing about it—no piety, no noble resignation, but the resistance of a child or an animal to an incomprehensible & ⟨incredible⟩ torment. I never was more distressed. The scene was pure pain, neither redeemed nor elevated by any sense of majestic meekness before decrees that must be to him divine. Not the right end for a life of such power, & long and sweeping triumph.

Gladstone no doubt sensed the same. He focused his fury into a long memorandum. With his usual powers of resilience he rallied himself and addressed the Cabinet next day for fifty minutes in a grave and dignified exposition of its follies in accepting the Admiralty's line on the navy estimates and on his personal position ('silent—and disgraced. A survival. $\frac{3}{4}$ of my life, a continuous effort for economy'), and he brought forward an alternative plan for gradual naval expansion.

Following Gladstone's exposition, his retirement was overtly discussed in Cabinet in his presence, a remarkable and humiliating moment:

Rosebery pressed for prompt decision; the govmt. wd be broken up either way: either Spencer & others wd. be obliged to go, or Mr. G. and others who thought with him wd. go; it was not a situation that permitted suspension until Feb. 15. For this was the question:– was Mr. G. to leave now, or at the end of the session. After some talk, I [Morley] made the suggestion that we should now adjourn, and then informally among ourselves consider whether there ought to be a Cabinet for definite decision this week or whether the retirement shd. be postponed until February. The wearied, dejected, and perplexed men flew to this solution, and off we went.*

It is clear from his journal that Gladstone was very close to resigning at this moment in early January 1894: 'My family, within *viva voce*, are made aware. . . . Fuller conversation with my children. It is hard for them to understand.' A stop-gap compromise emerged on 10 January:

J. Morley with much activity, last night, & today after a long conversation with me prosecuted & brought into action the plan for time. I am to go to Biarritz on Saturday. The Estimates will be prepared departmentally as usual. The session will be wound up shortly after Feb. 12. No Cabinet at present.

Next day he noted:

I am now like the sea in swell after a storm, bodily affected, but mentally pretty well anchored. It is bad: but oh how infinitely better than to be implicated in that [navy] plan!

* Morley's diary, 9 January 1894.

So Gladstone was sent to exile in France, and the Prime Minister spent a month in the country whose navy was the chief force against which the defence estimates were intended to guard.

Just before leaving for Biarritz, Gladstone had a further examination of his eyes by Granger, the Chester oculist who had treated him following the gingerbread assault. When Gladstone, in response to a report in the *Pall Mall Gazette* that his resignation was imminent, issued a statement from Biarritz *via* his secretary, Algernon West, that no decision had been made but that 'the condition of his sight and hearing have in his judgment, made relief from public cares desirable', Granger was tricked by a reporter into making a public statement about his patient, giving his view that Gladstone's eyesight did not in itself require his resignation. Hardly surprisingly, Gladstone was incensed at this intervention—which seemed a further conspiracy against his arranging his retirement on his own terms.

With Gladstone removed to the Grand Hotel in Biarritz, correspondents and emissaries—in particular Acton, who accompanied him to France—tried to help him change his mind. He responded by setting down his thoughts in a memorandum remarkable in the annals of British radical writing:

The Plan

I deem it to be in excess of public expectation
I know it to be in excess of all precedent
It entails unjust taxation
It endangers sound finance
I shall not minister to the alarming aggression of the professional elements[?]
    to the weakness of alarmism
    to the unexampled manoeuvres of party
not lend a hand to dress Liberalism in Tory clothes.
I shall not break to pieces the continuous action of my political life, nor trample on the tradition received from every colleague who has ever been my teacher
Above all I cannot & will not add to the perils & the coming calamities of Europe by an act of militarism which will be found to involve a policy, and which excuses thus the militarism of Germany, France or Russia. England's providential part is to help peace, and liberty of which peace is the nurse; this policy is the foe of both. I am ready to see England dare[?] the world in arms: but not to see England help to set the world in arms.
My full intention is that of silence till the matter is settled in the regular course of sessional proceedings; when they are at an end, in the event of new circumstances and prolonged controversy, I may consider my duty afresh, upon the principle which guides me throughout, namely that of choosing the ultimate good and the smallest present evil. The smallest of all the present evils is the probable disparagement of myself (for surmise will arise, and probably will not be put down): great and certain evils are the danger to the party, and new uncertainties for

Ireland. But these in my opinion are inherent in the plan itself, and would not be averted were it possible for me to say aye to it.*

To keep Gladstone from resigning, Acton was a good card to play, but he was not a trump. His lack of executive experience meant that he could count for little in Gladstone's mind on the particular point at issue. He could, and did, put the immediate question of the naval estimates in the wider context of the future of Liberalism and the implication for that future if Gladstone resigned to oppose a policy which a Liberal Cabinet was prepared to execute. Gladstone was already aware of this aspect of the question and Acton's urgings probably gave him greater pause. After making no significant progress in Biarritz, Acton returned to London and then sent a detailed refutation of Gladstone's arguments to be read to him by his daughter Mary, Acton's long-term friend and correspondent.

Two days after Acton's memorandum had been read to him in Biarritz by Mary Drew, Gladstone began seriously to bring forward the quite different matter of the House of Lords, already adumbrated in correspondence. A dissolution on the Lords—'whether the people of the U.K. are or are not to be self-governing people'—would, he argued, unite the Cabinet and the party. Certainly the conduct of the Lords since 1892 had posed this as a major question for the future of Liberalism. It was, however, one which would require a very careful selection of timing: in Gladstone's own terminology, the question did not yet seem 'ripe'. From Gladstone's own point of view, an immediate dissolution on the Lords had the great advantage of deferring decisions on the navy estimates until after the election.

'Final Cabinet' and Last Speech in the Commons

Gladstone thus returned to London from Biarritz on 10 February 1894 with two routes to resignation open, and one to a further round of political activity. He had two reasons for retiring—his eyesight and the navy estimates—and the *ballon* of a dissolution at the end of the session on the question of the Lords. It was a flexible position for one whose political career most of his Cabinet assumed was over. He pressed the Lords dissolution to the fore just before his return, and it was at once clear that the Cabinet was uniformly hostile.

It was obvious that Gladstone was not returning simply to chair the Cabinet in a routine way. He, and its members, expected a *dénouement*. He found the session not ended, but extended because of the Lords' amendments to the Employers Liability and Local Government Bills. Morley told him on his return that if he (Gladstone) resigned on the navy plan, he (Morley) would resign also: this was in effect a reminder that a resignation

* 20 Jan. 94. His view of the growth of 'militarism' was confirmed by a visit to the opening of the Kiel Canal in June 1895; 'this means war!' he exclaimed on seeing the German fleet.

on the navy would harm the Irish cause. This probably was a trump card. More than anything, it is likely to have encouraged Gladstone to give several reasons rather than a single cause for his departure.

At the Cabinet on 12 February, however, Gladstone chaired the meeting as if nothing had happened, or was expected to happen, and made no comment in his journal. Morley described the scene:

Cabinet met at noon. Everybody there, full of expectation. Mr G. easy and cheerful. In the most matter-of-fact way he opened the fateful sitting. Ripon, he sd., had something to say about N.S. Wales . . . it was agreed to in a minute. . . . Next we passed to Employers' Liability. Asquith stated his point: with admirable clearness. Then to Parish Councils. About twenty minutes on this. That brought us to the end of the agenda. Now the moment had come. The declaration of his final purpose must now be made. ⟨The cruel suspense of all these weeks was now at an end⟩ We drew in our breaths. Mr G. moved in his seat—gathered up his notes— and in a dry voice with a touch of a sigh of relief in it sd., 'I suppose that brings us to an end for to-day.' Out we trooped, like schoolboys dismissed from their hour of class. Never was dramatic surprise more perfect.*

By the time of the Cabinet dinner on 17 February it had been made clear to him by colleagues *via* Sir Algernon West, his private secretary, that some sort of announcement was expected. Gladstone noted in his journal:

Cabinet dinner. All. I believe it was expected I should say something. But from my point of view there is nothing to be said.†

Next day Gladstone started work on an article on the Atonement, a clear sign that his mind had moved past the point of retirement. By this time it was apparent both that the Lords were pressing forward with their substantial amendments to the Employers' Liabilities Bill and the Local Government Bill and that there was no support for defiant action by the Cabinet.

As the Session drifted to its end, Gladstone alerted Sir Henry Ponsonby, the Queen's Secretary who had worked so hard to contain the Queen's hostility, that it was 'probable' that when it ended 'I may have a communication to make to Her Majesty'—the first of several papers 'connected with the coming events'.‡ Gladstone's aim was to prepare the Queen for his resignation while trying to get her not to tell the Tories that it was impending. He needed to be sure that what he said would not go 'beyond H.M.'. The Queen in reply refused to 'bind herself to preserve secrecy on a

* Morley's diary, 12 February 1894.
† 17 Feb. 94. Morley noted in his diary on 12 February, further to his account of the non-resignation Cabinet that day: 'Three hours later, sitting on the bench between Mr G. and Asquith I recd. a card for a Cabinet dinner on Saturday. The others got theirs by & bye. Nobody had heard a word of this. What a curious ⟨silent⟩ move. Doubtless he means to make this an occasion for telling us he is off, and being a dinner, he will not have to report to the Queen. The delay for a week makes our position in respect of reconstruction, budget, and other business, almost impracticable.'
‡ 21 Feb. 94.

matter of which she knew nothing and asked for some hint . . .'. It required little imagination on the Queen's part as to what Gladstone had in mind, but she was determinedly and unpleasantly unhelpful throughout the process of the retirement for which she had so long wished and worked.

It would be easy to see these manœuvres as an example of Gladstonian over-elaboration. Gladstone's request for an assurance of secrecy may have seemed offensive but Victoria's recent record suggested that it was necessary: vital amendments by the Lords on various bills were still pending and Tory tactics might be affected if Gladstone's resignation was known to be definite. Gladstone's need to ask for secrecy and Victoria's refusal of it was a sharp example of her marked political partisanship. It was an exceptional situation when the sovereign would not agree to accept a confidence from her Prime Minister.

Eventually, Gladstone cut the knot by writing to the Queen, on 27 February, of his intention to retire when the business of the Session was concluded. His resignation was 'on physical grounds'.* Next day during an audience of about half-an-hour—'doubtless my last in an official capacity'—he told her that 'if we had the Speech Council on Saturday my definitive letter might go to her on that day',† as indeed it did. Gladstone had done as he told Spencer in January he would do: resigned at the end of the Session.

His final Cabinet was on Thursday, 1 March 1894, the last of 556 he had chaired. It was not simply a formal farewell. The Cabinet gave in to the Lords' amendments to the Local Government Bill: '*Accept and protest? We adopt this*'‡ and the end-of-Session Queen's Speech was agreed to. Gladstone's 'words in the Commons [later] today' were then discussed: he was urged to speak strongly against the Lords while announcing the capitulation, and he agreed to do so.

There then followed the moment anticipated for so long—at least since 1880—by his Liberal colleagues. They were too upset to manage it well, and the scene became known as 'the blubbering Cabinet'. Kimberley, the senior member of the Cabinet, began to speak but broke down. He managed to finish his few simple sentences. Harcourt, also weeping, read out a long letter which he had already sent to Gladstone and to which he had had a reply.§ It spoilt the dignity of the occasion, but it reflected the character of the Cabinet. Gladstone, Morley noted, 'sat quite composed and still. The emotion of the Cabinet did not gain him for an instant.'¶ Gladstone noted:

* 27 Feb. 94n.
† 28 Feb. 94.
‡ 1 Mar. 94.
§ 25 Feb. 94.
¶ Morley's diary, 1 March 1894.

Final Cabinet 12–1$\frac{3}{4}$. A really moving scene.*

The Cabinet ended. Gladstone 'went slowly out of one door, while we with downcast looks and oppressed hearts filed out by the other; much as men walk away from the graveside'.†

In what can hardly have been an easy occasion for him, Gladstone went for the last time to the House of Commons and sat through his last question-time. He then spoke on the Lords' amendments to the Local Government Bill, withdrawing opposition to them 'under protest'. This was no formal epilogue. Gladstone was put up by the Cabinet to conduct an awkward retreat and in effect to announce the defeat of his own plan for a dissolution against the Lords. He did so, as so often before, by covering an immediate defeat by a call to action in a future crusade—it was 'a controversy which, when once raised, must go forward to an issue'‡—and his speech helped to limit the Radical vote against the Cabinet's decision to 37—a typically ambivalent conclusion to Gladstone's relations with Radicalism. As the House emptied, Gladstone with characteristic politeness stayed in his place to listen to the ramblings of Lord Randolph Churchill.

The House had sensed something unusual, but the Cabinet had not 'leaked' and Gladstone remained, of course, a stickler to the last for constitutional form:

I tried to follow the wish of the Cabinet: with a good conscience. The House showed feeling: but of course I made no outward sign.§

* 1 Mar. 94. For the final Cabinet, see *The Gladstone Diaries*, Vol. XIII, Appendix I and Lord Rosebery, 'Mr. Gladstone's last Cabinet', *History Today* (December 1951 and January 1952).

† Morley's diary, 1 March 1894.

‡ 4*H* 21. 1151 (1 March 1894).

§ 1 Mar. 94.

CHAPTER XVI

'Successive snapping of the threads'

'Mr. Gladstone'—Queen Victoria—Friends and the Gladstone Court—The Gladstone 'Children'—Catherine Gladstone—Laura Thistlethwayte: Old Age and Death—Books, St Deiniol's, and Writing in Retirement—Gladstone's 'Autobiography'—Bishop Butler's Works—Money and Posterity—'Successive snapping of the threads'—Death—Rites of Passage

The blessings of family life continue to be poured in the largest measure upon my unworthy head. Even my temporal affairs have thriven.

Still old age is appointed for the gradual loosening or successive snapping of the threads. I visited Ld Stratford at Froom Park(?) when he was 90 or 91 or thereabouts. He said to me 'It is not a blessing'.*

'Mr. Gladstone'

Gladstone never again entered the House of Commons, in which he had first set foot as an MP sixty-one years previously, in 1833. He again declined the Queen's offer of a peerage, and made it clear to his wife that in his view she should likewise decline a peerage for herself.† He thus died plain 'Mr.', an almost unique reticence for a Prime Minister.‡ To accept a title at the same time as declaring the House of Lords the central political question of the future would not, in the history of the British political élite's attempts to come to terms with constitutional change, have been an exceptional or even an unusual irony. But its refusal went beyond mere consistency. For all the many honours he had recommended for others, Gladstone always saw himself as a commoner. His veneration for hereditary land tenure and the social system that accompanied it was well-established. But despite the fact that he had at various times owned most of the Glynne family's lands in Flintshire, he always saw himself as outside the British tradition of aristocratic absorption. He was always a guest at

---

* Diary for 29 Dec. 96.

† To Mrs Gladstone, 21 Mar. 94.

‡ Of non-titled Prime Ministers, Henry Pelham, the younger Pitt, Spencer Perceval, and Canning died in office. There have been three others (George Grenville, Bonar Law, and Ramsay MacDonald) who had a period after holding the premiership during which they might have taken a title—in Bonar Law's case a very brief one.

Hawarden: it was not his home. It was entirely in character that, in encouraging his wife to resist the offer of a new peerage, he should in the same letter suggest she revive her claim to a dormant one. It was a thin line of distinction, but it was one which sharply illustrated Gladstone's curious relationship to the political class. To be both a leading executive politician—a man from the heart of the Oxford establishment with all the necessary credentials of experience and authority—and for several political generations the dominant voice in the party of progress, gave Gladstone a force unrivalled in the history of progressive politics. It was not the least ironic feature of Gladstone's long career that the last part of it was devoted to the promotion of a policy which he deemed and which from the perspective of a century later does seem conservative and conducive to the strength of the monarchy.

Queen Victoria

The Queen, of course, would have none of Gladstone's protestations. When he warned her during his last administration in a huge memorandum that 'in the powerful social circles with which Your Majesty has ordinary personal intercourse' the views of her 'actual advisers' (i.e. the Liberal government) were barely represented, and that this could not but be dangerous to the monarchy, she only acknowledged receipt of it under pressure from her secretary, the long-suffering Henry Ponsonby. Gladstone and Ponsonby, a Liberal, continued to shield the Queen. Her response was to assert her powers at least as energetically as in her dealings with earlier Gladstonian administrations. At the same time she expected—as Gladstone put it—'a party with whom she has publicly advertised her disgust at having anything to do'* to get a good settlement for her financially incompetent son, Alfred Duke of Edinburgh, when he decided to go to live in Germany as Duke of Saxe-Coburg. Gladstone sometimes referred to his relationship with her as a reason for leaving office. It is certainly the case that freedom from her constant importunities was the most pleasurable aspect of his retirement from the premiership. His relations with the Prince of Wales, despite the Tranby Croft gambling scandal in 1890, continued to be frequent and satisfactory and he found the Duke of York—the future George V—'not only likeable but perhaps loveable'.†

Notoriously, the Queen did not ask her most experienced Prime Minister for his advice as to his successor. Ponsonby, perhaps with the Queen's knowledge, sounded out Gladstone on this before his final audience, but the latter refused to discuss the matter unless the inquiry was clearly 'from her and in her name ... otherwise my lips must be sealed'. Gladstone's

* To Harcourt, 14 Sept. 93.
† 16 Feb. 93.

stiffness was partly a matter of constitutional rectitude—precedent certainly suggested that he was right to expect formally to be asked—afforced throughout the episode by his sense that the Crown was darkened by a dank Unionist shadow.* But the episode was also, as he realized, symptomatic of a more general malaise. Even discounting the Queen's hostility to Liberalism, Gladstone thought, there was in his relations with her 'something of mystery, which I have not been able to fathom, and probably never shall'.† In the fortnight after his resignation he was preoccupied in conversation and on paper with the Queen's behaviour towards him, for he felt he had been dismissed with the 'same brevity' used in 'settling a tradesman's bill'.‡ He was still worrying about the episode in 1896, dreaming about having breakfast with Victoria§ and noting that his family was, after his death, 'to keep in the background the personal relations of the Queen and myself in these later years, down to 1894 when they died a kind of natural death'.¶ It was the Queen's personal discourtesy to him and to Catherine Gladstone which rankled, not her constitutional failure to ask his advice as to his successor.

Gladstone smarted at the Queen's handling of his retirement. If that was her intention, it was ignominious. If it was not, it showed a marked limitation in her capacity as a constitutional monarch.

Friends and the Gladstone Court

The effort of his final government left Gladstone and his wife more exhausted than perhaps they first realized. Colds, coughs, diarrhoea, fatigue, deafness, the impending cataract operation, meant doctors were in constant attendance on them both: 'what a couple!' Moreover, they were, outside Hawarden Castle, nomadic. None of the Gladstone children had a house in London, suitable for parental use. After the sale of the lease of 73 Harley Street in 1882, the Gladstones had no London base, except when entitled to live in 10 Downing Street (in 1894 Rosebery delayed moving in to take account of this). For accommodation in the south they thus relied on the 'Gladstone court', that small group of rich relatives and friends who effectively looked after them in the later 1880s and through the 1890s

---

* Gladstone's preference was Spencer, at first glance an ironic choice, for it was Spencer's naval programme that had caused the row leading up to Gladstone's resignation. But Spencer was of all the Cabinet, more so perhaps than Morley, the person most committed to Home Rule. Morley noted in his diary on 4 January 1894, when the navy row was at its height, Gladstone's 'extraordinary ejaculation, "Under certain circs., Kimberley."!'

† 10 Mar. 94.   ‡ 10 Mar. 94.

§ This dream—and Gladstone very seldom recorded having dreamt—was one of two in his lifetime involving people: the other was of Disraeli (see 3 July 64). His dream about having breakfast with Victoria may have had a sexual dimension, for he records having 'a small perturbation as to the how and where of access'. 'Reserved for access' was the phrase he had used in 1839 to describe his virginity on marriage (see 14 June 39). For sexual dreams about royalty, see W. Ronald D. Fairbairn, 'The effect of the king's death [George V] upon patients undergoing analysis' (1936) in his *Psychoanalytic studies of the personality* (1952).   ¶ 2 Jan. 96.

(except when Gladstone was Prime Minister): the Aberdeens with their house at Dollis Hill, then regarded as north of London; Lucy Cavendish and the Rendels in central London; George Armitstead in London and Brighton. These arrangements cannot have been easy on either side— 'Moving in and out of furnished houses is a serious affair after 80'—but the alternative of a London house or flat—a return perhaps to Albany—was not sought on a permanent basis. Gladstone noted in 1887: 'to Dollis Hill: a refuge for my shrinking timidity, unwilling at 77 to begin a new London house'. 10 St James's Square—a vast and hardly suitable establishment, later Chatham House—was rented for six months in 1890, but the experiment was not repeated.

Rendel and Armitstead, moreover, arranged and paid for most of the Gladstones' trips abroad which became a settled feature of the routine of their old age. Rendel hosted their visit to the south of France in 1887 and to Italy in 1888, Armitstead their stays in Biarritz when for a time it replaced Cannes as their French wintering place in the 1890s, despite the fact that Gladstone was initially blackballed from the British club there.* One or other of them made the hotel arrangements. They booked the carriages for the Gladstones' day trips and sometimes for more extensive expeditions, including one to Lourdes in January 1892. Sometimes both Rendel and Armitstead were in attendance together.

They were, from Gladstone's point of view, a convenient choice as companions. Neither had real political ambition or sharp intellectual power. But both were Liberal in politics, wealthy, interested in politics but largely outside the inner circle of active policy makers. Armitstead had been Liberal MP for Dundee and Rendel, like Gladstone an Oxonian Anglican, was Liberal MP for Montgomeryshire until 1894. Each got on amiably with the Gladstones, genially advancing the old man's flow of conversation with a prompt or a question and happily taking their turns at the evening game of backgammon which, almost as much as Church-going, was a regular part of Gladstone's daily round in his later years. They acted as companions almost in the professional, Victorian sense, except that they, not Gladstone, paid. Their relationship to him was thus easy. They were both 'old shoes'. Someone like Acton or Morley might be more stimulating for a day or so. But neither Acton nor Morley could become 'old shoes' in the way that Rendel and Armitstead did. Angry almost to the point of fury over the navy estimates in December 1893, Gladstone retired with Armitstead (a bachelor) to Lion Mansions, Brighton (Catherine Gladstone being ill at Hawarden) and the two of them spent Christmas week with Helen Gladstone at the seaside. Armitstead, particularly, seems to have been a calming crony. Like Catherine Gladstone they are frequently mentioned in the diary but no more than mentioned: like her, Gladstone took them for

* For the blackballing—the club reversed its initial decision—see 17 Dec. 91n.

granted. Unusual among Gladstone's close friends, both were successful business men, Rendel in the armament and engineering firm of Armstrongs of Newcastle, Armitstead in the Baltic trade in his family's firm.

Various other friends attempted a similar role but were rather obviously using Gladstone to advance their interests. Andrew Carnegie, the Scottish-American steel magnate, offered 'as a Loan "any sum" needful to place me in a state of abundance, without interest, repayable at my death, if my estate would well bear it; if not, then to be cancelled altogether'. Gladstone considered the offer 'entirely disinterested' but 'of course, with gratitude, I declined it altogether' and tried to interest Carnegie in the Liberals' election fund.* For a man expecting (in 1887) again to be Prime Minister this was clearly prudent, for to have been thus beholden to the world's most flamboyant capitalist could hardly have been seen as disinterested. Sir Edward Watkin's sponsorship of Gladstone's Paris visit in 1889 as part of his campaign for the Channel Tunnel and Sir Donald Currie's lending of his steamships for Gladstonian voyages are lesser examples. But Stuart Rendel and George Armitstead were not intrusive in this way. Both were capable of giving a political nudge—Rendel on Welsh affairs, keeping Gladstone in touch with Welsh MPs† and acting as a broker on the Welsh church question, Armitstead introducing Gladstone to Labour MPs—but their advantage was that they were political messengers rather than players. 'Attendant lords' was exactly their position, for Gladstone ennobled Rendel in his final honours list and Campbell-Bannerman saw to Armitstead in 1906.

A different sort of case was Lionel Tollemache, who saw himself as Gladstone's 'proxy-Boswell', though Gladstone hardly saw himself as Tollemache's Johnson. When in Biarritz he enjoyed an intellectual joust with Tollemache and noted of him: 'he in particular is a very interesting person.' But talking to Tollemache was like talking in the All Souls Common Room: suitable for a literary show but not a confidence. Gladstone showed one side of his intellectual fascination to Tollemache, and he did so in such depth as to indicate a considerable compliment. Even so, Tollemache with his ready pen was a man to be watchful of.‡

The Gladstone 'Children'

Parallel to the sustaining work of Rendel and Armitstead was the assistance of the Gladstone 'children', now in their 40s and 50s. They had what Gladstone aptly called (with respect to Hallam Tennyson) a 'filial career'.§

* 12 June 87.
† He was consulted by Gladstone on his important speech at Swansea; see 3 June 87. Gladstone used him to contact the Welsh MPs during the Parnell crisis; see 26 Nov. 90.
‡ For him, see Asa Briggs's introduction to *Gladstone's Boswell*, a reprint (1984) of the third edition of L. A. Tollemache, *Talks with Mr. Gladstone* (1903).
§ To Hallam Tennyson, 8 Oct. 92.

The lives of six of the seven living children were lived, whether by occupation or relationship, within a context largely of their parents' making: that is, their emotional focus remained parental. Several of them attempted non-filial careers or married, but in almost every case these were confirmations of their parents' interests rather than departures. William and Catherine Gladstone spread a long and subtle shadow.

Willy, the owner of Hawarden, and consequently the central figure of the familial support-network for his parents, died from a brain tumour in June 1891.* That he was seriously ill rather than cantankerous began to become clear from March 1889, but the probability of his death does not seem to have been fully grasped by his parents. When his son's illness entered its final stage, Gladstone was with J. J. Colman at Lowestoft, recuperating from influenza. Catherine Gladstone left for London on 'her holy errand'. The news of Willy's imminent death was kept from his father, who travelled next day to London only in time to see 'the dear remains'. Gladstone's failure to see his son alive for a last time reflected their curious relationship. In terms of time spent together, Willy was probably the closest of the children to his father, yet there was always a sense of distance between them: that same unstated sense that the son had not come 'up-to-scratch' that had existed in the mind of Sir John Gladstone about *his* eldest son, Tom, William's last living sibling, who died in 1889 just as the seriousness of Willy's condition first became apparent.

Willy's unexpected death immediately caused confusion in the arrangements made for the succession to the Hawarden estates. In order for them to remain wholly within the Gladstone family, it was arranged that their ownership should revert to W. E. Gladstone, who had very briefly owned them in 1875, so as to exclude Catherine Gladstone's niece, Gertrude Glynne, now wife of the choleric Lord Penrhyn, who disputed the reversion, eventually unsuccessfully. For the second time in his life, William Gladstone was thus briefly laird of Hawarden. That he should own his wife's family estates as a result of the death of his son was a cruel irony.†

Gladstone enjoyed a cheerful relationship with his grandson William, who became the heir of Hawarden as a result of his father's death. The cross-generational link (and the discounting of W. H. Gladstone even before his death) was marked by the last of Millais's portraits of W. E. Gladstone, begun in 1889. The least successful of the series, it shows Gladstone in a formal setting holding his top hat with his grandson by his side, the latter sporting a 'Little Lord Fauntleroy' suit (Gladstone had read the book and met Frances Hodgson Burnett in Italy).‡ The picture was

---

* For him, see Michael Bentley, 'Gladstone's Heir', *English Historical Review* (October 1992).

† Changes were then made to the testamentary dispositions of Stephen Gladstone, the second son, lest the young W. G. C. Gladstone (the heir to Hawarden whose affairs were administered by his uncles as trustees), should die childless. This was prudent, as he was killed in the First World War, married but without an heir.　　　　　　　‡ See 12, 16 Nov. 87, 19 Jan. 88.

finished, by odd coincidence, just as W. H. Gladstone died. 'Dossie' Drew (Mary's daughter) was the grandchild whose company the Prime Minister especially enjoyed; her disregard for convention was similar to Catherine Gladstone's and she is often described by her grandfather as being 'in great force'.

Increasingly Gladstone relied on his third son, Henry Neville Gladstone, now permanently returned from India, for business arrangements. Henry married Maud, daughter of Stuart Rendel, and thus the business links between the families were formalized. Henry and Herbert both continued to take turns with their sisters Mary and Helen at supporting their parents and acting as their father's private secretary. Herbert and Helen remained unmarried. Helen's decision to decline the Principalship of Royal Holloway College and stay on at Newnham College, Cambridge, meant that she had some time to take her turn with Mary in what became after 1894 the role of nurse. Newnham was rewarded by a visit from the former Prime Minister, a notable event for a young college (see the photograph in this volume). Gladstone planted a tree, soon afterwards destroyed, probably by a Tory undergraduate; he presented instead an oak reared in the grounds of Hawarden, which still flourishes.

Between them, Gladstone's children had made up for the clerical career for which he had sometimes yearned. Stephen was Rector of Hawarden and remained so, despite doubts about his calling which made him often restless and sometimes inclined to resign his valuable charge. His father's instinctive reaction was to try to link him to Hawarden in a different way— and one which would have put him much more directly under his control— by offering him at £300 p.a. the wardenship of the embryonic St Deiniol's Library.* This came to nothing, but his advice seems to have played a part in persuading Stephen to continue during a period of severe doubt in 1893. Agnes and Mary were both married to priests and Mary's unhealthy husband, Harry Drew, was wholly absorbed into the Gladstonian circle, becoming curate of Hawarden and acting Warden of St Deiniol's Library. Of the children, only Agnes Wickham lived her life largely outside the context of her parents' activities. But she was not wholly outside them, for her father's patronage made her husband, Edward, dean of Lincoln in 1894, one of his last acts of ecclesiastical patronage.

When out of office—as on previous occasions—Gladstone did not employ a secretary. His correspondence increased as his capacity to deal with it diminished. His failing sight meant he had to have much of it read to him and though he continued to write most of his letters he no longer made his own copies of the important ones. His daily routine required the processing of his vast post and he also needed the repose which reading gave

---

* To S. E. Gladstone, 8 Apr. 93. Stephen took some time to recover from this crisis; see 17 June 93.

him. Increasingly he depended for the latter on a reader. Without a secretary (though Spencer Lyttelton sometimes helped with the post) these duties fell largely on his 'children'—especially but not solely on Mary and Helen.

Gladstone and his wife thus created a set of extraordinarily powerful family ties, which, because he was Prime Minister, necessarily existed largely on Gladstone's terms. Those terms were generous. The children were well supported financially and large capital sums were made over to them in the 1890s. The parents' company was scarcely dull or their life unexciting. The nature of obligation was understood and not stated. Overt requests for help never had to be made. The 'children' seem to have arranged their rotas willingly enough. But Henry, Herbert, Mary, and Helen must sometimes have wondered how their lives would have developed if their father had employed a couple of secretaries.

Catherine Gladstone

Catherine Gladstone remains an enigmatic figure. Her illnesses and insomnia suggest a more complex character than the cheerful, slightly scatty chatterbox she is usually depicted as. What she knew of her husband's sexual temptations, we do not know. Had she seen the scars on his back when in the 1840s and 1850s he used the scourge after meeting prostitutes? What was her view of the regular letters to and fro to Laura Thistlethwayte and the visits to 15 Grosvenor Square and later to Laura's cottage in Hampstead? Certainly the view that the Gladstones' marriage was a matter of *simple* happiness is not one tenable by a systematic reader of her husband's diaries. But, in the 1890s at least, with Gladstone in his seventies and eighties and work with the prostitutes virtually ended*—the last recorded encounter was in the nervous days just before resignation as Prime Minister†—she had to deal with a less restless husband. Gladstone recorded much about himself and about most of his regular habits, including in his later years a good deal about his bowels (the 'lower department', as he called it). But for all its intimate detail, his diary is completely silent about his sexual relations with his wife. This is hardly surprising, but it means a central aspect of their lives is unrecoverable.

In an age when the public position of women was fast changing, Catherine Gladstone was an important icon, her own commemorative plate next to her husband's on many a sideboard. She was the first woman regularly to sit on the platform at political speeches. She energetically organized various homes and hostels, especially for children, and was an unembarrassable fundraiser. She was the first President of the Women's Liberal Federation, a role which led her into difficulties and finally to

---

* 15 and 17 June 92 are the penultimate examples of encounters with prostitutes. Significantly Gladstone refers to being 'accosted', i.e. the initiative was the prostitutes', not, as in the past, his.
† 24 Feb. 94.

resignation in the face of demands from Lady Carlisle and others that the Federation be more active in demanding women's suffrage.* She always opposed her husband's suggestions of resignation and retirement from politics—and her illness and absence from him in December 1893 meant that she was not able to calm his fury at the naval expansion proposals.† Catherine Gladstone ran the Gladstone court with a firm but discreet hand. Like that of many political wives of the period, her influence in shaping the character of the political as well as the domestic *ménage* was as important as it is hard to document. Gladstone's comments in the diary usually present her as distanced from the political world, in accordance with his view of the proper sphere of femininity (as when he thought the Royal Commission on the Poor Laws was not the proper place for 'the first canter' of women on such bodies):‡ in fact, she was an integral part of his political world.

Laura Thistlethwayte: Old Age and Death

From the late 1860s to the mid-1880s, Laura Thistlethwayte and her *salon* had provided something of an antithesis to the Gladstonian circle. In the late 1880s and early 1890s she no longer did. Though Gladstone would never have admitted it directly, her frequent importunities, her invitations to lunch and dinner, her presents and her requests for letters became something of a nuisance. He commented to his wife, she 'has cooked up a habit of much fuss about small things'.§ In 1887 the indebted A. F. Thistlethwayte died through a revolver wound—perhaps a suicide but perhaps, as Gladstone and the world decided, an accident, for he was wont to summon his servants by firing his pistol at the ceiling of his bedroom.¶ For all that Gladstone had discussed with Laura the disappointments of her marriage, he may have felt ill at ease with her as a widow. She set up house in Woodbine Cottage in Hampstead with Melita Ponsonby, sister to the Queen's Secretary, as a quasi-companion. Catherine Gladstone was introduced to her for the first time in 1887, twenty-two years after he began his often daily correspondence with her, and subsequently sometimes accompanied her husband on his not very frequent visits to that curious *ménage*. Gladstone guarded his flank with respect to possible developments as he and Laura Thistlethwayte aged. Gladstone twice examined with Lord

* See 22 May 89n., 17, 27 Apr. 92, 1 May 92. This episode merits further investigation. For it, see E. A. Pratt, *Catherine Gladstone* (1898), ch. xiii.

† Even so, Rosebery told Morley he was confident there would be no crisis, being 'sure that domestic influence wd. be too strong'; see Morley's diary, 9 Jan. 1894.

‡ To Fowler, 8 Dec. 92: 'I would rather give the ladies their first canter on some subject less arduous, & where there would be less danger of their being led astray by the emotional elements of the case.'

§ To Mrs Gladstone, 19 Dec. 93.

¶ 24 Aug. 87ff. His death certificate stated as 'Cause of death' after receipt of a Coroner's certificate: 'Pistol Shot Wound in Head Accidentally when carrying a loaded pistol[;] found in a helpless condition on the floor and died in 14 Hours.'

Rothschild the correspondence of Disraeli with Mrs Brydges Willyams.* It cannot have escaped him that similar scenes would be played out after his death over his own papers.

In 1893:

Burned my box of Mrs Thistlethwayte's older letters. I had marked them to be returned: but I do not know what would become of them. They would lead to misapprehension: it was in the main a one-sided correspondence: not easy to understand.†

He did not, however, attempt to recover his letters to her, which could not but astonish those who read them and dismay members of his family. Much of his correspondence with her is published in Appendices to Volumes VIII and XII of *The Gladstone Diaries*. The correspondence confirms the cooling in their relationship, at any rate on his side. After the Thistlethwaytes became involved in a series of debt actions by Mr Padwick, a well-known Paddington gambler and money-lender,‡ Gladstone changed his salutation from 'Dear Spirit' to 'Dear Mrs Thistlethwayte' or, more often, opened the letter without any form of address. Laura Thistlethwayte had acquired anonymity. The likelihood—at one point acute—of Gladstone's name and letters being mentioned in the debt actions passed, and the possibility receded of Laura's lavish presents to him being publicly given as a cause of A. F. Thistlethwayte's inability to pay Padwick. But the old intimacy never really revived.

His trust in her discretion was, however, justified. Despite genteel poverty (though like many such she had in fact significant assets) and a life ultimately solitary and rather miserable, Laura Thistlethwayte never traded on her intimacy with the Prime Minister, even posthumously. When she died in 1894, she did not embarrass him with gifts left in her will, and there was no mention in it of his large correspondence with her, almost all of which she had preserved. She left her cottage to be a North London St Deiniol's, 'a Retreat for Clergymen of all denominations true believers in my God and Saviour and literary men'.§ Gladstone was not an executor, though he had advised her over her affairs after her husband's death. The correspondence was probably recovered by H. N. Gladstone from her chief executor, Lord Edward Pelham-Clinton, son of the Duke of Newcastle (who had with Arthur Kinnaird introduced Gladstone to Laura Thistlethwayte in the 1860s) and of Lady Susan Opdebeck, the former Lady Lincoln, whose life after she returned from exile on the Continent and until her death in 1889 seems to have become entwined with Laura

* 17 Mar. 88, 28 Feb. 91. Mrs Brydges Willyams enjoyed the same sort of relationship to Disraeli with respect to money as Mrs Thistlethwayte did to Gladstone with respect to sex.
† 25 Feb. 93.
‡ See above, pp. 321–2.
§ Will of Laura Thistlethwayte in Somerset House.

Thistlethwayte's.* Thus did two of Gladstone's private preoccupations of the 1860s—the fate of the Newcastle Estates, of which he was a trustee, and the condition of Laura Thistlethwayte's moral being, of which he also saw himself as a trustee—come into a curious congruity.†

Gladstone's last recorded visit to Laura Thistlethwayte was with his wife in May 1894 just before Laura's death: 'We drove to Mrs T's to inquire. Bad account.'‡ She died three weeks later, just after Gladstone suspended regular entries in his diaries because of his operation for cataract. There is thus no Gladstonian epilogue to her life: he may have been relieved not to have to write one. He did not reopen his journal—as he did for some subsequent events—to record his views. Her death coincided with a miserable period of his own life and with 'Mrs Th.' his duty, as he saw it, was all-ended. He did not attend her funeral, probably being unable to do so as the usual treatment after a cataract operation was a fortnight in bed with the eyes bandaged.

Books, St Deiniol's, and Writing in Retirement

The wretched five months' period following his resignation in March 1894 showed the 84-year-old Gladstone in marked physical decline, increasingly dependent on his Lear-like coterie as he moved from residence to residence in the south of England, not returning to Hawarden until August. He and his wife discussed arrangements for their funerals,§ and Gladstone wrote verses on death.¶ In the midst of it, on 24 May, he had an operation for the removal of cataract in his right eye. The effect of the operation was 'disabling'.‖ Cataract at once developed in the left eye and a second operation was judged inadvisable. Though there was some later revival in his eyesight, 1894 effectively saw the end of his ability for sustained reading, always a central part of his daily routine, however busy. His sight had, as we have seen, been for a considerable time in decline, but, though it had annoyed him, it had (except in 1892–3) not

---

* The intertwined relationships of Newcastle, his divorced wife Susan, Laura Thistlethwayte, and Gladstone merit further attention.

† The Thistlethwayte entry in Burke's *Landed Gentry* (1858 ed. only: the information is dropped in subsequent editions) shows Laura Thistlethwayte's mother, Laura Jane Seymour, to have been the illegitimate daughter of the third Marquis of Hertford, the notorious libertine. It has always been known that her father, Capt. R. H. Bell, was probably a bailiff on the Hertfords' estates in Co. Antrim, but this information makes much clearer the reason for the presence of Laura Thistlethwayte's portrait in the Wallace Collection (Wallace being another of Hertford's illegitimate descendants, inheriting Hertford's picture collection and his Irish estates). It is also better evidence than the unsubstantiated rumours that Laura Thistlethwayte was herself Hertford's daughter and it clarifies the various references to the Hertfords and the Wallaces in Gladstone's letters to her. I am obliged to Mrs. Jean Gilliland for this information.

‡ 4 May 94. Her death certificate gave 'Acute Renal congestion' as the 'Cause of death', and gave her age as 62, though her date of birth is normally given as c. 1829.

§ 28 Mar. 94.   ¶ 13 July 94.

‖ 19 July 94.

very seriously inconvenienced him, if the extraordinary level at which his reading and writing was maintained in the late 1880s and early 1890s is taken as a measure.

Throughout his life Gladstone used the Waverley novels as a base-point of departure for his reading, but he was none the less 'up' with the new style of best-seller which by its introduction of a new sexual tone moved sharply away from the Scottian framework of reference within which so much Victorian fiction had been written and read. Gladstone read Marie Corelli and met her to discuss her work (she hoped for but did not get a review).* He deplored Zola with a vehemence directed at no other author in the entire diary, but read a good deal of him: *La Terre* was 'the most loathsome of all books in the picture it presents', *Nana* 'a dreadful and revolting delineation', *Piping Hot* 'that wretched book' (rather curiously, 'a yellow-backed Zola' caught the eye of the visitor to the Humanities Room in St Deiniol's Library).† A theme in Gladstone's comments on such works was the de-Christifying of morality: thus Zola's *La Bête Humaine* 'I think . . . shows what would be a world without Christ' and Hardy's *Tess of the D'Urbervilles* was 'a deplorable anticipation of a world without a Gospel'. Less violent in language, but similar in sentiment, was his reaction to Mrs Humphry Ward's *Robert Elsmere* (1888); in this case, however, he marked respect for the author's motivation by reviewing the book, which was dedicated to the memory of T. H. Green and Laura Lyttelton, Catherine Gladstone's niece-by-marriage. His review, ironically, helped make it an improbable best-seller.

He caught up with some works surprisingly little read despite his regular trawling of the classics (read 'Bunyan's *Pilgrim's Progress*: a clear cut object-ivity reminding one of Dante')‡ and made acquaintance with what were then less obvious authors: 'Read . . . Kipling's *Light that failed* . . . read Kipling (bad)' and 'O[live] Schreiner's *Dreams*—Mary kindly read aloud to me in evg—*but*.'

Such works were just the tips of several very large icebergs. The volume of different works read by Gladstone in the late 1880s and early 1890s is as heavy as at any time in his life and his recording of them constitutes a considerable proportion of his journal's text. More perhaps tended to be pamphlets or light fiction and Gladstone's classical writings rested on critical reading in part out-of-date. But, just as his political life was fuller than his apparent preoccupation with Ireland might lead us to expect, so his reading and the correspondence which accompanied it kept him

* See 31 May, 4 June, 6 and 10 Aug. 89.

† See *In the evening of his days. A study of Mr Gladstone in retirement. With some account of St Deiniol's Library and Hostel* (1896), 117 (anonymous, but probably by W. T. Stead).

‡ In an autobiographical fragment, Gladstone records *The Pilgrim's Progress* as one of the books read or read to him as a boy, i.e. before he was 15, the age at which his surviving journal begins; *Autobiographica*, i. 19.

abreast of a wide range of subjects and authors. One example may suffice: his reading of Pareto and subsequent correspondence in Italian on free trade, protectionism, and political economy, which looked forward to the debate on corporatism which has in its various forms constituted the focus of much twentieth-century politico-economic dispute.*

Gladstone's huge accumulation of books had long posed a problem. As early as 1845, in the months after his resignation over Maynooth, he had made a catalogue of his collection, dividing it into three parts: (*a*) Theology, ecclesiastical history, and biography; (*b*) Secular literature: English language; (*c*) Secular literature: Foreign languages including Classics. As we have seen, his response to loss of office in 1886 was to start work on what became St Deiniol's Library, and by 1895 a temporary iron building had been finished on the same site as the present library, built on principles of maximum-density storage which Gladstone developed.† It was accompanied by a hostel for those coming to use the library. The library initially contained about 20,000 books. Readers could also borrow books from the 'Temple of Peace', which became merely 'the Castle section' of the main library. The only stipulation was that readers should not quote the many, sometimes salty, annotations which Gladstone wrote in pencil in the margins of his books. The Trustees of St Deiniol's Library met informally in October 1895 and on 1 January 1896 the Trust Deed formally establishing the library was signed, Gladstone making over £30,000 as an endowment together with the hostel, the 'Iron Library' and a large field which he had bought from the Ecclesiastical Commissioners to allow for expansion. St Deiniol's Library, carefully developed after Gladstone's death by its Trustees and Wardens, is a remarkable monument to Victorian culture, its mixture of the Spartan, the cosy, and the eclectic splendidly emphasizing the Gladstonian view that knowledge and understanding are both demanding to achieve and fun to get.

Final retirement from executive politics gave Gladstone at last a clear run for his writing. This he had maintained through the years of opposition, 1886–1892, at what was an astonishing rate. Books on the classics and the Bible, articles on current affairs, Egyptology, Ireland, the United States, Italy, the design of bookcases, and a wide range of other subjects rushed from his pen. 'An Academic Sketch', his Romanes Lecture, the first of the series, delivered at Oxford on 24 October 1892, gave him more trouble than anything else he published. Its final preparations coincided with the crisis over Uganda and Gladstone's correspondence at the time

* See 27, 30 Apr. 92.

† See his 'On books and the housing of them', *Nineteenth Century* (March 1890); fertile as ever, he explained these principles in the context of the space-problems of the Bodleian Library, designing on the spot (during a visit) a scheme for moving stack cases similar to those built for the underground store below Radcliffe Square in Oxford; see E. W. B. Nicholson, 'Mr. Gladstone and the Bodleian' (1898). See also above, p. 301.

was an odd amalgam of Occam, Dante, Gerald Portal, and Frederick Lugard. The family was mobilized as research assistants; Acton was summoned; Oxford scholars such as Hastings Rashdall were alerted. Gladstone was determined to offer a scholastic piece worthy of the occasion.* It was as if he was again preparing for Schools. Scholarly work was maintained through the final government, with a translation of Horace worked on in odd moments and, as we shall shortly see, work on the edition of Bishop Butler, the long-planned, chief objective of Gladstone's retirement, began immediately after his resignation as Prime Minister.

Gladstone's 'Autobiography'

For posterity, the most intriguing of Gladstone's later writings was his autobiography, begun at Dalmeny during the 1892 election campaign: 'Being almost shut out from reading [following the attack on him in Chester] . . . I turn to writing . . . and I made today an actual beginning of that quasi Autobiography which Acton has so strongly urged upon me.'† He continued at intervals until 1897 but it was never completed.‡ Though it might be thought that the keeping of his diary could be seen as anticipating an autobiography, this would be a twentieth-century assumption. Though many Victorian politicians kept diaries, virtually none of them published one or an autobiography derived from one. The idea that Gladstone should write his autobiography seems to have been external, and to have come from three very different sources. First, and not surprisingly, publishers. In 1887 Cassell offered £5,000 for the copyright of Gladstone's autobiography and in 1891 the Century Company of Putnam New York offered £25,000 for serialization and what it anticipated would amount to two octavo volumes. Gladstone was thus well-placed, with an international offer, to break another mould and become the first Prime Minister to make a large sum by writing about having been Prime Minister. He was encouraged in this by Andrew Carnegie, with whom he forged quite close links in the 1880s. Carnegie, of course, liked money. He also energetically promoted Anglo-Americanism, and he probably saw the publication of Gladstone's autobiography as a further step in mutual understanding. That work was bound to be strongly attractive to Americans, for it would appear to tell a tale of escape from conservative, monarchic church-and-statism to liberal individualism. It was very probably Carnegie who in 1887 engineered an

* See Robert Blake, 'Gladstone, Disraeli, and Queen Victoria: the Centenary Romanes Lecture delivered . . . 10 November 1992' (1993).

† 8 July 92.

‡ Gladstone had stated his suggestive but ambivalent views about autobiography in the pamphlet written as a retrospect to his 'great and glaring change' with respect to church establishment, *A chapter of autobiography* (1868): 'Autobiography is commonly interesting; but there can, I suppose, be little doubt that, as a general rule, it should be posthumous. The close of an active career supplies an obvious exception: for this resembles the gentle death which, according to ancient fable, was rather imparted than inflicted by the tender arrows of Apollo and Artemis.'

American offer of £100,000 (according to E. W. Hamilton, usually a reliable witness about financial matters) for Gladstone's political autobiography,* a gigantic sum by the standards of the day—Disraeli had been paid £10,000 in 1881 for his autobiographical novel, *Endymion*, and that was thought to be a record for a work of fiction.† Carnegie was also involved in the 1891 offer from Century. The third, and least likely encouragement came from Acton. Like Carnegie, Acton was fascinated by Gladstone's capacity to maintain a sense of freedom of will and of destiny while at the same time being a supreme man of politics.

The autobiography was, as we have seen, begun at Dalmeny in a moment grabbed during the 1892 election campaign. This was to be its fate. Gladstone never allocated it a time for sustained writing. As far as can be discovered, it had no plan. Brief segments were written at odd moments, though when collected together they amount to a substantial body of writing.‡ After he finished writing daily entries in his diary, Gladstone sometimes wrote autobiographical fragments as an alternative, but never very systematically. In some of them he set down what were clearly intended as points for posterity, giving his version of events and singling out individuals for criticism—especially Henry Manning, Lord Rosebery, and the Queen—in a way conspicuously absent from his daily journal. It cannot be said that he wrote 'an autobiography' but he did leave papers on a series of episodes, mostly dealing with early life, with religious development, with particular individuals, and with political crises. Even so, their influence on Gladstonian biography has been pervasive. Morley started with them and most have subsequently followed. Though the diary provided help with dating, it is not the foundation document for the autobiography. Indeed, the autobiographical fragments are written in juxtaposition to the diary, as if Gladstone in old age regretted his decision to record in the diary a life seen as routine and therefore wrote later accounts of dramatic episodes and political crises which he had not written about at the time.

Neither Gladstone's autobiography nor his long journal records a joke. Gladstone was not a funny person, though his intensity often caused amusement. J. A. Godley, one of his private secretaries, recalled the moment when, on receiving a telegram announcing the Sultan's surrender to the Concert's terms in 1880, Gladstone 'exclaimed with indescribable

---

* Diary of Edward Hamilton, in the British Library, 22 July 1887; Hamilton, who advised against acceptance, noted that Gladstone was tempted by the sum, which would pay off the debts of the Hawarden estate. Unfortunately, there is no file for these various offers and references to them are widely scattered. There seem to be no copies of Gladstone's replies to them. It may be that he made no copies (unlikely given the sums involved) or that a file was lost, possibly during the writing of Morley's biography.

† Robert Blake, *Disraeli* (1966), 734.

‡ Collected and published as volume i of *The Prime Minister's Papers: W. E. Gladstone*, ed. J. Brooke and M. Sorensen, 4v. (1971–81).

fervour: "Thank God! Then I can go down by the 2.45".' This, we may be sure, was said with no sense of irony. Gladstone was not droll, and his conversation and letters were as literally intended as Disraeli's were ironic—so at least was the view of contemporaries on which we must rely, for the detection of irony is one of the most difficult of historical exercises. But Gladstone was by no means humourless. He excelled in the Commons' tradition of witty repartee through Latin quotation and he often used humour as a weapon in debate. He was a fluent writer of comic verses and like many Victorians he enjoyed puns.

The following story brings the classicism and the puns together: on the Gladstones' Irish visit in 1877, Lord Fitzwilliam brought in J. P. Mahaffy, the noted Dublin classical scholar and wit, to amuse his distinguished guest. Mahaffy brought along Browning's recently published translation of Aeschylus's *Agamemnon*. Gladstone deplored Browning's rendering for 'in belly's strict necessity'. Mahaffy recalled: 'Fitzwilliam came to us and said, "I know your conversation must be most interesting but I am obliged to interrupt you for my lady is waiting". "Certainly," said Mr. Gladstone, and then turning to me added, "This is indeed 'in belly's strict necessity'." I think it was the only joke, certainly the best I ever heard him make.'* As Godley remarked, Gladstone 'thoroughly enjoyed a joke, but the jokes he enjoyed were not the best ones', even though he often moved the Commons 'to long and hearty laughter' and in private life 'could be excruciatingly amusing, playful, and full of fun'. An example of this was his habit, when arriving punctually for dinner at Hawarden and finding the rest of the family late, of singing 'a mysterious chant' which echoed round the Castle until the family and guests gathered.† Another was his habit of breaking out into popular songs during dinner at Hawarden as well as after it.

Gladstone was thus not always earnest, though he often was. Homer, eternal punishment and the other topics of passionate interest about which he liked to talk were alleviated by bursts of humour and song. Even so, as his diary and autobiography show, it was neither humour nor irony which kept Gladstone going.

Bishop Butler's Works

The day after resigning as Prime Minister Gladstone resumed work on his edition of Bishop Butler. His decision that in retirement the completion of this edition should take precedence over the finishing of his 'Autobiography' had, none the less, a strong autobiographical element to it. For his edition of the early eighteenth-century bishop's works was in part an

* W. B. Stanford and R. B. McDowell, *Mahaffy* (1971), 97; another recorded joke is also a pun, on Tait/eight: A. C. Tait was the laziest man on earth because each day he rose a Tait and went to bed a Tait; see David W. Bebbington, *William Ewart Gladstone* (1993), 243.

† See K., [J. A. Godley, Lord Kilbracken], *Reminiscences 1847–1916* (privately printed, 1916), 110, 171.

intellectual and moral *credo*, a statement of his philosophical view of the role of the individual in the destiny of mankind. Gladstone found in Butler a fixed point of reference; reading him he felt 'like one resting on the wings of a great strong bird, when it takes an excursion in mid-air, and is felt to mount as easily as it will descend'.* His reliance on Butler had an element of paradox to it, for the point of Butler's approach was the assertion of probability and experience rather than of absolutes. The certainty which Gladstone gained from Butler was the certainty of a method which stressed the primacy 'of reason, and of the common sense which we rightly accept as our guide in all the interests and incidents of life'. For Gladstone, evidence, reason, and commonsense all suggested the truth of 'the Christian religion' and primarily that part of it known as the Church of England.

Butler emphasized to Gladstone the significance of individuality, experience, and duty in public life: an individual was a moral agent, active not passive, constantly responsible for the terrible consequences of action, but equipped to deal with them through the capacity and redemption provided by God. Gladstone's life as a public figure who at every moment of his career felt moved to initiate is exemplified by this passage in which he summarizes his understanding of Butler's argument:

Our Almighty Father is continually, aye every day and hour, calling upon us, almost compelling us, to act. Now acting is not the mere discharge of an outward function. It is a continuing process, in which we are responsible throughout. What is meant by being responsible? It is meant that we expose ourselves to consequences flowing from our actions. These are (say) of two kinds. First, there is alteration of environment: which implies that in the future actings, which cannot be escaped, we shall have to cast our account anew with circumstances. The second cuts deeper still. It is that our action modifies, that is to say progressively but silently alters, from time to time, and eventually shapes, our own mind and character.†

Butler's inductivism—his absence of systematic theology—was inherently and characteristically Anglican. Though it fitted strangely with the absolute positions sometimes taken up by Gladstone with respect to public life it was in general a convenient creed for a politician and enabled him to bring a sense of method to the necessarily complex business of trying to establish reasoned positions in the constant flux of 'events'. It offered a means of arguing principled propositions in a context recognized to be one of change. As the Church of England was defined by the character of its past and the experiences of its members, more than by its theology, so the governance and constitution of the United Kingdom was defined by history and practice rather than by reference to a deductive model such as that of the United States. In this context Butler was a Christianized development

* W. E. Gladstone, *Studies subsidiary to the works of Bishop Butler* (1896), 249.
† Ibid., p. 9.

of the inductive wisdom of Aristotle. As we have seen, Gladstone went through a period of reliance on an Idealist and deductive approach to the State and the Church in the 1830s, influenced by Plato.* But in the 1840s Butler asserted his influence as Gladstone went through the chastisement of learning by experience in the Peel governments of 1841–6 the impracticability of trying to apply a deductive model in the context of British politics. From that time Gladstone had seen Butler's method—'Probability as the guide of life'—as his means of bringing into intellectual coherence the velocity of change in public life and of shaping that life into more than a succession of haphazard incidents.

The edition of Butler's *Works* in two volumes, accompanied by *Studies subsidiary to the works of Bishop Butler*, was published by the Clarendon Press of Oxford University in 1896. Though to Gladstone it was the fulfilment of an intention formed in the 1840s, to contemporaries it seemed something of an oddity.† To Butlerian scholars it was old-fashioned in its approach and out-of-date in aspects of its scholarship. As parts of it had been written in 1845 and published in 1879 this was hardly surprising. Gladstone's range of reference in fact showed the extent to which, as a general reader, he could claim a fair all-round competence. But, in entering upon an edition of an author who had in the mid-nineteenth century been the hegemonic Oxford text and was still of central philosophical and theological interest to specialists, he could not expect but to be judged at the highest level of criticism. Moreover, the assumption that an editor was an apologist and that the purpose of the edition was to demonstrate that Butler was 'right' jarred in the 1890s. For Gladstone's aim was to argue for Butler's rightness as a religious philosopher—implicitly therefore criticizing the Evangelical and to some extent also the Tractarian tradition—while protecting the Christian element in Butler's thought from the use of him made by Unitarians, utilitarians and agnostics such as Walter Bagehot, Sarah Hennell, James Martineau, Leslie Stephen, and Matthew Arnold (a predominantly mid-Victorian group of Butlerian critics, no longer in the van of philosophical debate). To the intelligentsia more generally, the edition and the *Studies* were a reminder of an older intellectual world of religious certainties, when what was at issue were the details of theological interpretation, not the legitimacy of Christianity itself. To the Asquith generation, 'experience' had come to mean the probability that God did not exist. Butler had provided Gladstone and many of his generation with categories of argument and means of appraisal of evidence which were of profound value to him and to many of his colleagues as public figures. But

---

* See above, Part I, chapters 2 and 3.

† See Jane Garnett, 'Bishop Butler and the *Zeitgeist*: Butler and the development of Christian moral philosophy in Victorian Britain' in C. Cunliffe, ed., *Joseph Butler's moral and religious thought* (1922), 74 ff.

for those at the forefront of public life in *fin de siècle* Britain, those categories had ceased to seem of relevance.

Money and Posterity

In no respect is a human-being more responsible—in the Butlerian sense—than in getting and spending. In not writing and selling his autobiography Gladston forwent, as we have seen, a substantial sum of money. Even if we discount the £100,000 offer reported by E. W. Hamilton, it seems clear that he could have earned £25,000 for it without difficulty. This would have been more than the whole of his life-time literary earnings, which he calculated (to the end of 1896) at £18,836. Of this, Gladstone estimated that £4,750 had come from the pamphlets and articles on the Vatican controversy in 1874–5. Well-selling though Gladstone's pamphlets were, his steady literary income came from periodical articles and reviews. He made more from one review in the *Fortnightly* or the *Contemporary* than he did from any of his scholarly books. The *North American Review* paid best, with his piece on Home Rule and the Duke of Argyll in September 1892 earning £315, his highest recorded fee for an article.

Gladstone's literary earnings were an important element of an account always short of ready cash, for they were, in periods of Tory government, his only earned income. In the later years of his life, however, his financial position eased, partly because he no longer had a London house. For most of his life, Gladstone made an annual assessment of his finances in late December, usually between Christmas Day and his birthday on the 29th. He made the last of these on 31 December 1891.

In 1891, his moveable personalty (i.e. disposable goods) was £11,250, composed of pictures, works of art and ivories (£6,000), furniture (£800), library (£2,500, but difficult to calculate because of the split between his own books and those given to St Deiniol's Library). His other property—made up of bonds, shares, and money on loan or in the bank, for he no longer owned land—was worth £73,700. Of this £3,800 was in various forms of bank accounts and loans and the rest in bonds and shares—i.e. about £70,000.

This portfolio was invested in railways and bonds. He had £18,600 in the Highland Railway, £12,000 in the Darjeeling Railway,* £4,600 in the Grand Trunk, and £3,350 still in his old favourite and great mistake the Metropolitan and District (the line which as we shall see transferred his coffin across London). In bonds, he had £12,000 in Brazilian Loan at 80 and,

---

* An assessment of Gladstone's 'Investments in Calcutta' made by H. N. Gladstone in December 1889 shows his father owning, in addition to the Darjeeling Railway shares, debentures in Hoogly Mills worth 56,000 rupees and Rangoon Tramway Preference $6\frac{1}{2}\%$ worth 30,000 rupees—his Calcutta investments, including the Darjeeling shares, being then worth £15,798. So the 1891 figures might be a slight underestimate; or Gladstone may have sold the Hoogly and Rangoon shares by then.

remarkably, his largest holding was £19,400 in the Egyptian Tribute Loan, the bonds which in 1882 had made up more than a third of his portfolio. In 1891 they still constituted 27 per cent of it. The stock now stood at 97—it had been 42 when bought in 1875, 57 in the summer of 1882, and 82 after he had invaded Egypt, so Gladstone had done well out of his investment, more than doubling its value in less than twenty years—a good performance for a government bond but a questionable one for a Prime Minister directly involved in the central act which increased its value. Since 1882 he had realized part of the profit on what at its zenith had been £51,500 of 'Egyptians'. 62 per cent of his holdings were thus in overseas stocks and bonds—a 'gentlemanly capitalist' indeed. Divided another way, 55 per cent were in railways. It was a conservative portfolio.

This final financial assessment shows Gladstone in his eighties to have been a rich man. But he was not nearly so rich as he had been in his seventies, when his annual assessment was usually for around £290,000 (and once, in 1881, reached £390,000). This was because he practised a deliberate policy of 'gradually divesting myself of the chief part of it'. In this he agreed with the philosophy of wealth put forward by Andrew Carnegie, though he differed from Carnegie in supporting inheritance of land by members of the landed class.* Gladstone did not consider himself a member of that class and in 1882 he gave all his Flintshire estates (except a field called Collins Meadow) with various other gifts, to an overall value of about £261,500, to his eldest son in exchange for an annuity of £3,400 p.a. In 1890, he distributed £43,000 among his children and paid £7,200 for the advowson of Liverpool (with the right to appoint the rector of that city). The purchase was a rare self-indulgence. In 1896 he endowed St Deiniol's Library with £30,000 and distributed further sums to his children, so that each surviving son had had in all £27,000 and each surviving daughter £15,000, a total of £105,000. The gender distinction was characteristically Victorian.

These large distributions were exceptional. They came on top of the charitable donations Gladstone gave throughout his life—almost always in the form of small gifts, but sometimes more extensive support for the education of children or students thought deserving in some particular way. In the 1870s Gladstone normally gave about £1,200 p.a. in such donations. In office again in the 1880s this rose accordingly to nearly £2,000 p.a. For it was his intention to give away at least 10 per cent of his income, a purpose established by his occasional calculations in his account book, which show that he knew that he was giving between 12 and 14 per cent in charitable donations. By the end of 1896 Gladstone had effectively given away most of his money and many of his possessions and after his death his will was eventually proved at £58,569/7/8, the sum being made up chiefly

* See W. E. Gladstone, 'Mr Carnegie's "Gospel of Wealth": a review and a recommendation', *Nineteenth Century* (November 1890).

from the valuation of his various collections and the money kept back for running Hawarden Castle in his final years.*

'Successive snapping of the threads'

On 23 May 1894 Gladstone wrote the last routine entry of his journal: from that day onwards the entries are episodic. The occasion was his cataract operation; but nonresumption when his sight partially recovered shows the cause to have been deeper. For fifty years, Gladstone had discussed in his journal his impending retirement from politics. When at last it came, he was content to see the journal go with the politics: 'retirement from active business in the world ... affords a good opportunity for breaking off the commonly dry daily Journal, or ledger as it might almost be called ...'.† For Gladstone's diary had been chiefly a record not of reflection but of process—of the process of corresponding, reading and participating in public life broadly understood in the Victorian manner. It had of course also recorded what the twentieth century would see as 'private' religious observance and study, but which Gladstone saw as a natural part of a healthy society and of civic behaviour: the daily walk to church at Hawarden and participation in the services there was a public affirmation, and a good citizen read the literature of his or her day.

Physical decline and a sense of conclusion thus ended the daily diary entries. Gladstone enjoyed 'the relief from the small grind of the Daily Journal'.‡ It was a 'grind' which he had maintained virtually without a break since July 1825; there are therefore about 25,200 entries in the daily journal (as he usually called it). Gladstone's formulaic style of diary writing evolved early on—a daily recording of religious observance, correspondence, reading, political and similar activity, details of travel and family matters, and an occasional, terse observation. On holiday and on other exceptional occasions he sometimes expanded the last to a more substantial passage. In 1826 his birthday entry (29 December) mentions the need for 'retrospect' and in 1827 he began the habit of a birthday reflection on sin. At no time (save for the separately kept travel diaries) does the daily diary read as if its author thought he or anyone else would publish it. Though he spent much time in his later years on the cataloguing and ordering of his papers, he left, as far as is known, no instructions about what was to become of his diary. Probably he knew it should not be destroyed, but that its existence posed a problem, and a problem of a kind he would not wish to discuss with his wife or children. For, as we shall

---

* Gladstone's will divided his estate, after various specific dispositions, into sections. His wife got one section and his children the rest, in the same ratios as his distribution in December 1896; i.e. two sections for each son, one section for each daughter.

† Memorandum printed at 25 July 94; it is characteristic that Gladstone says more in a memorandum about breaking off the daily entries than he does in the journal itself.

‡ 17 Dec. 94.

shortly see, Gladstone was well aware of the rumours about his sexual activities and must have known that after his death, there would, sooner or later, be a book and a scandal. Left with the journal, the family in 1928 presented it and its ancillary papers (including the letters to and from Laura Thistlethwayte) to the Archbishop of Canterbury (at that time Randall Davidson) to own *ex officio*.*

The regular daily diary thus runs from 16 July 1825 to 23 May 1894. But in December 1894, Gladstone revived the journal for the limited purpose of recording the daily reading which sustained his intellectual interests, in particular work on the Butler edition. But it was too much. After about two weeks and 'a fall over one of the drawers of my writing table, on my fore-head, with the whole weight of my body', he noted pathetically (after begin-ning a short list of authors and books): 'Il male Occhio [the bad eye]. No. I *cannot* do it.'†

Short passages follow about his and Catherine's health, the Queen's rudeness to Catherine, the progress of the Butler edition, travel, the death of Archbishop Benson in Hawarden Church during a service, the signing of the Trust Deed for St Deiniol's, the new will, and the distribution of his assets to his children or St Deiniol's. He made his last major speech, on Turkish atrocities in Armenia, on 24 September 1896 in Hengler's Circus, Liverpool.

As his eighty-seventh birthday approached, Gladstone made an import-ant move in the process of winding down the coil of life. On 7 December 1896 he made what became known in the family as the 'Declaration': a statement of his marital fidelity. In it—one of the most dramatic private documents in any Prime Minister's papers—Gladstone refers to 'rumours which I believe were at one time afloat' (probably a reference to those in the summer of 1886) and to 'the times when I shall not be here to answer for myself' as the reasons for making the 'Declaration'.‡ Included inferentially

---

* Since then, the 41 volumes (mostly pott octavo) have been in Lambeth Palace Library, except (*a*) during the Second World War, when the Librarian of Lambeth, Claude Jenkins, took the volumes for safe keeping to Christ Church, Oxford, where he was a Professor, hiding them in the wine-cellar under his rooms; (*b*) during the editing of the diaries for publication, when M. R. D. Foot or myself occasionally had a volume in charge, and when relevant volumes were moved to the cupboard in Duke Humfrey in the Bodleian Library, Oxford. More detail on the journal's remark-able history will be found in M. R. D. Foot's 'Introduction' to Volume I of *The Gladstone Diaries*.

† 24 Dec. 94.

‡ It reads in full:

'With reference to rumours which I believe were at one time afloat, though I know not with what degree; [*sic*] of currency: and also with reference to the times when I shall not be here to answer for myself; I desire to record my solemn declaration and assurance, as in the sight of God and before His judgment seat, that at no period of my life have I been guilty of the act which is known as that of infidelity to the marriage bed.

I limit myself to this negation, and I record it with my dear Son Stephen, both as the eldest surviving of our sons, and as my pastor. It will be for him to retain or use it, confidentially unless necessity should require more, which is unlikely: and in any case making it known to his brothers.

WEG Dec. 7. 1896'

in these must have been a decision not to destroy his daily journal. For the journal—already well-known to the family and the Gladstone circle but not yet read by any of its members—contained abundant evidence not merely of temptation but of acts variously interpretable. So also did the correspondence with Laura Thistlethwayte. When Gladstone stated in the 'Declaration' both that 'at no period of my life have I been guilty of the act which is known as that of infidelity to the marriage bed' and that 'I limit myself to this negation', he made a qualification whose force is apparent to any reader of his journal, especially for the years 1845 to 1875. The preserved journal supports the 'negation', but emphasizes its qualified character.*

Having made the 'Declaration'—heavily enveloped, sealed, and given to Stephen, his eldest son, and 'my pastor'—Gladstone determined on his 87th birthday to write the last entry in his journal, for 'old age is appointed for the gradual loosening or successive snapping of the threads'.

'Retrospect' had been a theme of the birthday entries from 1826, since a birthday—especially for one of Evangelical origins—was a moment of spiritual and temporal reckoning as well as a time for celebration. It was thus fitting and deliberate that on 29 December 1896—sixteen months and one birthday before his death—Gladstone finished his diary.

This was his conclusion:

My long and tangled life this day concludes its 87th year. My Father died four days short of that term. I know of no other life so long in the Gladstone family, and my profession has been that of politicians, or more strictly Ministers of State, an extremely shortlived race, when their scene of action has been in the House of Commons: Lord Palmerston being the only complete exception.

In the last twelvemonth, eyes and ears may have declined, but not materially. The occasional constriction of the chest is the only inconvenience that can be

---

* The 'limited' negation in the 'Declaration' and the extensive evidence in the diaries of the degree to which Gladstone was sexually tempted by prostitutes and courtesans meant that neither the journal nor the 'Declaration' were offered as evidence in the Wright trial of January 1927. In his *Portraits and Criticisms* (1925), Captain Peter E. Wright wrote of Gladstone that it was his custom 'in public to speak the language of the highest and strictest principle, and in private to pursue and possess every sort of woman'. Unable to sue for libel of the dead, Herbert Gladstone provoked Wright to sue him for libel, his defence being that the charges he publicly made against Wright's character were justified by the fact that Wright's statement about the Prime Minister was a calumny. Charles Russell, the Gladstones' solicitor, persuaded Herbert and Henry Gladstone (against their initial inclination) not to offer the journal, and perhaps the 'Declaration', as evidence. If part of the journal was quoted, the whole of it would have to be made available, and although it could be used to show that Wright's use of the word 'possess' was unsupported—and indeed denied by Gladstone's 'Declaration'—the fact of extensive temptation and self-flagellation would be revealed, would cause a public sensation, and would to a degree exonerate Wright. As it was, the foreman of the jury interrupted Norman Birkett, Herbert Gladstone's counsel, to add to its verdict for the defendant that 'the jury wish to add that in their unanimous opinion the evidence that has been placed before them has completely vindicated the high moral character of the late Mr. W. E. Gladstone'; Charles Russell had given shrewd advice. For the Wright case, see Herbert Gladstone, *After Thirty Years* (1928), app. v, Foot, op. cit., p. cxxxiii, and extensive papers in Lambeth MSS.

called new. I am not without hope that Cannes may have a mission to act upon it. Catherine is corporally better than she was twelve months ago.

As to work I have finished my labours upon Butler, have made or rather remade my Will, have made progress with 'Olympian Religion' and good progress with a new Series of Gleanings, and have got St. Deiniol's very near its launch upon the really difficult and critical part of the undertaking.

The blessings of family life continue to be poured in the largest measure upon my unworthy head. Even my temporal affairs have thriven.

Still old age is appointed for the gradual loosening or successive snapping of the threads. I visited Ld Stratford at Froom Park(?) [sc. Frant Court] when he was 90 or 91 or thereabouts. He said to me 'It is not a blessing'.

As to politics I think the basis of my mind is laid principally in finance and philanthropy. The prospects of the first are darker than I have ever known them. Those of the second are black also: but with more hope of some early dawn.

I do not enter on interior matters. It is so easy to write, but to write honestly nearly impossible.

Lady Grosvenor gave me today a delightful present of a small Crucifix. I am rather too independent of symbol.

Adieu old year. Lord have mercy.

WEG D. 29. 1896.

Death

Having by the end of 1896 made these various dispositions—intellectual, financial, and moral—Gladstone clearly felt he had discharged his chief earthly obligations. But death was not to be so tidy.

This book has been written as an interpretation of Gladstone's own writings. It has by no means shown him as he wished to be seen, but it has used his words as its point of departure. With the ending of his diary, we move to a different perspective: we can report observations of Gladstone in his dying years; but it is necessarily an external report. For he, so often the assiduous recorder, in the Evangelical tradition, of the details of death of members of his family and close friends, naturally left no record of his own, nor, as he might have done, did he try to record his immediate movement towards it.

Gladstone's death was a serious matter for the English-speaking, the European, and the Imperial world. The manner of it encouraged interest, for Gladstone took a long time to die. Having finished his diary, he, his wife, and their coterie went to Cannes for the early months of 1897. There they met the Queen, who was staying at Cimiez. Something of a reconciliation took place, Gladstone felt, though he also noted that 'to speak frankly, it seemed to me that the Queen's peculiar faculty and habit of conversation had disappeared'. Uniquely in his recollection of fifty years of meeting her, she shook hands with him. This spell in France was the last holiday the Gladstones had without nurses and doctors in constant attendance. Not surprisingly for a person who had so successfully kept at bay the most annoying features of old age, Gladstone was irritated when at last they caught up with him; a young neighbour left an interesting description of William and Catherine Gladstone at Cannes in 1897:

He and his devoted wife never missed the morning services on Sunday.... In my seat immediately behind theirs I fancied I could almost see the reflection of my face in the shiny surface of Mrs. Gladstone's ancient cloak, for she never paid the least attention to her clothes.... One Sunday, returning from the altar rail, the old, partially blind man stumbled at the chancel step. One of the clergy sprang involuntarily to his assistance, but retreated with haste, so withering was the fire which flashed from those failing eyes.*

The Gladstones returned to Hawarden at the end of March and he spent the summer of 1897 in his usual way, still speaking at local events, still corresponding, still intervening against the Tories on the Eastern Question (in a public letter to the Duke of Westminster), still finding work on his 'autobiography' interrupted by a variety of causes. He no longer walked daily to the 8.00 a.m. service in Hawarden Church or read the lessons at the services he did attend, but he still took a daily stroll in Hawarden Park with Petz, his black Pomeranian dog. Though clearly frail, he could still receive the Prince of Wales and the Colonial Premiers—in Britain for the Jubilee—at Hawarden and he could still travel, visiting George Armitstead in Perthshire in the autumn. Up to this point, Gladstone seemed to his friends an old but healthy man. Only heavy discharges of what seemed a peculiar form of catarrh suggested a change from the aches, pains, deafness, and impeded sight with which he had lived for years.

On his return to Hawarden, he had what seemed to be a bad attack of the facial neuralgia which had spasmodically afflicted him since his forties.† A decline in interest in public affairs was observed. His correspondence on matters of the day, which he knew would mostly be immediately published, ceased to flow. His doctor, Samuel Habershon, and the family encouraged him to winter in Cannes with the Rendels and from the end of November 1897 to mid-February 1898 he was at the Château de Thorenc, Rendel's

---

* *Alice Ravenhill—the memoirs of an educational pioneer* (1951), 88; I am obliged to Nancy Blakestad for this reference.

† Friends, accustomed to Gladstone's resilience, found it hard to recognize that anything was wrong, or, indeed, that his permanent presence in their lives might soon end; Edward Hamilton met the Gladstones on their way to Cannes and noted in his diary, embarrassingly patronizingly as it turned out: 'Mr. G.... complained that the neuralgia which had taken hold of one side of his face was most distressing and completely incapacitated him for serious writing or reading. He has always made the most of his ailments, partly due to the extraordinary immunity from troubles which he has enjoyed during his long life; so one must make allowance for some exaggeration; and I tried to persuade him that all his neuralgia would fly at the sight of Cannes. Apart from glumness and depression I could see no sign of increased failure either mentally or physically'; EHD, 24 November 1897.

villa so often used in earlier days to recuperate from insomnia or exhaustion from a heavy parliamentary Session.

Cannes had, in the past, always meant recuperation. But the early months of 1898 must have been agonizing for Gladstone. The spasmodic pain in his face increased. He took opiates but refused close medical examination. His daughter, Mary, regretted that 'he has been allowed to drop *all* occupations and work, and the whole of his great unimpaired brain is turned on his own ailments'.* His chief solace was listening to music, and friends were brought in to play to him. He managed an interview for the *Daily Telegraph*, which was published on 5 January 1898 as 'Personal Recollections of Arthur H. Hallam': his last literary publication thus being a cautious record of his most famous friendship and a veiled correction to Tennyson. When it was clear that Cannes had not brought its usual relief, he was transferred to Bournemouth, the move to Britain implying the likelihood of death, although no diagnosis had yet been made (and 'different air' was the reason publicly given for the return from France). In Bournemouth, Habershon found a swelling on the palate. He summoned the leading cancer surgeon, Sir Thomas Smith, on 18 March and cancer was diagnosed. An announcement was made to the press, Gladstone was moved to Hawarden on 22 March and his rather public death began. But, assisted by Nurse Kate Pitts, Gladstone's strong body refused to yield. Weak, clearly in intense pain despite the narcotics and with his mind at times muddled, he did not die. He calculated the number of days lost through illness in the course of his life ('*dies non*' as he used to call them in the diary) and was pleased by how small a percentage of his life they formed. He quoted hymns to his visitors, especially Newman's 'Praise to the Holiest in the Height'. He was well enough to dictate to his daughter Helen the following elegant answer—and his last public statement—to a message of 'sorrow and affection' from the Vice-Chancellor of the University of Oxford, writing on behalf of its Hebdomadal Council (established by Gladstone's Oxford Act of 1854):

There is no expression of Christian sympathy that I value more than that of the ancient University of Oxford, the God-fearing and God-sustaining University of Oxford. I served her perhaps mistakenly, but to the best of my ability. My most earnest prayers are hers to the uttermost and to the last.

On 9 April he went out of the house for the last time, on the 18th he came down to dinner for the last time, and after that he ceased to come downstairs at all, though still getting up each day to lie on the sofa. Soon, he was told to stay in bed. At this time, G. H. Wilkinson, Bishop of St Andrews,

---

* *Mary Gladstone*, 443 (11 February 1898). She added, with a note of alarm: 'if we are to face *years* of this time of invalidism (like Bismarck), we ought to equip ourselves for it'.

ministered to him in addition to Stephen Gladstone. He recorded his ministry thus:

Shall I ever forget the last Friday in Passion Week, when I gave him the last Holy Communion that I was allowed to administer to him? It was early in the morning. He was obliged to be in bed, and he was ordered to remain there, but the time had come for the confession of sin and the receiving of absolution. Out of his bed he came. Alone he knelt in the presence of his God till the absolution had been spoken, and the sacred elements received.*

This is the last recorded occasion on which Gladstone made his Communion. Surprisingly, there is no mention of the administration of the elements when he was dying.

Despite the doctors, Gladstone continued to get up for a short time on most days. On 12 May it was noticed that this small exertion exhausted him and by Tuesday, 17 May, it was clear that death must be close. Early on Wednesday morning he seemed about to die, and the family collected around his bed. But, rather characteristically, he rallied and they had to wait. Later that day, his breathing steadied and the pallor of his face freshened. He was able to show occasional recognition of the presence of his relatives. But for the most part he was barely conscious. At two-thirty o'clock on the morning of Thursday, 19 May, Ascension Day, a change was noticed. The family was again gathered and just after five o'clock that morning, with nine members of the family and three doctors around the bed—Catherine Gladstone kneeling at her husband's right hand—Gladstone was pronounced dead.† He had probably been unconscious for several hours.‡ The stentorian voice of Stephen Gladstone intoning the prayers for the dying and the dead echoed throughout the corridors of the castle. It was in keeping with his life that Gladstone's death was inferred by the reporters, waiting in the smoking room underneath his bedroom, through the hearing of prayers. But it was out of character of him to die just too late to catch the morning editions: special editions of the London papers brought the news to the capital.

---

* A. J. Mason, *Memoir of G. H. Wilkinson, Bishop of St Andrews* (1909), ii. 271. It is unlikely that 'confession' here means more than the general confession made in the Communion Service, for Gladstone was a life-long opponent of private confession in the Church of England.

† Those in the bedroom at the time of death were: Catherine, Herbert and Helen Gladstone; Stephen Gladstone and his wife Annie; Henry Gladstone and his wife Maud; Mary and Harry Drew; Agnes Wickham; Drs Habershon, Biss, and Dobie. Nurse Pitts may have been present also.

‡ The death was registered by Helen Gladstone on 23 May; Gladstone's occupation was recorded as 'Privy Councillor' and the cause of death as 'Syncope Senility', certified by Hubert Biss, M.B. This is consistent with the descriptions of Gladstone's final days; 'syncope' simply means failure of the action of the heart; 'senility' was used in the nineteenth century to denote the infirmity of extreme old age, rather than actual loss of mental faculties.

Rites of Passage

On the afternoon of Gladstone's death, the Commons met and adjourned, A. J. Balfour giving notice of an Address to the Queen praying for a public funeral and a public memorial in Westminster Abbey. Next day, the Address was approved by both Houses and tributes were made. Being in office, these were initiated by the Tories, who seem to have found the task easier than Gladstone did in 1881 on the death of Disraeli.

Herbert Gladstone, on behalf of the family, accepted the offer of a public funeral. His father had left three directions in his will of 1896 as to his burial: an absolute requirement that he should not be interred where Catherine Gladstone might not ultimately be interred also;* the very Gladstonian instruction—reminiscent of his qualified statements on his various political retirements—that his burial was 'to be very simple and also private unless they [i.e. his Executors] shall consider that there are conclusive reasons to the contrary'; and, lastly, that 'on no account should any laudatory inscription be placed over me'. Herbert told Lord Salisbury, the Prime Minister, of these requirements, stating that in the family's view public reaction constituted a 'conclusive reason', and urging that his mother's state of health required that there be no significant delay in holding the funeral.

On a white sheet embroidered 'Requiescat in Pace', Gladstone's body was laid as if for an academic occasion, dressed in sub-fusc and the scarlet robes of his Oxford Doctorate of Civil Law *honoris causa*—awarded to him in the Sheldonian Theatre in 1848—and with his mortar board with its black silk tassel laid on his chest, and placed just above his hands which were clasped with his fingers tightly intertwined. A red silk handkerchief recently given by the Armenians as a gesture of thanks covered his feet. The body, thus prepared, was placed for view in the 'Temple of Peace', his study at Hawarden Castle, and between two and three thousand people filed past the body there. W. B. Richmond's drawing, made at this time and reproduced in this volume, shows the pain and decline of his final months.† The doctoral robes seem odd to the twentieth-century reader.

* This may have been agreed between William and Catherine Gladstone when they discussed their funerals in 1894; see 28 Mar. 94. But it is not clear how much the family had received detailed suggestions from Gladstone about his funeral; the names of the pall-bearers, for example, seem to have been chosen by the 'children'. Herbert Gladstone's letter to Salisbury, 21 May 1898, and much other material is in *The passing of Gladstone. His life, death, and burial* (1898): chiefly reprinted reports from the Liberal paper, the *Daily News*, which was kept very well-informed by the family and the many Liberals who visited the Castle at the time of or immediately after the death. The account of Gladstone's death in it, and in *The Times* on 20 May 1898, was taken from a detailed statement written for the reporters by Mary Drew and now in Hawn P.

† Richmond reported in the *Daily News*, 23 May 1898, that 'the expression . . . seems almost to attain nobility almost joyous'; but the sketch suggests otherwise; see *The passing of Gladstone*, 35. Richmond's sketch is dedicated to Gladstone's nurse, Kate Pitts.

They represented Gladstone's lingering relationship with his university and the world of learning; his Privy Council uniform, with its implication that he was a mere politician, would have struck the wrong note.* At a different level, the academical gown was a striking choice, for the whole of his life had been conducted as if sitting a series of tests and examinations set by his Maker: 'for, gold is tried in the fire and acceptable men in the furnace of adversity.'

Four days later, on 25 May, Gladstone's body—still in its red doctor's robes but now sealed in a simple oak coffin†—was pulled on a hand bier by colliers, estate workmen, tenants, and labourers of Hawarden to Hawarden Church, where a Communion Service was held, and then to Broughton Hall railway station. The engine 'Gladstone' pulled the coaches with the coffin, its attendants, and the reporters overnight to London, the swiftness of its arrival there confirming the central significance of railways to the public life of Gladstone. On coming in to Willesden, the coaches were transferred to the Underground (the District Line) and thence to Westminster Station; Victorians saw no indignity in a coffin for a state funeral arriving by Underground. The coffin was then taken across the road to Westminster Hall. There was thus no procession through the streets of London: the crowds were to come to the coffin, not the coffin to the crowds, and there was consequently no need for martial display or troops lining the streets.

From 6 a.m. to 8 p.m. on Thursday and Friday, 26 and 27 May, the closed coffin lay in state in Westminster Hall. Over a quarter of a million people were estimated to have viewed it. There were no soldiers guarding the coffin, no batons, coronets, ribbons, or honours on top of it. 'Mostly up from the provinces' was one observer's impression of the crowds,‡ and this would not have been surprising, given the distribution of the Liberal vote. Among those who filed through was Thomas Hardy who described the scene to his sister, typically catching the demotic detail:

---

* The reference to Oxford in Gladstone's laying-out clothes was deliberate; Mary Drew recorded: 'The Oxford robes were put on, & he lay on his bed like a king . . . and looking exactly as at the Sheldonian in 1892 [the Romanes Lecture], the last time he wore them' (diary of Mary Drew, Add MS 46264, 23 May 1898). See the photograph reproduced in this volume.

† Some of the family were keen for the coffin to be open during the lying-in-state in Westminster Hall. They were persuaded of the undesirability of this by Hamilton, who took a week off his duties at the Treasury to liaise between the family and the Duke of Norfolk who, as Earl Marshal, was in charge of the arrangements in London; Hamilton considered that an open coffin 'would no doubt be thought "un-English" and without precedent'; EHD, 23 May 1898. Hamilton had in fact started work on the arrangements before Gladstone had died, acting on advice about the will from Herbert Gladstone, who had clearly decided at an early stage for a state funeral. The precedents were murky; Palmerston had died and been buried in the Abbey, but during the Recess; Nelson's and Wellington's funerals had been in St Paul's and had, naturally, been martial affairs. The *longuers* of the Wellington funeral had given a number of lessons of what not to do.

‡ *The selected letters of Somerville and Ross*, ed. Gifford Lewis (1989), 245.

I went to see Gladstone 'lying in state' this morning—though it can hardly be called in state—so plain, even to bareness was the whole scene—a plain oak coffin on a kind of altar covered with a black cloth, a tall candle at each corner, a cross, & 'requiescat in pace' embroidered on the *white* pall under the coffin. Two carpenters in front of me said 'a rough job—$\frac{3}{4}$ panels, & $1\frac{1}{4}$ framing' referring to the coffin, which was made by the village carpenter at Hawarden. The scene however, was impressive, as being in Westminster Hall, & close to where his voice had echoed for 50 years.*

The funeral was held in Westminster Abbey on the morning of Saturday, 28 May, nine days after the death. The family, Edward Hamilton and the Earl Marshal had moved quickly and effectively. Being a state funeral, the long procession into the Abbey of the Lords, the Commons, other dignitaries and the family was necessarily laced with heralds, but theirs and those of the policemen lining the short route were almost the only uniforms. The Guard of Honour was provided by Eton schoolboys. The ten pall-bearers were Gladstone's two old cronies, George Armitstead and Stuart Rendel; three members of his last Cabinet: Lord Kimberley (the only survivor of his first Cabinet still in politics), Sir William Harcourt, and Lord Rosebery; the Duke of Rutland who, as Lord John Manners, had been his fellow MP in Newark, his first constituency;† A. J. Balfour and Lord Salisbury; and the two royal Princes with whom he had been particularly friendly, the Prince of Wales and his son, the Duke of York (the future George V).‡ It was a fair sample of the masculine and secular side of Gladstone's public life. The absence of John Morley from the list reflected, perhaps, family sensitivity to his agnosticism.§ The hymns were Toplady's 'Rock of Ages' (which Gladstone had translated into Latin), Watts's 'Oh God, our help in ages past', and Newman's 'Praise to the Holiest in the Height', which had been on Gladstone's lips as he slipped in and out of consciousness in his last days. Evangelical, national, and Tractarian: the mix of hymns was appropriate. The coffin was placed in an earth grave in the statesmen's corner of the Abbey, with room for Catherine Gladstone, who followed her

* *Thomas Hardy: selected letters*, ed. M. Millgate (1990), 123. The coffin was unguarded while the public filed by it; at night, Anglican laity and clergy kept a vigil.

† The Duke of Argyll was invited but was unable to be present; Manners took his place. Argyll made a public explanation to show that his absence was not intended to reflect his recent political differences with Gladstone; *The Times*, 27 May 1898, 4f.

‡ The Queen, in a final flash of hostility, 'took the Prince of Wales to task for being a pall-bearer. She asks whether there are any precedents for Royal mourners, and on whose advice the Prince and the Duke of York acted. The Prince telegraphed back that there was no precedent and that he took no advice—the circumstances were *un*precedented, and he would and should never forget what a friend to Royalty Mr. G. had been'; EHD, 27 May 1898.

§ Harcourt was, in personal terms, not a suitable choice, for he was one of the few colleagues in a lifetime of office who really exasperated Gladstone. Lord Spencer would have been personally more appropriate. But as Leader of the Liberal party Harcourt could hardly be omitted and the Liberal leaders among Gladstone's pall-bearers could hardly all be members of the House of Lords!

husband to it in 1900. The grave lies between the statues of Peel and Disraeli, placed with no doubt unconscious irony so that the angle of the head of the latter gazes permanently across it. When Mrs Gladstone thanked the pall-bearers as she led the family from the Abbey, the Prince of Wales made a point of saying a few words. Many took the gesture as an apology for his mother for, by what the Queen told Lord Salisbury was 'entirely an oversight', the *Court Circular* had failed to notice Gladstone's death. On the day of the funeral, the Queen sent a polite telegram—*en clair*—to the widow, for the monarch did not attend public funerals.

The proceedings at Hawarden, the lying-in-state, and the funeral were throughout resolutely religious and civilian. The absence of uniforms and weapons was a striking contrast to the tone of Europe in 1898. Gladstone's death occasioned the last great set-piece of Victorian Liberalism. The Gladstone family managed it quietly and well.

Epilogue

It is not difficult to see the latter part of Gladstone's public life as a failure, and his sense of imperfectibility encouraged him to do so also: religion on the wane, the free-trade order of the mid-century giving way to militarism and protectionism which the Concert of Europe was powerless to prevent, Britain bloated by imperial expansions, Home Rule unachieved, the Liberal party divided. And in certain moods Gladstone certainly felt himself to be 'a dead man, one fundamentally a Peel–Cobden man' whose time had passed.

Yet when we place him and his generation in a longer chronological context their record was remarkable. Gladstone was a chief agent in the process by which the Anglican university élite adapted itself and public life to the requirements of an industrial age while substantially maintaining traditional institutions and securing, for the most part, its own dominant political position. In the European context of the time it was uniquely successful in so doing. From the 1840s, Gladstone's view had been that this could only be achieved by sometimes dramatic measures—legislative and administrative proposals usually deeply shocking to conservative opinion. He had rarely been reluctant to propose such initiatives and in most cases was able to carry them through. The notable exception to the latter was Home Rule for Ireland, the greatest and most dramatic of Gladstone's proposals of radical conservatism.

This achievement was based on a coherent methodology of politics which skilfully fused theory and practice. Gladstone did not subscribe to the view that politics is merely a process, its content irrelevant. On the contrary, he held very firmly that the content of policy, the concepts that underpinned it, and the process of achieving it through political action were organically related. To remove any of the elements was to corrupt the whole: concepts—'abstract resolutions'—were useless without formulation as to content and means of achievement; policies whose contents were unprincipled led to disaster; a process of politics removed from ideas and their related policies meant sterility in the body politic. It was the special function of the executive politician to hold these three elements in balance. Gladstone found the method of the 'big bill' the best way of bringing all three into coherence and by the subsequent controversy it generated linking the activities of Parliament dramatically and rhetorically with the interests of the country, legitimizing the former and enlivening the latter.

Politics and ideology, the focus of public discussion, necessarily changed as times changed, for politics was a second-order and largely secular activity whose nature was not, like theological dogma, set in stone. In a long life in politics, Gladstone was not always consistent in his policies, nor did he seek to be. His recognition of this—and the way he explained it—bewildered some of his contemporaries. A degree of inconsistency because of short-term political difficulties is the necessary occasional refuge of any politician. But Gladstone's political philosophy of learning by experience provided for a reasoned change in his political position on a number of major questions: church and state in the 1830s and 1840s, tariffs in the 1840s and 1850s, political reform in the 1860s, Ireland in the 1870s and 1880s. His consistency was, he contended, one of method of change rather than maintenance of content. Indeed the acknowledgement of the need to change, to move on, in the imperfect world of politics was, Gladstone thought, the best preparation for distinguishing between what required changing and what was best kept.

Representative government is founded on the assumption of change: it is a means of arranging and legitimizing it. A chief purpose of such a system is to debate such changes, to reach conclusions upon them, and then to state those conclusions in laws and administrative acts validated by the community through its representatives. Such a system, and especially one such as the British where the executive and the legislature was fused, makes very high demands on its practitioners. None gave more to it than Gladstone in a life-time's work as an 'old Parliamentary hand'.

Three aspects of Gladstone's career have proved of especial significance for posterity.

First, the minimal state in whose construction he played so large a part proved remarkably enduring in practice and even more so in the rhetoric of public life in this country. Here, once he had established it, Gladstone experienced nothing which suggested a need to modify or to amend, only from time to time a need to perfect and to systematize. The powerful, almost schematic model of this state was of striking simplicity considering the complexity of the society to which it was applied. It was based on Treasury control and public accountability, a sharp and fundamental distinction between economic development and the government's duty as raiser and spender of revenue, and free trade in currency and commerce providing a moral as well as a fiscal context for development. Despite his Butlerian emphasis on the role of individual agency in shaping public life, Gladstone had an almost Marxian sense of State-structure, seen at its strongest in this area of the codification of the minimal state. The late-twentieth century Chancellor carrying his budget to the Commons in Gladstone's battered dispatch case—which he used to carry the 1853 budget—is making no mere symbolic reference to the past. Free trade remained intact until the First World War and staged a strong resurgence after it; the budgetary strategy which accompanied it lasted even longer, enduring long after it ceased to be an appropriate mechanism for the economy it claimed not to affect.

The character which Gladstone and those with him gave to the free-trade state was one of un-British rigidity. Free-trade absolutism was in marked contrast to the usual fluidity of British politics, exemplified by their adaptability in constitutional matters. When the Cabinet debated whether the registration of sellers of foreign meat would be a condoning of protectionism, it showed a bizarre fascination with dogmatic purism. The Gladstonian distinction between state and economy proved a heavy and distorting mill-stone around the nation's neck, and one that proved very hard to remove. When J. M. Keynes wrote that we 'are usually the slaves of some defunct economist' he probably meant Ricardo; but he could have better written 'defunct politician' and meant Gladstone. For it was the institutionalization and politicization of free-trade theory which were the vital elements in its remarkable hold on British political culture, and Gladstone had deliberately undertaken and achieved both. Keynes's *The General Theory* with its emphasis on imperfection, the psychological aspects of markets, the need to apply experience and to experiment, was quite consistent with an application to economics of Joseph Butler's theory of probability. It was a supreme irony that Keynes's book was designed, in effect, to undermine the intellectual foundations of the model of minimal state organization in whose construction Gladstone—that arch-Butlerian—had played so central a role. *The General Theory* (1936) was the response of progressive twentieth-century Liberalism to Gladstonian economics. H. N. Gladstone commissioned F. W. Hirst's *Gladstone as financier and economist* (1931) to counter the influence of the Liberal Summer Schools from which Keynes's book emerged. It was remarkable, but true, that the tradition Hirst described was not merely of historic interest but still the dominant ethos in the Treasury.

Gladstone and his generation accepted the implication of the concept of the minimal state: welfare—in its broadest sense—must be provided by voluntary agencies. He was an energetic participant in helping this system to function, taking part in a range of trusts, schools, hospitals, and other sorts of voluntary societies and raising money for them from others and from his own funds. The image of the young President of the Board of Trade slipping out to oversee a ragged school in Bedfordbury (off Trafalgar Square) represents the dedication of a generation of public figures to a view of 'active citizenry' which was energetically committed but ultimately inadequate.

Second, and in marked contrast to the inflexibility of the minimal state, Gladstone's evolving view of the constitution—so arrestingly stated in 1886—posed a question which challenged the next century in almost every decade: how far was the unitary constitution of the United Kingdom of

Great Britain and Ireland sustainable? Most of Ireland went its way out of the Union, the United Kingdom offering an agreed Home Rule settlement only after the constitutional movement in Ireland had been stranded by British inaction. The length of time Irish Home Rulers had been prepared to wait and their remarkable electoral solidity until 1914 testified to the strength of their commitment. Within Great Britain, no settled formulation for the devolution of power from Westminster was found. There was an unresolved conflict between Home Rule and regional devolution. The former would be an admission of the status of local and historic nationalism and thus would relate to existing local patriotisms; the latter would largely ignore or even cut across nationality, would set aside the discrepancy of size between England and her neighbouring countries, and would be administratively neater. The nationalism that Home Rule sought to accommodate was never as homogeneous as the Home Rulers claimed; the administrative convenience of regional devolution lacked sufficient passion to succeed.

Gladstone's view that the unitary constitution was not sustainable was confirmed, not by devolution, but by Britain's signing the Treaty of Rome, thus merging its sovereignty with other European states in a dramatic constitutional change accompanied by financial transfer arrangements similar to those negotiated between Gladstone and Parnell in 1886. In recognizing that constitutions can represent nationalities and their interests in a variety of ways and at several levels, the European Union was based on just the sort of flexible and evolving constitutional arrangements which the Home Rule bills were intended to introduce. The British within the European Union accepted a status not exactly of Home Rule, but one closer to Home Rule than to independence. But the English remained unwilling to make similar changes within what remained of the United Kingdom. Ironically, Gladstone's 'mighty heave in the body politic'—a major change in the character of British sovereignty—was achieved upwards from Westminster, by a Unionist cession of power to the European Union, but not downwards within the United Kingdom itself.

Third, the politics of 'The Platform' of which Gladstone was the dominant exponent offered one solution to the question of how a governing élite could legitimize itself in the wider political franchises established by 1832, 1867 and 1884. The enfranchisement of 'capable citizens' (in Gladstone's phrase of 1884), the assumption that a healthy political community depended on their active involvement in politics and the development of the mass meeting rationally addressed and nationally reported was a concept of democracy important for the Western world, and influential in it. Gladstone also had a prescient sense that a political culture of 'capable citizenry' was one whose passing Liberalism would not long survive and that the leaders of the working-class organizations emerging at the end of his life could either develop or frustrate the democracy which it had made possible.

'Working the institutions' of the country—the day-to-day duty of the executive politician—had therefore always to be done in the context of this wider awareness, and those workings should be willingly explained and defended in the wider court of public opinion as well as in the traditional forum of Parliament.

Liberals, of course, saw the Liberal party as the natural agent of this process. The Liberal party which Gladstone helped to build was a rare and transitory phenomenon. It was not a 'party' in the twentieth-century sense: it had no formal structure and no membership. It achieved a degree of political integration unparalleled in Europe. It was constituted by a mutual association of class and religion whose delicate balance was the envy of its European equivalents. At its fullest, it comprised the Whigs, the free-trading commercial and industrial middle classes, and the working class's 'labour aristocracy' (a term now out of favour with historians but an accurate description of the working-class people the Liberals set out especially to attract). It contained the whole of the religious spectrum of the day, from Roman Catholics through a ballast of Anglicans to Nonconformists; and to all of these it also attached the secularists and the Jews.

The Liberal party was thus a double rainbow of class and religion, and, like rainbows, depended on especial conditions of light: in this case upon a political culture which especially represented positive political self-consciousness. Gladstone was the chief facet of the prism through which the light of late-Victorian Liberalism gained coherence and, as we have often seen, he was a successful articulator of that political self-consciousness. Despite his cautions about the future, Gladstone was a powerful optimist. Though often full of alarms, and in the late 1870s almost a Cassandra, he could none the less make a gloomy warning seem a step forward, the proclamation of the warning being in itself a public atonement. And he had in abundance the capacity—required of any public figure of real staying power—to see victory in defeat. His private verdict on the defeat of the first Government of Ireland Bill was that 'Upon the whole we have more ground to be satisfied with the progress made, than to be disappointed at the failure.' One's immediate reaction is that such a remark is pure self-deception. But the historian is not a Prime Minister. Gladstone had the capacity—useful in any party and vital in the 'party of progress'—to move onwards even when seeming to be thrust back.

Organization around a dominant charismatic leader is obviously a danger to a political movement. Gladstone sensed this in his constant protestations of the temporary character of his political return, and the point was highlighted by the doldrums of Liberalism after 1894. Yet, operating very much within the Gladstonian tradition of platform rhetoric, the Liberals were able to launch their spectacular if temporary Edwardian resurgence on the very Gladstonian issue of free-trade. Moreover, the issue of constitutional reform provided a significant though limited basis for co-operation with the various elements of what became the Labour party, just the sort of co-operation which Continental Liberals failed to develop with their socialist equivalents. The twenty years after Gladstone's final retirement saw, with the development and then predominance of a notion of 'positive welfare', as sharp a discontinuity in British public policy as had occurred since the repeal of the Corn Laws in 1846: Gladstonian issues—free trade, Home Rule, the Lords—gave, however unintended, a continuity to British politics generally and one of especial value to the 'party of progress'. The traditional areas of Gladstonian reforming concern provided the Liberal party with a coherence in the twentieth century which balanced the ructions which the adoption of 'positive welfare' policies so often caused.

From the longer-term perspective of the late twentieth century—when twenty years at Cabinet level is an exceptional achievement and politicians claim to be little else—it is the range, depth and extent of Gladstone's public life and of the political culture which made it possible which is so striking and so alien. Though it is the combination of Gladstonian attributes which now seems so remarkable—executive politician, orator, scholar, author and, as Lord Salisbury called him, 'great Christian statesman'—its bedrock was a hard political professionalism. Gladstone was an exceptionally determined, resilient, and resourceful politician who was hardly ever caught out and, when he was caught, was at his most formidable. He used this professionalism to engage public life over the full range of his interests. Rarely in a representative political system can one person have had such a capacity to dominate the agenda of politics over so extended a period. Gladstone was able to do so because on the whole he moved with the mind of his age and indeed represented some of its chief characteristics. He was not like Churchill, in a restless battle against the tendencies of his century, but represented Victorianism more completely than any other person in public life, and certainly much more than the Queen. Even in his hostility to further acquisition of imperial responsibilities in areas of non-British settlement—which Gladstone saw as encumbering, corrupting, diverting the proper focus of British attention which was the domestic economy—he represented a strong if ineffective tradition and his oratory, more than his actions, was a potent link between the British Liberal tradition and its fast-developing colonial and Indian equivalents. Since the empire was, even by the 1890s, a community of sentiment, that was a far more significant force for practical co-operation than the various schemes of economic and federal union which became fashionable among some of the supposed friends of empire in that decade.

To a curious extent, therefore, an assessment of Gladstone is a personification of an assessment of Britain's moment in world history. In offering freedom, representative government, free-trade economic progress, international co-operation through discussion and arbitration, probity in government and in society generally, as the chief objectives of public life, and in an ideology which combined and harmonized them, Gladstone offered much to the concept of a civilized society of nations. As the twenty-first century approaches, the Victorian world order, complex though aspects of it were, has a hard simplicity which starkly contrasts with the ambiguities of our own times. The Gladstonian moment showed much of what was best about public life at the start of the modern age. But it was a moment only. With the self-confidence and the articulation went a curious absence of self-awareness, an inability to sense that what seemed to be the establishment of 'normal' standards was in the world's context a very abnormal undertaking, hard to sustain and likely to be brief.

References

CHAPTERS I and II were written for *Gladstone *1809–1874* (1986). References to their footnotes will be found below. The other chapters were first published—largely but not wholly in their present form—as introductions to volumes of *The Gladstone Diaries with Cabinet Minutes and Prime-Ministerial Correspondence*. Full references will be found in the relevant volume of the *Diaries*; I have retained for this volume only those footnotes of general interest, or notes which establish a diary-date of particular importance.

The following is the correlation between the chapters of this book and the printed Introductions: in Part I, Chapters III and IV (1840–1854) introduce Volumes III and IV (1974); Chapters V and VI (1855–1868), Volumes V and VI (1978); Chapters VII–IX (1869–1874), Volumes VII and VIII (1982). In Part II, Chapters I–III (1875–1880) introduce Volume IX (1986); Chapters IV–XII (1881–1886), Volumes X and XI (1990); and Chapters XIII–XVI (1887–1896) introduce Volumes XII and XIII (1994).

Notes to Chapter I

1. S. G. Checkland, *The Gladstones. A family biography 1764–1851* (1971) contains an exhaustive account of the making of the family's finances, based on the huge family archive, now at St Deiniol's Library. See Checkland's Appendix II for a summary of the fortune.
2. 19 Apr. 60; all references to Gladstone's *Diaries* are in this form. In the references below, 'Add MS' refers to Additional Manuscripts in the British Library, among which are the Gladstone Papers, and 'Hawn P' to the manuscripts in St Deiniol's Library, Hawarden.
3. Gladstone's recollection in 1892, quoted in J. Brooke and M. Sorensen, eds., *The Prime Minister's Papers: W. E. Gladstone. i. Autobiographical memoranda* (1971), 16; henceforth *Autobiographica*.
4. Checkland, op. cit., 233–4.
5. G. W. E. Russell, *Mr. Gladstone's religious development. A paper read in Christ Church, May 5, 1899* (1899), 7, quoted in P. Butler, *Gladstone: church state and tracturianism. A study of his religious ideas and attitudes, 1809–1859* (1982), 12. Russell's evidence was a letter (not now extant) from Mrs Gladstone in 1818 or 1819, 'communicated' by J. Macdonald of Edinburgh. I have benefited from discussions with Perry Butler and from teaching a class on 'Church and State' for many years with John Walsh, to whom I am also grateful for his comments on this and the next chapter. I am similarly obliged to Marilyn Butler.
6. *Autobiographica*, ii. 61.
7. R. I. and S. Wilberforce, *The life of William Wilberforce* (1838), iv. 83 (Wilberforce was a friend of Gladstone's mother, see *Autobiographica*, i. 15); 29 Dec. 31.
8. *Autobiographica*, i. 140; see Butler, op. cit., 14.

9. W. E. Gladstone, 'The Evangelical movement: its parentage, progress and issue' (1879), in *Gleanings of past years* (1879), vii. 219. Applied to John Gladstone, this was a slightly unfair remark, as he built up a good collection of paintings. For the guns, see J. Morley, *The life of William Ewart Gladstone* (1903), i. 10–11.

10. *Autobiographica*, i. 13.

11. Ibid., 21. See also Butler, op. cit., 14.

12. See Add MSS 44715–8.

13. Gladstone to A. C. Benson, 26 August 1897, in A. C. Benson, *Fasti Etones* (1899), 501, 505.

14. Printed list of membership in Add MS 44717, f. 105.

15. Gladstone to his father, 25 June 1826, Hawn P 222.

16. See Gladstone to his father, 7 July 1826, in *Etoniana* (1938), 340; *Etoniana* reprinted accurately extracts from a number of Gladstone's letters home from Eton, the originals of which are at St Deiniol's. Extracts from the selection were reprinted in P. S. H. Lawrence, *The encouragement of learning* (1980). For Gladstone's later recollection, see C. Milnes Gaskell, *An Eton Boy* (1939), xvi.

17. Benson, *Fasti Etones*, 502; Gaskell, though of Unitarian background, was also a strong Canningite; he was a Tory MP 1832–68, holding office as a whip during Peel's government 1841–6.

18. See below p. 179.

19. Benson, *Fasti Etones*, 502.

20. J. Kolb, ed., *The letters of Arthur Henry Hallam* (1981), 49. This splendid edition contains Hallam's copious letters to Gladstone; unfortunately few of Gladstone's to Hallam have survived. Gladstone's recollections in old age are in his 'Personal recollections of Arthur H. Hallam', *Daily Telegraph*, 5 January 1898, 9.

21. Kolb, *Hallam*, 77 (13–14 September 1826).

22. Ibid., 220.

23. See T. H. Vail Motter, *The writings of Arthur Hallam* (1943) and Henry Hallam's in this respect very candid memoir of his son in *Remains in verse and prose of Arthur Henry Hallam* (1834).

24. Vail Motter, op. cit., 45; the probable attribution of Gladstone as the subject seems quite right, especially given the date of composition—May 1829—and the poem's slightly nostalgic tone, reflecting the chronology of disintegration of intimacy quoted above. Vail Motter is clearly right in stating (p. 35) that the subject of the poem 'My bosom-friend' must be Gaskell and not Gladstone.

25. 1 July 26; 4 July 26; 10 Feb. 27.

26. F. H. Doyle, *Miscellaneous Verses* (1840), 25.

27. 2 Mar. 27; see also Checkland, op. cit., 114.

28. 26 Nov. 25.

29. 18 Dec. 26; 12 Mar., 14 June 27. Epitomes of Gibbon and of Hume are in Add MSS 44717, 44724, and 44792.

30. 3 June 27.

31. 4 May 26 and Kolb, *Hallam*, 108, 169.

32. Begun on 14 January 1827, just before his Confirmation. Doyly and Mant may have been used at the school's suggestion: in Newman's novel, *Loss and Gain* (1848), 3, Charles Reding at Eton fell 'into the hands of an excellent tutor, who, while he instructed him in the old Church-of-England principles of Mant and Doyley, gave his mind a religious impression . . .'. In Gladstone's annotated copy, 'St. Saviour's College', where Reding goes after Eton, is noted as 'Ch.Ch.'.

33. 4 Feb. 27. The five volumes of Blair's *Sermons* (Gladstone had the 1822 edition) begun on 23 October 1825 were read together with Sumner on Sundays throughout 1826 and later. Blair's influential *Rhetoric* (1783) was read on weekdays. For him, see R. B. Sher, *Church and University in the Scottish Enlightenment* (1985).

34. 24 Sept., 1 Oct. 26.

35. 1 Feb. 27.

36. C. Milnes Gaskell, *Records of an Eton schoolboy* (1883), 85.

37. 2 Dec. 27.

38. Recollections of C. J. Canning in Gaskell, *Records of an Eton schoolboy*, 100.

39. Gladstone to his father, 3 November 1824; Hawn P 222; on the timing of his entry to Christ Church probably as a Commoner, rather than as a Gentleman Commoner.

40. Gladstone to his sister Anne, 17 November 1828, Hawn P 745.

41. Gladstone, 'Classical Education' [1835], Add MS 44725, f. 70; J. H. Newman, 'The Tamworth Reading Room' (1841) in *Discussions and arguments* (1872), 275.

42. See 24 Jan.–11 Apr. 28; the character of the Turner household is suggested by the presence of Miss Sumner, J. B. Sumner's sister. On the other hand, Turner introduced Gladstone to Edward Craig, a high Calvinist preaching in Edinburgh, whom Gladstone visited almost daily during a stay in Edinburgh in April–May 1828; see Butler, op. cit., 20–1.

43. Gaskell, *Records of an Eton schoolboy*, 140.

44. Add MS 44719, f. 246; n.d.

45. Gladstone to his father, 15 September [1831], Hawn P 222.

46. *Letters to M.G. & H.G. by John Ruskin with a preface by . . . G. Wyndham* (1903), 15.

47. Add MS 44808.

48. C. R. L. F[letcher], *Mr. Gladstone at Oxford 1890* (1908), 16.

49. Gladstone to his father, 27 September 1829, Hawn P 222; 'It was Hallam's communication concerning the Cambridge Society that first gave me the idea of going about to different people here with the idea of getting one similar to it set on foot among ourselves.'

50. Gladstone to his mother, 20 January 1830, Hawn P 394.

51. Gladstone to his mother, 19 February 1830, Hawn P 394.

52. See 21 Mar. 36 and Morley, i. 161.

53. Gladstone to his father, 31 May 1831, Hawn P 222.

Notes to Chapter II

1. 16 Aug. 40.
2. Correspondence in Hawn P 223 and 637; possibly with a view to keeping the seat open for Tom Gladstone, whom he praised later in the letter, John Gladstone (while leaving the decision open to William) told the Duke that William 'will complete his 23rd year in December and altho' his mind is matured beyond his years, yet I doubt if his experience is sufficient to justify his thus early entering upon such serious and responsible duties as Your Grace holds out to him'; William, however, accepted by return of post from Italy. For this defence of pocket boroughs, see W. E. Gladstone, 'The County Franchise and Mr. Lowe thereon' (1877), reprinted in *Gleanings of Past Years* (1879), i. 136.
3. Gladstone to his sister Helen, 23 October 1831; to his father, 7 May [1831], Hawn P 222.
4. Gladstone to his mother, 7 April 1835, Hawn P 394 f. 214; Butler, 53n.
5. *Autobiographica*, i. 37.
6. Meeting of 12 June 1830, Add MS 44804, f. 42.
7. 'Report and proceedings of the opening of the Liverpool Collegiate Institution' (1843), 13. For the Reform Bill, see his notes for his Oxford Union speech and his 'Letter to Mr. Grant' (unpublished) in Add MS 44721, ff. 28, 86.
8. Memorandum of March 1829, now in Hawn P, printed in D. C. Lathbury, *Correspondence on Church and Religion of William Ewart Gladstone* (1910), i. 2–3.
9. Butler, 26–7; 3–4 Aug. 30.
10. 12 Aug. 30; letters of August 1830 printed in Morley, i. 635; the originals are in Hawn P 222.
11. Add MS 44719, f. 216. The authorities Gladstone quotes in this memorandum are Mant and Paley.
12. Letter of 7 January 1832 in *Autobiographica*, i, App. 2.
13. See the important thesis by Richard Brent, 'The emergence of Liberal Anglican Politics: the Whigs and the Church 1830–1841' (Oxford, 1984).
14. Section on Church and State in Gladstone's Oxford Union speech on the Reform Bill, 16 May 1831; notes in Add MS 44721, f. 23.
15. 'Report . . . of the Liverpool Collegiate Institution' (1843), 10.
16. For the continental dimension, see A. Vidler, *Prophecy and Papacy* (1954), ch. 4 and W. G. Roe, *Lamennais and England* (1966), ch. 4.
17. Add MS 44722–8. A. F. Robbins, *The early public life of . . . Gladstone* (1894) has much well-researched detail on Gladstone's constituency and parliamentary activities.
18. *Nottingham Journal*, 22 Dec. 1832; 3 and 5 June 32.
19. 19 Feb. 35; Add MS 44724, f. 4 and *Autobiographica*, ii. 21.
20. 20 Nov. 35. See his reading lists set out following 28 Feb. 38, and Owen Chadwick, 'Young Gladstone and Italy' in P. Jagger, ed., *Gladstone, Politics and Religion* (1985). Aristotle's *Politics* was begun in the previous Recess, in August 1834.
21. Paper of 26 October 1835, Add MS 44724, f. 203; 4 Mar. 38; 'Speech on Irish Church Temporalities Bill, 31 March 1835' (extracted from 'The Mirror of Parliament'); 31 Mar. 35.

22. Add MS 44719, f. 115; the essay continues with many other similarly balanced comparisons. *Phaedo* was the main Platonic text read as an undergraduate. For Plato and Aristotle in Oxford, see D. Newsome, *Two Classes of Men. Platonism and English Romantic Thought* (1974). I am obliged to Dr Julia Annas for her comments on Gladstone's essay.

23. 'On the Principle of Government', begun on 24 May 31; Add MS 44721, f. 3.

24. 'Of the law of social obligation', of 16 December 1835, Add MS 44725, f. 183.

25. Notes on Aristotle's *Politics*, 1835, Add MS 44723, f. 125^v. Gladstone repeated this comparison, with a slightly more Aristotelian leaning, to his son in 1860, Lathbury, op. cit., ii. 164, quoted in Newsome, op. cit., 74. See also Agatha Ramm, 'Gladstone's Religion', *Historical Journal* (1985) and R. J. Helmstadter, 'Conscience and Politics: Gladstone's First Book' in B. L. Kinzer, ed., *The Gladstonian Turn of Mind* (1985), both published after this chapter was written; I do not go the whole way with Professor Helmstadter's views on Gladstone's Aristotelianism, but he has written a powerful essay on the basis of the published sources.

26. 8 Feb. 32.

27. For an interesting gloss on this, see O. Chadwick, op. cit., 69. For his Oxford notes on Roman Catholicism, see Add MS 44719, f. 191.

28. 29 and 31 Mar. 32; 8 Oct. 38.

29. 15 Apr. 32.

30. 13 May 32; it is important to note that Gladstone went to the Prayer Book to look into 'the details of the system'; he was *not*, as Magnus thought, 'idly examining the *Occasional Offices'* (see Magnus, 12).

31. W. E. Gladstone, 'Speech on Irish Church Temporalities Bill, 31 March 1835' (extracted from 'The Mirror of Parliament'). See also his speech of 29 June 1840, published in pamphlet form as 'Speech of W. E. Gladstone, esq., M.P., in the House of Commons, Monday, June 29, 1840' (1840); inadequately reported in *Hansard*.

32. See H. C. G. Matthew, 'Gladstone, Vaticanism, and the Question of the East', in D. Baker, ed., *Studies in Church History*, xv. 417 (1978).

33. Gladstone's annotated copy of Arnold's pamphlet, dated 'January 1833' (the month of publication) is in St Deiniol's Library, as is his annotated copy of Arnold's important 'Postscript'.

34. Note of 27 Oct. 1836, Add MS 44727, f. 178. See 20, 27 Aug., 29–31 Oct. 37. See also 24–6 Feb. 36. Gladstone's copy of Coleridge's *Church and State*, with marginal annotations, proof corrections and an added quotation, is in St Deiniol's Library.

35. 24 Mar. 34 (fly leaf).

36. *The State* (1838), 6, 17–18.

37. *Church Principles*, 3.

38. *The State* (1838), 312.

39. 'Speech on Irish Church Temporalities Bill, 31 March 1835' (extracted from 'The Mirror of Parliament'), 8.

40. Notes of 1838 on Palmer (e.g. criticizing his over-confident demarcation between which Churches' members can be saved) in Add MS 44728, f. 138ff.

41. *The State* (1838), 312.

42. *Church Principles*, as quoted in D. Nicholls, 'Gladstone and the Anglican Critics of Newman', in J. D. Bastable, *Newman and Gladstone* (1978), 121–4.

43. Paper of 25 February 1836, Add MS 44726, f. 21.

44. For an interesting exposition of Butler's influential arguments on this point, see J. R. Lucas, 'Butler's Philosophy of Religion Vindicated' (1978), 8. For the passage on politics of 11 Dec. 1835, see Add MS 44725, ff. 108–9.

45. For the Scottish Church, see note of 25 Aug. 1838, Add MS 44728, f. 141; see also *The State* (1838), ch. 3. For the Irish Union, see 'Speech on Irish Church Temporalities Bill, 31 March 1835' (extracted from 'The Mirror of Parliament'), 9.

46. 19 Apr. 39 and letter to Russell, 12 April 1870 in *Diaries*, vii. 275; quoted in Morley, i. 130.

47. Butler, op. cit., 68–9.

48. 1 May 38. See also Gladstone's strong defence of the cathedrals on Puseyite lines in his 'Speech . . . in the House of Commons, Monday, June 29, 1840' (1840) on the Ecclesiastical Duties and Revenues Bill, reprinted from *The Mirror of Parliament*. For this aspect of Pusey, see H. C. G. Matthew, 'Edward Bouverie Pusey: from Scholar to Tractarian', *Journal of Theological Studies* (1981).

49. J. S. Mill to G. d'Eichthal, 27 December 1839, in F. E. Mineka, ed., *The Earlier Letters of John Stuart Mill 1812–1848* (1963), ii. 416.

50. Notes on Aristotle, 1835, Add MS 44723, f. 120. Speech on disfranchisement of Liverpool freemen, 1 March 1833, *H* xxii. 474.

51. Article intended for *Dublin University Magazine*, written in May 1834, Add MS 44681, f. 12. On 17 May 34, Gladstone noted: 'finished my paper: a sorry affair'; doubtless he therefore did not submit it for publication.

52. 18 June 34.

53. Add MS 44728, f. 28 and Lathbury ii. 433.

54. Letter of 18 December 1835, in Magnus, 27, which gives a good description of the affair.

55. Verses written in September 1837, Add MS 44727, f. 175, partly quoted in Richard Shannon, *Gladstone* (1982), i. 63.

56. 14 Nov. 37; 31 Jan. 38; and Magnus, 30.

57. M. R. D. Foot's translation of Gladstone's Italian diary entry, 28 Apr. 38.

58. 23 May and 4 June 38.

59. 3 Dec. 35ff.

60. 23 July 38; 29 Jan. 38.

61. 30 Jan.–1 Feb. 36.

62. In Magnus, 38–9.

63. 6 Feb. 39.

64. 8–15 June 39.

65. 14 June 39.

66. 15, 27 July 39.

67. 'Report of the Liverpool Collegiate Institution' (1843); John Gladstone was a chief contributor to the Institution.

68. This, and subsequent figures, are taken from the 'Secret Account Book' and from the 'Rough Books' in the Hawarden Papers.

69. Memorandum of 18 September 1836, Add MS 44726, f. 147.

70. Add MSS 44779–81.

71. Note of 25 March 1838, Add MS 44728, f. 36.

72. Paper dated 5 May 1839, Add MS 44728, f. 254.

73. Letter of 4 September 1826, the third of his *Liverpool Courier* letters, Add MS 44718, f. 74; *Nottingham Journal*, 11 August 1832; pamphlet dated 21 November 1834, Add MS 44723, f. 306; see 20–1 Nov. 34. There are notes made in 1835 on 'Free Trade and Toryism', but these are on the legislation of the 17th and 18th centuries; Add MS 44724, f. 205.

74. Correspondence of January 1841 in Add MS 44135, f. 1ff. and part in Morley, i. 232, 239; it is unclear on the MS whether the italicization is Gladstone's or Cobden's.

75. W. E. Gladstone, 'Course of commercial policy at home and abroad', *Foreign and Colonial Review* (Jan. 1843), 264.

76. Undated paper, probably 1839; Add MS 44728, f. 336; 24 Mar. 34.

Gladstone's Papers

GLADSTONE'S life is well covered in MSS collections. His vast archive is preserved in three parts. First, the British Library holds what A. Tilney Bassett, the family archivist, selected in the 1930s as the public section of the papers (described in their own volume of the British Library Catalogue of Additions to the Manuscripts, *The Gladstone Papers* (1953)). These papers were given to the British Museum by the Gladstone family, with important additions in the 1970s. The British Library papers are supplemented, on deposit, by Gladstone's copies of his letters to the Queen and her replies. Second, deposited in St Deiniol's Library, Hawarden, and produced in Clwyd Record Office across the churchyard, is the family section of the papers, containing much of Gladstone's 'minor' political material as well as the papers of many of the other members of the family; this collection is described by C. J. Williams in 'Handlist of the Glynne–Gladstone MSS in St Deiniol's Library, Hawarden' (*List and Index Society* (1990)). Third, in Lambeth Palace Library, are Gladstone's daily diaries, various ancillary papers, and his correspondence with Laura Thistlethwayte. Letters from Gladstone are to be found in virtually all late nineteenth-century collections. Much of the political material in the British Library (including some in collections other than the Gladstone Papers) and a small amount of that at St Deiniol's is now available on microfilm as *Papers of the Prime Ministers of Great Britain, Series Eight: The Papers of William Ewart Gladstone*, edited by H. C. G. Matthew for Research Publications, Reading.

Gladstone is well documented in editions of his papers and publications. *The Gladstone Diaries with Cabinet Minutes and Prime-Ministerial Correspondence*, 14 vols. (1968–94) ed. M. R. D. Foot and H. C. G. Matthew, contains the whole of his daily diary, and also the minutes of the Cabinets he chaired and a large selection of letters written during his four governments. The index (Volume XIV) is a starting-point for research into almost any aspect of his life and contains details of the 22,000 people he notes as meeting or corresponding with, a subject index, a bibliography of his own works and a bibliography of his life-time's reading as recorded in his diaries, some 20,000 titles. The other chief primary sources are: Philip Guedella, *Gladstone and Palmerston* (1928) and *The Queen and Mr. Gladstone*, 2 vols. (1933); Agatha Ramm, *The political correspondence of Mr. Gladstone and Lord Granville*, 4 vols. (1952–62); J. Brooke and M. Sorensen, *The Prime Ministers' Papers: W. E. Gladstone*, 4 vols. (1971–81), which includes Gladstone's 'autobiography'; D. C. Lathbury, *Correspondence on church and religion of W. E. Gladstone*, 2 vols. (1914); *The Gladstone Papers* (1930); A. Tilney Bassett, *Gladstone to his wife* (1936) and his edition of *Gladstone's Speeches* (1916); *The Speeches and Public Addresses of W. E. Gladstone*, ed. A. W. Hutton and H. J. Cohen (only the last two volumes, X and XI, were published, 1892–4); Gladstone published many of his speeches, sometimes in a gathered form, notably *Speeches on parliamentary reform* (1866) and a series on each

Midlothian campaign (the first series was reprinted in 1971, ed. M. R. D. Foot; the others are important, but hard to obtain). W. E. Gladstone, *Gleanings of past years*, 7 vols. (1879) and *Later Gleanings* (1897, 2nd edn. 1898) are Gladstone's own selections of his reviews, pamphlets, and articles.

Chronology

1809	29 December	Born in Liverpool
1821–7		At Eton
1825		Begins keeping a diary
1828–31		At Oxford University
1829		Death of Anne Gladstone
1832	February–July	On the Continent; Rome
	December	Elected for Newark: Gladstone, 887; Handley, 798; Wilde, 726
1833	June	Maiden speech
1834	December	Junior Lord of the Treasury
1835	January	Under Secretary for War and the Colonies
	April	Out of office Proposes to Caroline Farquhar
	September	Death of mother Intense study at Fasque
1836		Start of close relationship with Hope and Manning
1837	April	Returned unopposed for Newark (defeated at Manchester: Thomson, 4158; Philips, 3759; Gladstone, 2224).
	November	Proposes to Lady Frances Douglas
1838	August	Abroad; Rome, Sicily, Naples
	December	*The State in its Relations with the Church*
1839	January	Back in England
	July	Marries Catherine Glynne
1840	November	*Church Principles considered in their results*
1841	April	Fourth, revised edition of *The State* published in 2 vols.
	July	Re-elected for Newark: Gladstone, 633; Lord J. Manners, 630; Hobhouse, 394
	September	Vice-President of Board of Trade
1842		Revision of tariffs
1843	January	'The Course of Commercial Policy at Home and Abroad' in *Foreign and Quarterly Review* (anon.)
	May	President of the Board of Trade
1844	July	Railways Bill
1845	January	Resigns from Cabinet. Begins attending meetings of 'the engagement'
	March	*Remarks upon recent commercial legislation*
	September–November	In Germany: with Helen Gladstone; moral crisis; meets Döllinger
	December	Colonial Secretary (retiring from Newark seat)
1846	June	Out of office
1847	August	Elected for Oxford University (two seats): Inglis, 1700; Gladstone, 997; Round, 824
	December	Oak Farm bankruptcy

1848	April	Serves as special constable during Chartist meetings
1849	July–August	In Italy, following Lady Lincoln
1850	April	Death of Catherine Jessy
	June	*Remarks on the Royal Supremacy* (on the Gorham case)
	October	In Naples
1851	February	Back in Britain. Intense rescue work
	April	Hope and Manning apostasize
	April, July	*First* and *Second Letter to Aberdeen*
	December	Death of Sir J. Gladstone 'On the functions of laymen in the Church' and translation of Farini, *The Roman State*, 4 vols.
1852	January	*An examination of the official reply of the Neapolitan government*
	July	Re-elected for Oxford University: Inglis, 1369; Gladstone, 1108; Marsham, 758.
	December	Speeches on free trade, Disraeli's budget Chancellor of the Exchequer
1853	January	Re-elected for Oxford University: Gladstone, 1022; Perceval, 898
	April	First budget
1854	March	Second budget
	April	Oxford University Bill
	May	War Budget
1855	February	Out of office
1856	September	'The declining efficiency of Parliament' in *Quarterly*
1857	August	Opposes Divorce Bill
1858	March	*Studies on Homer and the Homeric Age*, 3 vols.
	November	Lord High Commissioner Extraordinary for Ionian Islands
1859	February	Returned unopposed for Oxford University
	March	Back in Britain
	April	Returned unopposed for Oxford University
	June	Chancellor of the Exchequer
	July	Re-elected for Oxford University: Gladstone, 1050; Chandos, 859
	November	Elected Lord Rector of Edinburgh University
1860	February	Budget and Cobden Treaty
1861	February	Post Office Savings Bill
1862	October	Newcastle speech on American Civil War
1864	March	Government Annuity Bill
	May	'Pale of the Constitution' speech Start of contact with Laura Thistlethwayte
1865	July	Defeated at Oxford University: Heathcote, 3236; Gathorne Hardy, 1904; Gladstone, 1724 Elected for S. Lancashire, three seats: Egerton, 9171; Turner, 8806; Gladstone, 8786; Leigh, 8476; Thompson, 7703; Heywood, 7653
	October	Death of Palmerston: Russell Prime Minister
1866	March	Reform Bill
	June	Out of office on resignation of Russell's government Exchequer and Audit Act

1866	October	In Rome
1867	February	Back in Britain
	December	Speeches in Lancashire
1868	March	Supports Compulsory Church Rates Abolition Bill
		Moves resolutions for Irish Church disestablishment
	November	Elected for Greenwich, two seats: Salomons, 6684; Gladstone, 6386; Parker, 4704; Mahon, 4372
		A Chapter of Autobiography
		Defeated in S.W. Lancashire: Cross, 7729; Turner, 7676; Gladstone, 7415; Grenfell, 6939
	December	Prime Minister
1869	March	Irish Church Disestablishment Bill
	August	*Juventus Mundi*
	October	Intense correspondence with Laura Thistlethwayte
1870	February	Irish Land Bill
	March	Elementary Education Bill
	October	'Germany, France and England', on Franco-Prussian War, anon. in *Edinburgh Review*
1871	July	Abolition of purchase by royal warrant
1872	September	Alabama claims arbitration award
1873	February	Irish Universities Bill
	March	Unsuccessfully offers resignation of government
	June–July	Government rocked by scandals
	August	Chancellor of Exchequer as well as Prime Minister
1874	January	Dissolves Parliament
	February	Re-elected for Greenwich: Boord, 6193; Gladstone, 5968 (Liberal); Liardet, 5561; Langley, 5525 (Liberal)
		Resignation as Prime Minister and quasi-resignation as Liberal leader
	June	Death of Sir S. Glynne
	July	Resolutions on Public Worship Regulation Bill
	September	In Germany with Döllinger
	November	*The Vatican Decrees*
	December	Writes letter formally resigning as Liberal leader
1875	January	Retirement from leadership publicly announced
	February	Publishes *Vaticanism: an answer to replies and reproofs*
		Attends large meeting of Nonconformists
	March	Sells lease of 11 Carlton House Terrace
1876	February	Speaks on Suez Canal share purchase
		Buys 73 Harley Street
	April	Death of George Lyttelton
	April–June	Publishes articles on Homerology
	September	*The Bulgarian Horrors and the Question of the East*
		Speech at Blackheath on the atrocities
		Northumbrian visit and speeches
	November–December	Writes articles on Eastern Question
		Homeric Synchronism
1877	January	Speeches on the Eastern Question
		Tour of the West Country
	January–March	Writes articles on the Eastern Question

1877	May	Moves Resolutions on the Eastern Question Speech at inaugural meeting of National Liberal Federati-on
	July	Another tour of the West Country
	August	'Aggression on Egypt and Freedom in the East', *Nineteenth Century*
	October–November	Visit to Ireland
	November	Elected Rector of Glasgow University
1878	February	'The Peace to Come', *Nineteenth Century* Jingo mob breaks Gladstone's Harley Street windows
	March	'The Paths of Honour and of Shame', *Nineteenth Century* Announces he will not stand again in Greenwich
	May–July	Attacks Disraeli's imperial policies
	September	'England's Mission', *Nineteenth Century* 'Kin beyond Sea', *North American Review*
	December	Speaks on Afghan War *Primer of Homer*
1879	January	Accepts nomination for Midlothian
	July	'The Evangelical Movement', *British Quarterly Review*
	September–October	In Bavaria and North Italy
	November	Opens Midlothian Campaign
	December	*Gleanings of Past Years 1843–1879*, 7 vols.
1880	March	Midlothian speeches
	April	Elected for Midlothian: Gladstone, 1579; Lord Dalkeith, 1368; and for Leeds: Gladstone, 24,622; Barran (Liberal), 23,674; Jackson (Tory), 13,331; Wheelhouse (Tory), 11,965 Prime Minister and Chancellor of the Exchequer
	July	Compensation for Disturbance (Ireland) Bill
1880	August	Serious fever Cruise on *Grantully Castle*; visits Dublin
	December	Boer War begins Irish Land Bill planned
1881	February	Bad fall in snow in Downing Street Majuba Hill defeat
	April	Budget Introduces second Irish Land Bill Death of Beaconsfield (Disraeli)
	August	Convention of Pretoria
	October	Arrest of Parnell
1882	February	Bradlaugh affair
	April	Plans for retirement 73 Harley Street sold
	May	'Kilmainham Treaty'; Parnell released Phoenix Park murders Arrears Bill; Coercion Bill
	July	Alexandria bombarded; Egypt to be invaded
	September	Cairo captured; Arabi imprisoned
	October	Introduces new procedures for Commons Plans for retirement
	December	Cedes Exchequer to Childers; insomnia starts

1883	January	Severe insomnia; convalescent in Cannes
	March	Returns to London
	June	Suez Canal negotiations
	September	Cruise in *Pembroke Castle* to Scandinavia
	November–December	Preparation of Reform Bill
1884	January	London Convention on Transvaal
		Sudan to be evacuated; Gordon sent
	February	Introduces Reform Bill
	June	Reform Bill passes Commons
	July	Reform Bill rejected by Lords
	August	Scottish tour
	September	Wolseley's expedition to rescue Gordon
	November	Liberal–Tory talks on redistribution
		Attends spiritualist séances
	December	Introduces Redistribution Bill
1885	February	Fall of Khartoum and death of Gordon
	April	Penjdeh crisis
		Vote of credit
	May	Central Board plan for Ireland defeated in Cabinet
	June	Defeat of government on budget
		Resignation
	July	Contacts with Parnell opened on Irish government
		Loss of voice and electric shock treatment
	August	Norwegian cruise on *Sunbeam*
		Writes election pamphlet
	November	'Proposed Constitution for Ireland' sent by Parnell
		Home Rule Bill sketched
		Re-elected for Midlothian: Gladstone, 7879; Dalrymple, 3248; Liberals, 333; Tories, 251; Home Rulers, 86
1885	December	'Hawarden Kite'
		Proposal for co-operation with Tories on Home Rule rejected
1886	January	Prime Minister and Lord Privy Seal
	February	Home Rule Bill and Land Bill prepared
	March	Chamberlain and Trevelyan resign
	April	Introduces First Home Rule Bill and Third Land Bill
	June	Home Rule Bill defeated in Commons
		General election: Tories, 316; Liberals, 196; dissentient Liberals, 74; Home Rulers, 86
		Returned unopposed for Midlothian and Leith Burghs
		Resigns premiership
	August	*The Irish Question: History of an Idea; Lessons of the Election*
1887	January	'*Locksley Hall* and the Jubilee', *Nineteenth Century*
	June	Welsh tour; speech at Swansea
	September	Speech on Mitchelstown affair
1888	January–February	In Italy
	May	'Robert Elsmere and the battle of belief', *Nineteenth Century*
	September	At Eisteddfod
	December	In Italy

1889	February	Returns to London
	June	Tour of West Country
	July	Golden Wedding
	September	Attends French Revolution centenary in Paris
1890	August	Death of Döllinger
	October	Tour of Scotland
	November	O'Shea divorce proceedings
	December	Fall of Parnell
		Impregnable Rock of Holy Scripture
		Landmarks of Homeric Study
1891	July	Death of W. H. Gladstone
	October	'The Newcastle Programme'
	December	In Biarritz
1892	February	Returns to London
	June	Eye wounded by attack in Chester
		Midlothian Campaign
		Elected for Midlothian: Gladstone, 5845; Wauchope, 5155
	July	Begins writing of 'autobiography'
	August	Prime Minister and Lord Privy Seal
	September	Uganda crisis
	October	Romanes Lecture at Oxford
	December	In Biarritz
1893	January	Returns to London
	February	Introduces Second Home Rule Bill
	May–July	Home Rule Bill in Committee
	September	Home Rule Bill passes Commons; rejected by Lords
	October	Matabele war
	November	Navy 'scare' starts
1894	January–February	In Biarritz
	March	Final Cabinet and last Commons speech
		Resigns premiership
	May	Cataract operation on right eye
		Death of Laura Thistlethwayte
1895	June	Cruise in *Tantallon Castle* to Germany
1896	February	*The Works of Bishop Butler*, 2v.
		Studies Subsidiary to Bishop Butler
	September	Speech on Armenia
1897	January	In Cannes
	March	Returns to Hawarden
	November	In Cannes
		Later Gleanings
1898	February	Returns from Cannes
		In Bournemouth
	March	Returns to Hawarden
	19 May	Dies at Hawarden
	26–7 May	Lying in state in Westminster Hall
	28 May	Buried in Westminster Abbey

*   *   *   *   *   *

1898	Morley commissioned as biographer
1900	Death of Catherine Gladstone, buried in Westminster Abbey
1903	Morley's *Life of William Ewart Gladstone*, 3 vols.

Index

Readers who wish to follow up in more detail incidents and episodes described in this book will find the Index volume (i.e. Volume XIV) of *The Gladstone Diaries with Cabinet Minutes and Prime Ministerial Correspondence* a convenient starting point. It contains a large Subject Index to the text which contains much of the evidence on which this biographical study is based.

There is an extensive listing below for Gladstone, William Ewart; for his writings and publications, *see* Gladstone, William Ewart, works.

à Kempis, Thomas, 318
Abbas II, 598
Abdur Rahman, 379 ff.
Abercorn, *Lord*, 21
Aberdeen, *Lord*, *see* Gordon
Aberdeen, speech at, 203
    Freedom of, 229
Aberdeen coalition, 77, 82–6, 104–6, 121, 123, 137, 154, 181
Aberystwyth, college at, 204
Abyssinia, 192, 220
Acland, A. H. D. (formerly Troyte), 21, 22, 90
Acland, A. H. D., 583
Acland, *Sir* Henry, 594
Acland, *Sir* Thomas Dyke, 21, 22, 45, 90, 91, 218, 475, 482, 541 n., 583 n.
Acton, *Sir* John, *Lord Acton*, 150, 167–8, 175, 195, 249, 326, 356, 509, 517, 529, 533, 537, 547, 581, 584, 603–4, 611, 621, 622; Plate 29(b)
Adam, W. P., 138, 288, 291, 292, 299, 306
Adams, C., 189
Adderley, C. B., 75
Additional Curates Society, 45
Admiralty, 111, 218, 225, 396, 397, 600 ff.
Adullamites, 134, 141, 142
advertising, 300
Aeschylus, *Agamemnon*, 623
Afghanistan, 303, 307, 354, 355, 374, 379–81, 401, 459, 461, 513
Africa, 275–6, 377, 397, 402–9
    Boer Wars, 402, 406
    East, 402 ff., 595–600
    scramble for, 402–10, 595–600
    South, 270, 282, 288, 307, 402–9, 599–600
    telegraph to, 221
    West, 227
    see also Berlin Conference, Cape Colony, Egypt, Gold Coast, Orange Free State, Sudan, Transvaal, Uganda
Agnostics, 339
agriculture, 335, 416, 437 ff., 485
    ministry of, 417

Ainsworth, H., 131
Akerman, J. W., 405
Alabama, case of, 179, 188–90
Albania, 165, 167
Albany, the, 53, 57
Albert, Lake, 276, 390, 598
Albert, *Prince*, 83, 143, 210
Alexander, L. C., 277 n.
Alexandria, bombardment of, 366, 375, 385, 389 ff.
Alford, *Lady* Marion, 326
Algeria, 382, 390, 409 n., 300
Alhambra Music Hall, 323–4
Ali Pasha, 273
All Saints, Margaret Street, 96
All Souls College, Oxford, 554–5, 556, 612
Allen, W., 132
alliances, 375, 410 ff.
Alsace-Loraine, 187 ff.
Althorp House, 234
Anderson, Mary, 529
Anderson *Sir* W. G., 151
Anglo-Catholicism, *see* Tractarianism
Anglo-German Agreement (1890), 595, 597
Anglo-Turkish Convention (1878), 379
Angra Pequeña, 403, 404
Annual Register, 209, 547 n.
Anstice, J., 21, 22–3, 28
Anti-Corn-Law League, 56, 76–9, 181, 577
apostacy, 47, 69–70, 248
apostolicity, 261–2
Applegarth, R., 131, 132
Arabi Pasha, 374, 383–9, 450
Argyll, *duke of*, *see* Campbell
Arians, 262
Aristotle, 20, 32–6, 39, 41, 42, 77, 92, 155, 156, 306, 571, 650–2
Armenia, 629, 635
Armitstead, George, 563 n., 572, 611–12, 632, 637
Armstrong & Co., 612
army, 189, 341, 375, 384, 390–401, 411
    see also militarism

Army Regulation Bill (1871), 211, 213
Arnauld, Agnès *and* Angélique, 158
Arnold, Matthew, 238, 625
Arnold, Thomas, 30, 38–9, 54, 55, 253, 263
Arrears Bill (1882), 359, 386, 453–6
artisans, 103, 133, 140–2
Artists at Home, 541
Ashbourne Act (1885), 474, 496, 499
Ashley, A. E. M., 147
Asia, Central, 377–82, 401, 462
Asquith, H. H., 240, 290, 583, 588 n., 605, 625
Asquith, Margot, *see* Tennant
Aston Hall purchase, 245–7
atheism, 339
Athens, 164–5
   British School in, 524
Augustine, St., 32, 184, 275
Austin, Alfred, 595
Austria-Hungary, 108, 167, 562
   see also Hapsburg Empire
Australia, 404, 502
   Gladstone's voice recorded for, 552

Babbington, Churchill, 320
backgammon, 611
Bacup, 288
Baden, 87, 89, 92
Bagehot, Walter, 151, 178, 225, 238, 258, 319, 512, 625
Balfour, Arthur James, 237, 313, 436, 482–3, 526, 544, 635, 637
ballast heavers, 102
Balliol College, 47
ballot, 295, 414, 577
Balmoral Castle, 143, 234, 236, 539
Baltic, 3, 85
Bampton Lectures, 301
Bank Charter Act (1844), 118, 171
Bank of England, *see* England, Bank of
Bankruptcy Bill (1883), 424
Baring, T. G., *Lord* Northbrook, 364, 365, 380 ff., 393, 411–12, 494
Baring, *Sir* Evelyn, *Lord* Cromer, 370, 395–8, 598
Barkly, *Sir* H., 193
Barron, H. P. T., 277 n.
Bashi-Bazouks, 273
Bauer, Karoline, 527
Bavaria, 184, 186, 547
Baxter, R. Dudley, 127, 236
B.B.C., 552
Beach, *Sir* Michael Hicks, 109, 420, 422, 433, 461
Bechuanaland, 408, 412
Bedford, *Duke and Duchess of*, 357
Bedfordbury ragged school and chapel of ease, 97, 641

Bee Hive, 225
Beesly, E. S., 225
Belgium, 186–7, 410, 561
Bell, *Captain* R. H., 618 n.
Bellamarine, *St.* R., 40
Ben Macdhui, ascent of, 539
Bennett, née Ramsden, *cousin*, 248, 328
Benson, A. C., 252
Benson, *Archbishop* E. W., 270 ff., 629
Bentham, J., 62
Berber, 398 ff.
Berlin, Congress of (1878), 267, 269, 300
Berlin Conference (1884), 402–4, 409
Bermuda, 191
Bernhardt, Sarah, 324
Berthomier, M., 9
Bessborough Commission, 439 ff., 444, 495
Biarritz, 602–4, 611, 612
Biggar, 3, 101
Biggar, J. G., 440
bimetallism, 416 n.
Bingley Hall, Birmingham, 551
Birkenhead, 527
Birkett, *Sir* Norman, 630 n.
Birks, *Mrs.*, 314
Birmingham, 88, 175, 229, 551
birth control, 90, 569, 571, 576
Biscoe, R., 28
Bismarck, Herbert, 404
Bismarck, Otto von, 186–7, 221, 246, 274, 334, 392, 403–4, 409 n., 410–11, 633 n.
Biss, *Dr.* Hubert, 634 n.
Blackheath, speeches at, 229–30
Blackie, J. Stuart, 495 n.
Blackstone, *Sir* W., 32
Blaine, James, 569
Blair, Hugh, 15–16, 649
Blantyre, *Lord*, 315
Blenheim Palace, 150
Blomfield, C. J., 45
Blouett, L. P., 515 n.
Blunt, Wilfrid Scawen, 383 ff., 386
Bluntschli, J. C., 274
Board of Trade, *see* Trade
Bodleian Library, Oxford, 620 n., 629 n.
Bolingbroke, *Lord*, 32
Bolton, 288
Bolton, *Mrs.*, 541
bondholders, 384–5, 387–9, 392 ff.
Bonifazio, 314
Bonn Conferences, 264–5
Boord, T. W., 229
Bootle, 9
Borough Franchise Bill (1861), 139
Bournemouth, 633
Boveridge, 241
Boydell, J., 89

Bradlaugh, Charles, 209, 294, 339, 371, 422
Bradley, G. G., 521
Bramston, John, 403 n.
Brand, Speaker H. B. W., *Lord Hampden*, 141, 164, 423, 424
Brandes, George, 286
Brassey, *Lady*, 530
Brassey, Thomas, *Baron Brassey*, 132, 475, 518
Brazilian Loan, 626
Breadalbane, *Lord*, 310
Brett, W. B., *Lord Esher*, 216
Bridges, Robert, 595
Bright, John, 81, 138, 176–7, 181–2, 186, 192, 195, 196, 198, 205, 216, 229, 235, 352 n., 356, 364, 366, 368, 384, 386, 389, 400, 410, 439, 441, 443, 494, 507, 541
Brighton, 540, 601, 611
  sea too warm at, 151
British Critic, 63
British and Foreign Schools Society, 205
British Museum, 98, 283, 327
British North America Act (1867), 468, 477, 479
British Quarterly Review, 319
British South Africa Company, 599–600
Broad Church, 30, 55, 84, 154–6, 200, 213, 239, 260, 271, 493 ff., 522, 545
  see also Noetics
Broadhurst, Henry, 419, 494
Broadlands, 149
Brodrick, G. C., 258, 296
Bronkhorstspruit, 406
Brougham, H., *Lord Brougham*, 149
Brougham Hall, 149
Broughton Hall station, 636
Brown, J. Baldwin, 262
Browne, *Bishop* E. H., 521–2
Browning, Robert, 326, 519, 623
Bruce, H. A., *Lord Aberdare*, 138, 176
Bruce, I., 21
Bryce, James, 485, 561, 583, 588 n.
Buckle, G. E., 513 n.
Buddhists, 64
budgets
  1853: 76, 79, 81, 92, 95, 99, 113–14, 116, 121–4, 126–7, 137, 139, 222
  1857: 112, 126–7
  1860: 113–14, 116, 121, 124–5, 126, 137, 139, 222
  1861: 124
  1863: 214
  1864: 214
  1866: 111
  1867: 143
  1869: 220
  1871: 219
  1873: 418

1874: 123, 222–7
1881: 418
1882: 415, 417
1885: 418–20, 433, 461
Bulgaria and Bulgarian atrocities, 167, 254, 259, 266 ff., 273 ff., 279 ff., 292 ff., 311, 376 n., 594
  Exarchate of, 277 ff.
Bulteel, Henry, 25
Bunyan, John, 619
Burdett, *Sir* Francis, 13
Burials Bill, 174
Burke, Edmund, 26, 27, 35, 174, 201, 202, 469, 483, 547
Burke, Thomas, 435, 455
Burn, W. L., 104
Burne-Jones, E. C., 314, 324, 326, 519
Burnet, Gilbert, 14
Burnett, Frances Hodgson, 613
Burnett, Gregory, 162
Burns, John, 574
Butler, *Bishop* Joseph, 18, 20–1, 41, 55, 61, 239, 255, 257, 260, 284, 304, 343, 344, 347 n., 486, 553, 621, 623–5, 631, 641
Butler, *General Sir* William, 515
Butt, Isaac, 438–9
Butterfield, William, 90, 96
Byron, *see* Gordon
Bywater, Jane, 91

cab, Gladstone knocked down by, 553 n.
cabinet, 66–9, 73, 76, 97, 102, 104, 141, 184–8, 208–10, 214 ff., 219 ff., 226–9, 230, 234, 236, 336, 346, 354–9, 362, 364–72, 402, 422 ff., 439 ff., 541, 578; Plate 20
  East Africa and, 596 ff.
  education and, 203 ff.
  Egypt and, 385 ff., 597 ff.
  ex-cabinet, 254, 564
  finance and 106, 109 ff., 170 ff.
  Gladstone's final, 578, 604–7
  Gladstone's retirement discussed by, 602
  Gordon and, 394–401
  Home Rule test for, 491–3
  inner group of, 369
  Ireland and, 198, 485–6, 490–505
  Irish church and, 195–7
  leaks from, 367
  minutes of, 178 ff., 370–1
  embryonic office of, 236
  seating of, 369–70
Caesarism, 301–3
Cairns, Hugh, *Lord Cairns*, 195
Calcutta, 315, 378
Calder, West, 310, 311
Cambridge, 8, 9, 12, 18, 457
Cambridge, *Duke of*, 211–12, 301

Cambridge, University of, 18, 85, 178, 208–11, 583
  Apostles, 21, 151
  see also Trinity and Newnham Colleges
Campbell, George, 197, 238
Campbell, George Douglas, *Duke of Argyll*, 104, 114, 149–50, 176–7, 190, 204, 238, 258, 364, 365, 366, 369, 380, 444, 446, 447, 581, 637 n.
Campbell, P. W., 310
Campbell-Bannerman, *Sir* Henry, 177, 433, 460, 494, 588 n., 612
Camperdown, H.M.S., 600
Canada, 32, 73, 146, 188, 189, 190–2, 404, 406, 468, 477, 479, 480, 501, 502
  railways of, 389 n.
  see also British North America Act
Cannes, 355, 363, 370, 537, 540, 611, 632–3
Canning, George, 4, 6, 8–9, 17, 20, 27, 71, 273, 349, 585, 608 n., 649
Canning, Stratford, *Lord Stratford de Redcliffe*, 266, 283, 555 n., 608, 631
Canterbury Association, 534
Canton, bombardment of, 386
Cape Colony, 192–3
capital, exports of, 417, 499, 598
Capodistria, *Count*, 167
Cardiff, 551
Cardwell, Edward, *Lord Cardwell*, 176–7, 189, 192, 210–12, 222–3, 226–7, 232, 236, 390, 537, 601
Carl Rosa Opera Company, 530
Carlisle, *Lady*, 616
Carlton Club, 31, 83, 105
Carlton Gardens, No. 4, 313
Carlton House Terrace
  No. 11: 225, 245, 247, 253, 313–14
  No. 13: 53, 159
  No. 23: 313
Carmichael, *Sir* James, 393 n., 534
Carnarvon, *Lord, see* Herbert
Carnegie, Andrew, 569, 284 on., 584, 612, 621–2, 627
Carpenter, *Bishop* Boyd, 545
Caruso, Enrico, 254
Carrington, *Lord*, 552
Cassell, *Messrs.*, 621
Castlereagh, *Lord*, 478
Catholic Apostolic Church, 25
Catholic Emancipation, 10, 13–14, 23, 27, 305, 414
caucus, 295–6, 302–3, 361
Cavendish, *Lady* Frederick (Lucy Cavendish, *née* Lyttelton), 161–2, 235, 236, 327 n., 366, 533, 540 n., 611
Cavendish, *Lord* Frederick, 160, 235, 236, 337, 366, 416 n., 435, 455, 533; Plate 25

Cavendish, S. C., *Lord Hartington, 8th Duke of Devonshire*, 176, 177, 201, 253, 283, 288, 289–90, 324, 352, 353, 355, 364 ff., 371, 385, 386, 393, 395 ff., 416 n., 368, 458, 489, 533, 559, 568, 578 n., 584; Plate 25
  Home Rule and, 475 ff., 488, 493, 494
  offered Exchequer by Gladstone, 367
  redistribution and, 427 ff.
Cavour, *Count*, 167–8
Cecil, *Lady* Gwendolen, 492
Cecil, *Lord* Robert A. T. G., *Marquis of Salisbury*, 112, 224, 225, 235, 237, 270, 332, 336, 351, 356, 372, 382, 416, 419 n., 516, 558, 568, 586, 587, 591, 595, 635, 637, 638, 644; Plates 24, 26
  absence of policy for Ireland of, 483
  franchise, redistribution and, 429 ff., 281
  governments of, 461–2, 472, 474, 485, 548, 595
  ill to deal with, 433–4
  Ireland and, 474, 478, 481–5, 497 ff.
  narrow cynicism of, 478
Celtic revival, 567
central government expenditure, 111, 124, 414 ff.
Central Liberal Association, 361
Century Company, New York, 621–2
Cervantes, 528
Cesarewitch race, 544
Cetewayo, Chief, 407
Ceylon, 64
Chalmers, Thomas, 7, 15, 32, 39–40, 77
Chamberlain, Joseph, 225, 295–6, 357, 364–9, 377, 410, 417, 420, 422, 424, 425, 441, 456, 459–60, 462, 474, 476 ff., 482, 489, 493–4, 495, 496, 498, 500, 507, 541, 548, 549, 587, 590; Plate 26(a)
  Round Table talks and, 559–60
champagne, 524
Channel tunnel, 412, 612
Chaplin, Henry, 347 n.
charity, 48, 54, 90–5, 116, 158 ff., 627–8
Charity Organization Society, 172, 340
Charles I, 151
Charterhouse, 98
Chartists, 102, 104, 131, 335, 437
Chatham House, 611
Chester, 230, 351
  Gladstone attacked in, 580–1, 603
Chester Chronicle, 226
Chesterfield, Lord, 176
Chevalier, M., 187
Chick, S., 302 n.
Childers, H. C. E., 138, 223, 224, 355, 453, 474, 495, 534
China, 65, 66, 80, 151
china, Gladstone's collection of 151

Christ Church, Oxford, 5, 9, 16–23, 33, 47, 48–9, 50, 74, 138, 151, 159, 161, 176, 252, 365, 538, 583 n., 585
Canterbury quadrangle of, 21
portrait of Gladstone for, 519–21
Christian socialism, 325
Christianity, 1, 15, 21, 26, 155–7, 255 ff., 342 ff., 375, 434, 490, 549, 570, 571–2, 624 ff.
spiritualism and, 545–6
Christie, Manson and Woods, 314
Chronicles of Eri, 546
Church and State, see *The State in its Relations with the Church* under Gladstone: works
Church of England, 1, 7, 8, 18, 22–3, 29, 32–3, 37–43, 44–7, 50, 55, 57, 61–7, 70–2, 73, 76, 87–8, 104–6, 116–7, 168, 171, 176, 193 ff., 205, 212–15, 245–50, 254 ff., 261, 294–5, 338–9, 364–5, 521–3, 578, 624 ff.
clergy of, 348, 521 ff.
Church of Scotland, 4, 44, 204, 294–5, 327, 364, 465–6
Church Pastoral Aid-Society, 45
church patronage, 212–14, 521–3
Church Quarterly Review, 319
church rates, 44, 84, 104, 141–2, 414
Churchill, J. W., *Duke of Marlborough*, 150
Churchill, *Lord* Randolph, 112, 474, 482, 526, 548, 607
Churchill, Winston S., 587, 644
Cimiez, 631
citizenship, 312, 346 ff., 464, 641–2
'civic individuality', European distinctiveness of, 184–5
civil service, 65, 84–5, 110, 174, 176, 212, 231
Civil War, 522
Clarendon, see Hyde or Villiers
claret, see 'Gladstone claret'
Clarendon Press, 319, 625
Clark, *Sir* Andrew, 234, 535–9, 593, 600
class, 115 ff., 122 ff., 214 ff., 222–5, 228, 247, 345–50, 417–18, 482, 511, 549, 570, 571–76, 643–3
wealthy classes, 304 ff., 511
see also middle classes and working classes
Clayden, P. W., 307
Clemenceau, Georges, 537
clergy, patronage and, 521 ff.
Clergy Relief Bill, 91
clerisy, 13, 63, 65, 85, 295
Clewer, House of Mercy at, 91, 97, 159
Clinton, *Lord* Edward Pelham-, 617
Clinton, Henry, *4th Duke of Newcastle*, 24, 46, 650
Clinton, Henry, *Lord Lincoln, 5th Duke of Newcastle*, 21, 24, 70, 80, 137, 138–9, 159, 169, 203, 239, 240, 241, 543, 584, 617–18
Clinton, Susan, *Lady* Lincoln, 80, 88

see also Opdebeck
Cliveden House, 149–50, 160, 168
closure, 208, 423 ff., 470
Club, The, 361, 524
coalwhippers, 102
Coalwhippers Act (1843), 342
Cobbett, William, 238
Cobden, Richard, 56, 75, 76, 111, 113, 133, 135, 137, 151, 182, 375, 410, 415, 528, 574, 639
Cobden Treaty (1860), *see* French commercial treaty
Cody, 'Buffalo Bill', 529–30
Cohen, H. J., 553
Cole, F., 21
Cole, O. B., 21
Colenso, J. W., 152
Coleridge, J. T., 90, 238
Coleridge, S. T., 13, 39–41, 55, 57, 62–5, 85, 255, 295, 318, 555
Coliseum Theatre, 97
collectivism, 336, 342
Colley, Sir E., 406
Collins, Elizabeth, 93, 94
Collings, Jesse, 419, 485, 494
Collins Meadow, 627
Colman, J. J., 613; Plate 30(c)
Cologne, 328
colonial bishoprics, 74
Colonial Bishoprics Fund, 98, 152, 377
Colonial Office, 31, 32, 60, 73–4, 108, 111, 165 ff., 180, 190–3, 402 ff., 595 ff.
colonies, 358, 375–7, 402–10, 561, 567, 644
Colonial Reform Association, 75
Colvin, *Sir* A., 383 ff.
Coollattin, 437–8
Combe Hurst, 540
Combe Warren, 540
Commerce, Ministry of, 417
Commons, House of, 10, 22, 24, 31, 32, 43–4, 46, 50, 70–1, 82, 83, 88, 91, 106, 117, 121, 122, 126, 128, 137, 139, 144, 164, 176, 177, 178, 194 ff., 204, 208, 228, 230, 233, 234–6, 238, 266, 270, 287, 296–7, 301, 311, 339, 345, 354, 359 ff., 401, 412, 489, 535, 563–4, 588–9, 590–91, 635, 637, 640
Gladstone as Leader of, 524–6, 551, 578
Gladstone's final speech in, 607, 608
Grand Committees of, 423 ff., 582
Prime Minister's Question Time and, 525
procedural reform of, 422–5
spiritualism and, 544
Compensation for Disturbance Bill (1880), 439 ff.
Concert of Europe, 183–8, 258, 269, 271 ff., 276 ff., 336, 350, 375 ff., 391 ff., 410–11, 622, 638
concurrent endowment, 41, 44, 45, 68, 194–6

Confederacy, 135–6, 164
Congregationalists, 138, 262, 295
Connaught, 438
Constantinople, 369
    Conference of, 269, 385–6
constitutionalism, 509, 574–5
Conservatism, 1, 24 ff., 29 ff., 42 ff., 48, 55–8,
    81, 103–8, 201–3, 228, 267 ff., 511 ff.
    see also Tory Party
Conservatives, *see* Tory Party
consols, 187, 246,
Conspiracy and Protection of Property Act
    (1875), 216
Contagious Diseases Acts, 158, 178, 521
Contemporary Review, 263, 319, 569, 626
conveyance duty, 220
cookery, 300
Copenhagen, 518
Corelli, Marie, 619
Corfu, 165 ff.
Cork Constitution, 162–3
Corn Laws and corn duty, 55–8, 66, 73, 75–9,
    100, 124, 220, 292, 349, 353, 414, 550,
    577, 644
Corry, Montagu, 323 n.
cost of living index, sketched by Gladstone,
    215
Country Bank Notes Issue Bill, 118, 151
County Boards, plans for, 218–19
Court, the, 178 ff., 209–11, 609 ff.
Court Circular, 638
Courtney, L. H., 513 n.
Cowan, *Sir* John, 362, 363
Cowper, *Lord*, 449, 454
Cowper, *Miss*, 159
Cowper-Temple Amendment, 205
Coxe, W., 14
Craig, E., 649
Crawford divorce case, 586 n.
Credit, Votes of, 382, 393, 401, 419–20
Creighton, Mandell, 523
Crepaz, Adele, 576
cricket, Gladstone playing, 16
Crimean War, 85–6, 99, 102, 103, 105, 121, 126,
    182, 266, 273, 276–7, 390
Crimes Act (1882), 359, 386, 459, 461
Criminal Law Amendment Act (1871), 123,
    216–17
Criminal Law Procedure Amendment Act
    (India), 378–9
Criterion Theatre, 400
Crofters Act (1886), 495
Croker, J. W., 528
Cross, J. W., 529
Crystal Palace, 268, 297
Cuddesdon, 22, 28
Cullen, Cardinal P., 200, 202

Culture and Anarchy, 238
Currie, Bertram W., 535 n., 540 n., 584 n.
Currie, *Sir* Donald, 405, 518, 535, 540, 612
customs and excise duties, 124–7
Cyprus, 307

Daily News, 484, 537, 635 n.
Daily Telegraph, 135–6, 138, 230–32, 278 n., 300,
    633
Dale, *Mrs.*, *see* Summerhayes
Dalkeith, *Lord*, 289, 292
Dalmahoy, 49
Dalmeny House, 310, 479, 581, 583, 622
Dante, 32, 548, 619, 620
Darbyshire, Samuel, 138, 368
Darjeeling Railway, 626
Darwinism, 239
Davidson, *Mrs.*, 543
Davidson, *Archbishop* Randall, 629
Davitt, Michael, 443, 565
Days, Alfred, 287
death duties, 123, 125, 219, 223, 224, 415
deaths, 327–9, 434, 455, 568, 593, 616, 618, 629,
    631 ff.
de Girardin, E., 326
de Laveleye, E., 263, 319, 467
de Lesseps, F., 382 ff., 392, 419
de Lisle, A. Phillipps, 264, 294
de Lisle, Margaret, 317
de Montfort, Simon, 291
deductivism, 342–3, 446, 466, 469, 547, 561,
    624–5
Defoe, Daniel, 528
Delane, J. T., 231
demagoguism of tories, 347
Denison, G. A., 152
Denmark, 561, 562
Dent, Palmer & Co., 387 n.
Depression of Trade, Royal Commission on,
    372, 416
Derry Lodge, 539
devolution, 438 ff., 478 ff., 500 ff.
diary, *see* Gladstone, journal of
Dicey, A. V., 469–70, 478, 483, 501, 547
Dicey, Edward, 275 n.
Dickens, Charles, 528
Dictionary of National Biography, 556
Dilke, *Sir* Charles, 104, 209, 334, 364, 365, 366,
    367, 369, 377, 408, 410, 420, 459–60, 462,
    514, 578, 586
    Crawford divorce case and, 542, 586 n.
    franchise and, 430 ff.
    local government and, 421 ff.
Dillon, John, 440, 447 n., 448–50, 454
Dingwall, 8
disestablishment, 463 ff., 476, 493, 496, 572,
    576

Disraeli, B., *Earl of Beaconsfield*, 9, 10, 45, 60, 69, 77–9, 81, 82–3, 107, 110, 111, 121, 126, 128, 136–7, 141–4, 163, 172, 178, 192, 195, 202, 208, 210, 215, 216, 218–22, 228, 237, 247, 255, 257, 265, 266, 267–70, 286–92, 293, 303 ff., 308, 323, 332, 333, 351, 354, 364, 370, 374, 377, 382, 410–12, 415, 419 n., 420, 423, 433, 481, 517, 528, 610 n., 617; Plate 6
  death of, 536, 635
  Endymion (1881), fee for, 622
  portrait of, 520
  statue of, 638
Dissenters Chapels Bill (1844), 68
Divorce Act (1857), 161, 248, 339
Dobie, *Dr.*, 634 n.
Dod's Parliamentary Companion, 169
Dodson, J. G., *Lord Monk Bretton*, 364, 365, 421–2
Döllinger, J. J. I. von, 185, 248, 249, 264–5, 326, 328, 547–8; Plate 29
Dollis Hill, 462, 507, 540, 611
Dolomites, 326
Douglas, *Lady* Frances, 49
Doyle, *Sir* F. H. C., 10, 13, 21, 52, 257, 648
D'Oyly, G., 15, 649
D'Oyly Carte Company, 530
dreams, 47–8, 610
Dresden, 165
Drew, Dorothy ('Dossie'), *grand-daughter*, 614
Drew, Revd. Harry, *son-in-law*, 492, 533, 614, 634 n.
Drew, Mary, *née* Gladstone, *daughter*, 80, 95–6, 161, 315, 324, 325 n., 492, 519, 522, 529, 530, 532–3, 604, 614–15, 633, 634 n., 636 n.; Plate 7 (c)
Drumguish, 234
Dual Control, 382 ff., 387 ff., 392
Dublin, 435, 437, 438, 440, 450, 455, 490, 535–6, 582
  see also Phoenix Park
Dublin Castle, 198, 459, 460, 468, 485, 495, 589
Dublin, University of, 201, 479
Dublin University Magazine, 652
Dudley, *Lord*, *see* Ward
Duff, Alexander, 318
Dun, Finlay, 437–8
Duncan, *Mrs.*, 545, 546
Dundee, 551
Dunrobin, 95, 149
Durdans, The, Epsom, 539–40
Dyce, William, 156–9, 314, 543

Earle, Ralph, 163
Eason, H. L., 291 n.
East Africa Company, 596
East Indies, 53

Eastern Churches, 158, 167, 239, 254, 264 ff., 277 ff.
Eastern Question, 86, 257, 267–71, 272–92, 293 ff., 307–8, 323, 390–1, 632
Eaton Hall, 149, 482
Ecclesiastical Commissioners, 620
Ecclesiastical Titles Act (1851), 79, 339
Echo, 231
Economist, The, 225
economy, 414–20, 644
  recession in, 372
  working of, 114 ff., 170–3
ecumenism, 183–4, 239, 262 ff., 328
Edinburgh, 8, 49, 129, 294, 306, 310–11, 351, 555
Edinburgh, University of, 129
  Chancellorships and Lord Rectorship of, 129, 200
Edinburgh Review, 62, 98, 183, 203
Edinburgh, *Duke of*, 594, 599, 609
Edison, Thomas, 552
Education, 45, 116–17, 146, 173, 180, 371
  Education Act (1870), 203–6, 207, 219, 263, 340
  Irish, 44, 199–203
  Scottish, 203–4, 208
  see also Scotland
Edward VII, *formerly Prince of Wales*, 209 ff., 514, 609, 632, 637–8
Egerton, *Lady* L., 435
Egerton, T., 21
Eglinton, William, 544–5, 546
Egypt, 266, 275–6, 307, 355, 370, 372, 374, 379, 382–94, 395, 396 ff., 408–9, 412, 415, 424, 430, 450, 459, 512, 534, 537, 597–9, 600
  occupation of, 382–94
  settlement of, 390–4, 597–8
  Tribute Loan of, 266 n., 387–9, 626–7
  see also Alexandria, Dual Control, Sudan
Eighty Club, 361
Eisteddfod, Gladstone speaks at, 214, 551
'Elijah's Mantle', 526
Eliot, George, 61, 131, 237, 250, 528, 529
  see also *Felix Holt* and *Middlemarch*
Ellice, E., 237
Employers and Workmen Act (1875), 216
Employers Liability Bill (1894), 604–7
Ems, 51
Endowed Schools Amendment Act (1874), 176
Endowed Schools Bill (1869), 204
Endymion, 622
Enfield, *Lady*, 546
'Engagement' The, 22, 47, 72, 90–5, 96, 97, 157
Engels, Friedrich, 214, 315
England, Bank of, 106, 118
English Hymnal, Gladstone's hymn in, 54
Erastianism, 65

estimates, 127–8, 219–22, 226–7, 592, 600–4
étatism, 338 ff.
Eton College, 5, 9–16, 37, 48, 49, 50, 150, 155,
    159, 252–3, 521, 551, 637
Eton Miscellany, 12, 43
European Union, 505, 642
Evangelicalism, 6–8, 15, 19, 22, 25, 27–9, 47,
    48, 54, 72, 83, 94, 96–7, 156, 158, 159,
    271, 282–92, 315, 323, 328, 522, 545, 625,
    630, 631, 637
Evicted Tenants Bill (1893), 591
Ewart, William, 5
Exchequer, 60, 76–7, 80, 83, 94, 106, 108,
    109–28, 222–8, 230
Exchequer and Audit Act (1866), 106, 109
Exhibition, 1851, Commissioners of, 98, 143
expenditure, 341, 418 ff., 589–90
experience, 257, 466, 470, 624–5, 640

Factory Acts, 118
Factory Bill, education clauses of (1843), 67
faggot votes, 299 ff.
Farini, L. C., 95, 98, 248
Farquhar, Caroline, Gladstone's relationship
    with, 31, 49–50, 52, 194
Farquhar, *Sir* Thomas, 29
Farquhar, Walter, 49
Farr, W. W., 555 n.
Farrar, F. W., 260
Fasque, 4, 6, 31–2, 34, 48, 61, 78, 96, 97, 100–1,
    163, 230, 244–5, 328
    St Andrew's Chapel of, 97, 100
Fawcett, Henry, 319
Felix Holt, 131
federalism, 502, 549, 565, 644
Fenianism and Fenians, 144–5, 188, 196,
    436 ff., 506, 565
feudalism, 574
Fiji, annexation of, 192–3
finance, 307–9, 333 ff., 415 ff., 503 ff.
Finance Bill (1853), 344 n.
Finance, Ministry of, 106, 110, 117, 171, 418
Financial Reform Association, 5, 121, 122, 368
Fine Arts Club, 157
Finsbury Central, 379
fire insurance duty, 220
fiscal policy, 55–8, 66, 75–9, 82, 88, 103–5,
    170–3, 174, 214 ff., 340 ff., 640 ff.
Fish, Hamilton, 188–9
Fitzwilliam, *Lord*, 437–8, 623
flagellation, 92–5, 158, 243
Fletcher, C. R. L., 554–5
Flintshire, 50, 127, 164, 217, 245–7, 360, 627
Florence, 166
Foreign and Colonial Review, 98
foreign policy, 113, 180, 182–8, 350, 374–82,
    402 ff., 410–13, 512, 595–600

principles of, 374 ff.
Foreigners Enlistment Bill, 99
Forster, *Sir* Charles, 524
Forster, W. E., 138, 204–5, 226, 364, 366, 369 n.,
    441, 444, 448–9, 452–4, 487, 555 n.
Fort Portal, 597
Fortescue, C. S. P., *Lord Carlingford*, 145–6,
    174, 194 ff., 197, 199, 364, 365, 366,
    368–9, 417, 446, 456, 494
Forth Bridge, 363
Fortnightly Review, 296, 626
Fowler, H. H., 583
Fowler, W., 199
France, 24, 41, 57, 111–13, 116, 124, 182–8, 221,
    246, 382 ff., 386, 390, 392, 402, 409–11,
    561, 568–9, 597–8, 603, 611, 612, 631–3
    commercial treaty with (1860), 111–13, 116,
        124, 151, 182–3, 186, 334, 392
    renewal of (1870), 183
    militarism in, 603
    Franco-Prussian war, 181, 183–8, 191, 203,
        210–11, 232, 246
franchise, 295 ff., 305–6, 335, 344, 345 ff., 353,
    361, 362, 371, 419, 425–34, 442, 456,
    572–3, 576 ff., 642
    see also Redistribution Act, representation,
        Representation of the People Act
'Free Breakfast Table', 224
Free Church of Scotland, 204, 294–5, 465, 466
free contract, 335 ff.
free trade, 55–8, 73, 75–9, 82, 100, 105–9,
    124–6, 134–7, 138, 170–3, 182–3, 190–2,
    214–15, 257, 272, 325, 333 ff., 342, 349,
    377, 392, 410–11, 559, 568–71, 572, 578,
    599, 640 ff.
Free Trade League, 224
Freeman, E. A., 523
Freeman's Journal, 196
French Revolution, 551, 568–9
Frere, *Sir* Bartle, 405, 406
Freshfield, *Mr.*, 244
Friendly Societies, 118, 171, 216, 614
Froude, J. A., 92, 135, 498 n., 546
Fuad Pasha, 273
Furniss, Harry, 254
Future Punishment, 259–60

Gaisford, *Dean*, 84
Gallie, W. B., 487 n.
Galway contract, 110, 162
gardening, 300
Gardiner, S. R., 523
Garendon, monastery at, 237
Garibaldi, G., 109
Garter, filling of, 212–15
Gas Stokers' case, 216–17
Gaskell, J. Milnes-, 11, 12, 16, 19, 237, 528, 648

Gavan Duffy, C., 441
general elections,
    1880, 310–11, 512
    1885, 472 ff., 481, 493
    1886, 507–8, 547
    1892, 579–81
    1906, 580
Geneva arbitration, 188–90
George III, 430
George V, 436, 513 n., 609, 637
George, Henry, 357
Germany, 57, 124, 182–8, 203–4, 236–9, 326–7,
    334, 376, 392, 402–5, 408 ff., 467, 572,
    595 ff., 600
    militarism in, 603
    see also Prussia
Gibbon, Edward, 15, 648
Gibraltar, 165, 191
Gibson T. Milner-, 114
Gilbert, J. T., 546
Gilbert, W. S., 325
Giorgione, 314
Gladstone, Agnes, *daughter, see* Wickham
Gladstone, Anne Mackenzie, *mother*, 4, 6–7,
    25, 49, 52, 251
Gladstone, Anne Mackenzie, *sister*, 4–6, 52,
    328
Gladstone, Annie, *daughter-in-law*, 634 n.
Gladstone, Catherine, *née* Glynne, *wife*, 50–6,
    88–9, 91, 94, 95, 100, 160, 161–5, 240,
    244–7, 259, 310, 312, 321, 531 ff., 535 ff.,
    540, 543, 593, 610, 611, 613–16, 618,
    628–35, 634, 635–8; Plates 3, 12(c), 17
    death of, 637–8
    enigma of, 615–16
    family of, 50
    iconic status of, 615
    insomnia of, 536–7
    known as 'Cathie', 321
    marriage of 53
    peerage and, 608–9
    platform, presence on, 310, 615
    President of Women's National Liberal
        Federation, 578, 615–16
    suitors of, 52
    wooing of, 51 ff.
Gladstone, Catherine Jessy, *daughter*, 96, 101,
    243; Plate 7(b)
Gladstone, Elizabeth, *sister-in-law*, 150, 163
Gladstone, Gertrude, *daughter-in-law*, 315
Gladstone, Helen, *daughter*, 161, 315–16, 533,
    544, 611, 614–15, 633, 634 n.
Gladstone, Helen Jane, *sister*, 5, 51, 78, 88–9,
    92, 95, 100, 161, 248, 257, 328–9
Gladstone, Henry Neville ('Harry'), *son*, 148,
    161, 244, 314, 315, 333, 378, 386, 513 n.,
    532, 614–15, 617, 630 n., 634 n., 641

Gladstone, Herbert John, *son*, 93, 161, 244, 315,
    351 n., 362, 434, 513 n., 532, 573, 614–15,
    630 n., 634 n., 635; Plate 7(d), 28(b)
    Hawarden Kite and, 483–4, 532
    Ireland and, 452, 457 n., 477, 532
Gladstone, Ida, *niece*, 244–5
Gladstone, Jessy, *see* Gladstone, Catherine
    Jessy
Gladstone, Sir John, *father*, 3–4, 8–9, 15, 24,
    28, 46, 49, 52, 76, 78, 88–9, 100–1, 131,
    156, 163, 556, 613, 630, 650 ff.; Plate 2
Gladstone John Neilson, *brother*, 5, 28, 36, 56,
    163
Gladstone, Mary, *see* Drew
Gladstone, Mary Ellen, *sister-in-law*, 163
Gladstone, Maud, *daughter-in-law*, 614, 634 n.
Gladstone, Robertson, *brother*, 5, 10, 49, 50, 88,
    163, 212, 245, 327, 328, 368
Gladstone, Revd. Stephen Edward, *son*, 93, 161,
    244, 315, 532, 540, 543, 614, 629–30, 634
Gladstone, Sir Thomas, *brother*, 4, 5, 9, 10, 101,
    163, 230, 244–5, 328, 473, 613, 650
Gladstone, William Ewart. *This entry is a guide*
    to his chief activities, interests, and
    attributes; detailed references will be found
    under other relevant entries.

    absence of political machine of, 296
    abstract resolutions, dislike of, 465, 480, 639
    accent of, 552, 584
    actor's craft and, 530–1, 584
    admires Home Rulers' assiduity, 525–6
    ambitions of, 107–8
    apostasy, hatred of, 328
    aristocracy, plans to reconstruct, 210–12
    art collection of, 314, 626
    attack on in Chester, 580–1
    'aureoniophone' used by, 538
    autobiography of, 555, 581, 621–3, 626
    axes of, 317
    backgammon, passion for, 611
    banking, views of, 118 ff.
    Berlin Conference and, 409 ff. big bills,
        use of, 359 ff., 371, 447, 488–9, 639
    birth control, hatred of, 90, 569, 571, 576
    Bismarck and, 411–12
    blackballed at British club in Biarritz, 611
    boisterousness of, 530–1
    bondholder, role as, 387–9, 626–7
    book catalogue of, 620
    bowels, problems with, 615
    Broad Church, complex relationship to,
        38 ff., 154–7, 213, 239, 545
    budgets of, 79, 103–35, 219–29, 416
    Bulgaria and, 254–95
    bullying by, 328–9
    Butler, *Bishop*, study of, 257, 260, 284, 304,
        343–4, 486, 553, 621, 623–5, 631, 641

Gladstone, William Ewart (*cont.*)
Cabinet, management of, 79, 110–14, 175, 176–82, 197, 204, 207–9, 234–6, 364–72, 402 ff., 422 ff., 471–80, 491 ff., 507–8, 582–7, 590, 604–7
Canada and, 468
capacity to change of, 329
career of, 255–7
cataract operation of, 593, 618
character, view of, 319–20
charismatic politics of, 302–3, 311–12, 643–4
charitable donations of, 627–8
chewing of food by, 556
children of, 313, 315–16, 612–15, 627, 629–30
china, collection of, 151
church patronage and, 212–16, 521–3
churchgoing of, 317, 628, 632
civil service and, 84–5, 175–6
classes, duties of, 231, 133–6, 142, 231, 348 ff.
clergyman, offering to become, 22, 28
clubs, reluctant to enter and little use for, 235, 361
coherent policies of, 373, 638 ff.
collars of, 254; Plate 21(b)
collected speeches of, 553
colonies, interest in, 73–5, 190–3, 374 ff.
colonial alarmism, views on, 403
commoner, view of himself as, 608–9
Commons, lengthy attendances at, 234–5, 237–8, 359–61, 524–6, 585
company of women, enjoyment of, 525
comparison with Chamberlain by, 368
composure of, 606
Concert of Europe and, 182–90, 271 ff., 410, 639
concurrent endowment, hostility to, 41, 194–6, 199–205
confirmation of, 16
conservatism of, 23, 24–58, 61–9, 81–6, 87–8, 104–9, 177, 202–3, 333, 501, 506, 562
conservatism, view of failure of, 347 ff.
constituencies held:
    Newark (1832–45), 24, 31, 45–6, 251–2
    Oxford University (1847–65), 70–3, 82, 83–5, 129, 163, 262–3, 294
    Lancashire, S. (1865–8), 129, 133–4, 141, 145–7
    Greenwich (1868–80), 147, 222, 229–30, 253, 291
    Leeds (1880), 291, 315, 567, 532
    Midlothian (1880–95), 290–2, 293–312, 351, 507, 580
    Leith Burghs (1886), 507
constitutional orthodoxy of, 486, 607
conversation of, 530–1
correspondence, organization of, 233, 235–6, 241, 534–5, 557, 614–15

cosmopolitanism of, 569–70
cost of living index, proposes introduction of, 214–15
courage of, 337
Court, dealings with, 143, 176–82, 511 ff., 609 ff.
courtships of, 49–50
cow, mad, attacked by, 581
cricket, played at Eton, 16
daily round as Prime Minister of, 233 ff., 527 ff.
death of, 631–34; Plate 32
    certificate of, 634 n.
    expectation of, 535, 548
debator, performance as, 10 ff., 21–2, 43–4, 233, 235, 238–9, 292 ff.
'Declaration' of, 543, 629–30
demophil rather than demogogue, 230
devotions of, 6–8, 15–16, 22, 25, 26–9, 37–8, 54–5, 96–8, 148, 157–8, 237
dispositions to children of, 627
dissolution (1874), decides on, 217, 218, 224–9
divorce, hostility to, 578, 586 n.
dreams of, 47–8, 610
Eastern Question and, 257, 266–90, 377–401
eclectic and gallimaufrous nature of, 16, 34, 95, 99–100, 238, 530 ff.
economy, view of, 414 ff., 573, 640 ff.
ecumenism and, 165, 182–5, 262 ff., 328
'Egypt for the Egyptians' and, 382–94, 598
Eiffel Tower, speech at top of, 568
'Engagement', involvement in, 90–5
epic nature of his career, 1, 250, 638 ff.
'Epitomes', construction of, 15, 20
étatism of, 117–20, 125, 171–4, 338
evangelicalism and, 6–9, 15–16, 27–9, 54, 71–2, 83
evolution and, 486, 490
excessive office-holding of, 415
executive politician, function of, 638
expediency, not governed by, 373
expenditure, views on, 418 ff., 640 ff.
experience, guiding importance of, 466, 623–5
eyesight of, 301, 535 ff., 583, 601–4, 610, 629
    cataract operation on, 610, 618
    impeded by attack in Chester, 580–1
failure of ?, 638
family affairs of, 53–5, 87–97, 98, 100–1, 104, 149–65, 244–7, 531 ff., 612 ff.
fanatic, viewed by Victoria, 579 n.
fear of revolution of, 23, 29–30
final cabinet of, 578, 604–7
final retirement of, 600–7, 620
finance, uses to unify government, 220 ff., 249

finances of, 5, 53–4, 245–7, 313 ff., 626–8
fingers of, 255
fingerstall of, 255
fitness of, 254–5, 317, 553 ff., 583–4
flagellation, self-inflicted, 92 ff., 104, 157, 243
foreign policy, principles of, 108–9, 182–90, 374 ff.
form, a stickler for, 607
franchise, conservative view of, 425–33
free trade and fiscal policies of, 55 ff., 75–83, 100–2, 114–20, 214 ff., 344 ff., 416 ff., 568 ff., 639 ff.
French, studying and speaking in, 9, 551, 568
friendships, male: Anstice, 22–3
    Gaskell, 11, 237
    Hallam, 11–13, 240
    Hope, 47 ff., 69–70, 73, 93, 157, 185, 198, 199, 202, 205, 243, 248, 249, 286, 295, 329, 460, 555, 556, 622
    female: Duchess of Sutherland, 95, 149–50, 241
    Novikoff, 322–3, 458, Summerhayes, 158–9, 542–3
    Thistlethwayte, 159–60, 235, 239–44, 543–4, 616–18
funeral of, 618
galvanism, treatment by, 538
gentlemanly capitalism of, 627
Germany, African expansion welcomed, 376, 403 ff.
Gladstonism defined, 337–50, 559, 638 ff.
Gladstonian Court, support to of, 610–12
golden moments, sense of, 343–4, 454, 508, 510
Gordon, warning about, 396
gossip, little interest in, 179, 221
as Grand Old Man, 400
grand-children of, 613–14
Granville's debts, organizes payment of, 584
Grillion's Club, 361
hair of, 254
Harvard, declines invitation to, 319
'Hawarden Kite' and, 483–5
Hawarden estates, again briefly owner of, 613
height of, 254
high-risk strategy of, 450 ff.
Highchurchmanship of, 332–3
historicism of, 342 ff., 446, 495
holidays of, 149–51
home rule and, 435 ff., 450 ff., 462 ff., 478 ff., 486, 488–510, 581–2, 587–92, 642
    conservative emphasis of, 486
humour of, 622–3
hymns by, 54
as icon, 363, 550, 556

Idealism of, 38 ff., 62–9, 73, 118, 255, 295
illnesses and accidents of
    cancer of the cheek, 557, 632–4
    chronic laryngeal catarrh, 280–1
    colds, 548, 554, 557, 610
    deafness, 610
    diarrhoea, 234, 535, 536, 610
    erysipelas, 95
    falls, 406
    influenza, 557, 613
    insomnia, 355, 492, 523, 536–7, 554, 557
    lumbago, 283, 355, 535
    myaesthenia laryngis, 538–9
    nervous exhaustion, 196
    neuralgia, 535, 557, 632
    overaction of the bowels, 400
    shoots of own finger, 96
    skin disease, 400
    'tightness in the chest', 234
    voice impaired, 363, 449–50, 462, 474–5, 507, 535, 537–9
ill-temper of, 248
imperfection, sense of, 342, 638, 641
imperialism and, 374–410, 595–600
India and, 377 ff.
indispensability to the Whigs of, 228–9, 357–9
individualism and, 509, 571–2
inequalitarianism of, 325
influence of the classics on, 9 ff., 20 ff., 33 ff., 74, 148, 152–7, 247
interventionist views of, 375 ff., 386–7
Ireland and, 44, 65; 68–9, 142–8, 193–203, 209, 435–62, 463–90, 494–510, 558–68, 581–2, 587–92
    dominance of, 548 ff.
    finance of, humiliated by, 589–90
    reading on, 546–7
    visits to, 437 ff., 535–6
Islam and, 377 ff., 395 ff.
ivories of, 626
journal of, 2, 7, 49–50, 51, 59, 67, 74, 79, 82, 88, 89, 95–100, 104, 148, 150, 151, 157, 234, 244, 256, 283, 285, 314, 317 ff., 330, 460, 464, 492, 543, 546–7, 553, 556, 557, 583, 621, 622, 628, 629–30
    end of, 618, 628–31; Plate 31
    length of, 628–9
journalism of, 318–19, 620, 626
'Kilmainham Treaty' and, 453 ff.
labour representation and, 571–6
Land League and, 438–55
land purchase and, 443 ff.
leadership of Liberal party of, 339 ff., 486–90, 558–78, 582 ff., 643–4
Lear-like coterie of, 618
legislation, concept of, 345 ff.

Gladstone, William Ewart (*cont.*)
    letter-writing, political use of, 541
    liberal-toryism of, 341–2
    liberalism, relationship to, 25–6, 68–86,
        104–9, 128–48, 168–9, 179, 186, 188,
        207–9, 223–32, 329, 415 ff., 558 ff.,
        638 ff.
    library and papers of, 101, 151, 236, 238, 240,
        243, 555–6
    literary productivity and earnings of,
        317–19, 552–3, 619–21, 626
    loan for life offered to, 612
    local government and, 420 ff., 607
    Lords, House of, and, 486 ff., 591–2, 604–7
    lying-in-state of, 635–7
    marital fidelity of, 629 ff.
    marriage of, 50–8, 89–95, 160 ff., 244–7
        view of, 567–8, 578
    martial enthusiasm of, 389–90
    Maynooth and, 68–70, 435, 438, 506, 560 n.,
        620
    memory, failing powers of, 557
    methodology of politics of, 639 ff.
    middle-class, sees himself as, 53, 212
    Midlothian and, 290–2, 293–312
    militarism, fear of, 603
    modern novels, view of, 619
    moderation, ferocity of, 142
    monarchism, respect for, 512–16, 609–10
    money, *see* Gladstone, finances of
    mountain climbing by, 539
    moveable personalty of, 626
    Murray's dictionary, aids financially, 523–4
    mythic status of, 556
    national politician, development of, 128–35,
        137–9
    nations, equal rights of, 375 ff.
    navy and, 410–13, 600–4
    Newcastle Estates, trustee of, 543, 617–18
    Newcastle Programme and, 560, 572–5, 576
    nicknames: 'Mr. Tipple', 16
        'Merrypebble', 180
    nomadic life of, 540, 610 ff.
    non-Utopianism of, 342–3
    'Obstruction and Devolution', paper on by,
        440
    O'Connell, reappraisal of view of, 560–1
    offices held by:
        Board of Trade, Vice-President and
            President (1841–5), 65–8, 77–8
        Colonial Secretary (1845–6), 73–5, 190
        Colonial Under-Secretary (1834–5), 31
        Exchequer, Chancellor of (1852–5), 76, 79,
            82–6, 103–28
        (1859–66), 103–48, 170–2, 219–20
        (1873–4), 222–8
        (1880–2), 309, 340, 354, 355, 359, 414–5

Ionian Islands, Lord High Commissioner
    of (1858–9), 107, 164–7
Leader of the Commons (1865–6,
    1868–74, 1880–5, 1886, 1892–4), 139–41,
    206, 208–9, 355, 359, 371, 414, 423–5,
    512, 524–6, 585 ff.
Lord Privy Seal, 419, 585 n.
Prime Minister (1868–74), 103, 147–8,
    170 ff.
Prime Minister (1880–5), 338, 352 ff.,
    415 ff.
Prime Minister (1886), 492 ff.
Prime Minister (1892–4), 579 ff.
Treasury, Commissioner of (1834), 31
old age and, 168–9, 330 ff., 530–1, 549 ff.,
    556–7, 583–4, 593, 610 ff., 622, 630–4
'old Parliamentary hand', 524–6, 591
Olympian religion, plans for book on, 320,
    548, 553
operas seen by, 323, 530
optimism of, 327, 336 ff., 507, 548, 567, 585
Ossian, interest in, 14
over-elaboration of, 606
Oxford University, attendance at, 16–33
pacification of Ireland and, 471, 496 ff., 501
painters and, 519 ff.
pall-bearers of, 637
papers, private, storage and use of, 555–6
parliamentary reform and, 23, 24–7, 77, 85,
    139–42, 226, 420–34
Parnell and, 448 ff., 471 ff.
    talks with, 503, 562 ff.
    view of, 455–8, 563–8
party meetings, use of, 363–4, 590
patronage, exercise of by, 212–14, 516–24,
    614
paupers, concern for, 214
payment of M.P.s and, 572 ff.
'peculiar position' of, 358–9
Peel, debt to, 78–9, 101
'Peel–Cobden man', a, 574, 639
peerage declined by, 461, 608–9
peerage, views on, 516–19, 608–9
Pentecostalism, hostility to, 25
'People's William', known as, 135–6, 230
permanence, yearning for, 172–3
physical decline of, 556–7, 583–4
platform speaking and, 295 ff., 550–1, 642–3
'plot' against, 357 n.
Poet Laureateship and, 594–5
politician, view of role of, 43–7, 59–61, 72,
    172–3, 179–80, 228, 342, 511 ff., 556, 559,
    571–72, 581, 624–5, 630, 639–45
pornography, reading of and temptation by,
    90 ff.
portfolio of, 387–9, 626–7
portraits of, 313, 326, 519–21, 613–14; Plate 22

post, burden of, 316 ff., 534–5
poverty and, 309–10
power base of, 345
Pre-Raphaelism of, 157–60, 243, 324–5, 519
press, awareness and use of, 135–7, 229–32
probate value of estate of, 627–8
professionalism of, 644
Professorship of Ancient History of, 541; Plate 19
progress, view of, 337, 343, 348–9
progressive politics, dominance of, 609, 643–4
prostitutes, dealings with, 88, 89–100, 157–60, 241–4, 321 ff., 541–3, 615
public opinion, sense of, 114, 229–32, 344 ff., 464, 481–2, 604
puns, delight in, 623
question-time in Commons and, 525
radical conservatism of, 333–4, 639
radicalism of, 366
railways, 67, 119–20
ramblings of, 601–2
reading of, 14 ff., 20, 31–2, 77, 98–100, 131, 237–9, 317–18, 527 ff., 546–7, 569, 618–21
Rectorship of Glasgow University of, 289, 292, 304, 307, 325
relaxations of, 527 ff.
relics, understanding of use of, 363
republicanism, stiffles, 209–10
'rescue work' of, 88, 89–100, 157–60, 241–4, 321 ff., 541 ff., 615
resignations and retirement, actual, threatened or desired, 68–70, 72, 112, 141, 170, 207, 228, 245–50, 253 ff., 270, 289, 330 ff., 352, 354–7, 461, 531, 556, 592–3, 600–7, 616, 620, 628
ripeness, concept of, 343–4, 464, 481–2, 604
Romanes Lecture of, 551, 581
Round Table conferences and, 559–60
Royal Academy, professor of, 325
as sage, 553 ff.
schooling of, 5–16
Scott, enthusiasm for, 14, 97, 524–9, 537, 555, 619
sculling at Eton, 16
séances, attendance at, 544–6
secretariat of, 316 ff., 533–5, 614–15
self-awareness, curious absence of, 645
self-knowledge, search for, 553
sex and, 321–3, 578, 610 n., 615, 629–30
shields Queen from her folly, 515 ff.
shrewd political sense of, 353
singing of, 530, 623
sophism, self-awareness of, 94
South Africa and, 402–8, 599–600
speeches outside Parliament of, 130, 133–5, 141, 164, 229–32, 270, 272, 283, 284,

293–312, 449–50, 538, 550–2, 553–4, 642–3
spiritualism and, 544–6
stamina of, 538–9, 581
state funeral of, 635–8
strawberries used for insomnia by, 537
successor, not consulted by Victoria about, 609–10
Sudan and, 394 ff.
supposed priapism of, 71 n.
swimming, enjoys, 151
taxation and, 104–28, 217–27, 418
telephone, use by, 316
temptations of, 91–5, 156–60, 239–44
theatre and, 267, 300, 323–4, 529–30, 557
Thistlethwayte, Laura, relationship with, 321 ff., 543 ff., 616–18
tory party, contempt for, 482
totemic role of, 550 ff.
Tractarianism and, 27 ff., 54–5, 63–5, 69–75, 89–100, 157–8, 196, 205, 235, 237, 248–50, 637
treefelling by, 254, 288, 317, 352, 527, 541, 553; Plate 27
treeplanting by, 614; Plate 23
Turkey and, 266–91, 307–8, 382 ff., 391 ff., 561–2
Turkish Empire, only visit to, 167
Uganda and, 595–8
Ulster and, 486–8
undergraduate days, 16–24
United States and, 64, 99, 124, 133–4, 140, 146, 162, 163–4, 179, 182, 188–90, 191, 249, 276, 480, 552, 565, 569–70, 621–2, 624
unselfconsciousness of ?, 530–1
Victoria, relations with, 97, 138, 143–8, 209–12, 222, 370, 508, 511–16, 578, 586, 605–6, 609–10, 631–2
posthumous hostility of, 637, 638
visits abroad:
  (1832), 36–7
  (1838–9), 37, 50–1
  (1845), 88, 89, 92, 328
  (1849), 80, 89
  (1850–1), 80–1
  (1858–9), 107, 164–8
  (1866–7), 141, 167–8
  (1874), 249, 326
  (1879), 324, 326–7, 328
  (1883), 518, 523, 537
  (1886), 547–8
  (1889), 551, 568–9, 612
  (1894), 602–4
  (1897–8), 631–3
voice of, recordings of, 551–2
walks of, 254, 539

Gladstone, William Ewart (*cont.*)
  wealth of, 313–15, 318–19, 626–8
  weekending of, 149–51, 235–7, 539 ff.
  weight of, 254
  Welsh language, view of, 151, 214
  West Africa and, 409
  West Country, tour of, 551
  Whigs, close and familiar links with, 366–7,
    509
  Whigs, complains at feebleness of, 357–8
  will of, 627–8, 629, 635
  women, view of, 343 n., 428–9, 576–8, 616
  words, use of, 296 ff., 553–6
  works, published or unpublished, arranged
    by date of composition/publication:
  Liverpool Courier, letters to (1826), 55
  Eton Miscellany (1828), 12
  'On eloquence' (1827), 300
  'The doctrine of conversion' (1830), 29
  'On the principle of government' (1831),
    34
  pamphlet on reform, unpublished (1831),
    27
  Liverpool Courier, letters to (1833), 25
  article for *Dublin University Magazine*
    (unpublished, 1834), 46
  'On the laws of social obligation' (1835),
    34–5
  'Prevalent theories of government' (1835),
    35
  'Public speaking' (1836), 43
  The State in its Relations with the Church
    (1838, 4th edn. in 2 vols. 1841), 33, 40–3,
    47, 60–5, 68–9, 73, 77, 81, 183, 202, 464
  Church principles considered in their results
    (1840), 33, 36 ff., 40–3, 46, 61, 62, 138,
    262, 263–4
  'Course of commercial policy at home
    and abroad' (1843), 57, 76, 257
  review of W. G. Ward (1845), 72
  'Probability as the guide of conduct'
    (1845, 1879), 61, 260, 625
  Manual of Prayers from the Liturgy (1845), 97
  homoionyms, dictionary of (*c.*1848), 85
  'Remarks on the Royal Supremacy'
    (1850), 73
  review of Leopardi (1850), 80
  Letters to Lord Aberdeen (1851), 80–1
  translation of Farini, *Lo Stato Romano*, 4
    vols. (1851–4), 95, 98, 248
  *Examination of the official reply of the
    Neapolitan government* (1852), 81
  'Functions of Laymen in the Church'
    (1852), 74
  review of Montalembert (1852), 95
  'Declining efficiency of Parliament'
    (unpublished article, 1856), 105, 117

  'On the place of Homer in classical
    education and in historical enquiry'
    (1857), 153
  Studies on Homer and the Homeric Age (3
    vols., 1858), 61, 74, 152 ff., 265, 318–19,
    320, 326, 548
  review of Tennyson (1859), 160
  Translations (1861), 152, 162
  'Iliad', translation of (1860s), 154
  concordance to Aristotle (1860s), 156
  'Trochaic Version of Aristotle' (1860s), 156
  'Shield of Achilles' (1864), 156
  Speeches and Addresses (1865), 1
  review of *Ecce Homo* (1868), 152, 156–7
  A Chapter of Autobiography (1868), 144, 145,
    174, 462, 463, 508, 621 n.
  Juventus Mundi (1869), 152, 156, 203, 238
  'Germany, France, and England',
    Edinburgh Review (1870), 182 ff., 203, 232
  'Letter to Schenck' (1872), in *Harper's*
    (1876), 189–90
  'Ritualism and Ritual' (1874), 249
  review of Yonge, *J. C. Patteson* (1874), 249
  The Vatican Decrees (1874), 185, 249, 259 ff.
  Introductory letter to E. de Laveleye,
    Protestantism and Catholicism (1875), 319
  'Is the Church of England worth
    preserving?' (1875), 261
  'The Bulgarian Horrors and the Question
    of the East' (1876), 269, 277, 280, 283–4,
    287, 318 n., 324
  'The courses of religious thought' (1876),
    261
  'The Hellenic Factor' (1876), 278, 281
  Homeric Synchronism (1876), 259, 318
  review of Trevelyan's *Macaulay* (1876),
    319–20
  'Aggression on Egypt and Freedom in the
    East' (1877), 275 ff., 386
  'Lessons in Massacre' (1877), 284
  'Montenegro' (1877), 325
  'Piracy in Borneo' (1877), 288
  Review of Sir G. C. Lewis, *Essay on
    authority* (1877), 261
  'The Sclavonic Provinces of the Ottoman
    Empire' (1877), 274 n., 279 ff.
  'Electoral Facts' (1878), 351
  'England's Mission' (1878), 275–6, 308,
    319, 351 n.
  'Kin beyond Sea' (1878), 275–6, 319
  'Last words on the county franchise'
    (1878), 349 n.
  'The Paths of Honour and of Shame'
    (1878), 284
  'The Peace to Come' (1878), 280 ff.
  'Postscriptum on the county franchise'
    (1878), 304 n., 347 ff.

Primer of Homer (1878), 318
'The slicing of Hector' (1878), 319
'The Evangelical Movement' (1879), 251, 285
Gleanings of Past Years, 7v. (1879), 318
'Dawn of creation and of worship' (1885), 477, 486
'On the Liberal Party' (1885), 476, 485
The Irish question (1886), 463 ff., 499, 508, 547
'Ingram's History of the Irish Union' (1887), 561
'Lessons of Irish history in the eighteenth century' (1887), 561
'"Locksley Hall" and the Jubilee' (1887), 337, 548
'Mr Lecky and political morality' (1887), 561
Review of volumes v and vi of W. E. H. Lecky's *History of England in the eighteenth century* (1887), 561
'Daniel O'Connell' (1888), 560
'A reply to Dr. Ingram' (1888), 561
'Robert Elsmere and the battle of belief' (1888), 619
'Free Trade' (1890), 569–70
'Home Rule for Ireland. An appeal to the Tory Householder' (1890), 561
'Mr. Carnegie's "Gospel of Wealth": a review and a recommendation' (1890), 627
'On books and the housing of them' (1890), 620
'The rights and responsibilities of labour' (1890), 574–5
'An Academic Sketch' (Romanes Lecture, 1892), 581, 620–1
'Letter to Samuel Smith on women's suffrage' (1892), 577
Special Aspects of the Irish Question (1892), 560 n., 561 n., 565 n.
'A Vindication of Home Rule. A reply to the Duke of Argyll' (1892), 581, 626
The Odes of Horace (1894), 581
'The Phoenician elements in the Homeric poems' (Address to Oriental Congress, 1894), 581
'True and false conceptions of the Atonement' (1894), 605
Studies subsidiary to the works of Bishop Butler (begun 1845, published 1896), 61, 260, 624–5, 631
The works of . . . Joseph Butler, edited by W. E. Gladstone, 2v. (1896), 621, 623–5, 631
Later Gleanings (1897), 553, 631
'Personal recollections of Arthur H. Hallam' (1898), 633

Gladstone, William Glynne Charles, *grandson*, 532, 613–14
Gladstone, William Henry, *son*, 98, 136, 150, 161, 162, 244, 247, 258, 315, 324, 416 n., 507, 532 ff., 540; Plate 15(a)
  death of, 532, 613–14
'Gladstone claret' 113
'Gladstone's Rock', Snowdon, 551
Gladstones, Thomas, *grandfather*, 3
Gladstonian Court, 610–12
Gladstonism defined, 337–50, 639–45
Glasgow, 129
Glasgow University, 289, 292, 304, 307
Glenalmond, Trinity College, 61, 97, 100, 245
glove trade, 113
Glyn, G. G., *Lord Wolverton*, 175, 176, 208, 219, 227, 231, 237, 290, 314, 351, 352, 361, 461–2, 472–3, 482, 493, 505, 537, 540, 541 n.
Glynne, Catherine, *see* Gladstone
Glynne, Gertrude, 613
Glynne, Henry, *brother-in-law*, 50, 162–3, 244
Glynne, Sir Stephen, *brother-in-law*, 10, 50–1, 53, 127, 151, 162, 244–5, 247, 258, 556; Plate 13
Glynne Arms, Hawarden, 581 n.
God, 6, ff., 27 ff., 89 ff., 285–6, 292, 331 ff., 344, 376, 406, 553, 557, 581, 624 ff., 629–30
Godley, J. A., *Lord Kilbracken*, 313, 316, 517, 622, 623
Godley, J. R., 534
Goethe, J. W. von, 318
gold, 415–16, 503
Gold Coast, 192, 226
Goodwin, *Bishop*, 545
Gordon, Arthur, *Lord Stanmore*, 134, 161, 236, 249
Gordon, Charles George, 370, 392, 393, 394–401, 430, 459, 515, 596
Gordon, George, *Lord Aberdeen*, 2, 31, 75, 77, 82 ff., 99, 101, 105, 137, 138, 173, 236, 493, 540, 611
Gordon, George, *Lord Byron*, 50
Gorst, Sir J. E., 175, 295
Gortchakoff circular, 187 ff.
Goschen, G. J., 172, 176–7, 217–18, 226, 227, 232, 302, 474–5, 491, 494
Gouraud, Colonel, 552
Government of Ireland Bill (1886), 422, 465, 469 n., 472, 487, 489, 490, 508, 517, 531, 539, 587–8
  defeat of, 490, 506–7, 535, 643
  draft and sketch of, 463, 469 n., 479–81, 483, 488 n.
  financial clauses of a boon to Ireland, 503–5
  potential for repeal of, 470
  preparation of, 494–505

Government of Ireland Bill (1886) (*cont.*)
  see also Home Rule, Parnell
Government of Ireland Bill (1893), 558, 561 n.,
  563 ff., 587–92
  miscalculated financial settlement of,
    589–90
  plan for revival of in 1894, 591, 592
  see also Home Rule
Government of Ireland Act (1920), 508
Gower, Freddy Leveson, 539, 584 n.
Gower, George Leveson, 366, 533–4
Gower, G. G. Leveson, *Lord Granville*, 15, 141,
  176–9, 180, 190–2, 195–6, 209, 221,
  226–7, 235, 249, 253, 277, 283, 287,
  289–90, 299, 324, 352–3, 355, 358, 360,
  364, 366, 380 ff., 416, 435, 451, 471 n.,
  482, 493, 533, 541, 566, 579; Plate 25
  debts of, 584
  decline of, 402, 493, 584
  Sudan and, 396 ff.
Gower, Harriet Leveson, *Duchess of Sutherland*,
  95, 130, 150, 241, 315, 366; Plate 12(b)
Graham, *Sir* James, 67, 101, 137, 138
Gramsci, A., 13
Grand Trunk Railway, 626
Granger, F. M., 603
Grant, C., 254
grants-in-aid, 217, 219, 420 ff.
Grantully Castle, 535
Granville, *Lord, see* Gower
Graphic, The, 303
Gray, *Sir* John, 196, 198, 199
'Great Depression', 415–16
Great Orme, 151
Greece, 74, 155, 165–6, 277 ff., 354, 572
Green, J. R., 318
Green, *Revd.* S. F., 522
Green, T. H., 619
Grattan, Henry, 440, 468, 546
Greenwich constituency, 147, 164, 175, 229–30,
  253, 283, 284, 291
Grenville, George, 608 n.
Grenville, Thomas, 90
Greville, Charles, 546
Grey, *Earl*, 433
Grey, *General* Charles, 143, 147, 194
Grey, H. G., *3rd Earl Grey*, 75, 176
Grillion's Club, 520, 524–5
Grimston, E. H., 21
Grossmith, George, 530
Grosvenor, *Lady*, 531
Grosvenor, H. L., *Duke of Westminster*, 294, 517,
  632
Grosvenor, *Lord* Richard, 360–1, 416 n., 457,
  468, 473, 478
Grosvenor Gallery, 325
Guedella, Philip, 513

guillotine, 424, 470, 590
Guinness, *Sir* Arthur, 313, 314
Gurdon William Brampton, secretary, 164, 210
Gwyn, Nell, 540

Habeas Corpus, 440
Habershon, *Dr.* Samuel, 632–4
Haddo House, 363
Hagley, 90, 94, 130, 161
Hall, C. Newman, 131, 138, 262
Hallam, Arthur, 11–16, 21, 47, 240, 324–5, 633,
  648, 650
Hallam, Henry, 522
Hamilton, E. W., 370, 383–4 n., 411 n., 456 n.,
  473 n., 494, 515, 517, 522, 530, 534–5,
  589 n., 621–2, 626
  Gladstone's death and, 632 n., 635–7
  Gladstone's 'rescue work' and, 542
Hamilton, *Lord* George, 601 ff.
Hamilton, Janet, 132
Hamilton, *Sir* Robert, 485, 494–5
Hamilton, *Bishop* Walter Kerr, 22, 49, 534
Hamlet, 323
Hampden, *Bishop* R. D., 18, 19, 23, 71
Hannah, J., 145
Hansard, 296
Hapsburg Empire, dual monarchy in, 501
Harcourt, *Sir* William, 248, 360, 364, 365, 369,
  372, 493, 495, 498, 541 n., 559, 560, 564,
  566, 582, 583, 585, 589, 606, 637
Hardie, James Keir, 571
Hardy Thomas, 619, 636–7
Harley Street, No. 73, 290–1, 313–14, 355, 540,
  610
Harper's New Monthly Magazine, 189
Harrison, Benjamin, 21
Hartington, *Lord, see* Cavendish
Hartmann, Eduard von, 544
Hartmann, *Mrs.* Emma, 544
Harvard University, 319
Hastings, *Miss* H., 159
Hatfield House, 150, 235, 237
Hatherley, *Lord, see* Wood
Hawarden Castle and estate, 50, 53, 59, 89, 90,
  95, 100, 101, 147, 150–- 2, 158, 161, 181,
  195, 201, 222, 234, 238, 245, 249, 258–9,
  313 ff., 324–6, 351, 355, 368, 416, 437,
  460, 461, 482, 526, 529, 532 ff., 548, 553,
  565, 608–9, 613–14, 623, 628
  Gladstone's death at, 632–6
  mad cow attack at, 581
  Octagon of, 543, 555
  Parnell's visit to, 563 ff.
  political gatherings at, 541
  rents of, 438
  'Temple of Peace' of, 317, 541, 620, 635;
    Plates 19, 32

Hawarden Church, 52
'Hawarden Kite', 483–5, 494, 532
Hawtrey, E. C., 556
Healy, T. M., 436, 454
Heathcote, *Sir* William, 108, 213
Heligoland, 595, 597
Henderson, Fred, 595
Hennell, Sarah, 625
Henri, T., 535
Hepburn, Walter, 300
Herat, 380
Herbert, H. H. M., *Lord Carnarvon*, 225, 242,
    405, 412, 474, 482–3, 495
Herder, J. G. von, 40
Herschell, F., *Lord Herschell*, 494, 583, 588 n.
Hertford, *Marquis of*, 618 n.
Hervey, *Lord* A. C., 211
Heygate, W. E., 158
Heywood, J., 164
Hicks Pasha, 392, 395
High-Churchmanship, 27, 40, 41, 45, 54, 62–3,
    71, 205, 262 ff., 271 ff., 282, 285–6,
    332–3, 338 ff., 350, 522, 545, 583 n.
Highland Railway, 626
Hinsley, F. H., 272
Hirst, F. W., 641
historicism, 445, 446, 495, 547
Hobbes, Thomas, 20, 40
Hodgkinson's amendment (1867), 142
Holborn restaurant, 551
Holker Hall, 399
Holland, 561
Holland, Henry Scott, 325
Holyoake, G. J., 132, 263 n.
Home Office, 222
Home Rule, 254, 344, 358, 360, 435, 462–90,
    532, 546–7, 548 ff., 570, 582, 587–92, 601,
    638, 642
    colonial model for, 502
    conservative character of, 550
    disestablishment and, 463 ff.
    an essentially contested concept, 487
    intellectual assumptions underpinning,
        467 ff.
    Liberal party and, 486–90, 581–2, 587–92
    naturalness of, 560 ff.
    no conversion by Gladstone to, 464
    primacy of, 558 ff., 578, 581–2
    Resolution for, 506 n., 582
    Tory bill for encouraged, 481–2, 565
    see also Government of Ireland Bills
Home Rule Association, 202
Home Rule Bills, *see* Government of Ireland
    Bills
Home Rule Party/Parnellites, 360, 369 n.,
    422 ff., 432, 433, 436–7, 444 ff., 452, 456,
    458–9, 461–2, 270, 477, 481 ff., 485,

505–6, 509, 525–6, 558 ff., 562 ff., 580,
    587, 588–9, 642
    Parnell split and, 565–8
Homer, 20, 61, 74, 148, 152 ff., 247, 259, 289,
    551, 623
    Thesaurus of, 320
homoionyms, dictionary of, 88
Hook, W. F., 205
Hope, A. J. Beresford-, 265
Hope-Scott, James, 11, 47, 67, 69–70, 93, 157,
    236, 240, 243, 329, 528
Horace, 258, 579, 581, 591, 621
Horse Guards, 211
Hotel Cecil, 492 n.
Hottentots, 497
house duty, 106, 123, 218, 223
household suffrage, 139 ff., 172, 175, 215, 230,
    425 ff., 574
Houses of Mercy, 578
Hughes, J., 214
Hughes, Thomas, 216
humanitarianism, 294 ff.
Hume, David, 14–15, 26, 32, 648
humour, Gladstone's sense of, 622–3
Hunt, J. H. Leigh, 136
Hunt, T. Leigh, 136, 230–1
Huskisson, William, 27, 55
Hutton, A. W., 553
Hutton, G. C., 465 n.
Huxley, T. H., 11, 483, 490, 547
Hyde, Edward, *1st. Earl of Clarendon*, 14, 15
hymns by Gladstone, 54

Iceland, 562
Idealism, 39–45, 62–5, 118, 255, 260, 624–5
Ilbert Bill, 378–9
Illustrated London News, 303
Immaculate Conception, 264
Imperial Federation League, 403
Imperialism, 267–8, 281–2, 307–11, 350, 372,
    374 ff., 389 ff., 419, 468, 561, 595–600,
    644
income and property tax, 99, 106, 112, 116,
    120 ff., 139, 220, 222 ff., 415 ff.
    Select Committee on (1851), 123
Independent Labour Party, 595
India, 108, 190, 270, 275–6, 308, 354, 365,
    377–82, 391, 394, 396, 467, 594, 644
    see also Afghanistan
Indian National Congress, 378–9, 437
indirect taxes, 415 ff., 461, 502
inductivism, 342–3, 624
inflation, underpins growth, 215, 221, 226
Inglis, *Sir* Robert Harry, 38, 57, 72
Ingram, J. Dunbar, 561
Ingram, *Mrs.* Meynell, 541
International, Second, 570, 571

Inverary Castle, 149, 446
Iolanthe, 530
Ionian Islands, 107, 108, 136, 161, 164–7,
   356 n., 396
Ireland, 37, 38, 44, 46, 65, 66, 68 ff., 76, 129, 133,
   134, 136, 139, 142 ff., 164, 193 ff., 209 ff.,
   249, 268, 281–2, 335 ff., 344, 350, 351,
   354, 372–3, 385, 424, 433, 546–7, 557,
   619, 642
   Central Board scheme for, 459 ff., 472–4
   coercion in, 446 ff., 453 ff., 485
   creditworthiness of, 498 ff.
   disestablishment in, 104, 129, 144 ff.
   expenditure and, 419
   franchise and, 425 ff.
   home rule and, 450 ff., 478 ff.
   land purchase and, 443 ff., 452–3, 459, 461,
      480–1, 486, 495–500, 587–8
   local government for, 421 ff.
   M.P.s, status of, 505 ff., 559, 563, 572 n.,
      587–91
   peasant proprietary for, 496 ff.
   railways in 120, 197–8
   Receiver General for, 481, 498, 499
   tenant right and, 445 ff., 497 ff.
   Three Fs. and, 441, 444–8, 451
   visits by Gladstone to, 437 ff., 535–6
   see also Govt. of Ireland bills; home rule
Irish Church Bill (1833), 31
Irish Church Bill (1869), 173, 174, 176, 193–6,
   204, 207, 231, 297, 349, 365, 436
Irish Church Resolutions (1868), 136, 142,
   146–7, 444
Irish Free State, 435–6
Irish Land Bill (1866), 145–6
Irish Land Act (1870), 193, 196 ff., 204, 206, 207,
   231, 242–3, 436, 439 ff., 465, 495
Irish Land Act (1881), 196, 359, 368, 371, 406,
   422, 441–51
Irish Land Bill (1886), 495–500, 587–8
Irish National League, 335, 458, 481, 498
Irish Reform Bill (1868), 143
Irish University Bill (1873), 180, 199 ff., 226,
   230, 436, 465
Irving, Edward, 25
Irving, *Sir* Henry, 267, 323, 529, 557
Isault, 565–8
Islam, 26 n., 395
Italy, 24, 36–7, 50–1, 80–1, 108–9, 137, 165,
   167–8, 467

Jack Sheppard, 131
Jackson, *Dean* Cyril, 16–18
James, Henry, *novelist*, 256, 528, 539
James, *Sir* Henry, 426, 541 n.
James, *Sir* Walter, *Lord Northbourne*, 97, 129,
   157, 235, 292, 534

Jane Eyre, 99
Jansenism, 158
Japan, 555 n.
Jenkins, *Canon* Claude, 629
Jenkinson, E. G., 485
Jenkinson, R. B., *Lord Liverpool*, 17
Jevons, W. S., 319
Jewell, J., 54
Jews, 278 n., 643
   see also Judaism
Jewish Chronicle, 376
Jewish disabilities, 25, 72–3, 102
Jingoism, 290–1, 333, 346, 349
Johnson, *Dr.* Samuel, 556, 612
Johnson-Clarendon Treaty (1869), 188
Jones, D., 214
Jones, Lloyd, 132
Joubert, P. J., 405
Journal of the Society for Physical Research, 544
Jowett, Benjamin, 84
Judaism, 325, 326
'Junta', the, 131–2

Kalahari desert, 409 n.
Kama Sutra, 528
Kampala, 596
Kapital, Das, 214
Keble, John, 63, 65, 71, 72, 77, 90, 93, 94, 238
Keble College, Oxford, 315, 462, 538
Kennedy, T. F., 99
Kenya, 595
   land purchase and, 496
Keogh judgement, 199–200
Kerrison, *Sir* E., 48
Keynes, J. M., 641
Khartoum, 374, 398 ff.
Kilbrandon Royal Commission, 508
Kilimanjaro, Mount, 408
Killarney, 437
'Kilmainham treaty', 368, 416, 436, 450, 453–6
Kimberley, *Lord, see* Wodehouse
Kincardineshire, constituency of, 230
King Lear, 1, 618
King's College, London, 98
Kingsley, Charles, 144
Kingussie, 234
Kinnaird, Arthur, 50–1, 159, 241, 617
Kipling, Rudyard, 595, 619
Knowles, J. T., 263, 319, 489, 552, 569
Knowsley House, 529, 530–1, 541
Kong Meng, L., 318
Kossuth, L., 157
Kruger, Paul, 405 ff.
Küchük Kainardji, Treaty of, 276

Labouchere, Henry du Pré, 332, 477, 478, 484,
   586–7

labour aristocracy, 140–2, 643
labour movement, 571–6, 612
labour questions, 571–6
Labour World, 565
Lamb, William, *Lord Melbourne*, 23, 210, 586
Lambeth Palace Library, 629
Lamennais, F. R. de, 30
Lancashire, South and South-West, constituency of, 129, 130, 133, 145–6, 151, 163, 164, 229
Land League, 335, 429, 436–55, 456, 481
Langtry, Lillie, 453, 529
Lansdell, *Revd.* Henry, 381
Lansdowne, *Lord*, 594
Laud, William, 54
Law, Andrew Bonar, 608 n.
Lawley, F. C., 161–2
Lawson, E. Levy-, 135–6, 231, 278 n.
Lawson, *Sir* Wilfrid, 375
Layard, *Sir* A. H., 278 n.
Leader, J. T., 21
League of Nations, 272, 570
leaks from Cabinet, 367, 607
Leamington spa, 6, 234
Lebanon, 562
Leben Jesu, Das, 156
Lecky, W. E. H., 318, 546, 561
Leeds, 291, 315, 351, 362, 449
Leeds Mercury, 296
Lefevre, J. G. Shaw, 365, 583
legislative programme, 355, 359–60, 370–1
Leicester Square chapel, 97, 157
Leighton, *Sir* Frederic, 519
Leith, 3, 129
Leith Burghs, constituency of, 507
Lenbach, F. von., 326; Plates 28(a), 29(a)
Leopardi, G., 80
Leopold, *Prince*, 368
Le Play, P. G. F., 477, 547
Levellers, 55
Levy-Lawson, *see* Lawson
Lewis, *Sir* George Cornewall, 74, 106, 108, 110, 112, 138, 261
Liberal catholics, 64
Liberal imperialism, 377, 389 ff., 410, 599
Liberal Unionists/dissentient Liberals, 507, 548, 580–1, 588
   Round Table talks and, 559–60
   see also Tory Party, Unionists
Liberalism, Liberals and Liberal Party, 1, 26, 36, 42, 55, 62, 71, 72, 75, 80 ff., 104 ff., 120, 126, 128–9, 134–5, 140 ff., 164, 169, 175–7, 201 ff., 206 ff., 212–14, 222 ff., 228 ff., 247, 249–50, 253 ff., 287, 288, 295 ff., 331–50, 352–3, 359–64, 367–8, 411, 414, 467, 475 ff., 570, 582–7, 638, 642–4

as agent of political integration, 574–6
dependence on Home Rule MPs of, 510
'faddists' and, 578
female franchise and, 576–8
franchise and, 425–33, 475–6
free trade and, 569–71
Ireland and, 436 ff., 462 ff., 485, 486–7, 488–90, 550 ff.
labour movement and, 571–6
navy and, 600–4
party meetings and, 363–4, 590
patronage and, 516–19, 521–4
split of, 506 ff.
transitory character of, 643
Ulster and, 487
see also Whigs
Liberation Society, 142
Liddell, H. G., 20, 21, 151, 519, 523
Liddon, H. P., 264–5
life insurance allowance, 122, 126
Light, 544
Lincoln, *Lord*, *see* Clinton
Lisle, Ambrose Phillipps de, 237, 249
List, Friedrich, 57
Listowel, *Lord*, 439
Littlebury's, Mill Hill, 540
Liverpool, 4–5, 7, 8, 61, 108, 121, 134, 141, 212, 238, 256, 293, 348, 349, 368, 629, 652
   advowson of bought by Gladstone, 627
   Brown Museum of, 314
Liverpool Courier, 55, 653
Livingstone, David, 397
Llandaff, 523, 537
Lloyd George, David, 109, 500, 576
lobby, foundation of, 367
local government, 172, 218, 371, 415, 420–5, 452–3, 460, 466, 467, 471, 512, 576
Local Government Bill (1894), 604–7
Locke, John, 15, 32, 35, 62, 63
Lockwood, Frank, 565
lodgers, 428 ff.
Lohengrin, 323
London, 8, 51, 53, 130, 134, 158, 160, 226, 236, 253, 304, 331, 417–18, 483, 542, 634
   Gladstone Park, 540
   Government of London Bills, 360, 421 ff., 471
London, Convention of (1884), 408
London Library, 98
London Polytechnic, 159
London, University of, 583
Lopes, *Sir* M., 217–8
Lords, House of, 114, 124, 176, 208, 211, 344, 347, 392, 429 ff., 486, 505, 509–10, 514–15, 516–19, 549, 558, 586, 591–2, 605–7, 608–9, 644
   dissolution, Gladstone hopes for, 604–7

Lourdes, 611
Lowden, *Miss*, 160
Lowe, Robert, 133, 174, 181, 214, 219–20, 222, 223, 348
Lowestoft, 613
Lucy, H. W., 297, 585
Ludlow, J. M., 132
Lugard, Frederick, 620–1
Lushington, H., 21
Lyceum Theatre, 529
Lycurgus, *Bishop*, 265, 278 n.
Lyttelton, George W., *Lord Lyttelton, wife's brother-in-law*, 52, 75, 88, 130, 152, 161, 162, 266, 319, 327–8, 556
Lyttelton, Laura, 619
Lyttelton, Lucy, *see* Cavendish
Lyttelton, Mary, *née* Glynne (*sister-in-law*), 50, 52, 161–2
Lyttelton, Spencer, 533, 615
Lyttelton, Sybella (*formerly* Mildmay), 162
Lytton, E. Bulwer, 136, 166

Maamtrasna murders, 474
Macaulay, T. B., *Lord Macaulay*, 29, 45, 62, 114, 266, 319–20, 329, 337, 390, 518
McCarthy, Justin, 566–7
MacColl, Malcolm, 264–5, 542
Macdonald, J., 251
MacDonald, James Ramsay, 436, 608 n.
Machiavelli, N., 489
Macgregor, D., 555 n.
Mackarness, J. F., 213
MacKenzie, *Sir* Alexander, 530
McKinnon, *Sir* William, 597
Macmillan, Alexander, 318
Madagascar, 403
Magee College, 201
Mahaffy, J. P., 623
Mahdi, The, 394 ff.
'Maiden Tribute' campaign, 541–2
Maiwand, battle of, 380
Majuba Hill, battle of, 400, 406, 513
Malet, *Sir* E. B., 383 ff.
Malory, Thomas, 160
malt tax, 106, 220, 415
Malta, 165, 191
Malthusianism, 21
Man, Isle of, 326
Manchester, 67, 102, 134, 203, 260, 297, 551, 552
Manners, *Lord* John, *Duke of Rutland*, 261, 637
Manning, *Cardinal* Henry Edward, 5, 11, 22, 47, 55, 67, 69–70, 73, 93, 157, 185, 198, 199, 202, 205, 243, 248, 249, 257, 263, 286, 295, 329, 460, 555 n., 556, 622
Mansion House, 362
Mant, Richard, 15–16, 649

Manzoni, A., 51
Margaret Chapel, 90, 96
Mark, *King*, 567
Marlborough, *Duke of, see* Churchill
Marlborough House, 210
marriage, 48–54
Married Women's Property Acts, 576
Marriott, C., 21
Marshall, Alfred, 319
Martin, J., 47
Martineau, James, 263, 338, 625
Marylebone Liberal Association, 302
Marx, Karl, 1, 214, 315, 640
Masheder, R., 258
Mashonaland, 599
masses, the, 348–50
masturbation, 48
Matabeleland, 599
match tax, 219
Maurice, F. D., 21, 22, 30
May, *Sir* Thomas Erskine, 370, 424
Mayall, J. P., 541
Mayhew, Henry, 88
Maynooth, 59, 68–9, 73, 76, 86, 89, 144, 194, 195, 435, 438, 506, 560 n., 620
Mazra, battle of, 380
Meade, Robert, 403 n., 404 n.
meat sellers, foreign, 641
Melbourne, *Lord, see* Lamb
Melly, George, 151, 164
Mentmore Towers, 149, 494
Merton College, Oxford, 47
Merv, 381
Mervousness, 381
Methodists, 45, 138, 295
Metropolis Churches Fund, 45
Metropolitan and District Railway, 245–6, 389 n., 626
Metropolitan Visiting Association, 97
Michelstown, 562
middle-class, 53, 121 ff., 212, 224 ff., 348 ff.
Middlemarch, 61, 233, 250
Midlothian Campaigns, 129, 270, 289–92, 293–312, 321, 351, 375, 378, 405, 415, 420, 440, 465 n., 507, 538, 540, 580
Mikado, The, 530
Milan, 167
Mildmay, H. St. J., 162
militarism, 603, 639
Mill, James, 26, 62
Mill, John Stuart, 26, 45, 77, 116, 122, 576 n., 652
Millais, *Sir* John, 519–21, 536, 613–14; Plate 22
Milman, H. H., 155
Milner, Alfred, 394
bungles Home Rule finance, 589–90
Milnes, R. Monckton, *Lord Houghton*, 90, 230, 233, 256, 524–5

Milton, John, 14, 524
minimal state, 102 ff., 336, 338, 340 ff., 377, 415 ff., 504, 640–1
Mochizuki, Kotaro, 555 n.
Mohammedanism, 64, 184
Mold, Eisteddfod at, 214
Moldavia, 85
Molesworth, *Sir* William, 60, 75, 81
Molière, 9
Mombasa, 596
'Monad', 553
Moncrieff, H., 21, 26
Monsell, Harriet, 159
Montalembert, C. F. R. de, 64, 95
Monte Cassino, 168
Montenegro, 354, 375, 441
Moody-Sankey revivalism, 262, 310
Moorhouse, *Revd.* James, 522
Mordaunt divorce case, 209
Morgan, J. E., 238
Morier, R. B. D., 323 n.
Morley, Arnold, 541 n., 566
Morley, John, 8, 62, 258–9, 259, 261, 344, 365, 473, 485, 493, 494, 505, 528, 566, 582–3, 588 n., 599, 601–7, 611, 616 n., 637
  biography of Gladstone by, 584, 622
  revolted by Gladstone, 583–4
Morning Herald, 91
Morning Post, 544–5
Morris, Lewis, 595
Morris, William, 594
Moses, 550, 560–1
Motley, J. L., 188
Muggletonians, 528
Müller, F. Max, 187
Mundella, A. J., 132, 216, 494, 583
Munich, 326
Municipal Corporations Act (1835), 467
Munster, Count, 404
Murray, James, 407 n., 523–4, 540
  Dictionary of, 523–4
Murray, John, 283, 318, 528–9
Murray's Handbook for Sicily, 51
Myers, A. J., 376 n.
Myers, F. W. H., 545

Naoroji, Dababhai, 379
Napier Royal Commission, 495
Naples, 51, 80–1, 96, 363, 366 n.
Napoleon I, 8, 116, 555
National Association for the Promotion of Social Science, 132
national insurance, 171
National Liberal Club, 361, 525
National Liberal Federation, 295, 298, 302, 361, 507, 547, 551, 560, 576
National Portrait Gallery, 98, 520

National Press Agency, 484
National Reform Union, 361
national religion, 23, 38–43, 44, 55, 57, 63–5, 68–9, 74–5, 245 ff., 266 ff.
National Society for the Education of the Poor, 45, 203
nationalism, 271, 281–3, 382 ff., 409, 441–2, 501, 570, 642
Naval Annual, 518
Navigation Acts, 77–8, 79, 414
navy, 290, 341, 375, 410–13, 600–4, 611
Negropontis affair, 278 n., 300 n.
New College, Oxford, 538
New Guinea, 372 n., 402, 403, 404, 409 n.
New York, 569
New Zealand, 73, 74–5, 190–1, 389 n., 534
Newark, 24, 31, 45–6, 57, 61, 101, 230, 637
Newcastle, 133–4, 188, 551
Newcastle, *Dukes of, see* Clinton
Newcastle Programme, 560, 572–4, 576
Newdigate Prize, 19
Newman, John Henry, 5, 6, 7, 18, 23, 30, 41, 48, 55, 64, 66, 69, 71, 92, 93, 144, 184, 201, 249, 262, 286, 324, 347, 553 n., 633, 637, 649
Newmania; or, Puseyism unmasked, 72
Newnham College, Cambridge, 316, 533, 544, 614; Plate 23
newspapers, 1, 130 ff., 135–7, 139, 130 ff., 296–301, 397–8, 554
  Gladstone's death and, 634
  see also paper duties
Nigeria, 403
Nineteenth Century, 263, 319, 489, 569
Noetics, 18, 38, 58
nonconformists, 41, 50, 68, 69, 94, 102, 138, 141, 145, 174, 181–2, 196, 205, 239, 291, 364–5, 568, 576, 643
Norfolk, *Duke of*, 212–3, 636 n.
Normans, 281
North American Review, 569, 571, 581, 626
Northcote, S. H., *Lord Iddesleigh*, 84, 151, 289, 308–9, 352 n., 401, 416, 424, 430, 431 n., 455, 526
Northumbria, 287
Norway, 501, 562
Nottingham, 551
Nottingham Journal, 31, 653
Novikov, Olga, 243, 322–3, 376 n., 458, 547 n.

Oak Farm, 50, 59, 61, 88–9, 91, 102, 130, 162, 213, 416
Oakeley, F., 96
O'Brien, R. Barry, 489, 546
Occam, 620
O'Connell, Daniel, 30, 67, 560–1
O'Donnell, F. H., 454

Ogilvy, Gillanders, 378
O'Keeffe, R., 200
Old Catholics, 248, 249, 257, 264
Old Mortality, 14, 97
Oldham, speech in, 132
Olympian religion, 320, 548, 553, 631
Oman, Charles, 554
Opdebeck, *Lady* Susan (*formerly Lady Lincoln*),
        543, 617–18
opium and laudanum, 65, 89
Orange Free State, 407
O'Rell, Max, 515 n.
O'Rourke, Revd. John, 560 n.
Orthodox Churches, *see* Eastern Churches
Osborne House, 492, 579
O'Shea, *Mrs.*, *see* Parnell
O'Shea, *Captain* William, 442, 454–7, 460, 563,
        568
Osman Digna, 399
Ossian, 14
Outram, Zadok, 593, 600
Overend and Gurney, 109
Oxford, University of, 16 ff., 27, 32, 36, 38–9,
        69, 70 ff., 82, 83 ff., 90, 92, 99, 101–2,
        128–9, 139, 145, 153, 200, 208–9, 234,
        294, 315, 335, 523, 538, 583, 609, 625, 633
    Gladstone's death and, 633, 635
    Regius History chair and, 523
    Sheldonian Theatre of, 551, 635
    see also Bodleian Library, Clarendon Press,
        and names of colleges
Oxford University Act (1854), 583, 633
Oxnam, N., 21

Pacifico, Don, 80, 81, 91, 101
Padwick, Henry, 321–2, 617
Paget, *Lord* C., 151
Pahlen, *Count*, 537
Pall Mall Gazette, 261, 412, 484, 541, 603
Palmer, R. R., *Lord Selborne*, 90, 176, 199, 216,
        258, 377, 493
Palmer, William, *of Worcester*, 30, 40, 41, 64,
        262, 651
Palmerston, *Lord*, *see* Temple
Panama Canal, 386
Panizzi, Antonio, 318, 327
Pantheists, 339
paper duties, 106, 113–14, 135
Pareto, V. I., 620
Paris, 324
    Gladstone's 1889 visit to, 551, 568–9, 612
Paris, *Comte de*, 537
Parish Councils Bill (1893–4), 588, 604–7
Parker, C. S., 528
Parnell, Anna, 449
Parnell, Charles Stewart, 424, 438, 440, 444,
        501, 562, 572 n., 580

arrest of, 448–56
character of, 448, 456, 487, 558
death of, 568
elusiveness of, 566
estate of visited by Gladstone, 438
financial clauses, negotiation of, 503 ff.
general election 1885 and, 481
Home Rule and, 471–8, 484, 487, 501, 503–5
land purchase and, 498, 562
manifesto of, 564, 567, 589 n.
Mrs O'Shea and, 457–8
O'Shea divorce and, 557, 563, 567–8, 586 n.
'proposed Constitution' of, 478–81, 487, 562
Parnell, Katharine (formerly O'Shea), 384,
        450 ff., 457–8, 473–6, 478 ff., 565–8
patronage, 175–6, 212 ff., 516 ff., 614
Patteson, J. C., 249
Pattison, Mark, 203
payment of M.P.s, 572 ff.
Peace Preservation Act, 439
Peel, Arthur Wellesley, 173
Peel, *Sir* Robert, 17, 20, 25, 30, 31, 38, 41, 45,
        58, 59, 65 ff., 76, 78–9, 81, 88, 91, 100 ff.,
        106, 110, 114, 121, 123, 126, 173, 190,
        213, 218, 236, 307, 308, 347, 410, 415,
        433, 478, 480, 486, 525, 528, 555 n.,
        560 n., 574, 585, 625, 638, 639
Peelites, 81, 82, 83, 85, 101, 102, 104 ff., 114,
        122–3, 125, 137 ff., 165, 169, 174, 176,
        199, 213, 224, 236, 334, 353, 415, 416,
        480, 486, 560 n.
Pelham, Henry, 608 n.
Pembroke Castle, 518
Pembroke lodge, 149
Pendjeh, 381, 401
Penmaenmawr, 138, 151, 152, 368
Penrhyn, *Lord*, 150, 613
Pentecostalism, 25
Perceval, Spencer, 608 n.
Persia, 380 ff.
Petz, the dog, 632
Philadelphia and Reading Railway, 245
Philiates, 167
Phillimore, *Sir* Robert, 22, 70, 99, 141, 151, 152,
        235, 271, 273, 289, 291, 314, 323, 337,
        355, 391, 531
Phoenix Park murders, 355, 366, 367 n., 434,
        457
phonograph, Gladstone's recordings for,
        551–2
Piedmont-Sardinia, 108, 167–8
Pilgrim's Progress, 619
Pitlochry, 591
Pitt *the Elder*, *Lord Chatham*, 404
Pitt *the Younger*, 14, 50, 83, 114, 187, 440, 463,
        477, 546, 508 n.
Pitts, *Nurse* Kate, 633, 634 n., 635 n.

Pius IX, 265, 555 n.
Plan of Campaign, 562
platform speaking, 102, 128 ff., 295 ff., 345–50, 642–3
Plato, 20, 33–6, 39, 204, 625
'ploutocracy', 212, 525
pluralism, 464
Plymouth, 551
Pobedonostsev, K. P., 277
pocket boroughs, 254
Poerio, Carlo, 80
Poet Laureateship, 594–5
pogroms, 376 n.
Poland, 277
political economy, 319, 372, 445, 551, 573
Ponsonby, Sir Henry, 491–2, 514–15, 519, 579 n., 586, 605, 609–10
Ponsonby, Melita, 616
Poor Laws, 309–10
  Royal Commission on, 616
Pope-Hennessy, Sir J., 568
pornography, 90, 92
Port Sunlight, 551
Portal, Gerald, 597, 620
Porter, Andrew, 455, 487
portfolio, 387–9, 626–7
Post Office, 317
Post Office Savings Bank, 117, 119, 131, 214, 221, 573
postcards, 316
Potter, Beatrix, 520
Potter, George, 132
Potter, Rupert, 520
Power, O'Connor, 439
Prague, 165
Pre-Raphaelitism, 155–8, 324–5, 519
press, see newspapers
Press Association, 296, 298, 300, 484
Preston, 363
Pretoria, Convention of (1881), 407 ff.
Price, Bonamy, 84
Primeval Man, 238
Primrose, A. P., Lord Rosebery, 292, 298, 299, 306, 310–11, 355, 358, 364, 366, 368, 369, 370, 400, 461, 508, 517 n., 531, 533, 537, 541, 579, 584, 600, 602, 610, 616 n., 622, 637
  as foreign secretary, 492–3, 584, 595–600
  Gladstone's portrait and, 520–1
  Gladstone's 'rescue work' and, 542
  Ireland and, 479, 481, 482
  Labour movement and, 572, 594
  The Durdans and, 539–40
Primrose, Henry, 366, 533
Primrose, Lady Peggy, 520
Privy Council, 45
Privy Seal, 419, 446, 585 n.

probability as guide to conduct, 624 ff.
progress, 337, 343, 348–9
property, rights and duties of, 26 ff.
proportional representation, 343 n.
prostitutes, 48, 59, 88, 90–5, 158–60, 242, 243–4, 321 ff., 541–3, 615
Protection of Person and Property Bill, 443, 453–4
protectionism, 334 ff., 567, 639, 641
Protectorates, 377, 391, 394, 397
Providence, see God
Provincial Councils Bill, 453
Prussia, 41
Psalms, 97
psephology, invented by Gladstone?, 164
Psychical Research, Society for, 544–5
Public Accounts Committee, 117, 418
Public Worship Regulation Act (1874), 247 ff., 254, 339, 523 n.
Purcell, E. S., 555 n., 556
purchase, abolition of, 210 ff.
Puritanism, 522
Pusey, Edward Bouverie, 45, 50, 55, 71–2, 93, 248, 264, 522, 538, 652
Pusey House, 538
Pythagoras, 553 n.

Quakers, 364
Quaritch, 160
Quarterly Review, 72, 95, 98, 105, 160, 167
Queen's University, 200
Quetta, 381
quinine, 535

race, 279 ff.
Radcliffe Trust and Camera, 98
Radical Programme, 465, 476
Radicals and Radicalism, 30, 60, 66, 75, 77, 81, 105, 106, 108, 111, 121, 127, 134, 137–8, 141, 169, 175, 181–2, 184, 210–1, 225, 228, 230, 333 ff., 366 ff., 412, 418, 459, 513, 515–16, 586 n., 603, 607
railways, 67, 88, 199–200, 310–11, 389 n., 398 ff., 555
  Gladstone's coffin and, 636
Railways Act (1844), 67, 199–20
Rainy, R., 466 n.
Ralli, Mrs., 324
Ramsay, Dean E. B., 49
Rashdall, Hastings, 621
rates and ratepayers, 217–19, 224–7
rationalism, 301 ff., 489, 554, 571–2
Ravenhill, Alice, 632
Rawson, W., 9
Reay, Lord, 310
Red Sea telegraph, 110
Redistribution Bill (1885), 335, 360, 371, 395, 401, 425–33, 459, 537

Redlich, J., 425 n.
Redmond, John, 454
Reform Bills and Acts:
  (1831–2), 19, 24–7, 58, 61, 128, 254
  (1854), 85
  (1866), 128, 131, 132, 133, 134, 136, 139 ff.,
    143, 163, 172, 199, 208, 329
  (1867–8), 128, 141–3, 164, 165, 172, 223–4,
    225
  (1884–5), 425 ff.
  see also Representation of the People Bill
Reform Club, 105, 235, 361, 525
Reform League, 104, 134, 142, 437
regionalism, 467 ff., 642
Regium Donum, 194
registration, 428 ff., 460, 475–6
Reid, J. J., 298, 310
Reid, T. Wemyss, 483–5
religious nationality, 271 ff., 279 ff., 294–5
religious pluralism, 338 ff.
Renan, E., 156–7
Rendel, Stuart, Lord Rendel, 572, 599 n.,
  611–12, 632, 637
Representation of the People (Franchise) Bill
  (1884), 342, 359–60, 371, 392, 425–33,
  459, 473, 518–19, 544, 576
  see also Reform Bills
representation, 346, 573–5, 640, 644
republicanism, 209–10, 229
'rescue work', 542–3
  see also prostitutes
residuum, 305–6
retrenchment, 573–4, 600–4, 640–1
Rhodes, Cecil John, 572 n., 599–600
Rhodesia, 599–600
Ribbon Men, 196
Ricardo, David, 76, 118, 342, 641
Ricasoli, Baron, 555 n.
Richard, Henry, 365 n.
Richardson, Ralph, 298, 310
Richmond, George, 520
Richmond, Sir William Blake, 520, 635; Plate
  30(b)
Ridgeway, Sir J. West, 593
Rigby, Miss, 159
Rigg, J. H., 262, 263
Riis, Jacob, 569
Ripon, Lord, see Robinson
Ritchie, Alex, 296–7
Robbins, A. F., 556 n.
Robert Elsmere, 619
Robinson, F. J., Lord Ripon, 66
Robinson, G. F. S., Lord de Grey, Lord Ripon,
  176–7, 204–5, 226, 249, 358, 365, 378–9,
  467, 494, 540, 583, 599
Robinson, Sir Hercules, 372 n.
Roden, Mr., 313

Roebuck, J. A., 75, 81, 120
Rogers, Dawson, 484
Roman Catholicism, 13, 16, 30 36–7, 41, 44, 45,
  47, 64, 68 ff., 80, 89 ff., 158, 163, 167,
  184 ff., 194 ff., 198 ff., 205, 237, 247 ff.,
  257, 259 ff., 263 ff., 317, 326, 328–9, 353,
  365, 414, 568, 643
Romanes Lecture, 551, 581, 620
Rome, 36–7, 47, 51, 161, 184
Rome, Treaty of, 642
Roosevelt, President, 552 n.
Rose, Miss, 160
Rosebery, Lord, see Primrose
Rothschild, Lord, 536, 616–17
Round, C. G., 70
Round Table talks, 559–60
Rousseau, J. J., 35
Royal Academy, 325, 536, 541
Royal Grants, 586
Royal Historical Society, 277 n.
Royal Holloway College, 533, 614
Royal Titles Act (1876), 266
Ruskin, John, 324–5, 594
Russell, Sir Charles, 630 n.
Russell, Lord John, Earl Russell, 44, 73, 75, 85,
  99, 138–9, 141–2, 143, 146, 149, 173, 176,
  180–1, 195, 210, 213, 273, 358, 365, 426,
  464–5, 508
Russia, 165 ff., 187, 190, 269 ff., 274 ff., 307, 322,
  376, 379 ff., 420
  militarism in, 603
Ruwenzori Mountains, 597

Sabellians, 262
St Asaph, 67, 213–14
St Barnabas, House of, in Soho, 80–1, 97
St Deiniol's Library, Hawarden, 238, 251, 548,
  553, 614, 617, 619, 620, 626, 627, 629, 631
St George's in the East, 130
St Helen's Convent, 163
St James's, Piccadilly, 54
St James's Square, No. 10, 611
St Martin's-in-the-Fields, 54
St Pancras Workhouse, 309–10
St Paul's, 210
St Peter's, Rome, 37
Salisbury, Lord, see Cecil
Salomons, D., 164, 229
Salt Hill Club, 16
San Stephano, Treaty of, 280, 291
Sandringham, 517
Sandhurst, Lady, 544 n., 545
Sardinia, see Piedmont
Satan, 286
Saunders, A. P., 22
Saunders, Sir Edwin, 535, 538
Saxe-Coburg and Gotha, Duke of, 594, 599, 609

Saxe-Meininge Court Theatre, 529
Saxons, 281
scandals, government weakened by, 221 ff., 234
Scandinavia, 426, 501
Schenck R. C., 179, 189–90
Scherer, Edmond, 326
Schiller, J. C. F. von, 149
Schleswig-Holstein, 143, 182, 561
school boards, 204
Schnadhorst, F., 361
Schreiner, Olive, 408, 619
Schumpeter, J., 123
Scialoja, A., 168
Scotland, 3, 4, 7, 8, 16, 38, 44, 53, 74, 129, 196,
        197, 202, 214, 247–8, 255, 335, 339, 363,
        438, 445, 505
    disestablishment and, 465 ff., 576
    education in, 173, 203–4
    franchise and, 425 ff.
    home rule and, 465 ff., 479, 500, 501, 502,
        505, 580, 582, 591
    local government in, 421 ff.
    railways of, 389 n.
    walks in, 254, 539
Scott, J. Hope-, see Hope
Scott, S., 245
Scott, W. F. Montagu-Douglas-, Duke of
        Buccleuch, 289, 292
Scott, Sir Walter, 14, 97, 528–9, 537, 555, 619
Scottish Church Patronage Bill, 247–8
Scottish Leader, 552 n.
Scottish National University, plan for, 129
Seaforth House, 4, 245, 328
Secret Service, 470–1, 490
Secreta Eucharistica, 96
secretaries, private, 531 ff., 533–5; Plate 18
    James Carmichael, 534
    J. A. Godley, 534, 622–3
    E. W. Hamilton, 370, 534–5
    G. Leveson-Gower, 366, 533–4
    Spencer Lyttelton, 533, 615
    Henry Primrose, 366, 533
    Horace Seymour, 533–4
    Sir Algernon West, 603, 605
secularism, 294–5, 342
Secularist Hymn Book, 210
Sedgwick, A., 238
Seeley, J. R., 152, 156–7, 545
Selborne, Lord, see Palmer
Selwyn, G., 12
Semon, Felix, 538
Septennial Act, 425
Serbia, 266
Seven Dials, 294
Seymour, Horace, 533–4
Shakers, 569
Shakespeare, W., 1, 14, 159, 323, 529, 557 n.

Shaw, William, 456
Shaw-Lefevre, G. J., 138
Sheehy, Father, 449
Sheil, R. L., 68
Shelley, Lady, 52
Shetland, 231
Shorthouse, J. H., 528
Shuvalov, Count, 322
Sicily, 51
Sidgwick, Mrs., 544, 545
silk trade, 113
Simeon, C., 9
Sinclair, Lucy, 159
Sistine Chapel, 37
slavery, 279, 349, 353, 377, 398, 497
Slavs, 265 ff., 322
Smiles, Samuel, 3–4, 131
Smith, Adam, 16, 21, 272, 415
Smith, Samuel, 577
Smith, Revd. Sydney, 527
Smith, Sir Thomas, 633
Smith, W. H., 452, 568
Smyth, P. J., 451–2
Sneyd, W., 237
Snowdon, 551
social contract of the mid-Victorian state,
        120 ff., 223
socialism, 342, 419, 509
Society for the Propagation of the Gospel, 130
South West Africa, 403
South African Federation, plans for, 193
    see also, Africa, South
Southbourne, Birmingham, 368
Southport, speech in, 134
Spain, 280
Spencer, Herbert, 238
Spencer, J. P., 5th. Earl Spencer, 234, 355, 358,
        364, 366, 369, 452, 460, 473, 474, 482,
        493, 498, 500, 532, 533, 541, 582, 588 n.,
        600–4, 606, 610 n., 637 n.; Plate 25
spiritualism, 544–6
Standard, The, 484
Stanley, Dean A. P., 521
Stanley, E. G., 14th Earl of Derby, 69, 74, 82,
        105–7, 126–7, 141, 179
Stanley, E. H., 15th Earl of Derby, 151, 242, 246,
        355, 358, 360, 364, 365, 369, 472, 494,
        514, 529, 530–1, 541
    colonial secretaryship of, 402 ff.
Stanley, Henry Morton, 597
Stanley, Mary, Lady Derby, 286
Stanley, Venetia, 242
Stansfeld, James, 138, 218
States General, 503
Stead, W. T., 136, 397, 411 n., 412, 541, 542,
        586 n.
Stephen, Sir James Fitzjames, 275 n.

Stephen, Leslie, 625
Stephenson, *Sir* Frederick, 399
Stevenson, Robert Louis, 528
Stopford, E. A., 195
Storks, *Sir* H., 165
Strahan, A., 319
Straight, *Mr.*, 216
Strangford, *Lady*, 266
Strauss, D. F., 156–7, 239
Strawberry Hill, 149
Suakin, 396 ff.
succession duties, 124
    see also death duties
Sudan, 355, 358, 374, 379, 392 ff., 394–401, 412,
    420, 459, 461, 462, 515, 596, 598
Suez Canal, 266, 267, 275–6, 379, 382 ff., 390 ff.,
    419
sugar duty, 124, 125, 222
suicide, 319, 327–8
Summerhayes, *Miss* (also 'Mrs Dale'), 156–8,
    314, 542–3
Sumner, *Miss*, 649
Sumner, J. B., 15, 649
Sunbeam, 475 ff., 518, 530, 538
Stubbs, William, 523
Sutherland, *Duchess of*, *see* Gower
suzerainty, 267, 281–2, 382 ff., 390, 407
Swan, Annie S., 528
Swansea, 551, 563, 612 n.
Swanwick, Hannah, 318
Sweden, 501, 562
Swift, Jonathan, 148
Swinburne, Algernon, 594
Sybil, 528
Syllabus Errorum (1864), 264

Tabberner, J. L., 127
Taft, *President*, 552 n.
Talbot, E. S., 264, 462, 538
Tait, A. C., 194–5, 213, 247, 522, 623 n.
Tanganyika, 409
Tannhäuser, 161
Tanzimat movement, 273
tariff treaties, 334, 570
taxation, 377, 415 ff., 461
    direct and indirect, 112 ff., 215, 219 ff.
    local, 208, 217 ff., 228
Taxation of Charities Bill (1863), 139
Taylor, J., 54
tea duty, 124, 125, 220
Tegernsee, 326
Tel-el-Kebir, battle of, 391
Telegraph Act (1868), 119, 171, 298
telephone, 316
Temple, Henry John, *Lord Palmerston*, 20, 81,
    104, 106, 107, 108, 109, 112, 114, 119–20,
    127–8, 136, 137, 139, 143, 145, 147, 149,

167, 173, 175, 182, 210, 220, 227, 248,
    297, 336, 365, 582, 630, 636 n.
Temple of Peace, 152, 635
Tenant League, 196
Tennant, Dorothy, 597
Tennant, Margot (later Asquith), 530–1
Tennant, Mariquita, 91
Tennyson, Alfred, *Lord Tennyson*, 11, 150,
    159–60, 243, 318, 320, 324–5, 336–7, 429,
    518–19, 555 n., 594–5
Tennyson, Hallam, 594, 612
Terry, Ellen, 519, 529, 557 n.
Test and Corporation Acts, 14, 414
theatre, 267, 283, 300, 323–4, 529–30
    national theatre, Gladstone supports, 323
'Third Order', 47, 90
Thirlwall, *Bishop* Connop, 153, 325
Thistlethwayte, *Captain* A. F., 159, 241, 321–2,
    538, 616, 617
Thistlethwayte, Laura, *née* Bell, 159–10, 235,
    239 ff., 254, 321–4, 538, 543–4, 559 n.,
    594, 616–18, 630; Plate 12
Thornton, C., 21
Thornton, *Sir* E., 189
Thring, *Sir* Henry, 194, 344, 421
Thucydides, 19, 20
Times, The, 64, 135, 231–2, 311, 437
tobacco duty, 125
Tocqueville, A. de, 32
Tollemache, Lionel, 612
Tomline, *Sir* G. P., 14
Toplady, A. M., 637
Tory Party, 4, 5, 10, 12, 13 ff., 23, 24 ff., 29 ff.,
    42, 45, 56, 58, 62, 65 ff., 77 ff., 81–2, 86,
    87–8, 105 ff., 119, 121, 122, 126–7, 144,
    172, 177–8, 190, 193, 208, 222, 225, 228,
    246, 247–8, 267 ff., 292, 303 ff., 335 ff.,
    412–3, 558, 580, 606, 614
    causes of success of, 511
    Central Office of, 295
    class basis of, 511
    clergy and, 521
    Fourth Party of, 526
    Imperial-State worship and, 464
    Ireland and, 439, 451, 452–3, 461–2, 464, 477,
        481–5, 491–2, 580
    peerage and, 516–17
    villa Tories, 432
Tosti, L., 168
Touchard-Lafosse, G., 528
Townshend, L., 10
Tractarianism, Anglo-Catholicism, Oxford
    Movement, 22, 45, 54–5, 60, 62 ff., 70–2,
    74–5, 81, 83, 89, 90 ff., 100, 104, 138, 141,
    144, 154, 157–8, 169, 196, 203 ff., 213,
    237, 247, 259 ff., 522, 637
    see also High-Churchmanship

Trade, Board of, 60, 66–8, 75 ff., 102, 110, 113, 120–1, 124
Trade Union Act (1871), 216–17
Trade Union Congress, 315–16
trade unions, 131–3, 215–17, 349, 353
Trafalgar Square riots, 417
Tranby Croft affair, 609
Transvaal, 354, 372, 404–8, 448
Treasury, 31, 103, 110 ff., 117, 151, 222, 335, 417 ff., 503–4, 524, 589
treefelling, 254, 288, 317, 352, 527, 541; Plate 27
treeplanting, 614; Plate 23
Trentham House, 149
Trevelyan, *Sir* C., 84
Trevelyan, G. O., 319, 369, 426, 489, 494, 559, 583, 587
Trinity College, Cambridge, 365, 545, 583
Trinity College, Dublin, 200 ff.
Tristram, 565–8
Trollope, Anthony, 237, 284, 305
Tucker, Josiah, 304
Tunis, 382
Tupper, Martin, 22
Turkestan, 380
Turks and Turkish Empire, 85, 167, 257, 266, 267–71, 271–92, 307–8, 382 ff., 391 ff., 561–2
Turner, J. M., 19, 649
Tutors' Association, 84
Tyneside, tour of, 130, 133
Tyrone by-election, 449

Uganda, 398, 594, 595–8, 620
Ulster, Northern Ireland, 282 n., 437, 445, 455, 486, 487–8, 505, 508
    home rule applied in, 508
    tenant right in, 197 ff., 202
Ultramontanism, 64, 184–8, 248–50, 264
'Unauthorised Programme', 494
Uncle Tom's Cabin, 99
unemployment, 415–16, 574
Unionism, 464, 465 n., 494, 507, 509–10, 551, 556, 558, 561–2, 579–80, 585–7, 590, 592
    danger to constitution of, 562
    dank shadow of, 610
    English votes and organic change and, 487
    gigantic mistake of, 463, 469, 477
    press and, 554, 562
Unitarians, 49, 138, 250, 262, 338 n., 364, 368, 625
United Nations, 272
United States of America, 64, 99, 124, 133–4, 140, 146, 162, 163–4, 179, 182, 188 ff., 249, 276, 480, 565, 569–70, 621–2, 624
    Gladstone's voice recorded for, 552
    see also Confederacy
Universities (Scotland) Act (1858), 129, 200

Utilitarianism, 26, 30, 60, 62, 63, 68, 77, 508, 625

Vanity Fair, 540 n.
Vansittart, N., 109
Vatican Council (1870) and Vaticanism, 167, 184–8, 200, 238, 239, 248–50, 254, 259, 282, 283, 294, 326, 329, 460, 626
Vaudois, 36–7
Vaughan, H. H., 21
Venetia, 108
Venice, 326
venture capitalism, 598–9
Vernacular Press Act, 378
Vickers, J., 258
Victoria, H.M.S., 600
Victoria, Lake, 276, 390, 595, 598
Victoria, *Princess*, 516
Victoria, *Queen*, 97, 138, 143 ff., 150, 178, 180, 181, 195, 209 ff., 222, 266, 267, 352–3, 363, 370, 380, 399, 401, 411, 485, 508, 572, 578, 594, 595 n., 622, 631–2, 637 n., 638, 644
    church patronage and, 522–4
    en clair telegrams of, 401, 638
    franchise and, 429 ff.
    Gladstone's dream about, 610
    Gladstone's final retirement and, 605–6, 609–10
    Ireland and, 491
    Letters of Queen Victoria, 513
    More Leaves from the Journal of a Life in the Highlands, 515
    partisanship of, 511–16, 578, 584, 600–1, 605–6, 609–10
    unpleasant unhelpfulness of, 605–6
Vienna, 165
Villiers, C. P., 543, 559
Villiers, G. W. F., *4th Earl of Clarendon*, 143, 144, 146, 176, 180, 184, 185, 186 ff., 196
Virgil, 258
Virginia, 163
virtual representation, 127, 223
voluntarism, 336 ff., 339 ff., 641
Votes of Credit, *see* Credit, Votes of
Vyner, *Mrs.*, 540

Waddesdon, 462
Waddington, W. H., 326–7
Wagner, Richard, 323, 530
Wakefield, Edward Gibbon, 75, 75
Waldegrave, *Lady*, 149, 241, 368
Wales, 38, 50, 67, 104, 129–30, 150–2, 213–14, 339, 467, 479, 500, 522–3, 576, 580, 582, 597, 612
Wales, *Prince of*, *see* Edward VII
Wallace, *General*, 528

Wallace Collection, 618 n.
Wallachia, 85
Walmer Castle, 135
Walpole, *Sir* Robert, 13, 14
Walpole, Spencer, 106
Walsall, 56
War Office, 111, 186–7, 192, 220–1, 222, 396 ff.
Warburton, W., 40
Ward, *Mrs.* Humphry, 619
Ward, W., *Lord Dudley*, 130, 213
Ward, W. G., 71, 72, 102
Warren, *Sir* Charles, 408
Washington Treaty of (1871), 189
Waterloo, field of, 36
Watkin, *Sir* Edward, 612
Watson *Sir* J., 129, 246
Watson, William, 595
Watson, W. L., 302
Watts, G. F., 519–20
Watts, Isaac, 637
Wauchope, Colonel, 580 n.
Waverley novels, 14, 619
Webb, Sidney, 409 n.
Weber, Max, 301–3, 319
WEG Essay Club, 21–2, 26, 90
Welby, *Sir* R., 494, 589
welfare, 641, 644
Wellesley, Arthur, *Duke of Wellington*, 27, 30
Wellesley, *Dean* G. V., 521–2
Wellington College, 315, 533
Wesley, John, 76
West, *Sir* Algernon, 164, 235, 431 n., 603, 605
West Indies, 3, 31, 32, 49, 73, 496–7
Westminster, *Duke of, see* Grosvenor
Westminster Bridge Station, 636
Westminster Hall, 636–7
Westminster Review, 26, 91
Whately, Richard, 30, 38, 39
Whigs, 14, 23, 25, 27, 30 ff., 37–8, 44, 50, 56, 58,
    61, 64, 66, 74, 77, 79, 81 ff., 105, 108, 110,
    113, 128, 130–1, 137–8, 143 ff., 149 ff.,
    172, 177, 180–2, 195 ff., 210, 229, 272,
    292, 296, 306, 334, 346, 348–9, 356,
    357–9, 360, 366 ff., 393, 406, 430, 439,
    444, 446, 465, 467, 469, 491, 493, 509,
    514 ff., 534, 575, 584, 643
Whitby, speech at, 229, 230, 231
Wickham, Agnes, *née* Gladstone, *daughter*, 95,
    161–3, 244, 315, 533, 614, 634 n.; Plate 7
    (a)
Wickham, Edward, *son-in-law*, 315, 614
Wicklow, County, 437–8
Wigram, Clive, 513
Wilberforce, Robert, 70, 248
Wilberforce, Samuel, 70, 213, 236, 248, 320, 528

Wilberforce, William, 7, 8, 647
Wilde, Oscar, 325
Wilkinson, *Bishop* G. H., 633–4
Willesden, 636
William IV, 555
Williams, P., 22
Willyams, *Mrs.* Brydges, 617
Wilson, *blackmailer*, 91–2
Wilson, Harold, 346
Windsor, 353, 516, 517
Winter, J. W., 405
Wintour, Anna, 12
Wiseman, Nicholas, 47
Witney Gazette, 552 n.
Woburn Abbey, 149
Wodehouse, J., *Lord Kimberley*, 176, 189, 192–3,
    357, 360, 364, 365, 406, 494, 495, 606,
    610 n., 637
Wollstonecraft, Mary, 528
Wolseley, *Sir* Garnet, *Lord Wolseley*, 192, 374,
    387 n., 389–90, 397, 399–401, 405, 515
Wolverton, *see* Glyn
women, social position of, 616
women, votes for, 343 n., 428–9, 576–8, 616
Women's National Liberal Federation, 578,
    615–16
Women's Suffrage Bill (1892), 578
Wood, *Sir* Charles, *Lord* Halifax, 83, 121, 176,
    180, 189, 201, 209
Wood, *Sir* Evelyn, 407, 457
Wood, *Revd. Sir* John Page, 457
Wood, W. Page, *Lord Hatherley*, 176
Woodall, W., 429 n.
Wordsworth, C., 19, 47, 264
Wordsworth, William, 555, 594–5
working classes, 102, 118, 125–6, 128 ff., 140 ff.,
    214 ff., 224 ff., 306 ff., 571 ff., 643
Working Classes Annuities Act (1864), 118,
    128, 131, 171
Wright, *Captain* Peter E., 93, 630 n.
Wrottesley, A., 213
Wyllie, James, 315

Yonge, Charlotte M., 249
Young, G. M., 92
Young, *Sir* J., *Lord Lisgar*, 165, 191
Young England, 45
Yorke, J. R., 315

Zanzibar, 390, 403, 408, 595, 597
Zetland, Lord, 439
Zobeir Pasha, 398, 535
Zola, Émile, 619
Zollverein, 334
Zululand, 405 ff.